A to ZOO
Subject Access to
Children's Picture Books

A to ZOO
Subject Access to Children's Picture Books

SECOND EDITION

● Carolyn W. Lima

R. R. BOWKER COMPANY
New York & London

To My Husband, John

Published by R. R. Bowker Company,
   a division of Reed Publishing USA
205 East Forty-second Street, New York, NY 10017
Copyright © 1986 by Reed Publishing USA, a division of
   Reed Holdings, Inc.
Printed and bound in the United States of America

Illustrations by Jean Catherine Lima

Library of Congress Cataloging-in-Publication Data

Lima, Carolyn W.
      A to zoo.

      Bibliography: p.
      Includes index.
      1. Picture-books for children—Bibliography.
2. Children's literature—Bibliography.   3. Catalogs,
Subject.   4. Libraries, Children's—Book lists.
5. Subject headings—Picture-books for children.
6. Subject headings—Children's literature.
I. Title.
Z1037.L715   1985   [PN1009.A1]   011'.62   85-26961
ISBN 0-8352-2134-2

Contents

Preface

The titles in *A to Zoo* (first edition) were based on the San Diego, California, Public Library's collection of picture books for children. This large and versatile collection remains typical of the best and most carefully chosen children's works acquired over a period of time. However, in the effort to ensure that the most up-to-date information was included in this second edition, other sources, including published reviews and, of course, the author's personal searches of titles and literature, were consulted. This expansion into other sources resulted in identifying many additional titles not recognized in the first edition. Additionally, and in response to requests from users of the first edition, the author has endeavored to include the many titles representing the movement toward early childhood education in areas of science, technology, social sciences and other nonfiction educational subject areas. Consequently, this second edition contains more than 8,500 titles cataloged under more than 600 subject headings.

The picture book, long a source of delight and learning for young readers, has gained even more importance during the past few years with the increase in emphasis on early childhood education and the growing need for supervised child care for working mothers. Teachers, librarians, and parents are finding the picture book to be an important learning and entertainment tool. But choosing the right book for a particular situation is time consuming and frustrating without some guidance. The right book is more easily selected when the subject is defined as a specific, rather than simply choosing the first title that appears to treat the subject from among the many thousands of books available.

It is no simple task to select the best book for any particular young reader, and many librarians, teachers, and parents do not have the time or materials to develop an intimate familiarity with the field. Consequently, it is hoped that this second edition of *A to Zoo: Subject Access to Children's Picture Books*, the first published comprehensive guide of its kind, will provide the necessary help and make the task easier.

The picture book, as broadly defined within the scope of this book, is a fiction or nonfiction title that has suitable vocabulary for preschool to grade two, with illustrations occupying as much or more space than the text.

For the reader's convenience, the Introduction: Genesis of the English-Language Picture Book, contained in the 1982 edition, is repeated in this edition. Developments of historical proportion have not been discerned in the intervening three years. Some trends, however, seem more evident: engineered and "pop-up" books are becoming more prolific; attention to the very young reader is reflected in a large number of "board books"—books with cardboard pages designed for tiny tots; and, there is a continued trend toward picture books of a serious nature, bearing a message or lesson, designed to accomplish some social purpose other than mere entertainment of the young reader.

HOW TO USE THIS BOOK

A to Zoo can be used to obtain information about children's picture books in two ways: to learn the titles, authors, and illustrators of books on a particular subject, such as farms or magic; or to ascertain the subject (or subjects) when only the title, author and title, or illustrator and title are known. For example, if the title *One wide river to cross* is known, this volume will enable the user to discover that the book is written by Barbara Emberley, illustrated by Ed Emberley, published by Prentice-Hall in 1966, that it also concerns animals and songs, and is a Caldecott award honor book.

For ease and convenience of reference use, *A to Zoo* is divided into five sections:

Subject Headings
Subject Guide
Bibliographic Guide
Title Index
Illustrator Index

SUBJECT HEADINGS: This section contains an alphabetical listing of the subjects cataloged in this book. To facilitate reference use, and because subjects are requested in a variety of terms, the listing of subject headings contains numerous cross-references. Subheadings are arranged alphabetically under each general topic, for example:

Animals (general topic)
Animals—anteaters (subheading)
Animals—antelopes (subheading)
Animals—apes *see* Animals—gorillas; Animals—monkeys (cross-reference)

SUBJECT GUIDE: The subject-arranged guide reflects the arrangement in the Subject Headings, alphabetically arranged by subject heading and subheading. Titles are listed alphabetically by author within each subject heading. Many books, of course, relate to more than one subject, and this comprehensive listing is meant to provide a means of identifying all those books that may contain information or material on a particular subject.

If, for example, the user wants books on the desert, the Subject Headings section will show that Desert is a subject classification. A look in the Subject Guide reveals that under Desert are sixteen titles listed by author in alphabetical order.

BIBLIOGRAPHIC GUIDE: This section gives bibliographic information for children's picture books included in this volume. It is arranged alphabetically by author, or by title when the author is unknown, and contains bibliographic information in this order: author, title, illustrator, miscellaneous notes when given, publisher and date of publication, and subjects, listed according to the alphabetical classification in the Subject Headings section. After finding that sixteen titles are listed in the Subject Guide under the desired subject of Desert, this section will show the complete date for each of the sixteen titles. For example:

> **Caudill, Rebecca**. *Wind, sand and sky* ill. by Donald
> Carrick. Dutton, 1976. Subj: Desert.
> Poetry, rhyme.

Joint authors are listed in alphabetical order with the title of the book and the name of the primary author or main entry. The user can then locate the main entry for complete bibliographic information. For example:

> **Ahlberg, Allan**. *Burglar Bill* (Ahlberg, Janet)

Bibliographic information for this title will be found in the Bibliographic Guide section under: Ahlberg, Janet.

Titles for an author who is both a single author and a joint author are interfiled alphabetically.

Where the author is not known, the entry is listed alphabetically by title with complete bibliographic information following the same format as given above.

Library of Congress conventions regarding the cataloged name of the author(s) have been followed in this edition. Thus, books published under the name Aliki are listed in alphabetical order under Aliki with cross-references for the actual name of the author, Brandenberg, Aliki Liacouras, to refer the user to the name preferred.

TITLE INDEX: This section contains an alphabetical listing of all titles in the book with authors in parentheses, such as:

> Wind, sand and sky (Caudill, Rebecca)

When multiple versions of the same title is listed, the illustrator's name is given with the author's name (when known). For example:

> The night before Christmas, ill. by Gyo Fujikawa (Moore, Clement C)
> The night before Christmas, ill. by Tasha Tudor (Moore, Clement C)

ILLUSTRATOR INDEX: This section contains an alphabetical listing of illustrators with titles and authors, such as:

> **Carrick, Donald.** Wind, sand and sky (Caudill, Rebecca)

Numerous titles may be listed under an illustrator's name. Titles will appear in alphabetical sequence.

Introduction
Genesis of the English-Language Picture Book

Each year increasing numbers of children's books are published, each one touched in some way by those that preceded it. But how or by what path did the unique genre known as children's picture books arrive at this present and prolific state? Certainly, to imagine a time when children's books did not exist takes more than a little effort. Probably the roots of what we know as children's literature lie in the stories and folktales told and retold through the centuries in every civilization since humans first learned to speak. These stories were narrated over and over as a sort of oral history, literature, and education.[1] But they were not intended, either primarily or exclusively, for children. It was only through the passing years, as the children who were at least part of any audience responded with interest and delight to these tales, and as adults found less leisure time to be entertained in an increasingly busy world, that the stories and folktales came to be regarded as belonging to the world of the child.

Book art or book illustration began with manuscripts—handwritten on parchment or other materials, rolled or scrolled, and later loosely bound into books—that were illuminated or "decorated in lively, vigorous and versatile styles."[2] In time, these decorations, some realistic, some intricate, some imaginative, took on the technological advances of other art forms, notably stained glass, and color was introduced to these illustrated texts.[3]

The children's books that existed in the Middle Ages, before the invention of movable type, were rarely intended to amuse the reader. They were, instead, mostly instructional and moralizing. Monastic teachers, writing essentially for the children of wealthy families, usually wrote in Latin and "began the tradition of didacticism that was to dominate children's books for hundreds of years."[4]

Children's books of that day frequently followed either the rhymed format or the question-and-answer form, both attributed to Aldhelm, abbot of Malmesbury.[5] An early encyclopedia, thought to be the work of Anselm (1033–1109), archbishop of Canterbury, addressed such subjects as "manners and customs, natural science, children's duties, morals, and religious precepts."[6] The books were intended for instruction and indoctrination in the principles of moral and religious belief and behavior,[7] an intent that persisted even after the invention of movable type. Indeed, "children were not born to live happy but to die holy, and true education lay in preparing the soul to meet its maker."[8]

Perhaps the first printed book that was truly intended for children, other than elementary Latin grammar texts, was the French *Les Contenances de la Table*, on the courtesies and manners of dining.[9] Printed and illustrated children's books in Europe followed the invention of printing in the fifteenth century.

Those first books were printed in lowercase letters, and "blank spaces were left on the page for initials and marginal decorations to be added in color by hand. In general, the effect was the same as in manuscript."[10] Some well-known and important artists of the time did the illustrations, using woodcuts, engravings, and lithographic processes.[11]

This combination of pictures and printed text, still with the intent of teaching and incorporating the earlier, but persistent dedication to moral and religious education, finally resulted in what is often assumed to be the first real children's picture book, in 1657—the *Orbis Pictus* of John Amos Comenius.[12] The simple idea by this Czechoslovakian author was that a child would learn most quickly by naming and showing the object at the same time, a seventeenth-century ABC! Noted for its many illustrations, the book contained the seeds of future children's publications, softening somewhat the earlier "harshness with which, in the unsympathetic age, the first steps of learning were always associated."[13]

In the English language, children's books followed a parallel pattern. William Caxton is given credit for a legacy to young readers by publishing *Aesop's Fables* (about 1484).[14] His stories, the first for English children in their own language, gave the lessons of The Fox and the Grapes and The Tortoise and the Hare to children of the fifteenth century and all who followed thereafter.

Nearly 200 years later, American authors and books for American children, in English, began to appear. Like English publications before them, these books reflected a basic profile of moral and religious education. American John Cotton's *Spiritual Milk for Boston Babes* (1646) was not an especially easy text for the young minds that had to master its Puritan lessons. Later came similar books such as *Pilgrim's Progress* by John Bunyan (1678), *The New England Primer* with its rhyming alphabet (1691), and *Divine and Moral Songs for Children* by Isaac Watts (1715).

In the early eighteenth century, a significant movement began in English children's books with the publication of *Robinson Crusoe* by Daniel Defoe (1715), a narrative that delighted children as well as adults. This innovation, utilizing children's books to carry more intricate messages, perhaps aimed at adults as well as older children, reflected a growing sophistication of society, and perhaps some shifting of purely religious or moral bases toward political morality. An all-time favorite with young readers, *Gulliver's Travels* by Jonathan Swift, published in 1726, illustrates this dual thrust. This work, embellished with a wit and rather pointed sarcasm that is sure to escape the young, nonetheless delighted children with the inhabitants of mythical lands and has managed to survive through the years. Perhaps the ultimate development of this trend is found in Lewis Carroll's *Alice's Adventures in Wonderland* (1865), which manages to be perfectly palatable and interesting to children, yet contains subtle lessons for adult society. Although based on earlier plays and vignettes that had been written only for the purpose of entertainment and use of imagination, *Alice*, and other books of the time, began to reflect a change in society's view of children and of reading materials suitable for children.

The English translation of *Tales of Mother Goose* by Charles Perrault in 1729 made moral lessons for young readers less didactic, but it was 1744 that "saw the real foundation of something today everywhere taken for granted—the production of books for children's enjoyment."[15] This book from a small book-stall in London was *A Little Pretty Pocket-Book*, "now famous as the first book for children published by John Newbery"[16] and may indeed be the first book recognizing children as people with intelligence and other human needs, notably the need for humor and entertainment.[17]

For the next 20 years or so, Newbery published well-illustrated and inexpensive little books for young readers. Soon other books designed especially for children followed this trend. Pictures became an essential and integral part of the book, somewhat downplaying the soul-saving educational harshness of earlier books and promoting amusement and enlightened education. Thomas Bewick's first book specifically intended for children, *A Pretty Book of Pictures for Little Masters and Misses, or Tommy Trip's History of Beasts and Birds*, was published in 1779; and its particular effort represented major strides in the refinement of woodcuts used for book illustration. Bewick "developed better tools for this work, made effective use of the white line, and carried the woodcut to a new level of beauty."[18] His efforts and those of his brother John not only achieved a high level of artistic achievement for woodcuts, but had a more lasting effect on illustrators and illustrations for children's books. "An interesting by-product of the Bewicks' contribution is that artists of established reputation began to sign their pictures for children's books."[19] Some talented artists lovingly produced children's books with special artistic achievement, although their principal skills may have been directed toward adults. For example, William Blake, an artist and poet of considerable renown, published *Songs of Innocence* in 1789. "The artist wrote the verses, illustrated them, engraved, hand-colored, and bound the book."[20] The garlands and scrolls were lovingly engraved, and "he gave it color and beautifully drawn figures of people, especially children. The pictures are not realistic but delicate fantasies, almost dreamlike in character. . . . But here are color and a tender perception of the artless grace of children."[21]

Such loving dedication did not long enjoy a singular place in publishing history. Before long commercialism entered the scene and, although some very dedicated people in America and England alike continued to develop books for children, some hackwork also appeared. "Publishers, realizing that children formed a new and somewhat undiscriminating market, were quick to take advantage of the fact. Having chosen a suitable title, and having available some spare woodcut blocks that might be sufficiently relevant for a juvenile book, a publisher would commission a story or series of tales to be woven around the illustrations. One of the results of this was that illustrations of different proportions might be used in the same story, while on other occasions it was clear that the pictures were by different hands. Sometimes the inclusion of a picture was obviously forced. A good example occurs in one of the editions of *Goody Two-Shoes*," attributed to Oliver Goldsmith.[22]

Fortunately, the "hacks" did not totally invade the field of children's picture books. Carefully designed works, crafted with an eye toward the complete and final unit, with special consideration for the means of reproduction, appeared under the guidance of innovative and bold publishers. Beautiful printing became the mark of publishers such as Edmund Evans, printer and artist in his own right, who with his special skill in color engraving published the works of Walter Crane, Randolph Caldecott, and Kate Greenaway. "The work of the three great English picture-book artists of the nineteenth century represents the best to be found in picture books for children in any era; the strength of design and richness of color and detail of Walter Crane's pictures; the eloquence, humor, vitality, and movement of Randolph Caldecott's art; and the tenderness, dignity, and grace of the very personal interpretation of Kate Greenaway's enchanted land of childhood."[23]

These three were indeed great names of the century in the history of children's picture books. The first nursery picture books of Walter Crane, an apprentice wood engraver, were *Sing a Song for Sixpense, The House That Jack Built, Dame Trot and Her Comical Cat,* and *The History of Cock Robin and Jenny Wren,* published by the firm of Warne in 1865 and 1866. Crane was one of the first of the modern illustrators who believed that text and illustrations should be in harmony, forming a complete unit.

Randolph Caldecott, who began drawing at age six, could make animals seemingly come alive on a page. During his short life (1846–1886), he illustrated numerous books for children with fine examples of fun and good humor such as *The Diverting History of John Gilpin, The Babes in the Wood,* and many others from about 1877 until near his death.

Kate Greenaway's simple verses made an appropriate accompaniment to her lovely drawings. *Under the Window* was her first picture book published by Routledge in 1878. Everywhere in her books are the flowers she so loved. She is probably best known for her *Almanacs,* published between 1883 and 1897.

Like Crane, Caldecott, and Greenaway, the works of Beatrix Potter became as well known to American children as to English. Potter, a self-taught artist addicted to pets with charming characteristics, produced a number of tales for young children, the best known being *The Tale of Peter Rabbit* (1901), which presented the illustrations as an integral part of the story and marked a pivotal point in the development of the modern picture book in Europe.

The very excellence of the growing children's book field in England eclipsed the technologically inferior American product, virtually driving American efforts from the marketplace until nearly 15 years after World War I.[24] Meanwhile, the books of English artists such as L. Leslie Brooke, Arthur Rackham, Edmund Dulac, Charles Folkard, and others continued the tradition of excellence through the first three decades of the twentieth century.

Despite the superior English publications, "a self-conscious and systematic concern for children and the books they read had been growing in the United States."[25] Children's libraries and children's librarians appeared around the turn of the century. In 1916, the Bookshop for Boys and Girls was founded in Boston.[26] In 1924 the Bookshop published *The Horn Book Magazine,* "the first journal in the world to be devoted to the critical appraisal of children's books."[27] Another publication, *Junior Libraries,* made its appearance in 1954; this periodical later became *School Library Journal,* published by R. R. Bowker. In this area, the Americans were ten years ahead of Europeans.

Publishers and editors were becoming more and more oriented toward children's literature. In 1919, Macmillan established a Children's Book Department to be separate from its adult publishing line; other publishing houses began to do the same. Children's Book Week was instituted, an idea that started with Franklin K. Mathiews and was supported by Frederic G. Melcher. A landmark in children's book publishing was established in the United States in 1922 when Melcher, then chief editor of *Publishers Weekly*, proposed at the 1921 American Library Association meeting that a medal be awarded each year for the year's most distinguished contribution to American literature for children written by an American citizen or resident and published in the United States. Named for John Newbery, the medal was first awarded to Hendrik Willem van Loon for his book *The Story of Mankind*.

Melcher, who was always aware of the significance of books in the lives of children, later proposed the establishment of a similar award for picture books, named in honor of Randolph Caldecott whose pictures still delight today's children. Since 1938, the Caldecott Medal has been awarded annually by an awards committee of the American Library Association's Children's Services Division to the illustrator of the most distinguished American picture book for children published in the United States during the preceding year. Again, the recipient must reside in or be a citizen of the United States.

The end of the 1920s marked the newly emerging prominence of the modern children's picture book in America. Mainly imported from Europe until that time, children's picture books now began to be published in America. William Nicholson's *Clever Bill* (1927) was followed the next year by one of the most successful picture books of all time, *Millions of Cats* by Wanda Gág. The perfect marriage of the rhythmic prose and flowing movement of her dramatic black-and-white drawings tell a simple, direct story with a folk flavor. This title is still included in the repertoire of today's storytellers and continues to be taken from the shelves by young readers.

The explosion of children's book publishing became known as "The Golden Thirties."[28] By 1930, many publishers had set up separate editing departments expressly for the purpose of publishing children's materials. The White House Conference on Child Health and Protection was held that year to study the plight of the child.[29] Improved technologies accelerated and economized book production. The stage was set for the modern picture book with its profuse illustration. Until this time there were only a few great children's books, illustrated with pictures that were largely an extension of the text. "Yet in a very few years, in respect to the books for the younger children, the artist has attained a place of equal importance with the writer."[30]

The period between the two world wars brought many foreign authors and illustrators to America to join and collaborate with American authors and artists. Their talents and varied backgrounds have contributed immensely to the changes in the picture book in America, which truly came into its own in this period of lower production costs. The years of the 1930s and into the 1940s produced a spectacular number and variety of profusely illustrated books for young children.[31] The many new authors and illustrators then beginning their careers in this developing field of children's picture books have continued to keep their places in the hearts of children: such familiar names as Marjorie Flack, Maud and Miska Petersham, Ingri and Edgar d'Aulaire, Ludwig Bemelmans, Theodor Geisel (Dr. Seuss), Marcia Brown, Feodor Rojankovsky, James Daugherty, Robert Lawson, Marguerite de Angeli, Virginia Lee Burton, Robert McCloskey, and many, many more.

The war years of the mid-1940s affected the progress of children's picture books with shortages of materials, priorities, poor quality paper, narrow margins, inferior bindings, and less color and illustration. However, the postwar years began a boom in children's publishing, adding to the list of talented authors and illustrators such names as Maurice Sendak, Brian Wildsmith, Trina Schart Hyman, Paul Galdone, Leo Politi, Ezra Jack Keats, Gyo Fujikawa, Arnold Lobel, and so many more.

Through the years, many factors have contributed to the growth, even explosion, of children's picture books—society's changing attitudes toward the child; the development of children's libraries, awards, councils, and studies; increasing interest in children's reading on the part of publishers, educators, and literary critics; changing technologies; and the development of American artists and authors. Today the picture book is a part of growing up, a teaching tool, an entertainment medium, a memory to treasure. Perhaps only imagination and the talent of the artist and author can define its limits.

Professionalism, curiosity on all subjects, and freedom of expression have brought the children's picture book into the 1980s with a bewildering array of materials from which to choose. Imaginary animals of the past and future line the shelves with the cats, dogs, horses, and dolphins of the modern day. Fantasy lands compete with tales of spaceships and astronauts; dreams of the future can be found with the realities of the past; picture books of all kinds for all kinds of children—and adults—to enjoy!

For the teacher, librarian, or parent who wishes to open this fantastic world of color and imagination for the child, some tool is necessary to put oneself in touch with the great number of possibilities for enjoyment in the picture book field today. *A to Zoo: Subject Access to Children's Picture Books* is designed with just this purpose in mind.

For those interested in exploring more deeply the world of children's publishing and the children's picture book, consult the list of suggested titles for further reading.

Further Reading

Alderson, Brian. *Looking at Picture Books 1973*. Chicago: Children's Book Council, 1974.

*Arbuthnot, May Hill, and Sutherland, Zena. *Children and Books*, 4th ed. Glenview, Ill.: Scott, Foresman, 1972.

Arbuthnot, May Hill et al., comps. *The Arbuthnot Anthology of Children's Literature*, 4th ed. Glenview, Ill.: Scott, Foresman, 1972; New York: Lothrop, 1976.

*Bader, Barbara. *American Picturebooks from Noah's Ark to the Beast Within*. New York: Macmillan, 1976.

Barchilon, Jacques, and Pettit, Henry. *The Authentic Mother Goose Fairy Tales and Nursery Rhymes*. Athens, Ohio: Swallow Press, 1960.

Barry, Florence V. *A Century of Children's Books*. London: Methuen, 1922.

*Bingham, Jane, and Scholt, Grayce, eds. *Fifteen Centuries of Children's Literature: An Annotated Chronology of British and American Works in Historical Context*. Westport, Conn.: Greenwood Press, 1980.

Bland, David. *A History of Book Illustration*, 2nd ed. London: Faber & Faber, 1969.

———. *The Illustration of Books*. London: Faber & Faber, 1962.

Bodger, Joan. *How the Heather Looks*. New York: Viking, 1965.

Braun, Saul. "Sendak Raises the Shade on Childhood." *New York Times Magazine*, June 7, 1970, p. 34+.

*Indicates especially recommended titles in this reading list.

Butler, Dorothy. *Babies Need Books*. New York: Atheneum, 1984.

Butler, Francelia, and Rotert, Richard W., eds. *Reflections on Literature for Children*. Hamden, Conn.: Shoe String Press, 1984.

Cianciolo, Patricia. *Illustrations in Children's Books*, 2nd ed. Dubuque, Iowa: William C. Brown, 1976.

Comenius, John Amos. *The Orbis Pictus of John Amos Comenius*. Detroit: Gale, 1968.

Crouch, Marcus. *Treasure Seekers and Borrowers: Children's Books in Britain 1900–1960*. London: Library Association, 1962.

Daniel, Eloise. *A Treasury of Books for Family Enjoyment: Books for Children from Infancy to Grade 2*. Pontiac, Mich.: Blue Engine Press, 1983.

Darling, Richard L. *The Rise of Children's Book Reviewing in America, 1865–1881*. New York: Bowker, 1968.

Darrell, Margery, ed. *Once Upon a Time: The Fairy-Tale World of Arthur Rackham*. New York: Viking, 1972.

Darton, F. J. H. *Children's Books in England: Five Centuries of Social Life*, 3rd ed. New York: Cambridge Univ. Press, 1982.

Demers, Patricia, ed. *A Garland from the Golden Age: Children's Literature from 1850–1900*. New York: Oxford Univ. Press, 1983.

Demers, R. A., and Moyles, R. G., eds. *From Instruction to Delight: An Anthology of Children's Literature to 1850*. New York: Oxford Univ. Press, 1982.

Duvoisin, Roger. "Children's Book Illustration: The Pleasure and Problems." *Top of the News* 22: 30 (Nov. 1965).

Earle, Alice Morse. *Child Life in Colonial Days*. New York: Macmillan, 1899.

Eckenstein, Lina. *Comparative Studies in Nursery Rhymes*. London: Duckworth, 1906; Detroit: Gale, 1968.

Egoff, Sheila; Stubbs, G. T.; and Ashley, L. F., eds. *Only Connect: Readings on Children's Literature*. New York: Oxford Univ. Press, 1969.

Ellis, Alec. *A History of Children's Reading and Literature*. Elmsford, N.Y.: Pergamon Press, 1968.

Eyre, Frank. *British Children's Books in the Twentieth Century*. New York: Dutton, 1973.

———. *Twentieth Century Children's Books*. Cambridge, Mass.: Robert Bentley, 1953.

Field, Louise F. *The Child and His Book: Some Account of the History and Progress of Children's Literature in England*. Detroit: Gale, 1968.

Fisher, Margery Turner. *Intent upon Reading: A Critical Appraisal of Modern Fiction for Children*. Leicester, England: Brockhampton Press, 1961.

———. *Who's Who in Children's Books: A Treasury of the Familiar Characters of Childhood*. New York: Holt, 1975.

Fox, Geoffrey Percival, and others, eds. *Writers, Critics, and Children: Articles from Children's Literature in Education*. New York: Agathon Press, 1976.

*Freeman, Ruth Sunderlin. *Children's Picture Books, Yesterday and Today*. Watkins Glen, N.Y.: Century House, 1967.

Gillespie, John T., and Gilbert, Christine B., eds. *Best Books for Children: Preschool Through the Middle Grades*, 3rd ed. New York: Bowker, 1985.

Gillespie, Margaret C., and Connor, John W. *Creative Growth Through Literature for Children and Adolescents*. Columbus, Ohio: Merrill, 1975.

Gottlieb, Gerald. *Early Children's Books and Their Illustration*. Boston: Godine, 1975.

Green, Percy B. *A History of Nursery Rhymes*. Detroit: Gale, 1968.

Green, Roger Lancelyn. *Tellers of Tales: British Authors of Children's Books from 1800 to 1964*. New York: Watts, 1965.

*Greenaway, Kate. *The Kate Greenaway Treasury*. Cleveland: World, 1967.

Halsey, Rosalie V. *Forgotten Books of the American Nursery*. Detroit: Gale, 1969.

*Haviland, Virginia, comp. *Children and Literature: Views and Reviews*. Glenview, Ill.: Scott, Foresman, 1973.

———. *Children's Literature: A Guide to Reference Sources*. Washington, D.C.: Library of Congress, 1966; first supplement, 1972.

Huber, Miriam Blanton. *Story and Verse for Children*, 3rd ed. New York: Macmillan, 1965.

*Hürlimann, Bettina. *Three Centuries of Children's Books in Europe*. Ed. and trans. by Brian W. Alderson. London: Oxford Univ. Press, 1967; Cleveland: World, 1968.

James, Philip. *Children's Books of Yesterday.* Ed. by C. Geoffrey Holme. London and New York: Studio, 1933; Detroit: Gale, 1976.

Jan, Isabelle. *On Children's Literature.* Ed. by Catherine Storr. New York: Schocken Books, 1974.

Kiefer, Monica. *American Children Through Their Books, 1700–1835.* Philadelphia: Univ. of Pennsylvania Press, 1948, 1970.

Klemin, Diana. *The Illustrated Book.* New York: Potter, 1970.

Lanes, Selma G. "The Art of Maurice Sendak: A Diversity of Influences Inform an Art for Children," *Artform* IX (May 1971): 70–73.

Leif, Irving P. *Children's Literature: A Historical and Contemporary Bibliography.* Troy, N.Y.: Whitston, 1977.

Lewis, John. *The Twentieth Century Book: Its Illustration and Design.* New York: Van Nostrand Reinhold, 1967.

Lukens, Rebecca J. *A Critical Handbook of Children's Literature,* 2nd ed. Glenview, Ill: Scott, Foresman, 1981.

Lystad, Mary. *From Dr. Mather to Dr. Seuss: Two Hundred Years of American Books for Children.* Cambridge, Mass.: Schenkman, 1980.

*MacCann, Donnarae, and Richard, Olga. *The Child's First Books.* New York: Wilson, 1973.

Mahoney, Ellen, and Wilcox, Leah. *Ready, Set, Read: Best Books to Prepare Preschoolers.* Metuchen, N.J.: Scarecrow, 1985.

Mahony, Bertha E.; Latimer, Louise P.; and Folmsbee, Beulah, comps. *Illustrators of Children's Books, 1744–1945.* Boston: Horn Book, 1947.

*Meigs, Cornelia; Eaton, Anne; Nesbitt, Elizabeth; and Viguers, Ruth Hill, eds. *A Critical History of Children's Literature.* New York: Macmillan, 1953; rev. ed., 1969.

Moore, Anne Carroll. *My Roads to Childhood.* Boston: Horn Book, 1961.

Moransee, Jesse R., ed. *Children's Prize Books.* Ridgewood, N.J.: K.G. Saur, 1983.

Muir, Percy. *English Children's Books, 1600–1900.* New York: Praeger, 1969.

*Newbery, John. *A Little Pretty Pocket-Book: A Facsimile.* London: Oxford Univ. Press, 1966; New York: Harcourt Brace Jovanovich, 1967.

Opie, Iona, and Opie, Peter, comps. *A Family Book of Nursery Rhymes.* New York: Oxford Univ. Press, 1964.

———. *The Oxford Dictionary of Nursery Rhymes.* New York: Oxford Univ. Press, 1951.

The Original Mother Goose's Melody, As First Issued by John Newbery, of London, about A.D. 1760. Reproduced in facsimile from the edition as reprinted by Isaiah Thomas of Worcester, Mass., about A.D. 1785, with introductory notes by William H. Whitmore. Detroit: Gale, 1969.

Pitz, Henry C. *Illustrating Children's Books: History, Technique, Production.* New York: Watson-Guptill, 1963.

Preschool Services and Parent Education Committee, Association for Library Service to Children. *Opening Doors for Preschool Children and Their Parents,* 2nd ed. Chicago: ALA, 1981.

Richard, Olga. "The Visual Language of the Picture Book." *Wilson Library Bulletin* (Dec. 1969).

Rosenbach, Abraham S. W. *Early American Children's Books with Bibliographical Descriptions of the Books in His Private Collection.* Foreword by A. Edward Newton. Portland, Maine: Southworth Press, 1933.

Sadker, Myra, and Sadker, David Miller. *Now Upon a Time: A Contemporary View of Children's Literature.* New York: Harper, 1977.

Salway, Lance, ed. *A Peculiar Gift.* New York: Penguin, 1976.

Sendak, Maurice. "Mother Goose's Garnishings." *Book Week.* Fall Children's Issue (Oct. 31, 1965); 5, 38–40; also printed in Haviland, *Children and Literature,* pp. 188–195.

Smith, Dora V. *Fifty Years of Children's Books, 1910–1960.* Urbana, Ill.: National Council of Teachers of English, 1963.

*Smith, Elva S. *The History of Children's Literature: A Syllabus with Selected Bibliographies,* rev. and enlarged by Margaret Hodges and Susan Steinfirst. Chicago: ALA, 1980.

Stott, Jon. *Children's Literature from A to Z: A Guide for Parents and Teachers*. New York: McGraw-Hill, 1984.

*Sutherland, Zena, and Arbuthnot, May Hill. *Children and Books*, 5th ed. Glenview, Ill.: Scott, Foresman, 1977.

Targ, William, ed. *Bibliophile in the Nursery*. Metuchen, N.J.: Scarecrow, 1969.

Thomas, Katherine Elwes. *The Real Personages of Mother Goose*. New York: Lothrop, 1930.

Thwaite, Mary. *From Primer to Pleasure in Reading*, 2nd ed. London: The Library Association, 1972; Boston: Horn Book, 1972.

Townsend, John Rowe. *Written for Children: An Outline of English-Language Children's Literature*, rev. ed. London: Penguin, 1974.

Viguers, Ruth Hill; Dalphin, Marcia; and Miller, Bertha Mahony, comps. *Illustrators of Children's Books, 1946–1956*. Boston: Horn Book, 1958.

Weitenkampf, Frank. *The Illustrated Book*. Cambridge, Mass.: Harvard Univ. Press, 1938.

Welch, D'Alte A. *A Bibliography of American Children's Books Printed Prior to 1821*. Worcester, Mass.: American Antiquarian Society, 1972.

*Whalley, Joyce Irene. *Cobwebs to Catch Flies: Illustrated Books for the Nursery and Schoolroom 1700–1900*. Berkeley: Univ. of California Press, 1975.

White, Dorothy M. Neal. *Books Before Five*. New York: Oxford Univ. Press, 1954.

White, Mary Lou. *Children's Literature: Criticism and Response*. Columbus, Ohio: Merrill, 1976.

*Wilkin, Binnie Tate. *Survival Themes in Fiction for Children and Young People*. Metuchen, N.J.: Scarecrow, 1978.

Notes

1. Caroline M. Hewins, "The History of Children's Books (1888)," in *Children and Literature: Views and Reviews*, ed. Virginia Haviland (Glenview, Ill: Scott, Foresman, 1973), p. 30

2. Donnarae MacCann and Olga Richard, *The Child's First Books: A Critical Study of Pictures and Texts* (New York: Wilson, 1973), p. 11.

3. Ibid.

4. Zena Sutherland and May Hill Arbuthnot, *Children and Books*, 5th ed. (Glenview, Ill.: Scott, Foresman, 1977), p. 37.

5. Ibid.

6. Ibid.

7. Ibid.

8. Bettina Hürlimann, *Three Centuries of Children's Books in Europe*, trans. and ed. Brian Alderson (London: Oxford Univ. Press, 1967), p. xii.

9. Sutherland and Arbuthnot, *Children and Books*, p. 37.

10. MacCann and Richard, *The Child's First Books*, p. 11.

11. Ibid.

12. Hürlimann, *Three Centuries of Children's Books in Europe*, pp. 127–129.

13. Ruth Sunderlin Freeman, *Children's Picture Books, Yesterday and Today* (Watkins Glen, N.Y.: Century House, 1967), p. 12.

14. May Hill Arbuthnot and Zena Sutherland, *Children and Books*, 4th ed. (Glenview, Ill.: Scott, Foresman, 1972), p. 52.

15. John Newbery, *A Little Pretty Pocket-Book: A Facsimile* (London: Oxford Univ. Press, 1966), p. 2.

16. Ibid., p. 3.

17. Ibid., p. 2.

18. Arbuthnot and Sutherland, *Children and Books*, pp. 53–54.

19. Ibid., p. 54.

20. Ibid.

21. Ibid.

22. Joyce Irene Whalley. *Cobwebs to Catch Flies: Illustrated Books for the Nursery and Schoolroom 1700–1900* (Berkeley: Univ. of California Press, 1975), p. 14.

23. Ruth Hill Viguers, "Introduction," in Kate Greenaway, *The Kate Greenaway Treasury* (Cleveland: World, 1967), p. 13.

24. Barbara Bader, *American Picturebooks from Noah's Ark to the Beast Within* (New York: Macmillan, 1976), p. 7.

25. Viguers, "Introduction," p. 39.

26. Ibid.

27. Ibid.

28. Sutherland and Arbuthnot, *Children and Books*, p. 122.

29. Binnie Tate Wilkin, *Survival Themes in Fiction for Children and Young People* (Metuchen, N.J.: Scarecrow, 1978), p. 21.

30. Cornelia Meigs, Anne Eaton, Elizabeth Nesbitt, and Ruth Hill Viguers, *A Critical History of Children's Literature* (New York: Macmilllan, 1953), p. 587.

31. Ibid., p. 438.

Subject Headings

Main headings, subheadings, and cross-references are arranged alphabetically and provide a quick reference to the subjects used in the Subject Guide section where author and title names appear under appropiate headings.

Aardvarks *see* Animals — aardvarks
ABC books
Accordion books *see* Format, unusual
Activities
Activities — babysitting
Activities — ballooning
Activities — bathing
Activities — cooking
Activities — dancing
Activities — digging
Activities — flying
Activities — gardening
Activities — jumping
Activities — knitting
Activities — painting
Activities — photographing
Activities — picnicking
Activities — playing
Activities — reading
Activities — shopping *see* Shopping
Activities — swinging
Activities — trading
Activities — traveling
Activities — vacationing
Activities — walking
Activities — weaving
Activities — whistling
Activities — working
Activities — writing
Adoption
Africa *see* Foreign lands — Africa
Afro-Americans *see* Ethnic groups in the U.S. — Afro-Americans
Aged *see* Old age
Airplane pilots *see* Careers — airplane pilots
Airplanes, airports
Airports *see* Airplanes, airports
Albatrosses *see* Birds — albatrosses
Alligators *see* Reptiles — alligators, crocodiles
Ambition *see* Character traits — ambition
American Indians *see* Ethnic groups in the U.S. — Indians
Amphibians *see* Frogs and toads; Reptiles

Anatomy
Angels
Anger *see* Emotions — anger
Animals
Animals — aardvarks
Animals — anteaters
Animals — apes *see* Animals — gorillas; Animals — monkeys
Animals — armadillos
Animals — badgers
Animals — bats
Animals — bears
Animals — beavers
Animals — bobcats
Animals — buffaloes
Animals — bulls, cows
Animals — camels
Animals — cats
Animals — cheetahs
Animals — chipmunks
Animals — cougars
Animals — coyotes
Animals — deer
Animals, dislike of *see* Behavior — animals, dislike of
Animals — dogs
Animals — dolphins
Animals — donkeys
Animals — elephants
Animals — endangered animals
Animals — foxes
Animals — gerbils
Animals — giraffes
Animals — goats
Animals — gorillas
Animals — groundhogs
Animals — guinea pigs
Animals — hamsters
Animals — hedgehogs
Animals — hippopotami
Animals — horses
Animals — hyenas
Animals — kangaroos
Animals — kinkajous
Animals — koala bears
Animals — leopards
Animals — lions
Animals — llamas
Animals — mice
Animals — moles
Animals — mongooses

Animals — monkeys
Animals — moose
Animals — mules
Animals — muskrats
Animals — octopuses *see* Octopuses
Animals — otters
Animals — pack rats
Animals — pigs
Animals — porcupines
Animals — possums
Animals — prairie dogs
Animals — rabbits
Animals — raccoons
Animals — rats
Animals — reindeer
Animals — rhinoceros
Animals — sea lions
Animals — seals
Animals — sheep
Animals — shrews
Animals — skunks
Animals — sloths
Animals — snails
Animals — squirrels
Animals — tapirs
Animals — tigers
Animals — walruses
Animals — water buffaloes
Animals — weasels
Animals — whales
Animals — wolves
Animals — worms
Animals — yaks
Animals — zebras
Antarctic *see* Foreign lands — Antarctic
Anteaters *see* Animals — anteaters
Anti-violence *see* Violence, anti-violence
Ants *see* Insects — ants
Apes *see* Animals — gorillas; Animals — monkeys
Appearance *see* Character traits — appearance
April Fools' Day *see* Holidays — April Fools' Day
Arabia *see* Foreign lands — Arabia
Arctic *see* Foreign lands — Arctic
Arguing *see* Behavior — fighting, arguing
Arithmetic *see* Counting

Armadillos *see* Animals — armadillos

Armenia *see* Foreign lands — Armenia

Art

Artists *see* Careers — artists

Astrology *see* Zodiac

Astronauts *see* Space and space ships

Australia *see* Foreign lands — Australia

Austria *see* Foreign lands — Austria

Authors, children *see* Children as authors

Automobiles

Autumn *see* Seasons — fall

Babies

Babysitting *see* Activities — babysitting

Bad day *see* Behavior — bad day

Badgers *see* Animals — badgers

Bakers *see* Careers — bakers

Bali *see* Foreign lands — Bali

Ballooning *see* Activities — ballooning

Balloons *see* Toys — balloons

Balls *see* Toys — balls

Barbers *see* Careers — barbers

Barns

Barons *see* Royalty

Baseball *see* Sports — baseball

Basketball *see* Sports — basketball

Bathing *see* Activities — bathing

Bats *see* Animals — bats

Bavaria *see* Foreign lands — Austria; Foreign lands — Germany

Beaches *see* Sea and seashore

Bears *see* Animals — bears

Beasts *see* Monsters

Beavers *see* Animals — beavers

Bedtime

Bees *see* Insects — bees

Beetles *see* Insects — beetles

Behavior

Behavior — animals, dislike of

Behavior — bad day

Behavior — boasting

Behavior — boredom

Behavior — bullying

Behavior — carelessness

Behavior — collecting things

Behavior — disbelief

Behavior — dissatisfaction

Behavior — fighting, arguing

Behavior — forgetfulness

Behavior — gossip

Behavior — greed

Behavior — growing up

Behavior — hiding

Behavior — hiding things

Behavior — hurrying

Behavior — imitation

Behavior — indifference

Behavior — losing things

Behavior — lost

Behavior — lying

Behavior — misbehavior

Behavior — mistakes

Behavior — misunderstanding

Behavior — nagging

Behavior — needing someone

Behavior — running away

Behavior — saving things

Behavior — secrets

Behavior — seeking better things

Behavior — sharing

Behavior — solitude

Behavior — stealing

Behavior — talking to strangers

Behavior — trickery

Behavior — unnoticed, unseen

Behavior — wishing

Behavior — worrying

Being different *see* Character traits — being different

Bicycling *see* Sports — bicycling

Bigotry *see* Prejudice

Birds

Birds — albatrosses

Birds — blackbirds

Birds — bluejays

Birds — buzzards

Birds — canaries

Birds — cardinals

Birds — chickens

Birds — cockatoos

Birds — cormorants

Birds — cranes

Birds — crows

Birds — doves

Birds — ducks

Birds — eagles

Birds — egrets

Birds — flamingos

Birds — geese

Birds — hawks

Birds — nightingales

Birds — ostriches

Birds — owls

Birds — parakeets, parrots

Birds — peacocks, peahens

Birds — pelicans

Birds — penguins

Birds — pigeons

Birds — puffins

Birds — ravens

Birds — robins

Birds — sandpipers

Birds — sea gulls

Birds — sparrows

Birds — storks

Birds — swallows

Birds — swans

Birds — toucans

Birds — turkeys

Birds — vultures

Birds — woodpeckers

Birds — wrens

Birthdays

Black Americans *see* Ethnic groups in the U.S. — Afro-Americans

Blackbirds *see* Birds — blackbirds

Blackouts *see* Power failure

Blindness *see* Handicaps — blindness

Blocks *see* Toys — blocks

Bluejays *see* Birds — bluejays

Board books *see* Format, unusual — cardboard pages

Boasting *see* Behavior — boasting

Boats, ships

Bobcats *see* Animals — bobcats

Boogey man *see* Monsters

Books *see* Activities — reading; Libraries

Boredom *see* Behavior — boredom

Bravery *see* Character traits — bravery

Bridges

Brothers *see* Family life; Sibling rivalry

Brownies *see* Elves and little people

Buffaloes *see* Animals — buffaloes

Bugs *see* Insects

Bulls *see* Animals — bulls, cows

Bullying *see* Behavior — bullying

Bumble bees *see* Insects — bees

Burglars *see* Crime

Burros *see* Animals — donkeys

Bus drivers *see* Careers — bus drivers

Buses

Butchers *see* Careers — butchers

Butterflies *see* Insects — butterflies, caterpillars

Buzzards *see* Birds — buzzards

Cab drivers *see* Careers — taxi drivers

Cable cars, trolleys

Cabs *see* Taxis

Caldecott award book

Caldecott award honor book

Camels *see* Animals — camels

Camping *see* Sports — camping

Canada *see* Foreign lands — Canada

Canaries see Birds —
canaries
Cardboard page books see
Format, unusual —
cardboard pages
Cardinals see Birds —
cardinals
Careers
Careers — airplane pilots
Careers — artists
Careers — bakers
Careers — barbers
Careers — bus drivers
Careers — butchers
Careers — cab drivers see
Careers — taxi drivers
Careers — carpenters
Careers — clockmakers
Careers — dentists
Careers — detectives
Careers — doctors
Careers — firefighters
Careers — fishermen
Careers — forest rangers see
Careers — park rangers
Careers — fortune tellers
Careers — garbage collectors
Careers — judges
Careers — librarians
Careers — maids
Careers — mail carriers
Careers — military
Careers — miners
Careers — nuns
Careers — nurses
Careers — park rangers
Careers — peddlers
Careers — physicians see
Careers — doctors
Careers — police officers
Careers — railroad
engineers
Careers — rangers see
Careers — park rangers
Careers — sailors see
Careers — military
Careers — seamstresses
Careers — shoemakers
Careers — soldiers see
Careers — military
Careers — tailors
Careers — taxi drivers
Careers — teachers
Careers — telephone
operators
Careers — train engineers
see Careers — railroad
engineers
Careers — truck drivers
Careers — veterinarians
Careers — waiters, waitresses
Careers — waitresses see
Careers — waiters,
waitresses
Careers — window cleaners
Careers — writers
Carelessness see Behavior —
carelessness
Caribbean Islands see
Foreign lands —
Caribbean Islands
Carnivals see Fairs

Carousels see
Merry-go-rounds
Carpenters see Careers —
carpenters
Cars see Automobiles
Caterpillars see Insects —
butterflies, caterpillars
Cats see Animals — cats
Cavemen
Caves
Chanukah see Holidays —
Hanukkah
Character traits
Character traits — ambition
Character traits —
appearance
Character traits — being
different
Character traits — bravery
Character traits —
cleanliness
Character traits — cleverness
Character traits —
completing things
Character traits —
compromising
Character traits — conceit
Character traits —
confidence
Character traits — cruelty to
animals see Character traits
— kindness to animals
Character traits — curiosity
Character traits — flattery
Character traits —
foolishness
Character traits — fortune
see Character traits — luck
Character traits — freedom
Character traits — generosity
Character traits —
helpfulness
Character traits — honesty
Character traits — incentive
see Character traits —
ambition
Character traits —
individuality
Character traits — kindness
Character traits — kindness
to animals
Character traits — laziness
Character traits — littleness
see Character traits —
smallness
Character traits — loyalty
Character traits — luck
Character traits — meanness
Character traits — optimism
Character traits — ostracism
see Character traits —
being different
Character traits — patience
Character traits —
perseverance
Character traits —
persistence
Character traits —
practicality
Character traits — pride
Character traits —
questioning

Character traits — selfishness
Character traits — shyness
Character traits — smallness
Character traits —
stubbornness
Character traits — vanity
Character traits —
willfulness
Cheetahs see Animals —
cheetahs
Chickens see Birds —
chickens
Children as authors
Children as illustrators
China see Foreign lands —
China
Chinese-Americans see
Ethnic groups in the U.S.
— Chinese-Americans
Chinese New Year see
Holidays — Chinese New
Year
Chipmunks see Animals —
chipmunks
Christmas see Holidays —
Christmas
Cinco de Mayo see Holidays
— Cinco de Mayo
Circus
City
Cleanliness see Character
traits — cleanliness
Cleverness see Character
traits — cleverness
Clockmakers see Careers —
clockmakers
Clocks
Clothing
Clouds see Weather —
clouds
Clowns, jesters
Clubs, gangs
Cockatoos see Birds —
cockatoos
Codes see Secret codes
Cold see Weather — cold
Collecting things see
Behavior — collecting
things
Color see Concepts — color
Columbus Day see Holidays
— Columbus Day
Communication
Communities, neighborhoods
Competition see Sibling
rivalry
Completing things see
Character traits —
completing things
Compromising see Character
traits — compromising
Computers see Machines
Conceit see Character traits
— conceit
Concepts
Concepts — color
Concepts — counting see
Counting
Concepts — distance
Concepts — in and out
Concepts — left and right
Concepts — measurement

Concepts — opposites
Concepts — perspective
Concepts — self *see*
Self-concept
Concepts — shape
Concepts — size
Concepts — speed
Concepts — up and down
Concepts — weight
Confidence *see* Character
traits — confidence
Conservation *see* Ecology
Cooking *see* Activities —
cooking
Cooks *see* Careers — bakers
Coral Islands *see* Foreign
lands — South Sea Islands
Cormorants *see* Birds —
cormorants
Cougars *see* Animals —
cougars
Counting
Countries, foreign *see*
Foreign lands
Country
Cowboys
Cows *see* Animals — bulls,
cows
Coyotes *see* Animals —
coyotes
Crabs *see* Crustacea
Cranes *see* Birds — cranes
Creatures *see* Goblins;
Monsters
Creeks *see* Rivers
Crickets *see* Insects —
crickets
Crime
Criminals *see* Crime; Prisons
Crippled *see* Handicaps
Crocodiles *see* Reptiles —
alligators, crocodiles
Crows *see* Birds — crows
Cruelty to animals *see*
Character traits —
kindness to animals
Crustacea
Cumulative tales
Curiosity *see* Character traits
— curiosity
Currency *see* Money
Cycles *see* Motorcycles;
Sports — bicycling
Czechoslovakia *see* Foreign
lands — Czechoslovakia

Dancing *see* Activities —
dancing
Dark *see* Night
Darkness — fear *see*
Emotions — fear
Dawn *see* Morning
Days of the week, months of
the year
Deafness *see* Handicaps —
deafness
Death
Deer *see* Animals — deer
Demons *see* Devil; Monsters
Denmark *see* Foreign lands
— Denmark

Dentists *see* Careers —
dentists
Department stores *see* Stores
Desert
Detective stories *see* Problem
solving
Detectives *see* Careers —
detectives
Devil
Dictionaries
Digging *see* Activities —
digging
Dinosaurs
Disbelief *see* Behavior —
disbelief
Dissatisfaction *see* Behavior
— dissatisfaction
Distance *see* Concepts —
distance
Diving *see* Sports — skin
diving
Divorce
Doctors *see* Careers —
doctors
Dogs *see* Animals — dogs
Dolls *see* Toys — dolls
Dolphins *see* Animals —
dolphins
Donkeys *see* Animals —
donkeys
Doves *see* Birds — doves
Down and up *see* Concepts
— up and down
Dragonflies *see* Insects
Dragons
Drawing games *see* Games
Dreams
Droughts *see* Weather —
droughts
Ducks *see* Birds — ducks
Dwarfs *see* Elves and little
people
Dying *see* Death

Eagles *see* Birds — eagles
Ears *see* Anatomy
Earth
Easter *see* Holidays —
Easter
Eating *see* Food
Ecology
Ecuador *see* Foreign lands —
Ecuador
Education *see* School
Eggs
Egrets *see* Birds — egrets
Egypt *see* Foreign lands —
Egypt
Egyptian language *see*
Hieroglyphics
Elderly *see* Old age
Elephants *see* Animals —
elephants
Elves and little people
Embarrassment *see* Emotions
— embarrassment
Emergencies *see* Hospitals
Emotions
Emotions — anger
Emotions — embarrassment
Emotions — envy, jealousy

Emotions — fear
Emotions — happiness
Emotions — hate
Emotions — jealousy *see*
Emotions — envy,
jealousy
Emotions — loneliness
Emotions — love
Emotions — sadness
Emotions — unhappiness *see*
Emotions — happiness;
Emotions — sadness
Emperors *see* Royalty
Endangered animals *see*
Animals — endangered
animals
Engineered books *see*
Format, unusual
England *see* Foreign lands —
England
Entertainment *see* Theater
Envy *see* Emotions — envy,
jealousy
Eskimos *see* Ethnic groups in
the U.S. — Eskimos
Ethnic groups in the U.S.
Ethnic groups in the U.S. —
Afro-Americans
Ethnic groups in the U.S. —
Black Americans *see* Ethnic
groups in the U.S. —
Afro-Americans
Ethnic groups in the U.S. —
Chinese-Americans
Ethnic groups in the U.S. —
Eskimos
Ethnic groups in the U.S. —
Indians
Ethnic groups in the U.S. —
Japanese-Americans
Ethnic groups in the U.S. —
Mexican-Americans
Ethnic groups in the U.S. —
Puerto Rican-Americans
Etiquette
Europe *see* Foreign lands —
Europe
Evening *see* Twilight
Experiments *see* Science
Eye glasses *see* Glasses
Eyes *see* Anatomy

Fables *see* Folk and fairy
tales
Faces *see* Anatomy
Fairies
Fairs
Fairy tales *see* Folk and fairy
tales
Fall *see* Seasons — fall
Families *see* Family life
Family life
Family life — brothers *see*
Family life; Sibling rivalry
Family life — fathers
Family life — grandparents,
great-grandparents
Family life — mothers
Family life — only child
Family life — sisters *see*
Family life; Sibling rivalry

Family life — stepchildren
see Divorce; Family life —
step families
Family life — stepfamilies
Family life — stepparents see
Divorce; Family life — step
families
Farms
Fathers see Family life —
fathers
Fear see Emotions — fear
Feeling see Senses
Feelings see Emotions
Feet see Anatomy
Fighting see Behavior —
fighting, arguing
Fingers see Anatomy
Finishing things see
Character traits —
completing things
Fire
Fire engines see Careers —
firefighters; Trucks
Firefighters see Careers —
firefighters
Fireflies see Insects —
fireflies
Fish
Fishermen see Careers —
fishermen
Fishing see Sports — fishing
Flamingos see Birds —
flamingos
Flattery see Character traits
— flattery
Fleas see Insects — fleas
Flies see Insects — flies
Floods see Weather — floods
Flowers
Flying see Activities — flying
Fog see Weather — fog
Fold out books see Format,
unusual
Folk and fairy tales
Food
Foolishness see Character
traits — foolishness
Football see Sports —
football
Foreign lands
Foreign lands — Africa
Foreign lands — Antarctic
Foreign lands — Arabia
Foreign lands — Arctic
Foreign lands — Armenia
Foreign lands — Australia
Foreign lands — Austria
Foreign lands — Bali
Foreign lands — Bavaria see
Foreign lands — Austria;
Foreign lands — Germany
Foreign lands — Canada
Foreign lands — Caribbean
Islands
Foreign lands — China
Foreign lands —
Czechoslovakia
Foreign lands — Denmark
Foreign lands — Ecuador
Foreign lands — Egypt
Foreign lands — England
Foreign lands — Europe

Foreign lands — France
Foreign lands — Germany
Foreign lands — Greece
Foreign lands — Greenland
Foreign lands — Guyana
Foreign lands — Holland
Foreign lands — Hungary
Foreign lands — India
Foreign lands — Ireland
Foreign lands — Israel
Foreign lands — Italy
Foreign lands — Japan
Foreign lands — Korea
Foreign lands — Lapland
Foreign lands — Lithuania
Foreign lands — Malaysia
Foreign lands — Mexico
Foreign lands — New
Guinea
Foreign lands — Norway
Foreign lands — Pakistan
Foreign lands — Panama
Foreign lands — Persia
Foreign lands — Peru
Foreign lands — Philippines
Foreign lands — Poland
Foreign lands — Portugal
Foreign lands — Puerto Rico
Foreign lands — Russia
Foreign lands — Scotland
Foreign lands — Siam see
Foreign lands — Thailand
Foreign lands — South
America
Foreign lands — South Sea
Islands
Foreign lands — Spain
Foreign lands — Sweden
Foreign lands — Switzerland
Foreign lands — Thailand
Foreign lands — Tibet
Foreign lands — Turkey
Foreign lands — Tyrol
Foreign lands — Ukraine
Foreign lands — Vatican
City
Foreign languages
Forest rangers see Careers
— park rangers
Forest, woods
Forgetfulness see Behavior
— forgetfulness
Format, unusual
Format, unusual —
cardboard pages
Fortune see Character traits
— luck
Fortune tellers see Careers
— fortune tellers
Fourth of July see Holidays
— Fourth of July
Foxes see Animals — foxes
France see Foreign lands —
France
Freedom see Character traits
— freedom
Friendship
Frogs and toads

Games
Gangs see Clubs, gangs

Garage sales
Garbage collectors see
Careers — garbage
collectors
Gardening see Activities —
gardening
Geese see Birds — geese
Generosity see Character
traits — generosity
Gerbils see Animals —
gerbils
Germany see Foreign lands
— Germany
Ghosts
Giants
Gilbert Islands see Foreign
lands — South Sea Islands
Giraffes see Animals —
giraffes
Glasses
Gnomes see Elves and little
people
Goats see Animals — goats
Goblins
Gorillas see Animals —
gorillas
Gossip see Behavior —
gossip
Grammar see Language
Grandparents see Family life
— grandparents,
great-grandparents
Grasshoppers see Insects —
grasshoppers
Great-grandparents see
Family life —
grandparents,
great-grandparents
Greece see Foreign lands —
Greece
Greed see Behavior — greed
Griffins see Mythical
creatures
Grocery stores see Shopping;
Stores
Groundhog Day see Holidays
— Groundhog Day
Groundhogs see Animals —
groundhogs
Growing up see Behavior —
growing up
Guinea pigs see Animals —
guinea pigs
Guns see Weapons
Guyana see Foreign lands —
Guyana
Gymnastics see Sports —
gymnastics
Gypsies

Hair
Halloween see Holidays —
Halloween
Hamsters see Animals —
hamsters
Handicaps
Handicaps — blindness
Handicaps — deafness
Hands see Anatomy
Hanukkah see Holidays —
Hanukkah

Happiness *see* Emotions — happiness

Hares *see* Animals — rabbits

Hate *see* Emotions — hate

Hawaii

Hawks *see* Birds — hawks

Health

Hearing *see* Senses

Heavy equipment *see* Machines

Hedgehogs *see* Animals — hedgehogs

Helicopters

Helpfulness *see* Character traits — helpfulness

Hens *see* Birds — chickens

Hibernation

Hiding *see* Behavior — hiding

Hiding things *see* Behavior — hiding things

Hieroglyphics

Hippopotami *see* Animals — hippopotami

Hobby horses *see* Toys — rocking horses

Hockey *see* Sports — hockey

Holidays

Holidays — April Fools' Day

Holidays — Chanukah *see* Holidays — Hanukkah

Holidays — Chinese New Year

Holidays — Christmas

Holidays — Cinco de Mayo

Holidays — Columbus Day

Holidays — Easter

Holidays — Fourth of July

Holidays — Groundhog Day

Holidays — Halloween

Holidays — Hanukkah

Holidays — Independence Day *see* Holidays — Fourth of July

Holidays — Mardi Gras *see* Mardi Gras

Holidays — Memorial Day

Holidays — Mother's Day

Holidays — New Year's

Holidays — Passover

Holidays — St. Patrick's Day

Holidays — Thanksgiving

Holidays — Valentine's Day

Holidays — Washington's Birthday

Holland *see* Foreign lands — Holland

Homes *see* Houses

Honesty *see* Character traits — honesty

Honey bees *see* Insects — bees

Horses *see* Animals — horses

Horses, rocking *see* Toys — rocking horses

Hospitals

Hotels

Houses

Humor

Hungary *see* Foreign lands — Hungary

Hunting *see* Sports — hunting

Hurrying *see* Behavior — hurrying

Hyenas *see* Animals — hyenas

Ice skating *see* Sports — ice skating

Iguanas *see* Reptiles — iguanas

Illness

Illusions, optical *see* Optical illusions

Illustrators, children *see* Children as illustrators

Imaginary friends *see* Imagination — imaginary friends

Imagination

Imagination — imaginary friends

Imitation *see* Behavior — imitation

In and out *see* Concepts — in and out

Incentive *see* Character traits — ambition

Independence Day *see* Holidays — Fourth of July

India *see* Foreign lands — India

Indians, American *see* Ethnic groups in the U.S. — Indians

Indifference *see* Behavior — indifference

Individuality *see* Character traits — individuality

Indonesian Archipelago *see* Foreign lands — South Sea Islands

Insects

Insects — ants

Insects — bees

Insects — beetles

Insects — butterflies, caterpillars

Insects — caterpillars *see* Insects — butterflies, caterpillars

Insects — crickets

Insects — fireflies

Insects — fleas

Insects — flies

Insects — gnats

Insects — grasshoppers

Insects — lady birds *see* Insects — ladybugs

Insects — ladybugs

Insects — lightning bugs *see* Insects — fireflies

Insects — mosquitoes

Insects — moths

Insects — praying mantis

Insects — wasps

Interracial marriage *see* Marriage, interracial

Ireland *see* Foreign lands — Ireland

Islands

Israel *see* Foreign lands — Israel

Italy *see* Foreign lands — Italy

Jail *see* Prisons

Japan *see* Foreign lands — Japan

Japanese-Americans *see* Ethnic groups in the U.S. — Japanese-Americans

Jealousy *see* Emotions — envy, jealousy

Jesters *see* Clowns, jesters

Jewish culture

Jobs *see* Careers

Jokes *see* Riddles

Judges *see* Careers — judges

Jumping *see* Activities — jumping

Jungle

Kangaroos *see* Animals — kangaroos

Kindness *see* Character traits — kindness

Kindness to animals *see* Character traits — kindness to animals

Kings *see* Royalty

Kinkajous *see* Animals — kinkajous

Kites

Knights

Knitting *see* Activities — knitting

Koala bears *see* Animals — koala bears

Korea *see* Foreign lands — Korea

Lady birds *see* Insects — ladybugs

Ladybugs *see* Insects — ladybugs

Language

Language, foreign *see* Foreign languages

Lapland *see* Foreign lands — Lapland

Laundry

Law *see* Careers — judges; Crime

Laziness *see* Character traits — laziness

Left and right *see* Concepts — left and right

Left-handedness

Legends *see* Folk and fairy tales

Leopards *see* Animals — leopards

Leprechauns *see* Elves and little people

Letters

Librarians *see* Careers — librarians

Libraries

Lighthouses
Lightning bugs *see* Insects
— fireflies
Lights
Lions *see* Animals — lions
Lithuania *see* Foreign lands
— Lithuania
Little people *see* Elves and
little people
Littleness *see* Character traits
— smallness
Lizards *see* Reptiles —
lizards
Llamas *see* Animals —
llamas
Lobsters *see* Crustacea
Loneliness *see* Emotions —
loneliness
Losing things *see* Behavior
— losing things
Lost *see* Behavior — lost
Love *see* Emotions — love
Loyalty *see* Character traits
— loyalty
Luck *see* Character traits —
luck
Lying *see* Behavior — lying

Machines
Magic
Maids *see* Careers — maids
Mail *see* Letters
Mail carriers *see* Careers —
mail carriers
Malaysia *see* Foreign lands —
Malaysia
Manners *see* Etiquette
Mardi Gras
Marionettes *see* Puppets
Markets *see* Stores
Marriage, interracial
Marriages *see* Weddings
Math *see* Counting
Meanness *see* Character traits
— meanness
Measurement *see* Concepts
— measurement
Mechanical men *see* Robots
Memorial Day *see* Holidays
— Memorial Day
Mermaids *see* Mythical
creatures
Merry-go-rounds
Mexican-Americans *see*
Ethnic groups in the U.S.
— Mexican-Americans
Mexico *see* Foreign lands —
Mexico
Mice *see* Animals — mice
Middle ages
Military *see* Careers —
military
Mimes *see* Clowns, jesters
Miners *see* Careers —
miners
Minorities *see* Ethnic groups
in the U.S.
Mirages *see* Optical illusions
Misbehavior *see* Behavior —
misbehavior
Missions

Mist *see* Weather — fog
Mistakes *see* Behavior —
mistakes
Misunderstanding *see*
Behavior —
misunderstanding
Moles *see* Animals — moles
Money
Mongooses *see* Animals —
mongooses
Monkeys *see* Animals —
monkeys
Monsters
Months of the year *see* Days
of the week, months of the
year
Moon
Moose *see* Animals — moose
Mopeds *see* Motorcycles
Morning
Mosquitoes *see* Insects —
mosquitoes
Mother Goose *see* Nursery
rhymes
Mothers *see* Family life —
mothers
Mother's Day *see* Holidays
— Mother's Day
Moths *see* Insects — moths
Motorcycles
Moving
Mules *see* Animals — mules
Multi-ethnic *see* Ethnic
groups in the U.S.
Multiple birth children *see*
Triplets; Twins
Muppets *see* Puppets
Museums
Music
Musical instruments *see*
Music
Muskrats *see* Animals —
muskrats
Mysteries *see* Problem solving
Mythical creatures

Nagging *see* Behavior —
nagging
Names
Napping *see* Sleep
Native Americans *see* Ethnic
groups in the U.S. —
Eskimos; Ethnic groups in
the U.S. — Indians
Nature
Needing someone *see*
Behavior — needing
someone
Neighborhoods *see*
Communities,
neighborhoods
New Guinea *see* Foreign
lands — New Guinea
New Year's *see* Holidays —
New Year's
Night
Nightingales *see* Birds —
nightingales
Nightmares *see* Bedtime;
Goblins; Monsters; Night;
Sleep

No text *see* Wordless
Noah *see* Religion — Noah
Noise, sounds
Norway *see* Foreign lands —
Norway
Noses *see* Anatomy
Numbers *see* Counting
Nuns *see* Careers — nuns
Nursery rhymes
Nursery school *see* School
Nurses *see* Careers — nurses

Oceans *see* Sea and seashore
Octopuses
Oil
Old age
Olympics *see* Sports —
Olympics
Only child *see* Family life —
only child
Opossums *see* Animals —
possums
Opposites *see* Concepts —
opposites
Optical illusions
Optimism *see* Character traits
— optimism
Orphans
Ostracism *see* Character traits
— being different
Ostriches *see* Birds —
ostriches
Otters *see* Animals — otters
Out and in *see* Concepts —
in and out
Owls *see* Birds — owls

Pack rats *see* Animals —
pack rats
Painters *see* Activities —
painting; Careers — artists
Painting *see* Activities —
painting
Pakistan *see* Foreign lands —
Pakistan
Panama *see* Foreign lands —
Panama
Panthers *see* Animals —
leopards
Paper
Parades
Parakeets *see* Birds —
parakeets, parrots
Park rangers *see* Careers —
park rangers
Parrots *see* Birds —
parakeets, parrots
Participation
Parties
Passover *see* Holidays —
Passover
Patience *see* Character traits
— patience
Peacocks, peahens *see* Birds
— peacocks, peahens
Peddlers *see* Careers —
peddlers
Pelicans *see* Birds —
pelicans

Penguins *see* Birds —
  penguins
Perseverance *see* Character
  traits — perseverance
Persia *see* Foreign lands —
  Persia
Persistence *see* Character
  traits — persistence
Perspective *see* Concepts —
  perspective
Peru *see* Foreign lands —
  Peru
Petroleum *see* Oil
Pets
Philippines *see* Foreign lands
  — Philippines
Phoenix *see* Mythical
  creatures
Photography *see* Activities —
  photographing
Physicians *see* Careers —
  doctors
Picnicking *see* Activities —
  picnicking
Pigeons *see* Birds — pigeons
Pigs *see* Animals — pigs
Pilots *see* Careers —
  airplane pilots
Pirates
Pixies *see* Elves and little
  people; Fairies
Planes *see* Airplanes, airports
Plants
Playing *see* Activities —
  playing
Plays *see* Theater
Poetry, rhyme
Poland *see* Foreign lands —
  Poland
Police officers *see* Careers —
  police officers
Poltergeists *see* Ghosts
Poor *see* Poverty
Pop-up books *see* Format,
  unusual
Porcupines *see* Animals —
  porcupines
Porpoise *see* Animals —
  dolphins
Portugal *see* Foreign lands —
  Portugal
Possums *see* Animals —
  possums
Poverty
Power failure
Practicality *see* Character
  traits — practicality
Prairie dogs *see* Animals —
  prairie dogs
Praying mantis *see* Insects —
  praying mantis
Prejudice
Pride *see* Character traits —
  pride
Princes *see* Royalty
Princesses *see* Royalty
Prisons
Problem solving
Progress
Puerto Rican-Americans *see*
  Ethnic groups in the U.S.
  — Puerto Rican-Americans

Puerto Rico *see* Foreign lands
  — Puerto Rico
Puffins *see* Birds — puffins
Pumas *see* Animals —
  cougars
Puppets
Puzzles *see* Rebuses; Riddles

Queens *see* Royalty
Questioning *see* Character
  traits — questioning
Quicksand *see* Sand

Rabbits *see* Animals —
  rabbits
Raccoons *see* Animals —
  raccoons
Racing *see* Sports — racing
Railroad engineers *see*
  Careers — railroad
  engineers
Railroads *see* Trains
Rain *see* Weather — rain
Rainbows *see* Weather —
  rainbows
Rangers *see* Careers — park
  rangers
Rats *see* Animals — rats
Ravens *see* Birds — ravens
Reading *see* Activities —
  reading
Rebuses
Reindeer *see* Animals —
  reindeer
Religion
Religion — Noah
Repetitive stories *see*
  Cumulative tales
Reptiles
Reptiles — alligators,
  crocodiles
Reptiles — crocodiles *see*
  Reptiles — alligators,
  crocodiles
Reptiles — iguanas
Reptiles — lizards
Reptiles — snakes
Reptiles — turtles
Rest *see* Sleep
Rhinoceros *see* Animals —
  rhinoceros
Rhyming text *see* Poetry,
  rhyme
Riddles
Right and left *see* Concepts
  — left and right
Rivers
Roads
Robbers *see* Crime
Robins *see* Birds — robins
Robots
Rockets *see* Space and space
  ships
Rocking horses *see* Toys —
  rocking horses
Rocks
Roosters *see* Birds —
  chickens
Royalty

Running *see* Sports —
  racing
Running away *see* Behavior
  — running away
Russia *see* Foreign lands —
  Russia

Sadness *see* Emotions —
  sadness
Safety
Sailors *see* Careers —
  military
Saint Patrick's Day *see*
  Holidays — St. Patrick's
  Day
Sand
Sandcastles *see* Sand
Sandman
Sandpipers *see* Birds —
  sandpipers
Saving things *see* Behavior
  — saving things
Scarecrows
School
Science
Scotland *see* Foreign lands —
  Scotland
Scuba diving *see* Sports —
  skin diving
Sea and seashore
Sea gulls *see* Birds — sea
  gulls
Sea lions *see* Animals — sea
  lions
Sea serpents *see* Monsters;
  Mythical creatures
Seahorses *see* Crustacea
Seals *see* Animals — seals
Seamstresses *see* Careers —
  seamstresses
Seashore *see* Sea and
  seashore
Seasons
Seasons — autumn *see*
  Seasons — fall
Seasons — fall
Seasons — spring
Seasons — summer
Seasons — winter
Secret codes
Secrets *see* Behavior —
  secrets
Seeing *see* Senses
Seeking better things *see*
  Behavior — seeking better
  things
Self-concept
Self-esteem *see* Self-concept
Self-image *see* Self-concept
Selfishness *see* Character
  traits — selfishness
Senses
Shadows
Shakespeare
Shape *see* Concepts — shape
Shaped books *see* Format,
  unusual
Sharing *see* Behavior —
  sharing
Sheep *see* Animals — sheep
Ships *see* Boats, ships

Shoemakers *see* Careers — shoemakers
Shopping
Shops *see* Stores
Shows *see* Theater
Shrews *see* Animals — shrews
Shyness *see* Character traits — shyness
Siam *see* Foreign lands — Thailand
Sibling rivalry
Sickness *see* Health; Illness
Sisters *see* Family life; Sibling rivalry
Size *see* Concepts — size
Skating *see* Sports — ice skating
Skiing *see* Sports — skiing
Skin diving *see* Sports — skin diving
Skunks *see* Animals — skunks
Sky
Sleep
Sleight-of-hand *see* Magic
Sloths *see* Animals — sloths
Smallness *see* Character traits — smallness
Smelling *see* Senses
Snails *see* Animals — snails
Snakes *see* Reptiles — snakes
Snow *see* Weather — snow
Snowmen
Snowplows *see* Machines
Society Islands *see* Foreign lands — South Sea Islands
Soldiers *see* Careers — military
Soldiers, toy *see* Toys — soldiers
Solitude *see* Behavior — solitude
Songs
Sounds *see* Noise, sounds
South America *see* Foreign lands — South America
South Sea Islands *see* Foreign lands — South Sea Islands
Space and space ships
Spain *see* Foreign lands — Spain
Sparrows *see* Birds — sparrows
Spectacles *see* Glasses
Speech *see* Language
Speed *see* Concepts — speed
Spelunking *see* Caves
Spiders
Split page books *see* Format, unusual
Spooks *see* Ghosts; Goblins
Sports
Sports — baseball
Sports — basketball
Sports — bicycling
Sports — camping
Sports — fishing
Sports — football
Sports — gymnastics

Sports — hockey
Sports — hunting
Sports — ice skating
Sports — Olympics
Sports — racing
Sports — skiing
Sports — skin diving
Sports — soccer
Sports — surfing
Sports — swimming
Sports — T-ball
Sports — tennis
Sports — wrestling
Spring *see* Seasons — spring
Squirrels *see* Animals — squirrels
St. Patrick's Day *see* Holidays — St. Patrick's Day
Stage *see* Theater
Stars
Stealing *see* Behavior — stealing
Steam shovels *see* Machines
Steamrollers *see* Machines
Stepchildren *see* Divorce; Family life — stepfamilies
Stepfamilies *see* Divorce; Family life — stepfamilies
Stepparents *see* Divorce; Family life — stepfamilies
Stones *see* Rocks
Stores
Storks *see* Birds — storks
Storms *see* Weather — storms
Streams *see* Rivers
Streets *see* Roads
String
Stubbornness *see* Character traits — stubbornness
Sullivan Islands *see* Foreign lands — South Sea Islands
Summer *see* Seasons — summer
Sun
Surfing *see* Sports — surfing
Swallows *see* Birds — swallows
Swans *see* Birds — swans
Sweden *see* Foreign lands — Sweden
Swimming *see* Sports — swimming
Swinging *see* Activities — swinging
Switzerland *see* Foreign lands — Switzerland

T-ball *see* Sports — T-ball
Tailors *see* Careers — tailors
Talking to strangers *see* Behavior — talking to strangers
Tapirs *see* Animals — tapirs
Tasting *see* Senses
Taxi drivers *see* Careers — taxi drivers
Taxis
Teachers *see* Careers — teachers

Teddy bears *see* Toys — teddy bears
Teeth
Telephone
Telephone operators *see* Careers — telephone operators
Television
Telling time *see* Clocks; Time
Temper tantrums *see* Emotions — anger
Tennis *see* Sports — tennis
Textless *see* Wordless
Thailand *see* Foreign lands — Thailand
Thanksgiving *see* Holidays — Thanksgiving
Theater
Tibet *see* Foreign lands — Tibet
Tigers *see* Animals — tigers
Time
Tin soldiers *see* Toys — soldiers
Toads *see* Frogs and toads
Tongue twisters
Tools
Tortoises *see* Reptiles — turtles
Toucans *see* Birds — toucans
Touching *see* Senses
Towns *see* City
Toys
Toys — balloons
Toys — balls
Toys — bears *see* Toys — teddy bears
Toys — blocks
Toys — dolls
Toys — hobby horses *see* Toys — rocking horses
Toys — pandas *see* Toys — teddy bears
Toys — rocking horses
Toys — soldiers
Toys — teddy bears
Toys — tin soldiers *see* Toys — soldiers
Toys — trains
Tractors *see* Machines
Trading *see* Activities — trading
Traffic signs
Train engineers *see* Careers — railroad engineers
Trains
Trains, toy *see* Toys — trains
Transportation
Traveling *see* Activities — traveling
Trees
Trickery *see* Behavior — trickery
Tricks *see* Magic
Triplets
Trolleys *see* Cable cars, trolleys
Trolls
Truck drivers *see* Careers — truck drivers

Trucks
Turkey *see* Foreign lands — Turkey
Turkeys *see* Birds — turkeys
Turtles *see* Reptiles — turtles
TV *see* Television
Twilight
Twins
Tyrol *see* Foreign lands — Tyrol

Ukraine *see* Foreign lands — Ukraine
Umbrellas
Unhappiness *see* Emotions — happiness; Emotions — sadness
UNICEF
Unicorns *see* Mythical creatures
U.S. History
Unnoticed *see* Behavior — unnoticed, unseen
Unseen *see* Behavior — unnoticed, unseen
Unusual format *see* Format, unusual
Up and down *see* Concepts — up and down

Vacationing *see* Activities — vacationing
Vacuum cleaners *see* Machines
Valentine's Day *see* Holidays — Valentine's Day
Values
Vampires *see* Monsters
Vanity *see* Character traits — vanity
Vatican City *see* Foreign lands — Vatican City
Veterinarians *see* Careers — veterinarians
Violence, anti-violence

Volcanoes
Vultures *see* Birds — vultures

Waiters *see* Careers — waiters, waitresses
Waitresses *see* Careers — waiters, waitresses
Walking *see* Activities — walking
Walruses *see* Animals — walruses
War
Washington's Birthday *see* Holidays — Washington's Birthday
Wasps *see* Insects — wasps
Watches *see* Clocks
Water buffaloes *see* Animals — water buffaloes
Weapons
Weasels *see* Animals — weasels
Weather
Weather — clouds
Weather — cold
Weather — droughts
Weather — floods
Weather — fog
Weather — mist *see* Weather — fog
Weather — rain
Weather — rainbows
Weather — snow
Weather — storms
Weather — wind
Weaving *see* Activities — weaving
Weddings
Weekdays *see* Days of the week, months of the year
Weight *see* Concepts — weight
Werewolves *see* Monsters
Whales *see* Animals — whales
Wheels

Whistling *see* Activities — whistling
Willfulness *see* Character traits — willfulness
Wind *see* Weather — wind
Windmills
Window cleaners *see* Careers — window cleaners
Winter *see* Seasons — winter
Wishing *see* Behavior — wishing
Witches
Wizards
Wolves *see* Animals — wolves
Woodchucks *see* Animals — groundhogs
Woodpeckers *see* Birds — woodpeckers
Woods *see* Forest, woods
Word games *see* Language
Wordless
Words *see* Language
Working *see* Activities — working
World
Worms *see* Animals — worms
Worrying *see* Behavior — worrying
Wrecking machines *see* Machines
Wrens *see* Birds — wrens
Wrestling *see* Sports — wrestling
Writers *see* Careers — writers
Writing *see* Activities — writing
Writing letters *see* Letters

Yaks *see* Animals — yaks

Zebras *see* Animals — zebras
Zodiac
Zoos

Subject Guide

This is a subject-arranged guide to picture books. Under appropiate subject headings and subheadings, titles appear alphabetically by author name, or by title when author is unknown. Complete bibliographic information for each title cited will be found in the Bibliographic Guide.

Aardvarks *see* Animals—aardvarks

ABC books

A is for alphabet
ABCDEF...
Abrons, Mary. For Alice a palace
Alda, Arlene. Arlene Alda's ABC
Alexander, Anne. ABC of cars and trucks
Anglund, Joan Walsh. A is for always
Anno, Mitsumasa. Anno's alphabet
  Anno's magical ABC
Arnosky, Jim. Mouse numbers and letters
  Mouse writing
Asch, Frank. Little Devil's ABC
Azarian, Mary. A farmer's alphabet
Balian, Lorna. Humbug potion
Barry, Katharina. A is for anything
Barry, Robert E. Animals around the world
Baskin, Leonard. Hosie's alphabet
Bayer, Jane. A my name is Alice
Beller, Janet. A-B-C-ing
Berenstain, Stan. The Berenstain's B book
Berger, Terry. Ben's ABC day
Bishop, Ann. Riddle-iculous rid-alphabet book
Black, Floyd. Alphabet cat
Bond, Jean Carey. A is for Africa
Boxer, Deborah. 26 ways to be somebody else
Boynton, Sandra. A is for angry
Brown, Judith Gwyn. Alphabet dreams
Brown, Marcia. All butterflies
  Peter Piper's alphabet

Brown, Margaret Wise. Sleepy ABC
Bruna, Dick. B is for bear
Brunhoff, Laurent de. Babar's ABC
Budd, Lillian. The pie wagon
Budney, Blossom. N is for nursery school
Burningham, John. John Burningham's ABC
Burton, Marilee Robin. Aaron awoke
Chardiet, Bernice. C is for circus
Charles, Donald. Shaggy dog's animal alphabet
Charlip, Remy. Handtalk
Chase, Catherine. An alphabet book
  Baby mouse learns his ABC's
Chess, Victoria. Alfred's alphabet walk
Chwast, Seymour. Still another alphabet book
Cleary, Beverly. The hullabaloo ABC
Cleaver, Elizabeth. ABC
Clifton, Lucille. The black B C's
Cohen, Peter Zachary. Authorized autumn charts of the Upper Red Canoe River country
Coletta, Irene. From A to Z
Cooney, Barbara. A garland of games and other diversions
Corbett, Scott. The mysterious Zetabet
Cremins, Robert. My animal ABC
Crews, Donald. We read A to Z
Crowther, Robert. The most amazing hide and seek alphabet book
Dauphin, Francine Legrand. A French A. B. C.
DeLage, Ida. ABC Easter bunny
  ABC triplets at the zoo
Delaunay, Sonia. Sonia Delaunay's alphabet
Duke, Kate. The guinea pig ABC
Duvoisin, Roger Antoine. A for the ark
Elchenberg, Fritz. Ape in cape
Elting, Mary. Q is for duck
Emberley, Ed. Ed Emberley's ABC
Falls, C B (Charles Buckles). ABC book
Farber, Norma. As I was crossing Boston Common
Feelings, Muriel. Jambo means hello

Fife, Dale. Adam's ABC

Floyd, Lucy. Agatha's alphabet, with her very own dictionary

Freeman, Don. Add-a-line alphabet

Fujikawa, Gyo. Gyo Fujikawa's A to Z picture book

Gág, Wanda. ABC bunny

Gantz, David. The genie bear with the light brown hair word book

Garten, Jan. The alphabet tale

Greenaway, Kate. A apple pie

Gretz, Susanna. Teddy bears ABC

Grossbart, Francine. A big city

Gundersheimer, Karen. A B C say with me

Gunning, Monica. The two Georges

Hague, Kathleen. Alphabears

Harada, Joyce. It's the ABC book

Harrison, Ted. A northern alphabet

Hillman, Priscilla. A Merry-Mouse Christmas A B C

Hoban, Tana. A B See!

Hoberman, Mary Ann. Nuts to you and nuts to me

Hoguet, Susan Ramsay. I unpacked my grandmother's trunk

Holabird, Katharine. The little mouse ABC

Holl, Adelaide. The ABC of cars, trucks and machines

Hyman, Trina Schart. A little alphabet

Ilsley, Velma. A busy day for Chris
M is for moving

Ipcar, Dahlov. I love my anteater with an A

Isadora, Rachel. City seen from A to Z

Jefferds, Vincent. Disney's elegant ABC book.

Jewell, Nancy. ABC cat

Johnson, Crockett. Harold's ABC

Kitchen, Bert. Animal alphabet

Kuskin, Karla. ABCDEFGHIJKLMNOPQRSTUVW-XYZ

Lalicki, Barbara. If there were dreams to sell

Lalli, Judy. Feelings alphabet

Leander, Ed. Q is for crazy

Lear, Edward. ABC
An Edward Lear alphabet
Nonsense alphabets
A little ABC book.

Little, Mary E. ABC for the library

Lobel, Arnold. On Market Street

Low, Joseph. Adam's book of odd creatures

McGinley, Phyllis. All around the town

McMillan, Bruce. The alphabet symphony

Manson, Beverlie. The fairies' alphabet book

Margalit, Avishai. The Hebrew alphabet book

Mayer, Mercer. Little Monster's alphabet book

Mendoza, George. The alphabet boat
Alphabet sheep
Norman Rockwell's American ABC

Merriam, Eve. Good night to Annie

Miles, Miska. Apricot ABC

Miller, Edna. Mousekin's ABC

Miller, Jane. Farm alphabet book

Milne, A A (Alan Alexander). Pooh's alphabet book

Moak, Allan. A big city ABC

Montresor, Beni. A for angel

Morice, Dave. A visit from St. Alphabet

Morse, Samuel French. All in a suitcase

Moss, Jeffrey. The Sesame Street ABC storybook

Mother Goose. In a pumpkin shell

Munari, Bruno. ABC

Musgrove, Margaret. Ashanti to Zulu.

Newberry, Clare Turlay. The kittens' ABC

Niland, Deborah. ABC of monsters

Obligado, Lilian. Faint frogs feeling feverish and other terrifically tantalizing tongue twisters

Ogle, Lucille. A B See

Oliver, Dexter. I want to be...

Oxenbury, Helen. Helen Oxenbury's ABC of things

Peaceable kingdom

Peppé, Rodney. The alphabet book

Petersham, Maud. An American ABC

Piatti, Celestino. Celestino Piatti's animal ABC

Rey, Hans Augusto. Curious George learns the alphabet
Look for the letters

Rojankovsky, Feodor. ABC, an alphabet of many things
Animals in the zoo

Rosario, Idalia. Idalia's project ABC

Ruben, Patricia. Apples to zippers

Scarry, Richard. Richard Scarry's ABC word book
Richard Scarry's great big schoolhouse

The Sea World alphabet book

Sendak, Maurice. Alligators all around

The Sesame Street book of letters

Seuss, Dr. Dr. Seuss's ABC
Hooper Humperdink...? Not him!

Shuttlesworth, Dorothy E. ABC of buses

Smith, William Jay. Puptents and pebbles

Steiner, Charlotte. Charlotte Steiner's ABC

Stevenson, James. Grandpa's great city tour

Waber, Bernard. An anteater named
Arthur
Walters, Marguerite. The city-country
ABC
Watson, Clyde. Applebet
Watson, Nancy Dingman. What does A
begin with?
Wild, Robin. The bears' ABC book
Williams, Garth. The big golden animal
ABC
Wilson, Barbara. ABC et/and 123
Yolen, Jane. All in the woodland early

Accordion books see Format, unusual

Activities

Alderson, Sue Ann. Bonnie McSmithers
is at it again!
Alexander, Sue. Witch, Goblin and
Ghost's book of things to do
Allington, Richard L. Feelings
Hearing
Looking
Smelling
Tasting
Touching
Andre, Evelyn M. Places I like to be
Arnold, Caroline. How do we have fun?
Azarian, Mary. A farmer's alphabet
Behrens, June. Can you walk the plank?
Beller, Janet. A-B-C-ing
Bennett, Jill. Days are where we live and
other poems
Brann, Esther. A book for baby
Brown, Elinor. The little story book
Brown, Margaret Wise. The little fur
family
Brunhoff, Jean de. Babar's anniversary
album
Bryant, Dean. Here am I
Buck, Pearl S (Pearl Sydenstricker).
Stories for little children
Bulla, Clyde Robert. Daniel's duck
Burdekin, Harold. A child's grace
Burningham, John. Skip trip
Sniff shout
Wobble pop
Calmenson, Stephanie. The
kindergarten book
Carlson, Nancy. Bunnies and their
hobbies
Cartlidge, Michelle. The bear's bazaar
A mouse's diary
Carton, Lonnie Caming. Mommies
Chernoff, Goldie Taub. Clay-dough,
play-dough
Just a box?
Pebbles and pods
Puppet party
Cole, Ann. I saw a purple cow
Purple cow to the rescue

Crume, Marion W. Let me see you try
Listen!
What do you say?
Delton, Judy. I'm telling you now
Dinosaurs and monsters
Ernst, Lisa Campbell. Sam Johnson and
the blue ribbon quilt
Erskine, Jim. Bert and Susie's messy tale
Fair, Sylvia. The bedspread
Faunce-Brown, Daphne. Snuffles' house
Flournoy, Valerie. The best time of day
Fujikawa, Gyo. My favorite thing
Surprise! Surprise!
Gibbons, Gail. The missing maple syrup
sap mystery
Gipson, Morrell. Hello, Peter
Goor, Ron. In the driver's seat
Hallinan, P K (Patrick K). I'm glad to be
me
Just being alone
Holzenthaler, Jean. My feet do
My hands can
Hynard, Julia. Percival's party
Hynard, Stephen. Snowy the rabbit
Jonas, Ann. When you were a baby
Le-Tan, Pierre. The afternoon cat
Lilly, Kenneth. Animal builders
Animal climbers
Animal jumpers
Animal runners
Animal swimmers
Lionni, Leo. Let's make rabbits
McKié, Roy. Snow
McNaughton, Colin. Autumn
Winter
Maestro, Betsy. Busy day
Mangin, Marie-France. Suzette and
Nicholas and the seasons clock
Masks and puppets
My day.
Myers, Arthur. Kids do amazing things
Nelson, Brenda. Mud fore sale
Noble, Trinka Hakes. The day Jimmy's
boa ate the wash
Parish, Peggy. I can — can you?
Peyo. What do smurfs do all day?
Pitcher, Caroline. Animals
Cars and boats
Rockwell, Harlow. I did it
Look at this
Ross, H L. Not counting monsters
Rubel, Nicole. Me and my kitty
Rukeyser, Muriel. More night
Scarry, Richard. Richard Scarry's busy
busy world
Simon, Norma. What do I do?
Thorne, Jenny. My uncle
Tudor, Tasha. A time to keep
Türk, Hanne. The rope skips Max
Vasiliu, Marcea. What's happening?
Winteringham, Victoria. Penguin day

Zalben, Jane Breskin. Oliver and Alison's week

Activities — babysitting

Abel, Ruth. The new sitter
Berenstain, Stan. The Berenstain bears and the sitter
Berman, Linda. The goodbye painting
Blaustein, Muriel. Baby Mabu and Auntie Moose
Brandenberg, Franz. Leo and Emily and the dragon
Carlson, Natalie Savage. Marie Louise's heyday
Carrick, Carol. The climb
Cazet, Denys. Big shoe, little shoe
Chalmers, Mary. Be good, Harry
Christelow, Eileen. Jerome the babysitter
Cole, William. What's good for a three-year-old?
Coombs, Patricia. Dorrie and the goblin
Crowley, Arthur. Bonzo Beaver
Finfer, Celentha. Grandmother dear
Greenberg, Barbara. The bravest babysitter
Harris, Robie H. Don't forget to come back
Hughes, Shirley. George the babysitter
Hurd, Edith Thacher. Hurry hurry! Stop, stop
Lawson, Annetta. The lucky yak
Moore, Lilian. Little Raccoon and no trouble at all
Newberry, Clare Turlay. T-Bone, the baby-sitter
Puner, Helen Walker. The sitter who didn't sit
Quackenbush, Robert M. Henry babysits
Rayner, Mary. Mr. and Mrs. Pig's evening out
Schick, Eleanor. Peter and Mr. Brandon
Sendak, Maurice. Outside over there
Van den Honert, Dorry. Demi the baby sitter
Wahl, Jan. Peter and the troll baby
Watson, Jane Werner. My friend the babysitter
Watson, Pauline. Curley Cat baby-sits
Wells, Rosemary. Stanley and Rhoda
Williams, Barbara. Jeremy isn't hungry
Zweifel, Frances. Animal baby-sitters

Activities — ballooning

Adams, Adrienne. The great Valentine's Day balloon race
Calhoun, Mary. Hot-air Henry
Coerr, Eleanor. The big balloon race
Geisert, Arthur. Pa's balloon and other pig tales
Goffe, Toni. Toby's animal rescue service
Quin-Harkin, Janet. Benjamin's balloon
Wegen, Ron. The balloon trip
Wildsmith, Brian. Bear's adventure

Activities — bathing

Alborough, Jez. Bare bear
Allen, Pamela. Mr. Archimedes' bath
Ambrus, Victor G. The Sultan's bath
Aulaire, Ingri Mortenson d'. Children of the northlights
Bethell, Jean. Bathtime.
Burningham, John. Time to get out of the bath, Shirley
Hazen, Barbara Shook. The me I see
Henkes, Kevin. Clean enough
Jackson, Ellen B. The bear in the bathtub
Lindbloom, Steven. Let's give kitty a bath!
Lindgren, Barbro. Sam's bath
McLeod, Emilie Warren. One snail and me
McPhail, David. Andrew's bath
Manushkin, Fran. Bubblebath!
Paterson, Diane. The bathtub ocean
Reavin, Sam. Hurray for Captain Jane!
Rudolph, Marguerita. Sharp and shiny
Slate, Joseph. The mean, clean, giant canoe machine
Willis, Jeanne. The tale of Georgie Grub
Yolen, Jane. No bath tonight
Zion, Gene. Harry, the dirty dog

Activities — cooking

Brown, Marcia. Skipper John's cook
Brunhoff, Laurent de. Babar learns to cook
Cauley, Lorinda Bryan. The bake-off Pease porridge hot
Cunliffe, John. The king's birthday cake
Da Rif, Andrea. The blueberry cake that little fox baked
De Paola, Tomie. Pancakes for breakfast
The popcorn book
Things to make and do for Valentine's Day
Devlin, Wende. Old Black Witch
Old Witch and the polka-dot ribbon
Old Witch rescues Halloween
Gibbons, Gail. The too-great bread bake book
Gretz, Susanna. Teddybears cookbook
Hitte, Kathryn. Mexicallie soup
Hoban, Lillian. Arthur's Christmas cookies
Kahl, Virginia. The Duchess bakes a cake

Kitt, Tamara. Sam and the impossible thing

Krasilovsky, Phyllis. The man who entered a contest

Lasker, Joe. Lentil soup

Lemerise, Bruce. Sheldon's lunch

Levitin, Sonia. Nobody stole the pie

Lindman, Maj. Flicka, Ricka, Dicka bake a cake

Lindsey, Treska. When Batistine made bread

Long, Earlene. Johnny's egg

Miller, Alice P. The mouse family's blueberry pie

Parker, Nancy Winslow. Love from Aunt Betty

Petie, Haris. The seed the squirrel dropped

Rice, Eve. Benny bakes a cake

Rockwell, Anne F. The Mother Goose cookie-candy book

Schwalje, Marjory. Mr. Angelo

Tornborg, Pat. The Sesame Street cookbook

Ungerer, Tomi. Zeralda's ogre

Young, Miriam Burt. The sugar mouse cake

Activities — dancing

Allen, Pamela. Bertie and the bear

Ambrus, Victor G. The seven skinny goats

Ancona, George. Dancing is

Andersen, H C (Hans Christian). The red shoes

Bianco, Margery Williams. The hurdy-gurdy man

Bornstein, Ruth Lercher. The dancing man

Bottner, Barbara. Messy
Myra

Charlot, Martin. Felisa and the magic tikling bird

Cox, David. Ayu and the perfect moon

De Paola, Tomie. Oliver Button is a sissy

Edelman, Elaine. Boom-de-boom

Fern, Eugene. Pepito's story

Getz, Arthur. Humphrey, the dancing pig

Grimm, Jacob. The twelve dancing princesses, ill. by Dennis Hockerman
The twelve dancing princesses, ill. by Errol LeCain
The twelve dancing princesses, ill. by Uri Shulevitz

Hoban, Russell. The dancing tigers

Hoffmann, E T A. The nutcracker

Holabird, Katharine. Angelina and the princess
Angelina ballerina

Hurd, Edith Thacher. I dance in my red pajamas

Isadora, Rachel. Max
My ballet class
Opening night

Maiorano, Robert. A little interlude

Marshall, James. George and Martha encore

Mayer, Mercer. The queen always wanted to dance

Nelson, Esther L. Holiday singing and dancing games

Oxenbury, Helen. The dancing class

Quin-Harkin, Janet. Peter Penny's dance

Sorine, Stephanie Riva. Our ballet class

Tallon, Robert. Handella

Activities — digging

Aliki. Digging up dinosaurs

Cleary, Beverly. The real hole

Kumin, Maxine. Speedy digs downside up

Perkins, Al. The digging-est dog

Activities — flying

Anderson, Lonzo. Mr. Biddle and the birds

Arabian Nights. The flying carpet

Aulaire, Ingri Mortenson d'. Wings for Per

Ayal, Ora. The adventures of Chester the chest

Benchley, Nathaniel. The flying lessons of Gerald Pelican

Bradfield, Roger. The flying hockey stick

Brenner, Barbara. The flying patchwork quilt

Brock, Emma Lillian. Surprise balloon

Brown, Marc. Wings on things

Brown, Margaret Wise. Streamlined pig

Coombs, Patricia. Dorrie and the Halloween plot

Duvoisin, Roger Antoine. Petunia takes a trip

Florian, Douglas. Airplane ride

Gramatky, Hardie. Loopy

Hays, Hoffman Reynolds. Charley sang a song

Hill, Eric. Up there

Hoban, Russell. Ace Dragon Ltd.

Hughes, Shirley. Up and up

Jenny, Anne. The fantastic story of King Brioche the First

Jeschke, Susan. Perfect the pig

Kaufmann, John. Flying giants of long ago

Kojima, Naomi. The flying grandmother

Kuskin, Karla. Just like everyone else

Peet, Bill. Merle the high flying squirrel

Phleger, Fred B. Ann can fly
Provensen, Alice. The glorious flight
Ransome, Arthur. The fool of the world
  and the flying ship
Ross, Pat. Your first airplane trip
Stevenson, James. Grandpa's great city
  tour
Titus, Eve. Anatole over Paris
Trez, Denise. Maila and the flying
  carpet
Ungerer, Tomi. The Mellops go flying
Valens, Evans G. Wingfin and Topple
Watson, Clyde. Midnight moon
Wende, Philip. Bird boy
West, Ian. Silas, the first pig to fly
Wheeling, Lynn. When you fly
Wolkstein, Diane. The cool ride in the
  sky
  The magic wings
Young, Miriam Burt. If I flew a plane

Activities — gardening

Aliki. Corn is maize
  The story of Johnny Appleseed
Barrett, Judi. Old MacDonald had an
  apartment house
Berson, Harold. Pop! goes the turnip
Bishop, Gavin. Mrs. McGinty and the
  bizarre plant
Brown, Marc. Your first garden book
Browne, Caroline. Mrs. Christie's
  farmhouse
Cavagnaro, David. The pumpkin people
Collier, Ethel. Who goes there in my
  garden?
Craft, Ruth. Carrie Hepple's garden
DeJong, Meindert. Nobody plays with a
  cabbage
De Paola, Tomie. Four stories for four
  seasons
Domanska, Janina. The best of the
  bargain
Farjeon, Eleanor. Mr. Garden
Firmin, Peter. Chicken stew
Fontaine, Jan. The spaghetti tree
Fujikawa, Gyo. Let's grow a garden
Goldin, Augusta. Where does your
  garden grow?
Hader, Berta Hoerner. Mister Billy's
  gun
Hall, Fergus. Groundsel
Ichikawa, Satomi. Suzanne and Nicholas
  in the garden
Ipcar, Dahlov. The land of flowers
Johnson, Hannah Lyons. From seed to
  jack-o'-lantern
Keeping, Charles. Joseph's yard
Krauss, Ruth. The carrot seed
Le Tord, Bijou. Rabbit seeds
Lord, John Vernon. Mr. Mead and his
  garden

Marino, Dorothy. Buzzy Bear in the
  garden
Moore, Inga. The vegetable thieves
Morgenstern, Elizabeth. The little
  gardeners
Muntean, Michaela. Alligator's garden
Pike, Norman. The peach tree
Rockwell, Anne F. How my garden grew
Rockwell, Harlow. The compost heap
Rylant, Cynthia. This year's garden
Sharpe, Sara. Gardener George goes to
  town
Shecter, Ben. Partouche plants a seed
Taylor, Judy. Sophie and Jack help out
Trimby, Elisa. Mr. Plum's paradise
Westcott, Nadine Bernard. The giant
  vegetable garden

Activities — jumping

Bright, Robert. My hopping bunny
Stephens, Karen. Jumping

Activities — knitting

Holl, Adelaide. Mrs. McGarrity's
  peppermint sweater
Laurin, Anne. Little things
Storr, Catherine. Hugo and his
  grandma

Activities — painting

Adams, Adrienne. The Easter egg artists
Asch, Frank. Bread and honey
Becker, Edna. Nine hundred buckets of
  paint
Beim, Jerrold. Jay's big job
Bromhall, Winifred. Mary Ann's first
  picture
Duvoisin, Roger Antoine. The house of
  four seasons
Freeman, Don. The chalk box story
Kessler, Leonard P. Mr. Pine's purple
  house
Menter, Ian. The Albany Road mural
Miller, Warren. Pablo paints a picture
Morris, Jill. The boy who painted the
  sun
Pinkwater, Daniel Manus. The big
  orange splot
Spier, Peter. Oh, were they ever happy!
Weisgard, Leonard. Mr. Peaceable
  paints

Activities — photographing

Manushkin, Fran. The perfect
  Christmas picture
Seguin-Fontes, Marthe. A wedding book
Tison, Annette. Animal hide-and-seek
Türk, Hanne. Snapshot Max
Villarejo, Mary. The tiger hunt

Vincent, Gabrielle. Smile, Ernest and Celestine
Watts, Mabel. Weeks and weeks
Willard, Nancy. Simple pictures are best

Activities — picnicking

Asch, Frank. Sand cake
Benjamin, Alan. A change of plans
Berger, Terry. The turtles' picnic and other nonsense stories
Bishop, Bonnie. Ralph rides away
Bowden, Joan Chase. The Ginghams and the backward picnic
Brandenberg, Franz. A picnic, hurrah!
Brunhoff, Laurent de. Babar's picnic
Chalmers, Mary. Here comes the trolley
  Mr. Cat's wonderful surprise
Coombs, Patricia. Dorrie and the weather-box
Daugherty, James Henry. The picnic
Dickinson, Mary. Alex's outing
Ets, Marie Hall. In the forest
Freschet, Berniece. The ants go marching
Goodall, John S. The surprise picnic
Gordon, Margaret. Wilberforce goes on a picnic
Graham, Bob. Libby, Oscar and me
Hines, Anna Grossnickle. Come to the meadow
Hurd, Edith Thacher. No funny business
Kennedy, Jimmy. The teddy bears' picnic
Knox-Wagner, Elaine. The oldest kid
Lathrop, Dorothy Pulis. Who goes there?
McCully, Emily Arnold. Picnic
Marshall, Edward. Three by the sea
Rappus, Gerhard. When the sun was shining
Robertson, Lilian. Picnic woods
Saunders, Susan. Charles Rat's picnic
  Fish fry
Schroeder, Binette. Tuffa and the picnic
Taylor, Judy. Sophie and Jack
Tether, Graham. Skunk and possum
Van Stockum, Hilda. A day on skates
Vincent, Gabrielle. Ernest and Celestine's picnic
Wasmuth, Eleanor. The picnic basket
Watson, Clyde. Hickory stick rag
Westcott, Nadine Bernard. The giant vegetable garden
Wheeler, Cindy. Marmalade's picnic
Wood, Joyce. Grandmother Lucy goes on a picnic
Yeoman, John. The bear's water picnic

Activities — playing

Adam, Barbara. The big big box
Agee, Jon. Ellsworth
Ahlberg, Janet. Funnybones
Alexander, Martha G. I'll be the horse if you'll play with me
Arnold, Caroline. How do we have fun?
Artis, Vicki Kimmel. Pajama walking
Asch, Frank. Rebecka
Aulaire, Ingri Mortenson d'. Children of the northlights
Ayal, Ora. Ugbu
Bauer, Helen. Good times in the park
Baugh, Dolores M. Slides
  Swings
Benét, William Rose. Angels
Bethell, Jean. Playmates
Bonsall, Crosby Newell. And I mean it, Stanley
  Piggle
Bram, Elizabeth. Saturday morning lasts forever
Breinburg, Petronella. Doctor Shawn
Brown, Myra Berry. First night away from home
Bruna, Dick. Miffy at the playground
  Miffy's dream
Carroll, Ruth. Where's the bunny?
Cartlidge, Michelle. Pippin and Pod
Christian, Mary Blount. The sand lot
Clymer, Eleanor Lowenton. The big pile of dirt
Cole, William. What's good for a four-year-old?
  What's good for a six-year-old?
Emecheta, Buchi. Nowhere to play
Ets, Marie Hall. Play with me
Fitzhugh, Louise. Bang, bang, you're dead
Fujikawa, Gyo. That's not fair!
Gelman, Rita Golden. Dumb Joey
Hann, Jacquie. Follow the leader
Herz, Irene. Hey! Don't do that!
Hillert, Margaret. Play ball
Hughes, Shirley. Alfie's feet
Jewell, Nancy. Try and catch me
Johnson, Mildred D. Wait, skates!
Keats, Ezra Jack. Skates
  The snowy day
Keeping, Charles. Willie's fire-engine
Kent, Jack. Joey
Krahn, Fernando. Robot-bot-bot
Lenski, Lois. Let's play house
Lindgren, Barbro. The wild baby goes to sea
Lipkind, William. Sleepyhead
McNulty, Faith. When a boy wakes up in the morning
McPhail, David. Pig Pig rides
Maestro, Betsy. Harriet at play
Marino, Dorothy. Edward and the boxes

Mayers, Patrick. Just one more block
Meeks, Esther K. The hill that grew
Merriam, Eve. Boys and girls, girls and boys
Mitchell, Cynthia. Halloweena Hecatee Playtime
Moss, Elaine. Polar
Oppenheim, Joanne. James will never die
Oram, Hiawyn. In the attic
Oxenbury, Helen. Playing
Pearson, Susan. That's enough for one day!
Raebeck, Lois. Who am I?
Rockwell, Anne F. I play in my room
  My back yard
Rudolph, Marguerita. Sharp and shiny
Russ, Lavinia. Alec's sand castle
Sendak, Maurice. Maurice Sendak's Really Rosie
  The sign on Rosie's door
Snyder, Zilpha Keatley. Come on, Patsy
Steiner, Charlotte. Kiki's play house
  Look what Tracy found
Todd, Kathleen. Snow
Turkle, Brinton. Obadiah the Bold
Udry, Janice May. Mary Ann's mud day
Viorst, Judith. Sunday morning
Waber, Bernard. Ira sleeps over
Wahl, Jan. Push Kitty
Wasmuth, Eleanor. An alligator day
Watanabe, Shigeo. I can ride it!
  I'm the king of the castle!
Wells, Rosemary. A lion for Lewis
Winthrop, Elizabeth. Bunk beds
  That's mine
Young, Miriam Burt. Jellybeans for breakfast
Ziner, Feenie. Counting carnival
Zolotow, Charlotte. The park book
  The white marble

Activities — reading

Baker, Betty. Worthington Botts and the steam machine
Bank Street College of Education. People read
Black, Irma Simonton. The little old man who could not read
Bruna, Dick. I can read difficult words
Cohen, Miriam. When will I read?
DiFiori, Lawrence. My first book
Duvoisin, Roger Antoine. Petunia
Friskey, Margaret. Mystery of the gate sign
Funk, Tom. I read signs
Giff, Patricia Reilly. The beast in Ms. Rooney's room
Gillham, Bill. The early words picture book
Goor, Ron. Signs

Hallinan, P K (Patrick K). Just open a book
Hoban, Lillian. Arthur's prize reader
Hoban, Tana. I read signs
  I read symbols
  I walk and read
Hurd, Edith Thacher. Johnny Lion's book
Hutchins, Pat. The tale of Thomas Mead
Kuskin, Karla. Watson, the smartest dog in the U.S.A.
Lexau, Joan M. Olaf reads
McLenighan, Valjean. One whole doughnut, one doughnut hole
McPhail, David. Fix-it
Maestro, Betsy. Harriet reads signs and more signs
Minsberg, David. The book monster
Most, Bernard. There's an ant in Anthony
Ormerod, Jan. Reading
Ormondroyd, Edward. Broderick
Pearson, Susan. That's enough for one day!
Ross, Pat. M and M and the big bag
Seuss, Dr. I can read with my eyes shut

Activities — shopping *see* Shopping

Activities — swinging

Anderson, Robin. Sinabouda Lily
Baugh, Dolores M. Swings
Marks, Marcia Bliss. Swing me, swing tree

Activities — trading

Andersen, H C (Hans Christian). The old man is always right
Bushey, Jerry. The barge book
De Regniers, Beatrice Schenk. Was it a good trade?
Dick Whittington and his cat. Dick Whittington, ill. by Edward Ardizzone
  Dick Whittington, ill. by Marcia Brown
  Dick Whittington, ill. by Anthony Maitland
  Dick Whittington, ill. by Kurt Werth
Gill, Bob. A balloon for a blunderbuss
Hirsh, Marilyn. The pink suit
Hughes, Shirley. David and dog
Langstaff, John M. The swapping boy
Shannon, George. The Piney Woods peddler
Stroyer, Poul. It's a deal
Watts, Mabel. Something for you, something for me

Activities — traveling

Arnold, Caroline. How do we travel?
Austin, Margot. Willamet way
Baum, Louis. JuJu and the pirate
Beatty, Hetty Burlingame. Moorland pony
Bemelmans, Ludwig. Quito express
Billout, Guy. By camel or by car
Blech, Dietlind. Hello Irina
Bolognese, Don. A new day
Borchers, Elisabeth. Dear Sarah
Brandenberg, Franz. Everyone ready?
Brann, Esther. 'Round the world
Bridgman, Elizabeth. How to travel with grownups
  Nanny bear's cruise
Bröger, Achim. Bruno takes a trip
Bromhall, Winifred. Johanna arrives
Brown, Margaret Wise. Three little animals
Bruna, Dick. The sailor
Brunhoff, Jean de. The travels of Babar
Bunting, Eve. The traveling men of Ballycoo
Caines, Jeannette. Just us women
Carle, Eric. The rooster who set out to see the world
Chalmers, Mary. Here comes the trolley
Chwast, Seymour. Tall city, wide country
Cooney, Barbara. Miss Ramphius
Davis, Maggie S. The best way to Ripton
Demi. The adventures of Marco Polo
Fairclough, Chris. Take a trip to China
  Take a trip to England
  Take a trip to Holland
  Take a trip to Israel
  Take a trip to Italy
  Take a trip to West Germany
Goodall, John S. Paddy goes traveling
Grahame, Kenneth. The open road
Gray, Genevieve. How far, Felipe?
Greene, Carla. A motor holiday
Haley, Patrick. The little person
Hurd, Thacher. Hobo dog
Isadora, Rachel. No, Agatha!
Isele, Elizabeth. Pooks
Janosch. The trip to Panama
Kesselman, Wendy. There's a train going by my window
Kessler, Leonard P. Mrs. Pinc takes a trip
Lenski, Lois. Davy goes places
Lewin, Hugh. Jafta — the journey
Loof, Jan. Uncle Louie's fantastic sea voyage
McCormack, John E. Rabbit travels
McToots, Rudi. The kid's book of games for cars, trains and planes
May, Charles Paul. High-noon rocket

Meddaugh, Susan. Maude and Claude go abroad
Rose, Gerald. PB takes a holiday
Schulz, Charles M. Bon voyage, Charlie Brown (and don't come back!!)
Seuss, Dr. I had trouble getting to Solla Sollew
Steger, Hans-Ulrich. Traveling to Tripiti
Suben, Eric. Pigeon takes a trip
Tapio, Pat Decker. The lady who saw the good side of everything
Türk, Hanne. Max packs
Ungerer, Tomi. Adelaide
Vevers, Gwynne. Animals that travel

Activities — vacationing

Adams, Adrienne. The Easter egg artists
Bemelmans, Ludwig. Hansi
Bond, Michael. Paddington at the seaside
Bornstein, Ruth Lercher. I'll draw a meadow
Briggs, Raymond. Father Christmas goes on holiday
Bright, Robert. Georgie and the noisy ghost
Brunhoff, Laurent de. Babar's cousin, that rascal Arthur
  Babar's mystery
Carrick, Carol. The washout
Cole, Joanna. The Clown-Arounds go on vacation
Du Bois, William Pène. Otto and the magic potatoes
Duvoisin, Roger Antoine. Petunia takes a trip
Everton, Macduff. El circo magico modelo
Fatio, Louise. The happy lion's vacation
Gili, Phillida. Fanny and Charles
Goodall, John S. Paddy Pork's holiday
Goyder, Alice. Holiday in Catland
Hale, Kathleen. Orlando and the water cats
Kellogg, Steven. Ralph's secret weapon
Kessler, Leonard P. Are we lost, daddy?
Lazard, Naomi. What Amanda saw
Levy, Elizabeth. Something queer on vacation
Lindman, Maj. Snipp, Snapp, Snurr and the red shoes
Lippman, Peter. The Know-It-Alls take a winter vacation
Schick, Eleanor. Summer at the sea
Stevenson, James. The Sea View Hotel
Thomson, Ruth. Peabody all at sea
Tobias, Tobi. At the beach
Weiss, Nicki. Weekend at Muskrat Lake
Williams, Jay. The city witch and the country witch

Activities — walking

Arnosky, Jim. Outdoors on foot
Aylesworth, Jim. Siren in the night
Brown, Margaret Wise. Four fur feet
Buchanan, Joan. It's a good thing
Buckley, Helen Elizabeth. Grandfather
  and I
De Regniers, Beatrice Schenk. Going for
  a walk
Hill, Eric. The park
  Spot's first walk
Hoban, Tana. I walk and read
Kingman, Lee. Peter's long walk
Klein, Leonore. Henri's walk to Paris
Lenski, Lois. I went for a walk
Lobe, Mira. The snowman who went for
  a walk
McNaughton, Colin. Walk rabbit walk
Ray, Deborah Kogan. The cloud
Sharmat, Marjorie Weinman. Burton
  and Dudley
Showers, Paul. The listening walk
Thomas, Ianthe. Walk home tired, Billy
  Jenkins
Tobias, Tobi. The dawdlewalk
Türk, Hanne. Rainy day Max
Tworkov, Jack. The camel who took a
  walk
Viorst, Judith. Try it again, Sam
Watanabe, Shigeo. I can take a walk!
Wood, Joyce. Grandmother Lucy goes
  on a picnic
Zolotow, Charlotte. One step, two...
  Say it!
  The summer night

Activities — weaving

Bang, Molly. Dawn
Blood, Charles L. The goat in the rug
Coombs, Patricia. Tilabel
Le Tord, Bijou. Picking and weaving
Selsam, Millicent E. Cotton
Yagawa, Sumiko. The crane wife

Activities — whistling

Alexander, Anne. I want to whistle
Ambrus, Victor G. The three poor
  tailors
Avery, Kay. Wee willow whistle
Bason, Lillian. Pick a raincoat, pick a
  whistle
Blackwood, Gladys Rourke. Whistle for
  Cindy
Keats, Ezra Jack. Whistle for Willie

Activities — working

Abelson, Danny. The Muppets take
  Manhattan
Alda, Arlene. Sonya's mommy works

Allen, Jeffrey. Mary Alice, operator
  number 9
Ardizzone, Edward. Paul, the hero of
  the fire
Arkin, Alan. Tony's hard work day
Armstrong, Louise. How to turn lemons
  into money
Asch, Frank. Good lemonade
Bach, Othello. Lilly, Willy and the
  mail-order witch
Baker, Betty. Turkey girl
Basso, Bill. The top of the pizzas
Beim, Jerrold. Jay's big job
Bethell, Jean. Three cheers for Mother
  Jones!
Blance, Ellen. Monster gets a job
Burton, Virginia Lee. Mike Mulligan
  and his steam shovel
Carle, Eric. Walter the baker
Clark, Ann Nolan. The little Indian
  basket maker
  The little Indian pottery maker
Delaney, Ned. Terrible things could
  happen
Delton, Judy. My mother lost her job
  today
Fleischman, Paul. The animal hedge
Florian, Douglas. People working
Gág, Wanda. Gone is gone
Gallo, Giovanni. The lazy beaver
Goffstein, M B (Marilyn Brooks). A
  writer
Goodall, John S. Paddy Pork: odd jobs
Hall, Donald. The ox-cart man
Harper, Anita. How we work
Heine, Helme. Merry-go-round
Hoban, Russell. Charlie the tramp
Horvath, Betty F. Jasper makes music
Kessler, Ethel. Night story
Krahn, Fernando. Robot-bot-bot
Lasker, Joe. Mothers can do anything
Lindsey, Treska. When Batistine made
  bread
McGowen, Tom. The only glupmaker in
  the U.S. Navy
Maestro, Betsy. Harriet at work
Martini, Teri. Cowboys
Merriam, Eve. Mommies at work
Mitchell, Joyce Slayton. My mommy
  makes money
Paterson, Diane. Soap and suds
Petrides, Heidrun. Hans and Peter
Puner, Helen Walker. Daddys, what
  they do all day
Ross, Jessica. Ms. Klondike
Sandberg, Inger. Come on out, Daddy!
Schick, Eleanor. Home alone
Skurzynski, Gloria. Martin by himself
Türk, Hanne. Raking leaves with Max

Activities — writing

Arnosky, Jim. Mouse writing
Felt, Sue. Rosa-too-little
Hoban, Lillian. Arthur's pen pal
Johnston, Johanna. That's right, Edie
Joslin, Sesyle. Dear dragon
Krauss, Ruth. I write it
Miles, Miska. The pointed brush...
Seuss, Dr. I can write!

Adoption

Buck, Pearl S (Pearl Sydenstricker).
    Welcome child
Bunin, Catherine. Is that your sister?
Caines, Jeannette. Abby
Chapman, Noralee. The story of
    Barbara
Lapsley, Susan. I am adopted
Livingston, Carole. "Why was I
    adopted?"
Milgram, Mary. Brothers are all the
    same
Rondell, Florence. The family that grew
Rosenberg, Maxine B. Being adopted
Sobol, Harriet Langsam. We don't look
    like our mom and dad
Stanek, Muriel. My little foster sister
Stein, Sara Bonnett. The adopted one
Udry, Janice May. Theodore's parents
Wasson, Valentina Pavlovna. The
    chosen baby

Africa *see* Foreign lands — Africa

Afro-Americans *see* Ethnic groups in the
    U.S. — Afro-Americans

Aged *see* Old age

Airplane pilots *see* Careers — airplane
    pilots

Airplanes, airports

Bagwell, Richard. This is an airport
Baker, Donna. I want to be a pilot
Barton, Byron. Airport
Baumann, Kurt. The paper airplane
Brenner, Anita. I want to fly
Brown, Margaret Wise. Streamlined pig
Cave, Ron. Airplanes
Firmin, Peter. Basil Brush goes flying
Florian, Douglas. Airplane ride
Gay, Michael. Little plane
Gramatky, Hardie. Loopy
Lenski, Lois. The little airplane
Nolan, Dennis. Wizard McBean and his
    flying machine
Olschewski, Alfred. We fly
Phleger, Fred B. Ann can fly
Provensen, Alice. The glorious flight

Ross, Pat. Your first airplane trip
Scarry, Richard. Richard Scarry's great
    big air book
Schulz, Charles M. Snoopy's facts and
    fun book about planes
Spier, Peter. Bored — nothing to do!
Thompson, Brenda. Famous planes
Ungerer, Tomi. The Mellops go flying
Wheeling, Lynn. When you fly
Young, Miriam Burt. If I flew a plane
Zaffo, George J. The big book of real
    airplanes
    The giant nursery book of things that
    go

Airports *see* Airplanes, airports

Albatrosses *see* Birds — albatrosses

Alligators *see* Reptiles — alligators,
    crocodiles

Ambition *see* Character traits —
    ambition

American Indians *see* Ethnic groups in
    the U.S. — Indians

Amphibians *see* Frogs and toads;
    Reptiles

Anatomy

Aliki. My hands
Bailey, Jill. Eyes
    Feet
    Mouths
    Noses
Bishop, Claire Huchet. The man who
    lost his head
Brenner, Barbara. Faces, faces, faces
Caputo, Robert. More than just pets
Castle, Sue. Face talk, hand talk, body
    talk
Chase, Catherine. Feet
Cole, Joanna. A bird's body
    A cat's body
Elkin, Benjamin. Gillespie and the
    guards
Emberley, Ed. Ed Emberley's crazy
    mixed-up face game
Goor, Ron. All kinds of feet
Gross, Ruth Belov. A book about your
    skeleton
Hazen, Barbara Shook. The me I see
Hirschmann, Linda. In a lick of a flick
    of a tongue
Holzenthaler, Jean. My feet do
    My hands can
Kilroy, Sally. Babies' bodies
Krauss, Ruth. Eyes, nose, fingers, toes

Moncure, Jane Belk. What your nose
knows!
My body
Perkins, Al. The ear book
Hand, hand, fingers, thumb
The nose book
Seuss, Dr. The eye book
The foot book
Showers, Paul. You can't make a move
without your muscles
Your skin and mine
Weiss, Leatie. Funny feet!
Yudell, Lynn Deena. Make a face

Angels

Andersen, H C (Hans Christian). The
red shoes
Benét, William Rose. Angels
Brown, Abbie Farwell. The Christmas
angel
Kavanaugh, James J. The crooked angel
Knight, Hilary. Angels and berries and
candy canes
Krahn, Fernando. A funny friend from
heaven
Lathrop, Dorothy Pulis. An angel in the
woods
Martin, Judith. The tree angel
Ness, Evaline. Marcella's guardian angel
Sawyer, Ruth. The Christmas Anna
angel
Thomas, Kathy. The angel's quest

Anger *see* Emotions — anger

Animals

Aardema, Verna. The vingananee and
the tree toad
What's so funny, Ketu?
Who's in Rabbit's house?
Why mosquitoes buzz in people's ears
Abisch, Roz. The clever turtle
Adler, David A. The carsick zebra and
other riddles
Aitken, Amy. Kate and Mona in the
jungle
Aldridge, Alan. The butterfly ball and
the grasshopper's feast
Aldridge, Josephine Haskell. The best
of friends
Alexander, Martha G. Pigs say oink
Aliki. Wild and woolly mammoths
Allamand, Pascale. The animals who
changed their colors
Allan, Ted. Willie the squowse
Allard, Harry. Bumps in the night
Allen, Gertrude E. Everyday animals
Allen, Jeffrey. Mary Alice, operator
number 9

Allen, Jonathan. A bad case of animal
nonsense
Allen, Linda. Mrs. Simkin's bed
Allen, Marjorie N. One, two, three -
ah-choo!
Allen, Martha Dickson. Real life
monsters
Allen, Pamela. Mr. Archimedes' bath
Who sank the boat?
Allen, Robert. The zoo book
Anno, Mitsumasa. Anno's animals
Applebaum, Stan. Going my way?
Ariane. Animal stories
Armour, Richard Willard. Animals on
the ceiling
Have you ever wished you were
something else?
Arnold, Caroline. Five nests
Pets without homes
Arnosky, Jim. A kettle of hawks, and
other wildlife groups
Aruego, José. Look what I can do
We hide, you seek
Asch, Frank. Bread and honey
Atwood, Margaret. Anna's pet
Aulaire, Ingri Mortenson d'. Animals
everywhere
Children of the northlights
B. B. Blacksheep and Company
Bahr, Robert. Blizzard at the zoo
Bailey, Jill. Eyes
Feet
Mouths
Noses
Baker, Betty. Latki and the lightning
lizard
Sonny-Boy Sim
Baker, Eugene. Bicycles
Fire
Home
Outdoors
School
Water
Baker, Jeffrey J W. Patterns of nature
Baker, Laura Nelson. The friendly
beasts
Bang, Betsy. The old woman and the
red pumpkin
The old woman and the rice thief
Bannon, Laura. The best house in the
world
Little people of the night
Red mittens
The scary thing
Barrett, Judi. Animals should definitely
not act like people
Animals should definitely not wear
clothing
Snake is totally tail
Barry, Robert E. Animals around the
world

Baruch, Dorothy. Kappa's tug-of-war with the big brown horse

Baskin, Leonard. Hosie's zoo

Bason, Lillian. Castles and mirrors and cities of sand

Batherman, Muriel. Animals live here

Battles, Edith. What does the rooster say, Yoshio?

Baugh, Dolores M. Let's see the animals

Bayer, Jane. A my name is Alice

Bayley, Nicola. One old Oxford ox

Baylor, Byrd. Desert voices
  We walk in sandy places

Beach, Stewart. Good morning, sun's up!

Beim, Jerrold. Eric on the desert

Belling the cat and other stories

Belloc, Hilaire. The bad child's book of beasts
  The bad child's book of beasts, and more beasts for worse children
  More beasts for worse children

Bellville, Rod. Large animal veterinarians

Belpré, Pura. Dance of the animals

Bemelmans, Ludwig. Rosebud

Benchley, Nathaniel. Running Owl the hunter

Bendick, Jeanne. Why can't I?

Berger, Terry. The turtles' picnic and other nonsense stories

Bernstein, Margery. Coyote goes hunting for fire
  The first morning

Berson, Harold. Why the jackal won't speak to the hedgehog

Bester, Roger. Guess what?

Bethell, Jean. Bathtime.
  Playmates

Bible, Charles. Hamdaani

Binzen, Bill. Alfred goes house hunting

Blough, Glenn O. Who lives in this meadow?

Bograd, Larry. Egon

Bohdal, Susi. Tom cat

Bonino, Louise. The cozy little farm

Boon, Emilie. Peterkin's wet walk

Borden, Beatrice Brown. Wild animals of Africa

Borg, Inga. Plupp builds a house

Boyd, Selma. I met a polar bear

Boynton, Sandra. A is for angry
  The going to bed book
  Moo, baa, lalala

Brady, Irene. A mouse named Mus

Brandenberg, Franz. Aunt Nina and her nephews and nieces

Branley, Franklyn M. Big tracks, little tracks

Brenner, Barbara. Ostrich feathers

Brett, Jan. Annie and the wild animals

Brice, Tony. Baby animals

Brierley, Louise. King Lion and his cooks

Brister, Hope. The cunning fox and other tales

Bro, Marguerite H. The animal friends of Peng-u

Brock, Emma Lillian. Nobody's mouse
  Surprise balloon

Brooke, L Leslie (Leonard Leslie).
  Johnny Crow's garden
  Johnny Crow's new garden
  Johnny Crow's party

Brown, Marc. Arthur goes to camp
  Arthur's April fool
  Arthur's Christmas
  Arthur's eyes
  Arthur's Halloween
  Arthur's Thanksgiving
  Arthur's Valentine
  The bionic bunny show
  The silly tail book
  The true Francine

Brown, Marcia. The blue jackal
  The bun
  Once a mouse...

Brown, Margaret Wise. Baby animals
  The big fur secret
  Don't frighten the lion
  The duck
  Fox eyes
  Once upon a time in pigpen and three other stories
  Streamlined pig
  They all saw it
  Three little animals
  Wait till the moon is full
  Where have you been?

Browner, Richard. Everyone has a name

Buck, Frank. Jungle animals

Buff, Mary. Forest folk

Bunting, Eve. Terrible things

Burningham, John. Mr. Gumpy's outing

Burton, Marilee Robin. The elephant's nest

Byars, Betsy Cromer. The groober

Calhoun, Mary. Euphonia and the flood

Calmenson, Stephanie. The kindergarten book
  Where will the animals stay?

Carle, Eric. 1, 2, 3 to the zoo

Carlson, Natalie Savage. Surprise in the mountains

Carrick, Carol. Patrick's dinosaurs

Carrick, Malcolm. I can squash elephants!

Catchpole, Clive. Deserts
  Grasslands
  Jungles
  Mountains

Cathon, Laura E. Tot Botot and his little flute

Cauley, Lorinda Bryan. The animal kids
The bake-off
The cock, the mouse and the little red hen

Cazet, Denys. The duck with squeaky feet
Lucky me

Chalmers, Audrey. Hundreds and hundreds of pancakes

Charles, Donald. Calico Cat at the zoo
Shaggy dog's animal alphabet

Chicken Little. Chicken Licken
Henny Penny, ill. by Paul Galdone
Henny Penny, ill. by William Stobbs

Chorao, Kay. Lemon moon

Christensen, Gardell Dano. Mrs. Mouse needs a house

Clewes, Dorothy. Henry Hare's boxing match
The wild wood

Climo, Shirley. The cobweb Christmas

Clymer, Ted. The horse and the bad morning

Coatsworth, Elizabeth. A peaceable kingdom, and other poems

Cober, Alan E. Cober's choice

Colby, C B (Carroll Burleigh). Who lives there?
Who went there?

Cole, William. I went to the animal fair

Colman, Hila. Watch that watch

Conklin, Gladys. I caught a lizard

Cooper, Gale. Unicorn moon

Cormack, M Grant. Animal tales from Ireland

Cortesi, Wendy W. Explore a spooky swamp

Cosgrove, Margaret. Wintertime for animals

Coville, Bruce. Sarah's unicorn

Craig, M Jean. Spring is like the morning

Cremins, Robert. My animal ABC
My animal Mother Goose

Cristini, Ermanno. In the pond
In the woods

Cross, Genevieve. A trip to the yard

Crowe, Robert L. Tyler Toad and the thunder

Croxford, Vera. All kinds of animals

Crump, Donald J. Creatures small and furry

Curry, Peter. Animals

Cutler, Ivor. The animal house

Dahl, Roald. The enormous crocodile

Daly, Kathleen N. Today's biggest animals
Unusual animals

Davis, Douglas F. There's an elephant in the garage

DeLage, Ida. ABC triplets at the zoo

Dennis, Suzanne E. Answer me that

Dennis, Wesley. Flip

De Paola, Tomie. Country farm
The hunter and the animals

De Regniers, Beatrice Schenk. It does not say meow!
May I bring a friend?

DiFiori, Lawrence. Baby animals

Dionetti, Michelle. The day Eli went looking for bear

Domanska, Janina. What do you see?

Domestic animals

Du Bois, William Pène. Bear circus
Bear party

Duff, Maggie. Dancing turtle

Duncan, Riana. A nutcracker in a tree

Dunn, Judy. The animals of Buttercup Farm

Durrell, Julie. Mouse tails

Duvoisin, Roger Antoine. A for the ark
The crocodile in the tree
Jasmine
Our Veronica goes to Petunia's farm
Petunia
Petunia and the song
Petunia, beware!
Petunia takes a trip
Petunia's treasure

Eichenberg, Fritz. Dancing in the moon

Elkin, Benjamin. Why the sun was late

Elting, Mary. Q is for duck

Emberley, Barbara. One wide river to cross

Erickson, Russell E. Warton's Christmas Eve adventure

Ets, Marie Hall. Another day
Beasts and nonsense
Elephant in a well
In the forest
Just me
Mister Penny
Mister Penny's circus
Play with me

Evans, Eva Knox. Sleepy time
Where do you live?

Farber, Norma. As I was crossing Boston Common
How the hibernators came to Bethlehem
How the left-behind beasts built Ararat
How to ride a tiger

Farm house

Fay, Hermann. My zoo

Fiddle-i-fee

Fife, Dale. The little park

Fischer, Hans. The birthday

Johnson, Crockett. We wonder what will Walter be? When he grows up

Kalman, Benjamin. Animals in danger

Kane, Henry B. Wings, legs, or fins

Kaufmann, John. Flying giants of long ago

Keats, Ezra Jack. Pet show!

Keller, Holly. Too big
  Will it rain?

Kent, Jack. Little Peep

Kepes, Juliet. Five little monkeys

Kessler, Ethel. Do baby bears sit in chairs?
  What's inside the box?

Kessler, Leonard P. The big mile race
  Do you have any carrots?
  Kick, pass, and run
  Old Turtle's winter games
  On your mark, get set, go!
  Super bowl

Kherdian, David. The animal

Kilroy, Sally. Animal noises

Kingman, Lee. Peter's long walk

Kipling, Rudyard. The elephant's child
  The miracle of the mountain

Kirn, Ann. Beeswax catches a thief

Kitchen, Bert. Animal alphabet

Koelling, Caryl. Animal mix and match

Koide, Tan. May we sleep here tonight?

Krahn, Fernando. The biggest Christmas tree on earth

Krauze, Andrzej. What's so special about today?

Krüss, James. 3 X 3

Kuchalla, Susan. Baby animals

Kuskin, Karla. The animals and the ark
  James and the rain
  Roar and more

Kwitz, Mary DeBall. When it rains

Lady Eden's School. Just how stories

Langstaff, John M. Over in the meadow

Lapp, Eleanor. The mice came in early this year

Lathrop, Dorothy Pulis. Who goes there?

Lazard, Naomi. What Amanda saw

Lenski, Lois. Animals for me
  Big little Davy

Lesser, Carolyn. The goodnight circle

Lewin, Betsy. Animal snackers

Lewis, Stephen. Zoo city

Lilly, Kenneth. Animal builders
  Animal climbers
  Animal jumpers
  Animal runners
  Animal swimmers
  Animals at the zoo
  Animals in the country
  Animals in the jungle
  Animals on the farm

Lionni, Leo. The biggest house in the world

Lipkind, William. The boy and the forest

Lippman, Peter. New at the zoo

The little red hen, ill. by Janina Domanska

The little red hen, ill. by Paul Galdone

The little red hen, ill. by Mel Pekarsky

The little red hen, ill. by Margot Zemach

Lobel, Anita. King Rooster, Queen Hen

Lobel, Arnold. Fables
  A holiday for Mister Muster
  A zoo for Mister Muster

Löfgren, Ulf. One-two-three

Low, Joseph. Adam's book of odd creatures

Lüton, Mildred. Little chicks' mothers and all the others

Lyfick, Warren. Animal tales

McCauley, Jane. The way animals sleep

McLeod, Emilie Warren. One snail and me

McNeer, May Yonge. Little Baptiste

McPhail, David. Andrew's bath

Maestro, Giulio. Leopard is sick
  One more and one less

Mann, Peggy. King Laurence, the alarm clock

Mari, Iela. Eat and be eaten

Marshall, James. Four little troubles
  Willis

Massie, Diane Redfield. The baby beebee bird

Mayer, Marianna. Beauty and the beast

Mayer, Mercer. Appelard and Liverwurst
  What do you do with a kangaroo?

Meeks, Esther K. Friendly farm animals.
  Something new at the zoo

Mendoza, George. Need a house? Call Ms. Mouse

Miklowitz, Gloria D. The zoo that moved

Miles, Miska. Noisy gander
  Sylvester Jones and the voice in the forest

Miller, Susanne Santoro. Prehistoric mammals

Mizumura, Kazue. If I were a cricket...

Moncure, Jane Belk. Riddle me a riddle

Moore, John. Granny Stickleback

Morrison, Sean. Is that a happy hippopotamus?

Morse, Samuel French. All in a suitcase

Mullins, Edward S. Animal limericks

Munari, Bruno. Animals for sale
  Bruno Munari's zoo
  The elephant's wish
  Who's there? Open the door

Murdocca, Sal. Tuttle's shell
Nakano, Hirotaka. Elephant blue
Nakatani, Chiyoko. The zoo in my
 garden
Nussbaum, Hedda. Animals build
 amazing homes
Obligado, Lilian. Faint frogs feeling
 feverish and other terrifically
 tantalizing tongue twisters
Old MacDonald had a farm, ill. by Mel
 Crawford
Old MacDonald had a farm, ill. by
 David Frankland
Old MacDonald had a farm, ill. by
 Abner Graboff
Old MacDonald had a farm, ill. by
 Tracey Campbell Pearson
Old MacDonald had a farm, ill. by
 Robert M. Quackenbush
Over in the meadow
Oxenbury, Helen. Friends
 Monkey see, monkey do
 729 curious creatures
 729 merry mix-ups
Oxford Scientific Films. Jellyfish and
 other sea creatures
Pack, Robert. Then what did you do?
Palazzo, Tony. Animal babies
 Animals 'round the mulberry bush
Palmer, Helen Marion. I was kissed by a
 seal at the zoo
 Why I built the boogle house
Palmer, Mary Babcock.
 No-sort-of-animal
Park, W B. The costume party
Parnall, Peter. Alfalfa Hill
Partridge, Jenny. Colonel Grunt
 Grandma Snuffles
 Hopfellow
 Mr. Squint
 Peterkin Pollensnuff
Paterson, Diane. If I were a toad
Payne, Joan Balfour. The stable that
 stayed
Peaceable kingdom
Peet, Bill. The ant and the elephant
 Farewell to Shady Glade
 The gnats of knotty pine
Peppé, Rodney. Little circus
Peters, Sharon. Animals at night
Petersham, Maud. The box with red
 wheels
Peterson, Esther Allen. Frederick's
 alligator
Peyo. The Smurfs and their woodland
 friends
Piatti, Celestino. Celestino Piatti's animal
 ABC
Pieńkowski, Jan. Homes
Pitcher, Caroline. Animals
Polushkin, Maria. Who said meow?

Potter, Beatrix. Appley Dapply's nursery
 rhymes
 Cecily Parsley's nursery rhymes
 Ginger and Pickles
 The tale of Peter Rabbit and other
 stories
 A treasury of Peter Rabbit and other
 stories
 Yours affectionately, Peter Rabbit
Pouyanne, Rési. What I see hidden by
 the pond
Prelutsky, Jack. The pack rat's day and
 other poems
Provensen, Alice. Our animal friends
 The year at Maple Hill Farm
Purcell, John Wallace. African animals
Quackenbush, Robert M. Calling Doctor
 Quack
 Detective Mole
 Detective Mole and the secret clues
 Detective Mole and the Tip-Top
 mystery
 Pete Pack Rat
Raskin, Ellen. And it rained
 Who, said Sue, said whoo?
Rey, Hans Augusto. Tit for tat
 Where's my baby?
Rey, Margaret Elisabeth Waldstein.
 Billy's picture
Rice, Eve. Sam who never forgets
Richter, Mischa. Quack?
Robinson, Irene Bowen. Picture book of
 animal babies
Robinson, W W (William Wilcox). On
 the farm
Rockwell, Anne F. The good llama
 Honk honk!
 Poor Goose
Rojankovsky, Feodor. Animals in the
 zoo
 Animals on the farm
 The great big animal book
 The great big wild animal book
Roscoe, William. The butterfly's ball
Rose, Anne. Spider in the sky
Roughsey, Dick. The giant devil-dingo
Rusling, Albert. The mouse and Mrs.
 Proudfoot
Russell, Solveig Paulson. What good is a
 tail?
Ryder, Joanne. Fog in the meadow
Saleh, Harold J. Even tiny ants must
 sleep
Sandberg, Inger. Nicholas' favorite pet
Scarry, Richard. Is this the house of
 Mistress Mouse?
 Richard Scarry's animal nursery tales
 Richard Scarry's great big mystery
 book
 Richard Scarry's mix or match
 storybook

Richard Scarry's Postman Pig and his busy neighbors

Schatz, Letta. The extraordinary tug-of-war

Schick, Eleanor. A surprise in the forest

Schongut, Emanuel. Look kitten

Schumacher, Claire. King of the zoo

Schweitzer, Iris. Hilda's restful chair

Seignobosc, Françoise. The big rain
  The story of Colette

Selberg, Ingrid. Nature's hidden world

Selsam, Millicent E. All kinds of babies
  Benny's animals and how he put them in order
  A first look at seashells
  Hidden animals
  Night animals
  When an animal grows

Sendak, Maurice. Very far away

Seuss, Dr. Mr. Brown can moo! Can you?
  Would you rather be a bullfrog?

Sharmat, Marjorie Weinman.
  Bartholomew the bossy
  Taking care of Melvin
  Walter the wolf

Shecter, Ben. Stone house stories

Short, Mayo. Andy and the wild ducks

Simon, Mina Lewiton. If you were an eel, how would you feel?

Simon, Seymour. Animal fact-animal fable

Singer, Isaac Bashevis. Why Noah chose the dove

Skaar, Grace Marion. What do the animals say?

Skorpen, Liesel Moak. All the Lassies

Slobodkin, Louis. Friendly animals
  Melvin, the moose child
  Our friendly friends

Slobodkina, Esphyr. The wonderful feast

Small, David. Imogene's antlers

Smith, Jim. The frog band and the onion seller
  The frog band and the owlnapper

Snyder, Dick. One day at the zoo
  Talk to me tiger

Spier, Peter. Gobble, growl, grunt
  The pet store

Spilka, Arnold. Little birds don't cry

Stadler, John. Animal cafe
  Gorman and the treasure chest

Steig, William. Sylvester and the magic pebble

Steinmetz, Leon. Clocks in the woods

Stevens, Carla. Hooray for pig!
  Pig and the blue flag
  Stories from a snowy meadow

Stevens, Janet. Animal fair

Stevenson, James. Clams can't sing
  We can't sleep

Stobbs, William. Animal pictures

Stone, Lynn M. Endangered animals

Stratemeyer, Clara Georgeanna. Pepper
Struppi

Szekeres, Cyndy. Long ago

Taylor, Mark. "Lamb," said the lion, "I am here."

Tensen, Ruth M. Come to the zoo!

Tester, Sylvia Root. Chase!

Thaler, Mike. It's me, hippo!

Thomas, Patricia. "Stand back," said the elephant, "I'm going to sneeze!"

Tison, Annette. Animal hide-and-seek
  Animals in color magic

Tomkins, Jasper. The catalog

Tresselt, Alvin R. The mitten

Tworkov, Jack. The camel who took a walk

Uchida, Yoshiko. The rooster who understood Japanese

Udry, Janice May. Is Susan here?

Ueno, Noriko. Elephant buttons

Van Woerkom, Dorothy. The rat, the ox and the zodiac

Varga, Judy. The monster behind Black Rock

Venino, Suzanne. Animals helping people

Vevers, Gwynne. Animal homes
  Animal parents
  Animals of the dark
  Animals that store food
  Animals that travel

Vigna, Judith. Couldn't we have a turtle instead?

Villarejo, Mary. The tiger hunt

A visit to a pond

Wahl, Jan. Pleasant Fieldmouse
  The Pleasant Fieldmouse storybook
  Pleasant Fieldmouse's Halloween party

Ward, Lynd. Nic of the woods

Ward, Nanda Weedon. The black sombrero
  The elephant that ga-lumphed

Wegen, Ron. Where can the animals go?

Weil, Ann. Animal families

Welber, Robert. Goodbye, hello

Wiese, Kurt. The thief in the attic

Wildsmith, Brian. Animal games
  Animal homes
  Animal shapes
  Animal tricks
  Brian Wildsmith's wild animals
  Python's party
  What the moon saw

Williams, Garth. The big golden animal ABC

Winter, Jeanette. The girl and the moon man

Wiseman, Bernard. Doctor Duck and
Nurse Swan
Little new kangaroo
Tails are not for painting
Woolley, Catherine. Andy and his fine
friends
Ylla. Animal babies
Yolen, Jane. The acorn quest
Dragon night and other lullabies
An invitation to the butterfly ball
Young animals in the zoo
Young domestic animals
Zalben, Jane Breskin. Basil and Hillary
Norton's nighttime
Zoll, Max Alfred. Animal babies
Zoo animals
Zweifel, Frances. Animal baby-sitters

Animals — aardvarks

Caple, Kathy. Inspector Aardvark and
the perfect cake

Animals — anteaters

Hall, Malcolm. The friends of Charlie
Ant Bear
Waber, Bernard. An anteater named
Arthur

Animals — apes see Animals — gorillas; Animals — monkeys

Animals — armadillos

Kipling, Rudyard. The beginning of the
armadilloes
Saunders, Susan. Charles Rat's picnic
Simon, Sidney B. The armadillo who
had no shell
Singer, Marilyn. Archer Armadillo's
secret room

Animals — badgers

Baker, Betty. Partners
Hoban, Russell. A baby sister for
Frances
A bargain for Frances
Bedtime for Frances
Best friends for Frances
A birthday for Frances
Bread and jam for Frances
Potter, Beatrix. The tale of Mr. Tod
Tompert, Ann. Badger on his own
Varley, Susan. Badger's parting gifts

Animals — bats

Freeman, Don. Hattie the backstage bat
Hoban, Russell. Lavina bat
Jarrell, Randall. A bat is born
Ungerer, Tomi. Rufus

Animals — bears

Alborough, Jez. Bare bear
Alexander, Martha G. And my mean
old mother will be sorry, Blackboard
Bear
Blackboard Bear
I sure am glad to see you, Blackboard
Bear
We're in big trouble, Blackboard Bear
Allen, Pamela. Bertie and the bear
Amoit, Pierre. Bijou the little bear.
Anglund, Joan Walsh. Cowboy and his
friend
The cowboy's Christmas
Asch, Frank. Bread and honey
Happy birthday, moon!
Just like daddy
Moon bear
Mooncake
Popcorn
Sand cake
Skyfire
Austin, Margot. Growl Bear
Bach, Alice. Millicent the magnificent
Warren Weasel's worse than measles
Barrett, John M. The bear who slept
through Christmas.
The Easter bear.
Barto, Emily N. Chubby bear
Bartoli, Jennifer. Snow on bear's nose
Benchley, Nathaniel. Red Fox and his
canoe
Benton, Robert. Don't ever wish for a
7-foot bear
Berenstain, Stan. The bear detectives
The bears' almanac
Bears in the night
Bears on wheels
The Berenstain bears and the messy
room
The Berenstain bears and the missing
dinosaur bone
The Berenstain bears and the sitter
The Berenstain bears and the spooky
old tree
The Berenstain bears and the truth
The Berenstain bears and too much
TV
The Berenstain bears' Christmas tree
The Berenstain bears' counting book
The Berenstain bears get in a fight
The Berenstain bears go to camp
The Berenstain bears go to school
The Berenstain bears go to the doctor
The Berenstain bears in the dark
The Berenstain bears' moving day
The Berenstain bears' science fair
The Berenstain bears' trouble with
money
The Berenstain bears visit the dentist
The Berenstain's B book

He bear, she bear
Inside outside upside down
Old hat, new hat
Bishop, Claire Huchet. Twenty-two
  bears
Boegehold, Betty. Bear underground
Bond, Michael. Paddington at the circus
  Paddington at the seaside
  Paddington at the tower
  Paddington's lucky day
Bonners, Susan. Panda
Bowden, Joan Chase. The bear's
  surprise party
Bridgman, Elizabeth. Nanny bear's
  cruise
Bright, Robert. Me and the bears
Brinckloe, Julie. Gordon's house
Browne, Anthony. Bear hunt
Bunting, Eve. The Valentine bears
Carleton, Barbee Oliver. Benny and the
  bear
Cartlidge, Michelle. The bear's bazaar
  Teddy trucks
Chevalier, Christa. The little bear who
  forgot
Dabcovich, Lydia. Sleepy bear
Degen, Bruce. Jamberry
Delton, Judy. Bear and Duck on the run
  Brimhall comes to stay
  Brimhall turns detective
  Brimhall turns to magic
  A pet for Duck and Bear
Dennis, Morgan. Burlap
Dorian, Marguerite. When the snow is
  blue
Duvoisin, Roger Antoine. Snowy and
  Woody
Eberle, Irmengarde. Bears live here
Fatio, Louise. The happy lion and the
  bear
Flack, Marjorie. Ask Mr. Bear
Fleishman, Seymour. Too hot in
  Potzburg
Flory, Jane. The bear on the doorstep
Foreman, Michael. Moose
Freeman, Don. Bearymore
Gage, Wilson. Cully Cully and the bear
Galdone, Joanna. The little girl and the
  big bear
Gantschev, Ivan. RumpRump
Gantz, David. The genie bear with the
  light brown hair word book
George, Jean Craighead. The grizzly
  bear with the golden ears
Ginsburg, Mirra. Two greedy bears
Gordon, Margaret. Wilberforce goes on
  a picnic
Gordon, Sharon. Christmas surprise

Grimm, Jacob. The bear and the
  kingbird
  Snow White and Rose Red, ill. by
  Adrienne Adams
  Snow-White and Rose-Red, ill. by
  Barbara Cooney
  Snow White and Rose Red, ill. by John
  Wallner
Guilfoile, Elizabeth. Nobody listens to
  Andrew
Hamsa, Bobbie. Your pet bear
Hansen, Carla. Barnaby Bear builds a
  boat
  Barnaby Bear vists the farm
Harlow, Joan Hiatt. Shadow bear
Hayes, Geoffrey. Patrick and Ted
  The secret inside
Hellsing, Lennart. The wonderful
  pumpkin
Hill, Eric. At home
  Baby bear's bedtime
  Good morning, baby bear
  My pets
  Up there
Hillert, Margaret. The three bears
Hoff, Syd. Grizzwold
Hoffman, Mary. Animals in the wild:
  panda
Holl, Adelaide. Small Bear builds a
  playhouse
  Small Bear solves a mystery
Isenberg, Barbara. The adventures of
  Albert, the running bear
  Albert the running bear's exercise
  book
Jackson, Ellen B. The bear in the
  bathtub
Janice. Little Bear marches in the St.
  Patrick's Day parade
  Little Bear's Christmas
  Little Bear's New Year's party
  Little Bear's pancake party
  Little Bear's Sunday breakfast
  Little Bear's Thanksgiving
Jennings, Michael. The bears who came
  to breakfix
Jeschke, Susan. Angela and Bear
  The devil did it
Jonas, Ann. Two bear cubs
Kraus, Robert. Milton the early riser
Krauss, Ruth. Bears
Kuchalla, Susan. Bears
Kuratomi, Chizuko. Mr. Bear and the
  robbers
Lapp, Eleanor. The blueberry bears
Lilly, Kenneth. Animals of the ocean
Lipkind, William. Nubber bear
Lisowski, Gabriel. Roncalli's magnificent
  circus
McCloskey, Robert. Blueberries for Sal
Mack, Stanley. Ten bears in my bed

McPhail, David. The bear's toothache
  Henry Bear's park
  Stanley Henry Bear's friend
Margolis, Richard J. Big bear, spare that
  tree
Marino, Dorothy. Buzzy Bear and the
  rainbow
  Buzzy Bear goes camping
  Buzzy Bear in the garden
  Buzzy Bear's busy day
Marshall, James. What's the matter with
  Carruthers?
Martin, Bill (William Ivan). Brown bear,
  brown bear, what do you see?
Mayer, Mercer. Two moral tales
Minarik, Else Holmelund. Father Bear
  comes home
  A kiss for Little Bear
  Little Bear
  Little Bear's friend
  Little Bear's visit
Monsell, Helen Albee. Paddy's
  Christmas
Muntean, Michaela. Bicycle bear
  The house that bear built
Murphy, Jill. Peace at last
  What next, baby bear!
Myers, Bernice. Herman and the bears
  and the giants
Naylor, Phyllis Reynolds. Old Sadie and
  the Christmas bear
Parker, Nancy Winslow. The ordeal of
  Byron B. Blackbear
Peet, Bill. Big bad Bruce
Pinkwater, Daniel Manus. The bear's
  picture
Pluckrose, Henry. Bears
Polushkin, Maria. Bubba and Bubba
Raphael, Elaine. Turnabout
Ressner, Phil. August explains
Rockwell, Anne F. A bear, a bobcat and
  three ghosts
  Boats
Rose, Gerald. PB takes a holiday
Ruck-Pauquèt, Gina. Mumble bear
Shannon, George. Lizard's song
Sharmat, Marjorie Weinman. I'm terrific
Siewert, Margaret. Bear hunt
Sivulich, Sandra Stroner. I'm going on a
  bear hunt
Skorpen, Liesel Moak. Outside my
  window
Steiner, Jörg. The bear who wanted to
  be a bear
Steptoe, John. Jeffrey Bear cleans up his
  act
Stevenson, James. The bear who had no
  place to go
Stubbs, Joanna. Happy Bear's day
Taylor, Mark. Henry the explorer

The three bears. Goldilocks and the
  three bears
  The story of the three bears, ill. by L.
  Leslie Brooke
  The story of the three bears, ill. by
  William Stobbs
The three bears, ill. by Paul Galdone
The three bears, ill. by Feodor
  Rojankovsky
Turkle, Brinton. Deep in the forest
Upham, Elizabeth. Little brown bear
  loses his clothes
Van Woerkom, Dorothy. Becky and the
  bear
Venable, Alan. The checker players
Vincent, Gabrielle. Bravo, Ernest and
  Celestine!
  Ernest and Celestine
  Ernest and Celestine's picnic
  Smile, Ernest and Celestine
Wahl, Jan. Sylvester Bear overslept
Ward, Andrew. Baby bear and the long
  sleep
Ward, Lynd. The biggest bear
Watanabe, Shigeo. How do I put it on?
  I can build a house!
  I can ride it!
  I can take a walk!
  I'm the king of the castle!
  What a good lunch!
  Where's my daddy?
Wild, Robin. The bears' ABC book
  The bears' counting book
Wildsmith, Brian. Bear's adventure
  The lazy bear
Williams, Leslie. A bear in the air
Winter, Paula. The bear and the fly
Wiseman, Bernard. Morris has a
  birthday party!
Yeoman, John. The bear's water picnic
Ylla. Polar bear brothers
  Two little bears
Yulya. Bears are sleeping
Zimnik, Reiner. The bear on the
  motorcycle
Zirbes, Laura. How many bears?

Animals — beavers

Barr, Cathrine. Little Ben
Bowen, Vernon. The lazy beaver
Crowley, Arthur. Bonzo Beaver
Gallo, Giovanni. The lazy beaver
Hamsa, Bobbie. Your pet beaver
Hoban, Russell. Charlie the tramp
Sheehan, Angela. The beaver
Tresselt, Alvin R. The beaver pond

Animals — bobcats

Rockwell, Anne F. A bear, a bobcat and
  three ghosts

Animals — buffaloes

Baker, Olaf. Where the buffaloes begin

Animals — bulls, cows

Barker, Melvern J. Country fair.
Bellville, Cheryl Walsh. Round-up
Bulla, Clyde Robert. Dandelion Hill
Carlson, Natalie Savage. Time for the white egret
Carrick, Donald. The deer in the pasture
Coats, Belle. Little maverick cow
Cole, Joanna. A calf is born
Cushman, Jerome. Marvella's hobby
Dennis, Wesley. Flip and the cows
Drescher, Henrik. Looking for Santa Claus
Du Bois, William Pène. Elisabeth the cow ghost
Ets, Marie Hall. The cow's party
Forrester, Victoria. The magnificent moo
Hader, Berta Hoerner. The story of Pancho and the bull with the crooked tail
Hancock, Sibyl. Old Blue
Koch, Dorothy Clarke. When the cows got out
Krasilovsky, Phyllis. The cow who fell in the canal
Leaf, Munro. The story of Ferdinand the bull
Lent, Blair. Pistachio
Meeks, Esther K. The curious cow
Merrill, Jean. Tell about the cowbarn, Daddy
Pellowski, Michael. Clara joins the circus
Scruton, Clive. Circus cow
Sewall, Marcia. The wee, wee mannie and the big, big coo
Thomas, Patricia. "There are rocks in my socks!" said the ox to the fox
Wildsmith, Brian. Daisy
Wiseman, Bernard. Oscar is a mama
Wright, Dare. Look at a calf

Animals — camels

Goodenow, Earle. The last camel
Hamsa, Bobbie. Your pet camel
McKee, David. The day the tide went out and out and out
Parker, Nancy Winslow. The Christmas camel
Peet, Bill. Pamela Camel
Tworkov, Jack. The camel who took a walk

Animals — cats

Adam, Barbara. The big big box

Althea. Jeremy Mouse and cat
Ambrus, Victor G. Grandma, Felix, and Mustapha Biscuit
Anderson, Douglas. Let's draw a story
Aulaire, Ingri Mortenson d'. Foxie, the singing dog
Averill, Esther. The fire cat
  Jenny and the cat club
  Jenny's adopted brothers
  Jenny's birthday book
  Jenny's first party
  Jenny's moonlight adventure
  When Jenny lost her scarf
Balian, Lorna. Leprechauns never lie
Barrows, Marjorie Wescott. Fraidy cat
Bascom, Joe. Malcolm Softpaws
  Malcolm's job
Bayley, Nicola. Crab cat
  Elephant cat
  Parrot cat
  Polar bear cat
  Spider cat
Beecroft, John. What? Another cat!
Berg, Jean Horton. The O'Learys and friends
  The wee little man
Bernhard, Josephine Butkowska. Lullaby
Berson, Harold. Raminagrobis and the mice
Black, Floyd. Alphabet cat
Blegvad, Lenore. Mr. Jensen and cat
  Mittens for kittens and other rhymes about cats
Boegehold, Betty. In the castle of cats
  Pawpaw's run
  Three to get ready
Bohdal, Susi. Tom cat
Bonsall, Crosby Newell. The case of the cat's meow
  I'll show you cats
  Listen, listen!
Bradbury, Bianca. The antique cat
  Muggins
  One kitten too many
Brandenberg, Franz. Aunt Nina and her nephews and nieces
  Aunt Nina's visit
  No school today!
  A picnic, hurrah!
  A robber! A robber!
Brett, Jan. Annie and the wild animals
Brewster, Patience. Ellsworth and the cats from Mars
Bright, Robert. Miss Pattie
Brown, Marc. The cloud over Clarence
Brown, Marcia. Felice
Brown, Margaret Wise. House of a hundred windows
  Night and day
  Pussycat's Christmas

Sneakers
When the wind blew
Brown, Myra Berry. Benjy's blanket
Bruna, Dick. Kitten Nell
Buck, Pearl S (Pearl Sydenstricker). The
   Chinese story teller
Buckmaster, Henrietta. Lucy and Loki
Bulla, Clyde Robert. Valentine cat
Burch, Robert. Joey's cat
Calhoun, Mary. Audubon cat
   Cross-country cat
   Hot-air Henry
   The nine lives of Homer C. Cat
   The witch of Hissing Hill
   The witch who lost her shadow
   Wobble the witch cat
Cameron, John. If mice could fly
Cameron, Polly. The cat who thought
   he was a tiger
Carle, Eric. Have you seen my cat?
Carlson, Natalie Savage. Spooky night
Carroll, Ruth. Old Mrs. Billups and the
   black cats
Cass, Joan E. The cat thief
   The cats go to market
Cate, Rikki. A cat's tale
Chalmers, Audrey. Fancy be good
   A kitten's tale
Chalmers, Mary. Be good, Harry
   Boats finds a house
   The cat who liked to pretend
   Come to the doctor, Harry
   George Appleton
   Merry Christmas, Harry
   Mr. Cat's wonderful surprise
   Take a nap, Harry
   Throw a kiss, Harry
Chapman, Jean. Moon-Eyes
Charles, Donald. Calico Cat at school
   Calico Cat at the zoo
   Calico Cat meets bookworm
   Calico Cat's exercise book
   Time to rhyme with Calico Cat
Chenery, Janet. Pickles and Jake
Clymer, Eleanor Lowenton. Horatio
   Horatio goes to the country
Coatsworth, Elizabeth. The giant golden
   book of cat stories
Cohn, Norma. Brother and sister
Cole, Joanna. A cat's body
Cook, Bernadine. Looking for Susie
Coombs, Patricia. The magician and
   McTree
Cooper, Jacqueline. Angus and the
   Mona Lisa
Costa, Nicoletta. The birthday party
   Dressing up
   A friend comes to play
   The missing cat
Craft, Ruth. Carrie Hepple's garden
Crawford, Phyllis. The blot

Cretan, Gladys Yessayan. Lobo and
   Brewster
Damjan, Mischa. The little prince and
   the tiger cat
Dauer, Rosamond. The 300 pound cat
Daugherty, Charles Michael. Wisher
Davis, Douglas F. There's an elephant in
   the garage
Degen, Bruce. Aunt Possum and the
   pumpkin man
DeJong, David Cornel. Looking for
   Alexander
Dennis, Morgan. Skit and Skat
De Regniers, Beatrice Schenk. Cats cats
   cats
   Everyone is good for something
   Picture book theater
Dick Whittington and his cat. Dick
   Whittington, ill. by Edward Ardizzone
   Dick Whittington, ill. by Marcia Brown
   Dick Whittington, ill. by Antony
   Maitland
   Dick Whittington, ill. by Kurt Werth
Dillon, Eilis. The cats' opera
Diska, Pat. Andy says ... Bonjour!
Douglas, Michael. Round, round world
Duvoisin, Roger Antoine. Veronica and
   the birthday present
Ets, Marie Hall. Mr. T. W. Anthony
   Woo
Evans, Eva Knox. That lucky Mrs.
   Plucky
The fat cat
Fatio, Louise. Marc and Pixie and the
   walls in Mrs. Jones's garden
Faunce-Brown, Daphne. Snuffles' house
Feder, Jane. Beany
Fischer-Nagel, Heiderose. A kitten is
   born
Fish, Hans. Pitschi, the kitten who
   always wanted to do something else
Flack, Marjorie. Angus and the cat
   William and his kitten
Flory, Jane. We'll have a friend for
   lunch
Foreman, Michael. Cat and canary
Forrester, Victoria. The magnificent
   moo
Fowler, Richard. Cat's story
Fremlin, Robert. Three friends
Fujikawa, Gyo. Shags finds a kitten
Gág, Flavia. Chubby's first year
Gág, Wanda. Millions of cats
Galdone, Paul. King of the cats
Gantos, Jack. Rotten Ralph
   Rotten Ralph's rotten Christmas
   Worse than Rotten Ralph
Ginsburg, Mirra. Kitten from one to ten
Godden, Rumer. A kindle of kittens
Goodall, John S. The surprise picnic

Gordon, Margaret. The supermarket mice

Goyder, Alice. Holiday in Catland
  Party in Catland

Grabianski, Janusz. Cats

Graham, Bob. Libby, Oscar and me

Griffith, Helen V. Alex and the cat
  Alex remembers
  More Alex and the cat

Hale, Kathleen. Orlando and the water cats
  Orlando buys a farm
  Orlando the frisky housewife

Haley, Gail E. The post office cat

Hawkins, Colin. Pat the cat

Hayes, Geoffrey. Elroy and the witch's child

Hazen, Barbara Shook. Tight times

Henrie, Fiona. Cats

Herriot, James. Moses the kitten

Hess, Lilo. A cat's nine lives

Hiller, Catherine. Abracatabby

Hillert, Margaret. The little runaway

Hoban, Russell. Flat cat

Hoban, Tana. One little kitten

Holmes, Efner Tudor. The Christmas cat

Hurd, Edith Thacher. Come and have fun
  No funny business
  The so-so cat

Hürlimann, Ruth. The proud white cat

Inkiow, Dimiter. Me and Clara and Casimir the cat

Ipcar, Dahlov. The cat at night
  The cat came back

Jack Sprat. The life of Jack Sprat, his wife and his cat

Janice. Minette

Jewell, Nancy. ABC cat

Jonah

Kahl, Virginia. Whose cat is that?

Kay, Helen. A stocking for a kitten

Keats, Ezra Jack. Hi, cat!
  Kitten for a day
  Psst, doggie

Kellogg, Steven. A rose for Pinkerton
  Tallyho, Pinkerton!

Kerr, Judith. Mog's Christmas

Kherdian, David. Country cat, city cat

Kipling, Rudyard. The cat that walked by himself

Knotts, Howard. The summer cat
  The winter cat

Koci, Marta. Katie's kitten

Koenig, Marion. The tale of fancy Nancy
  The wonderful world of night

Komoda, Beverly. Simon's soup

Krahn, Fernando. Catch that cat!

Krasilovsky, Phyllis. Scaredy cat

Kunhardt, Dorothy. Kitty's new doll

Kunhardt, Edith. Pat the cat

Landshoff, Ursula. Cats are good company

Lansdown, Brenda. Galumpf

Laskowski, Jerzy. Master of the royal cats

Lasson, Robert. Orange Oliver

Lawrence, John. Rabbit and pork

Lear, Edward. The owl and the pussy-cat, ill. by Barbara Cooney
  The owl and the pussy-cat, ill. by William Pène Du Bois
  The owl and the pussy-cat, ill. by Gwen Fulton
  The owl and the pussycat, ill. by Elaine Muis
  The owl and the pussy-cat, ill. by Owen Wood

Le-Tan, Pierre. The afternoon cat

Levitin, Sonia. All the cats in the world

Lewin, Betsy. Cat count

Lexau, Joan M. Come here, cat

Lindbloom, Steven. Let's give kitty a bath!

Lindgren, Barbro. Sam's ball

Lindman, Maj. Flicka, Ricka, Dicka and the three kittens

Lipkind, William. Russet and the two reds
  The two reds

Livermore, Elaine. Find the cat
  Three little kittens lost their mittens

Lobel, Arnold. The rose in my garden

MacArthur-Onslow, Annette Rosemary. Minnie

McMillan, Bruce. Kitten can...

McPhail, David. Great cat

Mandry, Kathy. The cat and the mouse and the mouse and the cat

Maris, Ron. My book

Marzollo, Jean. Uproar on Hollercat Hill

Maschler, Fay. T. G. and Moonie go shopping
  T. G. and Moonie have a baby
  T. G. and Moonie move out of town

Matthias, Catherine. I love cats

Mayer, Mercer. The great cat chase

Mayne, William. The patchwork cat

Meddaugh, Susan. Too short Fred

Minarik, Else Holmelund. Cat and dog

Modell, Frank. Seen any cats?

Moncure, Jane Belk. The talking tabby cat

Moore, Lilian. See my lovely poison ivy

Moskin, Marietta D. Lysbet and the fire kittens

Mother Goose. The three little kittens

The moving adventures of Old Dame Trot and her comical cat

Waber, Bernard. Mice on my mind
  Rich cat, poor cat
Wagner, Jenny. John Brown, Rose and
  the midnight cat
Wahl, Jan. Dracula's cat
  Push Kitty
Watson, Pauline. Curley Cat baby-sits
Weihs, Erika. Count the cats
Welch, Martha McKeen. Will that wake
  mother?
Wezel, Peter. The naughty bird
Wheeler, Cindy. Marmalade's nap
  Marmalade's picnic
  Marmalade's snowy day
  Marmalade's yellow leaf
Whitney, Alma Marshak. Leave Herbert
  alone
Wild, Robin. Spot's dogs and the alley
  cats
Wilson, Joyce Lancaster. Tobi
Withers, Carl. The tale of a black cat
Woolley, Catherine. The cat that joined
  the club
Wright, Dare. The doll and the kitten
  The lonely doll learns a lesson
  Look at a kitten
Wright, Josephine Lord. Cotton Cat and
  Martha Mouse
Yashima, Mitsu. Momo's kitten
Yeoman, John. Mouse trouble
Ylla. I'll show you cats
Young, Ed. Up a tree
Zimelman, Nathan. Mean Murgatroyd
  and the ten cats

Animals — cheetahs

Adamson, Joy. Pippa the cheetah and
  her cubs
Conklin, Gladys. Cheetahs, the swift
  hunters
Irvine, Georgeanne. Sasha the cheetah

Animals — chipmunks

Angelo, Valenti. The acorn tree
Conger, Marion. The chipmunk that
  went to church
Eberle, Irmengarde. A chipmunk lives
  here
Moore, Lilian. Little Raccoon and no
  trouble at all
Price, Dorothy E. Speedy gets around
Stevenson, James. Wilfred the rat
Williams, Barbara. Chester Chipmunk's
  Thanksgiving

Animals — cougars

Anderson, C W (Clarence Williams).
  Blaze and the mountain lion

Animals — coyotes

Baker, Betty. And me, coyote!
  Partners
Baylor, Byrd. Coyote cry
  Moon song
Bernstein, Margery. Coyote goes
  hunting for fire
Carrick, Carol. Two coyotes

Animals — deer

Bemelmans, Ludwig. Parsley
Boegehold, Betty. Small Deer's magic
  tricks
Buff, Mary. Dash and Dart
  Forest folk
Carrick, Donald. The deer in the
  pasture
Eberle, Irmengarde. Fawn in the woods
Frankel, Bernice. Half-As-Big and the
  tiger
Lindman, Maj. Snipp, Snapp, Snurr and
  the reindeer
Schlein, Miriam. Deer in the snow

Animals, dislike of see Behavior —
animals, dislike of

Animals — dogs

Adler, David A. My dog and the key
  mystery
Agee, Jon. Ellsworth
Alexander, Martha G. Bobo's dream
  Maggie's moon
Allen, Jeffrey. The secret life of Mr.
  Weird
Allen, Pamela. Bertie and the bear
Ambler, Christopher Gifford. Ten little
  foxhounds
Anderson, Douglas. Let's draw a story
Annett, Cora. The dog who thought he
  was a boy
Ardizzone, Edward. Tim's friend
  Towser
Asch, Frank. The last puppy
  Rebecka
Aulaire, Ingri Mortenson d'. Foxie, the
  singing dog
Austin, Margot. Trumpet
  Willamet way
Baker, Charlotte. Little brother
Baker, Jeannie. Home in the sky
Baker, Margaret. A puppy called
  Spinach
Bannon, Laura. Watchdog
Barr, Cathrine. Hound dog's bone
Barton, Byron. Jack and Fred
  Where's Al?
Batherman, Muriel. Some things you
  should know about my dog
Battles, Edith. The terrible terrier

Baumann, Kurt. Piro and the fire
brigade
Baylor, Byrd. Coyote cry
Beim, Lorraine. The little igloo
Belting, Natalia Maree. Verity Mullens
and the Indian
Bemelmans, Ludwig. Madeline's rescue
Benchley, Nathaniel. Snip
Benchley, Peter. Jonathan visits the
White House
Berends, Polly Berrien. Ladybug and
dog and the night walk
Beresford, Elisabeth. Snuffle to the
rescue
Bettina (Bettina Ehrlich). Pantaloni
Black, Irma Simonton. Big puppy and
little puppy
Blackwood, Gladys Rourke. Whistle for
Cindy
Blegvad, Lenore. Hark! Hark! The dogs
do bark, and other poems about dogs
Bliss, Corinne Demas. That dog Melly!
Blocksma, Mary. The pup went up
Bolognese, Elaine. The sleepy watchdog
Bonsall, Crosby Newell. And I mean it,
Stanley
Listen, listen!
Who's afraid of the dark?
Bontemps, Arna Wendell. The fast
sooner hound
Bornstein, Ruth Lercher. I'll draw a
meadow
Jim
Bottner, Barbara. Horrible Hannah
Bowden, Joan Chase. Boo and the flying
flews
Bradbury, Bianca. Mutt
Bradford, Ann. The mystery of the
blind writer
The mystery of the missing dogs
Brenner, Barbara. A dog I know
Bridgman, Elizabeth. A new dog next
door
Bridwell, Norman. Clifford goes to
Hollywood
Clifford's good deeds
Clifford's Halloween
Bright, Robert. Georgie and the little
dog
Bröger, Achim. Francie's paper puppy
Brown, Margaret Wise. Big dog, little
dog
The country noisy book
Don't frighten the lion
The indoor noisy book
The quiet noisy book
The winter noisy book
Bryan, Dorothy. Friendly little Jonathan
Just Tammie!
Buck, Pearl S (Pearl Sydenstricker). The
Chinese story teller

Buckley, Helen Elizabeth. Josie's
Buttercup
Buckmaster, Henrietta. Lucy and Loki
Burningham, John. Cannonball Simp
The dog
Calhoun, Mary. Houn' dog
Mrs. Dog's own house
Carlson, Nancy. Harriet and the garden
Harriet and the roller coaster
Harriet and Walt
Harriet's Halloween candy
Harriet's recital
Carrick, Carol. The accident
Ben and the porcupine
The foundling
Carroll, Ruth. What Whiskers did
Carter, Debby L. Clipper
Chalmers, Audrey. Hector and Mr.
Murfit
Charles, Donald. Shaggy dog's tall tale
Time to rhyme with Calico Cat
Chase, Catherine. Pete, the wet pet
Chenery, Janet. Pickles and Jake
Christian, Mary Blount. No dogs
allowed, Jonathan!
Ciardi, John. Scrappy the pup
Cohen, Miriam. Jim's dog Muffins
Cole, Joanna. My puppy is born
Cook, Marion B. Waggles and the dog
catcher
Coontz, Otto. The quite house
Cretan, Gladys Yessayan. Lobo and
Brewster
Dale, Ruth Bluestone. Benjamin — and
Sylvester also
Daly, Kathleen N. The Giant little
Golden Book of dogs
Daly, Maureen. Patrick visits the library
Damjan, Mischa. Atuk
Denison, Carol. A part-time dog for
Nick
Dennis, Morgan. Burlap
The pup himself
The sea dog
Skit and Skat
Doughtie, Charles. Gabriel Wrinkles, the
bloodhound who couldn't smell
Du Bois, William Pène. Giant Otto
Otto and the magic potatoes
Otto at sea
Otto in Africa
Otto in Texas
Dumas, Philippe. Laura, Alice's new
puppy
Laura and the bandits
Laura loses her head
Laura on the road
Dunn, Judy. The little puppy
Dupré, Ramona Dorrel. Too many dogs
Duvoisin, Roger Antoine. Day and night
Eastman, P D (Philip D). Go, dog, go!

Elkin, Benjamin. The big jump and other stories

Erickson, Phoebe. Just follow me

Ets, Marie Hall. Mr. T. W. Anthony Woo

Fechner, Amrei. I am a little dog

Fisher, Aileen. I like weather

Flack, Marjorie. Angus and the cat
 Angus and the ducks
 Angus lost

Foster, Sally. A pup grows up

Freeman, Don. Ski pup

Frith, Michael K. I'll teach my dog 100 words

Fujikawa, Gyo. Millie's secret
 Shags finds a kitten

Furchgott, Terry. Phoebe and the hot water bottles

Gackenbach, Dick. A bag full of pups
 Claude and Pepper
 Claude the dog
 The dog and the deep dark woods
 Pepper and all the legs
 What's Claude doing?

Gág, Wanda. Nothing at all

Gannett, Ruth S. Katie and the sad noise

Gerson, Corinne. Good dog, bad dog

Goodspeed, Peter. Hugh and Fitzhugh

Gordon, Sharon. What a dog!

Graham, Bob. Libby, Oscar and me

Graham, Margaret Bloy. Benjy and the barking bird
 Benjy's boat trip
 Benjy's dog house

Green, Phyllis. Bagdad ate it

Griffith, Helen V. Alex and the cat
 Alex remembers
 Mine will, said John
 More Alex and the cat

Grimm, Jacob. The horse, the fox, and the lion

Hamberger, John. Hazel was an only pet
 The lazy dog

Heine, Helme. Mr. Miller the dog

Henrie, Fiona. Dogs

Hill, Eric. Spot goes to school
 Spot's first walk

Hoban, Lillian. The laziest robot in zone one

Hoban, Russell. The stone doll of Sister Brute

Hoff, Syd. Barkley
 Lengthy

Holmes, Efner Tudor. Carrie's gift

Holt, Margaret. David McCheever's twenty-nine dogs

Hopkins, Lee Bennett. A dog's life

Hurd, Edith Thacher. The black dog who went into the woods
 Little dog, dreaming

Hurd, Thacher. Hobo dog

Hürlimann, Bettina. Barry

Inkiow, Dimiter. Me and Clara and Snuffy the dog

Ipcar, Dahlov. Black and white

Isele, Elizabeth. Pooks

Iwamura, Kazuo. Ton and Pon big and little
 Ton and Pon two good friends

Iwasaki, Chihiro. What's fun without a friend?

Janice. Angélique
 Mr. and Mrs. Button's wonderful watchdogs

Joerns, Consuelo. Oliver's escape

Johnson, Crockett. The blue ribbon puppies
 Terrible terrifying Toby

Jones, Rebecca C. The biggest, meanest, ugliest dog in the whole wide world

Kahl, Virginia. Away went Wolfgang
 Maxie

Keats, Ezra Jack. Kitten for a day
 My dog is lost!
 Psst, doggie
 Skates
 Whistle for Willie

Kellogg, Steven. Pinkerton, behave!
 A rose for Pinkerton
 Tallyho, Pinkerton!

Keyser, Marcia. Roger on his own

Kimura, Yasuko. Fergus and the sea monster

King, Deborah. Sirius and Saba

Koci, Marta. Blackie and Marie

Kopczynski, Anna. Jerry and Ami

Kraus, Robert. The detective of London

Kroll, Steven. Woof, woof!

Kumin, Maxine. What color is Caesar?

Kuskin, Karla. Watson, the smartest dog in the U.S.A.

Laskowski, Jerzy. Master of the royal cats

Lathrop, Dorothy Pulis. Puppies for keeps

Leaf, Munro. Noodle

Leichman, Seymour. Shaggy dogs and spotty dogs and shaggy and spotty dogs

Lenski, Lois. Davy and his dog
 Debbie and her dolls
 A dog came to school

Levy, Elizabeth. Something queer is going on

Lewis, Thomas P. Call for Mr. Sniff

Lexau, Joan M. Go away, dog

Lindgren, Barbro. Sam's bath

Lindman, Maj. Flicka, Ricka, Dicka and
  a little dog
  Snipp, Snapp, Snurr and the seven
  dogs
  Snipp, Snapp, Snurr and the yellow
  sled
Lipkind, William. Even Steven
  Finders keepers
Lopshire, Robert. Put me in the zoo
Machetanz, Sara. A puppy named Gia
Marie, Geraldine. The magic box
Marshak, Samuel. In the van
Marshall, James. Miss Dog's Christmas
  Speedboat
Martin, Charles E. Dunkel takes a walk
Martin, Sarah Catherine. The comic
  adventures of Old Mother Hubbard
  and her dog
  Old Mother Hubbard and her dog, ill.
  by Paul Galdone
  Old Mother Hubbard and her dog, ill.
  by Evaline Ness
Miles, Miska. Show and tell...
  Somebody's dog
Minarik, Else Holmelund. Cat and dog
Modell, Frank. Tooley! Tooley!
Morris, Terry Nell. Lucky puppy! Lucky
  boy!
Nakatani, Chiyoko. The day Chiro was
  lost
Newberry, Clare Turlay. Barkis
Otto, Svend. Taxi dog
Overbeck, Cynthia. Rusty the Irish
  setter
Oxenbury, Helen. Our dog
Pape, Donna Lugg. Doghouse for sale
Parker, Nancy Winslow. Cooper, the
  McNallys' big black dog
  Poofy loves company
Peet, Bill. The Whingdingdilly
Perkins, Al. The digging-est dog
Pfloog, Jan. Puppies
Politi, Leo. Emmet
  The nicest gift
Potter, Beatrix. The pie and the
  patty-pan
Prather, Ray. Double dog dare
Puppies and kittens
Rey, Margaret Elisabeth Waldstein.
  Pretzel
  Pretzel and the puppies
Rice, Eve. Benny bakes a cake
  Papa's lemonade and other stories
Robins, Joan. Addie meets Max
Rockwell, Anne F. Willie runs away
Rose, Mitchell. Norman
Ross, Tony. Towser and the terrible
  thing
Rowand, Phyllis. George
  George goes to town

Ruby-Spears Enterprises. The puppy's
  new adventures
Sandberg, Inger. Nicholas' favorite pet
Saunders, Susan. Wales' tale
Saxon, Charles D. Don't worry about
  Poopsie
Schroeder, Binette. Tuffa and her
  friends
  Tuffa and the bone
  Tuffa and the ducks
  Tuffa and the picnic
  Tuffa and the snow
Schulz, Charles M. Snoopy's facts and
  fun book about boats
  Snoopy's facts and fun book about
  farms
  Snoopy's facts and fun book about
  houses
  Snoopy's facts and fun book about
  nature
  Snoopy's facts and fun book about
  planes
  Snoopy's facts and fun book about
  seashores
  Snoopy's facts and fun book about
  seasons
  Snoopy's facts and fun book about
  trucks
Scott, Sally. Little Wiener
  There was Timmy!
Selsam, Millicent E. A first look at dogs
  How puppies grow
Sewall, Marcia. The little wee tyke
Sewell, Helen Moore. Birthdays for
  Robin
  Ming and Mehitable
Sharmat, Marjorie Weinman. Sasha the
  silly
Shortall, Leonard W. Andy, the dog
  walker
Shyer, Marlene Fanta. Stepdog
Singer, Marilyn. The dog who insisted
  he wasn't
Skaar, Grace Marion. Nothing but (cats)
  and all about (dogs)
  The very little dog
Skorpen, Liesel Moak. All the Lassies
  His mother's dog
  Old Arthur
Snoopy on wheels
Spier, Peter. Little dogs
Steig, William. Caleb and Kate
Steiner, Charlotte. Lulu
  Pete and Peter
Stern, Mark. It's a dog's life
Stratemeyer, Clara Georgeanna. Tuggy
Sugita, Yutaka. My friend Little John
  and me
Surany, Anico. Kati and Kormos
Tallon, Robert. Latouse my moose
Tanaka, Hideyuki. The happy dog

Taylor, Mark. The case of the missing kittens
 Old Blue, you good dog you
Taylor, Sydney. The dog who came to dinner
Thaler, Mike. My puppy
Thomson, Ruth. Peabody all at sea
 Peabody's first case
Titus, Eve. Anatole and the poodle
Turkle, Brinton. The sky dog
Udry, Janice May. Alfred
 What Mary Jo wanted
Untermeyer, Louis. The kitten who barked
Van Allsburg, Chris. The garden of Abdul Gasazi
Van den Honert, Dorry. Demi the baby sitter
Waber, Bernard. Bernard
Wagner, Jenny. John Brown, Rose and the midnight cat
Wahl, Jan. Frankenstein's dog
Walt Disney Productions. Tod and Copper.
 Tod and Vixey.
Ward, Lynd. Nic of the woods
Weiss, Harvey. The sooner hound
Whitney, Alex. The tiger that barks
Wiese, Kurt. The dog, the fox and the fleas
Wild, Robin. Spot's dogs and the alley cats
Wildsmith, Brian. Hunter and his dog
Wilhelm, Hans. A new home, a new friend
Williamson, Stan. The no-bark dog
Willoughby, Elaine Macmann. Boris and the monsters
Wirth, Beverly. Margie and me
Wold, Jo Anne. Well! Why didn't you say so?
Woolley, Catherine. The puppy who wanted a boy
Ziefert, Harriet. Sleepy dog
Zimelman, Nathan. Mean Murgatroyd and the ten cats
Zion, Gene. Harry and the lady next door
 Harry by the sea
 Harry, the dirty dog
 No roses for Harry
Zolotow, Charlotte. The poodle who barked at the wind

Animals — dolphins

Anderson, Lonzo. Arion and the dolphins
Benchley, Nathaniel. The several tricks of Edgar Dolphin
Lilly, Kenneth. Animals of the ocean
Morris, Robert A. Dolphin

Nakatani, Chiyoko. Fumio and the dolphins

Animals — donkeys

Æsop. The miller, his son and their donkey
Bates, H E. Achilles and Diana
 Achilles the donkey
Bettina (Bettina Ehrlich). Cocolo comes to America
 Cocolo's home
 Piccolo
Brown, Marcia. Tamarindo!
Bulla, Clyde Robert. The donkey cart
Calhoun, Mary. Old man Whickutt's donkey
Daugherty, Sonia. Vanka's donkey
Dumas, Philippe. Lucy, a tale of a donkey
 The story of Edward
Duvoisin, Roger Antoine. Donkey-donkey
Evans, Katherine. The man, the boy and the donkey
Gramatky, Hardie. Bolivar
Gray, Genevieve. How far, Felipe?
Grimm, Jacob. The donkey prince
Hale, Irina. Donkey's dreadful day
Hurd, Edith Thacher. Under the lemon tree
La Fontaine, Jean de. The miller, the boy and the donkey
McCrea, James. The king's procession
Ness, Evaline. Josefina February
Palazzo, Tony. Bianco and the New World
Raphael, Elaine. Donkey and Carlo
 Donkey, it's snowing
Seignobosc, Françoise. Chouchou
Showalter, Jean B. The donkey ride
Silver, Jody. Isadora
Steig, William. Farmer Palmer's wagon ride
 Sylvester and the magic pebble
Van Woerkom, Dorothy. Donkey Ysabel
Winter, Paula. Sir Andrew

Animals — elephants

Ambrus, Victor G. Mishka
Barner, Bob. Elephant facts
Bishop, Ann. The Ella Fannie elephant riddle book
Bohman, Nils. Jim, Jock and Jumbo
Boynton, Sandra. If at first...
Brunhoff, Jean de. Babar and Father Christmas
 Babar and his children
 Babar and Zephir
 Babar the king
 Babar's anniversary album

The story of Babar, the little elephant
The travels of Babar
Brunhoff, Laurent de. Babar and the
  ghost
  Babar and the Wully-Wully
  Babar comes to America
  Babar learns to cook
  Babar loses his crown
  Babar the magician
  Babar visits another planet
  Babar's ABC
  Babar's birthday surprise
  Babar's book of color
  Babar's castle
  Babar's cousin, that rascal Arthur
  Babar's fair will be opened next
    Sunday
  Babar's mystery
  Babar's picnic
  Babar's visit to Bird Island
Cantieni, Benita. Little Elephant and
  Big Mouse
Chorao, Kay. Kate's box
  Kate's car
  Kate's quilt
  Kate's snowman
Clifford, Eth. Why is an elephant called
  an elephant?
Cole, Babette. Nungu and the elephant
Cole, Joanna. Aren't you forgetting
  something, Fiona?
Delton, Judy. Penny wise, fun foolish
Domanska, Janina. Why so much noise?
DuBois, Ivy. Baby Jumbo
Elephants
Ets, Marie Hall. Elephant in a well
Fechner, Amrei. I am a little elephant
Fern, Eugene. What's he been up to
  now?
Foulds, Elfrida Vipont. The elephant
  and the bad baby
Freschet, Berniece. Elephant and
  friends
Greene, Carol. The insignificant
  elephant
Hamsa, Bobbie. Your pet elephant
Hewett, Joan. The mouse and the
  elephant
Hoff, Syd. Oliver
Hoffman, Mary. Animals in the wild
  elephant
Hogan, Inez. About Nono, the baby
  elephant
Irvine, Georgeanne. Elmer the elephant
Joslin, Sesyle. Baby elephant and the
  secret wishes
  Baby elephant goes to China
  Baby elephant's trunk
  Brave Baby Elephant
  Señor Baby Elephant, the pirate
Kipling, Rudyard. The elephant's child

Klein, Suzanne. An elephant in my bed
Kraus, Robert. Boris bad enough
Lawrence, John. Pope Leo's elephant
Lipkind, William. Chaga
Lobel, Arnold. Uncle Elephant
Löfgren, Ulf. The traffic stopper that
  became a grandmother visitor
McKee, David. Elmer, the story of a
  patchwork elephant
  Tusk tusk
McNulty, Faith. The elephant who
  couldn't forget
Maestro, Betsy. Around the clock with
  Harriet
  Harriet at home
  Harriet at play
  Harriet at school
  Harriet at work
  Harriet goes to the circus
  Harriet reads signs and more signs
  On the go
  On the town
  Where is my friend?
Martin, Bill (William Ivan). Smoky Poky
Mayer, Mercer. Ah-choo
Nakano, Hirotaka. Elephant blue
Patz, Nancy. Pumpernickel tickle and
  mean green cheese
Peet, Bill. The ant and the elephant
  Ella
  Encore for Eleanor
Perkins, Al. Tubby and the lantern
  Tubby and the Poo-Bah
Petersham, Maud. The circus baby
Platt, Kin. Big Max
Pluckrose, Henry. Elephants
Quigley, Lillian Fox. The blind men and
  the elephant
Rogers, Edmund. Elephants
Sadler, Marilyn. Alistair's elephant
Saxe, John Godfrey. The blind men and
  the elephant
Schlein, Miriam. Elephant herd
Seuss, Dr. Horton hatches the egg
  Horton hears a Who!
Simont, Marc. How come elephants?
Slobodkina, Esphyr. Pezzo the peddler
  and the circus elephant
Smath, Jerry. But no elephants
Steig, William. An eye for elephants
Tresselt, Alvin R. Smallest elephant in
  the world
Wahl, Jan. Hello, elephant
Ward, Nanda Weedon. The elephant
  that ga-lumphed
Weisgard, Leonard. Silly Willy Nilly
Wells, H G (Herbert George). The
  adventures of Tommy
Williamson, Hamilton. Little elephant
Ylla. The little elephant

Young, Miriam Burt. If I rode an
  elephant

Animals — endangered animals

Cromie, William J. Steven and the green
  turtle

Animals — foxes

Æsop. Three fox fables
Ambrus, Victor G. Country wedding
Anderson, Paul S. Red fox and the
  hungry tiger
Barr, Cathrine. Hound dog's bone
Bemelmans, Ludwig. Welcome home
Berson, Harold. Henry Possum
  Joseph and the snake
Brown, Marcia. The neighbors
Brown, Margaret Wise. Fox eyes
Buck, Pearl S (Pearl Sydenstricker). The
  little fox in the middle
Burningham, John. Harquin
Calhoun, Mary. Houn' dog
Carroll, Ruth. What Whiskers did
Chaucer, Geoffrey. Chanticleer and the
  fox
Christelow, Eileen. Henry and the red
  stripes
Cunningham, Julia. The vision of
  Francois the fox
Davis, Lavinia. Roger and the fox
Delton, Judy. Duck goes fishing
Domanska, Janina. The best of the
  bargain
DuBois, Ivy. Mother fox
Eberle, Irmengarde. Foxes live here
Fatio, Louise. The red bantam
Firmin, Peter. Basil Brush and a dragon
  Basil Brush and the windmills
  Basil Brush finds treasure
  Basil Brush gets a medal
  Basil Brush goes flying
Fox, Charles Philip. A fox in the house
The fox went out on a chilly night
Ginsburg, Mirra. Across the stream
  The fox and the hare
  Mushroom in the rain
  Two greedy bears
Grimm, Jacob. The horse, the fox, and
  the lion
  Mrs. Fox's wedding
Guzzo, Sandra E. Fox and Heggie
Hess, Lilo. Foxes in the woodshed
Hogrogian, Nonny. One fine day
Hurd, Edith Thacher. Under the lemon
  tree
Hutchins, Pat. Rosie's walk
Kent, Jack. Silly goose
Leverich, Kathleen. The hungry fox and
  the foxy duck

Lifton, Betty Jean. The many lives of
  Chio and Goro
Lindgren, Astrid. The tomten and the
  fox
Lionni, Leo. In the rabbitgarden
Lipkind, William. The Christmas bunny
  The little tiny rooster
Livermore, Elaine. Follow the fox
Marshall, Edward. Fox and his friends
  Fox at school
  Fox in love
  Fox on wheels
Meddaugh, Susan. Maude and Claude
  go abroad
Miles, Miska. The fox and the fire
Potter, Beatrix. The tale of Mr. Tod
Preston, Edna Mitchell. Squawk to the
  moon little goose
Roach, Marilynne K. Dune fox
Rockwell, Anne F. Big boss
Schlein, Miriam. The four little foxes
Selsam, Millicent E. A first look at dogs
Sharmat, Marjorie Weinman. The best
  Valentine in the world
Small, David. Eulalie and the hopping
  head
Steig, William. Doctor De Soto
  Roland, the minstrel pig
Thomas, Patricia. "There are rocks in
  my socks!" said the ox to the fox
Tompert, Ann. Little Fox goes to the
  end of the world
Varga, Judy. The mare's egg
Walt Disney Productions. Tod and
  Copper.
  Tod and Vixey.
Watson, Clyde. Father Fox's feast of
  songs
  Tom Fox and the apple pie
Weil, Lisl. Gillie and the flattering fox
Wells, Rosemary. Don't spill it again,
  James
Wiese, Kurt. The dog, the fox and the
  fleas

Animals — gerbils

Henrie, Fiona. Gerbils
Tobias, Tobi. Petey

Animals — giraffes

Brenner, Barbara. Mr. Tall and Mr.
  Small
Brunhoff, Laurent de. Serafina the
  giraffe
Cooke, Ann. Giraffes at home
Doughtie, Charles. High Henry... the
  cowboy who was too tall to ride a
  horse
Duvoisin, Roger Antoine. Periwinkle
Hamsa, Bobbie. Your pet giraffe

Irvine, Georgeanne. Georgie the Giraffe

Rey, Hans Augusto. Cecily G and the nine monkeys

Animals — goats

Allamand, Pascale. The little goat in the mountains

Ambrus, Victor G. The seven skinny goats
  The three poor tailors

Asbjørnsen, P C (Peter Christen). The three billy goats Gruff, ill. by Marcia Brown
  The three billy goats Gruff, ill. by Paul Galdone
  The three billy goats Gruff, ill. by William Stobbs

Berson, Harold. Balarin's goat

Blood, Charles L. The goat in the rug

Bornstein, Ruth Lercher. Of course a goat

Carigiet, Alois. Anton the goatherd

Chandoha, Walter. A baby goat for you

Chiefari, Janet. Kids are baby goats

Damjan, Mischa. The wolf and the kid

Daudet, Alphonse. The brave little goat of Monsieur Séguin

Dunn, Judy. The little goat

Fletcher, Elizabeth. The little goat

Grimm, Jacob. The wolf and the seven kids

Hillert, Margaret. The three goats

Hoff, Syd. Happy birthday, Henrietta!

Hogrogian, Nonny. Billy Goat and his well-fed friends

Kroll, Steven. The goat parade

Leaf, Munro. Gordon, the goat

Lipkind, William. Billy the kid

Mills, Alan. The hungry goat

Rappus, Gerhard. When the sun was shining

Sattler, Helen Roney. No place for a goat

Seignobosc, Françoise. Biquette, the white goat
  Springtime for Jeanne-Marie

Sharmat, Mitchell. Gregory, the terrible eater

Siddiqui, Ashraf. Bhombal Dass, the uncle of lion

Slobodkin, Louis. The polka-dot goat
  Up high and down low

Suhl, Yuri. The Purim goat

Tudor, Tasha. Corgiville fair

Watson, Nancy Dingman. The birthday goat

Wolkstein, Diane. The banza

Animals — gorillas

Browne, Anthony. Gorilla
  Willy the wimp

Conklin, Gladys. Little apes

Harrison, David Lee. Detective Bob and the great ape escape

Hazen, Barbara Shook. The gorilla did it!
  Gorilla wants to be the baby

Hoff, Syd. Julius

Howe, James. The day the teacher went bananas

Krahn, Fernando. The great ape

Meyers, Susan. The truth about gorillas

Schertle, Alice. The gorilla in the hall

Selsam, Millicent E. A first look at monkeys

Zimelman, Nathan. Positively no pets allowed

Animals — groundhogs

Cauley, Lorinda Bryan. The new house

Cohen, Carol L. Wake up, groundhog!

Coombs, Patricia. Tilabel

Delton, Judy. Groundhog's Day at the doctor

Hamberger, John. This is the day

Johnson, Crockett. Will spring be early?

Kesselman, Wendy. Time for Jody

McNulty, Faith. Woodchuck

Palazzo, Tony. Waldo the woodchuck,

Stanovich, Betty Jo. Hedgehog adventures

Tompert, Ann. Nothing sticks like a shadow

Watson, Wendy. Has winter come?

Animals — guinea pigs

Brooks, Andrea. The guinea pigs' adventure

Duke, Kate. The guinea pig ABC
  Guinea pigs far and near

Meshover, Leonard. The guinea pigs that went to school

Potter, Beatrix. The tale of Tuppeny

Pursell, Margaret Sanford. Polly the guinea pig

Animals — hamsters

Ambrus, Victor G. Grandma, Felix, and Mustapha Biscuit

Baker, Alan. Benjamin and the box
  Benjamin bounces back
  Benjamin's book
  Benjamin's dreadful dream

Blegvad, Lenore. The great hamster hunt

Claude-Lafontaine, Pascale. Monsieur Bussy, the celebrated hamster

Harris, Dorothy Joan. The school mouse
and the hamster

Animals — hedgehogs

Berson, Harold. Why the jackal won't
speak to the hedgehog
Brook, Judy. Tim mouse goes down the
stream
 Tim mouse visits the farm
Domanska, Janina. The best of the
bargain
Flot, Jeannette B. Princess Kalina and
the hedgehog
Guzzo, Sandra E. Fox and Heggie
Holden, Edith. The hedgehog feast
McClure, Gillian. Prickly pig
Myller, Lois. No! No!
Potter, Beatrix. The tale of Mrs.
Tiggy-Winkle
Ruck-Pauquèt, Gina. Little hedgehog
Stanovich, Betty Jo. Hedgehog
adventures
Stott, Rowena. The hedgehog feast
Yeoman, John. The bear's water picnic

Animals — hippopotami

Allen, Frances Charlotte. Little hippo
Bennett, Rainey. The secret hiding place
Bohman, Nils. Jim, Jock and Jumbo
Boynton, Sandra. But not the
hippopotamus
 Hester in the wild
 Hippos go berserk
Brown, Marcia. How, hippo!
Calmenson, Stephanie. The birthday hat
 Where is Grandma Potamus?
Chalmers, Audrey. Parade of Obash
Cole, Babette. Nungu and the
hippopotamus
Croswell, Volney. How to hide a
hippopotamus
Duvoisin, Roger Antoine. Lonely
Veronica
 Our Veronica goes to Petunia's farm
 Veronica
 Veronica and the birthday present
 Veronica's smile
The hippo
Kishida, Eriko. The hippo boat
Lasher, Faith B. Hubert Hippo's world
Lewin, Betsy. Hip, hippo, hooray!
Mahy, Margaret. The boy who was
followed home
Marshall, James. George and Martha
 George and Martha back in town
 George and Martha encore
 George and Martha one fine day
 George and Martha rise and shine
 George and Martha, tons of fun

Mayer, Mercer. Hiccup
 Oops
Panek, Dennis. Matilda Hippo has a big
mouth
Parker, Nancy Winslow. Love from
Uncle Clyde
Scarry, Richard. The adventures of
Tinker and Tanker
Slobodkin, Louis. Hustle and bustle
Sugita, Yutaka. Helena the unhappy
hippopotamus
Taylor, Judy. Sophie and Jack
 Sophie and Jack help out
Thaler, Mike. It's me, hippo!
 There's a hippopotamus under my bed
Wahl, Jan. Old Hippo's Easter egg
Young, Miriam Burt. Please don't feed
Horace

Animals — horses

Aarle, Thomas Van. Don't put your cart
before the horse race
Anderson, C W (Clarence Williams).
 Billy and Blaze
 Blaze and the forest fire
 Blaze and the gray spotted pony
 Blaze and the gypsies
 Blaze and the Indian cave
 Blaze and the lost quarry
 Blaze and the mountain lion
 Blaze and Thunderbolt
 Blaze finds forgotten roads
 Blaze finds the trail
 Blaze shows the way
 The crooked colt
 Linda and the Indians
 Lonesome little colt
 A pony for Linda
 A pony for three
 The rumble seat pony
Arundel, Jocelyn. Shoes for Punch
Asch, Frank. Goodnight horsey
Baker, Betty. Three fools and a horse
Balet, Jan B. Five Rollatinis
Barr, Cathrine. A horse for Sherry
Barrett, Lawrence Louis. Twinkle, the
baby colt.
Beatty, Hetty Burlingame. Bucking
horse
 Little Owl Indian
 Moorland pony
Bellville, Cheryl Walsh. Round-up
Bemelmans, Ludwig. Madeline in
London
Blech, Dietlind. Hello Irina
Bowden, Joan Chase. A new home for
Snow Ball
Brett, Jan. Fritz and the beautiful horses
Burningham, John. Humbert, Mister
Firkin and the Lord Mayor of
London

Burton, Virginia Lee. Calico the wonder horse

Chan, Chin-Yi. Good luck horse

Chandler, Edna Walker. Pony rider

Charmatz, Bill. The Troy St. bus

Cretien, Paul D. Sir Henry and the dragon

Cummings, W T (Walter Thies). The kid

Dennis, Wesley. Flip and the cows
Flip and the morning
Tumble, the story of a mustang

Ets, Marie Hall. Mr. Penny's race horse

Fain, James W. Rodeos

Farley, Walter. Little Black, a pony
Little Black goes to the circus

Fatio, Louise. Anna, the horse

Felton, Harold W. Pecos Bill and the mustang

Fregosi, Claudia. The happy horse

Friskey, Margaret. Indian Two Feet and his horse

Garbutt, Bernard. Roger, the rosin back

Gaston, Susan. New boots for Salvador

Gay, Zhenya. Wonderful things

Goble, Paul. The gift of the sacred dog
The girl who loved wild horses

Grabianski, Janusz. Horses

Greaves, Margaret. A net to catch the wind

Greydanus, Rose. Horses

Grimm, Jacob. The horse, the fox, and the lion

Gross, Ruth Belov. The girl who wouldn't get married

Hasler, Eveline. Martin is our friend

Hawkinson, John. Where the wild apples grow

Heilbroner, Joan. Robert the rose horse

Hoff, Syd. Chester
The horse in Harry's room

Inkiow, Dimiter. Me and Clara and Baldwin the pony

Ipcar, Dahlov. One horse farm
World full of horses

Jeffers, Susan. All the pretty horses

Keeping, Charles. Molly o' the moors

Kraus, Robert. Springfellow

Krauss, Ruth. Charlotte and the white horse

Krum, Charlotte. The four riders

La Farge, Phyllis. Joanna runs away

Lasell, Fen. Michael grows a wish

Lobel, Arnold. Lucille

Low, Alice. David's windows

McGinley, Phyllis. The horse who lived upstairs

Meeks, Esther K. Playland pony

Miles, Miska. Friend of Miguel

Miller, Jane. Birth of a foal

Otsuka, Yuzo. Suho and the white horse

Otto, Margaret Glover. The little brown horse

Paterson, Andrew Barton. Mulga Bill's bicycle

Peet, Bill. Cowardly Clyde

Pender, Lydia. Barnaby and the horses

Pluckrose, Henry. Horses

Primavera, Elise. Basil and Maggie

Rabinowitz, Sandy. A colt named mischief
What's happening to Daisy?

Richard, Jane. A horse grows up

Rounds, Glen. Once we had a horse
The strawberry roan

Sewell, Helen Moore. Peggy and the pony

Slobodkina, Esphyr. The wonderful feast

Thompson, Vivian Laubach. The horse that liked sandwiches

Ward, Lynd. The silver pony

Wondriska, William. The stop

Woolley, Catherine. Andy and the runaway horse
The horse with the Easter bonnet

Wright, Dare. Look at a colt

Yeoman, John. The young performing horse

Young, Miriam Burt. If I rode a horse

Zimnik, Reiner. The proud circus horse

Zolotow, Charlotte. I have a horse of my own

Animals — hyenas

Newberry, Clare Turlay. Lambert's bargain

Prelutsky, Jack. The mean old mean hyena

Animals — kangaroos

Braun, Kathy. Kangaroo and kangaroo

Brown, Margaret Wise. Young kangaroo

Du Bois, William Pène. The forbidden forest

Hamsa, Bobbie. Your pet kangaroo

Hurd, Edith Thacher. The mother kangaroo

Johnson, Crockett. Upside down

Kent, Jack. Joey

Pape, Donna Lugg. Where is my little Joey?

Payne, Emmy. Katy no-pocket

Sanchez, Jose Louis Garcia. Kangaroo

Selig, Sylvie. Kangaroo

Stonehouse, Bernard. Kangaroos

Townsend, Anita. The kangaroo

Ungerer, Tomi. Adelaide

Wiseman, Bernard. Little new kangaroo

Animals — kinkajous

Vandivert, William. Barnaby

Animals — koala bears

Du Bois, William Pène. Bear circus
  Bear party
Eberle, Irmengarde. Koalas live here
Levens, George. Kippy the koala
Quackenbush, Robert M. I don't want to
  go, I don't know how to act
Ruck-Pauquèt, Gina. Oh, that koala!
Snyder, Dick. One day at the zoo

Animals — leopards

Aardema, Verna. Half-a-ball-of-kenki
Ipcar, Dahlov. Stripes and spots
Irvine, Georgeanne. Lindi the leopard
Kepes, Juliet. Run little monkeys, run,
  run, run
Maestro, Giulio. Leopard is sick

Animals — lions

Adamson, Joy. Elsa
  Elsa and her cubs
Æsop. The lion and the mouse
Androcles and the lion
Balet, Jan B. Ned and Ed and the lion
Bannerman, Helen. The story of the
  teasing monkey
Bohman, Nils. Jim, Jock and Jumbo
Bridges, William. Lion Island
Brown, Margaret Wise. The sleepy little
  lion
Daugherty, James Henry. Andy and the
  lion
  The picnic
Davis, Douglas F. The lion's tail
Demarest, Chris L. Clemens' kingdom
Devlin, Wende. Aunt Agatha, there's a
  lion under the couch!
Du Bois, William Pène. Lion
Fatio, Louise. The happy lion
  The happy lion and the bear
  The happy lion in Africa
  The happy lion roars
  The happy lion's quest
  The happy lion's rabbits
  The happy lion's treasure
  The happy lion's vacation
  The three happy lions
Fechner, Amrei. I am a little lion
Freeman, Don. Dandelion
Galdone, Paul. Androcles and the lion
Gay, Zhenya. I'm tired of lions
Grimm, Jacob. The horse, the fox, and
  the lion
Hawkins, Mark. A lion under her bed

Hurd, Edith Thacher. Johnny Lion's
  bad day
  Johnny Lion's book
  Johnny Lion's rubber boots
Kishida, Eriko. The lion and the bird's
  nest
La Fontaine, Jean de. The lion and the
  rat
Mahy, Margaret. A lion in the meadow
Makower, Sylvia. Samson's breakfast
Mann, Peggy. King Laurence, the alarm
  clock
Michel, Anna. Little wild lion cub
Ness, Evaline. Fierce the lion
Newberry, Clare Turlay. Herbert the
  lion
Peet, Bill. Eli
  Hubert's hair-raising adventures
  Randy's dandy lions
Pluckrose, Henry. Lions and tigers
Siddiqui, Ashraf. Bhombal Dass, the
  uncle of lion
Siepmann, Jane. The lion on Scott
  Street
Skorpen, Liesel Moak. If I had a lion
Stephenson, Dorothy. How to scare a
  lion
Stewart, Elizabeth Laing. The lion twins
Townsend, Kenneth. Felix, the
  bald-headed lion
Varga, Judy. Miss Lollipop's lion
Zelinsky, Paul O. The lion and the stoat

Animals — llamas

Rockwell, Anne F. The good llama

Animals — mice

Æsop. The lion and the mouse
  The town mouse and the country
    mouse, ill. by Lorinda Bryan Cauley
  The town mouse and the country
    mouse, ill. by Paul Galdone
  The town mouse and the country
    mouse, ill. by Tom Garcia
Alexander, Sue. Dear Phoebe
Aliki. At Mary Bloom's
Allen, Laura Jean. Rollo and Tweedy
  and the case of the missing cheese
Althea. Jeremy Mouse and cat
Angelo, Nancy Carolyn Harrison.
  Camembert
Angelo, Valenti. The candy basket
Arnosky, Jim. Mouse numbers and
  letters
  Mouse writing
Augarde, Steve. Barnaby Shrew, Black
  Dan and... the mighty wedgwood
Balzano, Jeanne. The wee moose
Barklem, Jill. Autumn story
  The big book of Brambly Hedge

The secret staircase
Spring story
Summer story
Winter story
Barrows, Marjorie Wescott. The book of favorite Muggins Mouse stories
Muggins' big balloon
Muggins Mouse
Muggins takes off
Belpré, Pura. Perez and Martina
Berson, Harold. A moose is not a mouse
Raminagrobis and the mice
Blair, Anne Denton. Hurrah for Arthur!
Boegehold, Betty. Here's Pippa again!
Pippa Mouse
Pippa pops out!
Bond, Felicia. The Halloween performance
Boynton, Sandra. If at first...
Brady, Irene. A mouse named Mus
Wild mouse
Brandenberg, Franz. Everyone ready?
It's not my fault
Nice new neighbors
Six new students
What can you make of it?
Brenner, Barbara. Mr. Tall and Mr. Small
Bright, Robert. Georgie and the runaway balloon
Brook, Judy. Tim mouse goes down the stream
Tim mouse visits the farm
Brown, Palmer. Cheerful
Hickory
Something for Christmas
Burningham, John. Trubloff
Cameron, John. If mice could fly
Cantieni, Benita. Little Elephant and Big Mouse
Carle, Eric. Do you want to be my friend?
Cartlidge, Michelle. A mouse's diary
Pippin and Pod
Charles, Donald. Calico Cat's exercise book
Chase, Catherine. Baby mouse goes shopping
Baby mouse learns his ABC's
The mouse in my house
Christensen, Gardell Dano. Mrs. Mouse needs a house
Claret, Maria. Melissa Mouse
Coombs, Patricia. Mouse Café
Cressey, James. Max the mouse
Cunningham, Julia. A mouse called Junction
Dauer, Rosamond. Bullfrog grows up
Daugherty, James Henry. The picnic

Delessert, Etienne. How the mouse was hit on the head by a stone and so discovered the world
De Paola, Tomie. Charlie needs a cloak
De Regniers, Beatrice Schenk. Picture book theater
Doty, Roy. Old-one-eye meets his match
Durrell, Julie. Mouse tails
Ets, Marie Hall. Mr. T. W. Anthony Woo
Felix, Monique. The story of a little mouse trapped in a book
Fisher, Aileen. Sing, little mouse
Freeman, Don. The guard mouse
Norman the doorman
Freeman, Lydia. Pet of the Met
Freschet, Berniece. Bear mouse
Bernard of Scotland Yard
Futamata, Eigorō. How not to catch a mouse
Gackenbach, Dick. The perfect mouse
Gág, Wanda. Snippy and Snappy
Gantz, David. The genie bear with the light brown hair word book
Gili, Phillida. Fanny and Charles
Goodall, John S. Creepy castle
Gordon, Margaret. The supermarket mice
Goundaud, Karen Jo. A very mice joke book
Graham, John. I love you, mouse
Greene, Carol. A computer went a-courting
Gundersheimer, Karen. 1 2 3 play with me
Gurney, Nancy. The king, the mice and the cheese
Hale, Irina. Chocolate mouse and sugar pig
Hale, Linda. The glorious Christmas soup party
Hall, Malcolm. And then the mouse...
Harris, Dorothy Joan. The school mouse and the hamster
Harris, Leon A. The great picture robbery
Hawkinson, John. The old stump
Heathers, Anne. The thread soldiers
Hewett, Joan. The mouse and the elephant
Hillman, Priscilla. A Merry-Mouse book of favorite poems
A Merry-Mouse book of months
A Merry-Mouse Christmas A B C
The Merry-Mouse schoolhouse
Hoban, Lillian. It's really Christmas
The sugar snow spring
Hoban, Russell. Flat cat
Hoff, Carol. The four friends
Hoffmann, E T A. The nutcracker

Holabird, Katharine. Angelina and the
    princess
  Angelina ballerina
  The little mouse ABC
Holl, Adelaide. A mouse story
Houghton, Eric. The mouse and the
    magician
House mouse
Houston, John A. A mouse in my house
Howard, Jean G. Of mice and mice
Hurd, Edith Thacher. Come and have
    fun
Hürlimann, Ruth. The mouse with the
    daisy hat
Ivimey, John William. The complete
    version of ye three blind mice
Joerns, Consuelo. The foggy rescue
  The lost and found house
  The midnight castle
Jonah
Keenan, Martha. The mannerly
    adventures of Little Mouse
Kellogg, Steven. The island of the skog
Koenig, Marion. The tale of fancy
    Nancy
Kraus, Robert. Another mouse to feed
  I, Mouse
  Whose mouse are you?
Kumin, Maxine. Joey and the birthday
    present
Kuskin, Karla. What did you bring me?
Kwitz, Mary DeBall. Mouse at home
Layton, Aviva. The squeakers
Linch, Elizabeth Johanna. Samson
Lionni, Leo. Alexander and the wind-up
    mouse
  Frederick
  Geraldine, the music mouse
  The greentail mouse
  In the rabbitgarden
  Mouse days
  Theodore and the talking mushroom
  What?
  When?
  Where?
  Who?
  Words to talk about
Little, Mary E. Ricardo and the puppets
Lobel, Arnold. Martha, the movie
    mouse
  Mouse soup
  Mouse tales
  The rose in my garden
Low, Joseph. The Christmas grump
  Mice twice
McCully, Emily Arnold. Picnic
McNulty, Faith. Mouse and Tim
Mandry, Kathy. The cat and the mouse
    and the mouse and the cat
Manushkin, Fran. Moon dragon

Martin, Jacqueline Briggs. Bizzy Bones
    and Uncle Ezra
Mayer, Marianna. Alley oop!
Mendoza, George. Henri Mouse
  Need a house? Call Ms. Mouse
Miles, Miska. Mouse six and the happy
    birthday
Miller, Alice P. The mouse family's
    blueberry pie
Miller, Edna. Mousekin finds a friend
  Mousekin's ABC
  Mousekin's Christmas eve
  Mousekin's close call
  Mousekin's fables
  Mousekin's family
  Mousekin's golden house
  Mousekin's mystery
Moore, Inga. The vegetable thieves
Mouse house
Numeroff, Laura Joffe. If you give a
    mouse a cookie
Oakley, Graham. The church cat abroad
  The church mice adrift
  The church mice and the moon
  The church mice at bay
  The church mice at Christmas
  The church mice in action
  The church mice spread their wings
  The church mouse
Ormondroyd, Edward. Broderick
Peppé, Rodney. Cat and mouse
  The kettleship pirates
  The mice who lived in a shoe
Piers, Helen. The mouse book
Polushkin, Maria. Mother, Mother, I
    want another
Potter, Beatrix. The tailor of
    Gloucester
  The tale of Johnny Town-Mouse
  The tale of Mrs. Tittlemouse
  The tale of two bad mice
Potter, Russell. The little red ferry boat
Roach, Marilynne K. Two Roman mice
Roche, P K. Good-bye, Arnold!
Ross, Tony. Hugo and Oddsock
  Hugo and the bureau of holidays
  Hugo and the man who stole colors
Schermer, Judith. Mouse in house
Schlein, Miriam. Home, the tale of a
    mouse
Schoenherr, John. The barn
Seidler, Rosalie. Grumpus and the
    Venetian cat
Seignobosc, Françoise. Small-Trot
Selden, George. The mice, the monks
    and the Christmas tree
Simon, Sidney B. Henry, the
    uncatchable mouse
Smith, Jim. The frog band and
    Durrington Dormouse
Stanley, Diane. The conversation club

Animals — moles

Animals — mongooses

Animals — monkeys

Komoda, Beverly. Simon's soup
Mathiesen, Egon. Oswald, the monkey
Meshover, Leonard. The monkey that
  went to school
Olds, Helen Diehl. Miss Hattie and the
  monkey
Parish, Peggy. Jumper goes to school
Preston, Edna Mitchell. Monkey in the
  jungle
Reitveld, Jane Klatt. Monkey island
Rey, Hans Augusto. Cecily G and the
  nine monkeys
  Curious George
  Curious George gets a medal
  Curious George learns the alphabet
  Curious George rides a bike
  Curious George takes a job
Rey, Margaret Elisabeth Waldstein.
  Curious George flies a kite
  Curious George goes to the hospital
Rockwell, Anne F. The stolen necklace
Selsam, Millicent E. A first look at
  monkeys
Shi, Zhang Xiu. Monkey and the white
  bone demon
Slobodkina, Esphyr. Caps for sale
Suba, Susanne. The monkeys and the
  pedlar
Teleki, Geza. Aerial apes
Thaler, Mike. Moonkey
Whitehead, Patricia. Monkeys
Williamson, Hamilton. Monkey tale
Wolkstein, Diane. The cool ride in the
  sky

Animals — moose

Brown, Marc. Moose and goose
Foreman, Michael. Moose
Freschet, Berniece. Moose baby
Hoff, Syd. Santa's moose
McNeer, May Yonge. My friend Mac
Marshall, James. The guest
Platt, Kin. Big Max in the mystery of
  the missing moose
Seuss, Dr. Thidwick, the big-hearted
  moose
Slobodkin, Louis. Melvin, the moose
  child
Wiseman, Bernard. Morris has a
  birthday party!

Animals — mules

Beatty, Hetty Burlingame. Droopy
Snyder, Anne. The old man and the
  mule
Zemach, Margot. Jake and Honeybunch
  go to heaven

Animals — muskrats

Hoban, Russell. Harvey's hideout

Animals — octopuses see Octopuses

Animals — otters

Allen, Laura Jean. Ottie and the star
Benchley, Nathaniel. Oscar Otter
Hoban, Russell. Emmet Otter's jug-band
  Christmas
Shaw, Evelyn S. Sea otters
Sheehan, Angela. The otter
Tompert, Ann. Little Otter remembers
  and other stories
Wisbeski, Dorothy Gross. Pícaro, a pet
  otter

Animals — pack rats

Miller, Edna. Pebbles, a pack rat
Quackenbush, Robert M. Pete Pack Rat
Van Horn, William. Harry Hoyle's giant
  jumping bean

Animals — pigs

Alexander, Lloyd. Coll and his white pig
Allard, Harry. There's a party at Mona's
  tonight
Augarde, Steve. Pig
Baldner, Gaby. Joba and the wild boar
Berson, Harold. Truffles for lunch
Bishop, Claire Huchet. The truffle pig
Blegvad, Lenore. This little pig-a-wig
  and other rhymes about pigs
Bond, Felicia. Mary Betty Lizzie
  McNutt's birthday
  Poinsettia and her family
  Poinsettia and the firefighters
Boynton, Sandra. Hester in the wild
Brand, Millen. This little pig named
  Curly
Brock, Emma Lillian. Pig with a front
  porch
Brooke, L Leslie (Leonard Leslie). This
  little pig went to market
Brown, Judith Gwyn. Max and the
  truffle pig
Brown, Marc. Perfect pigs
Bruna, Dick. Poppy Pig goes to market
Brunhoff, Laurent de. The one pig with
  horns
Calhoun, Mary. The witch's pig
Calmenson, Stephanie. Never take a pig
  to lunch and other funny poems
  about animals
Chorao, Kay. Oink and Pearl
Cole, Brock. Nothing but a pig
Coontz, Otto. Starring Rosa
Craig, Helen. Susie and Alfred in the
  knight, the princess and the dragon
Cushman, Doug. Once upon a pig
Dubanevich, Arlene. Pigs in hiding
Dunrea, Olivier. Eddy B, pigboy

Dyke, John. Pigwig
  Pigwig and the pirates
Ernst, Lisa Campbell. The prize pig
  surprise
Erskine, Jim. Bert and Susie's messy tale
Fremlin, Robert. Three friends
Gackenbach, Dick. The pig who saw
  everything
Galdone, Paul. The amazing pig
Geisert, Arthur. Pa's balloon and other
  pig tales
Getz, Arthur. Humphrey, the dancing
  pig
Goodall, John S. The adventures of
  Paddy Pork
  The ballooning adventures of Paddy
  Pork
  Paddy goes traveling
  Paddy Pork odd jobs
  Paddy Pork's holiday
  Paddy under water
  Paddy's evening out
  Paddy's new hat
Hale, Irina. Chocolate mouse and sugar
  pig
Hauptmann, Tatjana. A day in the life
  of Petronella Pig
Hawkins, Colin. Mig the pig
Heine, Helme. The pigs' wedding
Hoban, Lillian. Mr. Pig and family
  Mr. Pig and Sonny too
Hoff, Syd. Happy birthday, Henrietta!
Hofstrand, Mary. Albion pig
  Home before midnight
Jeschke, Susan. Perfect the pig
Keller, Holly. Geraldine's blanket
Kent, Jack. Piggy Bank Gonzalez
Kroll, Steven. Pigs in the house
Laird, Donivee Martin. The three little
  Hawaiian pigs and the magic shark
Lawrence, John. Rabbit and pork
Lobel, Arnold. Small pig
  A treeful of pigs
Lorenz, Lee. A weekend in the country
McClenathan, Louise. The Easter pig
McPhail, David. Pig Pig goes to camp
  Pig Pig grows up
  Pig Pig rides
Maestro, Betsy. The guessing game
Marshall, James. Portly McSwine
  Yummers!
Mathews, Louise. The great take-away
Miles, Miska. This little pig
Oxenbury, Helen. Pig tale
Peck, Robert Newton. Hamilton
Peet, Bill. Chester the worldly pig
Pomerantz, Charlotte. The piggy in the
  puddle
Potter, Beatrix. The tale of Little Pig
  Robinson
  The tale of Pigling Bland

Rayner, Mary. Garth Pig and the ice
  cream lady
  Mr. and Mrs. Pig's evening out
  Mrs. Pig's bulk buy
Ross, Tony. The enchanted pig
Scarry, Richard. Richard Scarry's
  Peasant Pig and the terrible dragon
Sharmat, Mitchell. The seven sloppy
  days of Phineas Pig
Shecter, Ben. Partouche plants a seed
Slate, Joseph. The mean, clean, giant
  canoe machine
Steig, William. The amazing bone
  Farmer Palmer's wagon ride
  Roland, the minstrel pig
Stevens, Carla. Hooray for pig!
  Pig and the blue flag
Stobbs, William. This little piggy
Stolz, Mary Slattery. Emmett's pig
The three little pigs, ill. by Erik Blegvad
The three little pigs, ill. by Lorinda
  Bryan Cauley
The three little pigs, ill. by William Pène
  Du Bois
The three little pigs, ill. by Paul Galdone
The three little pigs, ill. by Rodney Peppé
The three little pigs, ill. by Irma Wilde
The three little pigs. The story of the
  three little pigs, ill. by L. Leslie
  Brooke
  The story of the three little pigs, ill. by
  William Stobbs
  The three pigs, ill. by Tony Ross
Tripp, Wallace. The tale of a pig
Ungerer, Tomi. Christmas eve at the
  Mellops
  The Mellops go diving for treasure
  The Mellops go flying
  The Mellops go spelunking
  The Mellops strike oil
Van Leeuwen, Jean. Amanda Pig and
  her big brother Oliver
  More tales of Oliver Pig
  Tales of Amanda Pig
  Tales of Oliver Pig
Waechter, Friedrich Karl. Three is
  company
Walker, Barbara K. Pigs and pirates
Watson, Pauline. Wriggles, the little
  wishing pig
Weiss, Ellen. Pigs in space
West, Ian. Silas, the first pig to fly
Weston, Martha. Peony's rainbow
Wild, Robin. Little Pig and the big bad
  wolf
Winthrop, Elizabeth. Sloppy kisses
Wiseman, Bernard. Don't make fun!
Wondriska, William. Mr. Brown and
  Mr. Gray
Yeoman, John. The bear's water picnic

Zakhoder, Boris Vladimirovich. How a
piglet crashed the Christmas party
Zalben, Jane Breskin. Basil and Hillary

Animals — porcupines

Annett, Cora. When the porcupine
moved in
Carrick, Carol. Ben and the porcupine
Massie, Diane Redfield. Tiny pin
The porcupine
Scarry, Patsy. Little Richard and Prickles
Schlein, Miriam. Lucky porcupine!
Stren, Patti. Hug me
Weiner, Beth Lee. Benjamin's perfect
solution

Animals — possums

Berson, Harold. Henry Possum
Burch, Robert. Joey's cat
Carlson, Natalie Savage. Marie Louise's
heyday
Conford, Ellen. Eugene the brave
Impossible, possum
Just the thing for Geraldine
Degen, Bruce. Aunt Possum and the
pumpkin man
Freschet, Berniece. Possum baby
Hoban, Russell. Nothing to do
Hurd, Thacher. Mama don't allow
Taylor, Mark. Old Blue, you good dog
you
Tether, Graham. Skunk and possum
Weiner, Beth Lee. Benjamin's perfect
solution
Winthrop, Elizabeth. Potbellied possums

Animals — prairie dogs

Baylor, Byrd. Amigo
Luttrell, Ida. Lonesome Lester

Animals — rabbits

Adams, Adrienne. The Christmas party
The Easter egg artists
The great Valentine's Day balloon race
Adler, David A. Bunny rabbit rebus
Æsop. The hare and the frogs
The hare and the tortoise
Anderson, Lonzo. Two hundred rabbits
Annett, Cora. When the porcupine
moved in
Balian, Lorna. Humbug rabbit
Barrett, John M. The Easter bear.
Bartoli, Jennifer. In a meadow, two
hares hide
Barton, Byron. Jack and Fred
Bate, Lucy. Little rabbit's loose tooth
Baumann, Hans. The hare's race
Becker, John Leonard. Seven little
rabbits

Berson, Harold. Pop! goes the turnip
Bianco, Margery Williams. The
velveteen rabbit, ill. by Allen
Atkinson
The velveteen rabbit, ill. by Michael
Hague
The velveteen rabbit, ill. by William
Nicholson
The velveteen rabbit, ill. by Ilse Plume
The velveteen rabbit, ill. by Tien
Bornstein, Ruth Lercher. Indian bunny
Bowden, Joan Chase. Bouncy baby
bunny finds his bed
Little grey rabbit
Bright, Robert. My hopping bunny
Brown, Marc. The bionic bunny show
What do you call a dumb bunny? and
other rabbit riddles, games, jokes and
cartoons
Brown, Marcia. The neighbors
Brown, Margaret Wise. The golden egg
book
Goodnight moon
Little chicken
The runaway bunny
Bruna, Dick. Miffy
Miffy at the beach
Miffy at the playground
Miffy at the seaside
Miffy at the zoo
Miffy goes to school
Miffy in the hospital
Miffy in the snow
Miffy's bicycle
Miffy's dream
Brunhoff, Laurent de. Gregory and
Lady Turtle in the valley of the music
trees
Caldwell, Mary. Morning, rabbit,
morning
Carlson, Nancy. Bunnies and their
hobbies
Loudmouth George and the big race
Loudmouth George and the cornet
Loudmouth George and the fishing
trip
Loudmouth George and the new
neighbors
Loudmouth George and the
sixth-grade bully
Carrick, Carol. A rabbit for Easter
Carroll, Ruth. What Whiskers did
Where's the bunny?
Cazet, Denys. Big shoe, little shoe
Christmas moon
Chalmers, Mary. Come for a walk with
me
Kevin
Chandoha, Walter. A baby bunny for
you

The hunt for rabbit's galosh
Seuss, Dr. The eye book
Sharmat, Marjorie Weinman. Thornton, the worrier
Spier, Peter. Little rabbits
Steiner, Charlotte. My bunny feels soft
Steiner, Jörg. Rabbit Island
Stevenson, James. Monty
Tarrant, Graham. Rabbits
Tompert, Ann. Nothing sticks like a shadow
Tresselt, Alvin R. Rabbit story
Trez, Denise. Rabbit country
Tripp, Wallace. My Uncle Podger
Van Woerkom, Dorothy. Harry and Shelburt
Wahl, Jan. Carrot nose
Doctor Rabbit's foundling
The five in the forest
Watson, Wendy. The bunnies' Christmas eve
Lollipop
Weil, Lisl. The candy egg bunny
Weisgard, Leonard. The funny bunny factory
Wells, Rosemary. Max's breakfast
Max's new suit
Wiese, Kurt. Happy Easter
Williams, Garth. The rabbits' wedding
Wolf, Ann. The rabbit and the turtle
Zakhoder, Boris Vladimirovich. Rosachok
Zolotow, Charlotte. The bunny who found Easter
Mr. Rabbit and the lovely present

Animals — raccoons

Bradford, Ann. The mystery at Misty Falls
The mystery of the missing raccoon
Brown, Margaret Wise. Wait till the moon is full
Duvoisin, Roger Antoine. Petunia, I love you
Freschet, Berniece. Five fat raccoons
Hess, Lilo. The curious raccoons
Hoban, Lillian. Here come raccoons
Johnson, Donna Kay. Brighteyes
McPhail, David. Stanley Henry Bear's friend
Miklowitz, Gloria D. Save that raccoon!
Miles, Miska. The raccoon and Mrs. McGinnis
Moore, Lilian. Little Raccoon and no trouble at all
Little Raccoon and the outside world
Little Raccoon and the thing in the pool
Morgan, Allen. Molly and Mr. Maloney
Noguere, Suzanne. Little raccoon

St George, Judith. The Halloween pumpkin smasher
Steiner, Barbara. But not Stanleigh
Wells, Rosemary. Timothy goes to school
Woolley, Catherine. The clever raccoon

Animals — rats

Annixter, Jane. Brown rats, black rats
Augarde, Steve. Barnaby Shrew, Black Dan and... the mighty wedgwood
Barnaby Shrew goes to sea
Berson, Harold. The rats who lived in the delicatessen
Black, Floyd. Alphabet cat
Browning, Robert. The pied piper of Hamelin
Cressey, James. Fourteen rats and a rat-catcher
Cunningham, Julia. A mouse called Junction
Doty, Roy. Old-one-eye meets his match
Erickson, Russell E. Warton and the traders
Hoban, Russell. Flat cat
Hurd, Thacher. Mystery on the docks
Kouts, Anne. Kenny's rat
La Fontaine, Jean de. The lion and the rat
McNaughton, Colin. The rat race
Miles, Miska. Wharf rat
Moore, Inga. Aktil's big swim
Murdocca, Sal. Tuttle's shell
Oakley, Graham. The church mice adrift
Pomerantz, Charlotte. The ballad of the long-tailed rat
Potter, Beatrix. The sly old cat
Ross, Tony. The pied piper of Hamelin
Saunders, Susan. Charles Rat's picnic
Schiller, Barbara. The white rat's tale
Sharmat, Marjorie Weinman. Mooch the messy
Stevenson, James. Wilfred the rat
Van Woerkom, Dorothy. The rat, the ox and the zodiac
Walt Disney Productions. Walt Disney's The adventures of Mr. Toad.
Yolen, Jane. Mice on ice
Zemach, Kaethe. The beautiful rat

Animals — reindeer

Hoff, Syd. Where's Prancer?
May, Robert Lewis. Rudolph the red-nosed reindeer

Animals — rhinoceros

Ardizzone, Edward. Diana and her rhinoceros
Johnson, Louise. Malunda

Kipling, Rudyard. How the rhinoceros
   got his skin
Maestro, Giulio. Just enough Rosie
Silverstein, Shel. Who wants a cheap
   rhinoceros?
Standon, Anna. The singing rhinoceros

Animals — sea lions

Hamsa, Bobbie. Your pet sea lion
Olds, Elizabeth. Plop plop ploppie
Schreiber, Georges. Bambino the clown

Animals — seals

Barr, Cathrine. Sammy seal ov the sircus
Duran, Bonté. The adventures of
   Arthur and Edmund
Freeman, Don. The seal and the slick
Hoff, Syd. Sammy the seal
Lilly, Kenneth. Animals of the ocean
The seal

Animals — sheep

Beskow, Elsa Maartman. Pelle's new suit
Brown, Margaret Wise. Little lost lamb
Coe, Lloyd. Charcoal
De Paola, Tomie. Charlie needs a cloak
Dunn, Judy. The little lamb
Ginsburg, Mirra. The strongest one of
   all
Hale, Sara Josepha. Mary had a little
   lamb
Ipcar, Dahlov. The land of flowers
Mendoza, George. Alphabet sheep
   Silly sheep and other sheepish rhymes
Miller, Jane. Lambing time
Peet, Bill. Buford, the little bighorn
Russell, Betty. Run sheep run
Ryder, Joanne. Beach party
Slobodkin, Louis. Up high and down
   low
Steiner, Charlotte. Red Ridinghood's
   little lamb
Weiss, Ellen. Clara the fortune-telling
   chicken

Animals — shrews

Augarde, Steve. Barnaby Shrew, Black
   Dan and... the mighty wedgwood
   Barnaby Shrew goes to sea
Carrick, Malcolm. Today is shrew's day

Animals — skunks

Hoban, Brom. Skunk Lane
Kitt, Tamara. A special birthday party
   for someone very special
Schlein, Miriam. What's wrong with
   being a skunk?
Schoenherr, John. The barn
Tether, Graham. Skunk and possum

Animals — sloths

Knight, Hilary. Sylvia the sloth

Animals — snails

Lord, John Vernon. Mr. Mead and his
   garden
Marshall, James. The guest
O'Hagan, Caroline. It's easy to have a
   snail visit you
Rockwell, Anne F. The story snail
Ryder, Joanne. Snail in the woods
   The snail's spell
Ungerer, Tomi. Snail, where are you?

Animals — squirrels

Angelo, Valenti. The acorn tree
Buff, Mary. Hurry, Skurry and Flurry
Crane, Donn. Flippy and Skippy
DeLage, Ida. The squirrel's tree party
Earle, Olive L. Squirrels in the garden
Fremlin, Robert. Three friends
Jones, Penelope. I didn't want to be nice
Lane, Margaret. The squirrel
Oxford Scientific Films. Grey squirrel
Palazzo, Tony. Federico, the flying
   squirrel
Peet, Bill. Merle the high flying squirrel
Potter, Beatrix. The tale of Squirrel
   Nutkin
   The tale of Timmy Tiptoes
Pratten, Albra. Winkie, the grey squirrel
St Tamara. Chickaree, a red squirrel
Schumacher, Claire. Nutty's Christmas
Shannon, George. The surprise
Sharmat, Marjorie Weinman. Attila the
   angry
   Sophie and Gussie
   The trip
Stage, Mads. The lonely squirrel
Stevenson, James. Wilfred the rat
Yeoman, John. The bear's water picnic
Young, Miriam Burt. Miss Suzy's Easter
   surprise
Zion, Gene. The meanest squirrel I ever
   met
Zweifel, Frances. Bony

Animals — tapirs

Maestro, Giulio. The tortoise's tug of war

Animals — tigers

Adams, Richard. The tyger voyage
Anderson, Paul S. Red fox and the
   hungry tiger
Bannerman, Helen. The story of little
   black Sambo
Barrows, Marjorie Wescott. Timothy
   Tiger
Canning, Kate. A painted tale

Dines, Glen. A tiger in the cherry tree
Domanska, Janina. Why so much noise?
Farber, Norma. How to ride a tiger
Fenner, Carol. Tigers in the cellar
Frankel, Bernice. Half-As-Big and the tiger
Hoban, Russell. The dancing tigers
Hoffman, Mary. Animals in the wild tiger
Ipcar, Dahlov. Stripes and spots
Justice, Jennifer. The tiger
Kepes, Juliet. Cock-a-doodle-doo
Kraus, Robert. Leo the late bloomer
Paul, Anthony. The tiger who lost his stripes
Pluckrose, Henry. Lions and tigers
Prelutsky, Jack. The terrible tiger
Rockwell, Anne F. Big boss
Rose, Gerald. The tiger-skin rug
Taylor, Mark. Henry explores the jungle
Tworkov, Jack. The camel who took a walk
Villarejo, Mary. The tiger hunt
Wahl, Jan. Tiger watch
Wersba, Barbara. Do tigers ever bite kings?
Whitney, Alex. Once a bright red tiger
The tiger that barks
Wolkstein, Diane. The banza

Animals — walruses

Bonsall, Crosby Newell. What spot?
Bridges, William. Ookie, the walrus who likes people
Hoff, Syd. Walpole
Stevenson, James. Winston, Newton, Elton, and Ed

Animals — water buffaloes

Gobhai, Mehlli. Lakshmi, the water buffalo who wouldn't

Animals — weasels

Bach, Alice. Warren Weasel's worse than measles
Lobel, Arnold. Mouse soup
Mathews, Louise. Cluck one
Zelinsky, Paul O. The lion and the stoat

Animals — whales

Applebaum, Neil. Is there a hole in your head?
Armour, Richard Willard. Sea full of whales
Behrens, June. Whalewatch!
Benchley, Nathaniel. The deep dives of Stanley Whale

Bulla, Clyde Robert. Jonah and the great fish
Clark, Harry. The first story of the whale
Climo, Shirley. The adventure of Walter
Conklin, Gladys. Journey of the gray whales
Duvoisin, Roger Antoine. The Christmas whale
Engle, Joanna. Cap'n kid goes to the South Pole
Haiz, Danah. Jonah's journey
Hudson, Eleanor. A whale of a rescue
Hurd, Edith Thacher. What whale? Where?
Hutton, Warwick. Jonah and the great fish
Johnston, Johanna. Whale's way
Jonah
King, Patricia. Mable the whale
Lent, Blair. John Tabor's ride
Lilly, Kenneth. Animals of the ocean
McCloskey, Robert. Bert Dow, deep-water man
Maestro, Giulio. The tortoise's tug of war
Phleger, Fred B. The whales go by
Pluckrose, Henry. Whales
Postgate, Oliver. Noggin and the whale
Roy, Ronald. A thousand pails of water
Selsam, Millicent E. A first look at whales
Siberell, Anne. Whale in the sky
Watanabe, Yuichi. Wally the whale who loved balloons

Animals — wolves

Ambrus, Victor G. Country wedding
Blades, Ann. Mary of mile 18
Damjan, Mischa. Atuk
The wolf and the kid
Daudet, Alphonse. The brave little goat of Monsieur Séguin
De Regniers, Beatrice Schenk. Red Riding Hood
Evans, Katherine. The boy who cried wolf
Firmin, Peter. Chicken stew
Friskey, Margaret. Indian Two Feet and the wolf cubs
Goble, Paul. The friendly wolf
Grimm, Jacob. Little red cap
Little Red Riding Hood, ill. by Frank Aloise
Little Red Riding Hood, ill. by Bernadette
Little Red Riding Hood, ill. by Gwen Connelly
Little Red Riding Hood, ill. by Paul Galdone

Little Red Riding Hood, ill. by Trina
Schart Hyman
The wolf and the seven kids
The wolf and the seven little kids
Gunthrop, Karen. Adam and the wolf
Harper, Wilhelmina. The gunniwolf
Hawkins, Colin. What time is it, Mr.
Wolf?
McClure, Gillian. What's the time, Rory
Wolf?
McPhail, David. A wolf story
Parish, Peggy. Granny, the baby and the
big gray thing
Peck, Robert Newton. Hamilton
Prokofiev, Sergei Sergeievitch. Peter and
the wolf, ill. by Warren Chappell
Peter and the wolf, ill. by Frans
Haacken
Peter and the wolf, ill. by Alan
Howard
Peter and the wolf, ill. by Charles
Mikolaycak
Peter and the wolf, ill. by Kozo
Shimizu
Rayner, Mary. Garth Pig and the ice
cream lady
Mr. and Mrs. Pig's evening out
Rockwell, Anne F. The wolf who had a
wonderful dream
Schick, Alice. Just this once
Selsam, Millicent E. A first look at dogs
Sharmat, Marjorie Weinman. Walter the
wolf
Storr, Catherine. Clever Polly and the
stupid wolf
The three little pigs, ill. by Erik Blegvad
The three little pigs, ill. by Lorinda
Bryan Cauley
The three little pigs, ill. by William Pène
Du Bois
The three little pigs, ill. by Paul Galdone
The three little pigs, ill. by Rodney Peppé
The three little pigs, ill. by Irma Wilde
The three little pigs. The story of the
three little pigs, ill. by L. Leslie
Brooke
The story of the three little pigs, ill. by
William Stobbs
The three pigs, ill. by Tony Ross
Wild, Robin. Little Pig and the big bad
wolf

Animals — worms

Ahlberg, Janet. The little worm book
O'Hagan, Caroline. It's easy to have a
worm visit you
Scarry, Richard. Richard Scarry's busy
houses
Wong, Herbert H. Our earthworms
Woolley, Catherine. Andy and the wild
worm

Animals — yaks

Lawson, Annetta. The lucky yak

Animals — zebras

Goodall, Daphne Machin. Zebras
Hadithi, Mwenye. Greedy zebra

Antarctic see Foreign lands — Antarctic

Anteaters see Animals — anteaters

Anti-violence see Violence, anti-violence

Ants see Insects — ants

Apes see Animals — gorillas; Animals
— monkeys

Appearance see Character traits —
appearance

April Fools' Day see Holidays — April
Fools' Day

Arabia see Foreign lands — Arabia

Arctic see Foreign lands — Arctic

Arguing see Behavior — fighting,
arguing

Arithmetic see Counting

Armadillos see Animals — armadillos

Armenia see Foreign lands — Armenia

Art

Anderson, Douglas. Let's draw a story
Angelo, Nancy Carolyn Harrison.
Camembert
Baker, Jeannie. Grandmother
Baylor, Byrd. When clay sings
Borten, Helen. Do you see what I see?
A picture has a special look
Brandenberg, Franz. What can you
make of it?
Bröger, Achim. Francie's paper puppy
Bromhall, Winifred. Mary Ann's first
picture
Browne, Anthony. Bear hunt
Bulla, Clyde Robert. Daniel's duck
Canning, Kate. A painted tale
Coatsworth, Elizabeth. Boston Bells
Cober, Alan E. Cober's choice
Cohen, Miriam. No good in art
Craig, Helen. Susie and Alfred in the
knight, the princess and the dragon
Dionetti, Michelle. Thalia Brown and
the blue bug

Elliott, Dan. Ernie's little lie
Emberley, Ed. Ed Emberley's big green drawing book
  Ed Emberley's big orange drawing book
  Ed Emberley's big purple drawing book
  Ed Emberley's crazy mixed-up face game
Emberley, Michael. More dinosaurs!
Emberley, Rebecca. Drawing with numbers and letters
Fifield, Flora. Pictures for the palace
Freeman, Don. Norman the doorman
Green, Marion. The magician who lived on the mountain
Harris, Leon A. The great picture robbery
Hurd, Edith Thacher. Wilson's world
Johnson, Crockett. Harold and the purple crayon
  A picture for Harold's room
Kesselman, Wendy. Emma
Kilroy, Sally. Copycat drawing book
Lionni, Leo. Let's make rabbits
McPhail, David. The magical drawings of Moony B. Finch
Mendoza, George. Henri Mouse
Menter, Ian. The Albany Road mural
Peet, Bill. Encore for Eleanor
Pinkwater, Daniel Manus. The bear's picture
Rauch, Hans-Georg. The lines are coming
Rey, Margaret Elisabeth Waldstein. Billy's picture
Sharon, Mary Bruce. Scenes from childhood
Türk, Hanne. Max the artlover
Villarejo, Mary. The art fair
Wolf, Janet. The best present is me
Zelinsky, Paul O. The lion and the stoat

Artists *see* Careers — artists

Astrology *see* Zodiac

Astronauts *see* Space and space ships

Australia *see* Foreign lands — Australia

Austria *see* Foreign lands — Austria

Authors, children *see* Children as authors

Automobiles

Alexander, Anne. ABC of cars and trucks
Aulaire, Ingri Mortenson d'. The two cars

Baugh, Dolores M. Trucks and cars to ride
Biro, Val. Gumdrop, the adventures of a vintage car
Bridwell, Norman. Clifford's good deeds
Burningham, John. Mr. Gumpy's motor car
Caines, Jeannette. Just us women
Cars and trucks
Cave, Ron. Automobiles
Cummings, W T (Walter Thies). Miss Esta Maude's secret
DiFiori, Lawrence. If I had a little car
Ets, Marie Hall. Little old automobile
Holl, Adelaide. The ABC of cars, trucks and machines
Janosch. The magic auto
Lenski, Lois. The little auto
Löfgren, Ulf. The traffic stopper that became a grandmother visitor
Maestro, Betsy. Traffic
Oxenbury, Helen. The car trip
Peet, Bill. Jennifer and Josephine
Peppé, Rodney. Little wheels
Petrie, Catherine. Hot Rod Harry
Pinkwater, Daniel Manus. Tooth-gnasher superflash
Pitcher, Caroline. Cars and boats
Rockwell, Anne F. Cars
Scarry, Huck. On the road
Scarry, Richard. The great big car and truck book
  Richard Scarry's cars and trucks and things that go
Spier, Peter. Bill's service station
Stobbs, William. A car called beetle
Wilkinson, Sylvia. Automobiles
Young, Miriam Burt. If I drove a car

Autumn *see* Seasons — fall

Babies

Ahlberg, Janet. The baby's catalogue
  Peek-a-boo!
Alexander, Martha G. Nobody asked me if I wanted a baby sister
  When the new baby comes, I'm moving out
Aliki. At Mary Bloom's
Ancona, George. It's a baby!
Andry, Andrew C. Hi, new baby
  How babies are made
Arnstein, Helene S. Billy and our new baby

Asch, Frank. Starbaby
Baker, Charlotte. Little brother
Baker, Gayle. Special delivery
Banish, Roslyn. I want to tell you about my baby
Bendick, Jeanne. What made you you?
Bernadette (Bernadette Watts). David's waiting day
Bolognese, Don. A new day
Brandenberg, Franz. Aunt Nina and her nephews and nieces
Brann, Esther. A book for baby
Brice, Tony. Baby animals
Brooks, Robert B. So that's how I was born
Burningham, John. Avocado baby
Byars, Betsy Cromer. Go and hush the baby
Chaffin, Lillie D. Tommy's big problem
Chess, Victoria. Poor Esmé
Clifton, Lucille. Everett Anderson's nine months long
Cole, Joanna. A calf is born
   How you were born
Dragonwagon, Crescent. Wind Rose
Flack, Marjorie. The new pet
Foulds, Elfrida Vipont. The elephant and the bad baby
Gill, Joan. Hush, Jon!
Girard, Linda Walvoord. You were born on your very first birthday
Greenberg, Barbara. The bravest babysitter
Greenfield, Eloise. She come bringing me that little baby girl
Gruenberg, Sidonie Matsner. The wonderful story of how you were born
Hamilton-Merritt, Jane. Our new baby
Hanson, Joan. I don't like Timmy
Hazen, Barbara Shook. Why couldn't I be an only kid like you, Wigger?
Helmering, Doris Wild. We're going to have a baby
Herter, Jonina. Eighty-eight kisses
Hirsh, Marilyn. Leela and the watermelon
   Where is Yonkela?
Hobson, Laura Z. "I'm going to have a baby!"
Hoffman, Rosekrans. Sister Sweet Ella
Holland, Viki. We are having a baby
Hush little baby, ill. by Aliki
Hush little baby, ill. by Jeanette Winter
Hush little baby, ill. by Margot Zemach
Jarrell, Mary. The knee baby
Keats, Ezra Jack. Peter's chair
Kilroy, Sally. Babies' bodies
   Baby colors
Krasilovsky, Phyllis. The very little boy
   The very little girl

Kraus, Robert. Big brother
Langstaff, Nancy. A tiny baby for you
Lasky, Kathryn. A baby for Max
Lexau, Joan M. Finders keepers, losers weepers
Lindgren, Astrid. I want a brother or sister
Malecki, Maryann. Mom and dad and I are having a baby!
Manushkin, Fran. Baby, come out!
Newberry, Clare Turlay. Cousin Toby T-Bone, the baby-sitter
Ormerod, Jan. 101 things to do with a baby
Oxenbury, Helen. Playing
Parish, Peggy. Granny, the baby and the big gray thing
Petersham, Maud. The box with red wheels
Politi, Leo. Rosa
Pursell, Margaret Sanford. A look at birth
Rice, Eve. What Sadie sang
Rushnell, Elaine Evans. My mom's having a baby
Schick, Eleanor. Peggy's new brother
Schlein, Miriam. Laurie's new brother
Sendak, Maurice. Outside over there
Shapp, Martha. Let's find out about babies
Sheffield, Margaret. Before you were born
   Where do babies come from?
Showers, Paul. A baby starts to grow
   Before you were a baby
Stein, Sara Bonnett. Making babies
   That new baby
Stevenson, James. Worse than Willy!
Vigna, Judith. Couldn't we have a turtle instead?
Williams, Barbara. Jeremy isn't hungry
Woolley, Catherine. Gus and the baby ghost
Zolotow, Charlotte. But not Billy
   Do you know what I'll do?

Babysitting see Activities — babysitting

Bad day see Behavior — bad day

Badgers see Animals — badgers

Bakers see Careers — bakers

Bali see Foreign lands — Bali

Ballooning see Activities — ballooning

Balloons see Toys — balloons

Balls see Toys — balls

Barbers *see* Careers — barbers

Barns

Brown, Margaret Wise. Big red barn
Carrick, Carol. The old barn
Climo, Lindee. Chester's barn
Merrill, Jean. Tell about the cowbarn, Daddy
Miles, Miska. The raccoon and Mrs. McGinnis
Schoenherr, John. The barn
Sewell, Helen Moore. Blue barns

Barons *see* Royalty

Baseball *see* Sports — baseball

Basketball *see* Sports — basketball

Bathing *see* Activities — bathing

Bats *see* Animals — bats

Bavaria *see* Foreign lands — Austria; Foreign lands — Germany

Beaches *see* Sea and seashore

Bears *see* Animals — bears

Beasts *see* Monsters

Beavers *see* Animals — beavers

Bedtime

Asch, Frank. Goodnight horsey
Aylesworth, Jim. Tonight's the night
Bang, Molly. Ten, nine, eight
  Wiley and the hairy man
Barrett, Judi. I hate to go to bed
Beckman, Kaj. Lisa cannot sleep
Berenstain, Stan. Bears in the night
Berridge, Celia. Grandmother's tales
Blocksma, Mary. Did you hear that?
Bond, Felicia. Poinsettia and the firefighters
Bottner, Barbara. There was nobody there
Bowden, Joan Chase. Bouncy baby bunny finds his bed
Bowers, Kathleen Rice. At this very minute
Boynton, Sandra. The going to bed book
Brown, Margaret Wise. A child's good night book
  Goodnight moon
Callen, Larry. Dashiel and the night
Cameron, Ann. Harry (the monster)

Chevalier, Christa. Spence and the sleepytime monster
Chorao, Kay. Lemon moon
Christelow, Eileen. Henry and the Dragon
Coatsworth, Elizabeth. Good night
Cole, William. Frances face-maker
Corddry, Thomas I. Kibby's big feat
Cosgrove, Stephen. Sleepy time bunny
Dahl, Roald. Dirty beasts
De Paola, Tomie. Fight the night
Engvick, William. Lullabies and night songs
Erskine, Jim. Bedtime story
Fox, Siv Cedering. The blue horse and other night poems
Gackenbach, Dick. Poppy the panda
Ginsburg, Mirra. Which is the best place?
Goffstein, M B (Marilyn Brooks). Sleepy people
Goodspeed, Peter. A rhinoceros wakes me up in the morning
Greenleaf, Ann. No room for Sarah
Harris, Dorothy Joan. Goodnight Jeffrey
Hawkins, Mark. A lion under her bed
Hill, Eric. Baby bear's bedtime
Hoban, Russell. Bedtime for Frances
  Goodnight
Hopkins, Lee Bennett. Go to bed!
Ipcar, Dahlov. The calico jungle
Jeffers, Susan. All the pretty horses
Johnston, Johanna. Edie changes her mind
Jonas, Ann. The quilt
Joslin, Sesyle. Brave Baby Elephant
Keller, Holly. Ten sleepy sheep
Kent, Jack. The once-upon-a-time dragon
Koide, Tan. May we sleep here tonight?
Kotzwinkle, William. The nap master
Krahn, Fernando. Sleep tight, Alex Pumpernickel
Kraus, Robert. Good night little one
  Good night Richard Rabbit
Krauss, Ruth. The bundle book
Kuskin, Karla. Night again
  A space story
Larrick, Nancy. When the dark comes dancing
Leaf, Munro. Boo, who used to be scared of the dark
Lesser, Carolyn. The goodnight circle
Levine, Joan. A bedtime story
Lifton, Betty Jean. Goodnight orange monster
Lippman, Peter. New at the zoo
Lloyd, Errol. Nandy's bedtime
Lobe, Mira. Valerie and the good-night swing
Mack, Stanley. Ten bears in my bed

Mählqvist, Stefan. I'll take care of the crocodiles

Marcin, Marietta. A zoo in her bed

Maris, Ron. My book

Marshall, James. What's the matter with Carruthers?

Marshall, Margaret. Mike

Marzollo, Jean. Close your eyes

Mayer, Mercer. Little Monster's bedtime book

There's a nightmare in my closet

Merriam, Eve. Good night to Annie

Milne, A A (Alan Alexander). Pooh's bedtime book

Montresor, Beni. Bedtime!

The moon's the north wind's cooky

Morris, Terry Nell. Good night, dear monster!

Murphy, Jill. What next, baby bear!

Orgel, Doris. Little John

Ormerod, Jan. Moonlight

Oxenbury, Helen. Good night, good morning

Peck, Richard. Monster night at Grandma's house

Petersham, Maud. Off to bed

Plath, Sylvia. The bed book

Pomerantz, Charlotte. All asleep
Posy

Preston, Edna Mitchell. Monkey in the jungle

Rice, Eve. Goodnight, goodnight

Richter, Mischa. To bed, to bed!

Robison, Deborah. No elephants allowed

Rockwell, Anne F. Buster and the bogeyman

Saltzberg, Barney. It must have been the wind

Schneider, Nina. While Susie sleeps

Schubert, Ingrid. There's a crocodile under my bed!

Sharmat, Marjorie Weinman. Goodnight, Andrew. Good night, Craig

Skorpen, Liesel Moak. Outside my window

Smith, Robert Paul. Nothingatall, nothingatall, nothingatall

Steiner, Charlotte. The sleepy quilt

Stevenson, James. We can't sleep
What's under my bed?

Strahl, Rudi. Sandman in the lighthouse

Strand, Mark. The planet of lost things

Sugita, Yutaka. Good night 1, 2, 3

Sussman, Susan. Hippo thunder

Swados, Elizabeth. Lullaby

Tobias, Tobi. Chasing the goblins away

Trez, Denise. Good night, Veronica

Türk, Hanne. Goodnight Max

Viorst, Judith. My mama says there aren't any zombies, ghosts, vampires, creatures, demons, monsters, fiends, goblins, or things

Waber, Bernard. Ira sleeps over

Watson, Clyde. Fisherman lullabies
Midnight moon

Whiteside, Karen. Lullaby of the wind

Winthrop, Elizabeth. Bunk beds

Yolen, Jane. Dragon night and other lullabies

Zalben, Jane Breskin. Norton's nighttime

Zolotow, Charlotte. Flocks of birds
The sleepy book
The summer night
Wake up and good night
When the wind stops

Bees see Insects — bees

Beetles see Insects — beetles

Behavior

Babbitt, Lorraine. Pink like the geranium

Beim, Jerrold. The swimming hole

Belloc, Hilaire. The bad child's book of beasts

Benchley, Nathaniel. Oscar Otter

Boegehold, Betty. Three to get ready

Carle, Eric. The grouchy ladybug

Caudill, Rebecca. Contrary Jenkins

Delton, Judy. I'm telling you now

Ets, Marie Hall. Bad boy, good boy
Play with me

Gackenbach, Dick. Hattie be quiet, Hattie be good

Gaeddert, Lou Ann Bigge. Noisy Nancy Nora

Gambill, Henrietta. Self-control

Harris, Robie H. Don't forget to come back

Hoban, Russell. Dinner at Alberta's

Hogrogian, Nonny. Carrot cake

Horvath, Betty F. Be nice to Josephine

Low, Joseph. Don't drag your feet...

Myller, Lois. No! No!

Ness, Evaline. Marcella's guardian angel

Panek, Dennis. Matilda Hippo has a big mouth

Parker, Nancy Winslow. Puddums, the Cathcarts' orange cat

Paterson, Diane. Wretched Rachel

Quackenbush, Robert M. I don't want to go, I don't know how to act

Ringi, Kjell. The winner

Sharmat, Marjorie Weinman. Scarlet Monster lives here

Stover, Jo Ann. If everybody did

Supraner, Robyn. Would you rather be a tiger?

Svendsen, Carol. Hulda

Wittels, Harriet. Things I hate!

Behavior — animals, dislike of

Bemelmans, Ludwig. Madeline and the bad hat

Kay, Helen. An egg is for wishing

Udry, Janice May. Alfred

Behavior — bad day

Andrews, F Emerson (Frank Emerson). Nobody comes to dinner

Berenstain, Stan. The Berenstain bears get in a fight

Duncan, Jane. Janet Reachfar and Chickabird

Fujikawa, Gyo. Sam's all-wrong day

Giff, Patricia Reilly. Today was a terrible day

Hoban, Russell. The sorely trying day

Hurd, Thacher. Mystery on the docks

Keith, Eros. Bedita's bad day

Krahn, Fernando. Here comes Alex Pumpernickel!

Lexau, Joan M. I should have stayed in bed

Oxenbury, Helen. The car trip

Sondheimer, Ilse. The boy who could make his mother stop yelling

Viorst, Judith. Alexander and the terrible, horrible, no good, very bad day

Vreeken, Elizabeth. One day everything went wrong

Wells, Rosemary. Unfortunately Harriet

Behavior — boasting

Augarde, Steve. Barnaby Shrew, Black Dan and...the mighty wedgwood

Bonsall, Crosby Newell. Mine's the best

Browne, Anthony. Look what I've got!

Carlson, Nancy. Loudmouth George and the big race

Loudmouth George and the cornet

Loudmouth George and the fishing trip

Loudmouth George and the new neighbors

Loudmouth George and the sixth-grade bully

Collins, Pat Lowery. My friend Andrew

Diot, Alain. Better, best, bestest

Duvoisin, Roger Antoine. See what I am

Ellentuck, Shan. A sunflower as big as the sun

Kepes, Juliet. The story of a bragging duck

Lopshire, Robert. I am better than you

Lund, Doris Herold. You ought to see Herbert's house

Miller, Warren. The goings on at Little Wishful

Osborn, Lois. My dad is really something

Pavey, Peter. I'm Taggarty Toad

Peterson, Esther Allen. Frederick's alligator

Raphael, Elaine. Turnabout

Schwartz, Amy. Her majesty, Aunt Essie

Behavior — boredom

Alexander, Martha G. We never get to do anything

Ayal, Ora. The adventures of Chester the chest

Delton, Judy. My mom hates me in January

Duvoisin, Roger Antoine. Veronica's smile

Hoban, Russell. Nothing to do

Krauss, Ruth. A good man and his good wife

McGovern, Ann. Nicholas Bentley Stoningpot III

McLaughlin, Lissa. Why won't winter go?

Oram, Hiawyn. In the attic

Raskin, Ellen. Nothing ever happens on my block

Reit, Seymour. The king who learned to smile

Spier, Peter. Bored - nothing to do!

Watts, Marjorie-Ann. Crocodile medicine

Woolley, Catherine. Mr. Turtle's magic glasses

Behavior — bullying

Alexander, Martha G. I sure am glad to see you, Blackboard Bear

Move over, Twerp

Berquist, Grace. The boy who couldn't roar

Bradbury, Bianca. One kitten too many

Bryant, Bernice. Follow the leader

Carlson, Nancy. Loudmouth George and the sixth-grade bully

Chapman, Carol. Herbie's troubles

Charlton, Elizabeth. Terrible tyrannosaurus

Christopher, Matt. Johnny no hit

Cohen, Miriam. Tough Jim

Janice. Angélique

Keats, Ezra Jack. Goggles

Kessler, Leonard P. Last one in is a rotten egg

Peet, Bill. Big bad Bruce

Roche, P K. Plaid bear and the rude
rabbit gang

Behavior — carelessness

Aliki. Keep your mouth closed, dear
Bottner, Barbara. Messy
Brown, Marc. The cloud over Clarence
Buchanan, Joan. It's a good thing
Carrick, Carol. A rabbit for Easter
Chislett, Gail. The rude visitors
Cleary, Beverly. Lucky Chuck
De Paola, Tomie. The quicksand book
  Strega Nona's magic lessons
Gackenbach, Dick. Binky gets a car
Gantos, Jack. Aunt Bernice
Ilsley, Velma. The pink hat
Mayer, Mercer. Oops
Moskin, Marietta D. Lysbet and the fire
  kittens
Panek, Dennis. Catastrophe Cat
Pender, Lydia. Barnaby and the horses

Behavior — collecting things

Beim, Lorraine. Lucky Pierre
Bram, Elizabeth. Woodruff and the
  clocks
Braun, Kathy. Kangaroo and kangaroo
Enderle, Judith A. Good junk
Evans, Eva Knox. That lucky Mrs.
  Plucky
Fox, Paula. Maurice's room
Gans, Roma. Rock collecting
Lewis, Naomi. The butterfly collector
Van Horn, William. Harry Hoyle's giant
  jumping bean
Weil, Lisl. To sail a ship of treasures

Behavior — disbelief

Cole, Brock. The king at the door
Gunthrop, Karen. Adam and the wolf

Behavior — dissatisfaction

Aliki. The twelve months
  The wish workers
Allen, Jeffrey. The secret life of Mr.
  Weird
Balet, Jan B. The king and the broom
  maker
Brewster, Patience. Nobody
Brock, Emma Lillian. Pig with a front
  porch
Brothers, Aileen. Sad Mrs. Sam Sack
Byars, Betsy Cromer. The groober
Chapman, Carol. The tale of Meshka
  the Kvetch
Clymer, Ted. The horse and the bad
  morning
Crowley, Arthur. The boogey man

Cushman, Doug. Nasty Kyle the
  crocodile
Dale, Ruth Bluestone. Benjamin - and
  Sylvester also
Day, Shirley. Waldo's back yard
Duvoisin, Roger Antoine. Petunia,
  beware!
Elborn, Andrew. Bird Adalbert
Ets, Marie Hall. The cow's party
Fish, Hans. Pitschi, the kitten who
  always wanted to do something else
Gackenbach, Dick. Mother Rabbit's son
  Tom
Gay, Zhenya. I'm tired of lions
Getz, Arthur. Humphrey, the dancing
  pig
Hille-Brandts, Lene. The little black hen
Hoban, Lillian. Stick-in-the-mud turtle
Johnson, Evelyne. The cow in the
  kitchen
Keats, Ezra Jack. Jennie's hat
McDermott, Gerald. The stonecutter
McGinley, Phyllis. The horse who lived
  upstairs
Massie, Diane Redfield. Walter was a
  frog
Olujic, Grozdana. Rose of
  Mother-of-Pearl
Palmer, Mary Babcock.
  No-sort-of-animal
Peet, Bill. The caboose who got loose
  The luckiest one of all
  The Whingdingdilly
Price, Roger. The last little dragon
Sadler, Marilyn. It's not easy being a
  bunny
Sarnoff, Jane. That's not fair
Sharmat, Marjorie Weinman. Grumley
  the grouch
Turnage, Sheila. Trout the magnificent
Wiesner, William. Turnabout
Yaffe, Alan. The magic meatballs
Zakhoder, Boris Vladimirovich.
  Rosachok
Zolotow, Charlotte. It's not fair

Behavior — fighting, arguing

Alexander, Martha G. I'll be the horse if
  you'll play with me
Beim, Lorraine. Two is a team
Berry, Joy Wilt. Fighting
Bonsall, Crosby Newell. Who's a pest?
Brandenberg, Franz. It's not my fault
Burningham, John. Mr. Gumpy's outing
Christian, Mary Blount. The sand lot
Dayton, Mona. Earth and sky
Gekiere, Madeleine. The frilly lily and
  the princess
Gilchrist, Theo E. Halfway up the
  mountain

Hoban, Russell. Harvey's hideout
  The sorely trying day
  Tom and the two handles
McKee, David. Tusk tusk
Minarik, Else Holmelund. No fighting,
  no biting!
Sharmat, Marjorie Weinman. I'm not
  Oscar's friend any more
  Rollo and Juliet...forever!
  Sometimes mama and papa fight
Slobodkin, Louis. Hustle and bustle
Steadman, Ralph. The bridge
Udry, Janice May. Let's be enemies
Venable, Alan. The checker players
Winthrop, Elizabeth. That's mine
Zolotow, Charlotte. The quarreling book
  The unfriendly book

Behavior — forgetfulness

Alexander, Sue. Witch, Goblin and
  sometimes Ghost
Aliki. Use your head, dear
Cole, Joanna. Aren't you forgetting
  something, Fiona?
Copp, James. Martha Matilda O'Toole
De Paola, Tomie. Strega Nona
Dines, Glen. A tiger in the cherry tree
Domanska, Janina. Palmiero and the
  ogre
Galdone, Joanna. Gertrude, the goose
  who forgot
Galdone, Paul. The magic porridge pot
Hutchins, Pat. Don't forget the bacon!
MacGregor, Ellen. Theodor Turtle
McNulty, Faith. The elephant who
  couldn't forget
Miles, Miska. Chicken forgets
Parish, Peggy. Be ready at eight
Patz, Nancy. Pumpernickel tickle and
  mean green cheese
Rogers, Paul. Forget-me-not
Schweninger, Ann. The hunt for
  rabbit's galosh
Weisgard, Leonard. Silly Willy Nilly

Behavior — gossip

Berson, Harold. The thief who hugged
  a moonbeam
Chicken Little. Chicken Licken
  Henny Penny, ill. by Paul Galdone
  Henny Penny, ill. by William Stobbs
Holl, Adelaide. The runaway giant
Hutchins, Pat. The surprise party
Kraus, Robert. Mert the blurt
Varga, Judy. The monster behind Black
  Rock
Zolotow, Charlotte. The hating book

Behavior — greed

Aliki. The eggs

Andersen, H C (Hans Christian). The
  woman with the eggs
Angelo, Valenti. The candy basket
Aulaire, Ingri Mortenson d'. Don't
  count your chicks
Aylesworth, Jim. Mary's mirror
Barker, Inga-Lil. Why teddy bears are
  brown
Bascom, Joe. Malcolm Softpaws
Battles, Edith. The terrible terrier
  The terrible trick or treat
Berson, Harold. The rats who lived in
  the delicatessen
Bolliger, Max. The golden apple
Bonsall, Crosby Newell. It's mine! A
  greedy book
Brenner, Barbara. Ostrich feathers
Brown, Marcia. The bun
Bunting, Eve. The man who could call
  down owls
Carlson, Nancy. Harriet's Halloween
  candy
Christian, Mary Blount. The devil take
  you, Barnabas Beane!
Cooper, Susan. The silver cow
Dauer, Rosamond. The 300 pound cat
De Paola, Tomie. Andy (that's my name)
Ernst, Lisa Campbell. The prize pig
  surprise
Evans, Katherine. The maid and her
  pail of milk
Ginsburg, Mirra. Two greedy bears
Green, Phyllis. Bagdad ate it
Grimm, Jacob. The fisherman and his
  wife, ill. by Monika Laimgruber
  The fisherman and his wife, ill. by
  Margot Zemach
  Mother Holly
Jacobs, Joseph. Hudden and Dudden
  and Donald O'Neary
Kuskin, Karla. What did you bring me?
Lionni, Leo. The biggest house in the
  world
Lorenz, Lee. Pinchpenny John
McClenathan, Louise. My mother sends
  her wisdom
McLenighan, Valjean. Three strikes and
  you're out
Mahy, Margaret. Rooms for rent
Matsutani, Miyoko. How the withered
  trees blossomed
Obrist, Jürg. The miser who wanted the
  sun
Peet, Bill. Kermit the hermit
Perkins, Al. King Midas and the golden
  touch
Porter, David Lord. Mine!
Roffey, Maureen. Look, there's my hat!
Ross, Tony. The greedy little cobbler
Stadler, John. Animal cafe
Stage, Mads. The greedy blackbird

Winthrop, Elizabeth. That's mine

Behavior — growing up

Alexander, Sue. Dear Phoebe
Allison, Alida. The toddler's potty book
Appell, Clara. Now I have a daddy
  haircut
Ardizzone, Edward. Paul, the hero of
  the fire
Aulaire, Ingri Mortenson d'. Too big
Barrett, Judi. I hate to take a bath
  I'm too small, you're too big
Bogot, Howard. I'm growing
Brentano, Clemens. Schoolmaster
  Whackwell's wonderful sons
Bromhall, Winifred. Bridget's growing
  day
Brown, Myra Berry. Benjy's blanket
Brown, Palmer. Hickory
Bruna, Dick. I can dress myself
Bryant, Bernice. Follow the leader
Bulla, Clyde Robert. Dandelion Hill
Chaffin, Lillie D. Tommy's big problem
Ciardi, John. Scrappy the pup
Cohen, Miriam. Jim meets the thing
Cooney, Nancy Evans. The blanket that
  had to go
Corey, Dorothy. Tomorrow you can
Dauer, Rosamond. Bullfrog grows up
Delton, Judy. The best mom in the
  world
Drescher, Joan. I'm in charge!
Faison, Eleanora. Becoming
Fassler, Joan. Don't worry dear
  The man of the house
Felt, Sue. Rosa-too-little
Fribourg, Marjorie G. Ching-Ting and
  the ducks
Hanson, Joan. I won't be afraid
Harris, Robie H. I hate kisses
Hayes, Geoffrey. Patrick and Ted
Hoban, Brom. Skunk Lane
Horner, Althea J. Little big girl
Hurwitz, Johanna. Superduper Teddy
Iverson, Genie. I want to be big
Johnson, Crockett. We wonder what will
  Walter be? When he grows up
Jonas, Ann. When you were a baby
Krasilovsky, Phyllis. The very little boy
  The very little girl
Kraus, Robert. Leo the late bloomer
Krauss, Ruth. The growing story
Lexau, Joan M. I hate red rover
McPhail, David. Pig Pig grows up
Massie, Diane Redfield. Tiny pin
Mordvinoff, Nicolas. Coral Island
Newberry, Clare Turlay. Percy, Polly
  and Pete
Otto, Svend. The giant fish and other
  stories
Parish, Peggy. I can - can you?

Pellowski, Anne. Stairstep farm
Power, Barbara. I wish Laura's mommy
  was my mommy
Schlein, Miriam. Billy, the littlest one
  Herman McGregor's world
  When will the world be mine?
Schwartz, Amy. Begin at the beginning
Sharmat, Marjorie Weinman.
  Bartholomew the bossy
Smith, Robert Paul. When I am big
Snyder, Zilpha Keatley. Come on, Patsy
Turkle, Brinton. Obadiah the Bold
Van Leeuwen, Jean. Amanda Pig and
  her big brother Oliver
Waber, Bernard. You're a little kid with
  a big heart
Welber, Robert. Goodbye, hello
Wells, Rosemary. Timothy goes to
  school
Wittman, Sally. A special trade
Young, Helen. A throne for Sesame
Zagone, Theresa. No nap for me
Zimelman, Nathan. If I were strong
  enough...
Zolotow, Charlotte. But not Billy
  May I visit?
  Someone new
  When I have a son

Behavior — hiding

Aruego, José. We hide, you seek
Chorao, Kay. Kate's box
Dubanevich, Arlene. Pigs in hiding
Greydanus, Rose. My secret hiding place
Matus, Greta. Where are you, Jason?
Turpin, Lorna. The sultan's snakes
Vigna, Judith. The hiding house
Zion, Gene. Hide and seek day

Behavior — hiding things

Allan, Ted. Willie the squowse
Bason, Lillian. Those foolish Molboes!
Baylor, Byrd. Your own best secret
  place
Croswell, Volney. How to hide a
  hippopotamus

Behavior — hurrying

Greydanus, Rose. Willie the slowpoke
Hurd, Edith Thacher. Hurry hurry!
Steiner, Charlotte. What's the hurry,
  Harry?

Behavior — imitation

Allamand, Pascale. The animals who
  changed their colors
Aruego, José. Look what I can do
Asch, Frank. Just like daddy

Barrett, Judi. Animals should definitely not act like people
Animals should definitely not wear clothing
Bendick, Jeanne. Why can't I?
Blakeley, Peggy. What shall I be tomorrow?
Buckmaster, Henrietta. Lucy and Loki
Calhoun, Mary. The nine lives of Homer C. Cat
Canning, Kate. A painted tale
Cauley, Lorinda Bryan. The animal kids
Charlton, Elizabeth. Terrible tyrannosaurus
Christian, Mary Blount. Swamp monsters
Clewes, Dorothy. Henry Hare's boxing match
Cole, Brock. Nothing but a pig
Farber, Norma. There goes feathertop!
Hallinan, P K (Patrick K). Where's Michael?
Heine, Helme. Mr. Miller the dog
Kellogg, Steven. A rose for Pinkerton
Kent, Jack. The once-upon-a-time dragon
Schwartz, Amy. Bea and Mr. Jones

Behavior — indifference

Hogrogian, Nonny. The hermit and Harry and me
Roy, Ronald. Three ducks went wandering
Sendak, Maurice. Pierre
Sharmat, Marjorie Weinman. I don't care
Watts, Mabel. The day it rained watermelons

Behavior — losing things

Ardizzone, Edward. The little girl and the tiny doll
Ayer, Jacqueline. Nu Dang and his kite
Bannon, Laura. Red mittens
Barrows, Marjorie Wescott. The funny hat
Bowden, Joan Chase. Who took the top hat trick?
Boyle, Constance. The story of little owl
Bromhall, Winifred. Middle Matilda
Brunhoff, Laurent de. Babar loses his crown
Burningham, John. The blanket
Chorao, Kay. Molly's lies
Molly's Moe
Coombs, Patricia. The lost playground
Kay, Helen. One mitten Lewis
Kellogg, Steven. The mystery of the magic green ball
The mystery of the missing red mitten

Lexau, Joan M. Finders keepers, losers weepers
Livermore, Elaine. Lost and found
Three little kittens lost their mittens
McGinley, Phyllis. Lucy McLockett
McNeely, Jeannette. Where's Izzy?
Mother Goose. The three little kittens
Munari, Bruno. Jimmy has lost his cap
Rogers, Paul. Forget-me-not
Ryder, Eileen. Winston's new cap
Sharmat, Marjorie Weinman. The trip
Upham, Elizabeth. Little brown bear loses his clothes
Walsh, Jill Paton. Lost and found
White, Florence Meiman. How to lose your lunch money

Behavior — lost

Anderson, C W (Clarence Williams). Blaze finds forgotten roads
Blaze finds the trail
Ayer, Jacqueline. Little Silk
Barklem, Jill. Autumn story
Bartoli, Jennifer. Snow on bear's nose
Barton, Byron. Where's Al?
Belting, Natalia Maree. Verity Mullens and the Indian
Bemelmans, Ludwig. Madeline and the gypsies
Benjamin, Alan. Ribtickle Town
Berson, Harold. Henry Possum
Boegehold, Betty. Pawpaw's run
Bograd, Larry. Lost in the store
Bolliger, Max. Sandy at the children's zoo
Bornstein, Ruth Lercher. Annabelle Jim
Bothwell, Jean. Paddy and Sam
Brewster, Patience. Ellsworth and the cats from Mars
Brown, Judith Gwyn. Max and the truffle pig
Brown, Marcia. Tamarindo!
Brown, Margaret Wise. Little lost lamb
Three little animals
Calmenson, Stephanie. Where is Grandma Potamus?
Carigiet, Alois. Anton the goatherd
Carle, Eric. Have you seen my cat?
Carrick, Carol. The highest balloon on the common
Cartlidge, Michelle. Pippin and Pod
Cohen, Miriam. Lost in the museum
Cole, Joanna. The Clown-Arounds go on vacation
Corddry, Thomas I. Kibby's big feat
Cummings, Betty Sue. Turtle
Erickson, Phoebe. Just follow me
Farber, Norma. Where's Gomer?
Flack, Marjorie. Angus lost
Fletcher, Elizabeth. The little goat

Francis, Frank. The magic wallpaper
Gay, Michael. Take me for a ride
Gay, Zhenya. Small one
Goble, Paul. The friendly wolf
Guilfoile, Elizabeth. Have you seen my
  brother?
Hader, Berta Hoerner. Lost in the zoo
Hill, Eric. Where's Spot?
Hirsh, Marilyn. Where is Yonkela?
Hoban, Lillian. The laziest robot in zone
  one
Joerns, Consuelo. The foggy rescue
  The forgotten bear
Jonas, Ann. Two bear cubs
Keats, Ezra Jack. My dog is lost!
Kessler, Leonard P. Are we lost, daddy?
Koci, Marta. Katie's kitten
Lisker, Sonia O. Lost
Livermore, Elaine. Follow the fox
Lobel, Arnold. Uncle Elephant
Lubell, Winifred. Rosalie, the bird
  market turtle
McCloskey, Robert. Blueberries for Sal
McCully, Emily Arnold. Picnic
Mendoza, George. Alphabet sheep
Miles, Miska. This little pig
Modell, Frank. Tooley! Tooley!
Nakatani, Chiyoko. The day Chiro was
  lost
Ohlsson, Ib. Cat alley
Parenteau, Shirley. I'll bet you thought I
  was lost
Peet, Bill. Ella
Politi, Leo. The nicest gift
Rey, Margaret Elisabeth Waldstein.
  Curious George goes to the hospital
Sauer, Julia Lina. Mike's house
Saxon, Charles D. Don't worry about
  Poopsie
Seignobosc, Françoise. Minou
  Springtime for Jeanne-Marie
Shortall, Leonard W. Andy, the dog
  walker
Slobodkin, Louis. Yasu and the
  strangers
Sotomayor, Antonio. Khasa goes to the
  fiesta
Standon, Anna. Little duck lost
Stevenson, James. Howard
Taylor, Mark. The case of the missing
  kittens
  Henry the castaway
  Henry the explorer
Vreeken, Elizabeth. The boy who would
  not say his name
Wold, Jo Anne. Well! Why didn't you
  say so?
Ylla. Two little bears
Young, Evelyn. The tale of Tai

Behavior — lying

Belloc, Hilaire. Matilda who told lies
  and was burned to death
Berenstain, Stan. The Berenstain bears
  and the truth
Brown, Marc. The true Francine
Chorao, Kay. Molly's lies
Christopher, Matt. Jackrabbit goalie
Collodi, Carlo. The adventures of
  Pinocchio
Elliott, Dan. Ernie's little lie
Evans, Katherine. The boy who cried
  wolf
Gackenbach, Dick. Crackle, Gluck and
  the sleeping toad
Helena, Ann. The lie
Lexau, Joan M. Finders keepers, losers
  weepers
Sharmat, Marjorie Weinman. A big fat
  enormous lie

Behavior — misbehavior

Agard, John. Dig away two-hole Tim
Alexander, Martha G. We're in big
  trouble, Blackboard Bear
Allard, Harry. Miss Nelson is back
  Miss Nelson is missing!
Ashley, Bernard. Dinner ladies don't
  count
Baker, Alan. Benjamin's book
  Benjamin's dreadful dream
Baker, Margaret. A puppy called
  Spinach
Beech, Caroline. Peas again for lunch
Beim, Jerrold. The taming of Toby
Belloc, Hilaire. Matilda who told lies
  and was burned to death
Bemelmans, Ludwig. Madeline and the
  bad hat
Berenstain, Stan. The Berenstain bears
  and the truth
Berry, Joy Wilt. Being destructive
  Being selfish
  Disobeying
  Fighting
  Throwing tantrums
  Whining
Blaustein, Muriel. Baby Mabu and
  Auntie Moose
Bradbury, Bianca. Muggins
Brown, Margaret Wise. Sneakers
Brunhoff, Laurent de. Babar's cousin,
  that rascal Arthur
Calhoun, Mary. The goblin under the
  stairs
Cartlidge, Michelle. Pippin and Pod
Chalmers, Audrey. Fancy be good
Chapman, Carol. Herbie's troubles
Chess, Victoria. Alfred's alphabet walk
Cole, William. That pest Jonathan

Colette. The boy and the magic
Collodi, Carlo. The adventures of
  Pinocchio
Crowley, Arthur. The boogey man
Dauer, Rosamond. My friend, Jasper
  Jones
Delaney, Ned. Rufus the doofus
Douglas, Barbara. Good as new
Eastman, P D (Philip D). Are you my
  mother?
Flack, Marjorie. The story about Ping
Froment, Eugène. The story of a round
  loaf
Gackenbach, Dick. Pepper and all the
  legs
Gág, Wanda. The sorcerer's apprentice
Galbraith, Kathryn Osebold. Katie did!
Gantos, Jack. Rotten Ralph
  Worse than Rotten Ralph
Gerson, Corinne. Good dog, bad dog
Goodall, John S. Naughty Nancy
Harper, Wilhelmina. The gunniwolf
Herz, Irene. Hey! Don't do that!
Hiller, Catherine. Argentaybee and the
  boonie
Hoban, Russell. How Tom beat Captain
  Najork and his hired sportsmen
Hodeir, André. Warwick's three bottles
Hogan, Inez. About Nono, the baby
  elephant
Inkiow, Dimiter. Me and Clara and
  Baldwin the pony
  Me and Clara and Snuffy the dog
Jameson, Cynthia. The clay pot boy
Jeffers, Susan. Wild Robin
Joosse, Barbara M. The thinking place
Keller, Beverly. When mother got the
  flu
Kent, Jack. The scribble monster
Koenig, Marion. The wonderful world
  of night
Krasilovsky, Phyllis. The man who
  entered a contest
Kroll, Steven. Otto
  Pigs in the house
Leaf, Munro. A flock of watchbirds
Levy, Elizabeth. Something queer on
  vacation
Lindgren, Barbro. The wild baby
Lipkind, William. Nubber bear
Lippman, Peter. The Know-It-Alls go to
  sea
  The Know-It-Alls help out
  The Know-It-Alls mind the store
  The Know-It-Alls take a winter
  vacation
Lobel, Arnold. Prince Bertram the bad
Lorimer, Janet. The biggest bubble in
  the world
McPhail, David. Andrew's bath

Mahiri, Jabari. The day they stole the
  letter J
Marshall, Edward. Fox and his friends
  Fox on wheels
Marshall, James. The cut-ups
  George and Martha back in town
Marzollo, Jean. Uproar on Hollercat
  Hill
Mayer, Mercer. Appelard and
  Liverwurst
Moremen, Grace E. No, no, Natalie
Morgan, Allen. Molly and Mr. Maloney
Myller, Lois. No! No!
Oana, Kay D. Shasta and the shebang
  machine
Oldfield, Pamela. Melanie Brown climbs
  a tree
Olson, Helen Kronberg. The strange
  thing that happened to Oliver
  Wendell Iscovitch
Oxenbury, Helen. The car trip
Parker, Nancy Winslow. Cooper, the
  McNallys' big black dog
  Poofy loves company
Paterson, Diane. Soap and suds
Pearson, Tracey Campbell. Sing a song
  of sixpence
Potter, Beatrix. The complete
  adventures of Peter Rabbit
  The tale of Benjamin Bunny
  The tale of Peter Rabbit, ill. by Margot
  Apple
  The tale of Peter Rabbit, ill. by Beatrix
  Potter
  The tale of two bad mice
Preston, Edna Mitchell. Horrible
  Hepzibah
  Squawk to the moon, little goose
Rabinowitz, Sandy. A colt named
  mischief
Rappus, Gerhard. When the sun was
  shining
Rice, Eve. Benny bakes a cake
Robison, Deborah. Your turn, doctor
Rockwell, Anne F. Honk honk!
Ruck-Pauquèt, Gina. Oh, that koala!
Sadler, Marilyn. Alistair's elephant
Schatell, Brian. Farmer Goff and his
  turkey Sam
Schumacher, Claire. King of the zoo
Sendak, Maurice. Where the wild things
  are
Smith, Janice Lee. The monster in the
  third dresser drawer and other
  stories about Adam Joshua
Tierney, Hanne. Where's your baby
  brother, Becky Bunting?
Van Allsburg, Chris. The garden of
  Abdul Gasazi
Vigna, Judith. Anyhow, I'm glad I tried
  She's not my real mother

Ward, Nick. Giant.
Watanabe, Yuichi. Wally the whale who
  loved balloons
Watson, Wendy. Lollipop
Wells, Rosemary. Good night, Fred
White, Florence Meiman. How to lose
  your lunch money
Williams, Barbara. Whatever happened
  to Beverly Bigler's birthday?
Wiseman, Bernard. Don't make fun!
Zemach, Margot. Jake and Honeybunch
  go to heaven
Zhitkov, Boris. How I hunted for the
  little fellows

Behavior — mistakes

Bonsall, Crosby Newell. The case of the
  dumb bells
Brandenberg, Franz. No school today!
Bridwell, Norman. Clifford's good deeds
Chevalier, Christa. Spence makes circles
Coombs, Patricia. Dorrie's play
Cresswell, Helen. Two hoots and the
  king
  Two hoots in the snow
Firmin, Peter. Basil Brush goes flying
Gág, Wanda. Gone is gone
Galdone, Paul. Obedient Jack
Hoff, Syd. Henrietta, the early bird
Jacobs, Joseph. Hereafterthis
Lexau, Joan M. It all began with a drip,
  drip, drip
Springstubb, Tricia. The magic guinea
  pig
Waber, Bernard. Nobody is perfick
Walker, Barbara K. New patches for old
Weiner, Beth Lee. Benjamin's perfect
  solution
Wiseman, Bernard. Tails are not for
  painting

Behavior — misunderstanding

Allard, Harry. The Stupids die
Berg, Jean Horton. The O'Learys and
  friends
Berson, Harold. Kassim's shoes
Bryant, Sara Cone. Epaminondas and
  his auntie
Carrick, Carol. Old Mother Witch
Dickinson, Mike. My dad doesn't even
  notice
Gackenbach, Dick. Arabella and Mr.
  Crack
  King Wacky
Hopkins, Lee Bennett. I loved Rose
  Ann
Kraus, Robert. Ladybug, ladybug!
Lionni, Leo. Fish is fish
McClintock, Marshall. A fly went by

Parish, Peggy. Amelia Bedelia
  Amelia Bedelia and the surprise
    shower
  Amelia Bedelia goes camping
  Amelia Bedelia helps out
  Come back, Amelia Bedelia
  Good work, Amelia Bedelia
  Play ball, Amelia Bedelia
  Teach us, Amelia Bedelia
  Thank you, Amelia Bedelia
Polushkin, Maria. Mother, Mother, I
  want another
Roberts, Sarah. Bert and the missing
  mop mix-up
Sharmat, Marjorie Weinman. Gila
  monsters meet you at the airport
Wiseman, Bernard. Morris has a
  birthday party!
Wold, Jo Anne. Well! Why didn't you
  say so?

Behavior — nagging

Dickinson, Mary. Alex's outing
Mahy, Margaret. Mrs. Discombobulous
Stalder, Valerie. Even the Devil is afraid
  of a shrew

Behavior — needing someone

Billam, Rosemary. Fuzzy rabbit
Bulla, Clyde Robert. The stubborn old
  woman
Guilfoile, Elizabeth. Nobody listens to
  Andrew
Hess, Lilo. A cat's nine lives
Hughes, Richard. Gertrude's child
Hughes, Shirley. Alfie gives a hand
Keats, Ezra Jack. Louie's search
Kent, Jack. There's no such thing as a
  dragon
Livermore, Elaine. Follow the fox
Lobel, Anita. A birthday for the princess
McPhail, David. Great cat
Morris, Terry Nell. Lucky puppy! Lucky
  boy!
Oppenheim, Joanne. On the other side
  of the river
Scott, Ann Herbert. On mother's lap
  Sam
Sendak, Maurice. Very far away
Singer, Marilyn. Pickle plan
Skorpen, Liesel Moak. Charles
Sugita, Yutaka. Helena the unhappy
  hippopotamus
Wells, Rosemary. Noisy Nora
Wolde, Gunilla. Betsy and the chicken
  pox

Behavior — running away

Adoff, Arnold. Where wild Willie?

Alexander, Martha G. And my mean old mother will be sorry, Blackboard Bear

Barrett, Lawrence Louis. Twinkle, the baby colt

Bates, H E. Achilles the donkey

Brown, Margaret Wise. The runaway bunny

Brunhoff, Jean de. The story of Babar, the little elephant

Burton, Virginia Lee. Choo choo

Carlson, Natalie Savage. Runaway Marie Louise

Carroll, Ruth. What Whiskers did

Clifton, Lucille. My brother fine with me

Coombs, Patricia. Lisa and the grompet

Dumas, Philippe. Lucy, a tale of a donkey

Duvoisin, Roger Antoine. The missing milkman

Freeman, Don. Beady Bear

Gackenbach, Dick. Claude and Pepper

Gianni, Peg. Alex, the amazing juggler

The gingerbread boy, ill. by Paul Galdone

The gingerbread boy, ill. by Joan Elizabeth Goodman

The gingerbread boy, ill. by William Curtis Holdsworth

The gingerbread boy. The gingerbread man

Goodall, John S. The adventures of Paddy Pork

Greene, Graham. The little train

Hale, Irina. Chocolate mouse and sugar pig

Hamilton, Morse. My name is Emily

Hanson, Joan. I'm going to run away

Heller, Wendy. Clementine and the cage

Hillert, Margaret. The little runaway

Hoban, Russell. A baby sister for Frances

Hogrogian, Nonny. Billy Goat and his well-fed friends

Hughes, Richard. Gertrude's child

Hyman, Robin. Casper and the rainbow bird

Isenberg, Barbara. The adventures of Albert, the running bear

Joerns, Consuelo. Oliver's escape

Knight, Hilary. Where's Wallace?

La Farge, Phyllis. Joanna runs away

Langner, Nola. By the light of the silvery moon

Lasker, Joe. The do-something day

Lisowski, Gabriel. Roncalli's magnificent circus

Lobel, Arnold. The man who took the indoors out
Small pig

McClure, Gillian. Fly home McDoo

McPhail, David. Stanley Henry Bear's friend

Marol, Jean-Claude. Vagabul escapes

Miles, Miska. This little pig

Oakley, Graham. Hetty and Harriet

Otto, Svend. Taxi dog

Parker, Nancy Winslow. The crocodile under Louis Finneberg's bed

Peet, Bill. Pamela Camel

Pittaway, Margaret. The rainforest children

Rockwell, Anne F. Willie runs away

Seligman, Dorothy Halle. Run away home

Sendak, Maurice. Very far away

Sharmat, Marjorie Weinman. Rex

Singer, Marilyn. Archer Armadillo's secret room

Waber, Bernard. Bernard

Wildsmith, Brian. Daisy

Woolaver, Lance. From Ben Loman to the sea

Wright, Dare. Edith and Mr. Bear

Yolen, Jane. The girl who loved the wind

Zimnik, Reiner. The bear on the motorcycle
The proud circus horse

Zion, Gene. Harry, the dirty dog

Zolotow, Charlotte. Big sister and little sister

Behavior — saving things

Brandenberg, Franz. What can you make of it?

Calhoun, Mary. The traveling ball of string

Delton, Judy. Penny wise, fun foolish

Foster, Doris Van Liew. A pocketful of seasons

Mayne, William. The patchwork cat

Behavior — secrets

Aardema, Verna. What's so funny, Ketu?

Allard, Harry. Miss Nelson has a field day

Auerbach, Marjorie. King Lavra and the barber

Bang, Molly. Dawn

Barklem, Jill. The secret staircase

Baylor, Byrd. Your own best secret place

Brandenberg, Franz. A secret for grandmother's birthday

Coombs, Patricia. The magician and McTree

Cummings, W T (Walter Thies). Miss Esta Maude's secret

Davis, Maggie S. Grandma's secret letter

Hughes, Shirley. Sally's secret

Krahn, Fernando. The secret in the dungeon

Lifton, Betty Jean. The secret seller

Behavior — seeking better things

Allen, Jeffrey. The secret life of Mr. Weird
Cole, Brock. Nothing but a pig
Cummings, W T. The kid
Demarest, Chris L. Benedict finds a home
Gackenbach, Dick. Little bug
Giff, Patricia Reilly. Next year I'll be special
Pittaway, Margaret. The rainforest children
Rose, Anne. As right as right can be
Williams, Vera B. A chair for my mother

Behavior — sharing

Albert, Burton. Mine, yours, ours
Azaad, Meyer. Half for you
Beim, Jerrold. The smallest boy in the class
Caudill, Rebecca. A pocketful of cricket
Corey, Dorothy. Everybody takes turns
We all share
Croll, Carolyn. Too many babas
Davis, Gibbs. The other Emily
Devlin, Wende. Cranberry Christmas
Ets, Marie Hall. The cow's party
Flory, Jane. The unexpected grandchild
Gackenbach, Dick. Claude the dog
Galdone, Paul. The magic porridge pot
Houston, John A. The bright yellow rope
Keats, Ezra Jack. Peter's chair
Klein, Norma. Visiting Pamela
Lesikin, Joan. Down the road
Lester, Helen. The wizard, the fairy and the magic chicken
Lindgren, Barbro. Sam's car
Sam's cookie
Maiorano, Robert. A little interlude
Noble, June. Two homes for Lynn
Ormerod, Jan. 101 things to do with a baby
Politi, Leo. Mr. Fong's toy shop
Porte, Barbara Ann. Harry's visit
Schulman, Janet. Jack the bum and the Halloween handout
Sharmat, Marjorie Weinman. The trip
Sherman, Ivan. I do not like it when my friend comes to visit
Spinelli, Eileen. Thanksgiving at Tappletons'
Stadler, John. Gorman and the treasure chest
Stage, Mads. The greedy blackbird
Stanek, Muriel. My little foster sister
Turkle, Brinton. Rachel and Obadiah
Vigna, Judith. The hiding house

Vincent, Gabrielle. Bravo, Ernest and Celestine!
Waber, Bernard. Bernard
Watson, Clyde. Tom Fox and the apple pie
Watts, Mabel. Something for you, something for me
Wezel, Peter. The good bird
Wilson, Christopher Bernard. Hobnob
Winthrop, Elizabeth. That's mine
Wright, Josephine Lord. Cotton Cat and Martha Mouse
Yolen, Jane. Spider Jane
Zolotow, Charlotte. The new friend

Behavior — solitude

Bennett, Rainey. The secret hiding place
Bulla, Clyde Robert. Keep running, Allen!
Carrick, Carol. Sleep out
Dragonwagon, Crescent. Katie in the morning
When light turns into night
Ehrlich, Amy. The everyday train
Hallinan, P K. Just being alone
Hayes, Geoffrey. Bear by himself
Henkes, Kevin. All alone
Keller, Beverly. Pimm's place
Keyser, Marcia. Roger on his own
Luttrell, Ida. Lonesome Lester
Morris, Jill. The boy who painted the sun
Reesink, Marijke. The princess who always ran away
Schertle, Alice. In my treehouse
Stubbs, Joanna. Happy Bear's day
Tresselt, Alvin R. I saw the sea come in
Yezback, Steven A. Pumpkinseeds

Behavior — stealing

Barr, Cathrine. Hound dog's bone
Carlson, Nancy. Loudmouth George and the sixth-grade bully
Cass, Joan E. The cat thief
Cate, Rikki. A cat's tale
Christian, Mary Blount. The doggone mystery
J. J. Leggett, secret agent
Cole, Joanna. The secret box
Cooper, Jacqueline. Angus and the Mona Lisa
Devlin, Wende. Cranberry Halloween
Dyke, John. Pigwig
The firebird
Foulds, Elfrida Vipont. The elephant and the bad baby
Ginsburg, Mirra. Striding slippers
Hare, Norma Q. Mystery at mouse house

Kroll, Steven. Amanda and the giggling ghost

Ross, Tony. Hugo and the man who stole colors

Behavior — talking to strangers

Boegehold, Betty. Hurray for Pippa!

Chlad, Dorothy. Strangers

De Regniers, Beatrice Schenk. Red Riding Hood

Grimm, Jacob. Little red cap
  Little Red Riding Hood, ill. by Frank Aloise
  Little Red Riding Hood, ill. by Bernadette
  Little Red Riding Hood, ill. by Gwen Connelly
  Little Red Riding Hood, ill. by Paul Galdone
  Little Red Riding Hood, ill. by Trina Schart Hyman

Joyce, Irma. Never talk to strangers

Meyer, Linda D. Safety zone

Potter, Beatrix. The tale of Little Pig Robinson

Vogel, Carole Garbuny. The dangers of strangers

Behavior — trickery

Æsop. Three fox fables

Allard, Harry. There's a party at Mona's tonight

Althea. Jeremy Mouse and cat

Annett, Cora. When the porcupine moved in

Barth, Edna. Jack-o'-lantern

Boegehold, Betty. Small Deer's magic tricks

Bowden, Joan Chase. Strong John

Brown, Marcia. The blue jackal

Browning, Robert. The pied piper of Hamelin

Calhoun, Mary. The pixy and the lazy housewife

Chicken Little. Chicken Licken
  Henny Penny, ill. by Paul Galdone
  Henny Penny, ill. by William Stobbs

Christelow, Eileen. Jerome the babysitter

Dines, Glen. Gilly and the wicharoo

Domanska, Janina. The best of the bargain

Duff, Maggie. Dancing turtle

Duvoisin, Roger Antoine. Petunia, I love you

Elkin, Benjamin. Gillespie and the guards

Evans, Katherine. The boy who cried wolf

Gage, Wilson. The crow and Mrs. Gaddy

Galdone, Paul. A strange servant

Grimm, Jacob. The horse, the fox, and the lion

Jennings, Michael. Robin Goodfellow and the giant dwarf

Joyce, James. The cat and the devil

Mirkovic, Irene. The greedy shopkeeper

Parker, Nancy Winslow. The crocodile under Louis Finneberg's bed

Potter, Beatrix. The pie and the patty-pan
  The story of Miss Moppet

Rockwell, Anne F. The gollywhopper egg

Turkle, Brinton. Do not open

Ungerer, Tomi. The beast of Monsieur Racine

Varga, Judy. The mare's egg

Wegen, Ron. Billy Gorilla

Wild, Robin. Spot's dogs and the alley cats

Wildsmith, Brian. Python's party

Woolley, Catherine. The clever raccoon

Zemach, Harve. The tricks of Master Dabble

Behavior — unnoticed, unseen

Bishop, Bonnie. No one noticed Ralph

Kroll, Steven. The candy witch

Udry, Janice May. How I faded away

Behavior — wishing

Aliki. I wish I was sick, too!
  The wish workers

Ayer, Jacqueline. A wish for little sister

Baker, Betty. My sister says
  Turkey girl

Baruch, Dorothy. I would like to be a pony and other wishes

Benchley, Nathaniel. The magic sled

Benton, Robert. Don't ever wish for a 7-foot bear

Beresford, Elisabeth. Jack and the magic stove

Berson, Harold. Truffles for lunch

Brett, Jan. Fritz and the beautiful horses

Bright, Robert. Me and the bears

Butcher, Julia. The sheep and the rowan tree

Chapman, Carol. Barney Bipple's magic dandelions

Chess, Victoria. Poor Esmé

Christensen, Jack. The forgotten rainbow

Clifton, Lucille. Three wishes

Coopersmith, Jerome. A Chanukah fable for Christmas

Daugherty, Charles Michael. Wisher

Dragonwagon, Crescent. Coconut

Friedrich, Priscilla. The wishing well in the woods

Fuchshuber, Annegert. The wishing hat

Gackenbach, Dick. Hattie rabbit

Greenberg, Polly. Oh, Lord, I wish I was a buzzard

Haas, Irene. The Maggie B

Himmelman, John. Amanda and the witch switch

Hoban, Lillian. It's really Christmas

Iwasaki, Chihiro. The birthday wish

Jaffe, Rona. Last of the wizards

Janosch. Just one apple

Kay, Helen. An egg is for wishing

Kent, Jack. Knee-high Nina

Kojima, Naomi. The flying grandmother

Krauss, Ruth. Mama, I wish I was snow. Child, you'd be very cold

Lasell, Fen. Michael grows a wish

Littledale, Freya. The snow child

Munari, Bruno. The elephant's wish

Orbach, Ruth. Please send a panda

Paterson, Diane. If I were a toad

Perkins, Al. King Midas and the golden touch

Power, Barbara. I wish Laura's mommy was my mommy

Reed, Kit. When we dream

Rosen, Winifred. Henrietta and the day of the iguana

Sachs, Marilyn. Fleet-footed Florence

Seignobosc, Françoise. Jeanne-Marie counts her sheep

Seuss, Dr. I wish that I had duck feet
Please try to remember the first of october!

Sewell, Helen Moore. Peggy and the pony

Shecter, Ben. The discontented mother

Shimin, Symeon. I wish there were two of me

Stevenson, James. The wish card ran out!

Tobias, Tobi. Jane wishing

Turkle, Brinton. Do not open

Varga, Judy. Janko's wish

Waber, Bernard. You're a little kid with a big heart

Watson, Pauline. Wriggles, the little wishing pig

Weisgard, Leonard. Who dreams of cheese?

Williams, Barbara. Someday, said Mitchell

Wolkstein, Diane. The magic wings

Zimelman, Nathan. To sing a song as big as Ireland

Zolotow, Charlotte. Someday

Behavior — worrying

Gross, Alan. Sometimes I worry... What if the teacher calls on me?

Herman, Charlotte. My mother didn't kiss me good-night

Levitin, Sonia. A single speckled egg

Marshall, James. Portly McSwine

Segal, Lore. The story of old Mrs. Brubeck and how she looked for trouble and where she found him

Sewall, Marcia. The cobbler's song

Sharmat, Marjorie Weinman. Thornton, the worrier

Being different *see* Character traits — being different

Bicycling *see* Sports — bicycling

Bigotry *see* Prejudice

Birds

Adoff, Arnold. Birds

Alexander, Martha G. Out! Out! Out!

Aliki. The wish workers

Allred, Mary. Grandmother Poppy and the funny-looking bird

Anderson, Lonzo. Mr. Biddle and the birds

Arnold, Caroline. Five nests

Arnosky, Jim. A kettle of hawks, and other wildlife groups
Mouse writing

Asch, Frank. Moon bear
Mooncake

Ayer, Jacqueline. A wish for little sister

Azaad, Meyer. Half for you

Bailey, Jill. Eyes
Feet
Mouths

Baker, Jeffrey J W. Patterns of nature

Bang, Betsy. Tutuni the tailor bird

Baskin, Leonard. Hosie's aviary

Baum, Willi. Birds of a feather

Beisert, Heide Helene. Poor fish

Borden, Beatrice Brown. Wild animals of Africa

Brenner, Barbara. Baltimore orioles

Bright, Robert. Georgie and the baby birds

Brock, Emma Lillian. The birds' Christmas tree

Bruna, Dick. Little bird tweet

Brunhoff, Laurent de. Babar's visit to Bird Island

Chönz, Selina. Florina and the wild bird

Coatsworth, Elizabeth. Under the green willow

Colby, C B (Carroll Burleigh). Who lives there?
  Who went there?
Cole, Joanna. A bird's body
Conklin, Gladys. If I were a bird
Cortesi, Wendy W. Explore a spooky swamp
Cristini, Ermanno. In the woods
Cross, Diana Harding. Some birds have funny names
Cross, Genevieve. A trip to the yard
Dalmais, Anne-Marie. The butterfly book of birds
Damjan, Mischa. Goodbye little bird
Darby, Gene. What is a bird?
Demarest, Chris L. Benedict finds a home
Eastman, P D (Philip D). Are you my mother?
  Flap your wings
Elborn, Andrew. Bird Adalbert
Fender, Kay. Odette!
Fisher, Aileen. We went looking
Fitzsimons, Cecilia. My first birds
Flanders, Michael. Creatures great and small
Freeman, Don. Fly high, fly low
French, Fiona. The blue bird
Freschet, Berniece. The little woodcock
Friskey, Margaret. Birds we know
Fujita, Tamao. The boy and the bird
Gans, Roma. Hummingbirds in the garden
  When birds change their feathers
Givens, Janet Eaton. Just two wings
Grimm, Jacob. The bear and the kingbird
Hader, Berta Hoerner. Mister Billy's gun
Hawkinson, Lucy. Birds in the sky
Ipcar, Dahlov. Bright barnyard
  "The song of the day birds" and "The song of the night birds"
John, Naomi. Roadrunner
Kantrowitz, Mildred. When Violet died
Kaufmann, John. Birds are flying
  Flying giants of long ago
Kishida, Eriko. The lion and the bird's nest
Krauss, Ruth. The happy egg
Kuchalla, Susan. Birds
Kumin, Maxine. Mittens in May
Lifton, Betty Jean. Joji and the Amanojaku
  Joji and the dragon
  Joji and the fog
Lionni, Leo. Inch by inch
  Tico and the golden wings
Lubell, Winifred. Rosalie, the bird market turtle

Lyfick, Warren. The little book of fowl jokes
McCauley, Jane. Baby birds and how they grow
Marshak, Samuel. The merry starlings
Massie, Diane Redfield. The baby beebee bird
Mayer, Mercer. Two moral tales
Munari, Bruno. Bruno Munari's zoo
  Tic, Tac and Toc
Ness, Evaline. Pavo and the princess
Oana, Kay D. Robbie and the raggedy scarecrow
Olds, Elizabeth. Feather mountain
Parnall, Peter. Alfalfa Hill
Peet, Bill. The pinkish, purplish, bluish egg
Postgate, Oliver. Noggin the king
Rockwell, Anne F. Honk honk!
Seidler, Rosalie. Grumpus and the Venetian cat
Selsam, Millicent E. Tony's birds
Seuss, Dr. Horton hatches the egg
  Thidwick, the big-hearted moose
Snoopy on wheels
Stage, Mads. The greedy blackbird
Stone, A Harris. The last free bird
Varley, Dimitry. The whirly bird
Velthuijs, Max. The painter and the bird
Waechter, Friedrich Karl. Three is company
Wezel, Peter. The good bird
  The naughty bird
Wildsmith, Brian. Brian Wildsmith's birds
Wolff, Ashley. A year of birds
Yolen, Jane. Spider Jane
Zolotow, Charlotte. Flocks of birds

Birds — albatrosses

Hoff, Syd. Albert the albatross

Birds — blackbirds

Duff, Maggie. Rum pum pum

Birds — bluejays

Angelo, Valenti. The acorn tree
Margolis, Richard J. Big bear, spare that tree

Birds — buzzards

Sandburg, Helga. Anna and the baby buzzard
Wolkstein, Diane. The cool ride in the sky

Birds — canaries

Foreman, Michael. Cat and canary

Birds — chickens (continued)

Freeman, Don. Quiet! There's a canary in the library
Heller, Wendy. Clementine and the cage

Birds — cardinals

Galinsky, Ellen. The baby cardinal

Birds — chickens

Allard, Harry. I will not go to market today
Ambrus, Victor G. The little cockerel
Aulaire, Ingri Mortenson d'. Don't count your chicks
  Foxie, the singing dog
Belpré, Pura. Santiago
Benchley, Nathaniel. The strange disappearance of Arthur Cluck
Berquist, Grace. Speckles goes to school
Bishop, Ann. Chicken riddle
Bond, Felicia. Christmas in the chicken coop
Boreman, Jean. Bantie and her chicks
Bourke, Linda. Ethel's exceptional egg
Boutwell, Edna. Red rooster
Brothers, Aileen. Jiffy, Miss Boo and Mr. Roo
Brown, Margaret Wise. Little chicken
Carle, Eric. The rooster who set out to see the world
Cazet, Denys. Lucky me
Chaucer, Geoffrey. Chanticleer and the fox
Chicken Little. Chicken Licken
  Henny Penny, ill. by Paul Galdone
  Henny Penny, ill. by William Stobbs
Chukovsky, Korney. Good morning, chick
Cole, Joanna. A chick hatches
Dumas, Philippe. Caesar, cock of the village
Edwards, Dorothy. A wet Monday
Ehrhardt, Reinhold. Kikeri or, The proud red rooster
Fatio, Louise. The red bantam
Firmin, Peter. Chicken stew
Freschet, Berniece. Where's Henrietta's hen?
Ginsburg, Mirra. Across the stream
  The chick and the duckling
  The golden goose
Hader, Berta Hoerner. Cock-a-doodle doo
Hartelius, Margaret A. The chicken's child
Heine, Helme. The most wonderful egg in the world
Hewett, Anita. The little white hen
Hille-Brandts, Lene. The little black hen
Hoff, Syd. Happy birthday, Henrietta!
  Henrietta, circus star
  Henrietta goes to the fair
  Henrietta, the early bird
  Henrietta's Halloween
  Merry Christmas, Henrietta!
Hutchins, Pat. Rosie's walk
Jackson, Jacqueline. Chicken ten thousand
Jaynes, Ruth M. Three baby chicks
Kent, Jack. Little Peep
Kepes, Juliet. Cock-a-doodle-doo
Kwitz, Mary DeBall. Little chick's breakfast
  Little chick's story
Lester, Helen. The wizard, the fairy and the magic chicken
Lexau, Joan M. Crocodile and hen
Lifton, Betty Jean. The many lives of Chio and Goro
Lindman, Maj. Flicka, Ricka, Dicka and the big red hen
Lipkind, William. The little tiny rooster
The little red hen, ill. by Janina Domanska
The little red hen, ill. by Paul Galdone
The little red hen, ill. by Mel Pekarsky
The little red hen, ill. by Margot Zemach
Little Tuppen
Littlefield, William. The whiskers of Ho Ho
Lloyd, Megan. Chicken tricks
Lobel, Anita. King Rooster, Queen Hen
Lobel, Arnold. How the rooster saved the day
McKelvey, David. Bobby the mostly silky
Mathews, Louise. Cluck one
Miles, Miska. Chicken forgets
Murphey, Sara. The animal hat shop
Oakley, Graham. Hetty and Harriet
O'Neill, Mary. Big red hen
Otto, Margaret Glover. The little brown horse
Polushkin, Maria. The little hen and the giant
Provensen, Alice. My little hen
Pursell, Margaret Sanford. Jessie the chicken
Rockwell, Anne F. The wonderful eggs of Furicchia
Scarry, Richard. Egg in the hole
Selsam, Millicent E. Egg to chick
Sherman, Nancy. Gwendolyn and the weathercock
  Gwendolyn the miracle hen
Sondergaard, Arensa. Biddy and the ducks
Uchida, Yoshiko. The rooster who understood Japanese
Van Horn, Grace. Little red rooster
Van Woerkom, Dorothy. Something to crow about

Waber, Bernard. How to go about laying an egg

Weil, Lisl. Gillie and the flattering fox

Weiss, Ellen. Clara the fortune-telling chicken

Williams, Garth. The chicken book

Birds — cockatoos

Cummings, W T (Walter Thies). Wickford of Beacon Hill

Birds — cormorants

Bunting, Eve. Magic and the night river

Birds — cranes

Bang, Molly. Dawn

Laurin, Anne. Perfect crane

The peasant's pea patch

Yagawa, Sumiko. The crane wife

Birds — crows

DeLage, Ida. The old witch and the crows

Freeman, Don. Cyrano the crow

Gage, Wilson. The crow and Mrs. Gaddy

Hazelton, Elizabeth Baldwin. Sammy, the crow who remembered

Huxley, Aldous. The crows of Pearblossom

Hyman, Robin. Casper and the rainbow bird

Birds — doves

Agostinelli, Maria Enrica. On wings of love

Freeman, Don. The turtle and the dove

Peet, Bill. The pinkish, purplish, bluish egg

Potter, Beatrix. The tale of the faithful dove

Sage, James. The boy and the dove

Singer, Isaac Bashevis. Why Noah chose the dove

Wolff, Ashley. The bells of London

Birds — ducks

Allen, Jeffrey. Mary Alice, operator number 9

Andersen, H C (Hans Christian). The ugly duckling, ill. by Adrienne Adams

The ugly duckling, ill. by Lorinda Bryan Cauley

The ugly duckling, ill. by Tadasu Izawa and Shigemi Hijikata

The ugly duckling, ill. by Johannes Larsen

The ugly duckling, ill. by Josef Palecek

Barnhart, Peter. The wounded duck

Bothwell, Jean. Paddy and Sam

Brown, Margaret Wise. The duck

The golden egg book

Cazet, Denys. The duck with squeaky feet

Conover, Chris. Six little ducks

Delton, Judy. Bear and Duck on the run

Duck goes fishing

A pet for Duck and Bear

Three friends find spring

Dunn, Judy. The little duck

Duvoisin, Roger Antoine. Two lonely ducks

Ellis, Anne Leo. Dabble Duck

Flack, Marjorie. Angus and the ducks

The story about Ping

Freschet, Berniece. Wood duck baby

Fribourg, Marjorie G. Ching-Ting and the ducks

Friskey, Margaret. Seven diving ducks

Georgiady, Nicholas P. Gertie the duck

Gerstein, Mordicai. Arnold of the ducks

Follow me!

Ginsburg, Mirra. Across the stream

The chick and the duckling

Goldin, Augusta. Ducks don't get wet

Hader, Berta Hoerner. Cock-a-doodle doo

Hillert, Margaret. The funny baby

Hurd, Edith Thacher. Last one home is a green pig

Isenbart, Hans-Heinrich. A duckling is born

Janice. Angélique

Kepes, Juliet. The story of a bragging duck

Leverich, Kathleen. The hungry fox and the foxy duck

Lorenz, Lee. A weekend in the country

McCloskey, Robert. Make way for ducklings

Miles, Miska. Noisy gander

Moore, Sheila. Samson Svenson's baby

Pomerantz, Charlotte. One duck, another duck

Potter, Beatrix. The tale of Jemima Puddle-Duck

Quackenbush, Robert M. Dig to disaster

Express train to trouble

Henry babysits

Stairway to doom

Richter, Mischa. Eric and Matilda Quack?

Roy, Ronald. Three ducks went wandering

Schroeder, Binette. Tuffa and the ducks

Seignobosc, Françoise. Springtime for Jeanne-Marie

Sewell, Helen Moore. Blue barns

Shaw, Evelyn S. Nest of wood ducks
Sheehan, Angela. The duck
Sondergaard, Arensa. Biddy and the ducks
Spier, Peter. Little ducks
Standon, Anna. Little duck lost
Stevenson, James. Howard
  Monty
Tafuri, Nancy. Have you seen my duckling?
Tudor, Bethany. Samuel's tree house Skiddycock Pond
Turska, Krystyna. The woodcutter's duck
Wahl, Jan. Old Hippo's Easter egg
Wildsmith, Brian. The little wood duck
Withers, Carl. The wild ducks and the goose
Wright, Dare. Edith and the duckling

Birds — eagles

Foreman, Michael. Moose

Birds — egrets

Carlson, Natalie Savage. Time for the white egret

Birds — flamingos

Rossetti, Christina Georgina. What is pink?
Zoll, Max Alfred. A flamingo is born

Birds — geese

Asch, Frank. MacGooses's grocery
Brown, Marc. Moose and goose
Bunting, Eve. Goose dinner
Burningham, John. Borka
Cauley, Lorinda Bryan. The goose and the golden coins
Chandoha, Walter. A baby goose for you
Duvoisin, Roger Antoine. Petunia
  Petunia and the song
  Petunia, beware!
  Petunia, I love you
  Petunia takes a trip
  Petunia's Christmas
  Petunia's treasure
Freeman, Don. Will's quill
Galdone, Joanna. Gertrude, the goose who forgot
Holmes, Efner Tudor. Amy's goose
Houston, James. Kiviok's magic journey
Illyés, Gyula. Matt the gooseherd
Kent, Jack. Silly goose
Koch, Dorothy Clarke. Gone is my goose
Lasell, Fen. Fly away goose

Low, Joseph. Benny rabbit and the owl
  Boo to a goose
Preston, Edna Mitchell. Squawk to the moon, little goose
Rockwell, Anne F. Poor Goose
Sewell, Helen Moore. Blue barns
Zijlstra, Tjerk. Benny and his geese

Birds — hawks

Baylor, Byrd. Hawk, I'm your brother

Birds — nightingales

Andersen, H C (Hans Christian). The emperor and the nightingale
  The emperor's nightingale
  The nightingale, ill. by Harold Berson
  The nightingale, ill. by Nancy Ekholm Burkert
Chase, Catherine. The nightingale and the fool

Birds — ostriches

Delton, Judy. Penny wise, fun foolish
Ylla. Look who's talking

Birds — owls

Benchley, Nathaniel. The strange disappearance of Arthur Cluck
Bennett, Rainey. After the sun goes down
Boyle, Constance. The story of little owl
Bunting, Eve. The man who could call down owls
Carey, Mary. The owl who loved sunshine
Cresswell, Helen. Two hoots and the king
  Two hoots in the snow
DeLage, Ida. The old witch and the crows
Delton, Judy. Duck goes fishing
Duvoisin, Roger Antoine. Day and night
Eastman, P D (Philip D). Sam and the firefly
Flower, Phyllis. Barn owl
Foster, Doris Van Liew. Tell me, Mr. Owl
Funazaki, Yasuko. Baby owl
Garelick, May. About owls
Goodenow, Earle. The owl who hated the dark
Hollander, John. A book of various owls
Kirn, Ann. I spy
Kraus, Robert. Owliver
Lane, Carolyn. The voices of Greenwillow Pond

Lear, Edward. The owl and the
  pussycat, ill. by Barbara Cooney
  The owl and the pussy-cat, ill. by Wil-
    liam Pène Du Bois
  The owl and the pussy-cat, ill. by
    Gwen Fulton
  The owl and the pussy-cat, ill. by
    Elaine Muis
  The owl and the pussy-cat, ill. by
    Owen Wood
Leonard, Marcia. Little owl leaves the
  nest
Lobel, Arnold. Owl at home
McKeever, Katherine. A family for
  Minerva
Maschler, Fay. T. G. and Moonie go
  shopping
  T. G. and Moonie have a baby
  T. G. and Moonie move out of town
Nicoll, Helen. Meg at sea
  Meg's eggs
Piatti, Celestino. The happy owls
Potter, Beatrix. The tale of Squirrel
  Nutkin
Scarry, Patsy. Little Richard and Prickles
Schären, Beatrix. Tillo
Schoenherr, John. The barn
Slobodkin, Louis. Wide-awake owl
Smith, Jim. The frog band and the
  owlnapper
Tompert, Ann. Badger on his own
Wildsmith, Brian. The owl and the
  woodpecker

Birds — parakeets, parrots

Augarde, Steve. Barnaby Shrew, Black
  Dan and... the mighty wedgwood
Banchek, Linda. Snake in, snake out
Baum, Louis. JuJu and the pirate
Bishop, Bonnie. No one noticed Ralph
  Ralph rides away
Blegvad, Lenore. The parrot in the
  garret and other rhymes about
  dwellings
Bradford, Ann. The mystery of the tree
  house
Cressey, James. Pet parrot
Dragonwagon, Crescent. Coconut
Gordon, Sharon. Pete the parakeet
Graham, Margaret Bloy. Benjy and the
  barking bird
Holman, Felice. Victoria's castle
Hyman, Robin. Casper and the rainbow
  bird
McDermott, Gerald. Papagayo, the
  mischief maker
Potter, Stephen. Squawky, the
  adventures of a Clasperchoice
Zacharias, Thomas. But where is the
  green parrot?
Zusman, Evelyn. The Passover parrot

Birds — peacocks, peahens

Alan, Sandy. The plaid peacock
Daniel, Doris Temple. Pauline and the
  peacock
Hamberger, John. The peacock who lost
  his tail
Kepes, Juliet. The seed that peacock
  planted
Peet, Bill. The spooky tail of Prewitt
  Peacock
Wittman, Sally. Pelly and Peak
  Plenty of Pelly and Peak

Birds — pelicans

Benchley, Nathaniel. The flying lessons
  of Gerald Pelican
Crane, Alan. Pepita bonita
Freeman, Don. Come again, pelican
Hewett, Joan. Fly away free
Lear, Edward. The pelican chorus
  The pelican chorus and the quangle
  wangle's hat
O'Reilly, Edward. Brown pelican at the
  pond
Wildsmith, Brian. Pelican
Wise, William. Nanette, the hungry
  pelican
Wittman, Sally. Pelly and Peak
  Plenty of Pelly and Peak

Birds — penguins

Bonners, Susan. A penguin year
Bright, Robert. Which is Willy?
Coldrey, Jennifer. Penguins
Fatio, Louise. Hector and Christina
  Hector penguin
Hamsa, Bobbie. Your pet penguin
Hogan, Paula Z. The penguin
Howe, Caroline Walton. Counting
  penguins
Johnston, Johanna. Penguin's way
Lilly, Kenneth. Animals of the ocean
Nichols, Cathy. Tuxedo Sam
The penguin
Sheehan, Angela. The penguin
Stevenson, James. Winston, Newton,
  Elton, and Ed
Weiss, Leatie. Funny feet!
Whitlock, Ralph. Penguins
Winteringham, Victoria. Penguin day

Birds — pigeons

Baker, Jeannie. Home in the sky
  Millicent
Benchley, Nathaniel. Walter the homing
  pigeon
Kingman, Lee. Pierre Pigeon
McClure, Gillian. Fly home McDoo
Peet, Bill. Fly, Homer, fly

Selden, George. Chester Cricket's
pigeon ride
Shulman, Milton. Prep, the little pigeon
of Trafalgar Square
Suben, Eric. Pigeon takes a trip

Birds — puffins

Bonsall, Crosby Newell. What spot?
Drew, Patricia. Spotter Puff
Hall, Pam. On the edge of the eastern
ocean
Lawson, Annetta. The lucky yak
Lewis, Naomi. Puffin

Birds — ravens

Aiken, Joan. Arabel and Mortimer
Grimm, Jacob. The seven ravens, ill. by
Felix Hoffmann
The seven ravens, ill. by Lisbeth
Zwerger

Birds — robins

Cock Robin. The courtship, merry
marriage, and feast of Cock Robin
and Jenny Wren
Flack, Marjorie. The restless robin
Hawkinson, John. Robins and rabbits
Kent, Jack. Round Robin
Stern, Elsie-Jean. Wee Robin's Christmas
song

Birds — sandpipers

Hurd, Edith Thacher. Sandpipers
Mendoza, George. The scribbler

Birds — sea gulls

Armitage, Ronda. The lighthouse
keeper's lunch
Carrick, Carol. Beach bird
Duvoisin, Roger Antoine. Snowy and
Woody
Ness, Evaline. Do you have the time,
Lydia?
Pursell, Margaret Sanford. Shelley the
sea gull
Turkle, Brinton. Thy friend, Obadiah

Birds — sparrows

Crabtree, Judith. The sparrow's story at
the king's command
Fregosi, Claudia. The pumpkin sparrow
Gerstein, Mordicai. Prince Sparrow
Selden, George. Sparrow socks

Birds — storks

Brown, Margaret Wise. Wheel on the
chimney
Gantschev, Ivan. Journey of the storks

Birds — swallows

Politi, Leo. Song of the swallows

Birds — swans

Andersen, H C (Hans Christian). The
ugly duckling, ill. by Adrienne
Adams
The ugly duckling, ill. by Lorinda
Bryan Cauley
The ugly duckling, ill. by Tadasu
Izawa and Shigemi Hijikata
The ugly duckling, ill. by Johannes
Larsen
The ugly duckling, ill. by Josef Palecek
The wild swans, ill. by Angela Barrett
The wild swans, ill. by Susan Jeffers
Canfield, Jane White. Swan cove
Grimm, Jacob. The six swans
Hillert, Margaret. The funny baby
Hogan, Paula Z. The black swan

Birds — toucans

McKee, David. Two can toucan

Birds — turkeys

Baker, Betty. Turkey girl
Balian, Lorna. Sometimes it's turkey
Kroll, Steven. One tough turkey
Schatell, Brian. Farmer Goff and his
turkey Sam
Sam's no dummy, Farmer Goff

Birds — vultures

Duvoisin, Roger Antoine. Petunia, I love
you
Peet, Bill. Eli
Ungerer, Tomi. Orlando, the brave
vulture
Wolkstein, Diane. The cool ride in the
sky

Birds — woodpeckers

Wildsmith, Brian. The owl and the
woodpecker

Birds — wrens

Brock, Emma Lillian. Mr. Wren's house
Cock Robin. The courtship, merry
marriage, and feast of Cock Robin
and Jenny Wren

Birthdays

Abrons, Mary. For Alice a palace
Alexander, Sue. World famous Muriel
Aliki. June 7!
Use your head, dear
Amoss, Berthe. It's not your birthday

Anderson, C W (Clarence Williams).
Billy and Blaze

Annett, Cora. The dog who thought he
was a boy

Armitage, Ronda. The bossing of Josie

Arthur, Catherine. My sister's silent
world

Asch, Frank. Happy birthday, moon!

Ashley, Bernard. Dinner ladies don't
count

Averill, Esther. Jenny's birthday book

Ayer, Jacqueline. A wish for little sister

Bannon, Laura. Manuela's birthday

Barklem, Jill. Spring story

Barrett, Judi. Benjamin's 365 birthdays

Bauer, Helen. Good times in the park

Bell, Norman. Linda's airmail letter

Bemelmans, Ludwig. Madeline in
London

Benchley, Peter. Jonathan visits the
White House

Beskow, Elsa Maartman. Peter in
Blueberry Land
Peter's adventures in Blueberry land

Bible, Charles. Jennifer's new chair

Billam, Rosemary. Fuzzy rabbit

Blocksma, Mary. Grandma Dragon's
birthday

Bond, Felicia. Mary Betty Lizzie
McNutt's birthday

Brandenberg, Franz. Aunt Nina and her
nephews and nieces
A secret for grandmother's birthday

Bromhall, Winifred. Mary Ann's first
picture

Browne, Anthony. Gorilla

Bruna, Dick. Tilly and Tess

Brunhoff, Laurent de. Babar's birthday
surprise
Serafina the giraffe

Buntain, Ruth Jaeger. The birthday
story

Bunting, Eve. The robot birthday

Calmenson, Stephanie. The birthday hat

Carle, Eric. The secret birthday message

Chalmers, Audrey. A birthday for
Obash

Chalmers, Mary. A hat for Amy Jean

Clifton, Lucille. Don't you remember?

Cole, William. What's good for a
three-year-old?

Coombs, Patricia. Dorrie and the
birthday eggs

Costa, Nicoletta. The birthday party

Cunliffe, John. The king's birthday cake

Daly, Maureen. Patrick visits the library

Da Rif, Andrea. The blueberry cake that
little fox baked

Davis, Lavinia. The wild birthday cake

Dayton, Laura. LeRoy's birthday circus

Duvoisin, Roger Antoine. Veronica and
the birthday present

Eberstadt, Isabel. What is for my
birthday?

Elkin, Benjamin. The loudest noise in
the world

Fern, Eugene. Birthday presents

Fischer, Hans. The birthday

Flack, Marjorie. Ask Mr. Bear

Fleischman, Paul. The birthday tree

Fowler, Richard. Inspector Smart gets
the message!

Freedman, Sally. Monster birthday party

Freeman, Don. The guard mouse
Mop Top

Gackenbach, Dick. Binky gets a car

Gantos, Jack. Swampy alligator

Glovach, Linda. The Little Witch's
birthday book

Goodall, John S. Shrewbettina's birthday

Gordon, Shirley. Happy birthday,
Crystal

Heide, Florence Parry. Treehorn's wish

Hertza, Ole. Tobias has a birthday

Hill, Eric. Spot's birthday party

Hillert, Margaret. The birthday car
Happy birthday, dear dragon

Hoban, Russell. A birthday for Frances

Hoff, Syd. Happy birthday, Henrietta!

Homme, Bob. The friendly giant's
birthday

Hughes, Shirley. Alfie gives a hand

Hutchins, Pat. The best train set ever
Happy birthday, Sam
King Henry's palace

Iwasaki, Chihiro. The birthday wish

Jaynes, Ruth M. What is a birthday
child?

Jones, Penelope. I didn't want to be nice

Kitt, Tamara. A special birthday party
for someone very special

Krauze, Andrzej. What's so special about
today?

Kumin, Maxine. Joey and the birthday
present

Lasell, Fen. Michael grows a wish

Laurence, Margaret. The Christmas
birthday story

Lenski, Lois. A surprise for Davy

Lewis, Thomas P. Call for Mr. Sniff

Lexau, Joan M. Go away, dog
Me day

Lindman, Maj. Flicka, Ricka, Dicka bake
a cake
Snipp, Snapp, Snurr and the red shoes

Little, Lessie Jones. I can do it by myself

Lobel, Anita. A birthday for the princess

Lowrey, Janette Sebring. Six silver
spoons

McCue, Lisa. Corduroy's party

McKee, David. King Rollo and the birthday

McNeill, Janet. The giant's birthday

Marie, Geraldine. The magic box

Miklowitz, Gloria D. Bearfoot boy

Miles, Miska. Mouse six and the happy birthday

Minarik, Else Holmelund. Little Bear

Moon, Grace Purdie. One little Indian

Morice, Dave. The happy birthday handbook

Munari, Bruno. The birthday present

Myers, Bernice. Charlie's birthday present

Myller, Rolf. How big is a foot?

Myrick, Jean Lockwood. Ninety-nine pockets

Ness, Evaline. Josefina February

Oxenbury, Helen. The birthday party

Parish, Peggy. Be ready at eight
Snapping turtle's all wrong day

Park, W B. Bakery business

Parker, Nancy Winslow. Love from Uncle Clyde

Peppé, Rodney. The kettleship pirates

Perkins, Al. Tubby and the lantern

Peters, Sharon. Happy birthday

Pomerantz, Charlotte. The half-birthday party

Prager, Annabelle. The surprise party

Quin-Harkin, Janet. Helpful Hattie

Rice, Eve. Benny bakes a cake

Rockwell, Anne F. Happy birthday to me

Sandberg, Inger. Nicholas' favorite pet

Seuss, Dr. Happy birthday to you!
Hooper Humperdink...? Not him!

Sewell, Helen Moore. Birthdays for Robin

Shannon, George. The surprise

Shimin, Symeon. A special birthday

Steiner, Charlotte. Birthdays are for everyone

Steptoe, John. Birthday

Stolz, Mary Slattery. Emmett's pig

Türk, Hanne. Happy birthday Max

Uchida, Yoshiko. Sumi's special happening

Waber, Bernard. Lyle and the birthday party

Watson, Nancy Dingman. The birthday goat
Tommy's mommy's fish

Williams, Barbara. Whatever happened to Beverly Bigler's birthday?

Williams, Vera B. Something special for me

Yashima, Tarō. Umbrella

Zimelman, Nathan. Once when I was five

Zolotow, Charlotte. Mr. Rabbit and the lovely present

Black Americans *see* Ethnic groups in the U.S. — Afro-Americans

Blackbirds *see* Birds — blackbirds

Blackouts *see* Power failure

Blindness *see* Handicaps — blindness

Blocks *see* Toys — blocks

Bluejays *see* Birds — bluejays

Board books *see* Format, unusual — cardboard pages

Boasting *see* Behavior — boasting

Boats, ships

Alexander, Anne. Boats and ships from A to Z

Allen, Pamela. Who sank the boat?

Anderson, Lonzo. Arion and the dolphins

Ardizzone, Edward. Little Tim and the brave sea captain
Ship's cook Ginger
Tim all alone
Tim and Charlotte
Tim and Ginger
Tim and Lucy go to sea
Tim in danger
Tim to the rescue
Tim's friend Towser
Tim's last voyage

Augarde, Steve. Barnaby Shrew goes to sea

Baker, Betty. My sister says

Bate, Norman. What a wonderful machine is a submarine

Benchley, Nathaniel. Red Fox and his canoe

Benjamin, Alan. A change of plans

Berenstain, Michael. The ship book

Bridgman, Elizabeth. Nanny bear's cruise

Brown, Judith Gwyn. The happy voyage

Brown, Marcia. Skipper John's cook

Bruna, Dick. The sailor

Burchard, Peter. The Carol Moran

Burningham, John. Mr. Gumpy's outing

Bushey, Jerry. The barge book

Calhoun, Mary. Euphonia and the flood

Campbell, Ann. Let's find out about boats

Carrick, Carol. The washout

Carryl, Charles Edward. A capital ship

Carter, Katharine. Ships and seaports

Chalmers, Mary. Boats finds a house
Cohen, Peter Zachary. Authorized autumn charts of the Upper Red Canoe River country
Crews, Donald. Harbor
DeLage, Ida. Pilgrim children on the Mayflower
Dennis, Morgan. The sea dog
De Paola, Tomie. Four stories for four seasons
Devlin, Harry. The walloping window blind
Domanska, Janina. I saw a ship a-sailing
Dorros, Arthur. Pretzels
Du Bois, William Pène. Otto at sea
Elting, Mary. The big book of real boats and ships
Flack, Marjorie. The boats on the river
Flora, James. Fishing with dad
Fry, Christopher. The boat that mooed
Gay, Michael. Little boat
Gibbons, Gail. Boat book
Goodall, John S. Jacko
Graham, Margaret Bloy. Benjy's boat trip
Gramatky, Hardie. Little Toot
  Little Toot on the Mississippi
  Little Toot on the Thames
  Little Toot through the Golden Gate
Haas, Irene. The Maggie B
Haley, Gail E. Noah's ark
Hansen, Carla. Barnaby Bear builds a boat
Hillert, Margaret. The yellow boat
Hurd, Edith Thacher. What whale? Where?
Isadora, Rachel. No, Agatha!
Joerns, Consuelo. The foggy rescue
Kellogg, Steven. The island of the skog
Kuskin, Karla. The animals and the ark
Lenski, Lois. The little sail boat
  Mr. and Mrs. Noah
Lindman, Maj. Sailboat time
Lippman, Peter. The Know-It-Alls go to sea
Loof, Jan. Uncle Louie's fantastic sea voyage
McCloskey, Robert. Bert Dow, deep-water man
McGovern, Ann. Nicholas Bentley Stoningpot III
McGowan, Alan. Sailing ships
Maestro, Betsy. Big city port
Mahy, Margaret. Sailor Jack and the twenty orphans
Marshall, James. Speedboat
Massie, Diane Redfield. The Komodo dragon's jewels
Meddaugh, Susan. Maude and Claude go abroad
Mendoza, George. The alphabet boat
Miles, Miska. No, no, Rosina

Partridge, Jenny. Hopfellow
Peppé, Rodney. The kettleship pirates
Perkins, Al. Tubby and the Poo-Bah
Petersen, David. Submarines
Pitcher, Caroline. Cars and boats
Potter, Beatrix. The tale of Little Pig Robinson
Potter, Russell. The little red ferry boat
Ransome, Arthur. The fool of the world and the flying ship
Reavin, Sam. Hurray for Captain Jane!
Reesink, Marijke. The golden treasure
Rettich, Margret. The voyage of the jolly boat
Rockwell, Anne F. Boats
Schulz, Charles M. Snoopy's facts and fun book about boats
Shecter, Ben. If I had a ship
Shortall, Leonard W. Tod on the tugboat
Spier, Peter. Noah's ark
Stevenson, Jocelyn. Jim Henson's Muppets at sea
Surany, Anico. Ride the cold wind
Swift, Hildegarde Hoyt. The little red lighthouse and the great gray bridge
Taylor, Mark. Henry the castaway
Thomson, Ruth. Peabody all at sea
Tudor, Bethany. Skiddycock Pond
Van Allsburg, Chris. The wreck of the Zephyr
Venable, Alan. The checker players
Vinton, Iris. Look out for pirates!
Williams, Vera B. Three days on a river in a red canoe
Young, Miriam Burt. If I sailed a boat
Zaffo, George J. The giant nursery book of things that go

Bobcats *see* Animals — bobcats

Boogey man *see* Monsters

Books *see* Activities — reading; Libraries

Boredom *see* Behavior — boredom

Bravery *see* Character traits — bravery

Bridges

Carlisle, Norman. Bridges
Lobel, Anita. Sven's bridge
Oppenheim, Joanne. On the other side of the river
Steadman, Ralph. The bridge
Swift, Hildegarde Hoyt. The little red lighthouse and the great gray bridge

Brothers *see* Family life; Sibling rivalry

Brownies *see* Elves and little people

Buffaloes *see* Animals — buffaloes

Bugs *see* Insects

Bulls *see* Animals — bulls, cows

Bullying *see* Behavior — bullying

Bumble bees *see* Insects — bees

Burglars *see* Crime

Burros *see* Animals — donkeys

Bus drivers *see* Careers — bus drivers

Buses

Blance, Ellen. Monster on the bus
Crews, Donald. School bus
Jewell, Nancy. Bus ride
Matthias, Catherine. Out the door
Nichols, Paul. Big Paul's school bus
Shuttlesworth, Dorothy E. ABC of buses
Wolcott, Patty. Double-decker,
    double-decker, double-decker bus
Young, Miriam Burt. If I drove a bus

Butchers *see* Careers — butchers

Butterflies *see* Insects — butterflies,
    caterpillars

Buzzards *see* Birds — buzzards

Cab drivers *see* Careers — taxi drivers

Cable cars, trolleys

Burton, Virginia Lee. Maybelle, the
    cable car
Chalmers, Mary. Here comes the trolley
Gramatky, Hardie. Sparky
MacCabe, Naomi. Cable car Joey
Taniuchi, Kota. Trolley

Cabs *see* Taxis

Caldecott award book

Aardema, Verna. Why mosquitoes buzz
    in people's ears
Alger, Leclaire. Always room for one
    more

Aulaire, Ingri Mortenson d'. Abraham
    Lincoln
Bemelmans, Ludwig. Madeline's rescue
Brown, Marcia. Once a mouse...
Brown, Margaret Wise. The little island
Burton, Virginia Lee. The little house
Cendrars, Blaise. Shadow
Chaucer, Geoffrey. Chanticleer and the
    fox
De Regniers, Beatrice Schenk. May I
    bring a friend?
Dick Whittington and his cat. Dick
    Whittington, ill. by Marcia Brown
Emberley, Barbara. Drummer Hoff
Ets, Marie Hall. Nine days to Christmas
Field, Rachel Lyman. Prayer for a child
Fish, Helen Dean. Animals of the Bible
A frog he would a-wooing go
    (folk-song). Frog went a-courtin'
Goble, Paul. The girl who loved wild
    horses
Hader, Berta Hoerner. The big snow
Haley, Gail E. A story, a story
Hall, Donald. The ox-cart man
Handforth, Thomas. Mei Li
Hodges, Margaret. Saint George and the
    dragon
Hogrogian, Nonny. One fine day
Keats, Ezra Jack. The snowy day
Lawson, Robert. They were strong and
    good
Lipkind, William. Finders keepers
Lobel, Arnold. Fables
McCloskey, Robert. Make way for
    ducklings
  Time of wonder
McDermott, Gerald. Arrow to the sun
Milhous, Katherine. The egg tree
Mosel, Arlene. The funny little woman
Musgrove, Margaret. Ashanti to Zulu
Ness, Evaline. Sam, Bangs, and
    moonshine
Perrault, Charles. Cinderella
Petersham, Maud. The rooster crows
Politi, Leo. Song of the swallows
Provensen, Alice. The glorious flight
Ransome, Arthur. The fool of the world
    and the flying ship
Robbins, Ruth. Baboushka and the three
    kings
Sendak, Maurice. Where the wild things
    are
Spier, Peter. Noah's ark
Steig, William. Sylvester and the magic
    pebble
Thurber, James. Many moons
Tresselt, Alvin R. White snow, bright
    snow
Udry, Janice May. A tree is nice
Van Allsburg, Chris. Jumanji
Ward, Lynd. The biggest bear
Zemach, Harve. Duffy and the devil

Caldecott award honor book

Alger, Leclaire. All in the morning early
Armer, Laura Adams. The forest pool
Artzybasheff, Boris. Seven Simeons
Baker, Olaf. Where the buffaloes begin
Bang, Molly. The grey lady and the
strawberry snatcher
  Ten, nine, eight
Baskin, Leonard. Hosie's alphabet
Baylor, Byrd. The desert is theirs
  Hawk, I'm your brother
  The way to start a day
  When clay sings
Belting, Natalia Maree. The sun is a
golden earring
Bemelmans, Ludwig. Madeline
Birnbaum, Abe. Green eyes
Brown, Marcia. Henry fisherman
  Skipper John's cook
  Stone soup
Brown, Margaret Wise. A child's good
night book
  Little lost lamb
  Wheel on the chimney
Buff, Mary. Dash and Dart
Cathon, Laura E. Tot Botot and his
little flute
Caudill, Rebecca. A pocketful of cricket
Chan, Chin-Yi. Good luck horse
Clark, Ann Nolan. In my mother's house
Crews, Donald. Freight train
  Truck
Dalgliesh, Alice. The Thanksgiving story
Daugherty, James Henry. Andy and the
lion
Davis, Lavinia. Roger and the fox
  The wild birthday cake
Dayrell, Elphinstone. Why the sun and
the moon live in the sky
De Angeli, Marguerite. The book of
nursery and Mother Goose rhymes
  Yonie Wondernose
De Paola, Tomie. Strega Nona
Dick Whittington and his cat, ill. by
Marcia Brown
Domanska, Janina. If all the seas were
one sea
Du Bois, William Pène. Bear party
  Lion
Eichenberg, Fritz. Ape in cape
Elkin, Benjamin. Gillespie and the
guards
Emberley, Barbara. One wide river to
cross
Ets, Marie Hall. In the forest
  Just me
  Mister Penny
  Mr. Penny's race horse
  Mr. T. W. Anthony Woo
  Play with me
Feelings, Muriel. Jambo means hello
  Menjo means one

Fish, Helen Dean. Four and twenty
blackbirds
Flack, Marjorie. The boats on the river
Ford, Lauren. The ageless story
The fox went out on a chilly night, ill.
by Peter Spier
Freeman, Don. Fly high, fly low
Gág, Wanda. Nothing at all
Goffstein, M B (Marilyn Brooks). Fish
for supper
Goudey, Alice E. The day we saw the
sun come up
  Houses from the sea
Graham, Al. Timothy Turtle
Grimm, Jacob. The Brementown
musicians, ill. by Ilse Plume
  Hansel and Gretel, ill. by Paul O.
  Zelinsky
  Little Red Riding Hood, ill. by Trina
  Schart Hyman
  Snow White and the seven dwarfs, ill.
  by Wanda Gág
Hader, Berta Hoerner. Cock-a-doodle
doo
  The mighty hunter
Hodges, Margaret. The wave
Hogrogian, Nonny. The contest
Holbrook, Stewart. America's Ethan
Allen
Holling, Holling C (Holling Clancy).
Paddle-to-the-sea
The house that Jack built, ill. by Anto-
nio Frasconi
Isadora, Rachel. Ben's trumpet
Jonas, Ann. Holes and peeks
Jones, Jessie Mae Orton. Small rain
Joslin, Sesyle. What do you say, dear?
Keats, Ezra Jack. Goggles
Kepes, Juliet. Five little monkeys
Kingman, Lee. Pierre Pigeon
Krauss, Ruth. The happy day
  A very special house
Leaf, Munro. Wee Gillis
Lionni, Leo. Alexander and the wind-up
mouse
  Frederick
  Inch by inch
  Swimmy
Lipkind, William. The two reds
Lobel, Arnold. Frog and Toad are
friends
  On Market Street
Low, Joseph. Mice twice
Macaulay, David. Castle
  Cathedral
McCloskey, Robert. Blueberries for Sal
  One morning in Maine
McDermott, Beverly Brodsky. The
Golem
McDermott, Gerald. Anansi the spider
McGinley, Phyllis. All around the town
  The most wonderful doll in the world

Malcolmson, Anne. The song of Robin Hood

Minarik, Else Holmelund. Little Bear's visit

Mother Goose, ill. by Tasha Tudor

Mother Goose. Mother Goose and nursery rhymes, ill. by Philip Reed

The three jovial huntsmen, ill. by Susan Jeffers

Newberry, Clare Turlay. April's kittens
Barkis
Marshmallow
T-Bone, the baby-sitter

Olds, Elizabeth. Feather mountain

Perrault, Charles. Puss in boots, ill. by Marcia Brown

Petersham, Maud. An American ABC

Politi, Leo. Juanita
Pedro, the angel of Olvera Street

Preston, Edna Mitchell. Pop Corn and Ma Goodness

Reyher, Becky. My mother is the most beautiful woman in the world
The world

Ryan, Cheli Durán. Hildilid's night

Rylant, Cynthia. When I was young in the mountains

Sawyer, Ruth. The Christmas Anna angel
Journey cake, ho!

Scheer, Julian. Rain makes applesauce

Schick, Eleanor. The little school at Cottonwood Corners

Schlein, Miriam. When will the world be mine?

Schreiber, Georges. Bambino the clown

Sendak, Maurice. In the night kitchen
Outside over there

Seuss, Dr. Bartholomew and the Oobleck
If I ran the zoo
McElligot's pool

Shulevitz, Uri. The treasure

Sleator, William. The angry moon

Steig, William. The amazing bone

Tafuri, Nancy. Have you seen my duckling?

Titus, Eve. Anatole
Anatole and the cat

Tom Tit Tot, ill. by Evaline Ness

Tresselt, Alvin R. Hide and seek fog
Rain drop splash

Tudor, Tasha. 1 is one

Turkle, Brinton. Thy friend, Obadiah

Udry, Janice May. The moon jumpers

Van Allsburg, Chris. The garden of Abdul Gasazi

Wheeler, Opal. Sing in praise
Sing Mother Goose

Wiese, Kurt. Fish in the air
You can write Chinese

Willard, Nancy. A visit to William Blake's inn

Williams, Vera B. A chair for my mother

Yashima, Tarō. Crow boy
Seashore story
Umbrella

Yolen, Jane. The emperor and the kite

Zemach, Harve. The judge

Zemach, Margot. It could always be worse

Zion, Gene. All falling down

Zolotow, Charlotte. Mr. Rabbit and the lovely present
The storm book

Camels see Animals — camels

Camping see Sports — camping

Canada see Foreign lands — Canada

Canaries see Birds — canaries

Cardboard page books see Format, unusual — cardboard pages

Cardinals see Birds — cardinals

Careers

Aitken, Amy. Ruby!

Arnold, Caroline. What is a community?
Who keeps us safe?
Who works here?

Azaad, Meyer. Half for you

Baker, Eugene. I want to be a computer operator

Bank Street College of Education. People read

Bauer, Caroline Feller. My mom travels a lot

Boxer, Deborah. 26 ways to be somebody else

Brentano, Clemens. Schoolmaster Whackwell's wonderful sons

Burnett, Carol. What I want to be when I grow up

Florian, Douglas. People working

Freeman, Don. The night the lights went out

Harper, Anita. How we work

Klein, Norma. Girls can be anything

Kraus, Robert. Owliver

Lasker, Joe. Mothers can do anything

Lenski, Lois. Lois Lenski's big book of Mr. Small

Le-Tan, Pierre. Timothy's dream book

Mayer, Mercer. Little Monster at work

Merriam, Eve. Mommies at work

Mitchell, Joyce Slayton. My mommy makes money

Morrison, Bill. Louis James hates school
Nichols, Paul. Big Paul's school bus
Oliver, Dexter. I want to be...
Oppenheim, Joanne. On the other side
of the river
Puner, Helen Walker. Daddys, what
they do all day
Rowe, Jeanne A. City workers
Sandberg, Inger. Come on out, Daddy!
Scarry, Richard. Richard Scarry's busiest
people ever
Richard Scarry's Postman Pig and his
busy neighbors
What do people do all day?
Seignobosc, Françoise. What do you
want to be?
The Sesame Street book of people and
things
Stewart, Robert S. The daddy book
Williams, Barbara. I know a salesperson
Winn, Marie. The man who made fine
tops

Careers — airplane pilots

Baker, Donna. I want to be a pilot
Barton, Byron. Airport
Greene, Carla. Railroad engineers and
airplane pilots
Young, Miriam Burt. If I flew a plane

Careers — artists

Adams, Adrienne. The great Valentine's
Day balloon race
Angelo, Nancy Carolyn Harrison.
Camembert
Miller, Warren. Pablo paints a picture
Payne, Joan Balfour. The stable that
stayed
Pinkwater, Daniel Manus. The bear's
picture
Sharon, Mary Bruce. Scenes from
childhood
Sloan, Carolyn. Carter is a painter's cat
Velthuijs, Max. The painter and the
bird
Ventura, Piero. The painter's trick
Weisgard, Leonard. Mr. Peaceable
prints

Careers — bakers

Caple, Kathy. Inspector Aardvark and
the perfect cake
Carle, Eric. Walter the baker
Craig, M Jean. The man whose name
was not Thomas
Green, Melinda. Bembelman's bakery
Kessler, Leonard P. Soup for the king
Worthington, Phoebe. Teddy bear baker
Young, Miriam Burt. The sugar mouse
cake

Careers — barbers

Appell, Clara. Now I have a daddy
haircut
Auerbach, Marjorie. King Lavra and the
barber
Barry, Robert E. Next please
Freeman, Don. Mop Top
Kunhardt, Dorothy. Billy the barber
Mahiri, Jabari. The day they stole the
letter J
Peet, Bill. Hubert's hair-raising
adventures
Rockwell, Anne F. My barber

Careers — bus drivers

Young, Miriam Burt. If I drove a bus

Careers — butchers

Yorinks, Arthur. Louis the fish

Careers — cab drivers *see* Careers — taxi drivers

Careers — carpenters

Adkins, Jan. Toolchest
Greene, Carla. I want to be a carpenter

Careers — clockmakers

Ardizzone, Edward. Johnny the
clockmaker

Careers — dentists

Barnett, Naomi. I know a dentist
Berenstain, Stan. The Berenstain bears
visit the dentist
Duvoisin, Roger Antoine. Crocus
Lapp, Carolyn. The dentists' tools
Richter, Alice Numeroff. You can't put
braces on spaces
Rockwell, Harlow. My dentist
Wolf, Bernard. Michael and the dentist

Careers — detectives

Berenstain, Stan. The bear detectives
Bonsall, Crosby Newell. The case of the
cat's meow
The case of the dumb bells
The case of the hungry stranger
The case of the scaredy cats
Lawrence, James. Binky Brothers and
the fearless four
Binky Brothers, detectives
Platt, Kin. Big Max
Big Max in the mystery of the missing
moose
Quackenbush, Robert M. Detective Mole
Detective Mole and the secret clues

Detective Mole and the Tip-Top
  mystery
Dig to disaster
Express train to trouble
Piet Potter returns
Piet Potter strikes again
Piet Potter to the rescue
Piet Potter's first case
Stairway to doom
Sharmat, Marjorie Weinman. Nate the
  Great
  Nate the Great and the lost list
  Nate the Great and the phony clue
  Nate the Great goes undercover
Thomson, Ruth. Peabody all at sea
  Peabody's first case

Careers — doctors

Arnold, Caroline. Who keeps us
  healthy?
Berenstain, Stan. The Berenstain bears
  go to the doctor
Breinburg, Petronella. Doctor Shawn
Charlip, Remy. "Mother, mother I feel
  sick"
Cobb, Vicki. How the doctor knows
  you're fine
Gilbert, Helen Earle. Dr. Trotter and
  his big gold watch
Goodsell, Jane. Katie's magic glasses
Greene, Carla. Doctors and nurses what
  do they do?
Lerner, Marguerite Rush. Doctors' tools
Marcus, Susan. Casey visits the doctor
Oxenbury, Helen. The checkup
Robison, Deborah. Your turn, doctor
Rockwell, Harlow. My doctor
Stein, Sara Bonnett. A hospital story
Viorst, Judith. The tenth good thing
  about Barney
Wahl, Jan. Doctor Rabbit's foundling
Wolde, Gunilla. Betsy and the doctor

Careers — firefighters

Averill, Esther. The fire cat
Barr, Jene. Fire snorkel number 7
Baumann, Kurt. Piro and the fire
  brigade
Bester, Roger. Fireman Jim
Bridwell, Norman. Clifford's good deeds
Brown, Margaret Wise. Five little
  firemen
  The little fireman
Bundt, Nancy. The fire station book
Bushey, Jerry. Building a fire truck
Chalmers, Mary. Throw a kiss, Harry
Elliott, Dan. A visit to the Sesame Street
  firehouse
Fast rolling fire trucks
Firehouse

Fisher, Leonard Everett. Pumpers,
  boilers, hooks and ladders
Gibbons, Gail. Fire! Fire!
Gramatky, Hardie. Hercules
Greene, Carla. What do they do?
  Policemen and firemen
Greydanus, Rose. Big red fire engine
Hansen, Jeff. Being a fire fighter isn't
  just squirtin' water
Hill, Mary Lou. My dad's a
  smokejumper
Homme, Bob. The friendly giant's book
  of fire engines
Keeping, Charles. Willie's fire-engine
Lenski, Lois. The little fire engine
Marston, Hope Irvin. Fire trucks
Rey, Hans Augusto. Curious George
Robinson, Nancy K. Firefighters!
Spiegel, Doris. Danny and Company 92
Spier, Peter. Firehouse
Weiss, Harvey. The sooner hound
Zaffo, George J. Big book of real fire
  engines

Careers — fishermen

Aldridge, Josephine Haskell.
  Fisherman's luck
Beim, Lorraine. Lucky Pierre
Brown, Marcia. Henry fisherman
Brown, Margaret Wise. The little
  fisherman
Bunting, Eve. Magic and the night river
Flora, James. Fishing with dad
Gramatky, Hardie. Nikos and the sea
  god
Matsutani, Miyoko. The fisherman
  under the sea
Miles, Miska. No, no, Rosina
Napoli, Guillier. Adventure of Mont
  Saint Michel
Parker, Dorothy D. Liam's catch
Rettich, Margret. The voyage of the
  jolly boat
Weil, Lisl. Gertie and Gus

Careers — forest rangers see Careers — park rangers

Careers — fortune tellers

Coombs, Patricia. Dorrie and the
  fortune teller
Jeschke, Susan. Firerose
Weiss, Ellen. Clara the fortune-telling
  chicken

Careers — garbage collectors

Zion, Gene. Dear garbage man

Careers — judges

Mirkovic, Irene. The greedy shopkeeper
Zemach, Harve. The judge

Careers — librarians

Baker, Donna. I want to be a librarian

Careers — maids

Parish, Peggy. Amelia Bedelia
  Amelia Bedelia and the surprise
    shower
  Amelia Bedelia goes camping
  Amelia Bedelia helps out
  Come back, Amelia Bedelia
  Good work, Amelia Bedelia
  Play ball, Amelia Bedelia
  Teach us, Amelia Bedelia
  Thank you, Amelia Bedelia

Careers — mail carriers

Beim, Jerrold. Country mailman
Buchheimer, Naomi. Let's go to a post
  office
Drummond, Violet H. The flying
  postman
Gibbons, Gail. The post office book
Haley, Gail E. The post office cat
Hedderwick, Mairi. Katie Morag
  delivers the mail
Maury, Inez. My mother the mail
  carrier
Scarry, Richard. Richard Scarry's
  Postman Pig and his busy neighbors

Careers — military

Ambrus, Victor G. Brave soldier
  Janosch
Brown, Marcia. Stone soup
Emberley, Barbara. Drummer Hoff
Greene, Carla. Soldiers and sailors what
  do they do?
Langstaff, John M. Soldier, soldier,
  won't you marry me?
McGowen, Tom. The only glupmaker in
  the U.S. Navy
Mahy, Margaret. Sailor Jack and the
  twenty orphans

Careers — miners

Brown, Margaret Wise. Two little
  miners

Careers — nuns

Routh, Jonathan. The Nuns go to Africa

Careers — nurses

Arnold, Caroline. Who keeps us
  healthy?
Greene, Carla. Doctors and nurses what
  do they do?
Kraus, Robert. Rebecca Hatpin
Stein, Sara Bonnett. A hospital story
Whitney, Alma Marshak. Just awful

Careers — park rangers

Hill, Mary Lou. My dad's a park ranger

Careers — peddlers

Crossley-Holland, Kevin. The pedlar of
  Swaffham
Jacobs, Joseph. The crock of gold
Rockwell, Anne F. A bear, a bobcat and
  three ghosts
Slobodkina, Esphyr. Caps for sale
  Pezzo the peddler and the circus
    elephant
  Pezzo the peddler and the thirteen silly
    thieves
Suba, Susanne. The monkeys and the
  pedlar

Careers — physicians *see* Careers —
doctors

Careers — police officers

Adelson, Leone. Who blew that whistle?
Ahlberg, Allan. Cops and robbers
Baker, Donna. I want to be a police
  officer
Brown, David. Someone always needs a
  policeman
Chapin, Cynthia. Squad car 55
Erdoes, Richard. Policemen around the
  world
Goodall, John S. Paddy's new hat
Greene, Carla. What do they do?
  Policemen and firemen
Guilfoile, Elizabeth. Have you seen my
  brother?
Keats, Ezra Jack. My dog is lost!
Lattin, Anne. Peter's policeman
Lenski, Lois. Policeman Small
McCloskey, Robert. Make way for
  ducklings
Schlein, Miriam. The amazing Mr.
  Pelgrew
Vreeken, Elizabeth. The boy who would
  not say his name

Careers — railroad engineers

Greene, Carla. Railroad engineers and
  airplane pilots
Lenski, Lois. The little train

Careers — rangers *see* Careers — park rangers

Careers — sailors *see* Careers — military

Careers — seamstresses

Lobel, Anita. The seamstress of Salzburg

Olds, Helen Diehl. Miss Hattie and the monkey

Careers — shoemakers

Gilbert, Helen Earle. Mr. Plum and the little green tree

Grimm, Jacob. The elves and the shoemaker
  The shoemaker and the elves

Ross, Tony. The greedy little cobbler

Sheldon, Aure. Of cobblers and kings

Careers — soldiers *see* Careers — military

Careers — tailors

Ambrus, Victor G. The three poor tailors

Galdone, Paul. The monster and the tailor

Grimm, Jacob. The brave little tailor, ill. by Mark Corcoran
  The brave little tailor, ill. by Svend Otto
  The brave little tailor, ill. by Daniel San Souci
  The valiant little tailor

Potter, Beatrix. The tailor of Gloucester

Careers — taxi drivers

Moore, Lilian. Papa Albert

Otto, Svend. Taxi dog

Ross, Jessica. Ms. Klondike

Careers — teachers

Allard, Harry. Miss Nelson is back
  Miss Nelson is missing!

Arnold, Caroline. Where do you go to school?

Cummings, W T (Walter Thies). Miss Esta Maude's secret

Feder, Paula Kurzband. Where does the teacher live?

Careers — telephone operators

Allen, Jeffrey. Mary Alice, operator number 9

Careers — train engineers *see* Careers — railroad engineers

Careers — truck drivers

Cartlidge, Michelle. Teddy trucks

Greene, Carla. Truck drivers what do they do?

Young, Miriam Burt. If I drove a truck

Careers — veterinarians

Bellville, Rod. Large animal veterinarians

Greene, Carla. Animal doctors what do they do?

Herriot, James. Moses the kitten

Hewett, Joan. Fly away free

Polhamus, Jean Burt. Doctor Dinosaur

Careers — waiters, waitresses

Peters, Sharon. Happy Jack

Careers — waitresses *see* Careers — waiters, waitresses

Careers — window cleaners

Rey, Hans Augusto. Curious George takes a job

Careers — writers

Goffstein, M B (Marilyn Brooks). A writer

Carelessness *see* Behavior — carelessness

Caribbean Islands *see* Foreign lands — Caribbean Islands

Carnivals *see* Fairs

Carousels *see* Merry-go-rounds

Carpenters *see* Careers — carpenters

Cars *see* Automobiles

Caterpillars *see* Insects — butterflies, caterpillars

Cats *see* Animals — cats

Cavemen

Hoff, Syd. Stanley

Seyton, Marion. The hole in the hill

Slobodkin, Louis. Dinny and Danny

Caves

Friedman, Estelle. Boy who lived in a cave
Ungerer, Tomi. The Mellops go spelunking

Chanukah *see* Holidays — Hanukkah

Character traits

Johnson, Crockett. The emperor's gift
Seignobosc, Françoise. Jeanne-Marie in gay Paris

Character traits — ambition

Balet, Jan B. Joanjo
Claude-Lafontaine, Pascale. Monsieur Bussy, the celebrated hamster
Graham, Al. Timothy Turtle
Gramatky, Hardie. Little Toot
Hochman, Sandra. The magic convention
Horwitz, Elinor Lander. Sometimes it happens
Kumin, Maxine. Speedy digs downside up
Ringi, Kjell. My father and I
Seignobosc, Françoise. What do you want to be?
Shecter, Ben. Hester the jester
Turska, Krystyna. The magician of Cracow
Uchida, Yoshiko. Sumi's prize

Character traits — appearance

Andersen, H C (Hans Christian). The ugly duckling, ill. by Adrienne Adams
  The ugly duckling, ill. by Lorinda Bryan Cauley
  The ugly duckling, ill. by Tadasu Izawa and Shigemi Hijikata
  The ugly duckling, ill. by Johannes Larsen
  The ugly duckling, ill. by Josef Paleček
Balestrino, Philip. Fat and skinny
Beim, Jerrold. Freckle face
Bonsall, Crosby Newell. Listen, listen!
Cohen, Burton. Nelson makes a face
Collins, Judith Graham. Josh's scary dad
Crowley, Arthur. The ugly book
Dellinger, Annetta. You are special to Jesus
De Paola, Tomie. Big Anthony and the magic ring
Elborn, Andrew. Bird Adalbert
Fatio, Louise. The happy lion and the bear
Freeman, Don. Dandelion

Girion, Barbara. The boy with the special face
Hale, Irina. Brown bear in a brown chair
Heine, Helme. The most wonderful egg in the world
Hillert, Margaret. The funny baby
Iké, Jane Hori. A Japanese fairy tale
Keller, Irene. The Thingumajig book of manners
McDermott, Gerald. The magic tree
Maestro, Betsy. On the town
Mayer, Marianna. Beauty and the beast
Mayer, Mercer. How the trollusk got his hat
Moore, Sheila. Samson Svenson's baby
Myers, Amy. I know a monster
Ness, Evaline. The girl and the goatherd
Numeroff, Laura Joffe. Amy for short
Ormondroyd, Edward. Theodore
Park, Ruth. When the wind changed
Primavera, Elise. Basil and Maggie
Ring, Elizabeth. Tiger lilies
Salus, Naomi Panush. My daddy's mustache
Scott, Natalie. Firebrand, push your hair out of your eyes
Small, David. Imogene's antlers
Stren, Patti. Mountain Rose
Yolen, Jane. Sleeping ugly

Character traits — being different

Andersen, H C (Hans Christian). The ugly duckling, ill. by Adrienne Adams
  The ugly duckling, ill. by Lorinda Bryan Cauley
  The ugly duckling, ill. by Tadasu Izawa and Shigemi Hijikata
  The ugly duckling, ill. by Johannes Larsen
  The ugly duckling, ill. by Josef Paleček
Aulaire, Ingri Mortenson d'. Nils
Beim, Jerrold. Freckle face
Blue, Rose. I am here: Yo estoy aqui
Brightman, Alan. Like me
Burningham, John. Borka
Carle, Eric. The mixed-up chameleon, 1975
  The mixed-up chameleon, 1984
Coombs, Patricia. The lost playground
Crossley-Holland, Kevin. The green children
Duvoisin, Roger Antoine. Our Veronica goes to Petunia's farm
  Veronica
Emberley, Ed. Rosebud
Fern, Eugene. Pepito's story
Heine, Helme. Superhare
Hillert, Margaret. The funny baby
Karlin, Nurit. The blue frog

Krasilovsky, Phyllis. The very tall little
  girl
Lerner, Marguerite Rush. Lefty, the
  story of left-handedness
Levine, Rhoda. Harrison loved his
  umbrella
Lionni, Leo. Cornelius
McGovern, Ann. Mr. Skinner's skinny
  house
McKelvey, David. Bobby the mostly silky
Peet, Bill. The spooky tail of Prewitt
  Peacock
Reesink, Marijke. The princess who
  always ran away
Rey, Margaret Elisabeth Waldstein.
  Spotty
Shub, Elizabeth. Dragon Franz
Simon, Norma. Why am I different?
Simon, Sidney B. The armadillo who
  had no shell

Character traits — bravery

Aitken, Amy. Ruby, the red knight
Aliki. George and the cherry tree
Andersen, H C (Hans Christian). The
  snow queen, ill. by Toma Bagdanovic
  The snow queen, ill. by June Atkin
  Corwin
  The snow queen, ill. by Susan Jeffers
  The snow queen, ill. by Errol Le Cain
Anglund, Joan Walsh. The brave
  cowboy
Ardizzone, Edward. Little Tim and the
  brave sea captain
  Paul, the hero of the fire
  Peter the wanderer
  Tim and Charlotte
  Tim to the rescue
Aulaire, Ingri Mortenson d'. Wings for
  Per
Averill, Esther. When Jenny lost her
  scarf
Baker, Betty. Latki and the lightning
  lizard
Baldner, Gaby. Joba and the wild boar
Bannon, Laura. Hat for a hero
Barr, Cathrine. Little Ben
Barrows, Marjorie Wescott. Fraidy cat
Baumann, Kurt. Piro and the fire
  brigade
Bawden, Nina. William Tell
Beim, Jerrold. Eric on the desert
Benchley, Nathaniel. The deep dives of
  Stanley Whale
Blegvad, Lenore. Anna Banana and me
Bornstein, Ruth Lercher. Jim
Brenner, Anita. A hero by mistake
Brook, Judy. Tim mouse goes down the
  stream
Brown, Margaret Wise. Streamlined pig

Burgert, Hans-Joachim. Samulo and the
  giant
Cameron, Ann. Harry (the monster)
Carleton, Barbee Oliver. Benny and the
  bear
Carlson, Nancy. Harriet and the roller
  coaster
Chaffin, Lillie D. We be warm till
  springtime comes
Charlton, Elizabeth. Jeremy and the
  ghost
Conford, Ellen. Eugene the brave
Coombs, Patricia. Molly Mullett
Coville, Bruce. The foolish giant
Craft, Ruth. Carrie Hepple's garden
De La Mare, Walter. Molly Whuppie
Dreifus, Miriam W. Brave Betsy
Dyke, John. Pigwig
Fatio, Louise. The red bantam
Fern, Eugene. The most frightened
  hero
Furchgott, Terry. Phoebe and the hot
  water bottles
Gantschev, Ivan. The Christmas train
Ginsburg, Mirra. The strongest one of
  all
Grasshopper to the rescue
Grimm, Jacob. The brave little tailor, ill.
  by Mark Corcoran
  The brave little tailor, ill. by Svend
  Otto
  The brave little tailor, ill. by Daniel
  SanSouci
  The valiant little tailor
Holl, Adelaide. Sir Kevin of Devon
Horvath, Betty F. Jasper and the hero
  business
Hürlimann, Bettina. Barry
Keller, Beverly. Pimm's place
Lexau, Joan M. It all began with a drip,
  drip, drip
Little, Lessie Jones. I can do it by myself
Low, Joseph. Benny rabbit and the owl
  Boo to a goose
Marshak, Samuel. The tale of a hero
  nobody knows
Matsutani, Miyoko. The witch's magic
  cloth
Mayer, Marianna. The unicorn and the
  lake
Mayer, Mercer. Liverwurst is missing
  Liza Lou and the Yeller Belly Swamp
Milne, A A (Alan Alexander).
  Winnie-the-Pooh
Peet, Bill. Cowardly Clyde
Polushkin, Maria. The little hen and the
  giant
Scarry, Richard. Peasant Pig and the
  terrible dragon
Schertle, Alice. The gorilla in the hall

Sewell, Helen Moore. Jimmy and
Jemima
Shire, Ellen. The mystery at number
seven, Rue Petite
Stevenson, Drew. The ballad of
Penelope Lou...and me
Taylor, Mark. Henry explores the
jungle
Henry explores the mountains
Henry the explorer
Titus, Eve. Anatole and the cat
Van Woerkom, Dorothy. Becky and the
bear
Wells, H G (Herbert George). The
adventures of Tommy
Wolkstein, Diane. The banza
Yolen, Jane. The acorn quest

Character traits — cleanliness

Adelborg, Ottilia. Clean Peter and the
children of Grubbylea
Bowling, David Louis. Dirty Dingy Daryl
Burch, Robert. The jolly witch
De Paola, Tomie. Marianna May and
Nursey
Dickinson, Mary. Alex's bed
Flot, Jeannette B. Princess Kalina and
the hedgehog
Gantos, Jack. Swampy alligator
Groves-Raines, Antony. The tidy hen
Hamsa, Bobbie. Dirty Larry
Hare, Lorraine. Who needs her?
Haseley, Dennis. The soap bandit
Hickman, Martha Whitmore. Eeps
creeps, it's my room!
Howells, Mildred. The woman who lived
in Holland
Hurd, Edith Thacher. Stop, stop
Jackson, Ellen B. The bear in the
bathtub
Krasilovsky, Phyllis. The man who did
not wash his dishes
Peters, Sharon. Messy Mark
Polushkin, Maria. Bubba and Bubba
Potter, Beatrix. The tale of Mrs.
Tittlemouse
Rockwell, Anne F. Nice and clean
Rudolph, Marguerita. Sharp and shiny
Sharmat, Marjorie Weinman. Mooch the
messy
Sharmat, Mitchell. The seven sloppy
days of Phineas Pig
Stanton, Elizabeth. The very messy
room
Willis, Jeanne. The tale of Georgie Grub

Character traits — cleverness

Aliki. The eggs
Anderson, Paul S. Red fox and the
hungry tiger

Ardizzone, Edward. Peter the wanderer
Asbjørnsen, P C (Peter Christen). The
three billy goats Gruff, ill. by Marcia
Brown
The three billy goats Gruff, ill. by Paul
Galdone
The three billy goats Gruff, ill. by
William Stobbs
Baker, Betty. And me, coyote!
Partners
Bang, Betsy. The old woman and the
red pumpkin
The old woman and the rice thief
Bang, Molly. Wiley and the hairy man
Bannerman, Helen. The story of little
black Sambo
Bason, Lillian. Those foolish Molboes!
Bemelmans, Ludwig. Welcome home
Benchley, Nathaniel. The several tricks
of Edgar Dolphin
Berson, Harold. How the devil got his
due
Joseph and the snake
Why the jackal won't speak to the
hedgehog
Bishop, Claire Huchet. The five Chinese
brothers
Boegehold, Betty. Pawpaw's run
Brett, Jan. Fritz and the beautiful horses
Brown, Marcia. The bun
Stone soup
Brown, Margaret Wise. Don't frighten
the lion
Burningham, John. Harquin
The shopping basket
Burton, Virginia Lee. Calico the wonder
horse
Byfield, Barbara Ninde. The haunted
churchbell
Calhoun, Mary. Cross-country cat
Cameron, John. If mice could fly
Cauley, Lorinda Bryan. The cock, the
mouse and the little red hen
Christelow, Eileen. Jerome the babysitter
Christian, Mary Blount. J. J. Leggett,
secret agent
Coatsworth, Elizabeth. Pika and the
roses
Crompton, Anne Eliot. The lifting stone
Damjan, Mischa. The wolf and the kid
Daniels, Guy. The Tsar's riddles
De La Mare, Walter. Molly Whuppie
Demi. Under the shade of the mulberry
tree
De Regniers, Beatrice Schenk. Catch a
little fox
Dickens, Frank. Boffo: the great
motorcycle race
Dines, Glen. Gilly and the wicharoo

Domanska, Janina. The best of the bargain
  King Krakus and the dragon
  Why so much noise?
Dos Santos, Joyce Audy. The diviner
Elkin, Benjamin. Gillespie and the guards
  Lucky and the giant
Erickson, Russell E. Warton and the traders
Ernst, Lisa Campbell. The prize pig surprise
Frankel, Bernice. Half-As-Big and the tiger
Freschet, Berniece. Elephant and friends
Galdone, Paul. The monkey and the crocodile
  What's in fox's sack?
Ginsburg, Mirra. The fisherman's son
Grimm, Jacob. The four clever brothers
Hillert, Margaret. The three goats
Hirsh, Marilyn. The Rabbi and the twenty-nine witches
Hooks, William H. Three rounds with rabbit
Hutton, Warwick. The nose tree
Huxley, Aldous. The crows of Pearblossom
Jaffe, Rona. Last of the wizards
Jameson, Cynthia. The house of five bears
Kennedy, Richard. The contests at Cowlick
Leverich, Kathleen. The hungry fox and the foxy duck
Lobel, Anita. The straw maid
Lobel, Arnold. How the rooster saved the day
  Mouse soup
Logue, Christopher. The magic circus
McClenathan, Louise. My mother sends her wisdom
McCormack, John E. Rabbit tales
Martin, Charles E. Dunkel takes a walk
Obrist, Jürg. The miser who wanted the sun
Parish, Peggy. Zed and the monsters
Parry, Marian. King of the fish
Paterson, Andrew Barton. The man from Ironbark
Paul, Anthony. The tiger who lost his stripes
Perrault, Charles. Puss in boots, ill. by Marcia Brown
  Puss in boots, ill. by Jean Claverie
  Puss in boots, ill. by Hans Fischer
  Puss in boots, ill. by Paul Galdone
  Puss in boots, ill. by Julia Noonan
  Puss in boots, ill. by Tony Ross
  Puss in boots, ill. by William Stobbs
  Puss in boots, ill. by Barry Wilkinson

Potter, Beatrix. The sly old cat
  The tale of the Flopsy Bunnies
Prokofiev, Sergei Sergeievitch. Peter and the wolf, ill. by Warren Chappell
  Peter and the wolf, ill. by Frans Haacken
  Peter and the wolf, ill. by Alan Howard
  Peter and the wolf, ill. by Charles Mikolaycak
  Peter and the wolf, ill. by Kozo Shimizu
Ransome, Arthur. The fool of the world and the flying ship
Rockwell, Anne F. Big boss
  The bump in the night
  The stolen necklace
Schatell, Brian. Sam's no dummy, Farmer Goff
Schatz, Letta. The extraordinary tug-of-war
Schulman, Janet. Jack the bum and the UFO
Sheldon, Aure. Of cobblers and kings
Siddiqui, Ashraf. Bhombal Dass, the uncle of lion
Simon, Sidney B. Henry, the uncatchable mouse
Singh, Jacquelin. Fat Gopal
Steig, William. Doctor De Soto
Storr, Catherine. Clever Polly and the stupid wolf
The three little pigs, ill. by Erik Blegvad
The three little pigs, ill. by Lorinda Bryan Cauley
The three little pigs, ill. by William Pène Du Bois
The three little pigs, ill. by Paul Galdone
The three little pigs, ill. by Rodney Peppé
The three little pigs, ill. by Irma Wilde
The three little pigs. The story of the three little pigs, ill. by L. Leslie Brooke
  The story of the three little pigs, ill. by William Stobbs
  The three pigs, ill. by Tony Ross
Van Woerkom, Dorothy. The rat, the ox and the zodiac
Walker, Barbara K. Teeny-Tiny and the witch-woman
Wetterer, Margaret. Patrick and the fairy thief
Wild, Robin. Little Pig and the big bad wolf
Williams, Jay. School for sillies
Wolkstein, Diane. The cool ride in the sky
Young, Ed. The terrible Nung Gwama
Zemach, Harve. Nail soup

Character traits — completing things

Flack, Marjorie. Angus and the cat
Ness, Evaline. Do you have the time,
 Lydia?
Petrides, Heidrun. Hans and Peter

Character traits — compromising

Hogrogian, Nonny. Carrot cake
Wildsmith, Brian. The owl and the
 woodpecker

Character traits — conceit

Bill, Helen. Shoes fit for a king
Brenner, Barbara. Mr. Tall and Mr.
 Small
Flack, Marjorie. Angus and the ducks
Grimm, Jacob. King Grisly-Beard
Peet, Bill. Ella
Sharmat, Marjorie Weinman. I'm terrific
Williams, Barbara. So what if I'm a sore
 loser?

Character traits — confidence

Adler, David A. Jeffrey's ghost and the
 leftover baseball team

Character traits — cruelty to animals
 see Character traits — kindness to
 animals

Character traits — curiosity

Adamson, Gareth. Old man up a tree
Alden, Laura. When?
Ames, Mildred. The wonderful box
Bang, Molly. Dawn
Bograd, Larry. Egon
Clark, Roberta. Why?
Climo, Shirley. The adventure of Walter
Demarest, Chris L. Clemens' kingdom
Fisher, Aileen. Anybody home?
Flack, Marjorie. Angus and the cat
 Angus and the ducks
Gackenbach, Dick. The pig who saw
 everything
Kipling, Rudyard. The elephant's child
Meeks, Esther K. The curious cow
Moncure, Jane Belk. Where?
Napoli, Guillier. Adventure of Mont
 Saint Michel
Pinkwater, Daniel Manus. Devil in the
 drain
Reece, Colleen L. What?
Rey, Hans Augusto. Curious George
 Curious George gets a medal
 Curious George learns the alphabet
 Curious George rides a bike
 Curious George takes a job

Rey, Margaret Elisabeth Waldstein.
 Curious George flies a kite
 Curious George goes to the hospital
Rylant, Cynthia. Miss Maggie
Waber, Bernard. Lorenzo
Zhitkov, Boris. How I hunted for the
 little fellows

Character traits — flattery

Æsop. Three fox fables
Chaucer, Geoffrey. Chanticleer and the
 fox

Character traits — foolishness

Bason, Lillian. Those foolish Molboes!
Gammell, Stephen. The story of Mr.
 and Mrs. Vinegar
Grimm, Jacob. Hans in luck, ill. by Paul
 Galdone
 Hans in luck, ill. by Felix Hoffmann
Johnson, Evelyne. The cow in the
 kitchen
Maitland, Antony. Idle Jack
Phillips, Louis. The brothers Wrong and
 Wrong Again
Scruton, Clive. Circus cow

Character traits — fortune see Character
 traits — luck

Character traits — freedom

Andersen, H C (Hans Christian). The
 emperor and the nightingale
 The emperor's nightingale
 The nightingale, ill. by Harold Berson
 The nightingale, ill. by Nancy Ekholm
 Burkert
Baylor, Byrd. Hawk, I'm your brother
Blaustein, Muriel. Baby Mabu and
 Auntie Moose
Bradford, Ann. The mystery of the
 missing raccoon
Brady, Irene. A mouse named Mus
Dennis, Wesley. Tumble, the story of a
 mustang
Fatio, Louise. Hector and Christina
Fujita, Tamao. The boy and the bird
Hawkinson, John. Where the wild
 apples grow
McPhail, David. A wolf story
Steiner, Jörg. Rabbit Island
Stern, Mark. It's a dog's life

Character traits — generosity

Ainsworth, Ruth. The mysterious Baba
 and her magic caravan
Aliki. The story of Johnny Appleseed
Anglund, Joan Walsh. Christmas is a
 time of giving

Bawden, Nina. St. Francis of Assisi
Bohanon, Paul. Golden Kate
Brown, Palmer. Something for
  Christmas
Chalmers, Mary. A hat for Amy Jean
Christian, Mary Blount. The devil take
  you, Barnabas Beane!
Chute, Beatrice Joy. Joy to Christmas
Erickson, Russell E. Warton and the
  traders
Farjeon, Eleanor. Mrs. Malone
Fontane, Theodore. Sir Ribbeck of
  Ribbeck of Havelland
Hoban, Russell. Emmet Otter's jug-band
  Christmas
  The mole family's Christmas
Houston, John A. The bright yellow
  rope
Hush little baby, ill. by Aliki
Hush little baby, ill. by Jeanette Winter
Hush little baby, ill. by Margot Zemach
Janice. Little Bear's Christmas
Johnson, Crockett. The emperor's gift
Lexau, Joan M. A house so big
Lindman, Maj. Snipp, Snapp, Snurr and
  the red shoes
Lionni, Leo. Tico and the golden wings
McClenathan, Louise. The Easter pig
Ness, Evaline. Josefina February
Rockwell, Anne F. Gogo's pay day
Shecter, Ben. If I had a ship
Silverstein, Shel. The giving tree

Character traits — helpfulness

Adelson, Leone. Who blew that whistle?
Adshead, Gladys L. Brownies - hush!
  Brownies - they're moving
Æsop. The lion and the mouse
Aliki. The two of them
Androcles and the lion
Baker, Betty. Partners
Bakken, Harold. The special string
Beim, Jerrold. Country mailman
Blair, Anne Denton. Hurrah for
  Arthur!
Bonsall, Crosby Newell. Who's a pest?
Bridwell, Norman. Clifford's good deeds
Bright, Robert. Georgie and the baby
  birds
  Georgie and the ball of yarn
  Georgie and the little dog
  Georgie and the runaway balloon
Brown, Myra Berry. Company's coming
  for dinner
Calhoun, Mary. Euphonia and the flood
  Jack the wise and the Cornish cuckoos
Clifton, Lucille. My friend Jacob
Cole, William. Aunt Bella's umbrella
Collier, Ethel. Who goes there in my
  garden?
Davis, Alice Vaught. Timothy turtle

Day, Shirley. Waldo's back yard
Devlin, Wende. Cranberry Christmas
Du Bois, William Pène. Bear circus
Ets, Marie Hall. Elephant in a well
Graham, Al. Timothy Turtle
Gray, Genevieve. Send Wendell
Green, Norma B. The hole in the dike
Greene, Laura. Help
Grimm, Jacob. The elves and the
  shoemaker
  Mother Holly
  The shoemaker and the elves
Herold, Ann Bixby. The helping day
Hill, Elizabeth Starr. Evan's corner
Holmes, Efner Tudor. Amy's goose
Houston, John A. The bright yellow
  rope
Hürlimann, Bettina. Barry
Kishida, Eriko. The lion and the bird's
  nest
Kraus, Robert. Herman the helper
  Rebecca Hatpin
La Fontaine, Jean de. The lion and the
  rat
Lindman, Maj. Flicka, Ricka, Dicka and
  the new dotted dress
  Snipp, Snapp, Snurr and the red shoes
Lloyd, Errol. Nini at carnival
Marcus, Susan. The missing button
  adventure
Marshall, James. What's the matter with
  Carruthers?
Mayer, Mercer. Just for you
Mayne, William. The blue book of hob
  stories
Nakano, Hirotaka. Elephant blue
Ness, Evaline. Pavo and the princess
Oxenbury, Helen. Mother's helper
Parker, Nancy Winslow. Cooper, the
  McNallys' big black dog
Partridge, Jenny. Peterkin Pollensnuff
Paul, Sherry. 2-B and the rock 'n roll
  band
Peet, Bill. The ant and the elephant
  Cyrus the unsinkable sea serpent
Potter, Beatrix. The tailor of
  Gloucester
Rayner, Mary. The rain cloud
Rockwell, Anne F. The bump in the
  night
  Can I help?
Seuss, Dr. Horton hatches the egg
Simon, Norma. What do I do?
Slobodkin, Louis. Dinny and Danny
Snow, Pegeen. Mrs. Periwinkle's
  groceries
Suhl, Yuri. The Purim goat
Udry, Janice May. Is Susan here?
Venino, Suzanne. Animals helping
  people
Waber, Bernard. Lyle, Lyle Crocodile

Williams, Barbara. Someday, said
Mitchell
Wolde, Gunilla. Betsy's fixing day
Zemach, Margot. To Hilda for helping

Character traits — honesty

Alexander, Lloyd. The truthful harp
Aliki. Diogenes
Ardizzone, Edward. Peter the wanderer
Gallant, Kathryn. The flute player of
Beppu
Matsuno, Masako. A pair of red clogs
Taro and the Tofu
Mayer, Mercer. How the trollusk got his
hat
Wilson, Julia. Becky

Character traits — incentive *see*
Character traits — ambition

Character traits — individuality

Alderson, Sue Ann. Bonnie McSmithers
is at it again!
Allamand, Pascale. The animals who
changed their colors
Anglund, Joan Walsh. Look out the
window
Baker, Jeannie. Millicent
Beim, Jerrold. Country train
Freckle face
Bright, Robert. Which is Willy?
Carey, Mary. The owl who loved
sunshine
Charlip, Remy. Hooray for me!
Conford, Ellen. Impossible, possum
Delaney, Ned. One dragon to another
Dellinger, Annetta. You are special to
Jesus
Delton, Judy. I'm telling you now
De Paola, Tomie. Oliver Button is a
sissy
Duvoisin, Roger Antoine. Jasmine
Fatio, Louise. Hector penguin
Gramatky, Hardie. Little Toot through
the Golden Gate
Horvath, Betty F. Will the real Tommy
Wilson please stand up?
Jaynes, Ruth M. What is a birthday
child?
Kuskin, Karla. Which horse is William?
Leaf, Munro. The story of Ferdinand
the bull
Levine, Rhoda. Harrison loved his
umbrella
Lionni, Leo. A color of his own
Pezzettino
Tico and the golden wings
Littledale, Freya. The magic plum tree
Lystad, Mary H. That new boy
McCormack, John E. Rabbit tales

McKee, David. Elmer, the story of a
patchwork elephant
Peet, Bill. Buford, the little bighorn
The spooky tail of Prewitt Peacock
Pinkwater, Daniel Manus. The big
orange splot
Reeves, James. Rhyming Will
Rubel, Nicole. Sam and Violet are twins
Sam and Violet go camping
Ruck-Pauquèt, Gina. Mumble bear
Sendak, Maurice. Pierre
Seuling, Barbara. The triplets
Sharmat, Marjorie Weinman. What are
we going to do about Andrew?
Silverstein, Shel. The missing piece
Simon, Norma. I know what I like
Why am I different?
Singer, Marilyn. The dog who insisted
he wasn't
Pickle plan
Slobodkin, Louis. Millions and millions
and millions
Tafuri, Nancy. Have you seen my
duckling?
Viorst, Judith. Try it again, Sam

Character traits — kindness

Aliki. The story of William Penn
Brown, Margaret Wise. Dr. Squash the
doll doctor
Calhoun, Mary. The thieving dwarfs
Cole, Brock. The king at the door
Coville, Bruce. The foolish giant
Sarah and the dragon
Davis, Maggie S. Grandma's secret letter
Fatio, Louise. The happy lion's rabbits
Gannett, Ruth S. Katie and the sad
noise
Hasler, Eveline. Martin is our friend
Heyward, Du Bose. The country bunny
and the little gold shoes
Kent, Jack. Clotilda
Lipkind, William. The magic feather
duster
Mizumura, Kazue. If I built a village
Munsch, Robert N. David's father
Newton, Patricia Montgomery. The five
sparrows
Noble, Trinka Hakes. Hansy's mermaid
Ormondroyd, Edward. Theodore
Peterson, Hans. Erik and the Christmas
horse
Postgate, Oliver. Noggin the king
Seuss, Dr. Horton hears a Who!
Small, David. Eulalie and the hopping
head
Stevens, Carla. Stories from a snowy
meadow
Ungerer, Tomi. Zeralda's ogre
Vigna, Judith. Anyhow, I'm glad I tried

Wells, H G (Herbert George). The adventures of Tommy

Zolotow, Charlotte. I know a lady

Character traits — kindness to animals

Allred, Mary. Grandmother Poppy and the funny-looking bird

Anderson, C W (Clarence Williams). Lonesome little colt
  The rumble seat pony

Androcles and the lion

Averill, Esther. Jenny's adopted brothers

Baker, Jeannie. Home in the sky

Barnhart, Peter. The wounded duck

Beatty, Hetty Burlingame. Moorland pony

Berson, Harold. Joseph and the snake

Brock, Emma Lillian. The birds' Christmas tree

Burch, Robert. The hunting trip

Carey, Mary. The owl who loved sunshine

Clewes Dorothy. The wild wood

Daugherty, James Henry. Andy and the lion

Drew, Patricia. Spotter Puff

Dunn, Judy. The little lamb

Duvoisin, Roger Antoine. The happy hunter

Freeman, Don. The seal and the slick

Galdone, Paul. Androcles and the lion

Georgiady, Nicholas P. Gertie the duck

Goffstein, M B (Marilyn Brooks). Natural history

Hader, Berta Hoerner. Mister Billy's gun

Harrison, David Lee. Little turtle's big adventure

Holmes, Efner Tudor. Amy's goose
  Carrie's gift

Keats, Ezra Jack. Jennie's hat

Kumin, Maxine. Mittens in May

Lathrop, Dorothy Pulis. Who goes there?

Levitin, Sonia. All the cats in the world

Lipkind, William. The boy and the forest

McNulty, Faith. Mouse and Tim

McPhail, David. The bear's toothache
  A wolf story

Miklowitz, Gloria D. Save that raccoon!

Moore, Sheila. Samson Svenson's baby

Nakatani, Chiyoko. Fumio and the dolphins

Newberry, Clare Turlay. Percy, Polly and Pete

Numeroff, Laura Joffe. If you give a mouse a cookie

Peet, Bill. Huge Harold

Roy, Ronald. A thousand pails of water

Sandburg, Helga. Anna and the baby buzzard

Severo, Emöke de Papp. The good-hearted youngest brother

Turkle, Brinton. Thy friend, Obadiah

Turska, Krystyna. The woodcutter's duck

Varley, Dimitry. The whirly bird

Ward, Lynd. The biggest bear

Waterton, Betty. A salmon for Simon

Wersba, Barbara. Do tigers ever bite kings?

Whitney, Alma Marshak. Leave Herbert alone

Wildsmith, Brian. Hunter and his dog

Wondriska, William. The stop

Yagawa, Sumiko. The crane wife

Character traits — laziness

Aylesworth, Jim. Hush up!

Baker, Betty. Partners

Bolognese, Elaine. The sleepy watchdog

Bowen, Vernon. The lazy beaver

Bright, Robert. Gregory, the noisiest and strongest boy in Grangers Grove

Du Bois, William Pène. Lazy Tommy pumpkinhead

Grimm, Jacob. Mother Holly

Holding, James. The lazy little Zulu

Krasilovsky, Phyllis. The man who did not wash his dishes

Lazy Jack

The little red hen, ill. by Janina Domanska

The little red hen, ill. by Paul Galdone

The little red hen, ill. by Mel Pekarsky

The little red hen, ill. by Margot Zemach

Lobel, Arnold. A treeful of pigs

Lorenz, Lee. Big Gus and Little Gus

Mathews, Louise. The great take-away

Pack, Robert. How to catch a crocodile

Papas, William. Taresh the tea planter

Schmidt, Eric von. The young man who wouldn't hoe corn

Sharmat, Marjorie Weinman. Burton and Dudley

Werth, Kurt. Lazy Jack

Wildsmith, Brian. The lazy bear

Character traits — littleness see Character traits — smallness

Character traits — loyalty

Aliki. The two of them

Ardizzone, Edward. Tim to the rescue

Bridwell, Norman. Clifford goes to Hollywood

Calhoun, Mary. The witch who lost her shadow

Collodi, Carlo. The adventures of
Pinocchio
Cooney, Barbara. Little brother and
little sister
Crompton, Anne Eliot. The winter wife
Hurd, Edith Thacher. Under the lemon
tree
Hutton, Warwick. Beauty and the beast
Lasker, Joe. He's my brother
McCrea, James. The king's procession
Potter, Beatrix. The tale of the faithful
dove
Springstubb, Tricia. My Minnie is a
jewel
Stanovich, Betty Jo. Hedgehog
adventures

Character traits — luck

Aldridge, Josephine Haskell.
Fisherman's luck
Aliki. Three gold pieces
Beim, Lorraine. Lucky Pierre
Bond, Michael. Paddington's lucky day
Brown, Margaret Wise. Wheel on the
chimney
Brown, Myra Berry. Best of luck
Cazet, Denys. Lucky me
Delton, Judy. I never win!
It happened on Thursday
Elkin, Benjamin. Lucky and the giant
Grimm, Jacob. Hans in luck, ill. by Paul
Galdone
Hans in luck, ill. by Felix Hoffmann
Hann, Jacquie. Up day, down day
Holland, Janice. You never can tell
Moeri, Louise. The unicorn and the
plow
Russell, Betty. Big store, funny door
Seuss, Dr. Did I ever tell you how lucky
you are?
Stafford, Kay. Ling Tang and the lucky
cricket
Walsh, Jill Paton. Lost and found

Character traits — meanness

Barth, Edna. Jack-o'-lantern
Bottner, Barbara. Mean Maxine
Burningham, John. Borka
Carrick, Carol. Old Mother Witch
Coville, Bruce. Sarah's unicorn
Freeman, Don. Tilly Witch
Gantos, Jack. Rotten Ralph's rotten
Christmas
Worse than Rotten Ralph
Glazer, Lee. Cookie Becker casts a spell
Himmelman, John. Amanda and the
witch switch
Hoban, Russell. Big John Turkle
The little Brute family

Jones, Rebecca C. The biggest, meanest,
ugliest dog in the whole wide world
Kidd, Bruce. Hockey showdown
McCrea, James. The magic tree
Mahy, Margaret. The boy with two
shadows
Manushkin, Fran. Hocus and Pocus at
the circus
Nickl, Peter. Ra ta ta tam
Prelutsky, Jack. The mean old mean
hyena
Price, Michelle. Mean Melissa
Seuss, Dr. How the Grinch stole
Christmas
Snyder, Anne. The old man and the
mule
Udry, Janice May. The mean mouse and
other mean stories
Zimelman, Nathan. Mean Murgatroyd
and the ten cats
Zion, Gene. The meanest squirrel I ever
met

Character traits — optimism

Alexander, Sue. Marc the Magnificent
Aliki. The twelve months
Atwood, Margaret. Anna's pet
Ayer, Jacqueline. The paper-flower tree
Chalmers, Audrey. A kitten's tale
Delton, Judy. My mother lost her job
today
Hall, Malcolm. The friends of Charlie
Ant Bear
Hoff, Syd. Oliver
Krauss, Ruth. The carrot seed
Lindgren, Astrid. Of course Polly can
do almost everything
Lionni, Leo. Theodore and the talking
mushroom
Peet, Bill. The Whingdingdilly
Piatti, Celestino. The happy owls
Rice, Inez. A long long time
Seuss, Dr. Would you rather be a
bullfrog?
Tapio, Pat Decker. The lady who saw
the good side of everything
Wiesner, William. Happy-Go-Lucky
Zakhoder, Boris Vladimirovich.
Rosachok

Character traits — ostracism see
Character traits — being different

Character traits — patience

Laurin, Anne. Little things
Steiner, Charlotte. What's the hurry,
Harry?
Weiss, Nicki. Waiting
Wells, Rosemary. Max's breakfast

Character traits — perseverance

Abisch, Roz. Sweet Betsy from Pike
Æsop. The miller, his son and their
  donkey
Alexander, Martha G. Move over,
  Twerp
  We never get to do anything
Aliki. A weed is a flower
Ambrus, Victor G. The little cockerel
  Mishka
Bethell, Jean. Hooray for Henry
Blades, Ann. Mary of mile 18
Boynton, Sandra. If at first...
Brenner, Barbara. Wagon wheels
Calhoun, Mary. Old man Whickutt's
  donkey
Conford, Ellen. Just the thing for
  Geraldine
Day, Shirley. Ruthie's big tree
Gray, Genevieve. How far, Felipe?
Hoff, Syd. Slugger Sal's slump
Jensen, Virginia Allen. Sara and the
  door
Kahl, Virginia. Maxie
Keats, Ezra Jack. John Henry
Lane, Carolyn. The voices of
  Greenwillow Pond
Lindgren, Astrid. Of course Polly can
  do almost everything
Piper, Watty. The little engine that
  could
Riordan, James. The three magic gifts
Skorpen, Liesel Moak. All the Lassies
Thomas, Kathy. The angel's quest
Ungerer, Tomi. The Mellops go
  spelunking
Watanabe, Shigeo. I can build a house!
  I can ride it!
  Where's my daddy?

Character traits — persistence

Bulla, Clyde Robert. The stubborn old
  woman

Character traits — practicality

Evans, Katherine. The man, the boy and
  the donkey
Gág, Wanda. Millions of cats
La Fontaine, Jean de. The miller, the
  boy and the donkey
Modell, Frank. One zillion valentines
Schlein, Miriam. The pile of junk

Character traits — pride

Andersen, H C (Hans Christian). The
  emperor's new clothes, ill. by Pamela
  Baldwin-Ford
  The emperor's new clothes, ill. by Erik
  Blegvad
  The emperor's new clothes, ill. by
  Virginia Lee Burton
  The emperor's new clothes, ill. by Jack
  and Irene Delano
  The emperor's new clothes, ill. by
  Birte Dietz
  The emperor's new clothes, ill. by Jack
  Kent
  The emperor's new clothes, ill. by
  Monika Laimgruber
  The emperor's new clothes, ill. by
  Anne F. Rockwell
  The emperor's new clothes, ill. by
  Nadine Bernard Westcott
  The red shoes
Bemelmans, Ludwig. Rosebud
Burningham, John. Humbert, Mister
  Firkin and the Lord Mayor of
  London
Calhoun, Mary. The runaway brownie
Clifton, Lucille. All us come cross the
  water
Dionetti, Michelle. Thalia Brown and
  the blue bug
Duvoisin, Roger Antoine. Crocus
  Petunia
Edwards, Dorothy. A wet Monday
Ehrhardt, Reinhold. Kikeri or, The
  proud red rooster
Friskey, Margaret. Indian Two Feet
  rides alone
Gackenbach, Dick. The dog and the
  deep dark woods
Hamberger, John. The peacock who lost
  his tail
Hürlimann, Ruth. The proud white cat
Keats, Ezra Jack. John Henry
McLenighan, Valjean. What you see is
  what you get
Politi, Leo. Mieko
Pomerantz, Charlotte. The ballad of the
  long-tailed rat
Sharmat, Marjorie Weinman. I'm terrific
Whitney, Alex. Once a bright red tiger
Winthrop, Elizabeth. Tough Eddie
Zimnik, Reiner. The proud circus horse

Character traits — questioning

Adler, David A. A little at a time
Alden, Laura. When?
Allard, Harry. May I stay?
Brown, Margaret Wise. Wait till the
  moon is full
Clark, Roberta. Why?
Deveaux, Alexis. Na-ni
Jacobs, Leland B. Is somewhere always
  far away?
Krauze, Andrzej. What's so special about
  today?
Lionni, Leo. Tico and the golden wings

Mahood, Kenneth. Why are there more questions than answers, Grandad?
Moncure, Jane Belk. Where?
Reece, Colleen L. What?
Simont, Marc. How come elephants?
Stover, Jo Ann. Why? Because
Vance, Eleanor Graham. Jonathan
Williams, Barbara. If he's my brother

Character traits — selfishness

Angelo, Valenti. The acorn tree
Barrett, John M. Oscar the selfish octopus
Bascom, Joe. Malcolm Softpaws
Berquist, Grace. The boy who couldn't roar
Berry, Joy Wilt. Being selfish
Bryant, Bernice. Follow the leader
Christian, Mary Blount. The devil take you, Barnabas Beane!
Coombs, Patricia. Mouse Café
Elkin, Benjamin. Lucky and the giant
Kahl, Virginia. The perfect pancake
Kraus, Robert. Rebecca Hatpin
Lipkind, William. Even Steven
  Finders keepers
Peet, Bill. The ant and the elephant
Reesink, Marijke. The golden treasure
Rudolph, Marguerita. I am your misfortune
Yolen, Jane. The acorn quest

Character traits — shyness

Brice, Tony. The bashful goldfish
Dines, Glen. A tiger in the cherry tree
Goffstein, M B (Marilyn Brooks). Neighbors
Hamilton, Morse. How do you do, Mr. Birdsteps?
Hogrogian, Nonny. Carrot cake
Keats, Ezra Jack. Louie
Keller, Beverly. Fiona's bee
Krasilovsky, Phyllis. The shy little girl
Lexau, Joan M. Benjie
Udry, Janice May. What Mary Jo shared
Wold, Jo Anne. Tell them my name is Amanda
Yashima, Tarō. Crow boy
  The youngest one
Zolotow, Charlotte. A tiger called Thomas

Character traits — smallness

Andersen, H C (Hans Christian).
  Thumbelina, ill. by Adrienne Adams
  Thumbelina, ill. by Susan Jeffers
  Thumbelina, ill. by Christian Willis Nigognossian
  Thumbelina, ill. by Gustaf Tenggren
  Thumbelina, ill. by Lisbeth Zwerger

Bang, Betsy. The cucumber stem
Beim, Jerrold. The smallest boy in the class
Bromhall, Winifred. Bridget's growing day
Cooper, Susan. The silver cow
Cuneo, Mary Louise. Inside a sandcastle and other secrets
De Paola, Tomie. Andy (that's my name)
Hoff, Syd. The littlest leaguer
Horvath, Betty F. Hooray for Jasper
Johnston, Johanna. Sugarplum
Kraus, Robert. The littlest rabbit
Kumin, Maxine. Sebastian and the dragon
Kuskin, Karla. Herbert hated being small
Lipkind, William. The little tiny rooster
Meddaugh, Susan. Too short Fred
Miles, Miska. No, no, Rosina
Orgel, Doris. On the sand dune
Priolo, Pauline. Piccolina and the Easter bells
Schlein, Miriam. Billy, the littlest one
Stanley, John. It's nice to be little
Tresselt, Alvin R. Smallest elephant in the world
Williams, Barbara. Someday, said Mitchell
Yolen, Jane. The emperor and the kite

Character traits — stubbornness

Beatty, Hetty Burlingame. Droopy
Bulla, Clyde Robert. The stubborn old woman

Character traits — vanity

Brown, Marcia. Once a mouse...
Brown, Margaret Wise. The duck
Kepes, Juliet. The story of a bragging duck
McCormack, John E. Rabbit tales
Marshall, James. George and Martha, tons of fun
Sharmat, Marjorie Weinman. Sasha the silly
Winter, Paula. Sir Andrew

Character traits — willfulness

Alexander, Sue. Nadia the willful
Quin-Harkin, Janet. Benjamin's balloon

Cheetahs *see* Animals — cheetahs

Chickens *see* Birds — chickens

Children as authors

Baskin, Leonard. Hosie's alphabet
  Hosie's aviary

Krauss, Ruth. Somebody else's nut tree, and other tales from children
Lady Eden's School. Just how stories
O'Reilly, Edward. Brown pelican at the pond
Pasley, L. The adventures of Madalene and Louisa
Phumla. Nomi and the magic fish
St Pierre, Wendy. Henry finds a home

Children as illustrators

De Paola, Tomie. Criss-cross applesauce
Pasley, L. The adventures of Madalene and Louisa

China *see* Foreign lands — China

Chinese-Americans *see* Ethnic groups in the U.S. — Chinese-Americans

Chinese New Year *see* Holidays — Chinese New Year

Chipmunks *see* Animals — chipmunks

Christmas *see* Holidays — Christmas

Cinco de Mayo *see* Holidays — Cinco de Mayo

Circus

Adler, David A. You think it's fun to be a clown!
Allen, Jeffrey. Bonzini! the tattooed man
Ambrus, Victor G. Mishka
Amoit, Pierre. Bijou the little bear.
Anno, Mitsumasa. Dr. Anno's midnight circus
Austin, Margot. Barney's adventure
Bach, Alice. Millicent the magnificent
Balet, Jan B. Five Rollatinis
Baningan, Sharon Stearns. Circus magic
Barr, Cathrine. Sammy seal ov the sircus
Barton, Byron. Harry is a scaredy-cat
Blance, Ellen. Monster goes to the circus
Bond, Michael. Paddington at the circus
Booth, Eugene. At the circus
Bowden, Joan Chase. Boo and the flying flews
Brown, Marc. Lenny and Lola
Burningham, John. Cannonball Simp
Cameron, Polly. The cat who thought he was a tiger
Chardiet, Bernice. C is for circus
Come to the circus
Coontz, Otto. A real class clown
Dayton, Laura. LeRoy's birthday circus
De Regniers, Beatrice Schenk. Circus

Du Bois, William Pène. The alligator case
Bear circus
Ets, Marie Hall. Mister Penny's circus
Everton, Macduff. El circo magico modelo
Farley, Walter. Little Black goes to the circus
Flack, Marjorie. Wait for William
Fox, Charles Philip. Come to the circus
Freeman, Don. Bearymore
Fremlin, Robert. Three friends
Garbutt, Bernard. Roger, the rosin back
Gascoigne, Bamber. Why the rope went tight
Goodall, John S. The adventures of Paddy Pork
Gramatky, Hardie. Homer and the circus train
Hale, Irina. Donkey's dreadful day
Herrmann, Frank. The giant Alexander and the circus
Hoff, Syd. Barkley
Henrietta, circus star
Oliver
Holl, Adelaide. Mrs. McGarrity's peppermint sweater
Hopkins, Lee Bennett. Circus! Circus!
Johnson, Crockett. Harold's circus
Johnson, Jane. Bertie on the beach
Lent, Blair. Pistachio
Lipkind, William. Circus rucus
Lisowski, Gabriel. Roncalli's magnificent circus
Logue, Christopher. The magic circus
Lopshire, Robert. Put me in the zoo
Maestro, Betsy. Busy day
Harriet goes to the circus
Maley, Anne. Have you seen my mother?
Marokvia, Merelle. A French school for Paul
Mayer, Mercer. Liverwurst is missing
Modell, Frank. Seen any cats?
Munari, Bruno. The circus in the mist
Myers, Bernice. Herman and the bears and the giants
Ness, Evaline. Fierce the lion
Palazzo, Tony. Bianco and the New World
Peet, Bill. Chester the worldly pig
Ella
Randy's dandy lions
Pellowski, Michael. Clara joins the circus
Peppé, Rodney. Circus numbers
Little circus
Petersham, Maud. The circus baby
Prelutsky, Jack. Circus
Quackenbush, Robert M. The man on the flying trapeze

Rey, Hans Augusto. Curious George rides a bike
  See the circus
Rounds, Glen. The day the circus came to Lone Tree
Schulz, Charles M. Life is a circus, Charlie Brown
Seignobosc, Françoise. Small-Trot
Seuss, Dr. If I ran the circus
Slobodkina, Esphyr. Pezzo the peddler and the circus elephant
Slocum, Rosalie. Breakfast with the clowns
Taylor, Mark. Henry explores the jungle
Tester, Sylvia Root. Parade!
Tresselt, Alvin R. Smallest elephant in the world
Varga, Judy. Circus cannonball
  Miss Lollipop's lion
Wahl, Jan. Sylvester Bear overslept
Wildsmith, Brian. Brian Wildsmith's circus
Zimnik, Reiner. The bear on the motorcycle
  The proud circus horse

City

Adoff, Arnold. Where wild Willie?
Asch, Frank. City sandwich
Asch, George. Linda
Baker, Jeannie. Home in the sky
  Millicent
Bank Street College of Education. Around the city
  Green light, go
  In the city
  My city
  Uptown, downtown
Barrett, Judi. Old MacDonald had an apartment house
Baylor, Byrd. The best town in the world
Bemelmans, Ludwig. Sunshine
Bergere, Thea. Paris in the rain with Jean and Jacqueline
Binzen, Bill. Carmen
Blance, Ellen. Monster comes to the city
Blue, Rose. How many blocks is the world?
Bowden, Joan Chase. Emilio's summer day
Bozzo, Maxine Zohn. Toby in the country, Toby in the city
Bright, Robert. Georgie to the rescue
Brock, Emma Lillian. Nobody's mouse
Brown, Marcia. The little carousel
Brown, Margaret Wise. Three little animals

Burton, Virginia Lee. Katy and the big snow
  The little house
  Maybelle, the cable car
Busch, Phyllis S. City lots
Chalmers, Mary. Kevin
Chwast, Seymour. Tall city, wide country
Clifton, Lucille. The boy who didn't believe in spring
  Everett Anderson's Christmas coming
Clymer, Eleanor Lowenton. The big pile of dirt
Colman, Hila. Peter's brownstone house
Corcos, Lucille. The city book
Crews, Donald. Parade
Crowell, Maryalicia. A horse in the house
Deveaux, Alexis. Na-ni
Duvoisin, Roger Antoine. Lonely Veronica
  Veronica
Ellis, Anne Leo. Dabble Duck
Fife, Dale. Adam's ABC
Finsand, Mary Jane. The town that moved
Florian, Douglas. The city
Fraser, Kathleen. Adam's world, San Francisco
Freeman, Don. Fly high, fly low
  The guard mouse
Gelman, Rita Golden. Dumb Joey
Gerstein, Mordicai. The room
Goodall, John S. The story of an English village
Gramatky, Hardie. Little Toot through the Golden Gate
Grifalconi, Ann. City rhythms
Grossbart, Francine. A big city
Guilfoile, Elizabeth. Have you seen my brother?
Hawkesworth, Jenny. The lonely skyscraper
Himler, Ronald. The girl on the yellow giraffe
Hoban, Tana. Is it red? Is it yellow? Is it blue?
Holl, Adelaide. A mouse story
Hopkins, Lee Bennett. I think I saw a snail
Ingle, Annie. The big city book
Isadora, Rachel. City seen from A to Z
Ivory, Lesley Anne. A day in London
  A day in New York
Jordan, June. Kimako's story
Kahn, Joan. Hi, Jock, run around the block
Keats, Ezra Jack. Apartment 3
  Goggles
  Hi, cat!

Keeping, Charles. Alfie finds the other
  side of the world
  Through the window
Kesselman, Wendy. Angelita
Lenski, Lois. Policeman Small
Lewin, Hugh. Jafta - the town
Lewis, Stephen. Zoo city
Lexau, Joan M. Benjie on his own
  Come here, cat
  Me day
Low, Alice. David's windows
McCloskey, Robert. Make way for
  ducklings
McGinley, Phyllis. All around the town
Maestro, Betsy. Big city port
Maestro, Giulio. The remarkable plant
  in apartment 4
Mayer, Mercer. Little Monster's
  neighborhood
Miles, Miska. No, no, Rosina
  Rolling the cheese
Mizumura, Kazue. If I built a village
Moak, Allan. A big city ABC
Morris, Jill. The boy who painted the
  sun
Nichols, Cathy. Tuxedo Sam
Ohlsson, Ib. Cat alley
Olds, Elizabeth. Little Una
Peet, Bill. Fly, Homer, fly
Perera, Lydia. Frisky
Pitt, Valerie. Let's find out about the
  city
Provensen, Alice. Town and country
Quackenbush, Robert M. City trucks
Raskin, Ellen. Franklin Stein
  Nothing ever happens on my block
Ressner, Phil. Dudley Pippin
Roach, Marilynne K. Two Roman mice
Rosario, Idalia. Idalia's project ABC
Rowe, Jeanne A. City workers
Sauer, Julia Lina. Mike's house
Scarry, Richard. Richard Scarry's
  Postman Pig and his busy neighbors
Schick, Eleanor. City green
  City in the winter
  One summer night
  Peter and Mr. Brandon
Scott, Ann Herbert. Let's catch a
  monster
Selden, George. Chester Cricket's
  pigeon ride
Shannon, George. Beanboy
Shecter, Ben. Emily, girl witch of New
  York
Simon, Norma. What do I do?
Sonneborn, Ruth A. Friday night is
  papa night
  I love Gram
  Lollipop's party
Sopko, Eugeh. Townsfolk and
  countryfolk

Steptoe, John. Uptown
Stevenson, James. Grandpa's great city
  tour
Thomas, Ianthe. Walk home tired, Billy
  Jenkins
Tresselt, Alvin R. It's time now!
Trimby, Elisa. Mr. Plum's paradise
Vasiliu, Marcea. What's happening?
Ventura, Piero. Piero Ventura's book of
  cities
Walters, Marguerite. The city-country
  ABC
Williams, Jay. The city witch and the
  country witch
Williamson, Mel. Walk on!
Wold, Jo Anne. Well! Why didn't you
  say so?
Yashima, Tarō. Umbrella
Yezback, Steven A. Pumpkinseeds
Zion, Gene. Dear garbage man
  Hide and seek day
Zolotow, Charlotte. One step, two...
  The park book

Cleanliness *see* Character traits —
  cleanliness

Cleverness *see* Character traits —
  cleverness

Clockmakers *see* Careers —
  clockmakers

Clocks

Aiken, Conrad. Tom, Sue and the clock
Ardizzone, Edward. Johnny the
  clockmaker
Berg, Jean Horton. The noisy clock
  shop
Bragdon, Lillian J. Tell me the time,
  please
Bram, Elizabeth. Woodruff and the
  clocks
Cohen, Carol L. Wake up, groundhog!
Colman, Hila. Watch that watch
Gibbons, Gail. Clocks and how they go
Gilbert, Helen Earle. Dr. Trotter and
  his big gold watch
Gordon, Sharon. Tick tock clock
Hutchins, Pat. Clocks and more clocks
McGinley, Phyllis. Wonderful time
Maestro, Betsy. Around the clock with
  Harriet
Pieńkowski, Jan. Time
Slobodkin, Louis. The late cuckoo
Steinmetz, Leon. Clocks in the woods

Clothing

Alda, Arlene. Matthew and his dad

Andersen, H C (Hans Christian). The emperor's new clothes, ill. by Pamela Baldwin-Ford
The emperor's new clothes, ill. by Erik Blegvad
The emperor's new clothes, ill. by Virginia Lee Burton
The emperor's new clothes, ill. by Jack and Irene Delano
The emperor's new clothes, ill. by Birte Dietz
The emperor's new clothes, ill. by Jack Kent
The emperor's new clothes, ill. by Monika Laimgruber
The emperor's new clothes, ill. by Anne F. Rockwell
The emperor's new clothes, ill. by Nadine Bernard Westcott
The red shoes
Anderson, Leone Castell. The wonderful shrinking shirt
Asch, Frank. Yellow, yellow
Azaad, Meyer. Half for you
Babbitt, Lorraine. Pink like the geranium
Bannon, Laura. Hat for a hero
Red mittens
Barrett, Judi. Animals should definitely not wear clothing
Peter's pocket
Barrows, Marjorie Wescott. The funny hat
Barton, Pat. A week is a long time
Beskow, Elsa Maartman. Pelle's new suit
Blos, Joan W. Martin's hats
Bowden, Joan Chase. A hat for the queen
Brandenberg, Franz. Leo and Emily
Brenner, Barbara. Somebody's slippers, somebody's shoes
Bromhall, Winifred. Middle Matilda
Bruna, Dick. I can dress myself
Bulette, Sara. The splendid belt of Mr. Big
Carrick, Malcolm. The extraordinary hatmaker
Chalmers, Mary. A hat for Amy Jean
Credle, Ellis. Down, down the mountain
Daly, Niki. Joseph's other red sock
De Paola, Tomie. Charlie needs a cloak
Duvoisin, Roger Antoine. Jasmine
Fisher, Leonard Everett. A head full of hats
Freeman, Don. Corduroy
A pocket for Corduroy
Fremlin, Robert. Three friends
Gackenbach, Dick. Poppy the panda
Hoberman, Mary Ann. I like old clothes
Holland, Isabelle. Kevin's hat

Hürlimann, Ruth. The mouse with the daisy hat
Hutchins, Pat. You'll soon grow into them, Titch
Iwamura, Kazuo. Tan Tan's hat
Tan Tan's suspenders
Jaynes, Ruth M. Benny's four hats
Jensen, Virginia Allen. Sara and the door
Kay, Helen. One mitten Lewis
Keats, Ezra Jack. Jennie's hat
Krasilovsky, Phyllis. The girl who was a cowboy
Kumin, Maxine. Mittens in May
Kuskin, Karla. The Philharmonic gets dressed
Lear, Edward. The quangle wangle's hat
Two laughable lyrics
LeRoy, Gen. Billy's shoes
Lexau, Joan M. Who took the farmer's hat?
Lloyd, Errol. Nini at carnival
Lobel, Anita. The seamstress of Salzburg
McClintock, Marshall. What have I got?
McKee, David. King Rollo and the new shoes
McLenighan, Valjean. What you see is what you get
Maestro, Betsy. On the town
Matsuno, Masako. A pair of red clogs
Mayer, Mercer. Two moral tales
Miklowitz, Gloria D. Bearfoot boy
Murphey, Sara. The animal hat shop
Myrick, Jean Lockwood. Ninety-nine pockets
Partridge, Jenny. Grandma Snuffles
Payne, Emmy. Katy no-pocket
Peppé, Rodney. Little dolls
Politi, Leo. Little Leo
Potter, Beatrix. The tale of Mrs. Tiggy-Winkle
Rice, Eve. New blue shoes
Rice, Inez. The March wind
Rudolph, Marguerita. How a shirt grew in the field
Ryder, Eileen. Winston's new cap
Scott, Ann Herbert. Big Cowboy Western
Selden, George. Sparrow socks
Sharmat, Marjorie Weinman. The trip
Shearer, John. The case of the sneaker snatcher
Silver, Jody. Isadora
Slobodkina, Esphyr. Caps for sale
Pezzo the peddler and the circus elephant
Pezzo the peddler and the thirteen silly thieves
Taback, Simms. Joseph had a little overcoat

Townsend, Kenneth. Felix, the
  bald-headed lion
Ungerer, Tomi. The hat
Ward, Nanda Weedon. The black
  sombrero
Watanabe, Shigeo. How do I put it on?
Weiss, Harvey. My closet full of hats
Weiss, Leatie. Funny feet!
Wells, Rosemary. Max's new suit
Westerberg, Christine. The cap that
  mother made
Woolley, Catherine. Gus was a gorgeous
  ghost
  The horse with the Easter bonnet
Zion, Gene. No roses for Harry

Clouds *see* Weather — clouds

Clowns, jesters

Adler, David A. You think it's fun to be
  a clown!
Allen, Jeffrey. Bonzini! the tattooed
  man
Amoit, Pierre. Bijou the little bear
Anno, Mitsumasa. Dr. Anno's midnight
  circus
Austin, Margot. Barney's adventure
Barr, Cathrine. Sammy seal ov the sircus
Bradford, Ann. The mystery of the
  midget clown
Burningham, John. Cannonball Simp
Cole, Joanna. The Clown-Arounds go
  on vacation
  Get well, Clown-Arounds!
Coontz, Otto. A real class clown
De Paola, Tomie. Sing, Pierrot, sing
Faulkner, Nancy. Small clown
Freeman, Don. Forever laughter
Krahn, Fernando. A funny friend from
  heaven
Lent, Blair. Pistachio
Marceau, Marcel. The story of Bip
Mendoza, George. The Marcel Marceau
  counting book
Olds, Elizabeth. Plop plop ploppie
Pellowski, Michael. Clara joins the circus
Petersham, Maud. The circus baby
Politi, Leo. Lito and the clown
Quackenbush, Robert M. The man on
  the flying trapeze
Rockwell, Anne F. Gogo's pay day
Schreiber, Georges. Bambino goes home
  Bambino the clown
Shecter, Ben. Hester the jester
Slocum, Rosalie. Breakfast with the
  clowns
Sobol, Harriet Langsam. Clowns
Thurber, James. Many moons

Clubs, gangs

Alexander, Sue. Seymour the prince
Bonsall, Crosby Newell. The case of the
  double cross
Bradford, Ann. The mystery at Misty
  Falls
  The mystery in the secret club house
  The mystery of the blind writer
  The mystery of the midget clown
  The mystery of the missing dogs
  The mystery of the square footsteps
  The mystery of the tree house
Kotzwinkle, William. The day the gang
  got rich
Myrick, Mildred. The secret three
Stanley, Diane. The conversation club

Cockatoos *see* Birds — cockatoos

Codes *see* Secret codes

Cold *see* Weather — cold

Collecting things *see* Behavior —
  collecting things

Color *see* Concepts — color

Columbus Day *see* Holidays —
  Columbus Day

Communication

Arnold, Caroline. How do we
  communicate?
Bohdal, Susi. Tom cat
Bonsall, Crosby Newell. The case of the
  dumb bells
Borchers, Elisabeth. Dear Sarah
Branley, Franklyn M. Timmy and the
  tin-can telephone
Brown, Margaret Wise. The big fur
  secret
Buchheimer, Naomi. Let's go to a post
  office
Charlip, Remy. Handtalk
Chukovsky, Korney. The telephone
Clifford, Eth. A bear before breakfast
Emberley, Ed. Green says go
Engdahl, Sylvia. Our world is earth
Gibbons, Gail. The post office book
Goor, Ron. Signs
Hoban, Tana. I read signs
  I read symbols
Joslin, Sesyle. Dear dragon
Potter, Beatrix. Yours affectionately,
  Peter Rabbit
Stanley, Diane. The conversation club
Telephones
Tolkien, J R R (John Ronald Reuel).
  The Father Christmas letters

Van Woerkom, Dorothy. Hidden messages

Communities, neighborhoods

Arnold, Caroline. What is a community?
  Where do you go to school?
  Who works here?
Blakeley, Peggy. Two little ducks

Competition *see* Sibling rivalry

Completing things *see* Character traits — completing things

Compromising *see* Character traits — compromising

Computers *see* Machines

Conceit *see* Character traits — conceit

Concepts

Albert, Burton. Mine, yours, ours
Balestrino, Philip. Hot as an ice cube
Berenstain, Stan. Inside outside upside down
Berkley, Ethel S. Ups and down
Bodger, Joan. Belinda's ball
Booth, Eugene. At the circus
  At the fair
  In the air
  In the garden
  In the jungle
  Under the ocean
Borten, Helen. Do you see what I see?
Brown, Marcia. Touch will tell
  Walk with your eyes
Browner, Richard. Look again!
Charosh, Mannis. Number ideas through pictures
Chase, Catherine. Hot and cold
Crews, Donald. Light
  We read A to Z
Cushman, Doug. Nasty Kyle the crocodile
Duke, Kate. Guinea pigs far and near
Emberley, Ed. Ed Emberley's amazing look through book
Fisher, Leonard Everett. Boxes! Boxes!
Freudberg, Judy. Some, more, most
Froman, Robert. Angles are easy as pie
  A game of functions
  Seeing things
Green, Mary McBurney. Is it hard? Is it easy?
Greene, Laura. Change
Hoban, Tana. Is it rough? Is it smooth? Is it shiny?
  Take another look
Jensen, Virginia Allen. What's that?

Johnson, Ryerson. Upstairs and downstairs
Kuskin, Karla. All sizes of noises
Lopshire, Robert. The biggest, smallest, fastest, tallest things you've ever heard of
Maestro, Betsy. Where is my friend?
Mayer, Mercer. Mine!
Peppé, Rodney. Odd one out
  Rodney Peppé's puzzle book
Rahn, Joan Elma. Holes
Ruben, Patricia. True or false?
Scarry, Richard. Richard Scarry's best first book ever
  Richard Scarry's great big schoolhouse
  The Sesame Street book of people and things
Supraner, Robyn. Giggly-wiggly, snickety-snick

Concepts — color

Abisch, Roz. Open your eyes
Allamand, Pascale. The animals who changed their colors
Asch, Frank. Yellow, yellow
Berger, Judith. Butterflies and rainbows
Bright, Robert. I like red
Brown, Margaret Wise. Red light, green light
Brunhoff, Laurent de. Babar's book of color
Campbell, Ann. Let's find out about color
Carle, Eric. The mixed-up chameleon, 1975
  The mixed-up chameleon, 1984
Charlip, Remy. Harlequin and the gift of many colors
Chermayeff, Ivan. Tomato and other colors
Clifford, Eth. Red is never a mouse
Dines, Glen. Pitadoe, the color maker
Duvoisin, Roger Antoine. The house of four seasons
  See what I am
Emberley, Ed. Green says go
Fisher, Leonard Everett. Boxes! Boxes!
Freeman, Don. The chalk box story
  A rainbow of my own
Gillham, Bill. Let's look for colors
Haskins, Ilma. Color seems
Hoban, Tana. Is it red? Is it yellow? Is it blue?
Kessler, Leonard P. Mr. Pine's purple house
Kilroy, Sally. Baby colors
Kirkpatrick, Rena K. Look at rainbow colors
Kumin, Maxine. What color is Caesar?
Lewis, Naomi. Once upon a rainbow

Lionni, Leo. A color of his own
  Little blue and little yellow
A little book of colors
Lobel, Arnold. The great blueness and
  other predicaments
Löfgren, Ulf. The color trumpet
Lopshire, Robert. Put me in the zoo
Maril, Lee. Mr. Bunny paints the eggs
Miller, J P (John Parr). Do you know
  color?
  Learn about colors with Little Rabbit
Pieńkowski, Jan. Colors
Pinkwater, Daniel Manus. The bear's
  picture
  The big orange splot
Podendorf, Illa. Color
Reiss, John J. Colors
Rogers, Margaret. Green is beautiful
Ross, Tony. Hugo and the man who
  stole colors
Rossetti, Christina Georgina. What is
  pink?
Scott, Rochelle. Colors, colors all around
Shub, Elizabeth. Dragon Franz
Spier, Peter. Oh, were they ever happy!
Steiner, Charlotte. My slippers are red
Stinson, Kathy. Red is best
Testa, Fulvio. If you take a paintbrush
Tison, Annette. The adventures of the
  three colors
Wolff, Robert Jay. Feeling blue
  Hello, yellow!
  Seeing red
Youldon, Gillian. Colors
Zacharias, Thomas. But where is the
  green parrot?
Zolotow, Charlotte. Mr. Rabbit and the
  lovely present

Concepts — counting *see* Counting

Concepts — distance

Tresselt, Alvin R. How far is far?

Concepts — in and out

Banchek, Linda. Snake in, snake out
Daughtry, Duanne. What's inside?
Ueno, Noriko. Elephant buttons

Concepts — left and right

Chase, Catherine. Feet
Stanek, Muriel. Left, right, left, right!

Concepts — measurement

Adler, David A. 3D, 2D, 1D
Branley, Franklyn M. How little and
  how much
Lionni, Leo. Inch by inch
Myller, Rolf. How big is a foot?

Srivastava, Jane Jonas. Area
Thompson, Brenda. The winds that
  blow

Concepts — opposites

Banchek, Linda. Snake in, snake out
Barrett, Judi. I'm too small, you're too
  big
Boynton, Sandra. Opposites
Gillham, Bill. Let's look for opposites
Hoban, Tana. Push-pull, empty-full
McLenighan, Valjean. Stop-go, fast-slow
McMillan, Bruce. Here a chick, there a
  chick
McNaughton, Colin. At home
  At playschool
  At the park
  At the party
  At the stores
Maestro, Betsy. Traffic
Matthias, Catherine. Over-under
Mendoza, George. The Sesame Street
  book of opposites with Zero Mostel
Provensen, Alice. Karen's opposites
Spier, Peter. Fast-slow, high-low
Watson, Carol. Opposites
Wildsmith, Brian. What the moon saw

Concepts — perspective

Adler, David A. 3D, 2D, 1D
Wakefield, Joyce. From where you are

Concepts — self *see* Self-concept

Concepts — shape

Adler, David A. 3D, 2D, 1D
Allen, Robert. Round and square
Atwood, Ann. The little circle
Berenstain, Stan. Old hat, new hat
Brown, Marcia. Listen to a shape
Budney, Blossom. A kiss is round
Charosh, Mannis. The ellipse
Craig, M Jean. Boxes
Crews, Donald. Ten black dots
Emberley, Ed. The wing on a flea
Friskey, Margaret. Three sides and the
  round one
Gillham, Bill. Let's look for shapes
Hatcher, Charles. What shape is it?
Hefter, Richard. The strawberry book
  of shapes
Hoban, Tana. Circles, triangles, and
  squares
  Is it red? Is it yellow? Is it blue?
  Round and round and round
  Shapes and things
Hughes, Peter. The emperor's oblong
  pancake
Jensen, Virginia Allen. Catching
Lionni, Leo. Pezzettino

Newth, Philip. Roly goes exploring
Pieńkowski, Jan. Shapes
Podendorf, Illa. Shapes, sides, curves
and corners
Reiss, John J. Shapes
Reit, Seymour. Round things
everywhere
Roberts, Cliff. The dot
Start with a dot
Salazar, Violet. Squares are not bad
Schlein, Miriam. Shapes
The Sesame Street book of shapes
Seuss, Dr. The shape of me and other
stuff
Shaw, Charles Green. It looked like spilt
milk
Silverstein, Shel. The missing piece
Stoddard, Sandol. Curl up small
Testa, Fulvio. If you look around
Watson, Carol. Shapes
Wildsmith, Brian. Animal shapes
Youldon, Gillian. Shapes

Concepts — size

Anno, Mitsumasa. The king's flower
Aulaire, Ingri Mortenson d'. Too big
Balian, Lorna. Where in the world is
Henry?
Barrett, Judi. I hate to take a bath
Berenstain, Stan. Old hat, new hat
Black, Irma Simonton. Big puppy and
little puppy
Blue, Rose. How many blocks is the
world?
Brown, Marcia. Once a mouse...
Brown, Margaret Wise. Big dog, little
dog
Bumble bugs and elephants
Bulette, Sara. The splendid belt of Mr.
Big
Cantieni, Benita. Little Elephant and
Big Mouse
Chalmers, Audrey. Hector and Mr.
Murfit
Craig, M Jean. Boxes
Croswell, Volney. How to hide a
hippopotamus
Hoban, Tana. Big ones, little ones
Is it red? Is it yellow? Is it blue?
Hutchins, Pat. Titch
Ipcar, Dahlov. The biggest fish in the
sea
The land of flowers
Kalan, Robert. Blue sea
Kraus, Robert. The little giant
Krauss, Ruth. A bouquet of littles
Kuskin, Karla. Herbert hated being
small
Lipkind, William. Chaga
Long, Earlene. Gone fishing
Peet, Bill. Huge Harold

Pieńkowski, Jan. Sizes
Shapp, Charles. Let's find out what's big
and what's small
Stoddard, Sandol. Curl up small
Ueno, Noriko. Elephant buttons
Watson, Carol. Sizes
Youldon, Gillian. Sizes

Concepts — speed

Schlein, Miriam. Fast is not a ladybug
Spier, Peter. Fast-slow, high-low

Concepts — up and down

Berkley, Ethel S. Ups and down
Johnson, Crockett. Upside down
Knight, Hilary. Sylvia the sloth
Seuss, Dr. A great day for up
Slobodkin, Louis. Up high and down
low
Zion, Gene. All falling down

Concepts — weight

Fischer, Vera Kistiakowsky. One way is
down
Schlein, Miriam. Heavy is a
hippopotamus

Confidence see Character traits —
confidence

Conservation see Ecology

Cooking see Activities — cooking

Cooks see Careers — bakers

Coral Islands see Foreign lands — South
Sea Islands

Cormorants see Birds — cormorants

Cougars see Animals — cougars

Counting

Adler, David A. Base five
Alexander, Anne. My daddy and I
Allen, Robert. Numbers a first counting
book
Ambler, Christopher Gifford. Ten little
foxhounds
Anno, Mitsumasa. Anno's counting book
Anno's counting house
Arnosky, Jim. Mouse numbers and
letters
Asch, Frank. Little Devil's 123
Baker, Bonnie Jeanne. A pear by itself
Baker, Jeannie. One hungry spider
Bang, Molly. Ten, nine, eight

Baum, Arline. One bright Monday
  morning
Bayley, Nicola. One old Oxford ox
Becker, John Leonard. Seven little
  rabbits
Berenstain, Stan. Bears on wheels
  The Berenstain bears' counting book
Bishop, Claire Huchet. Twenty-two
  bears
Blegvad, Lenore. One is for the sun
Boynton, Sandra. Hippos go berserk
Bridgman, Elizabeth. All the little
  bunnies
Bright, Robert. My red umbrella
Bruna, Dick. I know more about
  numbers
  Poppy Pig goes to market
Burningham, John. Count up
  Five down
  Just cats
  Pigs plus
  Read one
  Ride off
  The shopping basket
Carle, Eric. 1, 2, 3 to the zoo
  The rooster who set out to see the
  world
Charlip, Remy. Thirteen
Charosh, Mannis. Number ideas
  through pictures
Chwast, Seymour. Still another number
  book
Conover, Chris. Six little ducks
Corbett, Grahame. What number now?
Counting rhymes
Cretan, Gladys Yessayan. Ten brothers
  with camels
Crews, Donald. Ten black dots
Crowther, Robert. Hide and seek
  counting book
Dalmais, Anne-Marie. In my garden
Dayton, Laura. LeRoy's birthday circus
DeCaprio, Annie. One, two
Dodd, Lynley. The nickle nackle tree
Duvoisin, Roger Antoine. Two lonely
  ducks
Eichenberg, Fritz. Dancing in the moon
Elkin, Benjamin. Six foolish fishermen
Farber, Norma. Up the down elevator
Feelings, Muriel. Menjo means one
Fisher, Leonard Everett. Boxes! Boxes!
Freschet, Berniece. The ants go
  marching
  Where's Henrietta's hen?
Friskey, Margaret. Chicken Little,
  count-to-ten
  Seven diving ducks
Gantz, David. Captain Swifty counts to
  50
Gerstein, Mordicai. Roll over!
Gillham, Bill. Let's look for numbers

Ginsburg, Mirra. Kitten from one to ten
Gregor, Arthur S. One, two, three, four,
  five
Gretz, Susanna. Teddy bears ABC
  Teddy bears one to ten
Grimm, Jacob. Mrs. Fox's wedding
Gundersheimer, Karen. 1 2 3 play with
  me
Hay, Dean. Now I can count
Hoban, Russell. Ten what?
Hoban, Tana. Count and see
  1, 2, 3
Holt, Margaret. David McCheever's
  twenty-nine dogs
Howe, Caroline Walton. Counting
  penguins
Hutchins, Pat. 1 hunter
Ipcar, Dahlov. Brown cow farm
  Ten big farms
Kessler, Ethel. Two, four, six, eight
Kraus, Robert. Good night little one
  Good night Richard Rabbit
Krüss, James. 3 X 3
Langstaff, John M. Over in the meadow
Lasker, Joe. Lentil soup
Let's count and count out
Lewin, Betsy. Cat count
  Hip, hippo, hooray!
A little book of numbers
Livermore, Elaine. One to ten, count
  again
Löfgren, Ulf. One-two-three
Mack, Stanley. Ten bears in my bed
McLeod, Emilie Warren. One snail and
  me
Maestro, Betsy. Harriet goes to the
  circus
Maestro, Giulio. One more and one less
Marshall, Ray. Pop-up numbers #1
  Pop-up numbers #2
  Pop-up numbers #3
  Pop-up numbers #4
Martin, Bill (William Ivan). Sounds I
  remember
  Sounds of numbers
Mathews, Louise. Bunches and bunches
  of bunnies
  Cluck one
  The great take-away
Mayer, Marianna. Alley oop!
Mayer, Mercer. Little Monster's
  counting book
Meeks, Esther K. One is the engine, ill.
  by Ernie King
  One is the engine, ill. by Joe Rogers
Merrill, Jean. How many kids are hiding
  on my block?
Miller, Jane. Farm counting book
Milne, A A (Alan Alexander). Pooh's
  counting book
Morse, Samuel French. Sea sums

Noll, Sally. Off and counting
One rubber duckie
One, two, buckle my shoe
Over in the meadow
Oxenbury, Helen. Numbers of things
Pavey, Peter. One dragon's dream
Peppé, Rodney. Circus numbers
  Little numbers
Petie, Haris. Billions of bugs
Pieńkowski, Jan. Numbers
Pomerantz, Charlotte. One duck,
  another duck
Price, Christine. One is God
The pudgy fingers counting book
Rand, Ann. Little 1
Reiss, John J. Numbers
Rockwell, Norman. Norman Rockwell's
  counting book
Roll over!
Ross, H L. Not counting monsters
Sazer, Nina. What do you think I saw?
Scarry, Richard. Richard Scarry's best
  counting book ever
  Richard Scarry's great big schoolhouse
Seignobosc, Françoise. Jeanne-Marie
  counts her sheep
Sendak, Maurice. One was Johnny
  Seven little monsters
The Sesame Street book of numbers
Sitomer, Mindel. How did numbers
  begin?
Smith, Donald. Farm numbers 1, 2, 3
Stanek, Muriel. One, two, three for fun
Steiner, Charlotte. Five little finger
  playmates
Stobbs, Joanna. One sun, two eyes, and
  a million stars
Stobbs, William. This little piggy
Sugita, Yutaka. Good night 1, 2, 3
Szekeres, Cyndy. Cyndy Szekeres'
  counting book, 1 to 10
Testa, Fulvio. If you take a pencil
Thompson, Susan L. One more thing,
  dad
Tudor, Tasha. 1 is one
Wadsworth, Olive A. Over in the
  meadow
Warren, Cathy. The ten-alarm camp-out
Watson, Nancy Dingman. What is one?
Weihs, Erika. Count the cats
Wild, Robin. The bears' counting book
Williams, Garth. The chicken book
Wilson, Barbara. ABC et/and 123
Yolen, Jane. An invitation to the
  butterfly ball
Youldon, Gillian. Counting
  Numbers
Zaslavsky, Claudia. Count on your
  fingers African style
Ziner, Feenie. Counting carnival
Zirbes, Laura. How many bears?

Zolotow, Charlotte. One step, two...

Countries, foreign see Foreign lands

Country

Asch, Frank. Country pie
Atwood, Margaret. Anna's pet
Barklem, Jill. The big book of Brambly
  Hedge
Barton, Pat. A week is a long time
Bozzo, Maxine Zohn. Toby in the
  country, Toby in the city
Bröger, Achim. Francie's paper puppy
Brown, Margaret Wise. The country
  noisy book
Browne, Caroline. Mrs. Christie's
  farmhouse
Burton, Virginia Lee. The little house
Caudill, Rebecca. Contrary Jenkins
Chwast, Seymour. Tall city, wide
  country
Dale, Ruth Bluestone. Benjamin - and
  Sylvester also
Dickinson, Mary. Alex's outing
Hawkesworth, Jenny. The lonely
  skyscraper
Hodeir, André. Warwick's three bottles
Holl, Adelaide. A mouse story
Kingman, Lee. Peter's long walk
Lorenz, Lee. A weekend in the country
Payne, Joan Balfour. The stable that
  stayed
Pender, Lydia. Barnaby and the horses
Provensen, Alice. Town and country
Roach, Marilynne K. Two Roman mice
Sopko, Eugeh. Townsfolk and
  countryfolk
Teal, Valentine. The little woman
  wanted noise
Walters, Marguerite. The city-country
  ABC
Williams, Jay. The city witch and the
  country witch

Cowboys

Anderson, C W (Clarence Williams).
  Blaze and the Indian cave
  Blaze and the lost quarry
  Blaze and the mountain lion
  Blaze and Thunderbolt
  Blaze finds forgotten roads
  Blaze finds the trail
Anglund, Joan Walsh. The brave
  cowboy
  Cowboy and his friend
  The cowboy's Christmas
  Cowboy's secret life
Aulaire, Ingri Mortenson d'. Nils
Beatty, Hetty Burlingame. Bucking
  horse

Bishop, Ann. Wild Bill Hiccup's riddle book

Bright, Robert. Georgie goes west

Burton, Virginia Lee. Calico the wonder horse

Chandler, Edna Walker. Cattle drive
Cowboy Andy
Pony rider
Secret tunnel

Dewey, Ariane. Pecos Bill

Doughtie, Charles. High Henry... the cowboy who was too tall to ride a horse

Fain, James W. Rodeos

Felton, Harold W. Pecos Bill and the mustang

Fitzhugh, Louise. Bang, bang, you're dead

Greene, Carla. Cowboys what do they do?

Hancock, Sibyl. Old Blue

Hillert, Margaret. The little cowboy and the big cowboy

Kennedy, Richard. The contests at Cowlick

Krasilovsky, Phyllis. The girl who was a cowboy

Lenski, Lois. Cowboy Small

Martini, Teri. Cowboys

Moon, Dolly M. My very first book of cowboy songs

Quackenbush, Robert M. Pete Pack Rat

Scott, Ann Herbert. Big Cowboy Western

Ward, Nanda Weedon. The black sombrero

Wise, William. The cowboy surprise

Wood, Nancy C. Little wrangler

Cows see Animals — bulls, cows

Coyotes see Animals — coyotes

Crabs see Crustacea

Cranes see Birds — cranes

Creatures see Goblins; Monsters

Creeks see Rivers

Crickets see Insects — crickets

Crime

Adamson, Gareth. Old man up a tree

Ahlberg, Allan. Cops and robbers

Ahlberg, Janet. Burglar Bill

Allard, Harry. It's so nice to have a wolf around the house

Anderson, C W (Clarence Williams). Blaze and the gypsies

Berson, Harold. The thief who hugged a moonbeam

Blake, Quentin. Snuff

Bradford, Ann. The mystery in the secret club house
The mystery of the blind writer
The mystery of the tree house

Brandenberg, Franz. A robber! A robber!

Brenner, Anita. A hero by mistake

Bright, Robert. Georgie and the robbers

Brunhoff, Laurent de. Babar's mystery

Burton, Virginia Lee. Calico the wonder horse

Cass, Joan E. The cat thief

Christian, Mary Blount. The doggone mystery
J. J. Leggett, secret agent

Coombs, Patricia. Dorrie and the haunted house

Cressey, James. Max the mouse
Pet parrot

Daly, Niki. Vim, the rag mouse

Dumas, Philippe. Laura and the bandits

Duvoisin, Roger Antoine. Petunia and the song

Gage, Wilson. Down in the boondocks

Harris, Leon A. The great picture robbery

Heller, George. Hiroshi's wonderful kite

Heymans, Margriet. Pippin and Robber Grumblecroak's big baby

Hickman, Martha Whitmore. When can daddy come home?

Hogrogian, Nonny. The contest

Jacobs, Joseph. Hereafterthis

Janice. Mr. and Mrs. Button's wonderful watchdogs

Kirn, Ann. I spy

Kraus, Robert. The detective of London

Kroll, Steven. Woof, woof!

Levitin, Sonia. Nobody stole the pie

Levy, Elizabeth. Something queer at the ball park

Lobel, Anita. The straw maid

Lobel, Arnold. How the rooster saved the day

McKee, David. 123456789 Benn

McPhail, David. Stanley Henry Bear's friend

Massie, Diane Redfield. Chameleon the spy and the terrible toaster trap

Mathews, Louise. The great take-away

Mayer, Mercer. Liverwurst is missing

Miles, Miska. The raccoon and Mrs. McGinnis

Moore, John. Granny Stickleback

Parish, Peggy. The cat's burglar
Granny and the desperadoes

Partch, Virgil Franklin. The Christmas cookie sprinkle snitcher

Politi, Leo. Emmet
Reidel, Marlene. Jacob and the robbers
Rose, Gerald. The tiger-skin rug
Ruby-Spears Enterprises. The puppy's new adventures
Scarry, Richard. Richard Scarry's great big mystery book
Schulman, Janet. Jack the bum and the haunted house
Seabrooke, Brenda. The best burglar alarm
Shire, Ellen. The mystery at number seven, Rue Petite
Slobodkina, Esphyr. Pezzo the peddler and the thirteen silly thieves
Thomson, Ruth. Peabody all at sea
  Peabody's first case
Titus, Eve. Anatole and the thirty thieves
Ungerer, Tomi. The three robbers
Watson, Nancy Dingman. The birthday goat

Criminals see Crime; Prisons

Crippled see Handicaps

Crocodiles see Reptiles — alligators, crocodiles

Crows see Birds — crows

Cruelty to animals see Character traits — kindness to animals

Crustacea

Carrick, Carol. The blue lobster
Kipling, Rudyard. The crab that played with the sea
Morris, Robert A. Seahorse
Peet, Bill. Kermit the hermit
Yamaguchi, Tohr. Two crabs and the moonlight

Cumulative tales

Aardema, Verna. Bringing the rain to Kapiti Plain
  The riddle of the drum
Alger, Leclaire. Always room for one more
Aliki. June 7!
Asbjørnsen, P C (Peter Christen). The three billy goats Gruff, ill. by Marcia Brown
  The three billy goats Gruff, ill. by Paul Galdone
  The three billy goats Gruff, ill. by William Stobbs
Austin, Margot. Manuel's kite string

Baker, Betty. Little runner of the longhouse
  Rat is dead and ant is sad
Barton, Byron. Buzz, buzz, buzz
Berson, Harold. The boy, the baker, the miller and more
Bishop, Claire Huchet. Twenty-two bears
Blegvad, Erik. Burnie's hill
Bonne, Rose. I know an old lady
Boutwell, Edna. Red rooster
Bowden, Joan Chase. The bean boy
A boy went out to gather pears
Brand, Oscar. When I first came to this land
Brian Wildsmith's The twelve days of Christmas
Brown, Marcia. The bun
  The neighbors
Brown, Margaret Wise. The little brass band
Brown, Ruth. A dark, dark tale
Bryan, Ashley. Beat the story-drum, pum-pum
Bunting, Eve. The big cheese
Burningham, John. Mr. Gumpy's outing
Burton, Virginia Lee. Katy and the big snow
Carle, Eric. Pancakes, pancakes
Chicken Little. Chicken Licken
  Henny Penny, ill. by Paul Galdone
  Henny Penny, ill. by William Stobbs
Christian, Mary Blount. Nothing much happened today
Clifford, Eth. Why is an elephant called an elephant?
Cunliffe, John. The king's birthday cake
Delaney, A. The butterfly
Domanska, Janina. The turnip
Elkin, Benjamin. The king who could not sleep
  Such is the way of the world
  Why the sun was late
Emberley, Barbara. Drummer Hoff
Ets, Marie Hall. Elephant in a well
Evans, Eva Knox. Sleepy time
The fat cat
Fenton, Edward. The big yellow balloon
Fiddle-i-fee
Firmin, Peter. Basil Brush gets a medal
Flora, James. The day the cow sneezed
Foulds, Elfrida Vipont. The elephant and the bad baby
Gág, Wanda. Millions of cats
Galdone, Paul. The greedy old fat man
Garrison, Christian. Little pieces of the west wind
The gingerbread boy, ill. by Paul Galdone
The gingerbread boy, ill. by Joan Elizabeth Goodman

The gingerbread boy, ill. by William Curtis Holdsworth

The gingerbread boy. The gingerbread man

The golden goose

Grasshopper to the rescue

Grimm, Jacob. The table, the donkey and the stick

Heilbroner, Joan. This is the house where Jack lives

Hewett, Anita. The little white hen
The tale of the turnip

Hillert, Margaret. The three goats

Hogrogian, Nonny. One fine day

Hoguet, Susan Ramsay. I unpacked my grandmother's trunk

Home before midnight

The house that Jack built, ill. by Randolph Caldecott

The house that Jack built, ill. by Seymour Chwast

The house that Jack built, ill. by Antonio Frasconi

The house that Jack built, ill. by Rodney Peppé

Houston, John A. A mouse in my house

Hughes, Shirley. Alfie gets in first

Hush little baby, ill. by Aliki

Hush little baby, ill. by Jeanette Winter

Hush little baby, ill. by Margot Zemach

Hutchins, Pat. Don't forget the bacon!
Good night owl
Titch

Jacobs, Joseph. Johnny-cake, ill. by Emma Lillian Brock
Johnny-cake, ill. by William Stobbs

Jameson, Cynthia. The clay pot boy

Kahl, Virginia. Whose cat is that?

Kalan, Robert. Jump, frog, jump!

Krahn, Fernando. The mystery of the giant footprints

Krasilovsky, Phyllis. The cow who fell in the canal

Kroll, Steven. The tyrannosaurus game

Kuskin, Karla. A boy had a mother who bought him a hat

Lazy Jack

Lear, Edward. Whizz!

Lenski, Lois. Susie Mariar

Lexau, Joan M. Crocodile and hen

Lindman, Maj. Snipp, Snapp, Snurr and the buttered bread

The little red hen, ill. by Janina Domanska

The little red hen, ill. by Paul Galdone

The little red hen, ill. by Mel Pekarsky

The little red hen, ill. by Margot Zemach

Little Tuppen

Lobel, Anita. The pancake

Lobel, Arnold. The rose in my garden

Lorenz, Lee. Big Gus and Little Gus

McClintock, Marshall. A fly went by

Martin, Bill (William Ivan). Brown bear, brown bear, what do you see?

Murphey, Sara. The roly poly cookie

Noble, Trinka Hakes. The king's tea

Nolan, Dennis. Wizard McBean and his flying machine

Old MacDonald had a farm, ill. by Mel Crawford

Old MacDonald had a farm, ill. by David Frankland

Old MacDonald had a farm, ill. by Abner Graboff

Old MacDonald had a farm, ill. by Tracey Campbell Pearson

Old MacDonald had a farm, ill. by Robert M. Quackenbush

The old woman and her pig

Pack, Robert. Then what did you do?

Patrick, Gloria. This is...

Peet, Bill. The ant and the elephant

Petie, Haris. The seed the squirrel dropped

Prelutsky, Jack. The terrible tiger

Preston, Edna Mitchell. One dark night

Quackenbush, Robert M. No mouse for me

Raskin, Ellen. Ghost in a four-room apartment

Rockwell, Anne F. Honk honk!
Poor Goose

Sawyer, Ruth. Journey cake, ho!

Scott, William R. This is the milk that Jack drank

Seeger, Pete. The foolish frog

Segal, Lore. All the way home

Seuss, Dr. Green eggs and ham

Seymour, Dorothy Z. The tent

Shannon, George. Beanboy

Silverstein, Shel. A giraffe and a half

Skorpen, Liesel Moak. All the Lassies

Snow, Pegeen. Mrs. Periwinkle's groceries

Steger, Hans-Ulrich. Traveling to Tripiti

Stone, Rosetta. Because a little bug went ka-choo!

Suhl, Yuri. Simon Boom gives a wedding

Sutton, Eve. My cat likes to hide in boxes

Tolstoĭ, Alekseĭ Nikolaevich. The great big enormous turnip

Tresselt, Alvin R. Rain drop splash

The twelve days of Christmas. English folk song. Jack Kent's twelve days of Christmas

The twelve days of Christmas, ill. by Ilonka Karasz

The twelve days of Christmas, ill. by Erika Schneider

Tworkov, Jack. The camel who took a
walk
Ueno, Noriko. Elephant buttons
Varga, Judy. The monster behind Black
Rock
Wahl, Jan. Follow me cried Bee
Werth, Kurt. Lazy Jack
Wiesner, William. Happy-Go-Lucky
Wolkstein, Diane. The magic wings
Ziner, Feenie. Counting carnival
Zolotow, Charlotte. The quarreling book

Curiosity *see* Character traits — curiosity

Currency *see* Money

Cycles *see* Motorcycles; Sports —
bicycling

Czechoslovakia *see* Foreign lands —
Czechoslovakia

Dancing *see* Activities — dancing

Dark *see* Night

Darkness — fear *see* Emotions — fear

Dawn *see* Morning

Days of the week, months of the year

Borchers, Elisabeth. There comes a time
Carle, Eric. The very hungry caterpillar
Clifton, Lucille. Some of the days of
Everett Anderson
De Regniers, Beatrice Schenk. Little
Sister and the Month Brothers
Gág, Flavia. Chubby's first year
Hillman, Priscilla. A Merry-Mouse book
of months
Keenen, George. The preposterous
week
Lasker, Joe. Lentil soup
Lord, Beman. The days of the week
Provensen, Alice. The year at Maple
Hill Farm
Scarry, Richard. Richard Scarry's best
first book ever
Richard Scarry's great big schoolhouse
Sendak, Maurice. Chicken soup with
rice
Shulevitz, Uri. One Monday morning
Tafuri, Nancy. All year long
Tudor, Tasha. Around the year

Wolff, Ashley. A year of birds
Yolen, Jane. No bath tonight

Deafness *see* Handicaps — deafness

Death

Aliki. Mummies made in Egypt
Anders, Rebecca. A look at death
Baker, Betty. Rat is dead and ant is sad
Barker, Peggy. What happened when
grandma died
Barnhart, Peter. The wounded duck
Bartoli, Jennifer. Nonna
Beim, Jerrold. With dad alone
Benchley, Nathaniel. Snip
Bernstein, Joanne E. When people die
Brown, Margaret Wise. The dead bird
Bunting, Eve. The big red barn
The happy funeral
Carrick, Carol. The accident
Clifton, Lucille. Everett Anderson's
goodbye
Cock Robin. The courtship, merry
marriage, and feast of Cock Robin
and Jenny Wren
Cohen, Miriam. Jim's dog Muffins
Coutant, Helen. First snow
De Paola, Tomie. Nana upstairs and
Nana downstairs
Fassler, Joan. My grandpa died today
Hogan, Bernice. My grandmother died
but I won't forget her
Hoopes, Lyn Littlefield. Nana
Hurd, Edith Thacher. The black dog
who went into the woods
Jewell, Nancy. Time for Uncle Joe
Kantrowitz, Mildred. When Violet died
Keats, Ezra Jack. Maggie and the pirate
Kübler-Ross, Elisabeth. Remember the
secret
Mendoza, George. The hunter I might
have been
Osborn, Lois. My dad is really
something
Peavy, Linda. Allison's grandfather
Simon, Norma. We remember Philip
Stein, Sara Bonnett. About dying
Stevens, Carla. Stories from a snowy
meadow
Stevens, Margaret. When grandpa died
Tobias, Tobi. Petey
Townsend, Maryann. Pop's secret
Varley, Susan. Badger's parting gifts
Viorst, Judith. The tenth good thing
about Barney
Wahl, Jan. Tiger watch
Zolotow, Charlotte. My grandson Lew

Deer *see* Animals — deer

Demons *see* Devil; Monsters

Denmark *see* Foreign lands — Denmark

Dentists *see* Careers — dentists

Department stores *see* Stores

Desert

Baylor, Byrd. The desert is theirs
  Desert voices
  We walk in sandy places
Beim, Jerrold. Eric on the desert
Busch, Phyllis S. Cactus in the desert
Catchpole, Clive. Deserts
Caudill, Rebecca. Wind, sand and sky
Clark, Ann Nolan. The desert people
  Tia Maria's garden
Cretan, Gladys Yessayan. Ten brothers
  with camels
Holmes, Anita. The 100-year-old cactus
John, Naomi. Roadrunner
Keats, Ezra Jack. Clementina's cactus
McKee, David. The day the tide went
  out and out and out
Ungerer, Tomi. Orlando, the brave
  vulture
Wondriska, William. The stop

Detective stories *see* Problem solving

Detectives *see* Careers — detectives

Devil

Alger, Leclaire. Kellyburn Braes
Asch, Frank. Little Devil's ABC
  Little Devil's 123
Berson, Harold. How the devil got his
  due
Coombs, Patricia. The magic pot
Elwell, Peter. The king of the pipers
Galdone, Joanna. Amber day
Grimm, Jacob. The bearskinner
  The devil with the green hairs
Joyce, James. The cat and the devil
Pinkwater, Daniel Manus. Devil in the
  drain
Scribner, Charles. The devil's bridge
Stalder, Valerie. Even the Devil is afraid
  of a shrew
Turska, Krystyna. The magician of
  Cracow
Zemach, Harve. Duffy and the devil

Dictionaries

Daly, Kathleen N. The Macmillan
  picture wordbook
Floyd, Lucy. Agatha's alphabet, with her
  very own dictionary
Halsey, William D. The magic world of
  words

Hayward, Linda. The Sesame Street
  dictionary
Howard, Katherine. My first picture
  dictionary
Krensky, Stephen. My first dictionary
MacBean, Dilla Wittemore. Picture book
  dictionary
McIntire, Alta. Follett beginning to read
  picture dictionary
Parke, Margaret B. Young reader's
  color-picture dictionary
Rand McNally picturebook dictionary
Scarry, Richard. Richard Scarry's best
  word book ever
  Richard Scarry's storybook dictionary
Schulz, Charles M. The Charlie Brown
  dictionary
Seuss, Dr. The cat in the hat beginner
  book dictionary

Digging *see* Activities — digging

Dinosaurs

Aliki. Digging up dinosaurs
  Fossils tell of long ago
  My visit to the dinosaurs
Brown, Marc. Dinosaurs, beware!
Carrick, Carol. The crocodiles still wait
  Patrick's dinosaurs
Charlton, Elizabeth. Terrible
  tyrannosaurus
Cole, William. Dinosaurs and beasts of
  yore
Corbett, Scott. The foolish dinosaur
  fiasco
Craig, M Jean. Dinosaurs and more
  dinosaurs
Cutts, David. More about dinosaurs
Daly, Kathleen N. Dinosaurs
Dinosaurs and monsters
Eastman, David. The story of dinosaurs
Emberley, Michael. More dinosaurs!
Freedman, Russell. Dinosaurs and their
  young
Gordon, Sharon. Dinosaurs in trouble
Harrison, Sarah. In granny's garden
Hodgetts, Blake Christopher. Dream of
  the dinosaurs
Hoff, Syd. Danny and the dinosaur
Hurd, Edith Thacher. Dinosaur, my
  darling
Klein, Robin. Thing
Knight, David C. Dinosaur days
Kroll, Steven. The tyrannosaurus game
Lambert, David. Dinosaurs
Moseley, Keith. Dinosaurs
Most, Bernard. If the dinosaurs came
  back
  Whatever happened to the dinosaurs?
Nicoll, Helen. Meg's eggs
Parish, Peggy. Dinosaur time

Polhamus, Jean Burt. Dinosaur do's and don'ts
  Doctor Dinosaur
Ross, Wilda S. What did the dinosaurs eat?
Rubel, Nicole. Bruno Brontosaurus
Sant, Laurent Sauveur. Dinosaurs
Selsam, Millicent E. A first look at dinosaurs
Sharmat, Marjorie Weinman. Mitchell is moving
Simon, Seymour. The smallest dinosaurs
Slobodkin, Louis. Dinny and Danny
Sundgaard, Arnold. Jethro's difficult dinosaur
Woolley, Catherine. Quiet on account of dinosaur
Zallinger, Peter. Dinosaurs

Disbelief *see* Behavior — disbelief

Dissatisfaction *see* Behavior — dissatisfaction

Distance *see* Concepts — distance

Diving *see* Sports — skin diving

Divorce

Berger, Terry. How does it feel when your parents get divorced?
Bienenfeld, Florence. My mom and dad are getting a divorce
Caines, Jeannette. Daddy
Dragonwagon, Crescent. Always, always
Goff, Beth. Where's daddy?
Hazen, Barbara Shook. Two homes to live in
Jukes, Mavis. Like Jake and me
Lexau, Joan M. Me day
Lisker, Sonia O. Two special cards
Mayle, Peter. Divorce can happen to the nicest people
Noble, June. Two homes for Lynn
Perry, Patricia. Mommy and daddy are divorced
Peterson, Jeanne Whitehouse. That is that
Pursell, Margaret Sanford. A look at divorce
Rogers, Helen Spelman. Morris and his brave lion
Roy, Ronald. Breakfast with my father
Schuchman, Joan. Two places to sleep
Simon, Norma. The daddy days
Stein, Sara Bonnett. On divorce
Thomas, Ianthe. Eliza's daddy
Vigna, Judith. Daddy's new baby
  Grandma without me
  She's not my real mother

Doctors *see* Careers — doctors

Dogs *see* Animals — dogs

Dolls *see* Toys — dolls

Dolphins *see* Animals — dolphins

Donkeys *see* Animals — donkeys

Doves *see* Birds — doves

Down and up *see* Concepts — up and down

Dragonflies *see* Insects

Dragons

Aruego, José. The king and his friends
Bradfield, Roger. A good night for dragons
Brandenberg, Franz. Leo and Emily and the dragon
Buck, Pearl S (Pearl Sydenstricker). The dragon fish
Buckaway, C M. Alfred, the dragon who lost his flame
Chalmers, Mary. George Appleton
Christelow, Eileen. Henry and the Dragon
Coville, Bruce. Sarah and the dragon
Craig, M Jean. The dragon in the clock box
Cressey, James. The dragon and George
Cretien, Paul D. Sir Henry and the dragon
Davis, Reda. Martin's dinosaur
DeLage, Ida. The old witch and the dragon
Delaney, Ned. One dragon to another
De Paola, Tomie. The knight and the dragon
  The wonderful dragon of Timlin
Dewey, Ariane. Dorin and the dragon
Domanska, Janina. King Krakus and the dragon
Emberley, Ed. Klippity klop
Fassler, Joan. The man of the house
Firmin, Peter. Basil Brush and a dragon
Gág, Wanda. The funny thing
Garrison, Christian. The dream eater
Grimm, Jacob. The four clever brothers
Hillert, Margaret. Happy birthday, dear dragon
  Merry Christmas, dear dragon
Hoban, Russell. Ace Dragon Ltd.
Janosch. Just one apple
Jeschke, Susan. Firerose
Joerns, Consuelo. The midnight castle
Joslin, Sesyle. Dear dragon

Kent, Jack. The once-upon-a-time
  dragon
  There's no such thing as a dragon
Kimmel, Margaret Mary. Magic in the
  mist
Krahn, Fernando. The secret in the
  dungeon
Kumin, Maxine. Sebastian and the
  dragon
Lifton, Betty Jean. Joji and the dragon
Lobel, Arnold. Prince Bertram the bad
McCrea, James. The story of Olaf
Mahood, Kenneth. The laughing
  dragon
Mahy, Margaret. The dragon of an
  ordinary family
  A lion in the meadow
Manushkin, Fran. Moon dragon
Massie, Diane Redfield. The Komodo
  dragon's jewels
Murphy, Shirley Rousseau. Valentine
  for a dragon
Nash, Ogden. Custard and Company
  Custard the dragon and the wicked
  knight
Oksner, Robert M. The incompetent
  wizard
Pavey, Peter. One dragon's dream
Peet, Bill. How Droofus the dragon lost
  his head
Phillips, Louis. The brothers Wrong and
  Wrong Again
Price, Roger. The last little dragon
Rosen, Winifred. Dragons hate to be
  discreet
Rudchenko, Ivan. Ivanko and the
  dragon
Scarry, Richard. Richard Scarry's
  Peasant Pig and the terrible dragon
Sherman, Nancy. Gwendolyn the
  miracle hen
Shub, Elizabeth. Dragon Franz
Trez, Denise. The little knight's dragon
Van Woerkom, Dorothy. Alexandra the
  rock-eater
Varga, Judy. The dragon who liked to
  spit fire
Williams, Jay. Everyone knows what a
  dragon looks like
Woolley, Catherine. The popcorn
  dragon
Yolen, Jane. The acorn quest

Drawing games see Games

Dreams

Alexander, Martha G. Bobo's dream
Aylesworth, Jim. Tonight's the night
Balet, Jan B. Joanjo
Brown, Margaret Wise. Dream book
  The little farmer

Bruna, Dick. Miffy's dream
Callen, Larry. Dashiel and the night
Carroll, Lewis. The nursery "Alice"
Chorao, Kay. Lemon moon
Chwast, Seymour. Still another
  children's book
Coombs, Patricia. Dorrie and the
  dreamyard monsters
Craig, M Jean. What did you dream?
Crowley, Arthur. The wagon man
Dahl, Roald. Dirty beasts
Daugherty, Charles Michael. Wisher
Dennis, Wesley. Flip
Dewey, Ariane. Dorin and the dragon
Donaldson, Lois. Karl's wooden horse
Drescher, Henrik. Simon's book
Duvoisin, Roger Antoine. The missing
  milkman
Erskine, Jim. Bedtime story
Foreman, Michael. Land of dreams
Francis, Anna B. Pleasant dreams
Francis, Frank. The magic wallpaper
Gantos, Jack. Greedy Greeny
Garrison, Christian. The dream eater
Giff, Patricia Reilly. Next year I'll be
  special
Ginsburg, Mirra. Across the stream
Greenfield, Eloise. Africa dream
Greenwood, Ann. A pack of dreams
Hale, Irina. Donkey's dreadful day
Hayes, Geoffrey. The secret inside
Hodgetts, Blake Christopher. Dream of
  the dinosaurs
Hunter, Mollie. The knight of the
  golden plain
Hurd, Edith Thacher. Little dog,
  dreaming
Jacobs, Joseph. The crock of gold
Jennings, Michael. The bears who came
  to breakfix
Johnson, Jane. Bertie on the beach
Jonas, Ann. The quilt
Keats, Ezra Jack. Dreams
Keith, Eros. Nancy's backyard
Knotts, Howard. The lost Christmas
Kotzwinkle, William. The nap master
Krahn, Fernando. Sebastian and the
  mushroom
Le-Tan, Pierre. Visit to the North Pole
Low, Joseph. Don't drag your feet...
McPhail, David. Mistletoe
  The train
Mählqvist, Stefan. I'll take care of the
  crocodiles
Moeschlin, Elsa. The red horse
Montresor, Beni. Bedtime!
Orgel, Doris. Little John
Pavey, Peter. One dragon's dream
Reed, Kit. When we dream

Rockwell, Anne F. Buster and the bogeyman
   The wolf who had a wonderful dream
Sendak, Maurice. In the night kitchen
Shimin, Symeon. I wish there were two of me
Shulevitz, Uri. The treasure
Simons, Traute. Paulino
Stevens, Janet. Animal fair
Strand, Mark. The planet of lost things
Thorne, Jenny. My uncle
Trez, Denise. Good night, Veronica
Van Allsburg, Chris. Ben's dream
Ward, Lynd. The silver pony
Weisgard, Leonard. Who dreams of cheese?
Wende, Philip. Bird boy
Wersba, Barbara. Amanda dreaming
Zolotow, Charlotte. I have a horse of my own
   Someday

Droughts see Weather — droughts

Ducks see Birds — ducks

Dwarfs see Elves and little people

Dying see Death

Eagles see Birds — eagles

Ears see Anatomy

Earth

Asimov, Isaac. The best new things
Bernstein, Margery. Earth namer
Branley, Franklyn M. What makes day and night
Dayton, Mona. Earth and sky
Engdahl, Sylvia. Our world is earth
Leutscher, Alfred. Earth
Lewis, Claudia Louise. When I go to the moon
McNulty, Faith. How to dig a hole to the other side of the world
Simon, Seymour. Beneath your feet
   Earth

Easter see Holidays — Easter

Eating see Food

Ecology

Arneson, D J. Secret places
Baylor, Byrd. The desert is theirs
Beisert, Heide Helene. Poor fish
Bloome, Enid. The air we breathe!
   The water we drink!
Burton, Virginia Lee. The little house
Busch, Phyllis S. Puddles and ponds
Caputo, Robert. More than just pets
Carrick, Carol. A clearing in the forest
De Paola, Tomie. Michael Bird-Boy
Duvoisin, Roger Antoine. The happy hunter
Fife, Dale. The little park
Firmin, Peter. Basil Brush and the windmills
Freeman, Don. The seal and the slick
Hader, Berta Hoerner. The mighty hunter
Haley, Gail E. Noah's ark
Hamberger, John. The day the sun disappeared
Hoff, Syd. Grizzwold
Hurd, Edith Thacher. Wilson's world
Ichikawa, Satomi. Suzanne and Nicholas in the garden
Jewell, Nancy. Try and catch me
Kalman, Benjamin. Animals in danger
Leutscher, Alfred. Water
Mabey, Richard. Oak and company
Margolis, Richard J. Big bear, spare that tree
Meyer, Louis A. The clean air and peaceful contentment dirigible airline
Miles, Miska. Rabbit garden
Mizumura, Kazue. If I built a village
Murschetz, Luis. Mister Mole
Newton, James R. Forest log
Parnall, Peter. The great fish
Peet, Bill. The caboose who got loose
   Farewell to Shady Glade
   Fly, Homer, fly
   The gnats of knotty pine
   The wump world
Quackenbush, Robert M. Calling Doctor Quack
Ricciuti, Edward R. Donald and the fish that walked
Roach, Marilynne K. Dune fox
Seuss, Dr. The Lorax
Short, Mayo. Andy and the wild ducks
Shortall, Leonard W. Just-in-time Joey
Stone, A Harris. The last free bird
Torgersen, Don Arthur. The troll who lived in the lake
Tresselt, Alvin R. The beaver pond
   The dead tree
Wegen, Ron. Where can the animals go?

Ecuador see Foreign lands — Ecuador

Education *see* School

Eggs

Andersen, H C (Hans Christian). The woman with the eggs
Asch, Frank. MacGooses's grocery
Bourke, Linda. Ethel's exceptional egg
Brown, Margaret Wise. The golden egg book
Coombs, Patricia. Dorrie and the birthday eggs
Coontz, Otto. The quiet house
Eastman, P D (Philip D). Flap your wings
Eggs
Gordon, Sharon. Easter Bunny's lost egg
Heller, Ruth. Chickens aren't the only ones
Huxley, Aldous. The crows of Pearblossom
Kay, Helen. An egg is for wishing
Kent, Jack. The egg book
Krauss, Ruth. The happy egg
Kumin, Maxine. Eggs of things
Kwitz, Mary DeBall. Little chick's story
Lasell, Fen. Fly away goose
Lauber, Patricia. What's hatching out of that egg?
Levitin, Sonia. A single speckled egg
Lloyd, Megan. Chicken tricks
Long, Earlene. Johnny's egg
Mathews, Louise. Cluck one
Milgrom, Harry. Egg-ventures
Nicoll, Helen. Meg's eggs
O'Neill, Mary. Big red hen
Peet, Bill. The pinkish, purplish, bluish egg
Potter, Beatrix. The tale of Jemima Puddle-Duck
Pursell, Margaret Sanford. Jessie the chicken
Sprig the tree frog
Rockwell, Anne F. The gollywhopper egg
The wonderful eggs of Furicchia
Scarry, Richard. Egg in the hole
Schick, Eleanor. A surprise in the forest
Selsam, Millicent E. The bug that laid the golden eggs
Egg to chick
Seuss, Dr. Horton hatches the egg
Standon, Anna. Little duck lost
Stevenson, James. The great big especially beautiful Easter egg
Sundgaard, Arnold. Jethro's difficult dinosaur
Tresselt, Alvin R. The world in the candy egg
Waber, Bernard. How to go about laying an egg
Wahl, Jan. The five in the forest

Wright, Dare. Edith and the duckling

Egrets *see* Birds — egrets

Egypt *see* Foreign lands — Egypt

Egyptian language *see* Hieroglyphics

Elderly *see* Old age

Elephants *see* Animals — elephants

Elves and little people

Adshead, Gladys L. Brownies - hush!
Brownies - it's Christmas
Brownies - they're moving
Alden, Laura. Learning about fairies
Balian, Lorna. Leprechauns never lie
Barrie, J M (James M). Peter Pan
Baruch, Dorothy. Kappa's tug-of-war with the big brown horse
Bass, Donna. The tale of the dark crystal
Berenstain, Michael. The dwarks
Berg, Jean Horton. The wee little man
Beskow, Elsa Maartman. Peter in Blueberry Land
Peter's adventures in Blueberry land
Borg, Inga. Plupp builds a house
Bulette, Sara. The elf in the singing tree
Calhoun, Mary. The hungry leprechaun
The pixy and the lazy housewife
The runaway brownie
The thieving dwarfs
Chenault, Nell. Parsifal the Poddley
Cox, Palmer. Another Brownie book
The Brownies
Davis, Maggie S. Grandma's secret letter
De Paola, Tomie. The Prince of the Dolomites
De Regniers, Beatrice Schenk. Penny
Elves, fairies and gnomes
Fish, Helen Dean. When the root children wake up
Fujikawa, Gyo. Come follow me...to the secret world of elves and fairies and gnomes and trolls
Funai, Mamoru. Moke and Poki in the rain forest
Grimm, Jacob. The elves and the shoemaker
The shoemaker and the elves
Snow White, ill. by Bernadette
Snow White, ill. by Trina Schart Hyman
Snow White and Rose Red, ill. by Adrienne Adams
Snow-White and Rose-Red, ill. by Barbara Cooney
Snow White and Rose Red, ill. by John Wallner

Kennedy, Richard. The leprechaun's story

Krauss, Ruth. Everything under a mushroom

Kunnas, Mauri. Santa Claus and his elves

McLenighan, Valjean. You can go jump

Madden, Don. Lemonade serenade or the thing in the garden

May, Robert Lewis. Rudolph the red-nosed reindeer

Mayne, William. The blue book of hob stories

Minarik, Else Holmelund. The little giant girl and the elf boys

Moncure, Jane Belk. Happy healthkins
 The healthkin food train
 Healthkins exercise!
 Healthkins help

Norby, Lisa. The Herself the elf storybook

Shub, Elizabeth. Seeing is believing

Smith, Mary. Long ago elf

Steiner, Charlotte. Red Ridinghood's little lamb

Tom Thumb. Grimm Tom Thumb

Tom Thumb, ill. by L. Leslie Brooke

Tom Thumb, ill. by Dennis Hockerman

Tom Thumb, ill. by Felix Hoffmann

Tom Thumb, ill. by Lidia Postma

Tom Thumb, ill. by William Wiesner

Walt Disney Productions. Walt Disney's Snow White and the seven dwarfs

Zimelman, Nathan. To sing a song as big as Ireland

Embarrassment *see* Emotions — embarrassment

Emergencies *see* Hospitals

Emotions

Allington, Richard L. Feelings

Andersen, Karen Born. What's the matter, Sylvie, can't you ride?

Bach, Alice. The day after Christmas

Berger, Terry. How does it feel when your parents get divorced?
 I have feelings
 I have feelings too

Bienenfeld, Florence. My mom and dad are getting a divorce

Borten, Helen. Do you move as I do?

Brenner, Barbara. Faces, faces, faces

Brown, Tricia. Someone special, just like you

Calhoun, Mary. The witch who lost her shadow

Castle, Sue. Face talk, hand talk, body talk

Clifford, Eth. Your face is a picture

Clifton, Lucille. Everett Anderson's goodbye

Cohen, Miriam. Jim's dog Muffins

Cole, William. Frances face-maker

Conta, Marcia Maher. Feelings between brothers and sisters
 Feelings between friends
 Feelings between kids and grownups
 Feelings between kids and parents

Cunningham, Julia. A mouse called Junction

DeJong, Meindert. Nobody plays with a cabbage

Dragonwagon, Crescent. Rainy day together

Hann, Jacquie. Crybaby

Hazen, Barbara Shook. Happy, sad, silly, mad
 Two homes to live in

Helena, Ann. The lie

Hoban, Russell. La corona and the tin frog
 The stone doll of Sister Brute

Hopkins, Lee Bennett. I loved Rose Ann

Horvath, Betty F. Will the real Tommy Wilson please stand up?

Jewell, Nancy. Time for Uncle Joe

Kherdian, David. Right now

Knox-Wagner, Elaine. My grandpa retired today

Krauss, Ruth. The bundle book

Lalli, Judy. Feelings alphabet

Lewin, Hugh. Jafta
 Jafta - the journey
 Jafta - the town

McCrea, James. The magic tree

McGovern, Ann. Feeling mad, feeling sad, feeling bad, feeling glad

Mayer, Mercer. Mine!

Mayers, Patrick. Just one more block

Mendoza, George. The hunter I might have been

Mitchell, Cynthia. Playtime

Ness, Evaline. Pavo and the princess

Pursell, Margaret Sanford. A look at divorce

The Sesame Street book of people and things

Simon, Norma. How do I feel?

Stanton, Elizabeth. Sometimes I like to cry

Sussman, Susan. Hippo thunder

Tobias, Tobi. Moving day
 Petey

Tresselt, Alvin R. What did you leave behind?

Wittels, Harriet. Things I hate!

Wolde, Gunilla. This is Betsy

Yudell, Lynn Deena. Make a face

Emotions — anger

Alexander, Martha G. And my mean old mother will be sorry, Blackboard Bear
Aliki. We are best friends
Andrews, F Emerson (Frank Emerson). Nobody comes to dinner
Brunhoff, Laurent de. The one pig with horns
Du Bois, William Pène. Bear party
Hapgood, Miranda. Martha's mad day
I'm mad at you
Sharmat, Marjorie Weinman. Attila the angry
  I'm not Oscar's friend any more
  Rollo and Juliet...forever!
Simon, Norma. I was so mad!
Watson, Jane Werner. Sometimes I get angry
Zolotow, Charlotte. The quarreling book

Emotions — embarrassment

Alexander, Martha G. Sabrina
Boyd, Selma. The how
Bulla, Clyde Robert. Daniel's duck
Carlson, Nancy. Loudmouth George and the big race
Freeman, Don. Quiet! There's a canary in the library
Hirsh, Marilyn. The pink suit
Lexau, Joan M. I should have stayed in bed
Stanek, Muriel. Left, right, left, right!
Townsend, Kenneth. Felix, the bald-headed lion
Udry, Janice May. How I faded away

Emotions — envy, jealousy

Abisch, Roz. Mai-Ling and the mirror
Alexander, Martha G. Nobody asked me if I wanted a baby sister
  When the new baby comes, I'm moving out
Averill, Esther. Jenny's adopted brothers
Aylesworth, Jim. Mary's mirror
Bach, Alice. Millicent the magnificent
Baker, Charlotte. Little brother
Beim, Jerrold. Country mailman
Buck, Pearl S (Pearl Sydenstricker). The Chinese story teller
Bunting, Eve. Monkey in the middle
Burningham, John. Humbert, Mister Firkin and the Lord Mayor of London
Conford, Ellen. Why can't I be William?
Cretan, Gladys Yessayan. Lobo and Brewster
Gantos, Jack. Rotten Ralph's rotten Christmas
Gill, Joan. Hush, Jon!

Gordon, Shirley. Happy birthday, Crystal
Graham, Margaret Bloy. Benjy and the barking bird
Greenfield, Eloise. She come bringing me that little baby girl
Grimm, Jacob. Snow White, ill. by Bernadette
  Snow White, ill. by Trina Schart Hyman
Hazen, Barbara Shook. Why couldn't I be an only kid like you, Wigger?
Hoban, Russell. A baby sister for Frances
  A birthday for Frances
Lindgren, Astrid. I want a brother or sister
Lionni, Leo. Alexander and the wind-up mouse
McLenighan, Valjean. You can go jump
Mayer, Mercer. One frog too many
Miller, Warren. The goings on at Little Wishful
Ormondroyd, Edward. Theodore's rival
Osborn, Lois. My dad is really something
Peet, Bill. The luckiest one of all
Schick, Eleanor. Peggy's new brother
Shyer, Marlene Fanta. Stepdog
Skorpen, Liesel Moak. His mother's dog
Vigna, Judith. Couldn't we have a turtle instead?
Waber, Bernard. Lyle and the birthday party
Walt Disney Productions. Walt Disney's Snow White and the seven dwarfs
Zemach, Margot. To Hilda for helping
Zolotow, Charlotte. It's not fair

Emotions — fear

Alexander, Anne. Noise in the night
Alexander, Martha G. I'll protect you from the jungle beasts
  Maybe a monster
Alexander, Sue. Witch, Goblin and sometimes Ghost
Aylesworth, Jim. Siren in the night
Babbitt, Natalie. The something
Bannon, Laura. Little people of the night
  The scary thing
Barton, Byron. Harry is a scaredy-cat
Bonsall, Crosby Newell. Who's afraid of the dark?
Brenner, Anita. A hero by mistake
Brown, Margaret Wise. Night and day
Bunting, Eve. Terrible things
Byfield, Barbara Ninde. The haunted churchbell
Cameron, Ann. Harry (the monster)
Carlson, Nancy. Harriet's recital

Carrick, Carol. Dark and full of secrets
Chorao, Kay. Lester's overnight
Clifton, Lucille. Amifika
Cohen, Miriam. Jim meets the thing
Conford, Ellen. Eugene the brave
Credle, Ellis. Big fraid, little fraid
Crowe, Robert L. Clyde monster
Cunningham, Julia. A mouse called
    Junction
Devlin, Wende. Aunt Agatha, there's a
    lion under the couch!
Gackenbach, Dick. Harry and the
    terrible whatzit
Gay, Zhenya. Who's afraid?
Goodenow, Earle. The owl who hated
    the dark
Greenberg, Barbara. The bravest
    babysitter
Hamilton, Morse. Who's afraid of the
    dark?
Hanlon, Emily. What if a lion eats me
    and I fall into a hippopotamus' mud
    hole?
Hanson, Joan. I won't be afraid
Harlow, Joan Hiatt. Shadow bear
Hoban, Russell. Goodnight
Jonas, Ann. Holes and peeks
Joosse, Barbara M. Spiders in the fruit
    cellar
Keller, Beverly. Pimm's place
Kraus, Robert. Noel the coward
Leaf, Munro. Boo, who used to be
    scared of the dark
Lifton, Betty Jean. Goodnight orange
    monster
Low, Joseph. Benny rabbit and the owl
    Boo to a goose
Martin, Jacqueline Briggs. Bizzy Bones
    and Uncle Ezra
Mayer, Mercer. There's a nightmare in
    my closet
    You're the scaredy cat
Moore, Lilian. Little Raccoon and the
    thing in the pool
Nash, Ogden. The adventures of Isabel
Reed, Jonathan. Do armadillos come in
    houses?
Robison, Deborah. No elephants allowed
Ross, Pat. Your first airplane trip
Schertle, Alice. The gorilla in the hall
Seuss, Dr. The Sneetches, and other
    stories
Sharmat, Marjorie Weinman. Frizzy the
    fearful
Shortall, Leonard W. Tony's first dive
Smith, Janice Lee. The monster in the
    third dresser drawer and other
    stories about Adam Joshua
Stein, Sara Bonnett. About phobias
Stevenson, Drew. The ballad of
    Penelope Lou...and me

Stevenson, James. What's under my
    bed?
Stubbs, Joanna. With cat's eyes you'll
    never be scared of the dark
Trez, Denise. The royal hiccups
Turkle, Brinton. It's only Arnold
Udry, Janice May. Alfred
Viorst, Judith. My mama says there
    aren't any zombies, ghosts, vampires,
    creatures, demons, monsters, fiends,
    goblins, or things
Vogel, Ilse-Margaret. The don't be
    scared book
Wallace, Ian. Chin Chiang and the
    dragon's dance
Watson, Jane Werner. Sometimes I'm
    afraid
Williams, Gweneira Maureen. Timid
    Timothy, the kitten who learned to
    be brave
Winthrop, Elizabeth. Potbellied possums
Wolf, Bernard. Michael and the dentist
Wondriska, William. The stop
Zolotow, Charlotte. The storm book

Emotions — happiness

Asch, George. Linda
Bradbury, Bianca. Mutt
Low, Joseph. The Christmas grump
McCrea, James. The magic tree
Piatti, Celestino. The happy owls
Rice, Eve. What Sadie sang
Tapio, Pat Decker. The lady who saw
    the good side of everything
Tobias, Tobi. Jane wishing
Tripp, Paul. The strawman who smiled
    by mistake
Williams, Barbara. Someday, said
    Mitchell
Wondriska, William. Mr. Brown and
    Mr. Gray
Yabuki, Seiji. I love the morning

Emotions — hate

Brunhoff, Laurent de. The one pig with
    horns
Udry, Janice May. Let's be enemies
Zolotow, Charlotte. The hating book

Emotions — jealousy see Emotions — envy, jealousy

Emotions — loneliness

Alexander, Sue. Dear Phoebe
Aliki. We are best friends
Ardizzone, Edward. Lucy Brown and
    Mr. Grimes
Austin, Margot. Growl Bear
Battles, Edith. One to teeter-totter
Blegvad, Lenore. Mr. Jensen and cat

Bolliger, Max. The lonely prince
Brett, Jan. Annie and the wild animals
Bröger, Achim. Francie's paper puppy
Brown, Marcia. The little carousel
Buck, Pearl S (Pearl Sydenstricker). The little fox in the middle
Buntain, Ruth Jaeger. The birthday story
Chenault, Nell. Parsifal the Poddley
Chess, Victoria. Poor Esmé
Clewes, Dorothy. Happiest day
Coatsworth, Elizabeth. Lonely Maria
Conaway, Judith. I'll get even
Conger, Marion. The chipmunk that went to church
Coontz, Otto. The quiet house
Cummings, W T (Walter Thies). The kid
Duvoisin, Roger Antoine. Periwinkle
Ellis, Anne Leo. Dabble Duck
Fatio, Louise. The happy lion roars
Fujikawa, Gyo. Shags finds a kitten
Funazaki, Yasuko. Baby owl
Gág, Wanda. Nothing at all
Goffstein, M B (Marilyn Brooks). Goldie the dollmaker
  Neighbors
Keats, Ezra Jack. The trip
Kesselman, Wendy. Angelita
  Emma
Lukešová, Milena. The little girl and the rain
Luttrell, Ida. Lonesome Lester
McClure, Gillian. What's the time, Rory Wolf?
McGovern, Ann. Mr. Skinner's skinny house
  Nicholas Bentley Stoningpot III
McNeer, May Yonge. My friend Mac
Munthe, Adam John. I believe in unicorns
Murphy, Shirley Rousseau. Valentine for a dragon
Norton, Natalie. A little old man
Park, W B. The costume party
Sarton, May. Punch's secret
Schick, Eleanor. Home alone
Seignobosc, Françoise. The story of Colette
Skurzynski, Gloria. Martin by himself
Slate, Joseph. Lonely Lula cat
Sonneborn, Ruth A. Lollipop's party
Spang, Günter. Clelia and the little mermaid
Stage, Mads. The lonely squirrel
Stevenson, James. The bear who had no place to go
Stren, Patti. Hug me
Sugita, Yutaka. Helena the unhappy hippopotamus
Surany, Anico. Kati and Kormos

Walter, Mildred Pitts. My mama needs me
Yashima, Tarō. Crow boy
Zindel, Paul. I love my mother
Zolotow, Charlotte. Janey
  Three funny friends
  A tiger called Thomas

Emotions — love

Agostinelli, Maria Enrica. On wings of love
Alexander, Sue. Dear Phoebe
  Nadia the willful
Andersen, H C (Hans Christian). The snow queen, ill. by Toma Bogdanovic
  The snow queen, ill. by June Atkin Corwin
  The snow queen, ill. by Susan Jeffers
  The snow queen, ill. by Errol Le Cain
Anglund, Joan Walsh. Love is a special way of feeling
Bianco, Margery Williams. The velveteen rabbit, ill. by Allen Atkinson
  The velveteen rabbit, ill. by Michael Hague
  The velveteen rabbit, ill. by William Nicholson
  The velveteen rabbit, ill. by Ilse Plume
  The velveteen rabbit, ill. by Tien
Billam, Rosemary. Fuzzy rabbit
Boegehold, Betty. Pawpaw's run
Brown, Palmer. Something for Christmas
Buckley, Helen Elizabeth. Grandmother and I
Clifton, Lucille. Everett Anderson's goodbye
De Paola, Tomie. Helga's dowry
Dragonwagon, Crescent. Wind Rose
Dyke, John. Pigwig
Estes, Eleanor. A little oven
Fatio, Louise. The happy lion's treasure
Flack, Marjorie. Ask Mr. Bear
Freeman, Don. Corduroy
Gerstein, Mordicai. Prince Sparrow
Hazen, Barbara Shook. Even if I did something awful
Hoopes, Lyn Littlefield. When I was little
Jenkins, Jordan. Learning about love
Jewell, Nancy. The snuggle bunny
Lasky, Kathryn. I have four names for my grandfather
Lexau, Joan M. A house so big
McPhail, David. Sisters
Marshall, Edward. Fox in love
Mayer, Marianna. Beauty and the beast
Mayer, Mercer. Just for you
Mayne, William. The patchwork cat
Miles, Betty. Around and around... love

Mizumura, Kazue. If I were a cricket...
Otsuka, Yuzo. Suho and the white horse
Paterson, Diane. Wretched Rachel
Reinl, Edda. The little snake
Rowand, Phyllis. Every day in the year
Samuels, Barbara. Faye and Dolores
Scott, Ann Herbert. On mother's lap
Shecter, Ben. If I had a ship
Springstubb, Tricia. My Minnie is a
  jewel
Tudor, Tasha. Miss Kiss and the nasty
  beast
Wahl, Jan. Old Hippo's Easter egg
Zalben, Jane Breskin. A perfect nose for
  Ralph
Zindel, Paul. I love my mother
Zola, Meguido. Only the best
Zolotow, Charlotte. Do you know what
  I'll do?
  May I visit?
  Say it!
  The sky was blue

Emotions — sadness

Alexander, Sue. Nadia the willful
Allen, Frances Charlotte. Little hippo
Baker, Betty. Rat is dead and ant is sad
Bartoli, Jennifer. Nonna
De Paola, Tomie. Nana upstairs and
  Nana downstairs
Deveaux, Alexis. Na-ni
Low, Joseph. The Christmas grump
Sharmat, Marjorie Weinman. I don't
  care
Sugita, Yutaka. Helena the unhappy
  hippopotamus
Wolff, Ashley. The bells of London

Emotions — unhappiness see Emotions
— happiness; Emotions — sadness

Emperors see Royalty

Endangered animals see Animals —
endangered animals

Engineered books see Format, unusual

England see Foreign lands — England

Entertainment see Theater

Envy see Emotions — envy, jealousy

Eskimos see Ethnic groups in the U.S.
— Eskimos

Ethnic groups in the U.S.

Belpré, Pura. Santiago
Bettinger, Craig. Follow me, everybody

Blue, Rose. I am here: Yo estoy aqui
Brenner, Barbara. Faces, faces, faces
Clifford, Eth. Your face is a picture
Cohen, Miriam. Will I have a friend?
Crume, Marion W. Listen!
Greene, Roberta. Two and me makes
  three
Jaynes, Ruth M. Benny's four hats
  Friends! friends! friends!
  Tell me please! What's that?
  That's what it is!
  What is a birthday child?
Keats, Ezra Jack. My dog is lost!
Kesselman, Wendy. Angelita
Klein, Leonore. Just like you
Lansdown, Brenda. Galumpf
May, Julian. Why people are different
  colors
Merriam, Eve. Boys and girls, girls and
  boys
Merrill, Jean. How many kids are hiding
  on my block?
Reit, Seymour. Round things
  everywhere
Rosenberg, Maxine B. Being adopted
Simon, Norma. What do I say?
Sobol, Harriet Langsam. We don't look
  like our mom and dad
Solbert, Ronni. I wrote my name on the
  wall
Stanek, Muriel. One, two, three for fun
Udry, Janice May. What Mary Jo shared

Ethnic groups in the U.S. —
Afro-Americans

Adoff, Arnold. Big sister tells me that
  I'm black
  Where wild Willie?
Alexander, Martha G. Bobo's dream
  The story grandmother told
Aliki. A weed is a flower
Bang, Molly. Wiley and the hairy man
Beim, Jerrold. The swimming hole
Beim, Lorraine. Two is a team
Blue, Rose. Black, black, beautiful black
  How many blocks is the world?
Bonsall, Crosby Newell. The case of the
  cat's meow
  The case of the hungry stranger
Breinburg, Petronella. Doctor Shawn
  Shawn goes to school
  Shawn's red bike
Brenner, Barbara. Wagon wheels
Burch, Robert. Joey's cat
Caines, Jeannette. Abby
  Daddy
  Just us women
Calloway, Northern J. Northern J.
  Calloway presents Super-vroomer!

Clifton, Lucille. All us come cross the water
Amifika
The black B C's
The boy who didn't believe in spring
Don't you remember?
Everett Anderson's Christmas coming
Everett Anderson's friend
Everett Anderson's goodbye
Everett Anderson's nine months long
Everett Anderson's 1-2-3
Everett Anderson's year
My brother fine with me
My friend Jacob
Some of the days of Everett Anderson
Three wishes
Clymer, Eleanor Lowenton. Horatio
Dionetti, Michelle. Thalia Brown and the blue bug
Evans, Mari. Singing black
Fassler, Joan. Don't worry dear
Fife, Dale. Adam's ABC
Flournoy, Valerie. The best time of day
The twins strike back
Fraser, Kathleen. Adam's world, San Francisco
Freeman, Don. Corduroy
A pocket for Corduroy
George, Jean Craighead. The wentletrap trap
Gill, Joan. Hush, Jon!
Gray, Genevieve. Send Wendell
Greenberg, Polly. Oh, Lord, I wish I was a buzzard
Greenfield, Eloise. Daydreamers
First pink light
Me and Nessie
She come bringing me that little baby girl
Grifalconi, Ann. City rhythms
Hill, Elizabeth Starr. Evan's corner
Hoffman, Phyllis. Steffie and me
Hopkins, Lee Bennett. I think I saw a snail
Horvath, Betty F. Hooray for Jasper
Jasper and the hero business
Jasper makes music
Jensen, Virginia Allen. Sara and the door
Keats, Ezra Jack. Apartment 3
Dreams
Goggles
Hi, cat!
John Henry
A letter to Amy
Louie
Pet show!
Peter's chair
Skates
The snowy day
The trip

Whistle for Willie
Kirn, Ann. Beeswax catches a thief
Lansdown, Brenda. Galumpf
Lexau, Joan M. Benjie
Benjie on his own
I should have stayed in bed
Me day
The rooftop mystery
Lipkind, William. Four-leaf clover
McGovern, Ann. Black is beautiful
Mayer, Mercer. Liza Lou and the Yeller Belly Swamp
Merriam, Eve. Epaminondas
Monjo, F N. The drinking gourd
Nolan, Madeena Spray. My daddy don't go to work
Scott, Ann Herbert. Big Cowboy Western
Let's catch a monster
Sam
Selsam, Millicent E. Tony's birds
Sharmat, Marjorie Weinman. I don't care
Showers, Paul. Look at your eyes
Your skin and mine
Steptoe, John. Birthday
My special best words
Stevie
Uptown
Taylor, Sydney. The dog who came to dinner
Thomas, Ianthe. Eliza's daddy
Lordy, Aunt Hattie
Walk home tired, Billy Jenkins
Udry, Janice May. Mary Ann's mud day
Mary Jo's grandmother
What Mary Jo shared
What Mary Jo wanted
Walter, Mildred Pitts. My mama needs me
Williamson, Mel. Walk on!
Williamson, Stan. The no-bark dog
Wilson, Julia. Becky
Yezback, Steven A. Pumpkinseeds
Zemach, Margot. Jake and Honeybunch go to heaven
Ziner, Feenie. Counting carnival

Ethnic groups in the U.S. — Black Americans see Ethnic groups in the U.S. — Afro-Americans

Ethnic groups in the U.S. — Chinese-Americans

Behrens, June. Soo Ling finds a way
Bunting, Eve. The happy funeral
Politi, Leo. Mr. Fong's toy shop
Moy Moy
Wallace, Ian. Chin Chiang and the dragon's dance

Ethnic groups in the U.S. — Eskimos

Beim, Lorraine. The little igloo
Damjan, Mischa. Atuk
Harlow, Joan Hiatt. Shadow bear
Hopkins, Marjorie. Three visitors
Houston, James. Kiviok's magic journey
Machetanz, Sara. A puppy named Gia
Morrow, Suzanne Stark. Inatuck's friend
Parish, Peggy. Ootah's lucky day
San Souci, Robert D. Song of Sedna
Scott, Ann Herbert. On mother's lap
Wiesenthal, Eleanor. Let's find out
  about Eskimos

Ethnic groups in the U.S. — Indians

Abisch, Roz. 'Twas in the moon of
  wintertime
Aliki. Corn is maize
Anderson, C W (Clarence Williams).
  Linda and the Indians
Aulaire, Ingri Mortenson d'. Pocahontas
Baker, Betty. And me, coyote!
  Latki and the lightning lizard
  Little runner of the longhouse
  Rat is dead and ant is sad
  Three fools and a horse
  Turkey girl
Baker, Laura Nelson. O children of the
  wind and pines
Baker, Olaf. Where the buffaloes begin
Baylor, Byrd. The desert is theirs
  A God on every mountain top
  Hawk, I'm your brother
  Moon song
  When clay sings
Beatty, Hetty Burlingame. Little Owl
  Indian
Belting, Natalia Maree. Verity Mullens
  and the Indian
Benchley, Nathaniel. Red Fox and his
  canoe
  Running Owl the hunter
  Small Wolf
Bernstein, Margery. Coyote goes
  hunting for fire
  Earth namer
  How the sun made a promise and kept
  it
Bierhorst, John. The ring in the prairie
Blood, Charles L. The goat in the rug
Bornstein, Ruth Lercher. Indian bunny
Brock, Emma Lillian. One little Indian
  boy
Clark, Ann Nolan. The desert people
  In my mother's house
  The little Indian basket maker
  The little Indian pottery maker
Crompton, Anne Eliot. The winter wife
Day, Michael E. Berry Ripe Moon

De Paola, Tomie. The legend of the
  bluebonnet
Ehrlich, Amy. Zeek Silver Moon
Elting, Mary. The Hopi way
Flöthe, Louise Lee. The Indian and his
  pueblo
Friskey, Margaret. Indian Two Feet and
  his eagle feather
  Indian Two Feet and his horse
  Indian Two Feet and the wolf cubs
  Indian Two Feet rides alone
Fritz, Jean. The good giants and the
  bad Pukwudgies
Goble, Paul. Buffalo woman
  The friendly wolf
  The gift of the sacred dog
  The girl who loved wild horses
Gorsline, Marie. North American
  Indians
Hader, Berta Hoerner. The mighty
  hunter
Hays, Wilma Pitchford. Little Yellow
  Fur
Hood, Flora Mae. Living in Navajoland
Jagendorf, Moritz A. Kwi-na the eagle
Jones, Hettie. The trees stand shining
Leech, Jay. Bright Fawn and me
Longfellow, Henry Wadsworth.
  Hiawatha
  Hiawatha's childhood
McDermott, Gerald. Arrow to the sun
Mariana. Doki, the lonely papoose
Martin, Bill (William Ivan). Brave little
  Indian
Mobley, Jane. The star husband
Monjo, F N. The drinking gourd
  Indian summer
Moon, Grace Purdie. One little Indian
Parish, Peggy. Good hunting, Little
  Indian
  Granny and the Indians
  Granny, the baby and the big gray
  thing
  Little Indian
  Snapping turtle's all wrong day
Parnall, Peter. The great fish
Perrine, Mary. Salt boy
Robbins, Ruth. How the first rainbow
  was made
Rose, Anne. Spider in the sky
Siberell, Anne. Whale in the sky
Sleator, William. The angry moon
Stan-Padilla, Viento. Dream Feather
Toye, William. The fire stealer
Wheeler, M J. First came the Indians
Wondriska, William. The stop

Ethnic groups in the U.S. — Japanese-Americans

Copeland, Helen. Meet Miki Takino

Hawkinson, Lucy. Dance, dance,
　Amy-Chan!
Politi, Leo. Mieko
Yashima, Mitsu. Momo's kitten
Yashima, Tarō. Umbrella
　The youngest one

Ethnic groups in the U.S. —
Mexican-Americans

Adams, Ruth Joyce. Fidelia
Behrens, June. Fiesta!
Bolognese, Don. A new day
Ets, Marie Hall. Bad boy, good boy
　Gilberto and the wind
　Nine days to Christmas
Felt, Sue. Rosa-too-little
Fraser, James Howard. Los Posadas
Garrett, Helen. Angelo the naughty one
Hitte, Kathryn. Mexicallie soup
Jaynes, Ruth M. Melinda's Christmas
　stocking
　Tell me please! What's that?
　That's what it is!
　What is a birthday child?
Molnar, Joe. Graciela
Ormsby, Virginia H. Twenty-one
　children plus ten
Politi, Leo. Juanita
　The mission bell
　Pedro, the angel of Olvera Street
　Song of the swallows
Serfozo, Mary. Welcome Roberto!
　Bienvenido, Roberto!

Ethnic groups in the U.S. — Puerto
Rican-Americans

Belpré, Pura. Santiago
Blue, Rose. I am here: Yo estoy aqui
Bowden, Joan Chase. Emilio's summer
　day
Keats, Ezra Jack. My dog is lost!
Kesselman, Wendy. Angelita
Simon, Norma. What do I do?
　What do I say?
Sonneborn, Ruth A. Friday night is
　papa night
　Lollipop's party
　Seven in a bed

Etiquette

Ackley, Edith Flack. Please
　Thank you
Behrens, June. The manners book
Betz, Betty. Manners for moppets
Brown, Marc. Perfect pigs
Brown, Myra Berry. Company's coming
　for dinner
Duvoisin, Roger Antoine. Periwinkle
Hoban, Russell. Dinner at Alberta's
　The little Brute family

Joslin, Sesyle. Dear dragon
　What do you do, dear?
　What do you say, dear?
Keenan, Martha. The mannerly
　adventures of Little Mouse
Keller, Irene. The Thingumajig book of
　manners
Keller, John G. Krispin's fair
Leaf, Munro. A flock of watchbirds
　How to behave and why
　Manners can be fun
Lexau, Joan M. Cathy is company
Myller, Lois. No! No!
Parish, Peggy. Mind your manners
Petersham, Maud. The circus baby
Polhamus, Jean Burt. Dinosaur do's and
　don'ts
Potter, Beatrix. The sly old cat
Quackenbush, Robert M. I don't want to
　go, I don't know how to act
Scarry, Richard. Richard Scarry's please
　and thank you book
Seignobosc, Françoise. The thank-you
　book
Sherman, Ivan. I do not like it when my
　friend comes to visit
Slobodkin, Louis. Thank you - you're
　welcome
Smaridge, Norah. You know better than
　that
Stover, Jo Ann. If everybody did

Europe *see* Foreign lands — Europe

Evening *see* Twilight

Experiments *see* Science

Eye glasses *see* Glasses

Eyes *see* Anatomy

Fables *see* Folk and fairy tales

Faces *see* Anatomy

Fairies

Alden, Laura. Learning about fairies
Anderson, Lonzo. Two hundred rabbits
Barker, Cicely Mary. Berry flower fairies
　Blossom flower fairies
　Flower fairies of the seasons
　Spring flower fairies
　Summer flower fairies

Bate, Lucy. Little rabbit's loose tooth

Beim, Lorraine. Sasha and the samovar

Coombs, Patricia. Lisa and the grompet

Elves, fairies and gnomes

Enright, Elizabeth. Zeee

Fairy poems for the very young

Fujikawa, Gyo. Come follow me...to the secret world of elves and fairies and gnomes and trolls

Gardner, Mercedes. Scooter and the magic star

Gunther, Louise. A tooth for the tooth fairy

Hoffmann, E T A. The nutcracker

Jeschke, Susan. Mia, Grandma and the genie

Kent, Jack. Clotilda

Kroll, Steven. Loose tooth

Lester, Helen. The wizard, the fairy and the magic chicken

Mahy, Margaret. Pillycock's shop

Manson, Beverlie. The fairies' alphabet book

Newbolt, Henry John, Sir. Rilloby-rill

Wetterer, Margaret. Patrick and the fairy thief

Fairs

Barker, Melvern J. Country fair

Booth, Eugene. At the fair

Bourke, Linda. Ethel's exceptional egg

Brunhoff, Laurent de. Babar's fair will be opened next Sunday

Carrick, Carol. The highest balloon on the common

Chiefari, Janet. Kids are baby goats

Coombs, Patricia. Dorrie and the Witchville fair

Delton, Judy. Penny wise, fun foolish

Devlin, Wende. Old Witch and the polka-dot ribbon

Ets, Marie Hall. Mr. Penny's race horse

Gauch, Patricia Lee. On to Widecombe Fair

Hoff, Syd. Henrietta goes to the fair

Leech, Jay. Bright Fawn and me

Miles, Miska. Jump frog jump

Schatell, Brian. Farmer Goff and his turkey Sam

Seignobosc, Françoise. Jeanne-Marie at the fair

Stevens, Janet. Animal fair

Tudor, Tasha. Corgiville fair

Watson, Clyde. Tom Fox and the apple pie

Watson, Nancy Dingman. The birthday goat

Widdecombe Fair

Fairy tales *see* Folk and fairy tales

Fall *see* Seasons — fall

Families *see* Family life

Family life

Adoff, Arnold. Big sister tells me that I'm black

Black is brown is tan

Ma nDa La

Make a circle, keep us in

Ahlberg, Janet. The baby's catalogue

Peek-a-boo!

Aho, Jennifer J. Learning about sex

Alexander, Martha G. I'll be the horse if you'll play with me

Marty McGee's space lab, no girls allowed

Alexander, Sue. Dear Phoebe

Nadia the willful

Aliki. June 7!

Keep your mouth closed, dear

Allen, Laura Jean. Ottie and the star

Amoss, Berthe. Tom in the middle

Anderson, C W (Clarence Williams). Billy and Blaze

Anderson, Douglas. Let's draw a story

Anderson, Lonzo. The day the hurricane happened

Arkin, Alan. Tony's hard work day

Armitage, Ronda. The bossing of Josie

Don't forget, Matilda

One moonlit night

Arnstein, Helene S. Billy and our new baby

Arthur, Catherine. My sister's silent world

Aulaire, Ingri Mortenson d'. Children of the northlights

Nils

Avery, Kay. Wee willow whistle

Ayer, Jacqueline. A wish for little sister

Aylesworth, Jim. Siren in the night

Babbitt, Lorraine. Pink like the geranium

Bach, Alice. Millicent the magnificent

Baker, Betty. Little runner of the longhouse

Sonny-Boy Sim

Baker, Charlotte. Little brother

Balet, Jan B. The fence

Five Rollatinis

Banish, Roslyn. I want to tell you about my baby

Bartoli, Jennifer. Nonna

Bascom, Joe. Malcolm's job

Battles, Edith. One to teeter-totter

Beatty, Hetty Burlingame. Moorland pony

Beckman, Kaj. Lisa cannot sleep

Beim, Jerrold. Jay's big job

Beim, Lorraine. Lucky Pierre

De Paola, Tomie. The family Christmas tree book

De Regniers, Beatrice Schenk. The giant story
A little house of your own

Dragonwagon, Crescent. Rainy day together

Drescher, Joan. I'm in charge!
The marvelous mess
Your family, my family

Ehrlich, Amy. Zeek Silver Moon

Ets, Marie Hall. Bad boy, good boy

Fassler, Joan. One little girl

Felt, Sue. Rosa-too-little

Fenton, Edward. Fierce John

Fisher, Aileen. In one door and out the other

Flack, Marjorie. The new pet
Wait for William

Fleisher, Robbin. Quilts in the attic

Flournoy, Valerie. The best time of day
The twins strike back

Fox, Charles Philip. Mr. Stripes the gopher

Fraser, Kathleen. Adam's world, San Francisco

Friedman, Estelle. Boy who lived in a cave

Friedman, Ina R. How my parents learned to eat

Galbraith, Kathryn Osebold. Katie did!

Galdone, Paul. Obedient Jack

Gantos, Jack. Aunt Bernice

Gill, Joan. Hush, Jon!

Gobhai, Mehlli. Usha, the mouse-maiden

Goffstein, M B (Marilyn Brooks). Family scrapbook

Goldman, Susan. Cousins are special

Goudey, Alice E. The day we saw the sun come up

Gray, Catherine. Tammy and the gigantic fish

Gray, Genevieve. Send Wendell

Gray, Nigel. It'll all come out in the wash

Green, Phyllis. Uncle Roland, the perfect guest

Greenfield, Eloise. Me and Nessie

Griffith, Helen V. Mine will, said John

Gruenberg, Sidonie Matsner. The wonderful story of how you were born

Hague, Kathleen. The man who kept house

Hale, Kathleen. Orlando and the water cats

Hamilton-Merritt, Jane. Our new baby

Harris, Robie H. Don't forget to come back

Hautzig, Esther. At home

Hazelton, Elizabeth Baldwin. Sammy, the crow who remembered

Hazen, Barbara Shook. Even if I did something awful
Tight times

Heide, Florence Parry. The shrinking of Treehorn
Treehorn's treasure

Heller, Linda. Lily at the table

Helmering, Doris Wild. We're going to have a baby

Hickman, Martha Whitmore. When can daddy come home?

Hill, Elizabeth Starr. Evan's corner

Hill, Eric. At home

Hirsh, Marilyn. The pink suit

Hitte, Kathryn. Mexicallie soup

Hoban, Lillian. Arthur's prize reader
Mr. Pig and family

Hoban, Russell. A baby sister for Frances
Harvey's hideout
They came from Aargh!

Hobson, Laura Z. "I'm going to have a baby!"

Hoff, Syd. My Aunt Rosie

Hoffman, Phyllis. Steffie and me

Hoke, Helen L. The biggest family in the town

Holland, Viki. We are having a baby

Horvath, Betty F. Be nice to Josephine

Hughes, Shirley. David and dog
Moving Molly

Hurd, Edith Thacher. The mother kangaroo

Hutchins, Pat. Titch
You'll soon grow into them, Titch

Ionesco, Eugene. Story number 1

Iwasaki, Chihiro. Staying home alone on a rainy day

Jack Sprat. The life of Jack Sprat, his wife and his cat

Jarrell, Mary. The knee baby

Jewell, Nancy. Time for Uncle Joe

Jones, Penelope. I'm not moving!

Jukes, Mavis. Like Jake and me

Keats, Ezra Jack. Apartment 3
Louie's search
Peter's chair

Keller, Holly. Cromwell's glasses

Kellogg, Steven. Can I keep him?

Kessler, Leonard P. Are we lost, daddy?

Koch, Dorothy Clarke. I play at the beach

Krasilovsky, Phyllis. The very little boy
The very little girl
The very tall little girl

Kraus, Robert. Another mouse to feed
Big brother

Krauss, Ruth. The backward day

Lapsley, Susan. I am adopted

Sharmat, Marjorie Weinman.
  Goodnight, Andrew. Good night,
  Craig
 Sometimes mama and papa fight
 What are we going to do about
  Andrew?
Sharr, Christine. Homes
Showers, Paul. Me and my family tree
Shyer, Marlene Fanta. Stepdog
Simon, Norma. All kinds of families
 How do I feel?
 What do I say?
Skorpen, Liesel Moak. His mother's dog
Slobodkin, Louis. Clear the track
 Magic Michael
Smith, Lucia B. A special kind of sister
Sobol, Harriet Langsam. We don't look
 like our mom and dad
Sonneborn, Ruth A. Seven in a bed
Spinelli, Eileen. Thanksgiving at
 Tappletons'
Stanton, Elizabeth. The very messy
 room
Steig, William. Sylvester and the magic
 pebble
Stein, Sara Bonnett. The adopted one
 Making babies
 On divorce
 That new baby
Steiner, Charlotte. Daddy comes home
Steptoe, John. My special best words
Stevenson, James. "Could be worse!"
 Worse than Willy!
Stevenson, Robert Louis. The moon
Stock, Catherine. Sophie's bucket
Stoddard, Sandol. Curl up small
 The thinking book
Strathdee, Jean. The house that grew
Tallarico, Tony. At home
Tax, Meredith. Families
Taylor, Judy. Sophie and Jack
Thomson, Pat. Rhymes around the day
Thorne, Jenny. My uncle
Tierney, Hanne. Where's your baby
 brother, Becky Bunting?
Tobias, Tobi. At the beach
 Jane wishing
Todd, Kathleen. Snow
Tsow, Ming. A day with Ling
Udry, Janice May. Theodore's parents
 What Mary Jo wanted
Van Leeuwen, Jean. More tales of
 Oliver Pig
 Tales of Amanda Pig
 Tales of Oliver Pig
Van Woerkom, Dorothy. Alexandra the
 rock-eater
Vevers, Gwynne. Animal parents
Vigna, Judith. Couldn't we have a turtle
 instead?
 She's not my real mother

Viorst, Judith. Alexander and the
 terrible, horrible, no good, very bad
 day
 I'll fix Anthony
 Sunday morning
Wahl, Jan. Old Hippo's Easter egg
 Sylvester Bear overslept
Walter, Mildred Pitts. My mama needs
 me
Watson, Clyde. Catch me and kiss me
 and say it again
Watson, Pauline. Days with Daddy
Wegen, Ron. The balloon trip
Weil, Lisl. Gertie and Gus
Weiss, Nicki. Weekend at Muskrat Lake
Whitney, Alex. The tiger that barks
Wilhelm, Hans. A new home, a new
 friend
Williams, Barbara. If he's my brother
 So what if I'm a sore loser?
Williams, Vera B. A chair for my
 mother
 Music, music for everyone
 Something special for me
Winthrop, Elizabeth. Bunk beds
 I think he likes me
Wolde, Gunilla. Betsy and Peter are
 different
 Betsy and the vacuum cleaner
 Betsy's fixing day
 This is Betsy
Wyse, Lois. Two guppies, a turtle and
 Aunt Edna
Yaffe, Alan. The magic meatballs
Young, Evelyn. Wu and Lu and Li
Zemach, Margot. To Hilda for helping
Zimelman, Nathan. If I were strong
 enough...
Zolotow, Charlotte. Big sister and little
 sister
 Do you know what I'll do?
 If it weren't for you
 It's not fair
 May I visit?
 My grandson Lew
 The sky was blue
 Someone new
 The summer night
 When I have a son
 William's doll
Zusman, Evelyn. The Passover parrot

Family life — brothers *see* Family life;
  Sibling rivalry

Family life — fathers

Alda, Arlene. Matthew and his dad
Asch, Frank. Goodnight horsey
 Just like daddy
Baker, Betty. My sister says

Family life — grandparents, great-grandparents

Heller, Linda. The castle on Hester Street

Henriod, Lorraine. Grandma's wheelchair

Herter, Jonina. Eighty-eight kisses

Hest, Amy. The crack-of-dawn walkers

Hines, Anna Grossnickle. Come to the meadow

Hogan, Bernice. My grandmother died but I won't forget her

Hoopes, Lyn Littlefield. Nana

Hurd, Edith Thacher. I dance in my red pajamas

Hutchins, Pat. Happy birthday, Sam

Isadora, Rachel. Jesse and Abe

Jarrell, Mary. The knee baby

Jeschke, Susan. Mia, Grandma and the genie

Kay, Helen. A stocking for a kitten

Kessler, Ethel. Grandpa Witch and the magic doobelator

Kirk, Barbara. Grandpa, me and our house in the tree

Knotts, Howard. Great-grandfather, the baby and me

Knox-Wagner, Elaine. My grandpa retired today

Kojima, Naomi. The flying grandmother

Kraus, Robert. Rebecca Hatpin

Kroll, Steven. If I could be my grandmother
  Toot! Toot!

Langner, Nola. Freddy my grandfather

Lapp, Eleanor. In the morning mist

Lasky, Kathryn. I have four names for my grandfather
  My island grandma

Lenski, Lois. Debbie and her grandma

Lexau, Joan M. Benjie
  Benjie on his own

Locker, Thomas. Where the river begins

Low, Alice. David's windows

Mahood, Kenneth. Why are there more questions than answers, Grandad?

Mayer, Mercer. Little Monster at work

Minarik, Else Holmelund. Little Bear's visit

Newman, Shirlee. Tell me, grandma; tell me, grandpa

Orbach, Ruth. Please send a panda

Parish, Peggy. Granny and the desperadoes
  Granny and the Indians
  Granny, the baby and the big gray thing

Paterson, Diane. Hey, cowboy!

Peavy, Linda. Allison's grandfather

Peck, Richard. Monster night at Grandma's house

Pomerantz, Charlotte. Buffy and Albert

Raynor, Dorka. Grandparents around the world

Rockwell, Anne F. When I go visiting

Rosen, Winifred. Henrietta and the gong from Hong Kong

Roth, Susan L. Patchwork tales

Schlein, Miriam. Go with the sun

Shulevitz, Uri. Dawn

Skofield, James. Snow country

Sonneborn, Ruth A. I love Gram

Stanovich, Betty Jo. Big boy, little boy

Steiner, Charlotte. Kiki and Muffy

Stevens, Margaret. When grandpa died

Stevenson, James. "Could be worse!"
  The great big especially beautiful Easter egg
  The terrible Halloween night
  We can't sleep
  What's under my bed?
  Worse than Willy!

Storr, Catherine. Hugo and his grandma

Swayne, Samuel F. Great-grandfather in the honey tree

Townsend, Maryann. Pop's secret

Turkle, Brinton. It's only Arnold

Udry, Janice May. Mary Jo's grandmother

Vigna, Judith. Everyone goes as a pumpkin
  Grandma without me

Wahl, Jan. The fishermen

Wallace, Ian. Chin Chiang and the dragon's dance

Walsh, Jill Paton. Lost and found

Williams, Barbara. Kevin's grandma

Williams, Vera B. Music, music for everyone

Wolf, Janet. The best present is me

Wood, Audrey. The napping house

Wood, Joyce. Grandmother Lucy goes on a picnic
  Grandmother Lucy in her garden

Yolen, Jane. No bath tonight

Zhitkov, Boris. How I hunted for the little fellows

Zolotow, Charlotte. My grandson Lew
  William's doll

Family life — mothers

Alda, Arlene. Sonya's mommy works

Asch, Frank. Bread and honey

Baker, Gayle. Special delivery

Bauer, Caroline Feller. My mom travels a lot

Blaine, Marge. The terrible thing that happened at our house

Carton, Lonnie Caming. Mommies

Cole, Babette. The trouble with mom

Family life — only child

Family life — sisters *see* Family life; Sibling rivalry

Family life — stepchildren *see* Divorce; Family life — step families

Family life — step families

Family life — stepparents *see* Divorce; Family life — step families

Farms

Baruch, Dorothy. Kappa's tug-of-war with the big brown horse

Bellville, Cheryl Walsh. Round-up

Benchley, Nathaniel. The strange disappearance of Arthur Cluck

Blades, Ann. Mary of mile 18

Bohanon, Paul. Golden Kate

Bonino, Louise. The cozy little farm

Brand, Millen. This little pig named Curly

Brenner, Barbara. Wagon wheels

Bright, Robert. Georgie

Brook, Judy. Tim mouse visits the farm

Brown, Margaret Wise. Big red barn
  The little farmer
  The summer noisy book

Browne, Caroline. Mrs. Christie's farmhouse

Bruna, Dick. Farmer John
  Little bird tweet

Budbill, David. Christmas tree farm

Bulla, Clyde Robert. Dandelion Hill

Bunting, Eve. Goose dinner
  Winter's coming

Burton, Marilee Robin. Aaron awoke

Carlson, Natalie Savage. Time for the white egret

Carrick, Donald. The deer in the pasture
  Harold and the giant knight

Caudill, Rebecca. A pocketful of cricket

Chaucer, Geoffrey. Chanticleer and the fox

Child, Lydia Maria. Over the river and through the wood

Cleary, Beverly. The hullabaloo ABC

Clewes, Dorothy. Hide and seek

Climo, Lindee. Chester's barn

Coats, Belle. Little maverick cow

Collier, Ethel. I know a farm

Cook, Bernadine. Looking for Susie

Dalgliesh, Alice. The little wooden farmer

Daniel, Doris Temple. Pauline and the peacock

De Angeli, Marguerite. Yonie Wondernose

Dennis, Wesley. Flip
  Flip and the cows

De Paola, Tomie. Country farm

Dewey, Ariane. Febold Feboldson

DiFiori, Lawrence. The farm

Domanska, Janina. The turnip

Duncan, Jane. Janet Reachfar and Chickabird

Dunn, Judy. The animals of Buttercup Farm
  The little lamb

Dunrea, Olivier. Eddy B, pigboy

Duvoisin, Roger Antoine. The crocodile in the tree
  Crocus
  Jasmine
  Our Veronica goes to Petunia's farm
  Petunia
  Petunia and the song
  Petunia, beware!
  Petunia, I love you
  Petunia's treasure
  Two lonely ducks
  Veronica
  Veronica and the birthday present

Ets, Marie Hall. Mister Penny
  Mr. Penny's race horse
  Farm house

Fatio, Louise. The red bantam

Fleischman, Paul. The animal hedge

Flora, James. Grandpa's farm

Freedman, Russell. Farm babies

Freschet, Berniece. Where's Henrietta's hen?

Gackenbach, Dick. Crackle, Gluck and the sleeping toad
  The pig who saw everything

Gammell, Stephen. Once upon MacDonald's farm

Greeley, Valerie. Farm animals

Green, Mary McBurney. Everybody has a house and everybody eats

Greenberg, Polly. Oh, Lord, I wish I was a buzzard

Gunthrop, Karen. Rina at the farm

Hader, Berta Hoerner. Cock-a-doodle doo

Hale, Kathleen. Orlando buys a farm

Hall, Donald. The ox-cart man

Hansen, Carla. Barnaby Bear vists the farm

Haseley, Dennis. The old banjo

Hawes, Judy. Fireflies in the night

Hurd, Edith Thacher. Under the lemon tree

Hutchins, Pat. Rosie's walk

Ipcar, Dahlov. Bright barnyard
  Brown cow farm
  Hard scrabble harvest
  One horse farm
  Ten big farms

Isenbart, Hans-Heinrich. Baby animals on the farm

Israel, Marion Louise. The tractor on the farm

Jacobs, Joseph. Hereafterthis

Kent, Jack. Little Peep

Koch, Dorothy Clarke. When the cows got out

Kwitz, Mary DeBall. Little chick's breakfast

Lapp, Eleanor. The mice came in early this year

Fathers *see* Family life — fathers

Fear *see* Emotions — fear

Feeling *see* Senses

Feelings *see* Emotions

Feet *see* Anatomy

Fighting *see* Behavior — fighting, arguing

Fingers *see* Anatomy

Finishing things *see* Character traits — completing things

Fire

Anderson, C W (Clarence Williams). Blaze and the forest fire

Augarde, Steve. Pig

Averill, Esther. When Jenny lost her scarf

Baker, Eugene. Fire

Barr, Jene. Fire snorkel number 7

Baumann, Kurt. Piro and the fire brigade

Beatty, Hetty Burlingame. Little Owl Indian

Belloc, Hilaire. Matilda who told lies and was burned to death

Bernstein, Margery. Coyote goes hunting for fire

Bester, Roger. Fireman Jim

Bible, Charles. Jennifer's new chair

Bond, Ruskin. Flames in the forest

Brenner, Barbara. Mr. Tall and Mr. Small

Brown, Margaret Wise. The little fireman

De Regniers, Beatrice Schenk. Willy O'Dwyer jumped in the fire

Du Bois, William Pène. Otto and the magic potatoes

Elliott, Dan. A visit to the Sesame Street firehouse

Fire

Firehouse

Gramatky, Hardie. Hercules

Greene, Graham. The little fire engine

Haines, Gail Kay. Fire

Kirn, Ann. The tale of a crocodile

Lawrence, John. Pope Leo's elephant

Mahood, Kenneth. The laughing dragon

Miklowitz, Gloria D. Save that raccoon!

Miles, Miska. The fox and the fire

Moskin, Marietta D. Lysbet and the fire kittens

Newton, James R. A forest is reborn

Quackenbush, Robert M. There'll be a hot time in the old town tonight

Spiegel, Doris. Danny and Company 92

Taylor, Mark. Henry explores the mountains

Ungerer, Tomi. Adelaide
  The Mellops strike oil

Fire engines *see* Careers — firefighters; Trucks

Firefighters *see* Careers — firefighters

Fireflies *see* Insects — fireflies

Fish

Aliki. The long lost coelacanth and other living fossils

Arnosky, Jim. A kettle of hawks, and other wildlife groups

Aruego, José. Pilyo the piranha

Balet, Jan B. Joanjo

Beisert, Heide Helene. Poor fish

Brice, Tony. The bashful goldfish

Broekel, Ray. Dangerous fish

Brown, Margaret Wise. The little fisherman

Bruna, Dick. The fish

Buck, Pearl S (Pearl Sydenstricker). The dragon fish

Coatsworth, Elizabeth. Under the green willow

Cole, Joanna. A fish hatches

Cook, Bernadine. The little fish that got away

Cooper, Elizabeth K. The fish from Japan

Damjan, Mischa. The little sea horse

Darby, Gene. What is a fish?

Eastman, David. What is a fish?

Friedman, Judi. The eels' strange journey

Hall, Bill. Fish tale

Hawes, Judy. Shrimps

Hogan, Paula Z. The salmon

Ipcar, Dahlov. The biggest fish in the sea

Jacobs, Francine. Barracuda

Kalan, Robert. Blue sea

Laird, Donivee Martin. The three little Hawaiian pigs and the magic shark

Lionni, Leo. Fish is fish
  Swimmy

Oxford Scientific Films. Jellyfish and other sea creatures
  The stickleback cycle

Palmer, Helen Marion. A fish out of water

Parnall, Peter. The great fish

Parry, Marian. King of the fish

Phleger, Fred B. Red Tag comes back

Ricciuti, Edward R. Donald and the fish that walked

Schatell, Brian. Midge and Fred

Selsam, Millicent E. A first look at sharks
  Plenty of fish

Seuss, Dr. McElligot's pool
  One fish, two fish, red fish, blue fish

Shaw, Evelyn S. Fish out of school

Turnage, Sheila. Trout the magnificent

Valens, Evans G. Wingfin and Topple

Waber, Bernard. Lorenzo

Waechter, Friedrich Karl. Three is company

Wezel, Peter. The good bird

Wildsmith, Brian. Brian Wildsmith's fishes
Wong, Herbert H. My goldfish
Wyse, Lois. Two guppies, a turtle and Aunt Edna
Yorinks, Arthur. Louis the fish

Fishermen see Careers — fishermen

Fishing see Sports — fishing

Flamingos see Birds — flamingos

Flattery see Character traits — flattery

Fleas see Insects — fleas

Flies see Insects — flies

Floods see Weather — floods

Flowers

Anno, Mitsumasa. The king's flower
Baker, Jeffrey J W. Patterns of nature
Barker, Cicely Mary. Berry flower fairies
  Blossom flower fairies
  Flower fairies of the seasons
  Spring flower fairies
  Summer flower fairies
Chapman, Carol. Barney Bipple's magic dandelions
Cooney, Barbara. Miss Ramphius
Denver, John. The children and the flowers
De Paola, Tomie. The legend of the bluebonnet
Ellentuck, Shan. A sunflower as big as the sun
Fisher, Aileen. And a sunflower grew
  Petals yellow and petals red
Givens, Janet Eaton. Something wonderful happened
Harper, Wilhelmina. The gunniwolf
Heilbroner, Joan. Robert the rose horse
Heller, Ruth. The reason for a flower
Ipcar, Dahlov. The land of flowers
Kirkpatrick, Rena K. Look at flowers
Lerner, Carol. Flowers of a woodland spring
Lobel, Arnold. The rose in my garden
Selsam, Millicent E. A first look at flowers
Slobodkina, Esphyr. Pinky and the petunias
Steig, William. Rotten island
Sugita, Yutaka. The flower family
Williams, Barbara. Hello, dandelions!

Flying see Activities — flying

Fog see Weather — fog

Fold out books see Format, unusual

Folk and fairy tales

Aardema, Verna. Bringing the rain to Kapiti Plain
  Half-a-ball-of-kenki
  Ji-nongo-nongo means riddles
  Oh, Kojo! How could you!
  The riddle of the drum
  The vingananee and the tree toad
  Who's in Rabbit's house?
  Why mosquitoes buzz in people's ears
Abisch, Roz. The clever turtle
  Mai-Ling and the mirror
  Sweet Betsy from Pike
Adshead, Gladys L. Brownies - hush!
Æsop. Æsop's fables, ill. by Gaynor Chapman
  Æsop's fables, ill. by Heidi Holder
  Æsop's fables, ill. by Nick Price
  Æsop's fables, ill. by Alice and Martin Provensen
  Æsop's fables, ill. by Helen Siegl
  The fables of Æsop
  The hare and the frogs
  The hare and the tortoise
  The lion and the mouse
  The miller, his son and their donkey
  Once in a wood
  Tales from Æsop
  Three fox fables
  The town mouse and the country mouse, ill. by Lorinda Bryan Cauley
  The town mouse and the country mouse, ill. by Paul Galdone
  The town mouse and the country mouse, ill. by Tom Garcia
Afanas'ev, Aleksandr. Russian folk tales
Alden, Laura. Learning about fairies
Aleichem, Sholom. Hannukah money
Alexander, Lloyd. Coll and his white pig
  The king's fountain
  The truthful harp
Alger, Leclaire. All in the morning early
  Always room for one more
Aliki. Diogenes
  The eggs
  George and the cherry tree
  The story of Johnny Appleseed
  Three gold pieces
  The twelve months
Allard, Harry. May I stay?
Ambrus, Victor G. The little cockerel
  The seven skinny goats
  The Sultan's bath
  The three poor tailors
Andersen, H C (Hans Christian). The emperor and the nightingale
  The emperor's new clothes, ill. by Pamela Baldwin-Ford

Chapman, Carol. The tale of Meshka the Kvetch

Chapman, Gaynor. The luck child

Chapman, Jean. Moon-Eyes

Charles Prince of Wales. The old man of Lochnagar

Charlip, Remy. Harlequin and the gift of many colors

Charlot, Martin. Felisa and the magic tikling bird

Chase, Catherine. The nightingale and the fool

Chase, Richard. Jack and the three sillies

Chaucer, Geoffrey. Chanticleer and the fox

Chicken Little. Chicken Licken
  Henny Penny, ill. by Paul Galdone
  Henny Penny, ill. by William Stobbs

Christensen, Jack. The forgotten rainbow

Christian, Mary Blount. April fool

Coatsworth, Elizabeth. The giant golden book of cat stories

Cocagnac, A M (Augustin Maurice). The three trees of the Samurai

Cohen, Barbara. The demon who would not die
  Here come the Purim players!

Cole, Joanna. Bony-legs
  Golly Gump swallowed a fly

Collodi, Carlo. The adventures of Pinocchio

Conger, Lesley. Tops and bottoms

Conover, Chris. The wizard's daughter

Coombs, Patricia. The magic pot
  Tilabel

Cooney, Barbara. Little brother and little sister

Cooper, Susan. The silver cow

Cormack, M Grant. Animal tales from Ireland

Coville, Bruce. Sarah and the dragon

Credle, Ellis. Big fraid, little fraid

Crompton, Anne Eliot. The lifting stone
  The winter wife

Crossley-Holland, Kevin. The green children
  The pedlar of Swaffham

Cummings, E E. Fairy tales

Daniels, Guy. The Tsar's riddles

Daugherty, Sonia. Vanka's donkey

Davis, Douglas F. The lion's tail

Dayrell, Elphinstone. Why the sun and the moon live in the sky

Demi. Under the shade of the mulberry tree

De Paola, Tomie. Fin M'Coul
  The legend of Old Befana
  The legend of the bluebonnet
  The mysterious giant of Barletta

The Prince of the Dolomites

De Regniers, Beatrice Schenk. Everyone is good for something
  Little Sister and the Month Brothers
  Red Riding Hood

Dewey, Ariane. Febold Feboldson
  The fish Peri
  Pecos Bill
  The thunder god's son

Dick Whittington and his cat. Dick Whittington, ill. by Edward Ardizonne
  Dick Whittington, ill. by Marcia Brown
  Dick Whittington, ill. by Antony Maitland
  Dick Whittington, ill. by Kurt Werth

Dobbs, Rose. More once-upon-a-time stories
  Once-upon-a-time story book

Domanska, Janina. The best of the bargain
  Busy Monday morning
  King Krakus and the dragon
  Look, there is a turtle flying
  Marek, the little fool
  Palmiero and the ogre
  A scythe, a rooster and a cat
  The tortoise and the tree
  The turnip
  What happens next?
  Why so much noise?

Dos Santos, Joyce Audy. The diviner
  Henri and the Loup-Garou

Du Bois, William Pène. The hare and the tortoise and the tortoise and the hare

Duff, Maggie. Dancing turtle
  The princess and the pumpkin
  Rum pum pum

Dukas, P (Paul Abraham). The sorcerer's apprentice

Elkin, Benjamin. The big jump and other stories
  The king's wish and other stories
  Six foolish fishermen
  Such is the way of the world
  The wisest man in the world

Elwell, Peter. The king of the pipers

Emberley, Barbara. One wide river to cross

Evans, Katherine. The boy who cried wolf
  A bundle of sticks
  The maid and her pail of milk
  The man, the boy and the donkey

Felton, Harold W. Pecos Bill and the mustang

Fiddle-i-fee

The firebird, ill. by Moira Kemp

The firebird, ill. by Boris Zvorykin

Little Red Riding Hood, ill. by Trina
Schart Hyman
Mother Holly
Mrs. Fox's wedding
The musicians of Bremen
Rapunzel, ill. by Julia Ash
Rapunzel, ill. by Bert Dodson
Rapunzel, ill. by Trina Schart Hyman
Rumpelstiltskin, ill. by Jacqueline Ayer
Rumpelstiltskin, ill. by Donna Diamond
Rumpelstiltskin, ill. by John Wallner
The seven ravens, ill. by Felix
Hoffmann
The seven ravens, ill. by Lisbeth
Zwerger
The shoemaker and the elves
The six swans
The sleeping beauty, ill. by Warwick
Hutton
The sleeping beauty, ill. by Trina
Schart Hyman
Snow White, ill. by Bernadette
Snow White, ill. by Trina Schart
Hyman
Snow White and Rose Red, ill. by
Adrienne Adams
Snow-White and Rose-Red, ill. by
Barbara Cooney
Snow White and Rose Red, ill. by John
Wallner
Snow White and the seven dwarfs, ill.
by Wanda Gág
The table, the donkey and the stick
Three Grimms' fairy tales
The twelve dancing princesses, ill. by
Dennis Hockerman
The twelve dancing princesses, ill. by
Errol LeCain
The twelve dancing princesses, ill. by
Uri Shulevitz
The valiant little tailor
The wolf and the seven kids
The wolf and the seven little kids
Gross, Michael. The fable of the fig tree
Gross, Ruth Belov. The girl who
wouldn't get married
Guy, Rosa. Mother crocodile
Hadithi, Mwenye. Greedy zebra
Hague, Kathleen. The man who kept
house
Haley, Gail E. A story, a story
Hall, Amanda. The gossipy wife
Hall, Malcolm. And then the mouse...
Hallinan, P K (Patrick K). I'm thankful
each day!
Hazen, Barbara Shook. The sorcerer's
apprentice
Heller, Linda. Alexis and the golden
ring
Hewett, Anita. The little white hen
High on a hill

Hill, Eric. Spot's birthday party
Where's Spot?
Hillert, Margaret. The funny baby
The magic beans
The three bears
The three goats
Hinojosa, Francisco. The old lady who
ate people
Hirsh, Marilyn. Captain Jiri and Rabbi
Jacob
One little goat
The history of Mother Twaddle and the
marvelous achievements of her son
Jack
Hobzek, Mildred. We came
a-marching...1, 2, 3
Hodges, Margaret. Saint George and the
dragon
Hoffmann, E T A. The nutcracker
Hogrogian, Nonny. The contest
Holland, Janice. You never can tell
Houston, James. Kiviok's magic journey
Hürlimann, Ruth. The proud white cat
Hush little baby
Hutton, Warwick. Beauty and the beast
The nose tree
Ichikawa, Satomi. A child's book of
seasons
Sun through small leaves
Iké, Jane Hori. A Japanese fairy tale
Illyés, Gyula. Matt the gooseherd
I'm mad at you
Isele, Elizabeth. The frog princess
Jack and the beanstalk, ill. by Lorinda
Bryan Cauley
Jack and the beanstalk, ill. by Ed Parker
Jack and the beanstalk, ill. by Tony Ross
Jack and the beanstalk, ill. by William
Stobbs
Jacobs, Joseph. The crock of gold
Hereafterthis
Hudden and Dudden and Donald
O'Neary
Johnny-cake, ill. by Emma Lillian
Brock
Johnny-cake, ill. by William Stobbs
Master of all masters
Old Mother Wiggle-Waggle
The three sillies
Jagendorf, Moritz A. Kwi-na the eagle
Jameson, Cynthia. The clay pot boy
The house of five bears
A January fog will freeze a hog
Jaquith, Priscilla. Bo Rabbit smart for
true
Johnson, Crockett. Harold's fairy tale
Jones, Olive. A treasure box of fairy
tales
Keats, Ezra Jack. John Henry

Kent, Jack. Jack Kent's happy-ever-after
   book
   Jack Kent's hokus pokus bedtime book
Kirn, Ann. The tale of a crocodile
Koenig, Marion. The tale of fancy
   Nancy
Kurtycz, Marcos. Tigers and opossums
La Fontaine, Jean de. The hare and the
   tortoise
   The lion and the rat
   The miller, the boy and the donkey
   The north wind and the sun
Langstaff, John M. Oh, a-hunting we
   will go
   Ol' Dan Tucker
   On Christmas day in the morning
   Over in the meadow
   Soldier, soldier, won't you marry me?
   The swapping boy
   The two magicians
Lazy Jack
Lee, Jeanne M. The legend of the milky
   way
Lenski, Lois. Susie Mariar
Lent, Blair. John Tabor's ride
Lexau, Joan M. Crocodile and hen
   It all began with a drip, drip, drip
Lipkind, William. The magic feather
   duster
The little red hen, ill. by Janina
   Domanska
The little red hen, ill. by Paul Galdone
The little red hen, ill. by Mel Pekarsky
The little red hen, ill. by Margot
   Zemach
Little Tuppen
Littlefield, William. The whiskers of Ho
   Ho
Löfgren, Ulf. The boy who ate more
   than the giant and other Swedish
   folktales
Lorenz, Lee. Big Gus and Little Gus
   Pinchpenny John
   Scornful Simkin
Luenn, Nancy. The dragon kite
MacBeth, George. Jonah and the Lord
McDermott, Beverly Brodsky. The
   crystal apple
   The Golem
McDermott, Gerald. Anansi the spider
   Arrow to the sun
   Daughter of earth
   The stonecutter
   The voyage of Osiris
MacDonald, George. The light princess
McFarland, John. The exploding frog
   and other fables from Æsop
McHale, Ethel Kharasch. Son of
   thunder
McKee, David. The man who was going
   to mind the house

McLenighan, Valjean. Turtle and rabbit
   What you see is what you get
   You are what you are
   You can go jump
Maestro, Giulio. The tortoise's tug of
   war
Magnus, Erica. Old Lars
Maitland, Antony. Idle Jack
Malcolmson, Anne. The song of Robin
   Hood
Martin, Bill (William Ivan). Sounds of
   laughter
Martin, Rafe. The hungry tigress
Matsuno, Masako. Taro and the bamboo
   shoot
Matsutani, Miyoko. The fisherman
   under the sea
   The witch's magic cloth
Mayer, Marianna. Beauty and the beast
   My first book of nursery tales
Merriam, Eve. Epaminondas
Miller, Edna. Mousekin's fables
Milne, A A (Alan Alexander). Prince
   Rabbit
Mirkovic, Irene. The greedy shopkeeper
Mobley, Jane. The star husband
Molarsky, Osmond. The peasant and
   the fly
Moncure, Jane Belk. The talking tabby
   cat
Moon, Dolly M. My very first book of
   cowboy songs
Morel, Eve. Fairy tales
   Fairy tales and fables
Mosel, Arlene. Tikki Tikki Tembo
Mother Goose. London Bridge is falling
   down, ill. by Ed Emberley
   London Bridge is falling down, ill. by
   Peter Spier
Ness, Evaline. The girl and the goatherd
Newton, Patricia Montgomery. The five
   sparrows
Nikly, Michelle. The princess on the nut
Nister, Ernest. Little tales from long ago
Odoyevsky, Vladimir. Old Father Frost
The old-fashioned children's storybook
The old woman and her pig
Opie, Iona Archibald. A nursery
   companion
Oram, Hiawyn. Skittlewonder and the
   wizard
Over in the meadow
A paper of pins
Parnall, Peter. The great fish
Parry, Marian. King of the fish
Parsons, Virginia. Pinocchio and
   Gepetto
   Pinocchio and the money tree
   Pinocchio goes on the stage
   Pinocchio plays truant
The peasant's pea patch

Perrault, Charles. Cinderella, ill. by
  Sheilah Beckett
Cinderella, ill. by Marcia Brown
Cinderella, ill. by Paul Galdone
Cinderella, ill. by Emanuele Luzzati
Cinderella, ill. by Phil Smith
Puss in boots, ill. by Marcia Brown
Puss in boots, ill. by Jean Claverle
Puss in boots, ill. by Hans Fischer
Puss in boots, ill. by Paul Galdone
Puss in boots, ill. by Julia Noonan
Puss in boots, ill. by Tony Ross
Puss in boots, ill. by William Stobbs
Puss in boots, ill. by Barry Wilkinson
The sleeping beauty
Phumla. Nomi and the magic fish
Plume, Ilse. The story of Befana
Polushkin, Maria. Bubba and Bubba
The little hen and the giant
Prather, Ray. The ostrich girl
The prince who knew his fate
Prokofiev, Sergei Sergeievitch. Peter and
  the wolf, ill. by Warren Chappell
Peter and the wolf, ill. by Frans
  Haacken
Peter and the wolf, ill. by Alan
  Howard
Peter and the wolf, ill. by Charles
  Mikolaycak
Peter and the wolf, ill. by Kozo
  Shimizu
Quackenbush, Robert M. Clementine
She'll be comin' 'round the mountain
Skip to my Lou
There'll be a hot time in the old town
  tonight
Quigley, Lillian Fox. The blind men and
  the elephant
Raphael, Elaine. Turnabout
Reesink, Marijke. The golden treasure
The princess who always ran away
Riordan, James. The three magic gifts
Robbins, Ruth. Baboushka and the three
  kings
How the first rainbow was made
Robinson, Adjai. Femi and old
  grandaddie
Rockwell, Anne F. Bafana
The old woman and her pig and 10
  other stories
Poor Goose
The three bears
Thump thump thump!
The wolf who had a wonderful dream
The wonderful eggs of Furicchia
Rogers, Margaret. Green is beautiful
Ronay, Jadja. Ginger
Rose, Anne. Akimba and the magic cow
Pot full of luck
Spider in the sky
The triumphs of Fuzzy Fogtop

Ross, Tony. The enchanted pig
The pied piper of Hamelin
Roughsey, Dick. The giant devil-dingo
Rounds, Glen. The boll weevil
Casey Jones
Sweet Betsy from Pike
Rudchenko, Ivan. Ivanko and the
  dragon
Rudolph, Marguerita. I am your
  misfortune
Sahagun, Bernardino de. Spirit child
San Souci, Robert D. Song of Sedna
Sawyer, Ruth. Journey cake, ho!
Say, Allen. Once under the cherry
  blossom tree
Scarry, Richard. Richard Scarry's animal
  nursery tales
Schatz, Letta. The extraordinary
  tug-of-war
Schiller, Barbara. The white rat's tale
Scribner, Charles. The devil's bridge
Seeger, Pete. The foolish frog
Seuling, Barbara. The teeny tiny woman
Severo, Emöke de Papp. The
  good-hearted youngest brother
Sewall, Marcia. The little wee tyke
The wee, wee mannie and the big, big
  coo
Shannon, George. The Piney Woods
  peddler
Shi, Zhang Xiu. Monkey and the white
  bone demon
Showalter, Jean B. The donkey ride
Shub, Elizabeth. Seeing is believing
Shulevitz, Uri. The treasure
Siberell, Anne. Whale in the sky
Siddiqui, Ashraf. Bhombal Dass, the
  uncle of lion
Sleator, William. The angry moon
Slobodkin, Louis. Colette and the
  princess
Spier, Peter. The Erie Canal
The legend of New Amsterdam
The squire's bride
Stalder, Valerie. Even the Devil is afraid
  of a shrew
Stan-Padilla, Viento. Dream Feather
Steptoe, John. The story of jumping
  mouse
Stevens, Bryna. Borrowed feathers and
  other fables
Still, James. Jack and the wonder beans
Tarrant, Margaret. Fairy tales
Taylor, Mark. The bold fisherman
Old Blue, you good dog you
Tempest, P. How the cock wrecked the
  manor
Thompson, Harwood. The witch's cat
The three bears, ill. by Paul Galdone
The three bears, ill. by Feodor
  Rojankovsky

The three bears. Goldilocks and the three bears
  The story of the three bears, ill. by L. Leslie Brooke
  The story of the three bears, ill. by William Stobbs
The three little pigs, ill. by Erik Blegvad
The three little pigs, ill. by Lorinda Bryan Cauley
The three little pigs, ill. by William Pène Du Bois
The three little pigs, ill. by Paul Galdone
The three little pigs, ill. by Rodney Peppé
The three little pigs, ill. by Irma Wilde
The three little pigs. The story of the three little pigs, ill. by L. Leslie Brooke
  The story of the three little pigs, ill. by William Stobbs
  The three pigs, ill. by Tony Ross
Tolstoï, Aleksei Nikolaevich. The great big enormous turnip
Tom Thumb. Grimm Tom Thumb
Tom Thumb, ill. by L. Leslie Brooke
Tom Thumb, ill. by Dennis Hockerman
Tom Thumb, ill. by Felix Hoffmann
Tom Thumb, ill. by Lidia Postma
Tom Thumb, ill. by William Wiesner
Tom Tit Tot
Towle, Faith M. The magic cooking pot
Toye, William. The fire stealer
Tresselt, Alvin R. The mitten
Tripp, Wallace. The tale of a pig
Tsultim, Yeshe. The mouse king
Turkle, Brinton. Deep in the forest
Turska, Krystyna. The magician of Cracow
  The woodcutter's duck
Van Woerkom, Dorothy. Alexandra the rock-eater
  The queen who couldn't bake gingerbread
  The rat, the ox and the zodiac
  Sea frog, city frog
  Tit for tat
Varga, Judy. The mare's egg
Walker, Barbara K. New patches for old
Walt Disney Productions. Walt Disney's Snow White and the seven dwarfs
Weiss, Harvey. The sooner hound
Werth, Kurt. Lazy Jack
Westerberg, Christine. The cap that mother made
Widdecombe Fair
Wildsmith, Brian. The true cross
Williams, Jay. Petronella
  The practical princess
  The surprising things Maui did
Winter, Jeanette. The girl and the moon man

Wolf, Ann. The rabbit and the turtle
Wolkstein, Diane. The banza
  The cool ride in the sky
  The magic wings
  White wave
Yagawa, Sumiko. The crane wife
Yashima, Tarō. Seashore story
Yolen, Jane. The hundredth dove
  Sleeping ugly
Young, Ed. The rooster's horns
  The terrible Nung Gwama
Zelinsky, Paul O. The maid and the mouse and the odd-shaped house
Zemach, Harve. Duffy and the devil
  Nail soup
Zemach, Kaethe. The beautiful rat
Zemach, Margot. It could always be worse
  Jake and Honeybunch go to heaven
  The little tiny woman
Zijlstra, Tjerk. Benny and his geese
Zola, Meguido. The dream of promise

Food

Adler, David A. Bunny rabbit rebus
Allamand, Pascale. Cocoa beans and daisies
Allen, Laura Jean. Rollo and Tweedy and the case of the missing cheese
Ambrus, Victor G. Country wedding
Armitage, Ronda. Ice creams for Rosie
  The lighthouse keeper's lunch
Aronin, Ben. The secret of the Sabbath fish
Asch, Frank. Good lemonade
  Moon bear
  Popcorn
Azarian, Mary. The tale of John Barleycorn or, From barley to beer
Barklem, Jill. The secret staircase
Barrett, Judi. An apple a day
  Cloudy with a chance of meatballs
Basso, Bill. The top of the pizzas
Baugh, Dolores M. Supermarket
Benchley, Nathaniel. Walter the homing pigeon
Benedictus, Roger. Fifty million sausages
Benjamin, Alan. Ribtickle Town
Berson, Harold. Pop! goes the turnip
  The rats who lived in the delicatessen
Beskow, Elsa Maartman. Peter in Blueberry Land
  Peter's adventures in Blueberry land
Bethell, Jean. Hooray for Henry
Bishop, Claire Huchet. Pancakes - Paris
Black, Irma Simonton. Is this my dinner?
Bolliger, Max. The giants' feast
  The golden apple
Boutell, Clarence Burley. The fat baron

Brandenberg, Franz. Fresh cider and apple pie

Brierley, Louise. King Lion and his cooks

Bright, Robert. Gregory, the noisiest and strongest boy in Grangers Grove

Brown, Judith Gwyn. Max and the truffle pig

Brown, Marc. Pickle things

Brown, Marcia. Stone soup

Bruna, Dick. The fish

Budd, Lillian. The pie wagon

Burch, Robert. The hunting trip

Burningham, John. Avocado baby
The cupboard

Burt, Olive. Let's find out about bread

Calhoun, Mary. Audubon cat
The hungry leprechaun

Carle, Eric. Pancakes, pancakes
Walter the baker

Cauley, Lorinda Bryan. Pease porridge hot

Cazet, Denys. Lucky me

Chalmers, Audrey. Hundreds and hundreds of pancakes

Coatsworth, Elizabeth. Under the green willow

Coontz, Otto. Starring Rosa

Croll, Carolyn. Too many babas

Degen, Bruce. Jamberry

De Paola, Tomie. Pancakes for breakfast
The popcorn book

Devlin, Wende. Old Witch and the polka-dot ribbon

Flory, Jane. We'll have a friend for lunch

Fontaine, Jan. The spaghetti tree

Gackenbach, Dick. Mother Rabbit's son Tom

Gág, Wanda. The funny thing

Galdone, Paul. The magic porridge pot

Gantschev, Ivan. RumpRump

Gibbons, Gail. The missing maple syrup sap mystery

The gingerbread boy, ill. by Paul Galdone

The gingerbread boy, ill. by Joan Elizabeth Goodman

The gingerbread boy, ill. by William Curtis Holdsworth

The gingerbread boy. The gingerbread man

Goodall, John S. The surprise picnic

Greene, Ellin. Princess Rosetta and the popcorn man
The pumpkin giant

Gunthrop, Karen. Adam and the wolf

Gurney, Nancy. The king, the mice and the cheese

Hale, Irina. Chocolate mouse and sugar pig

Hale, Linda. The glorious Christmas soup party

Heller, Linda. Lily at the table

Hellsing, Lennart. The wonderful pumpkin

Hirsh, Marilyn. Leela and the watermelon

Hitte, Kathryn. Mexicallie soup

Hoban, Russell. Bread and jam for Frances
Dinner at Alberta's

Holden, Edith. The hedgehog feast

Holl, Adelaide. Small Bear solves a mystery

Hughes, Peter. The emperor's oblong pancake
The king who loved candy

Hutchins, Pat. Don't forget the bacon!

Jack Sprat. The life of Jack Sprat, his wife and his cat

Jacobs, Joseph. Johnny-cake, ill. by Emma Lillian Brock
Johnny-cake, ill. by William Stobbs

Janice. Little Bear's pancake party
Little Bear's Sunday breakfast

Kahl, Virginia. The Duchess bakes a cake
The perfect pancake
Plum pudding for Christmas

Kantor, MacKinlay. The preposterous week

Kessler, Leonard P. Do you have any carrots?
Soup for the king

Kitt, Tamara. Sam and the impossible thing

Komoda, Beverly. Simon's soup

Kwitz, Mary DeBall. Little chick's breakfast

Lapp, Eleanor. The blueberry bears

Lasker, Joe. Lentil soup

Lemerise, Bruce. Sheldon's lunch

Levitin, Sonia. Nobody stole the pie

Lewin, Betsy. Animal snackers

Lindsey, Treska. When Batistine made bread

Lobel, Anita. The pancake

McCloskey, Robert. Blueberries for Sal

McKee, David. King Rollo and the bread

Manushkin, Fran. Moon dragon

Marshall, James. Miss Dog's Christmas
Yummers!

Mayer, Mercer. Frog goes to dinner

Murphey, Sara. The roly poly cookie

Nordqvist, Sven. Pancake pie

Orbach, Ruth. Apple pigs

Oxenbury, Helen. Eating out

Paterson, Diane. Eat

Petie, Haris. The seed the squirrel dropped

Rayner, Mary. Mrs. Pig's bulk buy
Retan, Walter. The steam shovel that wouldn't eat dirt
Rice, Eve. Sam who never forgets
Rockwell, Anne F. The Mother Goose cookie-candy book
  The wolf who had a wonderful dream
Rockwell, Harlow. My kitchen
Ross, Wilda S. What did the dinosaurs eat?
Schwalje, Marjory. Mr. Angelo
Seuss, Dr. Green eggs and ham
  Scrambled eggs super!
Sharmat, Marjorie Weinman. Nate the Great
  Nate the Great and the lost list
  Nate the Great and the phony clue
  Nate the Great goes undercover
Sharmat, Mitchell. Gregory, the terrible eater
Slobodkina, Esphyr. The wonderful feast
Slocum, Rosalie. Breakfast with the clowns
Spier, Peter. Food market
Stadler, John. Animal cafe
Stamaty, Mark Alan. Minnie Maloney and Macaroni
Stevenson, Jocelyn. Red and the pumpkins
Testa, Fulvio. The land where the ice cream grows
Thompson, Vivian Laubach. The horse that liked sandwiches
Towle, Faith M. The magic cooking pot
Van Woerkom, Dorothy. Alexandra the rock-eater
Vevers, Gwynne. Animals that store food
Wallner, Alexandra. Munch
Wasmuth, Eleanor. The picnic basket
Watanabe, Shigeo. What a good lunch!
Watson, Clyde. Tom Fox and the apple pie
Watson, Nancy Dingman. Sugar on snow
Williams, Gweneira Maureen. Timid Timothy, the kitten who learned to be brave
Winthrop, Elizabeth. Potbellied possums
Woolley, Catherine. The popcorn dragon
Young, Miriam Burt. The sugar mouse cake

Foolishness see Character traits — foolishness

Football see Sports — football

Foreign lands

Aleichem, Sholom. Hannukah money
Allen, Thomas B. Where children live
Anglund, Joan Walsh. Love one another
Baylor, Byrd. The way to start a day
Berg, Leila. Folk tales for reading and telling
Borchers, Elisabeth. Dear Sarah
Brann, Esther. 'Round the world
Bridgman, Elizabeth. How to travel with grownups
Bryson, Bernarda. The twenty miracles of Saint Nicolas
De Regniers, Beatrice Schenk. Little Sister and the Month Brothers
Domanska, Janina. Marek, the little fool
Douglas, Michael. Round, round world
Goffstein, M B (Marilyn Brooks). Across the sea
Otto, Svend. The giant fish and other stories
Robb, Brian. My grandmother's djinn
Sandin, Joan. The long way to a new land
Schulz, Charles M. Bon voyage, Charlie Brown (and don't come back!!)
Van Woerkom, Dorothy. Alexandra the rock-eater

Foreign lands — Africa

Aardema, Verna. Bringing the rain to Kapiti Plain
  Half-a-ball-of-kenki
  Ji-nongo-nongo means riddles
  Oh, Kojo! How could you!
  The vingananee and the tree toad
  Who's in Rabbit's house?
  Why mosquitoes buzz in people's ears
Abisch, Roz. The clever turtle
Adamson, Joy. Elsa
  Elsa and her cubs
  Pippa the cheetah and her cubs
Adoff, Arnold. Ma nDa La
Arkin, Alan. Black and white
Arnott, Kathleen. Spiders, crabs and creepy crawlers
Aruego, José. We hide, you seek
Bemelmans, Ludwig. Rosebud
Bernheim, Marc. In Africa
  A week in Aya's world
Bernstein, Margery. The first morning
Berson, Harold. Kassim's shoes
  Why the jackal won't speak to the hedgehog
Bess, Clayton. The truth about the moon
Bible, Charles. Hamdaani
Bond, Jean Carey. A is for Africa
Borden, Beatrice Brown. Wild animals of Africa

Bryan, Ashley. Beat the story-drum, pum-pum
Carrick, Malcolm. I can squash elephants!
Cendrars, Blaise. Shadow
Cole, Babette. Nungu and the elephant
Nungu and the hippopotamus
Davis, Douglas F. The lion's tail
Dayrell, Elphinstone. Why the sun and the moon live in the sky
De Paola, Tomie. Bill and Pete
Domanska, Janina. The tortoise and the tree
Du Bois, William Pène. Otto in Africa
Economakis, Olga. Oasis of the stars
Elkin, Benjamin. Such is the way of the world
Fatio, Louise. The happy lion in Africa
Feelings, Muriel. Jambo means hello
Menjo means one
Fournier, Catharine. The coconut thieves
Graham, Lorenz B. Song of the boat
Greenfield, Eloise. Africa dream
Guy, Rosa. Mother crocodile
Hadithi, Mwenye. Greedy zebra
Haley, Gail E. A story, a story
Holding, James. The lazy little Zulu
Kirn, Ann. The tale of a crocodile
Laskowski, Jerzy. Master of the royal cats
Lewin, Hugh. Jafta
Jafta and the wedding
Jafta - the journey
Jafta - the town
Jafta's father
Jafta's mother
Lexau, Joan M. Crocodile and hen
McDermott, Gerald. Anansi the spider
Musgrove, Margaret. Ashanti to Zulu
Phumla. Nomi and the magic fish
Prather, Ray. The ostrich girl
Purcell, John Wallace. African animals
Robinson, Adjai. Femi and old grandaddie
Rose, Anne. Akimba and the magic cow
Pot full of luck
Routh, Jonathan. The Nuns go to Africa
Schatz, Letta. The extraordinary tug-of-war
Ward, Leila. I am eyes, ni macho
Zaslavsky, Claudia. Count on your fingers African style

Foreign lands — Antarctic

Bonners, Susan. A penguin year

Foreign lands — Arabia

Alexander, Sue. Nadia the willful

Arabian Nights. Arabian Nights entertainments

Foreign lands — Arctic

Bonsall, Crosby Newell. What spot?

Foreign lands — Armenia

Hogrogian, Nonny. The contest

Foreign lands — Australia

Paterson, Andrew Barton. Mulga Bill's bicycle
Waltzing Matilda
Pittaway, Margaret. The rainforest children
Roughsey, Dick. The giant devil-dingo
Wagner, Jenny. The bunyip of Berkeley's Creek

Foreign lands — Austria

Kahl, Virginia. Away went Wolfgang

Foreign lands — Bali

Cox, David. Ayu and the perfect moon

Foreign lands — Bavaria *see* Foreign lands — Austria; Foreign lands — Germany

Foreign lands — Canada

Blades, Ann. Mary of mile 18
Bonne, Rose. I know an old lady
Climo, Lindee. Chester's barn
Dos Santos, Joyce Audy. The diviner
Henri and the Loup-Garou
Holling, Holling C (Holling Clancy). Paddle-to-the-sea
Moak, Allan. A big city ABC
Ward, Lynd. The biggest bear
Nic of the woods
Woolaver, Lance. Christmas with the rural mail

Foreign lands — Caribbean Islands

Anderson, Lonzo. The day the hurricane happened
Izzard
Dobrin, Arnold Jack. Josephine's 'magination
George, Jean Craighead. The wentletrap trap
Ness, Evaline. Josefina February

Foreign lands — China

Abisch, Roz. Mai-Ling and the mirror

Andersen, H C (Hans Christian). The emperor and the nightingale
The emperor's nightingale
The nightingale, ill. by Harold Berson
The nightingale, ill. by Nancy Ekholm Burkert
Behrens, June. Soo Ling finds a way
Bishop, Claire Huchet. The five Chinese brothers
Bright, Robert. The travels of Ching
Bro, Marguerite H. The animal friends of Peng-u
Buck, Pearl S (Pearl Sydenstricker). The Chinese story teller
The dragon fish
Cheng, Hou-Tien. The Chinese New Year
Demi. The adventures of Marco Polo
Under the shade of the mulberry tree
Fairclough, Chris. Take a trip to China
Flack, Marjorie. The story about Ping
Foley, Bernice Williams. A walk among clouds
Fribourg, Marjorie G. Ching-Ting and the ducks
Fyson, Nance Lui. A family in China
Handforth, Thomas. Mei Li
High on a hill
Holland, Janice. You never can tell
Lee, Jeanne M. The legend of the milky way
Littlefield, William. The whiskers of Ho Ho
Lobel, Arnold. Ming Lo moves the mountain
Miles, Miska. The pointed brush...
Mosel, Arlene. Tikki Tikki Tembo
Perkins, Al. Tubby and the lantern
Shi, Zhang Xiu. Monkey and the white bone demon
Skipper, Mervyn. The fooling of King Alexander
Slobodkin, Louis. Moon Blossom and the golden penny
Stafford, Kay. Ling Tang and the lucky cricket
Stone, Jon. Big Bird in China
Van Woerkom, Dorothy. The rat, the ox and the zodiac
Wiese, Kurt. Fish in the air
Williams, Jay. Everyone knows what a dragon looks like
Wolkstein, Diane. The magic wings
White wave
Yolen, Jane. The emperor and the kite
The seeing stick
Young, Ed. The rooster's horns
The terrible Nung Gwama
Young, Evelyn. The tale of Tai Wu and Lu and Li

Foreign lands — Czechoslovakia

Bolliger, Max. The fireflies
Ginsburg, Mirra. How the sun was brought back to the sky
Marshak, Samuel. The Month-Brothers

Foreign lands — Denmark

Andersen, H C (Hans Christian). The snow queen
Bason, Lillian. Those foolish Molboes!
Blegvad, Lenore. Mr. Jensen and cat
Bodecker, N M (Nils Mogens). "It's raining," said John Twaining
Brande, Marlie. Sleepy Nicholas
A Christmas book
Conover, Chris. The wizard's daughter
Coombs, Patricia. The magic pot
Kent, Jack. Hoddy doddy
Lobel, Anita. King Rooster, Queen Hen

Foreign lands — Ecuador

Bemelmans, Ludwig. Quito express

Foreign lands — Egypt

Aliki. Mummies made in Egypt
Goodenow, Earle. The last camel
Laskowski, Jerzy. Master of the royal cats
McDermott, Gerald. The voyage of Osiris
The prince who knew his fate

Foreign lands — England

Ahlberg, Allan. Cops and robbers
Ambler, Christopher Gifford. Ten little foxhounds
Anno, Mitsumasa. Anno's Britain
Ardizzone, Edward. Lucy Brown and Mr. Grimes
Armitage, Ronda. Don't forget, Matilda
Azarian, Mary. The tale of John Barleycorn or, From barley to beer
Beatty, Hetty Burlingame. Moorland pony
Belting, Natalia Maree. Christmas folk
Summer's coming in
Bemelmans, Ludwig. Madeline in London
Bennett, Olivia. A Turkish afternoon
Bentley, Anne. The Groggs' day out
The Groggs have a wonderful summer
Bond, Michael. Paddington at the circus
Paddington at the seaside
Paddington at the tower
Paddington's lucky day
Brown, Ruth. A dark, dark tale
Burningham, John. Borka

Calhoun, Mary. The pixy and the lazy
housewife
The witch's pig
Christian, Mary Blount. April fool
Cole, Brock. The king at the door
Conger, Lesley. Tops and bottoms
Cooper, Susan. The silver cow
Cressey, James. The dragon and
George
Crompton, Margaret. The house where
Jack lives
Crossley-Holland, Kevin. The green
children
Davidson, Amanda. Teddy at the
seashore
Davis, Reda. Martin's dinosaur
Dick Whittington and his cat. Dick
Whittington, ill. by Edward Ardizzone
Dick Whittington, ill. by Marcia
Brown
Dick Whittington, ill. by Antony
Maitland
Dick Whittington, ill. by Kurt Werth
Dines, Glen. Gilly and the wicharoo
Drummond, Violet H. The flying
postman
Emecheta, Buchi. Nowhere to play
Fairclough, Chris. Take a trip to
England
Freeman, Don. The guard mouse
Will's quill
Freschet, Berniece. Bernard of Scotland
Yard
Gauch, Patricia Lee. On to Widecombe
Fair
Gerrard, Jean. Matilda Jane
Goodall, John S. An Edwardian
Christmas
An Edwardian summer
The story of an English village
Gramatky, Hardie. Little Toot on the
Thames
Haley, Gail E. The post office cat
Herrmann, Frank. The giant Alexander
The giant Alexander and the circus
Ivory, Lesley Anne. A day in London
Jacobs, Joseph. The crock of gold
Keeping, Charles. Alfie finds the other
side of the world
Through the window
Lawrence, John. The giant of Grabbist
Lodge, Bernard. Door to door
Menter, Ian. Carnival
Mother Goose. London Bridge is falling
down, ill. by Ed Emberley
London Bridge is falling down, ill. by
Peter Spier
Oakley, Graham. The church cat abroad
The church mice and the moon
The church mice at bay
The church mice spread their wings

The church mouse
Oldfield, Pamela. Melanie Brown climbs
a tree
Oxenbury, Helen. The queen and Rosie
Randall
Ross, Diana. The story of the little red
engine
Seuling, Barbara. The teeny tiny woman
Sewall, Marcia. The little wee tyke
Shulman, Milton. Prep, the little pigeon
of Trafalgar Square
Solomon, Joan. A present for Mum
Thompson, Harwood. The witch's cat
Widdecombe Fair
Willard, Barbara. To London! To
London!
Wolff, Ashley. The bells of London
Wood, Joyce. Grandmother Lucy in her
garden
Worthington, Phoebe. Teddy bear baker
Teddy bear coalman
Zemach, Harve. Duffy and the devil

Foreign lands — Europe

Bornstein, Ruth Lercher. The dancing
man
Sopko, Eugeh. Townsfolk and
countryfolk

Foreign lands — France

Allen, Laura Jean. Rollo and Tweedy
and the case of the missing cheese
Angelo, Nancy Carolyn Harrison.
Camembert
Bemelmans, Ludwig. Madeline
Madeline and the bad hat
Madeline and the gypsies
Madeline's rescue
Bergere, Thea. Paris in the rain with
Jean and Jacqueline
Berson, Harold. Barrels to the moon
Charles and Claudine
How the devil got his due
Joseph and the snake
Bishop, Claire Huchet. Pancakes - Paris
The truffle pig
Bring a torch, Jeannette, Isabella
Brown, Judith Gwyn. Max and the
truffle pig
Brunhoff, Jean de. The story of Babar,
the little elephant
Charlip, Remy. Harlequin and the gift
of many colors
Daudet, Alphonse. The brave little goat
of Monsieur Séguin
Dauphin, Francine Legrand. A French
A. B. C.
Diska, Pat. Andy says ... Bonjour!

Dumas, Philippe. Caesar, cock of the
    village
  Laura loses her head
  The story of Edward
Fatio, Louise. The happy lion
  The happy lion and the bear
  The happy lion in Africa
  The happy lion roars
  The happy lion's quest
  The happy lion's rabbits
  The happy lion's treasure
  The three happy lions
Fender, Kay. Odette!
Froment, Eugène. The story of a round
    loaf
Harris, Leon A. The great picture
    robbery
Hautzig, Esther. At home
  In the park
Ichikawa, Satomi. Suzanne and Nicholas
    at the market
  Suzanne and Nicholas in the garden
Joslin, Sesyle. Baby elephant's trunk
Klein, Leonore. Henri's walk to
    Paris
Lubell, Winifred. Rosalie, the bird
    market turtle
Marokvia, Merelle. A French school for
    Paul
Meddaugh, Susan. Maude and Claude
    go abroad
Moore, Lilian. Papa Albert
Napoli, Guillier. Adventure of Mont
    Saint Michel
Rider, Alex. A la ferme. At the farm
  Chez nous. At our house
Rockwell, Anne F. Poor Goose
  The wolf who had a wonderful dream
Schiller, Barbara. The white rat's tale
Scribner, Charles. The devil's bridge
Seignobosc, Françoise. The big rain
  Biquette, the white goat
  Chouchou
  Jeanne-Marie at the fair
  Jeanne-Marie counts her sheep
  Jeanne-Marie in gay Paris
  Minou
  Noël for Jeanne-Marie
  Springtime for Jeanne-Marie
Shecter, Ben. Partouche plants a seed
Slobodkin, Louis. Colette and the
    princess
Titus, Eve. Anatole
  Anatole and the cat
  Anatole and the piano
  Anatole and the Pied Piper
  Anatole and the poodle
  Anatole and the robot
  Anatole and the thirty thieves
  Anatole and the toyshop
  Anatole over Paris

Ungerer, Tomi. Adelaide
  The beast of Monsieur Racine
Vacheron, Edith. Here is Henri!
Weelen, Guy. The little red train

Foreign lands — Germany

Allard, Harry. May I stay?
Attenberger, Walburga. The little man
    in winter
  Who knows the little man?
Bechstein, Ludwig. The rabbit catcher
    and other fairy tales
Browning, Robert. The pied piper of
    Hamelin
Calhoun, Mary. The thieving dwarfs
Coombs, Patricia. Tilabel
Cooney, Barbara. Little brother and
    little sister
Fairclough, Chris. Take a trip to West
    Germany
Grimm, Jacob. The elves and the
    shoemaker
  The shoemaker and the elves
Harper, Wilhelmina. The gunniwolf
Hürlimann, Ruth. The proud white cat
Kahl, Virginia. Droopsi
  Maxie
Morgenstern, Elizabeth. The little
    gardeners
Ross, Tony. The pied piper of Hamelin
Spang, Günter. Clelia and the little
    mermaid
Van Woerkom, Dorothy. The queen
    who couldn't bake gingerbread

Foreign lands — Greece

Aliki. Diogenes
  The eggs
  Three gold pieces
  The twelve months
Anderson, Lonzo. Arion and the
    dolphins
Brown, Marcia. Tamarindo!
Delton, Judy. My Uncle Nikos
Walker, Barbara K. Pigs and pirates

Foreign lands — Greenland

Hertza, Ole. Tobias catches trout
  Tobias goes ice fishing
  Tobias goes seal hunting
  Tobias has a birthday

Foreign lands — Guyana

Agard, John. Dig away two-hole Tim

Foreign lands — Holland

Bouhuys, Mies. The lady of Stavoren
Bromhall, Winifred. Johanna arrives

Chasek, Judith. Have you seen
  Wilhelmina Krumpf?
Fairclough, Chris. Take a trip to
  Holland
Green, Norma B. The hole in the dike
Howells, Mildred. The woman who lived
  in Holland
Krasilovsky, Phyllis. The cow who fell in
  the canal
Reesink, Marijke. The golden treasure
Van Stockum, Hilda. A day on skates

Foreign lands — Hungary

Ambrus, Victor G. Brave soldier
  Janosch
  The three poor tailors
Brown, Margaret Wise. Wheel on the
  chimney
Ginsburg, Mirra. Two greedy bears
The good-hearted youngest brother
Illyés, Gyula. Matt the gooseherd
Severo, Emöke de Papp. The
  good-hearted youngest brother
Surany, Anico. Kati and Kormos
Varga, Judy. Janko's wish

Foreign lands — India

Alan, Sandy. The plaid peacock
Ambrus, Victor G. The Sultan's bath
Bang, Betsy. The cucumber stem
  The old woman and the red pumpkin
  The old woman and the rice thief
  Tutuni the tailor bird
Bannerman, Helen. Sambo and the
  twins
  The story of little black Sambo
Bond, Ruskin. Flames in the forest
Brown, Marcia. The blue jackal
  Once a mouse...
Cassedy, Sylvia. Moon-uncle,
  moon-uncle
Cathon, Laura E. Tot Botot and his
  little flute
Chase, Catherine. The nightingale and
  the fool
Domanska, Janina. Why so much noise?
Duff, Maggie. Rum pum pum
Gobhai, Mehlli. Lakshmi, the water
  buffalo who wouldn't
  Usha, the mouse-maiden
Hirsh, Marilyn. Leela and the
  watermelon
Kipling, Rudyard. The miracle of the
  mountain
Lexau, Joan M. It all began with a drip,
  drip, drip
Papas, William. Taresh the tea planter
Quigley, Lillian Fox. The blind men and
  the elephant
Rockwell, Anne F. The stolen necklace

Singh, Jacquelin. Fat Gopal
Slobodkin, Louis. The polka-dot goat
Towle, Faith M. The magic cooking pot
Trez, Denise. Maila and the flying
  carpet
Villarejo, Mary. The tiger hunt
Wahl, Jan. Tiger watch
Ward, Nanda Weedon. The elephant
  that ga-lumphed

Foreign lands — Ireland

Balian, Lorna. Leprechauns never lie
Bromhall, Winifred. Bridget's growing
  day
Bunting, Eve. Clancy's coat
Calhoun, Mary. The hungry leprechaun
Cormack, M Grant. Animal tales from
  Ireland
De Paola, Tomie. Fin M'Coul
Jacobs, Joseph. Hudden and Dudden
  and Donald O'Neary
Kennedy, Richard. The leprechaun's
  story
Parker, Dorothy D. Liam's catch
What do you feed your donkey on?
Zimelman, Nathan. To sing a song as
  big as Ireland

Foreign lands — Israel

Adler, David A. A picture book of Israel
Allstrom, Elizabeth C. Songs along the
  way
Brin, Ruth F. David and Goliath
  The story of Esther
Elkin, Benjamin. The wisest man in the
  world
Fairclough, Chris. Take a trip to Israel

Foreign lands — Italy

Androcles and the lion
Anno, Mitsumasa. Anno's Italy
Atene, Ann. The golden guitar
Basile, Giambattista. Petrosinella
Bettina (Bettina Ehrlich). Pantaloni
Bowden, Joan Chase. The bean boy
Brown, Marcia. Felice
Cauley, Lorinda Bryan. The goose and
  the golden coins
Chafetz, Henry. The legend of Befana
Chapman, Jean. Moon-Eyes
De Paola, Tomie. The clown of God
  The legend of Old Befana
  The mysterious giant of Barletta
  The Prince of the Dolomites
Fairclough, Chris. Take a trip to Italy
Galdone, Paul. Androcles and the lion
Plume, Ilse. The story of Befana
Politi, Leo. Little Leo
Priolo, Pauline. Piccolina and the Easter
  bells

Rockwell, Anne F. The wonderful eggs
of Furicchia
Seidler, Rosalie. Grumpus and the
Venetian cat
Titus, Eve. Anatole in Italy
Ungerer, Tomi. The hat

Foreign lands — Japan

Ashby, Gwynneth. Take a trip to Japan
Bang, Molly. Dawn
Bartoli, Jennifer. Snow on bear's nose
Baruch, Dorothy. Kappa's tug-of-war
with the big brown horse
Battles, Edith. What does the rooster
say, Yoshio?
Bunting, Eve. Magic and the night river
Cocagnac, A M (Augustin Maurice). The
three trees of the Samurai
Creekmore, Raymond. Fujio
Damjan, Mischa. The little prince and
the tiger cat
DeForest, Charlotte B. The prancing
pony
Dines, Glen. A tiger in the cherry tree
Don't tell the scarecrow
Fifield, Flora. Pictures for the palace
Fujita, Tamao. The boy and the bird
Gackenbach, Dick. The perfect mouse
Garrison, Christian. The dream eater
Heller, George. Hiroshi's wonderful kite
Iké, Jane Hori. A Japanese fairy tale
Laurin, Anne. Perfect crane
Lifton, Betty Jean. Joji and the
Amanojaku
Joji and the dragon
The many lives of Chio and Goro
The rice-cake rabbit
Luenn, Nancy. The dragon kite
McDermott, Gerald. The stonecutter
Matsuno, Masako. A pair of red clogs
Taro and the bamboo shoot
Taro and the Tofu
Matsutani, Miyoko. The fisherman
under the sea
The witch's magic cloth
Matsutani, Miyoko. How the withered
trees blossomed
Mosel, Arlene. The funny little woman
Nakatani, Chiyoko. Fumio and the
dolphins
Newton, Patricia Montgomery. The five
sparrows
Roy, Ronald. A thousand pails of water
Sasaki, Jeannie. Chōchō is for butterfly
Say, Allen. The bicycle man
Once under the cherry blossom tree
Slobodkin, Louis. Yasu and the
strangers
Uchida, Yoshiko. Sumi's prize
Sumi's special happening

Van Woerkom, Dorothy. Sea frog, city
frog
Yagawa, Sumiko. The crane wife
Yashima, Mitsu. Plenty to watch
Yashima, Tarō. Crow boy
The village tree

Foreign lands — Korea

Fregosi, Claudia. The pumpkin sparrow
Parry, Marian. King of the fish

Foreign lands — Lapland

Aulaire, Ingri Mortenson d'. Children of
the northlights
Borg, Inga. Plupp builds a house
Lindman, Maj. Snipp, Snapp, Snurr and
the red shoes
McHale, Ethel Kharasch. Son of
thunder
Stalder, Valerie. Even the Devil is afraid
of a shrew

Foreign lands — Lithuania

Rudolph, Marguerita. I am your
misfortune

Foreign lands — Malaysia

Kaye, Geraldine. The sea monkey

Foreign lands — Mexico

Aardema, Verna. The riddle of the
drum
Balet, Jan B. The fence
Bannon, Laura. Hat for a hero
Manuela's birthday
Watchdog
Blackmore, Vivien. Why corn is golden
Crane, Alan. Pepita bonita
De Gerez, Toni. My song is a piece of
jade
De Paola, Tomie. The Lady of
Guadalupe
Ets, Marie Hall. Nine days to Christmas
Everton, Macduff. El circo magico
modelo
Fraser, James Howard. Los Posadas
Grifalconi, Ann. The toy trumpet
Hader, Berta Hoerner. The story of
Pancho and the bull with the crooked
tail
Hinojosa, Francisco. The old lady who
ate people
Hitte, Kathryn. Mexicallie soup
Kent, Jack. The Christmas piñata
Kurtycz, Marcos. Tigers and opossums
Lewis, Thomas P. Hill of fire
Martin, Bill (William Ivan). My days are
made of butterflies
Miles, Miska. Friend of Miguel

Morrow, Elizabeth Cutter. The painted
pig
Politi, Leo. Lito and the clown
Rosa
Sahagun, Bernardino de. Spirit child
Ungerer, Tomi. Orlando, the brave
vulture

Foreign lands — New Guinea

Anderson, Robin. Sinabouda Lily

Foreign lands — Norway

Allard, Harry. May I stay?
Aulaire, Ingri Mortenson d'. Ola
The terrible troll-bird
Benchley, Nathaniel. Snorri and the
strangers
Grieg, E H (Edvard Hagerup). E. H.
Grieg's Peer Gynt
Hague, Kathleen. The man who kept
house
Magnus, Erica. Old Lars
The squire's bride
Wiesner, William. Happy-Go-Lucky
Turnabout

Foreign lands — Pakistan

Siddiqui, Ashraf. Bhombal Dass, the
uncle of lion

Foreign lands — Panama

Janosch. The trip to Panama

Foreign lands — Persia

Foley, Bernice Williams. The gazelle and
the hunter

Foreign lands — Peru

Dewey, Ariane. The thunder god's son

Foreign lands — Philippines

Aruego, José. A crocodile's tale
Look what I can do
Charlot, Martin. Felisa and the magic
tikling bird

Foreign lands — Poland

Adler, David A. The children of Chelm
Bernhard, Josephine Butkowska.
Lullaby
Nine cry-baby dolls
Din dan don, it's Christmas
Domanska, Janina. The best of the
bargain
Busy Monday morning
King Krakus and the dragon
Look, there is a turtle flying

Turska, Krystyna. The magician of
Cracow
The woodcutter's duck

Foreign lands — Portugal

Balet, Jan B. The gift
Joanjo

Foreign lands — Puerto Rico

Belpré, Pura. Dance of the animals
Perez and Martina
Martel, Cruz. Yagua days

Foreign lands — Russia

Afanas'ev, Aleksandr. Russian folk tales
Beim, Lorraine. Sasha and the samovar
Bider, Djemma. The buried treasure
Black, Algernon D. The woman of the
wood
Brown, Marcia. The neighbors
Stone soup
Campbell, M Rudolph. The talking
crocodile
Cohen, Barbara. The demon who would
not die
Cole, Joanna. Bony-legs
Daniels, Guy. The Tsar's riddles
Daugherty, Sonia. Vanka's donkey
De Regniers, Beatrice Schenk. Everyone
is good for something
Domanska, Janina. A scythe, a rooster
and a cat
The turnip
The firebird, ill. by Boris Zvorykin
Francis, Frank. Natasha's new doll
Fregosi, Claudia. Snow maiden
Galdone, Paul. A strange servant
Ginsburg, Mirra. The fisherman's son
The fox and the hare
Pampalche of the silver teeth
The strongest one of all
Which is the best place?
Hall, Amanda. The gossipy wife
Hautzig, Esther. At home
In the park
Heller, Linda. Alexis and the golden
ring
Isele, Elizabeth. The frog princess
Jameson, Cynthia. The clay pot boy
The house of five bears
McDermott, Beverly Brodsky. The
crystal apple
Marshak, Samuel. The tale of a hero
nobody knows
Odoyevsky, Vladimir. Old Father Frost
The peasant's pea patch
Polushkin, Maria. The little hen and the
giant

Prokofiev, Sergei Sergeievitch. Peter and
the wolf, ill. by Warren Chappell
Peter and the wolf, ill. by Frans
Haacken
Peter and the wolf, ill. by Alan
Howard
Peter and the wolf, ill. by Charles
Mikolaycak
Peter and the wolf, ill. by Kozo
Shimizu
Robbins, Ruth. Baboushka and the three
kings
Slobodkina, Esphyr. Boris and his
balalaika
Tolstoĭ, Alekseĭ Nikolaevich. The great
big enormous turnip
Varga, Judy. The mare's egg
Winter, Jeanette. The girl and the moon
man
Wiseman, Bernard. Little new kangaroo
Zhitkov, Boris. How I hunted for the
little fellows
Zimmerman, Andrea Griffing. Yetta, the
trickster

Foreign lands — Scotland

Alger, Leclaire. All in the morning early
Always room for one more
Kellyburn Braes
Blegvad, Erik. Burnie's hill
Calhoun, Mary. The runaway brownie
Cate, Rikki. A cat's tale
Charles Prince of Wales. The old man
of Lochnagar
Duncan, Jane. Janet Reachfar and
Chickabird
Fern, Eugene. The most frightened
hero
Hedderwick, Mairi. Katie Morag
delivers the mail
Jeffers, Susan. Wild Robin
Leaf, Munro. Wee Gillis
Lewis, Naomi. Puffin
Sewall, Marcia. The wee, wee mannie
and the big, big coo

Foreign lands — Siam *see* Foreign lands
— Thailand

Foreign lands — South America

Aruego, José. Pilyo the piranha
Frasconi, Antonio. The snow and the
sun, la nieve y el sol
Gramatky, Hardie. Bolivar
Maestro, Giulio. The tortoise's tug of
war
Maiorano, Robert. Francisco
Rockwell, Anne F. The good llama
Sotomayor, Antonio. Khasa goes to the
fiesta

Surany, Anico. Ride the cold wind

Foreign lands — South Sea Islands

Mordvinoff, Nicolas. Coral Island

Foreign lands — Spain

Duff, Maggie. The princess and the
pumpkin
García Lorca, Federico. The Lieutenant
Colonel and the gypsy
Hautzig, Esther. At home
In the park
Leaf, Munro. The story of Ferdinand
the bull
Oleson, Claire. For Pipita, an orange
tree

Foreign lands — Sweden

Beskow, Elsa Maartman. Children of the
forest
Pelle's new suit
Peter in Blueberry Land
Peter's adventures in Blueberry land
Lindgren, Astrid. Christmas in noisy
village
Christmas in the stable
The tomten
The tomten and the fox
Lindman, Maj. Flicka, Ricka, Dicka and
a little dog
Flicka, Ricka, Dicka and the new
dotted dress
Flicka, Ricka, Dicka bake a cake
Sailboat time
Snipp, Snapp, Snurr and the buttered
bread
Snipp, Snapp, Snurr and the magic
horse
Snipp, Snapp, Snurr and the reindeer
Snipp, Snapp, Snurr and the seven
dogs
Snipp, Snapp, Snurr and the yellow
sled
Peterson, Hans. Erik and the Christmas
horse
Westerberg, Christine. The cap that
mother made
Zemach, Harve. Nail soup

Foreign lands — Switzerland

Allamand, Pascale. Cocoa beans and
daisies
Baumann, Kurt. Piro and the fire
brigade
Bawden, Nina. William Tell
Carigiet, Alois. The pear tree, the birch
tree and the barberry bush
Chönz, Selina. A bell for Ursli
Florina and the wild bird

The snowstorm
Freeman, Don. Ski pup

Foreign lands — Thailand

Ayer, Jacqueline. Nu Dang and his kite
  The paper-flower tree
  A wish for little sister
Northrup, Mili. The watch cat

Foreign lands — Tibet

Tsultim, Yeshe. The mouse king

Foreign lands — Turkey

Bennett, Olivia. A Turkish afternoon
Dewey, Ariane. The fish Peri
Van Woerkom, Dorothy. Abu Ali
  The friends of Abu Ali
Walker, Barbara K. Teeny-Tiny and the
  witch-woman

Foreign lands — Tyrol

Bemelmans, Ludwig. Hansi

Foreign lands — Ukraine

Kay, Helen. An egg is for wishing
Lisowski, Gabriel. How Tevye became a
  milkman
Rudchenko, Ivan. Ivanko and the
  dragon
Rudolph, Marguerita. How a shirt grew
  in the field
Tresselt, Alvin R. The mitten

Foreign lands — Vatican City

Lawrence, John,. Pope Leo's elephant

Foreign languages

ABCDEF...
Alger, Leclaire. Kellyburn Braes
Anglund, Joan Walsh. Love one another
Baldner, Gaby. Joba and the wild boar
Blue, Rose. I am here: Yo estoy aqui
Dauphin, Francine Legrand. A French
  A. B. C.
De Gerez, Toni. My song is a piece of
  jade
Diska, Pat. Andy says ... Bonjour!
Du Bois, William Pène. The hare and
  the tortoise and the tortoise and the
  hare
Everton, Macduff. El circo magico
  modelo
Feelings, Muriel. Jambo means hello
  Menjo means one
Frasconi, Antonio. See again, say again
  See and say
  The snow and the sun, la nieve y el sol
Gunning, Monica. The two Georges
Hautzig, Esther. At home

In the park
The house that Jack built, ill. by Anto-
  nio Frasconi
Jaynes, Ruth M. Tell me please! What's
  that?
Joslin, Sesyle. Baby elephant goes to
  China
  Baby elephant's trunk
  Señor Baby Elephant, the pirate
Kahn, Michèle. My everyday Spanish
  word book
Keats, Ezra Jack. My dog is lost!
Matsutani, Miyoko. How the withered
  trees blossomed
Maury, Inez. My mother the mail
  carrier
Moore, Lilian. Papa Albert
Mother Goose. Mother Goose in French
  Mother Goose in Spanish
  Rimes de la Mere Oie
On the little hearth
Pomerantz, Charlotte. If I had a Paka
  The tamarindo puppy and other
  poems
Rider, Alex. A la ferme. At the farm
  Chez nous. At our house
Rosario, Idalia. Idalia's project ABC
Sasaki, Jeannie. Chōchō is for butterfly
Schaffer, Marion. I love my cat!
Serfozo, Mary. Welcome Roberto!
  Bienvenido, Roberto!
Simon, Norma. What do I say?
Steiner, Charlotte. A friend is "Amie"
Uchida, Yoshiko. The rooster who
  understood Japanese
Vacheron, Edith. Here is Henri!
Wiese, Kurt. You can write Chinese
Wilson, Barbara. ABC et/and 123
Zola, Meguido. The dream of promise

Forest rangers *see* Careers — park
rangers

Forest, woods

Adler, David A. Redwoods are the
  tallest trees in the world
Allen, Gertrude E. Everyday animals
Anglund, Joan Walsh. Nibble nibble
  mousekin
Armer, Laura Adams. The forest pool
Arneson, D J. Secret places
Beskow, Elsa Maartman. Children of the
  forest
Bond, Ruskin. Flames in the forest
Brady, Irene. A mouse named Mus
Buff, Mary. Dash and Dart
  Forest folk
Carrick, Carol. A clearing in the forest
Cristini, Ermanno. In the woods
Ets, Marie Hall. Another day
  In the forest

Friedman, Judi. Noises in the woods
Frost, Robert. Stopping by woods on a snowy evening
Greaves, Margaret. A net to catch the wind
Grimm, Jacob. Hansel and Gretel, ill. by Adrienne Adams
  Hansel and Gretel, ill. by Anthony Browne
  Hansel and Gretel, ill. by Susan Jeffers
  Hansel and Gretel, ill. by Paul O. Zelinsky
  Hansel and Gretel, ill. by Lisbeth Zwerger
Hill, Mary Lou. My dad's a smokejumper
Hyman, Trina Schart. The enchanted forest
Leister, Mary. The silent concert
Lerner, Carol. Flowers of a woodland spring
Lipkind, William. The boy and the forest
Lukešová, Milena. Julian in the autumn woods
Marshall, Edward. Troll country
Miklowitz, Gloria D. Save that raccoon!
Miles, Miska. The fox and the fire
  Sylvester Jones and the voice in the forest
Miller, Edna. Mousekin's ABC
  Mousekin's close call
Newton, James R. A forest is reborn
  Forest log
Paul, Anthony. The tiger who lost his stripes
Peet, Bill. Big bad Bruce
Peyo. The Smurfs and their woodland friends
Prather, Ray. The ostrich girl
Schick, Eleanor. A surprise in the forest
Slobodkin, Louis. Melvin, the moose child
Wahl, Jan. The five in the forest
Ward, Lynd. Nic of the woods
Yolen, Jane. All in the woodland early
Zalben, Jane Breskin. Norton's nighttime

Forgetfulness *see* Behavior — forgetfulness

Format, unusual

Ahlberg, Janet. Peek-a-boo!
Alexander, Martha G. 3 magic flip books
Anno, Mitsumasa. Anno's magical ABC
Barrows, Marjorie Wescott. Fraidy cat
  The funny hat
Benjamin, Alan. 1000 monsters

Brown, Marc. What do you call a dumb bunny? and other rabbit riddles, games, jokes and cartoons
Brown, Margaret Wise. The little fur family
Burlson, Joe. Space colony
Carle, Eric. The secret birthday message
  The very hungry caterpillar
  Watch out! A giant!
Chwast, Seymour. Tall city, wide country
Cremins, Robert. My animal ABC
  My animal Mother Goose
Crowther, Robert. Hide and seek counting book
  The most amazing hide and seek alphabet book
De Paola, Tomie. Country farm
Emberley, Ed. Ed Emberley's amazing look through book
Golden tales from long ago
Goodall, John S. The adventures of Paddy Pork
  The ballooning adventures of Paddy Pork
  Creepy castle
  An Edwardian Christmas
  An Edwardian summer
  Jacko
  The midnight adventures of Kelly, Dot and Esmeralda
  Naughty Nancy
  Paddy goes traveling
  Paddy Pork odd jobs
  Paddy Pork's holiday
  Paddy under water
  Paddy's evening out
  Paddy's new hat
  Shrewbettina's birthday
  The story of an English village
  The surprise picnic
Gorey, Edward. The tunnel calamity
Hauptmann, Tatjana. A day in the life of Petronella Pig
Hawkins, Colin. What time is it, Mr. Wolf?
Hill, Eric. Spot's first walk
The house that Jack built, ill. by Seymour Chwast
Hyman, Trina Schart. The enchanted forest
Jensen, Virginia Allen. Catching
Kunhardt, Edith. Pat the cat
Ladybug, ladybug, and other nursery rhymes
Lewis, Stephen. Zoo city
Lodge, Bernard. Door to door
  Rhyming Nell
McGowan, Alan. Sailing ships
Mari, Iela. Eat and be eaten
Marshall, Ray. Pop-up numbers #1
  Pop-up numbers #2

Pop-up numbers #3
Pop-up numbers #4
Milne, A A (Alan Alexander).
  Winnie-the-Pooh
Moseley, Keith. Dinosaurs
Munari, Bruno. The circus in the mist
  The elephant's wish
  Jimmy has lost his cap
  Tic, Tac and Toc
  Who's there? Open the door
Newell, Peter. Topsys and turvys
Newth, Philip. Roly goes exploring
Oakley, Graham. Graham Oakley's
  magical changes
Rey, Hans Augusto. Anybody at home?
  How do you get there?
  See the circus
  Where's my baby?
Roffey, Maureen. Home sweet home
Ruby-Spears Enterprises. The puppy's
  new adventures
Scarry, Huck. Looking into the Middle
  Ages
Scarry, Richard. Egg in the hole
  Richard Scarry's mix or match
  storybook
Selberg, Ingrid. Nature's hidden world
Seymour, Peter. How the weather works
Steiner, Charlotte. The climbing book
The Superman mix or match storybook
Taback, Simms. Joseph had a little
  overcoat
Tarrant, Graham. Rabbits
Tison, Annette. The adventures of the
  three colors
  Animal hide-and-seek
  Animals in color magic
  Inside and outside
The twelve days of Christmas. English
  folk song. The twelve days of Christ-
  mas, ill. by Erika Schneider
Waber, Bernard. The snake
Walters, Marguerite. The city-country
  ABC
Watson, Wendy. The bunnies' Christmas
  eve
Youldon, Gillian. Colors
  Counting
  Numbers
  Shapes
  Sizes

Format, unusual — cardboard pages

Aronin, Ben. The secret of the Sabbath
  fish
Bailey, Jill. Eyes
  Feet
  Mouths
  Noses
Bambi

Boynton, Sandra. But not the
  hippopotamus
  The going to bed book
  Moo, baa, lalala
  Opposites
Burningham, John. Count up
  The dog
  Five down
  Just cats
  Pigs plus
  Read one
  Ride off
Campbell, Rod. Look inside! All kinds
  of places
  Look inside! Land, sea, air
Cars and trucks
The caterpillar who turned into a
  butterfly.
Children's Television Workshop.
  Muppets in my neighborhood
Come to the circus.
Corbett, Grahame. Guess who?
  What number now?
  Who is hiding?
  Who is inside?
  Who is next?
Cosgrove, Stephen. Sleepy time bunny
Costa, Nicoletta. The birthday party
  Dressing up
  A friend comes to play
  The missing cat
DiFiori, Lawrence. Baby animals
  The farm
  If I had a little car
  My first book
  My toys
Domestic animals
Farm house
Fast rolling fire trucks
Fast rolling work trucks
Fechner, Amrei. I am a little dog
  I am a little elephant
  I am a little lion
Firehouse
Fitzsimons, Cecilia. My first birds
  My first butterflies
Fowler, Richard. Cat's story
Fujikawa, Gyo. Let's grow a garden
  Millie's secret
  My favorite thing
  Surprise! Surprise!
Greeley, Valerie. Farm animals
  Field animals
  Pets
  Zoo animals
Hands, Hargrave. Bunny sees
Hoban, Tana. 1, 2, 3
  What is it?
Johnson, John E. My first book of
  things

Friendship

Aldridge, Josephine Haskell. The best of friends

Alexander, Sue. Small plays for you and a friend
Witch, Goblin and sometimes Ghost

Aliki. We are best friends

Anderson, Paul S. Red fox and the hungry tiger

Anglund, Joan Walsh. Cowboy and his friend
A friend is someone who likes you

Ardizzone, Edward. Tim and Lucy go to sea

Artis, Vicki Kimmel. Pajama walking

Aruego, José. The king and his friends

Baker, Alan. Benjamin and the box

Baker, Betty. Partners

Battles, Edith. One to teeter-totter

Baylor, Byrd. Guess who my favorite person is

Beim, Jerrold. The swimming hole

Beim, Lorraine. Two is a team

Bell, Norman. Linda's airmail letter

Berends, Polly Berrien. Ladybug and dog and the night walk

Berenstain, Stan. The Berenstain bears' moving day

Berger, Terry. Friends

Bergstrom, Corinne. Losing your best friend

Binzen, Bill. Carmen

Blance, Ellen. Monster looks for a friend

Bliss, Corinne Demas. That dog Melly!

Bolliger, Max. The lonely prince

Bond, Felicia. Four Valentines in a rainstorm

Bonsall, Crosby Newell. It's mine! A greedy book
Piggle

Bottner, Barbara. Horrible Hannah
Mean Maxine

Boyd, Selma. The how

Bradbury, Bianca. One kitten too many

Brandenberg, Franz. Leo and Emily
Nice new neighbors

Breinburg, Petronella. Shawn goes to school

Briggs, Raymond. The snowman

Bright, Robert. Me and the bears

Brown, Marc. The cloud over Clarence

Brown, Myra Berry. Best friends
First night away from home

Brown, Palmer. Hickory

Bryan, Dorothy. Friendly little Jonathan

Buck, Pearl S (Pearl Sydenstricker). The little fox in the middle

Buntain, Ruth Jaeger. The birthday story

Bunting, Eve. Clancy's coat
Monkey in the middle

Burningham, John. The friend

Calhoun, Mary. The witch who lost her shadow

Carle, Eric. Do you want to be my friend?

Carrick, Malcolm. Today is shrew's day

Chorao, Kay. Molly's lies

Clifton, Lucille. Everett Anderson's friend
My friend Jacob
Three wishes

Cohen, Miriam. Best friends
First grade takes a test
Will I have a friend?

Cole, Brock. Nothing but a pig

Collins, Pat Lowery. Tumble, tumble, tumbleweed

Conford, Ellen. Why can't I be William?

Conta, Marcia Maher. Feelings between friends

Coontz, Otto. The quiet house

Costa, Nicoletta. A friend comes to play

Coville, Bruce. The foolish giant

Cunningham, Julia. A mouse called Junction

Damjan, Mischa. Goodbye little bird

Dauer, Rosamond. Bullfrog builds a house

De Bruyn, Monica. Lauren's secret ring

Degen, Bruce. The little witch and the riddle

Delaney, Ned. Bert and Barney

Delton, Judy. Duck goes fishing
A pet for Duck and Bear
Three friends find spring

De Paola, Tomie. Andy (that's my name)

De Regniers, Beatrice Schenk. May I bring a friend?

Dickinson, Mary. Alex and Roy

Drdek, Richard E. Horace the friendly octopus

Duvoisin, Roger Antoine. The crocodile in the tree
Periwinkle
Petunia
Petunia and the song
Petunia, I love you
Petunia's treasure

Ehrlich, Amy. Leo, Zack and Emmie

Ellis, Anne Leo. Dabble Duck

Fassler, Joan. Boy with a problem

Fatio, Louise. The happy lion
Hector and Christina

Felt, Sue. Hello-goodbye

Fern, Eugene. What's he been up to now?

Fink, Dale Borman. Mr. Silver and Mrs. Gold

Peet, Bill. Eli
Politi, Leo. Mr. Fong's toy shop
Raphael, Elaine. Donkey and Carlo
Raskin, Ellen. A & the
  Franklin Stein
Robins, Joan. Addie meets Max
Ross, Pat. Meet M and M
Rubin, Jeff. Baseball brothers
Rylant, Cynthia. Miss Maggie
Sarton, May. Punch's secret
Saunders, Susan. Charles Rat's picnic
Scarry, Patsy. Little Richard and Prickles
Schick, Eleanor. Making friends
Schreiber, Georges. Bambino goes home
Schroeder, Binette. Tuffa and her
  friends
Schulman, Janet. The big hello
Schumacher, Claire. King of the zoo
Schweitzer, Iris. Hilda's restful chair
Sharmat, Marjorie Weinman.
  Bartholomew the bossy
  Burton and Dudley
  Gladys told me to meet her here
  I'm not Oscar's friend any more
  Mitchell is moving
  Rollo and Juliet...forever!
  Scarlet Monster lives here
  Sophie and Gussie
  Taking care of Melvin
  The trip
Sherman, Ivan. I do not like it when my
  friend comes to visit
Slate, Joseph. Lonely Lula cat
Slobodkin, Louis. Dinny and Danny
Smaridge, Norah. Peter's tent
Spang, Günter. Clelia and the little
  mermaid
Steadman, Ralph. The bridge
Steiner, Charlotte. A friend is "Amie"
Steptoe, John. Stevie
Stevens, Carla. Stories from a snowy
  meadow
Stevenson, James. Howard
  Wilfred the rat
  The worst person in the world
Sugita, Yutaka. Helena the unhappy
  hippopotamus
Taylor, Mark. Old Blue, you good dog
  you
Tether, Graham. Skunk and possum
Thaler, Mike. It's me, hippo!
  Moonkey
Tripp, Paul. The strawman who smiled
  by mistake
Tudor, Bethany. Samuel's tree house
Udry, Janice May. Let's be enemies
Van Woerkom, Dorothy. Harry and
  Shelburt
Varley, Susan. Badger's parting gifts
Venable, Alan. The checker players
Vigna, Judith. The hiding house

Viorst, Judith. Rosie and Michael
Waber, Bernard. Ira sleeps over
  Lovable Lyle
  Nobody is perfick
Wade, Anne. A promise is for keeping
Waechter, Friedrich Karl. Three is
  company
Weil, Lisl. Gillie and the flattering fox
Weiss, Nicki. Maude and Sally
Wiesner, William. Tops
Wildsmith, Brian. The lazy bear
Wilhelm, Hans. A new home, a new
  friend
Williams, Barbara. Kevin's grandma
Winthrop, Elizabeth. Katharine's doll
  Sloppy kisses
Wittman, Sally. Pelly and Peak
  Plenty of Pelly and Peak
  A special trade
  The wonderful Mrs. Trumbly
Wolcott, Patty. Double-decker,
  double-decker, double-decker bus
Wolde, Gunilla. Betsy and Peter are
  different
Woolley, Catherine. Gus was a friendly
  ghost
  The popcorn dragon
Yashima, Tarō. The youngest one
Yeoman, John. Mouse trouble
Zalben, Jane Breskin. Oliver and
  Alison's week
Zelinsky, Paul O. The lion and the stoat
Zion, Gene. The meanest squirrel I ever
  met
Zolotow, Charlotte. The hating book
  Hold my hand
  Janey
  My friend John
  The new friend
  Three funny friends
  The unfriendly book
  The white marble

Frogs and toads

Æsop. The hare and the frogs
Alexander, Martha G. No ducks in our
  bathtub
Berson, Harold. Charles and Claudine
Canfield, Jane White. The frog prince
Carrick, Malcolm. Today is shrew's day
Charles, Robert Henry. The roundabout
  turn
Chenery, Janet. The toad hunt
Cortesi, Wendy W. Explore a spooky
  swamp
Dauer, Rosamond. Bullfrog builds a
  house
  Bullfrog grows up
Duke, Kate. Seven froggies went to
  school
Duvoisin, Roger Antoine. Periwinkle

Erickson, Russell E. Warton and the
  traders
 Warton's Christmas Eve adventure
Flack, Marjorie. Tim Tadpole and the
  great bullfrog
Freschet, Berniece. The old bullfrog
A frog he would a-wooing go
  (folk-song). Frog went a-courtin'
Gackenbach, Dick. Crackle, Gluck and
  the sleeping toad
Greydanus, Rose. Freddie the frog
Harrison, David Lee. The case of Og,
  the missing frog
Hawes, Judy. Spring peepers
 Why frogs are wet
Hoban, Russell. Jim Frog
Hogan, Paula Z. The frog
Kalan, Robert. Jump, frog, jump!
Karlin, Nurit. The blue frog
Keith, Eros. Rrra-ah
Kellogg, Steven. The mysterious tadpole
Kent, Jack. The caterpillar and the
  polliwog
Kepes, Juliet. Frogs, merry
Kraus, Robert. Mert the blurt
Kumin, Maxine. Eggs of things
Lane, Carolyn. The voices of
  Greenwillow Pond
Lane, Margaret. The frog
Lionni, Leo. Fish is fish
Lobel, Arnold. Days with Frog and
  Toad
 Frog and Toad all year
 Frog and Toad are friends
 Frog and Toad together
MacLachlan, Patricia. Moon, stars, frogs
  and friends
McLenighan, Valjean. You are what you
  are
McPhail, David. Captain Toad and the
  motorbike
Maris, Ron. Better move on, frog!
Massie, Diane Redfield. Walter was a
  frog
Mayer, Mercer. A boy, a dog, a frog
  and a friend
 A boy, a dog and a frog
 Frog goes to dinner
 Frog on his own
 Frog, where are you?
 One frog too many
Miles, Miska. Jump frog jump
Noll, Sally. Off and counting
Partridge, Jenny. Hopfellow
Pavey, Peter. I'm Taggarty Toad
Pendery, Rosemary. A home for
  Hopper
Potter, Beatrix. The tale of Mr. Jeremy
  Fisher
Pursell, Margaret Sanford. Sprig the
  tree frog

Rockwell, Anne F. Big boss
  Toad
Seeger, Pete. The foolish frog
Seuss, Dr. Would you rather be a
  bullfrog?
Small, David. Eulalie and the hopping
  head
Smith, Jim. The frog band and
  Durrington Dormouse
 The frog band and the onion seller
 The frog band and the owlnapper
Steig, William. Gorky rises
Steptoe, John. The story of jumping
  mouse
Stevenson, James. Monty
Stratemeyer, Clara Georgeanna. Frog
  fun
 Tuggy
Tresselt, Alvin R. Frog in the well
Turska, Krystyna. The woodcutter's
  duck
Van Woerkom, Dorothy. Sea frog, city
  frog
Wahl, Jan. Doctor Rabbit's foundling
Walt Disney Productions. Walt Disney's
  The adventures of Mr. Toad
Yeoman, John. The bear's water picnic
Yolen, Jane. Commander Toad and the
  big black hole
 Commander Toad and the planet of
  the grapes
 Commander Toad in space
Zakhoder, Boris Vladimirovich.
  Rosachok

Games

Agostinelli, Maria Enrica. I know
  something you don't know
Ahlberg, Janet. Each peach pear plum
 Peek-a-boo!
Alexander, Martha G. We never get to
  do anything
Allen, Jeffrey. The secret life of Mr.
  Weird
Anderson, Douglas. Let's draw a story
Anglund, Joan Walsh. The brave
  cowboy
 Cowboy's secret life
Anno, Mitsumasa. Anno's animals
 Anno's Britain
 Anno's counting house
 Anno's flea market
 Anno's Italy
 Anno's journey

Anno's magical ABC
Anno's U.S.A.
Topsy-turvies
Upside-downers
Applebaum, Neil. Is there a hole in your head?
Aruego, José. Look what I can do
We hide, you seek
Asch, Frank. Goodnight horsey
Battles, Edith. One to teeter-totter
Baylor, Byrd. Guess who my favorite person is
Beach, Stewart. Good morning, sun's up!
Behrens, June. Can you walk the plank?
Bonsall, Crosby Newell. The day I had to play with my sister
Piggle
Booth, Eugene. At the circus
At the fair
In the air
In the garden
In the jungle
Under the ocean
Brown, Marc. Finger rhymes
What do you call a dumb bunny? and other rabbit riddles, games, jokes and cartoons
Brown, Margaret Wise. The indoor noisy book
Byars, Betsy Cromer. Go and hush the baby
Carroll, Ruth. Where's the bunny?
Charlip, Remy. Arm in arm
Where is everybody?
Clark, Harry. The first story of the whale
Cohen, Peter Zachary. Authorized autumn charts of the Upper Red Canoe River country
Craig, M Jean. Boxes
Delaney, Ned. One dragon to another
Delton, Judy. I never win!
De Paola, Tomie. Andy (that's my name)
Things to make and do for Valentine's Day
De Regniers, Beatrice Schenk. What can you do with a shoe?
Dubanevich, Arlene. Pigs in hiding
Elting, Mary. Q is for duck
Emberley, Ed. Ed Emberley's crazy mixed-up face game
Klippity klop
The farmer in the dell
Fleisher, Robbin. Quilts in the attic
Fox, Dorothea Warren. Follow me the leader
French, Fiona. Hunt the thimble
Glazer, Tom. Do your ears hang low?
Eye winker, Tom Tinker, chin chopper

Glovach, Linda. The little Witch's black magic book of games
Go tell Aunt Rhody, ill. by Aliki
Go tell Aunt Rhody, ill. by Robert M. Quackenbush
Hahn, Hannelore. Take a giant step
Hann, Jacquie. Follow the leader
Hillert, Margaret. Play ball
Hoban, Russell. How Tom beat Captain Najork and his hired sportsmen
Hoff, Syd. The littlest leaguer
Hoguet, Susan Ramsay. I unpacked my grandmother's trunk
Hurd, Edith Thacher. Last one home is a green pig
Jameson, Cynthia. A day with Whisker Wickles
Johnson, Elizabeth. All in free but Janey
Kahn, Joan. Seesaw
Keeshan, Robert. She loves me, she loves me not
Koch, Dorothy Clarke. I play at the beach
Krauss, Ruth. The bundle book
Mama, I wish I was snow. Child, you'd be very cold
Kroll, Steven. The tyrannosaurus game
Let's count and count out
Lexau, Joan M. Every day a dragon
I hate red rover
Lipkind, William. Sleepyhead
Livermore, Elaine. Find the cat
Lost and found
One to ten, count again
Three little kittens lost their mittens
Lopshire, Robert. How to make snop snappers and other fine things
McToots, Rudi. The kid's book of games for cars, trains and planes
Maestro, Giulio. The tortoise's tug of war
Merrill, Jean. How many kids are hiding on my block?
Miles, Miska. Rolling the cheese
Milne, A A (Alan Alexander). Pooh's quiz book
Mitchell, Cynthia. Halloweena Hecatee
Montgomerie, Norah. This little pig went to market
Morris, Neil. Find the canary
Hide and seek
Search for Sam
Where's my hat?
Mother Goose. London Bridge is falling down, ill. by Ed Emberley
London Bridge is falling down, ill. by Peter Spier
Mother Goose in hieroglyphics
The three little kittens
Munari, Bruno. The birthday present

Myers, Amy. I know a monster
Nelson, Esther L. Holiday singing and
dancing games
Oram, Hiawyn. Skittlewonder and the
wizard
Oxenbury, Helen. The queen and Rosie
Randall
Patterson, Pat. Hickory dickory duck
Peppé, Rodney. Little games
Odd one out
Rodney Peppé's puzzle book
The pudgy pat-a-cake book
The pudgy peek-a-boo book
Raebeck, Lois. Who am I?
Rockwell, Norman. Norman Rockwell's
counting book
Sandberg, Inger. Little Anna saved
Selsam, Millicent E. Is this a baby
dinosaur? and other science picture
puzzles
Shaw, Charles Green. The blue guess
book
The guess book
It looked like spilt milk
Siewert, Margaret. Bear hunt
Sivulich, Sandra Stroner. I'm going on a
bear hunt
Steig, William. The bad speller
Steiner, Charlotte. Five little finger
playmates
Red Ridinghood's little lamb
Taylor, Mark. Old Blue, you good dog
you
Thwaite, Ann. The day with the Duke
Tison, Annette. Animal hide-and-seek
Ueno, Noriko. Elephant buttons
Ungerer, Tomi. One, two, where's my
shoe?
Snail, where are you?
Van Allsburg, Chris. Jumanji
Venable, Alan. The checker players
Weil, Lisl. Owl and other scrambles
Wildsmith, Brian. Animal games
Brian Wildsmith's puzzles
Withers, Carl. The tale of a black cat
The wild ducks and the goose
Yudell, Lynn Deena. Make a face
Zacharias, Thomas. But where is the
green parrot?
Zion, Gene. Hide and seek day
Jeffie's party

Gangs see Clubs, gangs

Garage sales

Rockwell, Anne F. Our garage sale

Garbage collectors see Careers —
garbage collectors

Gardening see Activities — gardening

Geese see Birds — geese

Generosity see Character traits —
generosity

Gerbils see Animals — gerbils

Germany see Foreign lands — Germany

Ghosts

Adler, David A. Jeffrey's ghost and the
leftover baseball team
Ahlberg, Janet. Funnybones
Alexander, Sue. More Witch, Goblin,
and Ghost stories
Witch, Goblin, and Ghost in the
haunted woods
Witch, Goblin and Ghost's book of
things to do
Witch, Goblin and sometimes Ghost
Allard, Harry. Bumps in the night
Benchley, Nathaniel. A ghost named
Fred
Bright, Robert. Georgie
Georgie and the baby birds
Georgie and the ball of yarn
Georgie and the buried treasure
Georgie and the little dog
Georgie and the magician
Georgie and the noisy ghost
Georgie and the robbers
Georgie and the runaway balloon
Georgie goes west
Georgie to the rescue
Georgie's Christmas carol
Georgie's Halloween
Brown, Marc. Spooky riddles
Brunhoff, Laurent de. Babar and the
ghost
Charlton, Elizabeth. Jeremy and the
ghost
Coombs, Patricia. Dorrie and the
screebit ghost
Cuyler, Margery. Sir William and the
pumpkin monster
DeLage, Ida. The old witch and the
ghost parade
Du Bois, William Pène. Elisabeth the
cow ghost
Eisenberg, Phyllis Rose. Don't tell me a
ghost story
Fife, Dale. Follow that ghost!
Flora, James. Grandpa's ghost stories
Friedrich, Priscilla. The marshmallow
ghosts
Gage, Wilson. Mrs. Gaddy and the ghost
Galdone, Joanna. The tailypo
Galdone, Paul. King of the cats
The monster and the tailor
Hancock, Sibyl. Esteban and the ghost

Johnston, Tony. Four scary stories

Kroll, Steven. Amanda and the giggling ghost

Levy, Elizabeth. Something queer at the haunted school

Lexau, Joan M. Millicent's ghost

Mooser, Stephen. The ghost with the Halloween hiccups

Nixon, Joan Lowery. The Thanksgiving mystery

Olson, Helen Kronberg. The strange thing that happened to Oliver Wendell Iscovitch

Raskin, Ellen. Ghost in a four-room apartment

Rockwell, Anne F. A bear, a bobcat and three ghosts

Ross, Pat. M and M and the haunted house game

Sandberg, Inger. Little ghost Godfry

Schulman, Janet. Jack the bum and the haunted house

Seuling, Barbara. The teeny tiny woman

Sharmat, Marjorie Weinman. Two ghosts on a bench

Wallace, Daisy. Ghost poems

Woolley, Catherine. Gus and the baby ghost

  Gus was a friendly ghost

  Gus was a gorgeous ghost

  Gus was a real dumb ghost

  What's a ghost going to do?

Zemach, Margot. The little tiny woman

Giants

Balian, Lorna. A sweetheart for Valentine

Benjamin, Alan. Ribtickle Town

Bodwell, Gaile. The long day of the giants

Bolliger, Max. The giants' feast

Bradfield, Roger. Giants come in different sizes

Briggs, Raymond. Jim and the beanstalk

Carle, Eric. Watch out! A giant!

Coville, Bruce. The foolish giant

Cunliffe, John. Sara's giant and the upside down house

Cushman, Doug. Giants

De La Mare, Walter. Molly Whuppie

De Paola, Tomie. Fin M'Coul

  The mysterious giant of Barletta

De Regniers, Beatrice Schenk. The giant story

Du Bois, William Pène. Giant Otto

  Otto and the magic potatoes

  Otto at sea

  Otto in Africa

  Otto in Texas

Elkin, Benjamin. Lucky and the giant

Foreman, Michael. The two giants

Fritz, Jean. The good giants and the bad Pukwudgies

Greene, Ellin. The pumpkin giant

Grimm, Jacob. The brave little tailor, ill. by Mark Corcoran

  The brave little tailor, ill. by Svend Otto

  The brave little tailor, ill. by Daniel SanSouci

  The valiant little tailor

Herrmann, Frank. The giant Alexander

  The giant Alexander and the circus

Hillert, Margaret. The magic beans

  The history of Mother Twaddle and the marvelous achievements of her son Jack

Homme, Bob. The friendly giant's birthday

  The friendly giant's book of fire engines

Jack and the beanstalk, ill. by Lorinda Bryan Cauley

Jack and the beanstalk, ill. by Ed Parker

Jack and the beanstalk, ill. by Tony Ross

Jack and the beanstalk, ill. by William Stobbs

Jennings, Michael. Robin Goodfellow and the giant dwarf

Kahl, Virginia. Giants, indeed!

Kraus, Robert. The little giant

Lawrence, John. The giant of Grabbist

Lobel, Arnold. Giant John

Löfgren, Ulf. The boy who ate more than the giant and other Swedish folktales

McNeill, Janet. The giant's birthday

Minarik, Else Holmelund. The little giant girl and the elf boys

Munsch, Robert N. David's father

Polushkin, Maria. The little hen and the giant

Sherman, Ivan. I am a giant

Still, James. Jack and the wonder beans

Tompert, Ann. Charlotte and Charles

Ungerer, Tomi. Zeralda's ogre

Ward, Nick. Giant

Wiesner, William. Tops

Yolen, Jane. The giant's farm

  The giants go camping

Gilbert Islands see Foreign lands — South Sea Islands

Giraffes see Animals — giraffes

Glasses

Brown, Marc. Arthur's eyes

Goodsell, Jane. Katie's magic glasses

Keller, Holly. Cromwell's glasses

Kessler, Leonard P. Mr. Pine's mixed-up signs

Lasson, Robert. Orange Oliver
Raskin, Ellen. Spectacles
Tusa, Tricia. Libby's new glasses
Wise, William. The cowboy surprise
Woolley, Catherine. Mr. Turtle's magic
  glasses

Gnomes see Elves and little people

Goats see Animals — goats

Goblins

Alden, Laura. Learning about fairies
Alexander, Sue. More Witch, Goblin,
  and Ghost stories
  Witch, Goblin, and Ghost in the
  haunted woods
  Witch, Goblin and Ghost's book of
  things to do
  Witch, Goblin and sometimes Ghost
Calhoun, Mary. The goblin under the
  stairs
Coombs, Patricia. Dorrie and the goblin
Haley, Gail E. Go away, stay away
Johnston, Tony. Four scary stories
Lifton, Betty Jean. Joji and the
  Amanojaku
Sendak, Maurice. Outside over there
Tobias, Tobi. Chasing the goblins away

Gorillas see Animals — gorillas

Gossip see Behavior — gossip

Grammar see Language

Grandparents see Family life —
  grandparents, great-grandparents

Grasshoppers see Insects —
  grasshoppers

Great-grandparents see Family life —
  grandparents, great-grandparents

Greece see Foreign lands — Greece

Greed see Behavior — greed

Griffins see Mythical creatures

Grocery stores see Shopping; Stores

Groundhog Day see Holidays —
  Groundhog Day

Groundhogs see Animals —
  groundhogs

Growing up see Behavior — growing
  up

Guinea pigs see Animals — guinea pigs

Guns see Weapons

Guyana see Foreign lands — Guyana

Gymnastics see Sports — gymnastics

Gypsies

Anderson, C W (Clarence Williams).
  Blaze and the gypsies
Bemelmans, Ludwig. Madeline and the
  gypsies
García Lorca, Federico. The Lieutenant
  Colonel and the gypsy
Kellogg, Steven. The mystery of the
  magic green ball
Mahy, Margaret. Mrs. Discombobulous
Oram, Hiawyn. Skittlewonder and the
  wizard

Hair

Abisch, Roz. The Pumpkin Heads
Appell, Clara. Now I have a daddy
  haircut
Bright, Robert. I like red
Freeman, Don. Mop Top
Goldin, Augusta. Straight hair, curly
  hair
Grimm, Jacob. Rapunzel, ill. by Julia
  Ash
  Rapunzel, ill. by Bert Dodson
  Rapunzel, ill. by Trina Schart Hyman
Hair
Kunhardt, Dorothy. Billy the barber
Quin-Harkin, Janet. Helpful Hattie
Rockwell, Anne F. My barber
Scott, Natalie. Firebrand, push your hair
  out of your eyes
Tether, Graham. The hair book
Townsend, Kenneth. Felix, the
  bald-headed lion

Halloween see Holidays — Halloween

Hamsters see Animals — hamsters

Handicaps

Arnold, Katrin. Anna joins in
Bradford, Ann. The mystery of the
  missing dogs
Brightman, Alan. Like me

Brown, Tricia. Someone special, just like you

Charlot, Martin. Felisa and the magic tikling bird

Clifton, Lucille. My friend Jacob

Fanshawe, Elizabeth. Rachel

Fassler, Joan. Howie helps himself
One little girl

Gold, Phyllis. Please don't say hello

Hasler, Eveline. Martin is our friend

Henriod, Lorraine. Grandma's wheelchair

Larsen, Hanne. Don't forget Tom

Lasker, Joe. He's my brother
Nick joins in

Rosenberg, Maxine B. My friend Leslie

Smith, Lucia B. A special kind of sister

Sobol, Harriet Langsam. My brother Steven is retarded

Stein, Sara Bonnett. About handicaps

Wahl, Jan. Button eye's orange

White, Paul. Janet at school

Wolf, Bernard. Don't feel sorry for Paul

Handicaps — blindness

Bradford, Ann. The mystery of the blind writer

Brighton, Catherine. My hands, my world

Cohen, Miriam. See you tomorrow

Jensen, Virginia Allen. Catching
Red thread riddles
What's that?

Johnson, Donna Kay. Brighteyes

Keats, Ezra Jack. Apartment 3

Litchfield, Ada B. A cane in her hand

Newth, Philip. Roly goes exploring

Quigley, Lillian Fox. The blind men and the elephant

Reuter, Margaret. My mother is blind

Sargent, Susan. My favorite place

Saxe, John Godfrey. The blind men and the elephant

Yolen, Jane. The seeing stick

Handicaps — deafness

Arthur, Catherine. My sister's silent world

Charlip, Remy. Handtalk

Gage, Wilson. Down in the boondocks

Litchfield, Ada B. A button in her ear

Mother Goose. Nursery rhymes from Mother Goose in signed English.

Wahl, Jan. Jamie's tiger

Wolf, Bernard. Anna's silent world

Hands *see* Anatomy

Hanukkah *see* Holidays — Hanukkah

Happiness *see* Emotions — happiness

Hares *see* Animals — rabbits

Hate *see* Emotions — hate

Hawaii

Funai, Mamoru. Moke and Poki in the rain forest

Laird, Donivee Martin. The three little Hawaiian pigs and the magic shark

Williams, Jay. The surprising things Maui did

Hawks *see* Birds — hawks

Health

Berger, Melvin. Why I cough, sneeze, shiver, hiccup and yawn

Borten, Helen. Do you move as I do?

Burnstein, John. Slim Goodbody

Cobb, Vicki. How the doctor knows you're fine

Gross, Ruth Belov. A book about your skeleton

Isenberg, Barbara. Albert the running bear's exercise book

Leaf, Munro. Health can be fun

Marcus, Susan. Casey visits the doctor

Marshall, Lyn. Yoga for your children

Moncure, Jane Belk. Happy healthkins
The healthkin food train
Healthkins exercise!
Healthkins help

Oxenbury, Helen. The checkup

Radlauer, Ruth Shaw. Of course, you're a horse!

Rockwell, Harlow. My doctor

Seuss, Dr. The tooth book

Hearing *see* Senses

Heavy equipment *see* Machines

Hedgehogs *see* Animals — hedgehogs

Helicopters

Drummond, Violet H. The flying postman

Firmin, Peter. Basil Brush goes flying

Petersen, David. Helicopters

Taylor, Mark. Henry explores the mountains

Zaffo, George J. The big book of real airplanes

Helpfulness *see* Character traits — helpfulness

Hens *see* Birds — chickens

Hibernation

Barrett, John M. The bear who slept through Christmas
Bartoli, Jennifer. Snow on bear's nose
Cohen, Carol L. Wake up, groundhog!
De Paola, Tomie. Four stories for four seasons
Evans, Eva Knox. Sleepy time
Fisher, Aileen. Where does everyone go?
Freeman, Don. Bearymore
Janice. Little Bear's Christmas
Kepes, Juliet. Frogs, merry
Kesselman, Wendy. Time for Jody
Krauss, Ruth. The happy day
McClure, Gillian. Prickly pig
Marshall, James. What's the matter with Carruthers?
Miller, Edna. Mousekin's golden house
Parker, Nancy Winslow. The ordeal of Byron B. Blackbear
Piers, Helen. Grasshopper and butterfly
Stott, Rowena. The hedgehog feast
Ward, Andrew. Baby bear and the long sleep
Watson, Wendy. Has winter come?
Yulya. Bears are sleeping

Hiding see Behavior — hiding

Hiding things see Behavior — hiding things

Hieroglyphics

Mother Goose. Mother Goose in hieroglyphics
The prince who knew his fate

Hippopotami see Animals — hippopotami

Hobby horses see Toys — rocking horses

Hockey see Sports — hockey

Holidays

Adler, David A. A picture book of Jewish holidays
Alexander, Sue. Small plays for special days
Belting, Natalia Maree. Summer's coming in
Berenstain, Stan. The bears' almanac
Cohen, Barbara. Here come the Purim players!
Cone, Molly. The Jewish Sabbath
Conger, Marion. The little golden holiday book

Fisher, Aileen. Arbor day
Skip around the year
Forrester, Victoria. Oddward
Glovach, Linda. The Little Witch's spring holiday book
Kumin, Maxine. Follow the fall
Menter, Ian. Carnival
Meyer, Elizabeth C. The blue china pitcher
Ross, Tony. Hugo and the bureau of holidays
Sotomayor, Antonio. Khasa goes to the fiesta
Tudor, Tasha. A time to keep
Zolotow, Charlotte. Over and over

Holidays — April Fools' Day

Brown, Marc. Arthur's April fool
Christian, Mary Blount. April fool
Kelley, Emily. April Fools' Day
Krahn, Fernando. April fools
Rockwell, Norman. Norman Rockwell's counting book
Wegen, Ron. Billy Gorilla

Holidays — Chanukah see Holidays — Hanukkah

Holidays — Chinese New Year

Cheng, Hou-Tien. The Chinese New Year
Handforth, Thomas. Mei Li
Politi, Leo. Moy Moy
Wallace, Ian. Chin Chiang and the dragon's dance
Young, Evelyn. The tale of Tai

Holidays — Christmas

Adams, Adrienne. The Christmas party
Adshead, Gladys L. Brownies - it's Christmas
Ahlberg, Allan. Cops and robbers
Aichinger, Helga. The shepherd
Andersen, H C (Hans Christian). The fir tree
Anglund, Joan Walsh. A Christmas book
Christmas is a time of giving
The cowboy's Christmas
Aoki, Hisako. Santa's favorite story
Ardizzone, Aingelda. The night ride
Armour, Richard Willard. The year Santa went modern
Bach, Alice. The day after Christmas
Baker, Laura Nelson. The friendly beasts
O children of the wind and pines
Balet, Jan B. The gift
Balian, Lorna. Bah! Humbug?
Barrett, John M. The bear who slept through Christmas

Barry, Robert E. Mr. Willowby's
Christmas tree
Belting, Natalia Maree. Christmas folk
Bemelmans, Ludwig. Hansi
Benchley, Nathaniel. The magic sled
Berenstain, Stan. The Berenstain bears'
Christmas tree
Blough, Glenn O. Christmas trees and
how they grow
Bolognese, Don. A new day
Bond, Felicia. Christmas in the chicken
coop
Bonsall, Crosby Newell. Twelve bells for
Santa
Brian Wildsmith's The twelve days of
Christmas
Briggs, Raymond. Father Christmas
Father Christmas goes on holiday
Bright, Robert. Georgie's Christmas
carol
Bring a torch, Jeannette, Isabella
Brock, Emma Lillian. The birds'
Christmas tree
Brown, Abbie Farwell. The Christmas
angel
Brown, Marc. Arthur's Christmas
Brown, Margaret Wise. Christmas in the
barn
The little fir tree
On Christmas Eve
Pussycat's Christmas
The steamroller
Brown, Palmer. Something for
Christmas
Bruna, Dick. Christmas
The Christmas book
Brunhoff, Jean de. Babar and Father
Christmas
Bryson, Bernarda. The twenty miracles
of Saint Nicolas
Budbill, David. Christmas tree farm
Burland, Brian. St. Nicholas and the tub
Carlson, Natalie Savage. Surprise in the
mountains
Cazet, Denys. Christmas moon
Chafetz, Henry. The legend of Befana
Chalmers, Mary. A Christmas story
Merry Christmas, Harry
Chapman, Jean. Moon-Eyes
A Christmas book
Chute, Beatrice Joy. Joy to Christmas
Clifton, Lucille. Everett Anderson's
Christmas coming
Climo, Shirley. The cobweb Christmas
Coatsworth, Elizabeth. The children
come running
Cooney, Barbara. The little juggler
Darling, Kathy. The mystery in Santa's
toyshop
Davidson, Amanda. Teddy's first
Christmas

De Paola, Tomie. The cat on the
Dovrefell
The Christmas pageant
The clown of God
The family Christmas tree book
The story of the three wise kings
Devlin, Wende. Cranberry Christmas
Din dan don, it's Christmas
Domanska, Janina. I saw a ship a-sailing
Donaldson, Lois. Karl's wooden horse
Drescher, Henrik. Looking for Santa
Claus
Duvoisin, Roger Antoine. The
Christmas whale
One thousand Christmas beards
Petunia's Christmas
Ephron, Delia. Santa and Alex
Erickson, Russell E. Warton's Christmas
Eve adventure
Ets, Marie Hall. Nine days to Christmas
Farber, Norma. How the hibernators
came to Bethlehem
Fatio, Louise. Anna, the horse
Fenner, Carol. Christmas tree on the
mountain
Fraser, James Howard. Los Posadas
Freeman, Jean Todd. Cynthia and the
unicorn
The friendly beasts and A partridge in a
pear tree
Gackenbach, Dick. Claude the dog
Gannett, Ruth S. Katie and the sad
noise
Gantos, Jack. Rotten Ralph's rotten
Christmas
Gantschev, Ivan. The Christmas train
Gikow, Louise. Sprocket's Christmas tale
Glovach, Linda. The little Witch's
Christmas book
Goodall, John S. An Edwardian
Christmas
Gordon, Sharon. Christmas surprise
Hale, Linda. The glorious Christmas
soup party
Haywood, Carolyn. A Christmas fantasy
Santa Claus forever
Hillert, Margaret. Merry Christmas,
dear dragon
Hillman, Priscilla. A Merry-Mouse
Christmas A B C
Hoban, Lillian. Arthur's Christmas
cookies
It's really Christmas
Hoban, Russell. Emmet Otter's jug-band
Christmas
The mole family's Christmas
Hoff, Syd. Merry Christmas, Henrietta!
Santa's moose
Where's Prancer?
Hoffmann, E T A. The nutcracker

Hoffmann, Felix. The story of
Christmas
Holm, Mayling Mack. A forest
Christmas
Holmes, Efner Tudor. The Christmas
cat
Hurd, Edith Thacher. Christmas eve
Hutchins, Pat. The best train set ever
King Henry's palace
The silver Christmas tree
Janice. Little Bear's Christmas
Jaynes, Ruth M. Melinda's Christmas
stocking
Johnson, Crockett. Harold at the North
Pole
Jones, Jessie Mae Orton. A little child
Joslin, Sesyle. Baby elephant and the
secret wishes
Jüchen, Aurel von. The Holy Night
Kahl, Virginia. Gunhilde's Christmas
booke
Plum pudding for Christmas
Keats, Ezra Jack. The little drummer
boy
Kent, Jack. The Christmas piñata
Kerr, Judith. Mog's Christmas
Knight, Hilary. Angels and berries and
candy canes
Knotts, Howard. The lost Christmas
Krahn, Fernando. The biggest
Christmas tree on earth
Kroll, Steven. Santa's crash-bang
Christmas
Kunnas, Mauri. Santa Claus and his
elves
Langstaff, John M. On Christmas day in
the morning
Lathrop, Dorothy Pulis. An angel in the
woods
Laurence, Margaret. The Christmas
birthday story
Linch, Elizabeth Johanna. Samson
Lindgren, Astrid. Christmas in noisy
village
Christmas in the stable
Of course Polly can do almost
everything
Lines, Kathleen. Once in royal David's
city
Lipkind, William. The Christmas bunny
Low, Joseph. The Christmas grump
McGinley, Phyllis. How Mrs. Santa Claus
saved Christmas
McPhail, David. Mistletoe
Manushkin, Fran. The perfect
Christmas picture
Mariana. The journey of Bangwell Putt
Marshall, James. Miss Dog's Christmas
Martin, Judith. The tree angel
May, Robert Lewis. Rudolph the
red-nosed reindeer

Miller, Edna. Mousekin's Christmas eve
Moeschlin, Elsa. The red horse
Mohr, Joseph. Silent night
Monsell, Helen Albee. Paddy's
Christmas
Moore, Clement C. The night before
Christmas, ill. by Tomie De Paola
The night before Christmas, ill. by Gyo
Fujikawa
The night before Christmas, ill. by
Anita Lobel
The night before Christmas, ill. by
Gustaf Tenggren
The night before Christmas, ill. by
Tasha Tudor
A visit from St. Nicholas
Naylor, Phyllis Reynolds. Old Sadie and
the Christmas bear
Newland, Mary Reed. Good King
Wenceslas
Noble, Trinka Hakes. Apple tree
Christmas
Nussbaumer, Mares. Away in a manger
Oakley, Graham. The church mice at
Christmas
Parker, Nancy Winslow. The Christmas
camel
Partch, Virgil Franklin. The Christmas
cookie sprinkle snitcher
Pearson, Susan. Karin's Christmas walk
Peet, Bill. Countdown to Christmas
Peterson, Hans. Erik and the Christmas
horse
Play and sing - it's Christmas!
Plume, Ilse. The story of Befana
Politi, Leo. The nicest gift
Pedro, the angel of Olvera Street
Rosa
Robbins, Ruth. Baboushka and the three
kings
Rockwell, Anne F. Bafana
Rowand, Phyllis. Every day in the year
Sahagun, Bernardino de. Spirit child
Sawyer, Ruth. The Christmas Anna
angel
Scarry, Richard. Richard Scarry's best
Christmas book ever!
Schenk, Esther M. Christmas time
Schumacher, Claire. Nutty's Christmas
Schweninger, Ann. Christmas secrets
Seignobosc, Françoise. Noël for
Jeanne-Marie
Selden, George. The mice, the monks
and the Christmas tree
Seuss, Dr. How the Grinch stole
Christmas
Spier, Peter. Peter Spier's Christmas!
Steiner, Charlotte. The climbing book
Stephenson, Dorothy. The night it
rained toys

Stern, Elsie-Jean. Wee Robin's Christmas song

Stock, Catherine. Sampson the Christmas cat

Tippett, James Sterling. Counting the days

Tolkien, J R R (John Ronald Reuel). The Father Christmas letters

Trent, Robbie. The first Christmas

Tudor, Tasha. The doll's Christmas
  Snow before Christmas

Türk, Hanne. Merry Christmas Max

Tutt, Kay Cunningham. And now we call him Santa Claus

The twelve days of Christmas. English folk song. Jack Kent's twelve days of Christmas

  The twelve days of Christmas, ill. by Ilonka Karasz

  The twelve days of Christmas, ill. by Erika Schneider

Ungerer, Tomi. Christmas eve at the Mellops

Vincent, Gabrielle. Ernest and Celestine

Wahl, Jan. The Muffletumps' Christmas party

Watson, Clyde. How Brown Mouse kept Christmas

Watson, Wendy. The bunnies' Christmas eve

Weil, Lisl. The story of the Wise Men and the Child

Weiss, Ellen. Things to make and do for Christmas

Wenning, Elisabeth. The Christmas mouse

Wild, Robin. Little Pig and the big bad wolf

Winthrop, Elizabeth. A child is born

Woolaver, Lance. Christmas with the rural mail

Woolley, Catherine. The puppy who wanted a boy

Zakhoder, Boris Vladimirovich. How a piglet crashed the Christmas party

Zolotow, Charlotte. The beautiful Christmas tree

Holidays — Cinco de Mayo

Bannon, Laura. Watchdog
Behrens, June. Fiesta!

Holidays — Columbus Day

Showers, Paul. Columbus Day

Holidays — Easter

Adams, Adrienne. The Easter egg artists
Armour, Richard Willard. The adventures of Egbert the Easter egg
Balian, Lorna. Humbug rabbit

Barrett, John M. The Easter bear

Benchley, Nathaniel. The strange disappearance of Arthur Cluck

Brown, Margaret Wise. The golden egg book
  The runaway bunny

Carrick, Carol. A rabbit for Easter

Cross, Genevieve. My bunny book

Darling, Kathy. The Easter bunny's secret

DeLage, Ida. ABC Easter bunny

Dunn, Judy. The little rabbit

Duvoisin, Roger Antoine. Easter treat

Friedrich, Priscilla. The Easter bunny that overslept

Gordon, Sharon. Easter Bunny's lost egg

Heyward, Du Bose. The country bunny and the little gold shoes

Hopkins, Lee Bennett. Easter buds are springing

Kay, Helen. An egg is for wishing

Kraus, Robert. Daddy Long Ears

Kroll, Steven. The big bunny and the Easter eggs

Littlefield, William. The whiskers of Ho Ho

McClenathan, Louise. The Easter pig

Maril, Lee. Mr. Bunny paints the eggs

Milhous, Katherine. The egg tree

Priolo, Pauline. Piccolina and the Easter bells

Tresselt, Alvin R. The world in the candy egg

Wahl, Jan. The five in the forest

Weil, Lisl. The candy egg bunny

Weisgard, Leonard. The funny bunny factory

Wiese, Kurt. Happy Easter

Woolley, Catherine. The horse with the Easter bonnet

Young, Miriam Burt. Miss Suzy's Easter surprise

Zolotow, Charlotte. The bunny who found Easter
  Mr. Rabbit and the lovely present

Holidays — Fourth of July

Shortall, Leonard W. One way
Zion, Gene. The summer snowman

Holidays — Groundhog Day

Cohen, Carol L. Wake up, groundhog!
Delton, Judy. Groundhog's Day at the doctor
Hamberger, John. This is the day
Johnson, Crockett. Will spring be early?
Kesselman, Wendy. Time for Jody
Palazzo, Tony. Waldo the woodchuck

Holidays — Halloween

Adams, Adrienne. A Halloween
  happening
  A woggle of witches
Anderson, Lonzo. The Halloween party
Asch, Frank. Popcorn
Averill, Esther. Jenny's moonlight
  adventure
Balian, Lorna. Humbug witch
Barth, Edna. Jack-o'-lantern
Battles, Edith. The terrible trick or treat
Beim, Jerrold. Sir Halloween
Benarde, Anita. The pumpkin smasher
Bond, Felicia. The Halloween
  performance
Borten, Helen. Halloween
Bradford, Ann. The mystery of the live
  ghosts
Bridwell, Norman. Clifford's Halloween
Bright, Robert. Georgie's Halloween
Brown, Marc. Arthur's Halloween
Calhoun, Mary. The witch of Hissing
  Hill
  Wobble the witch cat
Carlson, Natalie Savage. Spooky night
Carrick, Carol. Old Mother Witch
Cavagnaro, David. The pumpkin people
Charlton, Elizabeth. Jeremy and the
  ghost
Coombs, Patricia. Dorrie and the
  Halloween plot
Cooper, Paulette. Let's find out about
  Halloween
Corwin, Judith Hoffman. Halloween fun
Cuyler, Margery. Sir William and the
  pumpkin monster
Davis, Maggie S. Rickety witch
Degen, Bruce. Aunt Possum and the
  pumpkin man
DeLage, Ida. The old witch and her
  magic basket
Devlin, Wende. Cranberry Halloween
  Old Witch rescues Halloween
Embry, Margaret. The blue-nosed witch
Foster, Doris Van Liew. Tell me, Mr.
  Owl
Freeman, Don. Space witch
  Tilly Witch
Friedrich, Priscilla. The marshmallow
  ghosts
Gibbons, Gail. Halloween
Glovach, Linda. The little Witch's black
  magic book of disguises
  The little Witch's Halloween book
Greene, Carol. The thirteen days of
  Halloween
Greene, Ellin. The pumpkin giant
Hellsing, Lennart. The wonderful
  pumpkin
Hoff, Syd. Henrietta's Halloween
Hurd, Edith Thacher. The so-so cat

Hutchins, Pat. The best train set ever
Johnson, Hannah Lyons. From seed to
  jack-o'-lantern
Johnston, Tony. The vanishing
  pumpkin
Kahl, Virginia. Gunhilde and the
  Halloween spell
Keats, Ezra Jack. The trip
Kellogg, Steven. The mystery of the
  flying orange pumpkin
Kessler, Ethel. Grandpa Witch and the
  magic doobelator
Kessler, Leonard P. Riddles that rhyme
  for Halloween time
Kroll, Steven. The candy witch
Low, Alice. The witch who was afraid of
  witches
  Witch's holiday
Maestro, Giulio. Halloween howls
Manushkin, Fran. Hocus and Pocus at
  the circus
Marks, Burton. The spook book
Marshall, Edward. Space case
Massey, Jeanne. The littlest witch
Miller, Edna. Mousekin's golden house
Mooser, Stephen. The ghost with the
  Halloween hiccups
Nicoll, Helen. Meg and Mog
Nolan, Dennis. Witch Bazooza
Numeroff, Laura Joffe. Emily's bunch
Ott, John. Peter Pumpkin
Patterson, Lillie. Haunted houses on
  Halloween
Paul, Sherry. 2-B and the space visitor
Peters, Sharon. Trick or treat Halloween
Prager, Annabelle. The spooky
  Halloween party
Prelutsky, Jack. It's Halloween
Preston, Edna Mitchell. One dark night
Racioppo, Larry. Halloween
Rockwell, Anne F. A bear, a bobcat and
  three ghosts
Rose, David S. It hardly seems like
  Halloween
St George, Judith. The Halloween
  pumpkin smasher
Schertle, Alice. Hob Goblin and the
  skeleton
Schulman, Janet. Jack the bum and the
  Halloween handout
Schweninger, Ann. Halloween surprises
Scott, Ann Herbert. Let's catch a
  monster
Shaw, Richard. The kitten in the
  pumpkin patch
Slobodkin, Louis. Trick or treat
Stevenson, James. The terrible
  Halloween night
Vigna, Judith. Everyone goes as a
  pumpkin

Von Hippel, Ursula. The craziest
Halloween
Wahl, Jan. Pleasant Fieldmouse's
Halloween party
Watson, Jane Werner. Which is the
witch?
Wegen, Ron. The Halloween costume
party
Woolley, Catherine. Gus was a gorgeous
ghost
Young, Miriam Burt. The witch mobile
Zimmer, Dirk. The trick-or-treat trap
Zolotow, Charlotte. A tiger called
Thomas

Holidays — Hanukkah

Adler, David A. A picture book of
Hanukkah
 A picture book of Jewish holidays
Aleichem, Sholom. Hannukah money
Coopersmith, Jerome. A Chanukah
fable for Christmas
Goffstein, M B (Marilyn Brooks).
Laughing latkes

Holidays — Independence Day *see* Holidays — Fourth of July

Holidays — Mardi Gras *see* Mardi Gras

Holidays — Memorial Day

Scott, Geoffrey. Memorial Day

Holidays — Mother's Day

Howe, James. The case of the missing
mother

Holidays — New Year's

Andersen, H C (Hans Christian). The
little match girl
Janice. Little Bear's New Year's party
Modell, Frank. Goodbye old year, hello
new year

Holidays — Passover

Adler, David A. A picture book of
Jewish holidays
 A picture book of Passover
Hirsh, Marilyn. One little goat
Rosen, Anne. A family Passover
Zusman, Evelyn. The Passover parrot

Holidays — St. Patrick's Day

Bunting, Eve. St. Patrick's Day in the
morning
Calhoun, Mary. The hungry leprechaun
Janice. Little Bear marches in the St.
Patrick's Day parade

Zimelman, Nathan. To sing a song as
big as Ireland

Holidays — Thanksgiving

Balian, Lorna. Sometimes it's turkey
Brown, Marc. Arthur's Thanksgiving
Child, Lydia Maria. Over the river and
through the wood
Dalgliesh, Alice. The Thanksgiving story
Devlin, Wende. Cranberry Thanksgiving
Gibbons, Gail. Thanksgiving Day
Glovach, Linda. The little Witch's
Thanksgiving book
Hopkins, Lee Bennett. Merrily comes
our harvest in
Ipcar, Dahlov. Hard scrabble harvest
Janice. Little Bear's Thanksgiving
Kroll, Steven. One tough turkey
Lowitz, Sadyebeth. The pilgrims' party
Nixon, Joan Lowery. The Thanksgiving
mystery
Ott, John. Peter Pumpkin
Quackenbush, Robert M. Sheriff Sally
Gopher and the Thanksgiving caper
Spinelli, Eileen. Thanksgiving at
Tappletons'
Tresselt, Alvin R. Autumn harvest
Williams, Barbara. Chester Chipmunk's
Thanksgiving
Zion, Gene. The meanest squirrel I ever
met

Holidays — Valentine's Day

Adams, Adrienne. The great Valentine's
Day balloon race
Balian, Lorna. A sweetheart for
Valentine
Bond, Felicia. Four Valentines in a
rainstorm
Brown, Marc. Arthur's Valentine
Bulla, Clyde Robert. Valentine cat
Bunting, Eve. The Valentine bears
Cohen, Miriam. Bee my Valentine!
De Paola, Tomie. Things to make and
do for Valentine's Day
Greene, Carol. A computer went
a-courting
Guilfoile, Elizabeth. Valentine's Day
Keeshan, Robert. She loves me, she
loves me not
Kelley, True. A valentine for Fuzzboom
Krahn, Fernando. Little love story
Modell, Frank. One zillion valentines
Murphy, Shirley Rousseau. Valentine
for a dragon
Nixon, Joan Lowery. The Valentine
mystery
Prelutsky, Jack. It's Valentine's Day
Schultz, Gwen. The blue Valentine

Schweninger, Ann. The hunt for rabbit's galosh
Sharmat, Marjorie Weinman. The best Valentine in the world

Holidays — Washington's Birthday

Blair, Anne Denton. Hurrah for Arthur!
Bulla, Clyde Robert. Washington's birthday

Holland *see* Foreign lands — Holland

Homes *see* Houses

Honesty *see* Character traits — honesty

Honey bees *see* Insects — bees

Horses *see* Animals — horses

Horses, rocking *see* Toys — rocking horses

Hospitals

Baker, Gayle. Special delivery
Bemelmans, Ludwig. Madeline
Blance, Ellen. Monster goes to the hospital
Bruna, Dick. Miffy in the hospital
Ciliotta, Claire. "Why am I going to the hospital?"
Collier, James Lincoln. Danny goes to the hospital
Elliott, Ingrid Glatz. Hospital roadmap
Marino, Barbara Pavis. Eric needs stitches
Pope, Billy N. Your world let's visit the hospital
Rey, Margaret Elisabeth Waldstein. Curious George goes to the hospital
Shay, Arthur. What happens when you go to the hospital
Sobol, Harriet Langsam. Jeff's hospital book
Sonneborn, Ruth A. I love Gram
Stein, Sara Bonnett. A hospital story
Stone, Bernard. Emergency mouse
Tamburine, Jean. I think I will go to the hospital
Watts, Marjorie-Ann. Crocodile medicine
Weber, Alfons. Elizabeth gets well
Wolde, Gunilla. Betsy and the doctor

Hotels

Mahy, Margaret. Rooms for rent
Parkin, Rex. The red carpet
Stevenson, James. The Sea View Hotel

Houses

Adler, David A. The house on the roof
Alger, Leclaire. Always room for one more
Arkin, Alan. Tony's hard work day
Ayars, James Sterling. Caboose on the roof
Bannon, Laura. The best house in the world
Barton, Byron. Building a house
Becker, Edna. Nine hundred buckets of paint
Bemelmans, Ludwig. Sunshine
Binzen, Bill. Alfred goes house hunting
Blegvad, Lenore. The parrot in the garret and other rhymes about dwellings
Borg, Inga. Plupp builds a house
Bour, Danièle. The house from morning to night
Brown, Marcia. The neighbors
Brown, Margaret Wise. House of a hundred windows
  The wonderful house
Burton, Virginia Lee. The little house
Calhoun, Mary. Mrs. Dog's own house
Calmenson, Stephanie. Where will the animals stay?
Carter, Katharine. Houses
Cauley, Lorinda Bryan. The new house
Chase, Catherine. The mouse in my house
Christensen, Gardell Dano. Mrs. Mouse needs a house
Clymer, Eleanor Lowenton. The tiny little house
Colby, C B (Carroll Burleigh). Who lives there?
Colman, Hila. Peter's brownstone house
Crompton, Margaret. The house where Jack lives
Curry, Nancy. The littlest house
Cutler, Ivor. The animal house
Dauer, Rosamond. Bullfrog builds a house
De Regniers, Beatrice Schenk. A little house of your own
Erickson, Phoebe. Just follow me
Farm house
Feder, Paula Kurzband. Where does the teacher live?
Firehouse
Fisher, Aileen. Best little house
Flory, Jane. The bear on the doorstep
Friedman, Estelle. Boy who lived in a cave
Green, Mary McBurney. Everybody has a house and everybody eats
Greydanus, Rose. Tree house fun
Harper, Anita. How we live

Hoberman, Mary Ann. A house is a house for me

Hoff, Syd. Stanley

Holl, Adelaide. Small Bear builds a playhouse

Hughes, Shirley. Alfie gets in first
Sally's secret

Hunter, Norman. Professor Branestawn's building bust-up

Jaques, Faith. Tilly's house

Jaynes, Ruth M. The biggest house

Joerns, Consuelo. The lost and found house

Kaune, Merriman B. My own little house

Kirk, Barbara. Grandpa, me and our house in the tree

Krauss, Ruth. A very special house

Kroll, Steven. Pigs in the house

Kwitz, Mary DeBall. Rabbits' search for a little house

Lippman, Peter. The Know-It-Alls help out

McGovern, Ann. Mr. Skinner's skinny house

Maestro, Betsy. Harriet at home

Maris, Ron. Better move on, frog!

Mayer, Mercer. Little Monster at home

Mendoza, George. Need a house? Call Ms. Mouse

Miles, Betty. A house for everyone

Mizumura, Kazue. If I built a village

Mother Goose house

Mouse house

Muntean, Michaela. The house that bear built

Murphy, Shirley Rousseau. Tattie's river journey

Nolan, Dennis. Witch Bazooza

Nussbaum, Hedda. Animals build amazing homes

Palmer, Helen Marion. Why I built the boogle house

Pape, Donna Lugg. Doghouse for sale

Patterson, Lillie. Haunted houses on Halloween

Peppé, Rodney. The mice who lived in a shoe

Pieńkowski, Jan. Homes

Pinkwater, Daniel Manus. The big orange splot

Rey, Hans Augusto. Anybody at home?

Rockwell, Anne F. Nice and clean

Roffey, Maureen. Home sweet home

Ross, Pat. M and M and the haunted house game

Rusling, Albert. The mouse and Mrs. Proudfoot

Sattler, Helen Roney. No place for a goat

Scarry, Richard. Is this the house of Mistress Mouse?
Richard Scarry's busy houses

Schaaf, Peter. An apartment house close up

Schertle, Alice. In my treehouse

Schlein, Miriam. My house

Schulman, Janet. Jack the bum and the haunted house

Schulz, Charles M. Snoopy's facts and fun book about houses

Seuss, Dr. In a people house

Shapp, Martha. Let's find out about houses

Sharr, Christine. Homes

Shecter, Ben. Emily, girl witch of New York

Stern, Simon. Mrs. Vinegar

Strathdee, Jean. The house that grew

Tallarico, Tony. At home

Tison, Annette. Inside and outside

Tudor, Bethany. Samuel's tree house

Vevers, Gwynne. Animal homes

Watanabe, Shigeo. I can build a house!

Wildsmith, Brian. Animal homes

Woolley, Catherine. What's a ghost going to do?

Zelinsky, Paul O. The maid and the mouse and the odd-shaped house

Humor

Aardema, Verna. Oh, Kojo! How could you!
What's so funny, Ketu?
Who's in Rabbit's house?

Adams, Richard. The tyger voyage

Adamson, Gareth. Old man up a tree

Adler, David A. The children of Chelm

Æsop. The miller, his son and their donkey

Ahlberg, Janet. The little worm book

Alborough, Jez. Bare bear

Alexander, Martha G. Move over, Twerp

Alexander, Sue. World famous Muriel

Aliki. Digging up dinosaurs
The eggs

Allamand, Pascale. The animals who changed their colors

Allan, Ted. Willie the squowse

Allard, Harry. Miss Nelson has a field day
The Stupids die
The Stupids have a ball
The Stupids step out
There's a party at Mona's tonight

Allen, Jonathan. A bad case of animal nonsense

Allen, Linda. Mr. Simkin's grandma
Mrs. Simkin's bed

Allen, Marjorie N. One, two, three - ah-choo!

Allen, Pamela. Mr. Archimedes' bath

Ambrus, Victor G. Grandma, Felix, and Mustapha Biscuit
The seven skinny goats

Andersen, H C (Hans Christian). The emperor's new clothes, ill. by Pamela Baldwin-Ford
The emperor's new clothes, ill. by Erik Blegvad
The emperor's new clothes, ill. by Virginia Lee Burton
The emperor's new clothes, ill. by Jack and Irene DeLano
The emperor's new clothes, ill. by Birte Dietz
The emperor's new clothes, ill. by Jack Kent
The emperor's new clothes, ill. by Monika Laimgruber
The emperor's new clothes, ill. by Anne F. Rockwell
The emperor's new clothes, ill. by Nadine Bernard Westcott
The old man is always right

Anderson, Leone Castell. The wonderful shrinking shirt

Anno, Mitsumasa. Anno's Britain
Anno's counting house
Anno's flea market
Anno's Italy
Anno's journey
Anno's U.S.A.
Dr. Anno's midnight circus
Topsy-turvies
Upside-downers

Armour, Richard Willard. Animals on the ceiling

Arnosky, Jim. Outdoors on foot

Asch, Frank. Sand cake
Turtle tale

Aulaire, Ingri Mortenson d'. Don't count your chicks

Ayars, James Sterling. Caboose on the roof

Aylesworth, Jim. Hush up!

Baker, Alan. Benjamin bounces back
Benjamin's book
Benjamin's dreadful dream

Baker, Betty. Sonny-Boy Sim
Three fools and a horse
Worthington Botts and the steam machine

Bakken, Harold. The special string

Balian, Lorna. Leprechauns never lie

Barr, Cathrine. Hound dog's bone

Barrett, John M. The bear who slept through Christmas

Behn, Harry. What a beautiful noise

Belloc, Hilaire. The bad child's book of beasts

Bemelmans, Ludwig. Rosebud
Sunshine

Benchley, Nathaniel. Walter the homing pigeon

Benedictus, Roger. Fifty million sausages

Benjamin, Alan. 1000 monsters

Bennett, Jill. Roger was a razor fish and other poems
Tiny Tim

Benton, Robert. Don't ever wish for a 7-foot bear

Berenstain, Stan. Old hat, new hat

Bishop, Ann. Chicken riddle
The Ella Fannie elephant riddle book
Hey riddle riddle
Merry-go-riddle
Noah riddle?
Oh, riddlesticks!
The riddle ages
Riddle-iculous rid-alphabet book
Wild Bill Hiccup's riddle book

Bishop, Claire Huchet. The man who lost his head

Blake, Quentin. Mister Magnolia
Quentin Blake's nursery rhyme book

Bodecker, N M (Nils Mogens). "It's raining," said John Twaining
"Let's marry," said the cherry, and other nonsense poems
Snowman Sniffles and other verse

Bohman, Nils. Jim, Jock and Jumbo

Bonne, Rose. I know an old lady

Borten, Helen. Do you go where I go?

Bossom, Naomi. A scale full of fish and other turnabouts

Bowden, Joan Chase. The bean boy
Why the tides ebb and flow

Boynton, Sandra. If at first...

Bradfield, Roger. The flying hockey stick

Brecht, Bertolt. Uncle Eddie's moustache

Brenner, Barbara. A dog I know

Bridwell, Norman. The witch grows up

Briggs, Raymond. Jim and the beanstalk

Bright, Robert. Georgie and the baby birds
Georgie and the ball of yarn
Georgie and the buried treasure
Georgie and the little dog
Georgie and the magician
Georgie and the runaway balloon

Brock, Emma Lillian. Mr. Wren's house
Nobody's mouse
Skipping Island

Bröger, Achim. Little Harry

Brooke, L Leslie (Leonard Leslie).
  Johnny Crow's garden
  Johnny Crow's new garden
  Johnny Crow's party
Brothers, Aileen. Sad Mrs. Sam Sack
Brown, Jeff. Flat Stanley
Brown, Marc. Spooky riddles
  What do you call a dumb bunny? and
  other rabbit riddles, games, jokes and
  cartoons
Brown, Margaret Wise. Once upon a
  time in pigpen and three other
  stories
Browne, Caroline. Mrs. Christie's
  farmhouse
Bruna, Dick. Kitten Nell
Brunhoff, Laurent de. Serafina the
  giraffe
Bryant, Sara Cone. Epaminondas and
  his auntie
Buchanan, Joan. It's a good thing
Burningham, John. The shopping
  basket
Burroway, Janet. The truck on the track
Burton, Marilee Robin. The elephant's
  nest
Byfield, Barbara Ninde. The haunted
  churchbell
Calhoun, Mary. The nine lives of
  Homer C. Cat
  Old man Whickutt's donkey
  The traveling ball of string
Cameron, Polly. A child's book of
  nonsense
Carroll, Lewis. Jabberwocky
Carroll, Ruth. Old Mrs. Billups and the
  black cats
Caudill, Rebecca. Contrary Jenkins
Cerf, Bennett Alfred. Bennett Cerf's
  book of animal riddles
  Bennett Cerf's book of laughs
  Bennett Cerf's book of riddles
  More riddles
Chalmers, Audrey. Hundreds and
  hundreds of pancakes
Charlip, Remy. Arm in arm
  Fortunately
  "Mother, mother I feel sick"
  Thirteen
Chevalier, Christa. Spence makes circles
Christian, Mary Blount. Nothing much
  happened today
Chukovsky, Korney. The telephone
Ciardi, John. I met a man
Cole, Joanna. The Clown-Arounds go
  on vacation
  Get well, Clown-Arounds!
  Golly Gump swallowed a fly
Cole, William. Dinosaurs and beasts of
  yore
  I went to the animal fair

Collins, Judith Graham. Josh's scary dad
Coontz, Otto. Starring Rosa
Copp, James. Martha Matilda O'Toole
Craig, M Jean. The man whose name
  was not Thomas
Daugherty, James Henry. Andy and the
  lion
Davis, Maggie S. The best way to Ripton
Delaney, M C. The marigold monster
Delaney, Ned. Terrible things could
  happen
Dennis, Suzanne E. Answer me that
De Paola, Tomie. Bill and Pete
  Flicks
  Strega Nona
  Strega Nona's magic lessons
De Regniers, Beatrice Schenk. May I
  bring a friend?
Dorros, Arthur. Pretzels
Duvoisin, Roger Antoine. Petunia's
  Christmas
Ellentuck, Shan. Did you see what I
  said?
  A sunflower as big as the sun
Ets, Marie Hall. Beasts and nonsense
  Mister Penny
Evans, Katherine. The maid and her
  pail of milk
  The man, the boy and the donkey
Farber, Norma. There once was a
  woman who married a man
Fenton, Edward. The big yellow balloon
Flora, James. The day the cow sneezed
  Grandpa's farm
  My friend Charlie
Folsom, Marcia. Easy as pie
Freeman, Don. Forever laughter
Frith, Michael K. I'll teach my dog 100
  words
From King Boggen's hall to
  nothing-at-all
A frog he would a-wooing go
  (folk-song). Frog went a-courtin'
Fuchshuber, Annegert. The wishing hat
Gackenbach, Dick. The pig who saw
  everything
Gelman, Rita Golden. Hey, kid
The golden goose
Grimm, Jacob. Clever Kate
Hall, Donald. Andrew the lion farmer
Hall, Katy. Fishy riddles
Hample, Stoo. Stoo Hample's silly joke
  book
Hart, Jeanne McGahey. Scareboy
Heide, Florence Parry. The shrinking of
  Treehorn
Heilbroner, Joan. Robert the rose horse
Hirsh, Marilyn. Could anything be
  worse?
Hoban, Russell. A near thing for
  Captain Najork

Thank you, Amelia Bedelia

Park, W B. Bakery business

Parkin, Rex. The red carpet

Partch, Virgil Franklin. The VIP's
mistake book

Paterson, Diane. Eat
Smile for auntie

Patz, Nancy. Pumpernickel tickle and
mean green cheese

Pearson, Tracey Campbell. Sing a song
of sixpence

Peet, Bill. Big bad Bruce
Buford, the little bighorn
Chester the worldly pig
Countdown to Christmas
Cowardly Clyde
Eli
Hubert's hair-raising adventures
Huge Harold
Jennifer and Josephine
Kermit the hermit
Merle the high flying squirrel
Randy's dandy lions

Postgate, Oliver. Noggin and the whale
Noggin the king

Potter, Beatrix. The tale of Tom Kitten

Prather, Ray. Double dog dare

Prelutsky, Jack. The baby uggs are
hatching
The queen of Eene
The Random House book of poetry
for children
The snopp on the sidewalk and other
poems

Preston, Edna Mitchell. Horrible
Hepzibah
Pop Corn and Ma Goodness

Puner, Helen Walker. The sitter who
didn't sit

Quackenbush, Robert M. Detective Mole
Detective Mole and the secret clues
Detective Mole and the Tip-Top
mystery
Funny bunnies
Pete Pack Rat
What has Wild Tom done now?!!!

Raskin, Ellen. Franklin Stein
Nothing ever happens on my block

Reeves, James. Rhyming Will

Reid, Alastair. Supposing

Rey, Hans Augusto. Cecily G and the
nine monkeys
Curious George
Curious George gets a medal
Curious George rides a bike
Curious George takes a job
Elizabite, adventures of a carnivorous
plant
Tit for tat

Rey, Margaret Elisabeth Waldstein.
Billy's picture
Curious George flies a kite
Curious George goes to the hospital

Rosen, Michael. You can't catch me!

Rossner, Judith. What kind of feet does
a bear have?

Rounds, Glen. The day the circus came
to Lone Tree

Roy, Ronald. Three ducks went
wandering

Rusling, Albert. The mouse and Mrs.
Proudfoot

Saddler, Allen. The Archery contest
The king gets fit

Sage, Michael. Dippy dos and don'ts
If you talked to a boar

Sazer, Nina. What do you think I saw?

Scarry, Richard. Richard Scarry's
funniest storybook ever

Schatell, Brian. Midge and Fred

Scheer, Julian. Rain makes applesauce

Schmidt, Eric von. The young man who
wouldn't hoe corn

Schwalje, Marjory. Mr. Angelo

Sendak, Maurice. Pierre

Seuss, Dr. And to think that I saw it on
Mulberry Street
Bartholomew and the Oobleck
The cat in the hat
The cat in the hat beginner book
dictionary
The cat in the hat comes back!
The cat's quizzer
Did I ever tell you how lucky you are?
Dr. Seuss's ABC
Dr. Seuss's sleep book
The foot book
Fox in sox
A great day for up
Green eggs and ham
Happy birthday to you!
Hooper Humperdink...? Not him!
Hop on Pop
Horton hatches the egg
Horton hears a Who!
How the Grinch stole Christmas
I can lick 30 tigers today and other
stories
I can read with my eyes shut
I can write!
I had trouble getting to Solla Sollew
If I ran the circus
If I ran the zoo
In a people house
The king's stilts
The Lorax
McElligot's pool
Marvin K. Mooney, will you please go
now!
Mr. Brown can moo! Can you?

Oh say can you say?
Oh, the thinks you can think!
On beyond zebra
One fish, two fish, red fish, blue fish
Please try to remember the first of
octember!
Scrambled eggs super!
The shape of me and other stuff
The Sneetches, and other stories
There's a wocket in my pocket
Thidwick, the big-hearted moose
Wacky Wednesday
Shannon, George. Beanboy
Showalter, Jean B. The donkey ride
Silverstein, Shel. A giraffe and a half
Singer, Marilyn. The dog who insisted
he wasn't
Slobodkina, Esphyr. Caps for sale
Pezzo the peddler and the circus
elephant
Pezzo the peddler and the thirteen silly
thieves
Smith, Jim. The frog band and the
onion seller
The frog band and the owlnapper
Smith, Robert Paul. Jack Mack
Smith, William Jay. Puptents and
pebbles
Spier, Peter. Bored - nothing to do!
Oh, were they ever happy!
Spilka, Arnold. And the frog went
"Blah!"
A lion I can do without
A rumbudgin of nonsense
Spinelli, Eileen. Thanksgiving at
Tappletons'
Stamaty, Mark Alan. Minnie Maloney
and Macaroni
Steig, William. Farmer Palmer's wagon
ride
Stone, Rosetta. Because a little bug went
ka-choo!
Stroyer, Poul. It's a deal
Suba, Susanne. The monkeys and the
pedlar
Suhl, Yuri. Simon Boom gives a
wedding
Sundgaard, Arnold. Jethro's difficult
dinosaur
Tapio, Pat Decker. The lady who saw
the good side of everything
Thaler, Mike. The yellow brick toad
Thomas, Patricia. "Stand back," said the
elephant, "I'm going to sneeze!"
Tobias, Tobi. Jane wishing
Tomkins, Jasper. The catalog
Tripp, Wallace. My Uncle Podger
The twelve days of Christmas. English
folk song. Jack Kent's twelve days of
Christmas
Ueno, Noriko. Elephant buttons

Ungerer, Tomi. The beast of Monsieur
Racine
Crictor
Emile
Van der Meer, Ron. Oh Lord!
Van Woerkom, Dorothy. Abu Ali
Donkey Ysabel
The friends of Abu Ali
The queen who couldn't bake
gingerbread
Viorst, Judith. Sunday morning
Waber, Bernard. How to go about
laying an egg
Nobody is perfick
Wahl, Jan. Cabbage moon
Watanabe, Shigeo. What a good lunch!
Watson, Clyde. Hickory stick rag
Wiese, Kurt. Fish in the air
Wiesner, William. Happy-Go-Lucky
Turnabout
Willard, Nancy. Simple pictures are best
Williams, Barbara. Jeremy isn't hungry
Williams, Jay. School for sillies
Wiseman, Bernard. Tails are not for
painting
Yolen, Jane. The acorn quest
Zemach, Harve. The tricks of Master
Dabble
Zemach, Margot. It could always be
worse
Zimmerman, Andrea Griffing. Yetta, the
trickster

Hungary *see* Foreign lands — Hungary

Hunting *see* Sports — hunting

Hurrying *see* Behavior — hurrying

Hyenas *see* Animals — hyenas

Ice skating *see* Sports — ice skating

Iguanas *see* Reptiles — iguanas

Illness

Aliki. I wish I was sick, too!
Arnold, Katrin. Anna joins in
Bains, Rae. Hiccups, hiccups
Barrett, Judi. An apple a day
Berger, Melvin. Why I cough, sneeze,
shiver, hiccup and yawn
Brown, Margaret Wise. When the wind
blew

Bruna, Dick. Miffy in the hospital
Carrick, Carol. Old Mother Witch
Chalmers, Mary. Come to the doctor, Harry
Charlip, Remy. "Mother, mother I feel sick"
Christelow, Eileen. Henry and the red stripes
Ciliotta, Claire. "Why am I going to the hospital?"
Cole, Joanna. Get well, Clown-Arounds!
De Groat, Diane. Alligator's toothache
Delton, Judy. Groundhog's Day at the doctor
  It happened on Thursday
De Paola, Tomie. Now one foot, now the other
Duff, Maggie. The princess and the pumpkin
Duvoisin, Roger Antoine. The Christmas whale
Eberstadt, Isabel. What is for my birthday?
Elliott, Ingrid Glatz. Hospital roadmap
Fern, Eugene. Pepito's story
Fleischman, Sid. Kate's secret riddle
Gackenbach, Dick. Hattie be quiet, Hattie be good
  What's Claude doing?
Galbraith, Kathryn Osebold. Spots are special
Gretz, Susanna. Teddy bears cure a cold
Hewett, Joan. Fly away free
Holl, Adelaide. Small Bear solves a mystery
Hurd, Edith Thacher. Johnny Lion's bad day
Hutchins, Pat. The best train set ever
Jenkins, Jordan. Learning about love
Johnson, Louise. Malunda
Keller, Beverly. When mother got the flu
Knotts, Howard. The lost Christmas
Kroll, Steven. The big bunny and the Easter eggs
Lerner, Marguerite Rush. Dear little mumps child
  Michael gets the measles
  Peter gets the chickenpox
Lewin, Betsy. Hip, hippo, hooray!
Lexau, Joan M. Benjie on his own
Lobel, Arnold. A holiday for Mister Muster
MacLachlan, Patricia. Mama one, Mama two
  The sick day
McPhail, David. The bear's toothache
Maestro, Giulio. Leopard is sick
Mann, Peggy. King Laurence, the alarm clock
Marshall, James. Yummers!

Mayer, Mercer. Ah-choo
  Hiccup
Moss, Elaine. Polar
Nourse, Alan Edward. Lumps, bumps and rashes
Numeroff, Laura Joffe. Phoebe Dexter has Harriet Peterson's sniffles
Ostrovsky, Vivian. Mumps!
Polhamus, Jean Burt. Doctor Dinosaur
Quackenbush, Robert M. Calling Doctor Quack
Rockwell, Anne F. Sick in bed
Seignobosc, Françoise. Biquette, the white goat
Sharmat, Marjorie Weinman. I want mama
Shay, Arthur. What happens when you go to the hospital
Showers, Paul. No measles, no mumps for me
Sonneborn, Ruth A. I love Gram
Stein, Sara Bonnett. A hospital story
Stephenson, Dorothy. How to scare a lion
Thurber, James. Many moons
Trez, Denise. The royal hiccups
Udry, Janice May. Mary Jo's grandmother
Wahl, Jan. Jamie's tiger
Watts, Marjorie-Ann. Crocodile medicine
Weber, Alfons. Elizabeth gets well
Whitney, Alma Marshak. Just awful
Williams, Barbara. Albert's toothache
Williams, Vera B. Music, music for everyone
Wolde, Gunilla. Betsy and the chicken pox
  Betsy and the doctor
Yolen, Jane. Commander Toad and the planet of the grapes

Illusions, optical *see* Optical illusions

Illustrators, children *see* Children as illustrators

Imaginary friends *see* Imagination — imaginary friends

Imagination

Abisch, Roz. Open your eyes
Adam, Barbara. The big big box
Agee, Jon. Ellsworth
Aiken, Joan. Arabel and Mortimer
Aitken, Amy. Kate and Mona in the jungle
  Ruby!
  Ruby, the red knight

Alexander, Martha G. Bobo's dream
Marty McGee's space lab, no girls
allowed

Allen, Jeffrey. The secret life of Mr.
Weird

Andersen, H C (Hans Christian). The
emperor's new clothes, ill. by Pamela
Baldwin-Ford
The emperor's new clothes, ill. by Erik
Blegvad
The emperor's new clothes, ill. by
Virginia Lee Burton
The emperor's new clothes, ill. by Jack
and Irene DeLano
The emperor's new clothes, ill. by
Birte Dietz
The emperor's new clothes, ill. by Jack
Kent
The emperor's new clothes, ill. by
Monika Laimgruber
The emperor's new clothes, ill. by
Anne F. Rockwell
The emperor's new clothes, ill. by
Nadine Bernard Westcott

Anderson, C W (Clarence Williams).
Linda and the Indians

Anglund, Joan Walsh. Cowboy's secret
life

Anno, Mitsumasa. Anno's alphabet
Anno's animals
Anno's Britain
Anno's counting book
Anno's counting house
Anno's flea market
Anno's Italy
Anno's journey
Anno's magical ABC
Anno's U.S.A.
Dr. Anno's midnight circus
The king's flower
Topsy-turvies
Upside-downers

Armour, Richard Willard. Animals on
the ceiling

Asch, Frank. City sandwich
Goodnight horsey
Rebecka

Ayal, Ora. The adventures of Chester
the chest
Ugbu

Bach, Othello. Lilly, Willy and the
mail-order witch

Baker, Alan. Benjamin bounces back

Baker, Betty. My sister says

Balet, Jan B. Ned and Ed and the lion

Bang, Molly. The grey lady and the
strawberry snatcher

Bannon, Laura. The best house in the
world

Barrett, Judi. Cloudy with a chance of
meatballs
I hate to go to bed

Barry, Katharina. A bug to hug

Barthelme, Donald. The slightly
irregular fire engine

Baumann, Kurt. The paper airplane

Bayley, Nicola. Crab cat
Elephant cat
Parrot cat
Polar bear cat
Spider cat

Beech, Caroline. Peas again for lunch

Behrens, June. Can you walk the plank?

Beim, Jerrold. The taming of Toby

Benedictus, Roger. Fifty million
sausages

Benjamin, Alan. Ribtickle Town

Bennett, Rowena. The day is dancing
and other poems
Songs from around a toadstool table

Berenstain, Stan. The Berenstain bears
in the dark

Blakeley, Peggy. What shall I be
tomorrow?

Blegvad, Lenore. Anna Banana and me

Blocksma, Mary. The pup went up

Blos, Joan W. Martin's hats

Boegehold, Betty. Hurray for Pippa!
In the castle of cats

Bonsall, Crosby Newell. Tell me some
more

Boon, Emilie. Peterkin meets a star
Peterkin's wet walk

Bottner, Barbara. Mean Maxine
Myra
There was nobody there

Boutell, Clarence Burley. The fat baron

Bowers, Kathleen Rice. At this very
minute

Boyd, Selma. I met a polar bear

Brandenberg, Franz. Leo and Emily and
the dragon

Brenner, Anita. I want to fly

Bröger, Achim. Francie's paper puppy
Little Harry

Brooks, Gregory. Monroe's island

Brown, Paul. Merrylegs, the rocking
pony

Browne, Anthony. Look what I've got!

Bruce, Sheilah B. The radish day jubilee

Brunhoff, Laurent de. Gregory and
Lady Turtle in the valley of the music
trees

Buckaway, C M. Alfred, the dragon who
lost his flame

Budd, Lillian. The people on Long Ago
Street

Bulette, Sara. The elf in the singing tree

Burningham, John. Come away from the water, Shirley
  Time to get out of the bath, Shirley
  Would you rather...
Callen, Larry. Dashiel and the night
Carrick, Carol. Patrick's dinosaurs
Carroll, Lewis. The nursery "Alice"
Chalmers, Mary. The cat who liked to pretend
Charles Prince of Wales. The old man of Lochnagar
Chevalier, Christa. Spence and the sleepytime monster
Chislett, Gail. The rude visitors
Chorao, Kay. Lester's overnight
Collins, Pat Lowery. My friend Andrew
Cooper, Elizabeth K. The fish from Japan
Craig, Helen. Susie and Alfred in the knight, the princess and the dragon
Craig, M Jean. The dragon in the clock box
Cummings, E E. Fairy tales
Davis, Douglas F. There's an elephant in the garage
Delaney, A. Monster tracks?
De Regniers, Beatrice Schenk. Laura's story
  A little house of your own
  Waiting for mama
  What can you do with a shoe?
Devlin, Wende. Aunt Agatha, there's a lion under the couch!
Dickinson, Mary. Alex and Roy
Dickinson, Mike. My dad doesn't even notice
DiFiori, Lawrence. If I had a little car
D'Ignazio, Fred. Katie and the computer
Dobrin, Arnold Jack. Josephine's 'magination
Dorian, Marguerite. When the snow is blue
Drescher, Henrik. Looking for Santa Claus
Etherington, Frank. The spaghetti word race
Ets, Marie Hall. In the forest
Felix, Monique. The story of a little mouse trapped in a book
Fenner, Carol. Tigers in the cellar
Fenton, Edward. Fierce John
Firmin, Peter. Basil Brush and a dragon
Fontaine, Jan. The spaghetti tree
Francis, Frank. The magic wallpaper
Freeman, Don. The paper party
  Quiet! There's a canary in the library
Gackenbach, Dick. Harry and the terrible whatzit
Gage, Wilson. Mrs. Gaddy and the ghost
Galbraith, Kathryn Osebold. Spots are special

Glass, Andrew. My brother tries to make me laugh
Hamsa, Bobbie. Your pet bear
  Your pet beaver
  Your pet camel
  Your pet elephant
  Your pet giraffe
  Your pet kangaroo
  Your pet penguin
  Your pet sea lion
Hanlon, Emily. What if a lion eats me and I fall into a hippopotamus' mud hole?
Himler, Ronald. The girl on the yellow giraffe
Hoban, Russell. The flight of Bembel Rudzuk
  Goodnight
  The great gum drop robbery
Hoffmann, E T A. The nutcracker
Holman, Felice. Victoria's castle
Horwitz, Elinor Lander. Sometimes it happens
Hughes, Shirley. Up and up
Hunter, Mollie. The knight of the golden plain
Hurd, Edith Thacher. The white horse
Ionesco, Eugene. Story number 1
Janosch. Hey Presto! You're a bear!
Jeschke, Susan. Tamar and the tiger
Jewell, Nancy. Try and catch me
Johnson, Crockett. The blue ribbon puppies
  Ellen's lion
  Harold and the purple crayon
  Harold at the North Pole
  Harold's ABC
  Harold's circus
  Harold's fairy tale
  Harold's trip to the sky
  A picture for Harold's room
Johnson, Elizabeth. All in free but Janey
Johnson, Jane. Sybil and the blue rabbit
Keats, Ezra Jack. Dreams
  Regards to the man in the moon
  The trip
Keeping, Charles. Willie's fire-engine
Kellogg, Steven. Ralph's secret weapon
Knight, Hilary. Hilary Knight's the owl and the pussy-cat
Kojima, Naomi. The flying grandmother
Krauss, Ruth. A moon or a button
  Open house for butterflies
  Somebody else's nut tree, and other tales from children
  This thumbprint
  A very special house
Kroll, Steven. Are you pirates?
  Toot! Toot!
  The tyrannosaurus game
Kumin, Maxine. Follow the fall

Viorst, Judith. My mama says there aren't any zombies, ghosts, vampires, creatures, demons, monsters, fiends, goblins, or things
Vogel, Ilse-Margaret. The don't be scared book
Vreeken, Elizabeth. The boy who would not say his name
Watson, Clyde. Midnight moon
Watson, Jane Werner. The tall book of make-believe
Wells, Rosemary. Good night, Fred
  A lion for Lewis
Willard, Nancy. A visit to William Blake's inn
Winthrop, Elizabeth. Bunk beds
Woolley, Catherine. Andy and the wild worm
Yorinks, Arthur. Louis the fish
Young, Miriam Burt. Jellybeans for breakfast
Zimelman, Nathan. Once when I was five
Zolotow, Charlotte. When I have a son

Imagination — imaginary friends

Alexander, Martha G. And my mean old mother will be sorry, Blackboard Bear
  Blackboard Bear
  I sure am glad to see you, Blackboard Bear
  I'll protect you from the jungle beasts
  We're in big trouble, Blackboard Bear
Andrews, F Emerson (Frank Emerson). Nobody comes to dinner
Anglund, Joan Walsh. Cowboy and his friend
  The cowboy's Christmas
Bram, Elizabeth. There is someone standing on my head
Brewster, Patience. Nobody
Brighton, Catherine. My hands, my world
Brown, Palmer. The silver nutmeg
Dauer, Rosamond. My friend, Jasper Jones
Dillon, Barbara. The beast in the bed
Dinan, Carolyn. The lunch box monster
Greenfield, Eloise. Me and Nessie
Hazen, Barbara Shook. The gorilla did it!
  Gorilla wants to be the baby
Hiller, Catherine. Argentaybee and the boonie
Hoff, Syd. The horse in Harry's room
Jeschke, Susan. Angela and Bear
  The devil did it
Joosse, Barbara M. The thinking place
Krahn, Fernando. The creepy thing
Krensky, Stephen. The lion upstairs

Langner, Nola. By the light of the silvery moon
Morris, Terry Nell. Good night, dear monster!
Noble, June. Two homes for Lynn
Oram, Hiawyn. Ned and the Joybaloo
Pinkwater, Daniel Manus. Pickle creature
Ross, Tony. Hugo and Oddsock
St George, Judith. The Halloween pumpkin smasher
Steiner, Charlotte. Lulu
Thaler, Mike. My puppy
Watts, Marjorie-Ann. Zebra goes to school
Woolley, Catherine. Andy and his fine friends
Zolotow, Charlotte. Three funny friends

Imitation see Behavior — imitation

In and out see Concepts — in and out

Incentive see Character traits — ambition

Independence Day see Holidays — Fourth of July

India see Foreign lands — India

Indians, American see Ethnic groups in the U.S. — Indians

Indifference see Behavior — indifference

Individuality see Character traits — individuality

Indonesian Archipelago see Foreign lands — South Sea Islands

Insects

Adelson, Leone. Please pass the grass
Aldis, Dorothy. Quick as a wink
Aldridge, Alan. The butterfly ball and the grasshopper's feast
Arnosky, Jim. A kettle of hawks, and other wildlife groups
Barrett, Judi. Snake is totally tail
Belpré, Pura. Perez and Martina
Boegehold, Betty. Bear underground
Brouillette, Jeanne S. Moths
Colby, C B (Carroll Burleigh). Who lives there?
Cole, Joanna. Find the hidden insect
Conklin, Gladys. I caught a lizard
  We like bugs
  When insects are babies
Cristini, Ermanno. In the pond

Farber, Norma. Never say ugh to a bug
Fields, Alice. Insects
Gackenbach, Dick. Little bug
George, Jean Craighead. All upon a stone
Goudey, Alice E. Red legs
Griffen, Elizabeth. A dog's book of bugs
Ipcar, Dahlov. Bug city
Jaynes, Ruth M. That's what it is!
Kaufmann, John. Flying giants of long ago
Lionni, Leo. Inch by inch
Lobel, Arnold. Grasshopper on the road
Pasley, L. The adventures of Madalene and Louisa
Petie, Haris. Billions of bugs
Peyo. The Smurfs and their woodland friends
Rounds, Glen. The boll weevil
Selden, George. Chester Cricket's pigeon ride
Selsam, Millicent E. Backyard insects
  The bug that laid the golden eggs
Stone, Rosetta. Because a little bug went ka-choo!
Tison, Annette. Animal hide-and-seek
Van Woerkom, Dorothy. Hidden messages

Insects — ants

Cameron, Polly. "I can't," said the ant
Freschet, Berniece. The ants go marching
Myrick, Mildred. Ants are fun
Peet, Bill. The ant and the elephant
Pluckrose, Henry. Ants

Insects — bees

Baran, Tancy. Bees
Barton, Byron. Buzz, buzz, buzz
Galdone, Joanna. Honeybee's party
Hawes, Judy. Watch honeybees with me
Hogan, Paula Z. The honeybee
Keller, Beverly. Fiona's bee
Lobel, Arnold. The rose in my garden
Pluckrose, Henry. Bees and wasps
Wahl, Jan. Follow me cried Bee

Insects — beetles

Conklin, Gladys. I like beetles
Hoban, Russell. Jim Frog

Insects — butterflies, caterpillars

Aardema, Verna. Who's in Rabbit's house?
Abisch, Roz. Let's find out about butterflies
Aldridge, Alan. The butterfly ball and the grasshopper's feast

Carle, Eric. The very hungry caterpillar
Carrick, Malcolm. I can squash elephants!
The caterpillar who turned into a butterfly.
Conklin, Gladys. I like butterflies
  I like caterpillars
Cutts, David. Look...a butterfly
Darby, Gene. What is a butterfly?
Delaney, A. The butterfly
Delaney, Ned. One dragon to another
Fitzsimons, Cecilia. My first butterflies
Garelick, May. Where does the butterfly go when it rains?
Hogan, Paula Z. The butterfly
Kent, Jack. The caterpillar and the polliwog
Kipling, Rudyard. The butterfly that stamped
Lewis, Naomi. The butterfly collector
McClung, Robert. Sphinx
O'Hagan, Caroline. It's easy to have a caterpillar visit you
Piers, Helen. Grasshopper and butterfly
Pluckrose, Henry. Butterflies and moths
Roscoe, William. The butterfly's ball
Selsam, Millicent E. Terry and the caterpillars
Thompson, Susan L. Diary of a monarch butterfly
Wong, Herbert H. Our caterpillars

Insects — caterpillars see Insects — butterflies, caterpillars

Insects — crickets

Caudill, Rebecca. A pocketful of cricket
Kimmel, Eric A. Why worry?
Mizumura, Kazue. If I were a cricket...

Insects — fireflies

Berends, Polly Berrien. Ladybug and dog and the night walk
Bolliger, Max. The fireflies
Callen, Larry. Dashiel and the night
Eastman, P D (Philip D). Sam and the firefly
Harris, Louise Dyer. Flash, the life of a firefly
Hawes, Judy. Fireflies in the night
Knight, Hilary. A firefly in a fir tree
Ryder, Joanne. Fireflies

Insects — fleas

Wiese, Kurt. The dog, the fox and the fleas

Insects — flies

Aardema, Verna. Half-a-ball-of-kenki

Brandenberg, Franz. Fresh cider and
apple pie
Conklin, Gladys. I watch flies
Elkin, Benjamin. Why the sun was late
Kraus, Robert. The trouble with spider
McClintock, Marshall. A fly went by
Winter, Paula. The bear and the fly
Yolen, Jane. Spider Jane

Insects — gnats

Peet, Bill. The gnats of knotty pine

Insects — grasshoppers

Aldridge, Alan. The butterfly ball and
the grasshopper's feast
Du Bois, William Pène. Bear circus
Grasshopper to the rescue
Kimmel, Eric A. Why worry?
Lobel, Arnold. Grasshopper on the road
Newbolt, Henry John, Sir. Rilloby-rill
Piers, Helen. Grasshopper and butterfly

Insects — lady birds *see* Insects —
ladybugs

Insects — ladybugs

Berends, Polly Berrien. Ladybug and
dog and the night walk
Carle, Eric. The grouchy ladybug
Conklin, Gladys. Lucky ladybugs
Fisher, Aileen. We went looking
Hawes, Judy. Ladybug, ladybug, fly
away home
Kepes, Juliet. Lady bird, quickly
Kraus, Robert. Ladybug, ladybug!
Schlein, Miriam. Fast is not a ladybug
Sueyoshi, Akiko. Ladybird on a bicycle
Wong, Herbert H. My ladybug

Insects — lightning bugs *see* Insects —
fireflies

Insects — mosquitoes

Aardema, Verna. Why mosquitoes buzz
in people's ears
Oxford Scientific Films. Mosquito

Insects — moths

Pluckrose, Henry. Butterflies and moths

Insects — praying mantis

Conklin, Gladys. Praying mantis

Insects — wasps

Pluckrose, Henry. Bees and wasps

Interracial marriage *see* Marriage,
interracial

Ireland *see* Foreign lands — Ireland

Islands

Armitage, Ronda. Ice creams for Rosie
Brock, Emma Lillian. Skipping Island
Brown, Margaret Wise. The little island
Brunhoff, Laurent de. Babar's visit to
Bird Island
Coatsworth, Elizabeth. Lonely Maria
Kellogg, Steven. The island of the skog
Kessler, Leonard P. The pirates'
adventure on Spooky Island
King, Deborah. Sirius and Saba
Krahn, Fernando. The great ape
Lasky, Kathryn. My island grandma
McCloskey, Robert. Time of wonder
McGovern, Ann. Nicholas Bentley
Stoningpot III
McPhail, David. Great cat
Martin, Charles E. Island winter
Mordvinoff, Nicolas. Coral Island
Steig, William. Rotten island

Israel *see* Foreign lands — Israel

Italy *see* Foreign lands — Italy

Jail *see* Prisons

Japan *see* Foreign lands — Japan

Japanese-Americans *see* Ethnic groups
in the U.S. — Japanese-Americans

Jealousy *see* Emotions — envy, jealousy

Jesters *see* Clowns, jesters

Jewish culture

Adler, David A. The children of Chelm
The house on the roof
A picture book of Hanukkah
A picture book of Israel
A picture book of Jewish holidays
A picture book of Passover
Aleichem, Sholom. Hannukah money
Aronin, Ben. The secret of the Sabbath
fish
Bogot, Howard. I'm growing
Burstein, Chaya M. Joseph and Anna's
time capsule
Chapman, Carol. The tale of Meshka
the Kvetch

Cohen, Barbara. Gooseberries to oranges
Here come the Purim players!
Cone, Molly. The Jewish Sabbath
Coopersmith, Jerome. A Chanukah fable for Christmas
Eisenberg, Phyllis Rose. A mitzvah is something special
Fass, David E. The shofar that lost its voice
Fassler, Joan. My grandpa died today
Gershator, Phillis. Honi and his magic circle
Goffstein, M B (Marilyn Brooks). Goldie the dollmaker
Laughing latkes
Greene, Jacqueline Dembar. Butchers and bakers, rabbis and kings
Gross, Michael. The fable of the fig tree
Hirsh, Marilyn. Captain Jiri and Rabbi Jacob
Could anything be worse?
One little goat
The pink suit
The Rabbi and the twenty-nine witches
Where is Yonkela?
Levitin, Sonia. A sound to remember
Levy, Sara G. Mother Goose rhymes for Jewish children
Lisowski, Gabriel. How Tevye became a milkman
McDermott, Beverly Brodsky. The Golem
Margalit, Avishai. The Hebrew alphabet book
On the little hearth
Rosen, Anne. A family Passover
Schwartz, Amy. Mrs. Moskowitz and the Sabbath candlesticks
Segal, Lore. Tell me a Mitzi
Tell me a Trudy
Shulevitz, Uri. The magician
Suhl, Yuri. Simon Boom gives a wedding
Weilerstein, Sadie Rose. The best of K'tonton
Zemach, Margot. It could always be worse
Zola, Meguido. The dream of promise
Zusman, Evelyn. The Passover parrot

Jobs see Careers

Jokes see Riddles

Judges see Careers — judges

Jumping see Activities — jumping

Jungle

Aitken, Amy. Kate and Mona in the jungle
Booth, Eugene. In the jungle
Catchpole, Clive. Jungles
Corddry, Thomas I. Kibby's big feat
Lilly, Kenneth. Animals in the jungle
Van Allsburg, Chris. Jumanji

Kangaroos see Animals — kangaroos

Kindness see Character traits — kindness

Kindness to animals see Character traits — kindness to animals

Kings see Royalty

Kinkajous see Animals — kinkajous

Kites

Ayer, Jacqueline. Nu Dang and his kite
Brown, Marcia. The little carousel
Cooper, Elizabeth K. The fish from Japan
Heller, George. Hiroshi's wonderful kite
Luenn, Nancy. The dragon kite
Peet, Bill. Merle the high flying squirrel
Rey, Margaret Elisabeth Waldstein. Curious George flies a kite
Ruthstrom, Dorotha. The big kite contest
Titus, Eve. Anatole over Paris
Uchida, Yoshiko. Sumi's prize
Wiese, Kurt. Fish in the air
Yolen, Jane. The emperor and the kite

Knights

Blake, Quentin. Snuff
Boutell, Clarence Burley. The fat baron
Bradfield, Roger. A good night for dragons
Carrick, Donald. Harold and the giant knight
Cressey, James. The dragon and George
Cretien, Paul D. Sir Henry and the dragon
De Paola, Tomie. The knight and the dragon
The wonderful dragon of Timlin
Emberley, Ed. Klippity klop
Goodall, John S. Creepy castle

Haley, Gail E. The green man
Holl, Adelaide. Sir Kevin of Devon
Hunter, Mollie. The knight of the
  golden plain
Ipcar, Dahlov. Sir Addlepate and the
  unicorn
McCrea, James. The story of Olaf
Mayer, Mercer. Terrible troll
Peet, Bill. Cowardly Clyde
  How Droofus the dragon lost his head
Scarry, Huck. Looking into the Middle
  Ages
Trez, Denise. The little knight's dragon

Knitting *see* Activities — knitting

Koala bears *see* Animals — koala bears

Korea *see* Foreign lands — Korea

Lady birds *see* Insects — ladybugs

Ladybugs *see* Insects — ladybugs

Language

Baer, Edith. Words are like faces
Battles, Edith. What does the rooster
  say, Yoshio?
Berson, Harold. A moose is not a mouse
Bossom, Naomi. A scale full of fish and
  other turnabouts
Charlip, Remy. Handtalk
Clifford, Eth. A bear before breakfast
Ellentuck, Shan. Did you see what I
  said?
Folsom, Marcia. Easy as pie
Goodspeed, Peter. Hugh and Fitzhugh
Hoban, Tana. More than one
Johnston, Johanna. Speak up, Edie
Leaf, Munro. Grammar can be fun
Leeton, Will C. The Tower of Babel
Maestro, Betsy. On the go
Parish, Peggy. Amelia Bedelia
  Amelia Bedelia and the surprise
    shower
  Amelia Bedelia goes camping
  Amelia Bedelia helps out
  Come back, Amelia Bedelia
  Good work, Amelia Bedelia
  Play ball, Amelia Bedelia
  Teach us, Amelia Bedelia
  Thank you, Amelia Bedelia
Preiss, Byron. The first crazy word book
Rand, Ann. Sparkle and spin

Richardson, Jack E. Six in a mix
Sage, Michael. If you talked to a boar
Sattler, Helen Roney. Train whistle
Scarry, Richard. Richard Scarry's best
  story book ever
Sesame Street. Sesame Street sign
  language fun
  Sesame Street word book
Sherman, Ivan. Walking talking words
Steig, William. The bad speller
Steptoe, John. My special best words
Terban, Marvin. I think I thought
Tester, Sylvia Root. Never monkey with
  a monkey
  What did you say?
Wiesner, William. The Tower of Babel
Wildsmith, Brian. What the moon saw

Language, foreign *see* Foreign languages

Lapland *see* Foreign lands — Lapland

Laundry

Behrens, June. Soo Ling finds a way
Freeman, Don. A pocket for Corduroy
Ormondroyd, Edward. Theodore

Law *see* Careers — judges; Crime

Laziness *see* Character traits — laziness

Left and right *see* Concepts — left and
right

Left-handedness

Lerner, Marguerite Rush. Lefty, the
  story of left-handedness

Legends *see* Folk and fairy tales

Leopards *see* Animals — leopards

Leprechauns *see* Elves and little people

Letters

Bell, Norman. Linda's airmail letter
Keats, Ezra Jack. A letter to Amy
Seuss, Dr. On beyond zebra

Librarians *see* Careers — librarians

Libraries

Alexander, Martha G. How my library
  grew by Dinah
Baker, Donna. I want to be a librarian
Bartlett, Susan. A book to begin on
  libraries
Baugh, Dolores M. Let's take a trip

Bonsall, Crosby Newell. Tell me some more
Charles, Donald. Calico Cat meets bookworm
Daly, Maureen. Patrick visits the library
Daugherty, James Henry. Andy and the lion
Demarest, Chris L. Clemens' kingdom
De Paola, Tomie. The knight and the dragon
Felt, Sue. Rosa-too-little
Freeman, Don. Quiet! There's a canary in the library
Gay, Zhenya. Look!
Little, Mary E. ABC for the library
 Ricardo and the puppets
Rockwell, Anne F. I like the library
Sadler, Marilyn. Alistair in outer space
Sauer, Julia Lina. Mike's house
Tudor, Tasha. Mildred and the mummy

Lighthouses

Armitage, Ronda. The lighthouse keeper's lunch
Barker, Melvern J. Little island star
Myrick, Mildred. The secret three
Strahl, Rudi. Sandman in the lighthouse
Swift, Hildegarde Hoyt. The little red lighthouse and the great gray bridge

Lightning bugs see Insects — fireflies

Lights

Crews, Donald. Light

Lions see Animals — lions

Lithuania see Foreign lands — Lithuania

Little people see Elves and little people

Littleness see Character traits — smallness

Lizards see Reptiles — lizards

Llamas see Animals — llamas

Lobsters see Crustacea

Loneliness see Emotions — loneliness

Losing things see Behavior — losing things

Lost see Behavior — lost

Love see Emotions — love

Loyalty see Character traits — loyalty

Luck see Character traits — luck

Lying see Behavior — lying

Machines

Adkins, Jan. Heavy equipment
Baker, Betty. Worthington Botts and the steam machine
Baker, Eugene. I want to be a computer operator
Bate, Norman. Vulcan
 Who built the bridge?
 Who built the highway?
Baugh, Dolores M. Let's take a trip
Behn, Harry. All kinds of time
Benedictus, Roger. Fifty million sausages
Bradfield, Roger. The flying hockey stick
Brown, Margaret Wise. The steamroller
Burton, Virginia Lee. Katy and the big snow
 Mike Mulligan and his steam shovel
D'Ignazio, Fred. Katie and the computer
Du Bois, William Pène. Lazy Tommy pumpkinhead
Fleishman, Seymour. Too hot in Potzburg
Goor, Ron. In the driver's seat
Greene, Carol. A computer went a-courting
Henstra, Friso. Wait and see
Hoban, Tana. Dig, drill, dump, fill
Holl, Adelaide. The ABC of cars, trucks and machines
Hunter, Norman. Professor Branestawn's building bust-up
Ipcar, Dahlov. One horse farm
Israel, Marion Louise. The tractor on the farm
Löfgren, Ulf. The traffic stopper that became a grandmother visitor
Munsch, Robert N. Jonathan cleaned up then he heard a sound
Olney, Ross R. Construction giants
 Farm giants
Retan, Walter. The snowplow that tried to go south
 The steam shovel that wouldn't eat dirt
Rockwell, Anne F. Machines
Steadman, Ralph. The little red computer
Things that go word book

Wolde, Gunilla. Betsy and the vacuum cleaner

Young, Miriam Burt. If I drove a tractor

Zaffo, George J. The giant nursery book of things that work

Magic

Alexander, Martha G. 3 magic flip books

Alexander, Sue. Marc the Magnificent

Aliki. The wish workers

Andersen, H C (Hans Christian). The wild swans, ill. by Angela Barrett
  The wild swans, ill. by Susan Jeffers

Anderson, Lonzo. Two hundred rabbits

Anderson, Robin. Sinabouda Lily

Arabian Nights. The flying carpet

Armitage, Ronda. The bossing of Josie

Babbitt, Samuel F. The forty-ninth magician

Bach, Othello. Lilly, Willy and the mail-order witch

Balian, Lorna. Humbug potion

Baningan, Sharon Stearns. Circus magic

Bass, Donna. The tale of the dark crystal

Berenstain, Stan. The Berenstain bears and the sitter

Berson, Harold. Charles and Claudine
  The thief who hugged a moonbeam

Beskow, Elsa Maartman. Peter in Blueberry Land
  Peter's adventures in Blueberry land

Bianco, Margery Williams. The velveteen rabbit, ill. by Allen Atkinson
  The velveteen rabbit, ill. by Michael Hague
  The velveteen rabbit, ill. by William Nicholson
  The velveteen rabbit, ill. by Ilse Plume
  The velveteen rabbit, ill. by Tien

Blance, Ellen. Monster and the magic umbrella

Bowden, Joan Chase. Who took the top hat trick?

Brandenberg, Franz. Leo and Emily

Brenner, Barbara. The flying patchwork quilt

Bridwell, Norman. The witch grows up

Bright, Robert. Georgie and the magician

Brown, Abbie Farwell. Under the rowan tree

Brown, Marcia. Once a mouse...

Brunhoff, Laurent de. Babar the magician

Buck, Pearl S (Pearl Sydenstricker). The dragon fish

Buckaway, C M. Alfred, the dragon who lost his flame

Bunting, Eve. The man who could call down owls

Chapman, Carol. Barney Bipple's magic dandelions

Climo, Shirley. The cobweb Christmas

Cole, Babette. Nungu and the elephant

Cole, Joanna. Bony-legs

Colette. The boy and the magic

Conover, Chris. The wizard's daughter

Coombs, Patricia. Dorrie and the amazing magic elixir
  Dorrie and the blue witch
  Dorrie and the dreamyard monsters
  Dorrie and the weather-box
  Dorrie and the witch doctor
  Dorrie and the witch's imp
  Dorrie and the Witchville fair
  Dorrie and the wizard's spell
  Dorrie's magic
  The magic pot
  The magician and McTree

Cooper, Gale. Unicorn moon

Corbett, Scott. Dr. Merlin's magic shop
  The foolish dinosaur fiasco
  The great custard pie panic

Coville, Bruce. The foolish giant
  Sarah and the dragon

Degen, Bruce. The little witch and the riddle

Delton, Judy. Brimhall turns to magic

De Paola, Tomie. Big Anthony and the magic ring
  Strega Nona
  Strega Nona's magic lessons

Dewey, Ariane. Dorin and the dragon
  The fish Peri
  The thunder god's son

Dines, Glen. A tiger in the cherry tree

Domanska, Janina. Palmiero and the ogre

Dukas, P (Paul Abraham). The sorcerer's apprentice
  The firebird

Flot, Jeannette B. Princess Kalina and the hedgehog

Fuchshuber, Annegert. The wishing hat

Gackenbach, Dick. Ida Fanfanny

Gág, Wanda. Nothing at all
  The sorcerer's apprentice

Galdone, Paul. The magic porridge pot

Ginsburg, Mirra. Striding slippers

Glazer, Lee. Cookie Becker casts a spell
  The good-hearted youngest brother

Graves, Robert. Two wise children

Green, Marion. The magician who lived on the mountain

Grimm, Jacob. The donkey prince
  Rumpelstiltskin, ill. by Jacqueline Ayer
  Rumpelstiltskin, ill. by Donna Diamond

Rumpelstiltskin, ill. by John Wallner
The seven ravens, ill. by Felix
Hoffmann
The seven ravens, ill. by Lisbeth
Zwerger
The six swans
Snow White, ill. by Bernadette
Snow White, ill. by Trina Schart
Hyman
Snow White and Rose Red, ill. by
Adrienne Adams
Snow White and Rose Red, ill. by John
Wallner
Haller, Danita Ross. Not just any ring
Hazen, Barbara Shook. The sorcerer's
apprentice
Heide, Florence Parry. Treehorn's
treasure
Treehorn's wish
Heller, Linda. Alexis and the golden
ring
Hiller, Catherine. Abracatabby
Hochman, Sandra. The magic
convention
Hoffman, Rosekrans. Sister Sweet Ella
Houghton, Eric. The mouse and the
magician
Hunter, Mollie. The knight of the
golden plain
Hutton, Warwick. Beauty and the beast
Isele, Elizabeth. The frog princess
Janosch. Joshua and the magic fiddle
The magic auto
Jeschke, Susan. Angela and Bear
Firerose
Mia, Grandma and the genie
Rima and Zeppo
Johnston, Tony. The witch's hat
Kennedy, Richard. The porcelain man
Kepes, Juliet. The seed that peacock
planted
Kimmel, Margaret Mary. Magic in the
mist
Knight, Hilary. Hilary Knight's the owl
and the pussy-cat
Kroll, Steven. The candy witch
Fat magic
Kumin, Maxine. The wizard's tears
Langstaff, John M. The two magicians
Laurin, Anne. Perfect crane
Leichman, Seymour. The wicked wizard
and the wicked witch
Lindman, Maj. Snipp, Snapp, Snurr and
the magic horse
Lipkind, William. The boy and the
forest
The magic feather duster
Lobel, Anita. The troll music
Lopshire, Robert. It's magic
McDermott, Gerald. The magic tree

McLenighan, Valjean. Three strikes and
you're out
You can go jump
McPhail, David. The magical drawings
of Moony B. Finch
Mahiri, Jabari. The day they stole the
letter J
Marie, Geraldine. The magic box
Mayer, Mercer. Mrs. Beggs and the
wizard
Moncure, Jane Belk. Riddle me a riddle
Nicoll, Helen. Meg and Mog
Meg at sea
Meg on the moon
Meg's eggs
Nolan, Dennis. Wizard McBean and his
flying machine
Norby, Lisa. The Herself the elf
storybook
Oksner, Robert M. The incompetent
wizard
Peet, Bill. Countdown to Christmas
Phumla. Nomi and the magic fish
Postma, Lidia. The stolen mirror
The prince who knew his fate
Rockwell, Anne F. The story snail
The wonderful eggs of Furicchia
Ronay, Jadja. Ginger
Rose, Anne. Akimba and the magic cow
Ross, Tony. The enchanted pig
Sachs, Marilyn. Fleet-footed Florence
Saddler, Allen. The Archery contest
Severo, Emöke de Papp. The
good-hearted youngest brother
Shecter, Ben. Emily, girl witch of New
York
Shulevitz, Uri. The magician
Slobodkin, Louis. Magic Michael
Steig, William. The amazing bone
Caleb and Kate
Gorky rises
Sylvester and the magic pebble
Steptoe, John. The story of jumping
mouse
Stevenson, James. Yuck!
Stubbs, Joanna. With cat's eyes you'll
never be scared of the dark
Tempest, P. How the cock wrecked the
manor
Thaler, Mike. Madge's magic show
Tom Tit Tot
Towle, Faith M. The magic cooking pot
Tresselt, Alvin R. The world in the
candy egg
Trez, Denise. Maila and the flying
carpet
Turkle, Brinton. The magic of Millicent
Musgrave
Turska, Krystyna. The magician of
Cracow
Ungerer, Tomi. The hat

Van Allsburg, Chris. The garden of
Abdul Gasazi
Varga, Judy. Janko's wish
Waber, Bernard. You're a little kid with
a big heart
Walt Disney Productions. Walt Disney's
Snow White and the seven dwarfs
Woolley, Catherine. Mr. Turtle's magic
glasses
Wyler, Rose. Spooky tricks
Yaffe, Alan. The magic meatballs
Yolen, Jane. Mice on ice
Sleeping ugly

Maids *see* Careers — maids

Mail *see* Letters

Mail carriers *see* Careers — mail
carriers

Malaysia *see* Foreign lands — Malaysia

Manners *see* Etiquette

Mardi Gras

Lionni, Leo. The greentail mouse

Marionettes *see* Puppets

Markets *see* Stores

Marriage, interracial

Adoff, Arnold. Black is brown is tan

Marriages *see* Weddings

Math *see* Counting

Meanness *see* Character traits —
meanness

Measurement *see* Concepts —
measurement

Mechanical men *see* Robots

Memorial Day *see* Holidays —
Memorial Day

Mermaids *see* Mythical creatures

Merry-go-rounds

Ardizzone, Edward. Paul, the hero of
the fire
Brown, Marcia. The little carousel
Charles, Robert Henry. The roundabout
turn
Crews, Donald. Carousel
Perera, Lydia. Frisky

Thomas, Art. Merry-go-rounds

Mexican-Americans *see* Ethnic groups
in the U.S. — Mexican-Americans

Mexico *see* Foreign lands — Mexico

Mice *see* Animals — mice

Middle ages

Althea. Castle life
Azarian, Mary. The tale of John
Barleycorn or, From barley to beer
Bishop, Ann. The riddle ages
Cohen, Barbara. Here come the Purim
players!
Coombs, Patricia. The magician and
McTree
Cressey, James. The dragon and
George
Dick Whittington and his cat. Dick
Whittington, ill. by Edward Ardizzone
Dick Whittington, ill. by Marcia Brown
Dick Whittington, ill. by Antony
Maitland
Dick Whittington, ill. by Kurt
Werth
Kahl, Virginia. The Baron's booty
The Duchess bakes a cake
Gunhilde and the Halloween spell
Gunhilde's Christmas booke
The habits of rabbits
Phillips, Louis. The brothers Wrong and
Wrong Again
Scarry, Huck. Looking into the Middle
Ages
Scarry, Richard. Peasant Pig and the
terrible dragon
Tompert, Ann. Charlotte and Charles

Military *see* Careers — military

Mimes *see* Clowns, jesters

Miners *see* Careers — miners

Minorities *see* Ethnic groups in the U.S.

Mirages *see* Optical illusions

Misbehavior *see* Behavior —
misbehavior

Missions

Politi, Leo. The mission bell
Song of the swallows

Mist *see* Weather — fog

Mistakes *see* Behavior — mistakes

Kahl, Virginia. Giants, indeed!
  How do you hide a monster?
Kellogg, Steven. The island of the skog
  The mysterious tadpole
Kimura, Yasuko. Fergus and the sea
  monster
Kitt, Tamara. Sam and the impossible
  thing
Koelling, Caryl. Mad monsters mix and
  match
Krahn, Fernando. The mystery of the
  giant footprints
Lifton, Betty Jean. Goodnight orange
  monster
Logue, Christopher. The magic circus
Marshall, Edward. Four on the shore
Mayer, Mercer. Little Monster at home
  Little Monster at school
  Little Monster at work
  Little Monster's alphabet book
  Little Monster's bedtime book
  Little Monster's counting book
  Little Monster's neighborhood
  Liza Lou and the Yeller Belly Swamp
  Mrs. Beggs and the wizard
  Terrible troll
  There's a nightmare in my closet
Memling, Carl. What's in the dark?
Minsberg, David. The book monster
Monster poems
Moore, Lilian. See my lovely poison ivy
Morris, Terry Nell. Good night, dear
  monster!
Mosel, Arlene. The funny little woman
Murphy, Shirley Rousseau. Valentine
  for a dragon
Myers, Amy. I know a monster
Newsham, Wendy. The monster hunt
Niland, Deborah. ABC of monsters
Parish, Peggy. No more monsters for
  me!
  Zed and the monsters
Parker, Nancy Winslow. Love from
  Aunt Betty
Peck, Richard. Monster night at
  Grandma's house
Peet, Bill. Cyrus the unsinkable sea
  serpent
Pinkwater, Daniel Manus. I was a
  second grade werewolf
Prelutsky, Jack. The baby uggs are
  hatching
Rockwell, Anne F. Thump thump
  thump!
Ross, David. Gorp and the space pirates
  Space monster
  Space Monster Gorp and the runaway
  computer
Ross, H L. Not counting monsters
Ross, Tony. Towser and the terrible
  thing

Rudolph, Marguerita. I am your
  misfortune
Schroder, William. Pea soup and
  serpents
Selsam, Millicent E. Sea monsters of
  long ago
Sendak, Maurice. Seven little monsters
  Where the wild things are
Seymour, Peter. What's at the beach?
Sharmat, Marjorie Weinman. Scarlet
  Monster lives here
Smith, Janice Lee. The monster in the
  third dresser drawer and other
  stories about Adam Joshua
Steig, William. Rotten island
Steptoe, John. Daddy is a
  monster...sometimes
Stevenson, James. "Could be worse!"
Turkle, Brinton. Do not open
Ungerer, Tomi. The beast of Monsieur
  Racine
  Zeralda's ogre
Viorst, Judith. My mama says there
  aren't any zombies, ghosts, vampires,
  creatures, demons, monsters, fiends,
  goblins, or things
Wagner, Jenny. The bunyip of
  Berkeley's Creek
Wahl, Jan. Dracula's cat
  Frankenstein's dog
Watson, Pauline. Wriggles, the little
  wishing pig
Willoughby, Elaine Macmann. Boris and
  the monsters
Young, Ed. The terrible Nung Gwama
Zemach, Harve. The judge

Months of the year *see* Days of the
  week, months of the year

Moon

Alexander, Martha G. Maggie's moon
Asch, Frank. Happy birthday, moon!
  Moon bear
  Mooncake
Asimov, Isaac. The moon
Balet, Jan B. Amos and the moon
Baylor, Byrd. Moon song
Berenstain, Stan. The bears' almanac
Bess, Clayton. The truth about the
  moon
Branley, Franklyn M. The moon seems
  to change
  What the moon is like
Brown, Margaret Wise. Goodnight
  moon
  Wait till the moon is full
Cazet, Denys. Christmas moon
Dayrell, Elphinstone. Why the sun and
  the moon live in the sky

De Paola, Tomie. The Prince of the Dolomites

De Regniers, Beatrice Schenk. Willy O'Dwyer jumped in the fire

Freeman, Mae. The sun, the moon and the stars
  You will go to the moon

Fuchs, Erich. Journey to the moon

Gantschev, Ivan. The moon lake

Garelick, May. Look at the moon

Griffith, Helen V. Alex remembers

Janosch. Joshua and the magic fiddle

Lewis, Claudia Louise. When I go to the moon

Lifton, Betty Jean. The rice-cake rabbit

McDermott, Gerald. Anansi the spider
  Papagayo, the mischief maker

Manushkin, Fran. Moon dragon

Merrill, Jean. Emily Emerson's moon

Moche, Dinah L. The astronauts

Nicoll, Helen. Meg on the moon

Oakley, Graham. The church mice and the moon

Preston, Edna Mitchell. Squawk to the moon, little goose

Schweninger, Ann. The man in the moon as he sails the sky and other moon verse

Simon, Seymour. The moon

Sleator, William. The angry moon

Stevenson, Robert Louis. The moon

Thaler, Mike. Moonkey

Thurber, James. Many moons

Turska, Krystyna. The magician of Cracow

Udry, Janice May. The moon jumpers

Ungerer, Tomi. Moon man

Wahl, Jan. Cabbage moon

Watson, Clyde. Midnight moon

Wildsmith, Brian. What the moon saw

Willard, Nancy. The nightgown of the sullen moon

Winter, Jeanette. The girl and the moon man

Yamaguchi, Tohr. Two crabs and the moonlight

Ziegler, Ursina. Squaps the moonling

Moose see Animals — moose

Mopeds see Motorcycles

Morning

Anglund, Joan Walsh. Morning is a little child

Beach, Stewart. Good morning, sun's up!

Brown, Margaret Wise. A child's good morning book
  The quiet noisy book

Caldwell, Mary. Morning, rabbit, morning

Craig, M Jean. Spring is like the morning
  What did you dream?

Dennis, Wesley. Flip and the morning

Dragonwagon, Crescent. Katie in the morning

Hill, Eric. Good morning, baby bear

Himler, Ronald. Wake up, Jeremiah

Lapp, Eleanor. In the morning mist

McNulty, Faith. When a boy wakes up in the morning

Mann, Peggy. King Laurence, the alarm clock

Ormerod, Jan. Sunshine

Oxenbury, Helen. Good night, good morning

Polushkin, Maria. Morning

Ray, Deborah Kogan. Fog drift morning

Shulevitz, Uri. Dawn

Tafuri, Nancy. Early morning in the barn

Tworkov, Jack. The camel who took a walk

Yabuki, Seiji. I love the morning

Zolotow, Charlotte. Wake up and good night

Mosquitoes see Insects — mosquitoes

Mother Goose see Nursery rhymes

Mothers see Family life — mothers

Mother's Day see Holidays — Mother's Day

Moths see Insects — moths

Motorcycles

Cave, Ron. Motorcycles

Cleary, Beverly. Lucky Chuck

Dickens, Frank. Boffo: the great motorcycle race

McPhail, David. Captain Toad and the motorbike

Zimnik, Reiner. The bear on the motorcycle

Moving

Adshead, Gladys L. Brownies — they're moving

Aliki. We are best friends

Becker, Edna. Nine hundred buckets of paint

Berenstain, Stan. The Berenstain bears' moving day

Berg, Jean Horton. The O'Learys and friends

Bond, Felicia. Poinsettia and her family
Bottner, Barbara. Horrible Hannah
Brandenberg, Franz. Nice new
  neighbors
  What can you make of it?
Brown, Myra Berry. Pip moves away
Clymer, Eleanor Lowenton. A yard for
  John
Cohen, Barbara. Gooseberries to
  oranges
DeLage, Ida. The old witch finds a new
  house
Felt, Sue. Hello-goodbye
Finsand, Mary Jane. The town that
  moved
Fisher, Aileen. Best little house
Gretz, Susanna. Teddy bears' moving
  day
Hickman, Martha Whitmore. My friend
  William moved away
Hoff, Syd. Who will be my friends?
Hughes, Shirley. Moving Molly
Ilsley, Velma. M is for moving
Isadora, Rachel. The Potters' kitchen
Jennings, Michael. The bears who came
  to breakfix
Jones, Penelope. I'm not moving!
Keats, Ezra Jack. The trip
Lexau, Joan M. The rooftop mystery
Lobel, Arnold. Ming Lo moves the
  mountain
Lystad, Mary H. That new boy
Marshak, Samuel. In the van
Maschler, Fay. T. G. and Moonie move
  out of town
Milord, Sue. Maggie and the goodbye
  gift
Morris, Jill. The boy who painted the
  sun
Obrist, Jürg. Fluffy
Sandin, Joan. The long way to a new
  land
Schlein, Miriam. My house
Schulman, Janet. The big hello
Sharmat, Marjorie Weinman. Gila
  monsters meet you at the airport
  Mitchell is moving
  Scarlet Monster lives here
Singer, Marilyn. Archer Armadillo's
  secret room
Strathdee, Jean. The house that grew
Tobias, Tobi. Moving day
Watson, Wendy. Moving
Wilhelm, Hans. A new home, a new
  friend
Zolotow, Charlotte. Janey

Mules *see* Animals — mules

Multi-ethnic *see* Ethnic groups in the
  U.S.

Multiple birth children *see* Triplets;
  Twins

Muppets *see* Puppets

Museums

Aliki. My visit to the dinosaurs
Berenstain, Stan. The Berenstain bears
  and the missing dinosaur bone
Blance, Ellen. Monster goes to the
  museum
Cohen, Miriam. Lost in the museum
Freeman, Don. Norman the doorman
Gramatky, Hardie. Hercules
Hoff, Syd. Danny and the dinosaur
Papajani, Janet. Museums
Woolley, Catherine. Gus and the baby
  ghost

Music

Abisch, Roz. Sweet Betsy from Pike
  'Twas in the moon of wintertime
Alexander, Cecil Frances. All things
  bright and beautiful
Alexander, Lloyd. The truthful harp
Alger, Leclaire. Always room for one
  more
  Kellyburn Braes
Ambrus, Victor G. Mishka
  The seven skinny goats
Arkin, Alan. Black and white
Atene, Ann. The golden guitar
Azarian, Mary. The tale of John
  Barleycorn or, From barley to beer
Bach, Othello. Lilly, Willy and the
  mail-order witch
Baker, Laura Nelson. The friendly
  beasts
  O children of the wind and pines
Bascom, Joe. Malcolm's job
Behn, Harry. What a beautiful noise
Bianco, Margery Williams. The
  hurdy-gurdy man
Boesel, Ann Sterling. Sing and sing
  again
  Singing with Peter and Patsy
Bolliger, Max. The most beautiful song
Bonne, Rose. I know an old lady
Botwin, Esther. A treasury of songs for
  little children
Brian Wildsmith's The twelve days of
  Christmas
Bring a torch, Jeannette, Isabella
Brown, Margaret Wise. The little brass
  band
Bruna, Dick. The orchestra
Bulla, Clyde Robert. The donkey cart
Bunting, Eve. The traveling men of
  Ballycoo

Burningham, John. Trubloff

Carle, Eric. I see a song

Carryl, Charles Edward. A capital ship

Cathon, Laura E. Tot Botot and his
little flute

Colette. The boy and the magic

Conover, Chris. Six little ducks

Cummings, W T (Walter Thies). The
kid

Dalton, Alene. My new picture book of
songs

Dillon, Eilis. The cats' opera

Domanska, Janina. Busy Monday
morning

Engvick, William. Lullabies and night
songs

The farmer in the dell

Flack, Marjorie. The restless robin

Freeman, Lydia. Pet of the Met

The friendly beasts and A partridge in a
pear tree

Glazer, Tom. Do your ears hang low?
Eye winker, Tom Tinker, chin chopper
On top of spaghetti

Go tell Aunt Rhody

Goffstein, M B (Marilyn Brooks). A little
Schubert

Greene, Carol. A computer went
a-courting
Hinny Winny Bunco
The thirteen days of Halloween

Grifalconi, Ann. The toy trumpet

Hale, Sara Josepha. Mary had a little
lamb

Haseley, Dennis. The old banjo

Hoban, Russell. Emmet Otter's jug-band
Christmas

Horvath, Betty F. Jasper makes music

Hot cross buns, and other old street
cries

Howe, Caroline Walton. Teddy Bear's
bird and beast band

Hurd, Thacher. Mama don't allow

Hush little baby, ill. by Aliki

Hush little baby, ill. by Jeanette Winter

Hush little baby, ill. by Margot Zemach

I sing a song of the saints of God

Ipcar, Dahlov. The cat came back
"The song of the day birds" and "The
song of the night birds"

Isele, Elizabeth. Pooks

Ivimey, John William. The complete
version of ye three blind mice

Janosch. Joshua and the magic fiddle
Tonight at nine

Kahl, Virginia. Droopsi
Gunhilde's Christmas booke

Kapp, Paul. Cock-a-doodle-doo!
Cock-a-doodle-dandy!

Keats, Ezra Jack. Apartment 3
The little drummer boy

Kepes, Juliet. The seed that peacock
planted

Kimmel, Eric A. Why worry?

Langstaff, John M. Oh, a-hunting we
will go
Ol' Dan Tucker
On Christmas day in the morning
Soldier, soldier, won't you marry me?
The swapping boy
The two magicians

Lasker, David. The boy who loved
music

Lear, Edward. Edward Lear's nonsense
book
The pelican chorus
The pelican chorus and the quangle
wangle's hat

Lenski, Lois. At our house
Davy and his dog
Davy goes places
Debbie and her grandma
A dog came to school
I like winter
I went for a walk

Lionni, Leo. Frederick
Geraldine, the music mouse

Lobel, Anita. The troll music

Löfgren, Ulf. The flying orchestra

McCloskey, Robert. Lentil

McMillan, Bruce. The alphabet
symphony

Maiorano, Robert. A little interlude

Maril, Lee. Mr. Bunny paints the eggs

Mayer, Mercer. The queen always
wanted to dance

Mills, Alan. The hungry goat

Mother Goose. Mother Goose's rhymes
and melodies
Sing hey diddle diddle
Thirty old-time nursery songs

Nelson, Esther L. The funny songbook
Holiday singing and dancing games
The silly songbook

Newbolt, Henry John, Sir. Rilloby-rill

Newland, Mary Reed. Good King
Wenceslas

Nussbaumer, Mares. Away in a manger

Old MacDonald had a farm, ill. by Mel
Crawford

Old MacDonald had a farm, ill. by
David Frankland

Old MacDonald had a farm, ill. by
Abner Graboff

Old MacDonald had a farm, ill. by
Tracey Campbell Pearson

Old MacDonald had a farm, ill. by
Robert M. Quackenbush

On the little hearth

Perrault, Charles. Cinderella, ill. by
Emanuele Luzzati

Play and sing - it's Christmas!

Poston, Elizabeth. Baby's song book

Prokofiev, Sergei Sergeievitch. Peter and the wolf, ill. by Warren Chappell
Peter and the wolf, ill. by Frans Haacken
Peter and the wolf, ill. by Alan Howard
Peter and the wolf, ill. by Charles Mikolaycak
Peter and the wolf, ill. by Kozo Shimizu

Quackenbush, Robert M. Clementine
The man on the flying trapeze
Pop! goes the weasel and Yankee Doodle
She'll be comin' 'round the mountain
Skip to my Lou
There'll be a hot time in the old town tonight

Raposo, Joe. The Sesame Street song book

Rey, Hans Augusto. Humpty Dumpty and other Mother Goose songs

Robbins, Ruth. Baboushka and the three kings

Rounds, Glen. The boll weevil
Casey Jones
The strawberry roan
Sweet Betsy from Pike

Schaaf, Peter. The violin close up

Schackburg, Richard. Yankee Doodle

Schick, Eleanor. One summer night
A piano for Julie

Seeger, Pete. The foolish frog

Sendak, Maurice. Maurice Sendak's Really Rosie

Singer, Marilyn. Will you take me to town on strawberry day?

Slobodkin, Louis. Wide-awake owl

Spier, Peter. The Erie Canal

Stecher, Miriam B. Max, the music-maker

Steig, William. Roland, the minstrel pig

Stern, Elsie-Jean. Wee Robin's Christmas song

Stevenson, James. Clams can't sing

Taylor, Mark. The bold fisherman
Old Blue, you good dog you

Thomas, Ianthe. Willie blows a mean horn

Titus, Eve. Anatole and the piano
Anatole and the Pied Piper

Tudor, Tasha. Junior's tune

The twelve days of Christmas. English folk song. Jack Kent's twelve days of Christmas
The twelve days of Christmas, ill. by Ilonka Karasz
The twelve days of Christmas, ill. by Erika Schneider

Vincent, Gabrielle. Bravo, Ernest and Celestine!

Watson, Clyde. Father Fox's feast of songs
Fisherman lullabies

Wenning, Elisabeth. The Christmas mouse

Wheeler, Opal. Sing in praise
Sing Mother Goose

Widdecombe Fair

Williams, Vera B. Music, music for everyone

Winter, Jeanette. The girl and the moon man

Wolkstein, Diane. The banza

Yulya. Bears are sleeping

Zimelman, Nathan. To sing a song as big as Ireland

Musical instruments *see* Music

Muskrats *see* Animals — muskrats

Mysteries *see* Problem solving

Mythical creatures

Andersen, H C (Hans Christian). The little mermaid, ill. by Edward Frascino
The little mermaid, ill. by Dorothy Pulis Lathrop
The little mermaid, ill. by Josef Palacek

Aruego, José. The king and his friends

Asbjørnsen, P C (Peter Christen). The three billy goats Gruff, ill. by Marcia Brown
The three billy goats Gruff, ill. by Paul Galdone
The three billy goats Gruff, ill. by William Stobbs

Aulaire, Ingri Mortenson d'. The terrible troll-bird

Cooper, Gale. Unicorn moon

Coville, Bruce. Sarah and the dragon
Sarah's unicorn

Freeman, Jean Todd. Cynthia and the unicorn

Gilleo, Alma. Learning about monsters

Gramatky, Hardie. Nikos and the sea god

Hillert, Margaret. The three goats

Howe, James. How the Ewoks saved the trees

Ipcar, Dahlov. Sir Addlepate and the unicorn

Keeshan, Robert. She loves me, she loves me not

Malnig, Anita. The big strawberry book of questions and answers and facts and things

Mayer, Marianna. The unicorn and the
lake
Mayer, Mercer. Terrible troll
Moeri, Louise. The unicorn and the
plow
Munthe, Adam John. I believe in
unicorns
Noble, Trinka Hakes. Hansy's mermaid
Peet, Bill. Cyrus the unsinkable sea
serpent
 The pinkish, purplish, bluish egg
Robb, Brian. My grandmother's djinn
Rockwell, Anne F. Buster and the
bogeyman
Schroder, William. Pea soup and
serpents
Spang, Günter. Clelia and the little
mermaid
Todaro, John. Phillip the flower-eating
phoenix
Wagner, Jenny. The bunyip of
Berkeley's Creek

Nagging *see* Behavior — nagging

Names

Alexander, Martha G. Sabrina
Bayer, Jane. A my name is Alice
Beim, Jerrold. The smallest boy in the
class
Benton, Robert. Little brother, no more
Browner, Richard. Everyone has a name
Cross, Diana Harding. Some birds have
funny names
 Some plants have funny names
Davis, Gibbs. The other Emily
De Paola, Tomie. Andy (that's my name)
Dragonwagon, Crescent. Wind Rose
Hogan, Inez. About Nono, the baby
elephant
Low, Joseph. Adam's book of odd
creatures
McKee, David. Two can toucan
Mosel, Arlene. Tikki Tikki Tembo
Parish, Peggy. Little Indian
Raskin, Ellen. A & the
Rice, Eve. Ebbie
Tom Tit Tot
Vreeken, Elizabeth. The boy who would
not say his name
Waber, Bernard. But names will never
hurt me
Williams, Jay. I wish I had another
name

Wold, Jo Anne. Tell them my name is
Amanda

Napping *see* Sleep

Native Americans *see* Ethnic groups in
the U.S. — Eskimos; Ethnic groups in
the U.S. — Indians

Nature

Baylor, Byrd. The other way to listen
Hands, Hargrave. Bunny sees
Schulz, Charles M. Snoopy's facts and
fun book about nature
Seymour, Peter. What's at the beach?
Stone, Lynn M. Endangered animals
Ward, Leila. I am eyes, ni macho
Wildsmith, Brian. Seasons
Zolotow, Charlotte. Say it!
 The song
Zweifel, Frances. Animal baby-sitters

Needing someone *see* Behavior —
needing someone

Neighborhoods *see* Communities,
neighborhoods

New Guinea *see* Foreign lands — New
Guinea

New Year's *see* Holidays — New Year's

Night

Adoff, Arnold. Make a circle, keep us in
Ahlberg, Janet. Funnybones
Alexander, Anne. Noise in the night
Alexander, Martha G. Maggie's moon
 We're in big trouble, Blackboard Bear
Ardizzone, Aingelda. The night ride
Armitage, Ronda. One moonlit night
Artis, Vicki Kimmel. Pajama walking
Asch, Frank. Moon bear
Averill, Esther. Jenny's moonlight
adventure
Aylesworth, Jim. Tonight's the night
Babbitt, Natalie. The something
Bannon, Laura. Little people of the
night
Bennett, Rainey. After the sun goes
down
Berends, Polly Berrien. Ladybug and
dog and the night walk
Berenstain, Stan. Bears in the night
 The Berenstain bears in the dark
Berg, Jean Horton. The wee little man
Blocksma, Mary. Did you hear that?
Bolliger, Max. The fireflies
Bond, Felicia. Poinsettia and the
firefighters

Bonsall, Crosby Newell. Who's afraid of the dark?

Bradbury, Ray. Switch on the night

Brandenberg, Franz. A robber! A robber!

Brown, Margaret Wise. A child's good night book
Night and day
Wait till the moon is full

Brown, Myra Berry. Pip camps out

Budney, Blossom. After dark

Burningham, John. The blanket

Callen, Larry. Dashiel and the night

Cass, Joan E. The cat thief

Conford, Ellen. Eugene the brave

Cosgrove, Stephen. Sleepy time bunny

Credle, Ellis. Big fraid, little fraid

Crowe, Robert L. Clyde monster

DeLage, Ida. The old witch and the crows

Delton, Judy. A walk on a snowy night

Donaldson, Lois. Karl's wooden horse

Dragonwagon, Crescent. When light turns into night

Duvoisin, Roger Antoine. The missing milkman

Emberley, Barbara. Night's nice

Erskine, Jim. Bedtime story

Fenner, Carol. Tigers in the cellar

Fisher, Aileen. In the middle of the night

Freeman, Don. The night the lights went out

Garelick, May. Sounds of a summer night

Ginsburg, Mirra. The sun's asleep behind the hill
Where does the sun go at night?

Goodenow, Earle. The owl who hated the dark

Hamilton, Morse. Who's afraid of the dark?

Highwater, Jamake. Moonsong lullaby

Horwitz, Elinor Lander. When the sky is like lace

Hurd, Thacher. The quiet evening

Ipcar, Dahlov. The cat at night
"The song of the day birds" and "The song of the night birds"

Kauffman, Lois. What's that noise?

Keats, Ezra Jack. Dreams

Kessler, Ethel. Night story

Koenig, Marion. The wonderful world of night

Kraus, Robert. Good night little one
Good night Richard Rabbit

Larrick, Nancy. When the dark comes dancing

Leaf, Munro. Boo, who used to be scared of the dark

Lesser, Carolyn. The goodnight circle

Lexau, Joan M. Millicent's ghost

Lifton, Betty Jean. Goodnight orange monster

Lionni, Leo. When?

Lloyd, Errol. Nandy's bedtime

Matus, Greta. Where are you, Jason?

Mayer, Mercer. You're the scaredy cat

Memling, Carl. What's in the dark?
The moon's the north wind's cooky

Murphy, Jill. What next, baby bear!

Peck, Richard. Monster night at Grandma's house

Peters, Sharon. Animals at night

Preston, Edna Mitchell. Monkey in the jungle

Reidel, Marlene. Jacob and the robbers

Rice, Eve. Goodnight, goodnight

Rockwell, Anne F. The night we slept outside

Rowand, Phyllis. It is night

Rukeyser, Muriel. More night

Ryan, Cheli Durán. Hildilid's night

Ryder, Joanne. The snail's spell

Schlein, Miriam. Here comes night

Schneider, Nina. While Susie sleeps

Selsam, Millicent E. Night animals

Stubbs, Joanna. With cat's eyes you'll never be scared of the dark

Tobias, Tobi. Chasing the goblins away

Vevers, Gwynne. Animals of the dark

Wallace, Daisy. Ghost poems

Willard, Nancy. The nightgown of the sullen moon

Winthrop, Elizabeth. Potbellied possums

Zalben, Jane Breskin. Norton's nighttime

Zolotow, Charlotte. I have a horse of my own
Wake up and good night
When the wind stops
The white marble

Nightingales *see* Birds — nightingales

Nightmares *see* Bedtime; Goblins; Monsters; Night; Sleep

No text *see* Wordless

Noah *see* Religion — Noah

Noise, sounds

Alexander, Anne. Noise in the night

Alexander, Martha G. Pigs say oink

Allard, Harry. Bumps in the night

Allen, Pamela. Bertie and the bear

Aylesworth, Jim. Hush up!
Siren in the night

Bassett, Preston R. Raindrop stories

Behn, Harry. What a beautiful noise

Norway see Foreign lands — Norway

Noses *see* Anatomy

Numbers *see* Counting

Nuns *see* Careers — nuns

Nursery rhymes

B. B. Blacksheep and Company

Barchilon, Jacques. The authentic Mother Goose fairy tales and nursery rhymes

Bartlett, Robert Merrill. Jack Horner and song of sixpence

Baum, L Frank (Lyman Frank). Mother Goose in prose

Bayley, Nicola. Nicola Bayley's book of nursery rhymes

Blake, Pamela. Peep-show

Blake, Quentin. Quentin Blake's nursery rhyme book

Blegvad, Lenore. Hark! Hark! The dogs do bark, and other poems about dogs

  Mittens for kittens and other rhymes about cats

  This little pig-a-wig and other rhymes about pigs

Bodecker, N M (Nils Mogens). "It's raining," said John Twaining

Briggs, Raymond. Fee fi fo fum

  Ring-a-ring o' roses

  The white land

Brooke, L Leslie (Leonard Leslie). Oranges and lemons

  This little pig went to market

Brown, Marcia. Peter Piper's alphabet

Cakes and custard

Caldecott, Randolph. Hey diddle diddle, and Baby bunting

  Hey diddle diddle picture book

  Panjandrum picture book

  The Queen of Hearts

  Randolph Caldecott's favorite nursery rhymes

  Randolph Caldecott's John Gilpin and other stories

  Randolph Caldecott's picture book, no. 1

  Randolph Caldecott's picture book, no. 2

  Sing a song of sixpence

  The three jovial huntsmen

Cassedy, Sylvia. Moon-uncle, moon-uncle

Cauley, Lorinda Bryan. Pease porridge hot

Chorao, Kay. The baby's bedtime book

Clark, Leonard. Drums and trumpets

Cock Robin. The courtship, merry marriage, and feast of Cock Robin and Jenny Wren

Cope, Dawn. Humpty Dumpty's favorite nursery rhymes

Cremins, Robert. My animal Mother Goose

Dame Wiggins of Lee and her seven wonderful cats

De Angeli, Marguerite. The book of nursery and Mother Goose rhymes

DeForest, Charlotte B. The prancing pony

De Regniers, Beatrice Schenk. Catch a little fox

  Willy O'Dwyer jumped in the fire

Domanska, Janina. I saw a ship a-sailing

  If all the seas were one sea

Emberley, Barbara. Simon's song

Evans, Mari. Singing black

Fish, Helen Dean. Four and twenty blackbirds

Frankenberg, Lloyd. Wings of rhyme

From King Boggen's hall to nothing-at-all

Gipson, Morrell. Favorite nursery tales

Hale, Sara Josepha. Mary had a little lamb

The history of Little Tom Tucker

The house that Jack built, ill. by Randolph Caldecott

The house that Jack built, ill. by Seymour Chwast

The house that Jack built, ill. by Antonio Frasconi

The house that Jack built, ill. by Rodney Peppé

Humpty Dumpty and other first rhymes

Ivimey, John William. The complete version of ye three blind mice

Jack Sprat. The life of Jack Sprat, his wife and his cat

Kepes, Juliet. Lady bird, quickly

Kessler, Leonard P. The silly Mother Goose

Knapp, John II. A pillar of pepper and other Bible nursery rhymes

Ladybug, ladybug, and other nursery rhymes

Lee, Dennis. Alligator pie

Levy, Sara G. Mother Goose rhymes for Jewish children

Livermore, Elaine. Three little kittens lost their mittens

Marshak, Samuel. The merry starlings

Martin, Bill (William Ivan). Sounds I remember

Martin, Sarah Catherine. The comic

adventures of Old Mother Hubbard
and her dog
Old Mother Hubbard and her dog, ill.
by Paul Galdone
Old Mother Hubbard and her dog, ill.
by Evaline Ness
Mendoza, George. Silly sheep and other
sheepish rhymes
Montgomerie, Norah. This little pig
went to market
Mother Goose. The annotated Mother
Goose
Baa baa black sheep
The baby's lap book
Blessed Mother Goose
Brian Wildsmith's Mother Goose
Carolyn Wells' edition of Mother
Goose
The Charles Addams Mother Goose
A child's book of old nursery
rhymes
The Chinese Mother Goose rhymes
The city and country Mother Goose
Frank Baber's Mother Goose
The gay Mother Goose
Grafa' Grig had a pig
Gray goose and gander and other
Mother Goose rhymes
Gregory Griggs
Hey Diddle Diddle
Hurrah, we're outward bound!
In a pumpkin shell
Jack Kent's merry Mother Goose
James Marshall's Mother Goose
The Larousse book of nursery
rhymes
Lavender's blue
Little boy blue
The little Mother Goose
London Bridge is falling down, ill. by
Ed Emberley
London Bridge is falling down, ill. by
Peter Spier
Mother Goose and nursery rhymes
The Mother Goose book, ill. by Alice
and Martin Provensen
The Mother Goose book, ill. by Sonia
Roetter
Mother Goose in French
Mother Goose in hieroglyphics
Mother Goose in Spanish
Mother Goose melodies
Mother Goose nursery rhymes, ill. by
Arthur Rackham, 1969
Mother Goose nursery rhymes, ill. by
Arthur Rackham, 1975
Mother Goose rhymes
The Mother Goose treasury
Mother Goose's melodies
Mother Goose's melody

Mother Goose's rhymes and melodies
Nursery rhyme book
Nursery rhymes, ill. Douglas Gorsline
Nursery rhymes, ill. by Eloise Wilkin
Nursery rhymes from Mother Goose in
signed English
One I love, two I love, and other
loving Mother Goose rhymes
One misty moisty morning
The only true Mother Goose melodies
The piper's son
A pocket full of posies
The rainbow Mother Goose
The real Mother Goose
Richard Scarry's best Mother Goose
ever
Richard Scarry's favorite Mother Goose
rhymes
Rimes de la Mere Oie
Ring o' roses
The Sesame Street players present
Mother Goose
Sing a song of sixpence
Sing hey diddle diddle
Songs for Mother Goose
The tall Mother Goose
Thirty old-time nursery songs
The three jovial huntsmen
The three little kittens
To market! To market!, ill. by Emma
Lillian Brock
To market! To market!, ill. by Peter
Spier
Tom, Tom the piper's son
Twenty nursery rhymes
Willy Pogany's Mother Goose
Mother Goose, ill. by Roger Antoine
Duvoisin
Mother Goose, ill. by Miss Elliott
Mother Goose, ill. by C. B. Falls
Mother Goose, ill. by Gyo Fujikawa
Mother Goose, ill. by Vernon Grant
Mother Goose, ill. by Kate Greenaway
Mother Goose, ill. by Michael Hague
Mother Goose, ill. by Violet La Mont
Mother Goose, ill. by Arthur Rackham
Mother Goose, ill. by Frederick
Richardson, 1915
Mother Goose, ill. by Frederick
Richardson, 1976
Mother Goose, ill. by Gustaf Tenggren
Mother Goose, ill. by Tasha Tudor
Mother Goose house
The moving adventures of Old Dame
Trot and her comical cat
Nursery rhymes
One, two, buckle my shoe
Opie, Iona Archibald. A family book of
nursery rhymes
A nursery companion

The Oxford nursery rhyme book
Puffin book of nursery rhymes
Palazzo, Tony. Animals 'round the
mulberry bush
The parrot in the garret and other
rhymes about dwellings
Patterson, Pat. Hickory dickory duck
Pearson, Tracey Campbell. Sing a song
of sixpence
Peppé, Rodney. Cat and mouse
Hey riddle diddle
Petersham, Maud. The rooster crows
Potter, Beatrix. Appley Dapply's nursery
rhymes
Cecily Parsley's nursery rhymes
Rey, Hans Augusto. Humpty Dumpty
and other Mother Goose songs
Robbins, Ruth. The harlequin and
Mother Goose
Scarry, Richard. Richard Scarry's animal
nursery tales
Sendak, Maurice. Hector Protector, and
As I went over the water
Simple Simon
The story of Simple Simon
Stearns, Monroe. Ring-a-ling
Stobbs, William. This little piggy
Tarrant, Margaret. Nursery rhymes
Thomas, Katherine Elwes. The real
personages of Mother Goose
Thomson, Pat. Rhymes around the day
Tucker, Nicholas. Mother Goose abroad
Watson, Clyde. Father Fox's
pennyrhymes
Weil, Lisl. Mother Goose picture riddles
What do you feed your donkey on?
Wheeler, Opal. Sing Mother Goose
Wood, Ray. The American Mother
Goose
Fun in American folk rhymes

Nursery school *see* School

Nurses *see* Careers — nurses

Oceans *see* Sea and seashore

Octopuses

Barrett, John M. Oscar the selfish
octopus

Carrick, Carol. Octopus
Drdek, Richard E. Horace the friendly
octopus
Kraus, Robert. Herman the helper
Most, Bernard. My very own octopus
Shaw, Evelyn S. Octopus
Ungerer, Tomi. Emile
Waber, Bernard. I was all thumbs

Oil

Freeman, Don. The seal and the slick
Ungerer, Tomi. The Mellops strike oil

Old age

Allard, Harry. It's so nice to have a wolf
around the house
Ardizzone, Edward. Lucy Brown and
Mr. Grimes
Benchley, Nathaniel. Snip
Briggs, Raymond. Jim and the beanstalk
Edelman, Elaine. Boom-de-boom
Farber, Norma. How does it feel to be
old?
Fassler, Joan. My grandpa died today
Fender, Kay. Odette!
Fink, Dale Borman. Mr. Silver and Mrs.
Gold
Gammell, Stephen. Git along, old
Scudder
Goffstein, M B (Marilyn Brooks). Fish
for supper
Grimm, Jacob. The Bremen town
musicians, ill. by Donna Diamond
The Bremen town musicians, ill. by
Janina Domanska
The Bremen town musicians, ill. by
Paul Galdone
The Brementown musicians, ill. by Ilse
Plume
The horse, the fox, and the lion
The musicians of Bremen
Hoff, Syd. Barkley
Kahl, Virginia. Maxie
Keeping, Charles. Molly o' the moors
Klein, Leonore. Old, older, oldest
Knox-Wagner, Elaine. My grandpa
retired today
Kunhardt, Dorothy. Billy the barber
Littledale, Freya. The snow child
Peet, Bill. Smokey
Pomerantz, Charlotte. Buffy and Albert
Skorpen, Liesel Moak. Old Arthur
Snow, Pegeen. Mrs. Periwinkle's
groceries
Sonneborn, Ruth A. I love Gram
Taber, Anthony. Cats' eyes
Taylor, Mark. Old Blue, you good dog
you
Uchida, Yoshiko. Sumi's special
happening

Wittman, Sally. A special trade
Zolotow, Charlotte. I know a lady

Olympics *see* Sports — Olympics

Only child *see* Family life — only child

Opossums *see* Animals — possums

Opposites *see* Concepts — opposites

Optical illusions

Anno, Mitsumasa. Anno's alphabet
  Anno's counting book
  Anno's counting house
  Anno's flea market
  Anno's Italy
  Anno's journey
  Anno's magical ABC
  Dr. Anno's midnight circus
  Topsy-turvies
  Upside-downers
Doty, Roy. Eye fooled you
Emberley, Ed. The Wizard of Op
Gardner, Beau. The look again...and
  again, and again, and again book
  The turn about, think about, look
  about book

Optimism *see* Character traits —
  optimism

Orphans

Ardizzone, Edward. Lucy Brown and
  Mr. Grimes
The babes in the woods. The old ballad
  of the babes in the woods
Bemelmans, Ludwig. Madeline
  Madeline and the bad hat
  Madeline and the gypsies
  Madeline in London
  Madeline's rescue
Bulla, Clyde Robert. Poor boy, rich boy
Gottstein, M B (Marilyn Brooks). Goldie
  the dollmaker
Mahy, Margaret. Sailor Jack and the
  twenty orphans
Moore, Inga. The vegetable thieves
Thomas, Kathy. The angel's quest
Ungerer, Tomi. The three robbers

Ostracism *see* Character traits — being
  different

Ostriches *see* Birds — ostriches

Otters *see* Animals — otters

Out and in *see* Concepts — in and out

Owls *see* Birds — owls

Pack rats *see* Animals — pack rats

Painters *see* Activities — painting;
  Careers — artists

Painting *see* Activities — painting

Pakistan *see* Foreign lands — Pakistan

Panama *see* Foreign lands — Panama

Panthers *see* Animals — leopards

Paper

Gibbons, Gail. Paper, paper everywhere
Huff, Vivian. Let's make paper dolls
Milgrom, Harry. Paper science

Parades

Anderson, C W (Clarence Williams).
  The rumble seat pony
Bright, Robert. Hurrah for Freddie!
Chalmers, Audrey. Parade of Obash
Crews, Donald. Parade
Emberley, Ed. The parade book
Ets, Marie Hall. Another day
  In the forest
Flack, Marjorie. Wait for William
Holt, Margaret. David McCheever's
  twenty-nine dogs
Janice. Little Bear marches in the St.
  Patrick's Day parade
Kroll, Steven. The goat parade
Richter, Mischa. Eric and Matilda
Slobodkina, Esphyr. Pezzo the peddler
  and the circus elephant
Spier, Peter. Crash! bang! boom!
Ziner, Feenie. Counting carnival

Parakeets *see* Birds — parakeets,
  parrots

Park rangers *see* Careers — park
  rangers

Parrots *see* Birds — parakeets, parrots

Participation

Agostinelli, Maria Enrica. I know
  something you don't know
Barrett, Judi. What's left?

Bendick, Jeanne. Why can't I?
Bester, Roger. Guess what?
Black, Irma Simonton. Is this my
  dinner?
Booth, Eugene. At the circus
  At the fair
  In the air
  In the garden
  In the jungle
  Under the ocean
Brown, Marc. Finger rhymes
Brown, Margaret Wise. The country
  noisy book
  The indoor noisy book
  Noisy book
  The quiet noisy book
  The seashore noisy book
  The summer noisy book
  The winter noisy book
Cameron, Polly. "I can't," said the ant
Carroll, Ruth. Where's the bunny?
Charlip, Remy. Fortunately
Cole, William. Frances face-maker
Corbett, Grahame. Guess who?
  What number now?
  Who is hiding?
  Who is inside?
  Who is next?
Craig, M Jean. Boxes
Crume, Marion W. Let me see you try
  Listen!
  What do you say?
De Regniers, Beatrice Schenk. It does
  not say meow!
Elting, Mary. Q is for duck
Emberley, Ed. Ed Emberley's amazing
  look through book
  Klippity klop
Ets, Marie Hall. Just me
  Talking without words
French, Fiona. Hunt the thimble
Garten, Jan. The alphabet tale
Glazer, Tom. Do your ears hang low?
  Eye winker, Tom Tinker, chin chopper
Heilbroner, Joan. This is the house
  where Jack lives
Hewett, Anita. The tale of the turnip
Hoban, Tana. Look again
  Where is it?
The house that Jack built
Hutchins, Pat. Good night owl
Ipcar, Dahlov. Lost and found
Jaynes, Ruth M. Benny's four hats
Johnson, Ryerson. Let's walk up the wall
Kepes, Juliet. Run little monkeys, run,
  run, run
Kuskin, Karla. Roar and more
Löfgren, Ulf. One-two-three
MacGregor, Ellen. Theodor Turtle
Martin, Bill (William Ivan). Brave little
  Indian

Montgomerie, Norah. This little pig
  went to market
Ogle, Lucille. I hear
Paterson, Diane. If I were a toad
Patrick, Gloria. This is...
Seignobosc, Françoise. The things I like
Seuss, Dr. Mr. Brown can moo! Can
  you?
  Wacky Wednesday
Shaw, Charles Green. It looked like spilt
  milk
Siewert, Margaret. Bear hunt
Simon, Norma. What do I say?
Sivulich, Sandra Stroner. I'm going on a
  bear hunt
Skaar, Grace Marion. What do the
  animals say?
Skorpen, Liesel Moak. All the Lassies
Slobodkina, Esphyr. Caps for sale
  Pezzo the peddler and the circus
  elephant
  Pezzo the peddler and the thirteen silly
  thieves
Spier, Peter. Crash! bang! boom!
  Gobble, growl, grunt
Steiner, Charlotte. Five little finger
  playmates
Sutton, Eve. My cat likes to hide in
  boxes
Ueno, Noriko. Elephant buttons
Watanabe, Shigeo. How do I put it on?
Weil, Lisl. Owl and other scrambles
Yudell, Lynn Deena. Make a face

Parties

Adams, Adrienne. The Christmas party
  A Halloween happening
Allard, Harry. The Stupids have a ball
  There's a party at Mona's tonight
Anderson, Lonzo. The Halloween party
Asch, Frank. Popcorn
Averill, Esther. Jenny's birthday book
  Jenny's first party
Bible, Charles. Jennifer's new chair
Blance, Ellen. Monster has a party
Bonsall, Crosby Newell. Twelve bells for
  Santa
Bowden, Joan Chase. The bear's
  surprise party
Brooke, L Leslie (Leonard Leslie).
  Johnny Crow's party
Brown, Myra Berry. Company's coming
  for dinner
Cohen, Miriam. Tough Jim
Crothers, Samuel McChord. Miss
  Muffet's Christmas party
DeLage, Ida. The squirrel's tree party
Du Bois, William Pène. Bear party
Ets, Marie Hall. The cow's party
Freedman, Sally. Monster birthday party

Freeman, Don. Dandelion
  The paper party
Gackenbach, Dick. Annie and the mud
  monster
Galdone, Joanna. Honeybee's party
Gendel, Evelyn. Tortoise and turtle
  Tortoise and turtle abroad
Glovach, Linda. The Little Witch's
  birthday book
Gordon, Shirley. Happy birthday,
  Crystal
Goyder, Alice. Party in Catland
Hoff, Syd. Henrietta's Halloween
Hughes, Shirley. Alfie gives a hand
Hutchins, Pat. The surprise party
Hynard, Julia. Percival's party
Janice. Little Bear's New Year's party
  Little Bear's pancake party
Jones, Penelope. I didn't want to be nice
Keats, Ezra Jack. A letter to Amy
Lazard, Naomi. What Amanda saw
Lenski, Lois. A surprise for Davy
Lipkind, William. The Christmas bunny
McNaughton, Colin. At the party
Marks, Burton. The spook book
Meyer, Elizabeth C. The blue china
  pitcher
Oxenbury, Helen. The queen and Rosie
  Randall
Parish, Peggy. Amelia Bedelia and the
  surprise shower
Park, W B. The costume party
Potter, Beatrix. The sly old cat
Prager, Annabelle. The spooky
  Halloween party
  The surprise party
Quin-Harkin, Janet. Helpful Hattie
Stott, Rowena. The hedgehog feast
Wegen, Ron. The Halloween costume
  party
Wiseman, Bernard. Morris has a
  birthday party!
Zimmer, Dirk. The trick-or-treat trap
Zion, Gene. Jeffie's party

Passover see Holidays — Passover

Patience see Character traits — patience

Peacocks, peahens see Birds —
  peacocks, peahens

Peddlers see Careers — peddlers

Pelicans see Birds — pelicans

Penguins see Birds — penguins

Perseverance see Character traits —
  perseverance

Persia see Foreign lands — Persia

Persistence see Character traits —
  persistence

Perspective see Concepts — perspective

Peru see Foreign lands — Peru

Petroleum see Oil

Pets

Aiken, Joan. Arabel and Mortimer
Alexander, Martha G. No ducks in our
  bathtub
Allard, Harry. It's so nice to have a wolf
  around the house
Allen, Marjorie N. One, two, three -
  ah-choo!
Ardizzone, Edward. Diana and her
  rhinoceros
Arnold, Caroline. Pets without homes
Asch, Frank. The last puppy
Atwood, Margaret. Anna's pet
Baldner, Gaby. Joba and the wild boar
Bannon, Laura. Watchdog
Barton, Byron. Jack and Fred
Baylor, Byrd. Amigo
Beatty, Hetty Burlingame. Moorland
  pony
Belpré, Pura. Santiago
Benchley, Peter. Jonathan visits the
  White House
Bishop, Claire Huchet. The truffle pig
Blackwood, Gladys Rourke. Whistle for
  Cindy
Blance, Ellen. Monster buys a pet
Blegvad, Lenore. The great hamster
  hunt
Bliss, Corinne Demas. That dog Melly!
Boegehold, Betty. Pawpaw's run
Brenner, Barbara. The five pennies
Brett, Jan. Annie and the wild animals
Brice, Tony. The bashful goldfish
Brock, Emma Lillian. A pet for Barbie
Bröger, Achim. Bruno takes a trip
  Francie's paper puppy
Brothers, Aileen. Jiffy, Miss Boo and
  Mr. Roo
Brunhoff, Laurent de. Babar and the
  Wully-Wully
Carlson, Natalie Savage. Spooky night
Carrick, Carol. The accident
  A clearing in the forest
  The foundling
Carroll, Ruth. Pet tale
Chenery, Janet. Pickles and Jake
Christian, Mary Blount. Devin and
  Goliath
Cohen, Miriam. Jim's dog Muffins

Zimelman, Nathan. Positively no pets allowed

Zolotow, Charlotte. The poodle who barked at the wind

Zweifel, Frances. Bony

Philippines *see* Foreign lands — Philippines

Phoenix *see* Mythical creatures

Photography *see* Activities — photographing

Physicians *see* Careers — doctors

Picnicking *see* Activities — picnicking

Pigeons *see* Birds — pigeons

Pigs *see* Animals — pigs

Pilots *see* Careers — airplane pilots

Pirates

Baum, Louis. JuJu and the pirate

Burningham, John. Come away from the water, Shirley

Carryl, Charles Edward. A capital ship

Devlin, Harry. The walloping window blind

Dyke, John. Pigwig and the pirates

Graham, Mary Stuart Campbell. The pirates' bridge

Haseley, Dennis. The pirate who tried to capture the moon

Hutchins, Pat. One-eyed Jake

Joslin, Sesyle. Señor Baby Elephant, the pirate

Keats, Ezra Jack. Maggie and the pirate

Kessler, Leonard P. The pirates' adventure on Spooky Island

Kroll, Steven. Are you pirates?

Mahy, Margaret. Sailor Jack and the twenty orphans

Peppé, Rodney. The kettleship pirates

Perkins, Al. Tubby and the lantern

Roberts, Thom. Pirates in the park

Ross, David. Gorp and the space pirates

Thompson, Brenda. Pirates

Vinton, Iris. Look out for pirates!

Walker, Barbara K. Pigs and pirates

Pixies *see* Elves and little people; Fairies

Planes *see* Airplanes, airports

Plants

Adelson, Leone. Please pass the grass

Aliki. Corn is maize

Ayer, Jacqueline. The paper-flower tree

Baker, Jeffrey J W. Patterns of nature

Berson, Harold. Pop! goes the turnip

Bishop, Gavin. Mrs. McGinty and the bizarre plant

Blackmore, Vivien. Why corn is golden

Brown, Marc. Your first garden book

Bulla, Clyde Robert. A tree is a plant

Busch, Phyllis S. Cactus in the desert
Lions in the grass

Carle, Eric. The tiny seed

Chapman, Carol. Barney Bipple's magic dandelions

Cole, Joanna. Plants in winter

Craig, M Jean. Spring is like the morning

Credle, Ellis. Down, down the mountain

Cristini, Ermanno. In the pond

Cross, Diana Harding. Some plants have funny names

Cross, Genevieve. A trip to the yard

Darby, Gene. What is a plant?

Domanska, Janina. The turnip

Ellentuck, Shan. A sunflower as big as the sun

Fisher, Aileen. And a sunflower grew
As the leaves fall down
Mysteries in the garden
Now that spring is here
Plant magic
Prize performance
Seeds on the go
Swords and daggers
We went looking

Ginsburg, Mirra. Mushroom in the rain
The green grass grows all around

Greenberg, Polly. Oh, Lord, I wish I was a buzzard

Heller, Ruth. Plants that never ever bloom

Hewett, Anita. The tale of the turnip

Hillert, Margaret. The magic beans

The history of Mother Twaddle and the marvelous achievements of her son Jack

Hogan, Paula Z. The dandelion

Holmes, Anita. The 100-year-old cactus

Hutchins, Pat. Titch

Ipcar, Dahlov. Hard scrabble harvest

Johnson, Hannah Lyons. From seed to jack-o'-lantern

Jordan, Helene J. Seeds of wind and water

Kepes, Juliet. The seed that peacock planted

Kirkpatrick, Rena K. Look at leaves
Look at seeds and weeds

Krauss, Ruth. The carrot seed

Kuchalla, Susan. All about seeds

Le Tord, Bijou. Picking and weaving

Lewis, Naomi. Leaves

Little, Lessie Jones. I can do it by myself
The little red hen, ill. by Janina Domanska
The little red hen, ill. by Paul Galdone
The little red hen, ill. by Mel Pekarsky
The little red hen, ill. by Margot Zemach
Littledale, Freya. The magic plum tree
Maestro, Giulio. The remarkable plant in apartment 4
Miller, Judith Ransom. Nabob and the geranium
Nash, Ogden. The animal garden
Oleson, Claire. For Pipita, an orange tree
Petie, Haris. The seed the squirrel dropped
Pouyanne, Rési. What I see hidden by the pond
Rey, Hans Augusto. Elizabite, adventures of a carnivorous plant
Ring, Elizabeth. Tiger lilies
Ringi, Kjell. The sun and the cloud
Rockwell, Harlow. The compost heap
Rudolph, Marguerita. How a shirt grew in the field
Selberg, Ingrid. Nature's hidden world
Selsam, Millicent E. The amazing dandelion
　Cotton
　More potatoes!
　Seeds and more seeds
Shecter, Ben. Partouche plants a seed
Sugita, Yutaka. The flower family
Tolstoĭ, Alekseĭ Nikolaevich. The great big enormous turnip
Williams, Barbara. Hello, dandelions!
Wondriska, William. The tomato patch
Wong, Herbert H. My plant
Zion, Gene. The plant sitter
Zolotow, Charlotte. In my garden

Playing *see* Activities — playing

Plays *see* Theater

Poetry, rhyme

Aardema, Verna. Bringing the rain to Kapiti Plain
　The riddle of the drum
Abrons, Mary. For Alice a palace
Adams, Richard. The tyger voyage
Adelborg, Ottilia. Clean Peter and the children of Grubbylea
Adelson, Leone. Please pass the grass
Adler, David A. You think it's fun to be a clown!
Adoff, Arnold. Big sister tells me that I'm black
　Birds
　Black is brown is tan

Make a circle, keep us in
Tornado!
Where wild Willie?
Æsop. Once in a wood
Ahlberg, Allan. Cops and robbers
Ahlberg, Janet. Each peach pear plum
Peek-a-boo!
Aiken, Conrad. Tom, Sue and the clock
Alborough, Jez. Bare bear
Alderson, Sue Ann. Bonnie McSmithers is at it again!
Aldis, Dorothy. All together
　Before things happen
　Hello day
　Quick as a wink
Aldridge, Alan. The butterfly ball and the grasshopper's feast
Alexander, Anne. ABC of cars and trucks
　Boats and ships from A to Z
　I want to whistle
　My daddy and I
Alger, Leclaire. All in the morning early
　Kellyburn Braes
Allen, Jonathan. A bad case of animal nonsense
Allen, Pamela. Who sank the boat?
Allstrom, Elizabeth C. Songs along the way
Ambler, Christopher Gifford. Ten little foxhounds
Andre, Evelyn M. Places I like to be
Anglund, Joan Walsh. A Christmas book
　The Joan Walsh Anglund story book
　Morning is a little child
Armour, Richard Willard. The adventures of Egbert the Easter egg
　Animals on the ceiling
　Have you ever wished you were something else?
　Sea full of whales
　The year Santa went modern
Arnosky, Jim. A kettle of hawks, and other wildlife groups
Asch, Frank. City sandwich
　Country pie
Attenberger, Walburga. The little man in winter
　Who knows the little man?
Atwood, Ann. The little circle
Aylesworth, Jim. Mary's mirror
Azarian, Mary. The tale of John Barleycorn or, From barley to beer
The babes in the woods. The old ballad of the babes in the woods
Bach, Othello. Lilly, Willy and the mail-order witch
Baer, Edith. Words are like faces
Bang, Molly. Ten, nine, eight
Baningan, Sharon Stearns. Circus magic

Barker, Cicely Mary. Berry flower fairies
  Blossom flower fairies
  Flower fairies of the seasons
  Spring flower fairies
  Summer flower fairies
Barry, Katharina. A is for anything
  A bug to hug
Barry, Robert E. Animals around the
  world
  Mr. Willowby's Christmas tree
Barto, Emily N. Chubby bear
Baruch, Dorothy. I would like to be a
  pony and other wishes
Baskin, Leonard. Hosie's zoo
Baylor, Byrd. Amigo
  The desert is theirs
  Desert voices
  Everybody needs a rock
  The other way to listen
Behn, Harry. Crickets and bullfrogs and
  whispers of thunder
Belloc, Hilaire. The bad child's book of
  beasts, and more beasts for worse
  children
  Matilda who told lies and was burned
  to death
  More beasts for worse children
Belting, Natalia Maree. Christmas folk
  Summer's coming in
Bemelmans, Ludwig. Madeline
  Madeline and the bad hat
  Madeline and the gypsies
  Madeline in London
  Madeline's rescue
  Welcome home
Benét, William Rose. Angels
Benjamin, Alan. A change of plans
  Ribtickle Town
Bennett, Jill. Days are where we live and
  other poems
  Roger was a razor fish and other
  poems
  Tiny Tim
Bennett, Rainey. The secret hiding place
Bennett, Rowena. The day is dancing
  and other poems
  Songs from around a toadstool table
Berenstain, Stan. The bear detectives
  The bears' almanac
  The Berenstain bears and the missing
  dinosaur bone
  The Berenstain bears and the spooky
  old tree
  The Berenstain bears' Christmas tree
  He bear, she bear
Berg, Jean Horton. The wee little man
Berger, Judith. Butterflies and rainbows
Beskow, Elsa Maartman. Children of the
  forest
  Peter in Blueberry Land
  Peter's adventures in Blueberry land

Betz, Betty. Manners for moppets
Billy Boy
Black, Irma Simonton. Is this my
  dinner?
Blake, Quentin. Mister Magnolia
Blegvad, Erik. Burnie's hill
Blegvad, Lenore. One is for the sun
  The parrot in the garret and other
  rhymes about dwellings
Bodecker, N M (Nils Mogens). "Let's
  marry," said the cherry, and other
  nonsense poems
  Snowman Sniffles and other verse
Bodwell, Gaile. The long day of the
  giants
Boegehold, Betty. Pawpaw's run
Borchers, Elisabeth. There comes a time
Borten, Helen. Do you go where I go?
  Do you hear what I hear?
  Do you know what I know?
Bottner, Barbara. There was nobody
  there
Bouton, Josephine. Favorite poems for
  the children's hour
A boy went out to gather pears
Boynton, Sandra. But not the
  hippopotamus
  The going to bed book
  Hippos go berserk
  Moo, baa, lalala
Braun, Kathy. Kangaroo and kangaroo
Brecht, Bertolt. Uncle Eddie's
  moustache
Bridgman, Elizabeth. All the little
  bunnies
Bright, Robert. My hopping bunny
Brooke, L Leslie (Leonard Leslie).
  Johnny Crow's garden
  Johnny Crow's new garden
Brooks, Gwendolyn. Bronzeville boys
  and girls
Brown, Beatrice Curtis. Jonathan Bing,
  ill. by Judith Gwyn Brown
  Jonathan Bing, ill. by Pelagie Doane
Brown, Judith Gwyn. Alphabet dreams
Brown, Marc. Finger rhymes
  Pickle things
  The silly tail book
  Wings on things
  Witches four
Brown, Margaret Wise. Big red barn
  Four fur feet
  Nibble nibble
  Sleepy ABC
  Two little trains
  Where have you been?
  Whistle for the train
  The wonderful story book
Brown, Myra Berry. Best friends
  Best of luck
Brown, Palmer. The silver nutmeg

Browner, Richard. Everyone has a name
Browning, Robert. The pied piper of
  Hamelin
Bruce, Sheilah B. The radish day jubilee
Bruna, Dick. Christmas
  The fish
  Kitten Nell
  Little bird tweet
  The orchestra
  Poppy Pig goes to market
  Tilly and Tess
Bryan, Ashley. Beat the story-drum,
  pum-pum
Buckley, Helen Elizabeth. Josie and the
  snow
  Josie's Buttercup
Budney, Blossom. A kiss is round
Buell, Ellen Lewis. Read me a poem
Buff, Mary. Hurry, Skurry and Flurry
Burdekin, Harold. A child's grace
Burgunder, Rose. From summer to
  summer
Burnstein, John. Slim Goodbody
Burroway, Janet. The truck on the track
Calmenson, Stephanie. Never take a pig
  to lunch and other funny poems
  about animals
  Where will the animals stay?
Cameron, John. If mice could fly
Cameron, Polly. A child's book of
  nonsense
  "I can't," said the ant
Carroll, Lewis. Jabberwocky
Carton, Lonnie Caming. Mommies
Cate, Rikki. A cat's tale
Caudill, Rebecca. Wind, sand and sky
Cendrars, Blaise. Shadow
Chardiet, Bernice. C is for circus
Charles, Donald. Calico Cat meets
  bookworm
  Shaggy dog's animal alphabet
  Time to rhyme with Calico Cat
Charles, Robert Henry. The roundabout
  turn
Chönz, Selina. A bell for Ursli
  Florina and the wild bird
  The snowstorm
Chorao, Kay. The baby's bedtime book
Chukovsky, Korney. The telephone
Ciardi, John. I met a man
  The monster den
  You read to me, I'll read to you
Clark, Leonard. Drums and trumpets
Clifford, Eth. Red is never a mouse
Clifton, Lucille. The black B C's
  Everett Anderson's Christmas coming
  Everett Anderson's friend
  Everett Anderson's goodbye
  Everett Anderson's nine months long
  Everett Anderson's 1-2-3
  Everett Anderson's year

  Some of the days of Everett Anderson
Clithero, Sally. Beginning-to-read poetry
Coatsworth, Elizabeth. The children
  come running
  The giant golden book of cat stories
  A peaceable kingdom, and other
  poems
Cole, Joanna. Golly Gump swallowed a
  fly
Cole, William. Frances face-maker
  That pest Jonathan
  What's good for a four-year-old?
  What's good for a six-year-old?
  What's good for a three-year-old?
Coletta, Irene. From A to Z
Conover, Chris. Six little ducks
Cooney, Barbara. A garland of games
  and other diversions
Copp, James. Martha Matilda O'Toole
Counting rhymes
Craft, Ruth. The winter bear
Crowley, Arthur. Bonzo Beaver
  The wagon man
Cushman, Doug. Giants
  Once upon a pig
Dahl, Roald. Dirty beasts
Dalmais, Anne-Marie. In my garden
Dayton, Laura. LeRoy's birthday circus
Degen, Bruce. Jamberry
De Gerez, Toni. My song is a piece of
  jade
Delaunay, Sonia. Sonia Delaunay's
  alphabet
Dennis, Suzanne E. Answer me that
De Paola, Tomie. Songs of the fog
  maiden
De Regniers, Beatrice Schenk. A bunch
  of poems and verses
  Cats cats cats
  It does not say meow!
  May I bring a friend?
  Red Riding Hood
  Something special
  Was it a good trade?
Dodd, Lynley. The nickle nackle tree
Dodge, Mary Mapes. Mary Anne
The dog writes on the window with his
  nose, and other poems
Domanska, Janina. What do you see?
Don't tell the scarecrow
Dowers, Patrick. One day scene through
  a leaf
Driz, Ovsei. The boy and the tree
Eastwick, Ivy O. Cherry stones! Garden
  swings!
  Rainbow over all
Eberstadt, Isabel. What is for my
  birthday?
Edelman, Elaine. Boom-de-boom
Eichenberg, Fritz. Dancing in the moon
Elborn, Andrew. Bird Adalbert

Greenfield, Eloise. Daydreamers
Greenwood, Ann. A pack of dreams
Gregorich, Barbara. My friend goes left
Gundersheimer, Karen. Happy winter
Gunning, Monica. The two Georges
Haas, Irene. The Maggie B
Hague, Kathleen. Alphabears
Hall, Pam. On the edge of the eastern
  ocean
Hallinan, P K (Patrick K). Just open a
  book
  That's what a friend is
Hample, Stoo. Yet another big fat funny
  silly book
Harrison, David Lee. The case of Og,
  the missing frog
Harrison, Sarah. In granny's garden
Hawkins, Colin. Boo! Who?
  Mig the pig
Hazen, Barbara Shook. Where do bears
  sleep?
Heller, Ruth. The reason for a flower
Highwater, Jamake. Moonsong lullaby
Hill, Helen. Dusk to dawn
Hillman, Priscilla. A Merry-Mouse book
  of favorite poems
  A Merry-Mouse book of months
The history of Mother Twaddle and the
  marvelous achievements of her son
  Jack
Hoban, Russell. Goodnight
Hoban, Tana. One little kitten
  Where is it?
Hoberman, Mary Ann. The cozy book
  A house is a house for me
  I like old clothes
  Nuts to you and nuts to me
Hofstrand, Mary. Albion pig
Holl, Adelaide. Mrs. McGarrity's
  peppermint sweater
  Sir Kevin of Devon
Holland, Marion. A big ball of string
Hollander, John. A book of various owls
Hopkins, Lee Bennett. And God bless
  me
  Circus! Circus!
  A dog's life
  Easter buds are springing
  Go to bed!
  I think I saw a snail
  Merrily comes our harvest in
  Morning, noon and nighttime, too
  The sky is full of song
  Hot cross buns, and other old street
  cries
Houston, John A. The bright yellow
  rope
Howells, Mildred. The woman who lived
  in Holland
Hurd, Edith Thacher. Caboose
  Come and have fun

Hutchins, Pat. The wind blew
Hymes, Lucia. Oodles of noodles and
  other rhymes
If dragon flies made honey
Ilsley, Velma. A busy day for Chris
  The pink hat
Ipcar, Dahlov. Black and white
  The cat came back
  Hard scrabble harvest
Jacobs, Leland B. Is somewhere always
  far away?
Janosch. Tonight at nine
Jarrell, Randall. A bat is born
Jerome, Judson. I never saw...
Jewell, Nancy. ABC cat
Jones, Hettie. The trees stand shining
Jones, Jessie Mae Orton. Small rain
Kahl, Virginia. The Baron's booty
  The Duchess bakes a cake
  Gunhilde and the Halloween spell
  Gunhilde's Christmas booke
  The habits of rabbits
  How do you hide a monster?
  The perfect pancake
  Plum pudding for Christmas
Kahn, Joan. Hi, Jock, run around the
  block
Kalman, Benjamin. Animals in danger
Kavanaugh, James J. The crooked
  angel
Kessler, Ethel. Do baby bears sit in
  chairs?
Kessler, Leonard P. Riddles that rhyme
  for Halloween time
Kherdian, David. Country cat, city cat
Kitt, Tamara. Sam and the impossible
  thing
Klimowicz, Barbara. The strawberry
  thumb
Knight, Hilary. Hilary Knight's the owl
  and the pussy-cat
Koenner, Alfred. High flies the ball
Krauss, Ruth. Bears
  A bouquet of littles
  Everything under a mushroom
Kroll, Steven. Pigs in the house
Krüss, James. 3 X 3
Kumin, Maxine. Follow the fall
  Sebastian and the dragon
  Speedy digs downside up
  Spring things
  A winter friend
Kuskin, Karla. All sizes of noises
  The animals and the ark
  A boy had a mother who bought him a
  hat
  Herbert hated being small
  In the flaky frosty morning
  James and the rain
  Roar and more
  Sand and snow

Miles, Miska. Apricot ABC
Miller, Edna. Mousekin's ABC
Mitchell, Cynthia. Halloweena Hecatee
  Playtime
  Under the cherry tree
Mizumura, Kazue. If I were a cricket...
Moncure, Jane Belk. Happy healthkins
  The healthkin food train
  Healthkins exercise!
  Healthkins help
Monster poems
The moon's the north wind's cooky
Moore, Clement C. The night before
  Christmas, ill. by Tomie De Paola
  The night before Christmas, ill. by Gyo
  Fujikawa
  The night before Christmas, ill. by
  Anita Lobel
  The night before Christmas, ill. by
  Gustaf Tenggren
  The night before Christmas, ill. by
  Tasha Tudor
  A visit from St. Nicholas
Moore, Lilian. I feel the same way
  See my lovely poison ivy
Morice, Dave. Dot town
  A visit from St. Alphabet
Morrison, Bill. Squeeze a sneeze
Morrison, Sean. Is that a happy
  hippopotamus?
Morse, Samuel French. Sea sums
Moss, Jeffrey. The songs of Sesame
  Street in poems and pictures
Mullins, Edward S. Animal limericks
Muntean, Michaela. Bicycle bear
Nash, Ogden. The adventures of Isabel
  The animal garden
  A boy is a boy
  Custard and Company
  Custard the dragon and the wicked
  knight
Newberry, Clare Turlay. The kittens'
  ABC
Nolan, Dennis. Wizard McBean and his
  flying machine
Noll, Sally. Off and counting
O'Neill, Mary. Big red hen
Oppenheim, Joanne. Have you seen
  roads?
  Have you seen trees?
Orbach, Ruth. Apple pigs
Orgel, Doris. Merry merry FIBruary
Osborne, Valerie. One big yo to go
Over in the meadow
Oxenbury, Helen. Pig tale
Pack, Robert. How to catch a crocodile
  Then what did you do?
The parrot in the garret and other
  rhymes about dwellings
Partch, Virgil Franklin. The Christmas
  cookie sprinkle snitcher

Paterson, Andrew Barton. The man
  from Ironbark
  Mulga Bill's bicycle
Patrick, Gloria. This is...
Patz, Nancy. Moses supposes his toeses
  are roses and 7 other silly old rhymes
Pavey, Peter. One dragon's dream
Peaceable kingdom
Peck, Robert Newton. Hamilton
Peet, Bill. Ella
  Hubert's hair-raising adventures
  Huge Harold
  Kermit the hermit
  The luckiest one of all
  The pinkish, purplish, bluish egg
  Randy's dandy lions
  Smokey
Peppé, Rodney. Cat and mouse
  Hey riddle diddle
Perkins, Al. The digging-est dog
  The ear book
  Hand, hand, fingers, thumb
  The nose book
Petie, Haris. Billions of bugs
  The seed the squirrel dropped
Peyo. What do smurfs do all day?
Phillips, Louis. The upside down riddle
  book
Piatti, Celestino. Celestino Piatti's animal
  ABC
Plath, Sylvia. The bed book
Pomerantz, Charlotte. All asleep
  The ballad of the long-tailed rat
  If I had a Paka
  The piggy in the puddle
  The tamarindo puppy and other
  poems
Prelutsky, Jack. The baby uggs are
  hatching
  Circus
  It's Halloween
  It's Valentine's Day
  The mean old mean hyena
  The pack rat's day and other poems
  The queen of Eene
  Rainy rainy Saturday
  The Random House book of poetry
  for children
  The snopp on the sidewalk and other
  poems
  The terrible tiger
  What I did last summer
Preston, Edna Mitchell. Pop Corn and
  Ma Goodness
Prince, Pamela. The secret world of
  teddy bears
Provensen, Alice. Karen's opposites
Puner, Helen Walker. Daddys, what
  they do all day
  The sitter who didn't sit
Puppies and kittens

Smith, William Jay. Puptents and pebbles
  Typewriter town
Snow, Pegeen. A pet for Pat
Snyder, Zilpha Keatley. Come on, Patsy
Spier, Peter. Noah's ark
Spilka, Arnold. And the frog went
  "Blah!"
  A lion I can do without
  Little birds don't cry
  A rumbudgin of nonsense
Starbird, Kaye. The covered bridge
  house and other poems
Steig, William. An eye for elephants
Stephenson, Dorothy. The night it
  rained toys
Stevens, Janet. Animal fair
Stevenson, Drew. The ballad of
  Penelope Lou...and me
Stevenson, Robert Louis. A child's
  garden of verses, ill. by Erik Blegvad
  A child's garden of verses, ill. by
  Pelagie Doane
  A child's garden of verses, ill. by Toni
  Frissell
  A child's garden of verses, ill. by Gyo
  Fujikawa
  A child's garden of verses, ill. by Alica
  and Martin Provensen
  A child's garden of verses, ill. by Tasha
  Tudor
  A child's garden of verses, ill. by Brian
  Wildsmith
  The moon
Stobbs, William. This little piggy
Stoddard, Sandol. My very own special
  particular private and personal cat
Stone, Rosetta. Because a little bug went
  ka-choo!
Stover, Jo Ann. If everybody did
Sundgaard, Arnold. Jethro's difficult
  dinosaur
Supraner, Robyn. Would you rather be
  a tiger?
Sutton, Eve. My cat likes to hide in
  boxes
Svendsen, Carol. Hulda
Terban, Marvin. I think I thought
Tether, Graham. The hair book
Thomas, Gary. The best of the little
  books
Thomas, Patricia. "Stand back," said the
  elephant, "I'm going to sneeze!"
  "There are rocks in my socks!" said the
  ox to the fox
The three little pigs, ill. by Erik Blegvad
The three little pigs, ill. by William Pène
  Du Bois
Tippett, James Sterling. Counting the
  days
Trent, Robbie. The first Christmas
Tresselt, Alvin R. Follow the wind

Tudor, Tasha. Around the year
Udry, Janice May. A tree is nice
Vance, Eleanor Graham. Jonathan
Vogel, Ilse-Margaret. The don't be
  scared book
Wadsworth, Olive A. Over in the
  meadow
Wahl, Jan. Follow me cried Bee
Wakefield, Joyce. Ask a silly question
  From where you are
Wallace, Daisy. Ghost poems
Wallner, Alexandra. Munch
Watson, Clyde. Applebet
  Catch me and kiss me and say it again
  Father Fox's feast of songs
  Hickory stick rag
Watson, Jane Werner. The tall book of
  make-believe
Welber, Robert. Goodbye, hello
Wells, Rosemary. Don't spill it again,
  James
  Noisy Nora
Wersba, Barbara. Do tigers ever bite
  kings?
Weygant, Noemi. It's autumn!
  It's summer!
  It's winter!
What do you feed your donkey on?
Wheeling, Lynn. When you fly
Wild, Robin. Little Pig and the big bad
  wolf
Wildsmith, Brian. Animal tricks
Willard, Nancy. A visit to William
  Blake's inn
Williams, Garth. The chicken book
Williams, Jay. I wish I had another
  name
Wise, William. Nanette, the hungry
  pelican
Wiseman, Bernard. Little new kangaroo
Wittels, Harriet. Things I hate!
Woolaver, Lance. Christmas with the
  rural mail
  From Ben Loman to the sea
Wright, Josephine Lord. Cotton Cat and
  Martha Mouse
Yolen, Jane. An invitation to the
  butterfly ball
Zemach, Harve. The judge
Ziner, Feenie. Counting carnival
Zolotow, Charlotte. River winding
  Some things go together
  Summer is...

Poland *see* Foreign lands — Poland

Police officers *see* Careers — police
officers

Poltergeists *see* Ghosts

Poor *see* Poverty

Pop-up books *see* Format, unusual

Porcupines *see* Animals — porcupines

Porpoise *see* Animals — dolphins

Portugal *see* Foreign lands — Portugal

Possums *see* Animals — possums

Poverty

Alexander, Lloyd. The king's fountain
Ambrus, Victor G. The three poor
 tailors
Andersen, H C (Hans Christian). The
 little match girl
Balet, Jan B. The fence
Bettina (Bettina Ehrlich). Pantaloni
Brand, Oscar. When I first came to this
 land
De Paola, Tomie. Helga's dowry
Deveaux, Alexis. Na-ni
Hazen, Barbara Shook. Tight times
Hoban, Lillian. Stick-in-the-mud turtle
Keeping, Charles. Joseph's yard
McCrea, James. The king's procession
Maiorano, Robert. Francisco
Nolan, Madeena Spray. My daddy don't
 go to work
Rose, Anne. How does a czar eat
 potatoes?
Sawyer, Ruth. Journey cake, ho!
Sonneborn, Ruth A. Friday night is
 papa night
 Seven in a bed
Steptoe, John. Uptown

Power failure

Freeman, Don. The night the lights
 went out
Rockwell, Anne F. Blackout

Practicality *see* Character traits —
 practicality

Prairie dogs *see* Animals — prairie
 dogs

Praying mantis *see* Insects — praying
 mantis

Prejudice

Anders, Rebecca. A look at prejudice
 and understanding
Carlson, Nancy. Loudmouth George
 and the new neighbors

Pride *see* Character traits — pride

Princes *see* Royalty

Princesses *see* Royalty

Prisons

Hickman, Martha Whitmore. When can
 daddy come home?
McKee, David. 123456789 Benn

Problem solving

Adler, David A. The children of Chelm
 My dog and the key mystery
Alexander, Martha G. I'll protect you
 from the jungle beasts
 Move over, Twerp
 Out! Out! Out!
 We never get to do anything
 We're in big trouble, Blackboard Bear
Alexander, Sue. World famous Muriel
Allen, Laura Jean. Rollo and Tweedy
 and the case of the missing cheese
Ames, Mildred. The wonderful box
Armitage, Ronda. Ice creams for Rosie
 The lighthouse keeper's lunch
Arnosky, Jim. Mud time and more
Ashley, Bernard. Dinner ladies don't
 count
Bakken, Harold. The special string
Balet, Jan B. The fence
Barklem, Jill. The secret staircase
Barrett, Judi. What's left?
Barry, Katharina. A bug to hug
Beim, Lorraine. Two is a team
Benarde, Anita. The pumpkin smasher
Benchley, Nathaniel. A ghost named
 Fred
Berenstain, Stan. The bear detectives
 The Berenstain bears and the messy
 room
 The Berenstain bears and the missing
 dinosaur bone
Berg, Jean Horton. The O'Learys and
 friends
Bester, Roger. Guess what?
Blaine, Marge. The terrible thing that
 happened at our house
Bonsall, Crosby Newell. The case of the
 cat's meow
 The case of the double cross
 The case of the dumb bells
 The case of the hungry stranger
Booth, Eugene. At the circus
 At the fair
 In the air
 In the garden
 In the jungle
 Under the ocean
Bradford, Ann. The mystery at Misty
 Falls
 The mystery of the blind writer

The mystery of the midget clown
The mystery of the missing dogs
The mystery of the square footsteps
The mystery of the tree house
Brandenberg, Franz. A picnic, hurrah!
Branley, Franklyn M. Big tracks, little tracks
Bröger, Achim. Little Harry
Brown, Jeff. Flat Stanley
Brown, Margaret Wise. They all saw it
Brown, Palmer. The silver nutmeg
Browne, Anthony. Bear hunt
Bulette, Sara. The splendid belt of Mr. Big
Calhoun, Mary. Audubon cat
Carlson, Nancy. Harriet and the garden
Carrick, Carol. Ben and the porcupine
Cauley, Lorinda Bryan. The new house
Chaffin, Lillie D. Tommy's big problem
Chapman, Carol. Herbie's troubles
Christensen, Gardell Dano. Mrs. Mouse needs a house
Christian, Mary Blount. The doggone mystery
  J. J. Leggett, secret agent
Cleary, Beverly. The real hole
Clymer, Ted. The horse and the bad morning
Coombs, Patricia. Dorrie and the witches' camp
Cooney, Nancy Evans. The blanket that had to go
Cooper, Jacqueline. Angus and the Mona Lisa
Cressey, James. Fourteen rats and a rat-catcher
Darling, Kathy. The mystery in Santa's toyshop
De Paola, Tomie. Charlie needs a cloak
Dewey, Ariane. The fish Peri
Dickinson, Mary. Alex's bed
Domanska, Janina. The turnip
Du Bois, William Pène. The alligator case
Economakis, Olga. Oasis of the stars
Elkin, Benjamin. Such is the way of the world
Emberley, Ed. Rosebud
Farber, Norma. How the left-behind beasts built Ararat
Fassler, Joan. Boy with a problem
Feder, Paula Kurzband. Where does the teacher live?
Fife, Dale. Follow that ghost!
Fowler, Richard. Inspector Smart gets the message!
Fremlin, Robert. Three friends
Freschet, Berniece. Bernard of Scotland Yard
Gelman, Rita Golden. Professor Coconut and the thief

Gibbons, Gail. The missing maple syrup sap mystery
Gordon, Margaret. The supermarket mice
Hancock, Sibyl. Freaky Francie
Hare, Norma Q. Mystery at mouse house
Harrison, David Lee. Detective Bob and the great ape escape
Heide, Florence Parry. The shrinking of Treehorn
Hines, Anna Grossnickle. Maybe a band-aid will help
Hoban, Lillian. Arthur's funny money
Holman, Felice. Elisabeth, the treasure hunter
Horvath, Betty F. The cheerful quiet
Houston, John A. The bright yellow rope
  A mouse in my house
Johnston, Johanna. Edie changes her mind
Jonas, Ann. Holes and peeks
Keats, Ezra Jack. Goggles
  Whistle for Willie
Keenen, George. The preposterous week
Kellogg, Steven. The mystery of the missing red mitten
  The mystery of the stolen blue paint
Klimowicz, Barbara. The strawberry thumb
Kraus, Robert. The detective of London
Leonard, Marcia. Little owl leaves the nest
Levy, Elizabeth. Something queer at the ball park
  Something queer at the haunted school
  Something queer is going on
  Something queer on vacation
Lewis, Thomas P. Call for Mr. Sniff
Lexau, Joan M. Benjie
  Benjie on his own
Lobel, Arnold. On the day Peter Stuyvesant sailed into town
Low, Joseph. What if...?
McCloskey, Robert. Lentil
McKee, David. 123456789 Benn
Maestro, Betsy. The guessing game
Maiorano, Robert. Francisco
Marie, Geraldine. The magic box
Marshall, James. Four little troubles
Marshall, Margaret. Mike
Mayer, Mercer. What do you do with a kangaroo?
Miller, Edna. Mousekin's mystery
Molarsky, Osmond. The peasant and the fly
Munsch, Robert N. Jonathan cleaned up — then he heard a sound

Myrick, Jean Lockwood. Ninety-nine
pockets
Ness, Evaline. Do you have the time,
Lydia?
Nixon, Joan Lowery. The Thanksgiving
mystery
 The Valentine mystery
Oakley, Graham. The church mice in
action
Obrist, Jürg. They do things right in
Albern
Pape, Donna Lugg. Snoino mystery
Partridge, Jenny. Hopfellow
 Mr. Squint
 Peterkin Pollensnuff
Payne, Emmy. Katy no-pocket
Platt, Kin. Big Max
 Big Max in the mystery of the missing
moose
Quackenbush, Robert M. Detective Mole
 Detective Mole and the secret clues
 Detective Mole and the Tip-Top
mystery
 Dig to disaster
 Express train to trouble
 Piet Potter returns
 Piet Potter strikes again
 Piet Potter to the rescue
 Piet Potter's first case
 Stairway to doom
Robb, Brian. My grandmother's djinn
Robison, Deborah. Bye-bye, old buddy
 No elephants allowed
Schermer, Judith. Mouse in house
Schurr, Cathleen. The long and the
short of it
Segal, Lore. The story of old Mrs.
Brubeck and how she looked for
trouble and where she found him
Seuss, Dr. Did I ever tell you how lucky
you are?
 Hunches of bunches
Sharmat, Marjorie Weinman. Nate the
Great and the lost list
 Nate the Great goes undercover
Shearer, John. Billy Jo Jive and the case
of the midnight voices
 The case of the sneaker snatcher
Smith, Jim. The frog band and the
onion seller
Tallon, Robert. Handella
Taylor, Mark. The case of the missing
kittens
Thomas, Patricia. "There are rocks in
my socks!" said the ox to the fox
Thompson, Vivian Laubach.
Camp-in-the-yard
Thomson, Ruth. Peabody all at sea
 Peabody's first case
Titus, Eve. Anatole and the cat
 Anatole and the Pied Piper

Anatole and the poodle
Anatole and the robot
Anatole and the thirty thieves
Anatole and the toyshop
Anatole in Italy
Tolstoĭ, Alekseĭ Nikolaevich. The great
big enormous turnip
Türk, Hanne. Max versus the cube
 A surprise for Max
Van Horn, William. Twitchtoe, the
beastfinder
Wiseman, Bernard. Doctor Duck and
Nurse Swan
Wold, Jo Anne. Tell them my name is
Amanda
Woolley, Catherine. What's a ghost
going to do?
Wyse, Lois. Two guppies, a turtle and
Aunt Edna
Yolen, Jane. Mice on ice
Zemach, Margot. It could always be
worse
Zion, Gene. Harry and the lady next
door

Progress

Barton, Byron. Wheels
Burton, Virginia Lee. The little house
Coombs, Patricia. Dorrie and the
fortune teller
Duvoisin, Roger Antoine. Lonely
Veronica
Fife, Dale. The little park
Goodall, John S. The story of an
English village
Greene, Graham. The little fire engine
Harrison, David Lee. Little turtle's big
adventure
Hoban, Russell. Arthur's new power
Ipcar, Dahlov. One horse farm
Murschetz, Luis. Mister Mole
Peet, Bill. Countdown to Christmas
 Farewell to Shady Glade
 The wump world
Schulman, Janet. Jack the bum and the
UFO
Shecter, Ben. Emily, girl witch of New
York
Steiner, Jörg. The bear who wanted to
be a bear

Puerto Rican-Americans *see* Ethnic
groups in the U.S. — Puerto
Rican-Americans

Puerto Rico *see* Foreign lands — Puerto
Rico

Puffins *see* Birds — puffins

Pumas *see* Animals — cougars

Puppets

Abelson, Danny. The Muppets take
  Manhattan
Atene, Ann. The golden guitar
Brandenberg, Franz. Aunt Nina's visit
Bruce, Sheilah B. The radish day jubilee
Chernoff, Goldie Taub. Puppet party
Children's Television Workshop.
  Muppets in my neighborhood
Collodi, Carlo. The adventures of
  Pinocchio
Eaton, Su. Punch and Judy in the rain
Elliott, Dan. Ernie's little lie
  A visit to the Sesame Street firehouse
Freeman, Don. The paper party
Gates, Frieda. Glove, mitten, and sock
  puppets
Gikow, Louise. Sprocket's Christmas tale
Heymans, Margriet. Pippin and Robber
  Grumblecroak's big baby
Howe, James. The case of the missing
  mother
Keats, Ezra Jack. Louie
Klimowicz, Barbara. The strawberry
  thumb
Lerner, Sharon. Big Bird's copycat day
Little, Mary E. Ricardo and the puppets
Marks, Burton. Puppet plays and
  puppet-making
Masks and puppets
Moss, Jeffrey. The Sesame Street ABC
  storybook
  The songs of Sesame Street in poems
  and pictures
Mother Goose. The Sesame Street
  players present Mother Goose
Muntean, Michaela. Muppet babies
  through the year
The Muppet show book
One rubber duckie
Parsons, Virginia. Pinocchio and
  Gepetto
  Pinocchio and the money tree
  Pinocchio goes on the stage
  Pinocchio plays truant
Peters, Sharon. Puppet show
Politi, Leo. Mr. Fong's toy shop
Roberts, Sarah. Bert and the missing
  mop mix-up
Sesame Street. Ernie and Bert can...can
  you?
  Sesame Street sign language fun
  Sesame Street word book
Steiner, Charlotte. Pete's puppets
Stevenson, Jocelyn. Jim Henson's
  Muppets at sea
  Red and the pumpkins
Stone, Jon. Big Bird in China
Tornborg, Pat. The Sesame Street
  cookbook

Weiss, Ellen. Pigs in space
  You are the star of a Muppet
  adventure
Young, Ed. The rooster's horns

Puzzles *see* Rebuses; Riddles

Queens *see* Royalty

Questioning *see* Character traits —
  questioning

Quicksand *see* Sand

Rabbits *see* Animals — rabbits

Raccoons *see* Animals — raccoons

Racing *see* Sports — racing

Railroad engineers *see* Careers —
  railroad engineers

Railroads *see* Trains

Rain *see* Weather — rain

Rainbows *see* Weather — rainbows

Rangers *see* Careers — park rangers

Rats *see* Animals — rats

Ravens *see* Birds — ravens

Reading *see* Activities — reading

Rebuses

Adler, David A. Bunny rabbit rebus
Coletta, Irene. From A to Z
Mother Goose. Mother Goose in
  hieroglyphics
Partch, Virgil Franklin. The Christmas
  cookie sprinkle snitcher
  The VIP's mistake book
Weil, Lisl. Mother Goose picture riddles

Reindeer *see* Animals — reindeer

Religion

Adler, David A. A picture book of
  Hanukkah
 A picture book of Israel
Aichinger, Helga. The shepherd
Alexander, Cecil Frances. All things
  bright and beautiful
Aliki. Mummies made in Egypt
Allstrom, Elizabeth C. Songs along the
  way
Androcles and the lion
Anglund, Joan Walsh. A book of good
  tidings from the Bible
Aoki, Hisako. Santa's favorite story
Aulaire, Ingri Mortenson d'. The Lord's
  prayer
Baker, Betty. And me, coyote!
Balet, Jan B. The gift
Barker, Peggy. What happened when
  grandma died
Bawden, Nina. St. Francis of Assisi
Baylor, Byrd. The way to start a day
Best-loved Bible verses for children
Bible New Testament. The Lord's
  prayer
Bible New Testament Gospels. The first
  Christmas
Bible Old Testament Daniel. Shadrach,
  Meshack and Abednego
Bible Old Testament Psalms. The Lord
  is my shepherd, ill. by George Kraus
 The Lord is my shepherd, ill. by Tasha
  Tudor
Brin, Ruth F. David and Goliath
 The story of Esther
Brown, Margaret Wise. On Christmas
  Eve
Bruna, Dick. Christmas
Bulla, Clyde Robert. Jonah and the
  great fish
Burdekin, Harold. A child's grace
Chapman, Jean. Moon-Eyes
Chase, Catherine. The miracles at Cana
Cone, Molly. The Jewish Sabbath
Cooney, Barbara. A little prayer
Dellinger, Annetta. You are special to
  Jesus
De Paola, Tomie. The clown of God
 The Lady of Guadalupe
 The legend of Old Befana
 The story of the three wise kings
De Regniers, Beatrice Schenk. David
  and Goliath
Din dan don, it's Christmas
Douglas, Robert W. John Paul II
Farber, Norma. How the hibernators
  came to Bethlehem
Fass, David E. The shofar that lost its
  voice

Field, Rachel Lyman. Prayer for a child
First graces
First prayers, ill. by Anna Maria
  Magagna
First prayers, ill. by Tasha Tudor
Fisher, Leonard Everett. The seven days
  of creation
Fitch, Florence Mary. A book about God
Fraser, James Howard. Los Posadas
The friendly beasts and A partridge in a
  pear tree
Galdone, Paul. The first seven days
Garfield, Leon. King Nimrod's tower
 The writing on the wall
Goddard, Carrie Lou. Isn't it a wonder!
Graham, Lorenz B. David he no fear
 Every man heart lay down
 Hongry catch the foolish boy
 A road down in the sea
Gramatky, Hardie. Nikos and the sea
  god
Haiz, Danah. Jonah's journey
Hamil, Thomas Arthur. Brother Alonzo
Hillman, Priscilla. The Merry-Mouse
  book of prayers and graces
Hoffmann, Felix. The story of
  Christmas
Hopkins, Lee Bennett. And God bless
  me
Hutton, Warwick. Jonah and the great
  fish
I sing a song of the saints of God
Ife, Elaine. The childhood of Jesus
 Moses in the bulrushes
 Stories Jesus told
Jonah
Jones, Jessie Mae Orton. A little child
 Small rain
 This is the way
Jüchen, Aurel von. The Holy Night
Keats, Ezra Jack. God is in the
  mountain
 The little drummer boy
Kipling, Rudyard. The miracle of the
  mountain
Knapp, John II. A pillar of pepper and
  other Bible nursery rhymes
Laurence, Margaret. The Christmas
  birthday story
Leeton, Will C. The Tower of Babel
Levitin, Sonia. A sound to remember
Lexau, Joan M. More beautiful than
  flowers
Lindgren, Astrid. Christmas in the
  stable
Lines, Kathleen. Once in royal David's
  city
MacBeth, George. Jonah and the Lord
McDermott, Beverly Brodsky. Jonah
McDermott, Gerald. The voyage of
  Osiris

Marshall, Lyn. Yoga for your children
Miyoshi, Sekiya. Singing David
Nussbaumer, Mares. Away in a manger
Petersham, Maud. The Christ Child
Price, Christine. One is God
Reed, Allison. Genesis
Sahagun, Bernardino de. Spirit child
Schwartz, Amy. Mrs. Moskowitz and the Sabbath candlesticks
Seignobosc, Françoise. The thank-you book
Shulevitz, Uri. The magician
Stan-Padilla, Viento. Dream Feather
Taylor, Mark. "Lamb," said the lion, "I am here."
Thomas, Kathy. The angel's quest
Trent, Robbie. The first Christmas
Van der Meer, Ron. Oh Lord!
Vasiliu, Marcea. Everything is somewhere
Waddell, Helen. The story of Saul the king
Weil, Lisl. The story of the Wise Men and the Child
  The very first story ever told
Wheeler, Opal. Sing in praise
Wiesner, William. The Tower of Babel
Winthrop, Elizabeth. A child is born

Religion — Noah

Bolliger, Max. Noah and the rainbow
Chase, Catherine. Noah's ark
Delessert, Etienne. The endless party
De Paola, Tomie. Noah and the ark
Duvoisin, Roger Antoine. A for the ark
Farber, Norma. How the left-behind beasts built Ararat
  Where's Gomer?
Goffstein, M B (Marilyn Brooks). My Noah's ark
Graham, Lorenz B. God wash the world and start again
Haley, Gail E. Noah's ark
Haubensak-Tellenbach, Margrit. The story of Noah's ark
Hewitt, Kathryn. Two by two
Hutton, Warwick. Noah and the great flood
Ife, Elaine. Noah and the ark
Kuskin, Karla. The animals and the ark
Lenski, Lois. Mr. and Mrs. Noah
MacBeth, George. Noah's journey
Martin, Charles E. Noah's ark
Matias. Mr. Noah and the animals
Mee, Charles L. Noah
Palazzo, Tony. Noah's ark
Singer, Isaac Bashevis. Why Noah chose the dove
Smith, Elmer Boyd. The story of Noah's ark
Spier, Peter. Noah's ark

Webb, Clifford. The story of Noah
Wiesner, William. Noah's ark

Repetitive stories see Cumulative tales

Reptiles

Barrett, Judi. Snake is totally tail
Colby, C B (Carroll Burleigh). Who went there?
Cortesi, Wendy W. Explore a spooky swamp
Cristini, Ermanno. In the pond
Daly, Kathleen N. A child's book of snakes, lizards and other reptiles
Harris, Susan. Reptiles
Kuchalla, Susan. What is a reptile?
Pluckrose, Henry. Reptiles

Reptiles — alligators, crocodiles

Aliki. Keep your mouth closed, dear
  Use your head, dear
Aruego, José. A crocodile's tale
Brown, Ruth. Crazy Charlie
Campbell, M Rudolph. The talking crocodile
Carrick, Carol. The crocodiles still wait
Cazet, Denys. The duck with squeaky feet
Christelow, Eileen. Jerome the babysitter
Cushman, Doug. Nasty Kyle the crocodile
Dahl, Roald. The enormous crocodile
De Groat, Diane. Alligator's toothache
De Paola, Tomie. Bill and Pete
Dorros, Arthur. Alligator shoes
Du Bois, William Pène. The alligator case
Duvoisin, Roger Antoine. The crocodile in the tree
  Crocus
Eastman, P D (Philip D). Flap your wings
Galdone, Paul. The monkey and the crocodile
Gantos, Jack. Swampy alligator
Gross, Ruth Belov. Alligators and other crocodilians
Guy, Rosa. Mother crocodile
Hartelius, Margaret A. The chicken's child
Hoban, Russell. Arthur's new power
  Dinner at Alberta's
Hodeir, André. Warwick's three bottles
Holland, Isabelle. Kevin's hat
Hurd, Thacher. Mama don't allow
Kinnell, Galway. How the alligator missed breakfast
Kirn, Ann. The tale of a crocodile
Lexau, Joan M. Crocodile and hen
Lionni, Leo. Cornelius

McPhail, David. Alligators are awful (and they have terrible manners, too)
Mayer, Marianna. Alley oop!
Minarik, Else Holmelund. No fighting, no biting!
Muntean, Michaela. Alligator's garden
Pack, Robert. How to catch a crocodile
Parker, Nancy Winslow. The crocodile under Louis Finneberg's bed
Peterson, Esther Allen. Frederick's alligator
Pickett, Carla. Calvin Crocodile and the terrible noise
Rice, James. Gaston goes to Texas
Schubert, Ingrid. There's a crocodile under my bed!
Sendak, Maurice. Alligators all around
Shaw, Evelyn S. Alligator
Stevenson, James. Monty
Venable, Alan. The checker players
Waber, Bernard. Lovable Lyle
  Lyle and the birthday party
  Lyle finds his mother
  Lyle, Lyle Crocodile
Wasmuth, Eleanor. An alligator day
  The picnic basket
Watts, Marjorie-Ann. Crocodile medicine
Weiss, Ellen. Millicent Maybe

Reptiles — crocodiles *see* Reptiles — alligators, crocodiles

Reptiles — iguanas

Newfield, Marcia. Iggy
Rosen, Winifred. Henrietta and the day of the iguana

Reptiles — lizards

Anderson, Lonzo. Izzard
Baker, Betty. Latki and the lightning lizard
Carle, Eric. The mixed-up chameleon, 1975
  The mixed-up chameleon, 1984
Conklin, Gladys. I caught a lizard
Himmelman, John. Talester the lizard
Lionni, Leo. A color of his own
Lopshire, Robert. I am better than you
McNeely, Jeannette. Where's Izzy?
Massie, Diane Redfield. Chameleon the spy and the terrible toaster trap
  The Komodo dragon's jewels
Shannon, George. Lizard's song

Reptiles — snakes

Aardema, Verna. What's so funny, Ketu?
Appleby, Leonard. Snakes
Banchek, Linda. Snake in, snake out

Berson, Harold. Joseph and the snake
Carlson, Natalie Savage. Marie Louise and Christophe at the carnival
Forrester, Victoria. Oddward
Freschet, Berniece. The watersnake
Hoff, Syd. Slithers
Huxley, Aldous. The crows of Pearblossom
Lemerise, Bruce. Sheldon's lunch
Lesikin, Joan. Down the road
Lionni, Leo. In the rabbitgarden
Noble, Trinka Hakes. The day Jimmy's boa ate the wash
  Jimmy's boa bounces back
Oppenheim, Joanne. Mrs. Peloki's snake
Prather, Ray. The ostrich girl
Reinl, Edda. The little snake
Turpin, Lorna. The sultan's snakes
Ungerer, Tomi. Crictor
Waber, Bernard. The snake
Wildsmith, Brian. Python's party

Reptiles — turtles

Abisch, Roz. The clever turtle
Æsop. The hare and the tortoise
Asch, Frank. Turtle tale
Augarde, Steve. Barnaby Shrew, Black Dan and... the mighty wedgwood
  Barnaby Shrew goes to sea
Baumann, Hans. The hare's race
Brunhoff, Laurent de. Gregory and Lady Turtle in the valley of the music trees
Christian, Mary Blount. Devin and Goliath
Craig, Janet. Turtles
Cromie, William J. Steven and the green turtle
Cummings, Betty Sue. Turtle
Darby, Gene. What is a turtle?
Davis, Alice Vaught. Timothy turtle
Domanska, Janina. Look, there is a turtle flying
  The tortoise and the tree
Du Bois, William Pène. The hare and the tortoise and the tortoise and the hare
Emberley, Ed. Rosebud
Freeman, Don. The turtle and the dove
Freschet, Berniece. Turtle pond
Gendel, Evelyn. Tortoise and turtle
  Tortoise and turtle abroad
Goldsmith, Howard. Toto the timid turtle
Graham, Al. Timothy Turtle
Harrison, David Lee. Little turtle's big adventure
Hoban, Lillian. Stick-in-the-mud turtle
  Turtle spring
La Fontaine, Jean de. The hare and the tortoise

Lesikin, Joan. Down the road
Lubell, Winifred. Rosalie, the bird
  market turtle
MacGregor, Ellen. Theodor Turtle
McLenighan, Valjean. Turtle and rabbit
Maestro, Giulio. The tortoise's tug of
  war
Matsutani, Miyoko. The fisherman
  under the sea
Murdocca, Sal. Tuttle's shell
Parry, Marian. King of the fish
St Pierre, Wendy. Henry finds a home
Selsam, Millicent E. Let's get turtles
The turtle
Van Woerkom, Dorothy. Harry and
  Shelburt
Wiese, Kurt. The cunning turtle
Williams, Barbara. Albert's toothache
Wolf, Ann. The rabbit and the turtle
Woolley, Catherine. Mr. Turtle's magic
  glasses
Wyse, Lois. Two guppies, a turtle and
  Aunt Edna
Yashima, Tarō. Seashore story

Rest *see* Sleep

Rhinoceros *see* Animals — rhinoceros

Rhyming text *see* Poetry, rhyme

Riddles

Aardema, Verna. Ji-nongo-nongo means
  riddles
Adler, David A. The carsick zebra and
  other riddles
Bishop, Ann. Chicken riddle
  The Ella Fannie elephant riddle book
  Hey riddle riddle
  Merry-go-riddle
  Noah riddle?
  Oh, riddlesticks!
  The riddle ages
  Riddle-iculous rid-alphabet book
  Wild Bill Hiccup's riddle book
Brown, Marc. Spooky riddles
  What do you call a dumb bunny? and
  other rabbit riddles, games, jokes and
  cartoons
Cerf, Bennett Alfred. Bennett Cerf's
  book of animal riddles
  Bennett Cerf's book of laughs
  Bennett Cerf's book of riddles
  More riddles
Cole, Joanna. The Clown-Arounds go
  on vacation
  Get well, Clown-Arounds!
Crowley, Arthur. The wagon man
Daniels, Guy. The Tsar's riddles
Degen, Bruce. The little witch and the
  riddle

Delaney, M C. The marigold monster
Demi. Where is it?
De Regniers, Beatrice Schenk. It does
  not say meow!
Duncan, Riana. A nutcracker in a tree
Elkin, Benjamin. The wisest man in the
  world
Emberley, Ed. Ed Emberley's amazing
  look through book
Fleischman, Sid. Kate's secret riddle
Fletcher, Elizabeth. What am I?
Gay, Zhenya. What's your name?
Goundaud, Karen Jo. A very mice joke
  book
Gregorich, Barbara. My friend goes left
Grimm, Jacob. Rumpelstiltskin, ill. by
  Jacqueline Ayer
  Rumpelstiltskin, ill. by Donna Diamond
  Rumpelstiltskin, ill. by John Wallner
Hall, Katy. Fishy riddles
Hall, Malcolm. CariCATures
Hample, Stoo. Stoo Hample's silly joke
  book
  Yet another big fat funny silly book
High on a hill
Hoff, Syd. Syd Hoff's best jokes ever
Holman, Felice. Elisabeth, the treasure
  hunter
Jensen, Virginia Allen. Red thread
  riddles
Keller, Charles. Giggle puss
  The nutty joke book
  School daze
Kessler, Leonard P. Riddles that rhyme
  for Halloween time
Lewis, Naomi. The butterfly collector
Low, Joseph. Five men under one
  umbrella
  A mad wet hen and other riddles
Lyfick, Warren. Animal tales
  The little book of fowl jokes
McKié, Roy. The riddle book
Maestro, Giulio. Halloween howls
  A raft of riddles
  Riddle romp
Moncure, Jane Belk. Riddle me a riddle
Peppé, Rodney. Hey riddle diddle
Phillips, Louis. The upside down riddle
  book
Potter, Beatrix. The tale of Squirrel
  Nutkin
Romanoli, Robert. What's so funny?!!
Schwartz, Alvin. Ten copycats in a boat
  and other riddles
Selberg, Ingrid. Nature's hidden world
Seuss, Dr. The cat's quizzer
Thaler, Mike. The yellow brick toad
Thomas, Gary. The best of the little
  books
Türk, Hanne. Max versus the cube
Wakefield, Joyce. Ask a silly question

Zwetchkenbaum, G. The Peanuts shape
circus puzzle book
The Peanuts sleepy time puzzle book
The Snoopy farm puzzle book
Snoopy safari puzzle book

Right and left see Concepts — left and
right

Rivers

Brook, Judy. Tim mouse goes down the
stream
Bushey, Jerry. The barge book
Carrick, Carol. The brook
Dabcovich, Lydia. Follow the river
Flack, Marjorie. The boats on the river
Grahame, Kenneth. The river bank
Gramatky, Hardie. Little Toot on the
Mississippi
Grasshopper to the rescue
Holling, Holling C (Holling Clancy).
Paddle-to-the-sea
Keeping, Charles. Alfie finds the other
side of the world
Locker, Thomas. Where the river begins
Murphy, Shirley Rousseau. Tattie's river
journey
Oakley, Graham. The church mice
adrift

Roads

Bate, Norman. Who built the highway?
Kehoe, Michael. Road closed
Roennfeldt, Robert. A day on the
avenue

Robbers see Crime

Robins see Birds — robins

Robots

Bradford, Ann. The mystery of the
square footsteps
Bunting, Eve. The robot birthday
Greene, Carol. Robots
Hoban, Lillian. The laziest robot in zone
one
Krahn, Fernando. Robot-bot-bot
Kroll, Steven. Otto
Marshall, Edward. Space case
Marzollo, Jean. Jed's junior space patrol
Paul, Sherry. 2-B and the rock 'n roll
band
2-B and the space visitor
Titus, Eve. Anatole and the robot

Rockets see Space and space ships

Rocking horses see Toys — rocking
horses

Rocks

Baylor, Byrd. Everybody needs a rock
Gans, Roma. Rock collecting
Kehoe, Michael. The rock quarry book
Lionni, Leo. On my beach there are
many pebbles
Selsam, Millicent E. A first look at rocks

Roosters see Birds — chickens

Royalty

Aardema, Verna. The riddle of the
drum
Abrons, Mary. For Alice a palace
Aitken, Amy. Ruby, the red knight
Alexander, Lloyd. The king's fountain
Allen, Pamela. Bertie and the bear
Ambrus, Victor G. The Sultan's bath
Andersen, H C (Hans Christian). The
emperor's new clothes, ill. by Pamela
Baldwin-Ford
The emperor's new clothes, ill. by Erik
Blegvad
The emperor's new clothes, ill. by
Virginia Lee Burton
The emperor's new clothes, ill. by Jack
and Irene DeLano
The emperor's new clothes, ill. by
Birte Dietz
The emperor's new clothes, ill. by Jack
Kent
The emperor's new clothes, ill. by
Monika Laimgruber
The emperor's new clothes, ill. by
Anne F. Rockwell
The emperor's new clothes, ill. by
Nadine Bernard Westcott
The princess and the pea, ill. by Dick
Gackenbach
The princess and the pea, ill. by Paul
Galdone
The princess and the pea, ill. by Janet
Stevens
Anderson, Lonzo. Two hundred rabbits
Anno, Mitsumasa. The king's flower
Aruego, José. The king and his friends
Auerbach, Marjorie. King Lavra and the
barber
Babbitt, Samuel F. The forty-ninth
magician
Balet, Jan B. The king and the broom
maker
Bang, Betsy. Tutuni the tailor bird
Basile, Giambattista. Petrosinella
Beresford, Elisabeth. Jack and the magic
stove
Berson, Harold. The thief who hugged
a moonbeam
Bill, Helen. Shoes fit for a king
Bolliger, Max. The most beautiful song

Bowden, Joan Chase. A hat for the queen
  A new home for Snow Ball
Brenner, Barbara. The prince and the pink blanket
Brierley, Louise. King Lion and his cooks
Bright, Robert. Hurrah for Freddie!
Browne, Caroline. Mrs. Christie's farmhouse
Brunhoff, Jean de. Babar the king
Brunhoff, Laurent de. Babar's visit to Bird Island
Burningham, John. Time to get out of the bath, Shirley
Canfield, Jane White. The frog prince
Chapman, Gaynor. The luck child
Clifford, Eth. Why is an elephant called an elephant?
Cole, Brock. The king at the door
Conover, Chris. The wizard's daughter
Coombs, Patricia. Tilabel
Cooney, Barbara. Little brother and little sister
Cooper, Gale. Unicorn moon
Crabtree, Judith. The sparrow's story at the king's command
Cretien, Paul D. Sir Henry and the dragon
Cunliffe, John. The king's birthday cake
Damjan, Mischa. The little prince and the tiger cat
De La Mare, Walter. Molly Whuppie
De Paola, Tomie. The wonderful dragon of Timlin
De Regniers, Beatrice Schenk. May I bring a friend?
Dewey, Ariane. Dorin and the dragon
Domanska, Janina. King Krakus and the dragon
  Look, there is a turtle flying
Dos Santos, Joyce Audy. The diviner
Elkin, Benjamin. The big jump and other stories
  Gillespie and the guards
  The king who could not sleep
  The king's wish and other stories
  The loudest noise in the world
  The wisest man in the world
Espenscheid, Gertrude E. The oh ball
Fern, Eugene. The king who was too busy
The firebird
Fleischman, Sid. Longbeard the wizard
Flot, Jeannette B. Princess Kalina and the hedgehog
Foreman, Michael. War and peas
Freeman, Don. Forever laughter
Gackenbach, Dick. King Wacky
Galdone, Paul. The amazing pig
  The monster and the tailor

Gekiere, Madeleine. The frilly lily and the princess
Gianni, Peg. Alex, the amazing juggler
The golden goose
Greaves, Margaret. A net to catch the wind
Greene, Ellin. Princess Rosetta and the popcorn man
Grimm, Jacob. Cinderella, ill. by Nonny Hogrogian
  Cinderella, ill. by Svend Otto
  The donkey prince
  King Grisly-Beard
  Rapunzel, ill. by Julia Ash
  Rapunzel, ill. by Bert Dodson
  Rapunzel, ill. by Trina Schart Hyman
  Rumpelstiltskin, ill. by Jacqueline Ayer
  Rumpelstiltskin, ill. by Donna Diamond
  Rumpelstiltskin, ill. by John Wallner
  The twelve dancing princesses, ill. by Dennis Hockerman
  The twelve dancing princesses, ill. by Errol Le Cain
  The twelve dancing princesses, ill. by Uri Shulevitz
Gurney, Nancy. The king, the mice and the cheese
Haywood, Carolyn. The king's monster
Heine, Helme. King Bounce the 1st
  The most wonderful egg in the world
Hughes, Peter. The emperor's oblong pancake
  The king who loved candy
Hutchins, Pat. King Henry's palace
Joerns, Consuelo. The midnight castle
Johnson, Crockett. The emperor's gift
  The frowning prince
Kahl, Virginia. The Baron's booty
  The Duchess bakes a cake
  Gunhilde and the Halloween spell
  Gunhilde's Christmas booke
  The habits of rabbits
  Plum pudding for Christmas
Karlin, Nurit. A train for the king
Kessler, Leonard P. Soup for the king
Kroll, Steven. Fat magic
Langner, Nola. By the light of the silvery moon
Lasker, David. The boy who loved music
Laskowski, Jerzy. Master of the royal cats
Littledale, Freya. The magic plum tree
Lobel, Anita. A birthday for the princess
  The seamstress of Salzburg
  Sven's bridge
Lobel, Arnold. Prince Bertram the bad
McCrea, James. The king's procession
  The magic tree
McDermott, Gerald. The voyage of Osiris

McKee, David. King Rollo and the birthday
  King Rollo and the bread
  King Rollo and the new shoes
McLenighan, Valjean. What you see is what you get
  You are what you are
McNaughton, Colin. The rat race
Mahood, Kenneth. The laughing dragon
Matsutani, Miyoko. The fisherman under the sea
Mayer, Mercer. The queen always wanted to dance
Milne, A A (Alan Alexander). Prince Rabbit
Myller, Rolf. How big is a foot?
  Rolling round
Ness, Evaline. Pavo and the princess
Nikly, Michelle. The emperor's plum tree
  The princess on the nut
Noble, Trinka Hakes. The king's tea
Oram, Hiawyn. Skittlewonder and the wizard
Oxenbury, Helen. The queen and Rosie Randall
Peet, Bill. How Droofus the dragon lost his head
Perkins, Al. King Midas and the golden touch
Perrault, Charles. Cinderella, ill. by Marcia Brown
  Cinderella, ill. by Emanuele Luzzati
  Cinderella, ill. by Sheilah Beckett
  Cinderella, ill. by Paul Galdone
  Cinderella, ill. by Phil Smith
  Puss in boots, ill. by Marcia Brown
  Puss in boots, ill. by Jean Claverle
  Puss in boots, ill. by Hans Fischer
  Puss in boots, ill. by Paul Galdone
  Puss in boots, ill. by Julia Noonan
  Puss in boots, ill. by Tony Ross
  Puss in boots, ill. by William Stobbs
  Puss in boots, ill. by Barry Wilkinson
Postgate, Oliver. Noggin the king
The prince who knew his fate
Reesink, Marijke. The princess who always ran away
Reeves, James. Rhyming Will
Reit, Seymour. The king who learned to smile
Richter, Mischa. To bed, to bed!
Rose, Anne. How does a czar eat potatoes?
Ross, Tony. Towser and the terrible thing
Saddler, Allen. The Archery contest
  The king gets fit
Schiller, Barbara. The white rat's tale
Schwartz, Amy. Her majesty, Aunt Essie

Seuss, Dr. Bartholomew and the Oobleck
  The king's stilts
Sexton, Gwain. There once was a king
Shulevitz, Uri. One Monday morning
Skipper, Mervyn. The fooling of King Alexander
Slobodkin, Louis. Colette and the princess
Steig, William. Roland, the minstrel pig
Stephenson, Dorothy. The night it rained toys
Thurber, James. Many moons
Trez, Denise. Maila and the flying carpet
  The royal hiccups
Turpin, Lorna. The sultan's snakes
Van Woerkom, Dorothy. The queen who couldn't bake gingerbread
Varga, Judy. The dragon who liked to spit fire
Wahl, Jan. Cabbage moon
Wersba, Barbara. Do tigers ever bite kings?
Williams, Jay. The practical princess
  School for sillies
Yolen, Jane. The emperor and the kite
  The seeing stick
Young, Miriam Burt. The sugar mouse cake
Zemach, Harve. The tricks of Master Dabble

Running *see* Sports — racing

Running away *see* Behavior — running away

Russia *see* Foreign lands — Russia

Sadness *see* Emotions — sadness

Safety

Arnold, Caroline. Who keeps us safe?
Baker, Eugene. Bicycles
  Fire
  Home
  Outdoors
  School
  Water
Brown, Marc. Dinosaurs, beware!
Brown, Margaret Wise. Red light, green light

Chlad, Dorothy. Bicycles are fun to ride
  Matches, lighters, and firecrackers are
    not toys
  Poisons make you sick
Cleary, Beverly. Lucky Chuck
Emecheta, Buchi. Nowhere to play
Glovach, Linda. The little Witch's black
  magic book of games
Joyce, Irma. Never talk to strangers
Leaf, Munro. Safety can be fun
Lindgren, Barbro. Sam's lamp
McLeod, Emilie Warren. The bear's
  bicycle
Meyer, Linda D. Safety zone
Moss, Elaine. Polar
Myller, Lois. No! No!
Shortall, Leonard W. One way
Smaridge, Norah. Watch out!
Viorst, Judith. Try it again, Sam
Vogel, Carole Garbuny. The dangers of
  strangers

Sailors *see* Careers — military

Saint Patrick's Day *see* Holidays — St.
  Patrick's Day

Sand

Bason, Lillian. Castles and mirrors and
  cities of sand
Roach, Marilynne K. Dune fox
Watanabe, Shigeo. I'm the king of the
  castle!

Sandcastles *see* Sand

Sandman

Strahl, Rudi. Sandman in the lighthouse

Sandpipers *see* Birds — sandpipers

Saving things *see* Behavior — saving
  things

Scarecrows

Bolliger, Max. The wooden man
Farber, Norma. There goes feathertop!
Gordon, Sharon. Sam the scarecrow
Hart, Jeanne McGahey. Scareboy
Lifton, Betty Jean. Joji and the
  Amanojaku
  Joji and the dragon
  Joji and the fog
Miller, Edna. Pebbles, a pack rat
Oana, Kay D. Robbie and the raggedy
  scarecrow
Tripp, Paul. The strawman who smiled
  by mistake

School

Adelson, Leone. All ready for school
Alexander, Martha G. Move over,
  Twerp
  Sabrina
Allard, Harry. Miss Nelson has a field
  day
  Miss Nelson is back
  Miss Nelson is missing!
Annett, Cora. The dog who thought he
  was a boy
Arnold, Caroline. Where do you go to
  school?
Arnold, Katrin. Anna joins in
Ashley, Bernard. Dinner ladies don't
  count
Aulaire, Ingri Mortenson d'. Children of
  the northlights
  Nils
Babbitt, Lorraine. Pink like the
  geranium
Baker, Eugene. School
Behrens, June. Who am I?
Beim, Jerrold. The taming of Toby
Bemelmans, Ludwig. Madeline
Berenstain, Stan. The Berenstain bears
  go to school
Berquist, Grace. Speckles goes to school
Blance, Ellen. Monster at school
  Monster goes to school
Blue, Rose. How many blocks is the
  world?
  I am here Yo estoy aqui
Bond, Felicia. The Halloween
  performance
Boreman, Jean. Bantie and her chicks
Boyd, Selma. I met a polar bear
Bram, Elizabeth. I don't want to go to
  school
Brandenberg, Franz. No school today!
  Six new students
Breinburg, Petronella. Shawn goes to
  school
Brooks, Ron. Timothy and Gramps
Brown, Marc. Arthur's Valentine
  The true Francine
Bruna, Dick. Miffy goes to school
  The school
Buchheimer, Naomi. Let's go to a school
Budney, Blossom. N is for nursery
  school
Calmenson, Stephanie. The
  kindergarten book
Caudill, Rebecca. A pocketful of cricket
Charles, Donald. Calico Cat at school
Charmatz, Bill. The Troy St. bus
Chorao, Kay. Molly's lies
Christian, Mary Blount. Swamp
  monsters
Clewes, Dorothy. Happiest day

Udry, Janice May. What Mary Jo shared
Vigna, Judith. Anyhow, I'm glad I tried
Watson, Clyde. Hickory stick rag
Watts, Marjorie-Ann. Zebra goes to
  school
Welber, Robert. Goodbye, hello
Wells, Rosemary. Timothy goes to
  school
White, Florence Meiman. How to lose
  your lunch money
White, Paul. Janet at school
Whitney, Alma Marshak. Just awful
Winthrop, Elizabeth. Tough Eddie
Wiseman, Bernard. Tails are not for
  painting
Wittman, Sally. The wonderful Mrs.
  Trumbly
Wolde, Gunilla. Betsy's first day at
  nursery school
Wolf, Bernard. Adam Smith goes to
  school
Woolley, Catherine. Gus was a real
  dumb ghost
Yashima, Tarō. Crow boy

Science

Abisch, Roz. Let's find out about
  butterflies
Adler, David A. Redwoods are the
  tallest trees in the world
Aho, Jennifer J. Learning about sex
Aldridge, Alan. The butterfly ball and
  the grasshopper's feast
Aliki. Corn is maize
  Digging up dinosaurs
  Fossils tell of long ago
  The long lost coelacanth and other
    living fossils
  My hands
  A weed is a flower
  Wild and woolly mammoths
Allen, Gertrude E. Everyday animals
Allen, Martha Dickson. Real life
  monsters
Allen, Pamela. Mr. Archimedes' bath
  Who sank the boat?
Anderson, Lucia. The smallest life
  around us
Andry, Andrew C. How babies are
  made
Annixter, Jane. Brown rats, black rats
Applebaum, Stan. Going my way?
Appleby, Leonard. Snakes
Ariane. Small Cloud
Arnold, Caroline. The biggest living
  thing
  Five nests
  Sun fun
Aruego, José. Symbiosis
Asimov, Isaac. The best new things
  The moon

Baker, Gayle. Special delivery
Baker, Jeannie. One hungry spider
Baker, Jeffrey J W. Patterns of nature
Balestrino, Philip. Hot as an ice cube
Balian, Lorna. Where in the world is
  Henry?
Baran, Tancy. Bees
Barner, Bob. Elephant facts
Bartlett, Margaret Farrington. The clean
  brook
  Down the mountain
  Where the brook begins
Bason, Lillian. Castles and mirrors and
  cities of sand
Batherman, Muriel. Animals live here
Behrens, June. Whalewatch!
Bendick, Jeanne. All around you
  What made you you?
  Why can't I?
Berenstain, Stan. The Berenstain bears'
  science fair
Blank, Joani. A kid's first book about
  sex
Boegehold, Betty. Bear underground
Bonners, Susan. Panda
  A penguin year
Boreman, Jean. Bantie and her chicks
Brady, Irene. Wild mouse
Branley, Franklyn M. Air is all around
  you
  The big dipper
  Big tracks, little tracks
  A book of satellites for you
  Comets
  Eclipse
  Flash, crash, rumble and roll
  Floating and sinking
  Gravity is a mystery
  High sounds, low sounds
  Light and darkness
  The moon seems to change
  North, south, east and west
  The planets in our solar system
  Rain and hail
  The sky is full of stars
  Snow is falling
  The sun, our nearest star
  Sunshine makes the seasons
  Timmy and the tin-can telephone
  What makes day and night
  What the moon is like
Brooks, Robert B. So that's how I was
  born
Brouillette, Jeanne S. Moths
Budbill, David. Christmas tree farm
Burt, Olive. Let's find out about bread
Busch, Phyllis S. Cactus in the desert
  City lots
  Lions in the grass
  Once there was a tree
  Puddles and ponds

Hamberger, John. The day the sun disappeared

Harris, Louise Dyer. Flash, the life of a firefly

Harris, Susan. Creatures that look alike
Reptiles

Hawes, Judy. Fireflies in the night
Ladybug, ladybug, fly away home
Shrimps
Spring peepers
Watch honeybees with me
Why frogs are wet

Hawkinson, Lucy. Birds in the sky

Heller, Ruth. Chickens aren't the only ones

Hess, Lilo. The curious raccoons
Foxes in the woodshed

Hoffman, Mary. Animals in the wild: elephant
Animals in the wild: monkey
Animals in the wild: panda
Animals in the wild: tiger

Hogan, Paula Z. The black swan
The butterfly
The dandelion
The frog
The honeybee
The oak tree
The penguin
The salmon

Holmes, Anita. The 100-year-old cactus

House mouse

Howell, Ruth. Splash and flow

Hurd, Edith Thacher. The mother kangaroo
Sandpipers
Starfish

Isenbart, Hans-Heinrich. A duckling is born

Jackson, Jacqueline. Chicken ten thousand

Jacobs, Francine. Barracuda
Sewer Sam

Johnson, Hannah Lyons. From seed to jack-o'-lantern

Johnston, Johanna. Penguin's way
Whale's way

Jolliffe, Anne. From pots to plastics
Water, wind and wheels

Justice, Jennifer. The tiger

Kane, Henry B. Wings, legs, or fins

Kaufmann, John. Birds are flying
Flying giants of long ago

Kirkpatrick, Rena K. Look at flowers
Look at leaves
Look at magnets
Look at pond life
Look at rainbow colors
Look at seeds and weeds
Look at trees
Look at weather

Knight, David C. Dinosaur days

Kuchalla, Susan. All about seeds

Kumin, Maxine. Eggs of things

Lambert, David. Dinosaurs
The seasons

Landshoff, Ursula. Cats are good company

Lane, Margaret. The frog
The squirrel

Lauber, Patricia. What's hatching out of that egg?

Leutscher, Alfred. Earth
Water

Lilly, Kenneth. Animal builders
Animal climbers
Animal jumpers
Animal runners
Animal swimmers

Lloyd, David. Air

Mabey, Richard. Oak and company

McCauley, Jane. Baby birds and how they grow

McClung, Robert. Sphinx

McKeever, Katherine. A family for Minerva

McNulty, Faith. How to dig a hole to the other side of the world
Hurricane
Woodchuck

Malnig, Anita. The big strawberry book of questions and answers and facts and things

May, Charles Paul. High-noon rocket

Meshover, Leonard. The guinea pigs that went to school
The monkey that went to school

Meyers, Susan. The truth about gorillas

Milgrom, Harry. Egg-ventures
Paper science

Miller, Edna. Jumping bean

Miller, Judith Ransom. Nabob and the geranium

Miller, Susanne Santoro. Prehistoric mammals

Moche, Dinah L. The astronauts

Morris, Robert A. Dolphin
Seahorse

Moseley, Keith. Dinosaurs

Myrick, Mildred. Ants are fun

Newton, James R. A forest is reborn
Forest log

Nussbaum, Hedda. Animals build amazing homes

Oxford Scientific Films. Grey squirrel
Jellyfish and other sea creatures
Mosquito
The stickleback cycle

Palazzo, Janet. Our friend the sun

Parish, Peggy. Dinosaur time

Parker, Nancy Winslow. The ordeal of Byron B. Blackbear

Sea and seashore

Adkins, Jan. The art and industry of sandcastles

Allen, Laura Jean. Ottie and the star

Ardizzone, Edward. Little Tim and the brave sea captain
  Peter the wanderer
  Ship's cook Ginger
  Tim all alone
  Tim and Charlotte
  Tim and Ginger
  Tim and Lucy go to sea
  Tim in danger
  Tim to the rescue
  Tim's friend Towser
  Tim's last voyage

Asch, Frank. Sand cake
  Starbaby

Bate, Norman. What a wonderful machine is a submarine

Bennett, Rainey. The secret hiding place

Bentley, Anne. The Groggs have a wonderful summer

Blance, Ellen. Monster goes to the beach

Bond, Michael. Paddington at the seaside

Bonsall, Crosby Newell. Mine's the best

Booth, Eugene. Under the ocean

Bowden, Joan Chase. Why the tides ebb and flow

Bright, Robert. Georgie and the noisy ghost

Brown, Margaret Wise. The seashore noisy book

Bruna, Dick. Miffy at the beach
  Miffy at the seaside

Burningham, John. Come away from the water, Shirley

Carrick, Carol. Beach bird

Carter, Debby L. Clipper

Corney, Estelle. Pa's top hat

Craig, Janet. What's under the ocean?

Crane, Alan. Pepita bonita

Damjan, Mischa. The little sea horse

Davidson, Amanda. Teddy at the seashore

Domanska, Janina. If all the seas were one sea

Dos Santos, Joyce Audy. Sand dollar, sand dollar

Dyke, John. Pigwig and the pirates

Field, Eugene. Wynken, Blynken and Nod

Freeman, Don. Come again, pelican

Garelick, May. Down to the beach

George, Jean Craighead. The wentletrap trap

Gerrard, Jean. Matilda Jane

Goodall, John S. Paddy under water

Goudey, Alice E. Houses from the sea

Haas, Irene. The Maggie B

Hall, Katy. Fishy riddles

Hoff, Syd. Albert the albatross

Hurd, Edith Thacher. Starfish

Iwasaki, Chihiro. What's fun without a friend?

Jacobs, Francine. Sewer Sam

Johnson, Jane. Bertie on the beach

Joslin, Sesyle. Baby elephant goes to China

Kimura, Yasuko. Fergus and the sea monster

Kipling, Rudyard. The crab that played with the sea

Koch, Dorothy Clarke. I play at the beach

Kraus, Robert. Herman the helper

Kumin, Maxine. The beach before breakfast

Kuskin, Karla. Sand and snow

Levy, Elizabeth. Something queer on vacation

Lilly, Kenneth. Animals of the ocean

Lionni, Leo. On my beach there are many pebbles
  Swimmy

Lobel, Arnold. Uncle Elephant

Lund, Doris Herold. The paint-box sea

McCloskey, Robert. Bert Dow, deep-water man
  One morning in Maine
  Time of wonder

McKee, David. The day the tide went out and out and out

Mahy, Margaret. Sailor Jack and the twenty orphans

Matsutani, Miyoko. The fisherman under the sea

Mendoza, George. The scribbler

Morse, Samuel French. Sea sums

Nakatani, Chiyoko. Fumio and the dolphins

Napoli, Guillier. Adventure of Mont Saint Michel

Nicoll, Helen. Meg at sea

Olujic, Grozdana. Rose of Mother-of-Pearl

Orgel, Doris. On the sand dune

Oxenbury, Helen. Beach day

Oxford Scientific Films. Jellyfish and other sea creatures

Peet, Bill. Cyrus the unsinkable sea serpent
  Kermit the hermit

Phleger, Fred B. You will live under the sea

Ray, Deborah Kogan. Fog drift morning

Russ, Lavinia. Alec's sand castle

Russo, Susan. The ice cream ocean and other delectable poems of the sea

Ryder, Joanne. Beach party
  A wet and sandy day

Schick, Eleanor. Summer at the sea
Schlein, Miriam. The sun, the wind, the sea and the rain
Schulz, Charles M. Snoopy's facts and fun book about seashores
The Sea World alphabet book
Selsam, Millicent E. A first look at seashells
 Sea monsters of long ago
Seymour, Peter. What's at the beach?
Shaw, Evelyn S. Fish out of school
 Octopus
Simon, Mina Lewiton. Is anyone here?
Slobodkin, Louis. The seaweed hat
Smith, Raymond Kenneth. The long dive
Smith, Theresa Kalab. The fog is secret
Steiner, Charlotte. Listen to my seashell
Stevenson, James. Clams can't sing
Stevenson, Jocelyn. Jim Henson's Muppets at sea
Stock, Catherine. Sophie's bucket
Strahl, Rudi. Sandman in the lighthouse
Straker, Joan Ann. Animals that live in the sea
Taylor, Mark. The bold fisherman
Thompson, Brenda. The winds that blow
Tobias, Tobi. At the beach
Tresselt, Alvin R. Hide and seek fog
 I saw the sea come in
Turkle, Brinton. Do not open
 Obadiah the Bold
 The sky dog
Ungerer, Tomi. The Mellops go diving for treasure
Vinson, Pauline. Willie goes to the seashore
Waber, Bernard. I was all thumbs
Watson, Nancy Dingman. When is tomorrow?
Wegen, Ron. Sand castle
Woolaver, Lance. From Ben Loman to the sea
Yashima, Taro. Seashore story
Zion, Gene. Harry by the sea

Sea gulls see Birds — sea gulls

Sea lions see Animals — sea lions

Sea serpents see Monsters; Mythical creatures

Seahorses see Crustacea

Seals see Animals — seals

Seamstresses see Careers — seamstresses

Seashore see Sea and seashore

Seasons

Arnosky, Jim. Outdoors on foot
Barker, Cicely Mary. Flower fairies of the seasons
Berenstain, Stan. The bears' almanac
Beskow, Elsa Maartman. Children of the forest
Blegvad, Erik. Burnie's hill
Blocksma, Mary. Apple tree! Apple tree!
Branley, Franklyn M. Sunshine makes the seasons
Brown, Margaret Wise. The little island
Burningham, John. Seasons
Carrick, Carol. The old barn
Clifton, Lucille. Everett Anderson's year
De Paola, Tomie. Four stories for four seasons
Don't tell the scarecrow
Dow, Katharine. My time of year
Duvoisin, Roger Antoine. The house of four seasons
Farjeon, Eleanor. Around the seasons
Fisher, Aileen. As the leaves fall down
 Going barefoot
 I stood upon a mountain
 Like nothing at all
Foster, Doris Van Liew. A pocketful of seasons
Fox, Charles Philip. Mr. Stripes the gopher
Gackenbach, Dick. Ida Fanfanny
Gibbons, Gail. The seasons of Arnold's apple tree
Greydanus, Rose. Changing seasons
Haley, Gail E. Go away, stay away
 The green man
Hall, Bill. A year in the forest
Hall, Donald. The ox-cart man
Hall, Fergus. Groundsel
Howell, Ruth. Everything changes
Hurd, Edith Thacher. The day the sun danced
Ichikawa, Satomi. A child's book of seasons
Kwitz, Mary DeBall. Mouse at home
Lambert, David. The seasons
Lewis, Naomi. Leaves
Lionni, Leo. Mouse days
 When?
Lobel, Arnold. Frog and Toad all year
McDermott, Gerald. Daughter of earth
Mangin, Marie-France. Suzette and Nicholas and the seasons clock
Marshak, Samuel. The Month-Brothers
Miller, Edna. Mousekin's fables
Muntean, Michaela. Muppet babies through the year
Oppenheim, Joanne. Have you seen trees?

Provensen, Alice. A book of seasons
  The year at Maple Hill Farm
Roach, Marilynne K. Dune fox
Schulz, Charles M. Snoopy's facts and
  fun book about seasons
Tresselt, Alvin R. It's time now!
  Johnny Maple-Leaf
Tudor, Tasha. Around the year
Udry, Janice May. A tree is nice
Welber, Robert. Song of the seasons
Wellington, Anne. Apple pie
Wildsmith, Brian. Seasons
Wolff, Ashley. A year of birds
Wood, Joyce. Grandmother Lucy in her
  garden
Zolotow, Charlotte. In my garden
  The song

Seasons — autumn *see* Seasons — fall

Seasons — fall

Adelson, Leone. All ready for school
Allington, Richard L. Autumn
Barklem, Jill. Autumn story
Cavagnaro, David. The pumpkin people
Cohen, Peter Zachary. Authorized
  autumn charts of the Upper Red
  Canoe River country
Fregosi, Claudia. The happy horse
Griffith, Helen V. Alex remembers
Hopkins, Lee Bennett. Merrily comes
  our harvest in
Kumin, Maxine. Follow the fall
Lapp, Eleanor. The mice came in early
  this year
Lenski, Lois. Now it's fall
McNaughton, Colin. Autumn
Ott, John. Peter Pumpkin
Potter, Beatrix. The tale of Squirrel
  Nutkin
Taylor, Mark. Henry explores the
  mountains
Tresselt, Alvin R. Autumn harvest
  Johnny Maple-Leaf
Udry, Janice May. Emily's autumn
Weygant, Noemi. It's autumn!
Wheeler, Cindy. Marmalade's yellow leaf
Zolotow, Charlotte. Say it!

Seasons — spring

Allington, Richard L. Spring
Anglund, Joan Walsh. Spring is a new
  beginning
Barklem, Jill. Spring story
Barrett, John M. The Easter bear
Baum, Arline. One bright Monday
  morning
Beer, Kathleen Costello. What happens
  in the spring

Belting, Natalia Maree. Summer's
  coming in
Chönz, Selina. A bell for Ursli
Clifton, Lucille. The boy who didn't
  believe in spring
Cohen, Carol L. Wake up, groundhog!
Craig, M Jean. Spring is like the
  morning
Dabcovich, Lydia. Sleepy bear
Delton, Judy. Three friends find spring
Fish, Helen Dean. When the root
  children wake up
Fisher, Aileen. My mother and I
  Now that spring is here
Forrester, Victoria. The touch said hello
Glovach, Linda. The Little Witch's
  spring holiday book
Hoban, Lillian. The sugar snow spring
  Turtle spring
Hurd, Edith Thacher. The day the sun
  danced
Ichikawa, Satomi. Sun through small
  leaves
Janice. Little Bear's pancake party
Johnson, Crockett. Time for spring
  Will spring be early?
Kesselman, Wendy. Time for Jody
Krauss, Ruth. The happy day
Kumin, Maxine. Spring things
Lenski, Lois. Spring is here
Lerner, Carol. Flowers of a woodland
  spring
Levens, George. Kippy the koala
McNaughton, Colin. Spring
Schlein, Miriam. Little Red Nose
Seignobosc, Françoise. Springtime for
  Jeanne-Marie
Taylor, Mark. Henry the castaway
Wolkstein, Diane. The magic wings
Wood, Joyce. Grandmother Lucy in her
  garden
Woolaver, Lance. From Ben Loman to
  the sea
Zion, Gene. Really spring

Seasons — summer

Adelson, Leone. All ready for summer
Allington, Richard L. Summer
Barklem, Jill. Summer story
Beim, Jerrold. The swimming hole
Belting, Natalia Maree. Summer's
  coming in
Bentley, Anne. The Groggs have a
  wonderful summer
Berenstain, Stan. The Berenstain bears
  go to camp
Bowden, Joan Chase. Emilio's summer
  day
Brown, Margaret Wise. The summer
  noisy book

Burgunder, Rose. From summer to summer

Burn, Doris. The summerfolk

Cavagnaro, David. The pumpkin people

Chönz, Selina. Florina and the wild bird

Chwast, Seymour. Still another children's book

Farjeon, Eleanor. Mr. Garden

Firmin, Peter. Basil Brush finds treasure

Gans, Roma. Hummingbirds in the garden

Garelick, May. Down to the beach

Goodall, John S. An Edwardian summer

Knotts, Howard. The summer cat

Kuskin, Karla. Sand and snow

Lenski, Lois. On a summer day

Lund, Doris Herold. The paint-box sea

McCloskey, Robert. Time of wonder

McNaughton, Colin. Summer

Schick, Eleanor. One summer night
Summer at the sea

Stobbs, William. There's a hole in my bucket

Taylor, Mark. Henry explores the jungle

Thomas, Ianthe. Eliza's daddy
Lordy, Aunt Hattie

Weygant, Noemi. It's summer!

Yashima, Tarō. The village tree

Yolen, Jane. Milkweed days

Zion, Gene. Harry by the sea
The summer snowman

Zolotow, Charlotte. Summer is...

Seasons — winter

Adelson, Leone. All ready for winter

Allington, Richard L. Winter

Asch, Frank. Mooncake

Attenberger, Walburga. The little man in winter

Aulaire, Ingri Mortenson d'. Children of the northlights

Barklem, Jill. The secret staircase
Winter story

Barnhart, Peter. The wounded duck

Bartoli, Jennifer. In a meadow, two hares hide
Snow on bear's nose

Brown, Margaret Wise. The winter noisy book

Bruna, Dick. Miffy in the snow

Buckley, Helen Elizabeth. Josie and the snow

Bunting, Eve. Winter's coming

Burton, Virginia Lee. Katy and the big snow

Carlson, Natalie Savage. Surprise in the mountains

Carrick, Carol. Two coyotes

Chaffin, Lillie D. We be warm till springtime comes

Chönz, Selina. The snowstorm

Cole, Joanna. Plants in winter

Cosgrove, Margaret. Wintertime for animals

Coutant, Helen. First snow

Craft, Ruth. The winter bear

Dabcovich, Lydia. Sleepy bear

Delton, Judy. My mom hates me in January
Three friends find spring

Dionetti, Michelle. The day Eli went looking for bear

Fisher, Aileen. Where does everyone go?

Flack, Marjorie. Angus lost

Freedman, Russell. When winter comes

Freeman, Don. The night the lights went out

Frost, Robert. Stopping by woods on a snowy evening

Fujikawa, Gyo. That's not fair!

Gundersheimer, Karen. Happy winter

Hertza, Ole. Tobias goes ice fishing

Hoban, Russell. Some snow said hello

Hoff, Syd. When will it snow?

Hoopes, Lyn Littlefield. When I was little

Janosch. Dear snowman

Keats, Ezra Jack. The snowy day

Kessler, Leonard P. Old Turtle's winter games

Knotts, Howard. The winter cat

Krauss, Ruth. The happy day

Kumin, Maxine. A winter friend

Kuskin, Karla. In the flaky frosty morning
Sand and snow

Lapp, Eleanor. The mice came in early this year

Lathrop, Dorothy Pulis. Who goes there?

Lenski, Lois. I like winter

Linch, Elizabeth Johanna. Samson

Lindgren, Astrid. The tomten
The tomten and the fox

Littledale, Freya. The snow child

McLaughlin, Lissa. Why won't winter go?

McNaughton, Colin. Winter

Martin, Charles E. Island winter

Miller, Edna. Mousekin's golden house

Odoyevsky, Vladimir. Old Father Frost

Parnall, Peter. Alfalfa Hill

Radin, Ruth Yaffe. A winter place

Retan, Walter. The snowplow that tried to go south

Roberts, Bethany. Waiting for spring stories

Schick, Eleanor. City in the winter

Schlein, Miriam. Deer in the snow
Go with the sun

Taylor, Mark. Henry the explorer
Tudor, Tasha. Snow before Christmas
Turkle, Brinton. Thy friend, Obadiah
Udry, Janice May. Mary Jo's
  grandmother
Ward, Andrew. Baby bear and the long
  sleep
Watson, Wendy. Has winter come?
Weiss, Ellen. Clara the fortune-telling
  chicken
Weygant, Noemi. It's winter!

Secret codes

Balian, Lorna. Humbug potion
Bonsall, Crosby Newell. The case of the
  double cross
Myrick, Mildred. The secret three

Secrets *see* Behavior — secrets

Seeing *see* Senses

Seeking better things *see* Behavior —
  seeking better things

Self-concept

Appell, Clara. Now I have a daddy
  haircut
Bach, Alice. Warren Weasel's worse than
  measles
Behrens, June. Who am I?
Berger, Terry. I have feelings
Blume, Judy. The one in the middle is
  the green kangaroo
Brown, Ruth. Crazy Charlie
Browne, Anthony. Willy the wimp
Carle, Eric. The mixed-up chameleon,
  1975
  The mixed-up chameleon, 1984
Charlip, Remy. Hooray for me!
Charlot, Martin. Felisa and the magic
  tikling bird
Cohen, Miriam. No good in art
  So what?
DeLage, Ida. Am I a bunny?
De Regniers, Beatrice Schenk. Everyone
  is good for something
Fitzhugh, Louise. I am five
  I am three
Hallinan, P K (Patrick K). I'm glad to be
  me
  Where's Michael?
Karlin, Nurit. A train for the king
Keats, Ezra Jack. Peter's chair
  Whistle for Willie
Krauss, Ruth. The carrot seed
Kuskin, Karla. What did you bring me?
Leaf, Munro. Noodle
Levitin, Sonia. A sound to remember
Lionni, Leo. Pezzettino

Lipkind, William. The little tiny rooster
Palmer, Mary Babcock.
  No-sort-of-animal
Peet, Bill. Pamela Camel
Sadler, Marilyn. It's not easy being a
  bunny
Schick, Eleanor. Joey on his own
Sharmat, Marjorie Weinman. I'm terrific
  Taking care of Melvin
Simon, Norma. Why am I different?
Slobodkin, Louis. Magic Michael
Stren, Patti. Mountain Rose
Supraner, Robyn. Would you rather be
  a tiger?
Tobias, Tobi. Jane wishing
Turnage, Sheila. Trout the magnificent
Tusa, Tricia. Libby's new glasses
Udry, Janice May. How I faded away
Weiner, Beth Lee. Benjamin's perfect
  solution
Wold, Jo Anne. Tell them my name is
  Amanda
Wondriska, William. Puff
Zola, Meguido. The dream of promise

Self-esteem *see* Self-concept

Self-image *see* Self-concept

Selfishness *see* Character traits —
  selfishness

Senses

Aliki. My five senses
Allington, Richard L. Hearing
  Looking
  Smelling
  Tasting
  Touching
Borten, Helen. Do you hear what I
  hear?
  Do you know what I know?
  Do you see what I see?
Bram, Elizabeth. One day I closed my
  eyes and the world disappeared
Brenner, Barbara. Faces, faces, faces
Brighton, Catherine. My hands, my
  world
Brown, Marcia. Touch will tell
  Walk with your eyes
Doughtie, Charles. Gabriel Wrinkles, the
  bloodhound who couldn't smell
Gibson, Myra Tomback. What is your
  favorite thing to touch?
Hay, Dean. I see a lot of things
Hoban, Tana. Look again
Jaynes, Ruth M. Melinda's Christmas
  stocking
Lionni, Leo. What?
Moncure, Jane Belk. The look book
  Sounds all around
  A tasting party

The touch book
What your nose knows!
Ogle, Lucille. I hear
I spy with my little eye
Perkins, Al. The ear book
Pluckrose, Henry. Things we hear
Things we see
Things we touch
Quigley, Lillian Fox. The blind men and
the elephant
Shecter, Ben. The stocking doll
Showers, Paul. The listening walk
Look at your eyes
Teal, Valentine. The little woman
wanted noise

Shadows

Cendrars, Blaise. Shadow
Christelow, Eileen. Henry and the
Dragon
De Regniers, Beatrice Schenk. The
shadow book
Gackenbach, Dick. Mr. Wink and his
shadow, Ned
Goor, Ron. Shadows
McHargue, Georgess. Private zoo
Mahy, Margaret. The boy with two
shadows
Marol, Jean-Claude. Vagabul and his
shadow
Tompert, Ann. Nothing sticks like a
shadow

Shakespeare

Freeman, Don. Will's quill

Shape *see* Concepts — shape

Shaped books *see* Format, unusual

Sharing *see* Behavior — sharing

Sheep *see* Animals — sheep

Ships *see* Boats, ships

Shoemakers *see* Careers — shoemakers

Shopping

Allard, Harry. I will not go to market
today
Ardizzone, Edward. The little girl and
the tiny doll
Arnold, Caroline. What will we buy?
Baugh, Dolores M. Supermarket
Black, Irma Simonton. The little old
man who could not read
Bond, Michael. Paddington's lucky day
Brenner, Barbara. Somebody's slippers,
somebody's shoes

Calmenson, Stephanie. The birthday hat
Cass, Joan E. The cats go to market
Chase, Catherine. Baby mouse goes
shopping
Chorao, Kay. Molly's Moe
Edwards, Linda Strauss. The downtown
day
Gretz, Susanna. Teddy bears go
shopping
Greydanus, Rose. Susie goes shopping
Guzzo, Sandra E. Fox and Heggie
Hastings, Evelyn Beilhart. The
department store
Holt, Margaret. David McCheever's
twenty-nine dogs
Hutchins, Pat. Don't forget the bacon!
Ichikawa, Satomi. Suzanne and Nicholas
at the market
Lobel, Arnold. On Market Street
McPhail, David. The cereal box
Maschler, Fay. T. G. and Moonie go
shopping
Mother Goose. To market! To market!
Oxenbury, Helen. The shopping trip
Patz, Nancy. Pumpernickel tickle and
mean green cheese
Potter, Beatrix. The tale of Little Pig
Robinson
Rice, Eve. New blue shoes
Rockwell, Anne F. The supermarket
Ross, Pat. M and M and the big bag
Russell, Betty. Big store, funny door
Schick, Eleanor. Joey on his own
Solomon, Joan. A present for Mum
Spier, Peter. Food market

Shops *see* Stores

Shows *see* Theater

Shrews *see* Animals — shrews

Shyness *see* Character traits — shyness

Siam *see* Foreign lands — Thailand

Sibling rivalry

Alexander, Martha G. I'll be the horse if
you'll play with me
Marty McGee's space lab, no girls
allowed
Nobody asked me if I wanted a baby
sister
When the new baby comes, I'm
moving out
Amoss, Berthe. It's not your birthday
Tom in the middle
Armitage, Ronda. The bossing of Josie
Arnstein, Helene S. Billy and our new
baby
Baker, Betty. My sister says

Baker, Charlotte. Little brother
Beecroft, John. What? Another cat!
Benson, Ellen. Philip's little sister
Berenstain, Stan. The Berenstain bears get in a fight
Blume, Judy. The Pain and The Great One
Bonsall, Crosby Newell. Who's a pest?
Bottner, Barbara. Jungle day
Brandenberg, Franz. It's not my fault
Brothers and sisters are like that!
Bulla, Clyde Robert. Keep running, Allen!
Caines, Jeannette. Abby
Carlson, Nancy. Harriet and Walt
Castiglia, Julie. Jill the pill
Chalmers, Audrey. Fancy be good
Chenery, Janet. Wolfie
Chorao, Kay. Oink and Pearl
Clifton, Lucille. My brother fine with me
Conaway, Judith. I'll get even
Crowley, Arthur. Bonzo Beaver
Dragonwagon, Crescent. I hate my brother Harry
Drescher, Joan. The marvelous mess
Duncan, Lois. Giving away Suzanne
Edelman, Elaine. I love my baby sister (most of the time)
Eisenberg, Phyllis Rose. Don't tell me a ghost story
Etherington, Frank. The spaghetti word race
Fair, Sylvia. The bedspread
Flournoy, Valerie. The twins strike back
Galbraith, Kathryn Osebold. Katie did!
Gili, Phillida. Fanny and Charles
Ginsburg, Mirra. Two greedy bears
Greene, Carol. Hinny Winny Bunco
Greenfield, Eloise. She come bringing me that little baby girl
Grimm, Jacob. Cinderella, ill. by Nonny Hogrogian
Cinderella, ill. by Svend Otto
Hamilton, Morse. Big sisters are bad witches
My name is Emily
Hazen, Barbara Shook. If it weren't for Benjamin (I'd always get to lick the icing spoon)
Why couldn't I be an only kid like you, Wigger?
Helmering, Doris Wild. We're going to have a baby
Henriod, Lorraine. Grandma's wheelchair
Hoban, Lillian. Arthur's pen pal
Hoban, Russell. A baby sister for Frances
The battle of Zormla
The great gum drop robbery
Some snow said hello

They came from Aargh!
Hoopes, Lyn Littlefield. When I was little
Keller, Holly. Too big
Knox-Wagner, Elaine. The oldest kid
Lasky, Kathryn. A baby for Max
Leech, Jay. Bright Fawn and me
LeRoy, Gen. Billy's shoes
Lucky stiff!
Lexau, Joan M. The homework caper
Lindgren, Astrid. I want a brother or sister
Lobel, Anita. The seamstress of Salzburg
Low, Alice. The witch who was afraid of witches
McDaniel, Becky Bring. Katie did it
McPhail, David. Sisters
Mallett, Anne. Here comes Tagalong
Margolis, Richard J. Secrets of a small brother
Marshall, Edward. Four on the shore
Mayers, Patrick. Just one more block
Milgram, Mary. Brothers are all the same
Ormerod, Jan. 101 things to do with a baby
Ormondroyd, Edward. Theodore's rival
Paterson, Diane. Hey, cowboy!
Perrault, Charles. Cinderella, ill. by Sheilah Beckett
Cinderella, ill. by Marcia Brown
Cinderella, ill. by Paul Galdone
Cinderella, ill. by Emanuele Luzzati
Cinderella, ill. by Phil Smith
Politi, Leo. Rosa
Postma, Lidia. The stolen mirror
Ray, Deborah Kogan. Sunday morning we went to the zoo
Reesink, Marijke. The princess who always ran away
Riordan, James. The three magic gifts
Roche, P K. Good-bye, Arnold!
Webster and Arnold and the giant box
Rosen, Winifred. Henrietta and the gong from Hong Kong
Rushnell, Elaine Evans. My mom's having a baby
Ruthstrom, Dorotha. The big kite contest
Samuels, Barbara. Faye and Dolores
Sarnoff, Jane. That's not fair
Schick, Eleanor. Peggy's new brother
Schlein, Miriam. Laurie's new brother
Scott, Ann Herbert. On mother's lap
Sewell, Helen Moore. Jimmy and Jemima
Skorpen, Liesel Moak. His mother's dog
Smith, Lucia B. A special kind of sister
Stanek, Muriel. My little foster sister

Stevenson, James. Winston, Newton, Elton, and Ed
Worse than Willy!
Tierney, Hanne. Where's your baby brother, Becky Bunting?
Tudor, Tasha. Junior's tune
Turkle, Brinton. Rachel and Obadiah
Udry, Janice May. Thump and Plunk
Van Leeuwen, Jean. Amanda Pig and her big brother Oliver
Tales of Amanda Pig
Vigna, Judith. Daddy's new baby
Viorst, Judith. I'll fix Anthony
Wahl, Jan. Peter and the troll baby
Wells, Rosemary. Good night, Fred
Max's breakfast
Peabody
Stanley and Rhoda
Winthrop, Elizabeth. I think he likes me
That's mine
Wolde, Gunilla. Betsy and the chicken pox
Zolotow, Charlotte. If it weren't for you

Sickness *see* Health; Illness

Sisters *see* Family life; Sibling rivalry

Size *see* Concepts — size

Skating *see* Sports — ice skating

Skiing *see* Sports — skiing

Skin diving *see* Sports — skin diving

Skunks *see* Animals — skunks

Sky

Asch, Frank. Starbaby
Belting, Natalia Maree. The sun is a golden earring
Branley, Franklyn M. Comets
The sky is full of stars
Dayrell, Elphinstone. Why the sun and the moon live in the sky
Dayton, Mona. Earth and sky
Shaw, Charles Green. It looked like spilt milk

Sleep

Alexander, Martha G. I'll protect you from the jungle beasts
Andersen, H C (Hans Christian). The princess and the pea
Aylesworth, Jim. Tonight's the night
Beckman, Kaj. Lisa cannot sleep
Bottner, Barbara. There was nobody there
Brande, Marlie. Sleepy Nicholas

Bright, Robert. Me and the bears
Brown, Margaret Wise. A child's good night book
Sleepy ABC
The sleepy little lion
Brown, Myra Berry. First night away from home
Chalmers, Mary. Take a nap, Harry
Chorao, Kay. Lester's overnight
Ciardi, John. Scrappy the pup
Coker, Gylbert. Naptime
De Paola, Tomie. Fight the night
When everyone was fast asleep
Elkin, Benjamin. The king who could not sleep
Evans, Eva Knox. Sleepy time
Field, Eugene. Wynken, Blynken and Nod
Hazen, Barbara Shook. Where do bears sleep?
Heine, Helme. King Bounce the 1st
Hutchins, Pat. Good night owl
Jeffers, Susan. All the pretty horses
Kantrowitz, Mildred. Willy Bear
Keats, Ezra Jack. Dreams
Kotzwinkle, William. The nap master
Krahn, Fernando. Sleep tight, Alex Pumpernickel
Kraus, Robert. Good night little one
Good night Richard Rabbit
Milton the early riser
McCauley, Jane. The way animals sleep
Marino, Dorothy. Edward and the boxes
Massie, Diane Redfield. The baby beebee bird
Murphy, Jill. Peace at last
Ormerod, Jan. Moonlight
Plath, Sylvia. The bed book
Polushkin, Maria. Mother, Mother, I want another
Preston, Edna Mitchell. Monkey in the jungle
Reidel, Marlene. Jacob and the robbers
Rowand, Phyllis. It is night
Saleh, Harold J. Even tiny ants must sleep
Schneider, Nina. While Susie sleeps
Seuss, Dr. Dr. Seuss's sleep book
Simon, Norma. Where does my cat sleep?
Slobodkin, Louis. Wide-awake owl
Sonneborn, Ruth A. Seven in a bed
Stevenson, James. We can't sleep
Sugita, Yutaka. Good night 1, 2, 3
Tobias, Tobi. Chasing the goblins away
Trez, Denise. Good night, Veronica
Waber, Bernard. Ira sleeps over
Wahl, Jan. Sylvester Bear overslept
Weisgard, Leonard. Who dreams of cheese?
Wersba, Barbara. Amanda dreaming

Wheeler, Cindy. Marmalade's nap
Wood, Audrey. The napping house
Yolen, Jane. Dragon night and other
    lullabies
Yulya. Bears are sleeping
Zagone, Theresa. No nap for me
Ziefert, Harriet. Sleepy dog
Zolotow, Charlotte. The sleepy book

Sleight-of-hand *see* Magic

Sloths *see* Animals — sloths

Smallness *see* Character traits —
    smallness

Smelling *see* Senses

Snails *see* Animals — snails

Snakes *see* Reptiles — snakes

Snow *see* Weather — snow

Snowmen

Briggs, Raymond. The snowman
Chorao, Kay. Kate's snowman
Erskine, Jim. The snowman
Gordon, Sharon. Friendly snowman
Holl, Adelaide. The runaway giant
Janosch. Dear snowman
Johnson, Crockett. Time for spring
Kellogg, Steven. The mystery of the
    missing red mitten
Kuskin, Karla. In the flaky frosty
    morning
Lobe, Mira. The snowman who went for
    a walk
Zion, Gene. The summer snowman

Snowplows *see* Machines

Society Islands *see* Foreign lands —
    South Sea Islands

Soldiers *see* Careers — military

Soldiers, toy *see* Toys — soldiers

Solitude *see* Behavior — solitude

Songs

Abisch, Roz. Sweet Betsy from Pike
Alexander, Cecil Frances. All things
    bright and beautiful
Alger, Leclaire. All in the morning early
    Kellyburn Braes
Arkin, Alan. Black and white
Bangs, Edward. Yankee Doodle
Billy Boy

Boesel, Ann Sterling. Sing and sing
    again
  Singing with Peter and Patsy
Bonne, Rose. I know an old lady
Botwin, Esther. A treasury of songs for
    little children
Brand, Oscar. When I first came to this
    land
Brian Wildsmith's The twelve days of
    Christmas
Briggs, Raymond. The white land
Bring a torch, Jeannette, Isabella
Bulla, Clyde Robert. The donkey cart
Carryl, Charles Edward. A capital ship
Child, Lydia Maria. Over the river and
    through the wood
Conover, Chris. Six little ducks
Dalton, Alene. My new picture book of
    songs
Denver, John. The children and the
    flowers
De Regniers, Beatrice Schenk. Was it a
    good trade?
Devlin, Harry. The walloping window
    blind
Din dan don, it's Christmas
Domanska, Janina. Busy Monday
    morning
Duvoisin, Roger Antoine. Petunia and
    the song
Emberley, Barbara. One wide river to
    cross
  Simon's song
Engvick, William. Lullabies and night
    songs
The farmer in the dell
Fern, Eugene. Birthday presents
The fox went out on a chilly night
The friendly beasts and A partridge in a
    pear tree
A frog he would a-wooing go
    (folk-song). Frog went a-courtin'
Glazer, Tom. Do your ears hang low?
  Eye winker, Tom Tinker, chin chopper
  On top of spaghetti
Go tell Aunt Rhody, ill. by Aliki
Go tell Aunt Rhody, ill. by Robert M.
    Quackenbush
Graham, Al. Songs for a small guitar
The green grass grows all around
Greene, Carol. A computer went
    a-courting
  Hinny Winny Bunco
  The thirteen days of Halloween
Hirsh, Marilyn. One little goat
Hoban, Brom. Skunk Lane
Hoban, Lillian. Harry's song
Hobzek, Mildred. We came
    a-marching...1, 2, 3
Homme, Bob. The friendly giant's
    birthday

Hopkins, Lee Bennett. And God bless me

Hot cross buns, and other old street cries

Houston, John A. The bright yellow rope
A mouse in my house
A room full of animals

Hush little baby, ill. by Aliki

Hush little baby, ill. by Jeanette Winter

Hush little baby, ill. by Margot Zemach

I sing a song of the saints of God

Ipcar, Dahlov. The cat came back
"The song of the day birds" and "The song of the night birds"

Ivimey, John William. The complete version of ye three blind mice

Johnston, Mary Anne. Sing me a song

Kapp, Paul. Cock-a-doodle-doo! Cock-a-doodle-dandy!

Keats, Ezra Jack. The little drummer boy

Key, Francis Scott. The Star-Spangled Banner, ill. by Paul Galdone
The Star-Spangled Banner, ill. by Peter Spier

Kimmel, Eric A. Why worry?

Langstaff, John M. Oh, a-hunting we will go
Ol' Dan Tucker
On Christmas day in the morning
Over in the meadow
Soldier, soldier, won't you marry me?
The swapping boy
The two magicians

Lear, Edward. The pelican chorus
The pelican chorus and the quangle wangle's hat

Lenski, Lois. At our house
Davy and his dog
Davy goes places
Debbie and her grandma
A dog came to school
I like winter
I went for a walk
The life I live

Lord, Beman. The days of the week

Mack, Stanley. Ten bears in my bed

Maril, Lee. Mr. Bunny paints the eggs

Mills, Alan. The hungry goat

Mohr, Joseph. Silent night

Moon, Dolly M. My very first book of cowboy songs

Moss, Jeffrey. The songs of Sesame Street in poems and pictures

Mother Goose. London Bridge is falling down, ill. by Ed Emberley
London Bridge is falling down, ill. by Peter Spier
Mother Goose's melodies
Thirty old-time nursery songs

Nelson, Esther L. The funny songbook
Holiday singing and dancing games
The silly songbook

Newbolt, Henry John, Sir. Rilloby-rill

Newland, Mary Reed. Good King Wenceslas

Old MacDonald had a farm, ill. by Mel Crawford

Old MacDonald had a farm, ill. by David Frankland

Old MacDonald had a farm, ill. by Abner Graboff

Old MacDonald had a farm, ill. by Tracey Campbell Pearson

Old MacDonald had a farm, ill. by Robert M. Quackenbush

On the little hearth

Over in the meadow

A paper of pins

Paterson, Andrew Barton. Waltzing Matilda

Play and sing - it's Christmas!

Pomerantz, Charlotte. All asleep

Poston, Elizabeth. Baby's song book

Preston, Edna Mitchell. Pop Corn and Ma Goodness

Price, Christine. One is God

Quackenbush, Robert M. Clementine
The man on the flying trapeze
Pop! goes the weasel and Yankee Doodle
She'll be comin' 'round the mountain
Skip to my Lou
There'll be a hot time in the old town tonight

Raebeck, Lois. Who am I?

Raposo, Joe. The Sesame Street song book

Rey, Hans Augusto. Humpty Dumpty and other Mother Goose songs

Robbins, Ruth. Baboushka and the three kings

Roll over!

Rounds, Glen. The boll weevil
Casey Jones
The strawberry roan
Sweet Betsy from Pike

Schackburg, Richard. Yankee Doodle

Seeger, Pete. The foolish frog

Shannon, George. Lizard's song

Singer, Marilyn. Will you take me to town on strawberry day?

Slobodkin, Louis. Wide-awake owl

Spier, Peter. The Erie Canal

Stern, Elsie-Jean. Wee Robin's Christmas song

Stobbs, William. There's a hole in my bucket

Swados, Elizabeth. Lullaby

Taylor, Mark. The bold fisherman
Old Blue, you good dog you

The twelve days of Christmas. English folk song. Jack Kent's twelve days of Christmas

 The twelve days of Christmas, ill. by Ilonka Karasz

 The twelve days of Christmas, ill. by Erika Schneider

Watson, Clyde. Fisherman lullabies

Wenning, Elisabeth. The Christmas mouse

Wheeler, Opal. Sing in praise

 Sing Mother Goose

Widdecombe Fair

Wolff, Ashley. The bells of London

Yolen, Jane. Dragon night and other lullabies

Yulya. Bears are sleeping

Zemach, Harve. Mommy buy me a China doll.

Zolotow, Charlotte. The song

Sounds *see* Noise, sounds

South America *see* Foreign lands — South America

South Sea Islands *see* Foreign lands — South Sea Islands

Space and space ships

Alexander, Martha G. Marty McGee's space lab, no girls allowed

Asimov, Isaac. The best new things

Blocksma, Mary. Easy-to-make spaceships that really fly

Bogart, Bonnie. The Ewoks join the fight

Branley, Franklyn M. A book of satellites for you

 The planets in our solar system

Brewster, Patience. Ellsworth and the cats from Mars

Brunhoff, Laurent de. Babar visits another planet

Freeman, Don. Space witch

Freeman, Mae. You will go to the moon

Fuchs, Erich. Journey to the moon

Glass, Andrew. My brother tries to make me laugh

Johnson, Crockett. Harold's trip to the sky

Keats, Ezra Jack. Regards to the man in the moon

Kuskin, Karla. A space story

Marshall, Edward. Space case

Marzollo, Jean. Jed's junior space patrol

May, Charles Paul. High-noon rocket

Moche, Dinah L. The astronauts

Murphy, Jill. What next, baby bear!

Paul, Sherry. 2-B and the space visitor

Peet, Bill. The wump world

Podendorf, Illa. Space

Rey, Hans Augusto. Curious George gets a medal

Robison, Nancy. UFO kidnap

Ross, David. Gorp and the space pirates

 Space monster

 Space Monster Gorp and the runaway computer

Sadler, Marilyn. Alistair in outer space

Schulman, Janet. Jack the bum and the UFO

Star wars

Steadman, Ralph. The little red computer

Ungerer, Tomi. Moon man

Weiss, Ellen. Pigs in space

Yolen, Jane. Commander Toad and the big black hole

 Commander Toad and the planet of the grapes

 Commander Toad in space

Zaffo, George J. The giant book of things in space

Ziegler, Ursina. Squaps the moonling

Spain *see* Foreign lands — Spain

Sparrows *see* Birds — sparrows

Spectacles *see* Glasses

Speech *see* Language

Speed *see* Concepts — speed

Spelunking *see* Caves

Spiders

Aardema, Verna. The vingananee and the tree toad

Adelson, Leone. Please pass the grass

Baker, Jeannie. One hungry spider

Brandenberg, Franz. Fresh cider and apple pie

Chenery, Janet. Wolfie

Climo, Shirley. The cobweb Christmas

Conklin, Gladys. I caught a lizard

Crothers, Samuel McChord. Miss Muffet's Christmas party

Dallinger, Jane. Spiders

Freschet, Berniece. The web in the grass

Galdone, Joanna. Honeybee's party

George, Jean Craighead. All upon a stone

Goldin, Augusta. Spider silk

Graham, Margaret Bloy. Be nice to spiders

Joosse, Barbara M. Spiders in the fruit cellar

Kraus, Robert. The trouble with spider

McDermott, Gerald. Anansi the spider

Rose, Anne. Spider in the sky

Ryder, Joanne. The spiders dance
Selsam, Millicent E. A first look at
spiders
The spider's web
Wagner, Jenny. Aranea
Yolen, Jane. Spider Jane

Split page books see Format, unusual

Spooks see Ghosts; Goblins

Sports

Carrick, Carol. The climb
Creekmore, Raymond. Fujio
Kessler, Leonard P. Old Turtle's winter
games
Saddler, Allen. The Archery contest

Sports — baseball

Adler, David A. Jeffrey's ghost and the
leftover baseball team
Christian, Mary Blount. The sand lot
Christopher, Matt. Johnny no hit
Downing, Joan. Baseball is our game
Gordon, Sharon. Play ball, Kate!
Hillert, Margaret. Play ball
Hoff, Syd. The littlest leaguer
Slugger Sal's slump
Isadora, Rachel. Max
Kessler, Leonard P. Here comes the
strikeout
Old Turtle's baseball stories
Parish, Peggy. Play ball, Amelia Bedelia
Perkins, Al. Don and Donna go to bat
Rubin, Jeff. Baseball brothers
Rudolph, Marguerita. I am your
misfortune
Sachs, Marilyn. Fleet-footed Florence
Matt's mitt
Schulman, Janet. Camp Kee Wee's
secret weapon

Sports — basketball

Porte, Barbara Ann. Harry's visit
Shearer, John. The case of the sneaker
snatcher

Sports — bicycling

Andersen, Karen Born. What's the
matter, Sylvie, can't you ride?
Baker, Eugene. Bicycles
Baugh, Dolores M. Bikes
Bentley, Anne. The Groggs' day out
Blance, Ellen. Monster, Lady Monster
and the bike ride
Breinburg, Petronella. Shawn's red bike
Bruna, Dick. Miffy's bicycle
Chlad, Dorothy. Bicycles are fun to ride
Heine, Helme. Friends

McLeod, Emilie Warren. The bear's
bicycle
Muntean, Michaela. Bicycle bear
Myers, Bernice. Herman and the bears
and the giants
Paterson, Andrew Barton. Mulga Bill's
bicycle
Phleger, Fred B. Off to the races
Rey, Hans Augusto. Curious George
rides a bike
Say, Allen. The bicycle man
Sueyoshi, Akiko. Ladybird on a bicycle

Sports — camping

Armitage, Ronda. One moonlit night
Berenstain, Stan. The Berenstain bears
go to camp
Boynton, Sandra. Hester in the wild
Brown, Marc. Arthur goes to camp
Brown, Myra Berry. Pip camps out
Carrick, Carol. Sleep out
McPhail, David. Pig Pig goes to camp
Marino, Dorothy. Buzzy Bear goes
camping
Mayer, Mercer. Just me and my dad
You're the scaredy cat
Parish, Peggy. Amelia Bedelia goes
camping
Peters, Sharon. Fun at camp
Price, Dorothy E. Speedy gets around
Rockwell, Anne F. The night we slept
outside
Rubel, Nicole. Sam and Violet go
camping
Schulman, Janet. Camp Kee Wee's
secret weapon
Shearer, John. Billy Jo Jive and the case
of the midnight voices
Shulevitz, Uri. Dawn
Thompson, Vivian Laubach.
Camp-in-the-yard
Warren, Cathy. The ten-alarm camp-out
Williams, Vera B. Three days on a river
in a red canoe
Yolen, Jane. The giants go camping

Sports — fishing

Aldridge, Josephine Haskell.
Fisherman's luck
A peony and a periwinkle
Bettina (Bettina Ehrlich). Pantaloni
Cook, Bernadine. The little fish that got
away
Delton, Judy. Duck goes fishing
Elkin, Benjamin. Six foolish fishermen
Gelman, Rita Golden. Uncle Hugh
Goffstein, M B (Marilyn Brooks). Fish
for supper
Gray, Catherine. Tammy and the
gigantic fish

Hall, Bill. Fish tale
Hann, Jacquie. Up day, down day
Hertza, Ole. Tobias catches trout
  Tobias goes ice fishing
Ipcar, Dahlov. The biggest fish in the
  sea
Lapp, Eleanor. In the morning mist
Long, Earlene. Gone fishing
Marzollo, Jean. Amy goes fishing
Mayer, Mercer. A boy, a dog, a frog
  and a friend
  A boy, a dog and a frog
Miles, Miska. No, no, Rosina
Ness, Evaline. Sam, Bangs, and
  moonshine
Parker, Dorothy D. Liam's catch
Potter, Beatrix. The tale of Mr. Jeremy
  Fisher
Rey, Margaret Elisabeth Waldstein.
  Curious George flies a kite
Stevenson, Robert Louis. The moon
Surany, Anico. Ride the cold wind
Taylor, Mark. The bold fisherman
Thorne, Jenny. My uncle
Wahl, Jan. The fishermen
Waterton, Betty. A salmon for Simon
Watson, Nancy Dingman. Tommy's
  mommy's fish
Wildsmith, Brian. Pelican

Sports — football

Kessler, Leonard P. Kick, pass, and run
  Super bowl

Sports — gymnastics

Schulman, Janet. Jenny and the tennis
  nut
Stevens, Carla. Pig and the blue flag

Sports — hockey

Kidd, Bruce. Hockey showdown

Sports — hunting

Baker, Betty. Sonny-Boy Sim
Bemelmans, Ludwig. Parsley
Browne, Anthony. Bear hunt
Burch, Robert. The hunting trip
Burningham, John. Harquin
Calhoun, Mary. Houn' dog
Carrick, Donald. The deer in the
  pasture
De Paola, Tomie. The hunter and the
  animals
De Regniers, Beatrice Schenk. Catch a
  little fox
Dionetti, Michelle. The day Eli went
  looking for bear
Duvoisin, Roger Antoine. The happy
  hunter

Gage, Wilson. Cully Cully and the bear
Hader, Berta Hoerner. The mighty
  hunter
Hertza, Ole. Tobias goes seal hunting
Hoban, Russell. The dancing tigers
Kahl, Virginia. How do you hide a
  monster?
Kellogg, Steven. Tallyho, Pinkerton!
Kroll, Steven. One tough turkey
Langstaff, John M. Oh, a-hunting we
  will go
Mari, Iela. Eat and be eaten
Mendoza, George. The hunter I might
  have been
Parish, Peggy. Ootah's lucky day
Peet, Bill. Buford, the little bighorn
  The gnats of knotty pine
Steiner, Charlotte. Pete and Peter
Wahl, Jan. Tiger watch
Wildsmith, Brian. Hunter and his dog
Withers, Carl. The wild ducks and the
  goose

Sports — ice skating

Hoban, Lillian. Mr. Pig and Sonny too
Johnson, Mildred D. Wait, skates!
Lindman, Maj. Snipp, Snapp, Snurr and
  the yellow sled
Radin, Ruth Yaffe. A winter place
Van Stockum, Hilda. A day on skates
Yolen, Jane. Mice on ice

Sports — Olympics

Kessler, Leonard P. On your mark, get
  set, go!
Schulz, Charles M. You're the greatest,
  Charlie Brown

Sports — racing

Aarle, Thomas Van. Don't put your cart
  before the horse race
Adams, Adrienne. The great Valentine's
  Day balloon race
Æsop. The hare and the tortoise
Baumann, Hans. The hare's race
Benchley, Nathaniel. Walter the homing
  pigeon
Calloway, Northern J. Northern J.
  Calloway presents Super-vroomer!
Dickens, Frank. Boffo: the great
  motorcycle race
Hurd, Edith Thacher. Last one home is
  a green pig
Isenberg, Barbara. The adventures of
  Albert, the running bear
Kessler, Leonard P. The big mile race
La Fontaine, Jean de. The hare and the
  tortoise
McLenighan, Valjean. Turtle and rabbit
McNaughton, Colin. The rat race

Marshall, Edward. Fox on wheels
Moore, John. Granny Stickleback
Neuhaus, David. His finest hour
Otsuka, Yuzo. Suho and the white horse
Phleger, Fred B. Off to the races
Van Woerkom, Dorothy. Harry and
Shelburt

Sports — skiing

Calhoun, Mary. Cross-country cat
Freeman, Don. Ski pup
Lindman, Maj. Snipp, Snapp, Snurr and
the red shoes
Marol, Jean-Claude. Vagabul goes skiing
Peet, Bill. Buford, the little bighorn

Sports — skin diving

Carrick, Carol. Dark and full of secrets
Ungerer, Tomi. The Mellops go diving
for treasure

Sports — soccer

Christopher, Matt. Jackrabbit goalie

Sports — surfing

Ormondroyd, Edward. Broderick

Sports — swimming

Alexander, Martha G. We never get to
do anything
Beatty, Hetty Burlingame. Droopy
Beim, Jerrold. The swimming hole
Cohn, Norma. Brother and sister
Ginsburg, Mirra. The chick and the
duckling
Kessler, Leonard P. Last one in is a
rotten egg
Moore, Inga. Aktil's big swim
Shortall, Leonard W. Tony's first dive
Stevens, Carla. Hooray for pig!

Sports — T-ball

Gemme, Leila Boyle. T-ball is our game

Sports — tennis

Schulman, Janet. Jenny and the tennis
nut

Sports — wrestling

Stren, Patti. Mountain Rose

Spring see Seasons — spring

Squirrels see Animals — squirrels

St. Patrick's Day see Holidays — St.
Patrick's Day

Stage see Theater

Stars

Allen, Laura Jean. Ottie and the star
Asch, Frank. Starbaby
Boon, Emilie. Peterkin meets a star
Branley, Franklyn M. The big dipper
The sky is full of stars
Coatsworth, Elizabeth. Good night
Freeman, Mae. The sun, the moon and
the stars
Kuskin, Karla. A space story
Lee, Jeanne M. The legend of the milky
way
Mobley, Jane. The star husband
Radley, Gail. The night Stella hid the
stars
Slate, Joseph. The star rocker

Stealing see Behavior — stealing

Steam shovels see Machines

Steamrollers see Machines

Stepchildren see Divorce; Family life —
stepfamilies

Stepfamilies see Divorce; Family life —
stepfamilies

Stepparents see Divorce; Family life —
stepfamilies

Stones see Rocks

Stores

Baugh, Dolores M. Let's go
Supermarket
Bograd, Larry. Lost in the store
Cooper, Letice Ulpha. The bear who
was too big
Freeman, Don. Corduroy
Gibbons, Gail. Department store
Gordon, Margaret. The supermarket
mice
Hale, Kathleen. Orlando the frisky
housewife
Hastings, Evelyn Beilhart. The
department store
Hoff, Syd. Merry Christmas, Henrietta!
Lippman, Peter. The Know-It-Alls mind
the store
Lobel, Arnold. On Market Street
McNaughton, Colin. At the stores
Maschler, Fay. T. G. and Moonie go
shopping
Miller, Alice P. The little store on the
corner
Potter, Beatrix. Ginger and Pickles

Rockwell, Anne F. The supermarket
Sawyer, Jean. Our village shop
Scarry, Richard. Richard Scarry's great
  big mystery book
Solomon, Joan. A present for Mum
Spier, Peter. Food market
  The pet store
  The toy shop
Steiner, Jörg. The bear who wanted to
  be a bear
Williams, Barbara. I know a salesperson

Storks *see* Birds — storks

Storms *see* Weather — storms

Streams *see* Rivers

Streets *see* Roads

String

Bakken, Harold. The special string
Calhoun, Mary. The traveling ball of
  string
Heathers, Anne. The thread soldiers
Holland, Marion. A big ball of string

Stubbornness *see* Character traits —
  stubbornness

Sullivan Islands *see* Foreign lands —
  South Sea Islands

Summer *see* Seasons — summer

Sun

Arnold, Caroline. Sun fun
Baylor, Byrd. The way to start a day
Berenstain, Stan. The bears' almanac
Bernstein, Margery. How the sun made
  a promise and kept it
Branley, Franklyn M. Eclipse
  The planets in our solar system
  The sun, our nearest star
  Sunshine makes the seasons
Dayrell, Elphinstone. Why the sun and
  the moon live in the sky
De Regniers, Beatrice Schenk. Who likes
  the sun?
Elkin, Benjamin. Why the sun was late
Engelbrektson, Sune. The sun is a star
Freeman, Mae. The sun, the moon and
  the stars
Gibbons, Gail. Sun up, sun down
Ginsburg, Mirra. How the sun was
  brought back to the sky
  Where does the sun go at night?
Goudey, Alice E. The day we saw the
  sun come up
Greene, Carol. Shine, sun!

Hamberger, John. The day the sun
  disappeared
Hurd, Edith Thacher. The day the sun
  danced
Kinney, Jean. What does the sun do?
La Fontaine, Jean de. The north wind
  and the sun
Obrist, Jürg. The miser who wanted the
  sun
Ormerod, Jan. Sunshine
Palazzo, Janet. Our friend the sun
Ringi, Kjell. The sun and the cloud
Schlein, Miriam. The sun looks down
  The sun, the wind, the sea and the
  rain
Schneider, Herman. Follow the sunset
Shulevitz, Uri. Dawn
Tresselt, Alvin R. Sun up
Wildsmith, Brian. What the moon saw

Surfing *see* Sports — surfing

Swallows *see* Birds — swallows

Swans *see* Birds — swans

Sweden *see* Foreign lands — Sweden

Swimming *see* Sports — swimming

Swinging *see* Activities — swinging

Switzerland *see* Foreign lands —
  Switzerland

T-ball *see* Sports — T-ball

Tailors *see* Careers — tailors

Talking to strangers *see* Behavior —
  talking to strangers

Tapirs *see* Animals — tapirs

Tasting *see* Senses

Taxi drivers *see* Careers — taxi drivers

Taxis

Moore, Lilian. Papa Albert
Ross, Jessica. Ms. Klondike

Teachers *see* Careers — teachers

Teddy bears *see* Toys — teddy bears

Teeth

Austin, Margot. Trumpet
Barnett, Naomi. I know a dentist
Bate, Lucy. Little rabbit's loose tooth
Brown, Ruth. Crazy Charlie
Cooney, Nancy Evans. The wobbly tooth
De Groat, Diane. Alligator's toothache
Duvoisin, Roger Antoine. Crocus
Gunther, Louise. A tooth for the tooth
  fairy
Kroll, Steven. Loose tooth
McCloskey, Robert. One morning in
  Maine
McGinley, Phyllis. Lucy McLockett
McPhail, David. The bear's toothache
Pomerantz, Charlotte. The mango tooth
Quin-Harkin, Janet. Helpful Hattie
Richter, Alice Numeroff. You can't put
  braces on spaces
Ricketts, Michael. Teeth
Rockwell, Harlow. My dentist
Ross, Pat. Molly and the slow teeth
Seuss, Dr. The tooth book
Williams, Barbara. Albert's toothache
Wolf, Bernard. Michael and the dentist

Telephone

Allen, Jeffrey. Mary Alice, operator
  number 9
Telephones
Wyse, Lois. Two guppies, a turtle and
  Aunt Edna

Telephone operators *see* Careers —
  telephone operators

Television

Brown, Marc. The bionic bunny show
McPhail, David. Fix-it

Telling time *see* Clocks; Time

Temper tantrums *see* Emotions —
  anger

Tennis *see* Sports — tennis

Textless *see* Wordless

Thailand *see* Foreign lands — Thailand

Thanksgiving *see* Holidays —
  Thanksgiving

Theater

Alexander, Sue. Seymour the prince
  Small plays for special days

  Small plays for you and a friend
Brown, Marc. Arthur's Thanksgiving
Cazet, Denys. The duck with squeaky
  feet
Coombs, Patricia. Dorrie's play
De Paola, Tomie. The Christmas
  pageant
  Sing, Pierrot, sing
De Regniers, Beatrice Schenk. Picture
  book theater
Ets, Marie Hall. Another day
Freeman, Don. Hattie the backstage bat
  Will's quill
Freeman, Lydia. Pet of the Met
Frye, Dean. Days of sunshine, days of
  rain
Giff, Patricia Reilly. The almost awful
  play
Goodall, John S. Paddy's evening out
Grimm, Jacob. King Grisly-Beard
Hoffmann, E T A. The nutcracker
Isadora, Rachel. Jesse and Abe
  Opening night
Johnston, Johanna. Speak up, Edie
Layton, Aviva. The squeakers
Lobel, Arnold. Martha, the movie
  mouse
Maiorano, Robert. Backstage
Marks, Burton. Puppet plays and
  puppet-making
Martin, Judith. The tree angel
Oppenheim, Joanne. Mrs. Peloki's class
  play
Rose, Mitchell. Norman
Sage, James. The boy and the dove
Sendak, Maurice. Maurice Sendak's
  Really Rosie
Steiner, Charlotte. Kiki is an actress
Tallon, Robert. Handella
Yeoman, John. The young performing
  horse
Yolen, Jane. Mice on ice

Tibet *see* Foreign lands — Tibet

Tigers *see* Animals — tigers

Time

Abisch, Roz. Do you know what time it
  is?
Aiken, Conrad. Tom, Sue and the clock
Allen, Jeffrey. Mary Alice, operator
  number 9
Behn, Harry. All kinds of time
Bodwell, Gaile. The long day of the
  giants
Bragdon, Lillian J. Tell me the time,
  please
Carle, Eric. The grouchy ladybug
Colman, Hila. Watch that watch
Gibbons, Gail. Clocks and how they go

Gordon, Sharon. Tick tock clock
Hawkins, Colin. What time is it, Mr.
  Wolf?
Hay, Dean. Now I can count
Hoff, Syd. Henrietta, the early bird
Hutchins, Pat. Clocks and more clocks
McGinley, Phyllis. Wonderful time
Maestro, Betsy. Around the clock with
  Harriet
May, Charles Paul. High-noon rocket
Ness, Evaline. Do you have the time,
  Lydia?
Pieńkowski, Jan. Time
Scarry, Richard. Richard Scarry's great
  big schoolhouse
Schlein, Miriam. It's about time
Seignobosc, Françoise. What time is it,
  Jeanne-Marie?
Slobodkin, Louis. The late cuckoo
Steinmetz, Leon. Clocks in the woods
Watson, Nancy Dingman. When is
  tomorrow?
Ziner, Feenie. The true book of time
Zolotow, Charlotte. Over and over

Tin soldiers *see* Toys — soldiers

Toads *see* Frogs and toads

Tongue twisters

Bodecker, N M (Nils Mogens).
  Snowman Sniffles and other verse
Brown, Marcia. Peter Piper's alphabet
Monster poems
Obligado, Lilian. Faint frogs feeling
  feverish and other terrifically
  tantalizing tongue twisters
Patz, Nancy. Pumpernickel tickle and
  mean green cheese
Pomerantz, Charlotte. The piggy in the
  puddle
Schwartz, Alvin. Busy buzzing
  bumblebees
Smith, Robert Paul. Jack Mack
Thomas, Gary. The best of the little
  books

Tools

Adkins, Jan. Toolchest
Beim, Jerrold. Tim and the tool chest
Gibbons, Gail. Tool book
Kesselman, Judi R. I can use tools
Lerner, Marguerite Rush. Doctors' tools
Pluckrose, Henry. Things we cut
Rockwell, Anne F. The toolbox
Zaffo, George J. The giant nursery book
  of things that work

Tortoises *see* Reptiles — turtles

Toucans *see* Birds — toucans

Touching *see* Senses

Towns *see* City

Toys

Alexander, Martha G. The story
  grandmother told
Ardizzone, Aingelda. The night ride
Avery, Kay. Wee willow whistle
Ayer, Jacqueline. Nu Dang and his kite
Bambi
Beckman, Kaj. Lisa cannot sleep
Bianco, Margery Williams. The
  velveteen rabbit, ill. by Allen
  Atkinson
  The velveteen rabbit, ill. by Michael
  Hague
  The velveteen rabbit, ill. by William
  Nicholson
  The velveteen rabbit, ill. by Ilse Plume
  The velveteen rabbit, ill. by Tien
Billam, Rosemary. Fuzzy rabbit
Binzen, Bill. Alfred goes house hunting
Boegehold, Betty. Hurray for Pippa!
Bornstein, Ruth Lercher. Annabelle
Brandenberg, Franz. Aunt Nina and her
  nephews and nieces
Bright, Robert. Hurrah for Freddie!
Bryant, Dean. See the bear
Chorao, Kay. Kate's car
  Molly's Moe
Coombs, Patricia. The lost playground
Corbett, Grahame. Guess who?
  Who is hiding?
  Who is inside?
  Who is next?
Craig, M Jean. Boxes
Daly, Niki. Vim, the rag mouse
DiFiori, Lawrence. My toys
Dobrin, Arnold Jack. Josephine's
  'magination
Francis, Anna B. Pleasant dreams
Gackenbach, Dick. Poppy the panda
Gilbreath, Alice. Making toys that crawl
  and slide
  Making toys that swim and float
Greenleaf, Ann. No room for Sarah
Grifalconi, Ann. The toy trumpet
Hale, Irina. Chocolate mouse and sugar
  pig
Hillert, Margaret. The birthday car
Hoban, Russell. La corona and the tin
  frog
Hughes, Richard. Gertrude's child
Hughes, Shirley. David and dog
Johnson, Crockett. The blue ribbon
  puppies
  Ellen's lion
Johnson, Jane. Sybil and the blue rabbit

Jones, Harold. There and back again
Kahn, Joan. Seesaw
Kent, Jack. Piggy Bank Gonzalez
Lindgren, Barbro. Sam's car
  The wild baby goes to sea
Lionni, Leo. Alexander and the wind-up
  mouse
Low, Joseph. Don't drag your feet...
McCue, Lisa. Corduroy's toys
McPhail, David. Mistletoe
Marcin, Marietta. A zoo in her bed
Marshall, James. The cut-ups
My toy box.
Noll, Sally. Off and counting
Oxenbury, Helen. Playing
Peppé, Rodney. Little circus
  Little dolls
  Little games
  Little numbers
  Little wheels
Politi, Leo. Mr. Fong's toy shop
Pollock, Penny. Emily's tiger
Potter, Beatrix. The tale of two bad
  mice
The pudgy book of toys
Roche, P K. Plaid bear and the rude
  rabbit gang
Sandburg, Carl. The wedding
  procession of the rag doll and the
  broom handle and who was in it
Seuss, Dr. The king's stilts
Simons, Traute. Paulino
Smith, Raymond Kenneth. The long
  dive
  The long slide
Snoopy on wheels
Spier, Peter. The toy shop
Steger, Hans-Ulrich. Traveling to Tripiti
Stephenson, Dorothy. The night it
  rained toys
Thelen, Gerda. The toy maker
Titus, Eve. Anatole and the toyshop
Tudor, Bethany. Samuel's tree house
Vincent, Gabrielle. Ernest and Celestine
Wahl, Jan. Button eye's orange
  Jamie's tiger
Ward, Nick. Giant
White, Laurence B. Science toys and
  tricks

Toys — balloons

Barrows, Marjorie Wescott. Muggins' big
  balloon
Bonsall, Crosby Newell. Mine's the best
Bright, Robert. Georgie and the
  runaway balloon
Brock, Emma Lillian. Surprise balloon
Carrick, Carol. The highest balloon on
  the common
Chase, Catherine. My balloon
Fenton, Edward. The big yellow balloon

Mari, Iela. The magic balloon
Sharmat, Marjorie Weinman. I don't
  care
Watanabe, Yuichi. Wally the whale who
  loved balloons

Toys — balls

Espenscheid, Gertrude E. The oh ball
Hamberger, John. The lazy dog
Holl, Adelaide. The remarkable egg
Kellogg, Steven. The mystery of the
  magic green ball
Krahn, Fernando. The biggest
  Christmas tree on earth
Lindgren, Barbro. Sam's ball
McClintock, Marshall. Stop that ball
Maley, Anne. Have you seen my
  mother?

Toys — bears see Toys — teddy bears

Toys — blocks

Hutchins, Pat. Changes, changes
Mayers, Patrick. Just one more block
Winthrop, Elizabeth. That's mine

Toys — dolls

Ainsworth, Ruth. The mysterious Baba
  and her magic caravan
Ardizzone, Aingelda. The night ride
Ardizzone, Edward. The little girl and
  the tiny doll
Ayer, Jacqueline. Little Silk
Bannon, Laura. Katy comes next
  Manuela's birthday
Bernhard, Josephine Butkowska. Nine
  cry-baby dolls
Bright, Robert. The travels of Ching
Brown, Margaret Wise. Dr. Squash the
  doll doctor
Dodge, Mary Mapes. Mary Anne
Dreifus, Miriam W. Brave Betsy
Francis, Frank. Natasha's new doll
Gottstein, M B (Marilyn Brooks). Goldie
  the dollmaker
  Me and my captain
Hines, Anna Grossnickle. Maybe a
  band-aid will help
Hoban, Russell. The stone doll of Sister
  Brute
Huff, Vivian. Let's make paper dolls
Jaques, Faith. Tilly's house
Johnston, Johanna. Sugarplum
Keller, Holly. Geraldine's blanket
Kroll, Steven. The hand-me-down doll
Kunhardt, Dorothy. Kitty's new doll
Lenski, Lois. Debbie and her dolls
  Let's play house
Lexau, Joan M. The rooftop mystery

McGinley, Phyllis. The most wonderful doll in the world
Mariana. The journey of Bangwell Putt
Pincus, Harriet. Minna and Pippin
Politi, Leo. Rosa
Sandburg, Carl. The wedding procession of the rag doll and the broom handle and who was in it
Schulman, Janet. The big hello
Shecter, Ben. The stocking doll
Skorpen, Liesel Moak. Elizabeth
Steig, William. Yellow and pink
Tudor, Tasha. The doll's Christmas
Udry, Janice May. Emily's autumn
Wahl, Jan. The Muffletump storybook
  The Muffletumps
  The Muffletumps' Christmas party
  The Muffletumps' Halloween scare
Wells, Rosemary. Peabody
Wilson, Julia. Becky
Winthrop, Elizabeth. Katharine's doll
Wiseman, Bernard. Oscar is a mama
Wright, Dare. The doll and the kitten
  Edith and Midnight
  Edith and Mr. Bear
  Edith and the duckling
  The lonely doll
  The lonely doll learns a lesson
Zolotow, Charlotte. William's doll

Toys — hobby horses *see* Toys — rocking horses

Toys — pandas *see* Toys — teddy bears

Toys — rocking horses

Brown, Paul. Merrylegs, the rocking pony
Donaldson, Lois. Karl's wooden horse
Lindman, Maj. Snipp, Snapp, Snurr and the magic horse
Moeschlin, Elsa. The red horse
Roberts, Thom. Pirates in the park
Robertson, Lilian. Runaway rocking horse

Toys — soldiers

Andersen, H C (Hans Christian). The steadfast tin soldier, ill. by Thomas Di Grazia
  The steadfast tin soldier, ill. by Paul Galdone
  The steadfast tin soldier, ill. by Monika Laimgruber
  The steadfast tin soldier, ill. by Alain Vaes
  The swineherd, ill. by Erik Blegvad
  The swineherd, ill. by Lisbeth Zwerger

Brown, Margaret Wise. Dr. Squash the doll doctor
Heathers, Anne. The thread soldiers
Nicholson, William, Sir. Clever Bill

Toys — teddy bears

Alexander, Martha G. I'll protect you from the jungle beasts
Ardizzone, Aingelda. The night ride
Barker, Inga-Lil. Why teddy bears are brown
Behrens, June. The manners book
Boyle, Constance. The story of little owl
Brown, Myra Berry. First night away from home
Cooper, Letice Ulpha. The bear who was too big
Craft, Ruth. The winter bear
Davidson, Amanda. Teddy at the seashore
  Teddy's first Christmas
Davis, Douglas F. There's an elephant in the garage
Douglas, Barbara. Good as new
Flora, James. Sherwood walks home
The fox went out on a chilly night
Freeman, Don. Beady Bear
  Corduroy
  A pocket for Corduroy
Gretz, Susanna. Teddy bears ABC
  Teddy bears cure a cold
  Teddy bears go shopping
  Teddy bears' moving day
  Teddy bears one to ten
  Teddybears cookbook
Hague, Kathleen. Alphabears
Hale, Irina. Brown bear in a brown chair
Hayes, Geoffrey. Bear by himself
Hoban, Lillian. Arthur's honey bear
Howe, Caroline Walton. Teddy Bear's bird and beast band
Howe, Deborah. Teddy Bear's scrapbook
Joerns, Consuelo. The forgotten bear
Kantrowitz, Mildred. Willy Bear
Kennedy, Jimmy. The teddy bears' picnic
Le-Tan, Pierre. Visit to the North Pole
Lewis, Naomi. Once upon a rainbow
Lindgren, Barbro. Sam's teddy bear
McCue, Lisa. Corduroy's party
  Corduroy's toys
McLeod, Émilie Warren. The bear's bicycle
Marcus, Susan. The missing button adventure
Marzollo, Jean. Jed's junior space patrol
Milne, A A (Alan Alexander). Pooh's alphabet book
  Pooh's bedtime book

Broekel, Ray. Trains
  Trucks
Burton, Virginia Lee. Maybelle, the
  cable car
Campbell, Rod. Look inside! Land, sea,
  air
Cars and trucks
Cave, Ron. Airplanes
  Automobiles
  Motorcycles
Cleary, Beverly. Lucky Chuck
Crews, Donald. School bus
  Truck
Gay, Michael. Little truck
Gibbons, Gail. New road!
Gramatky, Hardie. Sparky
Hoberman, Mary Ann. How do I go?
Koren, Edward. Behind the wheel
Lenski, Lois. Davy goes places
  Lois Lenski's big book of Mr. Small
McNaught, Harry. The truck book
Marston, Hope Irvin. Big rigs
Munari, Bruno. The birthday present
Olschewski, Alfred. The wheel rolls over
Oppenheim, Joanne. Have you seen
  roads?
Potter, Russell. The little red ferry boat
Rey, Hans Augusto. How do you get
  there?
Scarry, Richard. Richard Scarry's cars
  and trucks and things that go
  Richard Scarry's hop aboard! Here we
  go!
Woolley, Catherine. I like trains
Young, Miriam Burt. If I drove a bus
  If I drove a car
  If I drove a train
  If I drove a truck
  If I flew a plane
Zaffo, George J. The big book of real
  airplanes
  The giant nursery book of things that
  go
  The giant nursery book of things that
  work

Traveling *see* Activities — traveling

Trees

Adler, David A. Redwoods are the
  tallest trees in the world
Aliki. The story of Johnny Appleseed
Andersen, H C (Hans Christian). The
  fir tree
Angelo, Valenti. The acorn tree
Arnold, Caroline. The biggest living
  thing
Baker, Jeffrey J W. Patterns of nature
Barker, Cicely Mary. Flower fairies of
  the seasons

Barry, Robert E. Mr. Willowby's
  Christmas tree
Bason, Lillian. Pick a raincoat, pick a
  whistle
Bemelmans, Ludwig. Parsley
Berenstain, Stan. The Berenstain bears
  and the spooky old tree
  The Berenstain bears' Christmas tree
Blocksma, Mary. Apple tree! Apple tree!
Blough, Glenn O. Christmas trees and
  how they grow
Bond, Felicia. Christmas in the chicken
  coop
Brown, Margaret Wise. The little fir tree
Budbill, David. Christmas tree farm
Bulla, Clyde Robert. A tree is a plant
Busch, Phyllis S. Once there was a tree
Butcher, Julia. The sheep and the
  rowan tree
Carigiet, Alois. The pear tree, the birch
  tree and the barberry bush
Cleary, Beverly. The real hole
Cole, Joanna. Plants in winter
Day, Shirley. Ruthie's big tree
DeLage, Ida. The squirrel's tree party
De Paola, Tomie. The family Christmas
  tree book
Fenner, Carol. Christmas tree on the
  mountain
Fisher, Aileen. Arbor day
  As the leaves fall down
  A tree with a thousand uses
Fleischman, Paul. The birthday tree
Garelick, May. The tremendous tree
  book
Gibbons, Gail. The missing maple syrup
  sap mystery
  The seasons of Arnold's apple tree
Gilbert, Helen Earle. Mr. Plum and the
  little green tree
Gordon, Sharon. Trees
Greydanus, Rose. Tree house fun
Hawkinson, John. The old stump
Hogan, Paula Z. The oak tree
Howe, James. How the Ewoks saved the
  trees
Hutchins, Pat. The silver Christmas tree
Kirk, Barbara. Grandpa, me and our
  house in the tree
Kirkpatrick, Rena K. Look at trees
Krahn, Fernando. The biggest
  Christmas tree on earth
Lewis, Naomi. Leaves
Lindgren, Astrid. Of course Polly can
  do almost everything
Löfgren, Ulf. The wonderful tree
Mabey, Richard. Oak and company
Margolis, Richard J. Big bear, spare that
  tree
Miles, Miska. Apricot ABC

Myers, Bernice. Charlie's birthday present
Newton, James R. Forest log
Nikly, Michelle. The emperor's plum tree
Noble, Trinka Hakes. Apple tree Christmas
Oana, Kay D. Robbie and the raggedy scarecrow
Oppenheim, Joanne. Have you seen trees?
Orbach, Ruth. Apple pigs
Peet, Bill. Merle the high flying squirrel
Petie, Haris. The seed the squirrel dropped
Pike, Norman. The peach tree
Schertle, Alice. In my treehouse
Stemp, Robin. Guy and the flowering plum tree
Thelen, Gerda. The toy maker
Tresselt, Alvin R. The dead tree
 Johnny Maple-Leaf
Tudor, Bethany. Samuel's tree house
Udry, Janice May. A tree is nice
Wiese, Kurt. The thief in the attic
Wong, Herbert H. Our tree
Yashima, Tarō. The village tree
Young, Ed. Up a tree
Zolotow, Charlotte. The beautiful Christmas tree

Trickery *see* Behavior — trickery

Tricks *see* Magic

Triplets

Brunhoff, Jean de. Babar and his children
Lindman, Maj. Flicka, Ricka, Dicka and a little dog
 Flicka, Ricka, Dicka and the big red hen
 Flicka, Ricka, Dicka and the new dotted dress
 Flicka, Ricka, Dicka and the three kittens
 Flicka, Ricka, Dicka bake a cake
 Snipp, Snapp, Snurr and the buttered bread
 Snipp, Snapp, Snurr and the magic horse
 Snipp, Snapp, Snurr and the red shoes
 Snipp, Snapp, Snurr and the reindeer
 Snipp, Snapp, Snurr and the seven dogs
 Snipp, Snapp, Snurr and the yellow sled
Seuling, Barbara. The triplets

Trolleys *see* Cable cars, trolleys

Trolls

Asbjørnsen, P C (Peter Christen). The three billy goats Gruff, ill. by Marcia Brown
 The three billy goats Gruff, ill. by Paul Galdone
 The three billy goats Gruff, ill. by William Stobbs
Aulaire, Ingri Mortenson d'. The terrible troll-bird
Berenstain, Michael. The troll book
De Paola, Tomie. The cat on the Dovrefell
 Helga's dowry
Fujikawa, Gyo. Come follow me...to the secret world of elves and fairies and gnomes and trolls
Hillert, Margaret. The three goats
Lindgren, Astrid. The tomten
 The tomten and the fox
Lobel, Anita. The troll music
Marshall, Edward. Troll country
Mayer, Mercer. Terrible troll
Schertle, Alice. Hob Goblin and the skeleton
Svendsen, Carol. Hulda
Torgersen, Don Arthur. The girl who tricked the troll
 The troll who lived in the lake
Tudor, Tasha. Corgiville fair
Wahl, Jan. Peter and the troll baby

Truck drivers *see* Careers — truck drivers

Trucks

Adkins, Jan. Heavy equipment
Alexander, Anne. ABC of cars and trucks
Barr, Jene. Fire snorkel number 7
Baugh, Dolores M. Trucks and cars to ride
Broekel, Ray. Trucks
Burroway, Janet. The truck on the track
Bushey, Jerry. Building a fire truck
Cars and trucks
Cartlidge, Michelle. Teddy trucks
Crews, Donald. Truck
Fast rolling fire trucks
Fast rolling work trucks
Fisher, Leonard Everett. Pumpers, boilers, hooks and ladders
Gay, Michael. Little truck
Gibbons, Gail. Trucks
Gramatky, Hardie. Hercules
Greene, Carla. Truck drivers: what do they do?
Greydanus, Rose. Big red fire engine
Holl, Adelaide. The ABC of cars, trucks and machines

Homme, Bob. The friendly giant's book of fire engines

Kessler, Ethel. Night story

McNaught, Harry. The truck book

Marston, Hope Irvin. Big rigs
  Fire trucks

Peppé, Rodney. Little wheels

Quackenbush, Robert M. City trucks

Robbins, Ken. Trucks of every sort

Rockwell, Anne F. Trucks

Scarry, Richard. The great big car and truck book
  Richard Scarry's cars and trucks and things that go

Schulz, Charles M. Snoopy's facts and fun book about trucks

Siebert, Diane. Truck song

Trucks

Wolfe, Robert L. The truck book

Young, Miriam Burt. If I drove a truck

Zaffo, George J. The giant nursery book of things that go

Turkey *see* Foreign lands — Turkey

Turkeys *see* Birds — turkeys

Turtles *see* Reptiles — turtles

TV *see* Television

Twilight

Udry, Janice May. The moon jumpers

Twins

Balet, Jan B. Ned and Ed and the lion

Bruna, Dick. Tilly and Tess

Cleary, Beverly. The real hole
  Two dog biscuits

Clymer, Eleanor Lowenton. Horatio goes to the country

Flournoy, Valerie. The twins strike back

Hoban, Lillian. Here come raccoons

Lawrence, James. Binky Brothers and the fearless four
  Binky Brothers, detectives

McDermott, Gerald. The magic tree

McKissack, Patricia C. Who is who?

Moore, Lilian. Little Raccoon and no trouble at all

Neasi, Barbara J. Just like me

Perkins, Al. Don and Donna go to bat

Rubel, Nicole. Sam and Violet are twins
  Sam and Violet go camping

Simon, Norma. How do I feel?

Stewart, Elizabeth Laing. The lion twins

Thompson, Vivian Laubach. Camp-in-the-yard

Yeoman, John. The young performing horse

Tyrol *see* Foreign lands — Tyrol

Ukraine *see* Foreign lands — Ukraine

Umbrellas

Blance, Ellen. Monster and the magic umbrella

Bright, Robert. My red umbrella

Cole, William. Aunt Bella's umbrella

Levine, Rhoda. Harrison loved his umbrella

Lipkind, William. Professor Bull's umbrella

Pinkwater, Daniel Manus. Roger's umbrella

Yashima, Tarō. Umbrella

Unhappiness *see* Emotions — happiness; Emotions — sadness

UNICEF

Coatsworth, Elizabeth. The children come running

Schulman, Janet. Jack the bum and the Halloween handout

Unicorns *see* Mythical creatures

U.S. history

Abisch, Roz. The Pumpkin Heads
  Sweet Betsy from Pike

Aliki. George and the cherry tree
  The many lives of Benjamin Franklin
  The story of Johnny Appleseed
  The story of William Penn
  A weed is a flower

Aulaire, Ingri Mortenson d'. Abraham Lincoln
  Pocahontas

Austin, Margot. Willamet way

Baker, Betty. The pig war

Bangs, Edward. Yankee Doodle

Belting, Natalia Maree. Verity Mullens and the Indian

Benchley, Nathaniel. George the drummer boy
  Sam the minute man
  Small Wolf
  Snorri and the strangers

Benchley, Peter. Jonathan visits the White House

Bethell, Jean. Three cheers for Mother Jones!

Waiters *see* Careers — waiters, waitresses

Waitresses *see* Careers — waiters, waitresses

Walking *see* Activities — walking

Walruses *see* Animals — walruses

War

Ambrus, Victor G. Brave soldier Janosch

Aulaire, Ingri Mortenson d'. Wings for Per

Benchley, Nathaniel. George the drummer boy
  Sam the minute man

Bishop, Claire Huchet. Pancakes - Paris

Bogart, Bonnie. The Ewoks join the fight

De Paola, Tomie. The mysterious giant of Barletta

Du Bois, William Pène. The forbidden forest

Fitzhugh, Louise. Bang, bang, you're dead

Foreman, Michael. War and peas

Gauch, Patricia Lee. Once upon a Dinkelsbühl

Holbrook, Stewart. America's Ethan Allen

Hughes, Peter. The king who loved candy

Phillips, Louis. The brothers Wrong and Wrong Again

Schick, Alice. The remarkable ride of Israel Bissell... as related to Molly the crow

Seuss, Dr. The butter battle book

Stone, Bernard. The charge of the mouse brigade

Washington's Birthday *see* Holidays — Washington's Birthday

Wasps *see* Insects — wasps

Watches *see* Clocks

Water buffaloes *see* Animals — water buffaloes

Weapons

Bolliger, Max. The wooden man

Duvoisin, Roger Antoine. The happy hunter

Emberley, Barbara. Drummer Hoff

Fitzhugh, Louise. Bang, bang, you're dead

Hader, Berta Hoerner. Mister Billy's gun

Wondriska, William. The tomato patch

Weasels *see* Animals — weasels

Weather

Allington, Richard L. Autumn
  Spring
  Summer
  Winter

Ardizzone, Edward. Tim to the rescue

Asch, Frank. Country pie

Barrett, Judi. Cloudy with a chance of meatballs

Baum, Arline. One bright Monday morning

Bell, Norman. Linda's airmail letter

Berenstain, Stan. The bears' almanac

Bolliger, Max. The wooden man

Branley, Franklyn M. Rain and hail

Brown, Margaret Wise. The little island

Burgert, Hans-Joachim. Samulo and the giant

Coombs, Patricia. Dorrie and the weather-box

Dewey, Ariane. Febold Feboldson

Fisher, Aileen. I like weather

Frye, Dean. Days of sunshine, days of rain

Gackenbach, Dick. Ida Fanfanny

Greenberg, Barbara. The bravest babysitter

A January fog will freeze a hog,

Jaynes, Ruth M. Benny's four hats

Kirkpatrick, Rena K. Look at weather

Lewin, Betsy. Hip, hippo, hooray!

McCloskey, Robert. Time of wonder

Marshak, Samuel. The Month-Brothers

Palazzo, Janet. What makes the weather

Pieńkowski, Jan. Weather

Rockwell, Anne F. Blackout

Schlein, Miriam. The sun, the wind, the sea and the rain

Seymour, Peter. How the weather works

Tresselt, Alvin R. Sun up

Vance, Eleanor Graham. Jonathan

Zolotow, Charlotte. The storm book

Weather — clouds

Ariane. Small Cloud

De Paola, Tomie. The cloud book

Greene, Carol. Hi, clouds

Freeman, Don. A rainbow of my own
Kirkpatrick, Rena K. Look at rainbow
 colors
Kwitz, Mary DeBall. When it rains
Marino, Dorothy. Buzzy Bear and the
 rainbow
Weston, Martha. Peony's rainbow
Williams, Leslie. A bear in the air
Zolotow, Charlotte. The storm book

Weather — snow

Bahr, Robert. Blizzard at the zoo
Barklem, Jill. Winter story
Bartoli, Jennifer. Snow on bear's nose
Benchley, Nathaniel. The magic sled
Branley, Franklyn M. Snow is falling
Brown, Margaret Wise. The winter
 noisy book
Bruna, Dick. Another story to tell
 Miffy in the snow
Buckley, Helen Elizabeth. Josie and the
 snow
Burningham, John. Trubloff
Burton, Virginia Lee. Katy and the big
 snow
Chönz, Selina. The snowstorm
Delaney, A. Monster tracks?
Delton, Judy. Brimhall turns detective
 A walk on a snowy night
Dorian, Marguerite. When the snow is
 blue
Greene, Carol. Snow Joe
Gunther, Louise. Anna's snow day
Hader, Berta Hoerner. The big snow
Hoban, Lillian. The sugar snow spring
Hoban, Russell. Some snow said hello
Hoff, Syd. When will it snow?
Iwasaki, Chihiro. The birthday wish
Janosch. Dear snowman
Keats, Ezra Jack. The snowy day
Krauss, Ruth. The happy day
Kuskin, Karla. In the flaky frosty
 morning
McKié, Roy. Snow
McPhail, David. Snow lion
Parnall, Peter. Alfalfa Hill
Raphael, Elaine. Donkey, it's snowing
Retan, Walter. The snowplow that tried
 to go south
Sasaki, Isao. Snow
Sauer, Julia Lina. Mike's house
Schick, Eleanor. City in the winter
Schlein, Miriam. Deer in the snow
Schroeder, Binette. Tuffa and the snow
Skofield, James. Snow country
Todd, Kathleen. Snow
Tresselt, Alvin R. White snow, bright
 snow
Tudor, Tasha. Snow before Christmas
Udry, Janice May. Mary Jo's
 grandmother

Watson, Nancy Dingman. Sugar on
 snow
Wheeler, Cindy. Marmalade's snowy day
Zion, Gene. The summer snowman
Zolotow, Charlotte. Hold my hand

Weather — storms

Adoff, Arnold. Make a circle, keep us in
 Tornado!
Aldridge, Josephine Haskell.
 Fisherman's luck
Anderson, Lonzo. The day the
 hurricane happened
Bahr, Robert. Blizzard at the zoo
Branley, Franklyn M. Flash, crash,
 rumble and roll
Crowe, Robert L. Tyler Toad and the
 thunder
Delton, Judy. A walk on a snowy night
Dennis, Morgan. The sea dog
Keats, Ezra Jack. Clementina's cactus
Keller, Holly. Will it rain?
McNulty, Faith. Hurricane
Marino, Dorothy. Good-bye
 thunderstorm
Noble, Trinka Hakes. Apple tree
 Christmas
Rettich, Margret. The voyage of the
 jolly boat
Sussman, Susan. Hippo thunder
Taylor, Judy. Sophie and Jack help out
Van Allsburg, Chris. The wreck of the
 Zephyr

Weather — wind

Ardizzone, Edward. Tim's last voyage
Brown, Margaret Wise. When the wind
 blew
Ets, Marie Hall. Gilberto and the wind
Garrison, Christian. Little pieces of the
 west wind
Greene, Carol. Please, wind?
Hutchins, Pat. The wind blew
Keats, Ezra Jack. A letter to Amy
La Fontaine, Jean de. The north wind
 and the sun
Lexau, Joan M. Who took the farmer's
 hat?
McKay, Louise. Marny's ride with the
 wind
Rice, Inez. The March wind
Saltzberg, Barney. It must have been the
 wind
Schick, Eleanor. City in the winter
Schlein, Miriam. The sun, the wind, the
 sea and the rain
Thompson, Brenda. The winds that
 blow
Tresselt, Alvin R. Follow the wind
 The wind and Peter

Ungerer, Tomi. The hat
Whiteside, Karen. Lullaby of the wind
Yolen, Jane. The girl who loved the
    wind
Zolotow, Charlotte. When the wind
    stops

Weaving *see* Activities — weaving

Weddings

Ambrus, Victor G. Country wedding
Balian, Lorna. A sweetheart for
    Valentine
Barklem, Jill. Summer story
Clarct, Maria. Melissa Mouse
Cock Robin. The courtship, merry
    marriage, and feast of Cock Robin
    and Jenny Wren
Coombs, Patricia. Mouse Café
De Paola, Tomie. Helga's dowry
Goodall, John S. Naughty Nancy
Grimm, Jacob. Mrs. Fox's wedding
    Rumpelstiltskin, ill. by Jacqueline Ayer
    Rumpelstiltskin, ill. by Donna Diamond
    Rumpelstiltskin, ill. by John Wallner
    Snow White and Rose Red, ill. by
        Adrienne Adams
    Snow White and Rose Red, ill. by John
        Wallner
Gross, Ruth Belov. The girl who
    wouldn't get married
Heine, Helme. The pigs' wedding
Hoban, Lillian. Mr. Pig and Sonny too
Hogrogian, Nonny. Carrot cake
Hürlimann, Ruth. The mouse with the
    daisy hat
Lewin, Hugh. Jafta and the wedding
Quin-Harkin, Janet. Peter Penny's dance
Sandburg, Carl. The wedding
    procession of the rag doll and the
    broom handle and who was in it
Seguin-Fontes, Marthe. A wedding book
The squire's bride
Suhl, Yuri. Simon Boom gives a
    wedding
Varga, Judy. Janko's wish
Williams, Barbara. Whatever happened
    to Beverly Bigler's birthday?
Williams, Garth. The rabbits' wedding
Wittman, Sally. The wonderful Mrs.
    Trumbly

Weekdays *see* Days of the week, months
    of the year

Weight *see* Concepts — weight

Werewolves *see* Monsters

Whales *see* Animals — whales

Wheels

Barton, Byron. Wheels
Berenstain, Stan. Bears on wheels
Myller, Rolf. Rolling round
Olschewski, Alfred. The wheel rolls over
Snoopy on wheels

Whistling *see* Activities — whistling

Willfulness *see* Character traits —
    willfulness

Wind *see* Weather — wind

Windmills

Yeoman, John. Mouse trouble

Window cleaners *see* Careers —
    window cleaners

Winter *see* Seasons — winter

Wishing *see* Behavior — wishing

Witches

Adams, Adrienne. A Halloween
    happening
    A woggle of witches
Alexander, Sue. More Witch, Goblin,
    and Ghost stories
    Witch, Goblin, and Ghost in the
        haunted woods
    Witch, Goblin and Ghost's book of
        things to do
    Witch, Goblin and sometimes Ghost
Anderson, Robin. Sinabouda Lily
Anglund, Joan Walsh. Nibble nibble
    mousekin
Armitage, Ronda. The bossing of Josie
Bach, Othello. Lilly, Willy and the
    mail-order witch
Balian, Lorna. Humbug potion
    Humbug witch
Basile, Giambattista. Petrosinella
Benarde, Anita. The pumpkin smasher
Berridge, Celia. Grandmother's tales
Berson, Harold. Charles and Claudine
Bridwell, Norman. The witch grows up
    The witch next door
Brown, Marc. Spooky riddles
    Witches four
Burch, Robert. The jolly witch
Calhoun, Mary. The witch of Hissing
    Hill
    The witch who lost her shadow
    The witch's pig
    Wobble the witch cat
Carlson, Natalie Savage. Spooky night
Cole, Babette. The trouble with mom
Cole, Joanna. Bony-legs

Cristini, Ermanno. In my garden
  In the woods
Daughtry, Duanne. What's inside?
Degen, Bruce. Aunt Possum and the
  pumpkin man
De Groat, Diane. Alligator's toothache
De Paola, Tomie. Country farm
  Flicks
  The hunter and the animals
  Pancakes for breakfast
  Sing, Pierrot, sing
Domestic animals
Emberley, Ed. Ed Emberley's big green
  drawing book
Felix, Monique. The story of a little
  mouse trapped in a book
Florian, Douglas. The city
Freeman, Don. Forever laughter
Fromm, Lilo. Muffel and Plums
Fuchs, Erich. Journey to the moon
Fujikawa, Gyo. Millie's secret
  My favorite thing
Goodall, John S. The adventures of
  Paddy Pork
  The ballooning adventures of Paddy
  Pork
  Creepy castle
  An Edwardian Christmas
  An Edwardian summer
  Jacko
  The midnight adventures of Kelly, Dot
  and Esmeralda
  Naughty Nancy
  Paddy goes traveling
  Paddy Pork odd jobs
  Paddy Pork's holiday
  Paddy under water
  Paddy's evening out
  Paddy's new hat
  Shrewbettina's birthday
  The story of an English village
  The surprise picnic
Gorey, Edward. The tunnel calamity
Greeley, Valerie. Farm animals
  Field animals
  Pets
  Zoo animals
Hamberger, John. The lazy dog
Hartelius, Margaret A. The chicken's
  child
Hauptmann, Tatjana. A day in the life
  of Petronella Pig
Heller, Linda. Lily at the table
Hill, Eric. At home
  The park
  Up there
Hoban, Tana. Big ones, little ones
  Circles, triangles, and squares
  Dig, drill, dump, fill
  Is it red? Is it yellow? Is it blue?
  Is it rough? Is it smooth? Is it shiny?

  Look again
  1, 2, 3
  Shapes and things
  Take another look
  What is it?
Hughes, Shirley. Up and up
Hutchins, Pat. Changes, changes
Hyman, Trina Schart. The enchanted
  forest
Keats, Ezra Jack. Clementina's cactus
  Kitten for a day
  Psst, doggie
  Skates
Kent, Jack. The egg book
Kilroy, Sally. Animal noises
Krahn, Fernando. April fools
  The biggest Christmas tree on earth
  Catch that cat!
  The creepy thing
  A funny friend from heaven
  The great ape
  Here comes Alex Pumpernickel!
  How Santa Claus had a long and
  difficult journey delivering his
  presents
  Little love story
  The mystery of the giant footprints
  Robot-bot-bot
  Sebastian and the mushroom
  The secret in the dungeon
  Sleep tight, Alex Pumpernickel
  Who's seen the scissors?
Lemke, Horst. Places and faces
Lewis, Stephen. Zoo city
Lilly, Kenneth. Animals in the country
Lionni, Leo. What?
  When?
  Where?
  Who?
Lisker, Sonia O. Lost
McCue, Lisa. Corduroy's party
  Corduroy's toys
McCully, Emily Arnold. Picnic
Mari, Iela. Eat and be eaten
  The magic balloon
Marol, Jean-Claude. Vagabul and his
  shadow
  Vagabul escapes
  Vagabul goes skiing
  Vagabul in the clouds
Mayer, Mercer. Ah-choo
  A boy, a dog, a frog and a friend
  A boy, a dog and a frog
  Bubble bubble
  Frog goes to dinner
  Frog on his own
  Frog, where are you?
  The great cat chase
  Hiccup
  One frog too many
  Oops

Words see Language

Working see Activities — working

World

Worms see Animals — worms

Worrying see Behavior — worrying

Wrecking machines see Machines

Wrens see Birds — wrens

Wrestling see Sports — wrestling

Writers see Careers — writers

Writing see Activities — writing

Writing letters see Letters

Yaks see Animals — yaks

Zebras see Animals — zebras

Zodiac

Fisher, Leonard Everett. Star signs
Van Woerkom, Dorothy. The rat, the ox
  and the zodiac

Zoos

Aitken, Amy. Kate and Mona in the
  jungle
Allen, Robert. The zoo book
Arthur, Catherine. My sister's silent
  world
Bahr, Robert. Blizzard at the zoo
Barry, Robert E. Next please
Baskin, Leonard. Hosie's zoo
Bauer, Helen. Good times in the park
Bishop, Bonnie. Ralph rides away
Blance, Ellen. Monster goes to the zoo
Blue, Rose. Black, black, beautiful black
Bolliger, Max. Sandy at the children's
  zoo
Bridges, William. Lion Island
Bright, Robert. Me and the bears
Brown, Margaret Wise. The big fur
  secret
  Don't frighten the lion
Bruna, Dick. Miffy at the zoo
Calmenson, Stephanie. Where will the
  animals stay?
Canning, Kate. A painted tale
Carle, Eric. 1, 2, 3 to the zoo
Carrick, Carol. Patrick's dinosaurs
Chalmers, Audrey. Hundreds and
  hundreds of pancakes
  Parade of Obash
Charles, Donald. Calico Cat at the zoo
Colonius, Lillian. At the zoo
Cutler, Ivor. The animal house
DeLage, Ida. ABC triplets at the zoo
Fatio, Louise. The happy lion
  The happy lion and the bear
  The happy lion in Africa
  The happy lion roars
  The happy lion's rabbits
  The happy lion's treasure
  Hector and Christina
  The three happy lions
Fay, Hermann. My zoo
Flora, James. Leopold, the see-through
  crumbpicker
Gordon, Shirley. Grandma zoo
Graham, Margaret Bloy. Be nice to
  spiders
Greeley, Valerie. Zoo animals
Greydanus, Rose. Animals at the zoo
Grosvenor, Donna. Zoo babies
Hader, Berta Hoerner. Lost in the
  zoo

Hanlon, Emily. What if a lion eats me
  and I fall into a hippopotamus' mud
  hole?
Harrison, David Lee. Detective Bob and
  the great ape escape
Hoff, Syd. Sammy the seal
Howe, James. The day the teacher went
  bananas
Irvine, Georgeanne. Bo the orangutan
  Elmer the elephant
  Georgie the giraffe
  Lindi the leopard
  The nursery babies
  Sasha the cheetah
  Tully the tree kangaroo
Isenberg, Barbara. The adventures of
  Albert, the running bear
Jacobs, Francine. Sewer Sam
Johnson, Louise. Malunda
Kishida, Eriko. The hippo boat
Knight, Hilary. Where's Wallace?
Lewis, Stephen. Zoo city
Lilly, Kenneth. Animals at the zoo
Lippman, Peter. New at the zoo
Lisker, Sonia O. Lost
Lobel, Arnold. A holiday for Mister
  Muster
  A zoo for Mister Muster
Loof, Jan. Uncle Louie's fantastic sea
  voyage
McGovern, Ann. Zoo, where are you?
Meeks, Esther K. Something new at the
  zoo
Miklowitz, Gloria D. The zoo that
  moved
Munari, Bruno. Bruno Munari's zoo
Oxenbury, Helen. Monkey see, monkey
  do
Palmer, Helen Marion. I was kissed by a
  seal at the zoo
Panek, Dennis. Catastrophe Cat at the
  zoo
Ray, Deborah Kogan. Sunday morning
  we went to the zoo
Reitveld, Jane Klatt. Monkey island
Rey, Hans Augusto. Curious George
  takes a job
  Feed the animals
Rice, Eve. Sam who never forgets
Rojankovsky, Feodor. Animals in the
  zoo
Roosevelt, Michelle Chopin. Zoo animals
Schumacher, Claire. King of the zoo
Seuss, Dr. If I ran the zoo
Snyder, Dick. One day at the zoo
  Talk to me tiger
Tensen, Ruth M. Come to the zoo!
Ylla. Look who's talking
Young, Miriam Burt. Please don't feed
  Horace

Bibliographic Guide

Arranged alphabetically by author's name in boldface (or by title, if the author is unknown), each entry includes title, illustrator, publisher, publication date, and subjects. Joint authors and their titles appear as short entries, with the main author name (in parentheses after the title) citing where the complete entry will be found. Where only an author and title are given, complete information is listed under the *title* as the main entry.

A is for alphabet by Cathy, Marly and Wendy; ill. by George Suyeoka. Scott, 1968. Subj: ABC books.

Aardema, Verna. *Bringing the rain to Kapiti Plain: a Nandi tale* ill. by Beatriz Vidal. Dial, 1981. Subj: Cumulative tales. Folk and fairy tales. Foreign lands – Africa. Poetry, rhyme. Weather – droughts. Weather – rain.

Half-a-ball-of-kenki: an Ashanti tale retold by Verna Aardema; ill. by Diane Stanley. Warne, 1979. Subj: Animals – leopards. Folk and fairy tales. Foreign lands – Africa. Insects – flies.

Ji-nongo-nongo means riddles ill. by Jerry Pinkney. Four Winds Pr., 1978. Subj: Folk and fairy tales. Foreign lands – Africa. Riddles.

Oh, Kojo! How could you! an Ashanti tale ill. by Marc Brown. Dial, 1984. Subj: Folk and fairy tales. Foreign lands – Africa. Humor.

The riddle of the drum: a tale from Tizapan, Mexico ill. by Tony Chen. Four Winds Pr., 1978. Subj: Cumulative tales. Folk and fairy tales. Foreign lands – Mexico. Poetry, rhyme. Royalty.

The vingananee and the tree toad: a Liberian tale ill. by Ellen Weiss. Warne, 1983. Subj: Animals. Folk and fairy tales. Foreign lands – Africa. Spiders.

What's so funny, Ketu? a Nuer tale ill. by Marc Brown. Dial, 1982. Subj: Animals. Behavior – secrets. Humor. Reptiles – snakes.

Who's in Rabbit's house? ill. by Leo and Diane Dillon. Dial Pr., 1977. Subj: Animals. Folk and fairy tales. Foreign lands – Africa. Humor. Insects – butterflies, caterpillars.

Why mosquitoes buzz in people's ears: a West African tale ill. by Leo and Diane Dillon. Dial Pr., 1975. Subj: Animals. Caldecott award book. Folk and fairy tales. Foreign lands – Africa. Insects – mosquitoes.

Aarle, Thomas Van. *Don't put your cart before the horse race* ill. by Bob Barner. Houghton, 1980. Subj: Animals – horses. Sports – racing.

ABCDEF... *in English and Spanish* ill. by Robert Tallon. Lion Pr., 1969. Subj: ABC books. Foreign languages.

Abel, Ray. *The new sitter* (Abel, Ruth)

Abel, Ruth. *The new sitter* by Ruth and Ray Abel; ill. by Ray Abel. Oxford Univ. Pr., 1950. Subj: Activities – babysitting.

Abelson, Danny. *The Muppets take Manhattan: a movie storybook* adapt. by Danny Abelson; ill. with photos. Random House, 1983. Subj: Activities – working. Puppets.

Abisch, Roslyn Kroop *see* Abisch, Roz

Abisch, Roz. *The clever turtle* ill. by Boche Kaplan. Prentice-Hall, 1969. Subj: Animals. Folk and fairy tales. Foreign lands – Africa. Reptiles – turtles.

Do you know what time it is? ill. by Boche Kaplan. Prentice-Hall, 1968. Subj: Time.

Let's find out about butterflies ill. by Boche Kaplan. Subj: Insects – butterflies, caterpillars. Science.

Mai-Ling and the mirror: a Chinese folktale ill. by Boche Kaplan. Prentice-Hall, 1969. Subj: Emotions – envy, jealousy. Folk and fairy tales. Foreign lands – China.

Open your eyes ill. by Boche Kaplan. Parents, 1964. Subj: Concepts – color. Imagination.

The Pumpkin Heads ill. by Boche Kaplan. Prentice-Hall, 1968. "Based on an anecdote from General history of Connecticut, by Reverend Samuel Peters." Subj: Hair. U.S. history.

Sweet Betsy from Pike by Roz Abisch and Boche Kaplan; ill. by Boche Kaplan. McCall's, 1970. Subj: Character traits – perseverance. Folk and fairy tales. Music. Songs. U.S. history.

'Twas in the moon of wintertime: the first American Christmas carol adapt. by Roz Abisch; ill. by Boche Kaplan. Prentice-Hall, 1969. Subj: Ethnic groups in the U.S. – Indians. Music.

Abrons, Mary. *For Alice a palace* ill. by Gertrude Barrer-Russell. W. R. Scott, 1966. Subj: ABC books. Birthdays. Poetry, rhyme. Royalty.

Ackley, Edith Flack. *Please* ill. by Telka Ackley. Stokes, 1941. Subj: Etiquette.

Thank you ill. by Telka Ackley. Stokes, 1942. Subj: Etiquette.

Adam, Barbara. *The big big box* ill. by author. Doubleday, 1960. Subj: Activities – playing. Animals – cats. Imagination.

Adams, Adrienne. *The Christmas party* ill. by author. Scribner's, 1978. Subj: Animals – rabbits. Holidays – Christmas. Parties.

The Easter egg artists ill. by author. Scribner's, 1976. Subj: Activities – painting. Activities – vacationing. Animals – rabbits. Holidays – Easter.

The great Valentine's Day balloon race ill. by author. Scribner's, 1980. Subj: Activities – ballooning. Animals – rabbits. Careers – artists. Holidays – Valentine's Day. Sports – racing.

A Halloween happening ill. by author. Scribner's, 1981. Subj: Holidays – Halloween. Parties. Witches.

Two hundred rabbits (Anderson, Lonzo)

A woggle of witches ill. by author. Scribner's, 1971. Subj: Holidays – Halloween. Witches.

Adams, Richard. *The tyger voyage* ill. by Nicola Bayley. Knopf, 1976. Subj: Animals – tigers. Humor. Poetry, rhyme.

Adams, Ruth Joyce. *Fidelia* ill. by author. Lothrop, 1970. Subj: Ethnic groups in the U.S. – Mexican-Americans.

Adamson, Gareth. *Old man up a tree* ill. by author. Abelard-Schuman, 1963. Subj: Character traits – curiosity. Crime. Humor.

Adamson, Joy. *Elsa* photos. by author. Pantheon, 1961. Subj: Animals – lions. Foreign lands – Africa.

Elsa and her cubs photos. by author. Harcourt, 1965. Subj: Animals – lions. Foreign lands – Africa.

Pippa the cheetah and her cubs photos. by author. Harcourt, 1971. Subj: Animals – cheetahs. Foreign lands – Africa.

Adelberg, Doris *see* Orgel, Doris

Adelborg, Ottilia. *Clean Peter and the children of Grubbylea* tr. by Ada Wallas; ill. by author. Platt, 1968. Subj: Character traits – cleanliness. Poetry, rhyme.

Adelson, Leone. *All ready for school* ill. by Kathleen Elgin. McKay, 1957. Subj: School. Seasons – fall.

All ready for summer ill. by Kathleen Elgin. McKay, 1955. Subj: Seasons – summer.

All ready for winter ill. by Kathleen Elgin. McKay, 1952. Subj: Seasons – winter.

Please pass the grass ill. by Roger Antoine Duvoisin. McKay, 1960. Subj: Insects. Plants. Poetry, rhyme. Spiders.

Who blew that whistle? ill. by Oscar Fabrès. W. R. Scott, 1946. Subj: Careers – police officers. Character traits – helpfulness.

Adkins, Jan. *The art and industry of sandcastles* ill. by author. Walker, 1971. Subj: Sea and seashore.

Heavy equipment ill. by author. Scribner's, 1980. Subj: Machines. Trucks.

Toolchest: a primer of woodcraft ill. by author. Walker, 1973. Subj: Careers – carpenters. Tools.

Adler, David A. *Base five* ill. by Larry Ross. Crowell, 1975. Subj: Counting.

Bunny rabbit rebus ill. by Madelaine Gill Linden. Crowell, 1983. Subj: Animals – rabbits. Food. Rebuses.

The carsick zebra and other riddles ill. by Tomie de Paola. Holiday, 1983. Subj: Animals. Riddles.

The children of Chelm ill. by Arthur Friedman. Bonium Books, 1980. Subj: Foreign lands – Poland. Humor. Jewish culture. Problem solving.

The house on the roof: a Sukkot story ill. by Marilyn Hirsh. Bonim, 1976. Subj: Houses. Jewish culture.

Jeffrey's ghost and the leftover baseball team ill. by Jean Jenkins. Holt, 1984. Subj: Character traits – confidence. Ghosts. Sports – baseball.

A little at a time ill. by author. Random House, 1976. Subj: Character traits – questioning. Family life – grandparents, great-grandparents.

My dog and the key mystery ill. by Byron Barton. Watts, 1982. Subj: Animals – dogs. Problem solving.

A picture book of Hanukkah ill. by Linda Heller. Holiday, 1982. Subj: Holidays – Hanukkah. Jewish culture. Religion.

A picture book of Israel ill. with photos. Holiday, 1984. Subj: Foreign lands – Israel. Jewish culture. Religion.

A picture book of Jewish holidays ill. by Linda Heller. Holiday, 1981. Subj: Holidays. Holidays – Hanukkah. Holidays – Passover. Jewish culture.

A picture book of Passover ill. by Linda Heller. Holiday, 1982. Subj: Holidays – Passover. Jewish culture.

Redwoods are the tallest trees in the world ill. by Kazue Mizumura. Crowell, 1978. Subj: Forest, woods. Science. Trees.

3D, 2D, 1D ill. by Harvey Weiss. Crowell, 1975. Subj: Concepts – measurement. Concepts – perspective. Concepts – shape.

You think it's fun to be a clown! ill. by Ray Cruz. Doubleday, 1980. Subj: Circus. Clowns, jesters. Poetry, rhyme.

Adler, Irene *see* Storr, Catherine

Adoff, Arnold. *Big sister tells me that I'm black* ill. by Lorenzo Lynch. Holt, 1976. Subj: Ethnic groups in the U.S. – Afro-Americans. Family life. Poetry, rhyme.

Birds ill. by Troy Howell. Lippincott, 1982. Subj: Birds. Poetry, rhyme.

Black is brown is tan ill. by Emily Arnold McCully. Harper, 1973. Subj: Family life. Marriage, interracial. Poetry, rhyme.

Ma nDa La ill. by Emily Arnold McCully. Harper, 1971. Subj: Family life. Foreign lands – Africa.

Make a circle, keep us in: poems for a good day ill. by Ronald Himler. Delacorte Pr., 1975. Subj: Family life. Night. Poetry, rhyme. Weather – storms.

Tornado! poems ill. by Ronald Himler. Delacorte Pr., 1977. Subj: Poetry, rhyme. Weather – storms.

Where wild Willie? ill. by Emily Arnold McCully. Harper, 1978. Subj: Behavior – running away. City. Ethnic groups in the U.S. – Afro-Americans. Poetry, rhyme.

Adshead, Gladys L. *Brownies - hush!* ill. by Elizabeth Orton Jones. Oxford Univ. Pr., 1938. Subj: Character traits – helpfulness. Elves and little people. Folk and fairy tales.

Brownies - it's Christmas ill. by Velma Ilsley. Oxford Univ. Pr., 1955. Subj: Elves and little people. Holidays – Christmas.

Brownies - they're moving ill. by Richard Lebenson. Walck, 1970. Subj: Character traits – helpfulness. Elves and little people. Moving.

Æsop. *Æesop's fables* sel. and ill. by Gaynor Chapman. Atheneum, 1972. Subj: Folk and fairy tales.

Æsop's fables ill. by Heidi Holder. Viking, 1981. Subj: Folk and fairy tales.

Æsop's fables sel. and adapt. by Louis Untermeyer; ill. by Alice and Martin Provensen. Golden Pr., 1965. Subj: Folk and fairy tales.

Æsop's fables retold by Carol Watson; ill. by Nick Price. Usborne, 1982. Subj: Folk and fairy tales.

Æsop's fables retold by Anne Terry White; ill. by Helen Siegl. Random House, 1964. Subj: Folk and fairy tales.

The donkey ride (Showalter, Jean B)

The fables of Æsop ed. by Ruth Spriggs; ill. by Frank Baber. Rand McNally, 1975. Subj: Folk and fairy tales.

The hare and the frogs adapt. and ill. by William Stobbs. Merrimack, 1979. Subj: Animals – rabbits. Folk and fairy tales. Frogs and toads.

The hare and the tortoise ill. by Paul Galdone. Whittlesey House, 1962. Subj: Animals – rabbits. Folk and fairy tales. Reptiles – turtles. Sports – racing.

The lion and the mouse: an Æsop fable ill. by Ed Young. Doubleday, 1980. Subj: Animals – lions. Animals – mice. Character traits – helpfulness. Folk and fairy tales.

The miller, his son and their donkey ill. by Roger Antoine Duvoisin. McGraw-Hill, 1962. Subj: Animals – donkeys. Character traits – perseverance. Humor. Folk and fairy tales.

Once in a wood: ten tales from Æsop adapt. and ill. by Eve Rice. Greenwillow, 1980. Subj: Folk and fairy tales. Poetry, rhyme.

Tales from Æsop retold and ill. by Harold Jones. Watts, 1982. Subj: Folk and fairy tales.

Three fox fables ill. by Paul Galdone. Seabury Pr., 1971. Subj: Animals – foxes. Behavior – trickery. Character traits – flattery. Folk and fairy tales.

The town mouse and the country mouse ill. by Lorinda Bryan Cauley. Putnam's, 1984. Subj: Animals – mice. Folk and fairy tales.

The town mouse and the country mouse ill. by Paul Galdone. McGraw-Hill, 1971. Subj: Animals – mice. Folk and fairy tales.

The town mouse and the country mouse ill. by Tom Garcia. Troll Assoc., 1979. Subj: Animals – mice. Folk and fairy tales.

Twelve tales from Æsop (Carle, Eric)

Afanas'ev, Aleksandr. *Russian folk tales* tr. by Robert Chandler; ill. by Ivan I. Bilibin. Random House, 1980. Subj: Folk and fairy tales. Foreign lands – Russia.

Agard, John. *Dig away two-hole Tim* ill. by Jennifer Northway. Bodley Head, 1982. Subj: Behavior – misbehavior. Foreign lands – Guyana.

Agee, Jon. *Ellsworth* ill. by author. Pantheon, 1983. Subj: Activities – playing. Animals – dogs. Imagination.

Agostinelli, Maria Enrica. *I know something you don't know* ill. by author. Watts, 1970. Translation of Ich weiss etwas, was du nicht weisst. Subj: Games. Participation.

On wings of love: the United Nations declaration of the rights of the child ill. by author. Collins World, 1979. Subj: Birds – doves. Emotions – love.

Ahlberg, Allan. *The baby's catalogue* (Ahlberg, Janet)

Burglar Bill (Ahlberg, Janet)

Cops and robbers ill. by Janet Ahlberg. Greenwillow, 1979. Subj: Careers – police officers. Crime. Foreign lands – England. Holidays – Christmas. Poetry, rhyme.

Each peach pear plum (Ahlberg, Janet)

Funnybones (Ahlberg, Janet)

The little worm book (Ahlberg, Janet)

Peek-a-boo! (Ahlberg, Janet)

Ahlberg, Janet. *The baby's catalogue* by Janet and Allan Ahlberg; ill. by authors. Little, 1983. Subj: Babies. Family life.

Burglar Bill by Janet and Allan Ahlberg; ill. by authors. Greenwillow, 1977. Subj: Crime.

Each peach pear plum: an "I spy" story by Janet and Allan Ahlberg; ill. by authors. Viking, 1978. Subj: Games. Poetry, rhyme.

Funnybones by Janet and Allan Ahlberg; ill. by authors. Greenwillow, 1981. Subj: Activities – playing. Ghosts. Night.

The little worm book by Janet and Allan Ahlberg; ill. by authors. Viking, 1980. Subj: Animals – worms. Humor.

Peek-a-boo! by Janet and Allan Ahlberg; ill. by authors. Viking, 1981. Subj: Babies. Family life. Format, unusual. Games. Poetry, rhyme.

Aho, Jennifer J. *Learning about sex: a guide for children and their parents* by Jennifer J. Aho and John W. Petras; ill. by Jennifer J. Aho. Holt, 1978. Subj: Family life. Science.

Aichinger, Helga. *The shepherd* ill. by author. Crowell, 1967. Subj: Holidays – Christmas. Religion.

Aiken, Conrad. *Tom, Sue and the clock* ill. by Julie Maas. Macmillan, 1966. Subj: Clocks. Poetry, rhyme. Time.

Aiken, Joan. *Arabel and Mortimer* ill. by Quentin Blake. Doubleday, 1981. Subj: Birds – ravens. Imagination. Pets.

Ainsworth, Ruth. *The mysterious Baba and her magic caravan* ill. by Joan Hickson. Deutsch, dist. by Elsevier-Dutton, 1980. Subj: Character traits – generosity. Toys – dolls.

Aitken, Amy. *Kate and Mona in the jungle* ill. by author. Bradbury Pr., 1981. Subj: Animals. Imagination. Jungle. Zoos.

Ruby! ill. by author. Bradbury Pr., 1979. Subj: Careers. Imagination.

Ruby, the red knight ill. by author. Bradbury Pr., 1983. Subj: Character traits – bravery. Imagination. Royalty.

Akens, Floyd *see* Baum, L. Frank (Lyman Frank)

Akers, Floyd *see* Baum, L. Frank (Lyman Frank)

Alan, Sandy. *The plaid peacock* ill. by Kelly Oechsli. Pantheon, 1965. Subj: Birds – peacocks, peahens. Foreign lands – India.

Albert, Burton. *Mine, yours, ours* ill. by Lois Axeman. Albert Whitman, 1977. Subj: Behavior – sharing. Concepts.

Alborough, Jez. *Bare bear* ill. by author. Knopf, 1984. Subj: Activities – bathing. Animals – bears. Humor. Poetry, rhyme.

Alda, Arlene. *Arlene Alda's ABC* photos. by author. Celestial Arts, 1981. Subj: ABC books.

Matthew and his dad photos. by author. Simon and Schuster, 1983. Subj: Clothing. Family life – fathers.

Sonya's mommy works photos. by author. Messner, 1982. Subj: Activities – working. Family life – mothers.

Alden, Laura. *Learning about fairies* ill. by Krystyna Stasiak. Childrens Pr., 1982. Subj: Elves and little people. Fairies. Folk and fairy tales. Goblins.

When? ill. by Lois Axeman. Childrens Pr., 1983. Subj: Character traits – curiosity. Character traits – questioning.

Alderson, Brian W. *Cakes and custard*

Alderson, Sue Ann. *Bonnie McSmithers is at it again!* ill. by Fiona Garrick. Tree Frog Pr., 1980. Subj: Activities. Character traits – individuality. Poetry, rhyme.

Aldis, Dorothy. *All together: a child's treasury of verse* ill. by Helen D. Jameson, Marjorie Flack and Margaret Freeman. Putnam's, 1952. Subj: Poetry, rhyme.

Before things happen ill. by Margaret Freeman. Putnam's, 1939. Subj: Poetry, rhyme.

Hello day ill. by Susan Elson. Putnam's, 1959. Subj: Poetry, rhyme.

Quick as a wink ill. by Peggy Westphal. Putnam's, 1960. Subj: Insects. Poetry, rhyme.

Aldridge, Alan. *The butterfly ball and the grasshopper's feast* by Alan Aldridge, with verses by William Plomer and nature notes by Richard Fitter; rev. by Edward G. Atkins; ill. by William Mulready. Grossman Pub., 1975. Subj: Animals. Insects. Insects – butterflies, caterpillars. Insects – grasshoppers. Poetry, rhyme. Science.

Aldridge, Josephine Haskell. *The best of friends* ill. by Betty Peterson. Parnassus, 1963. Subj: Animals. Friendship.

Fisherman's luck ill. by Ruth Robbins. Parnassus, 1966. Subj: Careers – fishermen. Character traits – luck. Sports – fishing. Weather – storms.

A peony and a periwinkle ill. by Ruth Robbins. Parnassus, 1961. Subj: Sports – fishing.

Aleichem, Sholom. *Hannukah money* ill. by Uri Shulevitz. Greenwillow, 1978. Subj: Folk and fairy tales. Foreign lands. Holidays – Hanukkah. Jewish culture.

Alexander, Anna Barbara Cooke *see* Alexander, Anne

Alexander, Anne. *ABC of cars and trucks* ill. by Ninon. Doubleday, 1956. Subj: ABC books. Automobiles. Poetry, rhyme. Trucks.

Boats and ships from A to Z ill. by Will Huntington. Rand McNally, 1961. Subj: Boats, ships. Poetry, rhyme.

I want to whistle ill. by Abner Graboff. Abelard-Schuman, 1958. Subj: Activities –·whistling. Poetry, rhyme.

My daddy and I ill. by Cyril Satorsky. Abelard-Schuman, 1961. Subj: Counting. Poetry, rhyme.

Noise in the night ill. by Abner Graboff. Rand McNally, 1960. Subj: Emotions – fear. Night. Noise, sounds.

Alexander, Cecil Frances. *All things bright and beautiful: a hymn* ill. by Leo Politi. Scribner's, 1962. Subj: Music. Religion. Songs.

Alexander, Lloyd. *Coll and his white pig* ill. by Evaline Ness. Holt, 1965. Subj: Animals – pigs. Folk and fairy tales.

The king's fountain ill. by Ezra Jack Keats. Dutton, 1971. Subj: Folk and fairy tales. Poverty. Royalty.

The truthful harp ill. by Evaline Ness. Holt, 1967. Subj: Character traits – honesty. Folk and fairy tales. Music.

Alexander, Martha G. *And my mean old mother will be sorry, Blackboard Bear* ill. by author. Dial Pr., 1972. Subj: Animals – bears. Behavior – running away. Emotions – anger. Imagination – imaginary friends.

Blackboard Bear ill. by author. Dial Pr., 1969. Subj: Animals – bears. Imagination – imaginary friends.

Bobo's dream ill. by author. Dial Pr., 1970. Subj: Animals – dogs. Dreams. Ethnic groups in the U.S. – Afro-Americans. Imagination. Wordless.

How my library grew by Dinah ill. by author. H. W. Wilson, 1982. Subj: Libraries.

I sure am glad to see you, Blackboard Bear ill. by author. Dial Pr., 1976. Subj: Animals – bears. Behavior – bullying. Imagination – imaginary friends.

I'll be the horse if you'll play with me ill. by author. Dial Pr., 1975. Subj: Activities – playing. Behavior – fighting, arguing. Sibling rivalry. Family life.

I'll protect you from the jungle beasts ill. by author. Dial Pr., 1973. Subj: Emotions – fear. Imagination – imaginary friends. Problem solving. Sleep. Toys – teddy bears.

Maggie's moon ill. by author. Dial Pr., 1982. Subj: Animals – dogs. Moon. Night.

Marty McGee's space lab, no girls allowed ill. by author. Dial Pr., 1981. Subj: Family life. Imagination. Sibling rivalry. Space and space ships.

Maybe a monster ill. by author. Dial Pr., 1968. Subj: Emotions – fear. Monsters.

Move over, Twerp ill. by author. Dial Pr., 1981. Subj: Behavior – bullying. Character traits – perseverance. Humor. Problem solving. School.

No ducks in our bathtub ill. by author. Dial Pr., 1973. Subj: Frogs and toads. Pets.

Nobody asked me if I wanted a baby sister ill. by author. Dial Pr., 1971. Subj: Babies. Emotions – envy, jealousy. Sibling rivalry.

Out! Out! Out! ill. by author. Dial Pr., 1968. Subj: Birds. Problem solving. Wordless.

Pigs say oink: a first book of sounds ill. by author. Random House, 1978. Subj: Animals. Noise, sounds.

Sabrina ill. by author. Dial Pr., 1971. Subj: Emotions – embarrassment. Names. School.

The story grandmother told ill. by author. Dial Pr., 1969. Subj: Ethnic groups in the U.S. – Afro-Americans. Family life – grandparents, great-grandparents. Toys.

3 magic flip books: The magic hat; The magic box; The magic picture ill. by author. Dial Pr., 1984. Subj: Format, unusual. Magic. Wordless.

We never get to do anything ill. by author. Dial Pr., 1970. Subj: Behavior – boredom. Character traits – perseverance. Games. Problem solving. Sports – swimming.

We're in big trouble, Blackboard Bear ill. by author. Dial Pr., 1980. Subj: Animals – bears. Behavior – misbehavior. Imagination – imaginary friends. Night. Problem solving.

When the new baby comes, I'm moving out ill. by author. Dial Pr., 1979. Subj: Babies. Emotions – envy, jealousy. Sibling rivalry.

Alexander, Sue. *Dear Phoebe* ill. by Eileen Christelow. Little, 1984. Subj: Animals – mice. Behavior – growing up. Emotions – loneliness. Emotions – love. Family life.

Marc the Magnificent ill. by Tomie de Paola. Pantheon, 1978. Subj: Character traits – optimism. Magic.

More Witch, Goblin, and Ghost stories ill. by Jeanette Winter. Pantheon, 1978. Subj: Ghosts. Goblins. Witches.

Nadia the willful ill. by Lloyd Bloom. Pantheon, 1983. Subj: Character traits – willfulness. Emotions – love. Emotions – sadness. Family life. Foreign lands – Arabia.

Seymour the prince ill. by Lillian Hoban. Pantheon, 1979. Subj: Clubs, gangs. Theater.

Small plays for special days ill. by Tom Huffman. Seabury Pr., 1977. Subj: Holidays. Theater.

Small plays for you and a friend ill. by Olivia Cole. Houghton, 1974. Subj: Friendship. Theater.

Witch, Goblin, and Ghost in the haunted woods ill. by Jeanette Winter. Pantheon, 1981. Subj: Ghosts. Goblins. Witches.

Witch, Goblin and Ghost's book of things to do ill. by Jeanette Winter. Pantheon, 1982. Subj: Activities. Ghosts. Goblins. Witches.

Witch, Goblin and sometimes Ghost ill. by Jeanette Winter. Pantheon, 1976. Subj: Behavior – forgetfulness. Emotions – fear. Friendship. Ghosts. Goblins. Witches.

World famous Muriel ill. by Chris L. Demarest. Little, 1984. Subj: Birthdays. Humor. Problem solving.

Alger, Leclaire. *All in the morning early* ill. by Evaline Ness. Holt, 1963. Subj: Caldecott award honor book. Folk and fairy tales. Foreign lands – Scotland. Poetry, rhyme. Songs.

Always room for one more ill. by Nonny Hogrogian. Holt, 1965. Children's story based on the Scottish ballad of the same title. Subj: Caldecott award book. Cumulative tales. Folk and fairy tales. Foreign lands – Scotland. Houses. Music.

Kellyburn Braes ill. by Evaline Ness. Harcourt, 1968. Subj: Devil. Foreign lands – Scotland. Foreign languages. Music. Poetry, rhyme. Songs.

Aliki. *At Mary Bloom's* ill. by author. Greenwillow, 1976. Subj: Animals – mice. Babies.

Corn is maize: the gift of the Indians ill. by author. Crowell, 1976. Subj: Activities – gardening. Ethnic groups in the U.S. – Indians. Plants. Science.

Digging up dinosaurs ill. by author. Crowell, 1981. Subj: Activities – digging. Dinosaurs. Humor. Science.

Diogenes: the story of the Greek philosopher ill. by author. Prentice-Hall, 1969. Subj: Character traits – honesty. Folk and fairy tales. Foreign lands – Greece.

The eggs: a Greek folk tale ill. by adapt. Pantheon, 1969. Subj: Behavior – greed. Character traits – cleverness. Folk and fairy tales. Foreign lands – Greece. Humor.

Fossils tell of long ago ill. by author. Crowell, 1972. Subj: Dinosaurs. Science.

George and the cherry tree ill. by author. Dial Pr., 1964. Subj: Character traits – bravery. Folk and fairy tales. U.S. history.

I wish I was sick, too! ill. by author. Greenwillow, 1976. Subj: Behavior – wishing. Illness.

June 7! ill. by author. Macmillan, 1972. Subj: Birthdays. Cumulative tales. Family life.

Keep your mouth closed, dear ill. by author. Dial Pr., 1966. Subj: Behavior – carelessness. Family life. Reptiles – alligators, crocodiles.

The long lost coelacanth and other living fossils ill. by author. Crowell, 1973. Subj: Fish. Science.

The many lives of Benjamin Franklin ill. by author. Prentice-Hall, 1977. Subj: U.S. history.

Mummies made in Egypt ill. by author. Crowell, 1979. Subj: Death. Foreign lands – Egypt. Religion.

My five senses ill. by author. Crowell, 1962. Subj: Senses.

My hands ill. by author. Crowell, 1962. Subj: Anatomy. Science.

My visit to the dinosaurs ill. by author. Crowell, 1969. Subj: Dinosaurs. Museums.

The story of Johnny Appleseed ill. by author. Prentice-Hall, 1963. Subj: Activities – gardening. Character traits – generosity. Folk and fairy tales. Trees. U.S. history.

The story of William Penn ill. by author. Prentice-Hall, 1964. Subj: Character traits – kindness. U.S. history.

Three gold pieces: a Greek folk tale ill. by author. Pantheon, 1967. Subj: Character traits – luck. Folk and fairy tales. Foreign lands – Greece.

The twelve months: a Greek folktale ill. by adapt. Greenwillow, 1978. Subj: Behavior – dissatisfaction. Character traits – optimism. Folk and fairy tales. Foreign lands – Greece.

The two of them ill. by author. Greenwillow, 1979. Subj: Character traits – helpfulness. Character traits – loyalty. Family life – grandparents, great-grandparents.

Use your head, dear ill. by author. Greenwillow, 1983. Subj: Behavior – forgetfulness. Birthdays. Reptiles – alligators, crocodiles.

We are best friends ill. by author. Greenwillow, 1982. Subj: Emotions – anger. Emotions – loneliness. Friendship. Moving.

A weed is a flower: the life of George Washington Carver ill. by author. Prentice-Hall, 1965. Subj: Character traits – perseverance. Ethnic groups in the U.S. – Afro-Americans. Science. U.S. history.

Wild and woolly mammoths ill. by author. Crowell, 1977. Subj: Animals. Science.

The wish workers ill. by author. Dial Pr., 1962. Subj: Behavior – dissatisfaction. Behavior – wishing. Birds. Magic.

Allamand, Pascale. *The animals who changed their colors* ill. by Elizabeth Watson Taylor. Morrow, 1979. Subj: Animals. Behavior – imitation. Character traits – individuality. Concepts – color. Humor.

Cocoa beans and daisies: how chocolate is made photos. by author. Warne, 1978. Subj: Food. Foreign lands – Switzerland.

The little goat in the mountains tr. by Michael Bullock; ill. by author. Warne, 1978. Subj: Animals – goats.

Allan, Ted. *Willie the squowse* ill. by Quentin Blake. Hastings, 1978. Subj: Animals. Behavior – hiding things. Humor. Money.

Allard, Harry. *Bumps in the night* ill. by James Marshall. Doubleday, 1979. Subj: Animals. Ghosts. Noise, sounds.

I will not go to market today ill. by James Marshall. Dial Pr., 1979. Subj: Birds – chickens. Shopping.

It's so nice to have a wolf around the house ill. by James Marshall. Doubleday, 1977. Subj: Crime. Old age. Pets.

May I stay? ill. by F. A. Fitzgerald. Prentice-Hall, 1977. Subj: Character traits – questioning. Folk and fairy tales. Foreign lands – Germany. Foreign lands – Norway.

Miss Nelson has a field day ill. by James Marshall. Houghton, 1985. Subj: Behavior – secrets. Humor. School.

Miss Nelson is back by Harry Allard and James Marshall; ill. by James Marshall. Houghton, 1982. Subj: Behavior – misbehavior. Careers – teachers. School.

Miss Nelson is missing! by Harry Allard and James Marshall; ill. by James Marshall. Houghton, 1977. Subj: Behavior – misbehavior. Careers – teachers. School.

The Stupids die ill. by James Marshall. Houghton, 1981. Subj: Behavior – misunderstanding. Humor.

The Stupids have a ball by Harry Allard and James Marshall; ill. by James Marshall. Houghton, 1978. Subj: Humor. Parties.

The Stupids step out ill. by James Marshall. Houghton, 1974. Subj: Humor.

There's a party at Mona's tonight ill. by James Marshall. Doubleday, 1981. Subj: Animals – pigs. Behavior – trickery. Humor. Parties.

Three is company (Waechter, Friedrich Karl)

Allen, Allyn *see* Eberle, Irmengarde

Allen, Frances Charlotte. *Little hippo* ill. by Laura Jean Allen. Putnam's, 1971. Subj: Animals – hippopotami. Emotions – sadness.

Allen, Gertrude E. *Everyday animals* ill. by author. Houghton, 1961. Subj: Animals. Forest, woods. Science.

Allen, Jeffrey. *Bonzini! the tattooed man* ill. by James Marshall. Little, 1976. Subj: Circus. Clowns, jesters.

Mary Alice, operator number 9 ill. by James Marshall. Little, 1975. Subj: Activities – working. Animals. Birds – ducks. Careers – telephone operators. Telephone. Time.

The secret life of Mr. Weird ill. by Ned Delaney. Little, 1982. Subj: Animals – dogs. Behavior – dissatisfaction. Behavior – seeking better things. Games. Imagination.

Allen, Jonathan. *A bad case of animal nonsense* ill. by author. Godine, 1981. Subj: Animals. Humor. Poetry, rhyme.

Allen, Laura Jean. *Ottie and the star* ill. by author. Harper, 1979. Subj: Animals – otters. Family life. Sea and seashore. Stars.

Rollo and Tweedy and the case of the missing cheese ill. by author. Harper, 1983. Subj: Animals – mice. Food. Foreign lands – France. Problem solving.

Allen, Linda. *Mr. Simkin's grandma* ill. by Loretta Lustig. Morrow, 1979. Subj: Family life – grandparents, great-grandparents. Humor.

Mrs. Simkin's bed ill. by Loretta Lustig. Morrow, 1980. Subj: Animals. Humor.

Allen, Marjorie N. *One, two, three - ah-choo!* ill. by Dick Gackenbach. Coward, 1980. Subj: Animals. Humor. Pets.

The remarkable ride of Israel Bissell... as related to Molly the crow (Schick, Alice)

Allen, Martha Dickson. *Real life monsters* ill. by author. Prentice-Hall, 1979. Subj: Animals. Monsters. Science.

Allen, Pamela. *Bertie and the bear* ill. by author. Coward, 1984. Subj: Activities – dancing. Animals – bears. Animals – dogs. Noise, sounds. Royalty.

Mr. Archimedes' bath ill. by author. Lothrop, 1980. Subj: Activities – bathing. Animals. Humor. Science.

Who sank the boat? ill. by author. Coward, 1983. Subj: Animals. Boats, ships. Poetry, rhyme. Science.

Allen, Robert. *Numbers: a first counting book* ill. by Mottke Weissman. Platt, 1968. Subj: Counting.

Round and square ill. by Philippe Thomas. Platt, 1965. Subj: Concepts – shape.

The zoo book: a child's world of animals photos. by Peter Sahula. Platt, 1968. Subj: Animals. Zoos.

Allen, Thomas B. *Where children live* ill. by author. Prentice-Hall, 1980. Subj: Foreign lands.

Allington, Richard L. *Autumn* by Richard L. Allington and Kathleen Krull; ill. by Bruce Bond. Raintree, 1981. Subj: Seasons – fall. Weather.

Feelings by Richard L. Allington and Kathleen Cowles; ill. by Brian Cody. Raintree, 1981. Subj: Activities. Emotions.

Hearing by Richard L. Allington and Kathleen Cowles; ill. by Wayne Dober. Raintree, 1981. Subj: Activities. Senses.

Looking by Richard L. Allington and Kathleen Cowles; ill. by Bill Bober. Raintree, 1981. Subj: Activities. Senses.

Smelling by Richard L. Allington and Kathleen Cowles; ill. by Rick Thrun. Raintree, 1981. Subj: Activities. Senses.

Spring by Richard L. Allington and Kathleen Krull; ill. by Lynn Uhde. Raintree, 1981. Subj: Seasons – spring. Weather.

Summer by Richard L. Allington and Kathleen Krull; ill. by Dennis Hockerman. Raintree, 1981. Subj: Seasons – summer. Weather.

Tasting by Richard L. Allington and Kathleen Cowles; ill. by Noel Spangler. Raintree, 1981. Subj: Activities. Senses.

Touching by Richard L. Allington and Kathleen Cowles; ill. by Yoshi Miyake. Raintree, 1981. Subj: Activities. Senses.

Winter by Richard L. Allington and Kathleen Krull; ill. by John Wallner. Raintree, 1981. Subj: Seasons – winter. Weather.

Allison, Alida. *The toddler's potty book* by Alida Allison and Paula Sapphire. Price Stern Sloan, 1981, 1979. Subj: Behavior – growing up.

Allred, Mary. *Grandmother Poppy and the funny-looking bird* ill. by Paul Behrens. Broadman Pr., 1981. Subj: Birds. Character traits – kindness to animals. Family life – grandparents, great-grandparents.

Allstrom, Elizabeth C. *Songs along the way* ill. by Mel Silverman. Abingdon Pr., 1961. Subj: Foreign lands – Israel. Poetry, rhyme. Religion.

Althea. *Castle life* ill. by Maureen Galvani. Merrimack, 1980. Subj: Middle ages.

Jeremy Mouse and cat ill. by author. Merrimack, 1980. Subj: Animals – cats. Animals – mice. Behavior – trickery.

Ambler, Christopher Gifford. *Ten little foxhounds.* Children's Pr., 1968. Subj: Animals – dogs. Counting. Foreign lands – England. Poetry, rhyme.

Ambrus, Gyozo Laszlo *see* Ambrus, Victor G.

Ambrus, Victor G. *Brave soldier Janosch* ill. by author. Harcourt, 1967. Subj: Careers – military. Foreign lands – Hungary. War.

Country wedding ill. by author. Addison-Wesley, 1975. Subj: Animals – foxes. Animals – wolves. Food. Weddings.

Grandma, Felix, and Mustapha Biscuit ill. by author. W. Morrow, 1982. Subj: Animals – cats. Animals – hamsters. Family life – grandparents, great-grandparents. Humor.

The little cockerel ill. by author. Harcourt, 1968. Subj: Birds – chickens. Character traits – perseverance. Folk and fairy tales.

Mishka ill. by author. Warne, 1978. Subj: Animals – elephants. Character traits – perseverance. Circus. Music.

The seven skinny goats ill. by author. Harcourt, 1969. Subj: Activities – dancing. Animals – goats. Folk and fairy tales. Humor. Music.

The Sultan's bath ill. by author. Oxford Univ. Pr., 1971. Subj: Activities – bathing. Folk and fairy tales. Foreign lands – India. Royalty.

The three poor tailors ill. by author. Harcourt, 1966. Subj: Activities – whistling. Animals – goats. Careers – tailors. Folk and fairy tales. Foreign lands – Hungary. Poverty.

Ames, Gerald. *Spooky tricks* (Wyler, Rose)

Ames, Mildred. *The wonderful box* ill. by Richard Cuffari. Dutton, 1978. Subj: Character traits – curiosity. Problem solving.

Ames, Rose *see* Wyler, Rose

Amoit, Pierre. *Bijou the little bear.* Coward, 1950. Subj: Animals – bears. Circus. Clowns, jesters.

Amoss, Berthe. *It's not your birthday* ill. by author. Harper, 1966. Subj: Birthdays. Sibling rivalry.

Tom in the middle ill. by author. Harper, 1968. Subj: Family life. Sibling rivalry.

Ancona, George. *Dancing is* ill. by author. Dutton, 1981. Subj: Activities – dancing.

Handtalk (Charlip, Remy)

It's a baby! ill. by author. Dutton, 1979. Subj: Babies.

Ancona, Mary Beth. *Handtalk* (Charlip, Remy)

Anders, Rebecca. *A look at death* photos. by Maria S. Forrai; foreword by Robert C. Slater. Lerner, 1978. Subj: Death.

A look at prejudice and understanding ill. by Maria S. Forrai. Lerner, 1976. Subj: Prejudice.

Andersen, H. C. (Hans Christian). *The emperor and the nightingale* ill. by James Watling. Troll Assoc., 1979. Subj: Birds – nightingales. Character traits – freedom. Folk and fairy tales. Foreign lands – China.

The emperor's new clothes ill. by Pamela Baldwin-Ford. Troll Assoc., 1979. Translation of Kejserens nye klæder. Subj: Character traits – pride. Clothing. Folk and fairy tales. Humor. Imagination. Royalty.

The emperor's new clothes ill. by Erik Blegvad. Harcourt, 1959. Translation of Kejserens nye klæder by Erik Blegvad. Subj: Character traits – pride. Clothing. Folk and fairy tales. Humor. Imagination. Royalty.

The emperor's new clothes ill. by Virginia Lee Burton. Houghton, 1949. Translation of Kejserens nye klæder. Subj: Character traits – pride. Clothing. Folk and fairy tales. Humor. Imagination. Royalty.

The emperor's new clothes ill. by Jack and Irene Delano. Random House, 1971. Translation of Kejserens nye klæder. Text adapted from Hans Christian Andersen and other sources by Jean Van Leeuwen. Subj: Character traits – pride. Clothing. Folk and fairy tales. Humor. Imagination. Royalty.

The emperor's new clothes ill. by Birte Dietz; tr. by M. R. James; adapt. by Jean Van Leeuwen. Van Nostrand, 1972. Translation of Kejserens nye klæder. Subj: Character traits – pride. Clothing. Folk and fairy tales. Humor. Imagination. Royalty.

The emperor's new clothes ill. by Jack Kent. Four Winds Pr., 1977. Adaptation of Kejserens nye klæder by Ruth Belov Gross. Subj: Character traits – pride. Clothing. Folk and fairy tales. Humor. Imagination. Royalty.

The emperor's new clothes ill. by Monika Laimgruber. Addison-Wesley, 1973. Translation of Kejserens nye klæder. Subj: Character traits – pride. Clothing. Folk and fairy tales. Humor. Imagination. Royalty.

The emperor's new clothes ill. by Anne F. Rockwell. Crowell, 1982. Translation of Kejserens nye klæder by H. W. Dulcken. Subj: Character traits – pride. Clothing. Folk and fairy tales. Humor. Imagination. Royalty.

The emperor's new clothes ill. by Nadine Bernard Westcott. Little, 1984. Subj: Character traits – pride. Clothing. Folk and fairy tales. Humor. Imagination. Royalty.

The emperor's nightingale tr. by Erik Haugaard; ill. by Georges Lemoine. Schocken, 1981. Subj: Birds – nightingales. Character traits – freedom. Folk and fairy tales. Foreign lands – China.

The fir tree ill. by Nancy Ekholm Burkert. Harper, 1970. Translation of Grantræet by H. W. Dulcken. Subj: Folk and fairy tales. Holidays – Christmas. Trees.

The little match girl ill. by Blair Lent. Houghton, 1968. Translation of Den lille pige med svovlstikkerne. Subj: Folk and fairy tales. Holidays – New Year's. Poverty.

The little mermaid tr. by Eva Le Gallienne; ill. by Edward Frascino. Harper, 1971. Subj: Folk and fairy tales. Mythical creatures.

The little mermaid ill. by Dorothy Pulis Lathrop. Macmillan, 1939. Subj: Folk and fairy tales. Mythical creatures.

The little mermaid ill. by Josef Paleček. Faber, 1981. Translation of Den lille havfrue by M. R. James. Subj: Folk and fairy tales. Mythical creatures.

The nightingale ill. by Harold Berson. Lippincott, 1962. Subj: Birds – nightingales. Character traits – freedom. Folk and fairy tales. Foreign lands – China.

The nightingale tr. by Eva Le Gallienne; ill. by Nancy Ekholm Burkert. Harper, 1965. Subj: Birds – nightingales. Character traits – freedom. Folk and fairy tales. Foreign lands – China.

The old man is always right ill. by Feodor Rojankovsky. Harper, 1940. Subj: Activities – trading. Folk and fairy tales. Humor.

The princess and the pea ill. by Dick Gackenbach. Macmillan, 1983. Subj: Folk and fairy tales. Royalty.

The princess and the pea ill. by Paul Galdone. Seabury Pr., 1978. Translation of Den prindsessen paa aerten. Subj: Folk and fairy tales. Royalty. Sleep.

The princess and the pea adapt. and ill. by Janet Stevens. Holiday, 1982. Subj: Folk and fairy tales. Royalty.

The red shoes tr. from Danish by Anthea Bell; ill. by Chihiro Iwasaki. Alphabet Pr., 1983. Subj: Activities – dancing. Angels. Character traits – pride. Clothing.

The snow queen ill. by Toma Bogdanovic. Scroll Pr., n.d. An adapt. by Naomi Lewis of Sneedrenningen. Subj: Character traits – bravery. Emotions – love. Folk and fairy tales. Foreign lands – Denmark.

The snow queen ill. by June Atkin Corwin. Atheneum, 1968. Subj: Character traits – bravery. Emotions – love. Folk and fairy tales.

The snow queen adapt. by Amy Ehrlich; ill. by Susan Jeffers. Dial Pr., 1982. Subj: Character traits – bravery. Emotions – love. Folk and fairy tales.

The snow queen adapt. by Naomi Lewis; ill. by Errol Le Cain. Viking, 1979. Subj: Character traits – bravery. Emotions – love. Folk and fairy tales.

The snow queen and other stories from Hans Andersen ill. by Edmund Dulac. Doubleday, 1976. Subj: Folk and fairy tales.

The steadfast tin soldier ill. by Thomas Di Grazia. Prentice-Hall, 1981. Subj: Folk and fairy tales. Toys – soldiers.

The steadfast tin soldier ill. by Paul Galdone. Houghton, 1979. Translation of Den standhaftige tinsoldat. Subj: Folk and fairy tales. Toys – soldiers.

The steadfast tin soldier ill. by Monika Laimgruber. Atheneum, 1971. Translation of Den standhaftige tinsoldat. Subj: Folk and fairy tales. Toys – soldiers.

The steadfast tin soldier ill. by Alain Vaës. Little, 1983. Translation of Den standhaftige tinsoldat. Subj: Folk and fairy tales. Toys – soldiers.

The swineherd ill. by Erik Blegvad. Harcourt, 1958. Translation of Den svinedrengen by Erik Blegvad. Subj: Folk and fairy tales. Toys – soldiers.

The swineherd ill. by Lisbeth Zwerger. Morrow, 1982. Translation of Den svinedrengen by Anthea Bell. Subj: Folk and fairy tales. Toys – soldiers.

Thumbelina ill. by Adrienne Adams. Scribner's, 1961. Translation of Tommelise by R. P. Keigwin. Subj: Character traits – smallness. Folk and fairy tales.

Thumbelina ill. by Susan Jeffers; retold by Amy Ehrlich. Dial Pr., 1979. Translation of Tommelise. Subj: Character traits – smallness. Folk and fairy tales.

Thumbelina ill. by Christine Willis Nigognos-sian. Troll Assoc., 1979. Translation of Tommelise. Subj: Character traits – smallness. Folk and fairy tales.

Thumbelina ill. by Gustaf Tenggren. Simon and Schuster, 1953. Translation of Tommelise. Subj: Character traits – smallness. Folk and fairy tales.

Thumbelina ill. by Lisbeth Zwerger. Morrow, 1980. Translation of Tommelise by Richard and Clara Winston. Subj: Character traits – smallness. Folk and fairy tales.

The ugly duckling ill. by Adrienne Adams. Scribner's, 1965. Translation of Den grimme ælling by R. P. Keigwin. Subj: Birds – ducks. Birds – swans. Character traits – appearance. Character traits – being different. Folk and fairy tales.

The ugly duckling ill. by Lorinda Bryan Cauley. Harcourt, 1979. Subj: Birds – ducks. Birds – swans. Character traits – appearance. Character traits – being different. Folk and fairy tales.

The ugly duckling ill. by Tadasu Izawa and Shigemi Hijikata. Grosset, 1971. Translation of Den grimme ælling by Phyllis Paleček. Subj: Birds – ducks. Birds – swans. Character traits – appearance. Character traits – being different. Folk and fairy tales.

The ugly duckling ill. by Johannes Larsen. Ward, 1956. Translation of Den grimme ælling by R. P. Keigwin. Subj: Birds – ducks. Birds – swans. Character traits – appearance. Character traits – being different. Folk and fairy tales.

The ugly duckling adapt. by Phyllis Hoffman; ill. by Josef Paleček. Abelard-Schuman, 1972. Subj: Birds – ducks. Birds – swans. Character traits – appearance. Character traits – being different. Folk and fairy tales.

The wild swans tr. from Danish by Naomi Lewis; ill. by Angela Barrett. Harper, 1984. Subj: Birds – swans. Folk and fairy tales. Magic.

The wild swans retold by Amy Ehrlich; ill. by Susan Jeffers. Dial Pr., 1981. Subj: Birds – swans. Folk and fairy tales. Magic.

The woman with the eggs adapt. by Jan Wahl; ill. by Ray Cruz. Crown, 1974. An adaptation of a poem by H. C. Andersen pub. in Den danske bondeven, 1836. Subj: Behavior – greed. Eggs. Folk and fairy tales.

Andersen, Karen Born. *What's the matter, Sylvie, can't you ride?* ill. by author. Dial Pr., 1981. Subj: Emotions. Sports – bicycling.

Anderson, Adrienne Adams *see* Adams, Adrienne

Anderson, C. W. (Clarence Williams). *Billy and Blaze* ill. by author. Macmillan, 1936. Subj: Animals – horses. Birthdays. Family life.

Blaze and the forest fire ill. by author. Macmillan, 1938. Subj: Animals – horses. Fire.

Blaze and the gray spotted pony ill. by author. Macmillan, 1968. Subj: Animals – horses.

Blaze and the gypsies ill. by author. Macmillan, 1937. Subj: Animals – horses. Crime. Gypsies.

Blaze and the Indian cave ill. by author. Macmillan, 1964. Subj: Animals – horses. Cowboys.

Blaze and the lost quarry ill. by author. Macmillan, 1966. Subj: Animals – horses. Cowboys.

Blaze and the mountain lion ill. by author. Macmillan, 1959. Subj: Animals – cougars. Animals – horses. Cowboys.

Blaze and Thunderbolt ill. by author. Macmillan, 1955. Subj: Animals – horses. Cowboys.

Blaze finds forgotten roads ill. by author. Macmillan, 1970. Subj: Animals – horses. Behavior – lost. Cowboys.

Blaze finds the trail ill. by author. Macmillan, 1950. Subj: Animals – horses. Behavior – lost. Cowboys.

Blaze shows the way ill. by author. Macmillan, 1969. Subj: Animals – horses.

The crooked colt ill. by author. Macmillan, 1954. Subj: Animals – horses.

Linda and the Indians ill. by author. Macmillan, 1952. Subj: Animals – horses. Ethnic groups in the U.S. – Indians. Imagination.

Lonesome little colt ill. by author. Macmillan, 1961. Subj: Animals – horses. Character traits – kindness to animals.

A pony for Linda ill. by author. Macmillan, 1951. Subj: Animals – horses.

A pony for three ill. by author. Macmillan, 1958. Subj: Animals – horses.

The rumble seat pony ill. by author. Macmillan, 1971. Subj: Animals – horses. Character traits – kindness to animals. Parades.

Anderson, Douglas. *Let's draw a story* ill. by author. Sterling, 1959. Subj: Animals – cats. Animals – dogs. Art. Family life. Games.

Anderson, John L. *see* Anderson, Lonzo

Anderson, Leone Castell. *The wonderful shrinking shirt* ill. by Irene Trivas. Albert Whitman, 1983. Subj: Clothing. Humor.

Anderson, Lonzo. *Arion and the dolphins* ill. by Adrienne Adams. Scribner's, 1978. Based on an ancient Greek legend. Subj: Animals – dolphins. Boats, ships. Folk and fairy tales. Foreign lands – Greece.

The day the hurricane happened ill. by Ann Grifalconi. Scribner's, 1974. Subj: Family life. Foreign lands – Caribbean Islands. Weather – storms.

The Halloween party ill. by Adrienne Adams. Scribner's, 1974. Subj: Holidays – Halloween. Parties.

Izzard ill. by Adrienne Adams. Scribner's, 1973. Subj: Foreign lands – Caribbean Islands. Reptiles – lizards.

Mr. Biddle and the birds ill. by Adrienne Adams. Scribner's, 1971. Subj: Activities – flying. Birds.

Two hundred rabbits by Lonzo Anderson and Adrienne Adams; ill. by Adrienne Adams. Viking, 1968. Subj: Animals – rabbits. Fairies. Magic. Royalty.

Anderson, Lucia. *The smallest life around us* ill. by Leigh Grant. Crown, 1978. Subj: Science.

Anderson, Neil *see* Beim, Jerrold

Anderson, Paul S. *Red fox and the hungry tiger* ill. by Robert Kraus. Addison-Wesley, 1962. Subj: Animals – foxes. Animals – tigers. Character traits – cleverness. Friendship.

Anderson, Robin. *Sinabouda Lily: a folk tale from Papua New Guinea* ill. by Jennifer Allen. Oxford Univ. Pr., 1979. Subj: Activities – swinging. Folk and fairy tales. Foreign lands – New Guinea. Magic. Witches.

Andre, Evelyn M. *Places I like to be* photos. by author. Abingdon Pr., 1980. Subj: Activities. Poetry, rhyme.

Andrews, F. Emerson (Frank Emerson). *Nobody comes to dinner* ill. by Lydia Dabcovich. Little, 1977. Subj: Behavior – bad day. Emotions – anger. Imagination – imaginary friends.

Andrews, Wayne. *Snow White and Rose Red* (Grimm, Jacob)

Androcles and the lion ill. by Janusz Grabianski. Watts, 1970. Subj: Animals – lions. Character traits – helpfulness. Character traits – kindness to animals. Folk and fairy tales. Foreign lands – Italy. Religion.

Andry, Andrew C. *Hi, new baby: a book to help your child learn about the new baby* by Andrew C. Andry and Suzanne C. Kratka; ill. by Thomas Di Grazia. Simon and Schuster, 1970. Subj: Babies.

How babies are made by Andrew C. Andry and Steven Schepp; ill. by Blake Hampton. Time-Life, 1968. Subj: Babies. Science.

Angeli, Marguerite De *see* De Angeli, Marguerite

Angelis, Nancy de *see* Angelo, Nancy Carolyn Harrison

Angelo, Nancy Carolyn Harrison. *Camembert* ill. by author. Houghton, 1958. Subj: Animals – mice. Art. Careers – artists. Foreign lands – France.

Angelo, Valenti. *The acorn tree* ill. by author. Viking, 1958. Subj: Animals – chipmunks. Animals – squirrels. Birds – bluejays. Character traits – selfishness. Trees.

The candy basket ill. by author. Viking, 1960. Subj: Animals – mice. Behavior – greed.

Anglund, Joan Walsh. *A is for always: an ABC book* ill. by author. Harcourt, 1968. Subj: ABC books.

A book of good tidings from the Bible ill. by author. Harcourt, 1965. Subj: Religion.

The brave cowboy ill. by author. Harcourt, 1959. Subj: Character traits – bravery. Cowboys. Games.

A Christmas book ill. by author. Random House, 1983. Subj: Holidays – Christmas. Poetry, rhyme.

Christmas is a time of giving ill. by author. Harcourt, 1961. Subj: Character traits – generosity. Holidays – Christmas.

Cowboy and his friend ill. by author. Harcourt, 1961. Subj: Animals – bears. Cowboys. Friendship. Imagination – imaginary friends.

The cowboy's Christmas ill. by author. Atheneum, 1972. Subj: Animals – bears. Cowboys. Holidays – Christmas. Imagination – imaginary friends.

Cowboy's secret life ill. by author. Harcourt, 1963. Subj: Cowboys. Games. Imagination.

A friend is someone who likes you ill. by author. Harcourt, 1958. Subj: Friendship.

The Joan Walsh Anglund story book ill. by author. Random House, 1978. Subj: Poetry, rhyme.

Look out the window ill. by author. Random, 1978. Subj: Character traits – individuality.

Love is a special way of feeling ill. by author. Harcourt, 1960. Subj: Emotions – love.

Love one another ill. by author. Determined Prod., 1981. Subj: Foreign lands. Foreign languages.

Morning is a little child: poems ill. by author. Harcourt, 1969. Subj: Morning. Poetry, rhyme.

Nibble nibble mousekin: a tale of Hansel and Gretel ill. by author. Harcourt, 1962. Subj: Folk and fairy tales. Forest, woods. Witches.

Spring is a new beginning ill. by author. Harcourt, 1963. Subj: Seasons – spring.

Annett, Cora. *The dog who thought he was a boy* ill. by Walter Lorraine. Houghton, 1965. Subj: Animals – dogs. Birthdays. School.

When the porcupine moved in ill. by Peter Parnall. Watts, 1971. Subj: Animals – porcupines. Animals – rabbits. Behavior – trickery.

Annixter, Jane. *Brown rats, black rats* by Jane and Paul Annixter; ill. by Gilbert Riswold. Prentice-Hall, 1977. Subj: Animals – rats. Science.

Annixter, Paul. *Brown rats, black rats* (Annixter, Jane)

Anno, Masaichiro. *Anno's magical ABC* (Anno, Mitsumasa)

Anno, Mitsumasa. *Anno's alphabet: an adventure in imagination* ill. by author. Crowell, 1975. Subj: ABC books. Imagination. Optical illusions.

Anno's animals ill. by author. Collins-World, 1979. Subj: Animals. Games. Imagination. Wordless.

Anno's Britain ill. by author. Philomel, 1982. Subj: Foreign lands – England. Games. Humor. Imagination. Wordless.

Anno's counting book ill. by author. Crowell, 1975. Subj: Counting. Imagination. Optical illusions.

Anno's counting house ill. by author. Philomel, 1982. Translation of 10-nin no yukai na hikkoshi. Subj: Counting. Games. Humor. Imagination. Optical illusions. Wordless.

Anno's flea market ill. by author. Philomel, 1984. Translation of Nomi no ichi. Subj: Games. Humor. Imagination. Optical illusions. Wordless.

Anno's Italy ill. by author. Collins-World, 1980. Japanese ed. entitled My journey II, a translation of Tabi no ehon, II. Subj: Foreign lands – Italy. Games. Humor. Imagination. Optical illusions. Wordless.

Anno's journey ill. by author. Collins-World, 1978. Pub. in 1977 under title: My journey, a translation of Tabi no ehon. Subj: Games. Humor. Imagination. Optical illusions. Wordless.

Anno's magical ABC: an anamorphic alphabet by Mitsumasa and Masaichiro Anno; ill. by authors. Putnam's, 1981. Subj: ABC books. Format, unusual. Games. Imagination. Optical illusions.

Anno's U.S.A. ill. by author. Philomel, 1983. Translation of Tabi no ehon, IV. Subj: Games. Humor. Imagination. Wordless.

Dr. Anno's midnight circus ill. by author. Weatherhill, 1972. Subj: Circus. Clowns, jesters. Humor. Imagination. Optical illusions. Wordless.

The king's flower ill. by author. Collins-World, 1979. Subj: Concepts – size. Flowers. Imagination. Royalty.

Topsy-turvies: pictures to stretch the imagination ill. by author. Weatherhill, 1970. Subj: Games. Humor. Imagination. Optical illusions. Wordless.

Upside-downers: more pictures to stretch the imagination adapt. into English by Meredith Weatherby and Susan Trumbull; ill. by author. Weatherhill, 1971. Subj: Games. Humor. Imagination. Optical illusions.

Aoki, Hisako. *Santa's favorite story* by Hisako Aoki and Ivan Gantschev; ill. by authors. Neugebauer, 1982. Subj: Holidays – Christmas. Religion.

Appell, Clara. *Now I have a daddy haircut* by Clara and Morey Appell; photos. by authors. Dodd, 1960. Subj: Behavior – growing up. Careers – barbers. Hair. Self-concept.

Appell, Morey. *Now I have a daddy haircut* (Appell, Clara)

Applebaum, Neil. *Is there a hole in your head?* ill. by author. Ivan Obolensky, 1963. Subj: Animals – whales. Games.

Applebaum, Stan. *Going my way?* by Stan Applebaum and Victoria Cox; ill. by Leonard W. Shortall. Harcourt, 1976. Subj: Animals. Science.

Appleby, Leonard. *Snakes* photos. by author. A & C Black, 1983. Subj: Reptiles – snakes. Science.

Arabian Nights. *Arabian Nights entertainments: the first book of tales of ancient Araby* comp. by Charles Mozley. Watts, 1960. Subj: Folk and fairy tales. Foreign lands – Arabia.

The flying carpet ill. by Marcia Brown. Scribner's, 1956. Subj: Activities – flying. Folk and fairy tales. Magic.

Ardizzone, Aingelda. *The night ride* ill. by Edward Ardizzone. Windmill, 1975. Subj: Holidays – Christmas. Night. Toys. Toys – dolls. Toys – teddy bears.

Ardizzone, Edward. *Diana and her rhinoceros* ill. by author. Walck, 1964. Subj: Animals – rhinoceros. Pets.

Johnny the clockmaker ill. by author. Walck, 1960. Subj: Careers – clockmakers. Clocks.

The little girl and the tiny doll ill. by author. Delacorte Pr., 1967. Subj: Behavior – losing things. Shopping. Toys – dolls.

Little Tim and the brave sea captain ill. by author. Walck, 1955. Subj: Boats, ships. Character traits – bravery. Sea and seashore.

Lucy Brown and Mr. Grimes ill. by author. Walck, 1970. A new version of a story published in 1937. Subj: Emotions – loneliness. Foreign lands – England. Old age. Orphans.

Nicholas and the fast-moving diesel ill. by author. Walck, 1959. Subj: Trains. Transportation.

Paul, the hero of the fire ill. by author. Walck, 1963. A new version of a story published in 1949. Subj: Activities – working. Behavior – growing up. Character traits – bravery. Merry-go-rounds.

Peter the wanderer ill. by author. Walck, 1963. Subj: Character traits – bravery. Character traits – cleverness. Character traits – honesty. Sea and seashore.

Ship's cook Ginger ill. by author. Macmillan, 1978. First published in London by Bodley Head, 1977. Subj: Boats, ships. Sea and seashore.

Tim all alone ill. by author. Oxford Univ. Pr., 1957. Subj: Boats, ships. Sea and seashore.

Tim and Charlotte ill. by author. Oxford Univ. Pr., 1951. Subj: Boats, ships. Character traits – bravery. Sea and seashore.

Tim and Ginger ill. by author. Walck, 1965. Subj: Boats, ships. Sea and seashore.

Tim and Lucy go to sea ill. by author. Walck, 1958. Subj: Boats, ships. Friendship. Sea and seashore.

Tim in danger ill. by author. Walck, 1953. Subj: Boats, ships. Sea and seashore.

Tim to the rescue ill. by author. Walck, 1949. Subj: Boats, ships. Character traits – bravery. Character traits – loyalty. Sea and seashore. Weather.

Tim's friend Towser ill. by author. Walck, 1962. Subj: Animals – dogs. Boats, ships. Sea and seashore.

Tim's last voyage ill. by author. Walck, 1972. Subj: Boats, ships. Sea and seashore. Weather – wind.

Ariane. *Animal stories* ill. by Feodor Rojankovsky. Western Pub., 1944. Subj: Animals.

Small Cloud ill. by Annie Gusman. Dutton, 1984. Subj: Folk and fairy tales. Science. Weather – clouds.

Arkin, Alan. *Black and white* music by Earl Robinson; ill. by author. Golden Pr., 1966. Subj: Foreign lands – Africa. Music. Songs.

Tony's hard work day ill. by James Stevenson. Harper, 1972. Subj: Activities – working. Family life. Houses.

Armalyte, Olimpija. *How the cock wrecked the manor* (Tempest, P)

Armer, Laura Adams. *The forest pool* ill. by author. Longman, 1938. Subj: Caldecott award honor book. Forest, woods.

Armitage, David. *Ice creams for Rosie* (Armitage, Ronda)

One moonlit night (Armitage, Ronda)

Armitage, Marcia. *Lupatelli's favorite nursery tales* ill. by Anthony Lupatelli. Grosset, 1977. Subj: Folk and fairy tales.

Armitage, Ronda. *The bossing of Josie* ill. by David Armitage. Elsevier-Dutton, 1980. Subj: Birthdays. Family life. Magic. Sibling rivalry Witches

Don't forget, Matilda ill. by David Armitage. Elsevier-Dutton, 1979. Subj: Family life. Foreign lands – England.

Ice creams for Rosie by Ronda and David Armitage; ill. by David Armitage. Elsevier-Dutton, 1981. Subj: Food. Islands. Problem solving.

The lighthouse keeper's lunch ill. by David Armitage. Elsevier-Dutton, 1979. Subj: Birds – sea gulls. Food. Lighthouses. Problem solving.

One moonlit night by Ronda and David Armitage; ill. by David Armitage. Dutton, 1983. Subj: Family life. Night. Sports – camping.

Armour, Richard Willard. *The adventures of Egbert the Easter egg* ill. by Paul Galdone. McGraw-Hill, 1965. Subj: Holidays – Easter. Poetry, rhyme.

Animals on the ceiling ill. by Paul Galdone. McGraw-Hill, 1966. Subj: Animals. Humor. Imagination. Poetry, rhyme.

Have you ever wished you were something else? ill. by Scott Gustafson. Children's Pr., 1983. Subj: Animals. Poetry, rhyme.

Sea full of whales ill. by Paul Galdone. McGraw-Hill, 1974. Subj: Animals – whales. Poetry, rhyme.

The year Santa went modern ill. by Paul Galdone. McGraw-Hill, 1964. Subj: Holidays – Christmas. Poetry, rhyme.

Armstrong, Louise. *How to turn lemons into money: a child's guide to economics* ill. by Bill Basso. Harcourt, 1976. Subj: Activities – working. Money.

Arneson, D. J. *Secret places* ill. by Peter Arnold. Holt, 1971. Subj: Ecology. Forest, woods.

Arnold, Caroline. *The biggest living thing* ill. by author. Carolrhoda Bks., 1983. Subj: Science. Trees.

Five nests ill. by Ruth Sanderson. Dutton, 1980. Includes index. Subj: Animals. Birds. Science.

How do we communicate? ill. by Ginger Giles. Watts, 1983. Subj: Communication.

How do we have fun? photos. by Ginger Giles. Watts, 1983. Subj: Activities. Activities – playing.

How do we travel? photos. by Ginger Giles. Watts, 1983. Subj: Activities – traveling. Transportation.

Pets without homes ill. by Richard Hewett. Clarion, 1983. Subj: Animals. Pets.

Sun fun ill. by author. Watts, 1981. Subj: Science. Sun.

What is a community? ill. by Carole Bertole. Watts, 1982. Subj: Careers. Communities, neighborhoods.

What will we buy? photos. by Ginger Giles. Watts, 1983. Subj: Money. Shopping.

Where do you go to school? ill. by Carole Bertole. Watts, 1982. Includes index. Subj: Careers – teachers. Communities, neighborhoods. School.

Who keeps us healthy? ill. by Carole Bertole. Watts, 1982. Subj: Careers – doctors. Careers – nurses.

Who keeps us safe? photos. by Carole Bertole. Watts, 1983. Subj: Careers. Safety.

Who works here? ill. by Carole Bertole. Watts, 1982. Subj: Careers. Communities, neighborhoods.

Arnold, Katrin. *Anna joins in* ill. by Renate Seelig. Abingdon Pr., 1983. Subj: Handicaps. Illness. School.

Arnosky, Jim. *A kettle of hawks, and other wildlife groups* ill. by author. Coward, 1979. Subj: Animals. Birds. Insects. Fish. Poetry, rhyme.

Mouse numbers and letters ill. by author. Harcourt, 1982. Subj: ABC books. Animals – mice. Counting. Wordless.

Mouse writing ill. by author. Harcourt, 1983. Subj: ABC books. Activities – writing. Animals – mice. Birds. Wordless.

Mud time and more: Nathaniel stories ill. by author. Addison-Wesley, 1979. Subj: Problem solving. Wordless.

Outdoors on foot ill. by author. Coward, 1978. Subj: Activities – walking. Humor. Seasons.

Arnott, Kathleen. *Spiders, crabs and creepy crawlers: two African folktales* ill. by Bette Davis. Garrard, 1978. Subj: Folk and fairy tales. Foreign lands – Africa.

Arnstein, Helene S. *Billy and our new baby* ill. by M. Jane Smyth. Human Sciences Pr., 1973. Subj: Babies. Family life. Sibling rivalry.

Aronin, Ben. *The secret of the Sabbath fish* ill. by Shay Rieger. Jewish Pub. Soc., 1979. Subj: Folk and fairy tales. Food. Format, unusual – cardboard pages. Jewish culture.

Arquette, Lois S. *see* Duncan, Lois

Arthur, Catherine. *My sister's silent world* ill. by Nathan Talbot. Children's Pr., 1979. Subj: Birthdays. Handicaps – deafness. Family life. Zoos.

Artis, Vicki Kimmel. *Pajama walking* ill. by Emily Arnold McCully. Houghton, 1981. Subj: Activities – playing. Friendship. Night.

Artzybasheff, Boris. *Seven Simeons* ill. by author. Viking, 1937. Subj: Caldecott award honor book.

Aruego, Ariane *see* Dewey, Ariane

Aruego, José. *A crocodile's tale: a Philippine folk story* by José Aruego and Ariane Dewey; ill. by authors. Scribner's, 1972. Subj: Folk and fairy tales. Foreign lands – Philippines. Reptiles – alligators, crocodiles.

The king and his friends ill. by author. Scribner's, 1969. Subj: Dragons. Friendship. Mythical creatures. Royalty.

Look what I can do ill. by author. Scribner's, 1971. Subj: Animals. Behavior – imitation. Folk and fairy tales. Foreign lands – Philippines. Games.

Pilyo the piranha ill. by author. Macmillan, 1971. Subj: Fish. Foreign lands – South America.

Symbiosis: a book of unusual friendships ill. by author. Scribner's, 1970. Subj: Science.

We hide, you seek by José Aruego and Ariane Dewey; ill. by authors. Greenwillow, 1979. Subj: Animals. Behavior – hiding. Foreign lands – Africa. Games.

Arundel, Anne *see* Arundel, Jocelyn

Arundel, Jocelyn. *Shoes for Punch* ill. by Wesley Dennis. McGraw-Hill, 1964. Subj: Animals – horses.

Asbjørnsen, P. C. (Peter Christen). *The squire's bride*

The three billy goats Gruff ill. by Marcia Brown. Harcourt, 1957. Subj: Animals – goats. Character traits – cleverness. Cumulative tales. Folk and fairy tales. Mythical creatures. Trolls.

The three billy goats Gruff ill. by Paul Galdone. Seabury Pr., 1973. Translation of De tre bukkene Bruse. Subj: Animals – goats. Character traits – cleverness. Cumulative tales. Folk and fairy tales. Mythical creatures. Trolls.

The three billy goats Gruff ill. by William Stobbs. McGraw-Hill, 1967. Subj: Animals – goats. Character traits – cleverness. Cumulative tales. Folk and fairy tales. Mythical creatures. Trolls.

Asch, Frank. *Bread and honey* ill. by author. Parents, 1981. Adapted from the author's Monkey face. Subj: Activities – painting. Animals. Animals – bears. Family life – mothers.

City sandwich ill. by author. Greenwillow, 1978. Subj: City. Imagination. Poetry, rhyme.

Country pie ill. by author. Greenwillow, 1979. Subj: Country. Poetry, rhyme. Weather.

Good lemonade ill. by author. Watts, 1976. Subj: Activities – working. Food.

Goodnight horsey ill. by author. Prentice-Hall, 1981. Subj: Animals – horses. Bedtime. Family life – fathers. Games. Imagination.

Happy birthday, moon! ill. by author. Prentice-Hall, 1982. Subj: Animals – bears. Birthdays. Moon.

Just like daddy ill. by author. Prentice-Hall, 1981. Subj: Animals – bears. Behavior – imitation. Family life – fathers.

The last puppy ill. by author. Prentice-Hall, 1980. Subj: Animals – dogs. Pets.

Little Devil's ABC ill. by author. Scribner's, 1979. Subj: ABC books. Devil.

Little Devil's 123 ill. by author. Scribner's, 1979. Subj: Counting. Devil.

MacGooses's grocery ill. by James Marshall. Dial Pr., 1978. Subj: Birds – geese. Eggs.

Moon bear ill. by author. Scribner's, 1978. Subj: Animals – bears. Birds. Food. Moon. Night.

Mooncake ill. by author. Prentice-Hall, 1983. Subj: Animals – bears. Birds. Moon. Seasons – winter.

Popcorn ill. by author. Parents, 1979. Subj: Animals – bears. Food. Holidays – Halloween. Parties.

Rebecka ill. by author. Harper, 1972. Subj: Activities – playing. Animals – dogs. Imagination.

Sand cake ill. by author. Parents, 1979. Subj: Activities – picnicking. Animals – bears. Humor. Sea and seashore.

Skyfire ill. by author. Prentice-Hall, 1984. Subj: Animals – bears. Weather – rainbows.

Starbaby ill. by author. Scribner's, 1980. Subj: Babies. Sea and seashore. Sky. Stars.

Turtle tale ill. by author. Dial Pr., 1978. Subj: Humor. Reptiles – turtles.

Yellow, yellow ill. by Mark Alan Stamaty. McGraw-Hill, 1971. Subj: Clothing. Concepts – color.

Asch, George. *Linda* ill. by author. McGraw-Hill, 1969. Subj: City. Emotions – happiness. Wordless.

Ash, Jutta. *Rapunzel* (Grimm, Jacob)

Ashby, Gwynneth. *Take a trip to Japan* ill. by author. Watts, 1980. Subj: Foreign lands – Japan.

Ashey, Bella *see* Breinburg, Petronella

Ashley, Bernard. *Dinner ladies don't count* ill. by Janet Duchesne. Watts, 1981. Subj: Behavior – misbehavior. Birthdays. Problem solving. School.

Asimov, Isaac. *The best new things* ill. by Symeon Shimin. Collins-World, 1971. Subj: Earth. Science. Space and space ships.

The moon ill. by Alex Ebel. Follett, 1967. Subj: Moon. Science.

Atene, Ann. *The golden guitar* ill. by author. Little, 1967. Subj: Foreign lands – Italy. Music. Puppets.

Atene, Anna *see* Atene, Ann

Attenberger, Walburga. *The little man in winter* ill. by author. Random House, 1972. Translation of Het mannetje in de winter. Subj: Foreign lands – Germany. Poetry, rhyme. Seasons – winter.

Who knows the little man? ill. by author. Random House, 1972. Translation of Wie kent dat kleine mannetje? Subj: Foreign lands – Germany. Poetry, rhyme.

Attenborough, Elizabeth. *Walk rabbit walk* (McNaughton, Colin)

Atwood, Ann. *The little circle* ill. by author. Scribner's, 1967. Subj: Concepts – shape. Poetry, rhyme.

Atwood, Margaret. *Anna's pet* by Margaret Atwood and Joyce Barkhouse; ill. by Ann Blades. Lorimer, 1980. Subj: Animals. Character traits – optimism. Country. Pets.

Auerbach, Marjorie. *King Lavra and the barber* ill. by author. Knopf, 1964. Subj: Behavior – secrets. Careers – barbers. Folk and fairy tales. Royalty.

Augarde, Stephen *see* Augarde, Steve

Augarde, Steve. *Barnaby Shrew, Black Dan and... the mighty wedgwood* ill. by author. Elsevier-Dutton, 1980. Subj: Animals – mice. Animals – rats. Animals – shrews. Behavior – boasting. Birds – parakeets, parrots. Reptiles – turtles.

Barnaby Shrew goes to sea ill. by author. Elsevier-Dutton, 1979. Subj: Animals – rats. Animals – shrews. Boats, ships. Reptiles – turtles.

Pig ill. by author. Bradbury Pr., 1977. Subj: Animals – pigs. Farms. Fire.

Aulaire, Edgar Parin d'. *Abraham Lincoln* (Aulaire, Ingri Mortenson d')

Animals everywhere (Aulaire, Ingri Mortenson d')

Children of the northlights (Aulaire, Ingri Mortenson d')

Don't count your chicks (Aulaire, Ingri Mortenson d')

East of the sun and west of the moon (Aulaire, Ingri Mortenson d')

Foxie, the singing dog (Aulaire, Ingri Mortenson d')

Nils (Aulaire, Ingri Mortenson d')

Ola (Aulaire, Ingri Mortenson d')

Pocahontas (Aulaire, Ingri Mortenson d')

The terrible troll-bird (Aulaire, Ingri Mortenson d')

Too big (Aulaire, Ingri Mortenson d')

The two cars (Aulaire, Ingri Mortenson d')

Wings for Per (Aulaire, Ingri Mortenson d')

Aulaire, Ingri Mortenson d'. *Abraham Lincoln* by Ingri and Edgar Parin d'Aulaire; ill. by authors. Doubleday, 1939. Subj: Caldecott award book. U.S. history.

Animals everywhere by Ingri and Edgar Parin d'Aulaire; ill. by authors. Doubleday, 1940. Subj: Animals.

Children of the northlights by Ingri and Edgar Parin d'Aulaire; ill. by authors. Viking, 1962. Subj: Activities – bathing. Activities – playing. Animals. Family life. Folk and fairy tales. Foreign lands – Lapland. School. Seasons – winter.

Don't count your chicks by Ingri and Edgar Parin d'Aulaire; ill. by authors. Doubleday, 1943. Subj: Behavior – greed. Birds – chickens. Folk and fairy tales. Humor.

East of the sun and west of the moon ed. by Ingri and Edgar Parin d'Aulaire; ill. by eds. Doubleday, 1969. Subj: Folk and fairy tales.

Foxie, the singing dog by Ingri and Edgar Parin d'Aulaire; ill. by authors. Doubleday, 1949. Subj: Animals – cats. Animals – dogs. Birds – chickens.

The Lord's prayer ill. by Ingri and Edgar Parin d'Aulaire. Protestant version. Doubleday, 1934. Subj: Religion.

The Lord's prayer ill. by Ingri and Edgar Parin d'Aulaire. Catholic version. Doubleday, 1934. Subj: Religion.

Nils by Ingri and Edgar Parin d'Aulaire; ill. by authors. Doubleday, 1948. Subj: Character traits – being different. Cowboys. Family life. School.

Ola by Ingri and Edgar Parin d'Aulaire; ill. by authors. Doubleday, 1932. Subj: Foreign lands – Norway.

Pocahontas by Ingri and Edgar Parin d'Aulaire; ill. by authors. Doubleday, 1946. Subj: Ethnic groups in the U.S. – Indians. U.S. history.

The terrible troll-bird by Ingri and Edgar Parin d'Aulaire; ill. by authors. Doubleday, 1976. Subj: Foreign lands – Norway. Mythical creatures. Trolls.

Too big by Ingri and Edgar Parin d'Aulaire; ill. by authors. Doubleday, 1945. Subj: Behavior – growing up. Concepts – size.

The two cars by Ingri and Edgar Parin d'Aulaire; ill. by authors. Doubleday, 1955. Subj: Automobiles.

Wings for Per by Ingri and Edgar Parin d'Aulaire; ill. by authors. Doubleday, 1944. Subj: Activities – flying. Character traits – bravery. Farms. War.

Austin, Margot. *Barney's adventure* ill. by author. Dutton, 1941. Subj: Circus. Clowns, jesters.

Growl Bear ill. by author. Dutton, 1951. Subj: Animals – bears. Emotions – loneliness.

Manuel's kite string ill. by author. Scribner's, 1943. Subj: Cumulative tales. Folk and fairy tales.

Trumpet ill. by author. Dutton, 1926. Subj: Animals – dogs. Teeth.

Willamet way ill. by author. Scribner's, 1941. Subj: Activities – traveling. Animals – dogs. U.S. history.

Averill, Esther. *The fire cat* ill. by author. Harper, 1960. Subj: Animals – cats. Careers – firefighters.

Jenny and the cat club ill. by author. Harper, 1973. Subj: Animals – cats.

Jenny's adopted brothers ill. by author. Harper, 1952. Subj: Animals – cats. Character traits – kindness to animals. Emotions – envy, jealousy.

Jenny's birthday book ill. by author. Harper, 1954. Subj: Animals – cats. Birthdays. Parties.

Jenny's first party ill. by author. Harper, 1948. Subj: Animals – cats. Parties.

Jenny's moonlight adventure ill. by author. Harper, 1949. Subj: Animals – cats. Holidays – Halloween. Night.

When Jenny lost her scarf ill. by author. Harper, 1951. Subj: Animals – cats. Character traits – bravery. Fire.

Avery, Kay. *Wee willow whistle* ill. by Winifred Bromhall. Knopf, 1947. Subj: Activities – whistling. Family life. Farms. Toys.

Ayal, Ora. *The adventures of Chester the chest* by Ora Ayal and Naomi Löw Nakao; ill. by Ora Ayal. Harper, 1982. Subj: Activities – flying. Behavior – boredom. Imagination.

Ugbu tr. by Naomi Löw Nakao; ill. by author. Harper, 1979. Subj: Activities – playing. Imagination.

Ayars, James Sterling. *Caboose on the roof* ill. by Bob Hodgell. Abelard-Schuman, 1956. Subj: Houses. Humor. Trains.

Contrary Jenkins (Caudill, Rebecca)

Ayer, Jacqueline. *Little Silk* ill. by author. Harcourt, 1970. Subj: Behavior – lost. Toys – dolls.

Nu Dang and his kite ill. by author. Harcourt, 1959. Subj: Behavior – losing things. Foreign lands – Thailand. Kites. Toys.

The paper-flower tree: a tale from Thailand ill. by author. Harcourt, 1962. Subj: Character traits – optimism. Foreign lands – Thailand. Plants.

A wish for little sister ill. by author. Harcourt, 1962. Subj: Behavior – wishing. Birds. Birthdays. Family life. Foreign lands – Thailand.

Aylesworth, Jim. *Hush up!* ill. by Glen Rounds. Holt, 1980. Subj: Character traits – laziness. Humor. Noise, sounds.

Mary's mirror ill. by Richard Egielski. Holt, 1982. Subj: Behavior – greed. Emotions – envy, jealousy. Poetry, rhyme.

Siren in the night ill. by Tom Centola. Albert Whitman, 1983. Subj: Activities – walking. Emotions – fear. Family life. Noise, sounds.

Tonight's the night ill. by John Wallner. Albert Whitman, 1981. Subj: Bedtime. Dreams. Night. Sleep.

Azaad, Meyer. *Half for you* ill. by Nāhīd Ḥaqī-qāt. Carolrhoda, 1971. Subj: Behavior – sharing. Birds. Careers. Clothing.

Azarian, Mary. *A farmer's alphabet* ill. by author. Godine, 1981. Subj: ABC books. Activities. Farms.

The tale of John Barleycorn or, From barley to beer: a traditional English ballad ill. by author. Godine, 1983. Subj: Folk and fairy tales. Food. Foreign lands – England. Middle ages. Music. Poetry, rhyme.

B. B. Blacksheep and Company: *a collection of favorite nursery rhymes* ill. by Nick Butterworth. Grosset, 1982. Subj: Animals. Nursery rhymes.

Babbitt, Lorraine. *Pink like the geranium* ill. by author. Children's Pr., 1973. Subj: Behavior. Clothing. Family life. School.

Babbitt, Natalie. *The something* ill. by author. Farrar, 1970. Subj: Emotions – fear. Monsters. Night.

Babbitt, Samuel F. *The forty-ninth magician* ill. by Natalie Babbitt. Pantheon, 1966. Subj: Magic. Royalty.

The babes in the woods. *The old ballad of the babes in the woods* ed. by Kathleen Lines; ill. by Edward Ardizzone. Walck, 1972. Derived from a Chapbook ed. published in 1640. Subj: Folk and fairy tales. Orphans. Poetry, rhyme.

Bach, Alice. *The day after Christmas* ill. by Mary Chalmers. Harper, 1975. Subj: Emotions. Holidays – Christmas.

Millicent the magnificent ill. by Steven Kellogg. Harper, 1978. Subj: Animals – bears. Circus. Emotions – envy, jealousy. Family life.

Warren Weasel's worse than measles ill. by Hilary Knight. Harper, 1980. Subj: Animals – bears. Animals – weasels. Self-concept.

Bach, Othello. *Lilly, Willy and the mail-order witch* ill. by Timothy Hildebrandt. Caedmon, 1983. Subj: Activities – working. Imagination. Magic. Music. Poetry, rhyme. Witches.

Bacon, Joan Chase *see* Bowden, Joan Chase

Baer, Edith. *Words are like faces* ill. by Karen Gundersheimer. Pantheon, 1980. Subj: Language. Poetry, rhyme.

Bagwell, Elizabeth. *This is an airport* (Bagwell, Richard)

Bagwell, Richard. *This is an airport* by Richard and Elizabeth Bagwell; photos. by Lee Balterman. Follett, 1967. Subj: Airplanes, airports. Transportation.

Bahr, Robert. *Blizzard at the zoo* ill. by Consuelo Joerns. Lothrop, 1982. Subj: Animals. Weather – snow. Weather – storms. Zoos.

Bailey, Jill. *Eyes* photos. by Jim Bailey. Putnam's, 1984. Subj: Anatomy. Animals. Birds. Format, unusual – cardboard pages.

Feet photos. by Jim Bailey. Putnam's, 1984. Subj: Anatomy. Animals. Birds. Format, unusual – cardboard pages.

Mouths photos. by Jim Bailey. Putnam's, 1984. Subj: Anatomy. Animals. Birds. Format, unusual – cardboard pages.

Noses photos. by Jim Bailey. Putnam's, 1984. Subj: Anatomy. Animals. Format, unusual – cardboard pages.

Bains, Rae. *Hiccups, hiccups* ill. by Otto Coontz. Troll Assoc., 1981. Subj: Illness.

Baker, Alan. *Benjamin and the box* ill. by author. Lippincott, 1978. Subj: Animals – hamsters. Friendship.

Benjamin bounces back ill. by author. Lippincott, 1978. Subj: Animals – hamsters. Humor. Imagination.

Benjamin's book ill. by author. Lothrop, 1983. Subj: Animals – hamsters. Behavior – misbehavior. Humor.

Benjamin's dreadful dream ill. by author. Lippincott, 1980. Subj: Animals – hamsters. Behavior – misbehavior. Humor.

Baker, Betty. *And me, coyote!* ill. by Maria Horvath. Macmillan, 1982. Subj: Animals – coyotes. Character traits – cleverness. Ethnic groups in the U.S. – Indians. Folk and fairy tales. Religion.

Latki and the lightning lizard ill. by Donald Carrick. Macmillan, 1979. Subj: Animals. Character traits – bravery. Ethnic groups in the U.S. – Indians. Folk and fairy tales. Reptiles – lizards.

Little runner of the longhouse ill. by Arnold Lobel. Harper, 1962. Subj: Cumulative tales. Ethnic groups in the U.S. – Indians. Family life.

My sister says ill. by Tricia Taggart. Macmillan, 1984. Subj: Behavior – wishing. Boats, ships. Family life – fathers. Imagination. Sibling rivalry.

Partners ill. by Emily Arnold McCully. Greenwillow, 1978. Subj: Animals – badgers. Animals – coyotes. Character traits – cleverness. Character traits – helpfulness. Character traits – laziness. Farms. Friendship.

The pig war ill. by Robert Lopshire. Harper, 1969. Subj: U.S. history.

Rat is dead and ant is sad: based on a Pueblo Indian tale ill. by Mamoru Funai. Harper, 1981. Subj: Cumulative tales. Death. Emotions – sadness. Ethnic groups in the U.S. – Indians. Folk and fairy tales.

Sonny-Boy Sim ill. by Susanne Suba. Rand McNally, 1948. Subj: Animals. Family life. Humor. Sports – hunting.

Three fools and a horse ill. by Glen Rounds. Macmillan, 1975. Subj: Animals – horses. Ethnic groups in the U.S. – Indians. Humor.

Turkey girl ill. by Harold Berson. Macmillan, 1983. Based on a traditional Zuni tale. Subj: Activities – working. Behavior – wishing. Birds – turkeys. Ethnic groups in the U.S. – Indians. Folk and fairy tales.

Worthington Botts and the steam machine ill. by Sal Murdocca. Macmillan, 1981. Subj: Activities – reading. Humor. Machines.

Baker, Bonnie Jeanne. *A pear by itself* ill. by author. Children's Pr., 1982. Subj: Counting.

Baker, Charlotte. *Little brother* ill. by author. McKay, 1959. Subj: Animals – dogs. Babies. Emotions – envy, jealousy. Family life. Sibling rivalry.

Baker, Donna. *I want to be a librarian* ill. by Richard Wahl. Children's Pr., 1978. Subj: Careers – librarians. Libraries.

I want to be a pilot ill. by Richard Wahl. Children's Pr., 1978. Subj: Careers – airplane pilots. Airplanes, airports.

I want to be a police officer ill. by Richard Wahl. Children's Pr., 1978. Subj: Careers – police officers.

Baker, Eugene. *Bicycles* ill. by Tom Dunnington. Creative Ed., 1980. Subj: Animals. Safety. Sports – bicycling.

Fire ill. by Tom Dunnington. Creative Ed., 1980. Subj: Animals. Fire. Safety.

Home ill. by Tom Dunnington. Creative Ed., 1980. Subj: Animals. Safety.

I want to be a computer operator ill. by Tom Dunnington. Children's Pr., 1973. Subj: Careers. Machines.

Outdoors ill. by Tom Dunnington. Creative Ed., 1980. Subj: Animals. Safety.

School ill. by Tom Dunnington. Creative Ed., 1980. Subj: Animals. Safety. School.

Water ill. by Tom Dunnington. Creative Ed., 1980. Subj: Animals. Safety.

Baker, Gayle. *Special delivery: a book for kids about cesarean and vaginal birth* ill. by Debra Hillyer. Chas. Franklin Pr., 1981. Subj: Babies. Family life – mothers. Hospitals. Science.

Baker, Jeannie. *Grandmother* ill. by author. Elsevier-Dutton, 1979. Subj: Art. Family life – grandparents, great-grandparents.

Home in the sky ill. by author. Greenwillow, 1984. Subj: Animals – dogs. Birds – pigeons. Character traits – kindness to animals. City.

Millicent ill. by author. Elsevier-Dutton, 1980. Subj: Birds – pigeons. Character traits – individuality. City.

One hungry spider ill. by author. Elsevier-Dutton, 1983. Subj: Counting. Science. Spiders.

Baker, Jeffrey J. W. *Patterns of nature* photos. by Jaroslav Salek. Doubleday, 1967. Subj: Animals. Birds. Flowers. Plants. Science. Trees.

Baker, Laura Nelson. *The friendly beasts* ill. by Nicolas Sidjakov. Parnassus, 1958. Adapt. from an old English Christmas carol of the same title. Subj: Animals. Holidays – Christmas. Music.

O children of the wind and pines ill. by Inez Storer. Lippincott, 1967. Subj: Ethnic groups in the U.S. – Indians. Holidays – Christmas. Music.

Baker, Margaret. *A puppy called Spinach* by Margaret and Mary Baker; ill. by Mary Baker. Dodd, 1939. Subj: Animals – dogs. Behavior – misbehavior.

Baker, Mary. *A puppy called Spinach* (Baker, Margaret)

Baker, Olaf. *Where the buffaloes begin* ill. by Stephen Gammell. Subj: Animals – buffaloes. Caldecott award honor book. Ethnic groups in the U.S. – Indians. Folk and fairy tales.

Bakken, Harold. *The special string* ill. by Mischa Richter. Prentice-Hall, 1981. Subj: Character traits – helpfulness. Humor. Problem solving. String. Wordless.

Baldner, Gaby. *Joba and the wild boar: Joba und das wildschwein* ill. by Gerhard Oberländer. Hastings, 1961. Text in English and German. Subj: Animals – pigs. Character traits – bravery. Foreign languages. Pets.

Balestrino, Philip. *Fat and skinny* ill. by Pam Makie. Crowell, 1975. Subj: Character traits – appearance.

Hot as an ice cube ill. by Tomie de Paola. Crowell, 1971. Subj: Concepts. Science.

Balet, Jan B. *Amos and the moon* ill. by author. Oxford Univ. Pr., 1948. Subj: Moon.

The fence: a Mexican tale ill. by author. Delacorte Pr., 1969. Translation of Der Zaun. Subj: Family life. Folk and fairy tales. Foreign lands – Mexico. Poverty. Problem solving.

Five Rollatinis ill. by author. Lippincott, 1959. Subj: Animals – horses. Circus. Family life.

The gift: a Portuguese Christmas tale ill. by author. Delacorte, 1967. Subj: Foreign lands – Portugal. Holidays – Christmas. Religion.

Joanjo: a Portuguese tale ill. by author. Delacorte Pr., 1967. Subj: Character traits – ambition. Dreams. Fish. Foreign lands – Portugal.

The king and the broom maker ill. by author. Delacorte, 1968. Translation of König und der Besenbinder. Subj: Behavior – dissatisfaction. Royalty.

Ned and Ed and the lion ill. by author. Oxford Univ. Pr., 1949. Subj: Animals – lions. Imagination. Twins.

Balian, Lorna. *Bah! Humbug?* ill. by author. Abingdon, 1977. Subj: Holidays – Christmas.

Humbug potion: an A B Cipher ill. by author. Abingdon, 1984. Subj: ABC books. Magic. Secret codes. Witches.

Humbug rabbit ill. by author. Abingdon, 1974. Subj: Animals – rabbits. Family life – grandparents, great-grandparents. Holidays – Easter.

Humbug witch ill. by author. Abingdon, 1965. Subj: Holidays – Halloween. Witches.

Leprechauns never lie ill. by author. Abingdon, 1980. Subj: Animals – cats. Elves and little people. Folk and fairy tales. Foreign lands – Ireland. Humor.

Sometimes it's turkey ill. by author. Abingdon, 1973. Subj: Birds – turkeys. Holidays – Thanksgiving.

A sweetheart for Valentine ill. by author. Abingdon, 1979. Subj: Giants. Holidays – Valentine's Day. Weddings.

Where in the world is Henry? ill. by author. Bradbury Pr., 1972. Subj: Concepts – size. Science.

Balzano, Jeanne. *The wee moose* ill. by Enrico Arno. Parents, 1964. Subj: Animals – mice. Farms.

Bambi ill. by Christa Stephan. Imported Pubs., 1983. Subj: Format, unusual – cardboard pages. Toys. Wordless.

Banbery, Fred. *Paddington at the circus* (Bond, Michael)

Banchek, Linda. *Snake in, snake out* ill. by Elaine Arnold. Crowell, 1978. Subj: Birds – parakeets, parrots. Concepts – in and out. Concepts – opposites. Reptiles – snakes. Wordless.

Bancroft, Laura *see* Baum, L. Frank (Lyman Frank)

Bang, Betsy. *The cucumber stem* ill. by Tony Chen. Greenwillow, 1980. Adapt. from a Bengali folk tale. Subj: Character traits – smallness. Folk and fairy tales. Foreign lands – India.

The old woman and the red pumpkin ill. by Molly Bang. Macmillan, 1975. Adapt. and tr. from a Bengali folk tale by Betsy Bang. Subj: Animals. Character traits – cleverness. Folk and fairy tales. Foreign lands – India.

The old woman and the rice thief ill. by Molly Bang. Greenwillow, 1978. Adapt. and tr. from a Bengali folk tale by Betsy Bang. Subj: Animals. Character traits – cleverness. Folk and fairy tales. Foreign lands – India.

Tutuni the tailor bird ill. by Molly Bang. Greenwillow, 1978. Adapt. and tr. from a Bengali folk tale by Betsy Bang. Subj: Birds. Folk and fairy tales. Foreign lands – India. Royalty.

Bang, Molly. *Dawn* ill. by author. Morrow, 1983. An adaptation of the Japanese folk tale: Tsuru Nyōbō. Also known as The Crane Wife. Subj: Activities – weaving. Behavior – secrets. Birds – cranes. Character traits – curiosity. Folk and fairy tales. Foreign lands – Japan.

The grey lady and the strawberry snatcher ill. by author. Four Winds Pr., 1980. Subj: Caldecott award honor book. Imagination. Wordless.

Ten, nine, eight ill. by author. Greenwillow, 1983. Subj: Bedtime. Caldecott award honor book. Counting. Poetry, rhyme.

Wiley and the hairy man: adapted from an American folk tale ill. by author. Macmillan, 1976. Subj: Bedtime. Character traits – cleverness. Ethnic groups in the U.S. – Afro-Americans. Folk and fairy tales. Monsters.

Bangs, Edward. *Yankee Doodle* ill. by Steven Kellogg. Parents, 1976. Subj: Songs. U.S. history.

Baningan, Sharon Stearns. *Circus magic* ill. by Katharina Maillard. Dutton, 1958. Subj: Circus. Magic. Poetry, rhyme.

Banish, Roslyn. *I want to tell you about my baby.* Wingbow Pr., 1982. Subj: Babies. Family life.

Bank Street College of Education. *Around the city* ill. by Aurelius Battaglia and others. Rev. ed. Macmillan, 1972. Subj: City.

Green light, go ill. by Jack Endewelt and others. Rev. ed. Subj: City. Traffic signs.

In the city ill. by Dan Dickas. Rev. ed. Macmillan, 1972. Subj: City.

My city ill. by Ron Becker and others. Macmillan, 1965. Subj: City.

People read ill. by Dan Dickas. Rev. ed. Macmillan, 1972. Subj: Activities – reading. Careers.

Uptown, downtown ill. by Ron Becker and others. Macmillan, 1965. Subj: City.

Bannerman, Helen. *Sambo and the twins* ill. by author. Lippincott, 1937. Subj: Folk and fairy tales. Foreign lands – India.

The story of little black Sambo ill. by author. Lippincott, 1943. Subj: Animals – tigers. Character traits – cleverness. Foreign lands – India.

The story of the teasing monkey ill. by author. Lippincott, 1907. Subj: Animals – lions. Animals – monkeys.

Bannon, Laura. *The best house in the world* ill. by author. Houghton, 1952. Subj: Animals. Houses. Imagination.

Hat for a hero: a Tarasean boy of Mexico ill. by author. Albert Whitman, 1954. Subj: Character traits – bravery. Clothing. Foreign lands – Mexico.

Katy comes next ill. by author. Albert Whitman, 1959. Subj: Toys – dolls.

Little people of the night ill. by author. Houghton, 1963. Subj: Animals. Emotions – fear. Night.

Manuela's birthday ill. by author. Albert Whitman, 1972. Orig. pub. in 1939. Subj: Birthdays. Foreign lands – Mexico. Toys – dolls.

Red mittens ill. by author. Houghton, 1946. Subj: Animals. Behavior – losing things. Clothing.

The scary thing ill. by author. Houghton, 1956. Subj: Animals. Emotions – fear.

Watchdog ill. by author. Albert Whitman, 1948. Subj: Animals – dogs. Foreign lands – Mexico. Holidays – Cinco de Mayo. Pets.

Baran, Tancy. *Bees* ill. by author. Grosset, 1971. Subj: Insects – bees. Science.

Barchilon, Jacques. *The authentic Mother Goose fairy tales and nursery rhymes.* Alan Swallow, 1960. Subj: Nursery rhymes.

Barker, Carol. *Achilles and Diana* (Bates, H E)

Achilles the donkey (Bates, H E)

Barker, Cicely Mary. *Berry flower fairies* ill. by author. Putnam's, 1981. Subj: Fairies. Flowers. Poetry, rhyme.

Blossom flower fairies ill. by author. Putnam's, 1981. Subj: Fairies. Flowers. Poetry, rhyme.

Flower fairies of the seasons ill. by author. Harper, 1984. First published in 1923. Subj: Fairies. Flowers. Poetry, rhyme. Seasons. Trees.

Spring flower fairies ill. by author. Putnam's 1981. Subj: Fairies. Flowers. Poetry, rhyme.

Summer flower fairies ill. by author. Putnam's, 1981. Subj: Fairies. Flowers. Poetry, rhyme.

Barker, George. *Why teddy bears are brown* (Barker, Inga-Lil)

Barker, Inga-Lil. *Why teddy bears are brown* by Inga-Lil and George Barker; ill. by authors. Crowell, 1946. Subj: Behavior – greed. Toys – teddy bears.

Barker, Melvern J. *Country fair.* Oxford Univ. Pr., 1955. Subj: Animals – bulls, cows. Fairs.

Little island star. Oxford Univ. Pr., 1954. Subj: Lighthouses.

Barker, Peggy. *What happened when grandma died* ill. by Patricia Mattozzi. Concordia, 1984. Subj: Death. Family life – grandparents, great-grandparents. Religion.

Barkhouse, Joyce. *Anna's pet* (Atwood, Margaret)

Barklem, Jill. *Autumn story* ill. by author. Putnam's, 1980. Subj: Animals – mice. Behavior – lost. Seasons – fall.

The big book of Brambly Hedge ill. by author. Putnam's, 1981. Subj: Animals – mice. Country.

The secret staircase ill. by author. Putnam's, 1983. Subj: Animals – mice. Behavior – secrets. Food. Problem solving. Seasons – winter.

Spring story ill. by author. Putnam's, 1980. Subj: Animals – mice. Birthdays. Seasons – spring.

Summer story ill. by author. Putnam's, 1980. Subj: Animals – mice. Seasons – summer. Weddings.

Winter story ill. by author. Putnam's, 1980. Subj: Animals – mice. Seasons – winter. Weather – snow.

Barner, Bob. *Elephant facts* ill. by author. Dutton, 1979. Subj: Animals – elephants. Science.

Barnett, Naomi. *I know a dentist* ill. by Linda Boehm. Putnam's, 1977. Subj: Careers – dentists. Teeth.

Barnhart, Peter. *The wounded duck* ill. by Adrienne Adams. Scribner's, 1979. Subj: Birds – ducks. Character traits – kindness to animals. Death. Seasons – winter.

Barr, Cathrine. *A horse for Sherry* ill. by author. Walck, 1963. Subj: Animals – horses. Farms.

Hound dog's bone ill. by author. Walck, 1961. Subj: Animals – dogs. Animals – foxes. Behavior – stealing. Humor.

Little Ben ill. by author. Walck, 1960. Subj: Animals – beavers. Character traits – bravery.

Sammy seal ov the sircus ill. by author. [1st initial teaching alphabet ed.] Walck, 1955, 1964. Subj: Animals – seals. Circus. Clowns, jesters.

Barr, Jene. *Fire snorkel number 7* ill. by Joe Rogers. Albert Whitman, 1965. Subj: Careers – firefighters. Fire. Trucks.

Barrett, John M. *The bear who slept through Christmas.* Ideals, 1980. Subj: Animals – bears. Hibernation. Holidays – Christmas. Humor.

The Easter bear. Children's Pr., 1981. Subj: Animals – bears. Animals – rabbits. Holidays – Easter. Seasons – spring.

Oscar the selfish octopus ill. by Joe Servello. Human Sciences Pr., 1978. Subj: Character traits – selfishness. Octopuses.

Barrett, Judi. *Animals should definitely not act like people* ill. by Ron Barrett. Atheneum, 1980. Subj: Animals. Behavior – imitation.

Animals should definitely not wear clothing ill. by Ron Barrett. Atheneum, 1974. Subj: Animals. Behavior – imitation. Clothing.

An apple a day ill. by Tim Lewis. Atheneum, 1973. Subj: Food. Illness.

Benjamin's 365 birthdays ill. by Ron Barrett. Atheneum, 1974. Subj: Birthdays.

Cloudy with a chance of meatballs ill. by Ron Barrett. Atheneum, 1978. Subj: Family life – grandparents, great-grandparents. Food. Imagination. Weather.

I hate to go to bed ill. by Ray Cruz. Four Winds Pr., 1977. Subj: Bedtime. Imagination.

I hate to take a bath ill. by Charles B. Slackman. Atheneum, 1981. Subj: Behavior – growing up. Concepts – size.

I'm too small, you're too big ill. by David S. Rose. Atheneum, 1981. Subj: Behavior – growing up. Concepts – opposite. Family life – fathers.

Old MacDonald had an apartment house ill. by Ron Barrett. Atheneum, 1969. Subj: Activities – gardening. City. Farms.

Peter's pocket ill. by Julia Noonan. Atheneum, 1974. Subj: Clothing.

Snake is totally tail ill. by L. S. Johnson. Atheneum, 1983. Subj: Animals. Insects. Reptiles.

What's left? ill. by author. Atheneum, 1983. Subj: Participation. Problem solving.

Barrett, Lawrence Louis. *Twinkle, the baby colt.* Knopf, 1945. Subj: Animals – horses. Behavior – running away.

Barrie, J. M. (James M.). *Peter Pan* ill. by Diane Goode. Random House, 1983. Subj: Elves and little people. Folk and fairy tales.

Barrows, Marjorie Wescott. *The book of favorite Muggins Mouse stories* ill. by Anne Sellers Leaf. Rand McNally, 1965. Subj: Animals – mice.

Fraidy cat ill. by Barbara Maynard. Rand McNally, 1942. Subj: Animals – cats. Character traits – bravery. Format, unusual.

The funny hat ill. by Norv Mink. Rand McNally, 1943. Subj: Behavior – losing things. Clothing. Format, unusual.

Muggins' big balloon ill. by Anne Sellers Leaf. Rand McNally, 1967. Subj: Animals – mice. Toys – balloons.

Muggins Mouse ill. by Anne Sellers Leaf. Rand McNally, 1965. Subj: Animals – mice.

Muggins takes off ill. by Anne Sellers Leaf. Rand McNally, 1964. Subj: Animals – mice.

Timothy Tiger ill. by Keith Ward. Rand McNally, 1943. Subj: Animals – tigers.

Barry, Katharina. *A is for anything* ill. by author. Harcourt, 1961. Subj: ABC books. Poetry, rhyme.

A bug to hug ill. by author. Harcourt, 1964. Subj: Imagination. Poetry, rhyme. Problem solving.

Barry, Robert E. *Animals around the world* ill. by author. McGraw Hill, 1967. Subj: ABC books. Animals. Poetry, rhyme.

Mr. Willowby's Christmas tree ill. by Paul Galdone. McGraw-Hill, 1963. Subj: Holidays – Christmas. Poetry, rhyme. Trees.

Next please ill. by author. Houghton, 1961. Subj: Careers – barbers. Zoos.

Barth, Edna. *Jack-o'-lantern* ill. by Paul Galdone. Seabury Pr., 1974. Subj: Behavior – trickery. Character traits – meanness. Folk and fairy tales. Holidays – Halloween.

Barthelme, Donald. *The slightly irregular fire engine: or, The hithering thithering djinn* ill. by author. Farrar, 1971. Collage ill. made from nineteenth-century engravings. Subj: Imagination.

Bartlett, Margaret Farrington. *The clean brook* ill. by Aldren Auld Watson. McGraw-Hill, 1960. Subj: Science.

Down the mountain: a book about the ever-changing soil ill. by Rhys Caparn. Addison-Wesley, 1963. Subj: Science.

Raindrop stories (Bassett, Preston R.)

Where the brook begins ill. by Aldren Auld Watson. Crowell, 1961. Subj: Science.

Bartlett, Robert Merrill. *Jack Horner and song of sixpence* ill. by Emily N. Barto. Longman, 1943. Subj: Nursery rhymes.

Bartlett, Susan. *A book to begin on libraries* ill. by Gioia Fiammenghi. Holt, 1964. Subj: Libraries.

Barto, Emily N. *Chubby bear* ill. by author. Longman, 1941. Subj: Animals – bears. Poetry, rhyme.

Bartoli, Jennifer. *In a meadow, two hares hide* ill. by Takeo Ishida; ed. by Kathy Pacini. Albert Whitman, 1978. Subj: Animals – rabbits. Seasons – winter.

Nonna ill. by Joan Drescher. Harvey House, 1975. Subj: Death. Emotions – sadness. Family life. Family life – grandparents, great-grandparents.

Snow on bear's nose: a story of a Japanese moon bear cub ed. by Caroline Rubin; ill. by Takeo Ishida. Albert Whitman, 1972. Subj: Animals – bears. Behavior – lost. Foreign lands – Japan. Hibernation. Seasons – winter. Weather – snow.

Barton, Byron. *Airport* ill. by author. Crowell, 1982. Subj: Airplanes, airports. Careers – airplane pilots. Transportation.

Building a house ill. by author. Greenwillow, 1981. Subj: Houses.

Buzz, buzz, buzz ill. by author. Macmillan, 1973. Subj: Cumulative tales. Insects – bees.

Harry is a scaredy-cat ill. by author. Macmillan, 1974. Subj: Circus. Emotions – fear.

Jack and Fred ill. by author. Macmillan, 1974. Subj: Animals – dogs. Animals – rabbits. Pets.

Wheels ill. by author. Crowell, 1979. Subj: Progress. Wheels.

Where's Al? ill. by author. Seabury Pr., 1972. Subj: Animals – dogs. Behavior – lost. Wordless.

Barton, Pat. *A week is a long time* ill. by Jutta Ash. Academy Chicago Ltd., 1980. Subj: Country. Clothing.

Baruch, Dorothy. *I would like to be a pony and other wishes* ill. by Mary Chalmers. Harper, 1959. Subj: Behavior – wishing. Poetry, rhyme.

Kappa's tug-of-war with the big brown horse: the story of a Japanese water imp ill. by Sanryo Sakai. Tuttle, 1962. Subj: Animals. Elves and little people. Farms. Folk and fairy tales. Foreign lands – Japan.

Bascom, Joe. *Malcolm Softpaws* ill. by author. Lippincott, 1958. Subj: Animals – cats. Behavior – greed. Character traits – selfishness.

Malcolm's job ill. by author. Lippincott, 1959. Subj: Animals – cats. Family life. Music.

Bashevis, Isaac *see* Singer, Isaac Bashevis

Basile, Giambattista. *Petrosinella: a Neapolitan Rapunzel* adapt. by John Edward Taylor; ill. by Diane Stanley. Warne, 1981. Subj: Folk and fairy tales. Foreign lands – Italy. Royalty. Witches.

Baskin, Leonard. *Hosie's alphabet* ill. by author; words by Hosea, Tobias and Lisa Baskin. Viking, 1972. Subj: ABC books. Caldecott award honor book. Children as authors.

Hosie's aviary ill. by author; words mostly by Tobias Baskin and others. Viking, 1979. Subj: Birds. Children as authors.

Hosie's zoo ill. by author; words by Tobias Baskin and others. Viking, 1981. Subj: Animals. Poetry, rhyme. Zoos.

Baskin, Tobias. *Hosie's aviary* (Baskin, Leonard)

Hosie's zoo (Baskin, Leonard)

Bason, Lillian. *Castles and mirrors and cities of sand* ill. by Allan Eitzen. Lothrop, 1968. Subj: Animals. Sand. Science.

Pick a raincoat, pick a whistle ill. by Allan Eitzen. Lothrop, 1966. Subj: Activities – whistling. Trees.

Those foolish Molboes! ill. by Margot Tomes. Coward, 1977. Subj: Behavior – hiding things. Character traits – cleverness. Character traits – foolishness. Folk and fairy tales. Foreign lands – Denmark.

Bass, Donna. *The tale of the dark crystal* ill. by Bruce McNally. Holt, 1982. Subj: Elves and little people. Folk and fairy tales. Magic. Monsters.

Bassett, Preston R. *Raindrop stories* by Preston R. Bassett and Margaret Farrington Bartlett; ill. by Jim Arnosky. Four Winds Pr., 1981. Subj: Noise, sounds. Weather – rain.

Basso, Bill. *The top of the pizzas* ill. by author. Dodd, 1977. Subj: Activities – working. Food. Monsters.

Bate, Lucy. *Little rabbit's loose tooth* ill. by Diane de Groat. Crown, 1975. Subj: Animals – rabbits. Fairies. Teeth.

Bate, Norman. *Vulcan* ill. by author. Scribner's, 1961. Subj: Machines.

What a wonderful machine is a submarine ill. by author. Scribner's, 1961. Subj: Boats, ships. Sea and seashore.

Who built the bridge? ill. by author. Crown, 1975. Subj: Machines.

Who built the highway? ill. by author. Scribner's, 1953. Subj: Machines. Roads.

Bates, H. E. *Achilles and Diana* by H. E. Bates and Carol Barker; ill. by Carol Barker. Dobson, 1963. Subj: Animals – donkeys.

Achilles the donkey by H. E. Bates and Carol Barker; ill. by Carol Barker. Watts, 1963. Subj: Animals – donkeys. Behavior – running away.

Batherman, Muriel. *Animals live here* ill. by author. Greenwillow, 1979. Subj: Animals. Science.

Some things you should know about my dog ill. by author. Prentice-Hall, 1976. Subj: Animals – dogs.

Battles, Edith. *One to teeter-totter* ill. by Rosalind Fry. Albert Whitman, 1973. Subj: Emotions – loneliness. Family life. Friendship. Games.

The terrible terrier ill. by Tom Funk. Addison-Wesley, 1972. Subj: Animals – dogs. Behavior – greed.

The terrible trick or treat ill. by Tom Funk. Addison-Wesley, 1970. Subj: Behavior – greed. Holidays – Halloween.

What does the rooster say, Yoshio? ill. by Toni Hormann. Albert Whitman, 1978. Subj: Animals. Foreign lands – Japan. Language.

Bauer, Caroline Feller. *My mom travels a lot* ill. by Nancy Winslow Parker. Warne, 1981. Subj: Careers. Family life – mothers.

Bauer, Helen. *Good times in the park* photos. by Hubert A. Lowman. Melmont, 1954. Subj: Activities – playing. Birthdays. Zoos.

Baugh, Dolores M. *Bikes* by Dolores M. Baugh and Marjorie P. Pulsifer; ill. by Eve Hoffmann. Rev. ed. Chandler, 1965. Subj: Sports – bicycling. Traffic signs.

Let's go by Dolores M. Baugh and Marjorie P. Pulsifer; ill. by Eve Hoffmann. Noble, 1970. Subj: Stores.

Let's see the animals by Dolores M. Baugh and Marjorie P. Pulsifer; ill. by Eve Hoffmann. Chandler, 1965. Subj: Animals.

Let's take a trip by Dolores M. Baugh and Marjorie P. Pulsifer; ill. by Richard Szumski and others. Chandler, 1965. Subj: Libraries. Machines.

Slides by Dolores M. Baugh and Marjorie P. Pulsifer; ill. by Eve Hoffmann. Noble, 1970. Subj: Activities – playing.

Supermarket by Dolores M. Baugh and Marjorie P. Pulsifer; ill. by Eve Hoffmann. Noble, 1970. Subj: Food. Shopping. Stores.

Swings by Dolores M. Baugh and Marjorie P. Pulsifer; ill. by Eve Hoffmann. Noble, 1970. Subj: Activities – playing. Activities – swinging.

Trucks and cars to ride by Dolores M. Baugh and Marjorie P. Pulsifer; ill. by Eve Hoffmann. Noble, 1970. Subj: Automobiles. Trucks. Transportation.

Baum, Arline. *One bright Monday morning* by Arline and Joseph Baum; ill. by Joseph Baum. Random House, 1962. Subj: Counting. Seasons – spring. Weather.

Baum, Joseph. *One bright Monday morning* (Baum, Arline)

Baum, L. Frank (Lyman Frank). *Mother Goose in prose* ill. by Maxfield Parrish. Bounty Books, 1901. Subj: Nursery rhymes.

Baum, Louis. *JuJu and the pirate* ill. by Philippe Matter. Harper, 1984. Subj: Activities – traveling. Birds – parakeets, parrots. Pirates.

Baum, Willi. *Birds of a feather* ill. by author. Addison-Wesley, 1969. Subj: Birds. Wordless.

Baumann, Hans. *The hare's race* ill. by Antoni Boratynski; tr. from the German by Elizabeth D. Crawford. Morrow, 1976. Subj: Animals – rabbits. Folk and fairy tales. Reptiles – turtles. Sports – racing.

Baumann, Kurt. *The paper airplane* ill. by Fulvio Testa. Little, 1982. Subj: Airplanes, airports. Imagination.

Piro and the fire brigade ill. by Jiri Bernard. Faber, 1981. Translation of: Piro und die Feuerwehr. Subj: Animals – dogs. Careers – firefighters. Character traits – bravery. Fire. Foreign lands – Switzerland.

Puss in boots (Perrault, Charles)

Bawden, Nina. *St. Francis of Assisi* ill. by Pascale Allamand. Lothrop, 1983. Subj: Character traits – generosity. Religion.

William Tell ill. by Pascale Allamand. Lothrop, 1981. Subj: Character traits – bravery. Folk and fairy tales. Foreign lands – Switzerland.

Bayer, Jane. *A my name is Alice* ill. by Steven Kellogg. Dial Pr., 1984. Subj: ABC books. Animals. Names.

Bayley, Nicola. *Crab cat* ill. by author. Knopf, 1984. Subj: Animals – cats. Imagination.

Elephant cat ill. by author. Knopf, 1984. Subj: Animals – cats. Imagination.

Nicola Bayley's book of nursery rhymes ill. by author. Knopf, 1975. Subj: Nursery rhymes.

One old Oxford ox ill. by author. Atheneum, 1977. Subj: Animals. Counting.

Parrot cat ill. by author. Knopf, 1984. Subj: Animals – cats. Imagination.

Polar bear cat ill. by author. Knopf, 1984. Subj: Animals – cats. Imagination.

Spider cat ill. by author. Knopf, 1984. Subj: Animals – cats. Imagination.

Baylor, Byrd. *Amigo* ill. by Garth Williams. Macmillan, 1963. Subj: Animals – prairie dogs. Pets. Poetry, rhyme.

The best town in the world ill. by Ronald Himler. Scribner's, 1983. Subj: City.

Coyote cry ill. by Symeon Shimin. Lothrop, 1972. Subj: Animals – coyotes. Animals – dogs.

The desert is theirs ill. by Peter Parnall. Scribner's, 1975. Subj: Caldecott award honor book. Desert. Ecology. Ethnic groups in the U.S. – Indians. Folk and fairy tales. Poetry, rhyme.

Desert voices ill. by Peter Parnall. Scribner's, 1981. Subj: Animals. Desert. Poetry, rhyme.

Everybody needs a rock ill. by Peter Parnall. Scribner's, 1974. Subj: Poetry, rhyme. Rocks.

A God on every mountain top: stories of southwest Indian sacred mountains ill. by Carol Brown. Scribner's, 1981. Subj: Ethnic groups in the U.S. – Indians. Folk and fairy tales.

Guess who my favorite person is ill. by Robert Andrew Parker. Scribner's, 1977. Subj: Friendship. Games.

Hawk, I'm your brother ill. by Peter Parnall. Scribner's, 1976. Subj: Birds – hawks. Caldecott award honor book. Character traits – freedom. Ethnic groups in the U.S. – Indians.

Moon song ill. by Ronald Himler. Scribner's, 1982. Subj: Animals – coyotes. Ethnic groups in the U.S. – Indians. Folk and fairy tales. Moon.

The other way to listen ill. by Peter Parnall. Scribner's, 1978. Subj: Nature. Poetry, rhyme.

The way to start a day ill. by Peter Parnall. Scribner's, 1978. Subj: Caldecott award honor book. Folk and fairy tales. Foreign lands. Religion. Sun.

We walk in sandy places ill. by Marilyn Schweitzer. Scribner's, 1976. Subj: Animals. Desert.

When clay sings ill. by Tom Bahti. Scribner's, 1972. Subj: Art. Caldecott award honor book. Ethnic groups in the U.S. – Indians.

Your own best secret place ill. by Peter Parnall. Scribner's, 1979. Subj: Behavior – hiding things. Behavior – secrets.

Beach, Stewart. *Good morning, sun's up!* ill. by Yutaka Sugita. Scroll Pr., 1970. German ed. has title: Guten Morgen, liebe Sonne! Subj: Animals. Games. Morning.

Beatty, Hetty Burlingame. *Bucking horse* ill. by author. Houghton, 1957. Subj: Animals – horses. Cowboys.

Droopy ill. by author. Houghton, 1954. Subj: Animals – mules. Character traits – stubbornness. Sports – swimming.

Little Owl Indian ill. by author. Houghton, 1951. Subj: Animals – horses. Ethnic groups in the U.S. – Indians. Fire.

Moorland pony ill. by author. Houghton, 1961. Subj: Activities – traveling. Animals – horses. Character traits – kindness to animals. Family life. Foreign lands – England. Pets.

Bechstein, Ludwig. *The rabbit catcher and other fairy tales* tr. and intro. by Randall Jarrell; ill. by Ugo Fontana. Macmillan, 1962. Subj: Folk and fairy tales. Foreign lands – Germany.

Becker, Edna. *Nine hundred buckets of paint* ill. by Margaret Bradfield. Abingdon Pr., 1945. Subj: Activities – painting. Houses. Moving.

Becker, John Leonard. *Seven little rabbits* ill. by Barbara Cooney. Walker, 1973. Subj: Animals – rabbits. Counting.

Becker, May Lamberton. *The rainbow Mother Goose* (Mother Goose)

Beckett, Hilary. *The rooster's horns:* (Young, Ed)

Beckman, Kaj *Lisa cannot sleep* ill. by Per Beckman. Watts, 1970. Subj: Bedtime. Family life. Sleep. Toys.

Bedford, A. N. (Annie North) *see* Watson, Jane Werner

Beech, Caroline. *Peas again for lunch* ill. by Gina Calleja. Annick Pr., 1981. Subj: Behavior – misbehavior. Imagination.

Beecroft, John. *What? Another cat!* ill. by Kurt Wiese. Dodd, 1960. Subj: Animals – cats. Sibling rivalry.

Beer, Kathleen Costello. *What happens in the spring.* National Geographic Soc., 1977. Subj: Seasons – spring.

Behn, Harry. *All kinds of time* ill. by author. Harcourt, 1950. Subj: Machines. Time.

Crickets and bullfrogs and whispers of thunder sel. by Lee Bennett Hopkins; ill. by author. Harcourt, 1984. Subj: Poetry, rhyme.

What a beautiful noise ill. by Harold Berson. Collins-World, 1970. Subj: Humor. Music. Noise, sounds.

Behrens, June. *Can you walk the plank?* ill. by Michele and Tom Grimm. Childrens Pr., 1976. Subj: Activities. Games. Imagination.

Fiesta! ill. by Scott Taylor. Childrens Pr., 1978. Subj: Ethnic groups in the U.S. – Mexican-Americans. Holidays – Cinco de Mayo.

The manners book: what's right, Ned? ill. by Michele and Tom Grimm. Childrens Pr., 1980. Subj: Etiquette. Toys – teddy bears.

Soo Ling finds a way ill. by Tarō Yashima. Children's Pr., 1965. Subj: Ethnic groups in the U.S. – Chinese-Americans. Family life – grandparents, great-grandparents. Foreign lands – China. Laundry.

Whalewatch! ill. by John Olguin. Childrens Pr., 1978. Photographs collected by John Olguin. Subj: Animals – whales. Science.

Who am I? ill. by Ray Ambraziunas. Elk Grove Pr., 1968. Subj: School. Self-concept.

Beim, Jerrold. *Country mailman* ill. by Leonard W. Shortall. Morrow, 1958. Subj: Careers – mail carriers. Character traits – helpfulness. Emotions – envy, jealousy.

Country train ill. by Leonard W. Shortall. Morrow, 1950. Subj: Character traits – individuality. Trains.

Eric on the desert ill. by Louis Darling. Morrow, 1953. Subj: Animals. Character traits – bravery. Desert.

Freckle face ill. by Barbara Cooney. Crowell, 1957. Subj: Character traits – appearance. Character traits – being different. Character traits – individuality.

Jay's big job ill. by Tracy Sugarman. Morrow, 1957. Subj: Activities – painting. Activities – working. Family life.

The little igloo (Beim, Lorraine)

Lucky Pierre (Beim, Lorraine)

Sasha and the samovar (Beim, Lorraine)

Sir Halloween ill. by Tracy Sugarman. Morrow, 1959. Subj: Holidays – Halloween.

The smallest boy in the class ill. by Meg Wohlberg. Morrow, 1949. Subj: Behavior – sharing. Character traits – smallness. Names.

The swimming hole ill. by Louis Darling. Morrow, 1950. Subj: Behavior. Ethnic groups in the U.S. – Afro-Americans. Friendship. Seasons – summer. Sports – swimming.

The taming of Toby ill. by Tracy Sugarman. Morrow, 1953. Subj: Behavior – misbehavior. Imagination. School.

Tim and the tool chest ill. by Tracy Sugarman. Morrow, 1951. Subj: Tools.

Two is a team (Beim, Lorraine)

With dad alone ill. by Don Sibley. Harcourt, 1954. Subj: Death. Family life – fathers.

Beim, Lorraine. *The little igloo* by Lorraine and Jerrold Beim; ill. by Howard Simon. Harcourt, 1941. Subj: Animals – dogs. Ethnic groups in the U.S. – Eskimos.

Lucky Pierre by Lorraine and Jerrold Beim; ill. by Howard Simon. Harcourt, 1940. Subj: Behavior – collecting things. Careers – fishermen. Character traits – luck. Family life.

Sasha and the samovar by Lorraine and Jerrold Beim; ill. by Rafaello Busoni. Harcourt, 1944. Subj: Fairies. Foreign lands – Russia.

Two is a team by Lorraine and Jerrold Beim; ill. by Ernest Crichlow. Harcourt, 1945. Subj: Behavior – fighting, arguing. Ethnic groups in the U.S. – Afro-Americans. Friendship. Problem solving.

Beisert, Heide Helene. *Poor fish* tr. from German by Marion Koenig; ill. by author. Harper, 1982. Subj: Birds. Ecology. Fish.

Bell, Anthea. *The brave little tailor* (Grimm, Jacob)

Goodbye little bird (Damjan, Mischa)

Mumble bear (Ruck-Pauquèt, Gina)

The proud white cat (Hürlimann, Ruth)

The red shoes (Andersen, H C (Hans Christian))

Sandman in the lighthouse (Strahl, Rudi)

The swineherd (Andersen, H C (Hans Christian))

The trip to Panama (Janosch)

Bell, Gina *see* Balzano, Jeanne

Bell, Janet *see* Clymer, Eleanor Lowenton

Bell, Norman. *Linda's airmail letter* ill. by Patricia Villemain. Follett, 1964. Subj: Birthdays. Friendship. Letters. Weather.

Bell-Zano, Gina *see* Balzano, Jeanne

Beller, Janet. *A-B-C-ing: an action alphabet.* Crown, 1984. Subj: ABC books. Activities.

Belling the cat and other stories retold by Leland B. Jacobs; ill. by Harold Berson. Golden Pr., 1960. Subj: Animals. Folk and fairy tales.

Belloc, Hilaire. *The bad child's book of beasts* ill. by Basil T. Blackwood [B.A.T.]. Knopf, 1965. Originally published in 1896. Subj: Animals. Behavior. Humor.

The bad child's book of beasts, and more beasts for worse children ill. by Harold Berson. Grosset, 1966. Subj: Animals. Poetry, rhyme.

Matilda who told lies and was burned to death ill. by Steven Kellogg. Dial Pr., 1970. Subj: Behavior – lying. Behavior – misbehavior. Fire. Poetry, rhyme.

More beasts for worse children ill. by Basil T. Blackwood [B.A.T.]. Knopf, 1966. Subj: Animals. Poetry, rhyme.

Bellville, Cheryl Walsh. *Large animal veterinarians* (Bellville, Rod)

Round-up photos. by author. Carolrhoda Books, 1982. Subj: Animals – bulls, cows. Animals – horses. Farms.

Bellville, Rod. *Large animal veterinarians* by Rod and Cheryl Walsh Bellville; photos. by authors. Carolrhoda Books, 1983. Subj: Animals. Careers – veterinarians.

Belpré, Pura. *Dance of the animals: a Puerto Rican folk tale* ill. by Paul Galdone. Warne, 1972. Subj: Animals. Folk and fairy tales. Foreign lands – Puerto Rico.

Perez and Martina: a Portorican folk tale ill. by Carlos Sanchez. Rev. ed. Warne, 1961. Originally pub. in 1960. Subj: Animals – mice. Folk and fairy tales. Foreign lands – Puerto Rico. Insects.

Santiago ill. by Symeon Shimin. Warne, 1969. Subj: Birds – chickens. Ethnic groups in the U.S. Ethnic groups in the U.S. – Puerto Rican-Americans. Pets.

Belting, Natalia Maree. *Christmas folk* ill. by Barbara Cooney. Holt, 1969. Subj: Foreign lands – England. Holidays – Christmas. Poetry, rhyme.

Summer's coming in ill. by Adrienne Adams. Holt, 1970. Subj: Foreign lands – England. Holidays. Poetry, rhyme. Seasons – spring. Seasons – summer.

The sun is a golden earring ill. by Bernarda Bryson. Holt, 1962. Subj: Caldecott award honor book. Folk and fairy tales. Sky.

Verity Mullens and the Indian ill. by Leonard Everett Fisher. Holt, 1960. Subj: Animals – dogs. Behavior – lost. Ethnic groups in the U.S. – Indians. U.S. history.

Bemelmans, Ludwig. *Hansi* ill. by author. Viking, 1934. Subj: Activities – vacationing. Foreign lands – Tyrol. Holidays – Christmas.

Madeline ill. by author. Viking, 1939. Subj: Caldecott award honor book. Foreign lands – France. Hospitals. Orphans. Poetry, rhyme. School.

Madeline and the bad hat ill. by author. Viking, 1956. Subj: Behavior – animals, dislike of. Behavior – misbehavior. Foreign lands – France. Orphans. Poetry, rhyme.

Madeline and the gypsies ill. by author. Viking, 1959. Subj: Behavior – lost. Foreign lands – France. Gypsies. Orphans. Poetry, rhyme.

Madeline in London ill. by author. Viking, 1961. Subj: Animals – horses. Birthdays. Foreign lands – England. Orphans. Poetry, rhyme.

Madeline's rescue ill. by author. Viking, 1953. Subj: Animals – dogs. Caldecott Award book. Foreign lands – France. Orphans. Poetry, rhyme.

Parsley ill. by author. Harper, 1955. Subj: Animals – deer. Sports – hunting. Trees.

Quito express ill. by author. Viking, 1938. Subj: Activities – traveling. Family life. Foreign lands – Ecuador. Trains.

Rosebud ill. by author. Random House, 1942. Subj: Animals. Character traits – pride. Folk and fairy tales. Foreign lands – Africa. Humor.

Sunshine ill. by author. Simon and Schuster, 1950. Subj: City. Family life. Houses. Humor.

Welcome home ill. by author. Harper, 1970. Based on a poem by Beverley Bogert. Subj: Animals – foxes. Character traits – cleverness. Poetry, rhyme.

Benarde, Anita. *The pumpkin smasher* ill. by author. Walker, 1972. Subj: Holidays – Halloween. Problem solving. Witches.

Benchley, Nathaniel. *The deep dives of Stanley Whale* ill. by Mischa Richter. Harper, 1973. Subj: Animals – whales. Character traits – bravery.

The flying lessons of Gerald Pelican ill. by Mamoru Funai. Harper, 1970. Subj: Activities – flying. Birds – pelicans.

George the drummer boy ill. by Don Bolognese. Harper, 1977. Subj: U.S. history. War.

A ghost named Fred ill. by Ben Shecter. Harper, 1968. Subj: Ghosts. Problem solving.

The magic sled ill. by Mel Furakawa. Harper, 1972. Subj: Behavior – wishing. Holidays – Christmas. Weather – snow.

Oscar Otter ill. by Arnold Lobel. Harper, 1966. Subj: Animals – otters. Behavior.

Red Fox and his canoe ill. by Arnold Lobel. Harper, 1964. Subj: Animals – bears. Boats, ships. Ethnic groups in the U.S. – Indians.

Running Owl the hunter ill. by Mamoru Funai. Harper, 1979. Subj: Animals. Ethnic groups in the U.S. – Indians.

Sam the minute man ill. by Arnold Lobel. Harper, 1969. Subj: U.S. history. War.

The several tricks of Edgar Dolphin ill. by Mamoru Funai. Harper, 1978. Subj: Animals – dolphins. Character traits – cleverness.

Small Wolf ill. by Joan Sandin. Harper, 1972. Subj: Ethnic groups in the U.S. – Indians. U.S. history.

Snip ill. by Irene Trivas. Doubleday, 1981. Subj: Animals – dogs. Death. Old age.

Snorri and the strangers ill. by Don Bolognese. Harper, 1976. Subj: Foreign lands – Norway. U.S. history.

The strange disappearance of Arthur Cluck ill. by Arnold Lobel. Harper, 1967. Subj: Birds – chickens. Birds – owls. Farms. Holidays – Easter.

Walter the homing pigeon ill. by Whitney Darrow, Jr. Harper, 1981. Subj: Birds – pigeons. Food. Humor. Sports – racing.

Benchley, Peter. *Jonathan visits the White House* ill. by Richard Bergere. McGraw-Hill, 1964. Subj: Animals – dogs. Birthdays. Pets. U.S. history.

Bendick, Jeanne. *All around you* foreword by Glenn O. Blough; ill. by author. McGraw-Hill, 1951. Subj: Science. World.

What made you you? ill. by author. McGraw-Hill, 1971. Subj: Babies. Science.

Why can't I? ill. by author. McGraw-Hill, 1969. Subj: Animals. Behavior – imitation. Participation. Science.

Benedictus, Roger. *Fifty million sausages* ill. by Kenneth Mahood. Elsevier-Dutton, 1979. Subj: Food. Humor. Imagination. Machines.

Benét, William Rose. *Angels* ill. by Constantin Alajalov. Crowell, 1947. Subj: Activities – playing. Angels. Poetry, rhyme.

Mother Goose

Benjamin, Alan. *A change of plans* ill. by Steven Kellogg. Four Winds Pr., 1982. Subj: Activities – picnicking. Boats, ships. Family life. Poetry, rhyme.

1000 monsters ill. by Sal Murdocca. Four Winds Pr., 1979. Subj: Format, unusual. Humor. Monsters.

Ribtickle Town ill. by Ann Schweninger. Four Winds Pr., 1983. Subj: Behavior – lost. Food. Giants. Imagination. Poetry, rhyme.

Bennett, Jill. *Days are where we live and other poems* ill. by Maureen Roffey. Lothrop, 1982. Subj: Activities. Poetry, rhyme.

Roger was a razor fish and other poems ill. by Maureen Roffey. Lothrop, 1981. Subj: Humor. Poetry, rhyme.

Tiny Tim: verses for children ill. by Helen Oxenbury. Delacorte Pr., 1982. Subj: Humor. Poetry, rhyme.

Bennett, Olivia. *A Turkish afternoon* photos. by Christopher Cormack. David and Charles, 1984. Subj: Family life. Foreign lands – England. Foreign lands – Turkey.

Bennett, Rainey. *After the sun goes down* ill. by author. Collins-World, 1961. Subj: Birds – owls. Night.

The secret hiding place ill. by author. Collins-World, 1960. Subj: Animals – hippopotami. Behavior – solitude. Poetry, rhyme. Sea and seashore.

Bennett, Rowena. *The day is dancing and other poems* ill. by Rainey Bennett. Follett, 1968. Subj: Imagination. Poetry, rhyme.

Songs from around a toadstool table ill. by Betty Fraser. Follett, 1967. Subj: Imagination. Poetry, rhyme.

Benson, Ellen. *Philip's little sister* ill. by Rachael Davis. Childrens Pr., 1979. Subj: Family life. Sibling rivalry.

Bentley, Anne. *The Groggs' day out* ill. by Roy Bentley. Elsevier-Dutton, 1981. Subj: Foreign lands – England. Sports – bicycling.

The Groggs have a wonderful summer by Anne and Roy Bentley; ill. by Roy Bentley. Elsevier-Dutton, 1980. Subj: Foreign lands – England. Sea and seashore. Seasons – summer.

Bentley, Roy. *The Groggs have a wonderful summer* (Bentley, Anne)

Benton, Robert. *Don't ever wish for a 7-foot bear* ill. by Sally Benton. Knopf, 1972. Subj: Animals – bears. Behavior – wishing. Humor.

Little brother, no more ill. by author. Knopf, 1960. Subj: Family life. Names.

Berends, Polly Berrien. *Ladybug and dog and the night walk* ill. by Cyndy Szekeres. Random House, 1980. Subj: Animals – dogs. Friendship. Insects – fireflies. Insects – ladybugs. Night.

Berenstain, Jan. *The bear detectives* (Berenstain, Stan)

The bears' almanac (Berenstain, Stan)

Bears in the night (Berenstain, Stan)

Bears on wheels (Berenstain, Stan)

The Berenstain bears and the messy room (Berenstain, Stan)

The Berenstain bears and the missing dinosaur bone (Berenstain, Stan)

The Berenstain bears and the sitter (Berenstain, Stan)

The Berenstain bears and the spooky old tree (Berenstain, Stan)

The Berenstain bears and the truth (Berenstain, Stan)

The Berenstain bears and too much TV (Berenstain, Stan)

The Berenstain bears' Christmas tree (Berenstain, Stan)

The Berenstain bears' counting book (Berenstain, Stan)

The Berenstain bears get in a fight (Berenstain, Stan)

The Berenstain bears go to camp (Berenstain, Stan)

The Berenstain bears go to school (Berenstain, Stan)

The Berenstain bears go to the doctor (Berenstain, Stan)

The Berenstain bears in the dark (Berenstain, Stan)

The Berenstain bears' moving day (Berenstain, Stan)

The Berenstain bears' science fair (Berenstain, Stan)

The Berenstain bears' trouble with money (Berenstain, Stan)

The Berenstain bears visit the dentist (Berenstain, Stan)

The Berenstain's B book (Berenstain, Stan)

He bear, she bear (Berenstain, Stan)

Inside outside upside down (Berenstain, Stan)

Old hat, new hat (Berenstain, Stan)

Berenstain, Michael. *The dwarks: book 1* ill. by author. Bantam, 1983. Subj: Elves and little people. Family life.

The ship book ill. by author. McKay, 1978. Subj: Boats, ships.

The troll book ill. by author. Random House, 1980. Subj: Folk and fairy tales. Trolls.

Berenstain, Stan. *The bear detectives: the case of the missing pumpkin* by Stan and Jan Berenstain; ill. by authors. Random House, 1975. Subj: Animals – bears. Careers – detectives. Poetry, rhyme. Problem solving.

The bears' almanac: a year in bear country; holidays, seasons, weather, actual facts about snow, wind, rain, thunder, lightning, the sun, the moon and lots more by Stan and Jan Berenstain; ill. by authors. Random House, 1973. Subj: Animals – bears. Holidays. Moon. Poetry, rhyme. Seasons. Sun. Weather.

Bears in the night by Stan and Jan Berenstain; ill. by authors. Random House, 1971. Subj: Animals – bears. Bedtime. Night. Noise, sounds.

Bears on wheels by Stan and Jan Berenstain; ill. by authors. Random House, 1969. Subj: Animals – bears. Counting. Wheels.

The Berenstain bears and the messy room by Stan and Jan Berenstain; ill. by authors. Random House, 1983. Subj: Animals – bears. Problem solving.

The Berenstain bears and the missing dinosaur bone by Stan and Jan Berenstain; ill. by authors. Random House, 1980. Subj: Animals – bears. Museums. Poetry, rhyme. Problem solving.

The Berenstain bears and the sitter by Stan and Jan Berenstain; ill. by authors. Random House, 1981. Subj: Activities – babysitting. Animals – bears. Magic.

The Berenstain bears and the spooky old tree by Stan and Jan Berenstain; ill. by authors. Random House, 1978. Subj: Animals – bears. Poetry, rhyme. Trees.

The Berenstain bears and the truth by Stan and Jan Berenstain; ill. by authors. Random House, 1983. Subj: Animals – bears. Behavior – lying. Behavior – misbehavior. Family life.

The Berenstain bears and too much TV by Stan and Jan Berenstain; ill. by authors. Random House, 1984. Subj: Animals – bears. Family life.

The Berenstain bears' Christmas tree by Stan and Jan Berenstain; ill. by authors. Random House, 1980. Subj: Animals – bears. Family life. Holidays – Christmas. Poetry, rhyme. Trees.

The Berenstain bears' counting book by Stan and Jan Berenstain; ill. by authors. Random House, 1976. Subj: Animals – bears. Counting.

The Berenstain bears get in a fight by Stan and Jan Berenstain; ill. by authors. Random House, 1982. Subj: Animals – bears. Behavior – bad day. Sibling rivalry.

The Berenstain bears go to camp by Stan and Jan Berenstain; ill. by authors. Random House, 1982. Subj: Animals – bears. Seasons – summer. Sports – camping.

The Berenstain bears go to school by Stan and Jan Berenstain; ill. by authors. Random House, 1978. Subj: Animals – bears. School.

The Berenstain bears go to the doctor by Stan and Jan Berenstain; ill. by authors. Random House, 1981. Subj: Animals – bears. Careers – doctors.

The Berenstain bears in the dark by Stan and Jan Berenstain; ill. by authors. Random House, 1982. Subj: Animals – bears. Family life. Imagination. Night.

The Berenstain bears' moving day by Stan and Jan Berenstain; ill. by authors. Random House, 1981. Subj: Animals – bears. Family life. Friendship. Moving.

The Berenstain bears' science fair by Stan and Jan Berenstain; ill. by authors. Random House, 1977. Subj: Animals – bears. Science.

The Berenstain bears' trouble with money by Stan and Jan Berenstain; ill. by authors. Random House, 1983. Subj: Animals – bears. Money.

The Berenstain bears visit the dentist by Stan and Jan Berenstain; ill. by authors. Random House, 1981. Subj: Animals – bears. Careers – dentists.

The Berenstain's B book by Stan and Jan Berenstain; ill. by authors. Random House, 1971. Subj: ABC books. Animals – bears.

He bear, she bear by Stan and Jan Berenstain; ill. by authors. Random House, 1974. Subj: Animals – bears. Poetry, rhyme.

Inside outside upside down by Stan and Jan Berenstain; ill. by authors. Random House, 1968. Subj: Animals – bears. Concepts.

Old hat, new hat by Stan and Jan Berenstain; ill. by authors. Random House, 1970. Subj: Animals – bears. Concepts – shape. Concepts – size. Humor.

Beresford, Elisabeth. *Jack and the magic stove* ill. by Rita van Bilsen. Hutchinson, 1984. Subj: Behavior – wishing. Folk and fairy tales. Royalty.

Snuffle to the rescue ill. by Gunvor Edwards. Penguin, 1975. Subj: Animals – dogs.

Berg, Jean Horton. *The little red hen*

The noisy clock shop ill. by Art Seiden. Grosset, 1950. Subj: Clocks. Noise, sounds.

The O'Learys and friends ill. by Mary Stevens. Follett, 1961. Subj: Animals – cats. Behavior – misunderstanding. Moving. Problem solving.

The wee little man ill. by Charles Geer. Follett, 1963. Subj: Animals – cats. Elves and little people. Night. Noise, sounds. Poetry, rhyme.

Berg, Leila. *Folk tales for reading and telling* ill. by George Him. Collins-World, 1966. Subj: Folk and fairy tales. Foreign lands.

Berger, Judith. *Butterflies and rainbows* by Judith Berger and Terry Landau; ill. by Carmen Lowhar. Bande House, 1982. Subj: Concepts – color. Poetry, rhyme.

Berger, Melvin. *Why I cough, sneeze, shiver, hiccup and yawn* ill. by Holly Keller. Crowell, 1983. Subj: Health. Illness.

Berger, Terry. *Ben's ABC day* photos. by Alice Kandell. Lothrop, 1982. Subj: ABC books.

Friends photos. by Alice Kandell. Messner, 1981. Subj: Friendship.

How does it feel when your parents get divorced? photos. by Miriam Shapiro. Messner, 1977. Subj: Divorce. Emotions. Family life.

I have feelings ill. by Howard Spivak. Behavioral, 1971. Subj: Emotions. Self-concept.

I have feelings too photos. by Michael E. Ach. Human Sciences Pr., 1979. Subj: Emotions.

The turtles' picnic and other nonsense stories ill. by Erkki Alanen. Crown, 1977. Subj: Activities – picnicking. Animals.

Bergere, Thea. *Paris in the rain with Jean and Jacqueline* ill. by Richard Bergere. McGraw-Hill, 1963. Subj: City. Foreign lands – France. Weather – rain.

Bergstrom, Corinne. *Losing your best friend* ill. by Patricia Rosamilia. Human Sciences Pr., 1980. Subj: Friendship.

Beris, Sandra. *The cat's surprise* (Seguin-Fontes, Marthe)

A wedding book (Seguin-Fontes, Marthe)

Berkley, Ethel S. *Ups and down: a first book of space* ill. by Kathleen Elgin. Addison-Wesley, 1951. Subj: Concepts. Concepts – up and down.

Berman, Linda. *The goodbye painting* ill. by Mark Hannon. Human Sciences Pr., 1983. Subj: Activities – babysitting.

Bernadette (Bernadette Watts). *David's waiting day* ill. by author. Prentice-Hall, 1978. Subj: Babies. Family life.

Green is beautiful (Rogers, Margaret)

Mother Holly (Grimm, Jacob)

Bernhard, Josephine Butkowska. *Lullaby: why the pussy-cat washes himself so often; a folk-tale adapted from the Polish* ill. by Irena Lorentowicz. Roy Pubs., 1944. Subj: Animals – cats. Folk and fairy tales. Foreign lands – Poland.

Nine cry-baby dolls ill. by Irena Lorentowicz. Roy Pubs., 1945. Subj: Folk and fairy tales. Foreign lands – Poland. Toys – dolls.

Bernheim, Evelyne. *In Africa* (Bernheim, Marc)

A week in Aya's world (Bernheim, Marc)

Bernheim, Marc. *In Africa* by Marc and Evelyne Bernheim; photos. by authors. Atheneum, 1973. Subj: Family life. Foreign lands – Africa.

A week in Aya's world: the Ivory Coast by Marc and Evelyne Bernheim; photos. by authors. Macmillan, 1970. Subj: Foreign lands – Africa.

Bernstein, Joanne E. *When people die* by Joanne E. Bernstein and Steven V. Gullo; photos. by Rosmarie Hauscherr. Dutton, 1977. Subj: Death.

Bernstein, Margery. *Coyote goes hunting for fire: a California Indian myth* by Margery Bernstein and Janet Kobrin; ill. by Ed Heffernan. Scribner's, 1974. Subj: Animals. Animals – coyotes. Ethnic groups in the U.S. – Indians. Fire. Folk and fairy tales.

Earth namer: a California Indian myth by Margery Bernstein and Janet Kobrin; ill. by Ed Heffernan. Scribner's, 1974. Subj: Earth. Ethnic groups in the U.S. – Indians. Folk and fairy tales.

The first morning: an African myth by Margery Bernstein and Janet Kobrin; ill. by Enid Warner Romanek. Scribner's, 1976. Subj: Animals. Folk and fairy tales. Foreign lands – Africa.

How the sun made a promise and kept it: a Canadian Indian myth retold by Margery Bernstein and Janet Kobrin; ill. by Ed Heffernan. Scribner's, 1974. Subj: Ethnic groups in the U.S. – Indians. Folk and fairy tales. Sun.

Berquist, Grace. *The boy who couldn't roar* ill. by Ruth Van Sciver. Abingdon Pr., 1960. Subj: Behavior – bullying. Character traits – selfishness.

Speckles goes to school ill. by Kathleen Elgin. Abingdon Pr., 1952. Subj: Birds – chickens. School.

Berridge, Celia. *Grandmother's tales* ill. by author. Elsevier-Dutton, 1981. Subj: Bedtime. Family life – grandparents, great-grandparents. Witches.

Berry, Joy Wilt. *Being destructive* ill. by John Costanza. Rev. ed. Childrens Pr., 1984. Subj: Behavior – misbehavior.

Being selfish ill. by John Costanza. Rev. ed. Childrens Pr., 1984. Subj: Behavior – misbehavior. Character traits – selfishness.

Disobeying ill. by John Costanza. Rev. ed. Childrens Pr., 1984. Subj: Behavior – misbehavior.

Fighting ill. by John Costanza. Rev. ed. Childrens Pr., 1984. Subj: Behavior – fighting, arguing. Behavior – misbehavior.

Throwing tantrums ill. by John Costanza. Rev. ed. Childrens Pr., 1984. Subj: Behavior – misbehavior.

Whining ill. by John Costanza. Rev. ed. Childrens Pr., 1984. Subj: Behavior – misbehavior.

Berson, Harold. *Balarin's goat* ill. by author. Crown, 1972. Subj: Animals – goats. Folk and fairy tales.

Barrels to the moon ill. by author. Coward, 1982. Subj: Folk and fairy tales. Foreign lands – France.

The boy, the baker, the miller and more ill. by author. Crown, 1974. "The story is based on a French folk tale called Un Morceau de pain." Subj: Cumulative tales. Folk and fairy tales.

Charles and Claudine ill. by adapt. Macmillan, 1980. Subj: Folk and fairy tales. Foreign lands – France. Frogs and toads. Magic. Witches.

Henry Possum ill. by author. Crown, 1973. Subj: Animals – foxes. Animals – possums. Behavior – lost.

How the devil got his due ill. by adapt. Crown, 1972. Subj: Character traits – cleverness. Devil. Folk and fairy tales. Foreign lands – France.

Joseph and the snake ill. by author. Macmillan, 1979. Subj: Animals – foxes. Character traits – cleverness. Character traits – kindness to animals. Folk and fairy tales. Foreign lands – France. Reptiles – snakes.

Kassim's shoes ill. by adapt. Crown, 1977. Subj: Behavior – misunderstanding. Folk and fairy tales. Foreign lands – Africa.

A moose is not a mouse ill. by author. Crown, 1975. Subj: Animals – mice. Language.

Pop! goes the turnip ill. by author. Grosset, 1966. Subj: Activities – gardening. Animals – rabbits. Food. Plants.

Raminagrobis and the mice ill. by author. Seabury Pr., 1966. Subj: Animals – cats. Animals – mice. Folk and fairy tales.

The rats who lived in the delicatessen ill. by author. Crown, 1976. Subj: Animals – rats. Behavior – greed. Food.

The thief who hugged a moonbeam ill. by author. Seabury Pr., 1972. Subj: Behavior – gossip. Crime. Magic. Royalty.

Truffles for lunch ill. by author. Macmillan, 1980. Subj: Animals – pigs. Behavior – wishing.

Why the jackal won't speak to the hedgehog: a Tunisian folk tale ill. by adapt. Seabury Pr., 1970. Subj: Animals. Animals – hedgehogs. Character traits – cleverness. Folk and fairy tales. Foreign lands – Africa.

Beskow, Elsa Maartman. *Children of the forest* adapt. from the Swedish by William Jay Smith; ill. by author. Delacorte Pr., 1969. Subj: Foreign lands – Sweden. Forest, woods. Poetry, rhyme. Seasons.

Pelle's new suit ill. by author. Harper, 1919. Subj: Animals – sheep. Clothing. Foreign lands – Sweden.

Peter in Blueberry Land ill. by author. Merrimack, 1984. A new ed. of a 100-year-old picture book. Subj: Birthdays. Elves and little people. Food. Foreign lands – Sweden. Magic. Poetry, rhyme.

Peter's adventures in Blueberry land adapt. by Sheila La Farge; ill. by author. Delacorte Pr., 1975. Pub. in Sweden in 1901. Subj: Birthdays. Elves and little people. Food. Foreign lands – Sweden. Magic. Poetry, rhyme.

Bess, Clayton. *The truth about the moon* ill. by Rosekrans Hoffman. Houghton, 1983. Subj: Folk and fairy tales. Foreign lands – Africa. Moon.

Best-loved Bible verses for children ill. by Anna Maria Magagna. Grosset, 1983. Subj: Religion.

Bester, Roger. *Fireman Jim* photos. by author. Crown, 1981. Subj: Careers – firefighters. Fire.

Guess what? photos. by author. Crown, 1980. Subj: Animals. Participation. Problem solving.

Bethell, Jean. *Bathtime.* Holt, 1979. Subj: Activities – bathing. Animals.

Hooray for Henry ill. by Sergio Leone. Grosset, 1966. Subj: Character traits – perseverance. Food.

Playmates photos. by author. Holt, 1981. Subj: Activities – playing. Animals.

Three cheers for Mother Jones! ill. by Kathleen Garry-McCord. Holt, 1980. Subj: Activities – working. U.S. history.

Bettina (Bettina Ehrlich). *Cocolo comes to America* ill. by author. Harper, 1949. Subj: Animals – donkeys.

Cocolo's home ill. by author. Harper, 1950. Subj: Animals – donkeys.

Of uncles and aunts ill. by author. Norton, 1964. Subj: Family life.

Pantaloni ill. by author. Harper, 1957. Subj: Animals – dogs. Foreign lands – Italy. Poverty. Sports – fishing.

Piccolo ill. by author. Harper, 1954. Subj: Animals – donkeys.

Bettinger, Craig. *Follow me, everybody* ill. by Edward S. Hollander. Doubleday, 1968. Subj: Ethnic groups in the U.S.

Betz, Betty. *Manners for moppets* ill. by author. Grosset, 1962. Subj: Etiquette. Poetry, rhyme.

Bianco, Margery Williams. *The hurdy-gurdy man* ill. by Robert Lawson. Gregg, 1980. Subj: Activities – dancing. Music.

The velveteen rabbit: or, How toys became real ill. by Allen Atkinson. Knopf, 1983. Subj: Animals – rabbits. Emotions – love. Folk and fairy tales. Magic. Toys.

The velveteen rabbit: or, How toys became real ill. by Michael Hague. Holt, 1983. Subj: Animals – rabbits. Emotions – love. Folk and fairy tales. Magic. Toys.

The velveteen rabbit: or, How toys became real ill. by William Nicholson. Doubleday, n.d. Subj: Animals – rabbits. Emotions – love. Folk and fairy tales. Magic. Toys.

The velveteen rabbit: or, How toys became real ill. by Ilse Plume. Godine, 1983. Subj: Animals – rabbits. Emotions – love. Folk and fairy tales. Magic. Toys.

The velveteen rabbit: or, How toys became real ill. by Tien. Simon and Schuster, 1983. Subj: Animals – rabbits. Emotions – love. Folk and fairy tales. Magic. Toys.

Bible, Charles. *Hamdaani: a traditional tale from Zanzibar* ill. by adapt. Holt, 1977. Subj: Animals. Folk and fairy tales. Foreign lands – Africa.

Jennifer's new chair ill. by author. Holt, 1978. Subj: Birthdays. Family life. Family life – grandparents, great-grandparents. Fire. Parties.

Bible. New Testament. *The Lord's prayer* ill. by George Kraus. Dutton, 1970. Subj: Religion.

Bible. New Testament. Gospels. *The first Christmas: from the Gospels according to Saint Luke and Saint Matthew* ill. by Barbara Neustadt. Crowell, 1960. Subj: Religion.

Bible. Old Testament. Daniel. *Shadrach, Meshack and Abednego* ill. by Paul Galdone. McGraw-Hill, 1965. Subj: Religion.

Bible. Old Testament. Psalms. *The Lord is my shepherd* ill. by George Kraus. Dutton, 1971. Subj: Religion.

The Lord is my shepherd: the twenty-third Psalm ill. by Tasha Tudor. Putnam, 1980. Subj: Religion.

Bider, Djemma. *The buried treasure* ill. by Debby L. Carter. Dodd, 1982. Subj: Folk and fairy tales. Foreign lands – Russia.

Bienenfeld, Florence. *My mom and dad are getting a divorce* ill. by Art Scott. EMC, 1980. Subj: Divorce. Emotions.

Bierhorst, John. *The ring in the prairie: a Shawnee legend* tr. by John Bierhorst; ill. by Leo and Diane Dillon. Dial Pr., 1970. Subj: Ethnic groups in the U.S. – Indians. Folk and fairy tales.

Spirit child (Sahagun, Bernardino de)

Bileck, Marvin. *Penny* (De Regniers, Beatrice Schenk)

Rain makes applesauce (Scheer, Julian)

Bill, Helen. *Shoes fit for a king* ill. by Louis Slobodkin. Watts, 1956. Subj: Character traits – conceit. Royalty.

Billam, Rosemary. *Fuzzy rabbit* ill. by Vanessa Julian-Ottie. Random House, 1984. Subj: Behavior – needing someone. Birthdays. Emotions – love. Toys.

Billout, Guy. *By camel or by car: a look at transportation* ill. by author. Prentice-Hall, 1979. Subj: Activities – traveling. Transportation.

Billy Boy verses sel. by Richard Chase; ill. by Glen Rounds. Children's Pr., 1966. Subj: Folk and fairy tales. Poetry, rhyme. Songs.

Binzen, Bill. *Alfred goes house hunting* ill. by author. Doubleday, 1974. Subj: Animals. Houses. Toys.

Carmen photos. by author. Coward, 1970. Subj: City. Friendship.

Birnbaum, Abe. *Green eyes* ill. by author. Western Pr., 1953. Subj: Caldecott award honor book.

Biro, B. S. *see* Biro, Val

Biro, Val. *Gumdrop, the adventures of a vintage car* ill. by author. Follett, 1966. Subj: Automobiles.

Bishop, Ann. *Chicken riddle* ill. by Jerry Warshaw. Albert Whitman, 1972. Subj: Birds – chickens. Humor. Riddles.

The Ella Fannie elephant riddle book ill. by Jerry Warshaw. Albert Whitman, 1974. Subj: Animals – elephants. Humor. Riddles.

Hey riddle riddle ill. by Jerry Warshaw. Albert Whitman, 1968. Subj: Humor. Riddles.

Merry-go-riddle ill. by Jerry Warshaw. Albert Whitman, 1973. Subj: Humor. Riddles.

Noah riddle? ill. by Jerry Warshaw. Albert Whitman, 1970. Subj: Humor. Riddles.

Oh, riddlesticks! ill. by Jerry Warshaw. Albert Whitman, 1976. Subj: Humor. Riddles.

The riddle ages ill. by Jerry Warshaw. Albert Whitman, 1977. Subj: Humor. Middle ages. Riddles.

Riddle-iculous rid-alphabet book ill. by Jerry Warshaw. Albert Whitman, 1971. Subj: ABC books. Humor. Riddles.

Wild Bill Hiccup's riddle book ed. by Caroline Rubin; ill. by Jerry Warshaw. Albert Whitman, 1969. Subj: Cowboys. Humor. Riddles.

Bishop, Bonnie. *No one noticed Ralph* ill. by Jack Kent. Doubleday, 1979. Subj: Behavior – unnoticed, unseen. Birds – parakeets, parrots.

Ralph rides away ill. by Jack Kent. Doubleday, 1979. Subj: Activities – picnicking. Birds – parakeets, parrots. Zoos.

Bishop, Claire Huchet. *The five Chinese brothers* by Claire Huchet Bishop and Kurt Wiese; ill. by Kurt Wiese. Coward, 1938. Subj: Character traits – cleverness. Family life. Folk and fairy tales. Foreign lands – China.

The man who lost his head ill. by Robert McCloskey. Viking, 1942. Subj: Anatomy. Humor.

Pancakes - Paris ill. by Georges Schreiber. Viking, 1947. Subj: Food. Foreign lands – France. War.

The truffle pig ill. by Kurt Wiese. Coward, 1971. Subj: Animals – pigs. Foreign lands – France. Pets.

Twenty-two bears ill. by Kurt Wiese. Viking, 1964. Subj: Animals – bears. Counting. Cumulative tales.

Bishop, Gavin. *Mrs. McGinty and the bizarre plant* ill. by author. Oxford Univ. Pr., 1983. Subj: Activities – gardening. Plants.

Black, Algernon D. *The woman of the wood: a tale from old Russia* ill. by Evaline Ness. Holt, 1973. Subj: Folk and fairy tales. Foreign lands – Russia.

Black, Floyd. *Alphabet cat* ill. by Carol Nicklaus. Elsevier-Dutton, 1979. Subj: ABC books. Animals – cats. Animals – rats.

Black, Irma Simonton. *Big puppy and little puppy* ill. by Theresa Sherman. Holiday, 1960. Subj: Animals – dogs. Concepts – size.

Is this my dinner? ill. by Rosalind Fry. Albert Whitman, 1972. Subj: Food. Participation. Poetry, rhyme.

The little old man who could not read ill. by Seymour Fleishman. Albert Whitman, 1968. Subj: Activities – reading. Shopping.

Blackmore, Vivien. *Why corn is golden: stories about plants* ill. by Susana Martínez-Ostos. Little, 1984. Subj: Folk and fairy tales. Foreign lands – Mexico. Plants.

Blackwood, Gladys Rourke. *Whistle for Cindy* ill. by author. Albert Whitman, 1952. Subj: Activities – whistling. Animals – dogs. Pets.

Blades, Ann. *Mary of mile 18* ill. by author. Scribner's, 1976. Subj: Animals – wolves. Character traits – perseverance. Farms. Foreign lands – Canada.

Blaine, Marge. *The terrible thing that happened at our house* ill. by John Wallner. Parents, 1975. Subj: Family life. Family life – mothers. Problem solving.

Blaine, Margery Kay *see* Blaine, Marge

Blair, Anne Denton. *Hurrah for Arthur! a Mount Vernon birthday party* ill. by Carol Watson. Seven Locks Pr., 1983. Subj: Animals – mice. Character traits – helpfulness. Holidays – Washington's Birthday.

Blake, Pamela. *Peep show: a little book of rhymes* ill. by author. Macmillan, 1973. Subj: Nursery rhymes.

Blake, Quentin. *Custard and Company* (Nash, Ogden)

Mister Magnolia ill. by author. Jonathan Cape, 1980. Subj: Humor. Poetry, rhyme.

Quentin Blake's nursery rhyme book ill. by author. Harper, 1984. Subj: Humor. Nursery rhymes.

Snuff ill. by author. Lippincott, 1973. Subj: Crime. Knights.

The story of the dancing frog ill. by author. Knopf, 1985. Subj: Folk and fairy tales.

Blakeley, Peggy. *Two little ducks* ill. by Kenzo Kobayashi. Alphabet Pr., 1984. Subj: Communities, neighborhoods.

What shall I be tomorrow? ill. by Helga Aichinger. Alphabet Pr., 1984. Subj: Behavior − imitation. Imagination.

Blance, Ellen. *Lady Monster has a plan* by Ellen Blance and Ann Cook; ill. by Quentin Blake. Bowmar, 1977. Subj: Monsters.

Lady Monster helps out by Ellen Blance and Ann Cook; ill. by Quentin Blake. Bowmar, 1977. Subj: Monsters.

Monster and the magic umbrella by Ellen Blance and Ann Cook; ill. by Quentin Blake. Bowmar, 1973. Subj: Magic. Monsters. Umbrellas.

Monster and the mural by Ellen Blance and Ann Cook; ill. by Quentin Blake. Bowmar, 1977. Subj: Monsters.

Monster and the surprise cookie by Ellen Blance and Ann Cook; ill. by Quentin Blake. Bowmar, 1977. Subj: Monsters.

Monster at school by Ellen Blance and Ann Cook; ill. by Quentin Blake. Bowmar, 1973. Subj: Monsters. School.

Monster buys a pet by Ellen Blance and Ann Cook; ill. by Quentin Blake. Bowmar, 1977. Subj: Monsters. Pets.

Monster cleans his house by Ellen Blance and Ann Cook; ill. by Quentin Blake. Bowmar, 1973. Subj: Monsters.

Monster comes to the city by Ellen Blance and Ann Cook; ill. by Quentin Blake. Bowmar, 1973. Subj: City. Monsters.

Monster gets a job by Ellen Blance and Ann Cook; ill. by Quentin Blake. Bowmar, 1977. Subj: Activities − working. Monsters.

Monster goes around the town by Ellen Blance and Ann Cook; ill. by Quentin Blake. Bowmar, 1977. Subj: Monsters.

Monster goes to school by Ellen Blance and Ann Cook; ill. by Quentin Blake. Bowmar, 1973. Subj: Monsters. School.

Monster goes to the beach by Ellen Blance and Ann Cook; ill. by Quentin Blake. Bowmar, 1977. Subj: Monsters. Sea and seashore.

Monster goes to the circus by Ellen Blance and Ann Cook; ill. by Quentin Blake. Bowmar, 1977. Subj: Circus. Monsters.

Monster goes to the hospital by Ellen Blance and Ann Cook; ill. by Quentin Blake. Bowmar, 1977. Subj: Hospitals. Monsters.

Monster goes to the museum by Ellen Blance and Ann Cook; ill. by Quentin Blake. Bowmar, 1973. Subj: Monsters. Museums.

Monster goes to the zoo by Ellen Blance and Ann Cook; ill. by Quentin Blake. Bowmar, 1973. Subj: Monsters. Zoos.

Monster has a party by Ellen Blance and Ann Cook; ill. by Quentin Blake. Bowmar, 1973. Subj: Monsters. Parties.

Monster, Lady Monster and the bike ride by Ellen Blance and Ann Cook; ill. by Quentin Blake. Bowmar, 1977. Subj: Monsters. Sports − bicycling.

Monster looks for a friend by Ellen Blance and Ann Cook; ill. by Quentin Blake. Bowmar, 1973. Subj: Friendship. Monsters.

Monster looks for a house by Ellen Blance and Ann Cook; ill. by Quentin Blake. Bowmar, 1973. Subj: Monsters.

Monster meets Lady Monster by Ellen Blance and Ann Cook; ill. by Quentin Blake. Bowmar, 1973. Subj: Monsters.

Monster on the bus by Ellen Blance and Ann Cook; ill. by Quentin Blake. Bowmar, 1973. Subj: Buses. Monsters.

Blank, Joani. *A kid's first book about sex* ill. by Marcia Quackenbush. Rev. ed. Down There Pr., 1983. Subj: Family life. Science.

Blaustein, Muriel. *Baby Mabu and Auntie Moose* ill. by author. Four Winds Pr., 1983. Subj: Activities − babysitting. Behavior − misbehavior. Character traits − freedom.

Blech, Dietlind. *Hello Irina* ill. by author. Holt, 1971. Translation of Allo Irina by Yaak Karsunke. Subj: Activities − traveling. Animals − horses.

Blegvad, Erik. *Burnie's hill: a traditional rhyme* ill. by author. Atheneum, 1977. Subj: Cumulative tales. Foreign lands − Scotland. Poetry, rhyme. Seasons.

The emperor's new clothes (Andersen, H C (Hans Christian))

One is for the sun (Blegvad, Lenore)

The swineherd (Andersen, H C (Hans Christian))

Blegvad, Lenore. *Anna Banana and me* ill. by Erik Blegvad. Atheneum, 1985. Subj: Character traits − bravery. Imagination.

The great hamster hunt ill. by Erik Blegvad. Harcourt, 1969. Subj: Animals − hamsters. Pets.

Hark! Hark! The dogs do bark, and other poems about dogs ill. by Erik Blegvad. Atheneum, 1975. Subj: Animals − dogs. Nursery rhymes.

Mr. Jensen and cat ill. by Erik Blegvad. Harcourt, 1965. Subj: Animals − cats. Emotions − loneliness. Foreign lands − Denmark.

Mittens for kittens and other rhymes about cats ill. by Erik Blegvad. Atheneum, 1974. Subj: Animals − cats. Nursery rhymes.

One is for the sun by Lenore and Erik Blegvad; ill. by Erik Blegvad. Harcourt, 1968. Subj: Counting. Poetry, rhyme.

The parrot in the garret and other rhymes about dwellings comp. by Lenore Blegvad; ill. by Erik Blegvad. Atheneum, 1982. Subj: Birds — parakeets, parrots. Houses. Poetry, rhyme.

This little pig-a-wig and other rhymes about pigs ill. by Erik Blegvad. Atheneum, 1978. Subj: Animals — pigs. Nursery rhymes.

Bliss, Austin. *That dog Melly!* (Bliss, Corinne Demas)

Bliss, Corinne Demas. *That dog Melly!* by Corinne Demas Bliss with Austin Bliss; photos. by Corinne Demas Bliss and Jim Judkis. Hastings, 1981. Subj: Animals — dogs. Friendship. Pets.

Bloch, Marie Halun. *Ivanko and the dragon* (Rudchenko, Ivan)

Blocksma, Dewey. *Easy-to-make spaceships that really fly* (Blocksma, Mary)

Blocksma, Mary. *Apple tree! Apple tree!* ill. by Sandra Cox Kalthoff. Childrens Pr., 1983. Subj: Seasons. Trees.

Did you hear that? ill. by Sandra Cox Kalthoff. Childrens Pr., 1983. Subj: Bedtime. Night. Noise, sounds.

Easy-to-make spaceships that really fly by Mary and Dewey Blocksma; ill. by Marisabina Russo. Prentice-Hall, 1983. Subj: Space and space ships.

Grandma Dragon's birthday ill. by Sandra Cox Kalthoff. Childrens Pr., 1983. Subj: Birthdays.

The pup went up ill. by Sandra Cox Kalthoff. Childrens Pr., 1983. Subj: Animals — dogs. Imagination.

Blood, Charles L. *The goat in the rug* ill. by Nancy Winslow Parker. Parents, 1976. Subj: Activities — weaving. Animals — goats. Ethnic groups in the U.S. — Indians.

Bloome, Enid. *The air we breathe!* ill. with photos. Doubleday, 1972. Subj: Ecology.

The water we drink! ill. with photos. Doubleday, 1971. Subj: Ecology.

Blos, Joan W. *Martin's hats* ill. by Marc Simont. Morrow, 1984. Subj: Clothing. Imagination.

Blough, Glenn O. *Christmas trees and how they grow* ill. by Jeanne Bendick. McGraw-Hill, 1961. Subj: Holidays — Christmas. Trees.

Who lives in this meadow? ill. by Jeanne Bendick. McGraw-Hill, 1961. Subj: Animals.

Blue, Rose. *Black, black, beautiful black* ill. by Emmett Wigglesworth. Watts, 1969. Subj: Ethnic groups in the U.S. — Afro-Americans. Zoos.

How many blocks is the world? ill. by Harold James. Watts, 1970. Subj: City. Concepts — size. Ethnic groups in the U.S. — Afro-Americans. Family life. School.

I am here: Yo estoy aqui ill. by Moneta Barnett. Watts, 1971. Subj: Character traits — being different. Ethnic groups in the U.S. Ethnic groups in the U.S. — Puerto Rican-Americans. Foreign languages. School.

Blume, Judy. *The one in the middle is the green kangaroo* ill. by Amy Aitken. Bradbury Pr., 1981. Subj: Family life. Self-concept.

The Pain and The Great One ill. by Irene Trivas. Bradbury Pr., 1984. Orig. pub. in Free to be... you and me, McGraw-Hill, 1974. Subj: Family life. Sibling rivalry.

Blutig, Eduard *see* Gorey, Edward

Blyth, Alan. *Cinderella* (Perrault, Charles)

Bodecker, N. M. (Nils Mogens). *Good night little one* (Kraus, Robert)

Good night Richard Rabbit (Kraus, Robert)

"It's raining," said John Twaining: Danish nursery rhymes ill. by author. Atheneum, 1973. Subj: Foreign lands — Denmark. Humor. Nursery rhymes.

"Let's marry," said the cherry, and other nonsense poems ill. by author. Atheneum, 1974. Subj: Humor. Poetry, rhyme.

Snowman Sniffles and other verse ill. by author. Atheneum, 1983. Subj: Humor. Poetry rhyme. Tongue twisters.

Bodger, Joan. *Belinda's ball* ill. by Mark Thurman. Atheneum, 1981. Subj: Concepts.

Bodwell, Gaile. *The long day of the giants* ill. by Leon Steinmetz. McGraw-Hill, 1975. Subj: Giants. Poetry, rhyme. Time.

Boegehold, Betty. *Bear underground* ill. by Jim Arnosky. Doubleday, 1980. Subj: Animals — bears. Insects. Science.

Here's Pippa again! ill. by Cyndy Szekeres. Knopf, 1975. Subj: Animals — mice.

Hurray for Pippa! ill. by Cyndy Szekeres. Knopf, 1980. Subj: Behavior — talking to strangers. Imagination. Toys.

In the castle of cats ill. by Jan Brett. Dutton, 1981. Subj: Animals — cats. Imagination.

Pawpaw's run ill. by Christine Price. Dutton, 1968. Subj: Animals — cats. Behavior — lost. Character traits — cleverness. Emotions — love. Pets. Poetry, rhyme.

Pippa Mouse ill. by Cyndy Szekeres. Knopf, 1973. Subj: Animals — mice.

Pippa pops out! ill. by Cyndy Szekeres. Knopf, 1979. Subj: Animals — mice.

Small Deer's magic tricks ill. by Jacqueline Chwast. Coward, 1977. Subj: Animals — deer. Behavior — trickery.

Three to get ready ill. by Mary Chalmers. Harper, 1965. Subj: Animals — cats. Behavior.

Boesel, Ann Sterling. *Sing and sing again* ill. by Louise Costello. Oxford Univ. Pr., 1938. Subj: Music. Songs.

Singing with Peter and Patsy ill. by Pelagie Doane. Oxford Univ. Pr., 1944. Subj: Music. Songs.

Bogart, Bonnie. *The Ewoks join the fight* ill. by Diane de Groat. Random House, 1983. Subj: Space and space ships. War.

Bogot, Howard. *I'm growing* by Howard Bogot and Daniel B. Syme; ill. by Janet Compere. Union of American Hebrew Congregations, 1982. Subj: Behavior – growing up. Jewish culture.

Bograd, Larry. *Egon* ill. by Dirk Zimmer. Macmillan, 1980. Subj: Animals. Character traits – curiosity.

Felix in the attic ill. by Dirk Zimmer. Harvey House, 1978. Subj: Family life.

Lost in the store ill. by Victoria Chess. Macmillan, 1981. Subj: Behavior – lost. Stores.

Bohanon, Paul. *Golden Kate* ill. by Gertrude Howe. Oxford Univ. Pr., 1943. Subj: Character traits – generosity. Farms.

Bohdal, Susi. *Tom cat* ill. by author. Doubleday, 1977. Subj: Animals. Animals – cats. Communication.

Bohman, Nils. *Jim, Jock and Jumbo* ill. by Einar Norelius. Dutton, 1946. Subj: Animals – elephants. Animals – hippopotami. Animals – lions. Humor.

Bois, Ivy Du *see* DuBois, Ivy

Bois, William Pène Du *see* Du Bois, William Pène

Bolliger, Max. *The fireflies* ill. by Jiří Trnka. Atheneum, 1970. Based on a Czechoslovakian story: Broučci, by Jan Karafiát, first published in 1875; translated by Roseanna Hoover. Subj: Family life. Folk and fairy tales. Foreign lands – Czechoslovakia. Insects – fireflies. Night.

The giants' feast ill. by Monica Laimgruber. Addison-Wesley, 1976. Translation of Das Reisenfest; English version by Barbara Willard. Subj: Food. Giants.

The golden apple ill. by Celestino Piatti. Atheneum, 1970. Translated by Roseanna Hoover. Subj: Behavior – greed. Family life. Food.

The lonely prince ill. by Jurg Obrist. Atheneum, 1982. Subj: Emotions – loneliness. Friendship.

The most beautiful song ill. by Jindra Capek. Little, 1981. Subj: Music. Royalty.

Noah and the rainbow: an ancient story tr. by Clyde Robert Bulla; ill. by Helga Aichinger. Crowell, 1972. Subj: Religion – Noah.

Sandy at the children's zoo tr. from German by Elisabeth Gemming; ill. by Klaus Brunner. Crowell, 1967. Subj: Behavior – lost. Zoos.

The wooden man ill. by Fred Bauer. Seabury Pr., 1974. Translation of Der Mann aus Holz. Subj: Scarecrows. Weapons. Weather.

Bolognese, Don. *Donkey and Carlo* (Raphael, Elaine)

Donkey, it's snowing (Raphael, Elaine)

A new day ill. by author. Delacorte Pr., 1970. Subj: Activities – traveling. Babies. Ethnic groups in the U.S. – Mexican-Americans. Family life. Holidays – Christmas.

The sleepy watchdog (Bolognese, Elaine)

Turnabout (Raphael, Elaine)

Bolognese, Elaine. *The sleepy watchdog* by Elaine and Don Bolognese; ill. by Don Bolognese. Lothrop, 1964. Subj: Animals – dogs. Character traits – laziness.

Bolton, Evelyn *see* Bunting, Eve

Bond, Felicia. *Christmas in the chicken coop* ill. by author. Crowell, 1983. Subj: Birds – chickens. Holidays – Christmas. Trees.

Four Valentines in a rainstorm ill. by author. Crowell, 1983. Subj: Friendship. Holidays – Valentine's Day.

The Halloween performance ill. by author. Crowell, 1983. Subj: Animals – mice. Holidays – Halloween. School.

Mary Betty Lizzie McNutt's birthday ill. by author. Crowell, 1983. Subj: Animals – pigs. Birthdays.

Poinsettia and her family ill. by author. Crowell, 1981. Subj: Animals – pigs. Family life. Moving.

Poinsettia and the firefighters ill. by author. Crowell, 1984. Subj: Animals – pigs. Bedtime. Night. Noise, sounds.

Bond, Jean Carey. *A is for Africa* ill. by author. Watts, 1969. Subj: ABC books. Foreign lands – Africa.

Bond, Michael. *Paddington at the circus* by Michael Bond and Fred Banbery; ill. by Fred Banbery. Random House, 1973. Subj: Animals – bears. Circus. Foreign lands – England.

Paddington at the seaside ill. by Fred Banbery. Random House, 1975. Subj: Activities – vacationing. Animals – bears. Foreign lands – England. Sea and seashore.

Paddington at the tower ill. by Fred Banbery. Random House, 1975. Subj: Animals – bears. Foreign lands – England.

Paddington's lucky day ill. by Fred Banbery. Random House, 1973. Subj: Animals – bears. Character traits – luck. Foreign lands – England. Shopping.

Bond, Ruskin. *Flames in the forest* ill. by Valerie Littlewood. Watts, 1981. Subj: Fire. Foreign lands – India. Forest, woods.

Bonino, Louise. *The cozy little farm* ill. by Angelia. Random House, 1946. Subj: Animals. Farms.

Bonne, Rose. *I know an old lady* ill. by Abner Graboff. Rand McNally, 1961. Music by Alan Mills. Subj: Cumulative tales. Folk and fairy tales. Foreign lands – Canada. Humor. Music. Songs.

Bonners, Susan. *Panda* ill. by author. Delacorte Pr., 1978. Subj: Animals – bears. Science.

A penguin year ill. by author. Delacorte Pr., 1981. Subj: Birds – penguins. Family life. Foreign lands – Antarctic. Science.

Bonsall, Crosby Newell. *And I mean it, Stanley* ill. by author. Harper, 1974. Subj: Activities – playing. Animals – dogs.

The case of the cat's meow ill. by author. Harper, 1965. Subj: Animals – cats. Careers – detectives. Ethnic groups in the U.S. – Afro-Americans. Problem solving.

The case of the double cross ill. by author. Harper, 1980. Subj: Clubs, gangs. Problem solving. Secret codes.

The case of the dumb bells ill. by author. Harper, 1966. Subj: Behavior – mistakes. Careers – detectives. Communication. Problem solving.

The case of the hungry stranger ill. by author. Harper, 1963. Subj: Careers – detectives. Ethnic groups in the U.S. – Afro-Americans. Problem solving.

The case of the scaredy cats ill. by author. Harper, 1971. Subj: Careers – detectives.

The day I had to play with my sister ill. by author. Harper, 1972. Subj: Family life. Games.

I'll show you cats (Ylla)

It's mine! A greedy book ill. by author. Harper, 1964. Subj: Behavior – greed. Friendship.

Listen, listen! by Crosby Newell Bonsall and Ylla; photos. by Ylla. Harper, 1961. Subj: Animals – cats. Animals – dogs. Character traits – appearance.

Look who's talking (Ylla)

Mine's the best ill. by author. Harper, 1973. Subj: Behavior – boasting. Sea and seashore. Toys – balloons.

Piggle ill. by author. Harper, 1973. Subj: Activities – playing. Friendship. Games.

Polar bear brothers (Ylla)

Tell me some more ill. by Fritz Siebel. Harper, 1961. Subj: Imagination. Libraries.

Twelve bells for Santa ill. by author. Harper, 1977. Subj: Holidays – Christmas. Parties.

What spot? ill. by author. Harper, 1963. Subj: Animals – walruses. Birds – puffins. Foreign lands – Arctic.

Who's a pest? ill. by author. Harper, 1962. Subj: Behavior – fighting, arguing. Character traits – helpfulness. Sibling rivalry.

Who's afraid of the dark? ill. by author. Harper, 1980. Subj: Animals – dogs. Emotions – fear. Night.

Bontemps, Arna Wendell. *The fast sooner hound* by Arna Wendell Bontemps and Jack Conroy; ill. by Virginia Lee Burton. Houghton, 1942. Subj: Animals – dogs. Trains.

Boon, Emilie. *Peterkin meets a star* ill. by author. Random House, 1984. Subj: Imagination. Stars.

Peterkin's wet walk ill. by author. Random House, 1984. Subj: Animals. Imagination. Weather – rain.

Booth, Eugene. *At the circus* ill. by Derek Collard. Raintree, 1977. Subj: Circus. Concepts. Games. Participation. Problem solving.

At the fair ill. by Derek Collard. Raintree, 1977. Subj: Concepts. Fairs. Games. Participation. Problem solving.

In the air ill. by Derek Collard. Raintree, 1977. Subj: Concepts. Games. Participation. Problem solving.

In the garden ill. by Derek Collard. Raintree, 1977. Subj: Concepts. Games. Participation. Problem solving.

In the jungle ill. by Derek Collard. Raintree, 1977. Subj: Concepts. Games. Jungle. Participation. Problem solving.

Under the ocean ill. by Derek Collard. Raintree, 1977. Subj: Concepts. Games. Participation. Problem solving. Sea and seashore.

Borack, Barbara. *Grandpa* ill. by Ben Shecter. Harper, 1967. Subj: Family life – grandparents, great-grandparents.

Borchers, Elisabeth. *Dear Sarah* tr. and adapt. from German by Elizabeth Shub; ill. by Wilhelm Schlote. Greenwillow, 1980. Subj: Activities – traveling. Communication. Foreign lands.

There comes a time tr. by Babette Deutsch; ill. by Dietlind Blech. Doubleday, 1969. Subj: Days of the week, months of the year. Poetry, rhyme.

Borden, Beatrice Brown. *Wild animals of Africa* photos. by author. Random House, 1982. Subj: Animals. Birds. Foreign lands – Africa.

Boreman, Jean. *Bantie and her chicks* ill. by June Hendrickson. Melmont, 1959. Subj: Birds – chickens. School. Science.

Borg, Inga. *Plupp builds a house* ill. by author. Warne, 1961. Subj: Animals. Elves and little people. Foreign lands – Lapland. Houses.

Bornstein, Ruth Lercher. *Annabelle* ill. by author. Crowell, 1978. Subj: Behavior – lost. Toys.

The dancing man ill. by author. Seabury Pr., 1978. Subj: Activities – dancing. Foreign lands – Europe.

I'll draw a meadow ill. by author. Harper, 1979. Subj: Activities – vacationing. Animals – dogs.

Indian bunny ill. by author. Childrens Pr., 1973. Subj: Animals – rabbits. Ethnic groups in the U.S. – Indians.

Jim ill. by author. Seabury Pr., 1978. Subj: Animals – dogs. Behavior – lost. Character traits – bravery.

Of course a goat ill. by author. Harper, 1980. Subj: Animals – goats. Family life.

Borten, Helen. *Do you go where I go?* ill. by author. Abelard-Schuman, 1972. Subj: Humor. Poetry, rhyme.

Do you hear what I hear? ill. by author. Abelard-Schuman, 1960. Subj: Noise, sounds. Poetry, rhyme. Senses.

Do you know what I know? ill. by author. Abelard-Schuman, 1970. Subj: Poetry, rhyme. Senses.

Do you move as I do? ill. by author. Abelard-Schuman, 1963. Subj: Emotions. Health.

Do you see what I see? ill. by author. Abelard-Schuman, 1959. Subj: Art. Concepts. Senses.

Halloween ill. by author. Crowell, 1965. Subj: Holidays – Halloween.

A picture has a special look ill. by author. Abelard-Schuman, 1961. Subj: Art.

Bossom, Naomi. *A scale full of fish and other turnabouts* ill. by author. Greenwillow, 1979. Subj: Humor. Language.

Boston. Children's Hospital Medical Center. *Curious George goes to the hospital* (Rey, Margaret Elisabeth Waldstein)

Bothwell, Jean. *Paddy and Sam* ill. by Margaret Ayer. Abelard-Schuman, 1952. Subj: Behavior – lost. Birds – ducks.

Bottner, Barbara. *Horrible Hannah* ill. by Joan Drescher. Crown, 1980. Subj: Animals – dogs. Friendship. Moving.

Jungle day: or, How I learned to love my nosey little brother ill. by author. Delacorte Pr., 1978. Subj: Sibling rivalry.

Mean Maxine ill. by author. Pantheon, 1980. Subj: Character traits – meanness. Friendship. Imagination.

Messy ill. by author. Delacorte Pr., 1979. Subj: Activities – dancing. Behavior – carelessness.

Myra ill. by author. Macmillan, 1979. Subj: Activities – dancing. Imagination.

There was nobody there ill. by author. Macmillan, 1978. Subj: Bedtime. Imagination. Poetry, rhyme. Sleep.

Botwin, Esther. *A treasury of songs for little children* ill. by Evelyn Urbanowich. Hart, 1954. Subj: Music. Songs.

Bouhuys, Mies. *The lady of Stavoren: a story from Holland* ill. by Francien Van Westering. Penguin, 1979. Subj: Folk and fairy tales. Foreign lands – Holland.

Bour, Danièle. *The house from morning to night* ill. by author. Kane, 1985. Subj: Houses.

Bourke, Linda. *Ethel's exceptional egg* ill. by author. Harvey House, 1977. Subj: Birds – chickens. Eggs. Fairs.

Boutell, Clarence Burley. *The fat baron* ill. by Frank Lieberman. Houghton, 1946. Subj: Food. Imagination. Knights.

Bouton, Josephine. *Favorite poems for the children's hour* ill. by Bonnie and Bill Rutherford; foreword by Carolyn Sherwin Bailey. Platt, 1967. Subj: Poetry, rhyme.

Boutwell, Edna. *Red rooster* ill. by Bernard Garbutt. Atheneum, 1950. Subj: Birds – chickens. Cumulative tales. Folk and fairy tales.

Bowden, Joan Chase. *The bean boy* ill. by Sal Murdocca. Macmillan, 1979. Subj: Cumulative tales. Folk and fairy tales. Foreign lands – Italy. Humor.

The bear's surprise party ill. by Jerry Scott. Golden Pr., 1975. Subj: Animals – bears. Parties.

Boo and the flying flews ill. by Don Leake. Western, 1974. Subj: Animals – dogs. Circus.

Bouncy baby bunny finds his bed ill. by Christine Westerberg. Western, 1977. Subj: Animals – rabbits. Bedtime.

Emilio's summer day ill. by Ben Shecter. Harper, 1966. Subj: City. Ethnic groups in the U.S. – Puerto Rican-Americans. Seasons – summer.

The Ginghams and the backward picnic ill. by Joane Koenig. Western, 1979. Subj: Activities – picnicking.

A hat for the queen ill. by Olindo Giacomini. Golden Pr., 1974. Subj: Clothing. Royalty.

Little grey rabbit ill. by Lorinda Bryan Cauley. Western, 1979. Subj: Animals – rabbits.

A new home for Snow Ball ill. by Jan Pyk. Western, 1979. Subj: Animals – horses. Royalty.

Strong John ill. by Sal Murdocca. Macmillan, 1980. Subj: Behavior – trickery. Folk and fairy tales.

Who took the top hat trick? ill. by Jim Cummins. Golden Pr., 1974. Subj: Behavior – losing things. Magic.

Why the tides ebb and flow ill. by Marc Brown. Houghton, 1979. Subj: Folk and fairy tales. Humor. Sea and seashore.

Bowen, Vernon. *The lazy beaver* ill. by Jim Davis. McKay, 1948. Subj: Animals – beavers. Character traits – laziness.

Bowers, Kathleen Rice. *At this very minute* ill. by Linda Shute. Little, 1983. Subj: Bedtime. Imagination.

Bowling, David Louis. *Dirty Dingy Daryl* ill. by Patricia Hendy Bowling. Inka Dinka Ink, 1981. Subj: Character traits – cleanliness.

Boxer, Deborah. *26 ways to be somebody else* ill. by author. Pantheon, 1960. Subj: ABC books. Careers.

A boy went out to gather pears: *an old verse* ill. by Felix Hoffmann. Harcourt, 1966. Subj: Cumulative tales. Poetry, rhyme.

Boyd, Pauline. *The how* (Boyd, Selma)

I met a polar bear (Boyd, Selma)

Boyd, Selma. *The how: making the best of a mistake* by Selma and Pauline Boyd; ill. by Peggy Luks. Human Sciences Pr., 1981. Subj: Emotions – embarrassment. Friendship.

I met a polar bear by Selma and Pauline Boyd; ill. by Patience Brewster. Lothrop, 1983. Subj: Animals. Imagination. School.

Boyle, Constance. *The story of little owl* ill. by author. Barron's, 1985. Subj: Behavior – losing things. Birds – owls. Toys – teddy bears.

Boynton, Sandra. *A is for angry* ill. by author. Workman, 1983. Subj: ABC books. Animals.

But not the hippopotamus ill. by author. Simon and Schuster, 1982. Subj: Animals – hippopotami. Format, unusual – cardboard pages. Poetry, rhyme.

The going to bed book ill. by author. Simon and Schuster, 1982. Subj: Animals. Bedtime. Format unusual – cardboard pages. Poetry, rhyme.

Hester in the wild ill. by author. Harper, 1979. Subj: Animals – hippopotami. Animals – pigs. Sports – camping.

Hippos go berserk ill. by author. Little, 1979. Subj: Animals – hippopotami. Counting. Poetry, rhyme.

If at first... ill. by author. Little, 1980. Subj: Animals – elephants. Animals – mice. Character traits – perseverance. Humor.

Moo, baa, lalala ill. by author. Simon and Schuster, 1982. Subj: Animals. Format unusual – cardboard pages. Noise, sounds. Poetry, rhyme.

Opposites ill. by author. Simon and Schuster, 1982. Subj: Concepts – opposites. Format unusual – cardboard pages.

Bozzo, Maxine Zohn. *Toby in the country, Toby in the city* ill. by Frank Modell. Greenwillow, 1982. Subj: City. Country.

Bradbury, Bianca. *The antique cat* ill. by Diana Thorne and Connie Moran. Winston, 1945. Subj: Animals – cats.

Muggins ill. by Diana Thorne. Houghton, 1944. Subj: Animals – cats. Behavior – misbehavior.

Mutt ill. by Mary Stevens. Houghton, 1974. Subj: Animals – dogs. Emotions – happiness.

One kitten too many ill. by Marie C. Nichols. Houghton, 1952. Subj: Animals – cats. Behavior – bullying. Friendship.

Bradbury, Ray. *Switch on the night* ill. by Madeleine Gekiere. Pantheon, 1955. Subj: Night.

Bradfield, Jolly Roger *see* Bradfield, Roger

Bradfield, Roger. *The flying hockey stick* ill. by author. Rand McNally, 1966. Subj: Activities – flying. Humor. Machines.

Giants come in different sizes ill. by author. Rand McNally, 1966. Subj: Giants. Wizards.

A good night for dragons ill. by author. Addison Wesley, 1967. Subj: Dragons. Knights.

Bradford, Ann. *The mystery at Misty Falls* by Ann Bradford and Kal Gezi; ill. by Mina Gow McLean. Children's Pr., 1980. Subj: Animals – raccoons. Clubs, gangs. Problem solving.

The mystery in the secret club house by Ann Bradford and Kal Gezi; ill. by Mina Gow McLean. Children's Pr., 1978. Subj: Clubs, gangs. Crime.

The mystery of the blind writer by Ann Bradford and Kal Gezi; ill. by Mina Gow McLean. Children's Pr., 1980. Subj: Animals – dogs. Clubs, gangs. Crime. Handicaps – blindness. Problem solving.

The mystery of the live ghosts by Ann Bradford and Kal Gezi; ill. by Mina Gow McLean. Children's Pr., 1978. Subj: Holidays – Halloween.

The mystery of the midget clown by Ann Bradford and Kal Gezi; ill. by Mina Gow McLean. Children's Pr., 1980. Subj: Clowns, jesters. Clubs, gangs. Problem solving.

The mystery of the missing dogs by Ann Bradford and Kal Gezi; ill. by Mina Gow McLean. Children's Pr., 1980. Subj: Animals – dogs. Clubs, gangs. Handicaps. Problem solving.

The mystery of the missing raccoon by Ann Bradford and Kal Gezi; ill. by Mina Gow McLean. Children's Pr., 1978. Subj: Animals – raccoons. Character traits – freedom.

The mystery of the square footsteps by Ann Bradford and Kal Gezi; ill. by Mina Gow McLean. Children's Pr., 1980. Subj: Clubs, gangs. Problem solving. Robots.

The mystery of the tree house by Ann Bradford and Kal Gezi; ill. by Mina Gow McLean. Children's Pr., 1980. Subj: Birds – parakeets, parrots. Clubs, gangs. Crime. Problem solving.

Brady, Irene. *A mouse named Mus* ill. by author. Houghton, 1972. Subj: Animals. Animals – mice. Character traits – freedom. Forest, woods.

Wild mouse ill. by author. Scribner's, 1976. Subj: Animals – mice. Science.

Bragdon, Lillian J. *Tell me the time, please* ill. by Frank and Margaret Phares. Lippincott, 1937. Subj: Clocks. Time.

Bragg, Michael. *The writing on the wall* (Garfield, Leon)

Bram, Elizabeth. *I don't want to go to school* ill. by author. Greenwillow, 1977. Subj: School.

One day I closed my eyes and the world disappeared ill. by author. Dial Pr., 1978. Subj: Senses.

Saturday morning lasts forever ill. by author. Dial Pr., 1978. Subj: Activities – playing.

There is someone standing on my head ill. by author. Dial Pr., 1979. Subj: Imagination – imaginary friends.

Woodruff and the clocks ill. by author. Dial Pr., 1980. Subj: Behavior – collecting things. Clocks.

Brand, Millen. *This little pig named Curly* ill. by John Hamberger. Crown, 1968. Subj: Animals – pigs. Farms.

Brand, Oscar. *When I first came to this land* ill. by Doris Burn. Putnam's, 1974. Subj: Cumulative tales. Folk and fairy tales. Poverty. Songs.

Brande, Marlie. *Sleepy Nicholas* adapted by Noel Streatfield; ill. by author. Follett, 1970. Subj: Foreign lands – Denmark. Sleep.

Brandenberg, Aliki *see* Aliki

Brandenberg, Franz. *Aunt Nina and her nephews and nieces* ill. by Aliki. Greenwillow, 1983. Subj: Animals. Animals – cats. Babies. Birthdays. Toys.

Aunt Nina's visit ill. by Aliki. Greenwillow, 1984. Subj: Animals – cats. Puppets.

Everyone ready? ill. by Aliki. Greenwillow, 1979. Subj: Activities – traveling. Animals – mice. Family life. Trains.

Fresh cider and apple pie ill. by Aliki. Macmillan, 1973. Subj: Food. Insects – flies. Spiders.

It's not my fault ill. by Aliki. Greenwillow, 1980. Subj: Animals – mice. Behavior – fighting, arguing. Family life. Sibling rivalry.

Leo and Emily ill. by Aliki. Greenwillow, 1981. Subj: Clothing. Friendship. Magic.

Leo and Emily and the dragon ill. by Aliki. Greenwillow, 1984. Subj: Activities – babysitting. Dragons. Imagination.

Nice new neighbors ill. by Aliki. Greenwillow, 1977. Subj: Animals – mice. Friendship. Moving.

No school today! ill. by Aliki. Subj: Animals – cats. Behavior – mistakes. School.

A picnic, hurrah! ill. by Aliki. Greenwillow, 1978. Subj: Activities – picnicking. Animals – cats. Problem solving. Weather – rain.

A robber! A robber! ill. by Aliki. Greenwillow, 1975. Subj: Animals – cats. Crime. Night. Noise, sounds.

A secret for grandmother's birthday ill. by Aliki. Greenwillow, 1975. Subj: Behavior – secrets. Birthdays. Family life – grandparents, great-grandparents.

Six new students ill. by Aliki. Greenwillow, 1978. Subj: Animals – mice. School.

What can you make of it? ill. by Aliki. Greenwillow, 1977. Subj: Animals – mice. Art. Behavior – saving things. Moving.

Branley, Franklyn M. *Air is all around you* ill. by Robert Galster. Crowell, 1962. Subj: Science.

The big dipper ill. by Ed Emberley. Crowell, 1962. Subj: Science. Stars.

Big tracks, little tracks ill. by Leonard P. Kessler. Crowell, 1960. Subj: Animals. Problem solving. Science.

A book of satellites for you ill. by Leonard P. Kessler. Rev. ed. Crowell, 1971. Subj: Science. Space and space ships.

Comets ill. by Giulio Maestro. Crowell, 1984. Subj: Science. Sky.

Eclipse: darkness in daytime ill. by Donald Crews. Crowell, 1973. Subj: Science. Sun.

Flash, crash, rumble and roll ill. by Ed Emberley. Crowell, 1964. Subj: Science. Weather – storms.

Floating and sinking ill. by Robert Galster. Crowell, 1967. Subj: Science.

Gravity is a mystery ill. by Don Madden. Harper, 1970. Subj: Science.

High sounds, low sounds ill. by Paul Showers. Crowell, 1967. Subj: Noise, sounds. Science.

How little and how much: a book about scales ill. by Byron Barton. Crowell, 1976. Subj: Concepts – measurement.

Light and darkness ill. by Reynold Ruffins. Crowell, 1975 Subj: Science.

The moon seems to change ill. by Helen Borten. Crowell, 1960. Subj: Moon. Science.

North, south, east and west ill. by Robert Galster. Crowell, 1966. Subj: Science.

The planets in our solar system ill. by Don Madden. Crowell, 1981. Subj: Science. Space and space ships. Sun. World.

Rain and hail ill. by Harriett Barton. Rev. ed. Crowell, 1983. Subj: Science. Weather. Weather – rain.

The sky is full of stars ill. by Felicia Bond. Crowell, 1981. Subj: Science. Sky. Stars.

Snow is falling ill. by Helen Stone. Crowell, 1963. Subj: Science. Weather – snow.

The sun, our nearest star ill. by Helen Borten. Crowell, 1961. Subj: Science. Sun.

Sunshine makes the seasons ill. by Shelley Freshman. Crowell, 1974. Subj: Science. Seasons. Sun.

Timmy and the tin-can telephone by Franklyn M. Branley and Eleanor K. Vaughan; ill. by Paul Galdone. Crowell, 1959. Subj: Communication. Science.

What makes day and night ill. by Helen Borten. Crowell, 1961. Subj: Earth. Science.

What the moon is like ill. by Vladimir Bobri. Crowell, 1963. Subj: Moon. Science.

Brann, Esther. *A book for baby* ill. by author. Macmillan, 1945. Subj: Activities. Babies. Family life.

'Round the world ill. by author. Macmillan, 1935. Subj: Activities – traveling. Foreign lands. World.

Braun, Kathy. *Kangaroo and kangaroo* ill. by Jim McMullan. Doubleday, 1965. Subj: Animals – kangaroos. Behavior – collecting things. Poetry, rhyme.

Brecht, Bertolt. *Uncle Eddie's moustache* ill. by Ursula Kirchberg. Pantheon, 1974. Translation of Onkel Ede hat einen Schnurrbart by Muriel Rukeyser. Subj: Humor. Poetry, rhyme.

Breda, Tjalmar see DeJong, David Cornel

Breinburg, Petronella. *Doctor Shawn* ill. by Errol Lloyd. Crowell, 1975. Subj: Activities – playing. Careers – doctors. Ethnic groups in the U.S. – Afro-Americans.

Shawn goes to school ill. by Errol Lloyd. Crowell, 1973. Subj: Ethnic groups in the U.S. – Afro-Americans. Friendship. School.

Shawn's red bike ill. by Errol Lloyd. Crowell, 1976. Subj: Ethnic groups in the U.S. – Afro-Americans. Sports – bicycling.

Brenner, Anita. *A hero by mistake* ill. by Jean Charlot. Addison-Wesley, 1953. Subj: Character traits – bravery. Crime. Emotions – fear.

I want to fly ill. by Lucienne Bloch. Addison-Wesley, 1943. Subj: Airplanes, airports. Imagination.

Brenner, Barbara. *Baltimore orioles* ill. by J. Winslow Higginbottom. Harper, 1974. Subj: Birds.

A dog I know ill. by Fred Brenner. Harper, 1983. Subj: Animals – dogs. Humor.

Faces, faces, faces photos. by George Ancona. Dutton, 1970. Subj: Anatomy. Emotions. Ethnic groups in the U.S. Senses.

The five pennies ill. by Erik Blegvad. Knopf, 1964. Subj: Money. Pets.

The flying patchwork quilt ill. by Fred Brenner. Addison-Wesley, 1965. Subj: Activities – flying. Magic.

Mr. Tall and Mr. Small ill. by Tomi Ungerer. Addison-Wesley, 1966. Subj: Animals – giraffes. Animals – mice. Character traits – conceit. Fire.

Ostrich feathers ill. by Vera B. Williams and Evelyn Armstrong. Parents, 1979. Subj: Animals. Behavior – greed.

The prince and the pink blanket ill. by Nola Langner. Four Winds Pr., 1980. Subj: Family life. Royalty.

Somebody's slippers, somebody's shoes ill. by Leslie Jacobs. Addison-Wesley, 1957. Subj: Clothing. Shopping.

The tremendous tree book (Garelick, May)

Wagon wheels ill. by Don Bolognese. Harper, 1978. Subj: Character traits – perseverance. Ethnic groups in the U.S. – Afro-Americans. Farms. U.S. history.

Brentano, Clemens. *Schoolmaster Whackwell's wonderful sons* ill. by Maurice Sendak. Random House, 1962. Subj: Behavior – growing up. Careers. Folk and fairy tales.

Brett, Jan. *Annie and the wild animals* ill. by author. Houghton, 1985. Subj: Animals. Animals – cats. Emotions – loneliness. Pets.

Fritz and the beautiful horses ill. by author. Houghton, 1981. Subj: Animals – horses. Behavior – wishing. Character traits – cleverness. Folk and fairy tales.

Brewster, Benjamin see Elting, Mary

Brewster, Patience. *Ellsworth and the cats from Mars* ill. by author. Houghton, 1981. Subj: Animals – cats. Behavior – lost. Space and space ships.

Nobody ill. by author. Houghton, 1982. Subj: Behavior – dissatisfaction. Imagination – imaginary friends.

Brian Wildsmith's The twelve days of Christmas ill. by Brian Wildsmith. Watts, 1972. Subj: Cumulative tales. Holidays – Christmas. Music. Songs.

Brice, Tony. *Baby animals* ill. by author. Rand McNally, 1945. Subj: Animals. Babies.

The bashful goldfish ill. by author. Rand McNally, 1942. Subj: Character traits – shyness. Fish. Pets.

Bridges, William. *Lion Island* photos. by Emmy Haas and Sam Dunton. Morrow, 1965. Subj: Animals – lions. Zoos.

Ookie, the walrus who likes people photos. by Emmy Haas and Sam Dunton. Morrow, 1962. Subj: Animals – walruses.

Bridgman, Elizabeth. *All the little bunnies: a counting book* ill. by author. Atheneum, 1977. Subj: Counting. Poetry, rhyme.

How to travel with grownups ill. by Eleanor Hazard. Crowell, 1980. Subj: Activities – traveling. Foreign lands.

Nanny bear's cruise ill. by author. Harper, 1981. Subj: Activities – traveling. Animals – bears. Boats, ships.

A new dog next door ill. by author. Harper, 1978. Subj: Animals – dogs.

Bridle, Martin. *Punch and Judy in the rain* (Eaton, Su)

Bridwell, Norman. *Clifford goes to Hollywood* ill. by author. Scholastic, 1981. Subj: Animals – dogs. Character traits – loyalty.

Clifford's good deeds ill. by author. Four Winds Pr., 1975. Subj: Animals – dogs. Automobiles. Behavior – mistakes. Careers – firefighters. Character traits – helpfulness.

Clifford's Halloween ill. by author. Four Winds Pr., 1967. Subj: Animals – dogs. Holidays – Halloween.

The witch grows up ill. by author. Scholastic, 1980. Subj: Humor. Magic. Witches.

The witch next door ill. by author. Four Winds Pr., 1966. Subj: Witches.

Brierley, Louise. *King Lion and his cooks* ill. by author. Holt, 1982. Subj: Animals. Food. Royalty.

Briggs, Raymond. *Father Christmas* ill. by author. Coward, 1973. Subj: Holidays – Christmas. Wordless.

Father Christmas goes on holiday ill. by author. Coward, 1975. Subj: Activities – vacationing. Holidays – Christmas. Wordless.

Fee fi fo fum ill. by author. Coward, 1964. Subj: Nursery rhymes.

Jim and the beanstalk ill. by author. Coward, 1970. Subj: Folk and fairy tales. Giants. Humor. Old age.

Ring-a-ring o' roses ill. by author. Coward, 1962. Subj: Nursery rhymes.

The snowman ill. by author. Random House, 1978. Subj: Friendship. Snowmen. Wordless.

The white land: a picture book of traditional rhymes and verses ill. by compiler. Coward, 1963. Subj: Nursery rhymes. Songs.

Bright, Robert. *Georgie* ill. by author. Doubleday, 1944. Subj: Family life. Farms. Ghosts.

Georgie and the baby birds ill. by author. Doubleday, 1983. Subj: Birds. Character traits – helpfulness. Ghosts. Humor.

Georgie and the ball of yarn ill. by author. Doubleday, 1983. Subj: Character traits – helpfulness. Ghosts. Humor.

Georgie and the buried treasure ill. by author. Doubleday, 1979. Subj: Ghosts. Humor.

Georgie and the little dog ill. by author. Doubleday, 1983. Subj: Animals – dogs. Character traits – helpfulness. Ghosts. Humor.

Georgie and the magician ill. by author. Doubleday, 1966. Subj: Ghosts. Humor. Magic.

Georgie and the noisy ghost ill. by author. Doubleday, 1971. Subj: Activities – vacationing. Ghosts. Noise, sounds. Sea and seashore.

Georgie and the robbers ill. by author. Doubleday, 1963. Subj: Crime. Ghosts.

Georgie and the runaway balloon ill. by author. Doubleday, 1983. Subj: Animals – mice. Character traits – helpfulness. Ghosts. Humor. Toys – balloons.

Georgie goes west ill. by author. Doubleday, 1973. Subj: Cowboys. Ghosts.

Georgie to the rescue ill. by author. Doubleday, 1956. Subj: City. Ghosts.

Georgie's Christmas carol ill. by author. Doubleday, 1975. Subj: Ghosts. Holidays – Christmas.

Georgie's Halloween ill. by author. Doubleday, 1958. Subj: Ghosts. Holidays – Halloween.

Gregory, the noisiest and strongest boy in Grangers Grove ill. by author. Doubleday, 1969. Subj: Character traits – laziness. Food. Noise, sounds.

Hurrah for Freddie! ill. by author. Doubleday, 1955. Subj: Parades. Royalty. Toys.

I like red ill. by author. Doubleday, 1955. Subj: Concepts – color. Hair.

Me and the bears ill. by author. Doubleday, 1951. Subj: Animals – bears. Behavior – wishing. Friendship. Sleep. Zoos.

Miss Pattie ill. by author. Doubleday, 1954. Subj: Animals – cats.

My hopping bunny ill. by author. Doubleday, 1971. Subj: Activities – jumping. Animals – rabbits. Poetry, rhyme.

My red umbrella ill. by author. Morrow, 1959. Subj: Counting. Umbrellas. Weather – rain.

The travels of Ching ill. by author. Addison-Wesley, 1943. Subj: Foreign lands – China. Toys – dolls.

Which is Willy? ill. by author. Doubleday, 1962. Subj: Birds – penguins. Character traits – individuality.

Brightman, Alan. *Like me* ill. by author. Little, 1976. Subj: Character traits – being different. Handicaps.

Brighton, Catherine. *My hands, my world* ill. by author. Macmillan, 1984. Subj: Handicaps – blindness. Imagination – imaginary friends. Senses.

Brin, Ruth F. *David and Goliath* ill. by H. Hechtkopf. Lerner, 1977. Subj: Foreign lands – Israel. Religion.

The story of Esther ill. by H. Hechtkopf. Lerner, 1976. Subj: Foreign lands – Israel. Religion.

Brinckloe, Julie. *Gordon's house* ill. by author. Doubleday, 1976. Subj: Animals – bears.

Bring a torch, Jeannette, Isabella ill. by Adrienne Adams. Scribner's, 1963. A provincial carol attributed to Nicholas Saboly, seventeenth century. Subj: Foreign lands – France. Holidays – Christmas. Music. Songs.

Brister, Hope. *The cunning fox and other tales* ill. by Henry C. Pitz. Knopf, 1943. Subj: Animals. Folk and fairy tales.

Bro, Marguerite H. *The animal friends of Peng-u* ill. by Seong Moy. Doubleday, 1965. Subj: Animals. Folk and fairy tales. Foreign lands – China.

Brock, Emma Lillian. *The birds' Christmas tree* ill. by author. Knopf, 1946. Subj: Birds. Character traits – kindness to animals. Holidays – Christmas.

Mr. Wren's house ill. by author. Knopf, 1944. Subj: Birds – wrens. Family life. Humor.

Nobody's mouse ill. by author. Knopf, 1938. Subj: Animals. City. Humor.

One little Indian boy ill. by author. Hale, 1932. Subj: Ethnic groups in the U.S. – Indians.

A pet for Barbie ill. by author. Knopf, 1947. Subj: Family life. Pets.

Pig with a front porch ill. by author. Knopf, 1937. Subj: Animals – pigs. Behavior – dissatisfaction.

A present for Auntie ill. by author. Knopf, 1939. Subj: Family life.

Skipping Island ill. by author. Knopf, 1958. Subj: Humor. Islands.

Surprise balloon ill. by author. Knopf, 1949. Subj: Activities – flying. Animals. Toys – balloons.

Brodsky, Beverly *see* McDermott, Beverly Brodsky

Broekel, Ray. *Dangerous fish* ill. with photos. Childrens Pr., 1982. Subj: Fish.

Trains ill. with photos. Children's Pr., 1981. Subj: Trains. Transportation.

Trucks ill. with photos. Childrens Pr., 1983. Subj: Trucks. Transportation.

Brogan, Peggy. *Sounds around the clock* (Martin, Bill (William Ivan))

Sounds I remember (Martin, Bill (William Ivan))

Sounds of home (Martin, Bill (William Ivan))

Sounds of laughter (Martin, Bill (William Ivan))

Sounds of numbers (Martin, Bill (William Ivan))

Bröger, Achim. *Bruno takes a trip* tr. from German by Caroline Gueritz; ill. by Gisela Kalow. Morrow, 1978. Subj: Activities – traveling. Pets. Trains.

Francie's paper puppy ill. by Michele Sambin; tr. from German. Alphabet Pr., 1984. Subj: Animals – dogs. Art. Country. Emotions – loneliness. Imagination. Pets.

Little Harry tr. from German by Elizabeth D. Crawford; ill. by Judy Morgan. Morrow, 1979. Subj: Humor. Imagination. Problem solving.

Bromhall, Winifred. *Bridget's growing day* ill. by author. Knopf, 1957. Subj: Behavior – growing up. Character traits – smallness. Foreign lands – Ireland.

Johanna arrives ill. by author. Knopf, 1941. Subj: Activities – traveling. Foreign lands – Holland.

Mary Ann's first picture ill. by author. Knopf, 1947. Subj: Activities – painting. Art. Birthdays.

Middle Matilda ill. by author. Knopf, 1962. Subj: Behavior – losing things. Clothing.

Brook, Judy. *Tim mouse goes down the stream* ill. by author. Lothrop, 1975. Subj: Animals – hedgehogs. Animals – mice. Character traits – bravery. Rivers.

Tim mouse visits the farm ill. by author. Lothrop, 1977. Subj: Animals – hedgehogs. Animals – mice. Farms.

Brooke, L. Leslie (Leonard Leslie). *Johnny Crow's garden* ill. by author. Warne, 1903. Subj: Animals. Humor. Poetry, rhyme.

Johnny Crow's new garden ill. by author. Warne, 1935. Subj: Animals. Humor. Poetry, rhyme.

Johnny Crow's party ill. by author. Warne, 1907. Subj: Animals. Humor. Parties.

Oranges and lemons ill. by author. Warne, 1913. Subj: Nursery rhymes.

This little pig went to market ill. by author. Warne, 1922. Subj: Animals – pigs. Nursery rhymes.

Brooks, Andrea. *The guinea pigs' adventure* ill. by author. Little, 1980. Subj: Animals – guinea pigs.

Brooks, Gregory. *Monroe's island* ill. by author. Bradbury Pr., 1979. Subj: Imagination.

Brooks, Gwendolyn. *Bronzeville boys and girls* ill. by Ronni Solbert. Harper, 1956. Subj: Poetry, rhyme.

Brooks, Robert B. *So that's how I was born* ill. by Susan Perl. Simon and Schuster, 1983. Subj: Babies. Family life. Science.

Brooks, Ron. *Timothy and Gramps* ill. by author. Bradbury Pr., 1978. Subj: Family life – grandparents, great-grandparents. School.

Brothers, Aileen. *Jiffy, Miss Boo and Mr. Roo* ill. by Audean Johnson. Follett, 1966. Subj: Birds – chickens. Pets.

Sad Mrs. Sam Sack ill. by Muriel and Jim Collins. Follett, 1963. Subj: Behavior – dissatisfaction. Family life. Humor.

Brothers and sisters are like that! ill. by Michael Hampshire. Crowell, 1971. Selected by The Child Study Association of America. Subj: Family life. Sibling rivalry.

Brouillette, Jeanne S. *Moths* ill. by Bill Barss. Follett, 1966. Subj: Insects. Science.

Brown, Abbie Farwell. *The Christmas angel* ill. by Reginald Birch. Houghton, 1910. Subj: Angels. Holidays – Christmas.

Under the rowan tree ill. by Maurice Day. Houghton, 1926. Subj: Folk and fairy tales. Magic.

Brown, Beatrice Curtis. *Jonathan Bing* ill. by Judith Gwyn Brown. Lothrop, 1968. Subj: Poetry, rhyme.

Jonathan Bing ill. by Pelagic Doane. Oxford Univ. Pr., 1937. Subj: Poetry, rhyme.

Brown, Daphne Faunce *see* Faunce-Brown, Daphne

Brown, David. *Someone always needs a policeman* ill. by author. Simon and Schuster, 1972. Subj: Careers – police officers.

Brown, Elinor. *The little story book* ill. by author. Oxford Univ. Pr., 1940. Subj: Activities.

Brown, Jeff. *Flat Stanley* ill. by Tomi Ungerer. Harper, 1961. Subj: Family life. Humor. Problem Solving.

Brown, Judith Gwyn. *Alphabet dreams* ill. by author. Prentice-Hall, 1976. Subj: ABC books. Poetry, rhyme.

The happy voyage ill. by author. Macmillan, 1965. Subj: Boats, ships.

Max and the truffle pig ill. by author. Abingdon, 1963. Subj: Animals – pigs. Behavior – lost. Food. Foreign lands – France.

Brown, Laurene Krasny. *The bionic bunny show* (Brown, Marc)

Brown, Marc. *Arthur goes to camp* ill. by author. Little, 1982. Subj: Animals. Sports – camping.

Arthur's April fool ill. by author. Little, 1983. Subj: Animals. Holidays – April Fools' Day.

Arthur's Christmas ill. by author. Little, 1984. Subj: Animals. Holidays – Christmas.

Arthur's eyes ill. by author. Little, 1979. Subj: Animals. Glasses.

Arthur's Halloween ill. by author. Little, 1982. Subj: Animals. Holidays – Halloween.

Arthur's Thanksgiving ill. by author. Little, 1983. Subj: Animals. Holidays – Thanksgiving. Theater.

Arthur's Valentine ill. by author. Little, 1980. Subj: Animals. Holidays – Valentine's Day. School.

The bionic bunny show by Marc Brown and Laurene Krasny Brown; ill. by Marc Brown. Little, 1984. Subj: Animals. Animals – rabbits. Television.

The cloud over Clarence ill. by author. Dutton, 1979. Subj: Animals – cats. Behavior – carelessness. Friendship.

Dinosaurs, beware! a safety guide by Marc Brown and Stephen Krensky; ill. by authors. Little, 1982. Subj: Dinosaurs. Safety.

Finger rhymes ill. by author. Dutton, 1980. Subj: Games. Participation. Poetry, rhyme.

Lenny and Lola ill. by author. Dutton, 1978. Subj: Circus.

Marc Brown's full house ill. by author. Addison-Wesley, 1977. Subj: Monsters.

Moose and goose ill. by author. Dutton, 1978. Subj: Animals – moose. Birds – geese.

Perfect pigs: an introduction to manners by Marc Brown and Stephen Krensky; ill. by authors. Little, 1983. Subj: Animals – pigs. Etiquette.

Pickle things ill. by author. Parents, 1980. Subj: Food. Poetry, rhyme.

The silly tail book ill. by author. Parents, 1983. Subj: Animals. Poetry, rhyme.

Spooky riddles ill. by author. Random House, 1983. Subj: Ghosts. Humor. Monsters. Riddles. Witches.

The true Francine ill. by author. Little, 1981. Subj: Animals. Behavior – lying. School.

What do you call a dumb bunny? and other rabbit riddles, games, jokes and cartoons ill. by author. Little, 1983. Subj: Animals – rabbits. Format, unusual. Games. Humor. Riddles.

Wings on things ill. by author. Random House, 1982. Subj: Activities – flying. Poetry, rhyme.

Witches four ill. by author. Parents, 1980. Subj: Poetry, rhyme. Witches.

Your first garden book ill. by author. Little, 1981. Subj: Activities – gardening. Plants.

Brown, Marcia. *All butterflies: an ABC* ill. by author. Scribner's, 1974. Subj: ABC books.

The blue jackal ill. by author. Scribner's, 1977. Subj: Animals. Behavior – trickery. Folk and fairy tales. Foreign lands – India.

The bun: a tale from Russia ill. by author. Harcourt, 1972. Subj: Animals. Behavior – greed. Character traits – cleverness. Cumulative tales. Folk and fairy tales.

Dick Whittington and his cat

Felice ill. by author. Scribner's, 1958. Subj: Animals – cats. Foreign lands – Italy.

Henry fisherman ill. by author. Scribner's, 1949. Subj: Caldecott award honor book. Careers – fishermen.

How, hippo! ill. by author. Scribner's, 1969. Subj: Animals – hippopotami.

Listen to a shape photos. by author. Watts, 1979. Subj: Concepts – shape.

The little carousel ill. by author. Scribner's, 1946. Subj: City. Emotions – loneliness. Kites. Merry-go-rounds. Money.

The neighbors ill. by author. Scribner's, 1967. "Text adapted from Afanas'yev." Subj: Animals – foxes. Animals – rabbits. Cumulative tales. Foreign lands – Russia. Houses.

Once a mouse... adapt. and ill. by author. Scribner's, 1961. An adaption of Hitopadeśa, a tale from ancient India. Subj: Animals. Caldecott award book. Character traits – vanity. Concepts – size. Folk and fairy tales. Foreign lands – India. Magic.

Peter Piper's alphabet ill. by author. Scribner's, 1959. Subj: ABC books. Nursery rhymes. Tongue twisters.

Skipper John's cook ill. by author. Scribner's, 1951. Subj: Activities – cooking. Boats, ships. Caldecott award honor book.

Stone soup ill. by author. Scribner's, 1947. Subj: Caldecott award honor book. Careers – military. Character traits – cleverness. Folk and fairy tales. Food. Foreign lands – Russia.

Tamarindo! ill. by author. Scribner's, 1960. Subj: Animals – donkeys. Behavior – lost. Foreign lands – Greece.

Touch will tell photos. by author. Watts, 1979. Subj: Concepts. Senses.

Walk with your eyes photos. by author. Watts, 1979. Subj: Concepts. Senses.

Brown, Margaret Wise. *Baby animals* ill. by Mary Cameron. Random House, 1941. Subj: Animals.

Big dog, little dog ill. by Leonard Weisgard. Doubleday, 1943. Subj: Animals – dogs. Concepts – size.

The big fur secret ill. by Robert de Veyrac. Harper, 1944. Subj: Animals. Communication. Zoos.

Big red barn ill. by Rosella Hartman. Addison-Wesley, 1956. Subj: Barns. Farms. Poetry, rhyme.

Bumble bugs and elephants ill. by Clement Hurd. Addison-Wesley, 1941. Subj: Concepts – size.

A child's good morning book ill. by Jean Charlot. Addison-Wesley, 1952. Subj: Morning.

A child's good night book ill. by Jean Charlot. Addison-Wesley, 1950. Subj: Bedtime. Caldecott award honor book. Night. Sleep.

Christmas in the barn ill. by Barbara Cooney. Crowell, 1952. Subj: Holidays – Christmas.

The country noisy book ill. by Leonard Weisgard. Harper, 1940. Subj: Animals – dogs. Country. Noise, sounds. Participation.

The dead bird ill. by Remy Charlip. W. R. Scott, 1958. Subj: Death.

Dr. Squash the doll doctor ill. by J. P. Miller. Simon and Schuster, 1952. Subj: Character traits – kindness. Toys – dolls. Toys – soldiers.

Don't frighten the lion ill. by H. A. Rey. Harper, 1942. Subj: Animals. Animals – dogs. Character traits – cleverness. Zoos.

Dream book ill. by Richard Floethe. Random House, 1950. Subj: Dreams.

The duck photos. by Ylla. Harper, 1953. Subj: Animals. Birds – ducks. Character traits – vanity.

Five little firemen by Margaret Wise Brown and Edith Thacher Hurd ill. by Tibor Gergely. Simon and Schuster, 1959. Subj: Careers – firefighters. Noise, sounds.

Four fur feet ill. by Remy Charlip. W. R. Scott, 1961. Subj: Activities – walking. Poetry, rhyme. World.

Fox eyes ill. by Garth Williams. Pantheon, 1977, 1951. Subj: Animals. Animals – foxes.

The golden egg book ill. by Leonard Weisgard. Simon and Schuster, 1947. Subj: Animals – rabbits. Birds – ducks. Eggs. Holidays – Easter.

Goodnight moon ill. by Clement Hurd. Harper, 1934. Subj: Animals – rabbits. Bedtime. Moon.

House of a hundred windows Cat and architecture by Robert de Veyrac; ill. by Henri Rousseau and others. Harper, 1945. Subj: Animals – cats. Houses.

The indoor noisy book ill. by Leonard Weisgard. Harper, 1942. Subj: Animals – dogs. Games. Noise, sounds. Participation.

The little brass band ill. by Clement Hurd. Harper, 1948. Subj: Cumulative tales. Music.

Little chicken ill. by Leonard Weisgard. Harper, 1943. Subj: Animals – rabbits. Birds – chickens.

The little farmer ill. by Esphyr Slobodkina. Addison-Wesley, 1948. Subj: Dreams. Farms.

The little fir tree ill. by Barbara Cooney. Crowell, 1954. Subj: Holidays – Christmas. Trees.

The little fireman ill. by Esphyr Slobodkina. Addison-Wesley, 1952. Subj: Careers – firefighters. Fire.

The little fisherman ill. by Dahlov Ipcar. Addison-Wesley, 1945. Subj: Careers – fishermen. Fish.

The little fur family ill. by Garth Williams. Harper, 1946. Subj: Activities. Format, unusual.

The little island ill. by Leonard Weisgard. Doubleday, 1946. Subj: Caldecott award book. Islands. Seasons. Weather.

Little lost lamb ill. by Leonard Weisgard. Doubleday, 1945. Subj: Animals – sheep. Behavior – lost. Caldecott award honor book.

Nibble nibble ill. by Leonard Weisgard. Addison-Wesley, 1959. Subj: Poetry, rhyme.

Night and day ill. by Leonard Weisgard. Harper, 1942. Subj: Animals – cats. Emotions – fear. Night.

Noisy book ill. by Leonard Weisgard. Harper, 1939. Subj: Noise, sounds. Participation.

On Christmas Eve ill. by Beni Montresor. W. R. Scott, 1961. Subj: Holidays – Christmas. Religion.

Once upon a time in pigpen and three other stories ill. by Ann Strugnell. Addison-Wesley, 1980. Subj: Animals. Humor.

Pussycat's Christmas ill. by Helen Stone. Harper, 1949. Subj: Animals – cats. Holidays – Christmas.

The quiet noisy book ill. by Leonard Weisgard. Harper, 1950. Subj: Animals – dogs. Morning. Noise, sounds. Participation.

Red light, green light ill. by Leonard Weisgard. Doubleday, 1944. Subj: Concepts – color. Safety. Traffic signs.

The runaway bunny ill. by Clement Hurd. Harper, 1942. Subj: Animals – rabbits. Behavior – running away. Holidays – Easter.

The seashore noisy book ill. by Leonard Weisgard. Harper, 1941. Subj: Noise, sounds. Participation. Sea and seashore.

SHHhhh . . . Bang: a whispering book ill. by Robert De Veyrac. Harper, 1943. Subj: Noise, sounds.

Sleepy ABC ill. by Esphyr Slobodkina. Lothrop, 1953. Subj: ABC books. Poetry, rhyme. Sleep.

The sleepy little lion ill. by Ylla. Harper, 1947. Subj: Animals – lions. Sleep.

Sneakers ill. by Jean Charlot. Addison-Wesley, 1979, 1955. Reissue of 1955 ed. published by W. R. Scott under title Seven stories about a cat named Sneakers. Subj: Animals – cats. Behavior – misbehavior.

The steamroller: a fantasy ill. by Evaline Ness. Walker, 1974. Published in 1938 in the author's collection, The fish with the deep sea smile. Subj: Holidays – Christmas. Machines.

Streamlined pig ill. by Kurt Wiese. Harper, 1938. Subj: Activities – flying. Airplanes, airports. Animals. Character traits – bravery.

The summer noisy book ill. by Leonard Weisgard. Harper, 1951. Subj: Farms. Noise, sounds. Participation. Seasons – summer.

They all saw it photos. by Ylla. Harper, 1944. Subj: Animals. Problem solving.

Three little animals ill. by Garth Williams. Harper, 1956. Subj: Activities – traveling. Animals. Behavior – lost. City.

Two little miners ill. by Edith Thacher Hurd. Simon and Schuster, 1949. Subj: Careers – miners.

Two little trains ill. by Jean Charlot. Addison-Wesley, 1949. Subj: Poetry, rhyme. Trains.

Wait till the moon is full ill. by Garth Williams. Harper, 1948. Subj: Animals. Animals – raccoons. Character traits – questioning. Moon. Night.

Wheel on the chimney by Margaret Wise Brown and Tibor Gergely; ill. by Tibor Gergely. Lippincott, 1954. Subj: Birds – storks. Caldecott award honor book. Character traits – luck. Foreign lands – Hungary.

When the wind blew ill. by Geoffrey Hayes. Harper, 1977, 1937. Subj: Animals – cats. Illness. Weather – wind.

Where have you been? ill. by Barbara Cooney. Reissue of Crowell, 1952 ed. Hastings House, 1981. Subj: Animals. Poetry, rhyme.

Whistle for the train ill. by Leonard Weisgard. Doubleday, 1956. Subj: Poetry, rhyme. Trains.

The winter noisy book ill. by Charles Green Shaw. Harper, 1947. Subj: Animals – dogs. Noise, sounds. Participation. Seasons – winter. Weather – snow.

The wonderful house ill. by J. P. Miller. Simon and Schuster, 1950. Subj: Houses.

The wonderful story book ill. by J. P. Miller. Simon and Schuster, 1948. Subj: Poetry, rhyme.

Young kangaroo ill. by Symeon Shimin. Addison-Wesley, 1955. Subj: Animals – kangaroos.

Brown, Myra Berry. *Benjy's blanket* ill. by Dorothy Marino. Watts, 1952. Subj: Animals – cats. Behavior – growing up.

Best friends ill. by Don Freeman. Golden Gate, 1967. Subj: Friendship. Poetry, rhyme.

Best of luck ill. by Don Freeman. Golden Gate, 1969. Subj: Character traits – luck. Poetry, rhyme.

Company's coming for dinner ill. by Dorothy Marino. Watts, 1960. Subj: Character traits – helpfulness. Etiquette. Parties.

First night away from home ill. by Dorothy Marino. Watts, 1960. Subj: Activities – playing. Friendship. Sleep. Toys – teddy bears.

Pip camps out ill. by Phyllis Graham. Golden Gate, 1966. Subj: Family life. Night. Sports – camping.

Pip moves away ill. by Pauline Jackson. Golden Gate, 1967. Subj: Family life. Moving.

Brown, Palmer. *Cheerful* ill. by author. Harper, 1957. Subj: Animals – mice.

Hickory ill. by author. Harper, 1978. Subj: Animals – mice. Behavior – growing up. Friendship.

The silver nutmeg ill. by author. Harper, 1956. Subj: Imagination – imaginary friends. Poetry, rhyme. Problem solving.

Something for Christmas ill. by author. Harper, 1958. Subj: Animals – mice. Character traits – generosity. Emotions – love. Holidays – Christmas.

Brown, Paul. *Merrylegs, the rocking pony* ill. by author. Scribner's, 1946. Subj: Imagination. Toys – rocking horses.

Brown, Ruth. *Crazy Charlie* ill. by author. Rourke, 1982. Subj: Reptiles – alligators, crocodiles. Self-concept. Teeth.

A dark, dark tale ill. by author. Dial Pr., 1981. Subj: Cumulative tales. Foreign lands – England.

Brown, Tricia. *Someone special, just like you* photos. by Fran Ortiz. Holt, 1984. Subj: Emotions. Handicaps.

Browne, Anthony. *Bear hunt* ill. by author. Atheneum, 1980. Subj: Animals – bears. Art. Problem solving. Sports – hunting.

Gorilla ill. by author. Watts, 1983. Subj: Animals – gorillas. Birthdays.

Look what I've got! ill. by author. Watts, 1980. Subj: Behavior – boasting. Imagination.

Willy the wimp ill. by author. Knopf, 1985. Subj: Animals – gorillas. Animals – monkeys. Self-concept.

Browne, Caroline. *Mrs. Christie's farmhouse* ill. by author. Doubleday, 1977. Subj: Activities – gardening. Country. Farms. Humor. Royalty.

Browner, Richard. *Everyone has a name* ill. by Emma Landau. Walck, 1961. Subj: Animals. Names. Poetry, rhyme.

Look again! ill. by Emma Landau. Atheneum, 1962. Subj: Concepts.

Browning, Robert. *The pied piper of Hamelin* ill. by Kate Greenaway. Warne, n.d. Subj: Animals – rats. Behavior – trickery. Folk and fairy tales. Foreign lands – Germany. Poetry, rhyme.

Bruce, Sheilah B. *The radish day jubilee* ill. by Lawrence DiFiori. Holt, 1983. Subj: Imagination. Poetry, rhyme. Puppets.

Bruna, Dick. *Another story to tell* ill. by author. Methuen, 1978. Subj: Weather – snow. Wordless.

B is for bear: an A-B-C ill. by author. Methuen, 1971. Subj: ABC books.

Christmas ill. by author. Doubleday, 1969. Translation of Kerstmis. English verse by Eve Merriam. Subj: Holidays – Christmas. Poetry, rhyme. Religion.

The Christmas book ill. by author. Methuen, 1964. Subj: Holidays – Christmas.

Farmer John ill. by author. Price, Stern, Sloan, 1984. Subj: Farms.

The fish ill. by author. Follett, 1963. English verse translated from the Dutch by Sandra Greifenstein. Subj: Fish. Food. Poetry, rhyme.

I can dress myself ill. by author. Methuen, 1977. Subj: Behavior – growing up. Clothing.

I can read difficult words ill. by author. Methuen, 1978. Subj: Activities – reading.

I know more about numbers ill. by author. Methuen, 1981. Subj: Counting.

Kitten Nell ill. by author. Follett, 1963. Subj: Animals – cats. Humor. Poetry, rhyme.

Little bird tweet ill. by author. Follett, 1963. Subj: Birds. Farms. Poetry, rhyme.

Miffy ill. by author. Follett, 1970. Translation of Nijntje. Subj: Animals – rabbits. Family life.

Miffy at the beach ill. by author. Methuen, 1980. Subj: Animals – rabbits. Sea and seashore.

Miffy at the playground ill. by author. Methuen, 1980. Subj: Activities – playing. Animals – rabbits.

Miffy at the seaside ill. by author. Follett, 1970. Translation of Nijntje aan zee. Subj: Animals – rabbits. Sea and seashore.

Miffy at the zoo ill. by author. Follett, 1970. Translation of Nijntje in de dierentuin. Subj: Animals – rabbits. Zoos.

Miffy goes to school ill. by author. Price, Stern, Sloan, 1984. Subj: Animals – rabbits. School.

Miffy in the hospital ill. by author. Methuen, 1978. Subj: Animals – rabbits. Hospitals. Illness.

Miffy in the snow ill. by author. Follett, 1970. Translation of Nijntje in de sneeuw. Subj: Animals – rabbits. Seasons – winter. Weather – snow.

Miffy's bicycle ill. by author. Price, Stern, Sloan, 1984. Subj: Animals – rabbits. Sports – bicycling.

Miffy's dream ill. by author. Methuen, 1980. Subj: Activities – playing. Animals – rabbits. Dreams.

The orchestra ill. by author. Price, Stern, Sloan, 1984. Subj: Music. Poetry, rhyme.

Poppy Pig goes to market ill. by author. Methuen, 1981. Subj: Animals – pigs. Counting. Poetry, rhyme.

The sailor ill. by author. Methuen, 1980. Subj: Activities – traveling. Boats, ships.

The school ill. by author. Methuen, 1980. Subj: School.

Tilly and Tess ill. by author. Follett, 1963. Subj: Birthdays. Poetry, rhyme. Twins.

Brunhoff, Jean de. *Babar and Father Christmas* tr. by Merle Haas; ill. by author. Random House, 1940. Translation of Babar et le Père Nöel. Subj: Animals – elephants. Holidays – Christmas.

Babar and his children tr. by Merle Haas; ill. by author. Random House, 1938. Subj: Animals – elephants. Triplets.

Babar and Zephir tr. from French by Merle Haas; ill. by author. Reprint of 1937 ed. Random House, 1942. Subj: Animals – elephants. Animals – monkeys.

Babar the king tr. by Merle Haas; ill. by author. Random House, 1935. Subj: Animals – elephants. Royalty.

Babar's anniversary album: 6 favorite stories by Jean de Brunhoff and Laurent de Brunhoff; ill. by authors. Random House, 1981. Subj: Activities. Animals – elephants.

The story of Babar, the little elephant tr. by Merle Haas; ill. by author. Random House, 1960. Subj: Animals – elephants. Behavior – running away. Foreign lands – France.

The travels of Babar tr. by Merle Haas; ill. by author. Random House, 1934, 1961. Subj: Activities – traveling. Animals – elephants.

Brunhoff, Laurent de. *Babar and the ghost* ill. by author. Random House, 1981. Subj: Animals – elephants. Ghosts.

Babar and the Wully-Wully ill. by author. Random House, 1975. Subj: Animals – elephants. Pets.

Babar comes to America tr. by M. Jean Craig; ill. by author. Random House, 1965. Translation of Babar en Amérique. Subj: Animals – elephants.

Babar learns to cook ill. by author. Random House, 1979. Subj: Activities – cooking. Animals – elephants.

Babar loses his crown ill. by author. Random House, 1967. Subj: Animals – elephants. Behavior – losing things.

Babar the magician ill. by author. Random House, 1980. Subj: Animals – elephants. Animals – monkeys. Magic.

Babar visits another planet tr. by Merle Haas; ill. by author. Random House, 1972. Translation of Babar sur la planète molle. Subj: Animals – elephants. Space and space ships.

Babar's ABC ill. by author. Random House, 1983. Subj: ABC books. Animals – elephants.

Babar's anniversary album (Brunhoff, Jean de)

Babar's birthday surprise ill. by author. Random House, 1970. Translation of Anniversaire de Babar. Subj: Animals – elephants. Birthdays.

Babar's book of color ill. by author. Random House, 1984. Subj: Animals – elephants. Concepts – color.

Babar's castle tr. by Merle Haas; ill. by author. Random House, 1962. Subj: Animals – elephants.

Babar's cousin, that rascal Arthur tr. by Merle Haas; ill. by author. Random House, 1948. Translation of Babar et ce coquin d'Arthur. A continuation of the Babar stories of Jean de Brunhoff. Subj: Activities – vacationing. Animals – elephants. Behavior – misbehavior.

Babar's fair will be opened next Sunday tr. by Merle Haas; ill. by author. Random House, 1954. Translation of La fête de Célesteville. Subj: Animals – elephants. Fairs.

Babar's mystery ill. by author. Random House, 1978. Subj: Activities – vacationing. Animals – elephants. Crime.

Babar's picnic ill. by author. Random House, 1959. Subj: Activities – picnicking. Animals – elephants.

Babar's visit to Bird Island ill. by author. Random House, 1952. Subj: Animals – elephants. Birds. Islands. Royalty.

Gregory and Lady Turtle in the valley of the music trees tr. by Richard Howard; ill. by author. Pantheon, 1971. Subj: Animals – Rabbits. Imagination. Reptiles – turtles.

The one pig with horns tr. from French by Richard Howard; ill. by author. Pantheon, 1979. Subj: Animals – pigs. Emotions – anger. Emotions – hate.

Serafina the giraffe ill. by author. Collins-World, 1961. Subj: Animals – giraffes. Birthdays. Humor.

Brustlein, Janice Tworkov *see* Janice

Bryan, Ashley. *Beat the story-drum, pum-pum* ill. by adapt. Atheneum, 1980. Subj: Cumulative tales. Folk and fairy tales. Foreign lands – Africa. Poetry, rhyme.

Bryan, Dorothy. *Friendly little Jonathan* by Dorothy and Marguerite Bryan; ill. by Marguerite Bryan. Dodd, 1939. Subj: Animals – dogs. Friendship.

Just Tammie! by Dorothy and Marguerite Bryan; ill. by Marguerite Bryan. Dodd, 1951. Subj: Animals – dogs.

Bryan, Marguerite. *Friendly little Jonathan* (Bryan, Dorothy)

Just Tammie! (Bryan, Dorothy)

Bryant, Bernice. *Follow the leader* ill. by author. Houghton, 1950. Subj: Behavior – bullying. Behavior – growing up. Character traits – selfishness.

Bryant, Dean. *Here am I* ill. by author. Rand McNally, 1947. Subj: Activities.

See the bear ill. by author. Rand McNally, 1947. Subj: Toys.

Bryant, Sara Cone. *Epaminondas* (Merriam, Eve)

Epaminondas and his auntie ill. by Inez Hogan. Houghton, 1938. Subj: Behavior – misunderstanding. Folk and fairy tales. Humor.

Bryson, Bernarda. *The twenty miracles of Saint Nicolas* ill. by author. Atlantic Monthly Pr., 1960. Subj: Folk and fairy tales. Foreign lands. Holidays – Christmas.

Buchanan, Joan. *It's a good thing* ill. by Barbara Di Lella. Firefly Pr., 1984. Subj: Activities – walking. Behavior – carelessness. Humor.

Buchheimer, Naomi. *Let's go to a post office* ill. by Ruth Van Sciver. Putnam's, 1957. Subj: Careers – mail carriers. Communication.

Let's go to a school ill. by Ruth Van Sciver. Putnam's, 1957. Subj: School.

Buck, Frank. *Jungle animals* by Frank Buck; text by Ferrin Fraser; ill. by Roger Vernam. Random House, 1945. Subj: Animals.

Buck, Pearl S. (Pearl Sydenstricker). *The Chinese story teller* ill. by Regina Shekerjian. John Day, 1971. Subj: Animals – cats. Animals – dogs. Emotions – envy, jealousy. Folk and fairy tales. Foreign lands – China.

The dragon fish ill. by Esther Broch Bird. John Day, 1944. Subj: Dragons. Fish. Folk and fairy tales. Foreign lands – China. Magic.

The little fox in the middle ill. by Robert Jones. Collier, 1966. Subj: Animals – foxes. Emotions – loneliness. Family life. Friendship.

Stories for little children ill. by Weda Yap. John Day, 1940. Subj: Activities.

Welcome child ill. by Alan D. Haas. John Day, 1963. Subj: Adoption.

Buckaway, C. M. *Alfred, the dragon who lost his flame* ill. by Sarie Jenkins. Firefly Pr., 1982. Subj: Dragons. Imagination. Magic.

Buckley, Helen Elizabeth. *Grandfather and I* ill. by Paul Galdone. Lothrop, 1959. Subj: Activities – walking. Family life – grandparents, great-grandparents.

Grandmother and I ill. by Paul Galdone. Lothrop, 1961. Subj: Emotions – love. Family life – grandparents, great-grandparents.

Josie and the snow ill. by Evaline Ness. Lothrop, 1964. Subj: Poetry, rhyme. Seasons – winter. Weather – snow.

Josie's Buttercup ill. by Evaline Ness. Lothrop, 1967. Subj: Animals – dogs. Poetry, rhyme.

Buckmaster, Henrietta. *Lucy and Loki* ill. by Barbara Cooney. Scribner's, 1958. Subj: Animals – cats. Animals – dogs. Behavior – imitation.

Budbill, David. *Christmas tree farm* ill. by Donald Carrick. Macmillan, 1974. Subj: Farms. Holidays – Christmas. Science. Trees.

Budd, Lillian. *The people on Long Ago Street* ill. by Marilyn Miller. Rand McNally, 1964. Subj: Family life – grandparents, great-grandparents. Imagination.

The pie wagon ill. by Marilyn Miller. Lothrop, 1960. Subj: ABC books. Food.

Budney, Blossom. *After dark* ill. by Tony Chen. Lothrop, 1975. Subj: Night.

A kiss is round ill. by Vladimir Bobri. Lothrop, 1954. Subj: Concepts – shape. Poetry, rhyme.

N is for nursery school ill. by Vladimir Bobri. Lothrop, 1956. Subj: ABC books. School.

Buell, Ellen Lewis. *Read me a poem: children's favorite poetry* ill. by Anna Maria Magagna. Grosset, 1965. Subj: Poetry, rhyme.

Buff, Conrad. *Dash and Dart* (Buff, Mary)

Forest folk (Buff, Mary)

Hurry, Skurry and Flurry (Buff, Mary)

Buff, Mary. *Dash and Dart* by Mary and Conrad Buff; ill. by authors. Viking, 1942. Subj: Animals – deer. Caldecott award honor book. Forest, woods.

Forest folk by Mary and Conrad Buff; ill. by authors. Viking, 1962. Subj: Animals. Animals – deer. Forest, woods.

Hurry, Skurry and Flurry by Mary and Conrad Buff; ill. by authors. Viking, 1954. Subj: Animals – squirrels. Poetry, rhyme.

Bulette, Sara. *The elf in the singing tree* ill. by Tom Dunnington. Follett, 1964. Reading consultant: Morton Botel. Subj: Elves and little people. Imagination.

The splendid belt of Mr. Big ill. by Lou Myers. Follett, 1964. Reading consultant: Morton Botel. Subj: Animals – monkeys. Clothing. Concepts – size. Problem solving.

Bulla, Clyde Robert. *Dandelion Hill* ill. by Bruce Degen. Dutton, 1982. Subj: Animals – bulls, cows. Behavior – growing up. Farms.

Daniel's duck ill. by Joan Sandin. Harper, 1979. Subj: Activities. Art. Emotions – embarrassment.

The donkey cart ill. by Lois Lenski. Harper, 1942. Subj: Animals – donkeys. Music. Songs.

Jonah and the great fish ill. by Helga Aichinger. Crowell, 1970. Subj: Animals – whales. Religion.

Keep running, Allen! ill. by Satomi Ichikawa. Crowell, 1978. Subj: Behavior – solitude. Sibling rivalry.

Noah and the rainbow (Bolliger, Max)

Poor boy, rich boy ill. by Marcia Sewall. Harper, 1982. Subj: Orphans.

The stubborn old woman ill. by Anne F. Rockwell. Crowell, 1980. Subj: Behavior – needing someone. Character traits – persistence. Character traits – stubbornness.

A tree is a plant ill. by Lois Lignell. Crowell, 1960. Subj: Plants. Trees.

Valentine cat ill. by Leonard Weisgard. Crowell, 1959. Subj: Animals – cats. Holidays – Valentine's Day.

Washington's birthday ill. by Don Bolognese. Crowell, 1967. Subj: Holidays – Washington's Birthday. U.S. history.

Bunce, William. *Freight trains* ill. by Lemuel B. Line. Putnam's, 1954. Subj: Trains.

Bundt, Nancy. *The fire station book* text by Jeff Linzer; photos. by Nancy Bundt. Carolrhoda Books, 1981. Subj: Careers – firefighters.

Bunin, Catherine. *Is that your sister? a true story of adoption* by Catherine Bunin and Sherry Bunin; ill. with photos. Pantheon, 1976. Subj: Adoption. Family life.

Bunin, Sherry. *Is that your sister?* (Bunin, Catherine)

Buntain, Ruth Jaeger. *The birthday story* ill. by Eloise Wilkin. Holiday, 1953. Subj: Birthdays. Emotions – loneliness. Friendship.

Bunting, A. E. *see* Bunting, Eve

Bunting, Anne Evelyn *see* Bunting, Eve

Bunting, Eve. *The big cheese* ill. by Sal Murdocca. Macmillan, 1977. Subj: Cumulative tales.

The big red barn ill. by Howard Knotts. Harcourt, 1979. Subj: Death. Family life.

Clancy's coat ill. by Lorinda Bryan Cauley. Warne, 1984. Subj: Foreign lands – Ireland. Friendship.

Goose dinner ill. by Howard Knotts. Harcourt, 1981. Subj: Birds – geese. Farms.

The happy funeral ill. by Vo-Dinh Mai. Harper, 1982. Subj: Death. Ethnic groups in the U.S. – Chinese-Americans. Family life – grandparents, great-grandparents.

Magic and the night river ill. by Allen Say. Harper, 1978. Subj: Birds – cormorants. Careers – fishermen. Family life – grandparents, great-grandparents. Foreign lands – Japan.

The man who could call down owls ill. by Charles Mikolaycak. Macmillan, 1984. Subj: Behavior – greed. Birds – owls. Magic.

Monkey in the middle ill. by Lynn Munsinger. Harcourt, 1984. Subj: Animals – monkeys. Emotions – envy, jealousy. Friendship.

The robot birthday ill. by Marie DeJohn. Dutton, 1980. Subj: Birthdays. Robots.

St. Patrick's Day in the morning ill. by Jan Brett. Houghton, 1980. Subj: Holidays – St. Patrick's Day.

Terrible things ill. by Stephen Gammell. Harper, 1980. Subj: Animals. Emotions – fear.

The traveling men of Ballycoo ill. by Kaethe Zemach. Harcourt, 1983. Subj: Activities – traveling. Music.

The Valentine bears ill. by Jan Brett. Seabury Pr., 1983. Subj: Animals – bears. Holidays – Valentine's Day.

Winter's coming ill. by Howard Knotts. Harcourt, 1977. Subj: Family life – grandparents, great-grandparents. Farms. Seasons – winter.

Burch, Robert. *The hunting trip* ill. by Susanne Suba. Scribner's, 1971. Subj: Character traits – kindness to animals. Family life. Food. Sports – hunting.

Joey's cat ill. by Don Freeman. Viking, 1969. Subj: Animals – cats. Animals – possums. Ethnic groups in the U.S. – Afro-Americans. Family life.

The jolly witch ill. by Leigh Grant. Dutton, 1975. Subj: Character traits – cleanliness. Witches.

Burchard, Peter. *The Carol Moran* ill. by author. Macmillan, 1958. Subj: Boats, ships.

Burdekin, Harold. *A child's grace* by Harold Burdekin and Ernest Claxton; the grace by Mrs. E. Rutter Leatham; photos. by Harold Burdekin. Dutton, 1938. Subj: Activities. Poetry, rhyme. Religion.

Burgert, Hans-Joachim. *Samulo and the giant* ill. by author. Holt, 1970. Subj: Character traits – bravery. Weather.

Burgess, Anthony. *The land where the ice cream grows* (Testa, Fulvio)

Burgunder, Rose. *From summer to summer* ill. by author. Viking, 1965. Subj: Poetry, rhyme. Seasons – summer.

Burland, Brian. *St. Nicholas and the tub* ill. by Joseph Low. Holiday, 1964. Subj: Folk and fairy tales. Holidays – Christmas.

Burlingham, Mary. *The climbing book* (Steiner, Charlotte)

Burlson, Joe. *Space colony* ill. by author. Putnam's, 1984. Subj: Format, unusual. Wordless.

Burn, Doris. *The summerfolk* ill. by author. Coward, 1968. Subj: Seasons – summer.

Burnett, Carol. *What I want to be when I grow up* ill. by Sheldon Secunda. Simon and Schuster, 1975. Created by George Mendoza and Sheldon Secunda. Subj: Careers.

Burningham, Helen Oxenbury *see* Oxenbury, Helen

Burningham, John. *Avocado baby* ill. by author. Crowell, 1982. Subj: Babies. Family life. Food.

The blanket ill. by author. Crowell, 1976, 1975. Subj: Behavior – losing things. Night.

Borka: the adventures of a goose with no feathers ill. by author. Random House, 1963. Subj: Birds – geese. Character traits – being different. Character traits – meanness. Foreign lands – England.

Cannonball Simp ill. by author. Bobbs-Merrill, 1966. Subj: Animals – dogs. Circus. Clowns, jesters.

Come away from the water, Shirley ill. by author. Crowell, 1977. Subj: Imagination. Pirates. Sea and seashore.

Count up: learning sets ill. by author. Viking, 1983. Subj: Counting. Format, unusual – cardboard pages.

The cupboard ill. by author. Crowell, 1977. Subj: Food.

The dog ill. by author. Crowell, 1975. Subj: Animals – dogs. Format, unusual – cardboard pages.

Five down: numbers as signs ill. by author. Viking, 1983. Subj: Counting. Format, unusual – cardboard pages.

The friend ill. by author. Crowell, 1975. Subj: Friendship.

Harquin: the fox who went down to the valley ill. by author. Bobbs-Merrill, 1968. Subj: Animals – foxes. Character traits – cleverness. Sports – hunting.

Humbert, Mister Firkin and the Lord Mayor of London ill. by author. Bobbs-Merrill, 1967. Subj: Animals – horses. Character traits – pride. Emotions – envy, jealousy.

John Burningham's ABC ill. by author. Bobbs-Merrill, 1977. Subj: ABC books.

Just cats: learning groups ill. by author. Viking, 1983. Subj: Counting. Format, unusual – cardboard pages.

Mr. Gumpy's motor car ill. by author. Macmillan, 1975, 1973. Subj: Automobiles. Weather – rain.

Mr. Gumpy's outing ill. by author. Macmillan, 1971. Subj: Animals. Behavior – fighting, arguing. Boats, ships. Cumulative tales.

Pigs plus: learning addition ill. by author. Viking, 1983. Subj: Counting. Format, unusual – cardboard pages.

Read one: numbers as words ill. by author. Viking, 1983. Subj: Counting. Format, unusual – cardboard pages.

Ride off: learning subtraction ill. by author. Viking, 1983. Subj: Counting. Format, unusual – cardboard pages.

Seasons ill. by author. Bobbs-Merrill, 1970. Subj: Seasons.

The shopping basket ill. by author. Crowell, 1980. Subj: Character traits – cleverness. Counting. Humor.

Skip trip ill. by author. Viking, 1984. Subj: Activities. Noise, sounds.

Sniff shout ill. by author. Viking, 1984. Subj: Activities. Noise, sounds.

Time to get out of the bath, Shirley ill. by author. Crowell, 1978. Subj: Activities – bathing. Imagination. Royalty.

Trubloff: the mouse who wanted to play the balalaika ill. by author. Random House, 1965. Subj: Animals – mice. Music. Weather – snow.

Wobble pop ill. by author. Viking, 1984. Subj: Activities. Noise, sounds.

Would you rather... ill. by author. Crowell, 1978. Subj: Imagination.

Burnstein, John. *Slim Goodbody: what can go wrong and how to be strong* ill. with photos. and drawings. McGraw-Hill, 1978. Subj: Health. Poetry, rhyme.

Burroway, Janet. *The truck on the track* ill. by John Vernon Lord. Bobbs-Merrill, 1970. Subj: Humor. Poetry, rhyme. Trucks.

Burstein, Chaya M. *Joseph and Anna's time capsule* ill. by Nancy Edwards Calder. Simon and Schuster, 1984. Subj: Jewish culture.

Burt, Olive. *Let's find out about bread* ill. by Mimi Korach. Watts, 1966. Subj: Food. Science.

Burton, Marilee Robin. *Aaron awoke: an alphabet story* ill. by author. Harper, 1982. Subj: ABC books. Farms.

The elephant's nest ill. by author. Harper, 1979. Subj: Animals. Humor. Wordless.

Burton, Virginia Lee. *Calico the wonder horse: or, the saga of Stewy Slinker* ill. by author. Houghton, 1941. Subj: Animals – horses. Character traits – cleverness. Cowboys. Crime.

Choo choo: the story of a little engine who ran away ill. by author. Houghton, 1937. Subj: Behavior – running away. Trains.

Katy and the big snow ill. by author. Houghton, 1943. Subj: City. Cumulative tales. Machines. Seasons – winter. Weather – snow.

The little house ill. by author. Houghton, 1939. Subj: Caldecott award book. City. Country. Ecology. Houses. Progress.

Maybelle, the cable car ill. by author. Houghton, 1939. Subj: Cable cars, trolleys. City. Transportation.

Mike Mulligan and his steam shovel ill. by author. Houghton, 1939. Subj: Activities – working. Machines.

Busch, Phyllis S. *Cactus in the desert* ill. by Harriett Barton. Crowell, 1979. Subj: Desert. Plants. Science.

City lots: living things in vacant spots photos. by Arline Strong. Collins-World, 1970. Subj: City. Science.

Lions in the grass: the story of the dandelion, a green plant photos. by Arline Strong. Collins-World, 1968. Subj: Plants. Science.

Once there was a tree: the story of the tree, a changing home for plants and animals photos. by Arline Strong. Collins-World, 1968. Subj: Science. Trees.

Puddles and ponds: living things in watery places photos. by Arline Strong. Collins-World, 1969. Subj: Ecology. Science.

Bushey, Jerry. *The barge book* photos. by author. Carolrhoda Books, 1984. Subj: Activities – trading. Boats, ships. Rivers.

Building a fire truck photos. by author. Carolrhoda Books, 1981. Subj: Careers – firefighters. Trucks.

Butcher, Julia. *The sheep and the rowan tree* ill. by author. Holt, 1984. Subj: Behavior – wishing. Trees.

Butterfield-Campbell, Jill. *The queen and Rosie Randall* (Oxenbury, Helen)

Byars, Betsy Cromer. *Go and hush the baby* ill. by Emily Arnold McCully. Viking, 1971. Subj: Babies. Family life. Games.

The groober ill. by author. Harper, 1967. Subj: Animals. Behavior – dissatisfaction.

Byfield, Barbara Ninde. *The haunted churchbell* ill. by author. Doubleday, 1971. Subj: Character traits – cleverness. Emotions – fear. Humor.

Caines, Jeannette. *Abby* ill. by Steven Kellogg. Harper, 1973. Subj: Adoption. Ethnic groups in the U.S. – Afro-Americans. Family life. Sibling rivalry.

Daddy ill. by Ronald Himler. Harper, 1977. Subj: Divorce. Ethnic groups in the U.S. – Afro-Americans. Family life – fathers.

Just us women ill. by Pat Cummings. Harper, 1982. Subj: Activities – traveling. Automobiles. Ethnic groups in the U.S. – Afro-Americans.

Window wishing ill. by Kevin Brooks. Harper, 1980. Subj: Family life – grandparents, great-grandparents.

Cakes and custard: *children's rhymes* comp. by Brian W. Alderson; ill. by Helen Oxenbury. Morrow, 1975, 1974. Subj: Nursery rhymes.

Caldecott, Randolph. *Hey diddle diddle, and Baby bunting* ill. by author. Warne, 1882. Subj: Nursery rhymes.

Hey diddle diddle picture book ill. by author. Warne, 1883. Subj: Nursery rhymes.

Panjandrum picture book ill. by author. Warne, 1885. Subj: Nursery rhymes.

The Queen of Hearts ill. by author. Warne, 1881. Subj: Nursery rhymes.

The Randolph Caldecott treasury sel. and ed. by Elizabeth T. Billington; ill. by author. Warne, 1978. Subj: Folk and fairy tales.

Randolph Caldecott's favorite nursery rhymes ill. by author. Castle Books, 1980. Subj: Nursery rhymes.

Randolph Caldecott's John Gilpin and other stories ill. by author. Warne, 1977. The diverting history of John Gilpin.—The house that Jack built.—The frog he would a-wooing go.—The milkmaid. Subj: Nursery rhymes.

Randolph Caldecott's picture book, no. 1 ill. by author. Warne, 1879. Subj: Nursery rhymes.

Randolph Caldecott's picture book, no. 2 ill. by author. Warne, 1879. Subj: Nursery rhymes.

Sing a song of sixpence ill. by author. New ed. Hart, 1977. Reprint of orig. Warne pub. between 1876 and 1886. Subj: Nursery rhymes.

The three jovial huntsmen ill. by author. Warne, 1880. Subj: Nursery rhymes.

Caldwell, Mary. *Morning, rabbit, morning* ill. by Ann Schweninger. Harper, 1982. Subj: Animals – rabbits. Morning.

Calhoun, Mary. *Audubon cat* ill. by Susan Bonners. Morrow, 1981. Subj: Animals – cats. Food. Problem solving.

Cross-country cat ill. by Erick Ingraham. Morrow, 1979. Subj: Animals – cats. Character traits – cleverness. Sports – skiing.

Euphonia and the flood ill. by Simms Taback. Parents, 1976. Subj: Animals. Boats, ships. Character traits – helpfulness. Weather – rain.

The goblin under the stairs ill. by Janet McCaffery. Morrow, 1968. Subj: Behavior – misbehavior. Folk and fairy tales. Goblins.

Hot-air Henry ill. by Erick Ingraham. Morrow, 1981. Subj: Activities – ballooning. Animals – cats.

Houn' dog ill. by Roger Antoine Duvoisin. Morrow, 1959. Subj: Animals – dogs. Animals – foxes. Sports – hunting.

The hungry leprechaun ill. by Roger Antoine Duvoisin. Harber, 1962. Subj: Elves and little people. Food. Foreign lands – Ireland. Holidays – St. Patrick's Day.

Jack the wise and the Cornish cuckoos ill. by Tasha Tudor. Morrow, 1978. Subj: Character traits – helpfulness. Folk and fairy tales.

Mrs. Dog's own house ill. by Janet McCaffery. Morrow, 1972. Subj: Animals – dogs. Houses.

The nine lives of Homer C. Cat ill. by Roger Antoine Duvoisin. Morrow, 1961. Subj: Animals – cats. Behavior – imitation. Humor.

Old man Whickutt's donkey ill. by Tomie de Paola. Parents, 1975. Subj: Animals – donkeys. Character traits – perseverance. Folk and fairy tales. Humor.

The pixy and the lazy housewife ill. by Janet McCaffery. Morrow, 1969. Subj: Behavior – trickery. Elves and little people. Folk and fairy tales. Foreign lands – England.

The runaway brownie ill. by Janet McCaffery. Morrow, 1967. Subj: Character traits – pride. Elves and little people. Folk and fairy tales. Foreign lands – Scotland.

The thieving dwarfs ill. by Janet McCaffery. Morrow, 1967. Subj: Character traits – kindness. Elves and little people. Folk and fairy tales. Foreign lands – Germany.

The traveling ball of string ill. by Janet McCaffery. Morrow, 1969. Subj: Behavior – saving things. Humor. String.

The witch of Hissing Hill ill. by Janet McCaffery. Morrow, 1964. Subj: Animals – cats. Holidays – Halloween. Witches.

The witch who lost her shadow ill. by Trinka Hakes Noble. Harper, 1979. Subj: Animals – cats. Character traits – loyalty. Emotions. Friendship. Witches.

The witch's pig: a Cornish folktale ill. by Tasha Tudor. Morrow, 1977. Subj: Animals – pigs. Folk and fairy tales. Foreign lands – England. Witches.

Wobble the witch cat ill. by Roger Antoine Duvoisin. Morrow, 1958. Subj: Animals – cats. Holidays – Halloween. Witches.

Callen, Larry. *Dashiel and the night* ill. by Leslie Morrill. Dutton, 1981. Subj: Bedtime. Dreams. Imagination. Insects – fireflies. Night.

Calloway, Northern J. *Northern J. Calloway presents Super-vroomer!* ill. by Sammis McLean. Doubleday, 1978. Written by Carol Hall; conceived by Northern J. Calloway. Subj: Ethnic groups in the U.S. – Afro-Americans. Sports – racing.

Calmenson, Stephanie. *The birthday hat* ill. by Susan Gantner. Grosset, 1983. Subj: Animals – hippopotami. Birthdays. Shopping.

The kindergarten book ill. by Beth Lee Weiner. Grosset, 1983. Subj: Activities. Animals. School.

Never take a pig to lunch and other funny poems about animals ill. by Hilary Knight. Doubleday, 1982. Subj: Animals – pigs. Poetry, rhyme.

Where is Grandma Potamus? ill. by Susan Gantner. Grosset, 1983. Subj: Animals – hippopotami. Behavior – lost.

Where will the animals stay? ill. by Ellen Appleby. Parents, 1983. Subj: Animals. Houses. Poetry, rhyme. Zoos.

Calvert, Elinor H. *see* Lasell, Fen

Cameron, Ann. *Harry (the monster)* ill. by Jeanette Winter. Pantheon, 1980. Subj: Bedtime. Character traits – bravery. Emotions – fear. Monsters.

Cameron, John. *If mice could fly* ill. by author. Atheneum, 1979. Subj: Animals – cats. Animals – mice. Character traits – cleverness. Poetry, rhyme.

Cameron, Polly. *The cat who thought he was a tiger* ill. by author. Coward, 1956. Subj: Animals – cats. Circus.

A child's book of nonsense ill. by author. Coward, 1960. Subj: Humor. Poetry, rhyme.

"I can't," said the ant: a second book of nonsense ill. by author. Coward, 1961. Subj: Family life. Insects – ants. Participation. Poetry, rhyme.

Campbell, Ann. *Let's find out about boats* ill. by author. Watts, 1967. Subj: Boats, ships.

Let's find out about color ill. by author. Watts, 1966. Subj: Concepts – color.

Campbell, M. Rudolph. *The talking crocodile* ill. by Judy Piussi-Campbell. Atheneum, 1968. Adapt. from Krokodil by Fyodor Dostoyevsky. Subj: Foreign lands – Russia. Reptiles – alligators, crocodiles.

Campbell, Rod. *Look inside! All kinds of places* ill. by author. Harper, 1983. Subj: Format, unusual – cardboard pages. Wordless.

Look inside! Land, sea, air ill. by author. Harper, 1983. Subj: Format, unusual – cardboard pages. Transportation. Wordless.

Canfield, Jane White. *The frog prince: a true story* ill. by Winn Smith. Harper, 1970. Subj: Frogs and toads. Royalty.

Swan cove ill. by Jo Polseno. Harper, 1978. Subj: Birds – swans.

Canning, Kate. *A painted tale* ill. by author. Barron's, 1979. Subj: Animals – tigers. Art. Behavior – imitation. Zoos.

Cantieni, Benita. *Little Elephant and Big Mouse* tr. by Oliver Gadsby; ill. by Fred Gächter. Alphabet Pr., 1981. Orig. title: Der Kleine Elefant und die Grosse Maus. Subj: Animals – elephants. Animals – mice. Concepts – size.

Caple, Kathy. *Inspector Aardvark and the perfect cake* ill. by author. Windmill, 1980. Subj: Animals – aardvarks. Careers – bakers.

Caprio, Annie De *see* DeCaprio, Annie

Caputo, Robert. *More than just pets: why people study animals* photos. by author. Coward, 1980. Subj: Anatomy. Ecology.

Cardoza, Lois S. *see* Duncan, Lois

Carey, Mary. *The owl who loved sunshine* ill. by Joe Giordano. Golden Pr., 1977. Subj: Birds – owls. Character traits – individuality. Character traits – kindness to animals.

Carigiet, Alois. *Anton the goatherd* ill. by author. Walck, 1966. Subj: Animals – goats. Behavior – lost.

The pear tree, the birch tree and the barberry bush ill. by author. Walck, 1967. Subj: Foreign lands – Switzerland. Trees.

Carle, Eric. *Do you want to be my friend?* ill. by author. Crowell, 1971. Subj: Animals – mice. Friendship. Wordless.

The grouchy ladybug ill. by author. Crowell, 1977. English title: The bad-tempered ladybird. Subj: Behavior. Insects – ladybugs. Time.

Have you seen my cat? ill. by author. Watts, 1973. Subj: Animals – cats. Behavior – lost.

I see a song ill. by author. Crowell, 1973. Subj: Music. Wordless.

The mixed-up chameleon ill. by author. Rev. ed. Crowell, 1984. Subj: Character traits – being different. Concepts – color. Reptiles – lizards. Self-concept.

The mixed-up chameleon ill. by author. Crowell, 1975. Subj: Character traits – being different. Concepts – color. Reptiles – lizards. Self-concept.

1, 2, 3 to the zoo ill. by author. Collins-World, 1969. Subj: Animals. Counting. Zoos.

Pancakes, pancakes ill. by author. Knopf, 1970. Subj: Cumulative tales. Food.

The rooster who set out to see the world ill. by author. Watts, 1972. Subj: Activities – traveling. Birds – chickens. Counting.

The secret birthday message ill. by author. Crowell, 1972. Subj: Birthdays. Format, unusual.

The tiny seed ill. by author. Crowell, 1970. Subj: Plants.

Twelve tales from Æsop ill. by adapt. Putnam's, 1980. Subj: Folk and fairy tales.

The very hungry caterpillar ill. by author. Collins-World, 1969. Subj: Days of the week, months of the year. Format, unusual. Insects – butterflies, caterpillars.

Walter the baker: an old story ill. by author. Knopf, 1972. Subj: Activities – working. Careers – bakers. Food.

Watch out! A giant! ill. by author. Collins-World, 1978. Subj: Format, unusual. Giants.

Carleton, Barbee Oliver. *Benny and the bear* ill. by Dagmar Wilson. Follett, 1960. Subj: Animals – bears. Character traits – bravery.

Carlisle, Clark *see* Holding, James

Carlisle, Madelyn. *Bridges* (Carlisle, Norman)

Carlisle, Norman. *Bridges* by Norman and Madelyn Carlisle; ill. with photos. Childrens Pr., 1983. Subj: Bridges.

Carlson, Maria. *Peter and the wolf* (Prokofiev, Sergei Sergeievitch)

Carlson, Nancy. *Bunnies and their hobbies* ill. by author. Carolrhoda Books, 1984. Subj: Activities. Animals – rabbits.

Harriet and the garden ill. by author. Carolrhoda Books, 1982. Subj: Animals – dogs. Problem solving.

Harriet and the roller coaster ill. by author. Carolrhoda Books, 1982. Subj: Animals – dogs. Character traits – bravery.

Harriet and Walt ill. by author. Carolrhoda Books, 1982. Subj: Animals – dogs. Sibling rivalry.

Harriet's Halloween candy ill. by author. Carolrhoda Books, 1982. Subj: Animals – dogs. Behavior – greed.

Harriet's recital ill. by author. Carolrhoda Books, 1982. Subj: Animals – dogs. Emotions – fear.

Loudmouth George and the big race ill. by author. Carolrhoda Books, 1983. Subj: Animals – rabbits. Behavior – boasting. Emotions – embarrassment.

Loudmouth George and the cornet ill. by author. Carolrhoda Books, 1983. Subj: Animals – rabbits. Behavior – boasting.

Loudmouth George and the fishing trip ill. by author. Carolrhoda Books, 1983. Subj: Animals – rabbits. Behavior – boasting.

Loudmouth George and the new neighbors ill. by author. Carolrhoda Books, 1983. Subj: Animals – rabbits. Behavior – boasting. Prejudice.

Loudmouth George and the sixth-grade bully ill. by author. Carolrhoda Books, 1983. Subj: Animals – rabbits. Behavior – boasting. Behavior – bullying. Behavior – stealing.

Carlson, Natalie Savage. *Marie Louise and Christophe at the carnival* ill. by José Aruego and Ariane Dewey. Scribner's, 1981. Subj: Animals – mongooses. Reptiles – snakes.

Marie Louise's heyday ill. by José Aruego and Ariane Dewey. Scribner's, 1975. Subj: Activities – babysitting. Animals – mongooses. Animals – possums.

Runaway Marie Louise ill. by José Aruego and Ariane Dewey. Scribner's, 1977. Subj: Animals – mongooses. Behavior – running away.

Spooky night ill. by Andrew Glass. Lothrop, 1982. Subj: Animals – cats. Holidays – Halloween. Pets. Witches.

Surprise in the mountains ill. by Elise Primavera. Harper, 1983. Subj: Animals. Holidays – Christmas. Seasons – winter.

Time for the white egret ill. by Charles Robinson. Scribner's, 1978. Subj: Animals – bulls, cows. Birds – egrets. Farms.

Carrick, Carol. *The accident* ill. by Donald Carrick. Seabury Pr., 1976. Subj: Animals – dogs. Death. Pets.

Beach bird by Carol and Donald Carrick; ill. by Donald Carrick. Dial Pr., 1973. Subj: Birds – sea gulls. Sea and seashore.

Ben and the porcupine ill. by Donald Carrick. Houghton, 1981. Subj: Animals – dogs. Animals – porcupines. Problem solving.

The blue lobster: a life cycle by Carol and Donald Carrick; ill. by Donald Carrick. Dial Pr., 1975. Subj: Crustacea. Science.

The brook by Carol and Donald Carrick; ill. by Donald Carrick. Macmillan, 1967. Subj: Rivers.

A clearing in the forest by Carol and Donald Carrick; ill. by Donald Carrick. Dial Pr., 1970. Subj: Ecology. Forest, woods. Pets.

The climb ill. by Donald Carrick. Houghton, 1980. Subj: Activities – babysitting. Sports.

The crocodiles still wait ill. by Donald Carrick. Houghton, 1980. Subj: Dinosaurs. Reptiles – alligators, crocodiles. Science.

Dark and full of secrets ill. by Donald Carrick. Houghton, 1984. Subj: Emotions – fear. Sports – skin diving.

The foundling ill. by Donald Carrick. Seabury Pr., 1977. Subj: Animals – dogs. Pets.

The highest balloon on the common by Carol and Donald Carrick; ill. by Donald Carrick. Greenwillow, 1977. Subj: Behavior – lost. Fairs. Toys – balloons.

Octopus ill. by Donald Carrick. Seabury Pr., 1978. Subj: Octopuses. Science.

The old barn ill. by Donald Carrick. Bobbs-Merrill, 1966. Subj: Barns. Seasons.

Old Mother Witch ill. by Donald Carrick. Seabury Pr., 1975. Subj: Behavior – misunderstanding. Character traits – meanness. Holidays – Halloween. Illness.

Patrick's dinosaurs ill. by Donald Carrick. Houghton, 1983. Subj: Animals. Dinosaurs. Imagination. Science. Zoos.

A rabbit for Easter ill. by Donald Carrick. Greenwillow, 1979. Subj: Animals – rabbits. Behavior – carelessness. Holidays – Easter.

Sleep out ill. by Donald Carrick. Seabury Pr., 1973. Subj: Behavior – solitude. Sports – camping. Weather – rain.

Two coyotes ill. by Donald Carrick. Houghton, 1982. Subj: Animals – coyotes. Science. Seasons – winter.

The washout ill. by Donald Carrick. Seabury Pr., 1978. Subj: Activities – vacationing. Boats, ships. Weather – rain.

Carrick, Donald. *Beach bird* (Carrick, Carol)

The blue lobster (Carrick, Carol)

The brook (Carrick, Carol)

The climb (Carrick, Carol)

The deer in the pasture ill. by author. Greenwillow, 1976. Subj: Animals – bulls, cows. Animals – deer. Farms. Sports – hunting.

Harold and the giant knight ill. by author. Houghton, 1982. Subj: Farms. Knights.

The highest balloon on the common (Carrick, Carol)

Carrick, Malcolm. *The extraordinary hatmaker* ill. by author. Grosset, 1977. Subj: Clothing.

Happy Jack ill. by author. Harper, 1979. Subj: Folk and fairy tales.

I can squash elephants! a Masai tale about monsters ill. by author. Viking, 1978. Subj: Animals. Folk and fairy tales. Foreign lands – Africa. Insects – butterflies, caterpillars. Monsters.

Today is shrew's day ill. by author. Harper, 1978. Subj: Animals – shrews. Friendship. Frogs and toads.

Carroll, Latrobe. *Pet tale* (Carroll, Ruth)

Carroll, Lewis. *Jabberwocky* ill. by Jane Breskin Zalben. Warne, 1977. Subj: Humor. Poetry, rhyme.

The nursery "Alice" intro. by Martin Gardner; ill. by Sir John Tenniel. McGraw-Hill, 1966. A facsimile of the 2d ed. (1890) of Carroll's adapt. of Alice's Adventures in Wonderland. Subj: Dreams. Imagination.

Carroll, Ruth. *Old Mrs. Billups and the black cats* ill. by author. Walck, 1961. Subj: Animals – cats. Humor.

Pet tale by Ruth and Latrobe Carroll; ill. by Ruth Carroll. Oxford Univ. Pr., 1949. Subj: Pets.

What Whiskers did ill. by author. Walck, 1965. Subj: Animals – dogs. Animals – foxes. Animals – rabbits. Behavior – running away. Wordless.

Where's the bunny? ill. by author. Walck, 1950. Subj: Activities – playing. Animals – rabbits. Games. Participation. Wordless.

Carryl, Charles Edward. *A capital ship: or, The walloping window-blind* ill. by Paul Galdone. McGraw-Hill, 1963. Subj: Boats, ships. Music. Pirates. Songs.

Cars and trucks ill. by Daisuke Yokoi. Simon and Schuster, 1984. Subj: Automobiles. Format, unusual – cardboard pages. Transportation. Trucks.

Carter, Debby L. *Clipper* ill. by author. Harper, 1981. Subj: Animals – dogs. Sea and seashore.

Carter, James *see* Mayne, William

Carter, Katharine. *Houses* ill. with photos. Childrens Pr., 1982. Subj: Houses.

Ships and seaports ill. with photos. Children's Pr., 1982 Subj: Boats, ships.

Carter, Phyllis Ann *see* Eberle, Irmengarde

Cartlidge, Michelle. *The bear's bazaar: a story craft book* ill. by author. Lothrop, 1980. Subj: Activities. Animals – bears.

A mouse's diary ill. by author. Lothrop, 1982. Subj: Activities. Animals – mice.

Pippin and Pod ill. by author. Pantheon, 1978. Subj: Activities – playing. Animals – mice. Behavior – lost. Behavior – misbehavior.

Teddy trucks ill. by author. Lothrop, 1982. Subj: Animals – bears. Careers – truck drivers. Trucks.

Carton, Lonnie Caming. *Mommies* ill. by Leslie Jacobs. Random House, 1960. Subj: Activities. Family life – mothers. Poetry, rhyme.

Cass, Joan E. *The cat thief* ill. by William Stobbs. Abelard-Schuman, 1961. Subj: Animals – cats. Behavior – stealing. Crime. Night.

The cats go to market ill. by William Stobbs. Abelard-Schuman, 1969. Subj: Animals – cats. Shopping.

Cassedy, Sylvia. *Moon-uncle, moon-uncle: rhymes from India* sel. and tr. by Sylvia Cassedy and Parvathi Thampi; ill. by Susanne Suba. Doubleday, 1973. Subj: Foreign lands – India. Nursery rhymes.

Castiglia, Julie. *Jill the pill* ill. by Steven Kellogg. Atheneum, 1979. Subj: Family life. Sibling rivalry.

Castillo, Violetta. *Animal babies* (Zoll, Max Alfred)

Castle, Sue. *Face talk, hand talk, body talk* ill. by Frances McLaughlin-Gill. Doubleday, 1977. Subj: Anatomy. Emotions.

Catchpole, Clive. *Deserts* ill. by Brian McIntyre. Dial Pr., 1984. Subj: Animals. Desert.

Grasslands ill. by Peter Snowball. Dial Pr., 1984. Subj: Animals.

Jungles ill. by Denise Finney. Dial Pr., 1984. Subj: Animals. Jungle.

Mountains ill. by Brian McIntyre. Dial Pr., 1984. Subj: Animals.

Cate, Rikki. *A cat's tale* ill. by Shirley Hughes. Harcourt, 1982. Subj: Animals – cats. Behavior – stealing. Foreign lands – Scotland. Poetry, rhyme.

The caterpillar who turned into a butterfly. Simon and Schuster, 1980. Subj: Format, unusual – cardboard pages. Insects – butterflies, caterpillars.

Cathon, Laura E. *Tot Botot and his little flute* ill. by Arnold Lobel. Macmillan, 1970. Subj: Animals. Caldecott award honor book. Foreign lands – India. Music.

Caudill, Rebecca. *Contrary Jenkins* by Rebecca Caudill and James Sterling Ayars; ill. by Glen Rounds. Holt, 1969. Subj: Behavior. Country. Humor.

A pocketful of cricket ill. by Evaline Ness. Holt, 1964. Subj: Behavior – sharing. Caldecott award honor book. Farms. Insects – crickets. School.

Wind, sand and sky ill. by Donald Carrick. Dutton, 1976 Subj: Desert. Poetry, rhyme.

Cauley, Lorinda Bryan. *The animal kids* ill. by author. Putnam's, 1979. Subj: Animals. Behavior – imitation.

The bake-off ill. by author. Putnam's, 1978. Subj: Activities – cooking. Animals.

The cock, the mouse and the little red hen ill. by adapt. Putnam's, 1982. Subj: Animals. Character traits – cleverness. Folk and fairy tales.

Goldilocks and the three bears (The three bears)

The goose and the golden coins ill. by adapt. Harcourt, 1981. Subj: Birds – geese. Folk and fairy tales. Foreign lands – Italy.

The new house ill. by author. Harcourt, 1981. Subj: Animals – groundhogs. Family life. Houses. Problem solving.

Pease porridge hot: a Mother Goose cookbook ill. by author. Putnam's, 1977. Subj: Activities – cooking. Food. Nursery rhymes.

Causley, Charles. *Dick Whittington* (Dick Whittington and his cat)

Cavagnaro, David. *The pumpkin people* by David Cavagnaro and Maggie Cavagnaro; ill. with photos. Scribner's, 1979. Subj: Activities – gardening. Holidays – Halloween. Seasons – fall. Seasons – summer.

Cavagnaro, Maggie. *The pumpkin people* (Cavagnaro, David)

Cave, Joyce. *Airplanes* (Cave, Ron)

Automobiles (Cave, Ron)

Motorcycles (Cave, Ron)

Cave, Ron. *Airplanes* by Ron and Joyce Cave; ill. by David West and others. Watts, 1982. Subj: Airplanes, airports. Transportation.

Automobiles by Ron and Joyce Cave; ill. by David West and others. Watts, 1982. Subj: Automobiles. Transportation.

Motorcycles by Ron and Joyce Cave; ill. by David West and others. Watts, 1982. Subj: Motorcycles. Transportation.

Cazet, Denys. *Big shoe, little shoe* ill. by author. Bradbury Pr., 1984. Subj: Activities – babysitting. Animals – rabbits. Family life – grandparents, great-grandparents.

Christmas moon ill. by author. Bradbury Pr., 1984. Subj: Animals – rabbits. Holidays – Christmas. Moon.

The duck with squeaky feet ill. by author. Bradbury Pr., 1980. Subj: Animals. Birds – ducks. Reptiles – alligators, crocodiles. Theater.

Lucky me ill. by author. Bradbury Pr., 1983. Subj: Animals. Birds – chickens. Character traits – luck. Food.

Cendrars, Blaise. *Shadow* tr. and ill. by Marcia Brown. Scribner's, 1982. Subj: Caldecott award book. Folk and fairy tales. Foreign lands – Africa. Poetry, rhyme. Shadows.

Cerf, Bennett Alfred. *Bennett Cerf's book of animal riddles* ill. by Roy McKié. Random House, 1964. Subj: Humor. Riddles.

Bennett Cerf's book of laughs ill. by Carl Rose. Random House, 1959. Subj: Humor. Riddles.

Bennett Cerf's book of riddles ill. by Roy McKié. Random House, 1960. Subj: Humor. Riddles.

More riddles ill. by Roy McKié. Random House, 1961. Subj: Humor. Riddles.

Chafetz, Henry. *The legend of Befana* ill. by Ronni Solbert. Houghton, 1958. Subj: Folk and fairy tales. Foreign lands – Italy. Holidays – Christmas.

Chaffin, Lillie D. *Tommy's big problem* ill. by Haris Petie. Lantern Pr., 1965. Subj: Babies. Behavior – growing up. Family life. Problem solving.

We be warm till springtime comes ill. by Lloyd Bloom. Macmillan, 1980. Subj: Character traits – bravery. Seasons – winter.

Chalmers, Audrey. *A birthday for Obash* ill. by author. Viking, 1952. First pub. in 1937. Subj: Birthdays.

Fancy be good ill. by author. Viking, 1941. Subj: Animals – cats. Behavior – misbehavior. Sibling rivalry.

Hector and Mr. Murfit ill. by author. Viking, 1953. Subj: Animals – dogs. Concepts – size.

Hundreds and hundreds of pancakes ill. by author. Viking, 1942. Subj: Animals. Food. Humor. Zoos.

A kitten's tale ill. by author. Viking, 1946. Subj: Animals – cats. Character traits – optimism.

Parade of Obash ill. by author. Oxford Univ. Pr., 1939. Subj: Animals – hippopotami. Parades. Zoos.

Chalmers, Mary. *Be good, Harry* ill. by author. Harper, 1967. Subj: Activities – babysitting. Animals – cats.

Boats finds a house ill. by author. Harper, 1958. Subj: Animals – cats. Boats, ships.

The cat who liked to pretend ill. by author. Harper, 1959. Subj: Animals – cats. Imagination.

A Christmas story ill. by author. Harper, 1956. Subj: Holidays – Christmas.

Come for a walk with me ill. by author. Harper, 1955. Subj: Animals – rabbits.

Come to the doctor, Harry ill. by author. Harper, 1981. Subj: Animals – cats. Illness.

George Appleton ill. by author. Harper, 1957. Subj: Animals – cats. Dragons.

A hat for Amy Jean ill. by author. Harper, 1956. Subj: Birthdays. Character traits – generosity. Clothing.

Here comes the trolley ill. by author. Harper, 1955. Subj: Activities – picnicking. Activities – traveling. Cable cars, trolleys.

Kevin ill. by author. Harper, 1957. Subj: Animals – rabbits. City.

Merry Christmas, Harry ill. by author. Harper, 1977. Subj: Animals – cats. Holidays – Christmas.

Mr. Cat's wonderful surprise ill. by author. Harper, 1961. Subj: Activities – picnicking. Animals – cats. Family life.

Take a nap, Harry ill. by author. Harper, 1964. Subj: Animals – cats. Family life. Sleep.

Throw a kiss, Harry ill. by author. Harper, 1958. Subj: Animals – cats. Careers – firefighters.

Chan, Chin-Yi. *Good luck horse* ill. by Plao Chan. Whittlesey House, 1943. Subj: Animals – horses. Caldecott award honor book.

Chandler, Edna Walker. *Cattle drive* ill. by Jack Merryweather. Benefic Pr., 1966. Subj: Cowboys.

Cowboy Andy ill. by Raymond Kinstler. Random House, 1959. Subj: Cowboys.

Pony rider ill. by Jack Merryweather. Benefic Pr., 1966. Subj: Animals – horses. Cowboys.

Secret tunnel ill. by Jack Merryweather. Benefic Pr., 1967. Subj: Cowboys.

Chandler, Robert. *Russian folk tales* (Afanas'ev, Aleksandr)

Chandoha, Walter. *A baby bunny for you* ill. by author. Collins, 1968. Subj: Animals – rabbits.

A baby goat for you ill. by author. Collins, 1968. Subj: Animals – goats.

A baby goose for you ill. by author. Collins, 1968. Subj: Birds – geese.

Chapin, Cynthia. *Squad car 55* ill. by Dale Fleming. Albert Whitman, 1966. Educational consultant: Jene Barr. Subj: Careers – police officers.

Chapman, Carol. *Barney Bipple's magic dandelions* ill. by Steven Kellogg. Dutton, 1977. Subj: Behavior – wishing. Flowers. Magic. Plants.

Herbie's troubles ill. by Kelly Oechsli. Dutton, 1981. Subj: Behavior – bullying. Behavior – misbehavior. Problem solving.

The tale of Meshka the Kvetch ill. by Arnold Lobel. Dutton, 1980. Subj: Behavior – dissatisfaction. Folk and fairy tales. Jewish culture.

Chapman, Gaynor. *The luck child* ill. by author. Atheneum, 1968. Based on a story of the Brothers Grimm. Subj: Folk and fairy tales. Royalty.

Chapman, Jean. *Moon-Eyes* ill. by Astra Lacis. McGraw-Hill, 1980. Subj: Animals – cats. Folk and fairy tales. Foreign lands – Italy. Holidays – Christmas. Religion.

Chapman, Noralee. *The story of Barbara* ill. by Helen S. Hull. John Knox Pr., 1963. Subj: Adoption.

Chardiet, Bernice. *C is for circus* ill. by Brinton Turkle. Walker, 1971. Subj: ABC books. Circus. Poetry, rhyme.

Charles Prince of Wales. *The old man of Lochnagar* ill. by Hugh Casson. Farrar, 1980. Subj: Folk and fairy tales. Foreign lands – Scotland. Imagination.

Charles, Donald. *Calico Cat at school* ill. by author. Children's Pr., 1981. Subj: Animals – cats. School.

Calico Cat at the zoo ill. by author. Children's Pr., 1981. Subj: Animals. Animals – cats. Zoos.

Calico Cat meets bookworm ill. by author. Children's Pr., 1978. Subj: Animals – cats. Libraries. Poetry, rhyme.

Calico Cat's exercise book ill. by author. Children's Pr., 1982. Subj: Animals – cats. Animals – mice.

Shaggy dog's animal alphabet ill. by author. Children's Pr., 1979. Subj: ABC books. Animals. Poetry, rhyme.

Shaggy dog's tall tale ill. by author. Children's Pr., 1980. Subj: Animals – dogs.

Time to rhyme with Calico Cat ill. by author. Children's Pr., 1978. Subj: Animals – cats. Animals – dogs. Poetry, rhyme.

Charles, Nicholas *see* Kuskin, Karla

Charles, Robert Henry. *The roundabout turn* ill. by L. Leslie Brooke. Warne, 1930. Subj: Frogs and toads. Merry-go-rounds. Poetry, rhyme.

Charlip, Remy. *Arm in arm* ill. by author. Parents, 1969. Subj: Games. Humor.

Fortunately ill. by author. Parents, 1964. Subj: Humor. Participation.

Handtalk: an ABC of finger spelling and sign language by Remy Charlip, Mary Beth and George Ancona; ill. by George Ancona. Parents, 1974. Subj: ABC books. Communication. Handicaps – deafness. Language.

Harlequin and the gift of many colors by Remy Charlip and Burton Supree; ill. by Remy Charlip. Parents, 1973. Subj: Concepts – color. Folk and fairy tales. Foreign lands – France.

Hooray for me! by Remy Charlip and Lilian Moore; ill. by Vera B. Williams. Parents, 1975. Subj: Character traits – individuality. Family life. Self-concept.

"Mother, mother I feel sick" by Remy Charlip and Burton Supree; ill. by Remy Charlip. Parents, 1966. Subj: Careers – doctors. Humor. Illness.

Thirteen by Remy Charlip and Jerry Joyner; ill. by Remy Charlip. Parents, 1975. Subj: Counting. Humor.

*The tree angel (*Martin, Judith)

Where is everybody? ill. by author. Addison-Wesley, 1957. Subj: Games. Weather – rain.

Charlot, Martin. *Felisa and the magic tikling bird* ill. by Martin Charlot from a story by Jodi Parry Belknap. Island Heritage, 1973. Subj: Activities – dancing. Folk and fairy tales. Foreign lands – Philippines. Handicaps. Self-concept.

Sunnyside up ill. by author. Weatherhill, 1972. Subj: Wordless.

Charlton, Elizabeth. *Jeremy and the ghost* ill. by Celia Reisman. Dandelion, 1979. Subj: Character traits – bravery. Ghosts. Holidays – Halloween.

Terrible tyrannosaurus ill. by Andrew Glass. Elsevier-Nelson, 1981. Subj: Behavior – bullying. Behavior – imitation. Dinosaurs.

Charmatz, Bill. *The Troy St. bus* ill. by author. Macmillan, 1977. Subj: Animals – horses. School.

Charosh, Mannis. *The ellipse* ill. by Leonard P. Kessler. Crowell, 1972. Subj: Concepts – shape. Science.

Number ideas through pictures ill. by Giulio Maestro. Crowell, 1975. Subj: Concepts. Counting.

Charters, Janet. *The general* by Janet Charters and Michael Foreman; ill. by Michael Foreman. Dutton, 1961. Subj: Violence, anti-violence.

Chase, Alice *see* McHargue, Georgess

Chase, Catherine. *An alphabet book* ill. by June Goldsborough. Dandelion, 1979. Subj: ABC books.

Baby mouse goes shopping ill. by Jill Elgin. Elsevier-Nelson, 1981. Subj: Animals – mice. Shopping.

Baby mouse learns his ABC's ill. by Jill Elgin. Dandelion, 1979. Subj: ABC books. Animals – mice.

Feet ill. by Susan Reiss. Dandelion, 1979. Subj: Anatomy. Concepts – left and right.

Hot and cold ill. by Gail Gibbons. Dandelion, 1979. Subj: Concepts.

The miracles at Cana ill. by Wayne Atkinson. Dandelion, 1979. Subj: Religion.

The mouse in my house ill. by Gail Gibbons. Dandelion, 1979. Subj: Animals – mice. Houses.

My balloon ill. by Gail Gibbons. Dandelion, 1979. Subj: Toys – balloons.

The nightingale and the fool ill. by Judith Cheng. Dandelion, 1979. Subj: Birds – nightingales. Folk and fairy tales. Foreign lands – India.

Noah's ark ill. by Elliot Ivenbaum. Dandelion, 1979. Subj: Religion – Noah.

Pete, the wet pet ill. by Gail Gibbons. Elsevier-Nelson, 1981. Subj: Animals – dogs. Family life.

Chase, Richard. *Billy Boy*

Jack and the three sillies ill. by Joshua Tolford. Houghton, 1950. Subj: Folk and fairy tales.

Chasek, Judith. *Have you seen Wilhelmina Krumpf?* ill. by Sal Murdocca. Lothrop, 1973. Subj: Foreign lands – Holland.

Chaucer, Geoffrey. *Chanticleer and the fox* adapt. and ill. by Barbara Cooney. Crowell, 1958. Adapt. of the "Nun's priest's tale" from the Canterbury tales. Subj: Animals – foxes. Birds – chickens. Caldecott award book. Character traits – flattery. Farms. Folk and fairy tales.

Chenault, Nell. *Parsifal the Poddley* ill. by Vee Guthrie. Little, 1960. Subj: Elves and little people. Emotions – loneliness. U.S. history.

Chenery, Janet. *Pickles and Jake* ill. by Lilian Obligado. Viking, 1975. Subj: Animals – cats. Animals – dogs. Pets.

The toad hunt ill. by Ben Shecter. Harper, 1967. Subj: Frogs and toads. Science.

Wolfie ill. by Marc Simont. Harper, 1969. Subj: Sibling rivalry. Spiders.

Cheng, Hou-Tien. *The Chinese New Year* ill. by author. Holt, 1976. Subj: Foreign lands – China. Holidays – Chinese New Year.

Chermayeff, Ivan. *Tomato and other colors* ill. by author. Prentice-Hall, 1981. Subj: Concepts – color.

Chernoff, Goldie Taub. *Clay-dough, play-dough* ill. and photos. by Margaret A. Hartelius. Walker, 1974. Subj: Activities.

Just a box? ill. by Margaret A. Hartelius. Walker, 1973. Subj: Activities.

Pebbles and pods: a book of nature crafts ill. by Margaret A. Hartelius. Walker, 1973. Subj: Activities.

Puppet party ill. by Margaret A. Hartelius. Walker, 1972. Subj: Activities. Puppets.

Chess, Victoria. *Alfred's alphabet walk* ill. by author. Greenwillow, 1979. Subj: ABC books. Behavior – misbehavior.

Poor Esmé ill. by author. Holiday, 1982. Subj: Babies. Behavior – wishing. Emotions – loneliness.

Chevalier, Christa. *The little bear who forgot* ed. by Kathleen Tucker; ill. by author. Albert Whitman, 1984. Subj: Animals – bears. Family life.

Spence and the sleepytime monster ill. by author. Albert Whitman, 1984. Subj: Bedtime. Imagination. Monsters.

Spence makes circles ill. by author. Albert Whitman, 1982. Subj: Behavior – mistakes. Humor.

Chevalier, Joan. *Suzette and Nicholas and the seasons clock* (Mangin, Marie-France)

Chicken Little. *Chicken Licken* ill. text by Kenneth McLeish; by Jutta Ash. Bradbury Pr., 1972. Subj: Animals. Behavior – gossip. Behavior – trickery. Birds – chickens. Cumulative tales. Folk and fairy tales.

Henny Penny ill. by Paul Galdone. Seabury Pr., 1968. Subj: Animals. Behavior – gossip. Behavior – trickery. Birds – chickens. Cumulative tales. Folk and fairy tales.

Henny Penny ill. by William Stobbs. Follett, 1968. Subj: Animals. Behavior – gossip. Behavior – trickery. Birds – chickens. Cumulative tales. Folk and fairy tales.

Chiefari, Janet. *Kids are baby goats* ill. with photos. Dodd, 1984. Subj: Animals – goats. Fairs.

Child, Lydia Maria. *Over the river and through the wood* ill. by Brinton Turkle. Coward, 1974. First published in 1844 as The boy's Thanksgiving Day in the 2d vol. of the author's Flowers for children. Subj: Family life – grandparents, great-grandparents. Farms. Holidays – Thanksgiving. Songs.

Child Study Association of America. *Brothers and sisters are like that!*

Children's Television Workshop. *Muppets in my neighborhood* ill. by Harry McNaught. Random House, 1977. Subj: Format, unusual – cardboard pages. Puppets.

The Sesame Street book of letters

The Sesame Street book of numbers

The Sesame Street book of opposites with Zero Mostel (Mendoza, George)

The Sesame Street book of people and things

The Sesame Street book of shapes

The Sesame Street players present Mother Goose (Mother Goose)

The Sesame Street song book (Raposo, Joe)

A visit to the Sesame Street firehouse (Elliott, Dan)

Chimaera see Farjeon, Eleanor

Chislett, Gail. *The rude visitors* ill. by Barbara Di Lella. Firefly Pr., 1984. Subj: Behavior – carelessness. Imagination.

Chlad, Dorothy. *Bicycles are fun to ride* ill. by Lydia Halverson. Children's Pr., 1984. Subj: Safety. Sports – bicycling.

Matches, lighters, and firecrackers are not toys ill. by Lydia Halverson. Children's Pr., 1982. Subj: Safety.

Poisons make you sick ill. by Lydia Halverson. Children's Pr., 1984. Subj: Safety.

Strangers ill. by Lydia Halverson. Children's Pr., 1982. Subj: Behavior – talking to strangers.

Chönz, Selina. *A bell for Ursli* ill. by Alois Carigiet. Walck, 1950. Subj: Foreign lands – Switzerland. Poetry, rhyme. Seasons – spring.

Florina and the wild bird tr. by Anne & Ian Serraillier; ill. by Alois Carigiet. Walck, 1966. Translation of Flurina und das Wildvöglein. Subj: Birds. Foreign lands – Switzerland. Poetry, rhyme. Seasons – summer.

The snowstorm ill. by Alois Carigiet. Walck, 1958. Translated from the German. Subj: Foreign lands – Switzerland. Poetry, rhyme. Seasons – winter. Weather – snow.

Chorao, Kay. *The baby's bedtime book* ill. by comp. Dutton, 1984. Subj: Nursery rhymes. Poetry, rhyme.

Kate's box ill. by author. Dutton, 1982. Subj: Animals – elephants. Behavior – hiding.

Kate's car ill. by author. Dutton, 1982. Subj: Animals – elephants. Toys.

Kate's quilt ill. by author. Dutton, 1982. Subj: Animals – elephants.

Kate's snowman ill. by author. Dutton, 1982. Subj: Animals – elephants. Snowmen.

Lemon moon ill. by author. Holiday, 1983. Subj: Animals. Bedtime. Dreams. Family life – grandparents, great-grandparents.

Lester's overnight ill. by author. Dutton, 1977. Subj: Emotions – fear. Family life. Imagination. Sleep.

Molly's lies ill. by author. Seabury Pr., 1979. Subj: Behavior – losing things. Behavior – lying. Friendship. School.

Molly's Moe ill. by author. Seabury Pr., 1976. Subj: Behavior – losing things. Shopping. Toys.

Oink and Pearl ill. by author. Harper, 1981. Subj: Animals – pigs. Sibling rivalry.

Christelow, Eileen. *Henry and the Dragon* ill. by author. Houghton, 1984. Subj: Animals – rabbits. Bedtime. Dragons. Shadows.

Henry and the red stripes ill. by author. Houghton, 1982. Subj: Animals – foxes. Animals – rabbits. Illness.

Jerome the babysitter ill. by author. Houghton, 1985. Subj: Activities – babysitting. Behavior – trickery. Character traits – cleverness. Reptiles – alligators, crocodiles.

Christensen, Gardell Dano. *Mrs. Mouse needs a house* ill. by author. Holt, 1958. Subj: Animals. Animals – mice. Houses. Problem solving.

Christensen, Jack. *The forgotten rainbow* by Jack and Lee Christensen; ill. by authors. Morrow, 1960. Subj: Behavior – wishing. Folk and fairy tales.

Christensen, Lee. *The forgotten rainbow* (Christensen, Jack)

Christenson, Larry. *The wonderful way that babies are made* ill. by Dwight Walles. Bethany House, 1982. Subj: Family life. Science.

Christian, Mary Blount. *April fool* ill. by Diane Dawson. Macmillan, 1982. Subj: Folk and fairy tales. Foreign lands – England. Holidays – April Fools' Day.

The devil take you, Barnabas Beane! ill. by Anne Burgess. Crowell, 1980. Subj: Behavior – greed. Character traits – generosity. Character traits – selfishness.

Devin and Goliath ill. by Normand Chartier. Addison-Wesley, 1974. Subj: Pets. Reptiles – turtles.

The doggone mystery ill. by Irene Trivas. Albert Whitman, 1980. Subj: Behavior – stealing. Crime. Problem solving.

J. J. Leggett, secret agent ill. by Jacquie Hann. Lothrop, 1978. Subj: Behavior – stealing. Character traits – cleverness. Crime. Problem solving.

No dogs allowed, Jonathan! ill. by Don Madden. Addison-Wesley, 1973. Subj: Animals – dogs.

Nothing much happened today ill. by Don Madden. Addison-Wesley, 1973. Subj: Cumulative tales. Humor.

The sand lot ill. by Dennis Kendrick. Harvey House, 1978. Subj: Activities – playing. Behavior – fighting, arguing. Sports – baseball.

Swamp monsters ill. by Marc Brown. Dial Pr., 1983. Subj: Behavior – imitation. Monsters. School.

A Christmas book tr. from Danish by Joan Tate; ill. by Svend Otto S. Larousse, 1982. Subj: Foreign lands – Denmark. Holidays – Christmas.

Christopher, Matt. *Jackrabbit goalie* ill. by Ed Parker. Little, 1978. Subj: Behavior – lying. Sports – soccer.

Johnny no hit ill. by Raymond Burns. Little, 1977. Subj: Behavior – bullying. Sports – baseball.

Chukovsky, Korney. *Good morning, chick* adapt. by Mirra Ginsburg; ill. by Byron Barton. Greenwillow, 1980. Subj: Birds – chickens. Noise, sounds.

The telephone adapt. from Russian by William Jay Smith in collaboration with Max Hayward; ill. by Blair Lent. Delacorte Pr., 1977. Subj: Communication. Humor. Poetry, rhyme.

Chute, Beatrice Joy. *Joy to Christmas* ill. by Erik Blegvad. Dutton, 1958. Subj: Character traits – generosity. Holidays – Christmas.

Chwast, Seymour. *Still another alphabet book* by Seymour Chwast and Martin Stephen Moskof; ill. by authors. McGraw-Hill, 1969. Subj: ABC books. Wordless.

Still another children's book by Seymour Chwast and Martin Stephen Moskof; ill. by authors. McGraw-Hill, 1972. Subj: Dreams. Seasons – summer.

Still another number book by Seymour Chwast and Martin Stephen Moskof; ill. by authors. McGraw-Hill, 1971. Subj: Counting.

Tall city, wide country: a book to read forward and backward ill. by author. Viking, 1983. Subj: Activities – traveling. City. Country. Format, unusual.

Ciardi, John. *I met a man* ill. by Robert Osborn. Houghton, 1961. Subj: Humor. Poetry, rhyme.

The monster den: or, Look what happened at my house - and to it ill. by Edward Gorey. Lippincott, 1966. Subj: Monsters. Poetry, rhyme.

Scrappy the pup ill. by Jane Miller. Lippincott, 1960. Subj: Animals – dogs. Behavior – growing up. Sleep.

You read to me, I'll read to you ill. by Edward Gorey. Lippincott, 1962. Subj: Poetry, rhyme.

Ciliotta, Claire. *"Why am I going to the hospital?"* by Claire Ciliotta and Carole Livingston; ill. by Dick Wilson. Lyle Stuart, 1982. Subj: Hospitals. Illness.

Claret, Maria. *Melissa Mouse* ill. by author. Barron's, 1985. Subj: Animals – mice. Weddings.

Clark, Ann Nolan. *The desert people* ill. by Allan Houser. Viking, 1962. Subj: Desert. Ethnic groups in the U.S. – Indians.

In my mother's house ill. by Velino Herrera. Viking, 1941. Subj: Caldecott award honor book. Ethnic groups in the U.S. – Indians. Family life.

The little Indian basket maker ill. by Harrison Begay. Melmont, 1955. Subj: Activities – working. Ethnic groups in the U.S. – Indians.

The little Indian pottery maker ill. by Don Perceval. Melmont, 1955. Subj: Activities – working. Ethnic groups in the U.S. – Indians.

Tia Maria's garden ill. by Ezra Jack Keats. Viking, 1963. Subj: Desert.

Clark, Harry. *The first story of the whale* ill. by author. Houghton, 1938. Subj: Animals – whales. Games. Science.

Clark, Leonard. *Drums and trumpets: poetry for the youngest* ill. by Heather Copley. Bodley Head, 1979. Subj: Nursery rhymes. Poetry, rhyme.

Clark, Roberta. *Why?* ill. by Lois Axeman. Children's Pr., 1983. Subj: Character traits – curiosity. Character traits – questioning.

Claude-Lafontaine, Pascale. *Monsieur Bussy, the celebrated hamster* ill. by Annick Delhumeau. McGraw-Hill, 1968. Delhumeau's name appeared first on the title page of the French ed. pub. under title: Bussy, le hamster doré. Subj: Animals – hamsters. Character traits – ambition.

Claxton, Ernest. *A child's grace* (Burdekin, Harold)

Clay, Helen. *Beetles* (Clay, Pat)

Clay, Pat. *Beetles* by Pat and Helen Clay; photos. by authors. A & C Black, 1983. Subj: Science.

Cleary, Beverly. *The hullabaloo ABC* ill. by Earl Thollander. Parnassus, 1960. Subj: ABC books. Farms. Noise, sounds.

Lucky Chuck ill. by J. Winslow Higginbottom. Morrow, 1984. Subj: Behavior – carelessness. Motorcycles. Safety. Transportation.

The real hole ill. by Mary Stevens. Morrow, 1960. Subj: Activities – digging. Problem solving. Trees. Twins.

Two dog biscuits ill. by Mary Stevens. Morrow, 1961. Subj: Twins.

Cleaver, Elizabeth. *ABC* ill. by author. Atheneum, 1985. Subj: ABC books.

Clewes, Dorothy. *Happiest day* ill. by Sofia. Coward, 1959. Subj: Emotions – loneliness. School.

Henry Hare's boxing match ill. by Patricia W. Turner. Coward, 1950. Subj: Animals. Behavior – imitation.

Hide and seek ill. by Sofia. Coward, 1960. Subj: Farms.

The wild wood ill. by Irene Hawkins. Coward, 1948. Subj: Animals. Character traits – kindness to animals

Clifford, David. *Your face is a picture* (Clifford, Eth)

Clifford, Eth. *A bear before breakfast* ill. by Kelly Oechsli. Putnam's, 1962. Subj: Communication. Language.

Red is never a mouse ill. by Bill Heckler. Bobbs-Merrill, 1960. Subj: Concepts – color. Poetry, rhyme.

Why is an elephant called an elephant? ill. by Jackie Lacy. Bobbs-Merrill, 1966. Subj: Animals – elephants. Cumulative tales. Royalty.

Your face is a picture by Eth and David Clifford; photos. by David Clifford; ed. consultant: Leo Fay. E. C. Seale, 1963. Subj: Emotions. Ethnic groups in the U.S.

Clifton, Lucille. *All us come cross the water* ill. by John Steptoe. Holt, 1973. Subj: Character traits – pride. Ethnic groups in the U.S. – Afro-Americans. School.

Amifika ill. by Thomas Di Grazia. Dutton, 1977. Subj: Emotions – fear. Ethnic groups in the U.S. – Afro-Americans. Family life. Family life – fathers.

The black B C's ill. by Don Miller. Dutton, 1970. Subj: ABC books. Ethnic groups in the U.S. – Afro-Americans. Poetry, rhyme.

The boy who didn't believe in spring ill. by Brinton Turkle. Dutton, 1973. Subj: City. Ethnic groups in the U.S. – Afro-Americans. Seasons – spring.

Don't you remember? ill. by Evaline Ness. Dutton, 1973. Subj: Birthdays. Ethnic groups in the U.S. – Afro-Americans. Family life.

Everett Anderson's Christmas coming ill. by Evaline Ness. Holt, 1971. Subj: City. Ethnic groups in the U.S. – Afro-Americans. Holidays – Christmas. Poetry, rhyme.

Everett Anderson's friend ill. by Ann Grifalconi. Holt, 1976. Subj: Ethnic groups in the U.S. – Afro-Americans. Friendship. Poetry, rhyme.

Everett Anderson's goodbye ill. by Ann Grifalconi. Holt, 1983. Subj: Death. Emotions. Emotions – love. Ethnic groups in the U.S. – Afro-Americans. Family life. Poetry, rhyme.

Everett Anderson's nine months long ill. by Ann Grifalconi. Holt, 1978. Subj: Babies. Ethnic groups in the U.S. – Afro-Americans. Family life. Poetry, rhyme.

Everett Anderson's 1-2-3 ill. by Ann Grifalconi. Holt, 1977. Subj: Ethnic groups in the U.S. – Afro-Americans. Family life. Poetry, rhyme.

Everett Anderson's year ill. by Ann Grifalconi. Holt, 1974. Subj: Ethnic groups in the U.S. – Afro-Americans. Poetry, rhyme. Seasons.

My brother fine with me ill. by Moneta Barnett. Holt, 1975. Subj: Behavior – running away. Ethnic groups in the U.S. – Afro-Americans. Family life. Sibling rivalry.

My friend Jacob ill. by Thomas Di Grazia. Dutton, 1980. Subj: Character traits – helpfulness. Ethnic groups in the U.S. – Afro-Americans. Friendship. Handicaps.

Some of the days of Everett Anderson ill. by Evaline Ness. Holt, 1970. Subj: Days of the week, months of the year. Ethnic groups in the U.S. – Afro-Americans. Family life. Poetry, rhyme.

Three wishes ill. by Stephanie Douglas. Viking, 1976. Subj: Behavior – wishing. Ethnic groups in the U.S. – Afro-Americans. Friendship.

Climo, Lindee. *Chester's barn* ill. by author. Tundra, 1982. Subj: Barns. Farms. Foreign lands – Canada.

Climo, Shirley. *The adventure of Walter* ill. by Ingrid Fetz. Atheneum, 1965. Subj: Animals – whales. Character traits – curiosity.

The cobweb Christmas ill. by Joe Lasker. Crowell, 1982. Subj: Animals. Holidays – Christmas. Magic. Spiders.

Clithero, Myrtle E. *see* Clithero, Sally

Clithero, Sally. *Beginning-to-read poetry* Follett, 1967. Subj: Poetry, rhyme.

Clymer, Eleanor Lowenton. *The big pile of dirt* ill. by Robert Shore. Holt, 1968. Subj: Activities – playing. City.

Horatio ill. by Robert M. Quackenbush. Atheneum, 1968. Subj: Animals – cats. Ethnic groups in the U.S. – Afro-Americans.

Horatio goes to the country ill. by Robert M. Quackenbush. Atheneum, 1978. Subj: Animals – cats. Twins.

The tiny little house ill. by Ingrid Fetz. Atheneum, 1964. Subj: Houses.

A yard for John ill. by Mildred Boyle. McBride, 1943. Subj: Moving.

Clymer, Ted. *The horse and the bad morning* by Ted Clymer and Miska Miles; ill. by Leslie Morrill. Dutton, 1982. Subj: Animals. Behavior – dissatisfaction. Problem solving.

Coats, Belle. *Little maverick cow* ill. by George Fulton. Scribner's, 1957. Subj: Animals – bulls, cows. Farms.

Coatsworth, Elizabeth. *Boston Bells* ill. by Manning Lee. Macmillan, 1952. Subj: Art. U.S. history.

The children come running: UNICEF greeting cards. Golden Pr., 1961. Subj: Holidays – Christmas. Poetry, rhyme. UNICEF

The giant golden book of cat stories ill. by Feodor Rojankovsky. Simon and Schuster, 1953. Subj: Animals – cats. Folk and fairy tales. Poetry, rhyme.

Good night ill. by José Aruego. Macmillan, 1972. Subj: Bedtime. Stars.

Lonely Maria ill. by Evaline Ness. Pantheon, 1960. Subj: Emotions – loneliness. Family life – grandparents, great-grandparents. Islands.

A peaceable kingdom, and other poems ill. by Fritz Eichenberg. Pantheon, 1958. Subj: Animals. Poetry, rhyme.

Pika and the roses ill. by Kurt Wiese. Pantheon, 1959. Subj: Animals – rabbits. Character traits – cleverness.

Under the green willow ill. by Janina Domanska. Macmillan, 1971. Subj: Birds. Fish. Food.

Cobb, Vicki. *How the doctor knows you're fine* ill. by Anthony Ravielli. Lippincott, 1973. Subj: Careers – doctors. Health.

Lots of rot ill. by Brian Schatell. Lippincott, 1981. Subj: Science.

Cobbett, Richard *see* Pluckrose, Henry

Cober, Alan E. *Cober's choice* ill. by author. Dutton, 1979. Subj: Animals. Art.

Cocagnac, A. M. (Augustin Maurice). *The three trees of the Samurai* adapt. from a Japanese no play; ill. by Alain Le Foll. Dial Pr., 1970. Subj: Folk and fairy tales. Foreign lands – Japan.

Cock Robin. *The courtship, merry marriage, and feast of Cock Robin and Jenny Wren: to which is added the doleful death of Cock Robin* ill. by Barbara Cooney. Scribner's, 1965. Subj: Birds – robins. Birds – wrens. Death. Nursery rhymes. Weddings.

Coe, Lloyd. *Charcoal* ill. by author. Crowell, 1946. Subj: Animals – sheep.

Coerr, Eleanor. *The big balloon race* ill. by Carolyn Croll. Harper, 1981. Subj: Activities – ballooning.

Cohen, Barbara. *The demon who would not die* ill. by Anatoly Ivanov. Atheneum, 1982. Subj: Folk and fairy tales. Foreign lands – Russia. Monsters.

Gooseberries to oranges ill. by Beverly Brodsky McDermott. Lothrop, 1982. Subj: Jewish culture. Moving.

Here come the Purim players! ill. by Beverly Brodsky McDermott. Lothrop, 1984. Subj: Folk and fairy tales. Holidays. Jewish culture. Middle ages.

Cohen, Burton. *Nelson makes a face* ill. by William Schroder. Lothrop, 1978. Subj: Character traits – appearance.

Cohen, Carol L. *Wake up, groundhog!* ill. by author. Crown, 1975. Subj: Animals – groundhogs. Clocks. Hibernation. Holidays – Groundhog Day. Seasons – spring.

Cohen, Daniel. *America's very own monsters* ill. by Tom Huffman. Dodd, 1982. Subj: Monsters.

Cohen, Miriam. *Bee my Valentine!* ill. by Lillian Hoban. Greenwillow, 1978. Subj: Holidays – Valentine's Day. School.

Best friends ill. by Lillian Hoban. Macmillan, 1971. Subj: Friendship. School.

First grade takes a test ill. by Lillian Hoban. Greenwillow, 1980. Subj: Friendship. School.

Jim meets the thing ill. by Lillian Hoban. Greenwillow, 1981. Subj: Behavior – growing up. Emotions – fear. Monsters. School.

Jim's dog Muffins ill. by Lillian Hoban. Greenwillow, 1984. Subj: Animals – dogs. Death. Emotions. Pets.

Lost in the museum ill. by Lillian Hoban. Greenwillow, 1979. Subj: Behavior – lost. Museums. School.

The new teacher ill. by Lillian Hoban. Macmillan, 1972. Subj: School.

No good in art ill. by Lillian Hoban. Greenwillow, 1980. Subj: Art. School. Self-concept.

See you tomorrow ill. by Lillian Hoban. Greenwillow, 1983. Subj: Handicaps – blindness. School.

So what? ill. by Lillian Hoban. Greenwillow, 1982. Subj: School. Self-concept.

Tough Jim ill. by Lillian Hoban. Macmillan, 1974. Subj: Behavior – bullying. Parties. School.

When will I read? ill. by Lillian Hoban. Greenwillow, 1977. Subj: Activities – reading. School.

Will I have a friend? ill. by Lillian Hoban. Macmillan, 1967. Subj: Ethnic groups in the U.S. Friendship. School.

Cohen, Peter Zachary. *Authorized autumn charts of the Upper Red Canoe River country* ill. by Tomic dc Paola. Athcncum, 1972. Subj: ABC books. Boats, ships. Games. Seasons – fall.

Cohn, Norma. *Brother and sister* ill. by author. Oxford Univ. Pr., 1942. Subj: Animals – cats. Sports – swimming.

Coker, Gylbert. *Naptime* ill. by author. Delacorte, 1978. Subj: School. Sleep.

Colby, C. B. (Carroll Burleigh). *Who lives there?* ill. by author. Atheneum, 1953. Subj: Animals. Birds. Houses. Insects. Science.

Who went there? ill. by author. Atheneum, 1953. Subj: Animals. Birds. Reptiles. Science.

Coldrey, Jennifer. *Penguins* photos. by Douglas Allan and others. André Deutsch, 1983. Subj: Birds – penguins.

Cole, Ann. *I saw a purple cow: and 100 other recipes for learning* by Ann Cole and others; ill. by True Kelley. Little, 1972. Subj: Activities.

Purple cow to the rescue by Ann Cole and Carolyn Haas; ill. by True Kelley. Little, 1982. Subj: Activities.

Cole, Babette. *Nungu and the elephant* ill. by author. McGraw-Hill, 1980. Subj: Animals – elephants. Foreign lands – Africa. Magic.

Nungu and the hippopotamus ill. by author. McGraw-Hill, 1979. Subj: Animals – hippopotami. Foreign lands – Africa.

The trouble with mom ill. by author. Coward, 1984. Subj: Family life – mothers. School. Witches.

Cole, Brock. *The king at the door* ill. by author. Doubleday, 1979. Subj: Behavior – disbelief. Character traits – kindness. Foreign lands – England. Royalty.

Nothing but a pig ill. by author. Doubleday, 1981. Subj: Animals – pigs. Behavior – imitation. Behavior – seeking better things. Friendship.

Cole, Davis *see* Elting, Mary

Cole, Joanna. *Aren't you forgetting something, Fiona?* ill. by Ned Delaney. Parents, 1984. Subj: Animals – elephants. Behavior – forgetfulness.

A bird's body photos. by Jerome Wexler. Morrow, 1982. Subj: Anatomy. Birds. Science.

Bony-legs ill. by Dirk Zimmer. Four Winds Pr., 1983. Subj: Folk and fairy tales. Foreign lands – Russia. Magic. Witches.

A calf is born photos. by Jerome Wexler. Morrow, 1975. Subj: Animals – bulls, cows. Babies. Science.

A cat's body photos by Jerome Wexler. Morrow, 1982. Subj: Anatomy. Animals – cats. Science.

A chick hatches photos. by Jerome Wexler. Morrow, 1976. Subj: Birds – chickens. Science.

The Clown-Arounds go on vacation ill. by Jerry Smath. Parents, 1984. Subj: Activities – vacationing. Behavior – lost. Clowns, jesters. Humor. Riddles.

Find the hidden insect by Joanna Cole and Jerome Wexler; photos. by Jerome Wexler. Morrow, 1979. Subj: Insects. Science.

A fish hatches photos. by Jerome Wexler. Morrow, 1978. Subj: Fish. Science.

Get well, Clown-Arounds! ill. by Jerry Smath. Parents, 1983. Subj: Clowns, jesters. Humor. Illness. Riddles.

Golly Gump swallowed a fly ill. by Bari Weissman. Parents, 1982. Subj: Folk and fairy tales. Humor. Poetry, rhyme.

How you were born photos. by Lennart Nilsson. Morrow, 1984. Subj: Babies. Family life. Science.

My puppy is born photos. by Jerome Wexler. Morrow, 1973. Subj: Animals – dogs. Science.

Plants in winter ill. by Kazue Mizumura. Crowell, 1973. Subj: Plants. Science. Seasons – winter. Trees.

The secret box ill. by Joan Sandin. Morrow, 1971. Subj: Behavior – stealing.

Cole, William. *Aunt Bella's umbrella* ill. by Jacqueline Chwast. Doubleday, 1970. Subj: Character traits – helpfulness. Umbrellas. Weather – rain.

Dinosaurs and beasts of yore ill. by Susanna Natti. Collins-World, 1979. Subj: Dinosaurs. Humor.

Frances face-maker ill. by Tomi Ungerer. Collins-World, 1963. Subj: Bedtime. Emotions. Family life. Participation. Poetry, rhyme.

I went to the animal fair ill. by Colette Rosselli. Collins-World, 1959. Subj: Animals. Humor.

I'm mad at you

That pest Jonathan ill. by Tomi Ungerer. Harper, 1970. Subj: Behavior – misbehavior. Family life. Poetry, rhyme.

What's good for a four-year-old? ill. by Tomi Ungerer. Holt, 1967. Subj: Activities – playing. Poetry, rhyme.

What's good for a six-year-old? ill. by Ingrid Fetz. Holt, 1965. Subj: Activities – playing. Poetry, rhyme.

What's good for a three-year-old? ill. by Lillian Hoban. Holt, 1974. Subj: Activities – babysitting. Birthdays. Poetry, rhyme.

Coletta, Hallie. *From A to Z* (Coletta, Irene)

Coletta, Irene. *From A to Z* by Irene and Hallie Coletta; ill. by Hallie Coletta. Prentice-Hall, 1979. Subj: ABC books. Poetry, rhyme. Rebuses.

Colette. *The boy and the magic* tr. by Christopher Fry; ill. by Gerard Hoffnung. Putnam's, 1965. Subj: Behavior – misbehavior. Magic. Music.

Collier, Ethel. *I know a farm* ill. by Honoré Guilbeau. Addison-Wesley, 1960. Subj: Farms.

Who goes there in my garden? ill. by Honoré Guilbeau. Abelard-Schuman, 1963. Subj: Activities – gardening. Character traits – helpfulness.

Collier, James Lincoln. *Danny goes to the hospital* ill. by Yale Joel. Norton, 1970. Subj: Hospitals.

Collins, Judith Graham. *Josh's scary dad* ill. by Diane Paterson. Abingdon Pr., 1983. Subj: Character traits – appearance. Humor.

Collins, Pat Lowery. *My friend Andrew* ill. by Howard Berelson. Prentice-Hall, 1981. Subj: Behavior – boasting. Imagination.

Tumble, tumble, tumbleweed ill. by Charles Robinson. Albert Whitman, 1982. Subj: Friendship. Pets.

Collodi, Carlo. *The adventures of Pinocchio* adapt. by Stephanie Spinner; ill. by Diane Goode. Random House, 1983. Subj: Behavior – lying. Behavior – misbehavior. Character traits – loyalty. Folk and fairy tales. Puppets.

Colman, Hila. *Peter's brownstone house* ill. by Leonard Weisgard. Morrow, 1963. Subj: City. Houses.

Watch that watch ill. by Leonard Weisgard. Morrow, 1962. Subj: Animals. Clocks. Time.

Colonius, Lillian. *At the zoo* by Lillian Colonius and Glen W. Schroeder; ill. by Glen W. Schroeder. Melmont, 1954. Subj: Zoos.

Come to the circus Simon and Schuster, 1980. Subj: Circus. Format, unusual – cardboard pages.

Conaway, Judith. *I'll get even* ill. by Mark Gubin. Raintree Pub., 1977. Subj: Emotions – loneliness. Sibling rivalry.

Cone, Molly. *The Jewish Sabbath* ill. by Ellen Raskin. Crowell, 1966. Subj: Holidays. Jewish culture. Religion.

Conford, Ellen. *Eugene the brave* ill. by John M. Larrecq. Little, 1978. Subj: Animals – possums. Character traits – bravery. Emotions – fear. Night.

Impossible, possum ill. by Rosemary Wells. Little, 1971. Subj: Animals – possums. Character traits – individuality.

Just the thing for Geraldine ill. by John M. Larrecq. Little, 1974. Subj: Animals – possums. Character traits – perseverance.

Why can't I be William? ill. by Philip Wende. Little, 1972. Subj: Emotions – envy, jealousy. Family life. Family life – only child. Friendship.

Conger, Lesley. *Tops and bottoms* ill. by Imero Gobbato. Four Winds Pr., 1970. Subj: Folk and fairy tales. Foreign lands – England. Monsters.

Conger, Marion. *The chipmunk that went to church* ill. by author. Simon and Schuster, 1952. Subj: Animals – chipmunks. Emotions – loneliness.

The little golden holiday book ill. by author. Simon and Schuster, 1951. Subj: Holidays.

Conklin, Gladys. *Cheetahs, the swift hunters* ill. by Charles Robinson. Holiday, 1976. Subj: Animals – cheetahs. Science.

I caught a lizard ill. by Artur Marokvia. Holiday, 1967. Subj: Animals. Insects. Reptiles – lizards. Science. Spiders.

I like beetles ill. by Jean Zallinger. Holiday, 1975. Subj: Insects – beetles. Science.

I like butterflies ill. by Barbara Latham. Holiday, 1960. Subj: Insects – butterflies, caterpillars. Science.

I like caterpillars ill. by Barbara Latham. Holiday, 1958. Subj: Insects – butterflies, caterpillars. Science.

I watch flies ill. by Jean Zallinger. Holiday, 1977. Subj: Insects – flies. Science.

If I were a bird ill. by Artur Marokvia. Holiday, 1965. Subj: Birds. Science.

Journey of the gray whales ill. by Leonard Everett Fisher. Holiday, 1974. Subj: Animals – whales. Science.

Little apes ill. by Joseph Cellini. Holiday, 1970. Subj: Animals – gorillas. Science.

Lucky ladybugs ill. by Glen Rounds. Holiday, 1968. Subj: Insects – ladybugs. Science.

Praying mantis: the garden dinosaur ill. by Glen Rounds. Holiday, 1978. Subj: Insects – praying mantis. Science.

We like bugs ill. by Artur Marokvia. Holiday, 1962. Subj: Insects. Science.

When insects are babies ill. by Artur Marokvia. Holiday, 1969. Subj: Insects. Science.

Conover, Chris. *Six little ducks* ill. by author. Crowell, 1976. Subj: Birds – ducks. Counting. Music. Poetry, rhyme. Songs.

The wizard's daughter: a Viking legend ill. by author. Little, 1984. Subj: Folk and fairy tales. Foreign lands – Denmark. Magic. Royalty.

Conroy, Jack. *The fast sooner hound* (Bontemps, Arna Wendell)

Conta, Marcia Maher. *Feelings between brothers and sisters* ill. by Jules M. Rosenthal. Raintree Pub., 1974. Subj: Emotions. Family life.

Feelings between friends ill. by Jules M. Rosenthal. Raintree Pub., 1974. Subj: Emotions. Friendship.

Feelings between kids and grownups ill. by Jules M. Rosenthal. Raintree Pub., 1974. Subj: Emotions.

Feelings between kids and parents ill. by Jules M. Rosenthal. Raintree Pub., 1974. Subj: Emotions. Family life.

Cook, Ann. *Lady Monster has a plan* (Blance, Ellen)

Lady Monster helps out (Blance, Ellen)

Monster and the magic umbrella (Blance, Ellen)

Monster and the mural (Blance, Ellen)

Monster and the surprise cookie (Blance, Ellen)

Monster at school (Blance, Ellen)

Monster buys a pet (Blance, Ellen)

Monster cleans his house (Blance, Ellen)

Monster comes to the city (Blance, Ellen)

Monster gets a job (Blance, Ellen)

Monster goes around the town (Blance, Ellen)

Monster goes to school (Blance, Ellen)

Monster goes to the beach (Blance, Ellen)

Monster goes to the circus (Blance, Ellen)

Monster goes to the hospital (Blance, Ellen)

Monster goes to the museum (Blance, Ellen)

Monster goes to the zoo (Blance, Ellen)

Monster has a party (Blance, Ellen)

Monster, Lady Monster and the bike ride (Blance, Ellen)

Monster looks for a friend (Blance, Ellen)

Monster looks for a house (Blance, Ellen)

Monster meets Lady Monster (Blance, Ellen)

Monster on the bus (Blance, Ellen)

Cook, Bernadine. *The little fish that got away* ill. by Crockett Johnson. Addison-Wesley, 1956. Subj: Fish. Sports – fishing.

Looking for Susie ill. by Judith Shahn. Addison-Wesley, 1959. Subj: Animals – cats. Family life. Farms.

Cook, Marion B. *Waggles and the dog catcher* ill. by Louis Darling. Morrow, 1951. Subj: Animals – dogs.

Cooke, Ann. *Giraffes at home* ill. by Robert M. Quackenbush. Harper, 1972. Subj: Animals – giraffes. Science.

Cooke, Barbara *see* Alexander, Anne

Coombs, Patricia. *Dorrie and the amazing magic elixir* ill. by author. Lothrop, 1974. Subj: Magic. Witches. Wizards.

Dorrie and the birthday eggs ill. by author. Lothrop, 1971. Subj: Birthdays. Eggs. Witches.

Dorrie and the blue witch ill. by author. Lothrop, 1964. Subj: Magic. Witches.

Dorrie and the dreamyard monsters ill. by author. Lothrop, 1977. Subj: Dreams. Magic. Monsters. Witches.

Dorrie and the fortune teller ill. by author. Lothrop, 1973. Subj: Careers – fortune tellers. Progress. Witches. Wizards.

Dorrie and the goblin ill. by author. Lothrop, 1972. Subj: Activities – babysitting. Goblins. Witches.

Dorrie and the Halloween plot ill. by author. Lothrop, 1976. Subj: Activities – flying. Holidays – Halloween. Witches.

Dorrie and the haunted house ill. by author. Lothrop, 1970. Subj: Crime. Witches. Wizards.

Dorrie and the screebit ghost ill. by author. Lothrop, 1979. Subj: Ghosts. Witches.

Dorrie and the weather-box ill. by author. Lothrop, 1966. Subj: Activities – picnicking. Magic. Weather. Witches.

Dorrie and the witch doctor ill. by author. Lothrop, 1967. Subj: Magic. Witches

Dorrie and the witches' camp ill. by author. Lothrop, 1983. Subj: Problem solving. Witches.

Dorrie and the witch's imp ill. by author. Lothrop, 1975. Subj: Magic. Witches.

Dorrie and the Witchville fair ill. by author. Lothrop, 1980. Subj: Fairs. Magic. Witches.

Dorrie and the wizard's spell ill. by author. Lothrop, 1968. Subj: Magic. Witches. Wizards.

Dorrie's magic ill. by author. Lothrop, 1962. Subj: Magic. Witches.

Dorrie's play ill. by author. Lothrop, 1965. Subj: Behavior – mistakes. Theater. Witches.

Lisa and the grompet ill. by author. Lothrop, 1970. Subj: Behavior – running away. Fairies. Family life.

The lost playground ill. by author. Lothrop, 1963. Subj: Behavior – losing things. Character traits – being different. Toys.

The magic pot ill. by author. Lothrop, 1977. Subj: Devil. Folk and fairy tales. Foreign lands – Denmark. Magic.

The magician and McTree ill. by author. Lothrop, 1984. Subj: Animals – cats. Behavior – secrets. Magic. Middle ages.

Molly Mullett ill. by author. Lothrop, 1975. Subj: Character traits – bravery. Monsters.

Mouse Café ill. by author. Lothrop, 1972. Subj: Animals – mice. Character traits – selfishness. Weddings.

Tilabel ill. by author. Lothrop, 1978. Subj: Activities – weaving. Animals – groundhogs. Folk and fairy tales. Foreign lands – Germany. Royalty.

Cooney, Barbara. *A garland of games and other diversions: an alphabet book* initial letters by Suzanne R. Morse; ill. by author. Holt, 1969. Subj: ABC books. Poetry, rhyme.

Little brother and little sister ill. by author. Doubleday, 1982. Subj: Character traits – loyalty. Folk and fairy tales. Foreign lands – Germany. Royalty. Witches.

The little juggler ill. by author. Hastings, 1982. Reprint of 1961 ed. Subj: Holidays – Christmas.

A little prayer ill. by author. Hastings, 1967. Subj: Religion.

Miss Rumphius ill. by author. Viking, 1982. Subj: Activities – traveling. Flowers.

Snow-White and Rose-Red (Grimm, Jacob)

Cooney, Nancy Evans. *The blanket that had to go* ill. by Diane Dawson. Putnam's, 1981. Subj: Behavior – growing up. Problem solving. School.

The wobbly tooth ill. by Marylin Hafner. Putnam's, 1978. Subj: Teeth.

Coontz, Otto. *The quiet house* ill. by author. Little, 1978. Subj: Animals – dogs. Eggs. Emotions – loneliness. Friendship.

A real class clown ill. by author. Little, 1979. Subj: Circus. Clowns, jesters. School.

Starring Rosa ill. by author. Little, 1980. Subj: Animals – pigs. Food. Humor.

Cooper, Elizabeth K. *The fish from Japan* ill. by Beth and Joe Krush. Harcourt, 1969. Subj: Fish. Imagination. Kites. Pets.

Cooper, Gale. *Unicorn moon* ill. by author. Dutton, 1984. Subj: Animals. Magic. Mythical creatures. Royalty.

Cooper, Jacqueline. *Angus and the Mona Lisa* ill. by author. Lothrop, 1981. Subj: Animals – cats. Behavior – stealing. Problem solving.

Cooper, Letice Ulpha. *The bear who was too big* ill. by Ruth Ives. Follett, 1963. Subj: Stores. Toys – teddy bears.

Cooper, Paulette. *Let's find out about Halloween* ill. by Errol Le Cain. Watts, 1972. Subj: Holidays – Halloween.

Cooper, Susan. *The silver cow: a Welsh tale* ill. by Warwick Hutton. Atheneum, 1983. Subj: Behavior – greed. Character traits – smallness. Folk and fairy tales. Foreign lands – England.

Coopersmith, Jerome. *A Chanukah fable for Christmas* ill. by Syd Hoff. Putnam's, 1969. Subj: Behavior – wishing. Holidays – Hanukkah. Jewish culture.

Cope, Dawn. *Humpty Dumpty's favorite nursery rhymes* comp. by Dawn and Peter Cope; ill. by Jessie M. King, Randolph Caldecott and others. Holt, 1981. Subj: Nursery rhymes.

Cope, Peter. *Humpty Dumpty's favorite nursery rhymes* (Cope, Dawn)

Copeland, Helen. *Meet Miki Takino* ill. by Kurt Werth. Lothrop, 1963. Subj: Ethnic groups in the U.S. – Japanese-Americans. Family life – grandparents, great-grandparents.

Copp, Andrew James *see* Copp, James

Copp, James. *Martha Matilda O'Toole* ill. by Steven Kellogg. Bradbury Pr., 1969. Originally appeared as a song in the author's phonorecord: Jim Copp tales. Subj: Behavior – forgetfulness. Humor. Poetry, rhyme. School.

Copp, Jim *see* Copp, James

Corbett, Grahame. *Guess who?* ill. by author. Dial Pr., 1982. Subj: Format, unusual – cardboard pages. Participation. Toys.

What number now? ill. by author. Dial Pr., 1982. Subj: Counting. Format, unusual – cardboard pages. Participation.

Who is hiding? ill. by author. Dial Pr., 1982. Subj: Format, unusual – cardboard pages. Participation. Toys.

Who is inside? ill. by author. Dial Pr., 1982. Subj: Format, unusual – cardboard pages. Participation. Toys.

Who is next? ill. by author. Dial Pr., 1982. Subj: Format, unusual – cardboard pages. Participation. Toys.

Corbett, Scott. *Dr. Merlin's magic shop* ill. by Joseph Mathieu. Little, 1973. Subj: Magic.

The foolish dinosaur fiasco ill. by Jon McIntosh. Little, 1978. Subj: Dinosaurs. Magic.

The great custard pie panic ill. by Joseph Mathieu. Little, 1974. Subj: Magic.

The mysterious Zetabet ill. by Jon McIntosh. Little, 1979. Subj: ABC books.

Corcos, Lucille. *The city book* ill. by author. Golden Pr., 1972. Subj: City.

Corddry, Thomas I. *Kibby's big feat* ill. by Quentin Blake. Follett, 1971. Subj: Bedtime. Behavior – lost. Jungle.

Corey, Dorothy. *Everybody takes turns* ill. by Lois Axeman. Albert Whitman, 1979. Subj: Behavior – sharing.

Tomorrow you can ill. by Lois Axeman. Albert Whitman, 1977. Subj: Behavior – growing up.

We all share ill. by Rondi Colette. Albert Whitman, 1980. Subj: Behavior – sharing.

Cormack, M. Grant. *Animal tales from Ireland* ill. by Vana Earle. John Day, 1955. First published in England, 1954. Subj: Animals. Folk and fairy tales. Foreign lands – Ireland.

Corney, Estelle. *Pa's top hat* ill. by Hilary Abrahams. Elsevier-Dutton, 1981. Subj: Sea and seashore. Trains.

Cornish, Sam. *Grandmother's pictures* ill. by Jeanne Johns. Bradbury Pr., 1974. Subj: Family life. Family life – grandparents, great-grandparents.

Corrin, Sara. *Mrs. Fox's wedding* (Grimm, Jacob)

Corrin, Stephen. *Mrs. Fox's wedding* (Grimm, Jacob)

Cortesi, Wendy W. *Explore a spooky swamp* ill. by Joseph H. Bailey. National Geographic Soc., 1979. Subj: Animals. Birds. Frogs and toads. Reptiles.

Corwin, Judith Hoffman. *Halloween fun* ill. by author. Messner, 1983. Subj: Holidays – Halloween.

Cosgrove, Margaret. *Wintertime for animals* ill. by author. Dodd, 1975. Subj: Animals. Science. Seasons – winter.

Cosgrove, Stephen. *Sleepy time bunny* by Stephen Cosgrove and Charles Reasoner. Price, Stern, Sloan, 1984. Subj: Animals – rabbits. Bedtime. Format, unusual – cardboard pages. Night.

Costa, Nicoletta. *The birthday party* ill. by author. Grosset, 1984. Subj: Animals – cats. Birthdays. Format, unusual – cardboard pages.

Dressing up ill. by author. Grosset, 1984. Subj: Animals – cats. Format, unusual – cardboard pages.

A friend comes to play ill. by author. Grosset, 1984. Subj: Animals – cats. Format, unusual – cardboard pages. Friendship.

The missing cat ill. by author. Grosset, 1984. Subj: Animals – cats. Format, unusual – cardboard pages.

Counting rhymes ill. by Corinne Malvern. Simon and Schuster, 1946. Subj: Counting. Poetry, rhyme.

Coutant, Helen. *First snow* ill. by Vo-Dinh Mai. Knopf, 1974. Subj: Death. Family life – grandparents, great-grandparents. Seasons – winter.

Coville, Bruce. *The foolish giant* by Bruce and Katherine Coville; ill. by Katherine Coville. Lippincott, 1978. Subj: Character traits – bravery. Character traits – kindness. Friendship. Giants. Magic.

Sarah and the dragon ill. by Beth Peck. Lippincott, 1984. Subj: Character traits – kindness. Dragons. Folk and fairy tales. Magic. Mythical creatures. Witches.

Sarah's unicorn by Bruce and Katherine Coville; ill. by authors. Lippincott, 1979. Subj: Animals. Character traits – meanness. Mythical creatures. Witches.

Coville, Katherine. *The foolish giant* (Coville, Bruce)

Sarah's unicorn (Coville, Bruce)

Cowles, Kathleen. *Feelings* (Allington, Richard L)

Hearing (Allington, Richard L)

Looking (Allington, Richard L)

Smelling (Allington, Richard L)

Tasting (Allington, Richard L)

Touching (Allington, Richard L)

Cox, David. *Ayu and the perfect moon* ill. by author. Subj: Activities – dancing. Foreign lands – Bali.

Cox, Palmer. *Another Brownie book* ill. by author. McGraw-Hill, 1967. Re-publication of the orig. 1890 ed. Subj: Elves and little people.

The Brownies: their book ill. by author. McGraw-Hill, 1967. Re-publication of the orig. 1887 ed. Subj: Elves and little people.

Cox, Victoria. *Going my way?* (Applebaum, Stan)

Crabtree, Judith. *The sparrow's story at the king's command* ill. by author. Oxford Univ. Pr., 1983. Subj: Birds – sparrows. Royalty.

Craft, Ruth. *Carrie Hepple's garden* ill. by Irene Haas. Atheneum, 1979. Subj: Activities – gardening. Animals – cats. Character traits – bravery.

The winter bear ill. by Erik Blegvad. Atheneum, 1974. Subj: Poetry, rhyme. Seasons – winter. Toys – teddy bears.

Craig, Helen. *Susie and Alfred in the knight, the princess and the dragon* ill. by author. Knopf, 1985. Subj: Animals – pigs. Art. Imagination.

Craig, Janet. *Turtles* ill. by Kathie Kelleher. Troll Assoc., 1982. Subj: Reptiles – turtles. Science.

What's under the ocean? ill. by Paul Harvey. Troll Assoc., 1982. Subj: Sea and seashore.

Craig, M. Jean. *Babar comes to America* (Brunhoff, Laurent de)

Boxes ill. by Joe Lasker. Norton, 1964. Subj: Concepts – shape. Concepts – size. Games. Participation. Toys.

Dinosaurs and more dinosaurs ill. by George Solonevich. Four Winds Pr., 1968. Subj: Dinosaurs. Science.

The donkey prince (Grimm, Jacob)

The dragon in the clock box ill. by Kelly Oechsli. Norton, 1962. Subj: Dragons. Family life. Imagination.

The man whose name was not Thomas ill. by Diane Stanley. Doubleday, 1981. Subj: Careers – bakers. Humor.

Spring is like the morning ill. by Don Almquist. Putnam's, 1965. Subj: Animals. Morning. Plants. Seasons – spring.

What did you dream? ill. by Margery Gill. Abelard-Schuman, 1964. Subj: Dreams. Morning.

Crane, Alan. *Pepita bonita* ill. by author. Nelson, 1942. Subj: Birds – pelicans. Foreign lands – Mexico. Sea and seashore.

Crane, Donn. *Flippy and Skippy* ill. by author. Winston, 1940. Subj: Animals – squirrels. Pets.

Crawford, Elizabeth D. *Baby animals on the farm* (Isenbart, Hans-Heinrich)

Blackie and Marie (Koci, Marta)

Hansel and Gretel (Grimm, Jacob)

The hare's race (Baumann, Hans)

Little Harry (Bröger, Achim)

Little red cap (Grimm, Jacob)

The seven ravens (Grimm, Jacob)

Crawford, Phyllis. *The blot: little city cat* ill. by Holling C. Holling. Cape, 1930. Subj: Animals – cats.

Crayder, Teresa *see* Colman, Hila

Credle, Ellis. *Big fraid, little fraid: a folktale* ill. by author. Macmillan, 1964. Subj: Emotions – fear. Folk and fairy tales. Night.

Down, down the mountain ill. by author. Nelson, 1934, 1961. Subj: Clothing. Family life. Plants.

Creekmore, Raymond. *Fujio* ill. by author. Macmillan, 1951. Subj: Foreign lands – Japan. Sports.

Cremins, Robert. *My animal ABC* ill. by author. Crown, 1983. Subj: ABC books. Animals. Format, unusual.

My animal Mother Goose ill. by author. Crown, 1983. Subj: Animals. Format, unusual. Nursery rhymes.

Cressey, James. *The dragon and George* ill. by Tamasin Cole. Prentice-Hall, 1979. Subj: Dragons. Foreign lands – England. Knights. Middle ages.

Fourteen rats and a rat-catcher ill. by Tamasin Cole. Prentice-Hall, 1978. Subj: Animals – rats. Family life. Problem solving.

Max the mouse ill. by Tamasin Cole. Prentice-Hall, 1979. Subj: Animals – mice. Crime.

Pet parrot ill. by Tamasin Cole. Prentice-Hall, 1979. Subj: Birds – parakeets, parrots. Crime.

Cresswell, Helen. *Two hoots and the king* ill. by Martine Blanc. Crown, 1978. Subj: Birds – owls. Behavior – mistakes.

Two hoots in the snow ill. by Martine Blanc. Crown, 1978. Subj: Birds – owls. Behavior – mistakes.

Cretan, Gladys Yessayan. *Lobo and Brewster* ill. by Patricia Coombs. Lothrop, 1971. Subj: Animals – cats. Animals – dogs. Emotions – envy, jealousy.

Ten brothers with camels ill. by Piero Ventura. Golden Pr., 1975. Subj: Counting. Desert.

Cretien, Paul D. *Sir Henry and the dragon* ill. by author. Follett, 1958. Subj: Animals – horses. Dragons. Knights. Royalty. Witches.

Crews, Donald. *Carousel* ill. by author. Greenwillow, 1982. Subj: Merry-go-rounds.

Freight train ill. by author. Greenwillow, 1978. Subj: Caldecott award honor book. Trains.

Harbor ill. by author. Greenwillow, 1982. Subj: Boats, ships.

Light ill. by author. Greenwillow, 1981. Subj: Concepts. Lights.

Parade ill. by author. Greenwillow, 1983. Subj: City. Parades.

School bus ill. by author. Greenwillow, 1984. Subj: Buses. School. Transportation.

Ten black dots ill. by author. Scribner's, 1968. Subj: Concepts – shape. Counting.

Truck ill. by author. Greenwillow, 1980. Subj: Caldecott award honor book. Transportation. Trucks. Wordless.

We read: A to Z ill. by author. Harper, 1967. Subj: ABC books. Concepts.

Crichton, Michael *see* Douglas, Michael

Cristini, Ermanno. *In my garden* by Ermanno Cristini and Luigi Puricelli; ill. by authors. Alphabet Pr., 1981. Orig title: Falter, Blumen, Tierre und Ich. Subj: Wordless.

In the pond by Ermanno Cristini and Luigi Puricelli; ill. by authors. Alphabet Pr., 1984. Subj: Animals. Insects. Plants. Reptiles.

In the woods by Ermanno Cristini and Luigi Puricelli; ill. by authors. Alphabet Pr., 1983. Subj: Animals. Birds. Forest, woods. Wordless.

Croll, Carolyn. *Too many babas* ill. by author. Harper, 1979. Subj: Behavior – sharing. Food.

Cromie, William J. *Steven and the green turtle* ill. by Tom Eaton. Harper, 1970. Subj: Animals – endangered animals. Reptiles – turtles. Science.

Crompton, Anne Eliot. *The lifting stone* ill. by Marcia Sewall. Holiday, 1978. Subj: Folk and fairy tales. Character traits – cleverness.

The winter wife: an Abenaki folktale ill. by Robert Andrew Parker. Little, 1975. Subj: Character traits – loyalty. Ethnic groups in the U.S. – Indians. Folk and fairy tales.

Crompton, Margaret. *The house where Jack lives* ill. by Margery Gill. Merrimack, 1980. Subj: Family life. Foreign lands – England. Houses.

Cross, Diana Harding. *Some birds have funny names* ill. by Jan Brett. Crown, 1981. Subj: Birds. Names.

Some plants have funny names ill. by Jan Brett. Crown, 1983. Subj: Names. Plants.

Cross, Genevieve. *My bunny book* ill. by Charles Clement. Doubleday, 1952. Subj: Animals – rabbits. Holidays – Easter.

A trip to the yard ill. by Marjorie Hartwell and Rachel Dixon. Doubleday, 1952. Subj: Animals. Birds. Plants.

Crossley-Holland, Kevin. *The green children* ill. by Margaret Gordon. Seabury Pr., 1968. Subj: Character traits – being different. Folk and fairy tales. Foreign lands – England.

The pedlar of Swaffham ill. by Margaret Gordon. Seabury Pr., 1971. Subj: Careers – peddlers. Folk and fairy tales.

Croswell, Volney. *How to hide a hippopotamus* ill. by author. Dodd, 1958. Subj: Animals – hippopotami. Behavior – hiding things. Concepts – size.

Crothers, Samuel McChord. *Miss Muffet's Christmas party* ill. by Olive M. Long. Houghton, 1929. Subj: Parties. Spiders.

Crowe, Robert L. *Clyde monster* ill. by Kay Chorao. Dutton, 1976. Subj: Emotions – fear. Monsters. Night.

Tyler Toad and the thunder ill. by Kay Chorao. Dutton, 1980. Subj: Animals. Noise, sounds. Weather – storms.

Crowell, Maryalicia. *A horse in the house* ill. by Leonard P. Kessler. Addison-Wesley, 1957. Subj: City. Pets.

Crowley, Arthur. *Bonzo Beaver* ill. by Annie Gusman. Houghton, 1980. Subj: Activities – babysitting. Animals – beavers. Poetry, rhyme. Sibling rivalry.

The boogey man ill. by Annie Gusman. Houghton, 1978. Subj: Behavior – dissatisfaction. Behavior – misbehavior. Family life. Monsters.

The ugly book ill. by Annie Gusman. Houghton, 1982. Subj: Character traits – appearance.

The wagon man ill. by Annie Gusman. Houghton, 1981. Subj: Dreams. Poetry, rhyme. Riddles.

Crowther, Robert. *Hide and seek counting book* ill. by author. Viking, 1981. Subj: Counting. Format, unusual.

The most amazing hide and seek alphabet book ill. by author. Viking, 1978. Subj: ABC books. Format, unusual.

Croxford, Vera. *All kinds of animals* ill. by author. Grosset, 1972. Orig. title: All sorts of animals (Hamlyn Pub. Group, 1968). Subj: Animals

Crume, Marion W. *Let me see you try* ill. by Jacques Rupp. Bowmar, 1968. Subj: Activities. Participation.

Listen! ill. by Cliff Rowe and Judy Houston. Bowmar, 1968. Subj: Activities. Ethnic groups in the U.S. Participation.

What do you say? ill. by Harvey Mandlin. Bowmar, 1967. Subj: Activities. Participation.

Crump, Donald J. *Creatures small and furry* ill. with photos. National Geographic Soc., 1983. Subj: Animals.

Cummings, Betty Sue. *Turtle* ill. by Susan Dodge. Atheneum, 1981. Subj: Behavior – lost. Pets. Reptiles – turtles.

Cummings, E. E. *Fairy tales* ill. by John Eaton. Harcourt, 1965. Subj: Folk and fairy tales. Imagination.

Cummings, W. T. (Walter Thies). *The kid* ill. by author. McGraw-Hill, 1960. Subj: Animals – horses. Behavior – seeking better things. Emotions – loneliness. Music.

Miss Esta Maude's secret ill. by author. McGraw-Hill, 1961. Subj: Automobiles. Behavior – secrets. Careers – teachers.

Wickford of Beacon Hill ill. by author. Subj: Birds – cockatoos.

Cuneo, Mary Louise. *Inside a sandcastle and other secrets* ill. by Jan Brett. Houghton, 1979. Subj: Character traits – smallness.

Cunliffe, John. *The king's birthday cake* ill. by Faith Jaques. Elsevier-Dutton, 1979. Subj: Activities – cooking. Birthdays. Cumulative tales. Royalty.

Sara's giant and the upside down house ill. by Hilary Abrahams. Elsevier-Dutton, 1980. Subj: Giants.

Cunningham, Julia. *A mouse called Junction* ill. by Michael Hague. Pantheon, 1980. Subj: Animals – mice. Animals – rats. Emotions. Emotions – fear. Friendship.

The vision of Francois the fox ill. by Nicholas Angelo. Pantheon, 1969. Subj: Animals – foxes.

Curry, Nancy. *The littlest house* ill. by Jacques Rupp. Bowmar, 1968. Subj: Family life. Houses.

Curry, Peter. *Animals* ill. by author. Price, Stern, Sloan, 1984. Subj: Animals.

Curtis Brown, Beatrice see Brown, Beatrice Curtis

Cushman, Doug. *Giants* ill. by comp. Platt, 1980. Subj: Giants. Poetry, rhyme.

Nasty Kyle the crocodile ill. by author. Grosset, 1983. Subj: Behavior – dissatisfaction. Concepts. Reptiles – alligators, crocodiles.

Once upon a pig ill. by comp. Grosset, 1982. Subj: Animals – pigs. Poetry, rhyme.

Cushman, Jerome. *Marvella's hobby* ill. by Prue Theobalds. Abelard-Schuman, 1962. Subj: Animals – bulls, cows. Trains.

Cutler, Ebbitt. *Paulino* (Simons, Traute)

Cutler, Ivor. *The animal house* ill. by Helen Oxenbury. Morrow, 1977, 1976. Subj: Animals. Houses. Zoos.

Cutts, David. *The gingerbread boy*

Look... a butterfly ill. by Eulala Conner. Troll Assoc., 1982. Subj: Insects – butterflies, caterpillars. Science.

More about dinosaurs ill. by Gregory C. Wenzel. Troll Assoc., 1982. Subj: Dinosaurs.

Cuyler, Margery. *Sir William and the pumpkin monster* ill. by Marsha Winborn. Holt, 1984. Subj: Ghosts. Holidays – Halloween.

D'Andrea, Annette Cole *see* Steiner, Barbara

D'Aulaire, Edgar Parin *see* Aulaire, Edgar Parin d'

D'Aulaire, Ingri Mortenson *see* Aulaire, Ingri Mortenson d'

Dabcovich, Lydia. *Follow the river* ill. by author. Dutton, 1980. Subj: Rivers.

Sleepy bear ill. by author. Dutton, 1982. Subj: Animals – bears. Seasons – spring. Seasons – winter.

Dahl, Roald. *Dirty beasts* ill. by Rosemary Fawcett. Farrar, 1983. Subj: Bedtime. Dreams. Monsters. Poetry, rhyme.

The enormous crocodile ill. by Quentin Blake. Knopf, 1978. Subj: Animals. Reptiles – alligators, crocodiles.

Dale, Ruth Bluestone. *Benjamin - and Sylvester also* ill. by J. B. Handelsman. McGraw-Hill, 1960. Subj: Animals – dogs. Behavior – dissatisfaction. Country.

Dalgliesh, Alice. *The little wooden farmer* ill. by Anita Lobel. Macmillan, 1968. First pub. in 1930. Subj: Farms.

The Thanksgiving story ill. by Helen Moore Sewell. Scribner's, 1954. Subj: Caldecott award honor book. Holidays – Thanksgiving. U.S. history.

Dallinger, Jane. *Spiders* photos. by Satoshi Kuribayashi. Lerner, 1981. Subj: Science. Spiders.

Dalmais, Anne-Marie. *The butterfly book of birds* ill. by Guy Michel. Two Continents, 1977. Subj: Birds.

In my garden: learning to count ill. by Genji. Two Continents, 1977. Subj: Counting. Poetry, rhyme.

Dalton, Alene. *My new picture book of songs* scores by Reah Allen; ill. by Gini Bunnell. Osmond Pub., 1979. Subj: Music. Songs.

Daly, Kathleen N. *A child's book of snakes, lizards and other reptiles* ill. by Lilian Obligado. Doubleday, 1980. Subj: Reptiles. Science.

Dinosaurs ill. by Tim and Greg Hildebrandt. Golden Pr., 1977. Subj: Dinosaurs.

The Giant little Golden Book of dogs ill. by Tibor Gergely. Simon and Schuster, 1957. Subj: Animals – dogs.

The Macmillan picture wordbook ill. by John Wallner. Macmillan, 1982. Subj: Dictionaries.

The three bears

Today's biggest animals ill. by Tim and Greg Hildebrandt. Golden Pr., 1977. Subj: Animals. Science.

Unusual animals ill. by Tim and Greg Hildebrandt. Golden Pr., 1977. Subj: Animals. Science.

Daly, Maureen. *Patrick visits the library* ill. by Paul Lantz. Dodd, 1961. Subj: Animals – dogs. Birthdays. Libraries.

Daly, Niki. *Joseph's other red sock* ill. by author. Atheneum, 1982. Subj: Clothing.

Vim, the rag mouse ill. by author. Atheneum, 1979. Subj: Crime. Toys.

Dame Wiggins of Lee and her seven wonderful cats ed. by John Ruskin; ill. by Robert Broomfield. McGraw-Hill, 1963. Ascribed to Richard Scrafton Sharpe and Mrs. Pearson. Endpapers: reproduction of Kate Greenaway drawings. Subj: Nursery rhymes.

Damjan, Mischa. *Atuk* ill. by Gian Casty. Pantheon, 1966. Subj: Animals – dogs. Animals – wolves. Ethnic groups in the U.S. – Eskimos.

Goodbye little bird tr. from German by Anthea Bell; ill. by Dorothée Duntze. Faber, 1983. Subj: Birds. Friendship.

The little prince and the tiger cat ill. by Ralph Steadman. McGraw-Hill, 1967. Subj: Animals – cats. Foreign lands – Japan. Royalty.

The little sea horse ill. by Riccardo Bellettati. Faber, 1983. Subj: Fish. Sea and seashore.

The wolf and the kid ill. by Max Velthuijs. McGraw-Hill, 1967. Subj: Animals – goats. Animals – wolves. Character traits – cleverness.

Daniel, Anne *see* Steiner, Barbara

Daniel, Doris Temple. *Pauline and the peacock* ill. by Barbara Brown Schoenewolf. E. C. Temple, 1980. Subj: Birds – peacocks, peahens. Family life. Farms. Science.

Daniels, Guy. *The Tsar's riddles: or, the wise little girl* ill. by Paul Galdone. McGraw-Hill, 1967. Subj: Character traits – cleverness. Folk and fairy tales. Foreign lands – Russia. Riddles.

Darby, Gene. *What is a bird?* ill. by Lucy and John Hawkinson. Benefic Pr., 1959. Subj: Birds. Science.

What is a butterfly? ill. by Lucy and John Hawkinson. Benefic Pr., 1958. Subj: Insects — butterflies, caterpillars. Science.

What is a fish? ill. by Lucy and John Hawkinson. Benefic Pr., 1958. Subj: Fish. Science.

What is a plant? ill. by Lucy and John Hawkinson. Benefic Pr., 1959. Subj: Plants. Science.

What is a turtle? ill. by Lucy and John Hawkinson. Benefic Pr., 1959. Subj: Reptiles — turtles. Science.

Da Rif, Andrea. *The blueberry cake that little fox baked* ill. by author. Atheneum, 1984. Subj: Activities — cooking. Birthdays.

Darling, Kathy. *The Easter bunny's secret* ill. by Kelly Oechsli. Garrard, 1978. Subj: Animals — rabbits. Holidays — Easter.

The mystery in Santa's toyshop ill. by Lori Pierson. Garrard, 1978. Subj: Holidays — Christmas. Problem solving.

Darling, Mary Kathleen *see* Darling, Kathy

Dasent, George W.. *The cat on the Dovrefell* (De Paola, Tomie)

Daudet, Alphonse. *The brave little goat of Monsieur Séguin: a picture story from Provence* ill. by Chiyoko Nakatani. Collins-World, 1968. Translation and adaptation of La chèvre de M. Séguin. Subj: Animals — goats. Animals — wolves. Foreign lands — France.

Dauer, Rosamond. *Bullfrog builds a house* ill. by Byron Barton. Greenwillow, 1977. Subj: Friendship. Frogs and toads. Houses.

Bullfrog grows up ill. by Byron Barton. Greenwillow, 1976. Subj: Animals — mice. Behavior — growing up. Frogs and toads.

My friend, Jasper Jones ill. by Jerry Joyner. Parents, 1977. Subj: Behavior — misbehavior. Imagination — imaginary friends.

The 300 pound cat ill. by Skip Morrow. Holt, 1981. Subj: Animals — cats. Behavior — greed.

Daugherty, Charles Michael. *Wisher* ill. by James Henry Daugherty. Viking, 1960. Subj: Animals — cats. Behavior — wishing. Dreams.

Daugherty, James Henry. *Andy and the lion* ill. by author. Viking, 1938. Subj: Animals — lions. Caldecott award honor book. Character traits — kindness to animals. Humor. Libraries.

The picnic: a frolic in two colors and three parts ill. by author. Viking, 1958. Subj: Activities — picnicking. Animals — lions. Animals — mice.

Daugherty, Sonia. *Vanka's donkey* ill. by James Henry Daugherty. Stokes, 1940. Subj: Animals — donkeys. Folk and fairy tales. Foreign lands — Russia.

Daughtry, Duanne. *What's inside?* photos. by author. Knopf, 1984. Subj: Concepts — in and out. Wordless.

Dauphin, Francine Legrand. *A French A. B. C.* ill. by author. Coward, 1947. Subj: ABC books. Foreign lands — France. Foreign languages.

David, Eugene. *Crystal magic* ill. by Abner Graboff. Prentice-Hall, 1965. Subj: Science.

Davidson, Amanda. *Teddy at the seashore* ill. by author. Holt, 1984. Originally published under title: Teddy at the seaside. Subj: Foreign lands — England. Sea and seashore. Toys — teddy bears.

Teddy's first Christmas ill. by author. Holt, 1982. Subj: Holidays — Christmas. Toys — teddy bears.

Davies, Sumiko *see* Sumiko

Davis, Alice Vaught. *Timothy turtle* ill. by Guy Brown Wiser. Harcourt, 1940. Subj: Character traits — helpfulness. Reptiles — turtles.

Davis, Douglas F. *The lion's tail* ill. by Ronald Himler. Atheneum, 1980. Subj: Animals — lions. Folk and fairy tales. Foreign lands — Africa.

There's an elephant in the garage ill. by Steven Kellogg. Dutton, 1979. Subj: Animals. Animals — cats. Imagination. Toys — teddy bears.

Davis, Gibbs. *The other Emily* ill. by Linda Shute. Houghton, 1984. Subj: Behavior — sharing. Names.

Davis, Lavinia. *Roger and the fox* ill. by Hildegard Woodward. Doubleday, 1947. Subj: Animals — foxes. Caldecott award honor book.

The wild birthday cake ill. by Hildegard Woodward. Doubleday, 1949. Subj: Birthdays. Caldecott award honor book.

Davis, Maggie S. *The best way to Ripton* ill. by Stephen Gammell. Holiday, 1982. Subj: Activities — traveling. Humor.

Grandma's secret letter ill. by John Wallner. Holiday, 1982. Subj: Behavior — secrets. Character traits — kindness. Elves and little people.

Rickety witch ill. by Kay Chorao. Holiday, 1984. Subj: Holidays — Halloween. Witches.

Davis, Reda. *Martin's dinosaur* ill. by Louis Slobodkin. Crowell, 1959. Subj: Dragons. Foreign lands — England.

Dawson, Linda. *Phoebe and the hot water bottles* (Furchgott, Terry)

Day, Michael E. *Berry Ripe Moon* ill. by Carol Whitmore. Tide Grass Pr., 1977. Subj: Ethnic groups in the U.S. — Indians.

Day, Shirley. *Ruthie's big tree* ill. by author. Firefly Pr., 1982. Subj: Character traits — perseverance. Trees.

Waldo's back yard ill. by author. Firefly Pr., 1984. Subj: Behavior — dissatisfaction. Character traits — helpfulness.

Dayrell, Elphinstone. *Why the sun and the moon live in the sky: an African folktale* ill. by Blair Lent. Houghton, 1968. First published in 1914 in the author's Folk stories from southern Nigeria, West Africa. Subj: Caldecott award honor book. Folk and fairy tales. Foreign lands — Africa. Moon. Sky. Sun.

Dayton, Laura. *LeRoy's birthday circus* ill. by Susan Huggins. Nelson, 1981. Subj: Birthdays. Circus. Counting. Poetry, rhyme.

Dayton, Mona. *Earth and sky* ill. by Roger Antoine Duvoisin. Harper, 1969. Subj: Behavior — fighting, arguing. Earth. Sky.

Dean, Leigh. *Two special cards* (Lisker, Sonia O)

De Angeli, Marguerite. *The book of nursery and Mother Goose rhymes* ill. by compiler. Doubleday, 1954. Subj: Caldecott award honor book. Nursery rhymes.

Yonie Wondernose: for three little Wondernoses, Nina, David and Kiki ill. by author. Doubleday, 1944. Subj: Caldecott award honor book. Family life. Farms.

De Brunhoff, Jean see Brunhoff, Jean de

De Brunhoff, Laurent see Brunhoff, Laurent de

De Bruyn, Monica. *Lauren's secret ring* ill. by author. Albert Whitman, 1980. Subj: Friendship.

DeCaprio, Annie. *One, two* ill. by Seymour Nydorf. Grosset, 1965. Designed by David Krieger. Subj: Counting.

DeForest, Charlotte B. *The prancing pony: nursery rhymes from Japan* adapted into English verse for children, with "Kusa-e"; ill. by Keiko Hida. Walker, 1968. Subj: Foreign lands — Japan. Nursery rhymes.

Degen, Bruce. *Aunt Possum and the pumpkin man* ill. by author. Harper, 1977. Subj: Animals — cats. Animals — possums. Holidays — Halloween. Wordless.

Jamberry ill. by author. Harper, 1983. Subj: Animals — bears. Food. Poetry, rhyme.

The little witch and the riddle ill. by author. Harper, 1980. Subj: Friendship. Magic. Riddles. Witches.

De Gerez, Toni. *My song is a piece of jade: poems of ancient Mexico in English and Spanish* ill. by William Stark. Little, 1984. Subj: Foreign lands — Mexico. Foreign languages. Poetry, rhyme.

De Groat, Diane. *Alligator's toothache* ill. by author. Crown, 1977. Subj: Illness. Reptiles — alligators, crocodiles. Teeth. Wordless.

DeJong, David Cornel. *Looking for Alexander* ill. by Harvey Weiss. Little, 1963. Subj: Animals — cats. Family life — grandparents, great-grandparents.

DeJong, Meindert. *Nobody plays with a cabbage* ill. by Thomas B. Allen. Harper, 1962. Subj: Activities — gardening. Emotions.

De Kay, Ormonde. *Rimes de la Mere Oie* (Mother Goose)

De La Fontaine, Jean see La Fontaine, Jean de

DeLage, Ida. *ABC Easter bunny* ill. by Ellen Sloan. Garrard, 1979. Subj: ABC books. Animals — rabbits. Holidays — Easter.

ABC triplets at the zoo ill. by Lori Pierson. Garrard, 1980. Subj: ABC books. Animals. Zoos.

Am I a bunny? ill. by Ellen Sloan. Garrard, 1978. Subj: Animals — rabbits. Self-concept.

The old witch and her magic basket ill. by Ellen Sloan. Garrard, 1978. Subj: Holidays — Halloween. Witches.

The old witch and the crows ill. by Marianne Smith. Garrard, 1983. Subj: Birds — crows. Birds — owls. Night. Witches.

The old witch and the dragon ill. by Unada. Garrard, 1979. Subj: Dragons. Witches.

The old witch and the ghost parade ill. by Jody Taylor. Garrard, 1978. Subj: Ghosts. Witches.

The old witch finds a new house ill. by Pat Paris. Garrard, 1979. Subj: Moving. Witches.

Pilgrim children on the Mayflower ill. by Bert Dodson. Garrard, 1980. Subj: Boats, ships. U.S. history.

The squirrel's tree party ill. by Tracy McVay. Garrard, 1978. Subj: Animals — squirrels. Parties. Trees.

De La Mare, Walter. *Molly Whuppie* ill. by Errol Le Cain. Farrar, 1983. Subj: Character traits — bravery. Character traits — cleverness. Giants. Royalty.

Delaney, A. *The butterfly* ill. by author. Crown, 1977. Subj: Cumulative tales. Insects — butterflies, caterpillars.

Monster tracks? ill. by author. Harper, 1981. Subj: Imagination. Weather — snow.

Delaney, M. C. *The marigold monster* ill. by Ned Delaney. Dutton, 1983. Subj: Humor. Monsters. Riddles.

Delaney, Ned. *Bert and Barney* ill. by author. Houghton, 1979. Subj: Friendship.

One dragon to another ill. by author. Houghton, 1976. Subj: Character traits — individuality. Dragons. Games. Insects — butterflies, caterpillars.

Rufus the doofus ill. by author. Houghton, 1978. Subj: Behavior — misbehavior. School.

Terrible things could happen ill. by author. Lothrop, 1983. Subj: Activities — working. Humor.

Delaunay, Sonia. *Sonia Delaunay's alphabet* ill. by author. Crowell, 1972. Subj: ABC books. Poetry, rhyme.

Delessert, Etienne. *The endless party* tr. by Jeffrey Tabberner; ill. by author. Oxford Univ. Pr., 1981. Subj: Religion — Noah.

How the mouse was hit on the head by a stone and so discovered the world text and ill. by Etienne Delessert in collaboration with Odie Mosimann; foreword by Jean Piaget; tr. by C. Ross Smith. Doubleday, 1971. Subj: Animals — mice. World.

Dellinger, Annetta. *You are special to Jesus* ill. by Jan Brett. Concordia, 1984. Subj: Character traits — appearance. Character traits — individuality. Religion.

Delton, Judy. *Bear and Duck on the run* ill. by Lynn Munsinger. Albert Whitman, 1984. Subj: Animals — bears. Birds — ducks.

The best mom in the world ill. by John Faulkner. Albert Whitman, 1979. Subj: Behavior — growing up. Family life — mothers.

Brimhall comes to stay ill. by Cyndy Szekeres. Lothrop, 1978. Subj: Animals — bears. Family life.

Brimhall turns detective ill. by Cherie R. Wyman. Carolrhoda, 1983. Subj: Animals — bears. Animals — rabbits. Weather — snow.

Brimhall turns to magic ill. by Bruce Degen. Lothrop, 1979. Subj: Animals — bears. Animals — rabbits. Magic.

Duck goes fishing ill. by Lynn Munsinger. Albert Whitman, 1983. Subj: Animals — foxes. Birds — ducks. Birds — owls. Friendship. Sports — fishing.

Groundhog's Day at the doctor ill. by Giulio Maestro. Parents, 1981. Subj: Animals — groundhogs. Holidays — Groundhog Day. Illness.

I never win! ill. by Cathy Gilchrist. Carolrhoda, 1981. Subj: Character traits — luck. Games.

I'm telling you now ill. by Lillian Hoban. Dutton, 1983. Subj: Activities. Behavior. Character traits — individuality.

It happened on Thursday ill. by June Goldsborough. Albert Whitman, 1978. Subj: Character traits — luck. Family life. Illness.

My mom hates me in January ill. by John Faulkner. Albert Whitman, 1977. Subj: Behavior — boredom. Seasons — winter.

My mother lost her job today ill. by Irene Trivas. Albert Whitman, 1980. Subj: Activities — working. Character traits — optimism. Family life — mothers.

My Uncle Nikos ill. by Marc Simont. Crowell, 1983. Subj: Family life. Foreign lands — Greece.

The new girl at school ill. by Lillian Hoban. Dutton, 1979. Subj: School.

Penny wise, fun foolish ill. by Giulio Maestro. Crown, 1977. Subj: Animals — elephants. Behavior — saving things. Birds — ostriches. Fairs.

A pet for Duck and Bear ill. by Lynn Munsinger. Albert Whitman, 1982. Subj: Animals — bears. Birds — ducks. Friendship. Pets.

Three friends find spring ill. by Giulio Maestro. Crown, 1977. Subj: Animals — rabbits. Birds — ducks. Friendship. Seasons — spring. Seasons — winter.

A walk on a snowy night ill. by Ruth Rosner. Harper, 1982. Subj: Night. Weather — snow. Weather — storms.

Del Vecchio, Ellen. *Big city port* (Maestro, Betsy)

Demarest, Chris L. *Benedict finds a home* ill. by author. Lothrop, 1982. Subj: Behavior — seeking better things. Birds.

Clemens' kingdom ill. by author. Lothrop, 1983. Subj: Animals — lions. Character traits — curiosity. Libraries.

Demi. *The adventures of Marco Polo* ill. by author. Holt, 1982. Subj: Activities — traveling. Foreign lands — China.

Under the shade of the mulberry tree ill. by author. Prentice-Hall, 1979. Subj: Character traits — cleverness. Folk and fairy tales. Foreign lands — China.

Where is it? ill. by author. Doubleday, 1979. Subj: Riddles.

Denison, Carol. *A part-time dog for Nick* ill. by Jane Miller. Dodd, 1959. Subj: Animals — dogs. Family life.

Dennis, Morgan. *Burlap* ill. by author. Viking, 1945. Subj: Animals — bears. Animals — dogs.

The pup himself ill. by author. Viking, 1943. Subj: Animals — dogs.

The sea dog ill. by author. Viking, 1958. Subj: Animals — dogs. Boats, ships. Weather — storms.

Skit and Skat ill. by author. Viking, 1952. Subj: Animals — cats. Animals — dogs.

Dennis, Suzanne E. *Answer me that* ill. by Owen Wood. Bobbs-Merrill, 1969. Subj: Animals. Humor. Poetry, rhyme.

Dennis, Wesley. *Flip* ill. by author. Viking, 1941. Subj: Animals. Dreams. Farms.

Flip and the cows ill. by author. Viking, 1942. Subj: Animals — bulls, cows. Animals — horses. Farms.

Flip and the morning ill. by author. Viking, 1951. Subj: Animals — horses. Morning.

Tumble, the story of a mustang ill. by author. Hastings, 1966. Subj: Animals – horses. Character traits – freedom.

Denver, John. *The children and the flowers* ill. by Randi Gullerud. Green Tiger Pr., 1979. Subj: Flowers. Songs.

De Paola, Thomas Anthony *see* De Paola, Tomie

De Paola, Tomie. *Andy (that's my name)* ill. by author. Prentice-Hall, 1973. Subj: Behavior – greed. Character traits – smallness. Friendship. Games. Names.

Big Anthony and the magic ring ill. by author. Harcourt, 1979. Subj: Character traits – appearance. Magic.

Bill and Pete ill. by author. Putnam's, 1978. Subj: Foreign lands – Africa. Humor. Reptiles – alligators, crocodiles. School.

The cat on the Dovrefell: a Christmas tale tr. by George W. Dasent; ill. by author. Putnam's, 1979. Subj: Holidays – Christmas. Trolls.

Charlie needs a cloak ill. by author. Prentice-Hall, 1973. Subj: Animals – mice. Animals – sheep. Clothing. Problem solving.

The Christmas pageant ill. by author. Winston Pr., 1978. Subj: Holidays – Christmas. Theater.

The cloud book ill. by author. Holiday, 1975. Subj: Weather – clouds.

The clown of God: an old story ill. by author. Harcourt, 1978. Subj: Foreign lands – Italy. Holidays – Christmas. Religion.

Country farm ill. by author. Putnam's, 1984. Subj: Animals. Farms. Format, unusual. Wordless.

Criss-cross applesauce photos. by B. A. King; ill. by the B. A. King children. Addison-Wesley, 1979. Subj: Children as illustrators.

The family Christmas tree book ill. by author. Holiday, 1980. Subj: Family life. Holidays – Christmas. Trees.

Fight the night ill. by author. Lippincott, 1968. Subj: Bedtime. Sleep.

Fin M'Coul: the giant of Knockmany Hill ill. by author. Holiday, 1981. Subj: Folk and fairy tales. Foreign lands – Ireland. Giants.

Flicks ill. by author. Harcourt, 1979. Subj: Humor. Wordless.

Four stories for four seasons ill. by author. Prentice-Hall, 1977. Subj: Activities – gardening. Boats, ships. Hibernation. Seasons.

Helga's dowry ill. by author. Harcourt, 1977. Subj: Emotions – love. Poverty. Trolls. Weddings.

The hunter and the animals ill. by author. Holiday, 1981. Subj: Animals. Sports – hunting. Wordless.

The knight and the dragon ill. by author. Putnam's, 1980. Subj: Dragons. Knights. Libraries.

The Lady of Guadalupe ill. by author. Holiday, 1980. Subj: Foreign lands – Mexico. Religion.

The legend of Old Befana ill. by author. Harcourt, 1980. Subj: Folk and fairy tales. Foreign lands – Italy. Religion.

The legend of the bluebonnet ill. by author. Putnam's, 1983. Subj: Ethnic groups in the U.S. – Indians. Flowers. Folk and fairy tales.

Marianna May and Nursey ill. by author. Holiday, 1983. Subj: Character traits – cleanliness.

Michael Bird-Boy ill. by author. Prentice-Hall, 1975. Subj: Ecology.

The mysterious giant of Barletta: an Italian folktale ill. by author. Harcourt, 1984. Subj: Folk and fairy tales. Foreign lands – Italy. Giants. War.

Nana upstairs and Nana downstairs ill. by author. Putnam's, 1973. Subj: Death. Emotions – sadness. Family life – grandparents, great-grandparents.

Noah and the ark ill. by author. Winston, 1983. Subj: Religion – Noah.

Now one foot, now the other ill. by author. Putnam's 1981. Subj: Family life – grandparents, great-grandparents. Illness.

Oliver Button is a sissy ill. by author. Harcourt, 1979. Subj: Activities – dancing. Character traits – individuality.

Pancakes for breakfast ill. by author. Harcourt, 1978. Subj: Activities – cooking. Food. Wordless.

The popcorn book ill. by author. Holiday, 1978. Subj: Activities – cooking. Food.

The Prince of the Dolomites ill. by author. Harcourt, 1980. Subj: Elves and little people. Folk and fairy tales. Foreign lands – Italy. Moon.

The quicksand book ill. by author. Holiday, 1977. Subj: Behavior – carelessness.

Sing, Pierrot, sing: a picture book in mime ill. by author. Harcourt, 1983. Subj: Clowns, jesters. Theater. Wordless.

Songs of the fog maiden ill. by author. Holiday, 1979. Subj: Poetry, rhyme.

The story of the three wise kings ill. by author. Putnam's, 1983. Subj: Holidays – Christmas. Religion.

Strega Nona: an old tale ill. by author. Prentice-Hall, 1975. Subj: Behavior – forgetfulness. Caldecott award honor book. Humor. Magic. Witches.

Strega Nona's magic lessons ill. by author. Harcourt, 1982. Subj: Behavior – carelessness. Humor. Magic. Witches.

Things to make and do for Valentine's Day ill. by author. Watts, 1976. Subj: Activities – cooking. Games. Holidays – Valentine's Day.

When everyone was fast asleep ill. by author. Holiday, 1976. Subj: Sleep.

The wonderful dragon of Timlin ill. by author. Bobbs-Merrill, 1966. Subj: Dragons. Knights. Royalty.

De Regniers, Beatrice Schenk. *A bunch of poems and verses* ill. by Mary Jane Dunton. Seabury Pr., 1977. Subj: Poetry, rhyme.

Catch a little fox: variations on a folk rhyme ill. by Brinton Turkle. Seabury Pr., 1979. Subj: Character traits – cleverness. Nursery rhymes. Sports – hunting.

Cats cats cats ill. by Bill Sokol. Pantheon, 1958. Subj: Animals – cats. Poetry, rhyme.

Circus photos. by Al Giese. Viking, 1966. Subj: Circus.

David and Goliath ill. by Richard M. Powers. Viking, 1965. Subj: Religion.

Everyone is good for something ill. by Margot Tomes. Houghton, 1980. Subj: Animals – cats. Folk and fairy tales. Foreign lands Russia. Self-concept.

The giant story ill. by Maurice Sendak. Harper, 1953. Subj: Family life. Giants.

Going for a walk ill. by author. Harper, 1982. Orig. title: The little book. Subj: Activities – walking.

It does not say meow! ill. by Paul Galdone. Seabury Pr., 1972. Subj: Animals. Participation. Poetry, rhyme. Riddles.

Laura's story ill. by Jack Kent. Atheneum, 1979. Subj: Imagination.

A little house of your own ill. by Irene Haas. Harcourt, 1954. Subj: Family life. Houses. Imagination.

Little Sister and the Month Brothers ill. by Margot Tomes. Seabury Pr., 1976. Subj: Days of the week, months of the year. Folk and fairy tales. Foreign lands.

May I bring a friend? ill. by Beni Montresor. Atheneum, 1964. Subj: Animals. Caldecott award book. Friendship. Humor. Poetry, rhyme. Royalty.

Penny by Beatrice Schenk de Regniers and Marvin Bileck; ill. by Marvin Bileck. Viking, 1966. Subj: Elves and little people.

Picture book theater: the mysterious stranger and the magic spell ill. by William Lahey Cummings. Seabury Pr., 1982. Subj: Animals – cats. Animals – mice. Theater. Wizards.

Red Riding Hood ill. by Edward Gorey. Atheneum, 1972. Retold in verse for boys and girls to read themselves. Subj: Animals – wolves. Behavior – talking to strangers. Folk and fairy tales. Poetry, rhyme.

The shadow book ill. by Isabel Gordon. Harcourt, 1960. Subj: Shadows.

Something special ill. by Irene Haas. Harcourt, 1958. Subj: Poetry, rhyme.

Waiting for mama ill. by Victoria de Larrea. Clarion, 1984. Subj: Imagination.

Was it a good trade? ill. by Irene Haas. Harcourt, 1956. Subj: Activities – trading. Poetry, rhyme. Songs.

What can you do with a shoe? ill. by Maurice Sendak. Harper, 1955. Subj: Games. Imagination.

Who likes the sun? ill. by Leona Pierce. Harcourt, 1961. Subj: Sun.

Willy O'Dwyer jumped in the fire variations on a folk rhyme ill. by Beni Montresor. Atheneum, 1968. Subj: Fire. Moon. Nursery rhymes. Witches.

Deutsch, Babette. *There comes a time* (Borchers, Elisabeth)

Deveaux, Alexis. *Na-ni* ill. by author. Harper, 1973. Subj: Character traits – questioning. City. Emotions – sadness. Poverty.

Devlin, Harry. *Aunt Agatha, there's a lion under the couch!* (Devlin, Wende)

Cranberry Christmas (Devlin, Wende)

Cranberry Thanksgiving (Devlin, Wende)

Old Black Witch (Devlin, Wende)

Old Witch and the polka-dot ribbon (Devlin, Wende)

Old Witch rescues Halloween (Devlin, Wende)

The walloping window blind: an old nautical tale ill. by author. Van Nostrand, 1968. Adapted from an old sea tune. Subj: Boats, ships. Pirates. Songs.

Devlin, Wende. *Aunt Agatha, there's a lion under the couch!* by Wende and Harry Devlin; ill. by authors. Van Nostrand, 1968. Subj: Animals – lions. Emotions – fear. Imagination.

Cranberry Christmas by Wende and Harry Devlin; ill. by authors. Parents, 1976. Subj: Behavior – sharing. Character traits – helpfulness. Holidays – Christmas.

Cranberry Halloween ill. by Harry Devlin. Four Winds Pr., 1982. Subj: Behavior – stealing. Holidays – Halloween.

Cranberry Thanksgiving by Wende and Harry Devlin; ill. by Harry Devlin. Parents, 1971. Subj: Holidays – Thanksgiving.

Old Black Witch by Wende and Harry Devlin; ill. by Harry Devlin. Encyclopaedia Brit., 1963. Subj: Activities – cooking. Witches.

Old Witch and the polka-dot ribbon by Wende and Harry Devlin; ill. by Harry Devlin. Parents, 1970. Subj: Activities – cooking. Fairs. Food. Witches.

Old Witch rescues Halloween by Wende and Harry Devlin; ill. by Harry Devlin. Parents, 1972. Subj: Activities – cooking. Holidays – Halloween. Witches.

Dewey, Ariane. *A crocodile's tale* (Aruego, José)

Dorin and the dragon ill. by author. Greenwillow, 1982. Subj: Dragons. Dreams. Magic. Royalty.

Febold Feboldson ill. by author. Greenwillow, 1984. Subj: Farms. Folk and fairy tales. Weather.

The fish Peri ill. by author. Macmillan, 1979. Subj: Folk and fairy tales. Foreign lands – Turkey. Magic. Problem solving.

Pecos Bill ill. by author. Greenwillow, 1983. Subj: Cowboys. Folk and fairy tales.

The thunder god's son: a Peruvian folktale ill. by author. Greenwillow, 1981. Subj: Folk and fairy tales. Foreign lands – Peru. Magic.

We hide, you seek (Aruego, José)

Diamond, Donna. *The Bremen town musicians* (Grimm, Jacob)

Rumpelstiltskin (Grimm, Jacob)

Dick Whittington and his cat retold and ill. by Marcia Brown. Scribner's, 1950. Subj: Activities – trading. Animals – cats. Caldecott award honor book. Folk and fairy tales. Foreign lands – England. Middle ages.

Dick Whittington and his cat retold by Eva Moore; ill. by Kurt Werth. Seabury Pr., 1974. Subj: Activities – trading. Animals – cats. Folk and fairy tales. Foreign lands – England. Middle ages.

Dick Whittington and his cat. *Dick Whittington* retold by Kathleen Lines; ill. by Edward Ardizzone. Walck, 1970. Subj: Activities – trading. Animals – cats. Folk and fairy tales. Foreign lands – England. Middle ages.

Dick Whittington: a story from England retold by Charles Causley; ill. by Antony Maitland. Penguin, 1979. Subj: Activities – trading. Animals – cats. Folk and fairy tales. Foreign lands – England. Middle ages.

Dickens, Frank. *Boffo: the great motorcycle race* ill. by author. Parents, 1978. Subj: Character traits – cleverness. Motorcycles. Sports – racing.

Dickinson, Mary. *Alex and Roy* ill. by Charlotte Firmin. Elsevier-Dutton, 1981. Subj: Friendship. Imagination.

Alex's bed ill. by Charlotte Firmin. Elsevier-Dutton, 1980. Subj: Character traits – cleanliness. Problem solving.

Alex's outing ill. by Charlotte Firmin. Dutton, 1983. Subj: Activities – picnicking. Behavior – nagging. Country.

Dickinson, Mike. *My dad doesn't even notice* ill. by author. Elsevier-Dutton, 1982. Subj: Behavior – misunderstanding. Imagination.

DiFiori, Lawrence. *Baby animals* ill. by author. Macmillan, 1983. Subj: Animals. Format, unusual – cardboard pages.

The farm ill. by author. Macmillan, 1983. Subj: Farms. Format, unusual – cardboard pages.

If I had a little car ill. by author. Golden Pr., 1985. Subj: Automobiles. Format, unusual – cardboard pages. Imagination.

My first book ill. by author. Macmillan, 1983. Subj: Activities – reading. Format, unusual – cardboard pages.

My toys ill. by author. Macmillan, 1983. Subj: Format, unusual – cardboard pages. Toys.

D'Ignazio, Fred. *Katie and the computer* ill. by Stan Gilliam. Creative Computing, 1980. Subj: Imagination. Machines.

Dillon, Barbara. *The beast in the bed* ill. by Chris Conover. Morrow, 1981. Subj: Imagination – imaginary friends. Monsters.

Dillon, Eilis. *The cats' opera* ill. by Kveta Vanecek. Bobbs-Merrill, 1963. Subj: Animals – cats. Music.

Din dan don, it's Christmas ill. by Janina Domanska. Greenwillow, 1975. Text is a rendition of an anonymous Polish Christmas carol. Subj: Foreign lands – Poland. Holidays – Christmas. Religion. Songs.

Dinan, Carolyn. *The lunch box monster* ill. by author. Faber, 1983. Subj: Imagination – imaginary friends. Monsters.

Dines, Glen. *Gilly and the wicharoo* ill. by author. Lothrop, 1968. Subj: Behavior – trickery. Character traits – cleverness. Foreign lands – England.

Pitadoe, the color maker ill. by author. Macmillan, 1959. Subj: Concepts – color. Wizards.

A tiger in the cherry tree ill. by author. Macmillan, 1958. Subj: Animals – tigers. Behavior – forgetfulness. Character traits – shyness. Foreign lands – Japan. Magic.

Dinosaurs and monsters ill. by Louise Nevett. Watts, 1984. Subj: Activities. Dinosaurs. Monsters.

Dionetti, Michelle. *The day Eli went looking for bear* ill. by Joyce Audy Dos Santos. Addison-Wesley, 1980. Subj: Animals. Family life – mothers. Seasons – winter. Sports – hunting.

Thalia Brown and the blue bug ill. by James Calvin. Addison-Wesley, 1979. Subj: Art. Character traits – pride. Ethnic groups in the U.S. – Afro-Americans.

Diot, Alain. *Better, best, bestest* ill. by Joel Naprstek. Dial Pr., 1977. Subj: Behavior – boasting. Family life – fathers.

Diska, Pat. *Andy says ... Bonjour!* ill. by Chris Jenkyns. Vanguard, 1954. Subj: Animals – cats. Foreign lands – France. Foreign languages.

Dobbs, Rose. *More once-upon-a-time stories* ill. by Flavia Gág. Random House, 1961. Subj: Folk and fairy tales.

Once-upon-a-time story book ill. by Walter Hodges. Random House, 1958. Subj: Folk and fairy tales.

Dobrin, Arnold Jack. *Josephine's 'magination* ill. by author. Four Winds Pr., 1973. Subj: Foreign lands – Caribbean Islands. Imagination. Toys.

Dodd, Lynley. *The nickle nackle tree* ill. by author. Macmillan, 1976. Subj: Counting. Poetry, rhyme.

Dodge, Mary Mapes. *Mary Anne* ill. by June Amos Grammer. Lothrop, 1983. Subj: Poetry, rhyme. Toys – dolls.

Dodgson, Charles Lutwidge *see* Carroll, Lewis

The dog writes on the window with his nose, and other poems collected by David Kherdian; ill. by Nonny Hogrogian. Four Winds Pr., 1977. Subj: Poetry, rhyme.

Domanska, Janina. *The best of the bargain* ill. by author. Greenwillow, 1977. Subj: Activities – gardening. Animals – foxes. Animals – hedgehogs. Behavior – trickery. Character traits – cleverness. Folk and fairy tales. Foreign lands – Poland.

Busy Monday morning ill. by author. Greenwillow, 1985. Subj: Folk and fairy tales. Foreign lands – Poland. Music. Songs.

I saw a ship a-sailing ill. by author. Macmillan, 1972. Subj: Boats, ships. Holidays – Christmas. Nursery rhymes.

If all the seas were one sea ill. by author. Macmillan, 1971. Subj: Caldecott award honor book Nursery rhymes. Sea and seashore.

King Krakus and the dragon ill. by author. Greenwillow, 1979. Subj: Character traits – cleverness. Dragons. Folk and fairy tales. Foreign lands – Poland. Royalty.

Look, there is a turtle flying ill. by author. Macmillan, 1968. Subj: Folk and fairy tales. Foreign lands – Poland. Reptiles – turtles. Royalty.

Marek, the little fool ill. by author. Greenwillow, 1982. Subj: Folk and fairy tales. Foreign lands.

Palmiero and the ogre ill. by author. Macmillan, 1967. Subj: Behavior – forgetfulness. Folk and fairy tales. Magic.

A scythe, a rooster and a cat ill. by author. Greenwillow, 1981. Subj: Folk and fairy tales. Foreign lands – Russia.

The tortoise and the tree ill. by author. Greenwillow, 1978. Subj: Folk and fairy tales. Foreign lands – Africa. Reptiles – turtles.

The turnip ill. by author. Macmillan, 1969. Subj: Cumulative tales. Farms. Folk and fairy tales. Foreign lands – Russia. Plants. Problem solving.

What do you see? ill. by author. Macmillan, 1974. Subj: Animals. Poetry, rhyme. World.

What happens next? ill. by author. Greenwillow, 1983. Subj: Folk and fairy tales.

Why so much noise? ill. by author. Harper, 1965. "Adaptation of the tale entitled 'The elephant has a bet with the tiger,' [as recorded] by Walter William Skeat." Subj: Animals – elephants. Animals – tigers. Character traits – cleverness. Folk and fairy tales. Foreign lands – India. Noise, sounds.

Domestic animals ill. with photos. Imported Pubs., 1983. Subj: Animals. Format, unusual – cardboard pages. Wordless.

Donaldson, Lois. *Karl's wooden horse* ill. by Annie Bergmann. Albert Whitman, 1970. Subj: Dreams. Holidays – Christmas. Night. Toys – rocking horses.

Don't tell the scarecrow: *and other Japanese poems* by Issa, Yayū, Kikaku and other Japanese poets; ill. by Tālivaldis Stubis. Four Winds Pr., 1970. Subj: Foreign lands – Japan. Poetry, rhyme. Seasons.

Dorian, Marguerite. *When the snow is blue* ill. by author. Lothrop, 1960. Subj: Animals – bears. Imagination. Weather – snow.

Dorros, Arthur. *Alligator shoes* ill. by author. Dutton, 1982. Subj: Reptiles – alligators, crocodiles.

Pretzels ill. by author. Greenwillow, 1981. Subj: Boats, ships. Humor.

Dorsky, Blanche. *Harry, a true story* ill. by Muriel Batherman. Prentice-Hall, 1977. Subj: Animals – rabbits. School.

Dos Santos, Joyce Audy. *The diviner* ill. by author. Lippincott, 1980. Subj: Character traits – cleverness. Folk and fairy tales. Foreign lands – Canada. Royalty.

Henri and the Loup-Garou ill. by author. Pantheon, 1982. Subj: Folk and fairy tales. Foreign lands – Canada. Monsters.

Sand dollar, sand dollar ill. by author. Lippincott, 1980. Subj: Sea and seashore.

Dostoyevsky, Fyodor. *The talking crocodile* (Campbell, M Rudolph)

Doty, Roy. *Eye fooled you: the big book of optical illusions* ill. by author. Macmillan, 1983. Subj: Optical illusions.

Old-one-eye meets his match ill. by author. Lothrop, 1978. Subj: Animals – mice. Animals – rats.

Doughtie, Charles. *Gabriel Wrinkles, the bloodhound who couldn't smell* ill. by Charles D. Saxon. Dodd, 1959. Subj: Animals – dogs. Senses.

High Henry the cowboy who was too tall to ride a horse ill. by Don Gregg. Dodd, 1960. Subj: Animals – giraffes. Cowboys.

Douglas, Barbara. *Good as new* ill. by Patience Brewster. Lothrop, 1982. Subj: Behavior – misbehavior. Family life – grandparents, great-grandparents. Toys – teddy bears.

Douglas, Michael. *Round, round world* ill. by author. Golden Pr., 1960. Subj: Animals – cats. Foreign lands. World.

Douglas, Robert W. *John Paul II: the Pilgrim Pope* ill., map and photos. Children's Pr., 1979. Subj: Religion.

Dow, Katharine. *My time of year* ill. by Walter Erhard. Walck, 1961. Subj: Seasons.

Dowdy, Mrs. Regera *see* Gorey, Edward

Dowers, Patrick. *One day scene through a leaf* ill. by author. Green Tiger Pr., 1981. Subj: Poetry, rhyme.

Downing, Joan. *Baseball is our game* ill. by Tony Freeman. Children's Pr., 1982. Subj: Sports – baseball.

Doyle, Donovan *see* Boegehold, Betty

Dragonwagon, Crescent. *Always, always* ill. by Arieh Zeldich. Macmillan, 1984. Subj: Divorce.

Coconut ill. by Nancy Tafuri. Harper, 1984. Subj: Behavior – wishing. Birds – parakeets, parrots.

I hate my brother Harry ill. by Dick Gackenbach. Harper, 1983. Subj: Sibling rivalry.

Katie in the morning ill. by Betsy Day. Harper, 1983. Subj: Behavior – solitude. Morning.

Rainy day together ill. by Lillian Hoban. Harper, 1971. Subj: Emotions. Family life. Family life – only child. Weather – rain.

When light turns into night ill. by Robert Andrew Parker. Harper, 1975. Subj: Behavior – solitude. Night.

Wind Rose ill. by Ronald Himler. Harper, 1976. Subj: Babies. Emotions – love. Names.

Drdek, Richard E. *Horace the friendly octopus* ill. by Joseph Veno. Allyn and Bacon, 1965. Reading consultants: William D. Sheldon and Mary C. Austin. Subj: Friendship. Octopuses.

Dreifus, Miriam W. *Brave Betsy* ill. by Sheila Greenwald. Putnam's, 1961. Subj: Character traits – bravery. School. Toys – dolls.

Drescher, Henrik. *Looking for Santa Claus* ill. by author. Lothrop, 1984. Subj: Animals – bulls, cows. Holidays – Christmas. Imagination.

Simon's book ill. by author. Lothrop, 1983. Subj: Dreams. Monsters.

Drescher, Joan. *I'm in charge!* ill. by author. Little, 1981. Subj: Behavior – growing up. Family life.

The marvelous mess ill. by author. Houghton, 1980. Subj: Family life. Sibling rivalry.

Your family, my family ill. by author. Walker, 1980. Subj: Family life.

Drew, Patricia. *Spotter Puff* ill. by author. Merrimack Book Serv., 1979. Subj: Birds – puffins. Character traits – kindness to animals.

Driz, Ovsei. *The boy and the tree* tr. by Joachim Neugroschel; ill. by Victor Pivovarov. Prentice-Hall, 1978. Subj: Poetry, rhyme.

Drummond, Violet H. *The flying postman* ill. by author. Walck, 1964. Subj: Careers – mail carriers. Foreign lands – England. Helicopters.

Dubanevich, Arlene. *Pigs in hiding* ill. by author. Four Winds Pr., 1983. Subj: Animals – pigs. Behavior – hiding. Games.

DuBois, Ivy. *Baby Jumbo* ill. by Elsie Wrigley. Grosset, 1977. Subj: Animals – elephants.

Mother fox ill. by Elsie Wrigley. Grosset, 1977. Subj: Animals – foxes.

Du Bois, William Pène. *The alligator case* ill. by author. Harper, 1966. Subj: Circus. Problem solving. Reptiles – alligators, crocodiles.

Bear circus ill. by author. Viking, 1971. Subj: Animals. Animals – koala bears. Character traits – helpfulness. Circus. Insects – grasshoppers.

Bear party ill. by author. Viking, 1951. Subj: Animals. Animals – koala bears. Caldecott award honor book. Emotions – anger. Parties.

Elisabeth the cow ghost ill. by author. Viking, 1964. Subj: Animals – bulls, cows. Ghosts.

The forbidden forest ill. by author. Harper, 1978. Subj: Animals – kangaroos. War.

Giant Otto ill. by author. Viking, n.d. Subj: Animals – dogs. Giants.

The hare and the tortoise and the tortoise and the hare: La liebre y la tortuga and La tortuga y la liebre by William Pène Du Bois and Lee Po; ill. by William Pène Du Bois. Doubleday, 1972. Subj: Animals – rabbits. Folk and fairy tales. Foreign languages. Reptiles – turtles.

Lazy Tommy pumpkinhead ill. by author. Harper, 1966. Subj: Character traits – laziness. Machines.

Lion ill. by author. Viking, 1957. Subj: Animals – lions. Caldecott award honor book.

Otto and the magic potatoes ill. by author. Viking, 1970. Subj: Activities – vacationing. Animals – dogs. Fire. Giants.

Otto at sea ill. by author. Viking, 1936. Subj: Animals – dogs. Boats, ships. Giants.

Otto in Africa ill. by author. Viking, 1961. Subj: Animals – dogs. Foreign lands – Africa. Giants.

Otto in Texas ill. by author. Viking, 1959. Subj: Animals – dogs. Giants.

Duff, Maggie. *Dancing turtle* ill. by Maria Horvath. Macmillan, 1981. Subj: Animals. Behavior – trickery. Folk and fairy tales.

The princess and the pumpkin: from a Majorcan tale ill. by Catherine Stock. Macmillan, 1980. Subj: Folk and fairy tales. Foreign lands – Spain. Illness.

Rum pum pum ill. by José Aruego. Macmillan, 1978. Subj: Birds – blackbirds. Folk and fairy tales. Foreign lands – India.

Duff, Margaret K. *see* Duff, Maggie

Dukas, P. (Paul Abraham). *The sorcerer's apprentice* Adapt. by Makoto Oishi; tr. by Ann Brannen; ill. by Ryohei Yanagihara. Gakken, 1971. Subj: Folk and fairy tales. Magic.

Duke, Kate. *The guinea pig ABC* ill. by author. Dutton, 1983. Subj: ABC books. Animals – guinea pigs.

Guinea pigs far and near ill. by author. Dutton, 1984. Subj: Animals – guinea pigs. Concepts.

Seven froggies went to school ill. by author. Dutton, 1985. Subj: Frogs and toads. School.

Dulcken, H. W. *The fir tree* (Andersen, H C (Hans Christian))

Dumas, Philippe. *Caesar, cock of the village* ill. by author. Prentice-Hall, 1979. Subj: Birds – chickens. Foreign lands – France.

Laura, Alice's new puppy ill. by author. David and Charles, 1979. Subj: Animals – dogs.

Laura and the bandits ill. by author. David and Charles, 1980. Subj: Animals – dogs. Crime.

Laura loses her head ill. by author. David and Charles, 1982. Subj: Animals – dogs. Family life – grandparents, great-grandparents. Foreign lands – France.

Laura on the road ill. by author. David and Charles, 1979. Subj: Animals – dogs.

Lucy, a tale of a donkey ill. by author. Prentice-Hall, 1980. Subj: Animals – donkeys. Behavior – running away.

The story of Edward ill. by author. Parents, 1977. Subj: Animals – donkeys. Foreign lands – France.

Duncan, Gregory *see* McClintock, Marshall

Duncan, Jane. *Janet Reachfar and Chickabird* ill. by Mairi Hedderwick. Seabury Pr., 1978. Subj: Behavior – bad day. Farms. Foreign lands – Scotland.

Duncan, Lois. *Giving away Suzanne* ill. by Leonard Weisgard. Dodd, 1964. Subj: Sibling rivalry.

Duncan, Riana. *A nutcracker in a tree: a book of riddles* ill. by author. Delacorte, 1981. Subj: Animals. Riddles.

Dunn, Judy. *The animals of Buttercup Farm* photos. by Phoebe Dunn. Random House, 1981. Subj: Animals. Farms.

The little duck ill. by Phoebe Dunn. Random House, 1978. Subj: Birds – ducks.

The little goat ill. by Phoebe Dunn. Random House, 1978. Subj: Animals – goats. Pets.

The little lamb ill. by Phoebe Dunn. Random House, 1977. Subj: Animals – sheep. Character traits – kindness to animals. Farms.

The little puppy photos. by Phoebe Dunn. Random House, 1984. Subj: Animals – dogs. Pets.

The little rabbit photos. by Phoebe Dunn. Random House, 1980. Subj: Animals – rabbits. Holidays – Easter. Pets.

Dunrea, Olivier. *Eddy B, pigboy* ill. by author. Atheneum, 1983. Subj: Animals – pigs. Farms.

Duplaix, Georges *see* Ariane

Dupré, Ramona Dorrel. *Too many dogs* ill. by Howard Baer. Follett, 1960. Subj: Animals – dogs.

Duran, Bonté. *The adventures of Arthur and Edmund: a tale of two seals* ill. by Quentin Blake. Atheneum, 1984. Subj: Animals – seals.

Durrell, Julie. *Mouse tails* ill. by author. Crown, 1985. Subj: Animals. Animals – mice.

Duvoisin, Roger Antoine. *A for the ark* ill. by author. Lothrop, 1952. Subj: ABC books. Animals. Religion – Noah.

The Christmas whale ill. by author. Knopf, 1945. Subj: Animals – whales. Holidays – Christmas. Illness.

The crocodile in the tree ill. by author. Knopf, 1973. Subj: Animals. Farms. Friendship. Reptiles – alligators, crocodiles.

Crocus ill. by author. Knopf, 1977. Subj: Careers – dentists. Character traits – pride. Farms. Reptiles – alligators, crocodiles. Teeth.

Day and night ill. by author. Knopf, 1960. Subj: Animals – dogs. Birds – owls.

Donkey-donkey ill. by author. Parents, 1968. Subj: Animals – donkeys.

Easter treat ill. by author. Knopf, 1954. Subj: Holidays – Easter.

The happy hunter ill. by author. Lothrop, 1961. Subj: Character traits – kindness to animals. Ecology. Sports – hunting. Violence, anti-violence. Weapons.

The house of four seasons ill. by author. Lothrop, 1956. Subj: Activities – painting. Concepts – color. Seasons.

Jasmine ill. by author. Knopf, 1973. Subj: Animals. Character traits – individuality. Clothing. Farms.

Lonely Veronica ill. by author. Knopf, 1963. Subj: Animals – hippopotami. City. Progress.

Marc and Pixie and the walls in Mrs. Jones's garden (Fatio, Louise)

The missing milkman ill. by author. Knopf, 1967. Subj: Behavior – running away. Dreams. Night.

One thousand Christmas beards ill. by author. Knopf, 1955. Subj: Holidays – Christmas.

Our Veronica goes to Petunia's farm ill. by author. Knopf, 1962. Subj: Animals. Animals – hippopotami. Character traits – being different. Farms.

Periwinkle ill. by author. Knopf, 1976. Subj: Animals – giraffes. Emotions – loneliness. Etiquette. Friendship. Frogs and toads.

Petunia ill. by author. Knopf, 1950. Subj: Activities – reading. Animals. Birds – geese. Character traits – pride. Farms. Friendship.

Petunia and the song ill. by author. Knopf, 1951. Subj: Animals. Birds – geese. Crime. Farms. Friendship. Noise, sounds. Songs.

Petunia, beware! ill. by author. Knopf, 1958. Subj: Animals. Behavior – dissatisfaction. Birds – geese. Farms.

Petunia, I love you ill. by author. Knopf, 1965. Subj: Animals – raccoons. Behavior – trickery. Birds – geese. Birds – vultures. Farms. Friendship.

Petunia takes a trip ill. by author. Knopf, 1953. Subj: Activities – flying. Activities – vacationing. Animals. Birds – geese.

Petunia's Christmas ill. by author. Knopf, 1952. Subj: Birds – geese. Holidays – Christmas. Humor.

Petunia's treasure ill. by author. Knopf, 1975. Subj: Animals. Birds – geese. Farms. Friendship.

See what I am ill. by author. Lothrop, 1974. Subj: Behavior – boasting. Concepts – color.

Snowy and Woody ill. by author. Knopf, 1979. Subj: Animals – bears. Birds – sea gulls.

Two lonely ducks ill. by author. Knopf, 1955. Subj: Birds – ducks. Counting. Farms.

Veronica ill. by author. Knopf, 1961. Subj: Animals – hippopotami. Character traits – being different. City. Farms.

Veronica and the birthday present ill. by author. Knopf, 1971. Subj: Animals – cats. Animals – hippopotami. Birthdays. Farms.

Veronica's smile ill. by author. Knopf, 1964. Subj: Animals – hippopotami. Behavior – boredom.

Dyke, John. *Pigwig* ill. by author. Methuen, 1978. Subj: Animals – pigs. Behavior – stealing. Character traits – bravery. Emotions – love.

Pigwig and the pirates ill. by author. Methuen, 1979. Subj: Animals – pigs. Pirates. Sea and seashore.

Dynely, James *see* Mayne, William

Earle, Olive L. *Squirrels in the garden* ill. by author. Morrow, 1963. Subj: Animals – squirrels.

Eastman, David. *The story of dinosaurs* ill. by Joel Snyder. Troll Assoc., 1982. Subj: Dinosaurs.

What is a fish? ill. by Lynn Sweat. Troll Assoc., 1982. Subj: Fish. Science.

Eastman, P. D. (Philip D.). *Are you my mother?* ill. by author. Random House, 1960. Subj: Behavior – misbehavior. Birds. Family life – mothers.

The cat in the hat beginner book dictionary (Seuss, Dr.)

Flap your wings ill. by author. Random House, 1969. Subj: Birds. Eggs. Reptiles – alligators, crocodiles.

Go, dog, go! ill. by author. Random House, 1961. Subj: Animals – dogs.

Sam and the firefly ill. by author. Random House, 1958. Subj: Birds – owls. Insects – fireflies.

Snow (McKié, Roy)

Eastman, Patricia. *Sometimes things change* ill. by Seymour Fleishman. Children's Pr., 1983. Subj: Science.

Eastwick, Ivy O. *Cherry stones! Garden swings! poems* ill. by Robert Jones. Abingdon Pr., 1962. Subj: Poetry, rhyme.

Rainbow over all ill. by Anne Siberell. McKay, 1970. Subj: Poetry, rhyme.

Eaton, Su. *Punch and Judy in the rain* by Su Eaton and Martin Bridle; ill. by authors. Hamish Hamilton, 1985. Subj: Puppets.

Eberle, Irmengarde. *Bears live here* ill. with photos. Doubleday, 1962. Subj: Animals – bears.

A chipmunk lives here ill. by Matthew Kalmenoff. Doubleday, 1966. Subj: Animals – chipmunks.

Fawn in the woods photos. by Lilo Hess. Crowell, 1962. Subj: Animals – deer.

Foxes live here ill. with photos. Doubleday, 1966. Subj: Animals – foxes.

Koalas live here ill. with photos. Doubleday, 1967. Subj: Animals – koala bears.

Eberstadt, Frederick. *What is for my birthday?* (Eberstadt, Isabel)

Eberstadt, Isabel. *What is for my birthday?* by Isabel and Frederick Eberstadt; ill. by Leonard Weisgard. Little, 1961. Subj: Birthdays. Illness. Poetry, rhyme.

Eckert, Horst *see* Janosch

Economakis, Olga. *Oasis of the stars* ill. by Blair Lent. Coward, 1965. Subj: Foreign lands – Africa. Problem solving.

Edelman, Elaine. *Boom-de-boom* ill. by Karen Gundersheimer. Pantheon, 1980. Subj: Activities – dancing. Old age. Poetry, rhyme.

I love my baby sister (most of the time) ill. by Wendy Watson. Lothrop, 1984. Subj: Sibling rivalry.

Edman, Polly. *Red thread riddles* (Jensen, Virginia Allen)

Edwards, Al see Nourse, Alan Edward

Edwards, Dorothy. *A wet Monday* by Dorothy Edwards and Jenny Williams; ill. by Jenny Williams. Morrow, 1975. Subj: Birds – chickens. Character traits – pride.

Edwards, Linda Strauss. *The downtown day* ill. by author. Pantheon, 1983. Subj: Shopping.

Eggs ill. by Esmé Eve. Grosset, 1971. Subj: Eggs.

Ehrhardt, Reinhold. *Kikeri or, The proud red rooster* ill. by Bernadette. Collins, 1969. Subj: Birds – chickens. Character traits – pride.

Ehrlich, Amy. *The everyday train* ill. by Martha G. Alexander. Dial Pr., 1977. Subj: Behavior – solitude. Trains.

Leo, Zack and Emmie ill. by Steven Kellogg. Dial Pr., 1981. Subj: Friendship. School.

The snow queen (Andersen, H C (Hans Christian))

Thumbelina (Andersen, H C (Hans Christian))

The wild swans (Andersen, H C (Hans Christian))

Zeek Silver Moon ill. by Robert Andrew Parker. Dial Pr., 1972. Subj: Ethnic groups in the U.S. – Indians. Family life.

Ehrlich, Bettina Bauer see Bettina

Eichenberg, Fritz. *Ape in cape* ill. by author. Harcourt, 1952. Subj: ABC books. Caldecott award honor book.

Dancing in the moon ill. by author. Harcourt, 1955. Subj: Animals. Counting. Poetry, rhyme.

Eisenberg, Lisa. *Fishy riddles* (Hall, Katy)

Eisenberg, Phyllis Rose. *Don't tell me a ghost story* ill. by Lynn Munsinger. Harcourt, 1982. Subj: Ghosts. Monsters. Sibling rivalry.

A mitzvah is something special ill. by Susan Jeschke. Harper, 1978. Subj: Family life – grandparents, great-grandparents. Jewish culture.

Elborn, Andrew. *Bird Adalbert* ill. by Susi Bohdal. Alphabet Pr., 1983. Subj: Behavior – dissatisfaction. Birds. Character traits – appearance. Poetry, rhyme.

Elkin, Benjamin. *The big jump and other stories* ill. by Katherine Evans. Random House, 1958. Subj: Animals – dogs. Folk and fairy tales. Royalty.

Gillespie and the guards ill. by James Henry Daugherty. Viking, 1956. Subj: Anatomy. Behavior – trickery. Caldecott award honor book. Character traits – cleverness. Royalty.

The king who could not sleep ill. by Victoria Chess. Parents, 1975. Subj: Cumulative tales. Poetry, rhyme. Royalty. Sleep.

The king's wish and other stories ill. by Leonard W. Shortall. Random House, 1960. Subj: Folk and fairy tales. Royalty.

The loudest noise in the world ill. by James Henry Daugherty. Viking, 1954. Subj: Birthdays. Noise, sounds. Royalty.

Lucky and the giant ill. by Katherine Evans. Children's Pr., 1962. Subj: Character traits – cleverness. Character traits – luck. Character traits – selfishness. Giants.

Six foolish fishermen ill. by Katherine Evans. Children's Pr., 1957. Based on a folktale in Ashton's Chap-Books of the 18th century. Subj: Counting. Folk and fairy tales. Sports – fishing.

Such is the way of the world ill. by Yōko Mitsuhashi. Parents, 1968. Subj: Animals – monkeys. Cumulative tales. Folk and fairy tales. Foreign lands – Africa. Problem solving.

Why the sun was late ill. by James Snyder. Parents, 1966. Subj: Animals. Cumulative tales. Insects – flies. Sun.

The wisest man in the world: a legend of ancient Israel retold by Benjamin Elkin; ill. by Anita Lobel. Parents, 1968. Subj: Folk and fairy tales. Foreign lands – Israel. Riddles. Royalty.

Ellen, Barbara. *Phillip the flower-eating phoenix* (Todaro, John)

Ellentuck, Shan. *Did you see what I said?* ill. by author. Doubleday, 1967. Subj: Humor. Language.

A sunflower as big as the sun ill. by author. Doubleday, 1968. Subj: Behavior – boasting. Flowers. Humor. Plants.

Elliott, Dan. *Ernie's little lie* ill. by Joseph Mathieu. Random House, 1983. Subj: Art. Behavior – lying. Puppets.

A visit to the Sesame Street firehouse: featuring Jim Henson's Sesame Street Muppets ill. by Joseph Mathieu. Random House, 1983. Subj: Careers – firefighters. Fire. Puppets.

Elliott, Ingrid Glatz. *Hospital roadmap: a book to help explain the hospital experience to young children* ill. by author. Resources for Children in Hospitals, 1982. Subj: Hospitals. Illness.

Elliott, Robert see Allen, Robert

Ellis, Anne Leo. *Dabble Duck* ill. by Sue Truesdell. Harper, 1984. Subj: Birds – ducks. City. Emotions – loneliness. Friendship.

Elting, Mary. *The big book of real boats and ships* ill. by George J. Zaffo. Grosset, 1951. Subj: Boats, ships.

The Hopi way ill. by Louis Mofsie. Lippincott, 1970. Subj: Ethnic groups in the U.S. – Indians.

Q is for duck: an alphabet guessing game by Mary Elting and Michael Folsom; ill. by Jack Kent. Houghton, 1980. Subj: ABC books. Animals. Games. Participation.

Elves, fairies and gnomes: *poems* sel. by Lee Bennett Hopkins; ill. by Rosekrans Hoffman. Knopf, 1980. Subj: Elves and little people. Fairies. Poetry, rhyme.

Elwell, Peter. *The king of the pipers* ill. by author. Macmillan, 1984. Subj: Devil. Folk and fairy tales.

Emberley, Barbara. *Drummer Hoff* ill. by Ed Emberley. Prentice-Hall, 1967. Adapted from a folk verse. Subj: Caldecott award book. Careers – military. Cumulative tales. Poetry, rhyme. Weapons.

Night's nice by Barbara and Ed Emberley; ill. by Ed Emberley. Doubleday, 1963. Subj: Night. Poetry, rhyme.

One wide river to cross ill. by Ed Emberley. Prentice-Hall, 1966. Includes unacc. melody. Adaptation of the American folk song. Subj: Animals. Caldecott award honor book. Folk and fairy tales. Poetry, rhyme. Songs.

Simon's song ill. by Ed Emberley. Prentice-Hall, 1969. Includes unacc. melody. Adaptation of the folk song Simple Simon. Subj: Nursery rhymes. Songs.

Emberley, Ed. *Ed Emberley's ABC* ill. by author. Little, 1978. Subj: ABC books.

Ed Emberley's amazing look through book ill. by author. Little, 1979. Subj: Concepts. Format, unusual. Participation. Riddles.

Ed Emberley's big green drawing book ill. by author. Little, 1979. Subj: Art. Wordless.

Ed Emberley's big orange drawing book ill. by author. Little, 1980. Subj: Art.

Ed Emberley's big purple drawing book ill. by author. Little, 1981. Subj: Art.

Ed Emberley's crazy mixed-up face game ill. by author. Little, 1981. Subj: Anatomy. Art. Games.

Green says go ill. by author. Little, 1968. Subj: Communication. Concepts – color.

Klippity klop ill. by author. Little, 1974. Subj: Dragons. Games. Knights. Participation.

Night's nice (Emberley, Barbara)

The parade book ill. by author. Little, 1962. Subj: Parades.

Rosebud ill. by author. Little, 1966. Subj: Character traits – being different. Problem solving. Reptiles – turtles.

The wing on a flea: a book about shapes ill. by author. Little, 1961. Subj: Concepts – shape. Poetry, rhyme.

The Wizard of Op ill. by author. Little, 1975. Subj: Optical illusions. Wizards.

Emberley, Edward Randolph *see* Emberley, Ed

Emberley, Michael. *More dinosaurs! and other prehistoric beasts* ill. by author. Little, 1983. Subj: Art. Dinosaurs.

Emberley, Rebecca. *Drawing with numbers and letters* ill. by author. Little, 1981. Subj: Art.

Embry, Margaret. *The blue-nosed witch* ill. by Carl Rose. Holiday, 1956. Subj: Holidays – Halloween. Witches.

Emecheta, Buchi. *Nowhere to play* ill. by Peter Archer. Schocken, 1981. Subj: Activities – playing. Foreign lands – England. Safety.

Emmett, Fredrick Rowland. *New world for Nellie* ill. by author. Harcourt, 1952. Subj: Trains.

Emmons, Ramona Ware. *Your world: let's visit the hospital* (Pope, Billy N)

Encking, Louise F. *The little gardeners* (Morgenstern, Elizabeth)

The toy maker (Thelen, Gerda)

Enderle, Judith A. *Good junk* ill. by Gail Gibbons. Elsevier-Nelson, 1981. Subj: Behavior – collecting things.

Engdahl, Sylvia. *Our world is earth* ill. by Don Sibley. Atheneum, 1979. Subj: Communication. Earth. Science.

Engelbrektson, Sune. *Gravity at work and play* ill. by Eric Carle. Holt, 1963. Subj: Science.

The sun is a star ill. by Eric Carle. Holt, 1963. Subj: Science. Sun.

Engle, Joanna. *Cap'n kid goes to the South Pole* ill. by Pat Paris. Random House, 1983. Subj: Animals – whales.

Engvick, William. *Lullabies and night songs* ed. by William Engvick; music by Alec Wilder; ill. by Maurice Sendak. Harper, 1965. Subj: Bedtime. Musc. Songs.

Enright, Elizabeth. *Zeee* ill. by Irene Haas. Houghton, 1965. Subj: Fairies.

Ephron, Delia. *Santa and Alex* ill. by Elise Primavera. Little, 1983. Subj: Holidays – Christmas.

Erdoes, Richard. *Policemen around the world* ill. by author. McGraw-Hill, 1968. Subj: Careers – police officers.

Erickson, Phoebe. *Just follow me* ill. by author. Follett, 1960. Subj: Animals – dogs. Behavior – lost. Houses.

Erickson, Russell E. *Warton and the traders* ill. by Lawrence DiFiori. Lothrop, 1979. Subj: Animals – rats. Character traits – cleverness. Character traits – generosity. Frogs and toads.

Warton's Christmas Eve adventure ill. by Lawrence DiFiori. Lothrop, 1977. Subj: Animals. Frogs and toads. Holidays – Christmas.

Ernst, Lisa Campbell. *The prize pig surprise* ill. by author. Lothrop, 1984. Subj: Animals – pigs. Behavior – greed. Character traits – cleverness.

Sam Johnson and the blue ribbon quilt ill. by author. Lothrop, 1983. Subj: Activities.

Erskine, Jim. *Bedtime story* ill. by Ann Schweninger. Crown, 1982. Subj: Bedtime. Dreams. Night.

Bert and Susie's messy tale ill. by author. Crown, 1979. Subj: Activities. Animals – pigs.

The snowman ill. by author. Crown, 1978. Subj: Snowmen.

Espenscheid, Gertrude E. *The oh ball* ill. by author. Crown, 1966. Subj: Royalty. Toys – balls.

Estes, Eleanor. *A little oven* ill. by author. Harper, 1966. Subj: Emotions – love.

Etherington, Frank. *The spaghetti word race* ill. by Gina Calleja. Firefly Pr., 1982. Subj: Imagination. Sibling rivalry.

Ets, Marie Hall. *Another day* ill. by author. Viking, 1953. Subj: Animals. Forest, woods. Parades. Theater.

Bad boy, good boy ill. by author. Crowell, 1967. Subj: Behavior. Ethnic groups in the U.S. – Mexican-Americans. Family life. School.

Beasts and nonsense ill. by author. Viking, 1952. Subj: Animals. Humor. Poetry, rhyme.

The cow's party ill. by author. Viking, 1958. Subj: Animals – bulls, cows. Behavior – dissatisfaction. Behavior – sharing. Parties.

Elephant in a well ill. by author. Viking, 1972. Subj: Animals. Animals – elephants. Character traits – helpfulness. Cumulative tales.

Gilberto and the wind ill. by author. Viking, 1963. Subj: Ethnic groups in the U.S. – Mexican-Americans. Weather – wind.

In the forest ill. by author. Viking, 1944. Subj: Activities – picnicking. Animals. Caldecott award honor book. Forest, woods. Imagination. Parades.

Just me ill. by author. Viking, 1965. Subj: Animals. Caldecott award honor book. Participation.

Little old automobile ill. by author. Viking, 1948. Subj: Automobiles.

Mister Penny ill. by author. Viking, 1935. Subj: Animals. Caldecott award honor book. Farms. Humor.

Mister Penny's circus ill. by author. Viking, 1961. Subj: Animals. Circus.

Mr. Penny's race horse ill. by author. Viking, 1956. Subj: Animals – horses. Caldecott award honor book. Fairs. Farms.

Mr. T. W. Anthony Woo ill. by author. Viking, 1951. Subj: Animals – cats. Animals – dogs. Animals – mice. Caldecott award honor book.

Nine days to Christmas ill. by author. Viking, 1959. Subj: Caldecott award book. Ethnic groups in the U.S. – Mexican-Americans. Foreign lands – Mexico. Holidays – Christmas.

Play with me ill. by author. Viking, 1955. Subj: Activities – playing. Animals. Behavior. Caldecott award honor book.

Talking without words ill. by author. Viking, 1968. Subj: Participation.

Evans, Eva Knox. *Sleepy time* ill. by Reed Champion. Houghton, 1962. Subj: Animals. Cumulative tales. Hibernation. Sleep.

That lucky Mrs. Plucky ill. by Jo Ann Stover. McKay, 1961 Subj: Animals – cats Behavior – collecting things.

Where do you live? ill. by Beatrice Darwin. Golden Pr., 1960. Subj: Animals.

Evans, Katherine. *The boy who cried wolf* ill. by author. Albert Whitman, 1960. Subj: Animals – wolves. Behavior – lying. Behavior – trickery. Folk and fairy tales.

A bundle of sticks ill. by author. Albert Whitman, 1962. A retelling of an Æsop fable. Subj: Folk and fairy tales.

The maid and her pail of milk ill. by author. Albert Whitman, 1959. Subj: Behavior – greed. Folk and fairy tales. Humor.

The man, the boy and the donkey ill. by author. Albert Whitman, 1958. Subj: Animals – donkeys. Character traits – practicality. Folk and fairy tales. Humor.

Evans, Mari. *Singing black* ill. by Ramon Price. Third World Pr., 1978. Subj: Ethnic groups in the U.S. – Afro-Americans. Nursery rhymes.

Evans, Mel. *The tiniest sound* ill. by Ed Young. Doubleday, 1969. Subj: Noise, sounds. Poetry, rhyme.

Everton, Macduff. *El circo magico modelo: Finding the magic circus* ill. by author. Carolrhoda Books, 1979. Subj: Activities – vacationing. Circus. Foreign lands – Mexico. Foreign languages.

Fain, James W. *Rodeos* ill. with photos. Children's Pr., 1983. Subj: Animals – horses. Cowboys.

Fair, Sylvia. *The bedspread* ill. by author. Morrow, 1982. Subj: Activities. Sibling rivalry.

Fairclough, Chris. *Take a trip to China* photos. by author. Watts, 1981. Subj: Activities – traveling. Foreign lands – China.

Take a trip to England photos. by author. Watts, 1982. Subj: Activities – traveling. Foreign lands – England.

Take a trip to Holland photos. by author. Watts, 1982. Subj: Activities – traveling. Foreign lands – Holland.

Take a trip to Israel photos. by author. Watts, 1981. Subj: Activities – traveling. Foreign lands – Israel.

Take a trip to Italy photos. by author. Watts, 1981. Subj: Activities – traveling. Foreign lands – Italy.

Take a trip to West Germany photos. by author. Watts, 1981. Subj: Activities – traveling. Foreign lands – Germany.

Fairy poems for the very young ill. by Beverlie Manson. Doubleday, 1982. Subj: Fairies. Poetry, rhyme.

Faison, Eleanora. *Becoming* ill. by Cecelia Ercin. Patterson Pr., 1981. Subj: Behavior – growing up.

Falls, C. B. (Charles Buckles). *ABC book* ill. by author. Doubleday, 1923. Subj: ABC books.

Fanshawe, Elizabeth. *Rachel* ill. by Michael Charlton. Dutton, 1975. Subj: Handicaps. School.

Farber, Norma. *As I was crossing Boston Common* ill. by Arnold Lobel. Dutton, 1975. Subj: ABC books. Animals. Poetry, rhyme.

How does it feel to be old? ill. by Trina Schart Hyman. Dutton, 1979. Subj: Old age.

How the hibernators came to Bethlehem ill. by Barbara Cooney. Walker, 1980. Subj: Animals. Holidays – Christmas. Poetry, rhyme. Religion.

How the left-behind beasts built Ararat ill. by Antonio Frasconi. Walker, 1978. Subj: Animals. Poetry, rhyme. Problem solving. Religion – Noah.

How to ride a tiger ill. by Claire Schumacher. Houghton, 1983. Subj: Animals. Animals – tigers. Poetry. rhyme.

Never say ugh to a bug ill. by José Aruego. Greenwillow, 1979. Subj: Insects. Poetry, rhyme.

Small wonders ill. by Kazue Mizumura. Coward, 1979. Subj: Poetry, rhyme.

There goes feathertop! ill. by Marc Brown. Unicorn-Dutton, 1979. Subj: Behavior – imitation. Poetry, rhyme. Scarecrows.

There once was a woman who married a man ill. by Lydia Dabcovich. Addison-Wesley, 1978. Subj: Humor. Noise, sounds. Poetry, rhyme.

Up the down elevator ill. by Annie Gusman. Addison-Wesley, 1979. Subj: Counting. Poetry, rhyme.

Where's Gomer? ill. by William Pène Du Bois. Dutton, 1974. Subj: Behavior – lost. Poetry, rhyme. Religion – Noah.

Farge, Phyllis La *see* La Farge, Phyllis

Farge, Sheila La *see* La Farge, Sheila

Farjeon, Eleanor. *Around the seasons: poems* ill. by Jane Paton. Walck, 1969. Subj: Poetry, rhyme. Seasons.

Mr. Garden ill. by Jane Paton. Walck, 1966. Subj: Activities – gardening. Seasons – summer.

Mrs. Malone ill. by Edward Ardizzone. Walck, 1962. Subj: Character traits – generosity. Poetry, rhyme.

Farley, Walter. *Little Black, a pony* ill. by James Schucker. Random House, 1961. Subj: Animals – horses.

Little Black goes to the circus ill. by James Schucker. Random House, 1963. Subj: Animals – horses. Circus.

Farm house ill. by Zokeisha; ed. by Kate Klimo. Simon and Schuster, 1983. Subj: Animals. Farms. Format, unusual – cardboard pages. Houses.

The farmer in the dell ill. by Diane Stanley. Little, 1978. Subj: Games. Music. Songs.

Fass, David E. *The shofar that lost its voice* ill. by Marlene Lobell Ruthen. Union of American Hebrew Cong., 1982. Subj: Jewish culture. Religion.

Fassler, Joan. *All alone with daddy* ill by Dorothy Lake Gregory. Behavioral, 1969. Subj: Family life – fathers.

Boy with a problem ill. by Stuart [i.e. Stewart] Kranz. Behavioral, 1971. Subj: Friendship. Problem solving.

Don't worry dear ill. by Stuart [i.e. Stewart] Kranz. Behavioral, 1971. Subj: Behavior – growing up. Ethnic groups in the U.S. – Afro-Americans.

Howie helps himself ill. by Joe Lasker. Albert Whitman, 1975. Subj: Handicaps.

The man of the house ill. by Peter Landa. Behavioral, 1969. Subj: Behavior – growing up. Dragons. Family life – mothers. Monsters.

My grandpa died today ill. by Stuart [i.e. Stewart] Kranz. Behavioral, 1971. Subj: Death. Family life – grandparents, great-grandparents. Jewish culture. Old age.

One little girl ill. by M. Jane Smyth. Behavioral, 1969. Subj: Family life. Handicaps.

Fast rolling fire trucks ill. by Carolyn Bracken. Grosset, 1984. Subj: Careers – firefighters. Format unusual – cardboard pages. Trucks.

Fast rolling work trucks ill. by Alan Singer. Grosset, 1984. Subj: Format, unusual – cardboard pages. Trucks.

The fat cat ill. by Jack Kent. Parents, 1971. Translated from the Danish by Jack Kent. Subj: Animals – cats. Cumulative tales.

Fatio, Louise. *Anna, the horse* ill. by Roger Antoine Duvoisin. Atheneum, 1951. Subj: Animals – horses. Holidays – Christmas.

The happy lion ill. by Roger Antoine Duvoisin. McGraw-Hill, 1954. Subj: Animals – lions. Foreign lands – France. Friendship. Zoos.

The happy lion and the bear ill. by Roger Antoine Duvoisin. McGraw-Hill, 1964. Subj: Animals – bears. Animals – lions. Character traits – appearance. Foreign lands – France. Zoos.

The happy lion in Africa ill. by Roger Antoine Duvoisin. McGraw-Hill, 1955. Subj: Animals – lions. Foreign lands – Africa. Foreign lands – France. Zoos.

The happy lion roars ill. by Roger Antoine Duvoisin. McGraw-Hill, 1957. Subj: Animals – lions. Emotions – loneliness. Foreign lands – France. Zoos.

The happy lion's quest ill. by Roger Antoine Duvoisin. McGraw-Hill, 1961. Subj: Animals – lions. Foreign lands – France.

The happy lion's rabbits ill. by Roger Antoine Duvoisin. McGraw-Hill, 1974. Subj: Animals – lions. Animals – rabbits. Character traits – kindness. Foreign lands – France. Zoos.

The happy lion's treasure ill. by Roger Antoine Duvoisin. McGraw-Hill, 1970. Subj: Animals – lions. Emotions – love. Foreign lands – France. Zoos.

The happy lion's vacation ill. by Roger Antoine Duvoisin. McGraw-Hill, 1967. Subj: Activities – vacationing. Animals – lions.

Hector and Christina ill. by Roger Antoine Duvoisin. McGraw-Hill, 1977. Subj: Birds – penguins. Character traits – freedom. Friendship. Zoos.

Hector penguin ill. by Roger Antoine Duvoisin. McGraw-Hill, 1973. Subj: Birds – penguins. Character traits – individuality.

Marc and Pixie and the walls in Mrs. Jones's garden ill. by Roger Antoine Duvoisin. McGraw-Hill, 1975. Subj: Animals – cats.

The red bantam ill. by Roger Antoine Duvoisin. McGraw-Hill, 1963. Subj: Animals – foxes. Birds – chickens. Character traits – bravery. Farms.

The three happy lions ill. by Roger Antoine Duvoisin. McGraw-Hill, 1959. Subj: Animals – lions. Foreign lands – France. Zoos.

Faulkner, Anne Irvin *see* Faulkner, Nancy

Faulkner, Nancy. *Small clown* ill. by Paul Galdone. Doubleday, 1960. Subj: Clowns, jesters.

Faunce-Brown, Daphne. *Snuffles' house* ill. by Frances Thatcher. Children's Pr., 1983. Subj: Activities. Animals – cats.

Fay, Hermann. *My zoo* ill. by author. Hubbard Sci., 1972. Subj: Animals. Zoos.

Fayon, Lavinia *see* Russ, Lavinia

Fechner, Amrei. *I am a little dog* tr. from German by Robert Kimber; ill. by author. Barron's, 1983. Subj: Animals – dogs. Format, unusual – cardboard pages.

I am a little elephant ill. by author. Barron's, 1983. Subj: Animals – elephants. Format, unusual – cardboard pages.

I am a little lion ill. by author. Barron's, 1983. Subj: Animals – lions. Format, unusual – cardboard pages.

Feder, Jane. *Beany* ill. by Karen Gundersheimer. Pantheon, 1979. Subj: Animals – cats.

Feder, Paula Kurzband. *Where does the teacher live?* ill. by Lillian Hoban. Dutton, 1979. Subj: Careers – teachers. Houses. Problem solving. School.

Feelings, Muriel. *Jambo means hello: Swahili alphabet book* ill. by Tom Feelings. Dial Pr., 1974. Subj: ABC books. Caldecott award honor book. Foreign lands – Africa. Foreign languages.

Menjo means one: Swahili counting book ill. by Tom Feelings. Dial Pr., 1972. Subj: Caldecott award honor book. Counting. Foreign lands – Africa. Foreign languages.

Feilen, John *see* May, Julian

Feinberg, Harold S. *Snail in the woods* (Ryder, Joanne)

Feistel, Sally. *The guinea pigs that went to school* (Meshover, Leonard)

The monkey that went to school (Meshover, Leonard)

Felix, Monique. *The story of a little mouse trapped in a book* ill. by author. Green Tiger Pr., 1980. Subj: Animals – mice. Imagination. Wordless.

Felt, Sue. *Hello-goodbye* ill. by author. Doubleday, 1960. Subj: Friendship. Moving.

Rosa-too-little ill. by author. Doubleday, 1950. Subj: Activities – writing. Behavior – growing up. Ethnic groups in the U.S. – Mexican-Americans. Family life. Libraries.

Felton, Harold W. *Pecos Bill and the mustang* ill. by Leonard W. Shortall. Prentice-Hall, 1965. Subj: Animals – horses. Cowboys. Folk and fairy tales.

Fender, Kay. *Odette! a bird in Paris* ill. by Philippe Dumas. Prentice-Hall, 1978. Subj: Birds. Foreign lands – France. Old age.

Fenner, Carol. *Christmas tree on the mountain* ill. by author. Harcourt, 1966. Subj: Holidays – Christmas. Trees.

Tigers in the cellar ill. by author. Harcourt, 1963. Subj: Animals – tigers. Imagination. Night.

Fenton, Edward. *The big yellow balloon* ill. by Ib Ohlsson. Doubleday, 1967. Subj: Cumulative tales. Humor. Toys – balloons.

Fierce John ill. by William Pène Du Bois. Doubleday, 1959. Subj: Family life. Imagination.

Fern, Eugene. *Birthday presents* ill. by author. Farrar, 1967. Includes the song Sing me (2 p.) Subj: Birthdays. Songs.

The king who was too busy ill. by author. Ariel, 1966. Subj: Royalty.

The most frightened hero ill. by author. Coward, 1961. Subj: Character traits – bravery. Foreign lands – Scotland.

Pepito's story ill. by author. Ariel, 1960. Subj: Activities – dancing. Character traits – being different. Illness.

What's he been up to now? ill. by author. Dial Pr., 1961. Subj: Animals – elephants. Friendship.

Ferraro, Renato. *Alex, the amazing juggler* (Gianni, Peg)

Ferro, Beatriz. *Caught in the rain* ill. by Michele Sambin. Doubleday, 1980. Subj: Weather – rain.

Fiddle-i-fee: *a traditional American chant* ill. by Diane Stanley. Little, 1979. Subj: Animals. Cumulative tales. Folk and fairy tales.

Field, Eugene. *Wynken, Blynken and Nod* ill. by Barbara Cooney. Hastings, 1964. Subj: Poetry, rhyme. Sea and seashore. Sleep.

Field, Rachel Lyman. *Prayer for a child* ill. by Elizabeth Orton Jones. Macmillan, 1944. Subj: Caldecott award book. Religion.

Fields, Alice. *Insects* ill. by David Hurrell. Watts, 1980. Subj: Insects.

Fife, Dale. *Adam's ABC* ill. by Don Robertson. Coward, 1971. Subj: ABC books. City. Ethnic groups in the U.S. – Afro-Americans.

Follow that ghost! ill. by Joan Drescher. Dutton, 1979. Subj: Ghosts. Problem solving.

The little park ill. by Janet LaSalle. Albert Whitman, 1973. Subj: Animals. Ecology. Progress.

Fifield, Flora. *Pictures for the palace* ill. by Nola Langner. Vanguard, 1957. Subj: Art. Foreign lands – Japan.

Finfer, Celentha. *Grandmother dear* by Celentha Finfer, Esther Wasserberg and Florence Weinberg; ill. by Roy Mathews. Follett, 1966. Subj: Activities – babysitting. Family life – grandparents, great-grandparents. Poetry, rhyme.

Fink, Dale Borman. *Mr. Silver and Mrs. Gold* ill. by Shirley Chan. Human Sciences Pr., 1980. Subj: Friendship. Old age.

Finsand, Mary Jane. *The town that moved* ill. by Reg Sandland. Carolrhoda, 1983. Subj: City. Moving.

Fire ill. by Michael Ricketts. Grosset, 1972. Subj: Fire.

The firebird retold and ill. by Moira Kemp. Godine, 1984. Subj: Behavior – stealing. Folk and fairy tales. Magic. Royalty.

The firebird: *and other Russian fairy tales* ill. by Boris Zvorykin; ed. by Jacqueline Onassis. Viking, 1978. Subj: Folk and fairy tales. Foreign lands – Russia.

Firehouse ill. by Zokeisha; ed. by Kate Klimo. Simon and Schuster, 1983. Subj: Careers – firefighters. Fire. Format, unusual – cardboard pages. Houses.

Firmin, Peter. *Basil Brush and a dragon* ill. by author. Prentice-Hall, 1978. Subj: Animals – foxes. Animals – moles. Dragons. Imagination.

Basil Brush and the windmills ill. by author. Prentice-Hall, 1980. Subj: Animals – foxes. Animals – moles. Ecology.

Basil Brush finds treasure ill. by author. Prentice-Hall, 1979. Subj: Animals – foxes. Animals – moles. Seasons – summer.

Basil Brush gets a medal ill. by author. Prentice-Hall, 1978. Subj: Animals – foxes. Animals – moles. Cumulative tales.

Basil Brush goes flying ill. by author. Prentice-Hall, 1977. Subj: Airplanes, airports. Animals – foxes. Animals – moles. Behavior – mistakes. Helicopters.

Chicken stew ill. by author. Merrimack, 1982. Subj: Activities – gardening. Animals – wolves. Birds – chickens.

Noggin and the whale (Postgate, Oliver)

Noggin the king (Postgate, Oliver)

First graces ill. by Tasha Tudor. Walck, 1955. Subj: Poetry, rhyme. Religion.

First prayers ill. by Anna Maria Magagna. Macmillan, 1983. Subj: Poetry, rhyme. Religion.

First prayers ill. by Tasha Tudor. Oxford Univ. Pr., 1952. Subj: Poetry, rhyme. Religion.

Fischer, Hans. *The birthday* ill. by author. Harcourt, 1954. Subj: Animals. Birthdays.

Puss in boots (Perrault, Charles)

Fischer, Vera Kistiakowsky. *One way is down: a book about gravity* ill. by Ward Brackett. Little, 1967. Subj: Concepts – weight. Science.

Fischer-Nagel, Andreas. *A kitten is born* (Fischer-Nagel, Heiderose)

Fischer-Nagel, Heiderose. *A kitten is born* by Heiderose and Andreas Fischer-Nagel; tr. from German by Andrea Mernan; photos. by authors. Putnam's, 1983. Subj: Animals – cats. Science.

Fischtrom, Harvey *see* Zemach, Harve

Fish, Hans. *Pitschi, the kitten who always wanted to do something else* ill. by author. Harcourt, 1953. Subj: Animals – cats. Behavior – dissatisfaction.

Fish, Helen Dean. *Animals of the Bible* ill. by Dorothy Pulis Lathrop. Lippincott, 1937. Subj: Caldecott award book.

Four and twenty blackbirds ill. by Robert Lawson. Stokes, 1937. Subj: Caldecott award honor book. Nursery rhymes.

When the root children wake up ill. by Sibylle Von Olfers. Lippincott, 1930. Subj: Elves and little people. Seasons – spring.

Fisher, Aileen. *And a sunflower grew* ill. by Trina Schart Hyman; lettering by Paul Taylor. Noble, 1977. Subj: Flowers. Plants. Poetry, rhyme. Science.

Anybody home? ill. by Susan Bonners. Crowell, 1980. Subj: Character traits – curiosity. Poetry, rhyme.

Arbor day ill. by Nonny Hogrogian. Crowell, 1965. Subj: Holidays. Trees.

As the leaves fall down ill. by Barbara Smith. Noble, 1977. Subj: Plants. Science. Seasons. Trees.

Best little house ill. by Arnold Spilka. Crowell, 1966. Subj: Houses. Moving. Poetry, rhyme.

Cricket in the thicket ill. by Feodor Rojankovsky. Scribner's, 1963. Subj: Poetry, rhyme.

Do bears have mothers too? ill. by Eric Carle. Crowell, 1973. Subj: Animals. Family life – mothers. Poetry, rhyme.

Going barefoot ill. by Adrienne Adams. Crowell, 1960. Subj: Poetry, rhyme. Seasons.

I like weather ill. by Janina Domanska. Crowell, 1963. Subj: Animals – dogs. Poetry, rhyme. Weather.

I stood upon a mountain ill. by Blair Lent. Crowell, 1979. Subj: Seasons. World.

I wonder how, I wonder why ill. by Carol Barker. Abelard-Schuman, 1963. Subj: Poetry, rhyme.

In one door and out the other: a book of poems ill. by Lillian Hoban. Crowell, 1969. Subj: Family life. Poetry, rhyme.

In the middle of the night ill. by Adrienne Adams. Crowell, 1965. Subj: Night. Poetry, rhyme.

In the woods, in the meadow, in the sky ill. by Margot Tomes. Scribner's, 1965. Subj: Poetry, rhyme.

Like nothing at all ill. by Leonard Weisgard. Crowell, 1962. Subj: Poetry, rhyme. Science. Seasons.

Listen, rabbit ill. by Symeon Shimin. Crowell, 1964. Subj: Animals – rabbits. Poetry, rhyme.

My mother and I ill. by Kazue Mizumura. Crowell, 1967. Subj: Family life – mothers. Poetry, rhyme. Seasons – spring.

Mysteries in the garden ill. by Ati Forberg; lettering by Paul Taylor. Noble, 1977. Subj: Plants. Poetry, rhyme. Science.

Now that spring is here ill. by Symeon Shimin; lettering by Paul Taylor. Noble, 1977. Subj: Plants. Poetry, rhyme. Science. Seasons – spring.

Petals yellow and petals red ill. by Albert John Pucci; lettering by Paul Taylor. Noble, 1977. Subj: Flowers. Poetry, rhyme. Science.

Plant magic ill. by Barbara Cooney; lettering by Paul Taylor. Noble, 1977. Subj: Plants. Poetry, rhyme. Science.

Prize performance ill by Margot Tomes. Noble, 1977. Subj: Plants. Poetry, rhyme. Science.

Rabbits, rabbits ill. by Gail Niemann. Harper, 1983. Subj: Animals – rabbits. Poetry, rhyme.

Seeds on the go ill. by Hans Zander; lettering by Paul Taylor. Noble, 1977. Subj: Plants. Poetry, rhyme. Science.

Sing, little mouse ill. by Symeon Shimin. Crowell, 1969. Subj: Animals – mice. Poetry, rhyme.

Skip around the year ill. by Gioia Fiammenghi. Crowell, 1967. Subj: Holidays. Poetry, rhyme.

Swords and daggers ill. by James Higa; lettering by Paul Taylor. Noble, 1977. Subj: Plants. Poetry, rhyme. Science.

A tree with a thousand uses ill. by James R. Endicott. Noble, 1977. Subj: Poetry, rhyme. Science. Trees.

We went looking ill. by Marie Angel. Crowell, 1968. Subj: Animals. Birds. Insects – ladybugs. Plants. Poetry, rhyme.

Where does everyone go? ill. by Adrienne Adams. Crowell, 1961. Subj: Animals. Hibernation. Poetry, rhyme. Seasons – winter.

Fisher, Leonard Everett. *Boxes! Boxes!* ill. by author. Viking, 1984. Subj: Concepts. Concepts – color. Counting. Poetry, rhyme.

A head full of hats ill. by author. Dial Pr., 1962. Subj: Clothing.

Pumpers, boilers, hooks and ladders: a book of fire engines ill. by author. Dial Pr., 1961. Subj: Careers – firefighters. Trucks.

The seven days of creation ill. by the author. Holiday, 1981. Adapted from the Bible. Subj: Religion.

Star signs ill. by author. Holiday, 1983. Subj: Folk and fairy tales. Zodiac.

Fitch, Florence Mary. *A book about God* ill. by Leonard Weisgard. Lothrop, 1953. Subj: Religion.

Fitter, Richard. *The butterfly ball and the grasshopper's feast* (Aldridge, Alan)

Fitzhugh, Louise. *Bang, bang, you're dead* by Louise Fitzhugh and Sandra Scoppetone; ill. by Louise Fitzhugh. Harper, 1969. Subj: Activities – playing. Cowboys. Violence, anti-violence. War. Weapons.

I am five ill. by author. Delacorte, 1978. Subj: Self-concept.

I am three ill. by Susanna Natti. Delacorte, 1982. Subj: Self-concept.

Fitzsimons, Cecilia. *My first birds* ill. by author. Harper, 1985. Subj: Birds. Format, unusual – cardboard pages.

My first butterflies ill. by author. Harper, 1985. Subj: Format, unusual – cardboard pages. Insects – butterflies, caterpillars.

Flack, Marjorie. *Angus and the cat* ill. by author. Doubleday, 1931. Subj: Animals – cats. Animals – dogs. Character traits – completing things. Character traits – curiosity.

Angus and the ducks ill. by author. Doubleday, 1930. Subj: Animals – dogs. Birds – ducks. Character traits – conceit. Character traits – curiosity.

Angus lost ill. by author. Doubleday, 1932. Subj: Animals – dogs. Behavior – lost. Seasons – winter.

Ask Mr. Bear ill. by author. Macmillan, 1932. Subj: Animals. Animals – bears. Birthdays. Emotions – love. Family life – mothers.

The boats on the river ill. by author. Viking, 1946. Subj: Boats, ships. Caldecott award honor book. Rivers.

The new pet ill. by author. Doubleday, 1943. Subj: Babies. Family life.

The restless robin ill. by author. Houghton, 1937. Subj: Birds – robins. Music.

The story about Ping ill. by Kurt Wiese. Viking, 1933. Subj: Behavior – misbehavior. Birds – ducks. Foreign lands – China.

Tim Tadpole and the great bullfrog ill. by author. Doubleday, 1934. Subj: Frogs and toads.

Wait for William ill. by Marjorie Flack and Richard A. Holberg. Houghton, 1934. Subj: Circus. Family life. Parades.

William and his kitten ill. by author. Houghton, 1938. Subj: Animals – cats.

Flanders, Michael. *Creatures great and small* ill. by Marcello Minale. Holt, 1965. Subj: Animals. Birds. Poetry, rhyme.

Fleischman, Paul. *The animal hedge* ill. by Lydia Dabcovich. Dutton, 1983. Subj: Activities – working. Farms. Folk and fairy tales.

The birthday tree ill. by Marcia Sewall. Harper, 1979. Subj: Birthdays. Trees.

Fleischman, Sid. *Kate's secret riddle* ill. by Barbara Bottner. Watts, 1977. Subj: Illness. Riddles.

Longbeard the wizard ill. by Charles Bragg. Little, 1970. Subj: Royalty. Wizards.

Fleisher, Robbin. *Quilts in the attic* ill. by Ati Forberg. Macmillan, 1978. Subj: Family life. Games.

Fleishman, Seymour. *Too hot in Potzburg* ill. by author. Walker, 1981. Subj: Animals – bears. Machines.

Fletcher, Elizabeth. *The little goat* ill. by Deborah and Kilmeny Niland. Grosset, 1977. Subj: Animals – goats. Behavior – lost.

What am I? ill. by Deborah and Kilmeny Niland. Grosset, 1977. Subj: Animals. Riddles.

Flora, James. *The day the cow sneezed* ill. by author. Harcourt, 1957. Subj: Animals. Cumulative tales. Humor.

Fishing with dad ill. by author. Harcourt, 1967. Subj: Boats, ships. Careers – fishermen.

Grandpa's farm: 4 tall tales ill. by author. Harcourt, 1965. Subj: Family life – grandparents, great-grandparents. Farms. Humor.

Grandpa's ghost stories ill. by author. Atheneum. Subj: Family life – grandparents, great-grandparents. Ghosts. Witches.

Leopold, the see-through crumbpicker ill. by author. Harcourt, 1961. Subj: Monsters. Zoos.

My friend Charlie ill. by author. Harcourt, 1964. Subj: Humor.

Sherwood walks home ill. by author. Harcourt, 1966. Subj: Toys – teddy bears.

Florian, Douglas. *Airplane ride* ill. by author. Crowell, 1984. Subj: Activities – flying. Airplanes, airports.

A bird can fly ill. by author. Greenwillow, 1980. Subj: Animals. Science.

The city ill. by author. Crowell, 1982. Subj: City. Wordless.

People working ill. by author. Crowell, 1983. Subj: Activities – working. Careers.

Flory, Jane. *The bear on the doorstep* ill. by Carolyn Croll. Houghton, 1980. Subj: Animals – bears. Animals – rabbits. Houses.

The unexpected grandchild ill. by Carolyn Croll. Houghton, 1977. Subj: Behavior – sharing. Family life – grandparents, great-grandparents.

We'll have a friend for lunch ill. by Carolyn Croll. Houghton, 1974. Subj: Animals – cats. Food. Friendship.

Flot, Jeannette B. *Princess Kalina and the hedgehog* adapt. by Frances Marshall; ill. by Dorothée Duntze. Faber, 1981. Subj: Animals – hedgehogs. Character traits – cleanliness. Folk and fairy tales. Magic. Royalty.

Flöthe, Louise Lee. *The Indian and his pueblo* ill. by Richard Floethe. Scribner's, 1960. Subj: Ethnic groups in the U.S. – Indians.

Flournoy, Valerie. *The best time of day* ill. by George Ford. Random House, 1979. Subj: Activities. Ethnic groups in the U.S. – Afro-Americans. Family life.

The twins strike back ill. by Diane de Groat. Dial Pr., 1980. Subj: Ethnic groups in the U.S. – Afro-Americans. Family life. Sibling rivalry. Twins.

Flower, Phyllis. *Barn owl* ill. by Cherryl Pape. Harper, 1978. Subj: Birds – owls. Science.

Floyd, Lucy. *Agatha's alphabet, with her very own dictionary* ill. by Dora Leder. Rand McNally, 1975. Subj: ABC books. Dictionaries.

Foley, Bernice Williams. *The gazelle and the hunter: a folk tale from Persia* ill. by Diana Magnuson. Children's Pr., 1980. Subj: Folk and fairy tales. Foreign lands – Persia.

A walk among clouds: a folk tale from China ill. by Mina Gow McLean. Children's Pr., 1980. Subj: Folk and fairy tales. Foreign lands – China.

Folsom, Marcia. *Easy as pie: a guessing game of sayings* by Marcia and Michael Folsom; ill. by Jack Kent. Houghton, 1985. Subj: Humor. Language.

Folsom, Michael. *Easy as pie* (Folsom, Marcia)

Q is for duck (Elting, Mary)

Fontaine, Jan. *The spaghetti tree* ill. by Anne Marshall Runyon. Talespinner, 1980. Subj: Activities – gardening. Food. Imagination.

Fontaine, Jean de La *see* La Fontaine, Jean de

Fontane, Theodore. *Sir Ribbeck of Ribbeck of Havelland* tr. from German by Elizabeth Shub; ill. by Nonny Hogrogian. Macmillan, 1969. Subj: Character traits – generosity. Poetry, rhyme.

Ford, George. *Walk on!* (Williamson, Mel)

Ford, Lauren. *The ageless story* ill. by author. Dodd, 1940. Subj: Caldecott award honor book.

Foreman, Michael. *Cat and canary* ill. by author. Dial Pr., 1985. Subj: Animals – cats. Birds – canaries.

The general (Charters, Janet)

Land of dreams ill. by author. Holt, 1982. Subj: Dreams.

Moose ill. by author. Pantheon, 1972. Subj: Animals – bears. Animals – moose. Birds – eagles. Violence, anti-violence.

The two giants ill. by author. Pantheon, 1967. Subj: Giants.

War and peas ill by author. Crowell, 1974. Subj: Royalty. War.

Forest, Charlotte B. De *see* DeForest, Charlotte B.

Forrester, Victoria. *The magnificent moo* ill. by author. Atheneum, 1983. Subj: Animals – bulls, cows. Animals – cats. Noise, sounds.

Oddward ill. by author. Atheneum, 1982. Subj: Holidays. Reptiles – snakes.

The touch said hello ill. by author. Atheneum, 1982. Subj: Seasons – spring.

Words to keep against the night ill. by author. Atheneum, 1983. Subj: Poetry, rhyme.

Foster, Doris Van Liew. *A pocketful of seasons* ill. by Tālivaldis Stubis. Lothrop, 1961. Subj: Behavior – saving things. Seasons.

Tell me, Mr. Owl ill. by Helen Stone. Lothrop, 1957. Subj: Birds – owls. Holidays – Halloween.

Foster, Marian Curtis *see* Mariana

Foster, Sally. *A pup grows up* photos. by author. Dodd, 1984. Subj: Animals – dogs. Pets.

Foulds, Elfrida Vipont. *The elephant and the bad baby* ill. by Raymond Briggs. Coward, 1969. Subj: Animals – elephants. Babies. Behavior – stealing. Cumulative tales.

Fournier, Catharine. *The coconut thieves* ill. by Janina Domanska. Scribner's, 1964. Subj: Animals. Folk and fairy tales. Foreign lands – Africa.

Fowler, Richard. *Cat's story* ill. by author. Grosset, 1985. Subj: Animals – cats. Format, unusual – cardboard pages. Poetry, rhyme.

Inspector Smart gets the message! ill. by author. Little, 1983. Subj: Birthdays. Problem solving.

Fowles, John. *Cinderella* (Perrault, Charles)

Fox, Charles Philip. *Come to the circus* photos. by author. Reilly and Lee, 1960. Subj: Circus.

A fox in the house photos. by author. Reilly and Lee, 1960. Subj: Animals – foxes.

Mr. Stripes the gopher photos. by author. Reilly and Lee, 1962. Subj: Animals. Family life. Seasons.

Fox, Dorothea Warren. *Follow me the leader* ill. by author. Parents, 1968. Subj: Games. Poetry, rhyme.

Fox, Paula. *Maurice's room* ill. by Ingrid Fetz. Macmillan, 1966. Subj: Behavior – collecting things.

Fox, Siv Cedering. *The blue horse and other night poems* ill. by Donald Carrick. Seabury Pr., 1979. Subj: Bedtime. Poetry, rhyme.

The fox went out on a chilly night ill. by Peter Spier. Doubleday, 1961. Subj: Animals – foxes. Caldecott award honor book. Folk and fairy tales. Songs. Toys – teddy bears.

Françoise *see* Seignobosc, Françoise

Frances, Esteban. *The thread soldiers* (Heathers, Anne)

Francis, Anna B. *Pleasant dreams* ill. by author. Holt, 1983. Subj: Dreams. Monsters. Toys.

Francis, Frank. *The magic wallpaper* ill. by author. Abelard-Schuman, 1970. Subj: Animals. Behavior – lost. Dreams. Imagination.

Natasha's new doll ill. by author. O'Hara, 1971. Subj: Folk and fairy tales. Foreign lands – Russia. Toys – dolls. Witches.

Frank, Josette. *More poems to read to the very young* ill. by Dagmar Wilson. Random House, 1968. Subj: Poetry, rhyme.

Frankel, Bernice. *Half-As-Big and the tiger* ill. by Leonard Weisgard. Watts, 1961. Subj: Animals – deer. Animals – tigers. Character traits – cleverness.

Frankenberg, Lloyd. *Wings of rhyme* ill. by Alan Benjamin. Funk & Wagnalls, 1967. Subj: Nursery rhymes. Poetry, rhyme.

Frasconi, Antonio. *See again, say again: a picture book in four languages* ill. by author. Harcourt, 1964. Subj: Foreign languages.

See and say: a picture book in four languages ill. by author. Harcourt, 1955. Subj: Foreign languages.

The snow and the sun, la nieve y el sol: a South American folk rhyme in two languages ill. by author. Harcourt, 1961. Subj: Folk and fairy tales. Foreign lands – South America. Foreign languages. Poetry, rhyme.

Fraser, Ferrin. *Jungle animals* (Buck, Frank)

Fraser, James Howard. *Los Posadas: a Christmas story* ill. by Nick De Grazia. Northland, 1963. Subj: Ethnic groups in the U.S. – Mexican-Americans. Foreign lands – Mexico. Holidays – Christmas. Religion.

Fraser, Kathleen. *Adam's world, San Francisco* ill. by Helen D. Hipshman. Albert Whitman, 1971. Subj: City. Ethnic groups in the U.S. – Afro-Americans. Family life.

Freedman, Russell. *Dinosaurs and their young* ill. by Leslie Morrill. Holiday, 1983. Subj: Dinosaurs.

Farm babies photos. by author. Holiday, 1981. Subj: Animals. Farms.

Hanging on: how animals carry their young ill. by author. Holiday, 1977. Subj: Animals. Science.

Tooth and claw: a look at animal weapons photos. by author. Holiday, 1980. Subj: Animals. Science.

When winter comes ill. by Pamela Johnson. Dutton, 1981. Subj: Animals. Science. Seasons – winter.

Freedman, Sally. *Monster birthday party* ill. by Diane Dawson. Albert Whitman, 1983. Subj: Birthdays. Monsters. Parties.

Freeman, Don. *Add-a-line alphabet* ill. by author. Golden Gate, 1968. Subj: ABC books. Animals.

Beady Bear ill. by author. Viking, 1954. Subj: Behavior – running away. Toys – teddy bears.

Bearymore ill. by author. Viking, 1976. Subj: Animals – bears. Circus. Hibernation.

The chalk box story ill. by author. Lippincott, 1976. Subj: Activities – painting. Concepts – color.

Come again, pelican ill. by author. Viking, 1961. Subj: Birds – pelicans. Sea and seashore.

Corduroy ill. by author. Viking, 1968. Subj: Clothing. Emotions – love. Ethnic groups in the U.S. – Afro-Americans. Stores. Toys – teddy bears.

Cyrano the crow ill. by author. Viking, 1960. Subj: Birds – crows.

Dandelion ill. by author. Viking, 1964. Subj: Animals – lions. Character traits – appearance. Parties. Weather – rain.

Fly high, fly low ill. by author. Viking, 1957. Subj: Birds. Caldecott award honor book. City.

Forever laughter ill. by author. Golden Gate, 1970. Subj: Humor. Clowns, Jesters. Royalty. Wordless.

The guard mouse ill. by author. Viking, 1967. Subj: Animals – mice. Birthdays. City. Foreign lands – England.

Hattie the backstage bat ill. by author. Viking, 1970. Subj: Animals – bats. Theater.

Mop Top ill. by author. Viking, 1955. Subj: Birthdays. Careers – barbers. Hair. Poetry, rhyme.

The night the lights went out ill. by author. Viking, 1958. Subj: Careers. Night. Power failure. Seasons – winter.

Norman the doorman ill. by author. Viking, 1959. Subj: Animals – mice. Art. Museums.

The paper party ill. by author. Viking, 1974. Subj: Imagination. Parties. Puppets.

Pet of the Met (Freeman, Lydia)

A pocket for Corduroy ill. by author. Viking, 1978. Subj: Clothing. Ethnic groups in the U.S. – Afro-Americans. Laundry. Toys – teddy bears.

Quiet! There's a canary in the library ill. by author. Golden Gate, 1969. Subj: Birds – canaries. Emotions – embarrassment. Imagination. Libraries.

A rainbow of my own ill. by author. Viking, 1966. Subj: Concepts – color. Weather – rainbows.

The seal and the slick ill. by author. Viking, 1974. Subj: Animals – seals. Character traits – kindness to animals. Ecology. Oil.

Ski pup ill. by author. Viking, 1963. Subj: Animals – dogs. Foreign lands – Switzerland. Sports – skiing.

Space witch ill. by author. Viking, 1959. Subj: Holidays – Halloween. Space and space ships. Witches.

Tilly Witch ill. by author. Viking, 1969. Subj: Character traits – meanness. Holidays – Halloween. Witches.

The turtle and the dove ill. by author. Viking, 1964. Subj: Birds – doves. Reptiles – turtles.

Will's quill ill. by author. Viking, 1975. Subj: Birds – geese. Foreign lands – England. Shakespeare. Theater.

Freeman, Ira. *The sun, the moon and the stars* (Freeman, Mae)

You will go to the moon (Freeman, Mae)

Freeman, Jean Todd. *Cynthia and the unicorn* ill. by Leonard Weisgard. Norton, 1967. Subj: Holidays – Christmas. Mythical creatures. Poetry, rhyme.

Freeman, Lydia. *Pet of the Met* ill. by Don Freeman. Viking, 1953. Subj: Animals – mice. Music. Theater.

Freeman, Mae. *The sun, the moon and the stars* by Mae and Ira Freeman; ill. by René Martin. Rev. ed. Random House, 1979. Subj: Moon. Science. Stars. Sun.

You will go to the moon ill. by Lee J. Ames. Rev. ed. Random House, 1971. Subj: Moon. Space and space ships.

Fregosi, Claudia. *The happy horse* ill. by author. Greenwillow, 1977. Subj: Animals – horses. Seasons – fall.

The pumpkin sparrow: adapt. from a Korean folktale ill. by author. Morrow, 1977. Subj: Birds – sparrows. Folk and fairy tales. Foreign lands – Korea.

Snow maiden ill. by author. Prentice-Hall, 1979. Subj: Folk and fairy tales. Foreign lands – Russia.

Fremlin, Robert. *Three friends* ill. by Wallace Tripp. Little, 1975. Subj: Animals – cats. Animals – pigs. Animals – squirrels. Circus. Clothing. Friendship. Problem solving.

French, Fiona. *The blue bird* ill. by author. Walck, 1972. Subj: Birds.

Hunt the thimble ill. by author. Oxford Univ. Pr., 1978. Subj: Games. Participation.

French, Paul *see* Asimov, Isaac

Freschet, Berniece. *The ants go marching* ill. by Stefan Martin. Scribner's, 1973. Subj: Activities – picnicking. Counting. Insects – ants. Poetry, rhyme.

Bear mouse ill. by Donald Carrick. Scribner's, 1973. Subj: Animals – mice. Science.

Bernard of Scotland Yard ill. by Gina Freschet. Scribner's, 1978. Subj: Animals – mice. Foreign lands – England. Problem solving.

Elephant and friends ill. by Glen Rounds. Scribner's, 1978. Subj: Animals – elephants. Character traits – cleverness.

Five fat raccoons ill. by Irene Brady. Scribner's, 1980. Subj: Animals – raccoons.

The little woodcock ill. by Leonard Weisgard. Scribner's, 1967. Subj: Birds. Science.

Moose baby ill. by Jim Arnosky. Putnam's, 1979. Subj: Animals – moose. Science.

The old bullfrog ill. by Roger Antoine Duvoisin. Scribner's, 1968. Subj: Frogs and toads.

Possum baby ill. by Jim Arnosky. Putnam's, 1978. Subj: Animals – possums.

Turtle pond ill. by Donald Carrick. Scribner's, 1971. Subj: Reptiles – turtles.

The watersnake ill. by Susanne Suba. Scribner's, 1979. Subj: Reptiles – snakes.

The web in the grass ill. by Roger Antoine Duvoisin. Scribner's, 1972. Subj: Spiders.

Where's Henrietta's hen? ill. by Lorinda Bryan Cauley. Putnam's, 1980. Subj: Animals. Birds – chickens. Counting. Farms.

Wood duck baby ill. by Jim Arnosky. Putnam's, 1983. Subj: Birds – ducks. Science.

Freudberg, Judy. *Some, more, most* ill. by Richard Hefter. Larousse, 1976. Subj: Concepts.

Fribourg, Marjorie G. *Ching-Ting and the ducks* ill. by Artur Marokvia. Sterling, 1957. Subj: Behavior – growing up. Birds – ducks. Foreign lands – China.

Friedman, Estelle. *Boy who lived in a cave* ill. by Theresa Sherman. Putnam's, 1960. Subj: Caves. Family life. Houses.

Friedman, Ina R. *How my parents learned to eat* ill. by Allen Say. Houghton, 1984. Subj: Family life.

Friedman, Judi. *The eels' strange journey* ill. by Gail Owens. Crowell, 1976. Subj: Fish. Science.

Noises in the woods ill. by John Hamberger. Dutton, 1979. Subj: Forest, woods. Noise, sounds.

Friedman, Warner. *Uncle Hugh* (Gelman, Rita Golden)

Friedrich, Otto. *The Easter bunny that overslept* (Friedrich, Priscilla)

The marshmallow ghosts (Friedrich, Priscilla)

The wishing well in the woods (Friedrich, Priscilla)

Friedrich, Priscilla. *The Easter bunny that overslept* by Priscilla and Otto Friedrich; ill. by Adrienne Adams. Lothrop, 1957. Subj: Holidays – Easter.

The marshmallow ghosts by Priscilla and Otto Friedrich; ill. by Louis Slobodkin. Lothrop, 1960. Subj: Ghosts. Holidays – Halloween.

The wishing well in the woods by Priscilla and Otto Friedrich; ill. by Roger Antoine Duvoisin. Lothrop, 1961. Subj: Animals. Behavior – wishing.

The friendly beasts and A partridge in a pear tree ill. by Virginia Parsons; calligraphy by Sheila Waters. Doubleday, 1977. Subj: Holidays – Christmas. Music. Religion. Songs.

Friskey, Margaret. *Birds we know* ill. with photos. Children's Pr., 1981. Subj: Birds. Science.

Chicken Little, count-to-ten ill. by Katherine Evans. Children's Pr., 1946. Subj: Counting.

Indian Two Feet and his eagle feather ill. by John and Lucy Hawkinson. Children's Pr., 1967. Subj: Ethnic groups in the U.S. – Indians.

Indian Two Feet and his horse ill. by Katherine Evans. Children's Pr., 1959. Subj: Animals – horses. Ethnic groups in the U.S. – Indians.

Indian Two Feet and the wolf cubs ill. by John Hawkinson. Children's Pr., 1971. Subj: Animals – wolves. Ethnic groups in the U.S. – Indians.

Indian Two Feet rides alone ill. by John Hawkinson. Children's Pr., 1980. Subj: Character traits – pride. Ethnic groups in the U.S. – Indians.

Mystery of the gate sign ill. by Katherine Evans. Children's Pr., 1958. Subj: Activities – reading. Animals – rabbits.

Seven diving ducks ill. by Jean Morey. Children's Pr., 1965. Subj: Birds – ducks. Counting.

Three sides and the round one ill. by Mary Gehr. Children's Pr., 1973. Subj: Concepts – shape.

Frith, Michael K. *I'll teach my dog 100 words* ill. by P. D. Eastman. Random House, 1973. Subj: Animals – dogs. Humor. Poetry, rhyme.

Some of us walk, some fly, some swim ill. by author. Random House, 1971. Subj: Animals. Science.

Fritz, Jean. *The good giants and the bad Pukwudgies* ill. by Tomie de Paola. Putnam's, 1982. Subj: Ethnic groups in the U.S. – Indians. Folk and fairy tales. Giants.

A frog he would a-wooing go (folk-song). *Frog went a-courtin'* adapt. and ill. by Feodor Rojankovsky. Harcourt, 1955. Subj: Caldecott award book. Frogs and toads. Humor. Songs.

From King Boggen's hall to nothing-at-all: *a collection of improbable houses and unusual places found in traditional rhymes and limericks* ill. by Blair Lent. Little, 1967. Subj: Animals. Humor. Nursery rhymes.

Froman, Robert. *Angles are easy as pie* ill. by Byron Barton. Crowell, 1976. Subj: Concepts.

A game of functions ill. by Enrico Arno. Crowell, 1975. Subj: Concepts.

Seeing things: a book of poems ill. by author; lettering by Ray Barber. Crowell, 1974. Subj: Concepts. Poetry, rhyme.

Froment, Eugène. *The story of a round loaf* adapt. and ill. by Kathleen Rebek. Prentice-Hall, 1979. Subj: Behavior – misbehavior. Foreign lands – France.

Fromm, Lilo. *Muffel and Plums* ill. by author. Macmillan, 1972. Subj: Animals. Wordless.

Frost, Erica *see* Supraner, Robyn

Frost, Robert. *Stopping by woods on a snowy evening* ill. by Susan Jeffers. Dutton, 1978. Subj: Forest, woods. Poetry, rhyme. Seasons – winter.

Fry, Christopher. *The boat that mooed* ill. by Leonard Weisgard. Macmillan, 1965. Subj: Boats, ships. Weather – fog.

The boy and the magic (Colette)

Frye, Dean. *Days of sunshine, days of rain* ill. by Roger Antoine Duvoisin. McGraw-Hill, 1965. Subj: Theater. Weather.

Fuchs, Erich. *Journey to the moon* ill. by author. Delacorte Pr., 1969. Translation of Hier Apollo 11. Subj: Moon. Space and space ships. Wordless.

Fuchshuber, Annegert. *The wishing hat* ill. by author. Morrow, 1977. Translation of Korbinian mit dem Wunschhut by Elizabeth D. Crawford. Subj: Behavior – wishing. Humor. Magic.

Fujikawa, Gyo. *Come follow me...to the secret world of elves and fairies and gnomes and trolls* ill. by author. Grosset, 1979. Subj: Elves and little people. Fairies. Poetry, rhyme. Trolls.

Gyo Fujikawa's A to Z picture book ill. by author. Grosset, 1974. Subj: ABC books.

Let's grow a garden ill. by author. Grosset, 1978. Subj: Activities – gardening. Format, unusual – cardboard pages.

Millie's secret ill. by author. Grosset, 1978. Subj: Animals – dogs. Format, unusual – cardboard pages. Wordless.

My favorite thing ill. by author. Grosset, 1978. Subj: Activities. Format, unusual – cardboard pages. Wordless.

Sam's all-wrong day ill. by author. Grosset, 1982. Subj: Behavior – bad day.

Shags finds a kitten ill. by author. Grosset, 1983. Subj: Animals – cats. Animals – dogs. Emotions – loneliness.

Surprise! Surprise! ill. by author. Grosset, 1978. Subj: Activities. Format, unusual – cardboard pages.

That's not fair! ill. by author. Grosset, 1983. Subj: Activities – playing. Seasons – winter.

Fujita, Tamao. *The boy and the bird* tr. from Japanese by Kiyoko Tucker; ill. by Chiyo Ono. Harper, 1972. Subj: Birds. Character traits – freedom. Foreign lands – Japan. Pets.

Funai, Mamoru. *Moke and Poki in the rain forest* ill. by author. Harper, 1972. Subj: Elves and little people. Hawaii.

Funazaki, Yasuko. *Baby owl* ill. by Shuji Tateishi. Methune, 1980. Subj: Birds – owls. Emotions – loneliness.

Funk, Thompson *see* Funk, Tom

Funk, Tom. *I read signs* ill. by author. Holiday, 1962. Subj: Activities – reading.

Furchgott, Terry. *Phoebe and the hot water bottles* by Terry Furchgott and Linda Dawson; ill. by Terry Furchgott. Elsevier-Dutton, 1979. Subj: Animals – dogs. Character traits – bravery. Pets.

Futamata, Eigorō. *How not to catch a mouse* ill. by author. Weatherhill, 1972. Translation of Nezumi wa tsukamaru ka. Subj: Animals. Animals – mice.

Fyson, Nance Lui. *A family in China* ill. with photos. Lerner, 1985. Orig. published by A & C Black, dist. by Global Library Mktg. Services, 1982 under the title: Chun Ling in China. Subj: Foreign lands – China.

Gackenbach, Dick. *Annie and the mud monster* ill. by author. Lothrop, 1982. Subj: Parties.

Arabella and Mr. Crack ill. by author. Macmillan, 1982. A retelling of Joseph Jacob's Master of all masters. Subj: Behavior – misunderstanding. Folk and fairy tales.

A bag full of pups ill. by author. Houghton, 1981. Subj: Animals – dogs.

Binky gets a car ill. by author. Houghton, 1983. Subj: Behavior – carelessness. Birthdays.

Claude and Pepper ill. by author. Coward, 1976. Subj: Animals – dogs. Behavior – running away.

Claude the dog ill. by author. Seabury Pr., 1974. Subj: Animals – dogs. Behavior – sharing. Holidays – Christmas.

Crackle, Gluck and the sleeping toad ill. by author. Seabury Pr., 1979. Subj: Behavior – lying. Farms. Frogs and toads.

The dog and the deep dark woods ill. by author. Harper, 1984. Subj: Animals – dogs. Character traits – pride.

Harry and the terrible whatzit ill. by author. Seabury Pr., 1977. Subj: Emotions – fear. Imagination. Monsters.

Hattie be quiet, Hattie be good ill. by author. Harper, 1977. Subj: Animals – rabbits. Behavior. Illness.

Hattie rabbit ill. by author. Harper, 1971. Subj: Animals – rabbits. Behavior – wishing.

Ida Fanfanny ill. by author. Harper, 1978. Subj: Magic. Seasons. Weather.

King Wacky ill. by author. Crown, 1984. Subj: Behavior – misunderstanding. Royalty.

Little bug ill. by author. Houghton, 1981. Subj: Behavior – seeking better things. Insects.

Mr. Wink and his shadow, Ned ill. by author. Harper, 1983. Subj: Shadows.

Mother Rabbit's son Tom ill. by author. Harper, 1978. Subj: Animals – rabbits. Behavior – dissatisfaction. Food. Pets.

Pepper and all the legs ill. by author. Seabury Pr., 1978. Subj: Animals – dogs. Behavior – misbehavior.

The perfect mouse: a Japanese tale ill. by author. Macmillan, 1984. Subj: Animals – mice. Folk and fairy tales. Foreign lands – Japan.

The pig who saw everything ill. by author. Seabury Pr., 1978. Subj: Animals – pigs. Character traits – curiosity. Farms. Humor.

Poppy the panda ill. by author. Houghton, 1984. Subj: Bedtime. Clothing. Toys.

What's Claude doing? ill. by author. Houghton, 1984. Subj: Animals – dogs. Illness.

Gadsby, Oliver. *Little Elephant and Big Mouse* (Cantieni, Benita)

Gaeddert, Lou Ann Bigge. *Noisy Nancy Nora* ill. by Gioia Fiammenghi. Doubleday, 1965. Subj: Behavior. Noise, sounds.

Gág, Flavia. *Chubby's first year* ill. by author. Holt, 1960. Subj: Animals – cats. Days of the week, months of the year.

Gág, Wanda. *ABC bunny* ill. by author; hand lettered by Howard Gág. Doubleday, 1965. Subj: ABC books. Animals – rabbits. Poetry, rhyme.

The funny thing ill. by author. Coward, 1929. Subj: Dragons. Food. Monsters.

Gone is gone ill. by author. Coward, 1935. Subj: Activities – working. Behavior – mistakes.

Jorinda and Joringel (Grimm, Jacob)

Millions of cats ill. by author. Coward, 1928. Subj: Animals – cats. Character traits – practicality. Cumulative tales.

Nothing at all ill. by author. Coward, 1941. Subj: Animals – dogs. Caldecott award honor book. Emotions – loneliness. Magic.

The six swans (Grimm, Jacob)

Snippy and Snappy ill. by author. Coward, 1931. Subj: Animals – mice.

The sorcerer's apprentice ill. by Margot Tomes. Coward, 1979. Subj: Behavior – misbehavior. Folk and fairy tales. Magic.

Gage, Wilson. *The crow and Mrs. Gaddy* ill. by Marylin Hafner. Greenwillow, 1984. Subj: Behavior – trickery. Birds – crows.

Cully Cully and the bear ill. by James Stevenson. Greenwillow, 1983. Subj: Animals – bears. Sports – hunting.

Down in the boondocks ill. by Glen Rounds. Greenwillow, 1977. Subj: Crime. Handicaps – deafness. Poetry, rhyme.

Mrs. Gaddy and the ghost ill. by Marylin Hafner. Greenwillow, 1979. Subj: Ghosts. Imagination.

Galbraith, Kathryn Osebold. *Katie did!* ill. by Ted Ramsey. Atheneum, 1982. Subj: Behavior – misbehavior. Family life. Sibling rivalry.

Spots are special ill. by Diane Dawson. Atheneum, 1976. Subj: Illness. Imagination.

Galdone, Joanna. *Amber day* ill. by Paul Galdone. McGraw-Hill, 1978. Subj: Devil. Folk and fairy tales.

Gertrude, the goose who forgot ill. by Paul Galdone. Watts, 1975. Subj: Behavior – forgetfulness. Birds – geese. Poetry, rhyme.

Honeybee's party ill. by Paul Galdone. Watts, 1972. Subj: Insects – bees. Parties. Spiders.

The little girl and the big bear ill. by Paul Galdone. Houghton, 1980. Subj: Animals – bears. Folk and fairy tales.

The tailypo: a ghost story ill. by Paul Galdone. Seabury Pr., 1977. Subj: Ghosts. Poetry, rhyme.

Galdone, Paul. *The amazing pig: an old Hungarian tale* ill. by author. Houghton, 1981. Subj: Animals – pigs. Folk and fairy tales. Royalty.

Androcles and the lion ill. by author. McGraw-Hill, 1970. Subj: Animals – lions. Character traits – kindness to animals. Folk and fairy tales. Foreign lands – Italy.

Counting carnival (Ziner, Feenie)

The first seven days ill. by Paul Galdone. Crowell, 1962. Subj: Religion.

The greedy old fat man: an American folk tale ill. by author. Houghton, 1983. Subj: Cumulative tales. Folk and fairy tales.

Hans in luck (Grimm, Jacob)

King of the cats: a ghost story by Joseph Jacobs; ill. by adapt. Houghton, 1980. Subj: Animals – cats. Folk and fairy tales. Ghosts.

The life of Jack Sprat, his wife and his cat (Jack Sprat)

The magic porridge pot ill. by Paul Galdone. Seabury Pr., 1976. Subj: Behavior – forgetfulness. Behavior – sharing. Folk and fairy tales. Food. Magic.

The monkey and the crocodile: a Jataka tale from India ill. by author. Seabury Pr., 1969. Subj: Animals – monkeys. Character traits – cleverness. Folk and fairy tales. Reptiles – alligators, crocodiles.

The monster and the tailor: a ghost story ill. by author. Houghton, 1982. An adaptation of Joseph Jacobs' The sprightly tailor. Subj: Careers – tailors. Ghosts. Monsters. Royalty.

Obedient Jack ill. by author. Watts, 1971. Subj: Behavior – mistakes. Family life. Folk and fairy tales.

A strange servant: a Russian folktale tr. by Blanche Ross; ill. by author. Knopf, 1977. Subj: Animals – rabbits. Behavior – trickery. Folk and fairy tales. Foreign lands – Russia.

The table, the donkey and the stick (Grimm, Jacob)

What's in fox's sack? ill. by author. Houghton, 1982. Subj: Character traits – cleverness. Folk and fairy tales.

Galinsky, Ellen. *The baby cardinal* photos. by author. Putnam's, 1977. Subj: Birds – cardinals.

Gallant, Kathryn. *The flute player of Beppu* ill. by Kurt Wiese. Coward, 1960. Subj: Character traits – honesty.

Gallaudet Pre-school Signed English Project. *Nursery rhymes from Mother Goose in signed English* (Mother Goose)

Gallo, Giovanni. *The lazy beaver* ill. by Ermanno Samsa; tr. from Italian by Jane Fior. Putnam's, 1983. Subj: Activities – working. Animals – beavers.

Gambill, Henrietta. *Self-control* ill. by Kathryn Hutton. Rev. ed. Children's Pr., 1982. Subj: Behavior.

Gammell, Stephen. *Git along, old Scudder* ill. by author. Lothrop, 1983. Subj: Old age.

Once upon MacDonald's farm ill. by author. Four Winds Pr., 1981. Subj: Animals. Farms.

The story of Mr. and Mrs. Vinegar ill. by author. Lothrop, 1982. Subj: Character traits – foolishness. Folk and fairy tales.

Gannett, Ruth S. *Katie and the sad noise* ill. by Ellie Simmons. Random House, 1961. Subj: Animals – dogs. Character traits – kindness. Holidays – Christmas. Noise, sounds.

Gans, Roma. *Hummingbirds in the garden* ill. by Grambs Miller. Crowell, 1969. Subj: Birds. Seasons – summer.

Rock collecting ill. by Holly Keller. Crowell, 1984. Subj: Behavior – collecting things. Rocks. Science.

When birds change their feathers ill. by Felicia Bond. Crowell, 1980. Subj: Birds. Science.

Gant, Elizabeth. *Little Red Riding Hood* (Grimm, Jacob)

Gant, Katherine. *Little Red Riding Hood* (Grimm, Jacob)

Gantos, Jack. *Aunt Bernice* ill. by Nicole Rubel. Houghton, 1978. Subj: Behavior – carelessness. Family life.

Greedy Greeny ill. by Nicole Rubel. Doubleday, 1979. Subj: Dreams. Monsters.

The perfect pal ill. by Nicole Rubel. Houghton, 1979. Subj: Animals. Pets.

Rotten Ralph ill. by Nicole Rubel. Houghton, 1976. Subj: Animals – cats. Behavior – misbehavior.

Rotten Ralph's rotten Christmas ill. by Nicole Rubel. Houghton, 1984. Subj: Animals – cats. Character traits – meanness. Emotions – envy, jealousy. Holidays – Christmas.

Swampy alligator ill. by Nicole Rubel. Windmill, 1980. Subj: Birthdays. Character traits – cleanliness. Reptiles – alligators, crocodiles.

The werewolf family ill. by Nicole Rubel. Houghton, 1980. Subj: Monsters.

Worse than Rotten Ralph ill. by Nicole Rubel. Houghton, 1978. Subj: Animals – cats. Behavior – misbehavior. Character traits – meanness.

Gantos, John Jr. *see* Gantos, Jack

Gantschev, Ivan. *The Christmas train* ill. by author; tr. from German by Karen M. Klockner. Little, 1984. Subj: Character traits – bravery. Holidays – Christmas. Trains.

Journey of the storks ill. by author. Alphabet Pr., 1983. Subj: Birds – storks.

The moon lake tr. by Oliver Gadsby; ill. by author. Alphabet Pr., 1981. Subj: Moon.

RumpRump ill. by author. Alphabet Pr., 1984. Subj: Animals – bears. Food. Friendship.

Santa's favorite story (Aoki, Hisako)

Gantz, David. *Captain Swifty counts to 50* ill. by author. Doubleday, 1982. Subj: Counting.

The genie bear with the light brown hair word book ill. by author. Doubleday, 1982. Subj: ABC books. Animals – bears. Animals – mice.

Garbutt, Bernard. *Roger, the rosin back* ill. by author. Hastings, 1961. Subj: Animals – horses. circus.

García Lorca, Federico. *The Lieutenant Colonel and the gypsy* tr. and ill. by Marc Simont. Doubleday, 1971. Subj: Foreign lands – Spain. Gypsies. Poetry, rhyme.

Gardner, Beau. *The look again...and again, and again, and again book* ill. by author. Lothrop, 1984. Subj: Optical illusions

The turn about, think about, look about book ill. by author. Lothrop, 1980. Subj: Optical illusions.

Gardner, Mercedes. *Scooter and the magic star* by Mercedes and Jean Shannon Smith; ill. by Bob Johnson. Atheneum, 1980. Subj: Fairies.

Garelick, May. *About owls* ill. by Tony Chen. Four Winds Pr., 1975. Subj: Birds – owls. Science.

Down to the beach ill. by Barbara Cooney. Four Winds Pr., 1973. Subj: Sea and seashore. Seasons – summer.

Look at the moon ill. by Leonard Weisgard. Addison-Wesley, 1969. Subj: Animals. Moon. Poetry, rhyme.

Sounds of a summer night ill. by Beni Montresor. Addison-Wesley, 1963. Subj: Night. Noise, sounds.

The tremendous tree book by May Garelick and Barbara Brenner; ill. by Fred Brenner. Four Winds Pr., 1979. Subj: Science. Trees.

Where does the butterfly go when it rains? ill. by Leonard Weisgard. Addison-Wesley, 1961. Subj: Insects – butterflies, caterpillars. Poetry, rhyme. Weather – rain.

Garfield, Leon. *King Nimrod's tower* ill. by Michael Bragg. Lothrop, 1982. Subj: Religion.

The writing on the wall by Leon Garfield and Michael Bragg; ill. by Michael Bragg. Lothrop, 1983. Subj: Religion.

Garfinkel, Bernard *see* Allen, Robert

Garrett, Helen. *Angelo the naughty one* ill. by Leo Politi. Viking, 1944. Subj: Ethnic groups in the U.S. – Mexican-Americans.

Garrison, Christian. *The dream eater* ill. by Diane Goode. Dutton, 1978. Subj: Dragons. Dreams. Foreign lands – Japan.

Little pieces of the west wind ill. by Diane Goode. Dutton, 1975. Subj: Cumulative tales. Weather – wind.

Garten, Jan. *The alphabet tale* ill. by Muriel Batherman. Random House, 1964. Subj: ABC books. Animals. Participation. Poetry, rhyme.

Gascoigne, Bamber. *Why the rope went tight* ill. by Christina Gascoigne. Lothrop, 1981. Subj: Circus.

Gaston, Susan. *New boots for Salvador* ill. by Lydia Schwartz. Ritchie, 1972. Subj: Animals – horses.

Gates, Frieda. *Glove, mitten, and sock puppets* ill. by author. Walker, 1978. Subj: Puppets.

Gauch, Patricia Lee. *The little friar who flew* ill. by Tomie de Paola. Putnam's, 1980. Subj: Folk and fairy tales.

On to Widecombe Fair ill. by Trina Schart Hyman. Putnam's, 1978. Subj: Fairs. Folk and fairy tales. Foreign lands – England.

Once upon a Dinkelsbühl ill. by Tomie de Paola. Putnam's, 1977. Subj: War.

Gay, Michael. *Little boat* ill. by author. Macmillan, 1985. Subj: Boats, ships.

Little plane ill. by author. Macmillan, 1985. Subj: Airplanes, airports.

Little truck ill. by author. Macmillan, 1985. Subj: Trucks. Transportation.

Take me for a ride ill. by author. Morrow, 1985. Subj: Behavior – lost.

Gay, Zhenya. *I'm tired of lions* ill. by author. Viking, 1961. Subj: Animals – lions. Behavior – dissatisfaction.

Look! ill. by author. Viking, 1952. Subj: Animals. Libraries. Poetry, rhyme.

Small one ill. by author. Viking, 1958. Subj: Animals – rabbits. Behavior – lost.

What's your name? ill. by author. Viking, 1955. Subj: Animals. Poetry, rhyme. Riddles.

Who's afraid? ill. by author. Viking, 1965. Subj: Emotions – fear.

Wonderful things ill. by author. Viking, 1954. Subj: Animals – horses.

Geisel, Theodor Seuss *see* Seuss, Dr.

Geisert, Arthur. *Pa's balloon and other pig tales* ill. by author. Houghton, 1984. Subj: Activities – ballooning. Animals – pigs.

Gekiere, Madeleine. *The frilly lily and the princess* ill. by author. Lippincott, 1960. Subj: Behavior – fighting, arguing. Royalty.

Gelman, Rita Golden. *Dumb Joey* ill. by Cheryl Pelavin. Holt, 1973. Subj: Activities – playing. City. Friendship.

Hey, kid ill. by Carol Nicklaus. Watts, 1977. Subj: Humor. Poetry, rhyme.

Professor Coconut and the thief ill. by Emily Arnold McCully. Holt, 1977. Subj: Animals – monkeys. Problem solving.

Uncle Hugh: a fishing story by Rita Golden Gelman and Warner Friedman; ill. by Eros Keith. Harcourt, 1978. Subj: Sports – fishing.

Gemme, Leila Boyle. *T-ball is our game* photos. by Richard Marshall. Children's Pr., 1978. Subj: Sports – T-ball.

Gemming, Elisabeth. *Sandy at the children's zoo* (Bolliger, Max)

Gendel, Evelyn. *Tortoise and turtle* ill. by Hilary Knight. Simon and Schuster, 1960. Subj: Animals. Parties. Reptiles – turtles.

Tortoise and turtle abroad ill. by Hilary Knight. Simon and Schuster, 1963. Subj: Animals. Parties. Reptiles – turtles.

George, Jean Craighead. *All upon a stone* ill. by Don Bolognese. Crowell, 1971. Subj: Insects. Science. Spiders.

The grizzly bear with the golden ears ill. by Tom Catania. Harper, 1982. Subj: Animals – bears.

The wentletrap trap ill. by Symeon Shimin. Dutton, 1978. Subj: Ethnic groups in the U.S. – Afro-Americans. Foreign lands – Caribbean Islands. Sea and seashore.

Georgiady, Nicholas P. *Gertie the duck* ill. by Dagmar Wilson. Follett, 1959. Subj: Birds – ducks. Character traits – kindness to animals.

Gerez, Toni De *see* De Gerez, Toni

Gergely, Tibor. *Wheel on the chimney* (Brown, Margaret Wise)

Gerrard, Jean. *Matilda Jane* ill. by Roy Gerrard. Farrar, 1983. Subj: Foreign lands – England. Sea and seashore.

Gerrard, Roy. *The Favershams* ill. by author. Farrar, 1983. Subj: Poetry, rhyme.

Gershator, Phillis. *Honi and his magic circle* ill. by Shay Rieger. Jewish Publication Society of America, 1980. Subj: Jewish culture.

Gerson, Corinne. *Good dog, bad dog* ill. by Emily Arnold McCully. Atheneum, 1983. Subj: Animals – dogs. Behavior – misbehavior. Pets.

Gerstein, Mordicai. *Arnold of the ducks* ill. by author. Harper, 1983. Subj: Birds – ducks.

Follow me! ill. by author. Morrow, 1983. Subj: Birds – ducks.

Prince Sparrow ill. by author. Four Winds Pr., 1984. Subj: Birds – sparrows. Emotions – love.

Roll over! ill. by author. Crown, 1984. Subj: Counting. Poetry, rhyme.

The room ill. by author. Harper, 1984. Subj: City.

Getz, Arthur. *Humphrey, the dancing pig* ill. by author. Dial Pr., 1980. Subj: Activities – dancing. Animals – pigs. Behavior – dissatisfaction.

Gezi, Kal. *The mystery at Misty Falls* (Bradford, Ann)

The mystery in the secret club house (Bradford, Ann)

The mystery of the blind writer (Bradford, Ann)

The mystery of the live ghosts (Bradford, Ann)

The mystery of the midget clown (Bradford, Ann)

The mystery of the missing dogs (Bradford, Ann)

The mystery of the missing raccoon (Bradford, Ann)

The mystery of the square footsteps (Bradford, Ann)

The mystery of the tree house (Bradford, Ann)

Gianni, Peg. *Alex, the amazing juggler* by Peg Gianni and Renato Ferraro; ill. by Peg Gianni. Holt, 1981. Subj: Behavior – running away. Royalty.

Gibbons, Gail. *Boat book* ill. by author. Holiday, 1983. Subj: Boats, ships.

Clocks and how they go ill. by author. Crowell, 1979. Subj: Clocks. Time.

Department store ill. by author. Crowell, 1984. Subj: Stores.

Fire! Fire! ill. by author. Crowell, 1984. Subj: Careers – firefighters.

Halloween ill. by author. Holiday, 1984. Subj: Holidays – Halloween.

The missing maple syrup sap mystery: or, How maple syrup is made ill. by author. Warne, 1979. Subj: Activities. Food. Problem solving. Trees.

New road! ill. by author. Crowell, 1983. Subj: Transportation.

Paper, paper everywhere ill. by author. Harcourt, 1983. Subj: Paper.

The post office book: mail and how it moves ill. by author. Crowell, 1982. Subj: Careers – mail carriers. Communication.

The seasons of Arnold's apple tree ill. by author. Harcourt, 1984. Subj: Seasons. Trees.

Sun up, sun down ill. by author. Harcourt, 1983. Subj: Science. Sun.

Thanksgiving Day ill. by author. Holiday, 1983. Subj: Holidays – Thanksgiving.

The too-great bread bake book ill. by author. Warne, 1980. Subj: Activities – cooking.

Tool book ill. by author. Holiday, 1982. Subj: Tools.

Trucks ill. by author. Crowell, 1981. Subj: Trucks.

Gibson, Josephine *see* Joslin, Sesyle

Gibson, Myra Tomback. *What is your favorite thing to touch?* ill. by author. Grosset, 1965. Subj: Poetry, rhyme. Senses.

Giesen, Rosemary. *Famous planes* (Thompson, Brenda)

Pirates (Thompson, Brenda)

Giff, Patricia Reilly. *The almost awful play* ill. by Susanna Natti. Viking, 1984. Subj: Theater.

The beast in Ms. Rooney's room ill. by Blanche Sims. Dell, 1984. Subj: Activities – reading. School.

Next year I'll be special ill. by Marylin Hafner. Dutton, 1980. Subj: Behavior – seeking better things. Dreams. School.

Today was a terrible day ill. by Susanna Natti. Viking, 1980. Subj: Behavior – bad day. School.

Gikow, Louise. *Sprocket's Christmas tale* ill. by Lisa McCue. Holt, 1984. Subj: Holidays – Christmas. Puppets.

Gilbert, Helen Earle. *Dr. Trotter and his big gold watch* ill. by Margaret Bradfield. Abingdon Pr., 1948. Subj: Careers – doctors. Clocks.

Mr. Plum and the little green tree ill. by Margaret Bradfield. Abingdon Pr., 1946. Subj: Careers – shoemakers. Trees.

Gilbreath, Alice. *Making toys that crawl and slide* ill. by Joe Rogers. Follett, 1978. Subj: Toys.

Making toys that swim and float ill. by Joe Rogers. Follett, 1978. Subj: Toys.

Gilchrist, Theo E. *Halfway up the mountain* ill. by Glen Rounds. Lippincott, 1978. Subj: Behavior – fighting, arguing. Poetry, rhyme.

Gili, Phillida. *Fanny and Charles: a regency escapade or, The trick that went wrong* ill. by author. Viking, 1983. Subj: Activities – vacationing. Animals – mice. Sibling rivalry.

Gill, Bob. *A balloon for a blunderbuss* by Bob Gill and Alastair Reid; ill. by Bob Gill. Harper, 1961. Subj: Activities – trading.

Gill, Joan. *Hush, Jon!* ill. by Tracy Sugarman. Doubleday, 1968. Subj: Babies. Emotions – envy, jealousy. Ethnic groups in the U.S. – Afro-Americans. Family life.

Gilleo, Alma. *Learning about monsters* ill. by Joe Van Severen. Children's Pr., 1982. Subj: Folk and fairy tales. Monsters. Mythical creatures.

Gillham, Bill. *The early words picture book* photos. by Sam Grainger. Coward, 1983. Subj: Activities – reading.

Let's look for colors by Bill Gillham and Susan Hulme; photos. by Jan Siegieda. Putnam's, 1984. Subj: Concepts – color.

Let's look for numbers by Bill Gillham and Susan Hulme; photos. by Jan Siegieda. Putnam's, 1984. Subj: Counting.

Let's look for opposites by Bill Gillham and Susan Hulme; photos. by Jan Siegieda. Putnam's, 1984. Subj: Concepts – opposites.

Let's look for shapes by Bill Gillham and Susan Hulme; photos. by Jan Siegieda. Putnam's, 1984. Subj: Concepts – shape.

The gingerbread boy. *The gingerbread man* retold by Barbara Ireson; ill. by Gerald Rose. Norton, 1963. Subj: Behavior – running away. Cumulative tales. Folk and fairy tales. Food.

The gingerbread boy ill. by Paul Galdone. Seabury Pr., 1975. Subj: Behavior – running away. Cumulative tales. Folk and fairy tales. Food. Poetry, rhyme.

The gingerbread boy retold by David Cutts; ill. by Joan Elizabeth Goodman. Troll Assoc., 1979. Subj: Behavior – running away. Cumulative tales. Folk and fairy tales. Food.

The gingerbread boy ill. by William Curtis Holdsworth. Farrar, 1968. Subj: Behavior – running away. Cumulative tales. Folk and fairy tales. Food.

Ginsburg, Mirra. *Across the stream* ill. by Nancy Tafuri. Greenwillow, 1982. Subj: Animals – foxes. Birds – chickens. Birds – ducks. Dreams.

The chick and the duckling ill. by José Aruego and Ariane Dewey. Macmillan, 1972. Translation of Tsyplenok i utenok by Vladimir Grigorévich Suteyev. Subj: Birds – chickens. Birds – ducks. Sports – swimming.

The fisherman's son ill. by Tony Chen. Greenwillow, 1979. Subj: Character traits – cleverness. Folk and fairy tales. Foreign lands – Russia.

The fox and the hare ill. by Victor Nolden. Crown, 1969. Subj: Animals. Animals – foxes. Animals – rabbits. Folk and fairy tales. Foreign lands – Russia. Friendship.

Good morning, chick (Chukovsky, Korney)

How the sun was brought back to the sky: adapted from a Slovenian folk tale ill. by José Aruego and Ariane Dewey. Macmillan, 1975. Subj: Folk and fairy tales. Foreign lands – Czechoslovakia. Sun.

Kitten from one to ten ill. by Giulio Maestro. Crown, 1980. Subj: Animals – cats. Counting. Poetry, rhyme.

Mushroom in the rain ill. by José Aruego and Ariane Dewey. Macmillan, 1974. Adapted from the Russian of Vladimir Grigorévich Suteyev. Subj: Animals. Animals – foxes. Plants. Weather – rain.

Ookie-Spooky ill. by Emily Arnold McCully. Crown, 1979. Subj: Monsters.

Pampalche of the silver teeth ill. by Rocco Negri. Crown, 1976. Subj: Folk and fairy tales. Foreign lands – Russia. Witches.

Striding slippers: an Udmurt tale ill. by Sal Murdocca. Macmillan, 1978. Subj: Behavior – stealing. Folk and fairy tales. Magic.

The strongest one of all ill. by José Aruego and Ariane Dewey. Greenwillow, 1977. Subj: Animals – sheep. Character traits – bravery. Foreign lands – Russia.

The sun's asleep behind the hill ill. by Paul O. Zelinsky. Greenwillow, 1982. Subj: Night. Poetry, rhyme.

Two greedy bears ill. by José Aruego and Ariane Dewey. Macmillan, 1976. Subj: Animals – bears. Animals – foxes. Behavior – greed. Foreign lands – Hungary. Sibling rivalry.

Where does the sun go at night? ill. by José Aruego and Ariane Dewey. Greenwillow, 1980. Subj: Night. Sun.

Which is the best place? ill. by Roger Antoine Duvoisin. Macmillan, 1976. Tr. from Gde luchshe by Pyotr Dubochkin. Subj: Bedtime. Foreign lands – Russia.

Gipson, Morrell. *Favorite nursery tales* ill. by S. D. Schindler. Doubleday, 1983. Subj: Nursery rhymes.

Hello, Peter ill. by Clement Hurd. Doubleday, 1948. Subj: Activities.

Girard, Linda Walvoord. *You were born on your very first birthday* ill. by Christa Kieffer. Albert Whitman, 1983. Subj: Babies. Science.

Girion, Barbara. *The boy with the special face* ill. by Heidi Palmer. Abingdon, 1978. Subj: Character traits – appearance.

Givens, Janet Eaton. *Just two wings* ill. by Susan Dodge. Atheneum, 1984. Subj: Birds.

Something wonderful happened ill. by Susan Dodge. Atheneum, 1982. Subj: Flowers.

Glass, Andrew. *My brother tries to make me laugh* ill. by author. Lothrop, 1984. Subj: Imagination. Space and space ships.

Glazer, Lee. *Cookie Becker casts a spell* ill. by Margot Apple. Little, 1980. Subj: Character traits – meanness. Magic.

Glazer, Tom. *Do your ears hang low? fifty more musical fingerplays* ill. by Mila Lazarevich. Doubleday, 1980. Subj: Games. Music. Participation. Songs.

Eye winker, Tom Tinker, chin chopper: fifty musical fingerplays ill. by Ronald Himler. Doubleday, 1974. Subj: Games. Music. Participation. Songs.

On top of spaghetti ill. by Tom Garcia. Doubleday, 1982. Subj: Music. Songs.

Glovach, Linda. *The little Witch's birthday book* ill. by author. Prentice-Hall, 1981. Subj: Birthdays. Parties. Witches.

The little Witch's black magic book of disguises ill. by author. Prentice-Hall, 1973. Subj: Holidays – Halloween. Witches.

The little Witch's black magic book of games ill. by author. Prentice-Hall, 1974. Subj: Games. Safety.

The little Witch's Christmas book ill. by author. Prentice-Hall, 1975. Subj: Holidays – Christmas. Witches.

The little Witch's Halloween book ill. by author. Prentice-Hall, 1975. Subj: Holidays – Halloween. Witches.

The little Witch's spring holiday book ill. by author. Prentice-Hall, 1983. Subj: Holidays. Seasons – spring. Witches.

The little Witch's Thanksgiving book ill. by author. Prentice-Hall, 1976. Subj: Holidays – Thanksgiving.

Go tell Aunt Rhody ill. by Aliki. Macmillan, 1974. Subj: Folk and fairy tales. Games. Songs.

Go tell Aunt Rhody ill. by Robert M. Quackenbush. Lippincott, 1973. Subj: Games. Music. Songs.

Gobhai, Mehlli. *Lakshmi, the water buffalo who wouldn't* ill. by author. Hawthorn, 1969. Subj: Animals – water buffaloes. Foreign lands – India.

Usha, the mouse-maiden ill. by author. Hawthorn, 1969. Subj: Family life. Folk and fairy tales. Foreign lands – India.

Goble, Paul. *Buffalo woman* ill. by author. Bradbury Pr., 1984. Subj: Ethnic groups in the U.S. – Indians. Folk and fairy tales.

The friendly wolf ill. by author. Dutton, 1974. Subj: Animals – wolves. Behavior – lost. Ethnic groups in the U.S. – Indians.

The gift of the sacred dog ill. by author. Bradbury Pr., 1980. Subj: Animals – horses. Ethnic groups in the U.S. – Indians. Folk and fairy tales.

The girl who loved wild horses ill. by author. Dutton, 1978. Subj: Animals – horses. Caldecott award book. Ethnic groups in the U.S. – Indians.

Goddard, Carrie Lou. *Isn't it a wonder!* ill. by Leigh Grant. Abingdon Pr., 1976. Subj: Religion.

Godden, Rumer. *A kindle of kittens* ill. by Lynne Byrnes. Viking, 1979. Subj: Animals – cats.

Goff, Beth. *Where's daddy?* ill. by Susan Perl. Beacon Pr., 1969. Subj: Divorce.

Goffe, Toni. *Toby's animal rescue service* ill. by author. David and Charles, 1982. Subj: Activities – ballooning. Animals.

Goffstein, M. B. (Marilyn Brooks). *Across the sea* ill. by author. Farrar, 1968. Subj: Foreign lands.

Family scrapbook ill. by author. Farrar, 1978. Subj: Family life.

Fish for supper ill. by author. Dial Pr., 1976. Subj: Caldecott award honor book. Family life – grandparents, great-grandparents. Old age. Sports – fishing.

Goldie the dollmaker ill. by author. Farrar, 1969. Subj: Emotions – loneliness. Jewish culture. Orphans. Toys – dolls.

Laughing latkes ill. by author. Farrar, 1981. Subj: Holidays – Hanukkah. Jewish culture.

A little Schubert ill. by author. Harper, 1972. Subj: Music.

Me and my captain ill. by author. Farrar, 1974. Subj: Toys – dolls.

My Noah's ark ill. by author. Harper, 1978. Subj: Religion – Noah.

Natural history ill. by author. Farrar, 1979. Subj: Animals. Character traits – kindness to animals.

Neighbors ill. by author. Harper, 1979. Subj: Character traits – shyness. Emotions – loneliness.

Sleepy people ill. by author. Farrar, 1966. Subj: Bedtime.

A writer ill. by author. Harper, 1984. Subj: Activities – working. Careers – writers.

Gold, Phyllis. *Please don't say hello* ill. by Carl Baker. Human Sci. Pr., 1975. Subj: Handicaps.

Goldberg, Phyllis *see* Gold, Phyllis

The golden goose ill. by William Stobbs. McGraw-Hill, 1967. Subj: Birds – chickens. Cumulative tales. Folk and fairy tales. Humor. Royalty.

Golden tales from long ago: *Like Grandpa, Only birds, The three kittens.* Delacorte, 1980. Anonymous stories published by Ernest Nister in London near the turn of the century. Subj: Format, unusual.

Goldfrank, Helen Colodny Kay *see* Kay, Helen

Goldin, Augusta. *Ducks don't get wet* ill. by Leonard P. Kessler. Crowell, 1965. Subj: Birds – ducks. Science.

Salt ill. by Robert Galster. Crowell, 1966. Subj: Science.

The shape of water ill. by Demi. Doubleday, 1979. Subj: Science.

Spider silk ill. by Joseph Low. Crowell, 1964. Subj: Science. Spiders.

Straight hair, curly hair ill. by Ed Emberley. Crowell, 1966. Subj: Hair. Science.

Where does your garden grow? ill. by Helen Borten. Crowell, 1967. Subj: Activities – gardening. Science.

Goldman, Susan. *Cousins are special* ill. by author. Albert Whitman, 1978. Subj: Family life.

Grandma is somebody special ed. by Caroline Rubin; ill. by author. Albert Whitman, 1976. Subj: Family life – grandparents, great-grandparents.

Goldner, Kathryn Allen. *The dangers of strangers* (Vogel, Carole Garbuny)

Goldsmith, Howard. *Toto the timid turtle* ill. by Shirley Chan. Human Sciences Pr., 1981. Subj: Reptiles – turtles.

Gomi, Taro. *Coco can't wait!* ill. by author. Morrow, 1984. Subj: Family life – grandparents, great-grandparents.

Goodall, Daphne Machin. *Zebras* ill. with photos. Raintree, 1978. Subj: Animals – zebras.

Goodall, John S. *The adventures of Paddy Pork* ill. by author. Harcourt, 1968. Subj: Animals – pigs. Behavior – running away. Circus. Format, unusual. Wordless.

The ballooning adventures of Paddy Pork ill. by author. Harcourt, 1969. Subj: Animals – pigs. Format, unusual. Wordless.

Creepy castle ill. by author. Atheneum, 1975. Subj: Animals – mice. Format, unusual. Knights. Monsters. Wordless.

An Edwardian Christmas ill. by author. Atheneum, 1978. Subj: Foreign lands – England. Format, unusual. Holidays – Christmas. Wordless.

An Edwardian summer ill. by author. Atheneum, 1976. Subj: Foreign lands – England. Format, unusual. Seasons – summer. Wordless.

Jacko ill. by author. Harcourt, 1971. Subj: Animals – monkeys. Boats, ships. Format, unusual. Wordless.

The midnight adventures of Kelly, Dot and Esmeralda ill. by author. Atheneum, 1972. Subj: Format, unusual. Wordless.

Naughty Nancy ill. by author. Atheneum, 1975. Subj: Behavior – misbehavior. Format, unusual. Weddings. Wordless.

Paddy goes traveling ill. by author. Atheneum, 1982. Subj: Activities – traveling. Animals – pigs. Format, unusual. Wordless.

Paddy Pork: odd jobs ill. by author. Atheneum, 1983. Subj: Activities – working. Animals – pigs. Format, unusual. Wordless.

Paddy Pork's holiday ill. by author. Atheneum, 1976. Subj: Activities – vacationing. Animals – pigs. Format, unusual. Wordless.

Paddy under water ill. by author. Atheneum, 1984. Subj: Animals – pigs. Format, unusual. Sea and seashore. Wordless.

Paddy's evening out ill. by author. Atheneum, 1973. Subj: Animals – pigs. Format, unusual. Theater. Wordless.

Paddy's new hat ill. by author. Atheneum, 1980. Subj: Animals – pigs. Careers – police officers. Format, unusual. Wordless.

Shrewbettina's birthday ill. by author. Harcourt, 1970. Subj: Birthdays. Format, unusual. Wordless.

The story of an English village ill. by author. Atheneum, 1979. Subj: City. Foreign lands – England. Format, unusual. Progress. Wordless.

The surprise picnic ill. by author. Atheneum, 1977. Subj: Activities – picnicking. Animals – cats. Food. Format, unusual. Wordless.

Goodenow, Earle. *The last camel* ill. by author. Walck, 1968. Subj: Animals – camels. Foreign lands – Egypt.

The owl who hated the dark ill. by author. Walck, 1969. Subj: Birds – owls. Emotions – fear. Night.

Goodsell, Jane. *Katie's magic glasses* ill. by Barbara Cooney. Subj: Careers – doctors. Glasses.

Goodspeed, Peter. *Hugh and Fitzhugh* ill. by Carol Nicklaus. Platt, 1974. Subj: Animals – dogs. Language.

A rhinoceros wakes me up in the morning: a bedtime tale ill. by Dennis Panek. Bradbury Pr., 1982. Subj: Animals. Bedtime. Poetry, rhyme.

Goor, Nancy. *All kinds of feet* (Goor, Ron)

In the driver's seat (Goor, Ron)

Shadows (Goor, Ron)

Signs (Goor, Ron)

Goor, Ron. *All kinds of feet* by Ron and Nancy Goor; photos. by authors. Crowell, 1984. Subj: Anatomy. Animals.

Backyard insects (Selsam, Millicent E)

In the driver's seat by Ron and Nancy Goor; photos. by authors. Crowell, 1982. Subj: Activities. Machines.

Shadows: here, there and everywhere by Ron and Nancy Goor; photos. by authors. Crowell, 1981. Subj: Shadows.

Signs by Ron and Nancy Goor; photos. by authors. Crowell, 1983. Subj: Activities – reading. Communication.

Gordon, Margaret. *The supermarket mice* ill. by author. Dutton, 1984. Subj: Animals – cats. Animals – mice. Problem solving. Stores.

Wilberforce goes on a picnic ill. by author. Morrow, 1982. Subj: Activities – picnicking. Animals – bears.

Gordon, Sharon. *Christmas surprise* ill. by John Magine. Troll Assoc., 1980. Subj: Animals – bears. Holidays – Christmas.

Dinosaurs in trouble ill. by Paul Harvey. Troll Assoc., 1980. Subj: Dinosaurs.

Easter Bunny's lost egg ill. by John Magine. Troll Assoc., 1980. Subj: Animals – rabbits. Eggs. Holidays – Easter.

Friendly snowman ill. by John Magine. Troll Assoc., 1980. Subj: Snowmen.

Pete the parakeet ill. by Paul Harvey. Troll Assoc., 1980. Subj: Birds – parakeets, parrots.

Play ball, Kate! ill. by Don Page. Troll Assoc., 1981. Subj: Sports – baseball.

Sam the scarecrow ill. by Don Silverstein. Troll Assoc., 1980. Subj: Scarecrows.

Three little witches ill. by Deborah Sims. Troll Assoc., 1980. Subj: Witches.

Tick tock clock ill. by Don Page. Troll Assoc., 1982. Subj: Clocks. Time.

Trees ill. by Irene Trivas. Troll Assoc., 1983. Subj: Trees.

What a dog! ill. by Deborah Sims. Troll Assoc., 1980. Subj: Animals – dogs.

Gordon, Shirley. *Crystal is my friend* ill. by Edward Frascino. Harper, 1978. Subj: Friendship. School.

Crystal is the new girl ill. by Edward Frascino. Harper, 1976. Subj: Friendship. School.

Grandma zoo ill. by Whitney Darrow, Jr. Harper, 1978. Subj: Animals. Family life – grandparents, great-grandparents. Zoos.

Happy birthday, Crystal ill. by Edward Frascino. Harper, 1981. Subj: Birthdays. Emotions – envy, jealousy. Parties.

Gorey, Edward. *The tunnel calamity* ill. by author. Putnam's, 1984. Subj: Format, unusual. Monsters. Wordless.

Gorham, Michael *see* Elting, Mary

Gorsline, Douglas. *North American Indians* (Gorsline, Marie)

Gorsline, Marie. *North American Indians* by Marie and Douglas Gorsline; ill. by authors. Random House, 1978. Subj: Ethnic groups in the U.S. – Indians. U.S. history.

Goudey, Alice E. *The day we saw the sun come up* ill. by Adrienne Adams. Scribner's, 1961. Subj: Caldecott award honor book. Family life. Sun.

The good rain ill. by Nora Spicer Unwin. Dutton, 1950. Subj: Weather – rain.

Houses from the sea ill. by Adrienne Adams. Scribner's, 1959. Subj: Caldecott award honor book. Sea and seashore.

Red legs ill. by Marie Nonnast. Scribner's, 1966. Subj: Insects.

Goundaud, Karen Jo. *A very mice joke book* ill. by Lynn Munsinger. Houghton, 1981. Subj: Animals – mice. Riddles.

Goyder, Alice. *Holiday in Catland* ill. by author. Crowell, 1979. Subj: Activities – vacationing. Animals – cats.

Party in Catland ill. by author. Crowell, 1979. Subj: Animals – cats. Parties.

Grabianski, Janusz. *Cats* ill. by author. Watts, 1966. Subj: Animals – cats.

Grabianski's wild animals ill. by author. Watts, 1969. Translation of Tiere der Wildnis. Subj: Animals.

Horses ill. by author. Watts, 1966. Subj: Animals – horses.

Graham, Al. *Songs for a small guitar* ill. by Tony Palazzo. Duell, 1962. Subj: Poetry, rhyme. Songs.

Timothy Turtle ill. by Tony Palazzo. Walck, 1946. Subj: Caldecott award honor book. Character traits – ambition. Character traits – helpfulness. Friendship. Reptiles – turtles.

Graham, Bob. *Libby, Oscar and me* ill. by author. Harper, 1985. Subj: Animals – cats. Animals – dogs. Activities – picnicking.

Graham, John. *A crowd of cows* ill. by Feodor Rojankovsky. Harcourt, 1968. Subj: Animals. Noise, sounds.

I love you, mouse ill. by Tomie de Paola. Harcourt, 1976. Subj: Animals. Animals – mice.

Graham, Lorenz B. *David he no fear* ill. by Ann Grifalconi. Crowell, 1971. Subj: Religion.

Every man heart lay down ill. by Colleen Browning. Crowell, 1970. Subj: Religion.

God wash the world and start again ill. by Clare Romano. Crowell, 1971. Subj: Religion – Noah.

Hongry catch the foolish boy ill. by James Brown, Jr. Crowell, 1973. Story first appeared in the author's How God fix Jonah, published in 1946. Subj: Religion.

A road down in the sea ill. by Gregorio Prestopino. Crowell, 1970. Subj: Religion.

Song of the boat ill. by Leo and Diane Dillon. Crowell, 1975. Subj: Foreign lands – Africa. Poetry, rhyme.

Graham, Margaret Bloy. *Be nice to spiders* ill. by author. Harper, 1967. Subj: Spiders. Zoos.

Benjy and the barking bird ill. by author. Harper, 1971. Subj: Animals – dogs. Birds – parakeets, parrots. Emotions – envy, jealousy.

Benjy's boat trip ill. by author. Harper, 1977. Subj: Animals – dogs. Boats, ships.

Benjy's dog house ill. by author. Harper, 1973. Subj: Animals – dogs.

Graham, Mary Stuart Campbell. *The pirates' bridge* ill. by Winifred Lubell. Lothrop, 1960. Subj: Pirates.

Grahame, Kenneth. *The open road* ill. by Beverley Gooding. Scribner's, 1980. Subj: Activities – traveling. Animals.

The river bank: from The wind in the willows ill. by Adrienne Adams. Scribner's, 1977. Subj: Animals. Rivers.

Gramatky, Hardie. *Bolivar* ill. by author. Putnam's, 1961. Subj: Animals – donkeys. Foreign lands – South America.

Hercules ill. by author. Putnam's, 1940. Subj: Careers – firefighters. Fire. Museums. Trucks.

Homer and the circus train ill. by author. Putnam's, 1957. Subj: Circus. Trains.

Little Toot ill. by author. Putnam's, 1939. Subj: Boats, ships. Character traits – ambition.

Little Toot on the Mississippi ill. by author. Putnam's, 1973. Subj: Boats, ships. Rivers.

Little Toot on the Thames ill. by author. Putnam's, 1964. Subj: Boats, ships. Foreign lands – England.

Little Toot through the Golden Gate ill. by author. Putnam's, 1975. Subj: Boats, ships. City. Character traits – individuality.

Loopy ill. by author. Putnam's, 1941. Subj: Activities – flying. Airplanes, airports.

Nikos and the sea god ill. by author. Putnam's, 1963. Subj: Careers – fishermen. Folk and fairy tales. Mythical creatures. Religion.

Sparky: the story of a little trolley car ill. by author. Putnam's, 1952. Subj: Cable cars, trolleys. Transportation.

Grant, Anne. *Danbury's burning! The story of Sybil Ludington's ride* ill. by Pat Howell. Walck, 1976. Subj: U.S. history.

Grant, Matthew G. *see* May, Julian

Grasshopper to the rescue: *a Georgian story* tr. from the Russian by Bonnie Carey; ill. by Tasha Tudor. Morrow, 1979. Subj: Character traits – bravery. Cumulative tales. Insects – grasshoppers. Rivers.

Graves, Robert. *Two wise children* ill. by Ralph Pinto. Delacorte, 1967. Subj: Magic.

Gray, Catherine. *Tammy and the gigantic fish* by Catherine and James Gray; ill. by William Joyce. Harper, 1983. Subj: Family life. Sports – fishing.

Gray, Genevieve. *How far, Felipe?* ill. by Ann Grifalconi. Harper, 1978. Subj: Activities – traveling. Animals – donkeys. Character traits – perseverance.

Send Wendell ill. by Symeon Shimin. McGraw-Hill, 1974. Subj: Character traits – helpfulness. Ethnic groups in the U.S. – Afro-Americans. Family life.

Gray, James. *Tammy and the gigantic fish* (Gray, Catherine)

Gray, Jenny *see* Gray, Genevieve

Gray, Nigel. *It'll all come out in the wash* ill. by Edward Frascino. Harper, 1979. Subj: Family life.

Grayson, Marion F. *Let's count and count out*

Greaves, Margaret. *A net to catch the wind* ill. by Stephen Gammell. Harper, 1979. Subj: Animals – horses. Forest, woods. Royalty.

Greeley, Valerie. *Farm animals* ill. by author. Harper, 1984. Subj: Animals. Farms. Format, unusual – cardboard pages. Wordless.

Field animals ill. by author. Harper, 1984. Subj: Animals. Format, unusual – cardboard pages. Wordless.

Pets ill. by author. Harper, 1984. Subj: Animals. Format, unusual – cardboard pages. Pets. Wordless.

Zoo animals ill. by author. Harper, 1984. Subj: Animals. Format, unusual – cardboard pages. Wordless. Zoos.

Green, Adam *see* Weisgard, Leonard

The green grass grows all around: *a traditional folk song* ill. by Hilde Hoffmann. Macmillan, 1968. Subj: Plants. Poetry, rhyme. Songs.

Green, Marion. *The magician who lived on the mountain* ill. by John Dyke. Children's Pr., 1978. Subj: Art. Magic.

Green, Mary McBurney. *Everybody has a house and everybody eats* ill. by Louis Klein. Abelard-Schuman, 1944. Subj: Farms. Houses.

Is it hard? Is it easy? ill. by Lucienne Bloch. Abelard-Schuman, 1948. Subj: Concepts.

Green, Melinda. *Bembelman's bakery* ill. by Barbara Seuling. Parents, 1978. Subj: Careers – bakers.

Green, Norma B. *The hole in the dike* ill. by Eric Carle. Crowell, 1974. Subj: Character traits – helpfulness. Foreign lands – Holland.

Green, Phyllis. *Bagdad ate it* ill. by Joel Schick. Watts, 1980. Subj: Animals – dogs. Behavior – greed.

Uncle Roland, the perfect guest ill. by Marybeth Farrell. Four Winds Pr., 1983. Subj: Family life.

Greenaway, Kate. *A apple pie* ill. by author. Warne, 1886. Subj: ABC books.

Marigold garden ill. by author. Warne, 1885. Subj: Poetry, rhyme.

Under the window ill. by author. Warne, 1879. Subj: Poetry, rhyme.

Greenberg, Barbara. *The bravest babysitter* ill. by Diane Paterson. Dial Pr., 1977. Subj: Activities – babysitting. Babies. Emotions – fear. Weather.

Greenberg, David. *Slugs* ill. by Victoria Chess. Little, 1983. Subj: Poetry, rhyme.

Greenberg, Polly. *Oh, Lord, I wish I was a buzzard* ill. by Aliki. Macmillan, 1968. Subj: Behavior – wishing. Ethnic groups in the U.S. – Afro-Americans. Farms. Plants.

Greene, Carla. *Animal doctors: what do they do?* ill. by Leonard P. Kessler. Harper, 1967. Subj: Careers – veterinarians.

Cowboys: what do they do? ill. by Leonard P. Kessler. Harper, 1972. Subj: Cowboys.

Doctors and nurses: what do they do? ill. by Leonard P. Kessler. Harper, 1963. Subj: Careers – doctors. Careers – nurses.

I want to be a carpenter ill. by Frances Eckart. Childrens Pr., 1959. Subj: Careers – carpenters.

A motor holiday ill. by Harold L. Van Pelt. Melmont, 1956. Subj: Activities – traveling.

Railroad engineers and airplane pilots: what do they do? ill. by Leonard P. Kessler. Harper, 1964. Subj: Careers – airplane pilots. Careers – railroad engineers.

Soldiers and sailors: what do they do? ill. by Leonard P. Kessler. Harper, 1963. Subj: Careers – military.

Truck drivers: what do they do? ill. by Leonard P. Kessler. Harper, 1967. Subj: Careers – truck drivers. Trucks.

What do they do? Policemen and firemen ill. by Leonard P. Kessler. Harper, 1962. Subj: Careers – firefighters. Careers – police officers.

Greene, Carol. *A computer went a-courting: a love song for Valentine's Day* ill. by Tom Dunnington. Children's Pr., 1983. Subj: Animals – mice. Holidays – Valentine's Day. Machines. Music. Songs.

Hi, clouds ill. by Gene Sharp. Children's Pr., 1983. Subj: Weather – clouds.

Hinny Winny Bunco ill. by Jeanette Winter. Harper, 1982. Subj: Music. Sibling rivalry. Songs.

The insignificant elephant ill. by Susan Gantner. Harcourt, 1985. Subj: Animals – elephants. Animals – rabbits.

Please, wind? ill. by Gene Sharp. Children's Pr., 1982. Subj: Weather – wind.

Rain! Rain! ill. by Larry Frederick. Children's Pr., 1982. Subj: Weather – rain.

Robots ill. with photos. Children's Pr., 1983. Subj: Robots.

Shine, sun! ill. by Gene Sharp. Children's Pr., 1983. Subj: Sun.

Snow Joe ill. by Paul Sharp. Children's Pr., 1982. Subj: Weather – snow.

The thirteen days of Halloween ill. by Tom Dunnington. Children's Pr., 1983. Subj: Holidays – Halloween. Music. Songs. Witches.

Greene, Ellin. *Princess Rosetta and the popcorn man* ill. by Trina Schart Hyman. Lothrop, 1971. From The Pot of Gold by Mary E. Wilkins. Subj: Folk and fairy tales. Food. Royalty.

The pumpkin giant ill. by Trina Schart Hyman. Lothrop, 1970. Orig. story by Mary E. Wilkins. Subj: Food. Giants. Holidays – Halloween.

Greene, Graham. *The little fire engine* ill. by Edward Ardizzone. Doubleday, 1973. Subj: Fire. Progress.

The little train ill. by Edward Ardizzone. Doubleday, 1973. Subj: Behavior – running away. Trains.

Greene, Jacqueline Dembar. *Butchers and bakers, rabbis and kings* ill. by Marilyn Hirsh. Kar-Ben Copies, 1984. Subj: Jewish culture.

Greene, Laura. *Change: getting to know about ebb and flow* ill. by Gretchen Mayo. Human Sciences Pr., 1981. Subj: Concepts.

Help: getting to know about needing and giving ill. by Gretchen Mayo. Human Sciences Pr., 1981. Subj: Character traits – helpfulness.

Greene, Roberta. *Two and me makes three* ill. by Paul Galdone. Coward, 1970. Subj: Ethnic groups in the U.S.

Greenfield, Eloise. *Africa dream* ill. by Carole Byard. John Day, 1977. Subj: Dreams. Foreign lands – Africa.

Daydreamers ill. by Tom Feelings. Dial Pr., 1981. Subj: Ethnic groups in the U.S. – Afro-Americans. Poetry, rhyme.

First pink light ill. by Moneta Barnett. Crowell, 1976. Subj: Ethnic groups in the U.S. – Afro-Americans. Family life – fathers.

I can do it by myself (Little, Lessie Jones)

Me and Nessie ill. by Moneta Barnett. Crowell, 1975. Subj: Ethnic groups in the U.S. – Afro-Americans. Family life. Imagination – imaginary friends.

She come bringing me that little baby girl ill. by John Steptoe. Lippincott, 1974. Subj: Babies. Emotions – envy, jealousy. Ethnic groups in the U.S. – Afro-Americans. Sibling rivalry.

Greenhill, Richard. *A family in China* (Fyson, Nance Lui)

Greenleaf, Ann. *No room for Sarah* ill. by author. Dodd, 1983. Subj: Bedtime. Toys.

Greenwood, Ann. *A pack of dreams* ill. by Bernard Colonna and Mary Elizabeth Gordon. Prentice-Hall, 1979. Subj: Dreams. Poetry, rhyme.

Gregor, Arthur S. *Animal babies* (Ylla)

The little elephant (Ylla)

One, two, three, four, five ill. by Robert Doisneau. Lippincott, 1956. Subj: Counting.

Gregorich, Barbara. *My friend goes left* ill. by Joyce John; ed. by Joan Hoffman. School Zone Pub., 1984. Subj: Poetry, rhyme. Riddles.

Greisman, Joan. *Things I hate!* (Wittels, Harriet)

Gretz, Susanna. *Teddy bears ABC* ill. by author. Follett, 1975. Subj: ABC books. Counting. Toys – teddy bears.

Teddy bears cure a cold ill. by Alison Sage. Four Winds Pr., 1985. Subj: Illness. Toys – teddy bears.

Teddy bears go shopping ill. by author. Four Winds Pr., 1982. Subj: Shopping. Toys – teddy bears.

Teddy bears' moving day ill. by author. Four Winds Pr., 1981. Subj: Moving. Toys – teddy bears.

Teddy bears one to ten ill. by author. Follett, 1969. Subj: Counting. Toys – teddy bears.

Teddybears cookbook by Susanna Gretz and Alison Sage; ill. by Susanna Gretz. Doubleday, 1978. Subj: Activities – cooking. Toys – teddy bears.

Greydanus, Rose. *Animals at the zoo* ill. by Susan Hall. Troll Assoc., 1980. Subj: Animals. Zoos.

Big red fire engine ill. by Paul Harvey. Troll Assoc., 1980. Subj: Careers – firefighters. Trucks.

Changing seasons ill. by Susan Hall. Troll Assoc., 1983. Subj: Seasons.

Freddie the frog ill. by Tom Garcia. Troll Assoc., 1980. Subj: Frogs and toads.

Horses ill. by Joel Snyder. Troll Assoc., 1983. Subj: Animals – horses.

My secret hiding place ill. by Paul Harvey. Troll Assoc., 1980. Subj: Behavior – hiding.

Susie goes shopping ill. by Margot Apple. Troll Assoc., 1980. Subj: Shopping.

Tree house fun ill. by Chris L. Demarest. Troll Assoc., 1980. Subj: Houses. Trees.

Willie the slowpoke ill. by Andrea Eberbach. Troll Assoc., 1980. Subj: Behavior – hurrying.

Grieg, E. H. (Edvard Hagerup). *E. H. Grieg's Peer Gynt* ill. by Yoshiharu Suzuki. Gakkenk, 1971. Adapt. by Makoto Oishi; tr. by Ann Brannen. Subj: Folk and fairy tales. Foreign lands – Norway.

Grifalconi, Ann. *City rhythms* ill. by author. Bobbs-Merrill, 1965. Subj: City. Ethnic groups in the U.S. – Afro-Americans.

The toy trumpet ill. by author. Bobbs-Merrill, 1968. Subj: Foreign lands – Mexico. Music. Toys.

Griffen, Elizabeth. *A dog's book of bugs* ill. by Peter Parnall. Atheneum, 1967. Subj: Insects.

Griffith, Helen V. *Alex and the cat* ill. by Joseph Low. Greenwillow, 1982. Subj: Animals – cats. Animals – dogs.

Alex remembers ill. by Donald Carrick. Greenwillow, 1983. Subj: Animals – cats. Animals – dogs. Moon. Seasons – fall.

Mine will, said John ill. by Muriel Batherman. Greenwillow, 1980. Subj: Animals – dogs. Family life. Pets.

More Alex and the cat ill. by Donald Carrick. Greenwillow, 1983. Subj: Animals – cats. Animals – dogs.

Grimm, Jacob. *The bear and the kingbird* by Jacob and Wilhelm Grimm; tr. by Lore Segal; ill. by Chris Conover. Farrar, 1979. Subj: Animals – bears. Birds. Folk and fairy tales.

The bearskinner by Jacob and Wilhelm Grimm; ill. by Felix Hoffmann. Atheneum, 1978. Translation of Der Bärenhäuter. Subj: Devil. Folk and fairy tales.

The brave little tailor by Jacob and Wilhelm Grimm; ill. by Mark Corcoran. Troll Assoc., 1979. Subj: Careers – tailors. Character traits – bravery. Folk and fairy tales. Giants.

The brave little tailor by Jacob and Wilhelm Grimm; tr. by Anthea Bell; ill. by Svend Otto S. Larousse, 1979. Subj: Careers – tailors. Character traits – bravery. Folk and fairy tales. Giants.

The brave little tailor by Jacob and Wilhelm Grimm; adapt. by Robert D. San Souci; ill. by Daniel San Souci. Doubleday, 1982. Subj: Careers – tailors. Character traits – bravery. Folk and fairy tales. Giants.

The Bremen town musicians by Jacob and Wilhelm Grimm; retold and ill. by Donna Diamond. Delacorte Pr., 1981. Subj: Animals. Folk and fairy tales. Old age.

The Bremen town musicians by Jacob and Wilhelm Grimm; tr. by Elizabeth Shub; ill. by Janina Domanska. Greenwillow, 1980. Subj: Animals. Folk and fairy tales. Old age.

The Bremen town musicians by Jacob and Wilhelm Grimm; ill. by Paul Galdone. McGraw-Hill, 1968. Tr. of Der Bremer Stadtmusikanten. Subj: Animals. Folk and fairy tales. Old age.

The Brementown musicians by Jacob and Wilhelm Grimm; retold and ill. by Ilse Plume. Doubleday, 1980. Subj: Animals. Caldecott award honor book. Folk and fairy tales. Old age.

Cinderella by Jacob and Wilhelm Grimm; retold and ill. by Nonny Hogrogian. Greenwillow, 1981. Subj: Folk and fairy tales. Royalty. Sibling rivalry.

Cinderella by Jacob and Wilhelm Grimm; tr. by Anne Rogers; ill. by Svend Otto S. Larouse, 1978. Subj: Folk and fairy tales. Sibling rivalry. Royalty.

Clever Kate by Jacob and Wilhelm Grimm; adapt. by Elizabeth Shub; ill. by Anita Lobel. Macmillan, 1973. Subj: Folk and fairy tales. Humor.

The devil with the green hairs by Jacob and Wilhelm Grimm; retold and ill. by Nonny Hogrogian. Knopf, 1983. Subj: Devil. Folk and fairy tales.

The donkey prince by Jacob and Wilhelm Grimm; adapt. by M. Jean Craig; ill. by Barbara Cooney. Doubleday, 1977. Subj: Animals – donkeys. Folk and fairy tales. Magic. Royalty. Wizards.

The elves and the shoemaker by Jacob and Wilhelm Grimm; ill. by Paul Galdone. Clarion, 1984. "Based on Lucy Crane's tr. from the German." Adaption of Wichtelmänner. Subj: Careers – shoemakers. Character traits – helpfulness. Elves and little people. Folk and fairy tales. Foreign lands – Germany.

The fisherman and his wife by Jacob and Wilhelm Grimm; tr. by Elizabeth Shub; ill. by Monika Laimgruber. Greenwillow, 1979. Subj: Behavior – greed. Folk and fairy tales.

The fisherman and his wife by Jacob and Wilhelm Grimm; tr. by Randall Jarrell; ill. by Margot Zemach. Farrar, 1980. Subj: Behavior – greed. Folk and fairy tales.

The four clever brothers by Jacob and Wilhelm Grimm; ill. by Felix Hoffmann. Harcourt, 1967. Subj: Character traits – cleverness. Dragons. Folk and fairy tales.

The golden bird: and other fairy tales by Jacob and Wilhelm Grimm; tr. by Randall Jarrell; ill. by Sandro Nardini. Macmillan, 1962. Subj: Folk and fairy tales.

Grimm Tom Thumb (Tom Thumb)

Hans in luck by Jacob and Wilhelm Grimm; retold and ill. by Paul Galdone. Parents, 1979. Translation of Hans in Glück. Subj: Character traits – foolishness. Character traits – luck. Folk and fairy tales.

Hans in luck by Jacob and Wilhelm Grimm; ed. and ill. by Felix Hoffmann. Atheneum, 1975. Translation of Hans in Glück. Subj: Character traits – foolishness. Character traits – luck. Folk and fairy tales.

Hansel and Gretel by Jacob and Wilhelm Grimm; tr. by Charles Scribner, Jr.; ill. by Adrienne Adams. Scribner's, 1975. Subj: Folk and fairy tales. Forest, woods. Witches.

Hansel and Gretel by Jacob and Wilhelm Grimm; ill. by Anthony Browne. Watts, 1982. Subj: Folk and fairy tales. Forest, woods. Witches.

Hansel and Gretel by Jacob and Wilhelm Grimm; ill. by Susan Jeffers. Dial Pr., 1980. Subj: Folk and fairy tales. Forest, woods. Witches.

Hansel and Gretel by Jacob and Wilhelm Grimm; retold by Rika Lesser; ill. by Paul O. Zelinsky. Dodd, 1984. Subj: Caldecott award honor book. Folk and fairy tales. Forest, woods.

Hansel and Gretel by Jacob and Wilhelm Grimm; tr. from the German by Elizabeth D. Crawford; ill. by Lisbeth Zwerger. Morrow, 1980. Subj: Folk and fairy tales. Forest, woods. Witches.

The horse, the fox, and the lion by Jacob and Wilhelm Grimm; ill. by Paul Galdone. Seabury Pr., 1968. Adapt. from The fox and the horse [De Fuchs und das Pferd]. Subj: Animals – dogs. Animals – foxes. Animals – horses. Animals – lions. Behavior – trickery. Folk and fairy tales. Old age.

Jorinda and Joringel by Jacob and Wilhelm Grimm; tr. by Elizabeth Shub; ill. by Adrienne Adams. Scribner's, 1968. Subj: Folk and fairy tales. Witches.

Jorinda and Joringel by Jacob and Wilhelm Grimm; retold by Wanda Gág; ill. by Margot Tomes. Coward, 1978. Subj: Folk and fairy tales. Witches.

King Grisly-Beard by Jacob and Wilhelm Grimm; tr. by Edgar Taylor; ill. by Maurice Sendak. Farrar, 1973. 1823 translation. Subj: Character traits – conceit. Folk and fairy tales. Royalty. Theater.

Little red cap by Jacob and Wilhelm Grimm; tr. from German by Elizabeth D. Crawford; ill. by Lisbeth Zwerger. Morrow, 1983. Subj: Animals – wolves. Behavior – talking to strangers. Folk and fairy tales.

Little Red Riding Hood by Jacob and Wilhelm Grimm; adapt. by Elizabeth and Katherine Gant; ill. by Frank Aloise. Abingdon Pr., 1969. Adapt. and music based on retelling of Rotkäppchen. Incl. melodies with texts, with piano acc. Subj: Animals – wolves. Behavior – talking to strangers. Folk and fairy tales.

Little Red Riding Hood by Jacob and Wilhelm Grimm; ill. by Bernadette. Collins-World, 1969. Subj: Animals – wolves. Behavior – talking to strangers. Folk and fairy tales.

Little Red Riding Hood by Jacob and Wilhelm Grimm; adapt. by Margaret Hillert; ill. by Gwen Connelly. Follett, 1982. Subj: Animals – wolves. Behavior – talking to strangers. Folk and fairy tales.

Little Red Riding Hood by Jacob and Wilhelm Grimm; ill. by Paul Galdone. McGraw-Hill, 1974. Adapt. from the retelling of Rotkäppchen. Subj: Animals – wolves. Behavior – talking to strangers. Folk and fairy tales.

Little Red Riding Hood by Jacob and Wilhelm Grimm; retold and ill. by Trina Schart Hyman. Holiday, 1983. Subj: Animals – wolves. Behavior – talking to strangers. Caldecott award honor book. Folk and fairy tales.

Mother Holly by Jacob and Wilhelm Grimm; ill. by Bernadette. Crowell, 1972. Based on the Grimm brothers' Frau Holle. Subj: Behavior – greed. Character traits – helpfulness. Character traits – laziness. Folk and fairy tales.

Mrs. Fox's wedding by Jacob and Wilhelm Grimm; retold by Sara and Stephen Corrin; ill. by Errol Le Cain. Doubleday, 1980. Subj: Animals – foxes. Counting. Folk and fairy tales. Weddings.

The musicians of Bremen by Jacob and Wilhelm Grimm; tr. by Anne Rogers; ill. by Svend Otto S. Larousse, 1974. Subj: Animals. Folk and fairy tales. Old age.

Rapunzel by Jacob and Wilhelm Grimm; retold and ill. by Jutta Ash. Holt, 1982. Subj: Folk and fairy tales. Hair. Royalty. Witches.

Rapunzel by Jacob and Wilhelm Grimm; ill. by Bert Dodson. Troll Assoc., 1979. Subj: Folk and fairy tales. Hair. Royalty. Witches.

Rapunzel by Jacob and Wilhelm Grimm; retold by Barbara Rogasky; ill. by Trina Schart Hyman. Holiday, 1982. Subj: Folk and fairy tales. Hair. Royalty. Witches.

Rumpelstiltskin by Jacob and Wilhelm Grimm; ill. by Jacqueline Ayer. Harcourt, 1967. Subj: Folk and fairy tales. Magic. Riddles. Royalty. Weddings.

Rumpelstiltskin by Jacob and Wilhelm Grimm; retold and ill. by Donna Diamond. Holiday, 1983. Subj: Folk and fairy tales. Magic. Riddles. Royalty. Weddings.

Rumpelstiltskin by Jacob and Wilhelm Grimm; ill. by John Wallner. Prentice-Hall, 1984. Subj: Folk and fairy tales. Magic. Riddles. Royalty. Weddings.

The seven ravens by Jacob and Wilhelm Grimm; ill. by Felix Hoffmann. Harcourt, 1963. Subj: Birds – ravens. Folk and fairy tales. Magic.

The seven ravens by Jacob and Wilhelm Grimm; tr. from German by Elizabeth D. Crawford; ill. by Lisbeth Zwerger. Morrow, 1981. Subj: Birds – ravens. Folk and fairy tales. Magic.

The shoemaker and the elves by Jacob and Wilhelm Grimm; ill. by Cynthia and William Birrer. Lothrop, 1983. Adapt. of Wichtelmänner. Subj: Careers – shoemakers. Character traits – helpfulness. Elves and little people. Folk and fairy tales. Foreign lands – Germany.

The six swans by Jacob and Wilhelm Grimm; retold by Wanda Gág; ill. by Margot Tomes. Coward, 1982. Subj: Birds – swans. Folk and fairy tales. Magic.

The sleeping beauty by Jacob and Wilhelm Grimm; retold and ill. by Warwick Hutton. Atheneum, 1979. Subj: Folk and fairy tales.

The sleeping beauty by Jacob and Wilhelm Grimm; retold and ill. by Trina Schart Hyman. Little, 1977. Subj: Folk and fairy tales.

Snow White by Jacob and Wilhelm Grimm; ill. by Bernadette. Faber, 1983. Subj: Elves and little people. Emotions – envy, jealousy. Folk and fairy tales. Magic. Witches.

Snow White by Jacob and Wilhelm Grimm; tr. from German by Paul Heins; ill. by Trina Schart Hyman. Little, 1975. Subj: Elves and little people. Emotions – envy, jealousy. Folk and fairy tales. Magic. Witches.

Snow White and Rose Red by Jacob and Wilhelm Grimm; tr. by Wayne Andrews; ill. by Adrienne Adams. Scribner's, 1964. Subj: Animals – bears. Elves and little people. Folk and fairy tales. Magic. Weddings.

Snow-White and Rose-Red adapt. and ill. by Barbara Cooney. Dial Pr., 1966. Subj: Animals – bears. Elves and little people. Folk and fairy tales.

Snow White and Rose Red by Jacob and Wilhelm Grimm; tr. by Andrew Lang; ill. by John Wallner. Prentice-Hall, 1984. Subj: Animals – bears. Elves and little people. Folk and fairy tales. Magic. Weddings.

Snow White and the seven dwarfs by Jacob and Wilhelm Grimm; ill. by Wanda Gág. Coward, 1938. Subj: Caldecott award honor book. Folk and fairy tales.

The table, the donkey and the stick adapt. and ill. by Paul Galdone. McGraw-Hill, 1976. Adapt. from a retelling of Das tapfere Schneiderlein. Subj: Cumulative tales. Folk and fairy tales.

Three Grimms' fairy tales: The fox and the geese; The magic porridge pot; The silver pennies by Jacob and Wilhelm Grimm; ill. by Bernadette. Little, 1981. Subj: Folk and fairy tales.

Tom Thumb

The twelve dancing princesses by Jacob and Wilhelm Grimm; ill. by Dennis Hockerman. Troll Assoc., 1979. Subj: Activities – dancing. Folk and fairy tales. Royalty.

The twelve dancing princesses by Jacob and Wilhelm Grimm; ill. by Errol Le Cain. Viking, 1978. Subj: Activities – dancing. Folk and fairy tales. Royalty.

The twelve dancing princesses by Jacob and Wilhelm Grimm; tr. by Elizabeth Shub; ill. by Uri Shulevitz. Scribner's, 1966. Subj: Activities – dancing. Folk and fairy tales. Royalty.

The valiant little tailor by Jacob and Wilhelm Grimm; ill. by Victor G. Ambrus. Oxford Univ. Pr., 1980. First pub. in 1971. Subj: Careers – tailors. Character traits – bravery. Folk and fairy tales. Giants.

Walt Disney's Snow White and the seven dwarfs (Walt Disney Productions)

The wolf and the seven kids by Jacob and Wilhelm Grimm; ill. by Kinuko Craft. Troll Assoc., 1979. Subj: Animals – goats. Animals – wolves. Folk and fairy tales.

The wolf and the seven little kids by Jacob and Wilhelm Grimm; tr. by Anne Rogers; ill. by Svend Otto S. Larousse, 1977. Subj: Animals – wolves. Folk and fairy tales.

Grimm, Wilhelm. *The bear and the kingbird* (Grimm, Jacob)

The bearskinner (Grimm, Jacob,)

The brave little tailor (Grimm, Jacob)

The Bremen town musicians (Grimm, Jacob)

Cinderella (Grimm, Jacob)

Clever Kate (Grimm, Jacob)

The devil with the green hairs (Grimm, Jacob)

The donkey prince (Grimm, Jacob)

The elves and the shoemaker (Grimm, Jacob)

The fisherman and his wife (Grimm, Jacob)

The four clever brothers (Grimm, Jacob)

The golden bird (Grimm, Jacob)

Grimm Tom Thumb (Tom Thumb)

Hans in luck (Grimm, Jacob)

Hansel and Gretel (Grimm, Jacob)

The horse, the fox, and the lion (Grimm, Jacob)

Jorinda and Joringel (Grimm, Jacob)

King Grisly-Beard (Grimm, Jacob)

Little red cap (Grimm, Jacob)

Little Red Riding Hood (Grimm, Jacob)

Mother Holly (Grimm, Jacob)

Mrs. Fox's wedding (Grimm, Jacob)

The musicians of Bremen (Grimm, Jacob)

Rapunzel (Grimm, Jacob)

Rumpelstiltskin (Grimm, Jacob)

The seven ravens (Grimm, Jacob)

The shoemaker and the elves (Grimm, Jacob)

The six swans (Grimm, Jacob)

The sleeping beauty (Grimm, Jacob)

Snow White (Grimm, Jacob)

Snow White and Rose Red (Grimm, Jacob)

Snow White and the seven dwarfs (Grimm, Jacob)

The table, the donkey and the stick (Grimm, Jacob)

Three Grimms' fairy tales (Grimm, Jacob)

Tom Thumb

The twelve dancing princesses (Grimm, Jacob)

The valiant little tailor (Grimm, Jacob)

The wolf and the seven kids (Grimm, Jacob)

The wolf and the seven little kids (Grimm, Jacob)

Groat, Diane *see* De Groat, Diane

Grode, Redway *see* Gorey, Edward

Gross, Alan. *Sometimes I worry...* ill. by Mike Venezia. Children's Pr., 1978. Subj: Behavior – worrying.

What if the teacher calls on me? ill. by Mike Venezia. Children's Pr., 1980. Subj: Behavior – worrying. School.

Gross, Michael. *The fable of the fig tree* ill. by Mila Lazarevich. Walck, 1975. Subj: Folk and fairy tales. Jewish culture.

Gross, Ruth Belov. *Alligators and other crocodilians* ill. with photos. Four Winds Pr., 1978. Subj: Reptiles – alligators, crocodiles. Science.

A book about your skeleton ill. by Deborah Robison. Hastings, 1979. Subj: Anatomy. Health.

The emperor's new clothes (Andersen, H C (Hans Christian))

The girl who wouldn't get married ill. by Jack Kent. Four Winds Pr., 1983. Subj: Animals – horses. Folk and fairy tales. Weddings.

Grossbart, Francine. *A big city* ill. by author. Harper, 1966. Subj: ABC books. City.

Grosvenor, Donna. *Zoo babies* ill. by author. National Geographical Soc., 1979. Subj: Animals. Zoos.

Grover, Eulalie Osgood. *Mother Goose*

Groves-Raines, Antony. *The tidy hen* ill. by author. Harcourt, 1961. Subj: Character traits – cleanliness.

Gruber, Ruth *see* Michaels, Ruth

Gruenberg, Sidonie Matsner. *The wonderful story of how you were born* ill. by Symeon Shimin. Rev. ed. Doubleday, 1970. Subj: Babies. Family life. Science.

Guilfoile, Elizabeth. *Have you seen my brother?* ill. by Mary Stevens. Follett, 1962. Subj: Behavior – lost. Careers – police officers. City.

Nobody listens to Andrew ill. by Mary Stevens. Follett, 1957. Subj: Animals – bears. Behavior – needing someone.

Valentine's Day ill. by Gordon Laite. Garrard, 1965. Subj: Holidays – Valentine's Day.

Gullo, Stephen V. *When people die* (Bernstein, Joanne E)

Gundersheimer, Karen. *A B C say with me* ill. by author. Harper, 1984. Subj: ABC books.

Happy winter ill. by author. Harper, 1982. Subj: Poetry, rhyme. Seasons – winter.

1 2 3 play with me ill. by author. Harper, 1984. Subj: Animals – mice. Counting.

Gunning, Monica. *The two Georges: Los dos Jorges* ill. by Veronica Mary Miracle. Blaine-Ethridge, 1976. Subj: ABC books. Foreign languages. Poetry, rhyme.

Gunther, Louise. *Anna's snow day* ill. by Paul Frame. Garrard, 1979. Subj: Weather – snow.

A tooth for the tooth fairy ill. by Jim Cummins. Garrard, 1978. Subj: Fairies. Teeth.

Gunthrop, Karen. *Adam and the wolf* ill. by Attilio Cassinelli. Doubleday, 1967. Translation of Il pulcino e il lupo. Subj: Animals – wolves. Behavior – disbelief. Food.

Rina at the farm ill. by Attilio Cassinelli. Doubleday, 1968. Subj: Farms.

Gurney, Eric. *The king, the mice and the cheese* (Gurney, Nancy)

Gurney, Nancy. *The king, the mice and the cheese* by Nancy and Eric Gurney; ill. by Jean Vallier. Random House, 1965. Subj: Animals – mice. Food. Royalty.

Guy, Rosa. *Mother crocodile* ill. by John Steptoe. Delacorte, 1981. Subj: Animals – monkeys. Folk and fairy tales. Foreign lands – Africa. Reptiles – alligators, crocodiles.

Guzzo, Sandra E. *Fox and Heggie* ill. by Kathy Parkinson. Albert Whitman, 1983. Subj: Animals – foxes. Animals – hedgehogs. Shopping.

Haas, Carolyn. *Purple cow to the rescue* (Cole, Ann)

Haas, Irene. *The Maggie B* ill. by author. Atheneum, 1975. Subj: Behavior – wishing. Boats, ships. Poetry, rhyme. Sea and seashore.

Haas, Merle. *Babar and Father Christmas* (Brunhoff, Jean de)

Babar and his children (Brunhoff, Jean de)

Babar and Zephir (Brunhoff, Jean de)

Babar the king (Brunhoff, Jean de)

Babar visits another planet (Brunhoff, Laurent de)

Babar's castle (Brunhoff, Laurent de)

Babar's cousin, that rascal Arthur (Brunhoff, Laurent de)

Babar's fair will be opened next Sunday (Brunhoff, Laurent de)

The story of Babar, the little elephant (Brunhoff, Jean de)

The travels of Babar (Brunhoff, Jean de)

Hader, Berta Hoerner. *The big snow* by Berta and Elmer Hader; ill. by authors. Macmillan, 1948. Subj: Caldecott award book. Weather – snow.

Cock-a-doodle doo: the story of a little red rooster by Berta and Elmer Hader; ill. by authors. Macmillan, 1939. Subj: Birds – chickens. Birds – ducks. Caldecott award honor book. Farms.

Lost in the zoo by Berta and Elmer Hader; ill. by authors. Macmillan, 1951. Subj: Behavior – lost. Zoos.

The mighty hunter by Berta and Elmer Hader; ill. by authors. Macmillan, 1943. Subj: Caldecott award honor book. Ecology. Ethnic groups in the U.S. – Indians. School. Sports – hunting.

Mister Billy's gun by Berta and Elmer Hader; ill. by authors. Macmillan, 1960. Subj: Activities – gardening. Birds. Character traits – kindness to animals. Violence, anti-violence. Weapons.

The story of Pancho and the bull with the crooked tail by Berta and Elmer Hader; ill. by authors. Oxford Univ. Pr., 1933. Subj: Animals – bulls, cows. Foreign lands – Mexico.

Hader, Elmer. *The big snow* (Hader, Berta Hoerner)

Cock-a-doodle doo (Hader, Berta Hoerner)

Lost in the zoo (Hader, Berta Hoerner)

The mighty hunter (Hader, Berta Hoerner)

Mister Billy's gun (Hader, Berta Hoerner)

The story of Pancho and the bull with the crooked tail (Hader, Berta Hoerner)

Hadithi, Mwenye. *Greedy zebra* ill. by Adrienne Kennaway. Little, 1984. Subj: Animals – zebras. Folk and fairy tales. Foreign lands – Africa.

Hague, Kathleen. *Alphabears: an ABC book* ill. by Michael Hague. Holt, 1984. Subj: ABC books. Poetry, rhyme. Toys – teddy bears.

The man who kept house by Kathleen and Michael Hague; ill. by Michael Hague. Harcourt, 1981. Subj: Family life. Folk and fairy tales. Foreign lands – Norway.

Hague, Michael. *The man who kept house* (Hague, Kathleen)

Mother Goose

Hahn, Hannelore. *Take a giant step* ill. by Margot Zemach. Little, 1960. Subj: Games.

Haines, Gail Kay. *Fire* ill. by Jacqueline Chwast. Morrow, 1975. Subj: Fire. Science.

What makes a lemon sour? ill. by Janet McCaffery. Morrow, 1977. Subj: Science.

Hair ill. by Christine Sharr. Wonder Books, 1971. Subj: Hair.

Haiz, Danah. *Jonah's journey* ill. by H. Hechtkopf. Lerner, 1973. Subj: Animals – whales. Religion.

Hale, Irina. *Brown bear in a brown chair* ill. by author. Atheneum, 1983. Subj: Character traits – appearance. Toys – teddy bears.

Chocolate mouse and sugar pig ill. by author. Atheneum, 1979. Subj: Animals – mice. Animals – pigs. Behavior – running away. Food. Toys.

Donkey's dreadful day ill. by author. Atheneum, 1982. Subj: Animals – donkeys. Circus. Dreams.

Hale, Kathleen. *Orlando and the water cats* ill. by author. Merrimack, 1979. Subj: Activities – vacationing. Animals – cats. Family life.

Orlando buys a farm ill. by author. Merrimack, 1980. Subj: Animals – cats. Farms.

Orlando the frisky housewife ill. by author. Merrimack, 1979. Subj: Animals – cats. Stores.

Hale, Linda. *The glorious Christmas soup party* ill. by author. Viking, 1962. Subj: Animals – mice. Food. Holidays – Christmas.

Hale, Sara Josepha. *Mary had a little lamb* ill. by Tomie de Paola. Holiday, 1984. Subj: Animals – sheep. Music. Nursery rhymes. School.

Haley, Gail E. *Go away, stay away* ill. by author. Scribner's, 1977. Subj: Goblins. Seasons.

The green man ill. by author. Scribner's, 1980. Subj: Knights. Seasons.

Jack Jouett's ride ill. by author. Viking, 1973. Subj: U.S. history.

Noah's ark ill. by author. Atheneum, 1971. Subj: Animals. Boats, ships. Ecology. Religion – Noah.

The post office cat ill. by author. Scribner's, 1976. Subj: Animals – cats. Careers – mail carriers. Foreign lands – England.

A story, a story ill. by author. Atheneum, 1970. Subj: Caldecott award book. Folk and fairy tales. Foreign lands – Africa.

Haley, Patrick. *The little person* ill. by Jonna Kool. East Eagle Pr., 1981. Subj: Activities – traveling.

Hall, Amanda. *The gossipy wife* ill. by author. Harper, 1984. Subj: Folk and fairy tales. Foreign lands – Russia.

Hall, Bill. *Fish tale* ill. by John E. Johnson. Norton, 1967. Subj: Fish. Sports – fishing.

A year in the forest ill. by Feodor Rojankovsky. McGraw-Hill, 1973. Subj: Animals. Seasons.

Hall, Carol. *Northern J. Calloway presents Supervroomer!* (Calloway, Northern J)

Hall, Donald. *Andrew the lion farmer* ill. by Jane Miller. Watts, 1959. Subj: Humor.

The ox-cart man ill. by Barbara Cooney. Viking, 1979. Subj: Activities – working. Caldecott award book. Farms. Seasons.

Hall, Fergus. *Groundsel* ill. by author. Merrimack, 1983. Subj: Activities – gardening. Seasons.

Hall, Katy. *Fishy riddles* by Katy Hall and Lisa Eisenberg; ill. by Simms Taback. Dial Pr., 1983. Subj: Humor. Riddles. Sea and seashore.

Hall, Malcolm. *And then the mouse...* ill. by Stephen Gammell. Four Winds Pr., 1980. Subj: Animals – mice. Folk and fairy tales.

CariCATures ill. by Bruce Degen. Coward, 1978. Subj: Animals. Riddles.

The friends of Charlie Ant Bear ill. by Alexandra Wallner. Coward, 1980. Subj: Animals – anteaters. Character traits – optimism.

Hall, Pam. *On the edge of the eastern ocean* ill. by author. Silver Burdett, 1982. Subj: Birds – puffins. Poetry, rhyme.

Haller, Danita Ross. *Not just any ring* ill. by Deborah Kogan Ray. Knopf, 1982. Subj: Magic.

Hallinan, P. K. (Patrick K.). *I'm glad to be me* ill. by author. Children's Pr., 1977. Subj: Activities. Family life – only child. Self-concept.

I'm thankful each day! ill. by author. Children's Pr., 1981. Subj: Folk and fairy tales.

Just being alone ill. by author. Children's Pr., 1976. Subj: Activities. Behavior – solitude. Family life – only child.

Just open a book ill. by author. Children's Pr., 1981. Subj: Activities – reading. Poetry, rhyme.

That's what a friend is ill. by author. Children's Pr., 1977. Subj: Friendship. Poetry, rhyme.

Where's Michael? ill. by author. Children's Pr., 1978. Subj: Behavior – imitation. Self-concept.

Halsey, William D. *The magic world of words: a very first dictionary* ed. by William D. Halsey and Christopher G. Morris. Macmillan, 1977. Subj: Dictionaries.

Hamberger, John. *The day the sun disappeared* ill. by author. Norton, 1964. Subj: Animals. Ecology. Science. Sun.

Hazel was an only pet ill. by author. Norton, 1968. Subj: Animals – dogs. Family life – only child. Pets.

The lazy dog ill. by author. Four Winds Pr., 1971. Subj: Animals – dogs. Toys – balls. Wordless.

The peacock who lost his tail ill. by author. Norton, 1967. Subj: Birds – peacocks, peahens. Character traits – pride.

This is the day ill. by author. Grosset, 1971. Subj: Animals – groundhogs. Holidays – Groundhog Day.

Hamil, Thomas Arthur. *Brother Alonzo* ill. by author. Macmillan, 1957. Subj: Religion.

Hamilton, Emily. *My name is Emily* (Hamilton, Morse)

Hamilton, Morse. *Big sisters are bad witches* ill. by Marylin Hafner. Greenwillow, 1981. Subj: Sibling rivalry. Witches.

How do you do, Mr. Birdsteps? ill. by Patience Brewster. Avon, 1983. Subj: Character traits – shyness.

My name is Emily by Morse and Emily Hamilton; ill. by Jenni Oliver. Greenwillow, 1979. Subj: Behavior – running away. Sibling rivalry.

Who's afraid of the dark? ill. by Patience Brewster. Avon, 1983. Subj: Emotions – fear. Night.

Hamilton-Merritt, Jane. *My first days of school* photos. by author. Simon and Schuster, 1982. Subj: School.

Our new baby photos. by author. Simon and Schuster, 1982. Subj: Babies. Family life.

Hammarberg, Dyan. *Rusty the Irish setter* (Overbeck, Cynthia)

Hample, Stoo. *Stoo Hample's silly joke book* ill. by author. Delacorte, 1978. Subj: Humor. Riddles.

Yet another big fat funny silly book ill. by author. Delacorte, 1980. Subj: Poetry, rhyme. Riddles.

Hamsa, Bobbie. *Dirty Larry* ill. by Paul Sharp. Children's Pr., 1983. Subj: Character traits – cleanliness.

Your pet bear ill. by Tom Dunnington. Children's Pr., 1980. Subj: Animals – bears. Imagination.

Your pet beaver ill. by Tom Dunnington. Children's Pr., 1980. Subj: Animals – beavers. Imagination.

Your pet camel ill. by Tom Dunnington. Children's Pr., 1980. Subj: Animals – camels. Imagination.

Your pet elephant ill. by Tom Dunnington. Children's Pr., 1980. Subj: Animals – elephants. Imagination.

Your pet giraffe ill. by Tom Dunnington. Children's Pr., 1982. Subj: Animals – giraffes. Imagination.

Your pet kangaroo ill. by Tom Dunnington. Children's Pr., 1980. Subj: Animals – kangaroos. Imagination.

Your pet penguin ill. by Tom Dunnington. Children's Pr., 1980. Subj: Birds – penguins. Imagination.

Your pet sea lion ill. by Tom Dunnington. Children's Pr., 1982. Subj: Animals – sea lions. Imagination.

Hancock, Sibyl. *Esteban and the ghost* ill. by Dirk Zimmer. Dial Pr., 1983. Adapted from The tinker and the ghost by Ralph Steele Boggs and Mary Gould Davis. Subj: Ghosts.

Freaky Francie ill. by Leonard W. Shortall. Prentice-Hall, 1979. Subj: Problem solving.

Old Blue ill. by Erick Ingraham. Putnam's, 1980. Subj: Animals – bulls, cows. Cowboys.

Handforth, Thomas. *Mei Li* ill. by author. Doubleday, 1938. Subj: Caldecott award book. Foreign lands – China. Holidays – Chinese New Year.

Hands, Hargrave. *Bunny sees* ill. by author. Grosset, 1985. Subj: Animals – rabbits. Format, unusual – cardboard pages. Nature.

Hanlon, Emily. *What if a lion eats me and I fall into a hippopotamus' mud hole?* ill. by Leigh Grant. Delacorte Pr., 1975. Subj: Emotions – fear. Imagination. Zoos.

Hann, Jacquie. *Crybaby* ill. by author. Four Winds Pr., 1979. Subj: Emotions.

Follow the leader ill. by author. Crown, 1982. Subj: Activities – playing. Games.

Up day, down day ill. by author. Four Winds Pr., 1978. Subj: Character traits – luck. Sports – fishing.

Hansen, Carla. *Barnaby Bear builds a boat* by Carla and Vilhelm Hansen; ill. by authors. Random House, 1979. Subj: Animals – bears. Boats, ships.

Barnaby Bear visits the farm by Carla and Vilhelm Hansen; ill. by authors. Random House, 1979. Subj: Animals – bears. Farms.

Hansen, Jeff. *Being a fire fighter isn't just squirtin' water* ill. by author. Vantage Pr., 1978. Subj: Careers – firefighters.

Hansen, Vilhelm. *Barnaby Bear builds a boat* (Hansen, Carla)

Barnaby Bear visits the farms (Hansen, Carla)

Hanson, Joan. *I don't like Timmy* ill. by author. Carolrhoda Books, 1972. Subj: Babies. Friendship.

I won't be afraid ill. by author. Carolrhoda Books, 1974. Subj: Behavior – growing up. Emotions – fear.

I'm going to run away ill. by author. Platt, 1978. Subj: Behavior – running away.

Hapgood, Miranda. *Martha's mad day* ill. by Emily Arnold McCully. Crown, 1977. Subj: Emotions – anger.

Harada, Joyce. *It's the ABC book* ill. by author. Heian Intl., 1982. Subj: ABC books.

Hare, Lorraine. *Who needs her?* ill. by author. Atheneum, 1983. Subj: Character traits – cleanliness.

Hare, Norma Q. *Mystery at mouse house* ill. by Stella Ormai. Garrard, 1980. Subj: Behavior – stealing. Problem solving.

Harlow, Joan Hiatt. *Shadow bear* ill. by Jim Arnosky. Doubleday, 1981. Subj: Animals – bears. Emotions – fear. Ethnic groups in the U.S. – Eskimos.

Harms, D. *The merry starlings* (Marshak, Samuel)

Harper, Anita. *How we live* ill. by Christine Roche. Harper, 1977. Subj: Houses.

How we work ill. by Christine Roche. Harper, 1977. Subj: Activities – working. Careers.

Harper, Wilhelmina. *The gunniwolf* ill. by William Wiesner. Dutton, 1967. Subj: Animals – wolves. Behavior – misbehavior. Flowers. Foreign lands – Germany.

Harris, Dorothy Joan. *Goodnight Jeffrey* ill. by Nancy Hannans. Warne, 1983. Subj: Bedtime.

The school mouse and the hamster ill. by Judy Clifford. Warne, 1979. Subj: Animals – hamsters. Animals – mice. School.

Harris, Leon A. *The great picture robbery* ill. by Joseph Schindelman. Atheneum, 1963. Subj: Animals – mice. Art. Crime. Foreign lands – France.

Harris, Louise Dyer. *Flash, the life of a firefly* by Louise Dyer Harris and Norman Dyer Harris; ill. by Henry B. Kane. Little, 1966. Subj: Insects – Fireflies. Science.

Harris, Norman Dyer. *Flash, the life of a firefly* (Harris, Louise Dyer)

Harris, Robie H. *Don't forget to come back* ill. by Tony DeLuna. Atheneum, 1963. Subj: Activities – babysitting. Behavior. Family life.

I hate kisses ill. by Diane Paterson. Knopf, 1981. Subj: Behavior – growing up.

Harris, Susan. *Creatures that look alike* ill. by Don Forrest. Watts, 1980. Subj: Animals. Science.

Reptiles ill. by Jim Robins. Watts, 1978. Subj: Reptiles. Science.

Harrison, David Lee. *The case of Og, the missing frog* ill. by Jerry Warshaw. Rand McNally, 1972. Subj: Frogs and toads. Poetry, rhyme.

Detective Bob and the great ape escape ill. by Ned Delaney. Parents, 1980. Subj: Animals – gorillas. Problem solving. Zoos.

Little turtle's big adventure ill. by J. P. Miller. Random House, 1969. Subj: Character traits – kindness to animals. Progress. Reptiles – turtles.

Harrison, Sarah. *In granny's garden* ill. by Mike Wilks. Holt, 1980. Subj: Animals. Dinosaurs. Poetry, rhyme.

Harrison, Ted. *A northern alphabet: A is for arctic* ill. by author. Tundra Books, 1982. Subj: ABC books.

Harrop, Beatrice. *Sing hey diddle diddle* (Mother Goose)

Hart, Jeanne McGahey. *Scareboy* ill. by Gerhardt Hurt. Parnassus, 1957. Subj: Humor. Scarecrows.

Hartelius, Margaret A. *The chicken's child* ill. by author. Doubleday, 1975. Subj: Birds – chickens. Reptiles – alligators, crocodiles. Wordless.

Haseley, Dennis. *The old banjo* ill. by Stephen Gammell. Macmillan, 1983. Subj: Farms. Music.

The pirate who tried to capture the moon ill. by Sue Truesdell. Harper, 1983. Subj: Pirates.

The soap bandit ill. by Jane Chambless-Rigie. Warne, 1984. Subj: Character traits – cleanliness.

Haskins, Ilma. *Color seems* ill. by author. Vanguard, 1973. Subj: Concepts – color.

Hasler, Eveline. *Martin is our friend* ill. by Dorothea Desmarowitz. Abingdon Pr., 1981. Subj: Animals – horses. Character traits – kindness. Handicaps.

Hastings, Evelyn Beilhart. *The department store* ill. by Lewis A. Ogan. Melmont, 1956. Subj: Shopping. Stores.

Hatcher, Charles. *What shape is it?* ill. by Gareth Adamson. Duell, 1966. Subj: Concepts – shape.

Haubensak-Tellenbach, Margrit. *The story of Noah's ark* ill. by Erna Emhardt. Crown, 1983. Subj: Religion – Noah.

Haugaard, Erik. *The emperor's nightingale* (Andersen, H C (Hans Christian))

Hauptmann, Tatjana. *A day in the life of Petronella Pig* ill. by author. Holt, 1982. Subj: Animals – pigs. Format, unusual. Wordless.

Hautzig, Esther. *At home: a visit in four languages* ill. by Aliki. Macmillan, 1969. Subj: Family life. Foreign lands – France. Foreign lands – Russia. Foreign lands – Spain. Foreign languages.

In the park: an excursion in four languages ill. by Ezra Jack Keats. Macmillan, 1968. Subj: Foreign lands – France. Foreign lands – Russia. Foreign lands – Spain. Foreign languages.

Hawes, Judy. *Fireflies in the night* ill. by Kazue Mizumura. Coward, 1963. Subj: Family life – grandparents, great-grandparents. Farms. Insects – fireflies. Science.

Ladybug, ladybug, fly away home ill. by Ed Emberley. Crowell, 1968. Subj: Insects – ladybugs. Science.

Shrimps ill. by Joseph Low. Crowell, 1967. Subj: Fish. Science.

Spring peepers ill. by Graham Booth. Crowell, 1975. Subj: Frogs and toads. Science.

Watch honeybees with me ill. by Helen Stone. Crowell, 1964. Subj: Insects – bees. Science.

Why frogs are wet ill. by Don Madden. Crowell, 1968. Subj: Frogs and toads. Science.

Hawkesworth, Jenny. *The lonely skyscraper* ill. by Emanuel Schongut. Doubleday, 1980. Subj: City. Country.

Hawkins, Colin. *Boo! Who?* by Colin and Jacqui Hawkins; ill. by authors. Holt, 1984. Subj: Poetry, rhyme.

Mig the pig by Colin and Jacqui Hawkins; ill. by Colin Hawkins. Putnam's, 1984. Subj: Animals – pigs. Poetry, rhyme.

Pat the cat by Colin and Jacqui Hawkins; ill. by Colin Hawkins. Putnam's, 1983. Subj: Animals – cats.

What time is it, Mr. Wolf? ill. by author. Putnam's, 1983. Subj: Animals – wolves. Format, unusual. Time.

Hawkins, Jacqui. *Boo! Who?* (Hawkins, Colin)

Mig the pig (Hawkins, Colin)

Pat the cat (Hawkins, Colin)

Hawkins, Mark. *A lion under her bed* ill. by Jean Vallario. Holt, 1978. Subj: Animals – lions. Bedtime.

Hawkinson, John. *Birds in the sky* (Hawkinson, Lucy)

The old stump ill. by author. Albert Whitman, 1965. Subj: Animals – mice. Trees.

Robins and rabbits by John and Lucy Hawkinson; ill. by John Hawkinson. Albert Whitman, 1960. Subj: Animals. Birds – robins.

Where the wild apples grow ill. by author. Albert Whitman, 1967. Subj: Animals – horses. Character traits – freedom.

Hawkinson, Lucy. *Birds in the sky* by Lucy and John Hawkinson; ill. by authors. Children's Pr., 1966. Subj: Birds. Science.

Dance, dance, Amy-Chan! ill. by author. Albert Whitman, 1964. Subj: Ethnic groups in the U.S. – Japanese-Americans.

Robins and rabbits (Hawkinson, John)

Hay, Dean. *I see a lot of things* ill. by author. Lion, 1966. Subj: Senses.

Now I can count ill. by author. Lion, 1968. Subj: Counting. Time.

Hay, Timothy *see* Brown, Margaret Wise

Hayes, Geoffrey. *Bear by himself* ill. by author. Harper, 1976. Subj: Behavior – solitude. Toys – teddy bears.

Elroy and the witch's child ill. by author. Harper, 1982. Subj: Animals – cats. Witches.

Patrick and Ted ill. by author. Four Winds Pr., 1984. Subj: Animals – bears. Behavior – growing up.

The secret inside ill. by author. Harper, 1980. Subj: Animals – bears. Dreams.

Hayes, William D. (William Dimmity). *Mexicali soup* (Hitte, Kathryn)

Haynes, Robert. *The elephant that ga-lumphed* (Ward, Nanda Weedon)

Hays, Daniel. *Charley sang a song* (Hays, Hoffman Reynolds)

Hays, Hoffman Reynolds. *Charley sang a song* by Hoffman and Daniel Hays; ill. by Uri Shulevitz. Harper, 1964. Subj: Activities – flying.

Hays, Wilma Pitchford. *Little Yellow Fur* ill. by Richard Cuffari. Coward, 1973. Subj: Ethnic groups in the U.S. – Indians.

Hayward, Linda. *The Sesame Street dictionary* ill. by Joseph Mathieu. Random House, 1980. Subj: Dictionaries.

Hayward, Max. *The telephone* (Chukovsky, Korney)

Haywood, Carolyn. *A Christmas fantasy* ill. by Glenys and Victor G. Ambrus. Morrow, 1972. Subj: Holidays – Christmas.

The king's monster ill. by Victor G. Ambrus. Morrow, 1980. Subj: Monsters. Royalty.

Santa Claus forever ill. by Glenys and Victor G. Ambrus. Morrow, 1983. Subj: Holidays – Christmas.

Hazelton, Elizabeth Baldwin. *Sammy, the crow who remembered* ill. by Ann Atwood. Scribner's, 1969. Subj: Birds – crows. Family life.

Hazen, Barbara Shook. *Even if I did something awful* ill. by Nancy Kincade. Atheneum, 1981. Subj: Emotions – love. Family life.

The gorilla did it! ill. by Ray Cruz. Atheneum, 1974. Subj: Animals – gorillas. Imagination – imaginary friends.

Gorilla wants to be the baby ill. by Jacqueline Bardner Smith. Atheneum, 1978. Subj: Animals – gorillas. Imagination – imaginary friends.

Happy, sad, silly, mad: a beginning book about emotions ill. by Elizabeth Dauber; ed. consultant: Mary Elting. Grosset, 1971. Subj: Emotions.

If it weren't for Benjamin (I'd always get to lick the icing spoon) ill. by Laura Hartman. Human Sciences Pr., 1979. Subj: Sibling rivalry.

The me I see ill. by Ati Forberg. Abingdon, 1978. Subj: Activities – bathing. Anatomy.

The sorcerer's apprentice ill. by Tomi Ungerer. Lancelot Pr., 1969. Subj: Folk and fairy tales. Magic.

Tight times ill. by Trina Schart Hyman. Viking, 1979. Subj: Animals – cats. Family life. Family life – only child. Poverty.

Two homes to live in ill. by Peggy Luks. Human Sciences Pr., 1978. Subj: Divorce. Emotions.

Where do bears sleep? ill. by Ian E. Staunton. Addison-Wesley, 1970. Subj: Animals. Poetry, rhyme. Sleep.

Why couldn't I be an only kid like you, Wigger? ill. by Leigh Grant. Atheneum, 1975. Subj: Babies. Emotions – envy, jealousy. Family life – only child. Sibling rivalry.

Heathers, Anne. *The thread soldiers* by Anne Heathers and Esteban Frances; ill. by Esteban Frances. Harcourt, 1960. Subj: Animals – mice. String. Toys – soldiers.

Hedderwick, Mairi. *Katie Morag delivers the mail* ill. by author. Merrimack, 1984. Subj: Careers – mail carriers. Foreign lands – Scotland.

Hefter, Richard. *The strawberry book of shapes* ill. by author. Larousse, 1976. Subj: Concepts – shape.

Heide, Florence Parry. *A monster is coming! A monster is coming!* by Florence Parry Heide and Roxanne Heide; ill. by Rachi Farrow. Watts, 1980. Subj: Monsters.

The shrinking of Treehorn ill. by Edward Gorey. Holiday, 1971. Subj: Family life. Humor. Problem solving.

Treehorn's treasure ill. by Edward Gorey. Holiday House, 1981. Subj: Family life. Magic. Money.

Treehorn's wish ill. by Edward Gorey. Holiday, 1984. Subj: Birthdays. Magic.

Heide, Roxanne. *A monster is coming! A monster is coming!* (Heide, Florence Parry)

Heilbroner, Joan. *Robert the rose horse* ill. by Philip Eastman. Random House, 1962. Subj: Animals – horses. Flowers. Humor.

This is the house where Jack lives ill. by Aliki. Harper, 1962. Subj: Cumulative tales. Participation.

Heine, Helme. *Friends* ill. by author. Atheneum, 1982. Subj: Animals. Friendship. Sports – bicycling.

King Bounce the 1st ill. by author. Alphabet Pr., 1982. Subj: Royalty. Sleep.

Merry-go-round ill. by author. Barron's, 1980. Subj: Activities – working.

Mr. Miller the dog ill. by author. Atheneum, 1980. Subj: Animals – dogs. Behavior – imitation.

The most wonderful egg in the world ill. by author. Atheneum, 1983. Subj: Birds – chickens. Character traits – appearance. Royalty.

The pigs' wedding ill. by author. Atheneum, 1979. Subj: Animals – pigs. Weddings.

Superhare ill. by author. Barron's, 1979. Subj: Animals – rabbits. Character traits – being different.

Heins, Paul. *Snow White* (Grimm, Jacob)

Helena, Ann. *The lie* ill. by Ellen Pizer. Raintree, 1977. Subj: Behavior – lying. Emotions. Friendship.

Heller, George. *Hiroshi's wonderful kite* ill. by Kyuzo Tsugami. Silver Burdett, 1968. Subj: Crime. Foreign lands – Japan. Kites.

Heller, Linda. *Alexis and the golden ring* ill. by author. Macmillan, 1980. Subj: Folk and fairy tales. Foreign lands – Russia. Magic.

The castle on Hester Street ill. by author. Jewish Pub. Soc., 1982. Subj: Family life – grandparents, great-grandparents.

Lily at the table ill. by author. Macmillan, 1979. Subj: Family life. Food. Wordless.

Heller, Ruth. *Animals born alive and well* ill. by author. Grosset, 1982. Subj: Animals.

Chickens aren't the only ones ill. by author. Grosset, 1981. Subj: Eggs. Science.

Plants that never ever bloom ill. by author. Grosset, 1984. Subj: Plants.

The reason for a flower ill. by author. Grosset, 1983. Subj: Flowers. Poetry, rhyme.

Heller, Wendy. *Clementine and the cage* ill. by Rex J. Irvine. Kalimát, 1980. Subj: Behavior – running away. Birds – canaries.

Hellsing, Lennart. *The wonderful pumpkin* ill. by Svend Otto S. Atheneum, 1976, 1975. Translation of Der underbara pumpan. Subj: Animals – bears. Food. Holidays – Halloween.

Helmering, Doris Wild. *I have two families* ill. by Heidi Palmer. Abingdon Pr., 1981. Subj: Family life – stepfamilies.

We're going to have a baby by Doris and John William Helmering; ill. by Robert H. Cassell. Abingdon Pr., 1978. Subj: Babies. Family life. Sibling rivalry.

Helmering, John William. *We're going to have a baby* (Helmering, Doris Wild)

Henkes, Kevin. *All alone* ill. by author. Greenwillow, 1981. Subj: Behavior – solitude.

Clean enough ill. by author. Greenwillow, 1982. Subj: Activities – bathing.

Henkle, Henrietta *see* Buckmaster, Henrietta

Henley, Karyn. *Hatch!* ill. by Susan Kennedy. Carolrhoda Books, 1980. Subj: Animals.

Henrie, Fiona. *Cats* photos. by Marc Henrie. Watts, 1980. Subj: Animals – cats. Pets.

Dogs photos. by Marc Henrie. Watts, 1980. Subj: Animals – dogs. Pets.

Gerbils photos. by Marc Henrie. Watts, 1980. Subj: Animals – gerbils. Pets.

Rabbits photos. by Marc Henrie. Watts, 1980. Subj: Animals – rabbits. Pets.

Henriod, Lorraine. *Grandma's wheelchair* ill. by Christa Chevalier. Albert Whitman, 1982. Subj: Family life – grandparents, great-grandparents. Handicaps. Sibling rivalry.

Henrioud, Charles *see* Matias

Henstra, Friso. *Wait and see* ill. by author. Addison-Wesley, 1978. Subj: Machines.

Herman, Charlotte. *My mother didn't kiss me good-night* ill. by Bruce Degen. Dutton, 1980. Subj: Behavior – worrying.

Herold, Ann Bixby. *The helping day* ill. by Victoria de Larrea. Coward, 1980. Subj: Character traits – helpfulness.

Herring, Ann. *Suho and the white horse* (Otsuka, Yuzo)

Herriot, James. *Moses the kitten* ill. by Peter Barrett. St. Martin's, 1984. Subj: Animals – cats. Careers – veterinarians.

Herrmann, Frank. *The giant Alexander* ill. by George Him. McGraw-Hill, 1965. Subj: Foreign lands – England. Giants.

The giant Alexander and the circus ill. by George Him. McGraw-Hill, 1966. Subj: Circus. Foreign lands – England. Giants.

Herter, Jonina. *Eighty-eight kisses* ill. with photos. Boss Books, 1978. Subj: Babies. Family life – grandparents, great-grandparents.

Hertza, Ole. *Tobias catches trout* tr. from Danish by Tobi Tobias; ill. by author. Carolrhoda Books, 1984. Subj: Foreign lands – Greenland. Sports – fishing.

Tobias goes ice fishing tr. from Danish by Tobi Tobias; ill. by author. Carolrhoda Books, 1984. Subj: Foreign lands – Greenland. Seasons – winter. Sports – fishing.

Tobias goes seal hunting tr. from Danish by Tobi Tobias; ill. by author. Carolrhoda Books, 1984. Subj: Foreign lands – Greenland. Sports – hunting.

Tobias has a birthday tr. from Danish by Tobi Tobias; ill. by author. Carolrhoda Books, 1984. Subj: Birthdays. Foreign lands – Greenland.

Herz, Irene. *Hey! Don't do that!* ill. by Lucinda McQueen. Prentice-Hall, 1978. Subj: Activities – playing. Animals. Behavior – misbehavior.

Hess, Lilo. *A cat's nine lives* ill. by author. Scribner's, 1984. Subj: Animals – cats. Behavior needing someone.

The curious raccoons photos. by author. Scribner's, 1968. Subj: Animals – raccoons. Science.

Foxes in the woodshed photos. by author. Scribner's, 1966. Subj: Animals – foxes. Science.

Rabbits in the meadow photos. by author. Crowell, 1963. Subj: Animals – rabbits.

Hest, Amy. *The crack-of-dawn walkers* ill. by Amy Schwartz. Macmillan, 1984. Subj: Family life – grandparents, great-grandparents.

Hewett, Anita. *The little white hen* ill. by William Stobbs. McGraw-Hill, 1963. Subj: Birds – chickens. Cumulative tales. Folk and fairy tales.

The tale of the turnip ill. by Margery Gill. McGraw-Hill, 1961. Subj: Cumulative tales. Participation. Plants.

Hewett, Joan. *Fly away free* photos. by Richard Hewett. Walker, 1981. Subj: Birds – pelicans. Careers – veterinarians. Illness.

The mouse and the elephant photos. by Richard Hewett. Little, 1977. Subj: Animals – elephants. Animals – mice.

Hewitt, Kathryn. *Two by two: the untold story* ill. by author. Harcourt, 1984. Subj: Religion – Noah.

Heymans, Margriet. *Pippin and Robber Grumble-croak's big baby* ill. by author. Addison-Wesley, 1973. Subj: Crime. Puppets.

Heyward, Du Bose. *The country bunny and the little gold shoes* ill. by Marjorie Flack. Houghton, 1939. Subj: Animals – rabbits. Character traits – kindness. Holidays – Easter.

Hickman, Martha Whitmore. *Eeps creeps, it's my room!* ill. by Mary Alice Baer. Abingdon Pr., 1984. Subj: Character traits – cleanliness.

My friend William moved away ill. by Bill Myers. Abingdon Pr., 1979. Subj: Friendship. Moving.

When can daddy come home? ill. by Francis Livingston. Abingdon Pr., 1983. Subj: Crime. Family life. Prisons.

Hicks, Eleanor B. *see* Coerr, Eleanor

High on a hill: *a book of Chinese riddles* sel. and ill. by Ed Young. Collins-World, 1980. Subj: Folk and fairy tales. Foreign lands – China. Riddles.

Highwater, Jamake. *Moonsong lullaby* photos. by Marcia Keegan. Lothrop, 1981. Subj: Night. Poetry, rhyme.

Hill, Donna. *Ms. Glee was waiting* ill. by Diane Dawson. Atheneum, 1978. Subj: School.

Hill, Elizabeth Starr. *Evan's corner* ill. by Nancy Grossman. Holt, 1967. Subj: Character traits – helpfulness. Ethnic groups in the U.S. – Afro-Americans. Family life.

Hill, Eric. *At home* ill. by author. Random House, 1983. Subj: Animals – bears. Family life. Wordless.

Baby bear's bedtime ill. by author. Random House, 1984. Subj: Animals – bears. Bedtime.

Good morning, baby bear ill. by author. Random House, 1984. Subj: Animals – bears. Morning.

My pets ill. by author. Random House, 1983. Subj: Animals – bears. Pets.

The park ill. by author. Random House, 1983. Subj: Activities – walking. Wordless.

Spot goes to school ill. by author. Putnam's, 1984. Subj: Animals – dogs. School.

Spot's birthday party ill. by author. Putnam's, 1982. Subj: Folk and fairy tales. Birthdays.

Spot's first walk ill. by author. Putnam's, 1981. Subj: Activities – walking. Animals – dogs. Format, unusual.

Up there ill. by author. Random House, 1983. Subj: Activities – flying. Animals – bears Wordless.

Where's Spot? ill. by author. Putnam's, 1980. Subj: Behavior – lost. Folk and fairy tales.

Hill, Helen. *Dusk to dawn: poems of night* sel. by Helen Hill and others; ill. by Anne Burgess. Crowell, 1981. Subj: Poetry, rhyme.

Hill, Mary Lou. *My dad's a park ranger* ill. by Tom De Hart. Children's Pr., 1978. Subj: Careers – park rangers.

My dad's a smokejumper ill. by Don Hendricks. Children's Pr., 1978. Subj: Careers – firefighters. Forest, woods.

Hill, Monica *see* Watson, Jane Werner

Hille-Brandts, Lene. *The little black hen* tr. and adapt. by Marion Koenig; ill. by Sigrid Heuck. Children's Pr., 1968. Translation of Die Henne Gudula. Subj: Behavior – dissatisfaction. Birds – chickens.

Hiller, Catherine. *Abracatabby* ill. by Victoria De Larrea. Coward, 1981. Subj: Animals – cats. Magic.

Argentaybee and the boonie ill. by Cyndy Szekeres. Coward, 1979. Subj: Behavior – misbehavior. Imagination – imaginary friends.

Hillerich, Robert L. *Rand McNally picturebook dictionary*

Hillert, Margaret. *The birthday car* ill. by Kelly Oechsli. Follett, 1966. Subj: Birthdays. Toys.

The funny baby ill. by Hertha Depper. Follett, 1966. The tale of The Ugly Duckling by H. C. Andersen. Subj: Birds – ducks. Birds – swans. Character traits – appearance. Character traits – being different. Folk and fairy tales.

Happy birthday, dear dragon ill. by Carl Kock. Follett, 1977. Subj: Birthdays. Dragons.

The little cowboy and the big cowboy ill. by Dan Siculan. Follett, 1980. Subj: Cowboys. Family life – fathers.

Little Red Riding Hood (Grimm, Jacob)

The little runaway ill. by Irv Anderson. Follett, 1966. Subj: Animals – cats. Behavior – running away.

The magic beans ill. by Mel Pekarsky. Follett, 1966. The tale of Jack and the beanstalk. Subj: Folk and fairy tales. Giants. Plants.

Merry Christmas, dear dragon ill. by Carl Kock. Follett, 1980. Subj: Dragons. Holidays – Christmas.

Play ball ill. by Dick Martin. Follett, 1978. Subj: Activities – playing. Games. Sports – baseball.

The three bears ill. by Irma Wilde. Follett, 1963. Subj: Animals – bears. Folk and fairy tales.

The three goats ill. by Mel Pekarsky. Follett, 1963. The tale of The three billy goats Gruff. Subj: Animals – goats. Character traits – cleverness. Cumulative tales. Folk and fairy tales. Mythical creatures. Trolls.

The three little pigs

Tom Thumb

The yellow boat ill. by Ed Young. Follett, 1966. Subj: Boats, ships.

Hillman, Priscilla. *A Merry-Mouse book of favorite poems* ill. by author. Doubleday, 1981. Subj: Animals – mice. Poetry, rhyme.

A Merry-Mouse book of months ill. by author. Doubleday, 1980. Subj: Animals – mice. Days of the week, months of the year. Poetry, rhyme.

The Merry-Mouse book of prayers and graces ill. by author. Doubleday, 1983. Subj: Religion.

A Merry-Mouse Christmas A B C ill. by author. Doubleday, 1980. Subj: ABC books. Animals – mice. Holidays – Christmas.

The Merry-Mouse schoolhouse ill. by author. Doubleday, 1982. Subj: Animals – mice. School.

Himler, Ronald. *The girl on the yellow giraffe* ill. by author. Harper, 1976. Subj: City. Imagination.

Wake up, Jeremiah ill. by author. Harper, 1979. Subj: Morning.

Himmelman, John. *Amanda and the witch switch* ill. by author. Viking, 1985. Subj: Behavior – wishing. Character traits – meanness. Witches.

Talester the lizard ill. by author. Dial Pr., 1982. Subj: Reptiles – lizards.

Hine, Sesyle Joslin *see* Joslin, Sesyle

Hines, Anna Grossnickle. *Come to the meadow* ill. by author. Houghton, 1984. Subj: Activities – picnicking. Family life – grandparents, great-grandparents.

Maybe a band-aid will help ill. by author. Dutton, 1984. Subj: Problem solving. Toys – dolls.

Taste the raindrops ill. by author. Greenwillow, 1983. Subj: Weather – rain.

Hinojosa, Francisco. *The old lady who ate people: frightening stories* ill. by Leonel Maciel. Little, 1984. Subj: Folk and fairy tales. Foreign lands – Mexico.

Hippel, Ursula Von *see* Von Hippel, Ursula

The hippo ill. by Caroline Binch. Rourke, 1983. Subj: Animals – hippopotami.

Hippopotamus, Eugene H. *see* Kraus, Robert

Hirschberg, J. Cotter. *My friend the babysitter* (Watson, Jane Werner)

Sometimes I get angry (Watson, Jane Werner)

Sometimes I'm afraid (Watson, Jane Werner)

Hirschmann, Linda. *In a lick of a flick of a tongue* ill. by Jeni Bassett. Dodd, 1980. Subj: Anatomy. Animals.

Hirsh, Marilyn. *Captain Jiri and Rabbi Jacob: from a Jewish folktale* ill. by author. Holiday, 1976. Subj: Folk and fairy tales. Jewish culture.

Could anything be worse? a Yiddish tale ill. by author. Holiday, 1974. Subj: Humor. Jewish culture.

Leela and the watermelon by Marilyn Hirsh and Maya Narayan; ill. by Marilyn Hirsh. Crown, 1971. Subj: Babies. Food. Foreign lands – India.

One little goat: a Passover song ill. by author. Holiday, 1979. Subj: Folk and fairy tales. Jewish culture. Holidays – Passover. Songs.

The pink suit ill. by author. Crown, 1970. Subj: Activities – trading. Emotions – embarrassment. Family life. Jewish culture.

The Rabbi and the twenty-nine witches ill. by author. Holiday, 1976. Subj: Character traits – cleverness. Jewish culture. Witches.

Where is Yonkela? ill. by author. Crown, 1969. Subj: Babies. Behavior – lost. Jewish culture.

The history of Little Tom Tucker ill. by Paul Galdone. McGraw-Hill, 1970. This version was published by J. Kendrew, York, England, ca. 1820. Subj: Nursery rhymes.

The history of Mother Twaddle and the marvelous achievements of her son Jack ill. by Paul Galdone. Seabury Pr., 1974. A verse version of Jack and the beanstalk, written by Basil T. Blackwood [B.A.T.] and pub. in 1807 by J. Harris, London. Subj: Folk and fairy tales. Giants. Plants. Poetry, rhyme.

Hitte, Kathryn. *Mexicallie soup* by Kathryn Hitte and William D. Hayes; ill. by Anne F. Rockwell. Parents, 1970. Subj: Activities – cooking. Ethnic groups in the U.S. – Mexican-Americans. Family life. Food. Foreign lands – Mexico.

Hoban, Brom. *Skunk Lane* ill. by author. Harper, 1983. Subj: Animals – skunks. Behavior – growing up. Songs.

Hoban, Lillian. *Arthur's Christmas cookies* ill. by author. Harper, 1972. Subj: Activities – cooking. Animals – monkeys. Holidays – Christmas.

Arthur's funny money ill. by author. Harper, 1981. Subj: Animals – monkeys. Money. Problem solving.

Arthur's honey bear ill. by author. Harper, 1973. Subj: Animals – monkeys. Toys – teddy bears.

Arthur's pen pal ill. by author. Harper, 1976. Subj: Activities – writing. Animals – monkeys. Sibling rivalry.

Arthur's prize reader ill. by author. Harper, 1978. Subj: Activities – reading. Animals – monkeys. Family life.

Harry's song ill. by author. Greenwillow, 1980. Subj: Animals – rabbits. Songs.

Here come raccoons ill. by author. Holt, 1977. Subj: Animals – raccoons. Twins.

It's really Christmas ill. by author. Greenwillow, 1982. Subj: Animals – mice. Behavior – wishing. Holidays – Christmas.

The laziest robot in zone one by Lillian and Phoebe Hoban; ill. by Lillian Hoban. Harper, 1983. Subj: Animals – dogs. Behavior – lost. Robots.

Mr. Pig and family ill. by author. Harper, 1980. Subj: Animals – pigs. Family life.

Mr. Pig and Sonny too ill. by author. Harper, 1977. Subj: Animals – pigs. Sports – ice skating. Weddings.

Stick-in-the-mud turtle ill. by author. Greenwillow, 1977. Subj: Behavior – dissatisfaction. Poverty. Reptiles – turtles.

The sugar snow spring ill. by author. Harper, 1973. Subj: Animals – mice. Seasons – spring. Weather – cold. Weather – snow.

Turtle spring ill. by author. Greenwillow, 1978. Subj: Reptiles – turtles. Seasons – spring.

Hoban, Phoebe. *The laziest robot in zone one* (Hoban, Lillian)

Hoban, Russell. *Ace Dragon Ltd.* ill. by Quentin Blake. Merrimack, 1981. Subj: Activities – flying. Dragons.

Arthur's new power ill. by Byron Barton. Crowell, 1978. Subj: Progress. Reptiles – alligators, crocodiles.

A baby sister for Frances ill. by Lillian Hoban. Harper, 1964. Subj: Animals – badgers. Behavior – running away. Emotions – envy, jealousy. Family life. Sibling rivalry.

A bargain for Frances ill. by Lillian Hoban. Harper, 1970. Subj: Animals – badgers. Friendship.

The battle of Zormla ill. by Colin McNaughton. Putnam's, 1982. Subj: Sibling rivalry.

Bedtime for Frances ill. by Garth Williams. Harper, 1960. Subj: Animals – badgers. Bedtime.

Best friends for Frances ill. by Lillian Hoban. Harper, 1969. Subj: Animals – badgers. Friendship.

Big John Turkle ill. by Martin Baynton. Holt, 1984. Subj: Character traits – meanness.

A birthday for Frances ill. by Lillian Hoban. Harper, 1968. Subj: Animals – badgers. Birthdays. Emotions – envy, jealousy.

Bread and jam for Frances ill. by Lillian Hoban. Harper, 1964. Subj: Animals – badgers. Food. School.

Charlie the tramp ill. by Lillian Hoban. Four Winds Pr., 1967. Subj: Activities – working. Animals – beavers.

La corona and the tin frog ill. by Nicola Bayley. Merrimack, 1981. Subj: Emotions. Toys.

The dancing tigers ill. by David Gentleman. Merrimack, 1981. Subj: Activities – dancing. Animals – tigers. Sports – hunting.

Dinner at Alberta's ill. by James Marshall. Crowell, 1975. Subj: Behavior. Etiquette. Food. Reptiles – alligators, crocodiles.

Emmet Otter's jug-band Christmas ill. by Lillian Hoban. Parents, 1971. Subj: Animals – otters. Character traits – generosity. Holidays – Christmas. Music.

Flat cat ill. by Clive Scruton. Putnam's, 1980. Subj: Animals – cats. Animals – mice. Animals – rats.

The flight of Bembel Rudzuk ill. by Colin McNaughton. Putnam's, 1982. Subj: Imagination.

Goodnight ill. by Lillian Hoban. Norton, 1966. Subj: Bedtime. Emotions – fear. Imagination. Poetry, rhyme.

The great gum drop robbery ill. by Colin McNaughton. Putnam's, 1982. Subj: Imagination. Sibling rivalry.

Harvey's hideout ill. by Lillian Hoban. Parents, 1969. Subj: Animals – muskrats. Behavior – fighting, arguing. Family life.

How Tom beat Captain Najork and his hired sportsmen ill. by Quentin Blake. Atheneum, 1974. Subj: Behavior – misbehavior. Games.

Jim Frog ill. by Martin Baynton. Holt, 1984. Subj: Frogs and toads. Insects – beetles.

Lavina bat ill. by Martin Baynton. Holt, 1984. Subj: Animals – bats.

The little Brute family ill. by Lillian Hoban. Macmillan, 1966. Subj: Character traits – meanness. Etiquette.

The mole family's Christmas ill. by Lillian Hoban. Parents, 1969. Subj: Animals – moles. Character traits – generosity. Holidays – Christmas.

A near thing for Captain Najork ill. by Quentin Blake. Atheneum, 1976. Subj: Humor.

Nothing to do ill. by Lillian Hoban. Harper, 1964. Subj: Animals – possums. Behavior – boredom.

Some snow said hello ill. by Lillian Hoban. Harper, 1963. Subj: Seasons – winter. Sibling rivalry. Weather – snow.

The sorely trying day ill. by Lillian Hoban. Harper, 1964. Subj: Behavior – bad day. Behavior – fighting, arguing.

The stone doll of Sister Brute ill. by Lillian Hoban. Macmillan, 1968. Subj: Animals – dogs. Emotions. Toys – dolls.

Ten what? a mystery counting book by Russell Hoban and Sylvie Selig; ill. by authors. Scribner's, 1974. Subj: Counting.

They came from Aargh! ill. by Colin McNaughton. Putnam's, 1981. Subj: Family life. Sibling rivalry.

Tom and the two handles ill. by Lillian Hoban. Harper, 1965. Subj: Behavior – fighting, arguing.

Hoban, Tana. *A B See!* photos. by author. Greenwillow, 1982. Subj: ABC books.

Big ones, little ones ill. by author. Greenwillow, 1976. Subj: Animals. Concepts – size. Wordless.

Circles, triangles, and squares ill. by author. Macmillan, 1974. Subj: Concepts – shape. Wordless.

Count and see ill. by author. Macmillan, 1972. Subj: Counting.

Dig, drill, dump, fill ill. by author. Greenwillow, 1975. Subj: Machines. Wordless.

I read signs photos. by author. Greenwillow, 1983. Subj: Activities – reading. Communication.

I read symbols photos. by author. Greenwillow, 1983. Subj: Activities – reading. Communication.

I walk and read photos. by author. Greenwillow, 1984. Subj: Activities – reading. Activities – walking.

Is it red? Is it yellow? Is it blue? photos. by author. Greenwillow, 1978. Subj: City. Concepts – color. Concepts – shape. Concepts – size. Wordless.

Is it rough? Is it smooth? Is it shiny? photos. by author. Greenwillow, 1984. Subj: Concepts. Wordless.

Look again ill. by author. Macmillan, 1971. Subj: Participation. Senses. Wordless.

More than one photos. by author. Greenwillow, 1981. Subj: Language.

One little kitten photos. by author. Greenwillow, 1979. Subj: Animals – cats. Poetry, rhyme.

1, 2, 3 photos. by author. Greenwillow, 1985. Subj: Counting. Format, unusual – cardboard pages. Wordless.

Push-pull, empty-full ill. by author. Macmillan, 1972. Subj: Concepts – opposites.

Round and round and round photos. by author. Greenwillow, 1983. Subj: Concepts – shape.

Shapes and things ill. by author. Macmillan, 1970. Subj: Concepts – shape. Wordless.

Take another look photos. by author. Greenwillow, 1981. Subj: Concepts. Wordless.

What is it? photos. by author. Greenwillow, 1985. Subj: Format, unusual – cardboard pages. Wordless.

Where is it? ill. by author. Macmillan, 1974. Subj: Animals – rabbits. Participation. Poetry, rhyme.

Hoberman, Mary Ann. *The cozy book* ill. by Tony Chen. Viking, 1982. Subj: Poetry, rhyme.

A house is a house for me ill. by Betty Fraser. Viking, 1978. Subj: Houses. Poetry, rhyme.

How do I go? by Mary Ann and Norman Hoberman; ill. by authors. Little, 1958. Subj: Transportation.

I like old clothes ill. by Jacqueline Chwast. Knopf, 1976. Subj: Clothing. Poetry, rhyme.

Nuts to you and nuts to me: an alphabet of poems ill. by Ronni Solbert. Knopf, 1974. Subj: ABC books. Poetry, rhyme.

Hoberman, Norman. *How do I go?* (Hoberman, Mary Ann)

Hobson, Bruce *see* Hadithi, Mwenye

Hobson, Laura Z. *"I'm going to have a baby!"* ill. by May Kirkham. John Day, 1967. Subj: Babies. Family life.

Hobzek, Mildred. *We came a-marching...1, 2, 3* ill. by William Pène Du Bois. Parents, 1978. Subj: Folk and fairy tales. Songs.

Hochman, Sandra. *The magic convention* ill. by Ben Shecter. Doubleday, 1971. Subj: Character traits – ambition. Magic.

Hodeir, André. *Warwick's three bottles* by André Hodeir and Tomi Ungerer; ill. by Tomi Ungerer. Grove Pr., 1966. Subj: Behavior – misbehavior. Country. Reptiles – alligators, crocodiles.

Hodges, Margaret. *Saint George and the dragon* ill. by Trina Schart Hyman. Little, 1984. Subj: Caldecott award book. Folk and fairy tales.

The wave ill. by Blair Lent. Houghton, 1964. Subj: Caldecott award honor book.

Hodgetts, Blake Christopher. *Dream of the dinosaurs* ill. by Victoria Hodgetts. Doubleday, 1978. Subj: Dinosaurs. Dreams.

Hoff, Carol. *The four friends* ill. by Jim Ponter. Follett, 1958. Subj: Animals. Animals – mice.

Hoff, Syd. *Albert the albatross* ill. by author. Harper, 1961. Subj: Birds – albatrosses. Sea and seashore.

Barkley ill. by author. Harper, 1975. Subj: Animals – dogs. Circus. Old age.

Chester ill. by author. Harper, 1961. Subj: Animals – horses.

Danny and the dinosaur ill. by author. Harper, 1958. Subj: Dinosaurs. Museums.

Grizzwold ill. by author. Harper, 1963. Subj: Animals – bears. Ecology.

Happy birthday, Henrietta! ill. by author. Garrard, 1983. Subj: Animals – pigs. Animals – goats. Birds – chickens. Birthdays.

Henrietta, circus star ill. by author. Garrard, 1978. Subj: Birds – chickens. Circus.

Henrietta goes to the fair ill. by author. Garrard, 1979. Subj: Birds – chickens. Fairs.

Henrietta, the early bird ill. by author. Garrard, 1978. Subj: Behavior – mistakes. Birds – chickens. Time.

Henrietta's Halloween ill. by author. Garrard, 1980. Subj: Birds – chickens. Holidays – Halloween. Parties.

The horse in Harry's room ill. by author. Harper, 1970. Subj: Animals – horses. Imagination – imaginary friends.

Julius ill. by author. Harper, 1959. Subj: Animals – gorillas.

Lengthy ill. by author. Putnam's, 1964. Subj: Animals – dogs.

The littlest leaguer ill. by author. Dutton, 1976. Subj: Character traits – smallness. Games. Sports – baseball.

Merry Christmas, Henrietta! ill. by author. Garrard, 1980. Subj: Birds – chickens. Holidays – Christmas. Stores.

My Aunt Rosie ill. by author. Harper, 1972. Subj: Family life.

Oliver ill. by author. Harper, 1960. Subj: Animals – elephants. Character traits – optimism. Circus.

Sammy the seal ill. by author. Harper, 1959. Subj: Animals – seals. Zoos.

Santa's moose ill. by author. Harper, 1979. Subj: Animals – moose. Holidays – Christmas.

Slithers ill. by author. Putnam's, 1968. Subj: Reptiles – snakes.

Slugger Sal's slump ill. by author. Dutton, 1979. Subj: Character traits – perseverance. Sports – baseball.

Stanley ill. by author. Harper, 1962. Subj: Cavemen. Houses.

Syd Hoff's best jokes ever ill. by author. Putnam's, 1978. Subj: Humor. Riddles.

Walpole ill. by author. Harper, 1977. Subj: Animals – walruses.

When will it snow? ill. by Mary Chalmers. Harper, 1971. Subj: Seasons – winter. Weather – snow.

Where's Prancer? ill. by author. Harper, 1960. Subj: Animals – reindeer. Holidays – Christmas.

Who will be my friends? ill. by author. Harper, 1960. Subj: Friendship. Moving.

Hoffman, Joan. *My friend goes left* (Gregorich, Barbara)

Hoffman, Mary. *Animals in the wild: elephant* ill. by author. Random House, 1984. Subj: Animals – elephants. Science.

Animals in the wild: monkey ill. by author. Random House, 1984. Subj: Animals – monkeys. Science.

Animals in the wild: panda ill. by author. Random House, 1984. Subj: Animals – bears. Science.

Animals in the wild: tiger ill. by author. Random House, 1984. Subj: Animals – tigers. Science.

Hoffman, Phyllis. *Steffie and me* ill. by Emily Arnold McCully. Harper, 1970. Subj: Ethnic groups in the U.S. – Afro-Americans. Family life. Friendship. School.

The ugly duckling (Andersen, H C (Hans Christian))

Hoffman, Rosekrans. *Sister Sweet Ella* ill. by author. Morrow, 1981. Subj: Babies. Family life. Magic.

Hoffmann, E. T. A. *The nutcracker* tr. by Ralph Manheim; ill. by Maurice Sendak. Crown, 1984. Subj: Activities – dancing. Animals – mice. Fairies. Folk and fairy tales. Holidays – Christmas. Imagination. Theater.

Hoffmann, Felix. *Hans in luck* (Grimm, Jacob)

The story of Christmas ill. by author. Atheneum, 1975. Subj: Holidays – Christmas. Religion.

Hofstrand, Mary. *Albion pig* ill. by author. Knopf, 1984. Subj: Animals – pigs. Poetry, rhyme.

Hogan, Bernice. *My grandmother died but I won't forget her* ill. by Nancy Munger. Abingdon, 1983. Subj: Death. Family life – grandparents, great-grandparents.

Hogan, Inez. *About Nono, the baby elephant* ill. by author. Dutton, 1947. Subj: Animals – elephants. Behavior – misbehavior. Names.

Hogan, Paula Z. *The black swan* ill. by Kinuko Craft. Raintree, 1979. Subj: Birds – swans. Science.

The butterfly ill. by Geri K. Strigenz. Raintree, 1979. Subj: Insects – butterflies, caterpillars. Science.

The dandelion ill. by Yoshi Miyake. Raintree, 1979. Subj: Plants. Science.

The frog ill. by Geri K. Strigenz. Raintree, 1979. Subj: Frogs and toads. Science.

The honeybee ill. by Geri K. Strigenz. Raintree, 1979. Subj: Insects – bees. Science.

The oak tree ill. by Kinuko Craft. Raintree, 1979. Subj: Science. Trees.

The penguin ill. by Geri K. Strigenz. Raintree, 1979. Subj: Birds – penguins. Science.

The salmon ill. by Yoshi Miyake. Raintree, 1979. Subj: Fish. Science.

Hogrogian, Nonny. *Billy Goat and his well-fed friends* ill. by author. Harper, 1972. Subj: Animals. Animals – goats. Behavior – running away.

Carrot cake ill. by author. Greenwillow, 1977. Subj: Animals – rabbits. Behavior. Character traits – compromising. Character traits – shyness. Weddings.

Cinderella (Grimm, Jacob)

The contest ill. by author. Greenwillow, 1976. Subj: Caldecott award honor book. Crime. Folk and fairy tales. Foreign lands – Armenia.

The devil with the green hairs (Grimm, Jacob)

The hermit and Harry and me ill. by author. Subj: Behavior – indifference. Friendship.

One fine day ill. by Nonny Hogrogian. Macmillan, 1971. Subj: Animals – foxes. Caldecott award book. Cumulative tales.

Hoguet, Susan Ramsay. *I unpacked my grandmother's trunk: a picture book game* ill. by author. Dutton, 1983. Subj: ABC books. Cumulative tales. Games.

Hoke, Helen L. *The biggest family in the town* ill. by Vance Locke. McKay, 1947. Subj: Family life.

Holabird, Katharine. *Angelina and the princess* ill. by Helen Craig. Crown, 1984. Subj: Activities – dancing. Animals – mice.

Angelina ballerina ill. by Helen Craig. Crown, 1983. Subj: Activities – dancing. Animals – mice.

The little mouse ABC ill. by Helen Craig. Simon and Schuster, 1983. Subj: ABC books. Animals – mice.

Holbrook, Stewart. *America's Ethan Allen* ill. by Lynd Ward. Houghton, 1949. Subj: Caldecott award honor book. U.S. history. War.

Holden, Edith. *The hedgehog feast* ill. by Edith Holden; words by Rowena Stott. Dutton, 1978. Subj: Animals – hedgehogs. Food.

Holding, James. *The lazy little Zulu* ill. by Aliki. Morrow, 1962. Subj: Character traits – laziness. Foreign lands – Africa.

Holl, Adelaide. *The ABC of cars, trucks and machines* ill. by William Dugan. American Heritage, 1970. Subj: ABC books. Automobiles. Machines. Trucks.

A mouse story: Minnikin, Midgie and Moppet ill. by Priscilla Hillman. Golden Pr., 1977. Subj: Animals – mice. City. Country.

Mrs. McGarrity's peppermint sweater ill. by Abner Graboff. Lothrop, 1966. Subj: Activities – knitting. Circus. Poetry, rhyme.

My father and I (Ringi, Kjell)

The rain puddle ill. by Roger Antoine Duvoisin. Lothrop, 1965. Subj: Animals. Weather – rain.

The remarkable egg ill. by Roger Antoine Duvoisin. Lothrop, 1968. Subj: Toys – balls.

The runaway giant ill. by Mamoru Funai. Lothrop, 1967. Subj: Behavior – gossip. Snowmen.

Sir Kevin of Devon ill. by Leonard Weisgard. Lothrop, 1963. Subj: Character traits – bravery. Knights. Poetry, rhyme.

Small Bear builds a playhouse ill. by Cyndy Szekeres. Garrard, 1978. Subj: Animals. Animals – bears. Houses.

Small Bear solves a mystery ill. by Lorinda Bryan Cauley. Garrard, 1979. Subj: Animals – bears. Food. Illness.

Holland, Isabelle. *Kevin's hat* ill. by Leonard Lubin. Lothrop, 1984. Subj: Clothing. Reptiles – alligators, crocodiles.

Holland, Janice. *You never can tell* ill. by adapt. Scribner's, 1963. Adapted from the tr. by Arthur W. Hummel from the book of Hual nan tzu, written before 122 B.C. Subj: Character traits – luck. Folk and fairy tales. Foreign lands – China.

Holland, Kevin Crossley see Crossley-Holland, Kevin

Holland, Marion. *A big ball of string* ill. by author. Random House, 1958. Subj: Poetry, rhyme. String.

Holland, Viki. *We are having a baby* ill. by author. Scribner's, 1972. Subj: Babies. Family life.

Hollander, John. *A book of various owls* ill. by Tomi Ungerer. Norton, 1963. Subj: Birds – owls. Poetry, rhyme.

Holling, Holling C. (Holling Clancy). *Paddle-to-the-sea* ill. by author. Houghton, 1941. Subj: Caldecott award honor book. Foreign lands – Canada. Rivers.

Holm, Mayling Mack. *A forest Christmas* ill. by author. Harper, 1977. Subj: Animals. Holidays – Christmas.

Holman, Felice. *Elisabeth, the treasure hunter* ill. by Erik Blegvad. Macmillan, 1964. Subj: Problem solving. Riddles.

Victoria's castle ill. by Lillian Hoban. Norton, 1966. Subj: Birds – parakeets, parrots. Humor. Imagination.

Holmes, Anita. *The 100-year-old cactus* ill. by Carol Lerner. Four Winds Pr., 1983. Subj: Desert. Plants. Science.

Holmes, Efner Tudor. *Amy's goose* ill. by Tasha Tudor. Crowell, 1977. Subj: Birds – geese. Character traits – helpfulness. Character traits – kindness to animals.

Carrie's gift ill. by Tasha Tudor. Collins-World, 1978. Subj: Animals – dogs. Character traits – kindness to animals.

The Christmas cat ill. by Tasha Tudor. Crowell, 1976. Subj: Animals – cats. Holidays – Christmas.

Holt, Margaret. *David McCheever's twenty-nine dogs* ill. by Walter Lorraine. Houghton, 1963. Subj: Animals – dogs. Counting. Parades. Shopping.

Holzenthaler, Jean. *My feet do* ill. by George Ancona. Dutton, 1979. Subj: Activities. Anatomy.

My hands can ill. by Nancy Tafuri. Dutton, 1978. Subj: Activities. Anatomy.

Home before midnight: *a traditional verse* ill. by Bobby Lewis. Lothrop, 1984. Subj: Animals – pigs. Cumulative tales.

Homme, Bob. *The friendly giant's birthday* ill. by Kim La Fave and Carol Snelling. CBC Merchandising, 1982. Subj: Birthdays. Giants. Songs.

The friendly giant's book of fire engines ill. by Kim La Fave and Carol Snelling. CBC Merchandising, 1981. Subj: Careers – firefighters. Giants. Trucks.

Hood, Flora Mae. *Living in Navajoland* ill. by Mamoru Funai. Putnam's, 1970. Subj: Ethnic groups in the U.S. – Indians.

Hooks, William H. *Three rounds with rabbit* ill. by Lissa McLaughlin. Lothrop, 1984. Subj: Animals – rabbits. Character traits – cleverness.

Hoopes, Lyn Littlefield. *Nana* ill. by Arieh Zeldich. Harper, 1981. Subj: Death. Family life – grandparents, great-grandparents.

When I was little ill. by Marcia Sewall. Dutton, 1983. Subj: Emotions – love. Seasons – winter. Sibling rivalry.

Hoover, Roseanna. *The golden apple* (Bolliger, Max)

Hopkins, Lee Bennett. *And God bless me: prayers, lullabies and dream-poems* ill. by Patricia Henderson Lincoln. Knopf, 1982. Subj: Poetry, rhyme. Religion. Songs.

Circus! Circus! ill. by John O'Brien. Knopf, 1982. Subj: Circus. Poetry, rhyme.

Crickets and bullfrogs and whispers of thunder (Behn, Harry)

A dog's life ill. by Linda Rochester Richards. Harcourt, 1983. Subj: Animals – dogs. Poetry, rhyme.

Easter buds are springing ill. by Tomie de Paola. Harcourt, 1979. Subj: Holidays – Easter. Poetry, rhyme.

Elves, fairies and gnomes

Go to bed! a book of bedtime poems ill. by Rosekrans Hoffman. Knopf, 1979. Subj: Bedtime. Poetry, rhyme.

I loved Rose Ann ill. by Ingrid Fetz. Knopf, 1976. Subj: Behavior – misunderstanding. Emotions.

I think I saw a snail: young poems for city seasons ill. by Harold James. Crown, 1969. Subj: City. Ethnic groups in the U.S. – Afro-Americans. Poetry, rhyme.

Merrily comes our harvest in: poems for Thanksgiving ill. by Ben Shecter. Harcourt, 1978. Subj: Holidays – Thanksgiving. Poetry, rhyme. Seasons – fall.

Morning, noon and nighttime, too ill. by Nancy Hannans. Harper, 1980. Subj: Poetry, rhyme.

The sky is full of song ill. by Dirk Zimmer. Harper, 1983. Subj: Poetry, rhyme.

Hopkins, Marjorie. *Three visitors* ill. by Anne F. Rockwell. Parents, 1967. Subj: Ethnic groups in the U.S. – Eskimos.

Horner, Althea J. *Little big girl* ill. by Patricia Rosamilia. Human Sciences Pr., 1983. Subj: Behavior – growing up.

Horvath, Betty F. *Be nice to Josephine* ill. by Pat Grant Porter. Watts, 1970. Subj: Behavior. Family life.

The cheerful quiet ill. by Jo Ann Stover. Watts, 1969. Subj: Noise, sounds. Problem solving.

Hooray for Jasper ill. by Fermin Rocker. Watts, 1966. Subj: Character traits – smallness. Ethnic groups in the U.S. – Afro-Americans.

Jasper and the hero business ill. by Don Bolognese. Watts, 1977. Subj: Character traits – bravery. Ethnic groups in the U.S. – Afro-Americans.

Jasper makes music ill. by Fermin Rocker. Watts, 1967. Subj: Activities – working. Ethnic groups in the U.S. – Afro-Americans. Music.

Will the real Tommy Wilson please stand up? ill. by Charles Robinson. Watts, 1969. Subj: Character traits – individuality. Emotions. Friendship.

Horwitz, Elinor Lander. *Sometimes it happens* ill. by Susan Jeschke. Harper, 1981. Subj: Character traits – ambition. Imagination.

When the sky is like lace ill. by Barbara Cooney. Lippincott, 1975. Subj: Night.

Hot cross buns, and other old street cries sel. by John M. Langstaff; ill. by Nancy Winslow Parker. Atheneum, 1978. Subj: Music. Poetry, rhyme. Songs.

Houghton, Eric. *The mouse and the magician* ill. by Faith Jaques. Elsevier-Dutton, 1979. Subj: Animals – mice. Magic. Wizards.

House mouse photos. by David Thompson. Putnam's, 1978. Subj: Animals – mice. Science.

The house that Jack built ill. by Randolph Caldecott. Avenel Books, n.d. Subj: Cumulative tales. Nursery rhymes.

The house that Jack built ill. by Seymour Chwast. Random House, 1973. Subj: Cumulative tales. Format, unusual. Nursery rhymes. Participation.

The house that Jack built ill. by Rodney Peppé. Delacorte Pr., 1970. Subj: Cumulative tales. Nursery rhymes.

The house that Jack built: *la maison que Jacques a batie* ill. by Antonio Frasconi. Harcourt, 1958. Subj: Caldecott award honor book. Cumulative tales. Foreign languages. Nursery rhymes.

Houston, James. *Kiviok's magic journey: an Eskimo legend* ill. by author. Atheneum, 1973. Subj: Birds – geese. Ethnic groups in the U.S. – Eskimos. Folk and fairy tales.

Houston, John A. *The bright yellow rope* ill. by Winnie Fitch. Addison-Wesley, 1973. Subj: Behavior – sharing. Character traits – generosity. Character traits – helpfulness. Poetry, rhyme. Problem solving. Songs.

A mouse in my house ill. by Winnie Fitch. Addison-Wesley, 1973. Subj: Animals – mice. Cumulative tales. Problem solving. Songs.

A room full of animals ill. by Winnie Fitch. Addison-Wesley, 1973. Subj: Animals. Songs.

Howard, Jean G. *Of mice and mice* ill. by author. Tidal Pr., 1978. Subj: Animals – mice.

Howard, Katherine. *Do you know color?* (Miller, J P (John Parr))

My first picture dictionary ill. by Huck Scarry. Random House, 1978. Subj: Dictionaries.

Howard, Richard. *Gregory and Lady Turtle in the valley of the music trees* (Brunhoff, Laurent de)

The one pig with horns (Brunhoff, Laurent de)

Howe, Caroline Walton. *Counting penguins* ill. by author. Harper, 1983. Subj: Birds – penguins. Counting.

Teddy Bear's bird and beast band ill. by author. Windmill, 1980. Subj: Music. Toys – teddy bears.

Howe, Deborah. *Teddy Bear's scrapbook* by Deborah and James Howe; ill. by David S. Rose. Atheneum, 1980. Subj: Toys – teddy bears.

Howe, James. *The case of the missing mother* ill. by William Cleaver. Random House, 1983. Subj: Holidays – Mother's Day. Puppets.

The day the teacher went bananas ill. by Lillian Hoban. Dutton, 1984. Subj: Animals – gorillas. School. Zoos.

How the Ewoks saved the trees: an old Ewok legend ill. by Walter Velez. Random House, 1984. Subj: Mythical creatures. Trees.

Teddy Bear's scrapbook (Howe, Deborah)

Howell, Ruth. *Everything changes* photos. by Arline Strong. Atheneum, 1968. Subj: Seasons.

Splash and flow photos. by Arline Strong. Atheneum, 1973. Subj: Science.

Howells, Mildred. *The woman who lived in Holland* ill. by William Curtis Holdsworth. Farrar, 1973. Text originally published in 1898 in St. Nicholas magazine under title: Going too far. Subj: Character traits – cleanliness. Foreign lands – Holland. Poetry, rhyme.

Hudson, Eleanor. *A whale of a rescue* ill. by Pat Paris. Random House, 1983. Subj: Animals – whales.

Huff, Vivian. *Let's make paper dolls* photos. by author. Harper, 1978. Subj: Paper. Toys – dolls.

Hughes, Peter. *The emperor's oblong pancake* ill. by Gerald Rose. Abelard-Schuman, 1961. Subj: Concepts – shape. Food. Royalty.

The king who loved candy ill. by Gerald Rose. Abelard-Schuman, 1964. Subj: Food. Royalty. War.

Hughes, Richard. *Gertrude's child* ill. by Rick Schreiter. Crown, 1966. Subj: Behavior – needing someone. Behavior – running away. Toys.

Hughes, Shirley. *Alfie gets in first* ill. by author. Lothrop, 1982. Subj: Cumulative tales. Houses.

Alfie gives a hand ill. by author. Lothrop, 1984. Subj: Behavior – needing someone. Birthdays. Parties.

Alfie's feet ill. by author. Lothrop, 1983. Subj: Activities – playing.

David and dog ill. by author. Prentice-Hall, 1978. Edition of 1977 published under title: Dogger. Subj: Activities – trading. Family life. Toys.

George the babysitter ill. by author. Prentice-Hall, 1978. Subj: Activities – babysitting.

Moving Molly ill. by author. Prentice-Hall, 1979. Subj: Family life. Moving.

Sally's secret ill. by author. Merrimack, 1980. Subj: Behavior – secrets. Houses.

Up and up ill. by author. Prentice-Hall, 1979. Subj: Activities – flying. Imagination. Wordless.

Hulme, Susan. *Let's look for colors* (Gillham, Bill)

Let's look for numbers (Gillham, Bill)

Let's look for opposites (Gillham, Bill)

Let's look for shapes (Gillham, Bill)

Humpty Dumpty and other first rhymes ill. by Betty Youngs. Bodley Head, 1980. Subj: Nursery rhymes.

Hunt, Joyce. *A first look at dinosaurs* (Selsam, Millicent E)

A first look at dogs (Selsam, Millicent E)

A first look at flowers (Selsam, Millicent E)

A first look at monkeys (Selsam, Millicent E)

A first look at rocks (Selsam, Millicent E)

A first look at seashells (Selsam, Millicent E)

A first look at sharks (Selsam, Millicent E)

A first look at spiders (Selsam, Millicent E)

A first look at whales (Selsam, Millicent E)

Hunter, Mollie. *The knight of the golden plain* ill. by Marc Simont. Harper, 1983. Subj: Dreams. Imagination. Knights. Magic.

Hunter, Norman. *Professor Branestawn's building bust-up* ill. by Gerald Rose. Merrimack, 1982. Subj: Houses. Humor. Machines.

Hurd, Edith Thacher. *The black dog who went into the woods* ill. by Emily Arnold McCully. Harper, 1980. Subj: Animals – dogs. Death. Pets.

Caboose ill. by Clement Hurd. Lothrop, 1950. Subj: Poetry, rhyme. Trains.

Christmas eve ill. by Clement Hurd. Harper, 1962. Subj: Animals. Holidays – Christmas.

Come and have fun ill. by Clement Hurd. Harper, 1962. Subj: Animals – cats. Animals – mice. Poetry, rhyme.

The day the sun danced ill. by Clement Hurd. Harper, 1965. Subj: Seasons. Seasons – spring. Sun.

Dinosaur, my darling ill. by Don Freeman. Harper, 1978. Subj: Dinosaurs.

Engine, engine number 9 ill. by Clement Hurd. Lothrop, 1940. Subj: Trains.

Five little firemen (Brown, Margaret Wise)

Hurry hurry! ill. by Clement Hurd. Harper, 1960. Subj: Activities – babysitting. Behavior – hurrying.

I dance in my red pajamas ill. by Emily Arnold McCully. Harper, 1982. Subj: Activities – dancing. Family life – grandparents, great-grandparents.

Johnny Lion's bad day ill. by Clement Hurd. Harper, 1970. Subj: Animals – lions. Illness.

Johnny Lion's book ill. by Clement Hurd. Harper, 1965. Subj: Activities – reading. Animals – lions.

Johnny Lion's rubber boots ill. by Clement Hurd. Harper, 1972. Subj: Animals – lions. Weather – rain.

Last one home is a green pig ill. by Clement Hurd. Harper, 1959. Subj: Animals – monkeys. Birds – ducks. Games. Sports – racing.

Little dog, dreaming by Edith Thacher Hurd and Thacher Hurd; ill. by Clement Hurd. Harper, 1967. Subj: Animals – dogs. Dreams.

The mother chimpanzee ill. by Clement Hurd. Little, 1978. Subj: Animals – monkeys. Family life – mothers.

The mother kangaroo ill. by Clement Hurd. Little, 1976. Subj: Animals – kangaroos. Family life. Science.

No funny business ill. by Clement Hurd. Harper, 1962. Subj: Activities – picnicking. Animals – cats.

Sandpipers ill. by Lucienne Bloch. Crowell, 1961. Subj: Birds – sandpipers. Science.

The so-so cat ill. by Clement Hurd. Harper, 1964. Subj: Animals – cats. Holidays – Halloween. Witches.

Starfish ill. by Lucienne Bloch. Crowell, 1962. Subj: Sea and seashore. Science.

Stop, stop ill. by Clement Hurd. Harper, 1961. Subj: Activities – babysitting. Character traits – cleanliness.

Under the lemon tree ill. by Clement Hurd. Little, 1980. Subj: Animals – donkeys. Animals – foxes. Character traits – loyalty. Farms.

What whale? Where? ill. by Clement Hurd. Harper, 1966. Subj: Animals – whales. Boats, ships.

The white horse ill. by Tony Chen. Harper, 1970. Subj: Imagination.

Wilson's world ill. by Clement Hurd. Harper, 1971. Subj: Art. Ecology.

Hurd, Thacher. *Hobo dog* ill. by author. Scholastic, 1980. Subj: Activities – traveling. Animals – dogs. Trains.

Little dog, dreaming (Hurd, Edith Thacher)

Mama don't allow ill. by author. Harper, 1984. Subj: Animals – possums. Music. Reptiles – alligators, crocodiles.

Mystery on the docks ill. by author. Harper, 1983. Subj: Animals – rats. Behavior – bad day.

The quiet evening ill. by author. Greenwillow, 1978. Subj: Night.

Hürlimann, Bettina. *Barry: the story of a brave St. Bernard* ill. by Paul Nussbaumer; tr. by Elizabeth D. Crawford. Harcourt, 1968. Subj: Animals – dogs. Character traits – bravery. Character traits – helpfulness.

Hürlimann, Ruth. *The mouse with the daisy hat* ill. by author. White, 1971. Subj: Animals – mice. Clothing. Weddings.

The proud white cat tr. by Anthea Bell; ill. by author. Morrow, 1977. Translation of Der stolze weisse Kater. Subj: Animals – cats. Character traits – pride. Folk and fairy tales. Foreign lands – Germany.

Hurwitz, Johanna. *Superduper Teddy* ill. by Susan Jeschke. Morrow, 1980. Subj: Behavior – growing up.

Hush little baby: a folk lullaby ill. by Aliki. Prentice-Hall, 1968. Subj: Babies. Character traits – generosity. Cumulative tales. Music. Songs.

Hush little baby ill. by Jeanette Winter. Pantheon, 1984. Subj: Babies. Character traits – generosity. Cumulative tales. Folk and fairy tales. Music. Songs.

Hush little baby ill. by Margot Zemach. Dutton, 1976. Subj: Babies. Character traits – generosity. Cumulative tales. Music. Songs.

Hutchins, Pat. *The best train set ever* ill. by author. Greenwillow, 1978. Subj: Birthdays. Holidays – Christmas. Holidays – Halloween. Illness.

Changes, changes ill. by author. Macmillan, 1971. Subj: Toys – blocks. Wordless.

Clocks and more clocks ill. by author. Macmillan, 1970. Subj: Clocks. Humor. Time.

Don't forget the bacon! ill. by author. Greenwillow, 1975. Subj: Behavior – forgetfulness. Cumulative tales. Food. Humor. Shopping.

Good night owl ill. by author. Macmillan, 1972. Subj: Cumulative tales. Noise, sounds. Participation. Sleep.

Happy birthday, Sam ill. by author. Greenwillow, 1978. Subj: Birthdays. Family life – grandparents, great-grandparents.

King Henry's palace ill. by author. Greenwillow, 1983. Subj: Birthdays. Holidays – Christmas. Royalty.

One-eyed Jake ill. by author. Greenwillow, 1979. Subj: Pirates.

1 hunter ill. by author. Greenwillow, 1982. Subj: Animals. Counting.

Rosie's walk ill. by author. Macmillan, 1968. Subj: Animals – foxes. Birds – chickens. Farms. Humor.

The silver Christmas tree ill. by author. Macmillan, 1974. Subj: Animals. Holidays – Christmas. Trees.

The surprise party ill. by author. Macmillan, 1969. Subj: Animals. Behavior – gossip. Parties.

The tale of Thomas Mead ill. by author. Greenwillow, 1980. Subj: Activities – reading.

Titch ill. by author. Macmillan, 1971. Subj: Concepts – size. Cumulative tales. Family life. Plants.

The wind blew ill. by author. Macmillan, 1974. Subj: Poetry, rhyme. Weather – wind.

You'll soon grow into them, Titch ill. by author. Greenwillow, 1983. Subj: Clothing. Family life.

Hutton, Warwick. *Beauty and the beast* retold and ill. by Warwick Hutton. Atheneum, 1985. Subj: Character traits – loyalty. Folk and fairy tales. Magic.

Jonah and the great fish ill. by adapt. Atheneum, 1984. Subj: Animals – whales. Religion.

Noah and the great flood ill. by author. Atheneum, 1977. Subj: Religion – Noah.

The nose tree ill. by adapt. Atheneum, 1981. Subj: Character traits – cleverness. Friendship. Folk and fairy tales. Witches.

The sleeping beauty (Grimm, Jacob)

Huxley, Aldous. *The crows of Pearblossom* ill. by Barbara Cooney. Random House, 1967. [Written in 1944.] Subj: Birds – crows. Character traits – cleverness. Eggs. Reptiles – snakes.

Hyman, Inge. *Casper and the rainbow bird* (Hyman, Robin)

Hyman, Robin. *Casper and the rainbow bird* by Robin and Inge Hyman; ill. by Yutaka Sugita. Barron's, 1979. Subj: Behavior – running away. Birds – crows. Birds – parakeets, parrots.

Hyman, Trina Schart. *The enchanted forest* ill. by author. Putnam's, 1984. Subj: Forest, woods. Format, unusual. Wordless.

A little alphabet ill. by author. Little, 1980. Subj: ABC books.

Little Red Riding Hood (Grimm, Jacob)

The sleeping beauty (Grimm, Jacob)

Hymes, James L. *Oodles of noodles and other rhymes* (Hymes, Lucia)

Hymes, Lucia. *Oodles of noodles and other rhymes* by Lucia and James L. Hymes, Jr.; ill. by authors. Addison-Wesley, 1964. Subj: Poetry, rhyme.

Hynard, Julia. *Percival's party* ill. by Frances Thatcher. Children's Pr., 1983. Subj: Activities. Parties.

Hynard, Stephen. *Snowy the rabbit* ill. by Frances Thatcher. Children's Pr., 1983. Subj: Activities. Animals – rabbits.

I sing a song of the saints of God ill. by Judith Gwyn Brown. Seabury Pr., 1981. An ill. version of Lesbia Scott's hymn, "I sing a song of the saints of God" written in 1929. Subj: Music. Religion. Songs.

Iannone, Jeanne Koppel *see* Balzano, Jeanne

Ichikawa, Satomi. *A child's book of seasons* ill. by author. Parents, 1976. Subj: Folk and fairy tales. Seasons.

Sun through small leaves: poems of spring ill. by comp. Collins-World, 1980. Subj: Folk and fairy tales. Seasons – spring.

Suzanne and Nicholas at the market ill. by author. Watts, 1977. Translation by Denise Sheldon of Suzette et Nicolas au marché. Subj: Shopping. Foreign lands – France.

Suzanne and Nicholas in the garden tr. by Denise Sheldon; ill. by author. Watts, 1976. Translation of Suzette et Nicolas dans leur jardin. Subj: Activities – gardening. Ecology. Foreign lands – France.

If dragon flies made honey: *poems* col. by David Kherdian; ill. by José Aruego and Ariane Dewey. Greenwillow, 1977. Subj: Poetry, rhyme.

Ife, Elaine. *The childhood of Jesus* ill. by Eric Rowe. Rourke, 1983. Subj: Religion.

Moses in the bulrushes ill. by Eric Rowe. Rourke, 1983. Subj: Religion.

Noah and the ark ill. by Russell Lee. Rourke, 1983. Subj: Religion – Noah.

Stories Jesus told ill. by Russell Lee. Rourke, 1983. Subj: Religion.

Iké, Jane Hori. *A Japanese fairy tale* by Jane Hori Iké and Baruch Zimmerman; ill. by Jane Hori Iké. Warne, 1982. Subj: Character traits – appearance. Folk and fairy tales. Foreign lands – Japan.

Illyés, Gyula. *Matt the gooseherd: a story from Hungary* ill. by Károly Reich. Penguin, 1979. Subj: Birds – geese. Folk and fairy tales. Foreign lands – Hungary.

Ilsley, Velma. *A busy day for Chris* ill. by author. Lippincott, 1957. Subj: ABC books. Poetry, rhyme.

M is for moving ill. by author. Walck, 1966. Subj: ABC books. Moving.

The pink hat ill. by author. Lippincott, 1956. Subj: Behavior – carelessness. Poetry, rhyme.

I'm mad at you: *verses* sel. by William Cole; ill. by George MacClain. Collins-World, 1978. Subj: Emotions – anger. Folk and fairy tales.

Ingle, Annie. *The big city book* ill. by Tim and Greg Hildebrandt. Platt, 1976. Subj: City.

Inkiow, Dimiter. *Me and Clara and Baldwin the pony* tr. from German by Paula McGuire; ill. by Traudl and Walter Reiner. Pantheon, 1980. Subj: Animals – horses. Behavior – misbehavior.

Me and Clara and Casimir the cat tr. from German by Paula McGuire; ill. by Traudl and Walter Reiner. Pantheon, 1979. Subj: Animals – cats.

Me and Clara and Snuffy the dog tr. from German by Paula McGuire; ill. by Traudl and Walter Reiner. Pantheon, 1980. Subj: Animals – dogs. Behavior – misbehavior.

Me and my sister Clara tr. from German by Paula McGuire; ill. by Traudl and Walter Reiner. Pantheon, 1979. Behavior – misbehavior.

Ionesco, Eugene. *Story number 1* ill. by Etienne Delessert; tr. by Calvin K. Towle. Crown, 1969. Subj: Family life. Imagination.

Ipcar, Dahlov. *Animal hide and seek* ill. by author. Addison-Wesley, 1947. Subj: Animals.

The biggest fish in the sea ill. by author. Viking, 1972. Subj: Concepts – size. Fish. Sports – fishing.

Black and white ill. by author. Knopf, 1963. Subj: Animals – dogs. Poetry, rhyme.

Bright barnyard ill. by author. Knopf, 1966. Subj: Animals. Birds. Farms.

Brown cow farm ill. by author. Doubleday, 1959. Subj: Animals. Counting. Farms.

Bug city ill. by author. Holiday, 1975. Subj: Insects.

The calico jungle ill. by author. Knopf, 1965. Subj: Animals. Bedtime.

The cat at night ill. by author. Doubleday, 1969. Subj: Animals – cats. Night.

The cat came back ill. by author. Knopf, 1971. Subj: Animals – cats. Music. Poetry, rhyme. Songs.

A flood of creatures ill. by author. Holiday, 1973. Subj: Animals. Weather – floods.

Hard scrabble harvest ill. by author. Doubleday, 1976. Subj: Farms. Holidays – Thanksgiving. Plants. Poetry, rhyme.

I like animals ill. by author. Knopf, 1960. Subj: Animals.

I love my anteater with an A ill. by author. Knopf, 1964. Subj: ABC books. Animals.

The land of flowers ill. by author. Viking, 1974. Subj: Activities – gardening. Animals – sheep. Concepts – size. Flowers.

Lost and found: a hidden animal book ill. by author. Doubleday, 1981. Subj: Animals. Participation.

One horse farm ill. by author. Doubleday, 1950. Subj: Animals – horses. Farms. Machines. Progress.

Sir Addlepate and the unicorn ill. by author. Doubleday, 1971. Subj: Knights. Mythical creatures.

"The song of the day birds" and "The song of the night birds" ill. by author. Doubleday, 1967. Subj: Birds. Music. Night. Songs.

Stripes and spots ill. by author. Doubleday, 1953. Subj: Animals – leopards. Animals – tigers.

Ten big farms ill. by author. Knopf, 1958. Subj: Counting. Farms.

Wild and tame animals ill. by author. Doubleday, 1962. Subj: Animals.

World full of horses ill. by author. Doubleday, 1955. Subj: Animals – horses.

Ireson, Barbara. *The gingerbread man* (The gingerbread boy)

Irvine, Georgeanne. *Bo the orangutan* photos. by Ron Garrison. Children's Pr., 1983. Subj: Animals – monkeys. Zoos.

Elmer the elephant photos. by Ron Garrison. Children's Pr., 1983. Subj: Animals – elephants. Zoos.

Georgie the giraffe photos. by Ron Garrison. Children's Pr., 1983. Subj: Animals – giraffes. Zoos.

Lindi the leopard photos. by Ron Garrison. Children's Pr., 1983. Subj: Animals – leopards. Zoos.

The nursery babies photos. by Ron Garrison. Children's Pr., 1983. Subj: Animals. Zoos.

Sasha the cheetah photos. by Ron Garrison. Children's Pr., 1982. Subj: Animals – cheetahs. Zoos.

Tully the tree kangaroo photos. by Ron Garrison. Children's Pr., 1983. Subj: Animals. Zoos.

Isadora, Rachel. *Ben's trumpet* ill. by author. Greenwillow, 1979. Subj: Caldecott award honor book.

City seen from A to Z ill. by author. Greenwillow, 1983. Subj: ABC books. City.

Jesse and Abe ill. by author. Greenwillow, 1981. Subj: Family life – grandparents, great-grandparents. Theater.

Max ill. by author. Macmillan, 1976. Subj: Activities – dancing. Sports – baseball.

My ballet class ill. by author. Greenwillow, 1980. Subj: Activities – dancing.

No, Agatha! ill. by author. Greenwillow, 1980. Subj: Activities – traveling. Boats, ships.

Opening night ill. by author. Greenwillow, 1984. Subj: Activities – dancing. Theater.

The Potters' kitchen ill. by author. Greenwillow, 1977. Subj: Moving.

Willaby ill. by author. Macmillan, 1977. Subj: School.

Isele, Elizabeth. *The frog princess* ill. by Michael Hague. Crowell, 1984. Subj: Folk and fairy tales. Foreign lands – Russia. Magic. Witches.

Pooks ill. by Chris L. Demarest. Lippincott, 1983. Subj: Activities – traveling. Animals – dogs. Music.

Isenbart, Hans-Heinrich. *Baby animals on the farm* tr. from German by Elizabeth D. Crawford; photos by Ruth Rau. Putnam's, 1984. Subj: Animals. Farms.

A duckling is born tr. by Catherine Edwards Sadler; photos. by Othmar Baumli. Putnam's, 1981. Subj: Birds – ducks. Science.

Isenberg, Barbara. *The adventures of Albert, the running bear* by Barbara Isenberg and Susan Wolf; ill. by Dick Gackenbach. Houghton, 1982. Subj: Animals – bears. Behavior – running away. Sports – racing. Zoos.

The adventures of Albert, the running bear (Isenberg, Barbara)

Albert the running bear's exercise book by Barbara Isenberg and Marjorie Jaffe; ill. by Diane de Groat. Houghton, 1984. Subj: Animals – bears. Health.

Israel, Marion Louise. *The tractor on the farm* ill. by Robert Dranko. Melmont, 1958. Subj: Farms. Machines.

Iverson, Genie. *I want to be big* ill. by David McPhail. Dutton, 1979. Subj: Behavior – growing up.

Ivimey, John William. *The complete version of ye three blind mice* ill. by Walton Corbould. Warne, 1909. Subj: Animals – mice. Music. Nursery rhymes. Songs.

Ivory, Lesley Anne. *A day in London* ill. by author. Burke, 1982. Subj: City. Foreign lands – England.

A day in New York ill. by author. Burke, 1982. Subj: City.

Iwamatsu, Jun *see* Yashima, Tarō

Iwamura, Kazuo. *Tan Tan's hat* ill. by author. Bradbury, 1983. Subj: Animals – monkeys. Clothing.

Tan Tan's suspenders ill. by author. Bradbury, 1983. Subj: Animals – monkeys. Clothing.

Ton and Pon: big and little ill. by author. Bradbury, 1984. Subj: Animals – dogs. Friendship.

Ton and Pon: two good friends ill. by author. Bradbury, 1984. Subj: Animals – dogs. Friendship.

Iwasaki, Chihiro. *The birthday wish* ill. by author. McGraw-Hill, 1974, 1972. Subj: Behavior – wishing. Birthdays. Weather – snow.

Staying home alone on a rainy day ill. by author. McGraw-Hill, 1968. Subj: Family life. Family life – only child. Weather – rain.

What's fun without a friend? ill. by author. McGraw-Hill, 1972. Subj: Animals – dogs. Sea and seashore.

Will you be my friend? ill. by author. McGraw-Hill, 1970. Subj: Friendship.

Jack and the beanstalk adapt. and ill. by Lorinda Bryan Cauley. Putnam's, 1983. Subj: Folk and fairy tales. Giants.

Jack and the beanstalk ill. by Ed Parker. Troll Assoc., 1979. Subj: Folk and fairy tales. Giants.

Jack and the beanstalk adapt. and ill. by Tony Ross. Delacorte, 1981. Subj: Folk and fairy tales. Giants.

Jack and the beanstalk ill. by William Stobbs. Dial Pr., 1966. Subj: Folk and fairy tales. Giants.

Jack Sprat. *The life of Jack Sprat, his wife and his cat* retold and ill. by Paul Galdone. McGraw-Hill, 1969. Subj: Animals – cats. Family life. Food. Nursery rhymes.

Jackson, Ellen B. *The bear in the bathtub* ill. by Margot Apple. Addison-Wesley, 1981. Subj: Activities – bathing. Animals – bears. Character traits – cleanliness.

Jackson, Jacqueline. *Chicken ten thousand* ill. by Barbara Morrow. Little, 1968. Subj: Birds – chickens. Science.

Jacobs, Francine. *Barracuda: tiger of the sea* ill. by Harriett Springer. Walker, 1981. Subj: Fish. Science.

Sewer Sam: the sea cow ill. by Harriett Springer. Walker, 1979. Subj: Animals. Science. Sea and seashore. Zoos.

Jacobs, Joseph. *The crock of gold, being "The pedlar of Swaffham"* ill. by William Stobbs. Follett, 1971. Subj: Careers – peddlers. Dreams. Folk and fairy tales. Foreign lands – England.

Hereafterthis ill. by Paul Galdone. McGraw-Hill, 1973. Subj: Animals. Behavior – mistakes. Crime. Farms. Folk and fairy tales.

Hudden and Dudden and Donald O'Neary ill. by Doris Burn. Coward, 1968. Subj: Behavior – greed. Folk and fairy tales. Foreign lands – Ireland.

Johnny-cake ill. by Emma Lillian Brock. Putnam's, 1967. Subj: Cumulative tales. Folk and fairy tales. Food.

Johnny-cake ill. by William Stobbs. Viking, 1972. Subj: Cumulative tales. Folk and fairy tales. Food.

Master of all masters ill. by Anne F. Rockwell. Grosset, 1972. Subj: Folk and fairy tales.

Old Mother Wiggle-Waggle ill. by William Stobbs. Bodley Head, 1980. Subj: Folk and fairy tales.

The three sillies ill. by Paul Galdone. Houghton, 1981. Subj: Folk and fairy tales.

Jacobs, Leland B. *Belling the cat and other stories*

Is somewhere always far away? ill. by John E. Johnson. Holt, 1967. Subj: Character traits – questioning. Poetry, rhyme.

Jaffe, Marjorie. *Albert the running bear's exercise book* (Isenberg, Barbara)

Jaffe, Rona. *Last of the wizards* ill. by Erik Blegvad. Simon and Schuster, 1961. Subj: Behavior – wishing. Character traits – cleverness.

Jagendorf, Moritz A. *Kwi-na the eagle and other Indian tales* ill. by Jack Endewelt; consultant: Carolyn W. Field. Silver Burdett, 1968. Subj: Ethnic groups in the U.S. – Indians. Folk and fairy tales.

Jameson, Cynthia. *The clay pot boy* ill. by Arnold Lobel. Coward, 1973. Subj: Behavior – misbehavior. Cumulative tales. Folk and fairy tales. Foreign lands – Russia.

A day with Whisker Wickles ill. by James Marshall. Coward, 1975. Subj: Animals – rabbits. Games.

The house of five bears ill. by Lorinda Bryan Cauley. Putnam's, 1978. Subj: Character traits – cleverness. Folk and fairy tales. Foreign lands – Russia.

Janice. *Angélique* ill. by Roger Antoine Duvoisin. McGraw-Hill, 1960. Subj: Animals – dogs. Behavior – bullying. Birds – ducks.

Little Bear marches in the St. Patrick's Day parade ill. by Mariana. Subj: Animals – bears. Holidays – St. Patrick's Day. Parades.

Little Bear's Christmas ill. by Mariana. Lothrop, 1964. Subj: Animals – bears. Character traits – generosity. Hibernation. Holidays – Christmas.

Little Bear's New Year's party ill. by Mariana. Lothrop, 1973. Subj: Animals – bears. Holidays – New Year's. Parties.

Little Bear's pancake party ill. by Mariana. Lothrop, 1960. Subj: Animals – bears. Food. Parties. Seasons – spring.

Little Bear's Sunday breakfast ill. by Mariana. Lothrop, 1958. Subj: Animals – bears. Food.

Little Bear's Thanksgiving ill. by Mariana. Lothrop, 1967. Subj: Animals – bears. Holidays – Thanksgiving.

Minette ill. by Alain. McGraw-Hill, 1959. Subj: Animals – cats.

Mr. and Mrs. Button's wonderful watchdogs ill. by Roger Antoine Duvoisin. Lothrop, 1978. Subj: Animals – dogs. Crime.

Janosch. *Dear snowman* ill. by author. Collins, 1969. Subj: Seasons – winter. Snowmen. Weather – snow.

Hey Presto! You're a bear! tr. by Klauss Flugge; ill. by author. Little, 1980. Subj: Imagination.

Joshua and the magic fiddle ill. by author. Collins, 1967. Subj: Magic. Moon. Music.

Just one apple tr. by Refna Wilkin; ill. by author. Walck, 1965. Subj: Behavior – wishing. Dragons.

The magic auto ill. by author. Crown, 1971. Translation of Das Regenauto. Subj: Automobiles. Magic.

Tonight at nine ill. by author. Walck, 1967. Translation of Heute um neune hinter der Scheune. Subj: Animals. Music. Poetry, rhyme.

The trip to Panama tr. by Anthea Bell; ill. by author. Little, 1978. Translation of Oh, wie schon ist Panama. Subj: Activities – traveling. Foreign lands – Panama.

A January fog will freeze a hog, *and other weather folklore* comp. and ed. by Hubert Davis; ill. by John Wallner. Crown, 1977. Subj: Folk and fairy tales. Weather.

Jaques, Faith. *Tilly's house* ill. by author. Atheneum, 1979. Subj: Houses. Toys – dolls.

Jaquith, Priscilla. *Bo Rabbit smart for true: folktales from the Gullah* ill. by Ed Young. Putnam's, 1981. Subj: Animals – rabbits. Folk and fairy tales. Noise, sounds.

Jarrell, Mary. *The knee baby* ill. by Symeon Shimin. Farrar, 1973. Subj: Babies. Family life. Family life – grandparents, great-grandparents.

Jarrell, Randall. *A bat is born* ill. by John Schoenherr. Doubleday, 1978. Subj: Animals – bats. Poetry, rhyme.

The fisherman and his wife (Grimm, Jacob)

The golden bird (Grimm, Jacob)

The rabbit catcher and other fairy tales (Bechstein, Ludwig)

Jaynes, Ruth M. *Benny's four hats* ill. by Harvey Mandlin. Bowmar, 1967. Subj: Clothing. Ethnic groups in the U.S. Participation. Weather.

The biggest house ill. by Jacques Rupp. Bowmar, 1968. Subj: Houses.

Friends! friends! friends! ill. by Harvey Mandlin. Bowmar, 1967. Subj: Ethnic groups in the U.S. Friendship. School.

Melinda's Christmas stocking ill. by Richard George. Bowmar, 1968. Subj: Ethnic groups in the U.S. – Mexican-Americans. Holidays – Christmas. Senses.

Tell me please! What's that? ill. by Harvey Mandlin. Bowmar, 1968. Subj: Animals. Ethnic groups in the U.S. Ethnic groups in the U.S. – Mexican-Americans. Foreign languages.

That's what it is! ill. by Harvey Mandlin. Bowmar, 1968. Subj: Ethnic groups in the U.S. Ethnic groups in the U.S. – Mexican-Americans. Insects.

Three baby chicks ill. by Harvey Mandlin. Bowmar, 1967. Subj: Birds – chickens. School.

What is a birthday child? ill. by Harvey Mandlin. Bowmar, 1967. Subj: Birthdays. Character traits – individuality. Ethnic groups in the U.S. Ethnic groups in the U.S. – Mexican-Americans.

Jeake, Samuel *see* Aiken, Conrad

Jefferds, Vincent. *Disney's elegant ABC book.* Simon and Schuster, 1983. Subj: ABC books.

Jeffers, Susan. *All the pretty horses* ill. by author. Macmillan, 1974. Subj: Animals – horses. Bedtime. Sleep.

The three jovial huntsmen (Mother Goose)

Wild Robin ill. by author. Dutton, 1976. Based on a tale in Little Prudy's fairy book by R. S. Clarke. Subj: Behavior – misbehavior. Foreign lands – Scotland.

Jenkins, Jordan. *Learning about love* ill. by Gene Ruggles. Children's Pr., 1979. Subj: Emotions – love. Family life – mothers. Illness.

Jennings, Michael. *The bears who came to breakfix* ill. by Tom Dunnington. Children's Pr., 1977. Subj: Animals – bears. Dreams. Family life – mothers. Moving.

Robin Goodfellow and the giant dwarf ill. by Tomie de Paola. McGraw-Hill, 1981. Subj: Behavior – trickery. Giants.

Jenny, Anne. *The fantastic story of King Brioche the First* ill. by Joycelyne Pache. Lothrop, 1970. Translation by Catherine Barton from La fantastique histoire du roi Brioche Ier. Subj: Activities – flying. School.

Jensen, Virginia Allen. *Cat alley* (Ohlsson, Ib)

Catching: a book for blind and sighted children with pictures to feel as well as to see ill. by author. Putnam's, 1984. Subj: Concepts – shape. Format, unusual. Handicaps – blindness.

Red thread riddles by Virginia Allen Jensen and Polly Edman; ill. by authors. Putnam's, 1980. Subj: Handicaps – blindness. Riddles.

Sara and the door ill. by Ann Strugnell. Addison-Wesley, 1977. Subj: Character traits – perseverance. Clothing. Ethnic groups in the U.S. – Afro-Americans.

What's that? ill. by Dorcas Woodbury Haller. Collins-World, 1979. Subj: Concepts. Handicaps – blindness.

Jerome, Judson. *I never saw ...* ill. by Helga Aichinger. Albert Whitman, 1974. Subj: Poetry, rhyme.

Jeschke, Susan. *Angela and Bear* ill. by author. Holt, 1979. Subj: Animals – bears. Imagination – imaginary friends. Magic.

The devil did it ill. by author. Holt, 1979. Subj: Animals – bears. Imagination – imaginary friends.

Firerose ill. by author. Holt, 1974. Subj: Careers – fortune tellers. Dragons. Humor. Magic.

Mia, Grandma and the genie ill. by author. Holt, 1978. Subj: Fairies. Family life – grandparents, great-grandparents. Magic.

Perfect the pig ill. by author. Holt, 1981. Subj: Activities – flying. Animals – pigs.

Rima and Zeppo ill. by author. Dutton, 1976. Subj: Magic. Witches.

Tamar and the tiger ill. by author. Holt, 1980. Subj: Imagination.

Jewell, Nancy. *ABC cat* ill. by Ann Schweninger. Harper, 1983. Subj: ABC books. Animals – cats. Poetry, rhyme.

Bus ride ill. by Ronald Himler. Harper, 1978. Subj: Buses.

The snuggle bunny ill. by Mary Chalmers. Harper, 1972. Subj: Animals – rabbits. Emotions – love.

Time for Uncle Joe ill. by Joan Sandin. Harper, 1981. Subj: Death. Emotions. Family life.

Try and catch me ill. by Leonard Weisgard. Harper, 1972. Subj: Activities – playing. Ecology. Friendship. Imagination.

Joerns, Consuelo. *The foggy rescue* ill. by author. Four Winds Pr., 1980. Subj: Animals – mice. Boats, ships. Behavior – lost.

The forgotten bear ill. by author. Four Winds Pr., 1978. Subj: Behavior – lost. Toys – teddy bears.

The lost and found house ill. by author. Four Winds Pr., 1979. Subj: Animals – mice. Houses.

The midnight castle ill. by author. Lothrop, 1983. Subj: Animals – mice. Dragons. Royalty.

Oliver's escape ill. by author. Four Winds Pr., 1981. Subj: Animals. Animals – dogs. Behavior – running away. Friendship.

John, Naomi. *Roadrunner* ill. by Peter and Virginia Parnall. Dutton, 1980. Subj: Birds. Desert.

Johnson, Crockett. *The blue ribbon puppies* ill. by author. Harper, 1958. Subj: Animals – dogs. Imagination. Toys.

Ellen's lion ill. by author. Harper, 1959. Subj: Imagination. Toys.

The emperor's gift ill. by author. Holt, 1965. Subj: Character traits. Character traits – generosity. Royalty.

The frowning prince ill. by author. Harper, 1959. Subj: Royalty.

Harold and the purple crayon ill. by author. Harper, 1955. Subj: Art. Humor. Imagination.

Harold at the North Pole ill. by author. Harper, 1957. Subj: Holidays – Christmas. Imagination.

Harold's ABC: another purple crayon adventure ill. by author. Harper, 1963. Subj: ABC books. Imagination.

Harold's circus ill. by author. Harper, 1959. Subj: Circus. Humor. Imagination.

Harold's fairy tale: further adventures with the purple crayon ill. by author. Harper, 1956. Subj: Folk and fairy tales. Imagination.

Harold's trip to the sky ill. by author. Harper, 1957. Subj: Imagination. Space and space ships.

A picture for Harold's room ill. by author. Harper, 1960. Subj: Art. Imagination.

Terrible terrifying Toby ill. by author. Harper, 1957. Subj: Animals – dogs.

Time for spring ill. by author. Harper, 1957. Subj: Seasons – spring. Snowmen.

Upside down ill. by author. Albert Whitman, 1969. Subj: Animals – kangaroos. Concepts – up and down. Humor. World.

We wonder what will Walter be? When he grows up ill. by author. Holt, 1964. Subj: Animals. Behavior – growing up.

Will spring be early? ill. by author. Crowell, 1959. Subj: Animals – groundhogs. Holidays – Groundhog Day. Seasons – spring.

Johnson, Donna Kay. *Brighteyes* ill. by author. Holt, 1978. Subj: Animals – raccoons. Handicaps – blindness.

Johnson, Elizabeth. *All in free but Janey* ill. by Trina Schart Hyman. Little, 1968. Subj: Games. Imagination.

Johnson, Evelyne. *The cow in the kitchen: a folk tale* ill. by Anthony Rao. Simon and Schuster, 1983. Subj: Behavior – dissatisfaction. Character traits – foolishness.

Johnson, Hannah Lyons. *From seed to jack-o'-lantern* photos. by Daniel Dorn. Lothrop, 1974. Subj: Activities – gardening. Holidays – Halloween. Plants. Science.

Johnson, Jane. *Bertie on the beach* ill. by author. Four Winds Pr., 1981. Subj: Circus. Dreams. Sea and seashore.

Sybil and the blue rabbit ill. by author. Doubleday, 1980. Subj: Imagination. Toys.

Johnson, John E. *My first book of things* ill. by author. Random House, 1979. Subj: Format, unusual – cardboard pages.

Johnson, Louise. *Malunda* ill. by Edward Durose. Carolrhoda, 1982. Subj: Animals – rhinoceros. Illness. Zoos.

Johnson, Mildred D. *Wait, skates!* ill. by Tom Dunnington. Children's Pr., 1983. Subj: Activities – playing. Sports – ice skating.

Johnson, Ryerson. *Let's walk up the wall* ill. by Eva Cellini. Holiday, 1967. Subj: Participation.

Upstairs and downstairs ill. by Lisl Weil. Crowell, 1962. Subj: Concepts.

Johnson, Walter Ryerson *see* Johnson, Ryerson

Johnston, Johanna. *Edie changes her mind* ill. by Paul Galdone. Putnam's, 1964. Subj: Bedtime. Problem solving.

Penguin's way ill. by Leonard Weisgard. Doubleday, 1962. Subj: Birds – penguins. Science.

Speak up, Edie ill. by Paul Galdone. Putman's, 1974. Subj: Language. Theater.

Sugarplum ill. by Marvin Bileck. Knopf, 1955. Subj: Character traits – smallness. Toys – dolls.

That's right, Edie ill. by Paul Galdone. Putnam's, 1966. Subj: Activities – writing.

Whale's way ill. by Leonard Weisgard. Doubleday, 1965. Subj: Animals – whales. Science.

Johnston, Mary Anne. *Sing me a song* ill. by John Magine. Children's Pr., 1977. Subj: Animals – rabbits. Songs.

Johnston, Tony. *Four scary stories* ill. by Tomie de Paola. Putnam's, 1978. Subj: Ghosts. Goblins. Monsters.

The vanishing pumpkin ill. by Tomie de Paola. Putnam's, 1983. Subj: Holidays – Halloween. Witches.

The witch's hat ill. by Margot Tomes. Putnam's, 1984. Subj: Magic. Witches.

Jolliffe, Anne. *From pots to plastics* ill. by author. Hawthorn, 1965. Subj: Science.

Water, wind and wheels ill. by author. Hawthorn, 1965. Subj: Science.

Jonah: *the complete text of Jonah from the Holy Bible, New International version* ill. by Kurt Mitchell. Crossway, 1981. Subj: Animals – mice. Animals – cats. Animals – whales. Religion.

Jonas, Ann. *Holes and peeks* ill. by author. Greenwillow, 1984. Subj: Caldecott award honor book. Emotions – fear. Problem solving.

The quilt ill. by author. Greenwillow, 1984. Subj: Bedtime. Dreams.

Two bear cubs ill. by author. Greenwillow, 1982. Subj: Animals – bears. Behavior – lost. Family life – mothers.

When you were a baby ill. by author. Greenwillow, 1982. Subj: Activities. Behavior – growing up.

Jones, Harold. *Tales from Æsop (Æsop)*

There and back again ill. by author. Atheneum, 1977. Subj: Toys.

Jones, Hettie, comp. *The trees stand shining: poetry of the North American Indians* ill. by Robert Andrew Parker. Dial Pr., 1971. Subj: Ethnic groups in the U.S. – Indians. Poetry, rhyme.

Jones, Jessie Mae Orton. *A little child: the Christmas miracle told in Bible verses* ill. by Elizabeth Orton Jones. Viking, 1946. Subj: Holidays – Christmas. Religion.

Small rain: verses from the Bible ill. by Elizabeth Orton Jones. Viking, 1943. Subj: Caldecott award honor book. Poetry, rhyme. Religion.

This is the way: prayers and precepts from world religions ill. by Elizabeth Orton Jones. Viking, 1951. Subj: Religion.

Jones, Olive. *A treasure box of fairy tales: Hansel and Gretel; Rapunzel; Jack and the bean stalk; and Aladdin* ill. by Francesca Crespi. Dial Pr., 1984. Four books boxed together. Subj: Folk and fairy tales.

Jones, Penelope. *I didn't want to be nice* ill. by Rosalie Orlando. Bradbury Pr., 1977. Subj: Animals – squirrels. Birthdays. Parties.

I'm not moving! ill. by Amy Aitken. Bradbury Pr., 1980. Subj: Family life. Moving.

Jones, Rebecca C. *The biggest, meanest, ugliest dog in the whole wide world* ill. by Wendy Watson. Macmillan, 1982. Subj: Animals – dogs. Character traits – meanness. Friendship.

Jong, David Cornel De *see* DeJong, David Cornel

Jong, Meindert De *see* DeJong, Meindert

Joosse, Barbara M. *Spiders in the fruit cellar* ill. by Kay Chorao. Knopf, 1983. Subj: Emotions – fear. Spiders.

The thinking place ill. by Kay Chorao. Knopf, 1982. Subj: Behavior – misbehavior. Imagination – imaginary friends.

Jordan, Helene J. *Seeds of wind and water* ill. by Nils Hogner. Crowell, 1962. Subj: Plants.

Jordan, June. *Kimako's story* ill. by Kay Burford. Houghton, 1981. Subj: City.

Joslin, Sesyle. *Baby elephant and the secret wishes* ill. by Leonard Weisgard. Harcourt, 1962. Subj: Animals – elephants. Holidays – Christmas.

Baby elephant goes to China ill. by Leonard Weisgard. Harcourt, 1963. Subj: Animals – elephants. Foreign languages. Sea and seashore.

Baby elephant's trunk ill. by Leonard Weisgard. Harcourt, 1961. Subj: Animals – elephants. Foreign lands – France. Foreign languages.

Brave Baby Elephant ill. by Leonard Weisgard. Harcourt, 1960. Subj: Animals – elephants. Bedtime.

Dear dragon: and other useful letter forms for young ladies and gentlemen engaged in everyday correspondence ill. by Irene Haas. Harcourt, 1962. Subj: Activities – writing. Communication. Dragons. Etiquette. Humor.

Señor Baby Elephant, the pirate ill. by Leonard Weisgard. Harcourt, 1962. Subj: Animals – elephants. Foreign languages. Pirates.

What do you do, dear? ill. by Maurice Sendak. Addison-Wesley, 1961. Subj: Etiquette. Humor.

What do you say, dear? ill. by Maurice Sendak. Addison-Wesley, 1958. Subj: Caldecott award honor book. Etiquette. Humor.

Joyce, Irma. *Never talk to strangers* ill. by George Buckett. Golden Pr., 1967. Subj: Behavior – talking to strangers. Humor. Safety.

Joyce, James. *The cat and the devil* ill. by Richard Erdoes. Dodd, 1965. Subj: Behavior – trickery. Devil.

Joyner, Jerry. *Thirteen* (Charlip, Remy)

Jüchen, Aurel von. *The Holy Night: the story of the first Christmas* tr. from German by Cornelia Schaeffer; ill. by Celestino Piatti. Atheneum, 1968. Subj: Holidays – Christmas. Religion.

Jukes, Mavis. *Like Jake and me* ill. by Lloyd Bloom. Knopf, 1984. Subj: Divorce. Family life.

Justice, Jennifer. *The tiger* ill. by Graham Allen. Watts, 1979. Subj: Animals – tigers. Science.

Kahl, Virginia. *Away went Wolfgang* ill. by author. Scribner's, 1954. Subj: Animals – dogs. Foreign lands – Austria.

The Baron's booty ill. by author. Scribner's, 1963. Subj: Middle ages. Poetry, rhyme. Royalty.

Droopsi ill. by author. Scribner's, 1958 Subj: Foreign lands – Germany. Music.

The Duchess bakes a cake ill. by author. Scribner's, 1955. Subj: Activities – cooking. Food. Middle ages. Poetry, rhyme. Royalty.

Giants, indeed! ill. by author. Scribner's, 1974. Subj: Giants. Monsters.

Gunhilde and the Halloween spell ill. by author. Scribner's, 1975. Subj: Holidays – Halloween. Middle ages. Poetry, rhyme. Royalty. Witches.

Gunhilde's Christmas booke ill. by author. Scribner's, 1972. Subj: Holidays – Christmas. Middle ages. Music. Poetry, rhyme. Royalty.

The habits of rabbits ill. by author. Scribner's, 1957. Subj: Animals – rabbits. Middle ages. Pets. Poetry, rhyme. Royalty.

Here is Henri! (Vacheron, Edith)

How do you hide a monster? ill. by author. Scribner's, 1971. Subj: Monsters. Poetry, rhyme. Sports – hunting.

Maxie ill. by author. Scribner's, 1956. Subj: Animals – dogs. Character traits – perseverance. Foreign lands – Germany. Old age.

The perfect pancake ill. by author. Scribner's, 1960. Subj: Character traits – selfishness. Food. Poetry, rhyme.

Plum pudding for Christmas ill. by author. Scribner's, 1956. Subj: Food. Holidays – Christmas. Poetry, rhyme. Royalty.

Whose cat is that? ill. by author. Scribner's, 1979. Subj: Animals – cats. Cumulative tales.

Kahn, Joan. *Hi, Jock, run around the block* ill. by Whitney Darrow, Jr. Harper, 1978. Subj: City. Poetry, rhyme.

Seesaw ill. by Crosby Newell Bonsall. Harper, 1964. Subj: Games. Toys.

Kahn, Michèle. *My everyday Spanish word book* tr. from French by Michael Mahler and Gwen Marsh; ill. by Benvenuti. Barron's, 1982. Subj: Foreign languages.

Kalan, Robert. *Blue sea* ill. by Donald Crews. Greenwillow, 1979. Subj: Concepts – size. Fish.

Jump, frog, jump! ill. by Byron Barton. Greenwillow, 1981. Subj: Cumulative tales. Frogs and toads.

Rain ill. by Donald Crews. Greenwillow, 1978. Subj: Weather – rain.

Kalman, Benjamin. *Animals in danger: poems from no man's valley* ill. by Cécile Curtis and Michael Jupp. Random House, 1982. Subj: Animals. Ecology. Poetry, rhyme.

Kandell, Alice. *Max, the music-maker* (Stecher, Miriam B)

Kane, Henry B. *Wings, legs, or fins* photos. and ill. by author. Knopf, 1966. Subj: Animals. Science.

Kantor, MacKinlay. *The preposterous week* ill. by Kurt Wiese. Putnam's, 1942. Subj: Food. Humor.

Kantrowitz, Mildred. *I wonder if Herbie's home yet* ill. by Tony DeLuna. Parents, 1971. Subj: Friendship.

When Violet died ill. by Emily Arnold McCully. Parents, 1973. Subj: Birds. Death.

Willy Bear ill. by Nancy Winslow Parker. Parents, 1976. Subj: School. Sleep. Toys – teddy bears.

Kaplan, Boche. *Sweet Betsy from Pike* (Abisch, Roz)

Kapp, Paul. *Cock-a-doodle-doo! Cock-a-doodle-dandy!* ill. by Anita Lobel. Harper, 1966. Subj: Music. Songs.

Kark, Nina Mary *see* Bawden, Nina

Karlin, Nurit. *The blue frog* ill. by author. Coward, 1983. Subj: Character traits – being different. Frogs and toads.

A train for the king ill. by author. Coward, 1983. Subj: Royalty. Self-concept.

Karsunke, Yaak. *Hello Irina* (Blech, Dietlind)

Kauffman, Lois. *What's that noise?* ill. by Allan Eitzen. Lothrop, 1965. Subj: Family life – fathers. Night. Noise, sounds.

Kaufmann, John. *Birds are flying* ill. by author. Crowell, 1979. Subj: Birds. Science.

Flying giants of long ago ill. by author. Crowell, 1984. Subj: Activities – flying. Animals. Birds. Insects. Science.

Kaune, Merriman B. *My own little house* ill. by author. Follett, 1957. Subj: Houses.

Kavanaugh, James J. *The crooked angel* ill. by Elaine Havelock. Nash, 1970. Subj: Angels. Poetry, rhyme.

Kay, Helen. *An egg is for wishing* ill. by Yaroslava. Abelard-Schuman, 1966. Subj: Behavior – animals, dislike of. Behavior – wishing. Eggs. Foreign lands – Ukraine. Holidays – Easter.

One mitten Lewis ill. by Kurt Werth. Lothrop, 1955. Subj: Behavior – losing things. Clothing.

A stocking for a kitten ill. by Yaroslava. Abelard-Schuman, 1965. Subj: Animals – cats. Family life – grandparents, great-grandparents.

Kay, Ormonde De *see* De Kay, Ormonde

Kaye, Geraldine. *The sea monkey: a picture story from Malaysia* ill. by Gay Galsworthy. Collins-World, 1968. Subj: Animals – monkeys. Foreign lands – Malaysia.

Keats, Ezra Jack. *Apartment 3* ill. by author. Macmillan, 1971. Subj: City. Ethnic groups in the U.S. – Afro-Americans. Family life. Handicaps – blindness. Music.

Clementina's cactus ill. by author. Viking, 1983. Subj: Desert. Weather – storms. Wordless.

Dreams ill. by author. Macmillan, 1974. Subj: Dreams. Ethnic groups in the U.S. – Afro-Americans. Imagination. Night. Sleep.

God is in the mountain ill. by author. Holt, 1966. Subj: Religion.

Goggles ill. by author. Macmillan, 1969. Subj: Behavior – bullying. Caldecott award honor book. City. Ethnic groups in the U.S. – Afro-Americans. Problem solving.

Hi, cat! ill. by author. Macmillan, 1970. Subj: Animals – cats. City. Ethnic groups in the U.S. – Afro-Americans.

Jennie's hat ill. by author. Harper, 1966. Subj: Behavior – dissatisfaction. Character traits – kindness to animals. Clothing.

John Henry ill. by author. Harper, 1965. Subj: Character traits – perseverance. Character traits – pride. Ethnic groups in the U.S. – Afro-Americans. Folk and fairy tales.

Kitten for a day ill. by author. Watts, 1974. Subj: Animals – cats. Animals – dogs. Wordless.

A letter to Amy ill. by author. Harper, 1968. Subj: Ethnic groups in the U.S. – Afro-Americans. Friendship. Letters. Parties. Weather – rain. Weather – wind.

The little drummer boy ill. by author. Macmillan, 1968. Words and music by Katherine Davis, Henry Onorati and Harry Simeonne. Subj: Holidays – Christmas. Music. Religion. Songs.

Louie ill. by author. Greenwillow, 1975. Subj: Character traits – shyness. Ethnic groups in the U.S. – Afro-Americans. Puppets.

Louie's search ill. by author. Four Winds Pr., 1980. Subj: Behavior – needing someone. Family life.

Maggie and the pirate ill. by author. Four Winds Pr., 1979. Subj: Death. Pets. Pirates.

My dog is lost! ill. by Ezra Jack Keats. Crowell, 1960. Subj: Animals – dogs. Behavior – lost. Careers – police officers. Ethnic groups in the U.S. Ethnic groups in the U.S. – Puerto Rican-Americans. Foreign languages.

Pet show! ill. by author. Macmillan, 1972. Subj: Animals. Ethnic groups in the U.S. – Afro-Americans. Pets.

Peter's chair ill. by author. Harper, 1967. Subj: Babies. Behavior – sharing. Ethnic groups in the U.S. – Afro-Americans. Family life. Friendship. Self-concept.

Psst, doggie ill. by author. Watts, 1973. Subj: Animals – cats. Animals – dogs. Wordless.

Regards to the man in the moon ill. by author. Four Winds Pr., 1981. Subj: Imagination. Space and space ships.

Skates ill. by author. Watts, 1972. Subj: Activities – playing. Animals – dogs. Ethnic groups in the U.S. – Afro-Americans. Humor. Wordless.

The snowy day ill. by author. Viking, 1962. Subj: Activities – playing. Caldecott award book. Ethnic groups in the U.S. – Afro-Americans. Seasons – winter. Weather – snow.

The trip ill. by author. Greenwillow, 1978. Subj: Emotions – loneliness. Ethnic groups in the U.S. – Afro-Americans. Holidays – Halloween. Imagination. Moving.

Whistle for Willie ill. by author. Viking, 1964. Subj: Activities – whistling. Animals – dogs. Ethnic groups in the U.S. – Afro-Americans. Problem solving. Self-concept.

Keenan, Martha. *The mannerly adventures of Little Mouse* ill. by Meri Shardin. Crown, 1977. Subj: Animals – mice. Etiquette.

Keenen, George. *The preposterous week* ill. by Stanley Mack. Dial Pr., 1971. Subj: Days of the week, months of the year. Humor. Problem solving.

Keeping, Charles. *Alfie finds the other side of the world* ill. by author. Watts, 1968. Subj: City. Foreign lands – England. Rivers. Weather – fog.

Joseph's yard ill. by author. Watts, 1969. Subj: Activities – gardening. Poverty.

Molly o' the moors: the story of a pony ill. by author. Collins, 1966. Subj: Animals – horses. Old age.

Through the window ill. by author. Watts, 1970. Subj: City. Foreign lands – England.

Willie's fire-engine ill. by author. Oxford Univ. Pr., 1980. Subj: Activities – playing. Careers – firefighters. Imagination.

Keeshan, Robert. *She loves me, she loves me not* ill. by Maurice Sendak. Harper, 1963. Subj: Games. Holidays – Valentine's Day. Mythical creatures.

Kehoe, Michael. *Road closed* photos. by author. Carolrhoda, 1982. Subj: Roads.

The rock quarry book photos. by author. Carolrhoda, 1981. Subj: Rocks.

Keigwin, R. P. *Thumbelina* (Andersen, H C (Hans Christian))

The ugly duckling (Andersen, H C (Hans Christian))

Keith, Eros. *Bedita's bad day* ill. by author. Harper, 1973. Subj: Behavior – bad day. Witches.

Nancy's backyard ill. by author. Harper, 1973. Subj: Dreams. Weather – rain.

Rrra-ah ill. by author. Bradbury Pr., 1969. Subj: Frogs and toads. Pets.

Keller, Beverly. *Fiona's bee* ill. by Diane Paterson. Coward, 1975. Subj: Character traits – shyness. Insects – bees.

Pimm's place ill. by Jacqueline Chwast. Coward, 1978. Subj: Behavior – solitude. Character traits – bravery. Emotions – fear.

When mother got the flu ill. by Maxie Chambliss. Coward, 1984. Subj: Behavior – misbehavior. Family life – mothers. Illness.

Keller, Charles. *Giggle puss: pet jokes for kids* ill. by Paul Coker, Jr. Prentice-Hall, 1977. Subj: Humor. Pets. Riddles.

The nutty joke book ill. by Jean-Claude Suarès. Prentice-Hall, 1978. Subj: Humor. Riddles.

School daze ill. by Sam Q. Weissman. Prentice-Hall, 1979. Subj: Humor. Riddles.

Keller, Holly. *Cromwell's glasses* ill. by author. Greenwillow, 1982. Subj: Animals – rabbits. Family life. Glasses.

Geraldine's blanket ill. by author. Greenwillow, 1984. Subj: Animals – pigs. Toys – dolls.

Ten sleepy sheep ill. by author. Greenwillow, 1983. Subj: Bedtime.

Too big ill. by author. Greenwillow, 1983. Subj: Animals. Sibling rivalry.

Will it rain? ill. by author. Greenwillow, 1984. Subj: Animals. Weather – rain. Weather – storms.

Keller, Irene. *The Thingumajig book of manners* ill. by Dick Keller. Children's Pr., 1981. Subj: Character traits – appearance. Etiquette.

Keller, John G. *Krispin's fair* ill. by Ed Emberley. Little, 1976. Subj: Etiquette. Friendship.

Kelley, Emily. *April Fools' Day* ill. by C. A. Nobens. Carolrhoda, 1983. Subj: Holidays – April Fools' Day.

Kelley, True. *A valentine for Fuzzboom* ill. by author. Houghton, 1981. Subj: Animals – rabbits. Holidays – Valentine's Day.

Kellogg, Stephen *see* Kellogg, Steven

Kellogg, Steven. *Can I keep him?* ill. by author. Dial Pr., 1971. Subj: Family life. Pets.

The island of the skog ill. by author. Dial Pr., 1973. Subj: Animals – mice. Boats, ships. Islands. Monsters.

The mysterious tadpole ill. by author. Dial Pr., 1977. Subj: Frogs and toads. Monsters. Pets.

The mystery of the flying orange pumpkin ill. by author. Dial Pr., 1980. Subj: Holidays – Halloween.

The mystery of the magic green ball ill. by author. Dial Pr., 1978. Subj: Behavior – losing things. Gypsies. Toys – balls.

The mystery of the missing red mitten ill. by author. Dial Pr., 1974. Subj: Behavior – losing things. Problem solving. Snowmen.

The mystery of the stolen blue paint ill. by author. Dial Pr., 1982. Subj: Problem solving.

Pinkerton, behave! ill. by author. Dial Pr., 1979. Subj: Animals – dogs.

Ralph's secret weapon ill. by author. Dial Pr., 1983. Subj: Activities – vacationing. Imagination.

A rose for Pinkerton ill. by author. Dial Pr., 1981. Subj: Animals – cats. Animals – dogs. Behavior – imitation.

Tallyho, Pinkerton! ill. by author. Dial Pr., 1982. Subj: Animals – cats. Animals – dogs. Sports – hunting.

Kemp, Moira. *The firebird*

Kennedy, Jimmy. *The teddy bears' picnic* ill. by Alexandra Day. Green Tiger Pr., 1983. Subj: Activities – picnicking. Toys – teddy bears.

Kennedy, Richard. *The contests at Cowlick* ill. by Marc Simont. Little, 1975. Subj: Character traits – cleverness. Cowboys. Humor.

The leprechaun's story ill. by Marcia Sewall. Dutton, 1979. Subj: Elves and little people. Foreign lands – Ireland.

The porcelain man ill. by Marcia Sewall. Little, 1976. Subj: Magic.

Kent, Jack. *The caterpillar and the polliwog* ill. by author. Prentice-Hall, 1982. Subj: Frogs and toads. Insects – butterflies, caterpillars.

The Christmas piñata ill. by author. Parents, 1975. Subj: Foreign lands – Mexico. Holidays – Christmas.

Clotilda ill. by author. Random House, 1978. Subj: Character traits – kindness. Fairies.

The egg book ill. by author. Macmillan, 1975. Subj: Eggs. Wordless.

Hoddy doddy ill. by author. Greenwillow, 1979. Subj: Foreign lands – Denmark. Humor.

Jack Kent's happy-ever-after book ill. by author. Random House, 1976. Subj: Folk and fairy tales.

Jack Kent's hokus pokus bedtime book ill. by author. Random House, 1979. Subj: Folk and fairy tales.

Joey ill. by author. Prentice-Hall, 1984. Subj: Activities – playing. Animals – kangaroos. Family life – mothers.

Knee-high Nina ill. by author. Doubleday, 1981. Subj: Behavior – wishing.

Little Peep ill. by author. Prentice-Hall, 1981. Subj: Animals. Birds – chickens. Farms.

The once-upon-a-time dragon ill. by author. Harcourt, 1982. Subj: Bedtime. Behavior – imitation. Dragons.

Piggy Bank Gonzalez ill. by author. Parents, 1979. Subj: Animals – pigs. Money. Toys.

Round Robin ill. by author. Prentice-Hall, 1982. Subj: Birds – robins.

The scribble monster ill. by author. Harcourt, 1981. Subj: Behavior – misbehavior.

Silly goose ill. by author. Prentice-Hall, 1983. Subj: Animals – foxes. Birds – geese.

Socks for supper ill. by author. Parents, 1978. Subj: Friendship.

There's no such thing as a dragon ill. by author. Golden Pr., 1975. Subj: Behavior – needing someone. Dragons.

Kepes, Juliet. *Cock-a-doodle-doo* ill. by author. Pantheon, 1978. Subj: Animals – tigers. Birds – chickens.

Five little monkeys ill. by author. Houghton, 1952. Subj: Animals. Animals – monkeys. Caldecott award honor book.

Frogs, merry ill. by author. Pantheon, 1961. Subj: Frogs and toads. Hibernation.

Lady bird, quickly ill. by author. Little, 1964. Subj: Insects – ladybugs. Nursery rhymes.

Run little monkeys, run, run, run ill. by author. Pantheon, 1974. Subj: Animals – leopards. Animals – monkeys. Participation.

The seed that peacock planted ill. by author. Little, 1967. Subj: Birds – peacocks, peahens. Magic. Music. Plants.

The story of a bragging duck ill. by author. Houghton, 1983. Subj: Behavior – boasting. Birds – ducks. Character traits – vanity.

Ker Wilson, Barbara *see* Wilson, Barbara

Kerr, Judith. *Mog's Christmas* ill. by author. Collins-World, 1976. Subj: Animals – cats. Holidays – Christmas.

Kerry, Lois *see* Duncan, Lois

Kesselman, Judi R. *I can use tools* by Judi R. Kesselman and Franklynn Peterson; ill. by Tomás Gonzales. Elsevier Nelson, 1981. Subj: Tools.

Kesselman, Wendy. *Angelita* ill. by Norma Holt. Hill and Wang, 1970. Subj: City. Emotions – loneliness. Ethnic groups in the U.S. Ethnic groups in the U.S. – Puerto Rican-Americans.

Emma ill. by Barbara Cooney. Doubleday, 1980. Subj: Art. Emotions – loneliness.

There's a train going by my window ill. by Tony Chen. Doubleday, 1982. Subj: Activities – traveling.

Time for Jody ill. by Gerald Dumas. Harper, 1975. Subj: Animals – groundhogs. Hibernation. Holidays – Groundhog Day. Seasons – spring.

Kessler, Ethel. *All aboard the train* by Ethel and Leonard P. Kessler; ill. by authors. Doubleday, 1964. Subj: Trains.

Do baby bears sit in chairs? by Ethel and Leonard P. Kessler; ill. by authors. Doubleday, 1961. Subj: Animals. Poetry, rhyme.

Grandpa Witch and the magic doobelator by Ethel and Leonard P. Kessler; ill. by Leonard P. Kessler. Macmillan, 1981. Subj: Family life – grandparents, great-grandparents. Holidays – Halloween. Witches.

Night story by Ethel and Leonard P. Kessler; ill. by Leonard P. Kessler. Macmillan, 1981. Subj: Activities – working. Night. Trucks.

Two, four, six, eight: a book about legs by Ethel and Leonard P. Kessler; ill. by Leonard P. Kessler. Dodd, 1980. Subj: Counting.

What's inside the box? ill. by Leonard P. Kessler. Dodd, 1978. Subj: Animals.

Kessler, Jascha. *Rose of Mother-of-Pearl* (Olujic, Grozdana)

Kessler, Leonard P. *All aboard the train* (Kessler, Ethel)

Are we lost, daddy? ill. by author. Grosset, 1967. Subj: Activities – vacationing. Behavior – lost. Family life. Family life – fathers.

The big mile race ill. by author. Greenwillow, 1983. Subj: Animals. Sports – racing.

Do baby bears sit in chairs? (Kessler, Ethel)

Do you have any carrots? ill. by Lori Pierson. Garrard, 1979. Subj: Animals. Food.

Grandpa Witch and the magic doobelator (Kessler, Ethel)

Here comes the strikeout ill. by author. Harper, 1965. Subj: Sports – baseball.

Kick, pass, and run ill. by author. Harper, 1966. Subj: Animals. Sports – football.

Last one in is a rotten egg ill. by author. Harper, 1969. Subj: Behavior – bullying. Sports – swimming.

Mr. Pine's mixed-up signs ill. by author. Grosset, 1961. Subj: Glasses.

Mr. Pine's purple house ill. by author. Grosset, 1965. Subj: Activities – painting. Concepts – color.

Mrs. Pine takes a trip ill. by author. Grosset, 1966. Subj: Activities – traveling.

Night story (Kessler, Ethel)

Old Turtle's baseball stories ill. by author. Greenwillow, 1982. Subj: Sports – baseball.

Old Turtle's winter games ill. by author. Greenwillow, 1983. Subj: Animals. Seasons – winter. Sports.

On your mark, get set, go! The first all-animal Olympics ill. by author. Harper, 1972. Subj: Animals. Sports – Olympics.

The pirates' adventure on Spooky Island ill. by author. Garrard, 1979. Subj: Islands. Pirates.

Riddles that rhyme for Halloween time ill. by author. Garrard, 1978. Subj: Holidays – Halloween. Poetry, rhyme. Riddles.

The silly Mother Goose ill. by author. Garrard, 1980. Subj: Nursery rhymes.

Soup for the king ill. by author. Grosset, 1969. Subj: Careers – bakers. Food. Royalty.

Super bowl ill. by author. Greenwillow, 1980. Subj: Animals. Sports – football.

Two, four, six, eight (Kessler, Ethel)

Key, Francis Scott. *The Star-Spangled Banner* ill. by Paul Galdone. Crowell, 1966. Subj: Songs. U.S. history.

The Star-Spangled Banner ill. by Peter Spier. Doubleday, 1973. Subj: Songs. U.S. history.

Keyser, Marcia. *Roger on his own* ill. by Diane Dawson. Crown, 1982. Subj: Animals – dogs. Behavior – solitude.

Kherdian, David. *The animal* ill. by Nonny Hogrogian. Knopf, 1984. Subj: Animals.

Country cat, city cat ill. by Nonny Hogrogian. Four Winds Pr., 1978. Subj: Animals – cats. Poetry, rhyme.

The dog writes on the window with his nose, and other poems

If dragon flies made honey

Right now ill. by Nonny Hogrogian. Knopf, 1983. Subj: Emotions.

Kidd, Bruce. *Hockey showdown* ill. by Leoung O'Young. Lorimer, 1980. Subj: Character traits – meanness. Sports – hockey.

Kilreon, Beth *see* Walker, Barbara K.

Kilroy, Sally. *Animal noises* ill. by author. Four Winds Pr., 1983. Subj: Animals. Format, unusual – cardboard pages. Noise, sounds. Wordless.

Babies' bodies ill. by author. Scholastic, 1983. Subj: Anatomy. Babies. Format, unusual – cardboard pages.

Baby colors ill. by author. Scholastic, 1983. Subj: Babies. Concepts – color. Format, unusual – cardboard pages.

Copycat drawing book ill. by author. Dial Pr., 1981. Subj: Art.

Noisy homes ill. by author. Scholastic, 1983. Subj: Format, unusual – cardboard pages. Noise, sounds.

Kimmel, Eric A. *Why worry?* ill. by Beth Cannon. Pantheon, 1979. Subj: Insects – crickets. Insects – grasshoppers. Music. Songs.

Kimmel, Margaret Mary. *Magic in the mist* ill. by Trina Schart Hyman. Atheneum, 1975. Subj: Dragons. Magic. Wizards.

Kimura, Yasuko. *Fergus and the sea monster* ill. by author. McGraw-Hill, 1978. Subj: Animals – dogs. Friendship. Monsters. Sea and seashore.

Kines, Pat Decker *see* Tapio, Pat Decker

King, Deborah. *Sirius and Saba* ill. by author. David and Charles, 1982. Subj: Animals – dogs. Islands.

King, Patricia. *Mable the whale* ill. by Katherine Evans. Follett, 1958. Subj: Animals – whales.

Kingman, Lee. *Peter's long walk* ill. by Barbara Cooney. Doubleday, 1953. Subj: Activities – walking. Animals. Country. Friendship.

Pierre Pigeon ill. by Arnold E. Bare. Houghton, 1943. Subj: Birds – pigeons. Caldecott award honor book.

Kinnell, Galway. *How the alligator missed breakfast* ill. by Lynn Munsinger. Houghton, 1982. Subj: Reptiles – alligators, crocodiles.

Kinney, Jean. *What does the sun do?* ill. by Cle Kinney. W. R. Scott, 1967. Subj: Sun.

Kinsey, Elizabeth *see* Clymer, Eleanor Lowenton

Kipling, Rudyard. *The beginning of the armadilloes* ill. by Charles Keeping. Harper, 1983. Subj: Animals – armadillos.

The butterfly that stamped ill. by Alan Baker. Harper, 1983. Subj: Insects – butterflies, caterpillars.

The cat that walked by himself ill. by William Stobbs. Harper, 1983. Subj: Animals – cats.

The crab that played with the sea ill. by Michael Foreman. Harper, 1983. Subj: Crustacea. Sea and seashore.

The elephant's child ill. by Lorinda Bryan Cauley. Harcourt, 1983. Subj: Animals. Animals – elephants. Character traits – curiosity.

How the rhinoceros got his skin ill. by Leonard Weisgard. Walker, 1974. Subj: Animals – rhinoceros.

The miracle of the mountain ill. by Willi Baum. Addison-Wesley, 1969. Adapted by Aroline Arnett Beecher Leach from The Miracle of Purun Bhagat, by Rudyard Kipling. Subj: Animals. Foreign lands – India. Religion.

Kirk, Barbara. *Grandpa, me and our house in the tree* ill. by author. Macmillan, 1978. Subj: Family life – grandparents, great-grandparents. Houses. Trees.

Kirkpatrick, Rena K. *Look at flowers* ill. by Annabel Milne and Peter Stebbing. Raintree, 1978. Subj: Flowers. Science.

Look at leaves ill. by Annabel Milne and Peter Stebbing. Raintree, 1978. Subj: Plants. Science.

Look at magnets ill. by Ann Knight. Raintree, 1978. Subj: Science.

Look at pond life ill. by Annabel Milne and Peter Stebbing. Raintree, 1978. Subj: Science.

Look at rainbow colors ill. by Anna Barnard. Raintree, 1978. Subj: Concepts – color. Science. Weather – rainbows.

Look at seeds and weeds ill. by Debbie King. Raintree, 1978. Subj: Plants. Science.

Look at trees ill. by Jo Worth and Ann Knight. Raintree, 1978. Subj: Science. Trees.

Look at weather ill. by Janetta Lewin. Raintree, 1978. Subj: Science. Weather.

Kirn, Ann. *Beeswax catches a thief: from a Congo folktale* ill. by author. Norton, 1968. Subj: Animals. Ethnic groups in the U.S. – Afro-Americans.

I spy ill. by author. Norton, 1965. Subj: Birds – owls. Crime.

The tale of a crocodile: from a Congo folktale ill. by author. Norton, 1968. Subj: Animals – rabbits. Fire. Folk and fairy tales. Foreign lands – Africa. Reptiles – alligators, crocodiles.

Kirtland, G. B. *see* Joslin, Sesyle

Kishida, Eriko. *The hippo boat* ill. by Chiyoko Nakatani. Collins, 1964. Subj: Animals – hippopotami. Weather – rain. Zoos.

The lion and the bird's nest ill. by Chiyoko Nakatani. Crowell, 1972. Subj: Animals – lions. Birds. Character traits – helpfulness. Friendship.

Kitchen, Bert. *Animal alphabet* ill. by author. Dial Pr., 1984. Subj: ABC books. Animals.

Kitt, Tamara. *Sam and the impossible thing* ill. by Brinton Turkle. Norton, 1967. Subj: Activities – cooking. Food. Monsters. Poetry, rhyme.

A special birthday party for someone very special ill. by Brinton Turkle. Norton, 1966. Subj: Animals – skunks. Birthdays.

Klein, Arthur Luce. *Puss in boots* (Perrault, Charles)

Klein, Leonore. *Henri's walk to Paris* ill. by Saul Bass. Addison-Wesley, 1962. Subj: Activities – walking. Foreign lands – France.

Just like you ill. by Audrey Walters. Harvey House, 1968. Subj: Ethnic groups in the U.S.

Old, older, oldest ill. by Leonard P. Kessler. Hastings, 1983. Subj: Old age.

Klein, Norma. *Girls can be anything* ill. by Roy Doty. Dutton, 1973. Subj: Careers.

Visiting Pamela ill. by Kay Chorao. Dial Pr., 1979. Subj: Behavior – sharing. Friendship.

Klein, Robin. *Thing* ill. by Alison Lester. Oxford Univ. Pr., 1983. Subj: Dinosaurs. Pets.

Klein, Suzanne. *An elephant in my bed* ill. by Sharleen Pederson. Follett, 1974. Subj: Animals – elephants.

Klimowicz, Barbara. *The strawberry thumb* ill. by Gloria Kamen. Abingdon Pr., 1968. Subj: Poetry, rhyme. Problem solving. Puppets.

Knapp, John II. *A pillar of pepper and other Bible nursery rhymes* ill. by Dianne Turner Deckert. Cook, 1982. Subj: Nursery rhymes. Religion.

Knight, David C. *Dinosaur days* ill. by Joel Schick. McGraw-Hill, 1977. Subj: Dinosaurs. Science.

Knight, Hilary. *Angels and berries and candy canes* ill. by author. Harper, 1963. Subj: Angels. Holidays – Christmas.

A firefly in a fir tree ill. by author. Harper, 1963. Subj: Insects – fireflies.

Hilary Knight's the owl and the pussy-cat ill. by author. Macmillan, 1983. Based on The owl and the pussy-cat by Edward Lear. Subj: Imagination. Magic. Poetry, rhyme.

Sylvia the sloth ill. by author. Harper, 1969. Subj: Animals – sloths. Concepts – up and down.

Where's Wallace? ill. by author. Harper, 1964. Subj: Animals – monkeys. Behavior – running away. Zoos.

Knotts, Howard. *Great-grandfather, the baby and me* ill. by author. Atheneum, 1978. Subj: Family life – grandparents, great-grandparents.

The lost Christmas ill. by author. Harcourt, 1978. Subj: Dreams. Holidays – Christmas. Illness.

The summer cat ill. by author. Harper, 1981. Subj: Animals – cats. Seasons – summer.

The winter cat ill. by author. Harper, 1972. Subj: Animals – cats. Seasons – winter.

Knox-Wagner, Elaine. *The best mom in the world* (Delton, Judy)

My grandpa retired today ill. by Charles Robinson. Albert Whitman, 1982. Subj: Emotions. Family life – grandparents, great-grandparents. Old age.

The oldest kid ill. by Gail Owens. Albert Whitman, 1981. Subj: Activities – picnicking. Sibling rivalry.

Kobayashi, Masako Matsuno *see* Matsuno, Masako

Kobeh, Ana García. *Tigers and opossums* (Kurtycz, Marcos)

Kobrin, Janet. *Coyote goes hunting for fire* (Bernstein, Margery)

Earth namer (Bernstein, Margery)

The first morning (Bernstein, Margery)

How the sun made a promise and kept it (Bernstein, Margery)

Koch, Dorothy Clarke. *Gone is my goose* ill. by Doris Lee. Holiday, 1956. Subj: Birds – geese.

I play at the beach ill. by Feodor Rojankovsky. Random House, 1955. Subj: Family life. Games. Sea and seashore.

When the cows got out ill. by Paul Lantz. Holiday, 1958. Subj: Animals – bulls, cows. Farms.

Koci, Marta. *Blackie and Marie* tr. from German by Elizabeth D. Crawford; ill. by author. Morrow, 1981. Subj: Animals – dogs. Friendship.

Katie's kitten ill. by author. Alphabet Pr., 1982. Subj: Animals – cats. Behavior – lost.

Koelling, Caryl. *Animal mix and match* ill. by Roger Beerworth. Delacorte, 1980. Subj: Animals. Format, unusual – cardboard pages.

Mad monsters mix and match ill. by Linda Griffith. Delacorte, 1980. Subj: Format, unusual – cardboard pages. Monsters.

Silly stories mix and match ill. by Carroll Andrus. Delacorte, 1980. Subj: Format, unusual – cardboard pages. Humor.

Koenig, Marion. *The little black hen* (Hille-Brandts, Lene)

Poor fish (Beisert, Heide Helene)

The tale of fancy Nancy: a Spanish folktale ill. by Klaus Ensikat. Merrimack, 1979. Subj: Animals – cats. Animals – mice. Folk and fairy tales.

The wonderful world of night ill. by David Parry. Grosset, 1969. Subj: Animals – cats. Behavior – misbehavior. Night.

Koenner, Alfred. *Be quite quiet beside the lake* tr. from German by Georgia Peet; ill. by Karl-Heinz Appelmann. Imported Pub., 1981. Subj: Format, unusual – cardboard pages. Noise, sounds.

High flies the ball by Alfred Koenner and Siegfried Linke; tr. from German by Georgia Peet; ill. by Siegfried Linke. Imported Pub., 1983. Subj: Format, unusual – cardboard pages. Poetry, rhyme.

Koffler, Camilla *see* Ylla

Koide, Tan. *May we sleep here tonight?* ill. by Yasuko Koide. Atheneum, 1983. Subj: Animals. Bedtime.

Kojima, Naomi. *The flying grandmother* ill. by author. Crowell, 1981. Subj: Activities – flying. Behavior – wishing. Family life – grandparents, great-grandparents. Imagination.

Komoda, Beverly. *Simon's soup* ill. by author. Parents, 1978. Subj: Animals – cats. Animals – monkeys. Food.

Kopczynski, Anna. *Jerry and Ami* ill. by author. Scribner's, 1963. Subj: Animals – dogs. Friendship.

Koren, Edward. *Behind the wheel* ill. by author. Holt, 1972. Subj: Transportation.

Kotzwinkle, William. *The day the gang got rich* ill. by Joe Servello. Viking, 1970. Subj: Clubs, gangs. Friendship.

The nap master ill. by Joe Servello. Harcourt, 1979. Subj: Bedtime. Dreams. Sleep.

Up the alley with Jack and Joe ill. by Joe Servello. Macmillan, 1974. Subj: Friendship.

Kouts, Anne. *Kenny's rat* ill. by Betty Fraser. Viking, 1970. Subj: Animals – rats. Pets.

Krahn, Fernando. *April fools* ill. by author. Dutton, 1974. Subj: Holidays – April Fools' Day. Humor. Wordless.

The biggest Christmas tree on earth ill. by author. Little, 1978. Subj: Animals. Holidays – Christmas. Toys – balls. Trees. Wordless.

Catch that cat! ill. by author. Dutton, 1978. Subj: Animals – cats. Wordless.

The creepy thing ill. by author. Houghton, 1982. Subj: Imagination – imaginary friends. Wordless.

A funny friend from heaven ill. by author. Lippincott, 1977. Subj: Angels. Clowns, jesters. Wordless.

The great ape: being the true version of the famous saga of adventure and friendship newly discovered ill. by author. Viking, 1978. Subj: Animals – gorillas. Friendship. Islands. Wordless.

Here comes Alex Pumpernickel! ill. by author. Little, 1981. Subj: Behavior – bad day. Wordless.

How Santa Claus had a long and difficult journey delivering his presents ill. by author. Delacorte Pr., 1970. Holidays - Christmas. Subj: Wordless.

Little love story ill. by author. Lippincott, 1976. Subj: Holidays – Valentine's Day. Wordless.

The mystery of the giant footprints ill. by author. Dutton, 1977. Subj: Cumulative tales. Monsters. Wordless.

Robot-bot-bot ill. by author. Dutton, 1979. Subj: Activities – playing. Activities – working. Robots. Wordless.

Sebastian and the mushroom ill. by author. Delacorte Pr., 1976. Subj: Dreams. Wordless.

The secret in the dungeon ill. by author. Houghton, 1983. Subj: Behavior – secrets. Dragons. Wordless.

Sleep tight, Alex Pumpernickel ill. by author. Little, 1982. Subj: Bedtime. Sleep. Wordless.

Who's seen the scissors? ill. by author. Dutton, 1975. Subj: Wordless.

Krasilovsky, Phyllis. *The cow who fell in the canal* ill. by Peter Spier. Doubleday, 1953. Subj: Animals – bulls, cows. Cumulative tales. Foreign lands – Holland.

The girl who was a cowboy ill. by Cyndy Szekeres. Doubleday, 1965. Subj: Clothing. Cowboys.

The man who did not wash his dishes ill. by Barbara Cooney. Doubleday, 1950. Subj: Character traits – cleanliness. Character traits – laziness.

The man who entered a contest ill. by Ury Salzman. Doubleday, 1980. Subj: Activities – cooking. Behavior – misbehavior.

Scaredy cat ill. by Ninon. Macmillan, 1959. Subj: Animals – cats.

The shy little girl ill. by Trina Schart Hyman. Houghton, 1970. Subj: Character traits – shyness. Friendship.

The very little boy ill. by Ninon. Doubleday, 1962. Subj: Babies. Behavior – growing up. Family life.

The very little girl ill. by Ninon. Doubleday, 1953. Subj: Babies. Behavior – growing up. Family life.

The very tall little girl ill. by Olivia Cole. Doubleday, 1969. Subj: Character traits – being different. Family life.

Kratka, Suzanne C. *Hi, new baby* (Andry, Andrew C)

Kraus, Bruce. *The detective of London* (Kraus, Robert)

Kraus, Robert. *Another mouse to feed* ill. by José Aruego and Ariane Dewey. Windmill, 1980. Subj: Animals – mice. Family life.

Big brother ill. by author. Parents, 1973. Subj: Animals – rabbits. Babies. Family life.

Boris bad enough ill. by José Aruego and Ariane Dewey. Dutton, 1976. Subj: Animals – elephants

Daddy Long Ears ill. by author. Simon and Schuster, 1970. Subj: Animals – rabbits. Holidays – Easter.

The detective of London by Robert and Bruce Kraus; ill. by Robert Byrd. Windmill-Dutton, 1978. Subj: Animals – dogs. Crime. Problem solving.

Good night little one by Robert Kraus and N. M. Bodecker; ill. by N. M. Bodecker. Dutton, 1972. Subj: Bedtime. Counting. Night. Sleep.

Good night Richard Rabbit by Robert Kraus and N. M. Bodecker; ill. by N. M. Bodecker. Dutton, 1972. Subj: Animals – rabbits. Bedtime. Counting. Night. Sleep.

Herman the helper ill. by José Aruego and Ariane Dewey. Dutton, 1974. Subj: Character traits – helpfulness. Octopuses. Sea and seashore.

I, Mouse ill. by author. Harper, 1958. Subj: Animals – mice.

Ladybug, ladybug! ill. by author. Harper, 1957. Subj: Behavior – misunderstanding. Friendship. Insects – ladybugs.

Leo the late bloomer ill. by José Aruego. Dutton, 1971. Subj: Animals – tigers. Behavior – growing up.

The little giant ill. by author. Harper, 1967. Subj: Concepts – size. Giants.

The littlest rabbit ill. by author. Harper, 1961. Subj: Animals – rabbits. Character traits – smallness.

Mert the blurt ill. by José Aruego and Ariane Dewey. Windmill, 1981. Subj: Behavior – gossip. Frogs and toads.

Milton the early riser ill. by José Aruego and Ariane Dewey. Dutton, 1972. Subj: Animals – bears. Sleep.

Noel the coward ill. by José Aruego and Ariane Dewey. Dutton, 1977. Subj: Emotions – fear.

Owliver ill. by José Aruego and Ariane Dewey. Dutton, 1974. Subj: Birds – owls. Careers.

Rebecca Hatpin ill. by Robert Byrd. Dutton, 1974. Subj: Careers – nurses. Character traits – helpfulness. Character traits – selfishness. Family life – grandparents, great-grandparents.

Springfellow ill. by Sam Savitt. Dutton, 1978. Subj: Animals – horses.

The three friends ill. by José Aruego and Ariane Dewey. Dutton, 1975. Subj: Friendship.

The trouble with spider ill. by author. Harper, 1962. Subj: Friendship. Insects – flies. Spiders.

Whose mouse are you? ill. by José Aruego. Macmillan, 1970. Subj: Animals – mice.

Krauss, Ruth. *The backward day* ill. by Marc Simont. Harper, 1950. Subj: Family life.

Bears ill. by Phyllis Rowand. Harper, 1948. Subj: Animals – bears. Poetry, rhyme.

A bouquet of littles ill. by Jane Flora. Harper, 1963. Subj: Concepts – size. Poetry, rhyme.

The bundle book ill. by Helen Stone. Harper, 1951. Subj: Bedtime. Emotions. Family life – mothers. Games.

The carrot seed ill. by Crockett Johnson. Harper, 1945. Subj: Activities – gardening. Character traits – optimism. Plants. Self-concept.

Charlotte and the white horse ill. by Maurice Sendak. Harper, 1955. Subj: Animals – horses.

Everything under a mushroom ill. by Margot Tomes. Four Winds Pr., 1974. Subj: Elves and little people. Poetry, rhyme.

Eyes, nose, fingers, toes ill. by Elizabeth Schneider. Harper, 1964. Subj: Anatomy.

A good man and his good wife ill. by Marc Simont. Harper, 1962. Subj: Behavior – boredom. Friendship.

The growing story ill. by Phyllis Rowand. Harper, 1947. Subj: Behavior – growing up.

The happy day ill. by Marc Simont. Harper, 1949. Subj: Caldecott award honor book. Hibernation. Seasons – spring. Seasons – winter. Weather – snow.

The happy egg ill. by Crockett Johnson. O'Hara, 1967. Subj: Birds. Eggs.

I write it ill. by Mary Chalmers. Harper, 1970. Subj: Activities – writing.

I'll be you and you be me ill. by Maurice Sendak. Harper, 1954. Subj: Friendship. Humor.

Mama, I wish I was snow. Child, you'd be very cold ill. by Ellen Raskin. Atheneum, 1962. Subj: Behavior – wishing. Games.

A moon or a button ill. by Remy Charlip. Harper, 1959. Subj: Imagination.

Open house for butterflies ill. by Maurice Sendak. Harper, 1960. Subj: Imagination.

Somebody else's nut tree, and other tales from children ill. by Maurice Sendak. Harper, 1958. Subj: Children as authors. Imagination.

This thumbprint ill. by author. Harper, 1967. Subj: Humor. Imagination.

A very special house ill. by Maurice Sendak. Harper, 1953. Subj: Caldecott award honor book. Houses. Imagination.

Krauze, Andrzej. *What's so special about today?* ill. by author. Lothrop, 1984. Subj: Animals. Birthdays. Character traits – questioning.

Krensky, Stephen. *Dinosaurs, beware!* (Brown, Marc)

The lion upstairs ill. by Leigh Grant. Atheneum, 1983. Subj: Imagination – imaginary friends.

My first dictionary ill. by George Ulrich. Houghton, 1980. Subj: Dictionaries.

Perfect pigs (Brown, Marc)

Kroll, Steven. *Amanda and the giggling ghost* ill. by Dick Gackenbach. Holiday, 1980. Subj: Behavior – stealing. Ghosts.

Are you pirates? ill. by Marylin Hafner. Pantheon, 1982. Subj: Imagination. Pirates.

The big bunny and the Easter eggs ill. by Janet Stevens. Holiday, 1982. Subj: Animals – rabbits. Holidays – Easter. Illness.

The candy witch ill. by Marylin Hafner. Holiday, 1979. Subj: Behavior – unnoticed, unseen. Holidays – Halloween. Magic. Witches.

Fat magic ill. by Tomie de Paola. Holiday, 1978. Subj: Magic. Royalty.

The goat parade ill. by Tim Kirk. Parents, 1983. Subj: Animals – goats. Parades.

The hand-me-down doll ill. by Evaline Ness. Holiday, 1983. Subj: Toys – dolls.

If I could be my grandmother ill. by Tasha Tudor. Pantheon, 1977. Subj: Family life – grandparents, great-grandparents.

Loose tooth ill. by Tricia Tusa. Holiday, 1984. Subj: Fairies. Teeth.

One tough turkey: a Thanksgiving story ill. by John Wallner. Holiday, 1982. Subj: Birds – turkeys. Holidays – Thanksgiving. Sports – hunting.

Otto ill. by Ned Delaney. Parents, 1983. Subj: Behavior – misbehavior. Robots.

Pigs in the house ill. by Tim Kirk. Parents, 1983. Subj: Animals – pigs. Behavior – misbehavior. Houses. Poetry, rhyme.

Santa's crash-bang Christmas ill. by Tomie de Paola. Holiday, 1977. Subj: Holidays – Christmas.

Toot! Toot! ill. by Anne F. Rockwell. Holiday, 1983. Subj: Family life – grandparents, great-grandparents. Imagination. Toys – trains. Trains.

The tyrannosaurus game ill. by Tomie de Paola. Holiday, 1976. Subj: Cumulative tales. Dinosaurs. Games. Imagination.

Woof, woof! ill. by Nicole Rubel. Dial Pr., 1983. Subj: Animals – dogs. Crime.

Krull, Kathleen. *Autumn* (Allington, Richard L)

Spring (Allington, Richard L)

Summer (Allington, Richard L)

Winter (Allington, Richard L)

Krum, Charlotte. *The four riders* ill. by Katherine Evans. Follett, 1953. Subj: Animals – horses.

Krush, Beth. *The fish from Japan* (Cooper, Elizabeth K)

Krüss, James. *3 X 3: Three by three* ill. by Eva Johanna Rubin; English text by Geoffrey Strachan. Macmillan, 1963. Subj: Animals. Counting. Poetry, rhyme.

Kübler-Ross, Elisabeth. *Remember the secret* ill. by Heather Preston. Celestial Arts, 1982. Subj: Death.

Kuchalla, Susan. *All about seeds* ill. by Jane McBee. Troll Assoc., 1982. Subj: Plants. Science.

Baby animals ill. by Joel Snyder. Troll Assoc., 1982. Subj: Animals.

Bears ill. by Kathie Kelleher. Troll Assoc., 1982. Subj: Animals – bears.

Birds ill. by Gary Britt. Troll Assoc., 1982. Subj: Birds.

What is a reptile? ill. by Paul Harvey. Troll Assoc., 1982. Subj: Reptiles.

Kumin, Maxine. *The beach before breakfast* ill. by Leonard Weisgard. Putnam's, 1964. Subj: Sea and seashore.

Eggs of things ill. by Leonard W. Shortall. Putnam's, 1963. Subj: Eggs. Frogs and toads. Humor. Science.

Follow the fall ill. by Artur Marokvia. Putnam's, 1961. Subj: Holidays. Imagination. Poetry, rhyme. Seasons – fall.

Joey and the birthday present by Maxine Kumin and Anne Sexton; ill. by Evaline Ness. McGraw-Hill, 1971. Subj: Animals – mice. Birthdays.

Mittens in May ill. by Eliott Gilbert. Putnam's, 1962. Subj: Birds. Character traits – kindness to animals. Clothing.

Sebastian and the dragon ill. by William D. Hayes. Putnam's, 1960. Subj: Character traits – smallness. Dragons. Poetry, rhyme.

Speedy digs downside up ill. by Ezra Jack Keats. Putnam's, 1964. Subj: Activities – digging. Character traits – ambition. Humor. Poetry, rhyme.

Spring things ill. by Artur Marokvia. Putnam's, 1961. Subj: Poetry, rhyme. Seasons – spring.

What color is Caesar? ill. by Evaline Ness. McGraw-Hill, 1978. Subj: Animals – dogs. Concepts – color.

A winter friend ill. by Artur Marokvia. Putnam's, 1961. Subj: Poetry, rhyme. Seasons – winter.

The wizard's tears by Maxine Kumin and Anne Sexton; ill. by Evaline Ness. McGraw-Hill, 1975. Subj: Magic. Wizards.

Kunhardt, Dorothy. *Billy the barber* ill. by William Pène Du Bois. Harper, 1961. Subj: Careers – barbers. Hair. Old age.

Kitty's new doll ill. by Lucinda McQueen. Golden Pr., 1984. Subj: Animals – cats. Toys – dolls.

Kunhardt, Edith. *Pat the cat* ill. by author. Golden Pr., 1984. Subj: Animals – cats. Format, unusual. Pets.

Kunnas, Mauri. *Santa Claus and his elves* by Mauri Kunnas; assisted by Tarja Kunnas; ill. by authors. Harmony, 1982. Translation of Joulupukki. Subj: Elves and little people. Holidays – Christmas.

Kunnas, Tarja. *Santa Claus and his elves* (Kunnas, Mauri)

Kuratomi, Chizuko. *Mr. Bear and the robbers* ill. by Kozo Kakimoto. Dial Pr., 1970. Subj: Animals – bears. Animals – rabbits.

Kurtycz, Marcos. *Tigers and opossums: animal legends* adapt. by Marcos Kurtycz and Ana García Kobeh; ill. by adaptors. Little, 1984. Subj: Folk and fairy tales. Foreign lands – Mexico.

Kuskin, Karla. *ABCDEFGHIJKLMNOPQRSTUVWXYZ* ill. by author. Harper, 1963. Subj: ABC books.

All sizes of noises ill. by author. Harper, 1962. Subj: Concepts. Noise, sounds. Poetry, rhyme.

The animals and the ark ill. by author. Harper, 1958. Subj: Animals. Boats, ships. Poetry, rhyme. Religion – Noah.

A boy had a mother who bought him a hat ill. by author. Houghton, 1976. Subj: Cumulative tales. Poetry, rhyme.

Herbert hated being small ill. by author. Houghton, 1979. Subj: Character traits – smallness. Concepts – size. Poetry, rhyme.

In the flaky frosty morning ill. by author. Harper, 1969. Subj: Poetry, rhyme. Seasons – winter. Snowmen. Weather – snow.

James and the rain ill. by author. Harper, 1957. Subj: Animals. Poetry, rhyme. Weather – rain.

Just like everyone else ill. by author. Harper, 1959. Subj: Activities – flying.

Night again ill. by author. Little, 1981. Subj: Bedtime.

The Philharmonic gets dressed ill. by Marc Simont. Harper, 1982. Subj: Clothing.

Roar and more ill. by author. Harper, 1956. Subj: Animals. Noise, sounds. Participation. Poetry, rhyme.

Sand and snow ill. by author. Harper, 1965. Subj: Poetry, rhyme. Sea and seashore. Seasons – summer. Seasons – winter.

A space story ill. by Marc Simont. Harper, 1978. Subj: Bedtime. Space and space ships. Stars.

Watson, the smartest dog in the U.S.A. ill. by author. Harper, 1968. Subj: Activities – reading. Animals – dogs.

What did you bring me? ill. by author. Harper, 1973. Subj: Animals – mice. Behavior – greed. Self-concept. Witches.

Which horse is William? ill. by author. Harper, 1959. Subj: Character traits – individuality. Imagination.

Kwitz, Mary DeBall. *Little chick's breakfast* ill. by Bruce Degen. Harper, 1983. Subj: Birds – chickens. Farms. Food.

Little chick's story ill. by Cyndy Szekeres. Harper, 1978. Subj: Birds – chickens. Eggs.

Mouse at home ill. by author. Harper, 1966. Subj: Animals – mice. Seasons.

Rabbits' search for a little house ill. by Lorinda Bryan Cauley. Crown, 1977. Subj: Animals – rabbits. Houses.

When it rains ill. by author. Follett, 1974. Subj: Animals. Poetry, rhyme. Weather – rain. Weather – rainbows.

Lady Eden's School. *Just how stories* ill. by Derek Steele. Merrimack, 1981. Subj: Animals. Children as authors.

Ladybug, ladybug, and other nursery rhymes ill. by Eloise Burns Wilkin. Random House, 1979. Subj: Format, unusual. Nursery rhymes.

La Farge, Phyllis. *Joanna runs away* ill. by Trina Schart Hyman. Holt, 1973. Subj: Animals – horses. Behavior – running away.

La Farge, Sheila. *The boy who ate more than the giant and other Swedish folktales* (Löfgren, Ulf)

Peter's adventures in Blueberry land (Beskow, Elsa Maartman)

La Fontaine, Jean de. *The hare and the tortoise* ill. by Brian Wildsmith. Watts, 1963. Subj: Animals – rabbits. Folk and fairy tales. Reptiles – turtles. Sports – racing.

The lion and the rat ill. by Brian Wildsmith. Watts, 1963. Subj: Animals – lions. Animals – rats. Character traits – helpfulness. Folk and fairy tales.

The miller, the boy and the donkey adapt. and ill. by Brian Wildsmith. Watts, 1969. "Based on a fable by La Fontaine." Subj: Animals – donkeys. Character traits – practicality. Folk and fairy tales. Humor.

The north wind and the sun ill. by Brian Wildsmith. Watts, 1964. Subj: Folk and fairy tales. Sun. Weather – wind.

Lafontaine, Pascale Claude *see* Claude-Lafontaine, Pascale

Lage, Ida De *see* DeLage, Ida

Laird, Donivee Martin. *The three little Hawaiian pigs and the magic shark* ill. by Carol Jossem. Bess Pr., 1981. Subj: Animals – pigs. Fish. Hawaii.

Lalicki, Barbara. *If there were dreams to sell* ill. by Margot Tomes. Lothrop, 1984. Subj: ABC books. Poetry, rhyme.

Lalli, Judy. *Feelings alphabet: an album of emotions from A to Z* photos. by Douglas L. Mason-Fry. Jalmar Pr., 1984. Subj: ABC books. Emotions.

La Mare, Walter De *see* De La Mare, Walter

Lambert, David. *Dinosaurs* ill. by Christopher Forsey and others. Watts, 1982. Subj: Dinosaurs. Science.

The seasons ill. with photos. Watts, 1983. Subj: Science. Seasons.

Landau, Terry. *Butterflies and rainbows* (Berger, Judith)

Landshoff, Ursula. *Cats are good company* ill. by author. Harper, 1983. Subj: Animals – cats. Pets. Science.

Lane, Carolyn. *The voices of Greenwillow Pond* ill. by Wallace Tripp. Houghton, 1972. Subj: Birds – owls. Character traits – perseverance. Frogs and toads.

Lane, Margaret. *The frog* ill. by Grahame Corbett. Dial Pr., 1981. Subj: Frogs and toads. Science.

The squirrel ill. by Kenneth Lilly. Dial Pr., 1981. Subj: Animals – squirrels. Science.

Lang, Andrew. *Nursery rhyme book* (Mother Goose)

Snow White and Rose Red (Grimm, Jacob)

Langner, Nola. *By the light of the silvery moon* ill. by author. Lothrop, 1983. Subj: Behavior – running away. Imagination – imaginary friends. Royalty.

Freddy my grandfather ill. by author. Four Winds Pr., 1979. Subj: Family life – grandparents, great-grandparents.

Langstaff, John M. *Hot cross buns, and other old street cries*

Oh, a-hunting we will go ill. by Nancy Winslow Parker. Atheneum, 1974. Subj: Folk and fairy tales. Music. Songs. Sports – hunting.

Ol' Dan Tucker ill. by Joe Krush. Harcourt, 1963. Subj: Folk and fairy tales. Music. Songs.

On Christmas day in the morning ill. by Antony Groves-Raines. Harcourt, 1959. Piano settings by Marshall Woodbridge. Subj: Folk and fairy tales. Holidays – Christmas. Music. Songs.

Over in the meadow ill. by Feodor Rojankovsky. Harcourt, 1957. Includes Over in the meadow (for voice and piano) by Marshall Woodbridge. Subj: Animals. Counting. Folk and fairy tales. Songs.

Soldier, soldier, won't you marry me? ill. by Anita Lobel. Doubleday, 1972. Subj: Careers – military. Folk and fairy tales. Music. Songs.

The swapping boy ill. by Beth and Joe Krush. Harcourt, 1960. Subj: Activities – trading. Folk and fairy tales. Music. Songs.

The two magicians ill. by Fritz Eichenberg. Atheneum, 1973. Adapt. by John Langstaff from an ancient ballad. Subj: Folk and fairy tales. Magic. Music. Songs. Witches.

Langstaff, Nancy. *A tiny baby for you* ill. by Suzanne Szasz. Harcourt, 1955. Subj: Babies.

Lansdown, Brenda. *Galumpf* ill. by Ernest Crichlow. Houghton, 1963. Subj: Animals – cats. Ethnic groups in the U.S. Ethnic groups in the U.S. – Afro-Americans. Pets.

Lapp, Carolyn. *The dentists' tools* ill. by George Overlie. Lerner, 1961. Subj: Careers – dentists.

Lapp, Eleanor. *The blueberry bears* ill. by Margot Apple. Albert Whitman, 1983. Subj: Animals – bears. Food.

In the morning mist ill. by David Cunningham. Albert Whitman, 1978. Subj: Family life – grandparents, great-grandparents. Morning. Sports – fishing.

The mice came in early this year ill. by David Cunningham. Albert Whitman, 1976. Subj: Animals. Farms. Seasons – fall. Seasons – winter.

Lapsley, Susan. *I am adopted* ill. by Michael Charlton. Bradbury Pr., 1974. Subj: Adoption. Family life.

Larrick, Nancy. *When the dark comes dancing: a bedtime poetry book* ill. by John Wallner. Putnam's, 1983. Subj: Bedtime. Night. Poetry, rhyme.

Larsen, Hanne. *Don't forget Tom* ill. with photos. Crowell, 1978. Subj: Handicaps.

Lasell, Fen. *Fly away goose* ill. by author. Houghton, 1965. Subj: Birds – geese. Eggs. Imagination.

Michael grows a wish ill. by author. Houghton, 1974. Subj: Animals – horses. Behavior – wishing. Birthdays.

Lasher, Faith B. *Hubert Hippo's world* ill. by Leonard Lee Rue, III. Children's Pr., 1971. Subj: Animals – hippopotami.

Lasker, David. *The boy who loved music* ill. by Joe Lasker. Viking, 1979. Subj: Music. Royalty.

Lasker, Joe. *The do-something day* ill. by author. Viking, 1982. Subj: Behavior – running away.

He's my brother ill. by author. Albert Whitman, 1974. Subj: Character traits – loyalty. Family life. Handicaps.

Lentil soup ill. by author. Albert Whitman, 1977. Subj: Activities – cooking. Counting. Days of the week, months of the year. Food.

Mothers can do anything ill. by author. Albert Whitman, 1972. Subj: Activities – working. Careers. Family life – mothers.

Nick joins in ill. by author. Albert Whitman, 1980. Subj: Handicaps. School.

Laskowski, Janina Domanska *see* Domanska, Janina

Laskowski, Jerzy. *Master of the royal cats* ill. by Janina Domanska. Seabury Pr., 1965. Subj: Animals – cats. Animals – dogs. Foreign lands – Africa. Foreign lands – Egypt. Royalty.

Lasky, Kathryn. *Agatha's alphabet, with her very own dictionary* (Floyd, Lucy)

A baby for Max photos. by Christopher G. Knight. Scribner's, 1984. Subj: Babies. Sibling rivalry.

I have four names for my grandfather ill. by Christopher G. Knight. Little, 1976. Subj: Emotions – love. Family life – grandparents, great-grandparents.

My island grandma ill. by Emily Arnold McCully. Warne, 1979. Subj: Family life – grandparents, great-grandparents. Islands.

Lasson, Robert. *Orange Oliver: the kitten who wore glasses* ill. by Chuck Hayden. McKay, 1957. Subj: Animals – cats. Farms. Glasses.

Lathrop, Dorothy Pulis. *An angel in the woods* ill. by author. Macmillan, 1947. Subj: Angels. Holidays – Christmas.

Puppies for keeps ill. by author. Macmillan, 1943. Subj: Animals – dogs. Pets.

Who goes there? ill. by author. Macmillan, 1935. Subj: Activities – picnicking. Animals. Character traits – kindness to animals. Seasons – winter.

Lattin, Anne. *Peter's policeman* ill. by Gertrude E. Espenscheid. Follett, 1958. Subj: Careers – police officers.

Lauber, Patricia. *What's hatching out of that egg?* ill. with photos. Crown, 1979. Subj: Eggs. Science.

Laurence, Margaret. *The Christmas birthday story* ill. by Helen Lucas. Knopf, 1980. Subj: Birthdays. Holidays – Christmas. Religion.

Laurin, Anne. *Little things* ill. by Marcia Sewall. Atheneum, 1978. Subj: Activities – knitting. Character traits – patience. Humor.

Perfect crane ill. by Charles Mikolaycak. Harper, 1981. Subj: Birds – cranes. Foreign lands – Japan. Magic.

Lawrence, James. *Binky Brothers and the fearless four* ill. by Leonard P. Kessler. Harper, 1970. Subj: Careers – detectives. Twins.

Binky Brothers, detectives ill. by Leonard P. Kessler. Harper, 1968. Subj: Careers – detectives. Twins.

Lawrence, John, *The giant of Grabbist* ill. by author. White, 1969. Subj: Foreign lands – England. Giants.

Pope Leo's elephant ill. by author. Collins-World, 1970, 1969. Subj: Animals – elephants. Fire. Foreign lands – Vatican City.

Rabbit and pork: rhyming talk ill. by author. Crowell, 1976. Subj: Animals – cats. Animals – pigs. Animals – rabbits. Poetry, rhyme.

Lawson, Annetta. *The lucky yak* ill. by Allen Say. Houghton, 1980. Subj: Activities – babysitting. Animals – yaks. Birds – puffins.

Lawson, Robert. *They were strong and good* ill. by author. Viking, 1940. Subj: Caldecott award book. Family life. U.S. history.

Layton, Aviva. *The squeakers* ill. by Louise Scott. Mosaic Pr., 1982. Subj: Animals – mice. Family life. Theater.

Lazard, Naomi. *What Amanda saw* ill. by Paul O. Zelinsky. Greenwillow, 1981. Subj: Activities – vacationing. Animals. Parties.

Lazy Jack ill. by Bert Dodson. Troll Assoc., 1979. Subj: Character traits – laziness. Cumulative tales. Folk and fairy tales.

Leach, Aroline Arnett Beecher. *The miracle of the mountain* (Kipling, Rudyard)

Leaf, Munro. *Boo, who used to be scared of the dark* ill. by author. Random House, 1948. Subj: Bedtime. Emotions – fear. Night.

A flock of watchbirds ill. by author. Lippincott, 1946. Subj: Behavior – misbehavior. Etiquette.

Gordon, the goat ill. by author. Lippincott, 1944. Subj: Animals – goats.

Grammar can be fun ill. by author. Lippincott, 1934. Subj: Language.

Health can be fun ill. by author. Stokes, 1943. Subj: Health.

How to behave and why ill. by author. Lippincott, 1946. Subj: Etiquette.

Manners can be fun ill. by author. Rev. ed. Lippincott, 1958. Subj: Etiquette.

Noodle ill. by author. Four Winds Pr., 1965. Subj: Animals – dogs. Self-concept.

Robert Francis Weatherbee ill. by author. Lippincott, 1935. Subj: School.

Safety can be fun ill. by author. New, rev. ed. Lippincott, 1961. Subj: Safety.

The story of Ferdinand the bull ill. by Robert Lawson. Viking, 1936. Subj: Animals – bulls, cows. Character traits – individuality. Foreign lands – Spain. Violence, anti-violence.

Wee Gillis ill. by Robert Lawson. Viking, 1938. Subj: Caldecott award honor book. Foreign lands – Scotland.

Leander, Ed. *Q is for crazy* ill. by Józef Sumichrast. Dial-Delacorte, 1977. Subj: ABC books.

Lear, Edward. *ABC* ill. by author. McGraw-Hill, 1965. Subj: ABC books. Poetry, rhyme.

A book of nonsense ill. by author. Metropolitan Museum of Art-Viking, 1980. Subj: Poetry, rhyme.

The dong with the luminous nose ill. by Edward Gorey. Addison-Wesley, 1969. Subj: Humor. Poetry, rhyme.

An Edward Lear alphabet ill. by Carol Newsom. Lothrop, 1983. Subj: ABC books.

Edward Lear's nonsense book ill. by Tony Palazzo. Doubleday, 1956. Subj: Humor. Music. Poetry, rhyme.

Hilary Knight's the owl and the pussy-cat (Knight, Hilary)

A Learical lexicon sel. by Myra Cohn Livingston; ill. by Joseph Low. Atheneum, 1985. Subj: Humor. Poetry, rhyme.

Lear's nonsense verses ill. by Tomi Ungerer. Grosset, 1967. Subj: Humor. Poetry, rhyme.

Limericks by Lear ill. by Lois Ehlert. Collins-World, 1965. Subj: Poetry, rhyme.

Nonsense alphabets ill. by Richard Scarry. Doubleday, 1962. Subj: ABC books. Poetry, rhyme.

The nutcrackers and the sugar-tongs ill. by Marcia Sewall. Little, 1978. Subj: Humor. Poetry, rhyme.

The owl and the pussy-cat ill. by Barbara Cooney. Little, 1969. First pub. in 1961. Subj: Animals – cats. Birds – owls. Poetry, rhyme.

The owl and the pussy-cat ill. by William Pène Du Bois. Doubleday, 1961. Subj: Animals – cats. Birds – owls. Poetry, rhyme.

The owl and the pussy-cat ill. by Gwen Fulton. Atheneum, 1977. Subj: Animals – cats. Birds – owls. Poetry, rhyme.

The owl and the pussycat ill. by Elaine Muis. Grosset, 1977. Subj: Animals – cats. Birds – owls. Poetry, rhyme.

The owl and the pussy-cat and other nonsense ill. by Owen Wood. Viking, 1979. Subj: Animals – cats. Birds – owls. Poetry, rhyme.

The pelican chorus ill. by Harold Berson. Parents, 1967. Subj: Birds – pelicans. Humor. Music. Poetry, rhyme. Songs.

The pelican chorus and the quangle wangle's hat ill. by Kevin W. Maddison. Viking, 1981. Subj: Birds – pelicans. Humor. Music. Poetry, rhyme. Songs.

The pobble who has no toes ill. by Kevin W. Maddison. Viking, 1977. Subj: Humor. Poetry, rhyme.

The quangle wangle's hat ill. by Helen Oxenbury. Watts, 1969. Subj: Clothing. Humor. Poetry, rhyme.

Two laughable lyrics: The pobble who has no toes, [and] The quangle wangle's hat ill. by Paul Galdone. Putnam's, 1966. Subj: Clothing. Humor. Poetry, rhyme.

Whizz! ill. by Janina Domanska. Macmillan, 1973. Completed by Ogden Nash. Subj: Cumulative tales. Humor. Poetry, rhyme.

Lee, Dennis. *Alligator pie* ill. by Frank Newfeld. Houghton, 1975. Subj: Nursery rhymes. Poetry, rhyme.

Lee, Jeanne M. *The legend of the milky way* ill. by author. Holt, 1982. Subj: Folk and fairy tales. Foreign lands – China. Stars.

Leech, Jay. *Bright Fawn and me* by Jay Leech and Zane Spencer; ill. by Glo Coalson. Crowell, 1979. Subj: Ethnic groups in the U.S. – Indians. Fairs. Sibling rivalry.

Leeton, Will C. *The Tower of Babel* ill. by Jeffrey K. Lindberg. Dandelion, 1979. Subj: Language. Religion.

Le Gallienne, Eva. *The little mermaid* (Andersen, H C (Hans Christian))

The nightingale (Andersen, H C (Hans Christian))

Leichman, Seymour. *Shaggy dogs and spotty dogs and shaggy and spotty dogs* ill. by author. Harcourt, 1973. Subj: Animals – dogs. Poetry, rhyme.

The wicked wizard and the wicked witch ill. by author. Harcourt, 1972. Subj: Magic. Poetry, rhyme. Witches. Wizards.

Leisk, David Johnson *see* Johnson, Crockett

Leister, Mary. *The silent concert* ill. by Yōko Mitsuhashi. Bobbs-Merrill, 1970. Subj: Forest, woods. Noise, sounds.

Lemerise, Bruce. *Sheldon's lunch* ill. by author. Parents, 1980. Subj: Activities – cooking. Food. Reptiles – snakes.

Lemke, Horst. *Places and faces* ill. by author. Scroll Pr., 1971. Translation of Vielerlei aus Stadt und Land. Subj: Wordless.

Lenski, Lois. *Animals for me* ill. by author. Walck, 1941. Subj: Animals.

At our house ill. by author. Walck, 1959. Music by Clyde Robert Bulla. Subj: Family life. Music. Songs.

Big little Davy ill. by author. Walck, 1956. Subj: Animals.

Cowboy Small ill. by author. Oxford Univ. Pr., 1949. Subj: Cowboys.

Davy and his dog ill. by author. Walck, 1957. Subj: Animals – dogs. Music. Songs.

Davy goes places ill. by author. Walck, 1961. Subj: Activities – traveling. Music. Songs. Transportation.

Debbie and her dolls ill. by author. Walck, 1970. Subj: Animals – dogs. Toys – dolls.

Debbie and her family ill. by author. Walck, 1969. Subj: Family life.

Debbie and her grandma ill. by author. Walck, 1967. Subj: Family life – grandparents, great-grandparents. Music. Songs.

Debbie goes to nursery school ill. by author. Walck, 1970. Subj: School.

A dog came to school ill. by author. Oxford Univ. Pr., 1955. Subj: Animals – dogs. Music. School. Songs.

I like winter ill. by author. Walck, 1950. Subj: Music. Poetry, rhyme. Seasons – winter. Songs.

I went for a walk ill. by author. Walck, 1958. Subj: Activities – walking. Music. Songs.

Let's play house ill. by author. Walck, 1944. Subj: Activities – playing. Toys – dolls.

The life I live: collected poems ill. by author. Walck, 1966. Subj: Poetry, rhyme. Songs.

The little airplane ill. by author. Walck, 1938. Subj: Airplanes, airports.

The little auto ill. by author. Oxford Univ. Pr., 1934. Subj: Automobiles.

The little family ill. by author. Doubleday, 1932. Subj: Family life.

The little farm ill. by author. Walck, 1942. Subj: Farms.

The little fire engine ill. by author. Oxford Univ. Pr., 1946. Subj: Careers – firefighters.

The little sail boat ill. by author. Walck, 1937, 1965. Subj: Boats, ships.

The little train ill. by author. Oxford Univ. Pr., 1940. Subj: Careers – railroad engineers. Trains.

Lois Lenski's big book of Mr. Small ill. by author. Walck, 1979. Subj: Careers. Transportation.

Mr. and Mrs. Noah ill. by author. Crowell, 1948. Subj: Boats, ships. Religion – Noah.

Now it's fall ill. by author. Walck, 1948. Subj: Poetry, rhyme. Seasons – fall.

On a summer day ill. by author. Oxford Univ. Pr., 1953. Subj: Poetry, rhyme. Seasons – summer.

Papa Small ill. by author. Walck, 1951. Subj: Family life. Family life – fathers.

Policeman Small ill. by author. Walck, 1962. Subj: Careers – police officers. City.

Spring is here ill. by author. Walck, 1945. Subj: Poetry, rhyme. Seasons – spring.

A surprise for Davy ill. by author. Walck, 1947. Subj: Birthdays. Parties.

Susie Mariar ill. by author. Walck, 1967. First pub. in 1939. Subj: Cumulative tales. Folk and fairy tales. Poetry, rhyme.

Lent, Blair. *John Tabor's ride* ill. by author. Little, 1966. Subj: Animals – whales. Folk and fairy tales. Humor.

Pistachio ill. by author. Little, 1964. Subj: Animals – bulls, cows. Circus. Clowns, jesters.

Leodhas, Sorche Nic *see* Alger, Leclaire

Leonard, Marcia. *Little owl leaves the nest* ill. by Carol Newsom. Bantam, 1984. Subj: Birds – owls. Problem solving.

Lerner, Carol. *Flowers of a woodland spring* ill. by author. Morrow, 1979. Subj: Flowers. Forest, woods. Seasons – spring.

Lerner, Marguerite Rush. *Dear little mumps child* ill. by George Overlie. Lerner, 1959. Subj: Illness. Poetry, rhyme.

Doctors' tools ill. by George Overlie. Rev. 2nd ed. Lerner, 1960. Subj: Careers – doctors. Tools.

Lefty, the story of left-handedness ill. by Roy André. Lerner, 1960. Subj: Character traits – being different. Left-handedness.

Michael gets the measles ill. by George Overlie. Lerner, 1959. Subj: Illness.

Peter gets the chickenpox ill. by George Overlie. Lerner, 1959. Subj: Illness.

Lerner, Sharon. *Big Bird's copycat day* featuring Jim Henson's Sesame Street Muppets; ill. by Jean-Pierre Jacquet. Random House, 1984. Subj: Puppets.

LeRoy, Gen. *Billy's shoes* ill. by J. Winslow Higginbottom. McGraw-Hill, 1981. Subj: Clothing. Sibling rivalry.

Lucky stiff! ill. by J. Winslow Higginbottom. McGraw-Hill, 1981. Subj: Humor. Sibling rivalry.

LeSieg, Theo *see* Seuss, Dr.

Lesikin, Joan. *Down the road* ill. by author. Prentice-Hall, 1978. Subj: Behavior – sharing. Reptiles – snakes. Reptiles – turtles.

Lesser, Carolyn. *The goodnight circle* ill. by Lorinda Bryan Cauley. Harcourt, 1984. Subj: Animals. Bedtime. Night.

Lesser, Rika. *Hansel and Gretel* (Grimm, Jacob)

Lester, Helen. *The wizard, the fairy and the magic chicken* ill. by Lynn Munsinger. Houghton, 1983. Subj: Behavior – sharing. Birds – chickens. Fairies. Friendship. Wizards.

Le-Tan, Pierre. *The afternoon cat* ill. by author. Pantheon, 1977. Subj: Activities. Animals – cats.

Timothy's dream book ill. by author. Farrar, 1978. Subj: Careers. Imagination.

Visit to the North Pole ill. by author. Crown, 1983. Subj: Dreams. Imagination. Toys – teddy bears.

Le Tord, Bijou. *Picking and weaving* ill. by author. Four Winds Pr., 1980. Subj: Activities – weaving. Plants.

Rabbit seeds ill. by author. Four Winds Pr., 1984. Subj: Activities – gardening. Animals – rabbits.

Let's count and count out comp. by Marion F. Grayson; ill. by Deborah Derr McClintock. Luce, 1975. Subj: Counting. Games. Poetry, rhyme.

Leutscher, Alfred. *Earth* ill. by John Butler. Dial Pr., 1983. Subj: Earth. Science.

Water ill. by Nick Hardcastle. Dial Pr., 1983. Subj: Ecology. Science.

Levens, George. *Kippy the koala* ill. by Crosby Newell Bonsall. Harper, 1960. Subj: Animals – koala bears. Poetry, rhyme. Seasons – spring.

Leverich, Kathleen. *The hungry fox and the foxy duck* ill. by Paul Galdone. Parents, 1979. Subj: Animals – foxes. Birds – ducks. Character traits – cleverness.

Levine, Joan. *A bedtime story* ill. by Gail Owens. Dutton, 1975. Subj: Bedtime.

Levine, Rhoda. *Harrison loved his umbrella* ill. by Karla Kuskin. Atheneum, 1964. Subj: Character traits – being different. Character traits – individuality. Umbrellas.

Levitin, Sonia. *All the cats in the world* ill. by Charles Robinson. Harcourt, 1982. Subj: Animals – cats. Character traits – kindness to animals.

Nobody stole the pie ill. by Fernando Krahn. Harcourt, 1980. Subj: Activities – cooking. Crime. Food.

A single speckled egg ill. by John M. Larrecq. Parnassus Pr., 1976. Subj: Behavior – worrying. Eggs. Farms.

A sound to remember ill. by Gabriel Lisowski. Harcourt, 1979. Subj: Jewish culture. Religion. Self-concept.

Levy, Elizabeth. *Nice little girls* ill. by Mordicai Gerstein. Delacorte Pr., 1974. Subj: School.

Something queer at the ball park ill. by Mordicai Gerstein. Delacorte, 1975. Subj: Crime. Problem solving.

Something queer at the haunted school ill. by Mordicai Gerstein. Delacorte, 1982. Subj: Ghosts. Problem solving. School.

Something queer is going on ill. by Mordicai Gerstein. Delacorte Pr., 1973. Subj: Animals – dogs. Problem solving.

Something queer on vacation ill. by Mordicai Gerstein. Delacorte, 1980. Subj: Activities – vacationing. Behavior – misbehavior. Problem solving. Sea and seashore.

Levy, Miriam F. *Adam's world, San Francisco* (Fraser, Kathleen)

Levy, Sara G. *Mother Goose rhymes for Jewish children* ill. by Jessie B. Robinson. Bloch, 1945. Subj: Jewish culture. Nursery rhymes.

Lewin, Betsy. *Animal snackers* ill. by author. Dodd, 1980. Subj: Animals. Food. Poetry, rhyme.

Cat count ill. by author. Dodd, 1981. Subj: Animals – cats. Counting. Poetry, rhyme.

Hip, hippo, hooray! ill. by author. Dodd, 1982. Subj: Animals – hippopotami. Counting. Illness. Weather.

Lewin, Hugh. *Jafta* ill. by Lisa Kopper. Carolrhoda, 1983. Subj: Emotions, Family life. Foreign lands – Africa.

Jafta and the wedding ill. by Lisa Kopper. Carolrhoda, 1983. Subj: Family life. Foreign lands – Africa. Weddings.

Jafta — the journey ill. by Lisa Kopper. Carolrhoda, 1984. Subj: Activities – traveling. Emotions. Foreign lands – Africa.

Jafta - the town ill. by Lisa Kopper. Carolrhoda, 1984. Subj: City. Emotions. Foreign lands – Africa.

Jafta's father ill. by Lisa Kopper. Carolrhoda, 1983. Subj: Family life – fathers. Foreign lands – Africa.

Jafta's mother ill. by Lisa Kopper. Carolrhoda, 1983. Subj: Family life – mothers. Foreign lands – Africa.

Lewis, Claudia Louise. *When I go to the moon* ill. by Leonard Weisgard. Macmillan, 1961. Subj: Earth. Moon.

Lewis, Lucia Z. *see* Anderson, Lucia

Lewis, Naomi. *The butterfly collector* ill. by Fulvio Testa. Prentice-Hall, 1979. Subj: Behavior – collecting things. Insects – butterflies, caterpillars. Poetry, rhyme. Riddles.

Leaves ill. by Fulvio Testa. Harper, 1983. Subj: Plants. Seasons. Trees.

Once upon a rainbow ill. by Gabriele Eichenauer. Jonathan Cape, 1982. Subj: Concepts – color. Poetry, rhyme. Toys – teddy bears.

Puffin ill. by Deborah King. Lothrop, 1984. Subj: Birds – puffins. Foreign lands – Scotland.

The snow queen (Andersen, H C (Hans Christian))

The wild swans (Andersen, H C (Hans Christian))

Lewis, Richard. *In a spring garden* ill. by Ezra Jack Keats. Dial Pr., 1965. A collection of haiku. Subj: Poetry, rhyme.

Lewis, Stephen. *Zoo city* ill. by author. Greenwillow, 1976. Subj: Animals. City. Format, unusual. Imagination. Wordless. Zoos.

Lewis, Thomas P. *Call for Mr. Sniff* ill. by Beth Lee Weiner. Harper, 1981. Subj: Animals – dogs. Birthdays. Problem solving.

Hill of fire ill. by Joan Sandin. Harper, 1971. Subj: Foreign lands – Mexico. Volcanoes.

Lewiton, Mina *see* Simon, Mina Lewiton

Lexau, Joan M. *Benjie* ill. by Don Bolognese. Dial Pr., 1964. Subj: Character traits – shyness. Ethnic groups in the U.S. – Afro-Americans. Family life. Family life – grandparents, great-grandparents. Problem solving.

Benjie on his own ill. by Don Bolognese. Dial Pr., 1970. Subj: City. Ethnic groups in the U.S. – Afro-Americans. Family life – grandparents, great-grandparents. Illness. Problem solving.

Cathy is company ill. by Aliki. Dial Pr., 1961. Subj: Etiquette. Friendship.

Come here, cat ill. by Steven Kellogg. Harper, 1973. Subj: Animals – cats. City.

Crocodile and hen ill. by Joan Sandin. Harper, 1969. Adaptation of Why the crocodile does not eat the hen, from Notes on the folklore of the Fjort (French Congo), by R. E. Dennett. Subj: Birds – chickens. Cumulative tales. Folk and fairy tales. Foreign lands – Africa. Reptiles – alligators, crocodiles.

Every day a dragon ill. by Ben Shecter. Harper, 1967. Subj: Family life. Family life – fathers. Games.

Finders keepers, losers weepers ill. by Tomie de Paola. Lippincott, 1967. Subj: Babies. Behavior – losing things. Behavior – lying. Family life.

Go away, dog ill. by Crosby Newell Bonsall. Harper, 1963. Subj: Animals – dogs. Birthdays.

The homework caper ill. by Syd Hoff. Harper, 1966. Subj: Sibling rivalry.

A house so big ill. by Syd Hoff. Harper, 1968. Subj: Character traits – generosity. Emotions – love. Family life – mothers. Imagination.

I hate red rover ill. by Gail Owens. Dutton, 1979. Subj: Behavior – growing up. Games.

I should have stayed in bed ill. by Syd Hoff. Harper, 1965. Subj: Behavior – bad day. Emotions – embarrassment. Ethnic groups in the U.S. – Afro-Americans.

It all began with a drip, drip, drip ill. by Joan Sandin. McCall, 1970. Subj: Behavior – mistakes. Character traits – bravery. Folk and fairy tales. Foreign lands – India.

Me day ill. by Robert Weaver. Dial Pr., 1971. Subj: Birthdays. City. Divorce. Ethnic groups in the U.S. – Afro-Americans. Family life. Family life – fathers.

Millicent's ghost ill. by Ben Shecter. Dial Pr., 1962. Subj: Ghosts. Night.

More beautiful than flowers ill. by Don Bolognese. Lippincott, 1966. Subj: Poetry, rhyme. Religion.

Olaf reads ill. by Harvey Weiss. Dial Pr., 1961. Subj: Activities – reading.

The rooftop mystery ill. by Syd Hoff. Harper, 1968. Subj: Ethnic groups in the U.S. – Afro-Americans. Moving. Toys – dolls.

Who took the farmer's hat? ill. by Fritz Siebel. Harper, 1963. Subj: Clothing. Farms. Weather – wind.

Lifton, Betty Jean. *Goodnight orange monster* ill. by Cyndy Szekeres. Atheneum, 1972. Subj: Bedtime. Emotions – fear. Monsters. Night.

Joji and the Amanojaku ill. by Eiichi Mitsui. Norton, 1965. Subj: Birds. Foreign lands – Japan. Goblins. Scarecrows.

Joji and the dragon ill. by Eiichi Mitsui. Morrow, 1957. Subj: Birds. Dragons. Foreign lands – Japan. Scarecrows.

Joji and the fog ill. by Eiichi Mitsui. Morrow, 1959. Subj: Birds. Scarecrows. Weather – fog.

The many lives of Chio and Goro ill. by Yasuo Segawa. Norton, 1968. Subj: Animals – foxes. Birds – chickens. Foreign lands – Japan.

The rice-cake rabbit ill. by Eiichi Mitsui. Norton, 1966. Subj: Animals – rabbits. Foreign lands – Japan. Moon.

The secret seller ill. by Etienne Delessert and Norma Holt. Norton, 1967. Subj: Behavior – secrets. Imagination.

Lilly, Kenneth. *Animal builders* ill. by author. Random House, 1984. Subj: Activities. Animals. Format, unusual – cardboard pages. Science.

Animal climbers ill. by author. Random House, 1984. Subj: Activities. Animals. Format, unusual – cardboard pages. Science.

Animal jumpers ill. by author. Random House, 1984. Subj: Activities. Animals. Format, unusual – cardboard pages. Science.

Animal runners ill. by author. Random House, 1984. Subj: Activities. Animals. Format, unusual – cardboard pages. Science.

Animal swimmers ill. by author. Random House, 1984. Subj: Activities. Animals. Format, unusual – cardboard pages. Science.

Animals at the zoo ill. by author. Simon and Schuster, 1982. Subj: Animals. Format, unusual – cardboard pages. Zoos.

Animals in the country ill. by author. Simon and Schuster, 1982. Subj: Animals. Format, unusual – cardboard pages. Wordless.

Animals in the jungle ill. by author. Simon and Schuster, 1982. Subj: Animals. Format, unusual – cardboard pages. Jungle.

Animals of the ocean ill. by author. Simon and Schuster, 1982. Subj: Animals – bears. Animals – dolphins. Animals – seals. Animals – whales. Birds – penguins. Format, unusual – cardboard pages. Sea and seashore.

Animals on the farm ill. by author. Simon and Schuster, 1982. Subj: Animals. Farms. Format, unusual – cardboard pages.

Linch, Elizabeth Johanna. *Samson* ill. by author. Harper, 1964. Subj: Animals – mice. Holidays – Christmas. Seasons – winter.

Lindbloom, Steven. *Let's give kitty a bath!* ill. by True Kelley. Addison-Wesley, 1982. Subj: Activities – bathing. Animals – cats.

Lindgren, Astrid. *Christmas in noisy village* by Astrid Lindgren and Ilon Wikland. Tr. by Florence Lamborn; ill. by Ilon Wikland. Viking, 1964. Subj: Foreign lands – Sweden. Holidays – Christmas.

Christmas in the stable ill. by Harald Wiberg. Coward, 1962. Subj: Foreign lands – Sweden. Holidays – Christmas Religion.

I want a brother or sister tr. from Swedish by Barbara Lucas; ill. by Ilon Wikland. Harcourt, 1981. Subj: Babies. Emotions – envy, jealousy. Sibling rivalry.

Of course Polly can do almost everything ill. by Ilon Wikland. Follett, 1978. Subj: Character traits – optimism. Character traits – perseverance. Holidays – Christmas. Trees.

The tomten ill. by Harald Wiberg. Coward, 1961. Adapt. from a poem by Victor Rydberg. Subj: Farms. Foreign lands – Sweden. Seasons – winter. Trolls.

The tomten and the fox adapt. from a poem by Karl-Erik Forsslund; ill. by Harald Wiberg. Coward, 1965. Subj: Animals – foxes. Foreign lands – Sweden. Seasons – winter. Trolls.

Lindgren, Barbro. *Sam's ball* ill. by Eva Eriksson. Morrow, 1983. Subj: Animals – cats. Toys – balls.

Sam's bath ill. by Eva Eriksson. Morrow, 1983. Subj: Activities – bathing. Animals – dogs.

Sam's car ill. by Eva Eriksson. Morrow, 1982. Subj: Behavior – sharing. Toys.

Sam's cookie ill. by Eva Eriksson. Morrow, 1982. Subj: Behavior – sharing. Pets.

Sam's lamp ill. by Eva Eriksson. Morrow, 1983. Subj: Safety.

Sam's teddy bear ill. by Eva Eriksson. Morrow, 1982. Subj: Toys – teddy bears.

The wild baby adapt. from Swedish by Jack Prelutsky; ill. by Eva Eriksson. Greenwillow, 1981. Subj: Behavior – misbehavior. Family life – mothers. Poetry, rhyme.

The wild baby goes to sea adapt. from Swedish by Jack Prelutsky; ill. by Eva Eriksson. Greenwillow, 1983. Subj: Activities – playing. Family life – mothers. Imagination. Toys.

Lindman, Maj. *Flicka, Ricka, Dicka and a little dog* ill. by author. Albert Whitman, 1946. Subj: Animals – dogs. Family life. Foreign lands – Sweden. Triplets.

Flicka, Ricka, Dicka and the big red hen ill. by author. Albert Whitman, 1960. Subj: Birds – chickens. Family life. Triplets.

Flicka, Ricka, Dicka and the new dotted dress ill. by author. Albert Whitman, 1939. Subj: Character traits – helpfulness. Family life. Foreign lands – Sweden. Triplets.

Flicka, Ricka, Dicka and the three kittens ill. by author. Albert Whitman, 1941. Subj: Animals – cats. Family life. Triplets.

Flicka, Ricka, Dicka bake a cake ill. by author. Albert Whitman, 1955. Subj: Activities – cooking. Birthdays. Family life. Foreign lands – Sweden. Triplets.

Sailboat time ill. by author. Albert Whitman, 1951. Subj: Boats, ships. Foreign lands – Sweden.

Snipp, Snapp, Snurr and the buttered bread ill. by author. Albert Whitman, 1934. Subj: Cumulative tales. Family life. Farms. Foreign lands – Sweden. Triplets.

Snipp, Snapp, Snurr and the magic horse ill. by author. Albert Whitman, 1935. Subj: Family life. Foreign lands – Sweden. Magic. Toys – rocking horses. Triplets.

Snipp, Snapp, Snurr and the red shoes ill. by author. Albert Whitman, 1932. Subj: Activities – vacationing. Birthdays. Character traits – generosity. Character traits – helpfulness. Family life. Foreign lands – Lapland. Sports – skiing. Triplets.

Snipp, Snapp, Snurr and the reindeer ill. by author. Albert Whitman, 1957. Subj: Animals – deer. Family life. Foreign lands – Sweden. Triplets.

Snipp, Snapp, Snurr and the seven dogs ill. by author. Albert Whitman, 1959. Subj: Animals – dogs. Family life. Foreign lands – Sweden. Triplets.

Snipp, Snapp, Snurr and the yellow sled ill. by author. Albert Whitman, 1936. Subj: Animals – dogs. Family life. Foreign lands – Sweden. Sports – ice skating. Triplets.

Lindsey, Treska. *When Batistine made bread* ill. by author. Macmillan, 1985. Subj: Activities – cooking. Activities – working. Food.

Lines, Kathleen. *Dick Whittington* (Dick Whittington and his cat)

Lavender's blue (Mother Goose)

The old ballad of the babes in the woods (The babes in the woods)

Once in royal David's city; a picture book of the Nativity, retold from the Gospels ill. by Harold Iones. Watts, 1956. Subj: Holidays – Christmas. Religion.

Link, Martin A. *The goat in the rug* (Blood, Charles L)

Linzer, Jeff. *The fire station book* (Bundt, Nancy)

Lionni, Leo. *Alexander and the wind-up mouse* ill. by author. Pantheon, 1969. Subj: Animals – mice. Caldecott award honor book. Emotions – envy, jealousy. Friendship. Toys.

The biggest house in the world ill. by author. Pantheon, 1968. Subj: Animals. Behavior – greed.

A color of his own ill. by author. Pantheon, 1975. Subj: Character traits – individuality. Concepts – color. Reptiles – lizards.

Cornelius ill. by author. Pantheon, 1983. Subj: Character traits – being different. Reptiles – alligators, crocodiles.

Fish is fish ill. by author. Pantheon, 1970. Subj: Behavior – misunderstanding. Fish. Friendship. Frogs and toads.

Frederick ill. by author. Pantheon, 1967. Subj: Animals – mice. Caldecott award honor book. Music.

Geraldine, the music mouse ill. by author. Pantheon, 1979. Subj: Animals – mice. Music.

The greentail mouse ill. by author. Pantheon, 1973. Subj: Animals – mice. Mardi Gras.

In the rabbitgarden ill. by author. Pantheon, 1975. Subj: Animals – foxes. Animals – mice. Reptiles – snakes.

Inch by inch ill. by author. Astor-Honor, 1960. Subj: Birds. Caldecott award honor book. Concepts – measurement. Insects.

Let's make rabbits ill. by author. Pantheon, 1982. Subj: Activities. Animals – rabbits. Art. Imagination.

Little blue and little yellow ill. by author. Astor-Honor, 1959. Subj: Concepts – color. Friendship.

Mouse days ill. by author. Pantheon, 1981. Subj: Animals – mice. Seasons.

On my beach there are many pebbles ill. by author. Astor-Honor, 1961. Subj: Rocks. Sea and seashore.

Pezzettino ill. by author. Pantheon, 1975. Subj: Character traits – individuality. Concepts – shape. Self-concept.

Swimmy ill. by author. Pantheon, 1963. Subj: Caldecott award honor book. Fish. Sea and seashore.

Theodore and the talking mushroom ill. by author. Pantheon, 1971. Subj: Animals – mice. Character traits – optimism.

Tico and the golden wings ill. by author. Pantheon, 1964. Subj: Birds. Character traits – generosity. Character traits – individuality. Character traits – questioning.

What? pictures to talk about ill. by author. Pantheon, 1983. Subj: Animals – mice. Format, unusual – cardboard pages. Senses. Wordless.

When? ill. by author. Pantheon, 1983. Subj: Animals – mice. Format, unusual – cardboard pages. Night. Seasons. Wordless.

Where? pictures to talk about ill. by author. Pantheon, 1983. Subj: Animals – mice. Format, unusual – cardboard pages. Humor. Wordless.

Who? pictures to talk about ill. by author. Pantheon Books, 1983. Subj: Animals – mice. Format, unusual – cardboard pages. Wordless.

Words to talk about ill. by author. Pantheon, 1985. Subj: Animals – mice. Format, unusual – cardboard pages.

Lipkind, William. *Billy the kid* by William Lipkind and Nicolas Mordvinoff; ill. by Nicolas Mordvinoff. Harcourt, 1964. Subj: Animals – goats.

The boy and the forest by William Lipkind and Nicolas Mordvinoff; ill. by Nicolas Mordvinoff. Harcourt, 1964. Subj: Animals. Character traits – kindness to animals. Forest, woods. Magic.

Chaga by William Lipkind and Nicolas Mordvinoff; ill. by Nicolas Mordvinoff. Harcourt, 1955. Subj: Animals – elephants. Concepts – size.

The Christmas bunny by William Lipkind and Nicolas Mordvinoff; ill. by Nicolas Mordvinoff. Harcourt, 1953. Subj: Animals – foxes. Animals – rabbits. Holidays – Christmas. Parties.

Circus rucus by William Lipkind and Nicolas Mordvinoff; ill. by Nicolas Mordvinoff. Harcourt, 1954. Subj: Circus.

Even Steven by William Lipkind and Nicolas Mordvinoff; ill. by Nicolas Mordvinoff. Harcourt, 1952. Subj: Animals – dogs. Character traits – selfishness.

Finders keepers by William Lipkind and Nicolas Mordvinoff; ill. by Nicolas Mordvinoff. Harcourt, 1951. Subj: Animals – dogs. Caldecott award book. Character traits – selfishness.

Four-leaf clover by William Lipkind and Nicolas Mordvinoff; ill. by Nicolas Mordvinoff. Harcourt, 1959. Subj: Ethnic groups in the U.S. – Afro-Americans.

The little tiny rooster by William Lipkind and Nicolas Mordvinoff; ill. by Nicolas Mordvinoff. Harcourt, 1960. Subj: Animals – foxes. Birds – chickens. Character traits – smallness. Self-concept.

The magic feather duster by William Lipkind and Nicolas Mordvinoff; ill. by Nicolas Mordvinoff. Harcourt, 1958. Subj: Character traits – kindness. Folk and fairy tales. Magic.

Nubber bear ill. by Roger Antoine Duvoisin. Harcourt, 1966. Subj: Animals – bears. Behavior – misbehavior.

Professor Bull's umbrella by William Lipkind and Georges Schreiber; ill. by George Schreiber. Viking, 1954. Subj: Umbrellas.

Russet and the two reds by William Lipkind and Nicolas Mordvinoff; ill. by Nicolas Mordvinoff. Harcourt, 1962. Subj: Animals – cats.

Sleepyhead by William Lipkind and Nicolas Mordvinoff; ill. by Nicolas Mordvinoff. Harcourt, 1957. Subj: Activities – playing. Games. Poetry, rhyme.

The two reds by William Lipkind and Nicolas Mordvinoff; ill. by Nicolas Mordvinoff. Harcourt, 1950. Subj: Animals – cats. Caldecott award honor book. Friendship.

Lippman, Peter. *The Know-It-Alls go to sea* ill. by author. Doubleday, 1982. Subj: Behavior – misbehavior. Boats, ships.

The Know-It-Alls help out ill. by author. Doubleday, 1982. Subj: Behavior – misbehavior. Houses.

The Know-It-Alls mind the store ill. by author. Doubleday, 1982. Subj: Behavior – misbehavior. Stores.

The Know-It-Alls take a winter vacation ill. by author. Doubleday, 1982. Subj: Activities – vacationing. Behavior – misbehavior.

New at the zoo ill. by author. Harper, 1969. Subj: Animals. Bedtime. Zoos.

Lisker, Sonia O. *Lost* ill. by author. Harcourt, 1975. Subj: Behavior – lost. Wordless. Zoos.

Two special cards by Sonia O. Lisker and Leigh Dean; ill. by Sonia O. Lisker. Harcourt, 1976. Subj: Divorce. Family life.

Lisowski, Gabriel. *How Tevye became a milkman* ill. by author. Holt, 1976. Subj: Foreign lands – Ukraine. Jewish culture.

Roncalli's magnificent circus ill. by author. Doubleday, 1980. Subj: Animals – bears. Behavior – running away. Circus.

Litchfield, Ada B. *A button in her ear* ill. by Eleanor Mill. Albert Whitman, 1976. Subj: Handicaps – deafness.

A cane in her hand ill. by Eleanor Mill. Albert Whitman, 1977. Subj: Handicaps – blindness.

A little ABC book. Simon and Schuster, 1980. Subj: ABC books. Format, unusual – cardboard pages.

A little book of colors. Simon and Schuster, 1982. Subj: Concepts – color. Format, unusual – cardboard pages.

A little book of numbers. Simon and Schuster, 1980. Subj: Counting. Format, unusual – cardboard pages.

Little, Lessie Jones. *I can do it by myself* by Lessie Jones Little and Eloise Greenfield; ill. by Carole Byard. Crowell, 1978. Subj: Birthdays. Character traits – bravery. Plants.

Little, Mary E. *ABC for the library* ill. by author. Atheneum, 1975. Subj: ABC books. Libraries.

Ricardo and the puppets ill. by author. Scribner's, 1958. Subj: Animals – mice. Libraries. Puppets.

Little red cap (Grimm, Jacob)

The little red hen ill. by Janina Domanska. Macmillan, 1973. Subj: Animals. Birds – chickens. Character traits – laziness. Cumulative tales. Farms. Folk and fairy tales. Plants.

The little red hen ill. by Paul Galdone. Seabury Pr., 1973. Subj: Animals. Birds – chickens. Character traits – laziness. Cumulative tales. Farms. Folk and fairy tales. Plants.

The little red hen retold by Jean Horton Berg; reading consultant: Morton Betel; ill. by Mel Pekarsky. Follett, 1963. Subj: Animals. Birds – chickens. Character traits – laziness. Cumulative tales. Farms. Folk and fairy tales. Plants.

The little red hen: *an old story* retold and ill. by Margot Zemach. Farrar, 1983. Subj: Character traits – laziness. Cumulative tales. Farms. Folk and fairy tales. Plants.

Little Red Riding Hood (Grimm, Jacob)

Little Tuppen *an old tale* ill. by Paul Galdone. Seabury Pr., 1967. Subj: Birds – chickens. Cumulative tales. Folk and fairy tales.

Littledale, Freya. *The magic plum tree* ill. by Enrico Arno. Crown, 1981. Subj: Character traits – individuality. Plants. Royalty.

The snow child ill. by Leon Steinmetz. Scholastic, 1978. Subj: Behavior – wishing. Old age. Seasons – winter.

Littlefield, William. *The whiskers of Ho Ho* ill. by Vladimir Bobri. Lothrop, 1958. Subj: Animals – rabbits. Birds – chickens. Folk and fairy tales. Foreign lands – China. Holidays – Easter.

Livermore, Elaine. *Find the cat* ill. by author. Houghton, 1973. Subj: Animals – cats. Games.

Follow the fox ill. by author. Houghton, 1981. Subj: Animals – foxes. Behavior – lost. Behavior – needing someone.

Lost and found ill. by author. Houghton, 1975. Subj: Behavior – losing things. Games.

One to ten, count again ill. by author. Houghton, 1973. Subj: Counting. Games.

Three little kittens lost their mittens ill. by author. Houghton, 1979. Subj: Animals – cats. Behavior – losing things. Games. Nursery rhymes.

Livingston, Carole. *"Why am I going to the hospital?"* (Ciliotta, Claire)

"Why was I adopted?" ill. by Arthur Robins; designed by Paul Walter. Lyle Stuart, 1978. Subj: Adoption. Family life.

Livingston, Myra Cohn. *A Learical lexicon* (Lear, Edward)

Lloyd, David. *Air* ill. by Peter Visscher. Dial Pr., 1982. Subj: Science.

Lloyd, Errol. *Nandy's bedtime* ill. by author. Merrimack, 1983. Subj: Bedtime. Night.

Nini at carnival ill. by author. Crowell, 1979. Subj: Character traits – helpfulness. Clothing.

Lloyd, Megan. *Chicken tricks* ill. by author. Harper, 1983. Subj: Birds – chickens. Eggs. Humor. Poetry, rhyme.

Lobe, Mira. *The snowman who went for a walk* tr. from German by Peter Carter; ill. by Winfried Opgenoorth. Morrow, 1984. Subj: Activities – walking. Snowmen.

Valerie and the good-night swing tr. from German by Peter Carter; ill. by Winfried Opgenoorth. Oxford Univ. Pr., 1983. Subj: Bedtime. Poetry, rhyme.

Lobel, Anita. *A birthday for the princess* ill. by author. Harper, 1973. Subj: Behavior – needing someone. Birthdays. Royalty.

King Rooster, Queen Hen ill. by author. Greenwillow, 1975. Subj: Animals. Birds – chickens. Foreign lands – Denmark.

The pancake ill. by author. Greenwillow, 1978. Subj: Cumulative tales. Food.

Potatoes, potatoes ill. by author. Greenwillow, 1967. Subj: Violence, anti-violence.

The seamstress of Salzburg ill. by author. Harper, 1970. Subj: Careers – seamstresses. Clothing. Royalty. Sibling rivalry.

The straw maid ill. by author. Greenwillow, 1983. Subj: Character traits – cleverness. Crime.

Sven's bridge ill. by author. Harper, 1965. Subj: Bridges. Royalty.

The troll music ill. by author. Harper, 1966. Subj: Magic. Music. Trolls.

Lobel, Arnold. *Days with Frog and Toad* ill. by author. Harper, 1979. Subj: Friendship. Frogs and toads.

Fables ill. by author. Harper, 1980. Subj: Animals. Caldecott award book.

Frog and Toad all year ill. by author. Harper, 1976. Subj: Friendship. Frogs and toads. Seasons.

Frog and Toad are friends ill. by author. Harper, 1970. Subj: Caldecott award honor book. Friendship. Frogs and toads.

Frog and Toad together ill. by author. Harper, 1971. Subj: Friendship. Frogs and toads.

Giant John ill. by author. Harper, 1964. Subj: Giants.

Grasshopper on the road ill. by author. Harper, 1978. Subj: Insects. Insects – grasshoppers.

The great blueness and other predicaments ill. by author. Harper, 1968. Subj: Concepts – color. Wizards.

A holiday for Mister Muster ill. by author. Harper, 1963. Subj: Animals. Illness. Zoos.

How the rooster saved the day ill. by Anita Lobel. Greenwillow, 1977. Subj: Birds – chickens. Character traits – cleverness. Crime.

Lucille ill. by author. Harper, 1964. Subj: Animals – horses. Humor.

The man who took the indoors out ill. by author. Harper, 1974. Subj: Behavior – running away.

Martha, the movie mouse ill. by author. Harper, 1966. Subj: Animals – mice. Poetry, rhyme. Theater.

Ming Lo moves the mountain ill. by author. Greenwillow, 1982. Subj: Foreign lands – China. Moving.

Mouse soup ill. by author. Harper, 1977. Subj: Animals – mice. Animals – weasels. Character traits – cleverness.

Mouse tales ill. by author. Harper, 1972. Subj: Animals – mice. Humor.

On Market Street ill. by Anita Lobel. Greenwillow, 1981. Subj: ABC books. Caldecott award honor book. Poetry, rhyme. Shopping. Stores.

On the day Peter Stuyvesant sailed into town ill. by author. Harper, 1971. Subj: Poetry, rhyme. Problem solving. U.S. history.

Owl at home ill. by author. Harper, 1975. Subj: Birds – owls.

Prince Bertram the bad ill. by author. Harper, 1963. Subj: Behavior – misbehavior. Dragons. Royalty. Witches.

The rose in my garden ill. by Anita Lobel. Greenwillow, 1984. Subj: Animals – cats. Animals – mice. Cumulative tales. Flowers. Insects – bees. Poetry, rhyme.

Small pig ill. by author. Harper, 1969. Subj: Animals – pigs. Behavior – running away. Farms.

A treeful of pigs ill. by Anita Lobel. Greenwillow, 1979. Subj: Animals – pigs. Character traits – laziness. Farms. Humor.

Uncle Elephant ill. by author. Harper, 1981. Subj: Animals – elephants. Behavior – lost. Family life. Sea and seashore.

A zoo for Mister Muster ill. by author. Harper, 1962. Subj: Animals. Zoos.

Locker, Thomas. *Where the river begins* ill. by author. Dial Pr., 1984. Subj: Family life – grandparents, great-grandparents. Rivers.

Lodge, Bernard. *Door to door* ill. by Maureen Roffey. Lothrop, 1980. Subj: Foreign lands – England. Format, unusual.

Rhyming Nell ill. by Maureen Roffey. Lothrop, 1979. Subj: Format, unusual. Poetry, rhyme. Witches.

Löfgren, Ulf. *The boy who ate more than the giant and other Swedish folktales* tr. from Swedish by Sheila La Farge; ill. by author. Collins-World, 1978. Subj: Folk and fairy tales. Giants. Humor.

The color trumpet ill. by author. Addison-Wesley, 1973. English text by Alison Winn; adapt. by Ray Broekel. Subj: Concepts – color.

The flying orchestra ill. by author. Addison-Wesley, 1973. English text by Alison Winn; adapt. by Ray Broekel. Subj: Music.

One-two-three ill. by author. Addison-Wesley, 1973. English text by Alison Winn; adapt. by Ray Brockel. Subj: Animals. Counting. Participation.

The traffic stopper that became a grandmother visitor ill. by author. Addison-Wesley, 1973. English text by Alison Winn; adapt. by Ray Broekel. Subj: Animals – elephants. Automobiles. Machines.

The wonderful tree ill. by author. Delacorte Pr., 1969. Subj: Imagination. Trees.

Logue, Christopher. *The magic circus* ill. by Wayne Anderson. Viking, 1979. Subj: Character traits – cleverness. Circus. Monsters.

Long, Earlene. *Gone fishing* ill. by Richard Eric Brown. Houghton, 1984. Subj: Concepts – size. Family life – fathers. Sports – fishing.

Johnny's egg photos. by Neal Slavin and Charles Mikolaycak. Addison-Wesley, 1980. Subj: Activities – cooking. Eggs.

Longfellow, Henry Wadsworth. *Hiawatha* ill. by Susan Jeffers. Dial Pr., 1983. Subj: Ethnic groups in the U.S. – Indians. Poetry, rhyme.

Hiawatha's childhood ill. by Errol Le Caine. Farrar, 1984. Subj: Ethnic groups in the U.S. – Indians. Poetry, rhyme.

Paul Revere's ride ill. by Nancy Winslow Parker. Greenwillow, 1985. Subj: Poetry, rhyme. U.S. history.

Loof, Jan. *Uncle Louie's fantastic sea voyage* ill. by author. Random House, 1978. Subj: Activities – traveling. Boats, ships. Zoos.

Lopshire, Robert. *The biggest, smallest, fastest, tallest things you've ever heard of* ill. by author. Crowell, 1980. Subj: Concepts.

How to make snop snappers and other fine things ill. by author. Greenwillow, 1977. Subj: Games.

I am better than you ill. by author. Harper, 1968. Subj: Behavior – boasting. Reptiles – lizards.

It's magic ill. by author. Macmillan, 1969. Subj: Magic.

Put me in the zoo ill. by author. Random House, 1960. Subj: Animals – dogs. Circus. Concepts – color. Poetry, rhyme.

Lorca, Federico García *see* García Lorca, Federico

Lord, Beman. *The days of the week* ill. by Walter Erhard. Walck, 1968. Subj: Days of the week, months of the year. Poetry, rhyme. Songs.

Lord, John Vernon. *Mr. Mead and his garden* ill. by author. Houghton, 1975. Subj: Activities – gardening. Animals – snails. Poetry, rhyme.

Lord, Nancy *see* Titus, Eve

Lorenz, Lee. *Big Gus and Little Gus* ill. by author. Prentice-Hall, 1982. Subj: Character traits – laziness. Cumulative tales. Folk and fairy tales.

Pinchpenny John ill. by author. Prentice-Hall, 1981. Subj: Behavior – greed. Folk and fairy tales.

Scornful Simkin ill. by author. Prentice-Hall, 1980. Subj: Folk and fairy tales.

A weekend in the country ill. by author. Prentice-Hall, 1984. Subj: Animals – pigs. Birds – ducks. Country.

Lorenzini, Carlo *see* Collodi, Carlo

Lorimer, Janet. *The biggest bubble in the world* ill. by Diane Paterson. Watts, 1982. Subj: Behavior – misbehavior.

Lorimer, Lawrence T. *Noah's ark* (Martin, Charles E)

Lourie, Helen *see* Storr, Catherine

Low, Alice. *The charge of the mouse brigade* (Stone, Bernard)

David's windows ill. by Tomie de Paola. Putnam's, 1974. Subj: Animals – horses. City. Family life – grandparents, great-grandparents.

Taro and the bamboo shoot (Matsuno, Masako)

The witch who was afraid of witches ill. by Karen Gundersheimer. Pantheon, 1978. Subj: Holidays – Halloween. Sibling rivalry. Witches.

Witch's holiday ill. by Tony Walton. Pantheon, 1971. Subj: Holidays – Halloween. Poetry, rhyme. Witches.

Low, Joseph. *Adam's book of odd creatures* ill. by author. Atheneum, 1962. Subj: ABC books. Animals. Names. Poetry, rhyme.

Benny rabbit and the owl ill. by author. Greenwillow, 1978. Subj: Birds – geese. Character traits – bravery. Emotions – fear. Farms.

Boo to a goose ill. by author. Atheneum, 1975. Subj: Birds – geese. Character traits – bravery. Emotions – fear. Farms.

The Christmas grump ill. by author. Atheneum, 1977. Subj: Animals – mice. Emotions – happiness. Emotions – sadness. Holidays – Christmas.

Don't drag your feet... ill. by author. Atheneum, 1983. Subj: Behavior. Dreams. Toys.

Five men under one umbrella ill. by author. Macmillan, 1975. Subj: Riddles.

A mad wet hen and other riddles ill. by author. Greenwillow, 1977. Subj: Riddles.

Mice twice ill. by author. Atheneum, 1980. Subj: Animals – mice. Caldecott award honor book.

What if...? fourteen encounters - some frightful, some frivolous - that might happen to anyone ill. by author. Atheneum, 1976. Subj: Problem solving.

Lowitz, Anson. *The pilgrims' party* (Lowitz, Sadyebeth)

Lowitz, Sadyebeth. *The pilgrims' party* by Sadyebeth and Anson Lowitz; ill. by Anson Lowitz. Lerner, 1931. Subj: Holidays – Thanksgiving. U.S. history.

Lowrey, Janette Sebring. *Six silver spoons* ill. by Robert M. Quackenbush. Harper, 1971. Subj: Birthdays. U.S. history.

Lubell, Cicil. *Rosalie, the bird market turtle* (Lubell, Winifred)

Lubell, Winifred. *Here comes daddy: a book for twos and threes* ill. by author. Addison Wesley, 1944. Subj: Family life – fathers.

I wish I had another name (Williams, Jay)

Rosalie, the bird market turtle by Winifred and Cicil Lubell; ill. by Winifred Lubell. Rand McNally, 1962. Subj: Behavior – lost. Birds. Foreign lands – France. Reptiles – turtles.

Lucas, Barbara. *I want a brother or sister* (Lindgren, Astrid)

Luenn, Nancy. *The dragon kite* ill. by Michael Hague. Harcourt, 1982. Subj: Folk and fairy tales. Foreign lands – Japan. Kites.

Lukešová, Milena. *Julian in the autumn woods* ill. by Jan Kudlacek. Holt, 1977. Subj: Forest, woods.

The little girl and the rain ill. by Jan Kudlacek. Holt, 1978. Subj: Emotions – loneliness. Weather – rain.

Lund, Doris Herold. *The paint-box sea* ill. by Symeon Shimin. McGraw-Hill, 1971. Subj: Poetry, rhyme. Sea and seashore. Seasons – summer.

You ought to see Herbert's house ill. by Steven Kellogg. McGraw-Hill, 1973. Subj: Behavior – boasting. Friendship.

Lüton, Mildred. *Little chicks' mothers and all the others* ill. by Mary Maki Rae. Viking, 1983. Subj: Animals. Farms. Poetry, rhyme.

Luttrell, Ida. *Lonesome Lester* ill. by Megan Lloyd. Harper, 1984. Subj: Animals – prairie dogs. Behavior – solitude. Emotions – loneliness.

Lyfick, Warren. *Animal tales* ill. by Joe Kohl. Harvey House, 1980. Subj: Animals. Riddles.

The little book of fowl jokes ill. by Chris Cummings. Harvey House, 1980. Subj: Birds. Riddles.

Lynch, Marietta. *Mommy and daddy are divorced* (Perry, Patricia)

Lynn, Patricia *see* Watts, Mabel

Lystad, Mary H. *That new boy* ill. by Emily Arnold McCully. Crown, 1973. Subj: Character traits – individuality. Friendship. Moving.

Mabey, Richard. *Oak and company* ill. by Clare Roberts. Greenwillow, 1983. Subj: Ecology. Science. Trees.

MacArthur-Onslow, Annette Rosemary. *Minnie* ill. by author. Rand McNally, 1971. Subj: Animals – cats.

Macaulay, David. *Castle* ill. by author. Houghton, 1977. Subj: Caldecott award honor book.

Cathedral ill. by author. Houghton, 1973. Subj: Caldecott award honor book.

MacBean, Dilla Wittemore. *Picture book dictionary* ill. by Pauline B. Adams. Children's Pr., 1962. Subj: Dictionaries.

MacBeth, George. *Jonah and the Lord* ill. by Margaret Gordon. Holt, 1970. Subj: Folk and fairy tales. Religion.

Noah's journey ill. by Margaret Gordon. Viking, 1966. Subj: Poetry, rhyme. Religion – Noah.

MacCabe, Lorin. *Cable car Joey* (MacCabe, Naomi)

MacCabe, Naomi. *Cable car Joey* by Naomi and Lorin MacCabe; ill. by authors. Stanford Univ. Pr., 1949. Subj: Cable cars, trolleys.

McCauley, Jane. *Baby birds and how they grow* ill. with photos. National Geographic Soc., 1983. Subj: Birds. Science.

The way animals sleep ill. with photos. National Geographic Soc., 1983. Subj: Animals. Sleep.

McClenathan, Louise. *The Easter pig* ill. by Rosekrans Hoffman. Morrow, 1982. Subj: Animals – pigs. Character traits – generosity. Holidays – Easter.

My mother sends her wisdom ill. by Rosekrans Hoffman. Morrow, 1979. Subj: Behavior – greed. Character traits – cleverness.

McClintock, Marshall. *A fly went by* ill. by Fritz Siebel. Random House, 1958. Subj: Behavior – misunderstanding. Cumulative tales. Insects – flies.

Stop that ball ill. by Fritz Siebel. Random House, 1959. Subj: Toys – balls.

What have I got? ill. by Leonard P. Kessler. Harper, 1961. Subj: Clothing. Imagination. Poetry, rhyme.

McClintock, Mike *see* McClintock, Marshall

McCloskey, Robert. *Bert Dow, deep-water man a tale of the sea in the classic tradition* ill. by author. Viking, 1963. Subj: Animals – whales. Boats, ships. Sea and seashore.

Blueberries for Sal ill. by author. Viking, 1948. Subj: Animals – bears. Behavior – lost. Caldecott award honor book. Family life. Food.

Lentil ill. by author. Viking, 1940. Subj: Music. Noise, sounds. Problem solving.

Make way for ducklings ill. by author. Viking, 1941. Subj: Birds – ducks. Caldecott award book. Careers – police officers. City.

One morning in Maine ill. by author. Viking, 1952. Subj: Caldecott award honor book. Family life. Sea and seashore. Teeth.

Time of wonder ill. by author. Viking, 1957. Subj: Caldecott award book. Islands. Sea and seashore. Seasons – summer. Weather.

McClung, Robert. *Sphinx: the story of a caterpillar* ill. by Carol Lerner. Rev. ed. Morrow, 1981. Subj: Insects – butterflies, caterpillars. Science.

McClure, Gillian. *Fly home McDoo* ill. by author. Dutton, 1980. Subj: Behavior – running away. Birds – pigeons.

Prickly pig ill. by author. Elsevier-Dutton, 1980. Subj: Animals – hedgehogs. Hibernation.

What's the time, Rory Wolf? ill. by author. Dutton, 1982. Subj: Animals – wolves. Emotions – loneliness. Friendship.

McCord, David. *The star in the pail* ill. by Marc Simont. Little, 1976. Subj: Poetry, rhyme.

McCormack, John E. *Rabbit tales* ill. by Jenni Oliver. Dutton, 1980. Subj: Animals – rabbits. Character traits – cleverness. Character traits – individuality. Character traits – vanity. Friendship. Imagination.

Rabbit travels ill. by Lynne Cherry. Dutton, 1984. Subj: Activities – traveling. Animals – rabbits. Friendship.

McCrea, James. *The king's procession* by James and Ruth McCrea; ill. by authors. Atheneum, 1963. Subj: Animals – donkeys. Character traits – loyalty. Poverty. Royalty.

The magic tree by James and Ruth McCrea; ill. by authors. Atheneum, 1965. Subj: Character traits – meanness. Emotions. Emotions – happiness. Royalty.

The story of Olaf by James and Ruth McCrea; ill. by authors. Atheneum, 1964. Subj: Dragons. Knights. Wizards.

McCrea, Ruth. *The king's procession* (McCrea, James)

The magic tree (McCrea, James)

The story of Olaf (McCrea, James)

McCready, Lady *see* Tudor, Tasha

McCready, Tasha Tudor *see* Tudor, Tasha

McCue, Lisa. *Corduroy's party* ill. by author. Viking, 1985. Subj: Birthdays. Format, unusual – cardboard pages. Toys – teddy bears. Wordless.

Corduroy's toys ill. by author. Viking, 1985. Subj: Format, unusual – cardboard pages. Toys. Toys – teddy bears. Wordless.

McCully, Emily Arnold. *Picnic* ill. by author. Harper, 1984. Subj: Activities – picnicking. Animals – mice. Behavior – lost. Wordless.

McDaniel, Becky Bring. *Katie did it* ill. by Lois Axeman. Children's Pr., 1983. Subj: Sibling rivalry.

McDermott, Beverly Brodsky. *The crystal apple: a Russian tale* ill. by author. Viking, 1974. Subj: Folk and fairy tales. Foreign lands – Russia. Imagination.

The Golem: a Jewish legend ill. by author. Lippincott, 1976. Subj: Caldecott award honor book. Folk and fairy tales. Jewish culture.

Jonah: an Old Testament story ill. by author. Lippincott, 1977. Subj: Religion.

McDermott, Gerald. *Anansi the spider: a tale from the Ashanti* ill. by author. Holt, 1972. Subj: Caldecott award honor book. Folk and fairy tales. Foreign lands – Africa. Moon. Spiders.

Arrow to the sun: a Pueblo Indian tale ill. by author. Viking, 1974. Subj: Caldecott award book. Ethnic groups in the U.S. – Indians. Folk and fairy tales.

Daughter of earth: a Roman myth ill. by author. Delacorte, 1984. Subj: Folk and fairy tales. Seasons.

The magic tree: a tale from the Congo ill. by author. Holt, 1973. Subj: Character traits – appearance. Magic. Twins.

Papagayo, the mischief maker ill. by author. Windmill, 1980. Subj: Birds – parakeets, parrots. Moon.

The stonecutter: a Japanese folk tale ill. by author. Viking, 1975. Subj: Behavior – dissatisfaction. Folk and fairy tales. Foreign lands – Japan.

The voyage of Osiris: a myth of ancient Egypt ill. by author. Windmill Books, 1977. Subj: Folk and fairy tales. Foreign lands – Egypt. Religion. Royalty.

MacDonald, George. *The light princess* ill. by Maurice Sendak. Farrar, 1969. Subj: Folk and fairy tales.

MacDonald, Golden see Brown, Margaret Wise

MacDonald, Greville see MacDonald, George

McFarland, John. *The exploding frog and other fables from Æsop* retold by John McFarland; ill. by James Marshall. Little, 1981. Subj: Folk and fairy tales.

McGillicuddy, Mr. see Abisch, Roz

McGinley, Phyllis. *All around the town* ill. by Helen Stone. Lippincott, 1948. Subj: ABC books. Caldecott award honor book. City. Poetry, rhyme.

The horse who lived upstairs ill. by Helen Stone. Lippincott, 1944. Subj: Animals – horses. Behavior – dissatisfaction.

How Mrs. Santa Claus saved Christmas ill. by Kurt Werth. Lippincott, 1963. Subj: Holidays – Christmas. Poetry, rhyme.

Lucy McLockett ill. by Helen Stone. Lippincott, 1958. Subj: Behavior – losing things. Family life. Poetry, rhyme. Teeth.

The most wonderful doll in the world ill. by Helen Stone. Lippincott, 1950. Subj: Caldecott award honor book. Toys – dolls.

Wonderful time ill. by John Alcorn. Lippincott, 1966. Subj: Clocks. Poetry, rhyme. Time.

McGovern, Ann. *Black is beautiful* photos. by Hope Wurmfeld. Four Winds Pr., 1969. Subj: Ethnic groups in the U.S. – Afro-Americans.

Feeling mad, feeling sad, feeling bad, feeling glad photos. by Hope Wurmfeld. Walker, 1977. Subj: Emotions. Poetry, rhyme.

Mr. Skinner's skinny house ill. by Mort Gerberg. Four Winds Pr., 1980. Subj: Character traits – being different. Emotions – loneliness. Houses.

Nicholas Bentley Stoningpot III ill. by Tomie de Paola. Holiday, 1982. Subj: Behavior – boredom. Boats, ships. Emotions – loneliness. Islands.

Too much noise ill. by Simms Taback. Houghton, 1967. Subj: Humor. Noise, sounds.

Zoo, where are you? ill. by Ezra Jack Keats. Harper, 1965. Subj: Zoos.

McGowan, Alan. *Sailing ships* by Alan McGowan and Ron van der Meer; ill. by Borje Svensson. Viking, 1984. Subj: Boats, ships. Format, unusual.

McGowen, Thomas see McGowen, Tom

McGowen, Tom. *The only glupmaker in the U.S. Navy* ill. by author. Albert Whitman, 1966. Subj: Activities – working. Careers – military.

MacGregor, Ellen. *Mr. Pingle and Mr. Buttonhouse* ill. by Paul Galdone. McGraw-Hill, 1957. Subj: Friendship.

Theodor Turtle ill. by Paul Galdone. McGraw-Hill, 1955. Subj: Behavior – forgetfulness. Participation. Reptiles – turtles.

McGuire, Paula. *Me and Clara and Baldwin the pony* (Inkiow, Dimiter)

Me and Clara and Casimir the cat (Inkiow, Dimiter)

Me and Clara and Snuffy the dog (Inkiow, Dimiter)

Me and my sister Clara (Inkiow, Dimiter)

McHale, Ethel Kharasch. *Son of thunder: an old Lapp tale* ill. by Ruth Lercher Bornstein. Children's Pr., 1974. Subj: Folk and fairy tales. Foreign lands – Lapland.

McHargue, Georgess. *Private zoo* ill. by Michael Foreman. Viking, 1975. Subj: Imagination. Shadows.

Machetanz, Fred. *A puppy named Gia* (Machetanz, Sara)

Machetanz, Sara. *A puppy named Gia* by Sara and Fred Machetanz; ill. by Fred Machetanz. Scribner's, 1957. Subj: Animals – dogs. Ethnic groups in the U.S. – Eskimos.

McIlwraith, Maureen Mollie Hunter see Hunter, Mollie

McIntire, Alta. *Follett beginning to read picture dictionary* ill. by Janet La Salle. Follett, 1959. Subj: Dictionaries.

Mack, Stan see Mack, Stanley

Mack, Stanley. *Ten bears in my bed: a goodnight countdown* ill. by author. Pantheon, 1974. Subj: Animals – bears. Bedtime. Counting. Songs.

McKay, George. *Marny's ride with the wind* (McKay, Louise)

McKay, Louise. *Marny's ride with the wind* by Louise and George McKay; ill. by Margaret Smetana. New Harbinger, 1979. Subj: Friendship. Weather – wind.

McKee, David. *The day the tide went out and out and out* ill. by author. Abelard-Schuman, 1975. Subj: Animals – camels. Desert. Sea and seashore.

Elmer, the story of a patchwork elephant ill. by author. McGraw-Hill, 1968. Subj: Animals – elephants. Character traits – individuality.

King Rollo and the birthday ill. by author. Little, 1979. Subj: Birthdays. Royalty.

King Rollo and the bread ill. by author. Little, 1979. Subj: Food. Royalty.

King Rollo and the new shoes ill. by author. Little, 1979. Subj: Clothing. Royalty.

The man who was going to mind the house: a Norwegian folk-tale ill. by author. Abelard-Schuman, 1973. Subj: Folk and fairy tales.

123456789 Benn ill. by author. McGraw-Hill, 1970. Subj: Crime. Prisons. Problem solving.

Tusk tusk ill. by author. Barron's, 1979. Subj: Animals – elephants. Behavior – fighting, arguing.

Two can toucan ill. by author. Abelard-Schuman, 1964. Subj: Birds – toucans. Names.

McKee, Douglas. *Good night, Veronica* (Trez, Denise)

Maila and the flying carpet (Trez, Denise)

The royal hiccups (Trez, Denise)

McKeever, Katherine. *A family for Minerva* photos. by author. Greey De Pencier Books, 1981. Subj: Birds – owls. Science.

McKelvey, David. *Bobby the mostly silky* ill. by author. Corona, 1984. Subj: Birds – chickens. Character traits – being different.

McKié, Roy. *The riddle book* ill. by author. Random House, 1978. Subj: Humor. Riddles.

Snow by Roy McKié and P. D. Eastman; ill. by P. D. Eastman. Random House, 1962. Subj: Activities. Poetry, rhyme. Weather – snow.

McKissack, Patricia C. *Who is who?* ill. by Elizabeth M. Allen. Children's Pr., 1983. Subj: Twins.

MacLachlan, Patricia. *Mama one, Mama two* ill. by Ruth Lercher Bornstein. Harper, 1982. Subj: Family life – mothers. Illness.

Moon, stars, frogs and friends ill. by Tomie de Paola. Pantheon, 1980. Subj: Friendship. Frogs and toads. Witches.

The sick day ill. by William Pène Du Bois. Pantheon, 1979. Subj: Family life. Illness.

McLaughlin, Lissa. *Why won't winter go?* ill. by author. Lothrop, 1983. Subj: Behavior – boredom. Seasons – winter.

McLeish, Kenneth. *Chicken Licken* (Chicken Little)

McLenighan, Valjean. *One whole doughnut, one doughnut hole* ill. by Steven Roger Cole. Childrens Pr., 1982. Subj: Activities – reading.

Stop-go, fast-slow ill. by Margrit Fiddle. Children's Pr., 1982. Subj: Concepts – opposites.

Three strikes and you're out ill. by Laurie Hamilton. Follett, 1980. Subj: Behavior – greed. Magic.

Turtle and rabbit ill. by Vernon McKissack. Follett, 1980. Subj: Animals – rabbits. Folk and fairy tales. Reptiles – turtles. Sports – racing.

What you see is what you get ill. by Dev Appleyard. Four Winds Pr., 1980. Subj: Character traits – pride. Clothing. Folk and fairy tales. Humor. Imagination. Royalty.

You are what you are ill. by Jack Reilly. Follett, 1977. Subj: Folk and fairy tales. Frogs and toads. Royalty.

You can go jump ill. by Jared D. Lee. Follett, 1977. Subj: Elves and little people. Emotions – envy, jealousy. Folk and fairy tales. Magic. Witches.

McLeod, Emilie Warren. *The bear's bicycle* ill. by David McPhail. Little, 1975. Subj: Safety. Sports – bicycling. Toys – teddy bears.

One snail and me: a book of numbers and animals and a bathtub ill. by Walter Lorraine. Little, 1961. Subj: Activities – bathing. Animals. Counting. Imagination.

McMillan, Bruce. *The alphabet symphony: an ABC book* photos. by author. Greenwillow, 1977. Subj: ABC books. Music.

Here a chick, there a chick photos. by author. Lothrop, 1983. Subj: Concepts – opposites.

Kitten can... photos. by author. Lothrop, 1984. Subj: Animals – cats.

McNaught, Harry. *The truck book* ill. by author. Random House, 1978. Subj: Transportation. Trucks.

McNaughton, Colin. *At home* ill. by author. Putnam's, 1982. Subj: Concepts – opposites. Format, unusual – cardboard pages.

At playschool ill. by author. Putnam's, 1982. Subj: Concepts – opposites. Format, unusual – cardboard pages. School.

At the park ill. by author. Putnam's, 1982. Subj: Concepts – opposites. Format, unusual – cardboard pages.

At the party ill. by author. Putnam's, 1982. Subj: Concepts – opposites. Format, unusual – cardboard pages. Parties.

At the stores ill. by author. Putnam's, 1982. Subj: Concepts – opposites. Format, unusual – cardboard pages. Stores.

Autumn ill. by author. Dutton, 1983. Subj: Activities. Format, unusual – cardboard pages. Seasons – fall.

The rat race: the amazing adventures of Anton B. Stanton ill. by author. Doubleday, 1978. Subj: Animals – rats. Royalty. Sports – racing.

Spring ill. by author. Dial Pr., 1984. Subj: Format, unusual – cardboard pages. Seasons – spring.

Summer ill. by author. Dial Pr., 1984. Subj: Format, unusual – cardboard pages. Seasons – summer.

Walk rabbit walk by Colin McNaughton and Elizabeth Attenborough; ill. by Colin McNaughton. Viking, 1977. Subj: Activities – walking. Animals – rabbits.

Winter ill. by author. Dutton, 1983. Subj: Activities. Format, unusual – cardboard pages. Seasons – winter.

McNeely, Jeannette. *Where's Izzy?* ill. by Bill Morrison. Follett, 1972. Subj: Behavior – losing things. Pets. Reptiles – lizards.

McNeer, May Yonge. *Little Baptiste* ill. by Lynd Ward. Houghton, 1954. Subj: Animals. Farms.

My friend Mac: the story of Little Baptiste and the moose ill. by Lynd Ward. Houghton, 1960. Subj: Animals – moose. Emotions – loneliness.

McNeill, Janet. *The giant's birthday* ill. by Walter Erhard. Walck, 1964. Subj: Birthdays. Giants.

McNulty, Faith. *The elephant who couldn't forget* ill. by Marc Simont. Harper, 1980. Subj: Animals – elephants. Behavior – forgetfulness.

How to dig a hole to the other side of the world ill. by Marc Simont. Harper, 1979. Subj: Earth. Imagination. Science.

Hurricane ill. by Gail Owens. Harper, 1983. Subj: Science. Weather – storms.

Mouse and Tim ill. by Marc Simont. Harper, 1978. Subj: Animals – mice. Character traits – kindness to animals. Pets.

When a boy wakes up in the morning ill. by Leonard Weisgard. Knopf, 1962. Subj: Activities – playing. Morning. Noise, sounds.

Woodchuck ill. by Joan Sandin. Harper, 1974. Subj: Animals – groundhogs. Science.

McPhail, David. *Alligators are awful (and they have terrible manners, too)* ill. by author. Doubleday, 1980. Subj: Humor. Reptiles – alligators, crocodiles.

Andrew's bath ill. by author. Little, 1984. Subj: Activities – bathing. Animals. Behavior – misbehavior.

The bear's toothache ill. by author. Little, 1972. Subj: Animals – bears. Character traits – kindness to animals. Illness. Teeth.

Captain Toad and the motorbike ill. by author. Atheneum, 1978. Subj: Frogs and toads. Motorcycles.

The cereal box ill. by author. Little, 1974. Subj: Family life. Humor. Imagination. Shopping.

Fix-it ill. by author. Dutton, 1984. Subj: Activities – reading. Television.

Great cat ill. by author. Dutton, 1982. Subj: Animals – cats. Behavior – needing someone. Islands.

Henry Bear's park ill. by author. Little, 1976. Subj: Animals – bears.

The magical drawings of Moony B. Finch ill. by author. Doubleday, 1978. Subj: Art. Magic.

Mistletoe ill. by author. Dutton, 1978. Subj: Dreams. Holidays – Christmas. Imagination. Toys.

Pig Pig goes to camp ill. by author. Dutton, 1983. Subj: Animals – pigs. Sports – camping.

Pig Pig grows up ill. by author. Dutton, 1980. Subj: Animals – pigs. Behavior – growing up.

Pig Pig rides ill. by author. Dutton, 1982. Subj: Activities – playing. Animals – pigs. Imagination.

Sisters ill. by author. Harcourt, 1984. Subj: Emotions – love. Sibling rivalry.

Snow lion ill. by author. Parents, 1983. Subj: Weather – snow.

Stanley: Henry Bear's friend ill. by author. Little, 1979. Subj: Animals – bears. Animals – raccoons. Behavior – running away. Crime.

The train ill. by author. Little, 1977. Subj: Dreams. Imagination. Toys – trains. Trains.

A wolf story ill. by author. Scribner, 1981. Subj: Animals – wolves. Character traits – freedom. Character traits – kindness to animals.

McToots, Rudi. *The kid's book of games for cars, trains and planes* ill. by author. Bantam, 1980. Subj: Activities – traveling. Games.

Madden, Don. *Lemonade serenade or the thing in the garden* ill. by author. Albert Whitman, 1966. Subj: Elves and little people. Noise, sounds.

Maestro, Betsy. *Around the clock with Harriet: a book about telling time* ill. by Giulio Maestro. Crown, 1984. Subj: Animals – elephants. Clocks. Time.

Big city port by Betsy Maestro and Ellen Del Vecchio; ill. by Giulio Maestro. Four Winds Pr., 1983. Subj: Boats, ships. City.

Busy day: a book of action words by Betsy and Giulio Maestro; ill. by Giulio Maestro. Crown, 1978. Subj: Activities. Circus.

Fat polka-dot cat and other haiku ill. by Giulio Maestro. Dutton, 1976. Subj: Poetry, rhyme.

The guessing game ill. by Giulio Maestro. Grosset, 1983. Subj: Animals – pigs. Problem solving.

Harriet at home ill. by Giulio Maestro. Crown, 1984. Subj: Animals – elephants. Format, unusual – cardboard pages. Houses.

Harriet at play ill. by Giulio Maestro. Crown, 1984. Subj: Activities – playing. Animals – elephants. Format, unusual – cardboard pages.

Harriet at school ill. by Giulio Maestro. Crown, 1984. Subj: Animals – elephants. Format, unusual – cardboard pages. School.

Harriet at work ill. by Giulio Maestro. Crown, 1984. Subj: Activities – working. Animals – elephants. Format, unusual – cardboard pages.

Harriet goes to the circus by Betsy and Giulio Maestro; ill. by Giulio Maestro. Crown, 1977. Subj: Animals – Elephants. Circus. Counting.

Harriet reads signs and more signs ill. by Giulio Maestro. Crown, 1981. Subj: Activities – reading. Animals – elephants.

On the go: a book of adjectives by Betsy and Giulio Maestro; ill. by authors. Crown, 1979. Subj: Animals – elephants. Language.

On the town: a book of clothing words by Betsy and Giulio Maestro; ill. by authors. Crown, 1983. Subj: Animals – elephants. Character traits – appearance. Clothing.

Traffic: a book of opposites ill. by Giulio Maestro. Crown, 1981. Subj: Automobiles. Concepts – opposites.

Where is my friend? ill. by Giulio Maestro. Crown, 1976. Subj: Animals – elephants. Concepts.

Maestro, Giulio. *Busy day* (Maestro, Betsy)

Halloween howls: riddles that are a scream ill. by author. Dutton, 1983. Subj: Holidays – Halloween. Riddles.

Harriet goes to the circus (Maestro, Betsy)

Just enough Rosie ill. by author. Grosset, 1983. Subj: Animals – rhinoceros. Humor.

Leopard is sick ill. by author. Greenwillow, 1978. Subj: Animals. Animals – leopards. Friendship. Illness.

On the go (Maestro, Betsy)

On the town (Maestro, Betsy)

One more and one less ill. by author. Crown, 1974. Subj: Animals. Counting.

A raft of riddles ill. by author. Dutton, 1982. Subj: Humor. Riddles.

The remarkable plant in apartment 4 ill. by author. Bradbury Pr., 1973. Subj: City. Humor. Plants.

Riddle romp ill. by author. Houghton, 1983. Subj: Riddles.

The tortoise's tug of war ill. by author. Bradbury Pr., 1971. Subj: Animals – tapirs. Animals – whales. Folk and fairy tales. Foreign lands – South America. Games. Reptiles – turtles.

Magnus, Erica. *Old Lars* ill. by author. Carolrhoda, 1984. Subj: Folk and fairy tales. Foreign lands – Norway.

Mahiri, Jabari. *The day they stole the letter J* ill. by Dorothy Carter. Third World Pr., 1981. Subj: Behavior – misbehavior. Careers – barbers. Magic.

Mählqvist, Stefan. *I'll take care of the crocodiles* ill. by Tord Nygren. Atheneum, 1979. Subj: Bedtime. Dreams.

Mahony, Elizabeth Winthrop *see* Winthrop, Elizabeth

Mahood, Kenneth. *The laughing dragon* ill. by author. Scribner's, 1970. Subj: Dragons. Fire. Humor. Royalty.

Why are there more questions than answers, Grandad? ill. by author. Bradbury Pr., 1974. Subj: Character traits – questioning. Family life – grandparents, great-grandparents.

Mahy, Margaret. *The boy who was followed home* ill. by Steven Kellogg. Watts, 1975. Subj: Animals – hippopotami. Humor. Witches.

The boy with two shadows ill. by Jenny Williams. Watts, 1971. Subj: Character traits – meanness. Shadows. Witches.

The dragon of an ordinary family ill. by Helen Oxenbury. Watts, 1969. Subj: Dragons.

A lion in the meadow ill. by Jenny Williams. Watts, 1969. Subj: Animals – lions. Dragons.

Mrs. Discombobulous ill. by Jan Brychta. Watts, 1969. Subj: Behavior – nagging. Family life. Gypsies.

Pillycock's shop ill. by Carol Baker. Watts, 1969. Subj: Fairies. Values.

Rooms for rent ill. by Jenny Williams. Watts, 1974. Subj: Behavior – greed. Hotels.

Sailor Jack and the twenty orphans ill. by Robert Bartelt. Watts, 1970. Subj: Boats, ships. Careers – military. Orphans. Pirates. Sea and seashore.

Maiorano, Robert. *Backstage* ill. by Rachel Isadora. Greenwillow, 1978. Subj: Theater.

Francisco ill. by Rachel Isadora. Macmillan, 1978. Subj: Foreign lands – South America. Poverty. Problem solving.

A little interlude ill. by Rachel Isadora. Coward, 1980. Subj: Activities – dancing. Behavior – sharing. Music.

Maitland, Antony. *Idle Jack* ill. by author. Farrar, 1979. Subj: Character traits – foolishness. Folk and fairy tales.

Makower, Sylvia. *Samson's breakfast* ill. by author. Watts, 1961. Subj: Animals – lions.

Malcolmson, Anne. *The song of Robin Hood* ill. by Virginia Lee Burton. Houghton, 1947. Subj: Caldecott award honor book. Folk and fairy tales.

Malecki, Maryann. *Mom and dad and I are having a baby!* ill. by author. Pennypress, 1982. Subj: Babies. Family life.

Maley, Anne. *Have you seen my mother?* ill. by Yutaka Sugita. Subj: Circus. Family life – mothers. Toys – balls.

Mallett, Anne. *Here comes Tagalong* ill. by Steven Kellogg. Parents, 1971. Subj: Family life. Friendship. Sibling rivalry.

Malnig, Anita. *The big strawberry book of questions and answers and facts and things* ill. by Sal Murdocca. Larousse, 1977. Subj: Mythical creatures. Science.

Mandry, Kathy. *The cat and the mouse and the mouse and the cat* ill. by Joe Toto. Pantheon, 1972. Subj: Animals – cats. Animals – mice. Friendship.

Manes, Esther. *The bananas move to the ceiling* by Esther and Stephen Manes; ill. by Barbara Samuels. Watts, 1983. Subj: Family life. Humor.

Manes, Stephen. *The bananas move to the ceiling* (Manes, Esther)

Mangin, Marie-France. *Suzette and Nicholas and the seasons clock* tr. from French by Joan Chevalier; ill. by Satomi Ichikawa. Putnam's, 1982. Subj: Activities. Seasons.

Manheim, Ralph. *The nutcracker* (Hoffmann, E T A)

Mann, Peggy. *King Laurence, the alarm clock* ill. by Ray Cruz. Doubleday, 1976. Subj: Animals. Animals – lions. Illness. Morning.

Manson, Beverlie. *The fairies' alphabet book* ill. by author. Doubleday, 1982. Subj: ABC books. Fairies.

Manushkin, Fran. *Baby, come out!* ill. by Ronald Himler. Harper, 1972. Orig. entitled Baby. Subj: Babies.

Bubblebath! ill. by Ronald Himler. Harper, 1974. Subj: Activities – bathing. Family life.

Hocus and Pocus at the circus ill. by Geoffrey Hayes. Harper, 1983. Subj: Character traits – meanness. Holidays – Halloween. Witches.

Moon dragon ill. by Geoffrey Hayes. Macmillan, 1982. Subj: Animals – mice. Dragons. Food. Moon.

The perfect Christmas picture ill. by Karen Ann Weinhaus. Harper, 1980. Subj: Activities – photographing. Family life. Holidays – Christmas.

Marceau, Marcel. *The Marcel Marceau counting book* (Mendoza, George)

The story of Bip ill. by author. Harper, 1976. Subj: Clowns, jesters. Imagination.

Marcin, Marietta. *A zoo in her bed* ill. by Sofia. Coward, 1963. Subj: Bedtime. Poetry, rhyme. Toys.

Marcus, Susan. *Casey visits the doctor* ill. by Deborah Drew-Brook. CBC Merchandising, 1982. Subj: Careers – doctors. Health.

The missing button adventure ill. by Hajime Sawada. CBC Merchandising, 1981 Subj: Character traits – helpfulness. Toys – teddy bears.

Mare, Walter De La *see* De La Mare, Walter

Margalit, Avishai. *The Hebrew alphabet book: Me-Alef 'ad Tav* ill. by author. Funk and Wagnalls, 1968. Subj: ABC books. Jewish culture.

Margolis, Richard J. *Big bear, spare that tree* ill. by Jack Kent. Greenwillow, 1980. Subj: Animals – bears. Birds – bluejays. Ecology. Trees.

Secrets of a small brother ill. by Donald Carrick. Macmillan, 1984. Subj: Poetry, rhyme. Sibling rivalry.

Mari, Iela. *Eat and be eaten* ill. by author. Barron's 1980. Subj: Animals. Format, unusual. Sports – hunting. Wordless.

The magic balloon ill. by author. S. G. Phillips, 1970. Subj: Toys – balloons. Wordless.

Mariana. *Doki, the lonely papoose* ill. by author. Lothrop, 1955. Subj: Ethnic groups in the U.S. – Indians.

The journey of Bangwell Putt ill. by author. Lothrop, 1965. Subj: Holidays – Christmas. Toys – dolls.

Marie. *Nursery rhymes* (Mother Goose)

Marie, Geraldine. *The magic box* ill. by Michele Chessare. Elsevier-Nelson, 1981. Subj: Animals – dogs. Birthdays. Magic. Problem solving.

Maril, Lee. *Mr. Bunny paints the eggs* ill. by Irena Lorentowicz. Roy Pub., 1945. Subj: Animals – rabbits. Concepts – color. Holidays – Easter. Music. Songs.

Marino, Barbara Pavis. *Eric needs stitches* photos. by Richard Rudinski. Addison-Wesley, 1979. Subj: Hospitals.

Marino, Dorothy. *Buzzy Bear and the rainbow* ill. by author. Watts, 1962. Subj: Animals – bears. Weather – rainbows.

Buzzy Bear goes camping ill. by author. Watts, 1964. Subj: Animals – bears. Sports – camping.

Buzzy Bear in the garden ill. by author. Watts, 1963, 1961. Subj: Activities – gardening. Animals – bears.

Buzzy Bear's busy day ill. by author. Watts, 1965. Subj: Animals – bears.

Edward and the boxes ill. by author. Lippincott, 1957. Subj: Activities – playing. Sleep.

Good-bye thunderstorm ill. by author. Lippincott, 1958. Subj: Weather – rain. Weather – storms.

Maris, Ron. *Better move on, frog!* ill. by author. Watts, 1982. Subj: Frogs and toads. Houses.

My book ill. by author. Watts, 1983. Subj: Animals – cats. Bedtime.

Marks, Burton. *Puppet plays and puppet-making: the plays - the puppets - the production* by Burton and Rita Marks; ill. with photos. Plays, 1982. Subj: Puppets. Theater.

The spook book by Burton and Rita Marks; ill. by Lisa Campbell Ernst. Lothrop, 1981. Subj: Holidays – Halloween. Parties.

Marks, Marcia Bliss. *Swing me, swing tree* ill. by David Berger. Little, 1959. Subj: Activities – swinging. Poetry, rhyme.

Marks, Rita. *Puppet plays and puppet-making* (Marks, Burton)

The spook book (Marks, Burton)

Marokvia, Merelle. *A French school for Paul* ill. by Artur Marokvia. Lippincott, 1963. Subj: Circus. Foreign lands – France. School.

Marol, Jean-Claude. *Vagabul and his shadow* ill. by author. Creative Education, 1983. Subj: Shadows. Wordless.

Vagabul escapes ill. by author. Creative Education, 1983. Subj: Behavior – running away. Wordless.

Vagabul goes skiing ill. by author. Creative Education, 1983. Subj: Sports – skiing. Wordless.

Vagabul in the clouds ill. by author. Creative Education, 1983. Subj: Weather – clouds. Wordless.

Marsh, Jeri. *Hurrah for Alexander* ill. by Joan Hanson. Carolrhoda Books, 1977. Subj: Humor.

Marshak, Samuel. *In the van* tr. from Russian by Margaret Wettlin; ill. by V. Lebedev. Imported Pub., 1983. Subj: Animals – dogs. Moving. Poetry, rhyme.

The merry starlings by Samuel Marshak with D. Harms; tr. from Russian by Dorian Rottenberg; ill. by Arieh Zeldich. Harper, 1983. Subj: Birds. Nursery rhymes. Poetry, rhyme.

The Month-Brothers: a Slavic tale tr. from Russian by Thomas P. Whitney; ill. by Diane Stanley. Morrow, 1983. Subj: Foreign lands – Czechoslovakia. Poetry, rhyme. Seasons. Weather.

The tale of a hero nobody knows tr. from Russian by Peter Tempest; ill. by Vassili Shulzhenko. Imported Pub., 1983. Subj: Character traits – bravery. Foreign lands – Russia. Poetry, rhyme.

Marshall, Douglas *see* McClintock, Marshall

Marshall, Edward. *Four on the shore* ill. by James Marshall. Dial Pr., 1985. Subj: Monsters. Sibling rivalry.

Fox and his friends ill. by James Marshall. Dial Pr., 1982. Subj: Animals – foxes. Behavior – misbehavior.

Fox at school ill. by James Marshall. Dial Pr., 1983. Subj: Animals – foxes. Humor. School.

Fox in love ill. by James Marshall. Dial Pr., 1982. Subj: Animals – foxes. Emotions – love.

Fox on wheels ill. by James Marshall. Dial Pr., 1983. Subj: Animals – foxes. Behavior – misbehavior. Sports – racing.

Space case ill. by James Marshall. Dial Pr., 1980. Subj: Holidays – Halloween. Robots. Space and space ships.

Three by the sea ill. by James Marshall. Dial Pr., 1981. Subj: Activities – picnicking. Friendship.

Troll country ill. by James Marshall. Dial Pr., 1980. Subj: Forest, woods. Trolls.

Marshall, Frances. *Princess Kalina and the hedgehog* (Flot, Jeannette B)

Marshall, James. *The cut-ups* ill. by author. Viking, 1984. Subj: Behavior – misbehavior. Toys.

Four little troubles ill. by author. Houghton, 1975. Subj: Animals. Problem solving.

George and Martha ill. by author. Houghton, 1972. Subj: Animals – hippopotami. Friendship.

George and Martha back in town ill. by author. Houghton, 1984. Subj: Animals – hippopotami. Behavior – misbehavior. Friendship.

George and Martha encore ill. by author. Houghton, 1973. Subj: Activities – dancing. Animals – hippopotami. Friendship.

George and Martha one fine day ill. by author. Houghton, 1978. Subj: Animals – hippopotami. Friendship.

George and Martha rise and shine ill. by author. Houghton, 1976. Subj: Animals – hippopotami. Friendship.

George and Martha, tons of fun ill. by author. Houghton, 1980. Subj: Animals – hippopotami. Character traits – vanity.

The guest ill. by author. Houghton, 1975. Subj: Animals – moose. Animals – snails. Friendship.

Miss Dog's Christmas ill. by author. Houghton, 1973. Subj: Animals – dogs. Food. Holidays – Christmas.

Miss Nelson is back (Allard, Harry)

Miss Nelson is missing! (Allard, Harry)

Portly McSwine ill. by author. Houghton, 1979. Subj: Animals – pigs. Behavior – worrying.

Speedboat ill. by author. Houghton, 1976. Subj: Animals – dogs. Boats, ships. Friendship.

The Stupids have a ball (Allard, Harry)

What's the matter with Carruthers? ill. by author. Houghton, 1972. Subj: Animals – bears. Bedtime. Character traits – helpfulness. Friendship. Hibernation.

Willis ill. by author. Houghton, 1974. Subj: Animals. Friendship.

Yummers! ill. by author. Houghton, 1973. Subj: Animals – pigs. Food. Illness.

Marshall, Lyn. *Yoga for your children* ill. with photos. Schocken, 1979. Subj: Health. Religion.

Marshall, Margaret. *Mike* ill. by Lorraine Spiro. Merrimack, 1983. Subj: Bedtime. Problem solving.

Marshall, Ray. *Pop-up numbers #1* by Ray Marshall and Korky Paul; ill. by authors. Dutton, 1984. Subj: Counting. Format, unusual.

Pop-up numbers #2 by Ray Marshall and Korky Paul; ill. by authors. Dutton, 1984. Subj: Counting. Format, unusual.

Pop-up numbers #3 by Ray Marshall and Korky Paul; ill. by authors. Dutton, 1984. Subj: Counting. Format, unusual.

Pop-up numbers #4 by Ray Marshall and Korky Paul; ill. by authors. Dutton, 1984. Subj: Counting. Format, unusual.

Marston, Hope Irvin. *Big rigs* ill. with photos. Dodd, 1979. Subj: Transportation. Trucks.

Fire trucks ill. with photos. Dodd, 1984. Subj: Careers – firefighters. Trucks.

Martel, Cruz. *Yagua days* ill. by Jerry Pinkney. Dial Pr., 1976. Subj: Family life. Foreign lands – Puerto Rico.

Martin, Bernard H. *Brave little Indian* (Martin, Bill (William Ivan))

Smoky Poky (Martin, Bill (William Ivan))

Martin, Bill (William Ivan). *Brave little Indian* by Bill Martin, Jr. and Bernard H. Martin; ill. by Bernard H. Martin. Tell-Well Pr., 1951. Subj: Ethnic groups in the U.S. – Indians. Participation.

Brown bear, brown bear, what do you see? ill. by Eric Carle. Holt, 1983. Subj: Animals – bears. Cumulative tales. Poetry, rhyme.

My days are made of butterflies adapted by William Ivan Martin, Jr.; written by Sano M. Galea'i Fa'apouli; ill. by Vic Herman. Holt, 1970. Subj: Foreign lands – Mexico.

Smoky Poky by Bill Martin, Jr. and Bernard H. Martin; ill. by Bernard H. Martin. Tell-Well Pr., 1947. Subj: Animals – elephants. Trains.

Sounds around the clock comp. by Bill Martin, Jr. in collaboration with Peggy Brogan. Holt, 1966. Subj: Noise, sounds. Poetry, rhyme.

Sounds I remember comp. by Bill Martin, Jr. in collaboration with Peggy Brogan. Holt, 1974. Subj: Counting. Noise, sounds. Nursery rhymes.

Sounds of home comp. by Bill Martin, Jr. in collaboration with Peggy Brogan. Holt, 1972. Subj: Noise, sounds. Poetry, rhyme.

Sounds of laughter comp. by Bill Martin, Jr. in collaboration with Peggy Brogan. Holt, 1972. Subj: Folk and fairy tales. Humor. Noise, sounds. Poetry, rhyme.

Sounds of numbers comp. by Bill Martin, Jr. in collaboration with Peggy Brogan. Holt, 1972. Subj: Counting. Noise, sounds. Poetry, rhyme.

Martin, Charles E. *Dunkel takes a walk* ill. by author. Greenwillow, 1983. Subj: Animals – dogs. Character traits – cleverness.

Island winter ill. by author. Greenwillow, 1984. Subj: Islands. Seasons – winter.

Noah's ark retold by Lawrence T. Lorimer; ill. by Charles E. Martin. Random House, 1978. Subj: Religion – Noah.

Martin, Diane. *Mister Mole* (Murschetz, Luis)

Martin, Frederic *see* Christopher, Matt

Martin, Jacqueline Briggs. *Bizzy Bones and Uncle Ezra* ill. by Stella Ormai. Lothrop, 1984. Subj: Animals – mice. Emotions – fear.

Martin, Janet *see* Allen, Robert

Martin, Judith. *The tree angel* by Judith Martin and Remy Charlip; ill. by Remy Charlip. Knopf, 1962. Subj: Angels. Holidays – Christmas. Theater.

Martin, Patricia Miles *see* Miles, Miska

Martin, Rafe. *The hungry tigress: and other traditional Asian tales* ill. by Richard Wehrman. Shambhala, 1984. Subj: Folk and fairy tales.

Martin, Sarah Catherine. *The comic adventures of Old Mother Hubbard and her dog* ill. by Arnold Lobel. Bradbury Pr., 1968. Subj: Animals – dogs. Nursery rhymes.

Old Mother Hubbard and her dog ill. by Paul Galdone. McGraw-Hill, 1960. Subj: Animals – dogs. Nursery rhymes.

Old Mother Hubbard and her dog ill. by Evaline Ness. Holt, 1972. Subj: Animals – dogs. Nursery rhymes.

Martini, Teri. *Cowboys* ill. with photos. Rev. ed. Children's Pr., 1981. Subj: Activities – working. Cowboys.

Marzollo, Claudio. *Jed's junior space patrol* (Marzollo, Jean)

Marzollo, Jean. *Amy goes fishing* ill. by Ann Schweninger. Dial Pr., 1980. Subj: Family life – fathers. Sports – fishing

Close your eyes ill. by Susan Jeffers. Dial Pr., 1978. Subj: Bedtime. Family life – fathers. Poetry, rhyme.

Jed's junior space patrol by Jean and Claudio Marzollo; ill. by David S. Rose. Dial Pr., 1982. Subj: Robots. Space and space ships. Toys – teddy bears.

Uproar on Hollercat Hill ill. by Steven Kellogg. Dial Pr., 1980. Subj: Animals – cats. Behavior – misbehavior. Poetry, rhyme.

Maschler, Fay. *T. G. and Moonie go shopping* ill. by Sylvie Selig. Doubleday, 1978. Subj: Animals – cats. Birds – owls. Shopping. Stores

T. G. and Moonie have a baby ill. by Sylvie Selig. Doubleday, 1979. Subj: Animals – cats. Birds – owls. Family life.

T. G. and Moonie move out of town ill. by Sylvia Selig. Doubleday, 1978. Subj: Animals – cats. Birds – owls. Moving.

Masks and puppets ill. by Louise Nevett. Watts, 1984. Subj: Activities. Puppets.

Massey, Jeanne. *The littlest witch* ill. by Adrienne Adams. Knopf, 1959. Subj: Holidays – Halloween. Witches.

Massie, Diane Redfield. *The baby beebee bird* ill. by author. Harper, 1963. Subj: Animals. Birds. Noise, sounds. Sleep.

Chameleon the spy and the terrible toaster trap ill. by author. Crowell, 1982. Subj: Crime. Reptiles – lizards.

Cockle stew and other rhymes ill. by author. Atheneum, 1967. Subj: Poetry, rhyme.

The Komodo dragon's jewels ill. by author. Macmillan, 1975. Subj: Boats, ships. Dragons. Reptiles – lizards.

Tiny pin ill. by author. Harper, 1964. Subj: Animals – porcupines. Behavior – growing up. Poetry, rhyme.

Walter was a frog ill. by author. Simon and Schuster, 1970. Subj: Behavior – dissatisfaction. Frogs and toads.

Mathews, Louise. *Bunches and bunches of bunnies* ill. by Jeni Bassett. Dodd, 1978. Subj: Animals – rabbits. Counting. Poetry, rhyme.

Cluck one ill. by Jeni Bassett. Dodd, 1982. Subj: Animals – weasels. Birds – chickens. Counting. Eggs.

The great take-away ill. by Jeni Bassett. Dodd, 1980. Subj: Animals – pigs. Character traits – laziness. Counting. Crime.

Mathiesen, Egon. *Oswald, the monkey* adapt. from Danish by Nancy and Edward Maze; ill. by author. Astor-Honor, 1959. Subj: Animals – monkeys.

Matias. *Mr. Noah and the animals: Monsieur Noe et les animaux* ill. by author. Walck, 1960. Subj: Religion – Noah.

Matsuno, Masako. *A pair of red clogs* ill. by Kazue Mizumura. Collins, 1960. Subj: Character traits – honesty. Clothing. Foreign lands – Japan.

Taro and the bamboo shoot: a Japanese tale ill. by Yasuo Segawa. Pantheon, 1964. Adapted from the Japanese by Alice Low. Subj: Folk and fairy tales. Foreign lands – Japan.

Taro and the Tofu ill. by Kazue Mizumura. Collins-World, 1962. Subj: Character traits – honesty. Foreign lands – Japan.

Matsutani, Miyoko. *The fisherman under the sea* English version by Alvin Tresselt; ill. by Chihiro Iwasaki. Parents, 1969. Translation of Urashima Tarō. Subj: Careers – fishermen. Folk and fairy tales. Foreign lands – Japan. Reptiles – turtles. Royalty. Sea and seashore.

How the withered trees blossomed ill. by Yasuo Segawa. Lippincott, 1969. Subj: Behavior – greed. Foreign lands – Japan. Foreign languages.

The witch's magic cloth English version by Alvin Tresselt; ill. by Yasuo Segawa. Parents, 1969. Subj: Character traits – bravery. Folk and fairy tales. Foreign lands – Japan. Witches.

Matthias, Catherine. *I love cats* ill. by Tom Dunnington. Children's Pr., 1983. Subj: Animals – cats.

Out the door ill. by Eileen Mueller Neill. Children's Pr., 1982. Subj: Buses. School.

Over-under ill. by Gene Sharp. Children's Pr., 1984. Subj: Concepts – opposites.

Matus, Greta. *Where are you, Jason?* ill. by author. Lothrop, 1974. Subj: Behavior – hiding. Imagination. Night.

Maury, Inez. *My mother the mail carrier: Mi mama la cartera* tr. by Norah E. Alemany; ill. by Tasha Tudor. Feminist Pr., 1976. Subj: Careers – mail carriers. Foreign languages.

May, Charles Paul. *High-noon rocket* ill. by Brinton Turkle. Holiday, 1966. Subj: Activities – traveling. Science. Space and space ships. Time.

May, Julian. *Why people are different colors* ill. by Symeon Shimin. Holiday, 1971. Subj: Ethnic groups in the U.S.

May, Robert Lewis. *Rudolph the red-nosed reindeer* ill. by Diana Magnuson. Four Winds Pr., 1980. Subj: Animals – reindeer. Elves and little people. Holidays – Christmas. Weather – fog.

Mayer, Marianna. *Alley oop!* ill. by Gerald McDermott. Holt, 1985. Subj: Animals – mice. Counting. Reptiles – alligators, crocodiles.

Beauty and the beast ill. by Mercer Mayer. Four Winds Pr., 1978. Subj: Animals. Character traits – appearance. Emotions – love. Folk and fairy tales.

Mine! (Mayer, Mercer)

My first book of nursery tales: five favorite bedtime tales ill. by William Joyce. Random House, 1983. Subj: Folk and fairy tales.

One frog too many (Mayer, Mercer)

The unicorn and the lake ill. by Michael Hague. Dial Pr., 1982. Subj: Character traits – bravery. Mythical creatures.

Mayer, Mercer. *Ah-choo* ill. by author. Dial Pr., 1976. Subj: Animals – elephants. Illness. Wordless.

Appelard and Liverwurst ill. by Steven Kellogg. Four Winds Pr., 1978. Subj: Animals. Behavior – misbehavior. Farms.

A boy, a dog, a frog and a friend ill. by author. Dial Pr., 1971. Subj: Friendship. Frogs and toads. Sports – fishing. Wordless.

A boy, a dog and a frog ill. by author. Dial Pr., 1967. Subj: Friendship. Frogs and toads. Sports – fishing. Wordless.

Bubble bubble ill. by author. Parents, 1973. Subj: Imagination. Wordless.

Frog goes to dinner ill. by author. Dial Pr., 1974. Subj: Food. Frogs and toads. Wordless.

Frog on his own ill. by author. Dial Pr., 1973. Subj: Frogs and toads. Wordless.

Frog, where are you? ill. by author. Dial Pr., 1969. Subj: Friendship. Frogs and toads. Wordless.

The great cat chase ill. by author. Four Winds Pr., 1974. Subj: Animals – cats. Wordless.

Hiccup ill. by author. Dial Pr., 1976. Subj: Animals – hippopotami. Illness. Wordless.

How the trollusk got his hat ill. by author. Golden Pr., 1979. Subj: Character traits – appearance. Character traits – honesty.

I am a hunter ill. by author. Dial Pr., 1969. Subj: Imagination.

Just for you ill. by author. Golden Pr., 1975. Subj: Character traits – helpfulness. Emotions – love. Family life – mothers.

Just me and my dad ill. by author. Golden Pr., 1977. Subj: Family life – fathers. Sports – camping.

Little Monster at home ill. by author. Golden Pr., 1978. Subj: Houses. Monsters.

Little Monster at school ill. by author. Golden Pr., 1978. Subj: Monsters. School.

Little Monster at work ill. by author. Golden Pr., 1978. Subj: Careers. Family life – grandparents, great-grandparents. Monsters.

Little Monster's alphabet book ill. by author. Golden Pr., 1978. Subj: ABC books. Monsters.

Little Monster's bedtime book ill. by author. Golden Pr., 1978. Subj: Bedtime. Monsters. Poetry, rhyme.

Little Monster's counting book ill. by author. Golden Pr., 1978. Subj: Counting. Monsters.

Little Monster's neighborhood ill. by author. Golden Pr., 1978. Subj: City. Monsters.

Liverwurst is missing ill. by Steven Kellogg. Four Winds Pr., 1981. Subj: Character traits – bravery. Circus. Crime.

Liza Lou and the Yeller Belly Swamp ill. by author. Parents, 1976. Subj: Character traits – bravery. Ethnic groups in the U.S. – Afro-Americans. Monsters.

Mine! by Mercer and Marianna Mayer; ill. by Mercer Mayer. Simon and Schuster, 1970. Subj: Concepts. Emotions.

Mrs. Beggs and the wizard ill. by author. Parents, 1973. Subj: Magic. Monsters. Wizards.

One frog too many by Mercer and Marianna Mayer; ill. by Mercer Mayer. Dial Pr., 1975. Subj: Emotions – envy, jealousy. Frogs and toads. Wordless.

Oops ill. by author. Dial Pr., 1977. Subj: Animals – hippopotami. Behavior – carelessness. Wordless.

The queen always wanted to dance ill. by author. Simon and Schuster, 1971. Subj: Activities – dancing. Humor. Music. Royalty.

Terrible troll ill. by author. Dial Pr., 1968. Subj: Imagination. Knights. Monsters. Mythical creatures. Trolls.

There's a nightmare in my closet ill. by author. Dial Pr., 1968. Subj: Bedtime. Emotions – fear. Monsters.

Two moral tales ill. by author. Four Winds Pr., 1974. Bear's new clothes.—Bird's new hat. Subj: Animals – bears. Birds. Clothing. Wordless.

What do you do with a kangaroo? ill. by author. Four Winds Pr., 1973. Subj: Animals. Humor. Problem solving.

You're the scaredy cat ill. by author. Parents, 1974. Subj: Emotions – fear. Night. Sports – camping.

Mayers, Patrick. *Just one more block* ill. by Lucy Hawkinson. Albert Whitman, 1970. Subj: Activities – playing. Emotions. Sibling rivalry. Toys – blocks.

Mayle, Peter. *Divorce can happen to the nicest people* ill. by Arthur Robins. Macmillan, 1980. Subj: Divorce. Family life.

Mayne, William. *The blue book of hob stories* ill. by Patrick Benson. Putnam's, 1984. Subj: Character traits – helpfulness. Elves and little people.

The patchwork cat ill. by Nicola Bayley. Knopf, 1981. Subj: Animals – cats. Behavior – saving things. Emotions – love.

Maze, Edward. *Oswald, the monkey* (Mathiesen, Egon)

Maze, Nancy. *Oswald, the monkey* (Mathiesen, Egon)

M'Bane, Phumla *see* Phumla

Meddaugh, Susan. *Maude and Claude go abroad* ill. by author. Houghton, 1980. Subj: Activities – traveling. Animals – foxes. Boats, ships. Foreign lands – France.

Too short Fred ill. by author. Houghton, 1978. Subj: Animals – cats. Character traits – smallness.

Mee, Charles L. *Noah* by Charles L. Mee, Jr.; ill. by Ken Munowitz. Harper, 1978. Subj: Religion – Noah.

Meeks, Esther K. *The curious cow* ill. by Mel Pekarsky. Follett, 1960. Also published in German as "Die neugierige Kuh"; in French as "La vache curieuse"; and in Spanish as "La Vaca curiosa." Subj: Animals – bulls, cows. Character traits – curiosity.

Friendly farm animals. Follett, 1965. Subj: Animals. Farms.

The hill that grew ill. by Lazlo Roth. Follett, 1959. Subj: Activities – playing.

One is the engine: a counting book ill. by Joe Rogers. Follett, 1947, 1972. Subj: Counting. Trains.

One is the engine ill. by Ernie King. Follett, 1956. Subj: Counting. Trains.

Playland pony ill. by Mary Miller Salem. Follett, 1951. Subj: Animals – horses.

Something new at the zoo ill. by Hazel Hoecker. Follett, 1957. Subj: Animals. Zoos.

Memling, Carl. *What's in the dark?* ill. by John E. Johnson. Parent's, 1971. Subj: Monsters. Night.

Mendoza, George. *The alphabet boat: a seagoing alphabet book* ill. by author. American Heritage, 1972. Subj: ABC books. Boats, ships.

Alphabet sheep ill. by Kathleen Reidy. Grosset, 1982. Subj: ABC books. Animals – sheep. Behavior – lost.

Henri Mouse ill. by Joelle Boucher. Viking, 1985. Subj: Animals – mice. Art.

The hunter I might have been photos. by De Wayne Dalrymple. Astor-Honor, 1968. Subj: Death. Emotions. Poetry, rhyme. Sports – hunting.

The Marcel Marceau counting book photos. by Milton H. Greene. Doubleday, 1971. Subj: Clowns, jesters.

Need a house? Call Ms. Mouse ill. by Doris Susan Smith. Grosset, 1981. Subj: Animals. Animals – mice. Houses.

Norman Rockwell's American ABC ill. by Norman Rockwell. Abrams, 1975. Subj: ABC books.

The scribbler ill. by Robert M. Quackenbush. Holt, 1971. Subj: Birds – sandpipers. Poetry, rhyme. Sea and seashore.

The Sesame Street book of opposites with Zero Mostel photos. by Sheldon Secunda; book design by Nicole Sekora-Mendoza. Platt, 1974. Subj: Concepts – opposites.

Silly sheep and other sheepish rhymes ill. by Kathleen Reidy. Grosset, 1982. Subj: Animals – sheep. Nursery rhymes.

What I want to be when I grow up (Burnett, Carol)

Menter, Ian. *The Albany Road mural* photos. by Will Guy. David and Charles, 1984. Subj: Activities – painting. Art.

Carnival photos. by Will Guy. David and Charles, 1983. Subj: Foreign lands – England. Holidays.

Meredith, Lucy. *The princess on the nut* (Nikly, Michelle)

Merriam, Eve. *Boys and girls, girls and boys* ill. by Harriet Sherman. Holt, 1972. Subj: Activities – playing. Ethnic groups in the U.S.

Christmas (Bruna, Dick)

Epaminondas ill. by Trina Schart Hyman. Follett, 1968. Originally published in 1938 as "Epaminondas and his Aunty" by Sara Cone Bryant. Subj: Ethnic groups in the U.S. – Afro-Americans. Folk and fairy tales.

Good night to Annie ill. by John Wallner. Four Winds Pr., 1980. Subj: ABC books. Bedtime.

Mommies at work ill. by Beni Montresor. Knopf, 1961. Subj: Activities – working. Careers. Family life – mothers.

Merrill, Jean. *Emily Emerson's moon* by Jean Merrill and Ronni Solbert; ill. by Ronni Solbert. Little, 1960. Subj: Family life. Moon.

How many kids are hiding on my block? by Jean Merrill and Frances Gruse Scott; ill. by Frances Gruse Scott. Albert Whitman, 1970. Subj: Counting. Ethnic groups in the U.S. Games.

Tell about the cowbarn, Daddy ill. by Lili Cassel-Wronker. Addison-Wesley, 1963. Subj: Animals – bulls, cows. Barns. Farms.

Merritt, Jane Hamilton *see* Hamilton-Merritt, Jane

Meshover, Leonard. *The guinea pigs that went to school* by Leonard Meshover and Sally Feistel; photos. by Eve Hoffmann. Follett, 1968. Subj: Animals – guinea pigs. School. Science.

The monkey that went to school by Leonard Meshover and Sally Feistel; photos. by Eve Hoffmann. Follett, 1978. Subj: Animals – monkeys. School. Science.

Meyer, Elizabeth C. *The blue china pitcher* ill. by author. Abingdon Pr., 1974. Subj: Holidays. Parties.

Meyer, June *see* Jordan, June

Meyer, Linda D. *Safety zone* ill. by Marina Megale. Chas. Franklin Pr., 1984. Subj: Behavior – talking to strangers. Safety.

Meyer, Louis A. *The clean air and peaceful contentment dirigible airline* ill. by author. Little, 1972. Subj: Ecology. Humor. Noise, sounds.

Meyers, Susan. *The truth about gorillas* ill. by John Hamberger. Dutton, 1980. Subj: Animals – gorillas. Science.

Michaels, Ruth. *The family that grew* (Rondell, Florence)

Michel, Anna. *Little wild lion cub* ill. by Tony Chen. Pantheon, 1981. Subj: Animals – lions.

Miklowitz, Gloria D. *Bearfoot boy* ill. by Jim Collins. Follett, 1964. Subj: Birthdays. Clothing.

Save that raccoon! ill. by St. Tamara. Harcourt, 1978. Subj: Animals – raccoons. Character traits – kindness to animals. Fire. Forest, woods.

The zoo that moved ill. by Don Madden. Follett, 1968. Subj: Animals. Zoos.

Miles, Betty. *Around and around... love* ill. with photos. Knopf, 1975. Subj: Emotions – love. Poetry, rhyme.

Having a friend ill. by Erik Blegvad. Knopf, 1958. Subj: Friendship.

A house for everyone ill. by Jo Lowery. Knopf, 1958. Subj: Houses.

Miles, Miska. *Apricot ABC* ill. by Peter Parnall. Little, 1969. Subj: ABC books. Poetry, rhyme. Trees.

Chicken forgets ill. by Jim Arnosky. Little, 1976. Subj: Behavior – forgetfulness. Birds – chickens. Humor.

The fox and the fire ill. by John Schoenherr. Little, 1966. Subj: Animals – foxes. Fire. Forest, woods.

Friend of Miguel ill. by Genia. Rand McNally, 1967. Subj: Animals – horses. Foreign lands – Mexico.

The horse and the bad morning (Clymer, Ted)

Jump frog jump ill. by Earl Thollander. Putnam's, 1965. Subj: Fairs. Frogs and toads.

Mouse six and the happy birthday ill. by Leslie Morrill. Dutton, 1978. Subj: Animals – mice. Birthdays. Family life – mothers.

No, no, Rosina ill. by Earl Thollander. Putnam's, 1964. Subj: Boats, ships. Careers – fishermen. Character traits – smallness. City. Sports – fishing.

Noisy gander ill. by Leslie Morrill. Dutton, 1978. Subj: Animals. Birds – ducks. Farms. Noise, sounds.

The pointed brush... ill. by Roger Antoine Duvoisin. Lothrop, 1959. Subj: Activities – writing. Foreign lands – China.

Rabbit garden ill. by John Schoenherr. Little, 1967. Subj: Animals – rabbits. Ecology.

The raccoon and Mrs. McGinnis ill. by Leonard Weisgard. Putnam's, 1961. Subj: Animals – raccoons. Barns. Crime.

The rice bowl pet ill. by Ezra Jack Keats. Crowell, 1962. Subj: Pets.

Rolling the cheese ill. by Alton Raible. Atheneum, 1966. Subj: City. Games.

Show and tell... ill. by Thomas Arthur Hamil. Putnam's, 1962. Subj: Animals – dogs. School.

Small rabbit ill. by Jim Arnosky. Little, 1977. Subj: Animals – rabbits.

Somebody's dog ill. by John Schoenherr. Little, 1973. Subj: Animals – dogs. Pets.

Sylvester Jones and the voice in the forest ill. by Leonard Weisgard. Lothrop, 1958. Subj: Animals. Forest, woods.

This little pig ill. by Leslie Morrill. Dutton, 1980. Subj: Animals – pigs. Behavior – lost. Behavior – running away. Farms.

Wharf rat ill. by John Schoenherr. Little, 1972. Subj: Animals – rats.

Milgram, Mary. *Brothers are all the same* ill. by Rosmarie Hauscherr. Dutton, 1978. Subj: Adoption. Family life. Sibling rivalry.

Milgrom, Harry. *Egg-ventures: first science experiments* ill. by Giulio Maestro. Dutton, 1974. Subj: Eggs. Science.

Paper science ill. by Dan Nevins. Walker, 1978. Subj: Paper. Science.

Milhous, Katherine. *The egg tree* ill. by author. Scribner's, 1950. Subj: Caldecott award book. Holidays – Easter.

Milius, Winifred *see* Lubell, Winifred

Miller, Albert *see* Mills, Alan

Miller, Alice P. *The little store on the corner* ill. by John Lawrence. Abelard-Schuman, 1961. Subj: Stores.

The mouse family's blueberry pie ill. by Carol Bloch. Elsevier-Nelson, 1981. Subj: Activities – cooking. Animals – mice.

Miller, Edna. *Jumping bean* ill. by author. Prentice-Hall, 1980. Subj: Science.

Mousekin finds a friend ill. by author. Prentice-Hall, 1967. Subj: Animals – mice. Friendship.

Mousekin's ABC ill. by author. Prentice-Hall, 1972. Subj: ABC books. Animals – mice. Forest, woods. Poetry, rhyme.

Mousekin's Christmas eve ill. by author. Prentice-Hall, 1965. Subj: Animals – mice. Holidays – Christmas.

Mousekin's close call ill. by author. Prentice-Hall, 1978. Subj: Animals – mice. Forest, woods.

Mousekin's fables ill. by author. Prentice-Hall, 1982. Subj: Animals – mice. Folk and fairy tales. Seasons.

Mousekin's family ill. by author. Prentice-Hall, 1969. Subj: Animals – mice. Family life.

Mousekin's golden house ill. by author. Prentice-Hall, 1964. Subj: Animals – mice. Hibernation. Holidays – Halloween. Seasons – winter.

Mousekin's mystery ill. by author. Prentice-Hall, 1983. Subj: Animals – mice. Problem solving.

Pebbles, a pack rat ill. by author. Prentice-Hall, 1976. Subj: Animals – pack rats. Scarecrows.

Miller, J. P. (John Parr). *Do you know color?* by J. P. Miller and Katherine Howard; ill. by J. P. Miller. Random House, 1979. Subj: Concepts – color.

Learn about colors with Little Rabbit ill. by author. Random House, 1984. Subj: Concepts – color.

Miller, Jane. *Birth of a foal* ill. by author. Lippincott, 1977. Subj: Animals – horses.

Farm alphabet book photos. by author. Prentice-Hall, 1984. Subj: ABC books. Farms.

Farm counting book photos. by author. Prentice-Hall, 1983. Subj: Counting. Farms.

Lambing time photos. by author. Methuen, 1978. Subj: Animals – sheep.

Miller, Judith Ransom. *Nabob and the geranium* ill. by Marilyn Neuhart. Golden Gate, 1967. Subj: Plants. Science.

Miller, Susanne Santoro. *Prehistoric mammals* ill. by Christopher Santoro. Messner, 1984. Subj: Animals. Science.

Miller, Warren. *The goings on at Little Wishful* ill. by Edward Sorel. Little, 1959. Subj: Behavior – boasting. Emotions – envy, jealousy.

Pablo paints a picture ill. by Edward Sorel. Little, 1959. Subj: Activities – painting. Careers – artists.

Mills, Alan. *The hungry goat* ill. by Abner Graboff. Rand McNally, 1964. Subj: Animals – goats. Humor. Music. Songs.

Milne, A. A. (Alan Alexander). *Pooh's alphabet book* ill. by E. H. Shepard. Dutton, 1976. Subj: ABC books. Toys – teddy bears.

Pooh's bedtime book ill. by E. H. Shepard; colored by Gail Owens. Dutton, 1980. Subj: Bedtime. Toys – teddy bears.

Pooh's counting book ill. by E. H. Shepard. Dutton, 1982. Subj: Counting. Toys – teddy bears.

Pooh's quiz book ill. by E. H. Shepard. Dutton, 1977. Subj: Games. Humor. Toys – teddy bears.

Prince Rabbit: and, The princess who could not laugh ill. by Mary Shepard. Dutton, 1967. Subj: Animals – rabbits. Folk and fairy tales. Royalty.

Winnie-the-Pooh: a pop-up book ill. by Chuck Murphy; engineering by Keith Moseley. Dutton, 1984. Subj: Character traits – bravery. Format, unusual. Toys – teddy bears.

Milord, Jerry. *Maggie and the goodbye gift* (Milord, Sue)

Milord, Sue. *Maggie and the goodbye gift* by Sue and Jerry Milord; ill. by authors. Lothrop, 1979. Subj: Family life. Moving.

Minarik, Else Holmelund. *Cat and dog* ill. by Fritz Siebel. Harper, 1960. Subj: Animals – cats. Animals – dogs.

Father Bear comes home ill. by Maurice Sendak. Harper, 1959. Subj: Animals – bears. Family life – fathers.

A kiss for Little Bear ill. by Maurice Sendak. Harper, 1959. Subj: Animals – bears.

Little Bear ill. by Maurice Sendak. Harper, 1957. Subj: Animals – bears. Birthdays.

Little Bear's friend ill. by Maurice Sendak. Harper, 1960. Subj: Animals – bears. Friendship.

Little Bear's visit ill. by Maurice Sendak. Harper, 1961. Subj: Animals – bears. Caldecott award honor book. Family life – grandparents, great-grandparents.

The little giant girl and the elf boys ill. by Garth Williams. Harper, 1963. Subj: Elves and little people. Giants.

No fighting, no biting! ill. by Maurice Sendak. Harper, 1958. Subj: Behavior – fighting, arguing. Reptiles – alligators, crocodiles.

Minsberg, David. *The book monster* ill. by Shelley Matheis. Littlebee Pr., 1982. Subj: Activities – reading. Monsters.

Mirkovic, Irene. *The greedy shopkeeper* ill. by Harold Berson. Harcourt, 1980. Translated and adapt. from a Serbian folk tale. Subj: Behavior – trickery. Careers – judges. Folk and fairy tales.

Mitchell, Cynthia. *Halloweena Hecatee* ill. by Eileen Browne. Crowell, 1979. Subj: Activities – playing. Games. Poetry, rhyme.

Playtime ill. by Satomi Ichikawa. Collins-World, 1978. Subj: Activities – playing. Emotions. Poetry, rhyme.

Under the cherry tree ill. by Satomi Ichikawa. Collins-World, 1979. Subj: Poetry, rhyme.

Mitchell, Joyce Slayton. *My mommy makes money* ill. by True Kelley. Little, 1984. Subj: Activities – working. Careers. Family life – mothers.

Miyoshi, Sekiya. *Singing David* ill. by author. Watts, 1969. Subj: Religion.

Mizumura, Kazue. *If I built a village* ill. by author. Crowell, 1971. Subj: Character traits – kindness. City. Ecology. Houses.

If I were a cricket... ill. by author. Crowell, 1973. Subj: Animals. Emotions – love. Insects – crickets. Poetry, rhyme.

If I were a mother ill. by author. Crowell, 1967. Subj: Family life – mothers.

Moak, Allan. *A big city ABC* ill. by author. Tundra (dist. by Scribner's), 1984. Subj: ABC books. City. Foreign lands – Canada.

Mobley, Jane. *The star husband* ill. by Anna Vojtech. Doubleday, 1979. Subj: Ethnic groups in the U.S. – Indians. Folk and fairy tales. Stars.

Moche, Dinah L. *The astronauts* ill. with photos. from NASA. Random House, 1979. Subj: Moon. Science. Space and space ships.

Modell, Frank. *Goodbye old year, hello new year* ill. by author. Greenwillow, 1984. Subj: Holidays – New Year's.

One zillion valentines ill. by author. Greenwillow, 1981. Subj: Character traits – practicality. Holidays – Valentine's Day.

Seen any cats? ill. by author. Greenwillow, 1979. Subj: Animals – cats. Circus.

Tooley! Tooley! ill. by author. Greenwillow, 1979. Subj: Animals – dogs. Behavior – lost. Humor.

Moe, Jørgen Engebretsen. *The three billy goats Gruff* (Asbjørnsen, P C (Peter Christen))

Moeri, Louise. *The unicorn and the plow* ill. by Diane Goode. Dutton, 1982. Subj: Character traits – luck. Farms. Mythical creatures.

Moeschlin, Elsa. *The red horse* ill. by author. Coward, 1944. Subj: Dreams. Holidays – Christmas. Toys – rocking horses.

Moffett, Martha A. *A flower pot is not a hat* ill. by Susan Perl. Dutton, 1972. Subj: Humor.

Mohr, Joseph. *Silent night* verses by Joseph Mohr; ill. by Susan Jeffers. Dutton, 1984. Orig. title: Stille Nacht, heilige Nacht. Subj: Holidays – Christmas. Songs.

Molarsky, Osmond. *The peasant and the fly* ill. by Katherine Coville. Harcourt, 1980. Subj: Folk and fairy tales. Problem solving.

Molnar, Joe. *Graciela: a Mexican-American child tells her story* photos. by author. Watts, 1972. Subj: Ethnic groups in the U.S. – Mexican-Americans.

Moncure, Jane Belk. *Happy healthkins* ill. by Lois Axeman. Children's Pr., 1982. Subj: Elves and little people. Health. Poetry, rhyme.

The healthkin food train ill. by Lois Axeman. Children's Pr., 1982. Subj: Elves and little people. Health. Poetry, rhyme.

Healthkins exercise! ill. by Lois Axeman. Children's Pr., 1982. Subj: Elves and little people. Health. Poetry, rhyme.

Healthkins help ill. by Lois Axeman. Children's Pr., 1982. Subj: Elves and little people. Health. Poetry, rhyme.

The look book ill. by Lois Axeman. Children's Pr., 1982. Subj: Senses.

Riddle me a riddle ill. by Marc Belenchia. Children's Pr., 1977. Subj: Animals. Magic. Riddles.

Sounds all around ill. by Lois Axeman. Children's Pr., 1982. Subj: Senses.

The talking tabby cat: a folk tale from France ill. by Helen Endres. Children's Pr., 1980. Subj: Animals – cats. Folk and fairy tales.

A tasting party ill. by Lois Axeman. Children's Pr., 1982. Subj: Senses.

The touch book ill. by Lois Axeman. Children's Pr., 1982. Subj: Senses.

What your nose knows! ill. by Lois Axeman. Children's Pr., 1982. Subj: Anatomy. Senses.

Where? ill. by Lois Axeman. Children's Pr., 1983. Subj: Character traits – curiosity. Character traits – questioning.

Monjo, F. N. *The drinking gourd* ill. by Fred Brenner. Harper, 1970. Subj: Ethnic groups in the U.S. – Afro-Americans. Ethnic groups in the U.S. – Indians. U.S. history.

Indian summer ill. by Anita Lobel. Harper, 1968. Subj: Ethnic groups in the U.S. – Indians. U.S. history.

The one bad thing about father ill. by Rocco Negri. Harper, 1970. Subj: Family life – fathers. U.S. history.

Poor Richard in France ill. by Brinton Turkle. Holt, 1973. Subj: U.S. history.

Rudi and the distelfink ill. by George Kraus. Windmill, 1972. Subj: Family life.

Monsell, Helen Albee. *Paddy's Christmas* ill. by Kurt Wiese. Knopf, 1942. Subj: Animals – bears. Holidays – Christmas.

Monster poems ed. by Daisy Wallace; ill. by Kay Chorao. Holiday House, 1976. Subj: Monsters. Poetry, rhyme. Tongue twisters.

Montgomerie, Norah. *This little pig went to market play rhymes* ill. by Margery Gill. Watts, 1967. Subj: Games. Nursery rhymes. Participation.

Montresor, Beni. *A for angel: Beni Montresor's ABC picture-stories* ill. by author. Knopf, 1969. Subj: ABC books.

Bedtime! ill. by author. Harper, 1978. Subj: Bedtime. Dreams.

Moon, Carl. *One little Indian* (Moon, Grace Purdie)

Moon, Dolly M. *My very first book of cowboy songs: 21 favorite songs in easy piano arrangements* ill. by Frederic Remington. Dover, 1982. Subj: Cowboys. Folk and fairy tales. Songs.

Moon, Grace Purdie. *One little Indian* by Grace and Carl Moon; ill. by Carl Moon. Albert Whitman, 1950. Subj: Birthdays. Ethnic groups in the U.S. – Indians.

The moon's the north wind's cooky: *night poems* comp. and ill. by Susan Russo. Lothrop, 1979. Subj: Bedtime. Night. Poetry, rhyme.

Moorat, Joseph. *Thirty old-time nursery songs* (Mother Goose)

Moore, Clement C. *The night before Christmas* ill. by Tomie de Paola. Holiday, 1980. Subj: Holidays – Christmas. Poetry, rhyme.

The night before Christmas ill. by Gyo Fujikawa. Grosset, 1961. Subj: Holidays – Christmas. Poetry, rhyme.

The night before Christmas ill. by Anita Lobel. Knopf, 1984. Subj: Holidays – Christmas. Poetry, rhyme.

The night before Christmas ill. by Gustaf Tenggren. Simon and Schuster, 1951. Subj: Holidays – Christmas. Poetry, rhyme.

The night before Christmas ill. by Tasha Tudor. Rand McNally, 1975. Subj: Holidays – Christmas. Poetry, rhyme.

A visit from St. Nicholas: 'Twas the night before Christmas ill. by Paul Galdone. McGraw-Hill, 1968. Subj: Holidays – Christmas. Poetry, rhyme.

Moore, Eva. *Dick Whittington and his cat*

Moore, Inga. *Aktil's big swim* ill. by author. Oxford Univ. Pr., 1981. Subj: Animals – rats. Sports – swimming.

The vegetable thieves ill. by author. Viking, 1984. Subj: Activities – gardening. Animals – mice. Orphans.

Moore, John. *Granny Stickleback* by John Moore and Martin Wright; ill. by authors. Hamish Hamilton, 1982. Subj: Animals. Crime. Sports – racing.

Moore, Lilian. *Hooray for me!* (Charlip, Remy)

I feel the same way ill. by Robert M. Quackenbush. Atheneum, 1967. Subj: Poetry, rhyme.

Little Raccoon and no trouble at all ill. by Gioia Fiammenghi. McGraw-Hill, 1972. Subj: Activities – babysitting. Animals – chipmunks. Animals – raccoons. Twins.

Little Raccoon and the outside world ill. by Gioia Fiammenghi. McGraw-Hill, 1965. Subj: Animals – raccoons.

Little Raccoon and the thing in the pool ill. by Gioia Fiammenghi. McGraw-Hill, 1963. Subj: Animals – raccoons. Emotions – fear.

Papa Albert ill. by Gioia Fiammenghi. Atheneum, 1964. Subj: Careers – taxi drivers. Family life. Foreign lands – France. Foreign languages. Taxis.

See my lovely poison ivy, and other verses about witches, ghosts and things ill. by Diane Dawson. Atheneum, 1975. Subj: Animals – cats. Monsters. Poetry, rhyme. Witches.

Moore, Sheila. *Samson Svenson's baby* ill. by Karen Ann Weinhaus. Harper, 1983. Subj: Birds – ducks. Character traits – appearance. Character traits – kindness to animals.

Mooser, Stephen. *The ghost with the Halloween hiccups* ill. by Tomie de Paola. Watts, 1977. Subj: Ghosts. Holidays – Halloween.

Mordvinoff, Nicolas. *Billy the kid* (Lipkind, William)

The boy and the forest (Lipkind, William)

Chaga (Lipkind, William)

The Christmas bunny (Lipkind, William)

Circus rucus (Lipkind, William)

Coral Island ill. by author. Doubleday, 1957. Subj: Behavior – growing up. Foreign lands – South Sea Islands. Islands.

Even Steven (Lipkind, William)

Finders keepers (Lipkind, William)

Four-leaf clover (Lipkind, William)

The little tiny rooster (Lipkind, William)

The magic feather duster (Lipkind, William)

Russet and the two reds (Lipkind, William)

Sleepyhead (Lipkind, William)

The two reds (Lipkind, William)

More, Caroline *see* Cone, Molly

Morel, Eve. *Fairy tales* ill. by Gyo Fujikawa. Grosset, 1980. Subj: Folk and fairy tales.

Fairy tales and fables ill. by Gyo Fujikawa. Grosset, 1970. Subj: Folk and fairy tales.

Moremen, Grace E. *No, no, Natalie* photos. by Geoffrey P. Fulton. Children's Pr., 1973. Subj: Animals – rabbits. Behavior – misbehavior. School.

Morgan, Allen. *Molly and Mr. Maloney* ill. by Maryann Kovalski. Kids Can Pr., 1982. Subj: Animals – raccoons. Behavior – misbehavior. Pets.

Morgenstern, Elizabeth. *The little gardeners* tr. from German by Elizabeth Morgenstern; retold by Louise F. Encking; ill. by Marigard Bantzer. Albert Whitman, 1933. Subj: Activities – gardening. Foreign lands – Germany.

Morice, Dave. *Dot town* ill. by author. Toothpaste Pr., 1982. Subj: Poetry, rhyme.

The happy birthday handbook ill. by author. Coffee House Pr., 1982. Subj: Birthdays.

A visit from St. Alphabet ill. by author. Coffee House Pr., 1980. Subj: ABC books. Poetry, rhyme.

Morris, Christopher G. *The magic world of words* (Halsey, William D)

Morris, Jill. *The boy who painted the sun* ill. by Geoff Hocking. Viking, 1984. Subj: Activities – painting. Behavior – solitude. City. Moving.

Morris, Neil. *Find the canary* by Neil Morris and Ting; ill. by Anna Clarke. Little, 1983. Subj: Games.

Hide and seek by Neil Morris and Ting; ill. by Anna Clarke. Little, 1983. Subj: Games.

Search for Sam by Neil Morris and Ting; ill. by Anna Clarke. Little, 1983. Subj: Games.

Where's my hat? by Neil Morris and Ting; ill. by Anna Clarke. Little, 1983. Subj: Games.

Morris, Robert A. *Dolphin* ill. by Mamoru Funai. Harper, 1975. Subj: Animals – dolphins. Science.

Seahorse ill. by Arnold Lobel. Harper, 1972. Subj: Crustacea. Science.

Morris, Terry Nell. *Good night, dear monster!* ill. by author. Knopf, 1980. Subj: Bedtime. Imagination – imaginary friends. Monsters.

Lucky puppy! Lucky boy! ill. by author. Knopf, 1980. Subj: Animals – dogs. Behavior – needing someone.

Morrison, Bill. *Louis James hates school* ill. by author. Houghton, 1978. Subj: Careers. School.

Squeeze a sneeze ill. by author. Houghton, 1977. Subj: Poetry, rhyme.

Morrison, Sean. *Is that a happy hippopotamus?* ill. by Aliki. Crowell, 1966. Subj: Animals. Humor. Noise, sounds. Poetry, rhyme.

Morrow, Elizabeth Cutter. *The painted pig* ill. by René D'Harnoncourt. Knopf, 1930. Subj: Foreign lands – Mexico.

Morrow, Suzanne Stark. *Inatuck's friend* ill. by Ellen Raskin. Little, 1968. Subj: Ethnic groups in the U.S. – Eskimos. Friendship.

Morse, Samuel French. *All in a suitcase* ill. by Barbara Cooney. Little, 1966. Subj: ABC books. Animals.

Sea sums ill. by Fuku Akino. Little, 1970. Subj: Counting. Poetry, rhyme. Sea and seashore. Weather – fog.

Mosel, Arlene. *The funny little woman* ill. by Blair Lent. Dutton, 1972. Based on The old woman and her dumpling by Lafcadio Hearn. Subj: Caldecott award book. Foreign lands – Japan. Monsters.

Tikki Tikki Tembo ill. by Blair Lent. Holt, 1968. Subj: Folk and fairy tales. Foreign lands – China. Names.

Moseley, Keith. *Dinosaurs a lost world* ill. by Robert Cremins. Putnam's, 1984. Subj: Dinosaurs. Format, unusual. Science.

Mosimann, Odie. *How the mouse was hit on the head by a stone and so discovered the world* (Delessert, Étienne)

Moskin, Marietta D. *Lysbet and the fire kittens* ill. by Margot Tomes. Coward, 1973. Subj: Animals – cats. Behavior – carelessness. Fire. U.S. history.

Moskof, Martin Stephen. *Still another alphabet book* (Chwast, Seymour)

Still another children's book (Chwast, Seymour)

Still another number book (Chwast, Seymour)

Moss, Elaine. *Polar* ill. by Jeannie Baker. Elsevier-Dutton, 1979. Subj: Activities – playing. Illness. Safety. Toys – teddy bears.

The story of Saul the king (Waddell, Helen)

Moss, Jeffrey. *The Sesame Street ABC storybook* featuring Jim Henson's Muppets; by Jeffrey Moss, Norman Stiles and Daniel Wilcox; ill. by Peter Cross and others. Random House, 1974. Subj: ABC books. Puppets.

The songs of Sesame Street in poems and pictures by Jeffrey Moss and others; ill. by Normand Chartier. Random House, 1983. Subj: Poetry, rhyme. Puppets. Songs.

Most, Bernard. *If the dinosaurs came back* ill. by author. Harcourt, 1978. Subj: Dinosaurs. Imagination.

My very own octopus ill. by author. Harcourt, 1980. Subj: Octopuses. Pets.

There's an ant in Anthony ill. by author. Morrow, 1980. Subj: Activities – reading.

Whatever happened to the dinosaurs? ill. by author. Harcourt, 1984. Subj: Dinosaurs.

Mostel, Zero. *The Sesame Street book of opposites with Zero Mostel* (Mendoza, George)

Mother Goose. *The annotated Mother Goose: nursery rhymes old and new* arranged and explained by William S. and Ceil Baring-Gould; chapter decorations by E. M. Simon; ill. by Walter Crane and others. Potter, 1962. Subj: Nursery rhymes.

Baa baa black sheep ill. by Sue Porter. Peter Bedrick Books (dist. by Harper), 1984. Subj: Format, unusual – cardboard pages. Nursery rhymes.

The baby's lap book ill. by Kay Chorao. Dutton, 1977. Subj: Nursery rhymes.

Blessed Mother Goose: favorite nursery rhymes for today's children ill. by Kaye Luke. House-Warven, 1951. Subj: Nursery rhymes.

Brian Wildsmith's Mother Goose ill. by Brian Wildsmith. Watts, 1964. Subj: Nursery rhymes.

Carolyn Wells' edition of Mother Goose ill. by Margeria Cooper and others. Doubleday, 1946. Subj: Nursery rhymes.

The Charles Addams Mother Goose ill. by Charles Addams. Harper, 1967. Subj: Nursery rhymes.

A child's book of old nursery rhymes ill. by Joan Walsh Anglund. Atheneum, 1973. Subj: Nursery rhymes.

The Chinese Mother Goose rhymes sel. and ed. by Robert Wyndham; ill. by Ed Young. Putnam's, 1982. Orig. pub. by World, 1968. Subj: Nursery rhymes.

The city and country Mother Goose ill. by Hilda Hoffmann. American Heritage, 1969. Subj: Nursery rhymes.

The comic adventures of Old Mother Hubbard and her dog (Martin, Sarah Catherine)

Frank Baber's Mother Goose Sel. by Ruth Spriggs; ill. by Frank Baber. Crown, 1976. Subj: Nursery rhymes.

The gay Mother Goose ill. by Françoise Seignobosc. Scribner's, 1938. Subj: Nursery rhymes.

Grafa' Grig had a pig, and other rhymes without reason from Mother Goose ill. by Wallace Tripp. Little, 1976. Subj: Nursery rhymes.

Gray goose and gander and other Mother Goose rhymes ill. by Anne F. Rockwell. Crowell, 1980. Subj: Nursery rhymes.

Gregory Griggs, and other nursery rhyme people sel. and ill. by Arnold Lobel. Greenwillow, 1978. Subj: Nursery rhymes.

Hey Diddle Diddle ill. by Nita Sowter. Peter Bedrick Books (dist. by Harper), 1984. Subj: Format, unusual – cardboard pages. Nursery rhymes.

Hurrah, we're outward bound! ill. by Peter Spier. Doubleday, 1968. Subj: Nursery rhymes.

In a pumpkin shell ill. by Joan Walsh Anglund. Harcourt, 1960. Subj: ABC books. Nursery rhymes.

Jack Kent's merry Mother Goose ill. by Jack Kent. Golden Pr., 1977. Subj: Nursery rhymes.

James Marshall's Mother Goose ill. by James Marshall. Farrar, 1979. Subj: Nursery rhymes.

The Larousse book of nursery rhymes ed. by Robert Owen; ill. with photos. Larousse, 1984. Ill. are full color photos. of tile pictures, painted during the late 19th and early 20th cents., created by the Royal Doulton Co., designed by Margaret Thompson, William Rowe and John H. McLennan. Subj: Nursery rhymes.

Lavender's blue: a book of nursery rhymes comp. by Kathleen Lines; ill. by Harold Jones. Oxford Univ. Pr., 1982. Subj: Nursery rhymes.

Little boy blue ill. by Nita Sowter. Peter Bedrick Books (dist. by Harper), 1984. Subj: Format, unusual – cardboard pages. Nursery rhymes.

The little Mother Goose ill. by Jessie Willcox Smith. Dodd, 1918. Subj: Nursery rhymes.

London Bridge is falling down ill. by Ed Emberley. Little, 1967. Subj: Folk and fairy tales. Foreign lands – England. Games. Nursery rhymes. Songs.

London Bridge is falling down ill. by Peter Spier. Doubleday, 1967. Subj: Folk and fairy tales. Foreign lands – England. Games. Nursery rhymes. Songs.

Mother Goose abroad (Tucker, Nicholas)

Mother Goose and nursery rhymes ill. by Philip Reed. Atheneum, 1963. Subj: Caldecott award honor book. Nursery rhymes.

The Mother Goose book ill. by Alice and Martin Provensen. Random House, 1976. Subj: Nursery rhymes.

The Mother Goose book gathered from many sources; ill. by Sonia Roetter. Peter Pauper Pr., 1946. Subj: Nursery rhymes.

Mother Goose in French: Poesies de la vraie Mere Oie tr. by Hugh Latham; ill. by Barbara Cooney. Crowell, 1964. Subj: Foreign languages. Nursery rhymes.

Mother Goose in hieroglyphics ill. by George S. Appleton. Houghton, 1962. Reproduction of the 1st ed. published in 1849. Subj: Games. Hieroglyphics. Nursery rhymes. Rebuses.

Mother Goose in Spanish: Poesias de la Madre Oca tr. by Alastair Reid and Anthony Kerrigan; ill. by Barbara Cooney. Crowell, 1968. Subj: Foreign languages. Nursery rhymes.

Mother Goose melodies intro. and bib. note by E. F. Bleiler; ill. with engravings. Facsimile ed. of the Munroe and Francis c.1833 version. Dover, 1970. Subj: Nursery rhymes.

Mother Goose nursery rhymes ill. by Arthur Rackham. Watts, 1969. Reprint of the 1913 ed. Subj: Nursery rhymes.

Mother Goose nursery rhymes ill. by Arthur Rackham. Viking, 1975. Subj: Nursery rhymes.

Mother Goose rhymes ed. by Watty Piper; ill. by Eulalie M. Banks and Lois Lenski. Platt, 1947, 1956. Subj: Nursery rhymes.

The Mother Goose treasury ill. by Raymond Briggs. Coward, 1966. Subj: Nursery rhymes.

Mother Goose's melodies: or, songs for the nursery ed. by William A. Wheeler. Houghton, 189?. Subj: Nursery rhymes. Songs.

Mother Goose's melody: or, sonnets for the cradle. Facsimile of John Newbery's collection of Mother Goose rhymes, reproduced from the earliest known perfect copy of the 1794 printing. Frederic G. Melcher, 1945. Subj: Nursery rhymes.

Mother Goose's rhymes and melodies ill. by J. L. Webb; music and melodies by E. I. Lane. Cassell, 1888. Subj: Music. Nursery rhymes.

Nursery rhyme book ill. by L. Leslie Brooke; ed. by Andrew Lang. Warne, 1897. Subj: Nursery rhymes.

Nursery rhymes sel. by Marie; ill. by Douglas Gorsline. Random House, 1977. Subj: Nursery rhymes.

Nursery rhymes ill. by Eloise Wilkin. Random House, 1979. Subj: Nursery rhymes.

Nursery rhymes from Mother Goose in signed English. Prepared under the supervision of the staff of the Pre-School Signed English Project: Barbara M. Kanapell and others. Gallaudet College Pr., 1972. Subj: Handicaps – deafness. Nursery rhymes.

Old Mother Hubbard and her dog (Martin, Sarah Catherine)

One I love, two I love, and other loving Mother Goose rhymes ill. by Nonny Hogrogian. Dutton, 1972. Subj: Nursery rhymes.

One misty moisty morning: rhymes from Mother Goose ill. by Mitchell Miller. Farrar, 1971. Subj: Nursery rhymes.

The only true Mother Goose melodies intro. by Edward Everett Hale. Lothrop, 1905. An exact and full-size reproduction of the original edition published and copyrighted in Boston in the year 1833 by Munroe and Francis. Subj: Nursery rhymes.

The piper's son ill. by Emily N. Barto. Longmans, 1942. Subj: Nursery rhymes.

A pocket full of posies ill. by Marguerite De Angeli. Doubleday, 1961. First pub. in 1954. Subj: Nursery rhymes.

The rainbow Mother Goose ed. with an intro. by May Lamberton Becker; ill. by Lili Cassel-Wronker. Collins-World, 1947. Subj: Nursery rhymes.

The real Mother Goose ill. by Blanche Fisher Wright. Rand McNally, 1916. Subj: Nursery rhymes.

The real personages of Mother Goose. (Thomas, Katherine Elwes)

Richard Scarry's best Mother Goose ever ill. by Richard Scarry. Golden Pr., 1964. Subj: Nursery rhymes.

Richard Scarry's favorite Mother Goose rhymes ill. by Richard Scarry. Golden Pr., 1976. Subj: Nursery rhymes.

Rimes de la Mere Oie: Mother Goose rhymes rendered into French by Ormonde De Kay, Jr.; ill. by Seymour Chwast, Milton Glaser, and Barry Zaid. Little, 1971. Subj: Foreign languages. Nursery rhymes.

Ring o' roses ill. by L. Leslie Brooke. Warne, 1923. Subj: Nursery rhymes.

The Sesame Street players present Mother Goose: featuring Jim Henson's Sesame Street Muppets ill. by Michael Smollin. Random House-Children's Television Workshop, 1982. Subj: Nursery rhymes. Puppets.

Sing a song of sixpence ill. by Margaret Chamberlain. Peter Bedrick Books (dist. by Harper), 1984. Subj: Format, unusual – cardboard pages. Nursery rhymes.

Sing hey diddle diddle: 66 nursery rhymes with their traditional tunes comp. by Beatrice Harrop; ill. by Frank Francis and Bernard Cheese. Sterling, 1983. Subj: Music. Nursery rhymes.

Songs for Mother Goose ill. by Maginel Wright Enright Barney; set to music by Sidney Homer. Macmillan, 1920. Subj: Nursery rhymes.

The tall Mother Goose ill. by Feodor Rojankovsky. Harper, 1942. Subj: Nursery rhymes.

Thirty old-time nursery songs ed. by Joseph Moorat; ill. by Paul Woodroffe. Norton, 1980. Orig. pub. in 1912. Subj: Music. Nursery rhymes. Songs.

The three jovial huntsmen ill. by Susan Jeffers. Bradbury Pr., 1973. Subj: Caldecott award honor book. Nursery rhymes.

The three little kittens ill. by Lorinda Bryan Cauley. Putnam's, 1982. Subj: Animals – cats. Behavior – losing things. Games. Nursery rhymes.

To market! To market! ill. by Emma Lillian Brock. Knopf, 1930. Subj: Nursery rhymes. Shopping.

To market! To market! ill. by Peter Spier. Doubleday, 1967. Subj: Nursery rhymes.

Tom, Tom the piper's son ill. by Paul Galdone. McGraw-Hill, 1964. Subj: Nursery rhymes.

Twenty nursery rhymes ill. by Philip Van Aver. Grabhorn-Hoyem, 1970. Subj: Nursery rhymes.

Willy Pogany's Mother Goose ill. by Willy Pogany. Nelson, 1928. Subj: Nursery rhymes.

Mother Goose: *a comprehensive collection of the rhymes* comp. by William Rose Benét; ill. by Roger Antoine Duvoisin. Heritage Pr., 1943. Subj: Nursery rhymes.

Mother Goose sel. by Phyllis Maurine Fraser; ill. by Miss Elliott. Simon and Schuster, 1942. Subj: Nursery rhymes.

Mother Goose ill. by C. B. Falls. Doubleday, 1924. Subj: Nursery rhymes.

Mother Goose ill. by Gyo Fujikawa. Grosset, 1967. Subj: Nursery rhymes.

Mother Goose *as told by Kellogg's singing lady* ill. by Vernon Grant. Kellogg Co., 1933. Subj: Nursery rhymes.

Mother Goose: *or, the old nursery rhymes* sel. by Phyllis Maurine Fraser; ill. by Kate Greenaway. Routledge, 1881. Illustrated as originally engraved and printed by Edmund Evans. Subj: Nursery rhymes.

Mother Goose: *a collection of classic nursery rhymes* sel. and ill. by Michael Hague. Holt, 1984. Subj: Nursery rhymes.

Mother Goose: *sixty-seven favorite rhymes* ill. by Violet La Mont. Simon and Schuster, 1957. Subj: Nursery rhymes.

Mother Goose: *the old nursery rhymes* ill. by Arthur Rackham. Subj: Nursery rhymes.

Mother Goose arranged and ed. by Eulalie Osgood Grover; ill. by Frederick Richardson. The Volland ed. Volland, 1915. Subj: Nursery rhymes.

Mother Goose re-arranged and edited in this form by Eulalie Osgood Grover; ill. by Frederick Richardson. The classic Volland ed. Rand McNally, 1976. Reprint of the 1971 ed. published by Hubbard Press, Northbrook, Ill. Subj: Nursery rhymes.

Mother Goose ill. by Gustaf Tenggren. Little, 1940. Subj: Nursery rhymes.

Mother Goose: *seventy-seven verses* ill. by Tasha Tudor. Walck, 1944. Subj: Caldecott award honor book. Nursery rhymes.

Mother Goose house ill. by Zokeisha; ed. by Kate Klimo. Simon and Schuster, 1983. Subj: Format, unusual – cardboard pages. Houses. Nursery rhymes.

Mouse house ill. by Zokeisha; ed. by Kate Klimo. Simon and Schuster, 1983. Subj: Animals – mice. Format, unusual – cardboard pages. Houses.

The moving adventures of Old Dame Trot and her comical cat ill. by Paul Galdone. McGraw-Hill, 1973. Subj: Animals – cats. Nursery rhymes.

Mozley, Charles. *Arabian Nights entertainments* (Arabian Nights)

Mude, O. *see* Gorey, Edward

Mullins, Edward S. *Animal limericks* ill. by author. Follett, 1966. Subj: Animals. Poetry, rhyme.

Munari, Bruno. *ABC* ill. by author. Collins-World, 1960. Subj: ABC books.

Animals for sale ill. by author. Collins-World, 1957. Subj: Animals.

The birthday present ill. by author. Collins-World, 1959. Subj: Birthdays. Games. Transportation.

Bruno Munari's zoo ill. by author. Collins-World, 1963. Subj: Animals. Birds. Zoos.

The circus in the mist ill. by author. Collins, 1968. Subj: Circus. Format, unusual. Weather – fog.

The elephant's wish ill. by author. Collins, 1959. First pub. in 1945. Subj: Animals. Behavior – wishing. Format, unusual.

Jimmy has lost his cap ill. by author. Collins, 1959. Subj: Behavior – losing things. Format, unusual.

Tic, Tac and Toc ill. by author. Collins-World, 1957. Subj: Birds. Format, unusual.

Who's there? Open the door tr. by Maria Cimino; ill. by author. Collins-World, 1957. Subj: Animals. Format, unusual.

Munsch, Robert N. *David's father* ill. by Michael Martchenko. Firefly Pr., 1983. Subj: Character traits – kindness. Giants.

Jonathan cleaned up - then he heard a sound: or, blackberry subway jam ill. by Michael Martchenko. Firefly Pr., 1981. Subj: Machines. Problem solving. Trains.

Muntean, Michaela. *Alligator's garden* ill. by Nicole Rubel. Dial Pr., 1984. Subj: Activities – gardening. Reptiles – alligators, crocodiles.

Bicycle bear ill. by Doug Cushman. Parents, 1983. Subj: Animals – bears. Poetry, rhyme. Sports – bicycling.

The house that bear built ill. by Nicole Rubel. Dial Pr., 1984. Subj: Animals – bears. Houses.

Muppet babies through the year ill. by Bruce McNally. Random House, 1984. Subj: Puppets. Seasons.

Munthe, Adam John. *I believe in unicorns* ill. by Elizabeth Falconer. Merrimack, 1980. Subj: Emotions – loneliness. Mythical creatures.

The Muppet show book ill. by Tudor Banus. Abrams, 1978. Subj: Puppets.

Murdocca, Sal. *Tuttle's shell* ill. by author. Lothrop, 1976. Subj: Animals. Animals – rats. Friendship. Reptiles – turtles.

Murphey, Sara. *The animal hat shop* reading consultant: Morton Botel; ill. by Mel Pekarsky. Follett, 1964. Subj: Animals – cats. Birds – chickens. Clothing.

The roly poly cookie reading consultant: Morton Botel; ill. by Leonard W. Shortall. Follett, 1963. Subj: Cumulative tales. Food.

Murphy, Jill. *Peace at last* ill. by author. Dial Pr., 1980. Subj: Animals – bears. Noise, sounds. Sleep.

What next, baby bear! ill. by author. Dial Pr., 1984. Subj: Animals – bears. Bedtime. Imagination. Night. Space and space ships.

Murphy, Shirley Rousseau. *Tattie's river journey* ill. by Tomie de Paola. Dial Pr., 1983. Subj: Houses. Rivers. Weather – rain.

Valentine for a dragon ill. by Kay Chorao. Atheneum, 1984. Subj: Dragons. Emotions – loneliness. Holidays – Valentine's Day. Monsters.

Murschetz, Luis. *Mister Mole* tr. by Diane Martin; ill. by author. Prentice-Hall, 1976. Translation of Der Maulwurf Grabowski. Subj: Animals – moles. Ecology. Progress.

Musgrove, Margaret. *Ashanti to Zulu.* Dial Pr., 1976. Subj: ABC books. Caldecott award book. Foreign lands – Africa.

My body ill. by Sue Porter. Harper, 1985. Subj: Anatomy. Format, unusual – cardboard pages. Wordless.

My day. Simon and Schuster, 1980. Subj: Activities. Format, unusual – cardboard pages.

My toy box. Simon and Schuster, 1980. Subj: Format, unusual – cardboard pages. Toys.

Myers, Amy. *I know a monster* ill. by author. Addison-Wesley, 1979. Subj: Character traits – appearance. Games. Monsters.

Myers, Arthur. *Kids do amazing things* ill. by Anthony Rao. Random House, 1980. Subj: Activities.

Myers, Bernice. *Charlie's birthday present* ill. by author. Scholastic, 1981. Subj: Birthdays. Trees.

Herman and the bears and the giants ill. by author. Scholastic, 1978. Subj: Animals – bears. Circus. Sports – bicycling.

Myller, Lois. *No! No!* ill. by Cyndy Szekeres. Simon and Schuster, 1971. Subj: Animals – hedgehogs. Behavior. Behavior – misbehavior. Etiquette. Family life. Safety.

Myller, Rolf. *How big is a foot?* ill. by author. Atheneum, 1962. Subj: Birthdays. Concepts – measurement. Humor. Royalty.

Rolling round ill. by author. Atheneum, 1963. Subj: Royalty. Wheels.

Myrick, Jean Lockwood. *Ninety-nine pockets* ill. by Haris Petie. Lantern Pr., 1966. Subj: Birthdays. Clothing. Problem solving.

Myrick, Mildred. *Ants are fun* ill. by Arnold Lobel. Harper, 1968. Subj: Insects — ants. Science.

The secret three ill. by Arnold Lobel. Harper, 1963. Subj: Clubs, gangs. Lighthouses. Secret codes.

Nagel, Andreas Fischer *see* Fischer-Nagel, Andreas

Nagel, Heiderose Fischer *see* Fischer-Nagel, Heiderose

Nakano, Hirotaka. *Elephant blue* tr. by Fukuinkan Shoten; ill. by author. Bobbs-Merrill, 1970. Subj: Animals. Animals — elephants. Character traits — helpfulness.

Nakao, Naomi Löw. *The adventures of Chester the chest* (Ayal, Ora)

Ugbu (Ayal, Ora)

Nakatani, Chiyoko. *The day Chiro was lost* ill. by author. Collins-World, 1969. Subj: Animals — dogs. Behavior — lost.

Fumio and the dolphins ill. by author. Addison-Wesley, 1970. First published in Japan by Fukuinkan-Shoten, Tokyo, 1969. Subj: Animals — dolphins. Character traits — kindness to animals. Foreign lands — Japan. Sea and seashore.

My day on the farm ill. by author. Crowell, 1976. Subj: Farms.

The zoo in my garden ill. by author. Crowell, 1973. Translation of Boku no uchi no dōbutsuen. Subj: Animals.

Napoli, Guillier. *Adventure of Mont Saint Michel* ill. by author. McGraw-Hill, 1966. Subj: Careers — fishermen. Character traits — curiosity. Foreign lands — France. Sea and seashore.

Narayan, Maya. *Leela and the watermelon* (Hirsh, Marilyn)

Nash, Ogden. *The adventures of Isabel* ill. by Walter Lorraine. Little, 1963. Subj: Emotions — fear. Humor. Poetry, rhyme.

The animal garden ill. by Hilary Knight. Lippincott, 1963. Subj: Humor. Plants. Poetry, rhyme.

A boy is a boy ill. by Arthur Shilstone. Watts, 1960. Subj: Humor. Poetry, rhyme.

Custard and Company sel. and ill. by Quentin Blake. Little, 1980. Subj: Dragons. Humor. Poetry, rhyme.

Custard the dragon and the wicked knight ill. by Linell Nash. Little, 1959. Subj: Dragons. Poetry, rhyme.

Naxt, Elsa Ruth *see* Watson, Jane Werner

Naylor, Phyllis Reynolds. *Old Sadie and the Christmas bear* ill. by Patricia Montgomery Newton. Atheneum, 1984. Subj: Animals — bears. Holidays — Christmas.

Neasi, Barbara J. *Just like me* ill. by Lois Axeman. Children's Pr., 1984. Subj: Twins.

Nelson, Brenda. *Mud fore sale* ill. by Richard Brown. Houghton, 1984. Subj: Activities. Friendship.

Nelson, Esther L. *The funny songbook* ill. by Joyce Behr. Sterling, 1984. Subj: Music. Songs.

Holiday singing and dancing games photos. by Shirley Zeiberg. Sterling, 1980. Subj: Activities — dancing. Games. Music. Songs.

The silly songbook ill. by Joyce Behr. Sterling, 1982. Subj: Music. Songs.

Ness, Evaline. *Do you have the time, Lydia?* ill. by author. Dutton, 1971. Subj: Birds — sea gulls. Character traits — completing things. Problem solving. Time.

Exactly alike ill. by author. Scribner's, 1964. Subj: Family life.

Fierce: the lion ill. by author. Holiday, 1980. Subj: Animals — lions. Circus.

The girl and the goatherd: or, this and that and thus and so ill. by author. Dutton, 1970. Subj: Character traits — appearance. Folk and fairy tales.

Josefina February ill. by author. Scribner's, 1963. Subj: Animals — donkeys. Birthdays. Character traits — generosity. Foreign lands — Caribbean Islands.

Marcella's guardian angel ill. by author. Holiday, 1979. Subj: Angels. Behavior.

Pavo and the princess ill. by author. Scribner's, 1964. Subj: Birds. Character traits — helpfulness. Emotions. Royalty.

Sam, Bangs, and moonshine ill. by author. Holt, 1966. Subj: Caldecott award book. Imagination. Sports — fishing.

Neuhaus, David. *His finest hour* ill. by author. Viking, 1984. Subj: Friendship. Sports — racing.

Newberry, Clare Turlay. *April's kittens* ill. by author. Harper, 1940. Subj: Animals — cats. Caldecott award honor book. Pets.

Barkis ill. by author. Harper, 1938. Subj: Animals — dogs. Caldecott award honor book. Pets.

Cousin Toby ill. by author. Harper, 1939. Subj: Babies.

Herbert the lion ill. by author. Harper, 1956. First pub. in 1931. Subj: Animals – lions. Pets.

The kittens' ABC verse and pictures by Clare Turlay Newberry. New and rev. ed.; completely redrawn. Harper, 1965. Subj: ABC books. Animals – cats. Poetry, rhyme.

Lambert's bargain ill. by author. Harper, 1941. Subj: Animals – hyenas.

Marshmallow ill. by author. Harper, 1942. Subj: Animals – cats. Animals – rabbits. Caldecott award honor book. Friendship.

Mittens ill. by author. Harper, 1937. Subj: Animals – cats.

Pandora ill. by author. Harper, 1944. Subj: Animals – cats.

Percy, Polly and Pete ill. by author. Harper, 1952. Subj: Animals – cats. Behavior – growing up. Character traits – kindness to animals. Pets.

Smudge ill. by author. Harper, 1948. Subj: Animals – cats.

T-Bone, the baby-sitter story and pictures by Clare Turlay Newberry. Harper, 1950. Subj: Activities – babysitting. Animals – cats. Babies. Caldecott award honor book.

Widget ill. by author. Harper, 1958. Subj: Animals – cats.

Newbolt, Henry John, Sir. *Rilloby-rill* ill. by Susanna Gretz. O'Hara, 1973. Subj: Insects – grasshoppers. Fairies. Music. Songs.

Newell, Crosby *see* Bonsall, Crosby Newell

Newell, Peter. *Topsys and turvys* ill. by author. Dover, 1965. Subj: Format, unusual. Humor.

Newfield, Marcia. *Iggy* ill. by Jacqueline Chwast. Houghton, 1972. Subj: Pets. Reptiles – iguanas.

Newland, Mary Reed. *Good King Wenceslas: a legend in music and pictures* ill. by author. Seabury Pr., 1980. Subj: Holidays – Christmas. Music. Songs.

Newman, Shirlee. *Tell me, grandma; tell me, grandpa* ill. by Joan Drescher. Houghton, 1979. Subj: Family life – grandparents, great-grandparents.

Newsham, Ian. *The monster hunt* (Newsham, Wendy)

Newsham, Wendy. *The monster hunt* by Wendy and Ian Newsham; ill. by authors. Hamish Hamilton, 1983. Subj: Monsters.

Newth, Philip. *Roly goes exploring: a book for blind and sighted children, in Braille and standard type, with pictures to feel as well as see.* Putnam's, 1981. Subj: Concepts – shape. Format, unusual. Handicaps – blindness.

Newton, James R. *A forest is reborn* ill. by Susan Bonners. Crowell, 1982. Subj: Fire. Forest, woods. Science.

Forest log ill. by Irene Brady. Crowell, 1980. Subj: Ecology. Forest, woods. Science. Trees.

Newton, Patricia Montgomery. *The five sparrows* ill. by author. Atheneum, 1982. Subj: Character traits – kindness. Folk and fairy tales. Foreign lands – Japan.

Nic Leodhas, Sorche *see* Alger, Leclaire

Nichols, Cathy. *Tuxedo Sam: a penguin of a different color* ill. by Haruo Takahashi. Random House, 1983. Subj: Birds – penguins. City.

Nichols, Paul. *Big Paul's school bus* ill. by William Marshall. Prentice-Hall, 1981. Subj: Buses. Careers. School.

Nicholson, William, Sir. *Clever Bill* ill. by author. Farrar, 1977. Subj: Toys – soldiers.

Nickl, Peter. *Ra ta ta tam* by Peter Nickl and Binette Schroeder; ill. by authors. Merrimack, 1984. Subj: Character traits – meanness. Format, unusual – cardboard pages. Trains.

Nicolas *see* Mordvinoff, Nicolas

Nicole *see* Ariane

Nicoll, Helen. *Meg and Mog* by Helen Nicoll and Jan Pieńkowski; ill. by Jan Pieńkowski. Atheneum, 1972. Subj: Animals – cats. Holidays – Halloween. Magic. Witches.

Meg at sea by Helen Nicoll and Jan Pieńkowski; ill. by Jan Pieńkowski. Harvey House, 1974. Subj: Animals – cats. Birds – owls. Magic. Sea and seashore. Witches.

Meg on the moon by Helen Nicoll and Jan Pieńkowski; ill. by Jan Pieńkowski. Harvey House, 1974. Subj: Animals – cats. Magic. Moon. Witches.

Meg's eggs by Helen Nicoll and Jan Pieńkowski; ill. by Jan Pieńkowski. Atheneum, 1972. Subj: Animals – cats. Birds – owls. Dinosaurs. Eggs. Magic. Witches.

Nikly, Michelle. *The emperor's plum tree* tr. from French by Elizabeth Shub; ill. by author. Greenwillow, 1982. Subj: Friendship. Royalty. Trees.

The princess on the nut: or, the curious courtship of the son of the princess on the pea tr. by Lucy Meredith; ill. by Jean Claverie. Faber, 1981. Subj: Folk and fairy tales. Royalty.

Niland, Deborah. *ABC of monsters* ill. by author. McGraw-Hill, 1978. Subj: ABC books. Monsters.

Nister, Ernest. *Little tales from long ago: Cat's cradle, The tale of a dog, Three friends, Three little maids* ill. by author. Delacorte Pr., 1979. Subj: Folk and fairy tales.

Nixon, Joan Lowery. *The Thanksgiving mystery* ill. by Jim Cummins. Albert Whitman, 1980. Subj: Ghosts. Holidays – Thanksgiving. Problem solving.

The Valentine mystery ill. by Jim Cummins. Albert Whitman, 1979. Subj: Holidays – Valentine's Day. Problem solving.

Noble, June. *Two homes for Lynn* ill. by Yuri Salzman. Holt, 1979. Subj: Behavior – sharing. Divorce. Family life. Imagination – imaginary friends.

Noble, Trinka Hakes. *Apple tree Christmas* ill. by author. Dial Pr., 1984. Subj: Holidays – Christmas. Trees. Weather – storms.

The day Jimmy's boa ate the wash ill. by Steven Kellogg. Dial Pr., 1980. Subj: Activities. Reptiles – snakes. School.

Hansy's mermaid ill. by author. Dial Pr., 1983. Subj: Character traits – kindness. Mythical creatures.

Jimmy's boa bounces back ill. by Steven Kellogg. Dial Pr., 1984. Subj: Humor. Reptiles – snakes.

The king's tea ill. by author. Dial Pr., 1979. Subj: Cumulative tales. Royalty.

Nodset, Joan L. *see* Lexau, Joan M.

Noguere, Suzanne. *Little raccoon* ill. by Tony Chen. Holt, 1981. Subj: Animals – raccoons.

Nolan, Dennis. *Witch Bazooza* ill. by author. Prentice-Hall, 1979. Subj: Holidays – Halloween. Houses. Witches.

Wizard McBean and his flying machine ill. by author. Prentice-Hall, 1977. Subj: Airplanes, airports. Cumulative tales. Magic. Poetry, rhyme. Wizards.

Nolan, Madeena Spray. *My daddy don't go to work* ill. by Jim LaMarche. Carolrhoda Books, 1978. Subj: Ethnic groups in the U.S. – Afro-Americans. Family life. Family life – fathers. Poverty.

Noll, Sally. *Off and counting* ill. by author. Greenwillow, 1984. Subj: Counting. Frogs and toads. Poetry, rhyme. Toys.

Norby, Lisa. *The Herself the elf storybook.* Scholastic, 1983. Subj: Elves and little people. Magic.

Nordqvist, Sven. *Pancake pie* ill. by author. Morrow, 1985. Subj: Animals – cats. Food.

North, George Captain *see* Stevenson, Robert Louis

Northrup, Mili. *The watch cat* ill. by Adrina Zanazanian; designed by Kent Salisbury. Bobbs-Merrill, 1968. Subj: Animals – cats. Foreign lands – Thailand.

Norton, Natalie. *A little old man* ill. by Will Huntington. Rand McNally, 1959. Subj: Emotions – loneliness.

Nourse, Alan Edward. *Lumps, bumps and rashes: a look at kids' diseases.* Watts, 1976. Subj: Illness.

Numeroff, Laura Joffe. *Amy for short* ill. by author. Macmillan, 1976. Subj: Character traits – appearance. Friendship.

Emily's bunch by Laura Joffe Numeroff and Alice Numeroff Richter; ill. by Laura Joffe Numeroff. Macmillan, 1978. Subj: Holidays – Halloween.

If you give a mouse a cookie ill. by Felicia Bond. Harper, 1985. Subj: Animals – mice. Character traits – kindness to animals.

Phoebe Dexter has Harriet Peterson's sniffles ill. by author. Greenwillow, 1977. Subj: Illness.

You can't put braces on spaces (Richter, Alice Numcroff)

Nursery rhymes ill. by Gertrude Elliott. Simon and Schuster, 1948. Subj: Nursery rhymes.

Nussbaum, Hedda. *Animals build amazing homes* ill. by Christopher Santoro. Random House, 1979. Subj: Animals. Houses. Science.

Nussbaumer, Mares. *Away in a manger: a story of the Nativity* by Mares and Paul Nussbaumer; ill. by Paul Nussbaumer. Harcourt, 1965. Translation of Ihr Kinderlein kommet. Subj: Holidays – Christmas. Music. Religion.

Nussbaumer, Paul. *Away in a manger:* (Nussbaumer, Mares)

Oakley, Graham. *The church cat abroad* ill. by author. Atheneum, 1973. Subj: Animals – cats. Animals – mice. Foreign lands – England.

The church mice adrift ill. by author. Atheneum, 1976. Subj: Animals – mice. Animals – rats. Rivers.

The church mice and the moon ill. by author. Atheneum, 1974. Subj: Animals – cats. Animals – mice. Foreign lands – England. Moon.

The church mice at bay ill. by author. Atheneum, 1978. Subj: Animals – cats. Animals – mice. Foreign lands – England.

The church mice at Christmas ill. by author. Atheneum, 1980. Subj: Animals – mice. Holidays – Christmas.

The church mice in action ill. by author. Atheneum, 1983. Subj: Animals – mice. Problem solving.

The church mice spread their wings ill. by author. Atheneum, 1975. Subj: Animals – cats. Animals – mice. Foreign lands – England.

The church mouse ill. by author. Atheneum, 1972. Subj: Animals – cats. Animals – mice. Foreign lands – England.

Graham Oakley's magical changes ill. by author. Atheneum, 1980. Subj: Format, unusual. Imagination. Wordless.

Hetty and Harriet ill. by author. Atheneum, 1982. Subj: Behavior – running away. Birds – chickens.

Oana, Kay D. *Robbie and the raggedy scarecrow* ill. by Jackie Stephens. Oddo, 1978. Subj: Birds. Scarecrows. Trees.

Shasta and the shebang machine ill. by Jackie Stephens. Oddo, 1978. Subj: Animals – cats. Behavior – misbehavior.

Obligado, Lilian. *Faint frogs feeling feverish and other terrifically tantalizing tongue twisters* ill. by author. Viking, 1983. Subj: ABC books. Animals. Tongue twisters.

Obrist, Jürg. *Fluffy: the story of a cat* ill. by author. Atheneum, 1981. Subj: Animals – cats. Moving.

The miser who wanted the sun ill. by author. Atheneum, 1984. Subj: Behavior – greed. Character traits – cleverness. Sun.

They do things right in Albern ill. by author. Atheneum, 1978. Subj: Animals – moles. Problem solving.

O'Cuilleanain, Eilis Dillon *see* Dillon, Eilis

Odoyevsky, Vladimir. *Old Father Frost* tr. from Russian by James Riordan; ill. by Vassili Shulzhenko. Imported Pubs., 1983. Subj: Folk and fairy tales. Foreign lands – Russia. Seasons – winter.

Ogle, Lucille. *A B See* by Lucille Ogle and Tina Thoburn; ill. by Ralph Stobart. McGraw-Hill, 1973. Subj: ABC books.

I hear by Lucille Ogle and Tina Thoburn; ill. by Eloise Wilkin. American Heritage, 1971. Subj: Noise, sounds. Participation. Senses.

I spy with my little eye ill. by Joe Kaufman. McGraw-Hill, 1970. Subj: Senses. Wordless.

O'Hagan, Caroline. *It's easy to have a caterpillar visit you* ill. by Judith Allan. Lothrop, 1980. Subj: Insects – butterflies, caterpillars. Pets.

It's easy to have a snail visit you ill. by Judith Allan. Lothrop, 1980. Subj: Animals – snails. Pets.

It's easy to have a worm visit you ill. by Judith Allan. Lothrop, 1980. Subj: Animals – worms. Pets.

O'Hare, Colette. *What do you feed your donkey on?*

Ohlsson, Ib. *Cat alley* tr. by Virginia Allen Jensen; ill. by author. Coward, 1971. Translation of Kattehuset. Subj: Behavior – lost. City.

Oishi, Makoto. *E. H. Grieg's Peer Gynt* (Grieg, E H (Edvard Hagerup))

Oksner, Robert M. *The incompetent wizard* ill. by Janet McCaffery. Morrow, 1965. Subj: Dragons. Magic. Wizards.

The old-fashioned children's storybook. Wanderer, 1980. Subj: Folk and fairy tales.

Old MacDonald had a farm ill. by Mel Crawford. Golden Pr., 1967. Subj: Animals. Cumulative tales. Farms. Music. Songs.

Old MacDonald had a farm ill. by David Frankland. Merrill, 1980. Subj: Animals. Cumulative tales. Farms. Music. Songs.

Old MacDonald had a farm ill. by Abner Graboff. Four Winds Pr., 1970. Subj: Animals. Cumulative tales. Farms. Music. Songs.

Old MacDonald had a farm ill. by Tracey Campbell Pearson. Dial Pr., 1984. Subj: Animals. Cumulative tales. Farms. Music. Songs.

Old MacDonald had a farm ill. by Robert M. Quackenbush. Lippincott, 1972. Subj: Animals. Cumulative tales. Farms. Music. Songs.

The old woman and her pig ill. by Paul Galdone. McGraw-Hill, 1960. Subj: Cumulative tales. Folk and fairy tales.

Oldfield, Pamela. *Melanie Brown climbs a tree* ill. by Carolyn Dinan. Faber, 1980. Subj: Behavior – misbehavior. Foreign lands – England.

Olds, Elizabeth. *Feather mountain* ill. by author. Houghton, 1951. Subj: Birds. Caldecott award honor book.

Little Una ill. by author. Scribner's, 1963. Subj: City.

Plop plop ploppie ill. by author. Scribner's, 1962. Subj: Animals – sea lions. Clowns, jesters.

Olds, Helen Diehl. *Miss Hattie and the monkey* ill. by Dorothy Marino. Follett, 1958. Subj: Animals – monkeys. Careers – seamstresses.

Oleson, Claire. *For Pipita, an orange tree* ill. by Margot Tomes. Doubleday, 1967. Subj: Foreign lands – Spain. Plants.

Oliver, Dexter. *I want to be...* by Dexter and Patricia Oliver; photos. by Dexter Oliver. Third World Pr., 1974. Subj: ABC books. Careers.

Oliver, Patricia. *I want to be...* (Oliver, Dexter)

Olney, Ross R. *Construction giants* ill. with photos. Atheneum, 1984. Subj: Machines.

Farm giants ill. with photos. Atheneum, 1982. Subj: Farms. Machines.

Olschewski, Alfred. *We fly* ill. by author. Little, 1967. Subj: Airplanes, airports.

The wheel rolls over ill. by author. Little, 1962. Subj: Transportation. Wheels.

Olson, Helen Kronberg. *The strange thing that happened to Oliver Wendell Iscovitch* ill. by Betsy Lewin. Dodd, 1983. Subj: Behavior – misbehavior. Ghosts. Humor.

Olujic, Grozdana. *Rose of Mother-of-Pearl* tr. from Serbo-Croatian by Grozdana Olujic and Jascha Kessler; ill. by Kathy Jacobi. Toothpaste Pr., 1983. Subj: Behavior – dissatisfaction. Sea and seashore.

On the little hearth tr. by Miriam Chaikin; ill. by Gabriel Lisowski; score by Mark Warshawski. Holt, 1978. Subj: Foreign languages. Jewish culture. Music. Songs.

Onassis, Jacqueline. *The firebird*

One rubber duckie: *a Sesame Street counting book* photos. by John E. Barrett. Random House, 1982. Subj: Counting. Puppets.

One, two, buckle my shoe ill. by Gail E. Haley. Doubleday, 1964. Subj: Counting. Nursery rhymes.

O'Neill, Mary. *Big red hen* ill. by Judy Piussi-Campbell. Doubleday, 1971. Subj: Birds – chickens. Eggs. Poetry, rhyme.

Opie, Iona Archibald. *A family book of nursery rhymes* comp. by Iona and Peter Opie; ill. by Pauline Baynes. Oxford Univ. Pr., 1964. Subj: Nursery rhymes.

A nursery companion by Iona and Peter Opie. Oxford Univ. Pr., 1980. Subj: Folk and fairy tales. Nursery rhymes.

The Oxford nursery rhyme book comp. by Iona and Peter Opie; ill. by Joan Hassall. Oxford Univ. Pr., 1955. Subj: Nursery rhymes.

Puffin book of nursery rhymes comp. by Iona and Peter Opie; ill. by Pauline Baynes. Penguin, 1963. Subj: Nursery rhymes.

Opie, Peter. *A family book of nursery rhymes* (Opie, Iona Archibald)

A nursery companion (Opie, Iona Archibald)

The Oxford nursery rhyme book (Opie, Iona Archibald)

Puffin book of nursery rhymes (Opie, Iona Archibald)

Oppenheim, Joanne. *Have you seen roads?* ill. by Gerard Nook. Addison-Wesley, 1969. Subj: Poetry, rhyme. Transportation.

Have you seen trees? ill. by Irwin Rosenhouse. Addison-Wesley, 1967. Subj: Poetry, rhyme. Seasons. Trees.

James will never die ill. by True Kelley. Dodd, 1982. Subj: Activities – playing.

Mrs. Peloki's class play ill. by Joyce Audy dos Santos. Dodd, 1984. Subj: School. Theater.

Mrs. Peloki's snake ill. by Joyce Audy dos Santos. Dodd, 1980. Subj: Reptiles – snakes. School.

On the other side of the river ill. by Aliki. Watts, 1972. Subj: Behavior – needing someone. Bridges. Careers.

Oram, Hiawyn. *In the attic* ill. by Satoshi Kitamura. Holt, 1985. Subj: Activities – playing. Behavior – boredom. Imagination.

Ned and the Joybaloo ill. by Satoshi Kitamura. Global Lib. Mktg. Serv., 1983. Subj: Imagination – imaginary friends.

Skittlewonder and the wizard ill. by Jenny Rodwell. Dial Pr., 1980. Subj: Folk and fairy tales. Games. Gypsies. Royalty. Witches. Wizards.

Orbach, Ruth. *Apple pigs* ill. by author. Collins-World, 1977. Subj: Food. Poetry, rhyme. Trees.

Please send a panda ill. by author. Collins-World, 1978. Subj: Behavior – wishing. Family life – grandparents, great-grandparents. Pets.

O'Reilly, Edward. *Brown pelican at the pond* ill. by Florence Strange. Manzanita, 1979. Subj: Birds – pelicans. Children as authors.

Orgel, Doris. *Little John* by Theodor Storm; retold from the German by Doris Orgel; ill. by Anita Lobel. Farrar, 1972. Subj: Bedtime. Dreams.

Merry merry FIBruary ill. by Arnold Lobel. Parents, 1978. Subj: Poetry, rhyme.

On the sand dune ill. by Leonard Weisgard. Harper, 1968. Subj: Character traits – smallness. Sea and seashore.

Ormerod, Jan. *Moonlight* ill. by author. Lothrop, 1982. Subj: Bedtime. Family life. Sleep. Wordless.

101 things to do with a baby ill. by author. Lothrop, 1984. Subj: Babies. Behavior – sharing. Sibling rivalry.

Reading ill. by author. Lothrop, 1985. Subj: Activities – reading. Family life – fathers.

Sunshine ill. by author. Lothrop, 1981. Subj: Morning. Sun. Wordless.

Ormondroyd, Edward. *Broderick* ill. by John M. Larrecq. Parnassus, 1969. Subj: Activities – reading. Animals – mice. Sports – surfing.

Theodore ill. by John M. Larrecq. Parnassus, 1966. Subj: Character traits – appearance. Character traits – kindness. Laundry. Toys – teddy bears.

Theodore's rival ill. by John M. Larrecq. Parnassus, 1971. Subj: Emotions – envy, jealousy. Sibling rivalry. Toys – teddy bears.

Ormsby, Virginia H. *Twenty-one children plus ten* ill. by author. Lippincott, 1971. Subj: Ethnic groups in the U.S. – Mexican-Americans. School.

Osborn, Lois. *My dad is really something* ill. by Rodney Pate. Albert Whitman, 1983. Subj: Behavior – boasting. Death. Emotions – envy, jealousy. Family life – fathers. Friendship.

Osborne, Valerie. *One big yo to go* ill. by Jiri Tibor Novak. Oxford Univ. Pr., 1981. Subj: Poetry, rhyme.

Ostrovsky, Vivian. *Mumps!* ill. by Rose Ostrovsky. Holt, 1978. Subj: Illness.

Otsuka, Yuzo. *Suho and the white horse: a legend of Mongolia* tr. by Ann Herring; ill. by Suekichi Akaba. Viking, 1981. Subj: Animals – horses. Emotions – love. Sports – racing.

Ott, John. *Peter Pumpkin* originated by Peter Coley; ill. by Ivan Chermayeff. Doubleday, 1963. Subj: Holidays – Halloween. Holidays – Thanksgiving. Seasons – fall.

Otto, Margaret Glover. *The little brown horse* ill. by Barbara Cooney. Knopf, 1959. Subj: Animals – cats. Animals – horses. Birds – chickens.

Otto, Svend. *The giant fish and other stories* by Svend Otto S; tr. from Danish by Joan Tate; ill. by author. Larousse, 1982. Subj: Behavior – growing up. Foreign lands.

Taxi dog by Svend Otto S; ill. by author. Parents, 1978. Subj: Animals – dogs. Behavior – running away. Careers – taxi drivers.

Over in the meadow ill. by Ezra Jack Keats. Four Winds Pr., 1971. Subj: Animals. Counting. Folk and fairy tales. Poetry, rhyme. Songs.

Overbeck, Cynthia. *Rusty the Irish setter* rev. English text by Cynthia Overbeck; original French text by Anne Marie Pajot; tr. by Dyan Hammarberg; photos. by Antoinette Barrère; ill. by L'Enc Matte. Carolrhoda Books, 1977. Original ed. published under title: Jimmy, le grand chien. Subj: Animals – dogs.

The winds that blow (Thompson, Brenda)

Oxenbury, Helen. *Beach day* ill. by author. Dial Pr., 1982. Subj: Family life. Format, unusual – cardboard pages. Sea and seashore. Wordless.

The birthday party ill. by author. Dial Pr., 1983. Subj: Birthdays.

The car trip ill. by author. Dial Pr., 1983. Subj: Automobiles. Behavior – bad day. Behavior – misbehavior.

The checkup ill. by author. Dial Pr., 1983. Subj: Careers – doctors. Health.

The dancing class ill. by author. Dial Pr., 1983. Subj: Activities – dancing.

Eating out ill. by author. Dial Pr., 1983. Subj: Food.

Family ill. by author. Simon and Schuster, 1981. Subj: Family life. Format, unusual – cardboard pages.

First day of school ill. by author. Dial Pr., 1983. Subj: Friendship. School.

Friends ill. by author. Simon and Schuster, 1981. Subj: Animals. Format, unusual – cardboard pages. Friendship.

Good night, good morning ill. by author. Dial Pr., 1982. Subj: Bedtime. Morning. Wordless.

Helen Oxenbury's ABC of things ill. by author. Watts, 1971. Subj: ABC books.

Monkey see, monkey do ill. by author. Dial Pr., 1982. Subj: Animals. Wordless. Zoos.

Mother's helper ill. by author. Dial Pr., 1982. Subj: Character traits – helpfulness. Family life – mothers. Wordless.

Numbers of things ill. by author. Watts, 1968. Subj: Counting.

Our dog ill. by author. Dial Pr., 1984. Subj: Animals – dogs. Pets.

Pig tale ill. by author. Morrow, 1974. Subj: Animals – pigs. Poetry, rhyme.

Playing ill. by author. Wanderer Books, 1981. Subj: Activities – playing. Babies. Format, unusual – cardboard pages. Toys.

The queen and Rosie Randall by Helen Oxenbury from an idea by Jill Butterfield-Campbell; ill. by author. Morrow, 1979. Subj: Foreign lands – England. Games. Parties. Royalty.

729 curious creatures ill. by author. Harper, 1980. Subj: Animals. Format, unusual – cardboard pages. Imagination.

729 merry mix-ups ill. by author. Harper, 1980. Subj: Animals. Format, unusual – cardboard pages. Imagination.

729 puzzle people ill. by author. Harper, 1980. Subj: Format, unusual – cardboard pages. Imagination.

The shopping trip ill. by author. Dial Pr., 1982. Subj: Format, unusual – cardboard pages. Shopping. Wordless.

Oxford Scientific Films. *Grey squirrel* photos. by George Bernard and John Paling. Putnam's, 1982. Subj: Animals – squirrels. Science.

Jellyfish and other sea creatures photos. by Peter Parks. Putnam's, 1982. Subj: Animals. Fish. Sea and seashore. Science.

Mosquito photos. by George Bernard and John Cooke. Putnam's, 1982. Subj: Insects – mosquitoes. Science.

The stickleback cycle photos. by David Thompson. Putnam's, 1979. Subj: Fish. Science.

Pène Du Bois, William *see* Du Bois, William Pène

Pacheco, Miguel Angel. *Kangaroo* (Sanchez, Jose Louis Garcia)

Pack, Robert. *How to catch a crocodile* ill. by Nola Langner. Knopf, 1964. Subj: Character traits – laziness. Imagination. Poetry, rhyme. Reptiles – alligators, crocodiles.

Then what did you do? ill. by Nola Langner. Macmillan, 1961. Subj: Animals. Cumulative tales. Humor. Poetry, rhyme.

Page, Eleanor *see* Coerr, Eleanor

Pajot, Anne Marie. *Rusty the Irish setter* (Overbeck, Cynthia)

Palazzo, Anthony D. *see* Palazzo, Tony

Palazzo, Janet. *Our friend the sun* ill. by Susan Hall. Troll Assoc., 1982. Subj: Science. Sun.

What makes the weather ill. by Paul Harvey. Troll Assoc., 1982. Subj: Weather.

Palazzo, Tony. *Animal babies* ill. by author. Doubleday, 1960. Subj: Animals.

Animals 'round the mulberry bush ill. by author. Doubleday, 1958. Subj: Animals. Nursery rhymes.

Bianco and the New World ill. by author. Viking, 1957. Subj: Animals – donkeys. Circus.

Federico, the flying squirrel ill. by author. Viking, 1951. Subj: Animals – squirrels.

Noah's ark ill. by author. Doubleday, 1955. Subj: Religion – Noah.

Waldo the woodchuck ill. by author. Duell, 1964. Subj: Animals – groundhogs. Holidays – Groundhog Day.

Paleček, Phyllis. *The ugly duckling* (Andersen, H C (Hans Christian))

Palmer, Helen Marion. *A fish out of water* ill. by P. D. Eastman. Random House, 1961. Subj: Fish. Humor.

I was kissed by a seal at the zoo photos. by Lynn Fayman. Random House, 1962. Subj: Animals. Humor. Zoos.

Why I built the boogle house photos. by Lynn Fayman. Random House, 1964. Subj: Animals. Houses. Pets.

Palmer, Mary Babcock. *No-sort-of-animal* ill. by Abner Graboff. Houghton, 1964. Subj: Animals. Behavior – dissatisfaction. Self-concept.

Panek, Dennis. *Catastrophe Cat* ill. by author. Bradbury Pr., 1978. Subj: Animals – cats. Behavior – carelessness.

Catastrophe Cat at the zoo ill. by author. Bradbury Pr., 1979. Subj: Animals – cats. Wordless. Zoos.

Matilda Hippo has a big mouth ill. by author. Bradbury Pr., 1980. Subj: Animals – hippopotami. Behavior.

Paola, Thomas Anthony *see* De Paola, Tomi

Paola, Tomi De *see* De Paola, Tomi

Papajani, Janet. *Museums* ill. with photos. Children's Pr., 1983. Subj: Museums.

Papas, William. *Taresh the tea planter* ill. by author. Collins-World, 1968. Subj: Character traits – laziness. Foreign lands – India.

Pape, D. L. *see* Pape, Donna Lugg

Pape, Donna Lugg. *Doghouse for sale* ill. by Tom Eaton. Garrard, 1979. Subj: Animals – dogs. Houses.

Snoino mystery ill. by William Hutchinson. Garrard, 1980. Subj: Problem solving.

Where is my little Joey? ill. by Tom Eaton. Garrard, 1978. Subj: Animals – kangaroos.

A paper of pins ill. by Margaret Gordon. Seabury Pr., 1975. Subj: Folk and fairy tales. Money. Songs.

Parenteau, Shirley. *I'll bet you thought I was lost* ill. by Lorna Tomei. Lothrop, 1981. Subj: Behavior – lost.

Parish, Peggy. *Amelia Bedelia* ill. by Fritz Siebel. Harper, 1963. Subj: Behavior – misunderstanding. Careers – maids. Humor. Language.

Amelia Bedelia and the surprise shower ill. by Fritz Siebel. Harper, 1966. Subj: Behavior – misunderstanding. Careers – maids. Humor. Language. Parties.

Amelia Bedelia goes camping ill. by Lynn Sweat. Greenwillow, 1985. Subj: Behavior – misunderstanding. Careers – maids. Humor. Language. Sports – camping.

Amelia Bedelia helps out ill. by Lynn Sweat. Greenwillow, 1979. Subj: Behavior – misunderstanding. Careers – maids. Humor. Language.

Be ready at eight ill. by Leonard P. Kessler. Macmillan, 1979. Subj: Behavior – forgetfulness. Birthdays.

The cat's burglar ill. by Lynn Sweat. Greenwillow, 1983. Subj: Animals – cats. Crime.

Come back, Amelia Bedelia ill. by Wallace Tripp. Harper, 1971. Subj: Behavior – misunderstanding. Careers – maids. Humor. Language.

Dinosaur time ill. by Arnold Lobel. Harper, 1974. Subj: Dinosaurs. Science.

Good hunting, Little Indian ill. by Leonard Weisgard. Addison-Wesley, 1962. Subj: Ethnic groups in the U.S. – Indians.

Good work, Amelia Bedelia ill. by Lynn Sweat. Greenwillow, 1976. Subj: Behavior – misunderstanding. Careers – maids. Humor. Language.

Granny and the desperadoes ill. by Steven Kellogg. Macmillan, 1970. Subj: Crime. Family life – grandparents, great-grandparents. Humor.

Granny and the Indians. ill. by Brinton Turkle. Macmillan, 1969. Subj: Ethnic groups in the U.S. – Indians. Family life – grandparents, great-grandparents. Humor.

Granny, the baby and the big gray thing ill. by Lynn Sweat. Macmillan, 1972. Subj: Animals – wolves. Babies. Ethnic groups in the U.S. – Indians. Family life – grandparents, great-grandparents. Humor.

I can - can you? ill. by Marylin Hafner. Greenwillow, 1984. Set of 4 books: level 1-4. Subj: Activities. Behavior – growing up. Format, unusual – cardboard pages.

Jumper goes to school ill. by Cyndy Szekeres. Simon and Schuster, 1969. Subj: Animals – monkeys. School.

Little Indian ill. by John E. Johnson. Simon and Schuster, 1968. Subj: Ethnic groups in the U.S. – Indians. Names.

Mind your manners ill. by Marylin Hafner. Greenwillow, 1978. Subj: Etiquette.

No more monsters for me! ill. by Marc Simont. Harper, 1981. Subj: Monsters. Pets.

Ootah's lucky day ill. by Mamoru Funai. Harper, 1970. Subj: Ethnic groups in the U.S. – Eskimos. Sports – hunting.

Play ball, Amelia Bedelia ill. by Wallace Tripp. Harper, 1972. Subj: Behavior – misunderstanding. Careers – maids. Humor. Language. Sports – baseball.

Snapping turtle's all wrong day ill. by John E. Johnson. Simon and Schuster, 1970. Subj: Birthdays. Ethnic groups in the U.S. – Indians.

Teach us, Amelia Bedelia ill. by Lynn Sweat. Greenwillow, 1977. Subj: Behavior – misunderstanding. Careers – maids. Humor. Language. School.

Thank you, Amelia Bedelia ill. by Fritz Siebel. Harper, 1964. Subj: Behavior – misunderstanding. Careers – maids. Humor. Language.

Too many rabbits ill. by Leonard P. Kessler. Macmillan, 1974. Subj: Animals – rabbits.

Zed and the monsters ill. by Paul Galdone. Doubleday, 1979. Subj: Character traits – cleverness. Monsters.

Park, Ruth. *When the wind changed* ill. by Deborah Niland. Coward, 1981. Subj: Character traits – appearance.

Park, W. B. *Bakery business* ill. by author. Little, 1983. Subj: Birthdays. Humor.

The costume party ill. by author. Little, 1983. Subj: Animals. Emotions – loneliness. Parties.

Parke, Margaret B. *Young reader's color-picture dictionary* ill. by Cynthia and Alvin Koehler. Grosset, 1958. Subj: Dictionaries.

Parker, Dorothy D. *Liam's catch* ill. by Robert Andrew Parker. Viking, 1972. Subj: Careers – fishermen. Foreign lands – Ireland. Sports – fishing.

Parker, Nancy Winslow. *The Christmas camel* ill. by author. Dodd, 1983. Subj: Animals – camels. Holidays – Christmas.

Cooper, the McNallys' big black dog ill. by author. Dodd, 1981. Subj: Animals – dogs. Behavior – misbehavior. Character traits – helpfulness.

The crocodile under Louis Finneberg's bed ill. by author. Dodd, 1978. Subj: Behavior – running away. Behavior – trickery. Reptiles – alligators, crocodiles.

Love from Aunt Betty ill. by author. Dodd, 1983. Subj: Activities – cooking. Monsters.

Love from Uncle Clyde ill. by author. Dodd, 1977. Subj: Animals – hippopotami. Birthdays.

The ordeal of Byron B. Blackbear ill. by author. Dodd, 1979. Subj: Animals – bears. Hibernation. Science.

Poofy loves company ill. by author. Dodd, 1980. Subj: Animals – dogs. Behavior – misbehavior.

Puddums, the Cathcarts' orange cat ill. by author. Atheneum, 1980. Subj: Animals – cats. Behavior.

Parkin, Rex. *The red carpet* ill. by author. Macmillan, 1948. Subj: Hotels. Humor.

Parnall, Peter. *Alfalfa Hill* ill. by author. Doubleday, 1975. Subj: Animals. Birds. Seasons – winter. Weather – snow.

The great fish ill. by author. Doubleday, 1973. Subj: Ecology. Ethnic groups in the U.S. – Indians. Fish. Folk and fairy tales.

Parry, Marian. *King of the fish* ill. by author. Macmillan, 1977. Subj: Animals – rabbits. Character traits – cleverness. Fish. Folk and fairy tales. Foreign lands – Korea. Reptiles – turtles.

Parsons, Virginia. *Pinocchio and Gepetto* ill. by adapt. McGraw-Hill, 1979. Subj: Folk and fairy tales. Puppets.

Pinocchio and the money tree ill. by adapt. McGraw-Hill, 1979. Subj: Folk and fairy tales. Puppets.

Pinocchio goes on the stage ill. by adapt. McGraw-Hill, 1979. Subj: Folk and fairy tales. Puppets.

Pinocchio plays truant ill. by adapt. McGraw-Hill, 1979. Subj: Folk and fairy tales. Puppets.

Partch, Virgil Franklin. *The Christmas cookie sprinkle snitcher* ill. by author. Windmill Books, 1969. Subj: Crime. Holidays – Christmas. Poetry, rhyme. Rebuses.

The VIP's mistake book ill. by author. Windmill Books, 1970. Subj: Humor. Rebuses.

Partridge, Jenny. *Colonel Grunt* ill. by author. Holt, 1982. Subj: Animals.

Grandma Snuffles ill. by author. Holt, 1983. Subj: Animals. Clothing.

Hopfellow ill. by author. Holt, 1982. Subj: Animals. Boats, ships. Frogs and toads. Problem solving.

Mr. Squint ill. by author. Holt, 1982. Subj: Animals. Problem solving.

Peterkin Pollensnuff ill. by author. Holt, 1982. Subj: Animals. Character traits – helpfulness. Problem solving.

Parvathi, Thampi. *Moon-uncle, moon-uncle* (Cassedy, Sylvia)

Pasley, L. *The adventures of Madalene and Louisa* by L. and M. S. Pasley; ill. by authors. Random House, 1980. Subj: Children as authors. Children as illustrators. Insects.

Pasley, M. S. *The adventures of Madalene and Louisa* (Pasley, L.)

Paterson, Andrew Barton. *The man from Ironbark* ill. by Quentin Hole. Collins-World, 1975. Subj: Character traits – cleverness. Poetry, rhyme.

Mulga Bill's bicycle ill. by Kilmeny and Deborah Niland. Parents, 1975. Subj: Animals – horses. Foreign lands – Australia. Poetry, rhyme. Sports – bicycling.

Waltzing Matilda ill. by Desmund Digby. Holt, 1970. Subj: Foreign lands – Australia. Songs.

Paterson, Diane. *The bathtub ocean* ill. by author. Dial Pr., 1979. Subj: Activities – bathing. Imagination.

Eat ill. by author. Dial Pr., 1975. Subj: Food. Humor.

Hey, cowboy! ill. by author. Knopf, 1983. Subj: Family life – grandparents, great-grandparents. Sibling rivalry.

If I were a toad ill. by author. Dial Pr., 1977. Subj: Animals. Behavior – wishing. Participation.

Smile for auntie ill. by author. Dial Pr., 1976. Subj: Humor.

Soap and suds ill. by author. Knopf, 1984. Subj: Activities – working. Behavior – misbehavior.

Wretched Rachel ill. by author. Dial Pr., 1978. Subj: Behavior. Emotions – love. Family life.

Paterson, Katherine. *The crane wife* (Yagawa, Sumiko)

Paton Walsh, Jill *see* Walsh, Jill Paton

Patrick, Gloria. *This is...* ill. by Joan Hanson. Carolrhoda Books, 1970. Subj: Cumulative tales. Participation. Poetry, rhyme.

Patterson, Lillie. *Haunted houses on Halloween* ill. by Doug Cushman. Garrard, 1979. Subj: Holidays – Halloween. Houses.

Patterson, Pat. *Hickory dickory duck: a book of very funny rhymes and picture puzzles* by Pat Patterson and Joe Weissmann. Greey de Pencier Books, 1982. Subj: Games. Nursery rhymes.

Patz, Nancy. *Moses supposes his toeses are roses and 7 other silly old rhymes* ill. by author. Harcourt, 1983. Subj: Poetry, rhyme.

Pumpernickel tickle and mean green cheese ill. by author. Watts, 1978. Subj: Animals – elephants. Behavior – forgetfulness. Humor. Shopping. Tongue twisters.

Paul, Anthony. *The tiger who lost his stripes* ill. by Michael Foreman. Harcourt, 1982. Subj: Animals – tigers. Character traits – cleverness. Forest, woods.

Paul, Korky. *Pop-up numbers #1* (Marshall, Ray)

Pop-up numbers #2 (Marshall, Ray)

Pop-up numbers #3 (Marshall, Ray)

Pop-up numbers #4 (Marshall, Ray)

Paul, Sherry. *2-B and the rock 'n roll band* ill. by Bob Miller. Children's Pr., 1981. Subj: Character traits – helpfulness. Robots.

2-B and the space visitor ill. by Bob Miller. Children's Pr., 1981. Subj: Holidays – Halloween. Robots. Space and space ships.

Pavey, Peter. *I'm Taggarty Toad* ill. by author. Bradbury Pr., 1980. Subj: Behavior – boasting. Frogs and toads. Imagination.

One dragon's dream ill. by author. Bradbury Pr., 1979. Subj: Counting. Dragons. Dreams. Poetry, rhyme.

Payne, Emmy. *Katy no-pocket* ill. by Hans Augusto Rey. Houghton, 1944. Subj: Animals – kangaroos. Clothing. Problem solving.

Payne, Joan Balfour. *The stable that stayed* ill. by author. Ariel, 1952. Subj: Animals. Careers – artists. Country.

Peaceable kingdom: *the Shaker abecedarius* ill. by Alice and Martin Provensen. Viking, 1978. Subj: ABC books. Animals. Poetry, rhyme.

Pearson, Susan. *Everybody knows that!* ill. by Diane Paterson. Dial Pr., 1978. Subj: Friendship. School.

Karin's Christmas walk ill. by Trinka Hakes Noble. Dial Pr., 1980. Subj: Family life. Holidays – Christmas.

That's enough for one day! ill. by Kay Chorao. Dial Pr., 1977. Subj: Activities – playing. Activities – reading.

Pearson, Tracey Campbell. *Sing a song of sixpence* ill. by author. Dial Pr., 1985. Subj: Behavior – misbehavior. Humor. Nursery rhymes.

The peasant's pea patch ill. by Robert M. Quackenbush; tr. by Guy Daniels. Delacorte Pr., 1971. Subj: Birds – cranes. Folk and fairy tales. Foreign lands – Russia.

Peavy, Linda. *Allison's grandfather* ill. by Ronald Himler. Scribner's, 1981. Subj: Death. Family life – grandparents, great-grandparents.

Peck, Richard. *Monster night at Grandma's house* ill. by Don Freeman. Viking, 1977. Subj: Bedtime. Family life – grandparents, great-grandparents. Monsters. Night.

Peck, Robert Newton. *Hamilton* ill. by Laura Lydecker. Little, 1976. Subj: Animals – pigs. Animals – wolves. Farms. Poetry, rhyme.

Peet, Bill. *The ant and the elephant* ill. by author. Little, 1972. Subj: Animals. Animals – elephants. Character traits – helpfulness. Character traits – selfishness. Cumulative tales. Insects – ants.

Big bad Bruce ill. by author. Houghton, 1977. Subj: Animals – bears. Behavior – bullying. Forest, woods. Humor. Witches.

Buford, the little bighorn ill. by author. Houghton, 1967. Subj: Animals – sheep. Character traits – individuality. Humor. Sports – hunting. Sports – skiing.

The caboose who got loose ill. by author. Houghton, 1971. Subj: Behavior – dissatisfaction Ecology. Trains.

Chester the worldly pig ill. by author. Houghton, 1965. Subj: Animals – pigs. Circus. Humor. World.

Countdown to Christmas ill. by author. Houghton, 1972. Subj: Holidays – Christmas. Humor. Magic. Progress.

Cowardly Clyde ill. by author. Houghton, 1979. Subj: Animals – horses. Character traits – bravery. Humor. Knights.

Cyrus the unsinkable sea serpent ill. by author. Houghton, 1975. Subj: Character traits – helpfulness. Monsters. Mythical creatures. Sea and seashore.

Eli ill. by author. Houghton, 1978. Subj: Animals – lions. Birds – vultures. Friendship. Humor.

Ella ill. by author. Houghton, 1964. Subj: Animals – elephants. Behavior – lost. Character traits – conceit. Circus. Poetry, rhyme.

Encore for Eleanor ill. by author. Houghton, 1981. Subj: Animals – elephants. Art.

Farewell to Shady Glade ill. by author. Houghton, 1966. Subj: Animals. Ecology. Progress.

Fly, Homer, fly ill. by author. Houghton, 1969. Subj: Birds – pigeons. City. Ecology.

The gnats of knotty pine ill. by author. Houghton, 1975. Subj: Animals. Ecology. Insects – gnats. Sports – hunting.

How Droofus the dragon lost his head ill. by author. Houghton, 1971. Subj: Dragons. Knights. Royalty.

Hubert's hair-raising adventures ill. by author. Houghton, 1959. Subj: Animals – lions. Careers – barbers. Humor. Poetry, rhyme.

Huge Harold ill. by author. Houghton, 1961. Subj: Animals – rabbits. Character traits – kindness to animals. Concepts – size. Humor. Poetry, rhyme.

Jennifer and Josephine ill. by author. Houghton, 1967. Subj: Animals – cats. Automobiles. Humor.

Kermit the hermit ill. by author. Houghton, 1965. Subj: Behavior – greed. Crustacea. Humor. Poetry, rhyme. Sea and seashore.

The luckiest one of all ill. by author. Houghton, 1982. Subj: Behavior – dissatisfaction. Emotions – envy, jealousy. Poetry, rhyme.

Merle the high flying squirrel ill. by author. Houghton, 1974. Subj: Activities – flying. Animals – squirrels. Humor. Kites. Trees.

Pamela Camel ill. by author. Houghton, 1984. Subj: Animals – camels. Behavior – running away. Self-concept.

The pinkish, purplish, bluish egg ill. by author. Houghton, 1963. Subj: Birds. Birds – doves. Eggs. Mythical creatures. Poetry, rhyme. Violence, anti-violence.

Randy's dandy lions ill. by author. Houghton, 1964. Subj: Animals – lions. Circus. Humor. Poetry, rhyme.

Smokey ill. by author. Houghton, 1962. Subj: Old age. Poetry, rhyme. Trains.

The spooky tail of Prewitt Peacock ill. by author. Houghton, 1973. Subj: Birds – peacocks, peahens. Character traits – being different. Character traits – individuality.

The Whingdingdilly ill. by author. Houghton, 1970. Subj: Animals – dogs. Behavior – dissatisfaction. Character traits – optimism. Witches.

The wump world ill. by author. Houghton, 1970. Subj: Ecology. Progress. Space and space ships.

Peet, Georgia. *Be quite quiet beside the lake* (Koenner, Alfred)

High flies the ball (Koenner, Alfred)

Peet, William Bartlett *see* Peet, Bill

Pellowski, Anne. *Stairstep farm: Anna Rose's story* ill. by Wendy Watson. Putnam's, 1981. Subj: Behavior – growing up. Family life. Farms.

Pellowski, Michael. *Clara joins the circus* ill. by True Kelley. Parents, 1981. Subj: Animals – bulls, cows. Circus. Clowns, jesters.

Pender, Lydia. *Barnaby and the horses* ill. by Alie Evers. Abelard-Schuman, 1961. Subj: Animals – horses. Behavior – carelessness. Country.

Pendery, Rosemary. *A home for Hopper* ill. by Robert M. Quackenbush. Morrow, 1971. Subj: Frogs and toads.

Pène Du Bois, William *see* Du Bois, William Pène

The penguin ill. by Norman Weaver. Rourke, 1983. Subj: Birds – penguins.

Penn, Ruth Bonn *see* Clifford, Eth

Peppé, Rodney. *The alphabet book* ill. by author. Four Winds Pr., 1968. Subj: ABC books.

Cat and mouse: a book of rhymes comp. and ill. by Rodney Peppé. Holt, 1973. Subj: Animals — cats. Animals — mice. Nursery rhymes. Poetry, rhyme.

Circus numbers: a counting book ill. by author. Delacorte Pr., 1969. Subj: Circus. Counting.

Hey riddle diddle ill. by author. Holt, 1971. Subj: Nursery rhymes. Poetry, rhyme. Riddles.

The kettleship pirates ill. by author. Lothrop, 1983. Subj: Animals — mice. Birthdays. Boats, ships. Imagination. Pirates.

Little circus ill. by author. Viking, 1984. Subj: Animals. Circus. Format, unusual — cardboard pages. Toys.

Little dolls ill. by author. Viking, 1984. Subj: Clothing. Format, unusual — cardboard pages. Toys.

Little games ill. by author. Viking, 1984. Subj: Format, unusual — cardboard pages. Games. Toys.

Little numbers ill. by author. Viking, 1984. Subj: Counting. Format, unusual — cardboard pages. Toys.

Little wheels ill. by author. Viking, 1984. Subj: Automobiles. Format, unusual — cardboard pages. Toys. Trucks.

The mice who lived in a shoe ill. by author. Lothrop, 1982. Subj: Animals — mice. Houses.

Odd one out ill. by author. Viking, 1974. Subj: Concepts. Games.

Rodney Peppé's puzzle book ill. by author. Viking, 1977. Subj: Concepts. Games.

Perera, Lydia. *Frisky* ill. by Oscar Liebman. Random House, 1966. Subj: City. Merry-go-rounds.

Peretz, Isaac Loeb. *The magician* (Shulevitz, Uri)

Perez, Carla. *Your turn, doctor* (Robison, Deborah)

Perkins, Al. *The digging-est dog* ill. by Eric Gurney. Random House, 1967. Subj: Activities — digging. Animals — dogs. Poetry, rhyme.

Don and Donna go to bat ill. by Barney Tobey. Random House, 1968. Subj: Sports — baseball. Twins.

The ear book ill. by William O'Brian. Random House, 1968. Subj: Anatomy. Poetry, rhyme. Senses.

Hand, hand, fingers, thumb ill. by Eric Gurney. Random House, 1969. Subj: Anatomy. Poetry, rhyme.

King Midas and the golden touch ill. by Harold Berson. Random House, 1970. Subj: Behavior — greed. Behavior — wishing. Royalty.

The nose book ill. by Roy McKie. Random House, 1970. Subj: Anatomy. Poetry, rhyme.

Tubby and the lantern ill. by Rowland B. Wilson. Random House, 1971. Subj: Animals — elephants. Birthdays. Foreign lands — China. Pirates.

Tubby and the Poo-Bah ill. by Rowland B. Wilson. Random House, 1972. Subj: Animals — elephants. Boats, ships.

Perrault, Charles. *Cinderella* adapt. by John Fowles; ill. by Sheilah Beckett. Little, 1974. Adapt. from Perrault's Cendrillon of 1697. Subj: Folk and fairy tales. Royalty. Sibling rivalry.

Cinderella: or, the little glass slipper ill. by Marcia Brown. Scribner's, 1954. Subj: Caldecott award book. Folk and fairy tales. Royalty. Sibling rivalry.

Cinderella ill. by Paul Galdone. McGraw-Hill, 1978. Subj: Folk and fairy tales. Royalty. Sibling rivalry.

Cinderella: the story of Rossini's opera adapt. by Alan Blyth; ill. by Emanuele Luzzati. Watts, 1982. Subj: Folk and fairy tales. Music. Royalty. Sibling rivalry.

Cinderella ill. by Phil Smith. Troll Assoc., 1979. Subj: Folk and fairy tales. Royalty. Sibling rivalry.

Puss in boots a free translation from the French; ill. by Marcia Brown. Scribner's, 1952. Subj: Animals — cats. Caldecott award honor book. Character traits — cleverness. Folk and fairy tales. Royalty.

Puss in boots retold by Kurt Baumann; ill. by Jean Claverie. Faber, 1982. Subj: Animals — cats. Character traits — cleverness. Folk and fairy tales. Royalty.

Puss in boots adapt. and ill. by Hans Fischer. Harcourt, 1959. Subj: Animals — cats. Character traits — cleverness. Folk and fairy tales. Royalty.

Puss in boots ill. by Paul Galdone. Seabury Pr., 1976. Subj: Animals — cats. Character traits — cleverness. Folk and fairy tales. Royalty.

Puss in boots adapt. by Arthur Luce Klein; ill. by Julia Noonan. Doubleday, 1970. Adaptation of Le Chat botté. Subj: Animals — cats. Character traits — cleverness. Folk and fairy tales. Foreign lands — France. Royalty.

Puss in boots: the story of a sneaky cat adapt. and ill. by Tony Ross. Delacorte Pr., 1981. Subj: Animals — cats. Character traits — cleverness. Folk and fairy tales. Royalty.

Puss in boots ill. by William Stobbs. McGraw-Hill, 1975. A retelling of Maître Chat. Subj: Animals — cats. Character traits — cleverness. Folk and fairy tales. Royalty.

Puss in boots ill. by Barry Wilkinson. Collins-World, 1969. Subj: Animals — cats. Character traits — cleverness. Folk and fairy tales. Royalty.

The sleeping beauty tr. and ill. by David Walker. Crowell, 1977. Subj: Folk and fairy tales.

Perrine, Mary. *Salt boy* ill. by Leonard Weisgard. Houghton, 1968. Subj: Ethnic groups in the U.S. – Indians.

Perry, Patricia. *Mommy and daddy are divorced* by Patricia Perry and Marietta Lynch; ill. by authors. Dial Pr., 1978. Subj: Divorce.

Peters, Sharon. *Animals at night* ill. by Paul Harvey. Troll Assoc., 1983. Subj: Animals. Night.

Fun at camp ill. by Irene Trivas. Troll Assoc., 1980. Subj: Sports – camping.

Happy birthday ill. by Paul Harvey. Troll Assoc., 1980. Subj: Birthdays.

Happy Jack ill. by Paul Harvey. Troll Assoc., 1980. Subj: Careers – waiters, waitresses.

Messy Mark ill. by Bill Morrison. Troll Assoc., 1980. Subj: Character traits – cleanliness.

Puppet show ill. by Alana Lee. Troll Assoc., 1980. Subj: Puppets.

Ready, get set, go! ill. by Irene Trivas. Troll Assoc., 1980. Subj: Animals – rabbits.

Stop that rabbit ill. by Don Silverstein. Troll Assoc., 1980. Subj: Animals – rabbits.

Trick or treat Halloween ill. by Susan Hall. Troll Assoc., 1980. Subj: Holidays – Halloween.

Petersen, David. *Helicopters* ill. with photos. Children's Pr., 1983. Subj: Helicopters.

Submarines ill. with photos. Children's Pr., 1984. Subj: Boats, ships.

Petersham, Maud. *An American ABC* by Maud and Miska Petersham; ill. by authors. Macmillan, 1941. Subj: ABC books. Caldecott award honor book. U.S. history.

The box with red wheels by Maud and Miska Petersham; ill. by authors. Macmillan, 1949. Subj: Animals. Babies. Farms.

The Christ Child by Maud and Miska Petersham; ill. by authors. Doubleday, 1931. Subj: Religion.

The circus baby by Maud and Miska Petersham; ill. by authors. Macmillan, 1950. Subj: Animals – elephants. Circus. Clowns, jesters. Etiquette.

Off to bed by Maud and Miska Petersham; ill. by authors. Macmillan, 1954. Subj: Bedtime.

The rooster crows by Maud and Miska Petersham; ill. by authors. Macmillan, 1945. Subj: Caldecott award book. Nursery rhymes.

Petersham, Miska. *An American ABC* (Petersham, Maud)

The box with red wheels (Petersham, Maud)

The Christ Child (Petersham, Maud)

The circus baby (Petersham, Maud)

Off to bed (Petersham, Maud)

The rooster crows (Petersham, Maud)

Peterson, Esther Allen. *Frederick's alligator* ill. by Susanna Natti. Crown, 1979. Subj: Animals. Behavior – boasting. Reptiles – alligators, crocodiles.

Peterson, Franklynn. *I can use tools* (Kesselman, Judi R)

Peterson, Hans. *Erik and the Christmas horse* tr. from the Swedish by Christine Hyatt; ill. by Ilon Wikland. Lothrop, 1970. Translation of Magnus, Lindberg och hästen Mari. Subj: Character traits – kindness. Foreign lands – Sweden. Holidays – Christmas.

Peterson, Jeanne Whitehouse. *That is that* ill. by Deborah Kogan Ray. Harper, 1979. Subj: Divorce.

Petie, Haris. *Billions of bugs* ill. by author. Prentice-Hall, 1975. Subj: Counting. Insects. Poetry, rhyme.

The seed the squirrel dropped ill. by author. Prentice-Hall, 1976. Subj: Activities – cooking. Cumulative tales. Food. Plants. Poetry, rhyme. Trees.

Petras, John W. *Learning about sex* (Aho, Jennifer J)

Petrides, Heidrun. *Hans and Peter* ill. by author. Harcourt, 1962. Subj: Activities – working. Character traits – completing things.

Petrie, Catherine. *Hot Rod Harry* ill. by Paul Sharp. Children's Pr., 1982. Subj: Automobiles.

Petty, Roberta *see* Petie, Haris

Peyo. *The Smurfs and their woodland friends* ill. by author. Random House, 1983. Subj: Animals. Forest, woods. Insects.

What do smurfs do all day? ill. by author. Random House, 1983. Subj: Activities. Poetry, rhyme.

Pfloog, Jan. *Kittens* ill. by author. Random House, 1977. Subj: Animals – cats. Format, unusual – cardboard pages.

Puppies ill. by author. Random House, 1979. Subj: Animals – dogs. Format, unusual – cardboard pages.

Phang, Ruth. *Patchwork tales* (Roth, Susan L)

Phillips, Jack *see* Sandburg, Carl

Phillips, Louis. *The brothers Wrong and Wrong Again* ill. by J. Winslow Higginbottom. McGraw-Hill, 1979. Subj: Character traits – foolishness. Dragons. Middle ages. War.

The upside down riddle book ill. by Beau Gardner. Lothrop, 1982. Subj: Poetry, rhyme. Riddles.

Phleger, Fred B. *Ann can fly* ill. by Robert Lopshire. Random House, 1959. Subj: Activities – flying. Airplanes, airports.

Off to the races by Fred B. and Marjorie Phleger; ill. by Leo Summers. Random House, 1968. Subj: Sports – bicycling. Sports – racing.

Red Tag comes back ill. by Arnold Lobel. Harper, 1961. Subj: Fish. Science.

The whales go by ill. by Paul Galdone. Random House, 1959. Subj: Animals – whales. Science.

You will live under the sea by Fred B. and Marjorie Phleger; ill. by Ward Brackett. Random House, 1966. Subj: Science. Sea and seashore.

Phleger, Marjorie. *Off to the races* (Phleger, Fred B)

You will live under the sea (Phleger, Fred B)

Phumla. *Nomi and the magic fish: a story from Africa* ill. by Carole Byard. Doubleday, 1973. Subj: Children as authors. Folk and fairy tales. Foreign lands – Africa. Magic.

Piatti, Celestino. *Celestino Piatti's animal ABC* English text by Jon Reid; ill. by author. Atheneum, 1966. Subj: ABC books. Animals. Poetry, rhyme.

The happy owls ill. by author. Atheneum, 1964. Subj: Birds – owls. Character traits – optimism. Emotions – happiness.

Pickett, Carla. *Calvin Crocodile and the terrible noise* ill. by Carroll Dolezal. Steck-Vaughn, 1972. Subj: Noise, sounds. Reptiles – alligators, crocodiles.

Piecewicz, Ann Thomas. *See what I caught!* ill. by Perf Coxeter. Prentice-Hall, 1974. Subj: Pets.

Pieńkowski, Jan. *Colors* ill. by author. Harvey House, 1974. Subj: Concepts – color.

Homes ill. by author. Messner, 1983. Subj: Animals. Houses.

Meg and Mog (Nicoll, Helen)

Meg at sea (Nicoll, Helen)

Meg on the moon (Nicoll, Helen)

Meg's eggs (Nicoll, Helen)

Numbers ill. by author. Harvey House, 1975. Subj: Counting.

Shapes ill. by author. Harvey House, 1975. Subj: Concepts – shape.

Sizes ill. by author. Messner, 1983. Orig. pub. by Harvey House, 1974. Subj: Concepts – size.

Time ill. by author. Messner, 1983. Subj: Clocks. Time.

Weather ill. by author. Messner, 1983. Subj: Weather.

Pierce, Jack. *The freight train book* photos. by author. Carolrhoda, 1980. Subj: Trains.

Piers, Helen. *Grasshopper and butterfly* ill. by Pauline Baynes. McGraw-Hill, 1975. Subj: Hibernation. Insects – butterflies, caterpillars. Insects – grasshoppers.

The mouse book photos. by author. Watts, 1968. Subj: Animals – mice.

Pike, Norman. *The peach tree* ill. by Robin and Patricia DeWitt. Stemmer House, 1983. Subj: Activities – gardening. Trees.

Pincus, Harriet. *Minna and Pippin* ill. by author. Farrar, 1972. Subj: Toys – dolls.

Pinkwater, Daniel Manus. *The bear's picture* ill. by author. Dutton, 1984. Subj: Animals – bears. Art. Careers – artists. Concepts – color.

The big orange splot ill. by author. Hastings, 1977. Subj: Activities – painting. Character traits – individuality. Concepts – color. Houses.

Devil in the drain ill. by author. Dutton, 1984. Subj: Character traits – curiosity. Devil.

I was a second grade werewolf ill. by author. Dutton, 1983. Subj: Imagination. Monsters.

Pickle creature ill. by author. Four Winds Pr., 1979. Subj: Imagination – imaginary friends.

Roger's umbrella ill. by James Marshall. Dutton, 1982. Subj: Animals – cats. Umbrellas.

Tooth-gnasher superflash ill. by author. Four Winds Pr., 1981. Subj: Automobiles. Imagination.

Piper, Watty. *The little engine that could* ill. by George and Doris Hauman. Platt, 1961. Retold from The pony engine, by Mable C. Bragg. This version first pub. in 1955. Subj: Character traits – perseverance. Trains.

Pitcher, Caroline. *Animals* ill. by Louise Nevett. Watts, 1983. Subj: Activities. Animals. Wordless.

Cars and boats ill. by Louise Nevett. Watts, 1983. Subj: Activities. Automobiles. Boats, ships. Wordless.

Pitt, Valerie. *Let's find out about the city* ill. by Sheila Granda. Watts, 1968. Subj: City.

Let's find out about the family ill. by Gloria Kamen. Watts, 1970. Subj: Family life.

Pittaway, Margaret. *The rainforest children* ill. by Heather Philpott. Oxford Univ. Pr., 1980. Subj: Behavior – running away. Behavior – seeking better things. Foreign lands – Australia.

Plath, Sylvia. *The bed book* ill. by Emily Arnold McCully. Harper, 1976. Subj: Bedtime. Poetry, rhyme. Sleep.

Platt, Kin. *Big Max* ill. by Robert Lopshire. Harper, 1965. Subj: Animals – elephants. Careers – detectives. Problem solving.

Big Max in the mystery of the missing moose ill. by Robert Lopshire. Harper, 1977. Subj: Animals – moose. Careers – detectives. Problem solving.

Play and sing - it's Christmas! *a piano book of easy-to-play carols* comp. by Brooke Minarik Varnum; ill. by Emily Arnold McCully. Macmillan, 1980. Subj: Holidays – Christmas. Music. Songs.

Plomer, William. *The butterfly ball and the grass-hopper's feast* (Aldridge, Alan)

Pluckrose, Henry. *Ants* ill. by Tony Weaver and David Cook. Watts, 1981. Subj: Insects – ants. Science.

Bears ill. by Richard Orr. Watts, 1979. Subj: Animals – bears. Science.

Bees and wasps ill. by Tony Swift and Norman Weaver. Watts, 1981. Subj: Insects – bees. Insects – wasps. Science.

Butterflies and moths ill. by Norman Weaver and others. Watts, 1981. Subj: Insects – butterflies, caterpillars. Insects – moths. Science.

Elephants ill. by Peter Barrett. Watts, 1979. Subj: Animals – elephants. Science.

Horses ill. by Peter Barrett and Maurice Wilson. Watts, 1979. Subj: Animals – horses. Science.

Lions and tigers ill. by Eric Tenny and Maurice Wilson. Archon Pr., 1979. Subj: Animals – lions. Animals – tigers. Science.

Reptiles ill. by Gary Hincks and others. Watts, 1981. Subj: Reptiles. Science.

Things we cut ill. by G. W. Hales. Watts, 1976. Subj: Tools.

Things we hear ill. by G. W. Hales. Watts, 1976. Subj: Senses.

Things we see ill. by G. W. Hales. Watts, 1976. Subj: Senses.

Things we touch ill. by G. W. Hales. Watts, 1976. Subj: Senses.

Whales ill. by Norman Weaver. Watts, 1979. Subj: Animals – whales. Science.

Plume, Ilse. *The Brementown musicians* (Grimm, Jacob)

The story of Befana: an Italian Christmas tale ill. by adapt. Godine, 1981. Subj: Folk and fairy tales. Foreign lands – Italy. Holidays – Christmas.

Po, Lee. *The hare and the tortoise and the tortoise and the hare* (Du Bois, William Pène)

Podendorf, Illa. *Color* ill. by Wayne Stuart. Children's Pr., 1971. Subj: Concepts – color.

Shapes, sides, curves and corners ill. by Frank Rakoncay. Children's Pr., 1970. Subj: Concepts – shape.

Space ill. with photos. Children's Pr., 1982. Subj: Space and space ships.

Polhamus, Jean Burt. *Dinosaur do's and don'ts* ill. by Steve O'Neill. Prentice-Hall, 1975. Subj: Dinosaurs. Etiquette.

Doctor Dinosaur ill. by Steve O'Neill. Prentice-Hall, 1981. Subj: Careers – veterinarians. Dinosaurs. Illness.

Politi, Leo. *Emmet* ill. by author. Scribner's, 1971. Subj: Animals – dogs. Crime.

Juanita ill. by author. Scribner's, 1948. Subj: Caldecott award honor book. Ethnic groups in the U.S. – Mexican-Americans.

Lito and the clown ill. by author. Scribner's, 1964. Subj: Animals – cats. Clowns, jesters. Foreign lands – Mexico. Pets.

Little Leo ill. by author. Scribner's, 1951. Subj: Clothing. Family life. Foreign lands – Italy.

Mieko ill. by author. Golden Gate Jr. Books, 1969. Subj: Character traits – pride. Ethnic groups in the U.S. – Japanese-Americans.

The mission bell ill. by author. Scribner's, 1953. Subj: Ethnic groups in the U.S. – Mexican-Americans. Missions.

Mr. Fong's toy shop ill. by author. Scribner's, 1978. Subj: Behavior – sharing. Ethnic groups in the U.S. – Chinese-Americans. Friendship. Puppets. Toys.

Moy Moy ill. by author. Scribner's, 1960. Subj: Ethnic groups in the U.S. – Chinese-Americans. Holidays – Chinese New Year.

The nicest gift ill. by author. Scribner's, 1973. Subj: Animals – dogs. Behavior – lost. Holidays – Christmas.

Pedro, the angel of Olvera Street ill. by author. Scribner's, 1946. Subj: Caldecott award honor book. Ethnic groups in the U.S. – Mexican-Americans. Holidays – Christmas.

Rosa ill. by author. Scribner's, 1963. Subj: Babies. Foreign lands – Mexico. Holidays – Christmas. Sibling rivalry. Toys – dolls.

Song of the swallows ill. by author. Scribner's, 1949. Subj: Birds – swallows. Caldecott award book. Ethnic groups in the U.S. – Mexican-Americans. Missions.

Pollock, Penny. *Emily's tiger* ill. by author. Paulist Pr., 1985. Subj: Pets. Toys.

Polushkin, Maria. *Bubba and Bubba: based on a Russian folktale* ill. by Diane de Groat. Crown, 1976. Subj: Animals – bears. Character traits – cleanliness. Folk and fairy tales.

The little hen and the giant ill. by Yuri Salzman. Harper, 1977. Subj: Birds – chickens. Character traits – bravery. Folk and fairy tales. Foreign lands – Russia. Giants.

Morning ill. by Bill Morrison. Four Winds Pr., 1983. Subj: Farms. Morning.

Mother, Mother, I want another ill. by Diane Dawson. Crown, 1978. Subj: Animals – mice. Behavior – misunderstanding. Family life – mothers. Sleep.

Who said meow? ill. by Giulio Maestro. Crown, 1975. An adaptation of Vladimir Grigorévich Suteev's Kto skazal "Mĩau"? Subj: Animals. Noise, sounds.

Pomerantz, Charlotte. *All asleep* ill. by Nancy Tafuri. Greenwillow, 1984. Subj: Bedtime. Poetry, rhyme. Songs.

The ballad of the long-tailed rat ill. by Marian Parry. Macmillan, 1975. Subj: Animals – cats. Animals – rats. Character traits – pride. Poetry, rhyme.

Buffy and Albert ill. by Yossi Abolafia. Greenwillow, 1982. Subj: Animals – cats. Family life – grandparents, great-grandparents. Old age.

The half-birthday party ill. by DyAnne DiSalvo-Ryan. Houghton, 1984. Subj: Birthdays.

If I had a Paka: poems of eleven languages ill. by Nancy Tafuri. Greenwillow, 1982. Subj: Foreign languages. Poetry, rhyme.

The mango tooth ill. by Marylin Hafner. Greenwillow, 1977. Subj: Family life. Teeth.

One duck, another duck ill. by José Aruego and Ariane Dewey. Greenwillow, 1984. Subj: Birds – ducks. Counting.

The piggy in the puddle ill. by James Marshall. Macmillan, 1974. Subj: Animals – pigs. Poetry, rhyme. Tongue twisters.

Posy ill. by Catherine Stock. Greenwillow, 1983. Subj: Bedtime. Family life.

The tamarindo puppy and other poems ill. by Byron Barton. Greenwillow, 1980. Subj: Foreign languages. Poetry, rhyme.

Pope, Billy N. *Your world: let's visit the hospital* by Billy N. Pope and Ramona Ware Emmons. Taylor, 1968. Subj: Hospitals.

The porcupine ill. by Patrick Oxenham. Rourke, 1983. Subj: Animals – porcupines.

Porte, Barbara Ann. *Harry's visit* ill. by Yossi Abolafia. Greenwillow, 1983. Subj: Behavior – sharing. Sports – basketball.

Porter, David Lord. *Mine!* ill. by author. Houghton, 1981. Subj: Behavior – greed.

Postgate, Oliver. *Noggin and the whale* by Oliver Postgate and Peter Firmin; ill. by Peter Firmin. White, 1967. Subj: Animals – whales. Humor.

Noggin the king by Oliver Postgate and Peter Firmin; ill. by Peter Firmin. White, 1965. Subj: Birds. Character traits – kindness. Humor. Royalty.

Postma, Lidia. *The stolen mirror* ill. by author. McGraw-Hill, 1976. Translation of De gestolen Spiegel. Subj: Imagination. Magic. Sibling rivalry.

Poston, Elizabeth. *Baby's song book* ill. by William Stobbs. Crowell, 1971. Subj: Music. Songs.

Potter, Beatrix. *Appley Dapply's nursery rhymes* ill. by author. Warne, 1917. Subj: Animals. Nursery rhymes.

Cecily Parsley's nursery rhymes ill. by author. Warne, 1922. Subj: Animals. Nursery rhymes.

The complete adventures of Peter Rabbit ill. by author. Warne, 1982. Subj: Animals – rabbits. Behavior – misbehavior.

Ginger and Pickles ill. by author. Warne, 1937. First pub. in 1909. Subj: Animals. Stores.

The pie and the patty-pan ill. by author. Warne, 1933. First pub. in 1905. Subj: Animals – cats. Animals – dogs. Behavior – trickery.

Rolly-polly pudding ill. by author. Warne, 1936. First pub. in 1908. Subj: Animals – cats.

The sly old cat ill. by author. Warne, 1971. Subj: Animals – cats. Animals – rats. Character traits – cleverness. Etiquette. Parties.

The story of fierce bad rabbit ill. by author. Warne, 1906. Subj: Animals – rabbits.

The story of Miss Moppet ill. by author. Warne, 1906. Subj: Animals – cats. Behavior – trickery.

The tailor of Gloucester ill. by author. Warne, 1931. Subj: Animals – mice. Careers – tailors. Character traits – helpfulness.

The tale of Benjamin Bunny ill. by author. Warne, 1904. Subj: Animals – rabbits. Behavior – misbehavior.

The tale of Jemima Puddle-Duck ill. by author. Warne, 1936. First pub. in 1910. Subj: Birds – ducks. Eggs.

The tale of Johnny Town-Mouse ill. by author. Warne, 1918. Subj: Animals – mice.

The tale of Little Pig Robinson ill. by author. Warne, 1930. Subj: Animals – pigs. Behavior – talking to strangers. Boats, ships. Shopping.

The tale of Mr. Jeremy Fisher ill. by author. Warne, 1934. Subj: Frogs and toads. Sports – fishing.

The tale of Mr. Tod ill. by author. Warne, 1939. First pub. in 1911. Subj: Animals – badgers. Animals – foxes. Animals – rabbits.

The tale of Mrs. Tiggy-Winkle ill. by author. Warne, 1905. Subj: Animals – hedgehogs. Clothing.

The tale of Mrs. Tittlemouse ill. by author. Warne, 1910. Subj: Animals – mice. Character traits – cleanliness.

The tale of Peter Rabbit ill. by Margot Apple. Troll Assoc., 1979. Subj: Animals – rabbits. Behavior – misbehavior.

The tale of Peter Rabbit ill. by author. Warne, 1902. Subj: Animals – rabbits. Behavior – misbehavior. Farms.

The tale of Peter Rabbit and other stories ill. by Allen Atkinson. Knopf, 1982. Subj: Animals.

The tale of Pigling Bland ill. by author. Warne, 1913, 1941. Subj: Animals – pigs.

The tale of Squirrel Nutkin ill. by author. Warne, 1903. Subj: Animals – squirrels. Birds – owls. Riddles. Seasons – fall.

The tale of the faithful dove ill. by Marie Angel. Warne, 1970. Subj: Birds – doves. Character traits – loyalty.

The tale of the Flopsy Bunnies ill. by author. Warne, 1909, 1937. Subj: Animals – rabbits. Character traits – cleverness.

The tale of Timmy Tiptoes ill. by author. Warne, 1911, 1939. Subj: Animals – squirrels.

The tale of Tom Kitten ill. by author. Warne, 1907. Subj: Animals – cats. H᾽ ᾽or.

The tale of Tuppeny ill. by Marie Angel. Warne, 1971. Subj: Animals – guinea pigs.

The tale of two bad mice ill. by author. Warne, 1904, 1934. Subj: Animals – mice. Behavior – misbehavior. Toys.

A treasury of Peter Rabbit and other stories ill. by author. Watts, 1978. Subj: Animals.

Yours affectionately, Peter Rabbit: miniature letters ill. by author. Warne, 1984. Subj: Animals. Communication.

Potter, Russell. *The little red ferry boat* ill. by Marjorie Hill. Holt, 1947. Subj: Animals – mice. Boats, ships. Transportation.

Potter, Stephen. *Squawky, the adventures of a Clasperchoice* ill. by George Him. Lippincott, 1964. Subj: Birds – parakeets, parrots.

Pouyanne, Rési. *What I see hidden by the pond* ill. by Gerda Muller. Two Continents, 1977. Subj: Animals. Plants. Science.

Power, Barbara. *I wish Laura's mommy was my mommy* ill. by Marylin Hafner. Lippincott, 1979. Subj: Behavior – growing up. Behavior – wishing. Family life – mothers.

Prager, Annabelle. *The spooky Halloween party* ill. by Tomie de Paola. Pantheon, 1981. Subj: Holidays – Halloween. Parties.

The surprise party ill. by Tomie de Paola. Pantheon, 1977. Subj: Birthdays. Parties.

Prather, Ray. *Double dog dare* ill. by author. Macmillan, 1975. Subj: Animals – dogs. Humor.

The ostrich girl ill. by author. Scribner's, 1978. Subj: Folk and fairy tales. Foreign lands – Africa. Forest, woods. Reptiles – snakes. Witches.

Pratten, Albra. *Winkie, the grey squirrel* ill. by Ralph S. Thompson. Oxford Univ. Pr., 1950. Subj: Animals – squirrels. Pets.

Preiss, Byron. *The first crazy word book: verbs* by Byron Preiss and Ralph Reese; ill. by Ralph Reese. Watts, 1982. Subj: Language.

Prelutsky, Jack. *The baby uggs are hatching* ill. by James Stevenson. Greenwillow, 1982. Subj: Humor. Imagination. Monsters. Poetry, rhyme.

Circus ill. by Arnold Lobel. Macmillan, 1974. Subj: Circus. Poetry, rhyme.

It's Halloween ill. by Marylin Hafner. Greenwillow, 1977. Subj: Holidays – Halloween. Poetry, rhyme.

It's Valentine's Day ill. by Yossi Abolafia. Greenwillow, 1983. Subj: Holidays – Valentine's Day. Poetry, rhyme.

The mean old mean hyena ill. by Arnold Lobel. Greenwillow, 1978. Subj: Animals – hyenas. Character traits – meanness. Poetry, rhyme.

The pack rat's day and other poems ill. by Margaret Bloy Graham. Macmillan, 1974. Subj: Animals. Poetry, rhyme.

The queen of Eene ill. by Victoria Chess. Greenwillow, 1978. Subj: Humor. Poetry, rhyme.

Rainy rainy Saturday ill. by Marylin Hafner. Greenwillow, 1980. Subj: Poetry, rhyme. Weather – rain.

The Random House book of poetry for children ill. by Arnold Lobel. Random House, 1983. Subj: Humor. Poetry, rhyme.

The snopp on the sidewalk and other poems ill. by Byron Barton. Greenwillow, 1977. Subj: Humor. Poetry, rhyme.

The terrible tiger ill. by Arnold Lobel. Macmillan, 1970. Subj: Animals – tigers. Cumulative tales. Poetry, rhyme.

What I did last summer ill. by Yossi Abolafia. Greenwillow, 1984. Subj: Poetry, rhyme.

The wild baby (Lindgren, Barbro)

The wild baby goes to sea (Lindgren, Barbro)

Preston, Edna Mitchell. *Horrible Hepzibah* ill. by Ray Cruz. Viking, 1971. Subj: Behavior – misbehavior. Humor.

Monkey in the jungle ill. by Clement Hurd. Viking, 1968. Subj: Animals – monkeys. Bedtime. Night. Sleep.

One dark night ill. by Kurt Werth. Viking, 1969. Subj: Cumulative tales. Holidays – Halloween.

Pop Corn and Ma Goodness ill. by Robert Andrew Parker. Viking, 1969. Subj: Caldecott award honor book. Humor. Poetry, rhyme. Songs. Weather – rain.

Squawk to the moon, little goose ill. by Barbara Cooney. Viking, 1974. Subj: Animals – foxes. Behavior – misbehavior. Birds – geese. Moon.

Price, Christine. *One is God: two old counting songs* ill. by author. Warne, 1970. Subj: Counting. Religion. Songs.

Price, Dorothy E. *Speedy gets around* ill. by Betsy Warren. Steck-Vaughn, 1965. Subj: Animals – chipmunks. Sports – camping.

Price, Michelle. *Mean Melissa* ill. by author. Bradbury Pr., 1977. Subj: Character traits – meanness. School.

Price, Roger. *The last little dragon* ill. by Mamoru Funai. Harper, 1969. Subj: Behavior – dissatisfaction. Dragons.

Primavera, Elise. *Basil and Maggie* ill. by author. Lippincott, 1983. Subj: Animals – horses. Character traits – appearance.

Prince, Pamela. *The secret world of teddy bears* photos. by Elaine Faris Keenan. Crown, 1983. Subj: Poetry, rhyme. Toys – teddy bears.

The prince who knew his fate: *an ancient Egyptian tale* tr. from hieroglyphs and ill. by Lise Manniche. Putnam's, 1982. Subj: Folk and fairy tales. Foreign lands – Egypt. Hieroglyphics. Magic. Royalty.

Priolo, Pauline. *Piccolina and the Easter bells* ill. by Rita Fava. Little, 1962. Subj: Character traits – smallness. Foreign lands – Italy. Holidays – Easter.

Prokofiev, Sergei Sergeievitch. *Peter and the wolf* ill. by Warren Chappell; foreword by Serge Koussevitsky; calligraphy by Hollis Holland. Knopf, 1940. Subj: Animals – wolves. Character traits – cleverness. Folk and fairy tales. Foreign lands – Russia. Music.

Peter and the wolf ill. by Frans Haacken. Watts, 1961. Subj: Animals – wolves. Character traits – cleverness. Folk and fairy tales. Foreign lands – Russia. Music.

Peter and the wolf ill. by Alan Howard. Transatlantic, 1954. Subj: Animals – wolves. Character traits – cleverness. Folk and fairy tales. Foreign lands – Russia. Music.

Peter and the wolf tr. by Maria Carlson; ill. by Charles Mikolaycak. Viking, 1982. Subj: Animals – wolves. Character traits – cleverness. Folk and fairy tales. Foreign lands – Russia. Music.

Peter and the wolf retold by Ann Herring; ill. by Kozo Shimizu; photos. by Yasugi Yajima. Gakken, 1971. Subj: Animals – wolves. Character traits – cleverness. Folk and fairy tales. Foreign lands – Russia. Music.

Provensen, Alice. *A book of seasons* by Alice and Martin Provensen; ill. by authors. Random House, 1976. Subj: Seasons.

The glorious flight: across the channel with Louis Blériot by Alice and Martin Provensen; ill. by authors. Viking, 1983. Subj: Activities – flying. Airplanes, airports. Caldecott award book.

Karen's opposites by Alice and Martin Provensen; ill. by authors. Golden Pr., 1963. Subj: Concepts – opposites. Poetry, rhyme.

My little hen by Alice and Martin Provensen; ill. by authors. Random House, 1973. Subj: Birds – chickens.

Our animal friends by Alice and Martin Provensen; ill. by authors. Random House, 1974. Subj: Animals. Farms.

An owl and three pussycats by Alice and Martin Provensen; ill. by authors. Atheneum, 1981. Subj: Family life. Farms. Pets.

Town and country by Alice and Martin Provensen; ill. by authors. Crown, 1984. Subj: City. Country.

The year at Maple Hill Farm by Alice and Martin Provensen; ill. by authors. Atheneum, 1978. Subj: Animals. Days of the week, months of the year. Farms. Seasons.

Provensen, Martin. *A book of seasons* (Provensen, Alice)

The glorious flight (Provensen, Alice)

Karen's opposites (Provensen, Alice)

My little hen (Provensen, Alice)

Our animal friends (Provensen, Alice)

An owl and three pussycats (Provensen, Alice)

Town and country (Provensen, Alice)

The year at Maple Hill Farm (Provensen, Alice)

The pudgy book of toys ill. by Julie Durrell. Grosset, 1983. Subj: Format, unusual – cardboard pages. Toys.

The pudgy fingers counting book ill. by Doug Cushman. Grosset, 1983. Subj: Counting. Format, unusual – cardboard pages.

The pudgy pals ill. by Kathy Wilburn. Grosset, 1983. Subj: Format, unusual – cardboard pages.

The pudgy pat-a-cake book ill. by Terri Super. Grosset, 1983. Subj: Format, unusual – cardboard pages. Games.

The pudgy peek-a-boo book ill. by Amye Rosenberg. Grosset, 1983. Subj: Format, unusual – cardboard pages. Games.

The pudgy rock-a-bye book ill. by Kathy Wilburn. Grosset, 1983. Subj: Format, unusual – cardboard pages.

Pulsifer, Marjorie P. *Bikes* (Baugh, Dolores M)

Let's go (Baugh, Dolores M)

Let's see the animals (Baugh, Dolores M)

Let's take a trip (Baugh, Dolores M)

Slides (Baugh, Dolores M)

Supermarket (Baugh, Dolores M)

Swings (Baugh, Dolores M)

Trucks and cars to ride (Baugh, Dolores M)

Puner, Helen Walker. *Daddys, what they do all day* ill. by Roger Antoine Duvoisin. Lothrop, 1946. Subj: Activities – working. Careers. Family life – fathers. Poetry, rhyme.

The sitter who didn't sit ill. by Roger Antoine Duvoisin. Lothrop, 1949. Subj: Activities – babysitting. Humor. Poetry, rhyme.

Puppies and kittens photos. by Walter Chandoha. Platt, 1983. Subj: Animals – cats. Animals – dogs. Format, unusual – cardboard pages. Poetry, rhyme.

Purcell, John Wallace. *African animals* ill. with photos. Rev. ed. Children's Pr., 1982. Subj: Animals. Foreign lands – Africa.

Puricelli, Luigi. *In my garden* (Cristini, Ermanno)

In the pond (Cristini, Ermanno)

In the woods (Cristini, Ermanno)

Pursell, Margaret Sanford. *Jessie the chicken* orig. tr. by Dyan Hammarberg; photos. by Claudie Fayn-Rodriguez; ill. by L'Enc Matte. Based on Anne Marie Pajot's Picota la poule. Subj: Birds – chickens. Eggs.

A look at birth ill. by Maria S. Forrai. Lerner, 1976. Subj: Babies. Science.

A look at divorce ill. by Maria S. Forrai. Lerner, 1976. Subj: Divorce. Emotions.

Polly the guinea pig orig. tr. by Dyan Hammarberg; photos. by Antoinette Barrére; ill. by L'enc Matte. Carolrhoda Books, 1977. Original ed. published under title: Amilcar le cochon d'Inde. Subj: Animals – guinea pigs. Pets. Science.

Shelley the sea gull tr. by Dyan Hammarberg; photos. by Jean Christian David, Guy Dhuit and Claudie Fayn-Rodriguez. Carolrhoda Books, 1977. Original ed. published under title: Gwelan le goeland. Subj: Birds – sea gulls. Pets. Science.

Sprig the tree frog tr. by Dyan Hammarberg; ill. by Yves Vial. Carolrhoda Books, 1977. Subj: Eggs. Frogs and toads. Science.

Quackenbush, Robert M. *Calling Doctor Quack* ill. by author. Lothrop, 1978. Subj: Animals. Ecology. Illness.

City trucks ill. by author. Albert Whitman, 1981. Subj: City. Trucks.

Clementine ill. by author. Lippincott, 1974. Subj: Folk and fairy tales. Music. Songs. U.S. history.

Detective Mole ill. by author. Lothrop, 1976. Subj: Animals. Animals – moles. Careers – detectives. Humor. Problem solving.

Detective Mole and the secret clues ill. by author. Lothrop, 1977. Subj: Animals. Animals – moles. Careers – detectives. Humor. Problem solving.

Detective Mole and the Tip-Top mystery ill. by author. Lothrop, 1978. Subj: Animals. Animals – moles. Careers – detectives. Humor. Problem solving.

Dig to disaster ill. by author. Prentice-Hall, 1982. Subj: Birds – ducks. Careers – detectives. Problem solving.

Express train to trouble ill. by author. Prentice-Hall, 1981. Subj: Birds – ducks. Careers – detectives. Problem solving.

First grade jitters ill. by author. Lippincott, 1982. Subj: Animals – rabbits. School.

Funny bunnies ill. by author. Houghton, 1984. Subj: Animals – rabbits. Humor.

Henry babysits ill. by author. Parents, 1983. Subj: Activities – babysitting. Birds – ducks.

I don't want to go, I don't know how to act ill. by author. Lippincott, 1983. Subj: Animals – koala bears. Behavior. Etiquette. Family life.

The man on the flying trapeze: the circus life of Emmett Kelly, Sr., told with pictures and song! ill. by author. Lippincott, 1975. Subj: Circus. Clowns, jesters. Music. Songs.

No mouse for me ill. by author. Watts, 1981. Subj: Cumulative tales. Pets.

Pete Pack Rat ill. by author. Lothrop, 1976. Subj: Animals. Animals – pack rats. Cowboys. Humor.

Piet Potter returns ill. by author. McGraw-Hill, 1980. Subj: Careers – detectives. Problem solving.

Piet Potter strikes again ill. by author. McGraw-Hill, 1981. Subj: Careers – detectives. Problem solving.

Piet Potter to the rescue ill. by author. McGraw-Hill, 1981. Subj: Careers – detectives. Problem solving.

Piet Potter's first case ill. by author. McGraw-Hill, 1980. Subj: Careers – detectives. Problem solving.

Pop! goes the weasel and Yankee Doodle ill. by author. Lippincott, 1976. Subj: Music. Poetry, rhyme. Songs. U.S. history.

She'll be comin' 'round the mountain ill. by author. Lippincott, 1973. Subj: Folk and fairy tales. Music. Songs.

Sheriff Sally Gopher and the Thanksgiving caper ill. by author. Lothrop, 1982. Subj: Holidays – Thanksgiving.

Skip to my Lou ill. by author. Lippincott, 1975. Subj: Folk and fairy tales. Music. Songs.

Stairway to doom ill. by author. Prentice-Hall, 1983. Subj: Birds – ducks. Careers – detectives. Problem solving.

There'll be a hot time in the old town tonight ill. by author. Lippincott, 1974. Subj: Fire. Folk and fairy tales. Music. Songs. U.S. history.

What has Wild Tom done now?!!! a story of Thomas Alva Edison ill. by author. Prentice-Hall, 1981. Subj: Humor. Science.

Quigley, Lillian Fox. *The blind men and the elephant* ill. by Janice Holland. Scribner's, 1959. Subj: Animals – elephants. Folk and fairy tales. Foreign lands – India. Handicaps – blindness. Senses.

Quin-Harkin, Janet. *Benjamin's balloon* ill. by Robert Censoni. Parents, 1979. Subj: Activities – ballooning. Character traits – willfulness.

Helpful Hattie ill. by Susanna Natti. Harcourt, 1983. Subj: Birthdays. Hair. Parties. Teeth.

Peter Penny's dance ill. by Anita Lobel. Dial Pr., 1976. Subj: Activities – dancing. Weddings. World.

Rabinowitz, Sandy. *A colt named mischief* ill. by author. Doubleday, 1979. Subj: Animals – horses. Behavior – misbehavior.

What's happening to Daisy? ill. by author. Harper, 1977. Subj: Animals – horses. Science.

Racioppo, Larry. *Halloween* photos. by author. Scribner's, 1980. Subj: Holidays – Halloween.

Radin, Ruth Yaffe. *A winter place* ill. by Mattie Lou O'Kelley. Little, 1982. Subj: Seasons – winter. Sports – ice skating.

Radlauer, Ruth Shaw. *Of course, you're a horse!* ill. by Abner Graboff and Sheila Greenwald. Abelard-Schuman, 1959. Subj: Health. Imagination.

Radley, Gail. *The night Stella hid the stars* ill. by John Wallner. Crown, 1978. Subj: Imagination. Stars.

Raebeck, Lois. *Who am I?* ill. by June Goldsborough. Follett, 1970. Subj: Activities – playing. Games. Songs.

Rael, Rick. *Baseball brothers* (Rubin, Jeff)

Rahn, Joan Elma. *Holes* photos. by author. Houghton, 1984. Subj: Concepts.

Rand, Ann. *Little 1* ill. by Paul Rand. Harcourt, 1962. Subj: Counting.

Sparkle and spin: a book about words ill. by Paul Rand. Harcourt, 1957. Subj: Language.

Rand McNally picturebook dictionary: *a thousand words to see and say* comp. by Robert L. Hillerich and others; ill. by Dan Siculan. Rand McNally, 1971. Subj: Dictionaries.

Ransome, Arthur. *The fool of the world and the flying ship* ill. by Uri Shulevitz. Farrar, 1968. Subj: Activities – flying. Boats, ships. Caldecott award book. Character traits – cleverness.

Raphael, Elaine. *Donkey and Carlo* by Elaine Raphael and Don Bolognese; ill. by authors. Harper, 1978. Subj: Animals – donkeys. Farms. Friendship.

Donkey, it's snowing by Elaine Raphael and Don Bolognese; ill. by authors. Harper, 1981. Subj: Animals – donkeys. Farms. Weather – snow.

Turnabout by Elaine Raphael and Don Bolognese; ill. by authors. Viking, 1980. Subj: Animals – bears. Behavior – boasting. Family life. Folk and fairy tales. Poetry, rhyme.

Raposo, Joe. *The Sesame Street song book* words and music by Joe Raposo and Jeffrey Moss; arrangements by Sy Oliver; ill. by Loretta Trezzo. Simon and Schuster, 1971. "Published in conjunction with Children's Television Workshop." Subj: Music. Songs.

Rappus, Gerhard. *When the sun was shining* ill. by author. Imported Pubs., 1983. Subj: Activities – picnicking. Animals – goats. Behavior – misbehavior. Wordless.

Raskin, Ellen. *A & the: or, William T. C. Baumgarten comes to town* ill. by author. Atheneum, 1970. Subj: Friendship. Names.

And it rained ill. by author. Atheneum, 1969. Subj: Animals. Weather – rain.

Franklin Stein ill. by author. Atheneum, 1972. Subj: City. Friendship. Humor. Imagination.

Ghost in a four-room apartment ill. by author. Atheneum, 1969. Subj: Cumulative tales. Family life. Ghosts. Poetry, rhyme.

Nothing ever happens on my block ill. by author. Atheneum, 1966. Subj: Behavior – boredom. City. Humor.

Spectacles ill. by author. Atheneum, 1968. Subj: Glasses. Imagination.

Who, said Sue, said whoo? ill. by author. Atheneum, 1973. Subj: Animals. Noise, sounds. Poetry, rhyme.

Rauch, Hans-Georg. *The lines are coming: a book about drawing* ill. by author. Scribner's, 1978. Subj: Art.

Ray, Deborah Kogan. *The cloud* ill. by author. Harper, 1984. Subj: Activities – walking. Weather – clouds.

Fog drift morning ill. by author. Harper, 1983. Subj: Morning. Sea and seashore.

Sunday morning we went to the zoo ill. by author. Harper, 1981. Subj: Family life. Sibling rivalry. Zoos.

Rayner, Mary. *Garth Pig and the ice cream lady* ill. by author. Atheneum, 1977. Subj: Animals – pigs. Animals – wolves.

Mr. and Mrs. Pig's evening out ill. by author. Atheneum, 1976. Subj: Activities – babysitting. Animals – pigs. Animals – wolves.

Mrs. Pig's bulk buy ill. by author. Atheneum, 1981. Subj: Animals – pigs. Food.

The rain cloud ill. by author. Atheneum, 1980. Subj: Character traits – helpfulness. Weather – clouds.

Raynor, Dorka. *Grandparents around the world* ed. by Caroline Rubin; photos. by author. Albert Whitman, 1977. Subj: Family life – grandparents, great-grandparents.

Reardon, Maureen. *Feelings between brothers and sisters* (Conta, Marcia Maher)

Feelings between friends (Conta, Marcia Maher)

Feelings between kids and grownups (Conta, Marcia Maher)

Feelings between kids and parents (Conta, Marcia Maher)

Reasoner, Charles. *Sleepy time bunny* (Cosgrove, Stephen)

Reavin, Sam. *Hurray for Captain Jane!* ill. by Emily Arnold McCully. Parents, 1971. Subj: Activities – bathing. Boats, ships. Imagination.

Red Riding Hood (De Regniers, Beatrice Schenk.)

Reece, Colleen L. *What?* ill. by Lois Axeman. Children's Pr., 1983. Subj: Character traits – curiosity. Character traits – questioning.

Reed, Allison. *Genesis: the story of creation* ill. by author. Schocken, 1981. Subj: Religion.

Reed, Jonathan. *Do armadillos come in houses?* ill. by Carol Nicklaus. Atheneum, 1981. Subj: Emotions – fear.

Reed, Kit. *When we dream* ill. by Yutaka Sugita. Hawthorn, 1966. Subj: Behavior – wishing. Dreams.

Reed, Lillian Craig *see* Reed, Kit

Reed, Mary M. *Biddy and the ducks* (Sondergaard, Arensa)

Reese, Ralph. *The first crazy word book* (Preiss, Byron)

Reesink, Marijke. *The golden treasure* ill. by Jaap Tol. Harcourt, 1968. Translation of Het vrouwtje van Stavoren. Subj: Boats, ships. Character traits – selfishness. Folk and fairy tales. Foreign lands – Holland.

The princess who always ran away ill. by Francoise Trésy. McGraw-Hill, 1981. Subj: Behavior – solitude. Character traits – being different. Folk and fairy tales. Royalty. Sibling rivalry.

Reeves, James. *Rhyming Will* ill. by Edward Ardizzone. McGraw-Hill, 1967. Subj: Character traits – individuality. Humor. Poetry, rhyme. Royalty.

Regniers, Beatrice De *see* De Regniers, Beatrice Schenk

Reich, Hanns. *Animal babies* (Zoll, Max Alfred)

Reid, Alastair. *A balloon for a blunderbuss* (Gill, Bob)

Supposing ill. by Abe Birnbaum. Little, 1960. Subj: Humor. Imagination.

Reid, Jon. *Celestino Piatti's animal ABC* (Piatti, Celestino)

Reidel, Marlene. *Jacob and the robbers* ill. by author. Atheneum, 1967. Subj: Crime. Night. Sleep.

Reinl, Edda. *The little snake* ill. by author. Alphabet Pr., 1982. Subj: Emotions – love. Reptiles – snakes.

Reiss, John J. *Colors* ill. by author. Bradbury Pr., 1969. Subj: Concepts – color.

Numbers ill. by author. Bradbury Pr., 1971. Subj: Counting.

Shapes ill. by author. Bradbury Pr., 1974. Subj: Concepts – shape.

Reit, Seymour. *The king who learned to smile* ill. by Gordon Laite. Golden Pr., 1960. Subj: Behavior – boredom. Royalty.

Round things everywhere photos. by Carol Basen. McGraw-Hill, 1969. Subj: Concepts – shape. Ethnic groups in the U.S.

Reitveld, Jane Klatt. *Monkey island* ill. by author. Viking, 1963. Subj: Animals – monkeys. Zoos.

Ressner, Phil. *August explains* ill. by Crosby Newell Bonsall. Harper, 1963. Subj: Animals – bears.

Dudley Pippin ill. by Arnold Lobel. Harper, 1965. Subj: City. Imagination.

Retan, Walter. *The snowplow that tried to go south* by Walter Retan [i.e. George Walters]; ill. by John Resko. Atheneum, 1950. Subj: Machines. Seasons – winter. Weather – snow.

The steam shovel that wouldn't eat dirt ill. by Roger Antoine Duvoisin. Atheneum, 1948. Subj: Food. Machines.

Rettich, Margret. *The voyage of the jolly boat* tr. from German by Joy Backhouse; ill. by author. Methuen, 1981. Subj: Boats, ships. Careers – fishermen. Weather – storms.

Reuter, Margaret. *My mother is blind* ill. by Philip Lanier. Children's Pr., 1979. Subj: Family life – mothers. Handicaps – blindness.

Rey, H. A. *see* Rey, Hans Augusto

Rey, Hans Augusto. *Anybody at home?* ill. by author. Houghton, 1942. Subj: Format, unusual. Houses.

Billy's picture (Rey, Margaret Elisabeth Waldstein)

Cecily G and the nine monkeys ill. by author. Houghton, 1942. Subj: Animals – giraffes. Animals – monkeys. Humor.

Curious George ill. by author. Houghton, 1941. Subj: Animals – monkeys. Careers – firefighters. Character traits – curiosity. Humor.

Curious George gets a medal ill. by author. Houghton, 1957. Subj: Animals – monkeys. Character traits – curiosity. Humor. Space and space ships.

Curious George goes to the hospital (Rey, Margaret Elisabeth Waldstein)

Curious George learns the alphabet ill. by author. Houghton, 1963. Subj: ABC books. Animals – monkeys. Character traits – curiosity.

Curious George rides a bike ill. by author. Houghton, 1952. Subj: Animals – monkeys. Character traits – curiosity. Circus. Humor. Sports – bicycling.

Curious George takes a job ill. by author. Houghton, 1947. Subj: Animals – monkeys. Careers – window cleaners. Character traits – curiosity. Humor. Zoos.

Elizabite, adventures of a carnivorous plant ill. by author. Harper, 1942. Subj: Humor. Plants. Poetry, rhyme.

Feed the animals ill. by author. Houghton, 1944. Subj: Poetry, rhyme. Zoos.

How do you get there? ill. by author. Houghton, 1941. Subj: Format, unusual. Transportation.

Humpty Dumpty and other Mother Goose songs ill. by author. Harper, 1943. Subj: Music. Nursery rhymes. Songs.

Look for the letters ill. by author. Harper, 1942. Subj: ABC books.

See the circus ill. by author. Houghton, 1956. Subj: Circus. Format, unusual. Poetry, rhyme.

Tit for tat ill. by author. Harper, 1942. Subj: Animals. Humor.

Where's my baby? ill. by author. Houghton, 1943. Subj: Animals. Format, unusual. Poetry, rhyme.

Rey, Margaret Elisabeth Waldstein. *Billy's picture* by Margaret and Hans Augusto Rey; ill. by Hans Augusto Rey. Harper, 1948. Subj: Animals. Art. Humor.

Curious George flies a kite ill. by Hans Augusto Rey. Houghton, 1958. Subj: Animals – monkeys. Character traits – curiosity. Humor. Kites. Sports – fishing.

Curious George goes to the hospital by Margaret and Hans Augusto Rey in collaboration with the Children's Hospital Medical Center, Boston; ill. by Hans Augusto Rey. Houghton, 1966. Subj: Animals – monkeys. Behavior – lost. Character traits – curiosity. Hospitals. Humor.

Pretzel ill. by Hans Augusto Rey. Harper, 1941. Subj: Animals – dogs.

Pretzel and the puppies ill. by Hans Augusto Rey. Harper, 1946. Subj: Animals – dogs.

Spotty ill. by Hans Augusto Rey. Harper, 1945. Subj: Animals – rabbits. Character traits – being different.

Reyher, Becky. *My mother is the most beautiful woman in the world* ill. by Ruth S. Gannett. Lothrop, 1945. Subj: Caldecott award honor book. Family life – mothers.

The world ill. by Ruth S. Gannett. Lothrop, 1945. Subj: Caldecott award honor book. World.

Ricciuti, Edward R. *An animal for Alan* pictures by Tom Eaton. Harper, 1970. Subj: Pets. Science.

Donald and the fish that walked ill. by Syd Hoff. Harper, 1974. Subj: Ecology. Fish. Science.

Rice, Eve. *Benny bakes a cake* ill. by author. Greenwillow, 1981. Subj: Activities – cooking. Animals – dogs. Behavior – misbehavior. Birthdays.

Ebbie ill. by author. Greenwillow, 1975. Subj: Family life. Names.

Goodnight, goodnight ill. by author. Greenwillow, 1980. Subj: Bedtime. Night.

New blue shoes ill. by author. Macmillan, 1975. Subj: Clothing. Family life – mothers. Shopping.

Papa's lemonade and other stories ill. by author. Greenwillow, 1976. Subj: Animals – dogs. Family life.

Sam who never forgets ill. by author. Greenwillow, 1977. Subj: Animals. Food. Zoos.

What Sadie sang ill. by author. Greenwillow, 1976. Subj: Babies. Emotions – happiness.

Rice, Inez. *A long long time* ill. by Robert M. Quackenbush. Lothrop, 1964. Subj: Character traits – optimism. Imagination.

The March wind ill. by Vladimir Bobri. Lothrop, 1957. Subj: Clothing. Imagination. Weather – wind.

Rice, James. *Gaston goes to Texas* ill. by author. Pelican, 1978. Subj: Poetry, rhyme. Reptiles – alligators, crocodiles.

Richard, Jane. *A horse grows up* ill. by Bert Hardy. Walker, 1972. Subj: Animals – horses. Science.

Richardson, Jack E. *Six in a mix* by Jack E. Richardson, Jr. and others; ill. by Carlos Alfonso and others. Benziger, 1971. Subj: Language.

Richter, Alice Numeroff. *Emily's bunch* (Numeroff, Laura Joffe)

You can't put braces on spaces by Alice Numeroff Richter and Laura Joffe Numeroff; ill. by Laura Joffe Numeroff. Greenwillow, 1979. Subj: Careers – dentists. Teeth.

Richter, Joan. *Professor Coconut and the thief* (Gelman, Rita Golden)

Richter, Mischa. *Eric and Matilda* ill. by author. Harper, 1967. Subj: Birds – ducks. Parades.

Quack? ill. by author. Harper, 1978. Subj: Animals. Birds – ducks. Noise, sounds.

To bed, to bed! ill. by author. Prentice-Hall, 1981. Subj: Bedtime. Royalty.

Ricketts, Michael. *Rain* ill. by author. Wonder Books, 1971. Subj: Weather – rain.

Teeth ill. by author. Grosset, 1971. Subj: Teeth.

Rider, Alex. *A la ferme. At the farm: learn-a-language book in French and English* ill. by Paul Davis. Doubleday, 1962. Subj: Farms. Foreign lands – France. Foreign languages.

Chez nous. At our house: learn-a-language book in French and English ill. by Isadore Seltzer. Doubleday, 1962. Subj: Family life. Foreign lands – France. Foreign languages.

Ridlon, Marci. *Kittens and more kittens* ill. by Liz Dauber. Follett, 1967. Subj: Animals – cats. Pets.

Riley, James Whitcomb. *Little Orphant Annie* ill. by Diane Stanley. Putnam's, 1983. Subj: Poetry, rhyme.

Ring, Elizabeth. *Tiger lilies: and other beastly plants* ill. by Barbara Bash. Walker, 1985. Subj: Character traits – appearance. Plants.

Ringi, Kjell. *My father and I* by Kjell Ringi and Adelaide Holl; ill. by Kjell Ringi. Watts, 1972. Subj: Character traits – ambition. Family life – fathers. Imagination.

The sun and the cloud ill. by author. Harper, 1971. Subj: Plants. Sun. Weather – clouds.

The winner ill. by author. Harper, 1969. Subj: Behavior. Wordless.

Riordan, James. *Old Father Frost* (Odoyevsky, Vladimir)

The three magic gifts ill. by Errol le Cain. Oxford Univ. Pr., 1980. Subj: Character traits – perseverance. Folk and fairy tales. Sibling rivalry.

Rister, Claude *see* Marshall, James

Roach, Marilynne K. *Dune fox* ill. by author. Little, 1977. Subj: Animals – foxes. Ecology. Sand. Seasons.

Two Roman mice by Horace; ill. by author. Crowell, 1975. Based on a version of Æsop's fable about the country mouse and the city mouse as it appeared in Horace's Satirae II, 6. Subj: Animals – mice. City. Country.

Robb, Brian. *My grandmother's djinn* ill. by author. Parents, 1978. Subj: Family life. Foreign lands. Mythical creatures. Problem solving.

Robbins, Ken. *Trucks of every sort* photos. by author. Crown, 1981. Subj: Trucks.

Robbins, Ruth. *Baboushka and the three kings* ill. by Nicolas Sidjakov; verse by Edith R. Thomas; music by Mary Clement Sanks. Parnassus, 1960. Adapted from a Russian folk tale. Subj: Caldecott award book. Folk and fairy tales. Foreign lands – Russia. Holidays – Christmas. Music. Poetry, rhyme. Songs.

The harlequin and Mother Goose: or, The magic stick ill. by Nicolas Sidjakov. Parnassus, 1965. Subj: Nursery rhymes.

How the first rainbow was made ill. by author. Houghton, 1980. Subj: Ethnic groups in the U.S. – Indians. Folk and fairy tales. Weather – rain.

Roberts, Bethany. *Waiting for spring stories* ill. by William Joyce. Harper, 1984. Subj: Animals – rabbits. Seasons – winter.

Roberts, Cliff. *The dot* ill. by author. Watts, 1960. Subj: Concepts – shape.

Start with a dot ill. by author. Watts, 1960. Subj: Concepts – shape. Poetry, rhyme.

Roberts, Sarah. *Bert and the missing mop mix-up* ill. by Joseph Mathieu. Random House, 1983. Subj: Behavior – misunderstanding. Puppets.

Roberts, Thom. *Pirates in the park* ill. by Harold Berson. Crown, 1973. Subj: Imagination. Pirates. Toys – rocking horses.

Robertson, Lilian. *Picnic woods* ill. by author. Harcourt, 1949. Subj: Activities – picnicking.

Runaway rocking horse ill. by author. Harcourt, 1948. Subj: Toys – rocking horses.

Robins, Joan. *Addie meets Max* ill. by Sue Truesdell. Harper, 1985. Subj: Animals – dogs. Friendship.

Robinson, Adjai. *Femi and old grandaddie* ill. by Jerry Pinkney. Coward, 1972. Subj: Folk and fairy tales. Foreign lands – Africa.

Robinson, Earl. *Black and white* (Arkin, Alan)

Robinson, Irene Bowen. *Picture book of animal babies* by Irene and W. W. Robinson; ill. by Irene Bowen Robinson. Macmillan, 1947. Subj: Animals.

Robinson, Nancy K. *Firefighters!* ill. with photos. Scholastic, 1979. Subj: Careers – firefighters.

Robinson, Thomas P. *Buttons* ill. by Peggy Bacon. Viking, 1938. Subj: Animals – cats.

Robinson, Tom *see* Robinson, Thomas P.

Robinson, W. W. (William Wilcox). *On the farm* ill. by Irene Bowen Robinson. Macmillan, 1939. Subj: Animals. Farms.

Picture book of animal babies (Robinson, Irene Bowen)

Robison, Deborah. *Bye-bye, old buddy* ill. by author. Houghton, 1983. Subj: Problem solving.

No elephants allowed ill. by author. Houghton, 1981. Subj: Bedtime. Emotions – fear. Problem solving.

Your turn, doctor by Deborah Robison and Carla Perez; ill. by Deborah Robison. Dial Pr., 1982. Subj: Behavior – misbehavior. Careers – doctors.

Robison, Nancy. *UFO kidnap* ill. by Edward Frascino. Lothrop, 1978. Subj: Space and space ships.

Roche, A. K. *see* Abisch, Roz

Roche, P. K. *Good-bye, Arnold!* ill. by author. Dial Pr., 1979. Subj: Animals – mice. Family life. Sibling rivalry.

Jump all the morning: a child's day in verses ill. by author. Viking, 1984. Subj: Poetry, rhyme.

Plaid bear and the rude rabbit gang ill. by author. Dial Pr., 1982. Subj: Behavior – bullying. Toys.

Webster and Arnold and the giant box ill. by author. Dial Pr., 1980. Subj: Imagination. Sibling rivalry.

Roche, Patrick K. *see* Roche, P. K.

Rockwell, Anne F. *Bafana: a Christmas story* ill. by author. Atheneum, 1974. Subj: Folk and fairy tales. Holidays – Christmas.

A bear, a bobcat and three ghosts ill. by author. Macmillan, 1977. Subj: Animals – bears. Animals – bobcats. Careers – peddlers. Ghosts. Holidays – Halloween.

Big boss ill. by author. Macmillan, 1975. Subj: Animals – foxes. Animals – tigers. Character traits – cleverness. Frogs and toads.

Blackout by Anne F. and Harlow Rockwell; ill. by authors. Macmillan, 1979. Subj: Family life. Power failure. Weather.

Boats ill. by author. Dutton, 1982. Subj: Animals – bears. Boats, ships.

The bump in the night ill. by author. Greenwillow, 1979. Subj: Character traits – cleverness. Character traits – helpfulness.

Buster and the bogeyman ill. by author. Four Winds Pr., 1978. Subj: Bedtime. Dreams. Mythical creatures.

Can I help? by Anne F. and Harlow Rockwell; ill. by authors. Macmillan, 1982. Subj: Character traits – helpfulness.

Cars ill. by author. Dutton, 1984. Subj: Automobiles.

Gogo's pay day ill. by author. Doubleday, 1978. Subj: Character traits – generosity. Clowns, jesters. Money.

The gollywhopper egg ill. by author. Macmillan, 1974. Subj: Behavior – trickery. Eggs. Farms.

The good llama ill. by author. World, 1963. Subj: Animals. Animals – llamas. Foreign lands – South America.

Happy birthday to me by Anne F. and Harlow Rockwell; ill. by authors. Macmillan, 1981. Subj: Birthdays.

Honk honk! ill. by author. Dutton, 1980. Subj: Animals. Behavior – misbehavior. Birds. Cumulative tales.

How my garden grew by Anne F. and Harlow Rockwell; ill. by authors. Macmillan, 1982. Subj: Activities – gardening.

I like the library ill. by author. Dutton, 1977. Subj: Libraries.

I love my pets by Anne F. and Harlow Rockwell; ill. by authors. Macmillan, 1982. Subj: Pets.

I play in my room by Anne F. and Harlow Rockwell; ill. by authors. Macmillan, 1981. Subj: Activities – playing.

Machines by Anne F. and Harlow Rockwell; ill. by Harlow Rockwell. Macmillan, 1972. Subj: Machines.

The Mother Goose cookie-candy book ill. by author. Random House, 1983. Subj: Activities – cooking. Food.

My back yard by Anne F. and Harlow Rockwell; ill. by authors. Macmillan, 1984. Subj: Activities – playing.

My barber by Anne F. and Harlow Rockwell; ill. by authors. Macmillan, 1981. Subj: Careers – barbers. Hair.

Nice and clean by Anne F. and Harlow Rockwell; ill. by authors. Macmillan, 1984. Subj: Character traits – cleanliness. Houses.

The night we slept outside by Anne F. and Harlow Rockwell; ill. by authors. Macmillan, 1983. Subj: Night. Sports – camping.

The old woman and her pig and 10 other stories ill. by adapt. Crowell, 1979. Subj: Folk and fairy tales.

Our garage sale ill. by Harlow Rockwell. Greenwillow, 1984. Subj: Garage sales.

Poor Goose: a French folktale ill. by author. Crowell, 1976. Subj: Animals. Birds – geese. Cumulative tales. Folk and fairy tales. Foreign lands – France.

Sick in bed by Anne F. and Harlow Rockwell; ill. by authors. Macmillan, 1982. Subj: Illness.

The stolen necklace: a picture story from India ill. by author. Collins-World, 1968. "Based on a tale from the Jataka." Subj: Animals – monkeys. Character traits – cleverness. Foreign lands – India.

The story snail ill. by author. Macmillan, 1974. Subj: Animals – snails. Magic.

The supermarket by Anne F. and Harlow Rockwell; ill. by authors. Macmillan, 1979. Subj: Shopping. Stores.

The three bears: and 15 other stories ill. by author. Crown, 1975. Subj: Folk and fairy tales.

Thump thump thump! ill. by author. Dutton, 1981. Subj: Folk and fairy tales. Monsters.

Toad by Anne F. and Harlow Rockwell; ill. by authors. Doubleday, 1972. Subj: Frogs and toads.

The toolbox by Anne F. and Harlow Rockwell; ill. by Harlow Rockwell. Macmillan, 1971. Subj: Tools.

Trucks ill. by author. Dutton, 1984. Subj: Trucks.

When I go visiting by Anne F. and Harlow Rockwell; ill. by authors. Macmillan, 1984. Subj: Family life – grandparents, great-grandparents.

Willie runs away ill. by author. Dutton, 1978. Subj: Animals – dogs. Behavior – running away.

The wolf who had a wonderful dream ill. by author. Crowell, 1973. Subj: Animals – wolves. Dreams. Folk and fairy tales. Food. Foreign lands – France.

The wonderful eggs of Furicchia: a picture story from Italy ill. by author. Collins-World, 1969. Subj: Birds – chickens. Eggs. Folk and fairy tales. Foreign lands – Italy. Magic.

Rockwell, Harlow. *Blackout* (Rockwell, Anne F)

Can I help? (Rockwell, Anne F)

The compost heap ill. by author. Doubleday, 1974. Subj: Activities – gardening. Plants.

Happy birthday to me (Rockwell, Anne F)

How my garden grew (Rockwell, Anne F)

I did it ill. by author. Macmillan, 1974. Subj: Activities.

I love my pets (Rockwell, Anne F)

I play in my room (Rockwell, Anne F)

Look at this ill. by author. Macmillan, 1978. Subj: Activities.

Machines (Rockwell, Anne F)

My back yard (Rockwell, Anne F)

My barber (Rockwell, Anne F)

My dentist ill. by author. Greenwillow, 1975. Subj: Careers – dentists. Teeth.

My doctor ill. by author. Macmillan, 1973. Subj: Careers – doctors. Health.

My kitchen ill. by author. Greenwillow, 1980. Subj: Food.

My nursery school ill. by author. Greenwillow, 1976. Subj: School.

Nice and clean (Rockwell, Anne F)

The night we slept outside (Rockwell, Anne F)

Sick in bed (Rockwell, Anne F)

The supermarket (Rockwell, Anne F)

Toad (Rockwell, Anne F)

The toolbox (Rockwell, Anne F)

When I go visiting (Rockwell, Anne F)

Rockwell, Norman. *Norman Rockwell's counting book* sel. by Glorina Taborin; ill. by author. Harmony Books, 1977. Subj: Counting. Games. Holidays – April Fools' Day.

Roennfeldt, Robert. *A day on the avenue* ill. by author. Viking, 1984. Subj: Roads. Wordless.

Roffey, Maureen. *Home sweet home* ill. by author. Coward, 1983. Subj: Format, unusual. Houses.

Look, there's my hat! ill. by author. Putnam's, 1985. Subj: Behavior – greed.

Rogasky, Barbara *Rapunzel* (Grimm, Jacob)

Rogers, Anne. *Cinderella* (Grimm, Jacob)

The musicians of Bremen (Grimm, Jacob)

The wolf and the seven little kids (Grimm, Jacob)

Rogers, Edmund. *Elephants* ill. with photos. Raintree, 1978. Subj: Animals – elephants.

Rogers, Helen Spelman. *Morris and his brave lion* ill. by Glo Coalson. McGraw-Hill, 1975. Subj: Divorce.

Rogers, Margaret. *Green is beautiful* by Margaret Rogers and Bernadette; ill. by Bernadette. State Mutual Books, 1982. Subj: Concepts – color. Folk and fairy tales.

Rogers, Paul. *Forget-me-not* ill. by Celia Berridge. Viking, 1984. Subj: Behavior – forgetfulness. Behavior – losing things.

Rojankovsky, Feodor. *ABC, an alphabet of many things* ill. by author. Golden Pr., 1970. Subj: ABC books.

Animals in the zoo ill. by author. Knopf, 1962. Subj: ABC books. Animals. Zoos.

Animals on the farm ill. by author. Knopf, 1962. Subj: Animals. Farms. Wordless.

The great big animal book ill. by author. Simon and Schuster, 1950. Subj: Animals. Farms.

The great big wild animal book ill. by author. Western, 1951. Subj: Animals.

Roll over! *a counting song* ill. by Merle Peek. Houghton, 1981. Subj: Counting. Songs.

Romanek, Enid Warner. *Teddy* ill. by author. Scribner's, 1978. Subj: Toys – teddy bears.

Romano, Louis G. *Gertie the duck* (Georgiady, Nicholas P)

Romanoli, Robert. *What's so funny?!!* ill. by Jerry Zimmerman. Grosset, 1978. Subj: Riddles.

Ronay, Jadja. *Ginger* ill. by Anthony Accardo. Magnolia, 1981. Subj: Folk and fairy tales. Magic.

Rondell, Florence. *The family that grew* by Florence Rondell and Ruth Michaels. Crown, 1965. Subj: Adoption.

Roosevelt, Michelle Chopin. *Zoo animals* ill. by author. Random House, 1983. Subj: Format, unusual – cardboard pages. Zoos.

Rosario, Idalia. *Idalia's project ABC: an urban alphabet book in English and Spanish* ill. by author. Holt, 1981. Subj: ABC books. City. Foreign languages.

Roscoe, William. *The butterfly's ball* ill. by Don Bolognese. McGraw-Hill, 1967. Subj: Animals. Insects – butterflies, caterpillars. Poetry, rhyme.

Rose, Anne. *Akimba and the magic cow: a folktale from Africa* ill. by Hope Meryman. Four Winds Pr., 1979. Subj: Folk and fairy tales. Foreign lands – Africa. Magic.

As right as right can be ill. by Arnold Lobel. Dial Pr., 1976. Subj: Behavior – seeking better things. Money.

How does a czar eat potatoes? ill. by Janosch. Lothrop, 1973. Subj: Poetry, rhyme. Poverty. Royalty.

Pot full of luck ill. by Margot Tomes. Lothrop, 1982. Subj: Folk and fairy tales. Foreign lands – Africa.

Spider in the sky ill. by Gail Owens. Harper, 1978. Based on the story How the Sun came from American Indian mythology by Alice Marriott and Carol K. Rachlin. Subj: Animals. Ethnic groups in the U.S. – Indians. Folk and fairy tales. Spiders.

The triumphs of Fuzzy Fogtop ill. by Tomie de Paola. Dial Pr., 1979. Subj: Folk and fairy tales.

Rose, David S. *It hardly seems like Halloween* ill. by author. Lothrop, 1983. Subj: Holidays – Halloween.

Rose, Gerald. *PB takes a holiday* ill. by author. Bodley Head, 1981. Subj: Activities – traveling. Animals – bears.

The tiger-skin rug ill. by author. Prentice-Hall, 1979. Subj: Animals – tigers. Crime.

Rose, Mitchell. *Norman* ill. by author. Simon and Schuster, 1970. Subj: Animals – dogs. Theater.

Rosen, Anne. *A family Passover* by Anne Rosen and others; photos. by Laurence Salzmann. Jewish Pub. Soc., 1980. Subj: Holidays – Passover. Jewish culture.

Rosen, Michael. *You can't catch me!* ill. by Quentin Blake. Elsevier-Dutton, 1982. Subj: Humor. Poetry, rhyme.

Rosen, Winifred. *Dragons hate to be discreet* ill. by Edward Koren. Knopf, 1978. Subj: Dragons. Imagination.

Henrietta and the day of the iguana ill. by Kay Chorao. Four Winds Pr., 1978. Subj: Behavior – wishing. Pets. Reptiles – iguanas.

Henrietta and the gong from Hong Kong ill. by Kay Chorao. Four Winds Pr., 1981. Subj: Family life – grandparents, great-grandparents. Sibling rivalry.

Rosenberg, David *see* Clifford, David

Rosenberg, Ethel *see* Clifford, Eth

Rosenberg, Maxine B. *Being adopted* photos. by George Ancona. Lothrop, 1984. Subj: Adoption. Ethnic groups in the U.S. Family life.

My friend Leslie: the story of a handicapped child photos. by George Ancona. Lothrop, 1983. Subj: Handicaps. School.

Rosenberg, Nancy Sherman *see* Sherman, Nancy

Ross, David. *Gorp and the space pirates* ill. by author. Walker, 1983. Subj: Monsters. Pirates. Space and space ships.

Space monster ill. by author. Walker, 1981. Subj: Monsters. Space and space ships.

Space Monster Gorp and the runaway computer ill. by author. Walker, 1984. Subj: Monsters. Space and space ships.

Ross, Diana. *The story of the little red engine* ill. by Leslie Wood. Transatlantic, 1947. Subj: Foreign lands – England. Trains.

Ross, George Maxim. *When Lucy went away* ill. by Ingrid Fetz. Dutton, 1976. Subj: Animals – cats. Pets.

Ross, H. L. *Not counting monsters* ill. by Doug Cushman. Platt, 1978. Subj: Activities. Counting. Monsters.

Ross, Jessica. *Ms. Klondike* ill. by author. Viking, 1977. Subj: Activities – working. Careers – taxi drivers. Taxis.

Ross, Joel. *Your first airplane trip* (Ross, Pat)

Ross, Pat. *M and M and the big bag* ill. by Marylin Hafner. Pantheon, 1981. Subj: Activities – reading. Shopping.

M and M and the haunted house game ill. by Marylin Hafner. Pantheon, 1980. Subj: Ghosts. Houses.

Meet M and M ill. by Marylin Hafner. Pantheon, 1980. Subj: Friendship.

Molly and the slow teeth ill. by Jerry Milord. Lothrop, 1980. Subj: School. Teeth.

Your first airplane trip by Pat and Joel Ross; ill. by Lynn Wheeling. Lothrop, 1981. Subj: Activities – flying. Airplanes, airports. Emotions – fear.

Ross, Tony. *The enchanted pig: an old Rumanian tale* ill. by author. Harper, 1983. Subj: Animals – pigs. Folk and fairy tales. Magic. Witches.

The greedy little cobbler ill. by author. Barron's, 1980. Subj: Behavior – greed. Careers – shoemakers.

Hugo and Oddsock ill. by author. Follett, 1978. Subj: Animals – mice. Imagination – imaginary friends.

Hugo and the bureau of holidays ill. by author. Follett, 1982. Subj: Animals – mice. Holidays.

Hugo and the man who stole colors ill. by author. Follett, 1982. Subj: Animals – mice. Behavior – stealing. Concepts – color.

The pied piper of Hamelin retold and ill. by Tony Ross. Lothrop, 1978. Subj: Animals – rats. Folk and fairy tales. Foreign lands – Germany.

Towser and the terrible thing ill. by author. Pantheon, 1984. Subj: Animals – dogs. Monsters. Royalty.

Ross, Wilda S. *What did the dinosaurs eat?* ill. by Elizabeth Schmidt. Coward, 1972. Subj: Dinosaurs. Food. Science.

Rossetti, Christina Georgina. *What is pink?* ill. by José Aruego. Macmillan, 1971. Subj: Birds – flamingos. Concepts – color. Poetry, rhyme.

Rossner, Judith. *What kind of feet does a bear have?* ill. by Irwin Rosenhouse. Bobbs-Merrill, 1963. Subj: Humor.

Roth, Susan L. *Patchwork tales* by Susan L. Roth and Ruth Phang; ill. by authors. Atheneum, 1984. Subj: Family life – grandparents, great-grandparents.

Rottenberg, Dorian. *The merry starlings* (Marshak, Samuel)

Roughsey, Dick. *The giant devil-dingo* ill. by author. Macmillan, 1973. Subj: Animals. Folk and fairy tales. Foreign lands – Australia.

Rounds, Glen. *The boll weevil* Ill. by author. Golden Gate, 1967. Subj: Folk and fairy tales. Insects. Music. Songs.

Casey Jones: the story of a brave engineer ill. by author. Golden Gate, 1968. Subj: Folk and fairy tales. Music. Songs. Trains.

The day the circus came to Lone Tree ill. by author. Holiday, 1973. Subj: Circus. Humor.

Once we had a horse ill. by author. Holiday, 1971. Subj: Animals – horses.

The strawberry roan ill. by comp. Golden Gate, 1970. Subj: Animals – horses. Music. Songs.

Sweet Betsy from Pike ill. by comp. Children's Pr., 1973. Subj: Folk and fairy tales. Music. Songs.

Routh, Jonathan. *The Nuns go to Africa* ill. by author. Bobbs-Merrill, 1971. Subj: Careers – nuns. Foreign lands – Africa.

Rowand, Phyllis. *Every day in the year* ill. by author. Little, 1959. Subj: Emotions – love. Holidays – Christmas.

George ill. by author. Little, 1956. Subj: Animals – dogs.

George goes to town ill. by author. Little, 1958. Subj: Animals – dogs.

It is night ill. by author. Harper, 1953. Subj: Night. Sleep.

Rowe, Cliff. *Listen!* (Crume, Marion W)

Rowe, Jeanne A. *City workers* Watts, 1969. Subj: Careers. City.

A trip through a school. Watts, 1969. Subj: School.

Roy, Ronald. *Breakfast with my father* ill. by Troy Howell. Houghton, 1980. Subj: Divorce. Family life.

A thousand pails of water ill. by Vo-Dinh Mai. Knopf, 1978. Subj: Animals – whales. Character traits – kindness to animals. Foreign lands – Japan.

Three ducks went wandering ill. by Paul Galdone. Seabury Pr., 1979. Subj: Behavior – indifference. Birds – ducks. Humor.

Rubel, Nicole. *Bruno Brontosaurus* ill. by author. Camelot, 1983. Subj: Dinosaurs.

Me and my kitty ill. by author. Macmillan, 1983. Subj: Activities. Animals – cats.

Sam and Violet are twins ill. by author. Camelot, 1981. Subj: Animals – cats. Character traits – individuality. Twins.

Sam and Violet go camping ill. by author. Camelot, 1981. Subj: Animals – cats. Character traits – individuality. Sports – camping. Twins.

Ruben, Patricia. *Apples to zippers: an alphabet book* ill. by author. Doubleday, 1976. Subj: ABC books.

True or false? ill. by author. Lippincott, 1978. Subj: Concepts.

Rubin, Caroline. *Snow on bear's nose* (Bartoli, Jennifer)

Tell them my name is Amanda (Wold, Jo Anne)

Wild Bill Hiccup's riddle book (Bishop, Ann)

Rubin, Jeff. *Baseball brothers* by Jeff Rubin and Rick Rael; ill. by Sandy Kossin. Lothrop, 1976. Subj: Friendship. Sports – baseball.

Ruby-Spears Enterprises. *The puppy's new adventures: hide and seek* ill. by Ruby-Spears Enterprises. Antioch, 1983. Subj: Animals – dogs. Crime. Format, unusual.

Ruck-Pauquèt, Gina. *Little hedgehog* ill. by Marianne Richter. Hastings, 1959. Subj: Animals – hedgehogs.

Mumble bear tr. by Anthea Bell; ill. by Erika Dietzsch-Capelle. Putnam's, 1980. Subj: Animals – bears. Character traits – individuality.

Oh, that koala! ill. by Anna Mossakowska. McGraw-Hill, 1979. Subj: Animals – koala bears. Behavior – misbehavior.

Rudchenko, Ivan. *Ivanko and the dragon: an old Ukrainian folk tale* tr. by Marie Halun Bloch; ill. by Yaroslava. Atheneum, 1969. Subj: Dragons. Folk and fairy tales. Foreign lands – Ukraine.

Rudolph, Marguerita. *How a piglet crashed the Christmas party* (Zakhoder, Boris Vladimirovich)

How a shirt grew in the field adapt. from the Russian of K. Ushinsky; ill. by Yaroslava. McGraw-Hill, 1967. Subj: Clothing. Foreign lands – Ukraine. Plants.

I am your misfortune: a Lithuanian folk tale ill. by Imero Gobbato. Seabury Pr., 1968. Subj: Character traits – selfishness. Folk and fairy tales. Foreign lands – Lithuania. Monsters. Sports – baseball.

Rosachok (Zakhoder, Boris Vladimirovich)

Sharp and shiny ill. by Susan Perl. McGraw-Hill, 1971. Subj: Activities – bathing. Activities – playing. Character traits – cleanliness.

Rudomin, Esther *see* Hautzig, Esther

Ruffins, Reynold. *My brother never feeds the cat* ill. by author. Scribner's, 1979. Subj: Family life.

Rukeyser, Muriel. *More night* ill. by Symeon Shimin. Harper, 1981. Subj: Activities. Night.

Uncle Eddie's moustache (Brecht, Bertolt)

Rushnell, Elaine Evans. *My mom's having a baby* ill. with drawings and photos. Grosset, 1978. Subj: Babies. Family life. Science. Sibling rivalry.

Ruskin, John. *Dame Wiggins of Lee and her seven wonderful cats*

Rusling, Albert. *The mouse and Mrs. Proudfoot* ill. by author. Prentice-Hall, 1985. Subj: Animals. Houses. Humor.

Russ, Lavinia. *Alec's sand castle* ill. by James Stevenson. Harper, 1972. Subj: Activities – playing. Imagination. Sea and seashore.

Russell, Betty. *Big store, funny door* ill. by Mary Gehr. Albert Whitman, 1955. Subj: Character traits – luck. Shopping.

Run sheep run ill. by Mary Gehr. Albert Whitman, 1952. Subj: Animals – sheep.

Russell, Sandra Joanne. *A farmer's dozen* ill. by author. Harper, 1982. Subj: Farms. Poetry, rhyme.

Russell, Solveig Paulson. *What good is a tail?* ill. by Ezra Jack Keats. Bobbs-Merrill, 1962. Subj: Animals. Science.

Russo, Susan. *The ice cream ocean and other delectable poems of the sea* ill. by author. Lothrop, 1984. Subj: Poetry, rhyme. Sea and seashore.

The moon's the north wind's cooky:

Ruthstrom, Dorotha. *The big kite contest* ill. by Lillian Hoban. Pantheon, 1980. Subj: Kites. Sibling rivalry.

Ryan, Cheli Durán. *Hildilid's night* ill. by Arnold Lobel. Macmillan, 1971. Subj: Caldecott award honor book. Night.

Ryder, Eileen. *Winklet goes to school* ill. by Stephanie Lang. John Godon Burke, 1982. Subj: School.

Winston's new cap ill. by Stephanie Lang. John Godon Burke, 1982. Subj: Behavior – losing things. Clothing.

Ryder, Joanne. *Beach party* ill. by Diane Stanley. Warne, 1982. Subj: Animals – sheep. Family life. Sea and seashore.

Fireflies ill. by Don Bolognese. Harper, 1977. Subj: Insects – fireflies. Science.

Fog in the meadow ill. by Gail Owens. Harper, 1979. Subj: Animals. Weather – fog.

Snail in the woods by Joanne Ryder with the assistance of Harold S. Feinberg; ill. by Jo Polseno. Harper, 1979. Subj: Animals – snails. Science.

The snail's spell ill. by Lynne Cherry. Warne, 1982. Subj: Animals – snails. Night.

The spiders dance ill. by Robert J. Blake. Harper, 1981. Subj: Science. Spiders.

A wet and sandy day ill. by Donald Carrick. Harper, 1977. Subj: Sea and seashore. Weather – rain.

Rylant, Cynthia. *Miss Maggie* ill. by Thomas Di Grazia. Dutton, 1983. Subj: Character traits – curiosity. Friendship.

This year's garden ill. by Mary Szilagyi. Bradbury Pr., 1984. Subj: Activities – gardening.

When I was young in the mountains ill. by Diane Goode. Dutton, 1982. Subj: Caldecott award honor book. Family life.

S-Ringi, Kjell *see* Ringi, Kjell

Sachs, Marilyn. *Fleet-footed Florence* ill. by Charles Robinson. Doubleday, 1981. Subj: Behavior – wishing. Magic. Sports – baseball.

Matt's mitt ill. by Hilary Knight. Doubleday, 1975. Subj: Sports – baseball.

Saddler, Allen. *The Archery contest* ill. by Joe Wright. Oxford Univ. Pr., 1983. Subj: Humor. Magic. Royalty. Sports.

The king gets fit ill. by Joe Wright. Oxford Univ. Pr., 1983. Subj: Humor. Royalty.

Sadler, Catherine Edwards. *A duckling is born* (Isenbart, Hans-Heinrich)

A flamingo is born (Zoll, Max Alfred)

Sadler, Marilyn. *Alistair in outer space* ill. by Roger Bollen. Prentice-Hall, 1984. Subj: Libraries. Space and space ships.

Alistair's elephant ill. by Roger Bollen. Prentice-Hall, 1983. Subj: Animals – elephants. Behavior – misbehavior.

It's not easy being a bunny ill. by Roger Bollen. Random House, 1983. Subj: Animals – rabbits. Behavior – dissatisfaction. Self-concept.

Sage, James. *The boy and the dove* photos. by Robert Doisneau. Workman, 1978. Subj: Birds – doves. Theater.

Sage, Juniper *see* Brown, Margaret Wise

Sage, Juniper *see* Hurd, Edith Thacher

Sage, Michael. *Dippy dos and don'ts* by Michael Sage and Arnold Spilka; ill. by Arnold Spilka. Viking, 1967. Subj: Humor. Poetry, rhyme.

If you talked to a boar ill. by Arnold Spilka. Lippincott, 1960. Subj: Humor. Language.

Sahagun, Bernardino de. *Spirit child: a story of the Nativity* tr. from the Aztec by John Bierhorst; ill. by Barbara Cooney. Morrow, 1984. Subj: Folk and fairy tales. Foreign lands – Mexico. Holidays – Christmas. Religion.

Sahagun, Fray B. *see* Sahagun, Bernardino de.

St. George, Judith. *The Halloween pumpkin smasher* ill. by Margot Tomes. Putnam's, 1978. Subj: Animals – raccoons. Holidays – Halloween. Imagination – imaginary friends.

St. Pierre, Wendy. *Henry finds a home* ill. by Barbara Eidlitz. Firefly Pr., 1981. Subj: Children as authors. Reptiles – turtles.

St. Tamara. *Chickaree, a red squirrel* ill. by author. Harcourt, 1980. Subj: Animals – squirrels. Science.

Salazar, Violet. *Squares are not bad* ill. by Harlow Rockwell. Golden Pr., 1967. Subj: Concepts – shape.

Saleh, Harold J. *Even tiny ants must sleep* ill. by Jerry Pinkney. McGraw-Hill, 1967. Subj: Animals. Poetry, rhyme. Sleep.

Saltzberg, Barney. *It must have been the wind* ill. by author. Harper, 1982. Subj: Bedtime. Noise, sounds. Weather – wind.

Salus, Naomi Panush. *My daddy's mustache* ill. by Tomie de Paola. Doubleday, 1979. Subj: Character traits – appearance.

Samuels, Barbara. *Faye and Dolores* ill. by author. Bradbury Pr., 1985. Subj: Emotions – love. Sibling rivalry.

Sanchez, Jose Louis Garcia. *Kangaroo* by Jose Louis Garcia Sanchez and Miguel Angel Pacheco; ill. by Nella Bosnia. H P Books, 1983. Subj: Animals – kangaroos.

Sandberg, Inger. *Come on out, Daddy!* by Inger and Lasse Sandberg; ill. by Lasse Sandberg. Delacorte Pr., 1971. Translation of Pappa, kom ut. Subj: Activities – working. Careers. Family life – fathers.

Little Anna saved by Inger and Lasse Sandberg; ill. by Lasse Sandberg. Lothrop, 1966. Subj: Games.

Little ghost Godfry by Inger and Lasse Sandberg; tr. by Nancy S. Leupold; ill. by Lasse Sandberg. Delacorte Pr., 1968. Subj: Ghosts.

Nicholas' favorite pet by Inger and Lasse Sandberg; ill. by Lasse Sandberg. Delacorte Pr., 1969. Translation of Niklas' önskedjur. Subj: Animals. Animals – dogs. Birthdays. Pets.

Sandberg, Lasse. *Come on out, Daddy!* (Sandberg, Inger)

Little Anna saved (Sandberg, Inger)

Little ghost Godfry (Sandberg, Inger)

Nicholas' favorite pet (Sandberg, Inger)

Sandburg, Carl. *The wedding procession of the rag doll and the broom handle and who was in it* ill. by Harriet Pincus. Harcourt, 1922. Subj: Toys. Toys – dolls. Weddings.

Sandburg, Charles August *see* Sandburg, Carl

Sandburg, Helga. *Anna and the baby buzzard* ill. by Brinton Turkle. Dutton, 1970. Subj: Birds – buzzards. Character traits – kindness to animals.

Sandin, Joan. *The long way to a new land* ill. by author. Harper, 1981. Subj: Family life. Foreign lands. Moving.

San Souci, Robert D. *The brave little tailor* (Grimm, Jacob)

Song of Sedna ill. by Daniel San Souci. Doubleday, 1981. Subj: Ethnic groups in the U.S. – Eskimos. Folk and fairy tales.

Sant, Laurent Sauveur. *Dinosaurs* ill. by author. Wonder Books, 1971. Subj: Dinosaurs.

Santos, Joyce Audy Dos *see* Dos Santos, Joyce Audy

Sapphire, Paula. *The toddler's potty book* (Allison, Alida)

Sargent, Susan. *My favorite place* by Susan Sargent and Donna Aaron Wirt; ill. by Allan Eitzen. Abingdon Pr., 1983. Subj: Handicaps – blindness.

Sarnoff, Jane. *That's not fair* ill. by Reynold Ruffins. Scribner's, 1980. Subj: Behavior – dissatisfaction. Family life. Sibling rivalry.

Sarton, May. *Punch's secret* ill. by Howard Knotts. Harper, 1974. Subj: Emotions – loneliness. Friendship.

Sasaki, Isao. *Snow* ill. by author. Viking, 1982. Subj: Trains. Weather – snow. Wordless.

Sasaki, Jeannie. *Chōchō is for butterfly: a Japanese-English primer* by Jeannie Sasaki and Frances Uyeda; ill. by authors. Uyeda Sasaki Art, 1975. Subj: Foreign lands – Japan. Foreign languages.

Sattler, Helen Roney. *No place for a goat* ill. by Bari Weissman. Elsevier-Nelson, 1981. Subj: Animals – goats. Houses.

Train whistle: a language in code ill. by Tom Funk. Lothrop, 1977. Subj: Language. Trains.

Sauer, Julia Lina. *Mike's house* ill. by Don Freeman. Viking, 1954. Subj: Behavior – lost. City. Libraries. Weather – snow.

Saunders, Susan. *Charles Rat's picnic* ill. by Robert Byrd. Dutton, 1983. Subj: Activities – picnicking. Animals – armadillos. Animals – rats. Friendship.

Fish fry ill. by S. D. Schindler. Viking, 1982. Subj: Activities – picnicking.

Wales' tale ill. by Marilyn Hirsh. Viking, 1980. Subj: Animals – dogs.

Savage, Kathleen. *Bear hunt* (Siewert, Margaret)

Sawyer, Jean. *Our village shop* ill. by Faith Jaques. Putnam's, 1984. Subj: Stores.

Sawyer, Ruth. *The Christmas Anna angel* ill. by Kate Seredy. Viking, 1944. Subj: Angels. Caldecott award honor book. Holidays – Christmas.

Journey cake, ho! ill. by Robert McCloskey. Viking, 1953. Subj: Caldecott award honor book. Cumulative tales. Folk and fairy tales. Poverty.

Saxe, John Godfrey. *The blind men and the elephant* ill. by Paul Galdone. McGraw-Hill, 1963. Subj: Animals – elephants. Handicaps – blindness.

Saxon, Charles D. *Don't worry about Poopsie* ill. by author. Dodd, 1958. Subj: Animals – dogs. Behavior – lost.

Saxon, Gladys Relyea *see* Seyton, Marion

Say, Allen. *The bicycle man* ill. by author. Houghton, 1982. Subj: Foreign lands – Japan. Sports – bicycling.

Once under the cherry blossom tree: an old Japanese tale ill. by author. Harper, 1974. Subj: Folk and fairy tales. Foreign lands – Japan.

Sazer, Nina. *What do you think I saw? a nonsense number book* ill. by Lois Ehlert. Pantheon, 1976. Subj: Counting. Humor. Poetry, rhyme.

Scarry, Huck. *Huck Scarry's steam train journey* ill. by author. Collins-World, 1979. Subj: Trains.

Looking into the Middle Ages ill. by author. Harper, 1985. Subj: Format, unusual. Knights. Middle ages.

On the road ill. by author. Putnam's, 1981. Subj: Automobiles.

Scarry, Patricia *see* Scarry, Patsy

Scarry, Patsy. *Little Richard and Prickles* ill. by Cyndy Szekeres. American Heritage, 1971. Subj: Animals – porcupines. Animals – rabbits. Birds – owls. Friendship.

Patsy Scarry's big bedtime storybook ill. by Cyndy Szekeres. Random House, 1980. Subj: Animals – rabbits.

Scarry, Richard. *The adventures of Tinker and Tanker* ill. by author. Doubleday, 1968. A reissue of Tinker and Tanker, Tinker and Tanker out West, and Tinker and Tanker and their space ship. Subj: Animals – hippopotami. Animals – rabbits.

Egg in the hole ill. by author. Golden Pr., 1967. Subj: Birds – chickens. Eggs. Format, unusual.

The great big car and truck book ill. by author. Golden Pr., 1951. Subj: Automobiles. Trucks.

Is this the house of Mistress Mouse? ill. by author. Golden Pr., 1964. Subj: Animals. Houses.

Peasant Pig and the terrible dragon ill. by author. Random House, 1980. Subj: Animals – pigs. Character traits – bravery. Middle ages.

Richard Scarry's ABC word book ill. by author. Random House, 1971. Subj: ABC books.

Richard Scarry's animal nursery tales ill. by author. Golden Pr., 1975. Subj: Animals. Folk and fairy tales. Nursery rhymes.

Richard Scarry's best Christmas book ever! ill. by author. Random House, 1981. Subj: Holidays – Christmas.

Richard Scarry's best counting book ever ill. by author. Random House, 1975. Subj: Counting.

Richard Scarry's best first book ever ill. by author. Random House, 1979. Subj: Concepts. Days of the week, months of the year.

Richard Scarry's best story book ever ill. by author. Golden Pr., 1968. Subj: Language.

Richard Scarry's best word book ever ill. by author. Golden Pr., 1963. Subj: Dictionaries.

Richard Scarry's busiest people ever ill. by author. Random House, 1976. Subj: Careers.

Richard Scarry's busy busy world ill. by author. Golden Pr., 1965. Subj: Activities.

Richard Scarry's busy houses ill. by author. Random House, 1981. Subj: Animals – worms. Format, unusual – cardboard pages. Houses.

Richard Scarry's cars and trucks and things that go ill. by author. Golden Pr., 1974. Subj: Automobiles. Transportation. Trucks.

Richard Scarry's funniest storybook ever ill. by author. Random House, 1972. Subj: Humor.

Richard Scarry's great big air book ill. by author. Random House, 1971. Subj: Airplanes, airports. Science.

Richard Scarry's great big mystery book ill. by author. Random House, 1969. Subj: Animals. Crime. Stores.

Richard Scarry's great big schoolhouse ill. by author. Random House, 1969. Subj: ABC books. Concepts. Counting. Days of the week, months of the year. School. Time.

Richard Scarry's hop aboard! Here we go! ill. by author. Golden Pr., 1972. Subj: Transportation.

Richard Scarry's Lowly Worm word book ill. by author. Random House, 1981. Subj: Format, unusual – cardboard pages.

Richard Scarry's mix or match storybook ill. by author. Random House, 1979. Subj: Animals. Format, unusual.

Richard Scarry's Peasant Pig and the terrible dragon ill. by author. Random House, 1980. Subj: Animals – pigs. Dragons.

Richard Scarry's please and thank you book ill. by author. Random House, 1973. Subj: Etiquette.

Richard Scarry's Postman Pig and his busy neighbors ill. by author. Random House, 1978. Subj: Animals. Careers. Careers – mail carriers. City.

Richard Scarry's storybook dictionary ill. by author. Golden Pr., 1966. Subj: Dictionaries.

What do people do all day? ill. by author. Random House, 1968. Subj: Careers.

Schaaf, Peter. *An apartment house close up* photos. by author. Four Winds Pr., 1980. Subj: Houses.

The violin close up photos. by author. Four Winds Pr., 1980. Subj: Music.

Schackburg, Richard. *Yankee Doodle* ill. by Ed Emberley. Prentice-Hall, 1965. Subj: Music. Songs. U.S. history.

Schaffer, Marion. *I love my cat!* ill. by Kathy Vanderlinden. Kids Can Pr., 1981. Subj: Animals – cats. Foreign languages. Pets.

Schären, Beatrix. *Tillo* Translated by Gwen Marsh. Addison-Wesley, 1974. Subj: Birds – owls.

Schatell, Brian. *Farmer Goff and his turkey Sam* ill. by author. Lippincott, 1982. Subj: Behavior – misbehavior. Birds – turkeys. Fairs.

Midge and Fred ill. by author. Lippincott, 1983. Subj: Fish. Humor.

Sam's no dummy, Farmer Goff ill. by author. Lippincott, 1984. Subj: Birds – turkeys. Character traits – cleverness.

Schatz, Letta. *The extraordinary tug-of-war* ill. by John Burningham. Follett, 1968. Subj: Animals. Character traits – cleverness. Folk and fairy tales. Foreign lands – Africa.

Whiskers, my cat ill. by Paul Galdone. McGraw-Hill, 1967. Subj: Animals – cats.

Scheer, Julian. *Rain makes applesauce* by Julian Scheer and Marvin Bileck; ill. by Marvin Bileck. Holiday, 1964. Subj: Caldecott award honor book. Humor. Weather – rain.

Schenk, Esther M. *Christmas time* ill. by Vera Stone Norman. Follett, 1931. Subj: Holidays – Christmas.

Schepp, Steven. *How babies are made* (Andry, Andrew C)

Schermer, Judith. *Mouse in house* ill. by author. Houghton, 1979. Subj: Animals – mice. Family life. Problem solving.

Schertle, Alice. *The gorilla in the hall* ill. by Paul Galdone. Lothrop, 1977. Subj: Animals – gorillas. Character traits – bravery. Emotions – fear.

Hob Goblin and the skeleton ill. by Katherine Coville. Lothrop, 1982. Subj: Holidays – Halloween. Trolls.

In my treehouse ill. by Meredith Dunham. Lothrop, 1983. Subj: Behavior – solitude. Houses. Trees.

Schick, Alice. *Just this once* by Alice and Joel Schick; ill. by Joel Schick. Lippincott, 1978. Subj: Animals – wolves. Pets.

The remarkable ride of Israel Bissell... as related to Molly the crow: being the true account of an extraordinary post rider who persevered by Alice Schick and Marjorie N. Allen; ill. by Joel Schick. Lippincott, 1976. Subj: U.S. history. War.

Schick, Eleanor. *City green* ill. by author. Macmillan, 1974. Subj: City. Poetry, rhyme.

City in the winter ill. by author. Macmillan, 1970. Subj: City. Family life – only child. Seasons – winter. Weather – snow. Weather – wind.

Home alone ill. by author. Dial Pr., 1980. Subj: Activities – working. Family life – mothers. Emotions – loneliness.

Joey on his own ill. by author. Dial Pr., 1982. Subj: Self-concept. Shopping.

The little school at Cottonwood Corners ill. by author. Harper, 1965. Subj: Caldecott award honor book. School. Wordless.

Making friends ill. by author. Macmillan, 1969. Subj: Friendship. Wordless.

One summer night ill. by author. Greenwillow, 1977. Subj: City. Music. Seasons – summer.

Peggy's new brother ill. by author. Macmillan, 1970. Subj: Babies. Emotions – envy, jealousy. Family life. Sibling rivalry.

Peter and Mr. Brandon ill. by Donald Carrick. Macmillan, 1973. Subj: Activities – babysitting. City.

A piano for Julie ill. by author. Greenwillow, 1984. Subj: Family life. Music.

Summer at the sea ill. by author. Greenwillow, 1979. Subj: Activities – vacationing. Family life – only child. Sea and seashore. Seasons – summer.

A surprise in the forest ill. by author. Harper, 1964. Subj: Animals. Eggs. Forest, woods.

Schick, Joel. *Just this once* (Schick, Alice)

Schiller, Barbara. *The white rat's tale* ill. by Adrienne Adams. Holt, 1967. Subj: Animals – rats. Folk and fairy tales. Foreign lands – France. Royalty.

Schilling, Betty. *Two kittens are born: from birth to two months* photos. by author. Holt, 1980. Subj: Animals – cats. Science.

Schlein, Miriam. *The amazing Mr. Pelgrew* ill. by Harvey Weiss. Abelard-Schuman, 1957. Subj: Careers – police officers.

Billy, the littlest one ill. by Lucy Hawkinson. Albert Whitman, 1966. Subj: Behavior – growing up. Character traits – smallness. Family life.

Deer in the snow ill. by Leonard P. Kessler. Abelard-Schuman, 1965. Subj: Animals – deer. Seasons – winter. Weather – snow.

Elephant herd ill. by Symeon Shimin. Addison-Wesley, 1954. Subj: Animals – elephants.

Fast is not a ladybug ill. by Leonard P. Kessler. Addison-Wesley, 1953. Subj: Concepts speed. Insects – ladybugs.

The four little foxes ill. by Louis Quintanilla. Addison-Wesley, 1953. Subj: Animals – foxes.

Go with the sun ill. by Symeon Shimin. Addison-Wesley, 1952. Subj: Family life – grandparents, great-grandparents. Seasons – winter.

Heavy is a hippopotamus ill. by Leonard P. Kessler. Addison-Wesley, 1954. Subj: Concepts – weight.

Here comes night ill. by Harvey Weiss. Albert Whitman, 1957. Subj: Night.

Herman McGregor's world ill. by Harvey Weiss. Albert Whitman, 1959. Subj: Behavior – growing up. World.

Home, the tale of a mouse ill. by E. Harper Johnson. Abelard-Schuman, 1958. Subj: Animals – mice.

It's about time ill. by Leonard P. Kessler. Addison-Wesley, 1955. Subj: Time.

Laurie's new brother ill. by Elizabeth Donald. Abelard-Schuman, 1961. Subj: Babies. Family life. Sibling rivalry.

Little Rabbit, the high jumper ill. by Theresa Sherman. Addison-Wesley, 1957. Subj: Animals – rabbits.

Little Red Nose ill. by Roger Antoine Duvoisin. Abelard-Schuman, 1955. Subj: Seasons – spring.

Lucky porcupine! ill. by Martha Weston. Four Winds Pr., 1980. Subj: Animals – porcupines. Science.

My family ill. by Harvey Weiss. Abelard-Schuman, 1960. Subj: Family life.

My house ill. by Joe Lasker. Albert Whitman, 1971. Subj: Family life. Houses. Moving.

The pile of junk ill. by Harvey Weiss. Abelard-Schuman, 1962. Subj: Character traits – practicality. Values.

Shapes ill. by Sam Berman. Addison-Wesley, 1952. Subj: Concepts – shape.

Something for now, something for later ill. by Leonard Weisgard. Harper, 1956. Subj: Farms.

The sun looks down ill. by Abner Graboff. Abelard-Schuman, 1954. Subj: Sun.

The sun, the wind, the sea and the rain ill. by Joe Lasker. Abelard-Schuman, 1960. Subj: Sea and seashore. Sun. Weather. Weather – rain. Weather – wind.

What's wrong with being a skunk? ill. by Ray Cruz. Four Winds Pr., 1974. Subj: Animals – skunks. Science.

When will the world be mine? The story of a snowshoe rabbit ill. by Jean Charlot. Addison-Wesley, 1953. Subj: Behavior – growing up. Caldecott award honor book.

Schmeltz, Susan Alton. *Pets I wouldn't pick* ill. by Ellen Appleby. Parents, 1982. Subj: Pets. Poetry, rhyme.

Schmidt, Eric von. *The young man who wouldn't hoe corn* ill. by author. Houghton, 1964. Subj: Character traits – laziness. Farms. Humor.

Schneider, Herman. *Follow the sunset* by Herman and Nina Schneider; ill. by Lucille Corcoe. Doubleday, 1952. Subj: Science. Sun. World.

Schneider, Nina. *Follow the sunset* (Schneider, Herman)

While Susie sleeps ill. by Dagmar Wilson. Addison-Wesley, 1948. Subj: Bedtime. Night. Sleep.

Schoenherr, John. *The barn* ill. by author. Little, 1968. Subj: Animals – mice. Animals – skunks. Barns. Birds – owls. Farms.

Schongut, Emanuel. *Look kitten* ill. by author. Simon and Schuster, 1983. Subj: Animals.

Schreiber, Georges. *Bambino goes home* ill. by author. Viking, 1959. Subj: Clowns, jesters. Friendship.

Bambino the clown ill. by author. Viking, 1947. Subj: Animals – sea lions. Caldecott award honor book. Clowns, jesters.

Professor Bull's umbrella (Lipkind, William)

Schroder, William. *Pea soup and serpents* ill. by author. Lothrop, 1977. Subj: Monsters. Mythical creatures. Weather – fog.

Schroeder, Binette. *Ra ta ta tam* (Nickl, Peter)

Tuffa and her friends ill. by author. Dial Pr., 1983. Subj: Animals – dogs. Format, unusual – cardboard pages. Friendship.

Tuffa and the bone ill. by author. Dial Pr., 1983. Subj: Animals – dogs. Format, unusual – cardboard pages.

Tuffa and the ducks ill. by author. Dial Pr., 1983. Subj: Animals – dogs. Birds – ducks. Format, unusual – cardboard pages.

Tuffa and the picnic ill. by author. Dial Pr., 1983. Subj: Activities – picnicking. Animals – dogs. Format, unusual – cardboard pages.

Tuffa and the snow ill. by author. Dial Pr., 1983. Subj: Animals – dogs. Format, unusual – cardboard pages. Weather – snow.

Schroeder, Glen W. *At the zoo* (Colonius, Lillian)

Schubert, Dieter. *There's a crocodile under my bed!* (Schubert, Ingrid)

Schubert, Ingrid. *There's a crocodile under my bed!* by Ingrid and Dieter Schubert; ill. by authors. McGraw-Hill, 1981. Subj: Bedtime. Reptiles – alligators, crocodiles.

Schuchman, Joan. *Two places to sleep* ill. by Jim LaMarche. Carolrhoda, 1979. Subj: Divorce. Family life.

Schulman, Janet. *The big hello* ill. by Lillian Hoban. Greenwillow, 1976. Subj: Friendship. Moving. Toys – dolls.

Camp Kee Wee's secret weapon ill. by Marylin Hafner. Greenwillow, 1979. Subj: Sports – baseball. Sports – camping.

Jack the bum and the Halloween handout ill. by James Stevenson. Greenwillow, 1977. Subj: Behavior – sharing. Holidays – Halloween. UNICEF

Jack the bum and the haunted house ill. by James Stevenson. Greenwillow, 1977. Subj: Crime. Ghosts. Houses.

Jack the bum and the UFO ill. by James Stevenson. Greenwillow, 1978. Subj: Character traits – cleverness. Progress. Space and space ships.

Jenny and the tennis nut ill. by Marylin Hafner. Greenwillow, 1978. Subj: Sports – gymnastics. Sports – tennis.

Schultz, Gwen. *The blue Valentine* ill. by Elizabeth Coberly. Rev. ed. Morrow, 1979. Orig. pub. in 1965. Subj: Holidays – Valentine's Day.

Schulz, Charles M. *Bon voyage, Charlie Brown (and don't come back!!)* ill. by author. Random House, 1980. Subj: Activities – traveling. Foreign lands.

The Charlie Brown dictionary based on the rainbow dictionary by Wendell W. Wright; asst. by Helene Laird; ill. by author. Random House, 1973. Subj: Dictionaries.

Life is a circus, Charlie Brown ill. by author. Random House, 1981. Subj: Circus.

Snoopy's facts and fun book about farms ill. by author. Random House, 1980. Subj: Animals – dogs. Farms.

Snoopy's facts and fun book about boats ill. by author. Random House, 1979. Subj: Animals – dogs. Boats, ships.

Snoopy's facts and fun book about houses ill. by author. Random House, 1979. Subj: Animals – dogs. Houses.

Snoopy's facts and fun book about nature ill. by author. Random House, 1979. Subj: Animals – dogs. Nature. Science.

Snoopy's facts and fun book about planes ill. by author. Random House, 1979. Subj: Animals – dogs. Airplanes, airports.

Snoopy's facts and fun book about seashores ill. by author. Random House, 1979. Subj: Animals – dogs. Sea and seashore.

Snoopy's facts and fun book about seasons ill. by author. Random House, 1979. Subj: Animals – dogs. Seasons.

Snoopy's facts and fun book about trucks ill. by author. Random House, 1979. Subj: Animals – dogs. Trucks.

You're the greatest, Charlie Brown ill. by author. Random House, 1979. Subj: Sports – Olympics.

Schumacher, Claire. *King of the zoo* ill. by author. Morrow, 1985. Subj: Animals. Behavior – misbehavior. Friendship. Zoos.

Nutty's Christmas ill. by author. Morrow, 1984. Subj: Animals – squirrels. Holidays – Christmas.

Schurr, Cathleen. *The long and the short of it* ill. by Dorothy Maas. Vanguard, 1950. Subj: Problem solving.

Schwalje, Marjory. *Mr. Angelo* ill. by Abner Graboff. Abelard-Schuman, 1960. Subj: Activities – cooking. Food. Humor.

Schwartz, Alvin. *Busy buzzing bumblebees: and other tongue twisters* ill. by Kathie Abrams. Harper, 1982. Subj: Tongue twisters.

Ten copycats in a boat and other riddles ill. by Marc Simont. Harper, 1980. Subj: Riddles.

Schwartz, Amy. *Bea and Mr. Jones* ill. by author. Bradbury Pr., 1982. Subj: Behavior – imitation. Family life – fathers.

Begin at the beginning ill. by author. Harper, 1983. Subj: Behavior – growing up.

Her majesty, Aunt Essie ill. by author. Bradbury Pr., 1984. Subj: Behavior – boasting. Royalty.

Mrs. Moskowitz and the Sabbath candlesticks ill. by author. Jewish Pub. Soc., 1985. Subj: Jewish culture. Religion.

Schwartz, Delmore. *"I am Cherry Alive," the little girl sang* ill. by Barbara Cooney. Harper, 1979. Subj: Poetry, rhyme.

Schweitzer, Iris. *Hilda's restful chair* ill. by author. Atheneum, 1982. Subj: Animals. Friendship.

Schweninger, Ann. *Christmas secrets* ill. by author. Viking, 1984. Subj: Animals – rabbits. Holidays – Christmas.

Halloween surprises ill. by author. Viking, 1984. Subj: Animals – rabbits. Holidays – Halloween.

The hunt for rabbit's galosh ill. by Kay Chorao. Doubleday, 1976. Subj: Animals – rabbits. Behavior – forgetfulness. Holidays – Valentine's Day.

The man in the moon as he sails the sky and other moon verse ill. by author. Dodd, 1979. Subj: Moon. Poetry, rhyme.

Scoppetone, Sandra. *Bang, bang, you're dead* (Fitzhugh, Louise)

Scott, Ann Herbert. *Big Cowboy Western* ill. by Richard Lewis. Lothrop, 1965. Subj: Clothing. Cowboys. Ethnic groups in the U.S. – Afro-Americans. Imagination.

Let's catch a monster ill. by H. Tom Hall. Lothrop, 1967. Subj: City. Ethnic groups in the U.S. – Afro-Americans. Holidays – Halloween.

On mother's lap ill. by Glo Coalson. McGraw-Hill, 1972. Subj: Behavior – needing someone. Emotions – love. Ethnic groups in the U.S. – Eskimos. Family life. Family life – mothers. Sibling rivalry.

Sam ill. by Symeon Shimin. McGraw-Hill, 1967. Subj: Behavior – needing someone. Ethnic groups in the U.S. – Afro-Americans. Family life.

Scott, Cora Annett *see* Annett, Cora

Scott, Frances Gruse. *How many kids are hiding on my block?* (Merrill, Jean)

Scott, Geoffrey. *Memorial Day* ill. by Peter E. Hanson. Carolrhoda, 1983. Subj: Holidays – Memorial Day.

Scott, Natalie. *Firebrand, push your hair out of your eyes* ill. by Sandra Smith. Carolrhoda Books, 1969. Subj: Character traits – appearance. Hair.

Scott, Rochelle. *Colors, colors all around* ill. by Leonard P. Kessler. Grosset, 1965. Subj: Concepts – color.

Scott, Sally. *Little Wiener* ill. by Beth Krush. Harcourt, 1951. Subj: Animals – dogs.

There was Timmy! ill. by Beth Krush. Harcourt, 1957. Subj: Animals – dogs.

Scott, William R. *This is the milk that Jack drank* adapt. from Mother Goose; ill. by Charles Green Shaw. Addison-Wesley, 1944. Subj: Cumulative tales.

Scribner, Charles. *The devil's bridge: a legend* retold by Charles Scribner, Jr.; ill. by Evaline Ness. Scribner's, 1978. Subj: Folk and fairy tales. Foreign lands – France. Devil.

Hansel and Gretel (Grimm, Jacob)

Scruton, Clive. *Circus cow* ill. by author. Random House, 1985. Subj: Animals – bulls, cows. Character traits – foolishness.

The Sea World alphabet book concept by Sally and Alan Sloan. Sea World Pr., 1979. Subj: ABC books. Sea and seashore.

Seabrooke, Brenda. *The best burglar alarm* ill. by Loretta Lustig. Morrow, 1978. Subj: Crime. Pets.

The seal ill. by Charlotte Knox. Rourke, 1983. Subj: Animals – seals.

Secunda, Sheldon. *What I want to be when I grow up* (Burnett, Carol)

Sedges, John *see* Buck, Pearl S. (Pearl Sydenstricker)

Seeger, Charles. *The foolish frog* (Seeger, Pete)

Seeger, Pete. *The foolish frog* by Pete Seeger and Charles Seeger; ill. by Miloslav Jágr; adapted and designed from Firebird Film by Gene Deitch. Macmillan, 1973. Subj: Cumulative tales. Folk and fairy tales. Frogs and toads. Music. Songs.

Segal, Lore. *All the way home* ill. by James Marshall. Farrar, 1973. Subj: Cumulative tales.

The bear and the kingbird (Grimm, Jacob)

The story of old Mrs. Brubeck and how she looked for trouble and where she found him ill. by Marcia Sewall. Pantheon, 1981. Subj: Behavior – worrying. Problem solving.

Tell me a Mitzi ill. by Harriet Pincus. Farrar, 1970. Subj: Family life. Jewish culture.

Tell me a Trudy ill. by Rosemary Wells. Farrar, 1977. Subj: Family life. Jewish culture.

Seguin-Fontes, Marthe. *The cat's surprise* adapt. by Sandra Beris; ill. by author. Larousse, 1983. Subj: Animals – cats.

A wedding book adapt. by Sandra Beris; ill. by author. Larousse, 1983. Subj: Activities – photographing. Weddings.

Seidler, Rosalie. *Grumpus and the Venetian cat* ill. by author. Atheneum, 1964. Subj: Animals – cats. Animals – mice. Birds. Foreign lands – Italy.

Seignobosc, Françoise. *The big rain* ill. by author. Scribner's, 1961. Subj: Animals. Farms. Foreign lands – France. Weather – rain.

Biquette, the white goat ill. by author. Scribner's, 1953. Subj: Animals – goats. Foreign lands – France. Illness.

Chouchou ill. by author. Scribner's, 1958. Subj: Animals – donkeys. Foreign lands – France.

Jeanne-Marie at the fair ill. by author. Scribner's, 1959. Subj: Fairs. Foreign lands – France.

Jeanne-Marie counts her sheep ill. by author. Scribner's, 1951. Subj: Behavior – wishing. Counting. Foreign lands – France.

Jeanne-Marie in gay Paris ill. by author. Scribner's, 1956. Subj: Character traits. Foreign lands – France.

Minou ill. by author. Scribner's, 1962. Subj: Animals – cats. Behavior – lost. Foreign lands – France.

Noël for Jeanne-Marie ill. by author. Scribner's, 1953. Subj: Foreign lands – France. Holidays – Christmas.

Small-Trot ill. by author. Scribner's, 1952. Subj: Animals – mice. Circus.

Springtime for Jeanne-Marie ill. by author. Scribner's, 1955. Subj: Animals – goats. Behavior – lost. Birds – ducks. Foreign lands – France. Seasons – spring.

The story of Colette ill. by author. Hale, 1940. Subj: Animals. Emotions – loneliness. Pets.

The thank-you book ill. by author. Scribner's, 1947. Subj: Etiquette. Religion.

The things I like ill. by author. Scribner's, 1960. Subj: Participation.

What do you want to be? ill. by author. Scribner's, 1957. Subj: Careers. Character traits – ambition.

What time is it, Jeanne-Marie? ill. by author. Scribner's, 1963. Subj: Time.

Selberg, Ingrid. *Nature's hidden world* ill. by Andrew Miller. Putnam's, 1984. Subj: Animals. Format, unusual. Plants. Science. Riddles.

Selden, George. *Chester Cricket's pigeon ride* ill. by Garth Williams. Farrar, 1981. Subj: Birds – pigeons. City. Insects.

The mice, the monks and the Christmas tree ill. by Jan Balet. Macmillan, 1963. Subj: Animals – mice. Holidays – Christmas.

Sparrow socks ill. by Peter Lippman. Harper, 1965. Subj: Birds – sparrows. Clothing.

Selig, Sylvie. *Kangaroo* ill. by author. Merrimack, 1980. Subj: Animals – kangaroos. Wordless.

Ten what? (Hoban, Russell)

Seligman, Dorothy Halle. *Run away home* ill. by Christine Hoffmann. Golden Gate, 1969. Subj: Behavior – running away. Family life.

Selsam, Millicent E. *All kinds of babies* ill. by Symeon Shimin. Four Winds Pr., 1967. Subj: Animals. Science.

The amazing dandelion photos. by Jerome Wexler. Morrow, 1977. Subj: Plants. Science.

Backyard insects by Millicent E. Selsam and Ronald Goor; ill. by Ron Goor. Four Winds Pr., 1983. Subj: Insects. Science.

Benny's animals and how he put them in order ill. by Arnold Lobel. Harper, 1966. Subj: Animals. Science.

The bug that laid the golden eggs photos. by Harold Krieger; ill. by John Kaufmann; designed by Lee Epstein. Harper, 1967. Subj: Eggs. Insects. Science.

Cotton photos. by Jerome Wexler and others. Morrow, 1982. Subj: Activities – weaving. Plants.

Egg to chick ill. by Barbara Wolff. Rev. ed. Harper, 1970. Subj: Birds – chickens. Eggs. Science.

A first look at dinosaurs by Millicent E. Selsam and Joyce Hunt; ill. by Harriett Springer. Walker, 1982. Subj: Dinosaurs.

A first look at dogs by Millicent E. Selsam and Joyce Hunt; ill. by Harriett Springer. Walker, 1981. Subj: Animals – dogs. Animals – foxes. Animals – wolves.

A first look at flowers by Millicent E. Selsam and Joyce Hunt; ill. by Harriett Springer. Walker, 1977. Subj: Flowers. Science.

A first look at monkeys by Millicent E. Selsam and Joyce Hunt; ill. by Harriett Springer. Walker, 1979. Subj: Animals – gorillas. Animals – monkeys. Science.

A first look at rocks by Millicent E. Selsam and Joyce Hunt; ill. by Harriett Springer. Walker, 1984. Subj: Rocks. Science.

A first look at seashells by Millicent E. Selsam and Joyce Hunt; ill. by Harriett Springer. Walker, 1983. Subj: Animals. Sea and seashore. Science.

A first look at sharks by Millicent E. Selsam and Joyce Hunt; ill. by Harriett Springer. Walker, 1979. Subj: Fish. Science.

A first look at spiders by Millicent E. Selsam and Joyce Hunt; ill. by Harriett Springer. Walker, 1983. Subj: Science. Spiders.

A first look at whales by Millicent E. Selsam and Joyce Hunt; ill. by Harriett Springer. Walker, 1980. Subj: Animals – whales. Science.

Greg's microscope ill. by Arnold Lobel. Harper, 1963. Subj: Science.

Hidden animals ill. by David Shapiro. Harper, 1969. First pub. in 1947. Subj: Animals.

How kittens grow photos. by Esther Bubley. Four Winds Pr., 1975. Subj: Animals – cats. Science.

How puppies grow photos. by Esther Bubley. Four Winds Pr., 1971. Subj: Animals – dogs. Science.

Is this a baby dinosaur? and other science picture puzzles. Harper, 1972. Subj: Games. Science.

Let's get turtles ill. by Arnold Lobel. Harper, 1965. Subj: Pets. Reptiles – turtles. Science.

More potatoes! ill. by Ben Shecter. Harper, 1972. Subj: Farms. Plants. School. Science.

Night animals ill. with photos. Four Winds Pr., 1980. Subj: Animals. Night.

Plenty of fish ill. by Erik Blegvad. Harper, 1960. Subj: Fish. Pets. Science.

Sea monsters of long ago ill. by John Hamberger. Four Winds Pr., 1978. Subj: Monsters. Sea and seashore.

Seeds and more seeds ill. by Tomi Ungerer. Harper, 1959. Subj: Plants. Science.

Terry and the caterpillars ill. by Arnold Lobel. Harper, 1962. Subj: Insects – butterflies, caterpillars. Science.

Tony's birds ill. by Kurt Werth. Harper, 1961. Subj: Birds. Ethnic groups in the U.S. – Afro-Americans. Science.

When an animal grows ill. by John Kaufmann. Harper, 1966. Subj: Animals. Science.

You see the world around you ill. by Greta Elgaard. Doubleday, 1963. Subj: Science.

Sendak, Maurice. *Alligators all around: an alphabet* ill. by author. Harper, 1962. Subj: ABC books. Reptiles – alligators, crocodiles.

Chicken soup with rice ill. by author. Harper, 1962. Subj: Days of the week, months of the year.

Hector Protector, and As I went over the water: two nursery rhymes ill. by author. Harper, 1965. Subj: Nursery rhymes.

In the night kitchen ill. by author. Harper, 1970. Subj: Caldecott award honor book. Dreams. Imagination.

Maurice Sendak's Really Rosie: starring the Nutshell Kids ill. by author; music by Carole King; design by Jane Byers Bierhorst. Harper, 1976. Subj: Activities – playing. Music. Theater.

One was Johnny: a counting book ill. by author. Harper, 1962. Subj: Counting.

Outside over there ill. by author. Harper, 1981. Subj: Activities – babysitting. Babies. Caldecott award honor book. Goblins.

Pierre: a cautionary tale in five chapters and a prologue ill. by author. Harper, 1962. Subj: Behavior – indifference. Character traits – individuality. Humor. Poetry, rhyme.

Seven little monsters ill. by author. Harper, 1977. Subj: Counting. Monsters. Poetry, rhyme.

The sign on Rosie's door ill. by author. Harper, 1960. Subj: Activities – playing. Imagination.

Very far away ill. by author. Harper, 1957. Subj: Animals. Behavior – needing someone. Behavior – running away.

Where the wild things are ill. by author. Harper, 1963. Subj: Behavior – misbehavior. Caldecott award book. Imagination. Monsters.

Serfozo, Mary. *Welcome Roberto! Bienvenido, Roberto!* ill. by John Serfozo. Follett, 1969. Subj: Ethnic groups in the U.S. – Mexican-Americans. Foreign languages.

Serraillier, Anne. *Florina and the wild bird* (Chönz, Selina)

Serraillier, Ian. *Florina and the wild bird* (Chönz, Selina)

Suppose you met a witch ill. by Ed Emberley. Little, 1973. Subj: Poetry, rhyme. Witches.

Sesame Street. *Ernie and Bert can...can you?* ill. by Michael Smollin. Random House, 1982. Subj: Format, unusual – cardboard pages. Puppets.

Sesame Street sign language fun ill. with photos. Random House, 1980. Subj: Language. Puppets.

Sesame Street word book ill. by Tom Leigh. Golden Pr., 1983. Subj: Language. Puppets.

The Sesame Street book of letters created in cooperation with the Children's Television Workshop, producers of Sesame Street. Designed by Charles I. Miller and James J. Harvin. Preschool Pr.; distributed in assoc. with Time-Life Books, 1970. Subj: ABC books.

The Sesame Street book of numbers created in cooperation with the Children's Television Workshop, producers of Sesame Street. Designed by Charles I. Miller and James J. Harvin. Preschool Pr.; distributed in assoc. with Time-Life Books, 1970. Subj: Counting.

The Sesame Street book of people and things created in cooperation with the Children's Television Workshop, producers of Sesame Street. Designed by Charles I. Miller and James J. Harvin. Preschool Pr.; distributed in assoc. with Time-Life Books, 1970. Subj: Careers. Concepts. Emotions.

The Sesame Street book of shapes created in cooperation with the Children's Television Workshop, producers of Sesame Street. Designed by Charles I. Miller and James J. Harvin. Preschool Pr.; distributed in assoc. with Time-Life Books, 1970. Subj: Concepts – shape.

Seuling, Barbara. *The teeny tiny woman: an old English ghost tale* ill. by author. Viking, 1976. Subj: Folk and fairy tales. Foreign lands – England. Ghosts.

The triplets ill. by author. Houghton, 1980. Subj: Character traits – individuality. Triplets.

Seuss, Dr. *And to think that I saw it on Mulberry Street* ill. by author. Vanguard, 1937. Subj: Humor. Imagination. Poetry, rhyme.

Bartholomew and the Oobleck ill. by author. Random House, 1949. Subj: Caldecott award honor book. Humor. Royalty.

The butter battle book ill. by author. Random House, 1984. Subj: Poetry, rhyme. War.

The cat in the hat ill. by author. Random House, 1957. Subj: Animals – cats. Humor. Poetry, rhyme.

The cat in the hat beginner book dictionary by the Cat himself and P. D. Eastman; ill. by Dr. Seuss. Random House, 1964. Subj: Dictionaries. Humor.

The cat in the hat comes back! ill. by author. Random House, 1958. Subj: Animals – cats. Humor. Poetry, rhyme.

The cat's quizzer ill. by author. Random House, 1976. Subj: Humor. Poetry, rhyme. Riddles.

Did I ever tell you how lucky you are? ill. by Richard Erdoes. Random House, 1973. Subj: Character traits – luck. Humor. Poetry, rhyme. Problem solving.

Dr. Seuss's ABC ill. by author. Random House, 1963. Subj: ABC books. Humor. Poetry, rhyme.

Dr. Seuss's sleep book ill. by author. Random House, 1962. Subj: Humor. Poetry, rhyme. Sleep.

The eye book ill. by Roy McKié. Random House, 1968. Subj: Anatomy. Animals – rabbits. Poetry, rhyme.

The foot book ill. by author. Random House, 1968. Subj: Anatomy. Humor. Poetry, rhyme.

Fox in sox ill. by author. Random House, 1965. Subj: Humor. Poetry, rhyme.

A great day for up ill. by Quentin Blake. Random House, 1974. Subj: Concepts – up and down. Humor. Poetry, rhyme.

Green eggs and ham ill. by author. Random House, 1960. Subj: Cumulative tales. Food. Humor. Poetry, rhyme.

Happy birthday to you! ill. by author. Random House, 1959. Subj: Birthdays. Humor. Poetry, rhyme.

Hooper Humperdink...? Not him! ill. by Charles E. Martin. Random House, 1976. Subj: ABC books. Birthdays. Humor. Poetry, rhyme.

Hop on Pop ill. by author. Random House, 1963. Subj: Humor. Poetry, rhyme.

Horton hatches the egg ill. by author. Random House, 1940. Subj: Animals – elephants. Birds. Character traits – helpfulness. Eggs. Humor. Poetry, rhyme.

Horton hears a Who! ill. by author. Random House, 1954. Subj: Animals – elephants. Character traits – kindness. Humor. Poetry, rhyme.

How the Grinch stole Christmas ill. by author. Random House, 1957. Subj: Character traits – meanness. Holidays – Christmas. Humor. Poetry, rhyme.

Hunches of bunches ill. by author. Random House, 1982. Subj: Poetry, rhyme. Problem solving.

I can lick 30 tigers today and other stories ill. by author. Random House, 1969. Subj: Humor. Poetry, rhyme.

I can read with my eyes shut ill. by author. Random House, 1978. Subj: Activities – reading. Humor. Poetry, rhyme.

I can write! a book by me, myself, with a little help from Theo. LeSeig and Roy McKié ill. by Roy McKié. Random House, 1971. Subj: Activities – writing. Humor. Poetry, rhyme.

I had trouble getting to Solla Sollew ill. by author. Random House, 1965. Subj: Activities – traveling. Humor. Poetry, rhyme.

I wish that I had duck feet ill. by Barney Tobey. Random House, 1965. Subj: Behavior – wishing. Poetry, rhyme.

If I ran the circus ill. by author. Random House, 1956. Subj: Circus. Humor. Poetry, rhyme.

If I ran the zoo ill. by author. Random House, 1950. Subj: Caldecott award honor book. Humor. Poetry, rhyme. Zoos.

In a people house ill. by Roy McKié. Random House, 1972. Subj: Houses. Humor. Poetry, rhyme.

The king's stilts ill. by author. Random House, 1939. Subj: Humor. Poetry, rhyme. Royalty. Toys.

The Lorax ill. by author. Random House, 1971. Subj: Ecology. Humor. Poetry, rhyme.

McElligot's pool ill. by author. Random House, 1947. Subj: Caldecott award honor book. Fish. Humor. Imagination. Poetry, rhyme.

Marvin K. Mooney, will you please go now! ill. by author. Random House, 1972. Subj: Humor. Poetry, rhyme.

Mr. Brown can moo! Can you? ill. by author. Random House, 1970. Subj: Animals. Humor. Noise, sounds. Participation. Poetry, rhyme.

Oh say can you say? ill. by author. Random House, 1979. Subj: Humor. Imagination. Poetry, rhyme.

Oh, the thinks you can think! ill. by author. Random House, 1975. Subj: Humor. Imagination. Poetry, rhyme.

On beyond zebra ill. by author. Random House, 1955. Subj: Humor. Letters. Poetry, rhyme.

One fish, two fish, red fish, blue fish ill. by author. Random House, 1960. Subj: Fish. Humor. Poetry, rhyme.

Please try to remember the first of octember! ill. by author. Random House, 1977. Subj: Behavior – wishing. Humor. Poetry, rhyme.

Scrambled eggs super! ill. by author. Random House, 1953. Subj: Food. Humor. Poetry, rhyme.

The shape of me and other stuff ill. by author. Random House, 1973. Subj: Concepts – shape. Humor. Poetry, rhyme.

The Sneetches, and other stories ill. by author. Random House, 1961. Subj: Emotions – fear. Humor. Poetry, rhyme.

There's a wocket in my pocket ill. by author. Random House, 1974. Subj: Humor. Poetry, rhyme.

Thidwick, the big-hearted moose ill. by author. Random House, 1948. Subj: Animals – moose. Birds. Humor. Poetry, rhyme.

The tooth book ill. by Roy McKié. Random House, 1981. Subj: Health. Poetry, rhyme. Teeth.

Wacky Wednesday ill. by George Booth. Random House, 1974. Subj: Humor. Participation. Poetry, rhyme.

Would you rather be a bullfrog? ill. by Roy McKié. Random House, 1975. Subj: Animals. Character traits – optimism. Frogs and toads.

Severo, Emöke de Papp. *The good-hearted youngest brother: an Hungarian folktale* ill. by Diane Goode. Bradbury Pr., 1981. Subj: Character traits – kindness to animals. Folk and fairy tales. Foreign lands – Hungary. Magic.

Sewall, Marcia. *The cobbler's song* ill. by author. Dutton, 1982. Subj: Behavior – worrying.

The little wee tyke: an English folktale ill. by author. Atheneum, 1979. Subj: Animals – dogs. Folk and fairy tales. Foreign lands – England.

The wee, wee mannie and the big, big coo: a Scottish folk tale ill. by author. Little, 1977. Subj: Animals – bulls, cows. Folk and fairy tales. Foreign lands – Scotland.

Sewell, Helen Moore. *Birthdays for Robin* ill. by author. Macmillan, 1943. Subj: Animals – dogs. Birthdays.

Blue barns ill. by author. Macmillan, 1933. Subj: Barns. Birds – ducks. Birds – geese. Farms.

Jimmy and Jemima ill. by author. Macmillan, 1940. Subj: Character traits – bravery. Sibling rivalry.

Ming and Mehitable ill. by author. Macmillan, 1936. Subj: Animals – dogs.

Peggy and the pony ill. by author. Oxford Univ. Pr., 1936. Subj: Animals – horses. Behavior – wishing.

Sexton, Gwain. *There once was a king* ill. by author. Scribner's, 1959. Subj: Poetry, rhyme. Royalty.

Seymour, Dorothy Z. *The tent* ill. by Nancé Holman. Grosset, 1965. Subj: Cumulative tales.

Seymour, Peter. *How the weather works* ill. by Sally Springer. Macmillan, 1985. Subj: Format, unusual. Weather.

What's at the beach? ill. by David A. Carter. Holt, 1985. Subj: Monsters. Nature. Sea and seashore.

Seyton, Marion. *The hole in the hill* ill. by Leonard W. Shortall. Follett, 1960. Subj: Cavemen. Family life.

Shannon, George. *Beanboy* ill. by Peter Sís. Greenwillow, 1984. Subj: City. Cumulative tales. Humor.

Lizard's song ill. by José Aruego and Ariane Dewey. Greenwillow, 1981. Subj: Animals – bears. Reptiles – lizards. Songs.

The Piney Woods peddler ill. by Nancy Tafuri. Greenwillow, 1982. Subj: Activities – trading. Folk and fairy tales.

The surprise ill. by José Aruego and Ariane Dewey. Greenwillow, 1983. Subj: Animals – squirrels. Birthdays.

Shapp, Charles. *Let's find out about babies* (Shapp, Martha)

Let's find out about houses (Shapp, Martha)

Let's find out what's big and what's small by Charles and Martha Shapp; ill. by Vana Earle. Watts, 1959. Subj: Concepts – size.

Shapp, Martha. *Let's find out about babies* by Martha and Charles Shapp and Sylvia Shepard; ill. by Jenny Williams. Watts, 1975. Subj: Babies. Science.

Let's find out about houses by Martha and Charles Shapp; ill. by Tomie de Paola. Watts, 1975. Subj: Houses.

Let's find out what's big and what's small (Shapp, Charles)

Sharmat, Marjorie Weinman. *Attila the angry* ill. by Lillian Hoban. Holiday, 1985. Subj: Animals – squirrels. Emotions – anger.

Bartholomew the bossy ill. by Normand Chartier. Macmillan, 1984. Subj: Animals. Behavior – growing up. Friendship.

The best Valentine in the world ill. by Lilian Obligado. Holiday, 1982. Subj: Animals – foxes. Holidays – Valentine's Day.

A big fat enormous lie ill. by David McPhail. Dutton, 1978. Subj: Behavior – lying.

Burton and Dudley ill. by Barbara Cooney. Holiday, 1975. Subj: Activities – walking. Character traits – laziness. Friendship.

Frizzy the fearful ill. by John Wallner. Holiday, 1983. Subj: Emotions – fear.

Gila monsters meet you at the airport ill. by Byron Barton. Macmillan, 1980. Subj: Behavior – misunderstanding. Moving.

Gladys told me to meet her here ill. by Edward Frascino. Harper, 1970. Subj: Friendship.

Goodnight, Andrew. Good night, Craig ill. by Mary Chalmers. Harper, 1969. Subj: Bedtime. Family life.

Grumley the grouch ill. by Kay Chorao. Holiday, 1980. Subj: Behavior – dissatisfaction.

I don't care ill. by Lillian Hoban. Macmillan, 1977. Subj: Behavior – indifference. Emotions – sadness. Ethnic groups in the U.S. – Afro-Americans. Toys – balloons.

I want mama ill. by Emily Arnold McCully. Harper, 1974. Subj: Family life – only child. Illness.

I'm not Oscar's friend any more ill. by Tony DeLuna. Dutton, 1975. Subj: Behavior – fighting, arguing. Emotions – anger. Friendship.

I'm terrific ill. by Kay Chorao. Holiday, 1977. Subj: Animals – bears. Character traits – conceit. Character traits – pride. Self-concept.

Mitchell is moving ill. by José Aruego and Ariane Dewey. Macmillan, 1978. Subj: Dinosaurs. Friendship. Moving.

Mooch the messy ill. by Ben Shecter. Harper, 1976. Subj: Animals – rats. Character traits – cleanliness.

Nate the Great ill. by Marc Simont. Coward, 1972. Subj: Careers – detectives. Food.

Nate the Great and the lost list ill. by Marc Simont. Coward, 1975. Subj: Careers – detectives. Food. Problem solving.

Nate the Great and the phony clue ill. by Marc Simont. Coward, 1977. Subj: Careers – detectives. Food.

Nate the Great goes undercover ill. by Marc Simont. Coward, 1974. Subj: Careers – detectives. Food. Problem solving.

Rex ill. by Emily Arnold McCully. Harper, 1967. Subj: Behavior – running away.

Rollo and Juliet . . . forever! ill. by Marylin Hafner. Doubleday, 1981. Subj: Behavior – fighting, arguing. Emotions – anger. Friendship.

Sasha the silly ill. by Janet Stevens. Holiday, 1984. Subj: Animals – dogs. Character traits – vanity.

Scarlet Monster lives here ill. by Dennis Kendrick. Harper, 1979. Subj: Behavior. Friendship. Monsters. Moving.

Sometimes mama and papa fight ill. by Kay Chorao. Harper, 1980. Subj: Behavior – fighting, arguing. Family life.

Sophie and Gussie ill. by Lillian Hoban. Macmillan, 1973. Subj: Animals – squirrels. Friendship.

Taking care of Melvin ill. by Victoria Chess. Holiday, 1980. Subj: Animals. Friendship. Self-concept.

Thornton, the worrier ill. by Kay Chorao. Holiday, 1978. Subj: Animals – rabbits. Behavior – worrying.

The trip: and other Sophie and Gussie stories ill. by Lillian Hoban. Macmillan, 1976. Subj: Animals – squirrels. Behavior – losing things. Behavior – sharing. Clothing. Friendship.

Two ghosts on a bench ill. by Nola Langner. Harper, 1982. Subj: Ghosts.

Walter the wolf ill. by Kelly Oechsli. Holiday, 1975. Subj: Animals. Animals – wolves. Violence, anti-violence.

What are we going to do about Andrew? ill. by Ray Cruz. Macmillan, 1980. Subj: Character traits – individuality. Family life.

Sharmat, Mitchell. *Gregory, the terrible eater* ill. by José Aruego and Ariane Dewey. Four Winds Pr., 1980. Subj: Animals – goats. Food.

The seven sloppy days of Phineas Pig ill. by Sue Truesdell. Harcourt, 1983. Subj: Animals – pigs. Character traits – cleanliness.

Sharon, Mary Bruce. *Scenes from childhood* ill. by author. Dutton, 1978. Subj: Art. Careers – artists.

Sharpe, Sara. *Gardener George goes to town* ill. by Susan Moxley. Harper, 1982. Subj: Activities – gardening.

Sharr, Christine. *Homes* ill. by author. Wonder Books, 1971. Subj: Family life. Houses.

Shaw, Charles Green. *The blue guess book* ill. by author. Addison-Wesley, 1942. Subj: Games.

The guess book ill. by author. Addison-Wesley, 1941. Subj: Games.

It looked like spilt milk ill. by author. Harper, 1947. Subj: Concepts – shape. Games. Imagination. Participation. Sky. Weather – clouds.

Shaw, Evelyn S. *Alligator* ill. by Frances Zweifel. Harper, 1972. Subj: Reptiles – alligators, crocodiles. Science.

Fish out of school ill. by Ralph Carpentier. Harper, 1970. Subj: Fish. Science. Sea and seashore.

Nest of wood ducks ill. by Cherryl Pape. Harper, 1976. Subj: Birds – ducks. Science.

Octopus ill. by Ralph Carpentier. Harper, 1971. Subj: Octopuses. Science. Sea and seashore.

Sea otters ill. by Cherryl Pape. Harper, 1980. Subj: Animals – otters. Science.

Shaw, Richard. *The kitten in the pumpkin patch* ill. by Jacqueline Kahane. Warne, 1973. Subj: Animals – cats. Holidays – Halloween. Witches.

Shay, Arthur. *What happens when you go to the hospital* ill. by author. Reilly and Lee, 1969. Subj: Hospitals. Illness.

Shearer, John. *Billy Jo Jive and the case of the midnight voices* ill. by Ted Shearer. Delacorte, 1982. Subj: Problem solving. Sports – camping.

The case of the sneaker snatcher ill. by Ted Shearer. Delacorte, 1977. Subj: Clothing. Problem solving. Sports – basketball.

Shecter, Ben. *Conrad's castle* ill. by author. Harper, 1967. Subj: Imagination.

The discontented mother ill. by author. Harcourt, 1980. Subj: Behavior – wishing.

Emily, girl witch of New York ill. by author. Dial Pr., 1963. Subj: City. Houses. Magic. Progress. Witches.

Hester the jester ill. by author. Harper, 1977. Subj: Character traits – ambition. Clowns, Jesters.

If I had a ship ill. by author. Doubleday, 1970. Subj: Boats, ships. Character traits – generosity. Emotions – love. Imagination.

Partouche plants a seed ill. by author. Harper, 1966. Subj: Activities – gardening. Animals – pigs. Foreign lands – France. Plants.

The stocking doll ill. by author. Harper, 1976. Subj: Senses. Toys – dolls.

Stone house stories ill. by author. Harper, 1973. Subj: Animals.

Sheehan, Angela. *The beaver* ill. by Graham Allen. Watts, 1979. Subj: Animals – beavers. Science.

The duck ill. by Maurice Pledger and Bernard Robinson. Warwick Pr., 1979. Subj: Birds – ducks. Science.

The otter ill. by Bernard Robinson. Warwick Pr., 1979. Subj: Animals – otters. Science.

The penguin ill. by Trevor Boyer. Watts, 1979. Subj: Birds – penguins. Science.

Sheffield, Margaret. *Before you were born* ill. by Sheila Bewley. Knopf, 1984. Subj: Babies. Science.

Where do babies come from? ill. by Sheila Bewley. Knopf, 1973. Subj: Babies. Science.

Sheldon, Aure. *Of cobblers and kings* ill. by Don Leake. Parents, 1978. Subj: Careers – shoemakers. Character traits – cleverness.

Shepard, Sylvia. *Let's find out about babies* (Shapp, Martha)

Sherman, Elizabeth *see* Friskey, Margaret

Sherman, Ivan. *I am a giant* ill. by author. Harcourt, 1975. Subj: Giants. Imagination.

I do not like it when my friend comes to visit ill. by author. Harcourt, 1973. Subj: Behavior – sharing. Etiquette. Friendship.

Walking talking words ill. by author. Harcourt, 1980. Subj: Language. Poetry, rhyme.

Sherman, Nancy. *Gwendolyn and the weathercock* ill. by Edward Sorel. Golden Pr., 1961. Subj: Birds – chickens. Farms. Poetry, rhyme. Weather – rain.

Gwendolyn the miracle hen ill. by Edward Sorel. Western Pub., 1961. Subj: Birds – chickens. Dragons. Poetry, rhyme.

Shi, Zhang Xiu. *Monkey and the white bone demon* tr. by Ye Ping Kuei; rev. by Jill Morris; ill. by Lin Zheng and others. Viking, 1984. Adapted from the 16th century novel, The pilgrimage to the west, by Wu Cheng En. Subj: Animals – monkeys. Folk and fairy tales. Foreign lands – China.

Shimin, Symeon. *I wish there were two of me* ill. by author. Warne, 1976. Subj: Behavior – wishing. Dreams. Imagination.

A special birthday ill. by author. McGraw-Hill, 1976. Subj: Birthdays. Wordless.

Shire, Ellen. *The mystery at number seven, Rue Petite* ill. by author. Random House, 1978. Subj: Character traits – bravery. Crime.

Short, Mayo. *Andy and the wild ducks* ill. by Paul M. Souza. Melmont, 1959. Subj: Animals. Ecology. Farms.

Shortall, Leonard W. *Andy, the dog walker* ill. by author. Morrow, 1968. Subj: Animals – dogs. Behavior – lost.

Just-in-time Joey ill. by author. Morrow, 1973. Subj: Ecology.

One way: a trip with traffic signs ill. by author. Prentice-Hall, 1975. Subj: Holidays – Fourth of July. Poetry, rhyme. Safety. Traffic signs.

Tod on the tugboat ill. by author. Morrow, 1971. Subj: Boats, ships.

Tony's first dive ill. by author. Morrow, 1972. Subj: Emotions – fear. Sports – swimming.

Shoten, Fukuinkan. *Elephant blue* (Nakano, Hirotaka)

Showalter, Jean B. *The donkey ride: an Æsop fable* ill. by Tomi Ungerer. Doubleday, 1967. Subj: Animals – donkeys. Folk and fairy tales. Humor.

Showers, Kay Sperry. *Before you were a baby* (Showers, Paul)

Showers, Paul. *A baby starts to grow* ill. by Rosalind Fray. Crowell, 1969. Subj: Babies. Science.

Before you were a baby by Paul Showers and Kay Sperry Showers; ill. by Ingrid Fetz. Crowell, 1968. Subj: Babies. Science.

Columbus Day ill. by Ed Emberley. Crowell, 1965. Subj: Holidays – Columbus Day. U.S. history.

The listening walk ill. by Aliki. Crowell, 1961. Subj: Activities – walking. Noise, sounds. Senses.

Look at your eyes ill. by Paul Galdone. Crowell, 1962. Subj: Ethnic groups in the U.S. – Afro-Americans. Senses.

Me and my family tree ill. by Don Madden. Crowell, 1978. Subj: Family life. Science.

No measles, no mumps for me ill. by Harriett Barton. Crowell, 1980. Subj: Illness. Science.

You can't make a move without your muscles ill. by Harriett Barton. Crowell, 1982. Subj: Anatomy. Science.

Your skin and mine ill. by Paul Galdone. Crowell, 1965. Subj: Anatomy. Ethnic groups in the U.S. – Afro-Americans.

Shub, Elizabeth. *The Bremen town musicians* (Grimm, Jacob)

Clever Kate (Grimm, Jacob)

Dear Sarah (Borchers, Elisabeth)

Dragon Franz text by Josef Guggenmos; adapt. by Elizabeth Shub; ill. by Ursula Konopka. Greenwillow, 1976. Orig. pub. in German under the title Franz, der Drache. Subj: Character traits – being different. Concepts – color. Dragons.

The emperor's plum tree (Nikly, Michelle)

The fisherman and his wife (Grimm, Jacob)

Jorinda and Joringel (Grimm, Jacob)

Seeing is believing ill. by Rachel Isadora. Greenwillow, 1979. Subj: Elves and little people. Folk and fairy tales.

Sir Ribbeck of Ribbeck of Havelland (Fontane, Theodore)

The twelve dancing princesses (Grimm, Jacob)

Why Noah chose the dove (Singer, Isaac Bashevis)

Shulevitz, Uri. *Dawn* ill. by author. Farrar, 1974. Subj: Family life – grandparents, great-grandparents. Morning. Sports – camping. Sun.

The magician adapt. from the Yiddish of Isaac Loeb Peretz by Uri Shulevitz; ill. by adapt. Macmillan, 1973. Subj: Jewish culture. Magic. Religion.

One Monday morning ill. by author. Scribner's, 1967. Subj: Days of the week, months of the year. Imagination. Royalty.

Rain rain rivers ill. by author. Farrar, 1969. Subj: Poetry, rhyme. Weather – rain.

The treasure ill. by author. Farrar, 1978. Subj: Caldecott award honor book. Dreams. Folk and fairy tales.

Shulman, Milton. *Prep, the little pigeon of Trafalgar Square* ill. by Dale Maxey. Random House, 1964. Subj: Birds – pigeons. Foreign lands – England.

Shuttlesworth, Dorothy E. *ABC of buses* ill. by Leonard W. Shortall. Doubleday, 1965. Subj: ABC books. Buses.

Shyer, Marlene Fanta. *Stepdog* ill. by Judith Schermer. Scribner's, 1983. Subj: Animals – dogs. Emotions – envy, jealousy. Family life.

Siberell, Anne. *Whale in the sky* ill. by author. Dutton, 1982. Subj: Animals – whales. Ethnic groups in the U.S. – Indians. Folk and fairy tales.

Sicotte, Virginia. *A riot of quiet* ill. by Edward Ardizzone. Holt, 1969. Subj: Imagination. Noise, sounds.

Siddiqui, Ashraf. *Bhombal Dass, the uncle of lion: a tale from Pakistan* ill. by Thomas Arthur Hamil. Macmillan, 1959. Subj: Animals – goats. Animals – lions. Character traits – cleverness. Folk and fairy tales. Foreign lands – Pakistan.

Siebert, Diane. *Truck song* ill. by Byron Barton. Crowell, 1984. Subj: Poetry, rhyme. Trucks.

Siepmann, Jane. *The lion on Scott Street* ill. by Clement Hurd. Oxford Univ. Pr., 1952. Subj: Animals – lions. Imagination.

Siewert, Margaret. *Bear hunt* by Margaret Siewert and Kathleen Savage; ill. by Leonard W. Shortall. Prentice-Hall, 1976. Subj: Animals – bears. Games. Participation. Toys – teddy bears.

Silver, Jody. *Isadora* ill. by author. Doubleday, 1981. Subj: Animals – donkeys. Clothing.

Silverstein, Shel. *A giraffe and a half* ill. by author. Harper, 1964. Subj: Cumulative tales. Humor. Poetry, rhyme.

The giving tree ill. by author. Harper, 1964. Subj: Character traits – generosity. Poetry, rhyme.

The missing piece ill. by author. Harper, 1976. Subj: Character traits – individuality. Concepts – shape.

Who wants a cheap rhinoceros? ill. by author. Rev. ed. Macmillan, 1983. Subj: Animals – rhinoceros. Poetry, rhyme.

Simon, Howard. *If you were an eel, how would you feel?* (Simon, Mina Lewiton)

Simon, Mina Lewiton. *If you were an eel, how would you feel?* by Mina and Howard Simon; ill. by Howard Simon. Follett, 1963. Subj: Animals.

Is anyone here? ill. by Howard Simon. Atheneum, 1967. Subj: Poetry, rhyme. Sea and seashore.

Simon, Norma. *All kinds of families* ill. by Joe Lasker. Albert Whitman, 1976. Subj: Family life.

The daddy days ill. by Abner Graboff. Abelard-Schuman, 1958. Subj: Divorce. Family life – fathers.

How do I feel? ill. by Joe Lasker. Albert Whitman, 1970. Subj: Emotions. Family life. Twins.

I know what I like ill. by Dora Leder. Albert Whitman, 1971. Subj: Character traits – individuality.

I was so mad! ill. by Dora Leder. Albert Whitman, 1974. Subj: Emotions – anger.

We remember Philip ill. by Ruth Sanderson. Albert Whitman, 1979. Subj: Death.

The wet world ill. by Jane Miller. Lippincott, 1954. Subj: Weather – rain.

What do I do? ill. by Joe Lasker. Albert Whitman, 1969. Subj: Activities. Character traits – helpfulness. City. Ethnic groups in the U.S. – Puerto Rican-Americans. School.

What do I say? ill. by Joe Lasker. Albert Whitman, 1967. Subj: Ethnic groups in the U.S. Ethnic groups in the U.S. – Puerto Rican-Americans. Family life. Foreign languages. Participation. School.

Where does my cat sleep? ill. by Dora Leder. Albert Whitman, 1982. Subj: Animals – cats. Sleep.

Why am I different? ill. by Dora Leder. Albert Whitman, 1976. Subj: Character traits – being different. Character traits – individuality. Self-concept.

Simon, Seymour. *Animal fact-animal fable* ill. by Diane de Groat. Crown, 1979. Subj: Animals.

Beneath your feet ill. by Daniel Nevins. Walker, 1977. Subj: Earth. Science.

Earth: our planet in space ill. with photos. Four Winds Pr., 1984. Subj: Earth.

The moon ill. with photos. Four Winds Pr., 1984. Subj: Moon.

The smallest dinosaurs ill. by Anthony Rao. Crown, 1982. Subj: Dinosaurs.

Simon, Sidney B. *The armadillo who had no shell* ill. by Walter Lorraine. Norton, 1966. Subj: Animals – armadillos. Character traits – being different.

Henry, the uncatchable mouse ill. by Nola Langner. Norton, 1964. Subj: Animals – mice. Character traits – cleverness.

Simons, Traute. *Paulino* tr. by Ebbitt Cutler; ill. by Susi Bohdal. Tundra (dist. by Scribner's), 1978. Subj: Dreams. Toys.

Simont, Marc. *How come elephants?* ill. by author. Harper, 1965. Subj: Animals – elephants. Character traits – questioning.

Simple Simon. *The story of Simple Simon* ill. by Paul Galdone. McGraw-Hill, 1966. "The version used in this book was published in London in 1840 by A. Park." Subj: Nursery rhymes.

Simple Simon ill. by Rodney Peppé. Holt, 1973. Subj: Nursery rhymes.

Singer, Isaac Bashevis. *Why Noah chose the dove* tr. by Elizabeth Shub; ill. by Eric Carle. Farrar, 1974. Subj: Animals. Birds – doves. Religion – Noah.

Singer, Marilyn. *Archer Armadillo's secret room* ill. by Beth Lee Weiner. Macmillan, 1985. Subj: Animals – armadillos. Behavior – running away. Moving.

The dog who insisted he wasn't ill. by Kelly Oechsli. Dutton, 1976. Subj: Animals – dogs. Character traits – individuality. Humor.

Pickle plan ill. by Steven Kellogg. Dutton, 1978. Subj: Behavior – needing someone. Character traits – individuality.

Will you take me to town on strawberry day? ill. by Trinka Hakes Noble. Harper, 1981. Subj: Music. Poetry, rhyme. Songs.

Singh, Jacquelin. *Fat Gopal* ill. by Demi. Harcourt, 1984. Subj: Character traits – cleverness. Poetry, rhyme. Foreign lands – India.

Sitomer, Harry. *How did numbers begin?* (Sitomer, Mindel)

Sitomer, Mindel. *How did numbers begin?* by Mindel and Harry Sitomer; ill. by Richard Cuffari. Crowell, 1976. Subj: Counting.

Sivulich, Sandra Stroner. *I'm going on a bear hunt* ill. by Glen Rounds. Dutton, 1973. Subj: Animals – bears. Games. Participation.

Skaar, Grace Marion. *Nothing but (cats) and all about (dogs)* ill. by author. Addison-Wesley, 1947. Subj: Animals – cats. Animals – dogs.

The very little dog: and, The smart little kitty by Grace Marion Skaar and Louise Phinney Woodcock; ill. by authors. Addison-Wesley, 1967. Subj: Animals – cats. Animals – dogs.

What do the animals say? ill. by author. Addison-Wesley, 1968. 1950 ed. published under title: What do they say! Subj: Animals. Noise, sounds. Participation.

Skipper, Mervyn. *The fooling of King Alexander* ill. by Gaynor Chapman. Atheneum, 1967. Originally published in The white man's garden, by Mervyn Skipper. London, Mathews, 1931. Subj: Foreign lands – China. Royalty.

Skofield, James. *All wet! All wet!* ill. by Diane Stanley. Harper, 1984. Subj: Weather – rain.

Snow country ill. by Laura Jean Allen. Harper, 1983. Subj: Family life – grandparents, great-grandparents. Farms. Weather – snow.

Skorpen, Liesel Moak. *All the Lassies* ill. by Bruce Martin Scott. Dial Pr., 1970. Subj: Animals. Animals – dogs. Character traits – perseverance. Cumulative tales. Family life – only child. Participation. Pets.

Charles ill. by Martha G. Alexander. Harper, 1971. Subj: Behavior – needing someone. Toys – teddy bears.

Elizabeth ill. by Martha G. Alexander. Harper, 1970. Subj: Toys – dolls.

His mother's dog ill. by M. E. Mullin. Harper, 1978. Subj: Animals – dogs. Emotions – envy, jealousy. Family life. Sibling rivalry.

If I had a lion ill. by Ursula Landshoff. Harper, 1967. Subj: Animals – lions. Imagination.

Old Arthur ill. by Wallace Tripp. Harper, 1972. Subj: Animals – dogs. Old age.

Outside my window ill. by Mercer Mayer. Harper, 1968. Subj: Animals – bears. Bedtime.

Skurzynski, Gloria. *Martin by himself* ill. by Lynn Munsinger. Houghton, 1979. Subj: Activities – working. Emotions – loneliness. Family life – mothers.

Slate, Joseph. *Lonely Lula cat* ill. by Bruce Degen. Harper, 1985. Subj: Animals – cats. Emotions – loneliness. Friendship.

The mean, clean, giant canoe machine ill. by Lynn Munsinger. Crowell, 1983. Subj: Activities – bathing. Animals – pigs. Witches.

The star rocker ill. by Dirk Zimmer. Harper, 1982. Subj: Poetry, rhyme. Stars.

Sleator, William. *The angry moon* ill. by Blair Lent. Little, 1970. Subj: Caldecott award honor book. Ethnic groups in the U.S. – Indians. Folk and fairy tales. Moon.

Sleep, baby, sleep: *an old cradle song* ill. by Trudi Oberhänsli. Atheneum, 1967. Includes melody with words.

Sloan, Carolyn. *Carter is a painter's cat* ill. by Fritz Wegner. Simon and Schuster, 1971. Subj: Animals – cats. Careers – artists.

Slobodkin, Louis. *Clear the track* ill. by author. Macmillan, 1945. Subj: Family life. Imagination. Poetry, rhyme. Trains.

Colette and the princess ill. by author. Dutton, 1965. Subj: Animals – cats. Folk and fairy tales. Foreign lands – France. Noise, sounds. Royalty.

Dinny and Danny ill. by author. Macmillan, 1951. Subj: Cavemen. Character traits – helpfulness. Dinosaurs. Friendship.

Friendly animals ill. by author. Vanguard, 1944. Subj: Animals. Poetry, rhyme.

Hustle and bustle ill. by author. Macmillan, 1962. Subj: Animals – hippopotami. Behavior – fighting, arguing.

The late cuckoo ill. by author. Vanguard, 1962. Subj: Clocks. Time.

Magic Michael ill. by author. Macmillan, 1944. Subj: Family life. Imagination. Magic. Self-concept.

Melvin, the moose child ill. by author. Macmillan, 1957. Subj: Animals. Animals – moose. Forest, woods.

Millions and millions and millions ill. by author. Vanguard, 1955. Subj: Character traits – individuality. Poetry, rhyme.

Moon Blossom and the golden penny ill. by author. Vanguard, 1963. Subj: Foreign lands – China. Money.

One is good, but two are better ill. by author. Vanguard, 1956. Subj: Poetry, rhyme.

Our friendly friends ill. by author. Vanguard, 1951. Subj: Animals.

The polka-dot goat ill. by author. Macmillan, 1964. Subj: Animals – goats. Foreign lands – India.

The seaweed hat ill. by author. Macmillan, 1947. Subj: Poetry, rhyme. Sea and seashore.

Thank you - you're welcome ill. by author. Vanguard, 1957. Subj: Etiquette

Trick or treat ill. by author. Macmillan, 1959. Subj: Holidays – Halloween.

Up high and down low ill. by author. Macmillan, 1960. Subj: Animals – goats. Animals – sheep. Concepts – up and down. Poetry, rhyme.

Wide-awake owl ill. by author. Macmillan, 1958. Subj: Birds – owls. Music. Sleep. Songs.

Yasu and the strangers ill. by author. Macmillan, 1965. Subj: Behavior – lost. Foreign lands – Japan.

Slobodkina, Esphyr. *Boris and his balalaika* ill. by Vladimir Bobri. Abelard-Schuman, 1964. Subj: Foreign lands – Russia.

Caps for sale ill. by author. Addison-Wesley, 1940. Subj: Animals – monkeys. Careers – peddlers. Clothing. Humor. Participation.

Pezzo the peddler and the circus elephant ill. by author. Abelard-Schuman, 1967. Subj: Animals – elephants. Careers – peddlers. Circus. Clothing. Humor. Parades. Participation.

Pezzo the peddler and the thirteen silly thieves ill. by author. Abelard-Schuman, 1970. Subj: Careers – peddlers. Clothing. Crime. Humor. Participation.

Pinky and the petunias ill. by author. Abelard-Schuman, 1959. Based on a story by Tamara Schildkraut. Subj: Animals – cats. Flowers.

The wonderful feast ill. by author. Lothrop, 1955. Subj: Animals. Animals – horses. Farms. Food.

Slocum, Rosalie. *Breakfast with the clowns* ill. by author. Viking, 1937. Subj: Circus. Clowns, jesters. Food.

Small, David. *Eulalie and the hopping head* ill. by author. Macmillan, 1982. Subj: Animals – foxes. Character traits – kindness. Frogs and toads.

Imogene's antlers ill. by author. Crown, 1985. Subj: Animals. Character traits – appearance.

Small, Ernest *see* Lent, Blair

Smaridge, Norah. *Peter's tent* ill. by Brinton Turkle. Viking, 1965. Subj: Friendship.

Watch out! ill. by Susan Perl. Abingdon Pr., 1965. Subj: Safety.

You know better than that ill. by Susan Perl. Abingdon Pr., 1973. Subj: Etiquette. Poetry, rhyme.

Smart, Christopher. *For I will consider my cat Jeoffry* ill. by Emily Arnold McCully. Atheneum, 1984. Subj: Animals – cats. Poetry, rhyme.

Smath, Jerry. *But no elephants* ill. by author. Parents, 1979. Subj: Animals – elephants. Pets.

Smith, Catriona Mary. *The long dive* (Smith, Raymond Kenneth)

The long slide (Smith, Raymond Kenneth)

Smith, Donald. *Farm numbers 1, 2, 3* ill. by author. Abingdon Pr., 1970. Subj: Counting. Farms.

Smith, Elmer Boyd. *The story of Noah's ark* ill. by author. Houghton, 1904. Subj: Religion – Noah.

Smith, Henry Lee. *Frog fun* (Stratemeyer, Clara Georgeanna)

Pepper (Stratemeyer, Clara Georgeanna)

Tuggy (Stratemeyer, Clara Georgeanna)

Smith, Janice Lee. *The monster in the third dresser drawer and other stories about Adam Joshua* ill. by Dick Gackenbach. Harper, 1981. Subj: Behavior – misbehavior. Emotions – fear. Monsters.

Smith, Jean Shannon. *Scooter and the magic star* (Gardner, Mercedes)

Smith, Jim. *The frog band and Durrington Dormouse* ill. by author. Little, 1977. Subj: Animals – mice. Frogs and toads.

The frog band and the onion seller ill. by author. Little, 1976. Subj: Animals. Frogs and toads. Humor. Problem solving.

The frog band and the owlnapper ill. by author. Little, 1981. Subj: Animals. Birds – owls. Frogs and toads. Humor.

Smith, Lucia B. *A special kind of sister* ill. by Chuck Hall. Holt, 1979. Subj: Family life. Handicaps. Sibling rivalry.

Smith, Mary. *Long ago elf* by Mary and Robert Alan Smith; ill. by authors. Follett, 1968. Subj: Elves and little people.

Smith, Raymond Kenneth. *The long dive* by Raymond Kenneth and Catriona Mary Smith; ill. by authors. Atheneum, 1978. Subj: Sea and seashore. Toys.

The long slide by Raymond Kenneth and Catriona Mary Smith; ill. by authors. Atheneum, 1977. Subj: Toys.

Smith, Robert Alan. *Long ago elf* (Smith, Mary)

Smith, Robert Paul. *Jack Mack* ill. by Erik Blegvad. Coward, 1960. Subj: Humor. Tongue twisters.

Nothingatall, nothingatall, nothingatall ill. by Alan E. Cober. Harper, 1965. Subj: Bedtime.

When I am big ill. by Lillian Hoban. Harper, 1965. Subj: Behavior – growing up.

Smith, Theresa Kalab. *The fog is secret* ill. by author. Prentice-Hall, 1966. Subj: Sea and seashore. Weather – fog.

Smith, William Jay. *Children of the forest* (Beskow, Elsa Maartman)

Puptents and pebbles: nonsense ABC ill. by Juliet Kepes. Little, 1959. Subj: ABC books. Humor. Poetry, rhyme.

The telephone (Chukovsky, Korney)

Typewriter town ill. by author. Dutton, 1960. Subj: Poetry, rhyme.

Sniff, Mr. *see* Abisch, Roz

Snoopy on wheels ill. by Charles M. Schulz. Random House, 1983. Subj: Animals – dogs. Birds. Toys. Wheels.

Snow, Pegeen. *Mrs. Periwinkle's groceries* ill. by Jerry Warshaw. Children's Pr., 1981. Subj: Character traits – helpfulness. Cumulative tales. Old age.

A pet for Pat ill. by Tom Dunnington. Children's Pr., 1984. Subj: Pets. Poetry, rhyme.

Snyder, Anne. *The old man and the mule* ill. by Mila Lazarevich. Holt, 1978. Subj: Animals – mules. Character traits – meanness.

Snyder, Dick. *One day at the zoo* photos. by author. Scribner's, 1960. Subj: Animals. Animals – koala bears. Zoos.

Talk to me tiger photos. by author; foreword by George H. Pournelle. Golden Gate, 1965. Subj: Animals. Zoos.

Snyder, Zilpha Keatley. *Come on, Patsy* ill. by Margot Zemach. Atheneum, 1982. Subj: Activities – playing. Behavior – growing up. Poetry, rhyme.

Sobol, Harriet Langsam. *Clowns* photos. by Patricia Agre. Coward, 1982. Subj: Clowns, jesters.

Jeff's hospital book photos. by Patricia Agre. Walck, 1975. Subj: Hospitals.

My brother Steven is retarded photos. by Patricia Agre. Macmillan, 1977. Subj: Handicaps.

We don't look like our mom and dad photos. by Patricia Agre. Coward, 1984. Subj: Adoption. Ethnic groups in the U.S. Family life.

Solbert, Romaine G. *see* Solbert, Ronni

Solbert, Ronni. *Emily Emerson's moon* (Merrill, Jean)

I wrote my name on the wall: sidewalk songs ill. by author. Little, 1971. Subj: Ethnic groups in the U.S.

Solomon, Joan. *A present for Mum* photos. by Joan and Ryan Solomon. Hamish Hamilton, 1982. Subj: Foreign lands – England. Shopping. Stores.

Sondergaard, Arensa. *Biddy and the ducks* by Arensa Sondergaard and Mary M. Reed; ill. by Doris Henderson and Marion Henderson. Heath, 1941. Subj: Birds – chickens. Birds – ducks.

Sondheimer, Ilse. *The boy who could make his mother stop yelling* ill. by Dee deRosa. Rainbow Pr., 1982. Subj: Behavior – bad day. Family life – mothers.

Sonneborn, Ruth A. *Friday night is papa night* ill. by Emily Arnold McCully. Viking, 1970. Subj: City. Ethnic groups in the U.S. – Puerto Rican-Americans. Family life – fathers. Poverty.

I love Gram ill. by Leo Carty. Viking, 1971. Subj: City. Family life – grandparents, great-grandparents. Hospitals. Illness. Old age.

Lollipop's party ill. by Brinton Turkle. Viking, 1967. Subj: City. Emotions – loneliness. Ethnic groups in the U.S. – Puerto Rican-Americans.

Seven in a bed ill. by Don Freeman. Viking, 1968. Subj: Ethnic groups in the U.S. – Puerto Rican-Americans. Family life. Poverty. Sleep.

Sopko, Eugeh. *Townsfolk and countryfolk* ill. by author. Faber, 1982. Subj: City. Country. Foreign lands – Europe.

Sorine, Stephanie Riva. *Our ballet class* photos. by Daniel S. Sorine. Knopf, 1981. Subj: Activities – dancing.

Sotomayor, Antonio. *Khasa goes to the fiesta* ill. by author. Doubleday, 1967. Subj: Behavior – lost. Foreign lands – South America. Holidays.

Spang, Günter. *Clelia and the little mermaid* ill. by Pepperl Ott. Abelard-Schuman, 1967. Translation of Clelia und die kleine Wassernixe. Subj: Emotions – loneliness. Foreign lands – Germany. Friendship. Mythical creatures.

Spangenburg, Judith Dunn *see* Dunn, Judy

Spanner, Helmut. *I am a little cat* tr. from German by Robert Kimber; ill. by author. Barron's, 1983. Subj: Animals – cats. Format, unusual – cardboard pages.

Spencer, Zane. *Bright Fawn and me* (Leech, Jay)

The spider's web photos. by John Cooke. Putnam's, 1978. Subj: Spiders. Science.

Spiegel, Doris. *Danny and Company 92* ill. by author. Coward, 1945. Subj: Careers – firefighters. Fire.

Spier, Peter. *Bill's service station* ill. by author. Doubleday, 1981. Subj: Automobiles. Format, unusual – cardboard pages.

Bored - nothing to do! ill. by author. Doubleday, 1978. Subj: Airplanes, airports. Behavior – boredom. Humor.

Crash! bang! boom! ill. by author. Doubleday, 1972. Subj: Noise, sounds. Parades. Participation.

The Erie Canal ill. by author. Doubleday, 1970. Subj: Folk and fairy tales. Music. Songs. U.S. history.

Fast-slow, high-low: a book of opposites ill. by author. Doubleday, 1972. Subj: Concepts – opposites. Concepts – speed.

Firehouse ill. by author. Doubleday, 1981. Subj: Careers – firefighters. Format, unusual – cardboard pages.

Food market ill. by author. Doubleday, 1981. Subj: Food. Format, unusual – cardboard pages. Shopping. Stores.

Gobble, growl, grunt ill. by author. Doubleday, 1971. Subj: Animals. Noise, sounds. Participation.

The legend of New Amsterdam ill. by author. Doubleday, 1979. Subj: Folk and fairy tales. U.S. history.

Little cats ill. by author. Doubleday, 1984. Subj: Animals – cats. Format, unusual – cardboard pages.

Little dogs ill. by author. Doubleday, 1984. Subj: Animals – dogs. Format, unusual – cardboard pages.

Little ducks ill. by author. Doubleday, 1984. Subj: Birds – ducks. Format, unusual – cardboard pages.

Little rabbits ill. by author. Doubleday, 1984. Subj: Animals – rabbits. Format, unusual – cardboard pages.

My school ill. by author. Doubleday, 1981. Subj: Format, unusual – cardboard pages. School.

Noah's ark ill. by author. Doubleday, 1977. Includes P. Spier's translation of The flood, by Jacobus Revius. Subj: Boats, ships. Caldecott award book. Poetry, rhyme. Religion – Noah. Wordless.

Oh, were they ever happy! ill. by author. Doubleday, 1978. Subj: Activities – painting. Concepts – color. Humor.

People ill. by author. Doubleday, 1980. Subj: World.

The pet store ill. by author. Doubleday, 1981. Subj: Animals. Format, unusual – cardboard pages. Pets. Stores.

Peter Spier's Christmas! ill. by author. Doubleday, 1983. Subj: Holidays – Christmas.

Peter Spier's rain ill. by author. Doubleday, 1982. Subj: Weather – rain. Wordless.

The toy shop ill. by author. Doubleday, 1981. Subj: Format, unusual – cardboard pages. Stores. Toys.

Spilka, Arnold. *And the frog went "Blah!"* ill. by author. Scribner's, 1972. Subj: Humor. Poetry, rhyme.

Dippy dos and don'ts (Sage, Michael)

A lion I can do without ill. by author. Walck, 1964. Subj: Humor. Poetry, rhyme.

Little birds don't cry ill. by author. Viking, 1965. Subj: Animals. Poetry, rhyme.

A rumbudgin of nonsense ill. by author. Scribner's, 1970. Subj: Humor. Poetry, rhyme.

Spinelli, Eileen. *Thanksgiving at Tappletons'* ill. by Maryann Cocca-Leffler. Addison-Wesley, 1982. Subj: Behavior – sharing. Family life. Holidays – Thanksgiving. Humor.

Spinner, Stephanie. *The adventures of Pinocchio* (Collodi, Carlo)

Spriggs, Ruth. *The fables of Æsop* (Æsop)

Frank Baber's Mother Goose (Mother Goose)

Springstubb, Tricia. *The magic guinea pig* ill. by Bari Weissman. Morrow, 1982. Subj: Behavior – mistakes. Witches.

My Minnie is a jewel ill. by Jim LaMarche. Carolrhoda, 1980. Subj: Character traits – loyalty. Emotions – love.

The squire's bride: *a Norwegian folk tale* orig. told by P. C. Asbjørnsen; ill. by Marcia Sewall. Atheneum, 1975. Subj: Folk and fairy tales. Foreign lands – Norway. Weddings.

Srivastava, Jane Jonas. *Area* ill. by Shelley Freshman. Crowell, 1974. Subj: Concepts – measurement.

Stadler, John. *Animal cafe* ill. by author. Bradbury Pr., 1980. Subj: Animals. Behavior – greed. Food.

Gorman and the treasure chest ill. by author. Bradbury Pr., 1984. Subj: Animals. Behavior – sharing.

Stafford, Kay. *Ling Tang and the lucky cricket* ill. by Louise Zibold. McGraw-Hill, 1944. Subj: Character traits – luck. Foreign lands – China.

Stage, Mads. *The greedy blackbird* ill. by author. John Godon Burke, 1981. Subj: Behavior – greed. Behavior – sharing. Birds.

The lonely squirrel ill. by author. John Godon Burke, 1980. Subj: Animals – squirrels. Emotions – loneliness.

Stalder, Valerie. *Even the Devil is afraid of a shrew: a folktale of Lapland* adapt. by Ray Brocket; ill. by Richard Eric Brown. Addison-Wesley, 1972. Subj: Behavior – nagging. Devil. Folk and fairy tales. Foreign lands – Lapland.

Stamaty, Mark Alan. *Minnie Maloney and Macaroni* ill. by author. Dial Pr., 1976. Subj: Food. Humor.

Standon, Anna. *Little duck lost* by Anna and Edward Cyril Standon; ill. by Edward Cyril Standon. Delacorte Pr., 1965. Subj: Behavior – lost. Birds – ducks. Eggs. Family life – mothers.

The singing rhinoceros ill. by Edward Cyril Standon. Coward, 1963. Subj: Animals – rhinoceros.

Standon, Edward Cyril. *Little duck lost* (Standon, Anna)

Stanek, Muriel. *Left, right, left, right!* ill. by Lucy Hawkinson. Albert Whitman, 1969. Subj: Concepts – left and right. Emotions – embarrassment.

My little foster sister ill. by Judith Cheng. Albert Whitman, 1981. Subj: Adoption. Behavior – sharing. Sibling rivalry.

One, two, three for fun ill. by Seymour Fleishman. Albert Whitman, 1967. Subj: Counting. Ethnic groups in the U.S.

Stang, Judit *see* Varga, Judy

Stanley, Diane. *The conversation club* ill. by author. Macmillan, 1983. Subj: Animals – mice. Clubs, gangs. Communication. Noise, sounds.

Stanley, John. *It's nice to be little* ill. by Jean Tamburine. Rand McNally, 1965. Subj: Character traits – smallness.

Stanovich, Betty Jo. *Big boy, little boy* ill. by Virginia Wright-Frierson. Lothrop, 1984. Subj: Family life – grandparents, great-grandparents.

Hedgehog adventures ill. by Chris L. Demarest. Lothrop, 1983. Subj: Animals – groundhogs. Animals – hedgehogs. Character traits – loyalty.

Stan-Padilla, Viento. *Dream Feather* ill. by author. Atheneum, 1980. Subj: Ethnic groups in the U.S. – Indians. Folk and fairy tales. Religion.

Stanton, Elizabeth. *Sometimes I like to cry* by Elizabeth and Henry Stanton; ill. by Richard Leyden. Albert Whitman, 1978. Subj: Emotions.

The very messy room by Elizabeth and Henry Stanton; ill. by Richard Leyden. Albert Whitman, 1978. Subj: Character traits – cleanliness. Family life.

Stanton, Henry. *Sometimes I like to cry* (Stanton, Elizabeth)

The very messy room (Stanton, Elizabeth)

Star wars: *the maverick moon* ill. by Walter Wright. Random House, 1979. Subj: Space and space ships.

Starbird, Kaye. *The covered bridge house and other poems* ill. by Jim Arnosky. Four Winds Pr., 1979. Subj: Poetry, rhyme.

Starret, William *see* McClintock, Marshall

Steadman, Ralph. *The bridge* ill. by author. Subj: Behavior – fighting, arguing. Bridges. Friendship.

The little red computer ill. by author. McGraw-Hill, 1969. Subj: Machines. Space and space ships.

Stearns, Monroe. *Ring-a-ling* ill. by Adolf Zabransky. Lippincott, 1959. Subj: Nursery rhymes.

Stecher, Miriam B. *Daddy and Ben together* photos. by Alice Kandell. Lothrop, 1981. Subj: Family life – fathers.

Max, the music-maker by Miriam B. Stecher and Alice Kandell; photos. by Alice Kandell. Lothrop, 1980. Subj: Music. Science.

Steele, Mary Quintard Govan *see* Gage, Wilson

Steger, Hans-Ulrich. *Traveling to Tripiti* tr. by Elizabeth D. Crawford; ill. by author. Harcourt, 1967. Subj: Activities – traveling. Cumulative tales. Toys. Toys – teddy bears.

Steig, William. *The amazing bone* ill. by author. Farrar, 1976. Subj: Animals – pigs. Caldecott award honor book. Magic.

The bad speller ill. by author. Windmill Books, 1970. Subj: Games. Language.

Caleb and Kate ill. by author. Farrar, 1977. Subj: Animals – dogs. Magic. Witches.

Doctor De Soto ill. by author. Farrar, 1982. Subj: Animals – foxes. Animals – mice. Character traits – cleverness.

An eye for elephants ill. by author. Windmill Books, 1970. Subj: Animals – elephants. Poetry, rhyme.

Farmer Palmer's wagon ride ill. by author. Farrar, 1974. Subj: Animals – donkeys. Animals – pigs. Humor.

Gorky rises ill. by author. Farrar, 1980. Subj: Frogs and toads. Magic.

Roland, the minstrel pig ill. by author. Windmill Books, 1968. Subj: Animals – foxes. Animals – pigs. Music. Royalty.

Rotten island ill. by author. Rev. ed. of The bad island issued in 1969. Godine, 1984. Subj: Flowers. Islands. Monsters.

Sylvester and the magic pebble ill. by author. Windmill Books, 1969. Subj: Animals. Animals – donkeys. Caldecott award book. Family life. Magic.

Yellow and pink ill. by author. Farrar, 1984. Subj: Toys – dolls.

Stein, Sara Bonnett. *About dying: an open family book for parents and children together* by Sara Bonnett Stein, in cooperation with Gilbert W. Kliman [et al.]; photos. by Dick Frank; graphic design by Michael Goldberg. Walker, 1974. Subj: Death.

About handicaps: an open family book for parents and children together by Sara Bonnett Stein, in cooperation with Gilbert W. Kliman [et al.]; photos. by Dick Frank; graphic design by Michael Goldberg. Walker, 1974. Subj: Handicaps.

About phobias: an open family book for parents and children together Thomas R. Holman, consultant; photos. by Erika Stone. Walker, 1979. Subj: Emotions – fear. Family life – fathers.

The adopted one: an open family book for parents and children together Thomas R. Holman, consultant; photos. by Erika Stone. Walker, 1979. Subj: Adoption. Family life.

Cat ill. by Manuel Garcia. Harcourt, 1985. Subj: Animals – cats. Science.

A child goes to school photos. by Don Connors. Doubleday, 1978. Subj: School.

A hospital story: an open family book for parents and children together photos. by Doris Pinney; graphic design by Michel Goldberg. Walker, 1974. Subj: Careers – doctors. Careers – nurses. Hospitals. Illness.

Making babies: an open family book for parents and children together by Sara Bonnett Stein, in cooperation with Gilbert W. Kliman [et al.]; photos. by Doris Pinney; graphic design by Michael Goldberg. Walker, 1974. Subj: Babies. Family life.

Mouse ill. by Manuel Garcia. Harcourt, 1985. Subj: Animals – mice. Science.

On divorce: an open family book for parents and children together Thomas R. Holman, consultant; photos. by Erika Stone. Walker, 1979. Subj: Divorce. Family life.

That new baby: an open family book for parents and children together by Sara Bonnett Stein, in cooperation with Gilbert W. Kliman [et al.]; photos by Dick Frank; graphic design by Michael Goldberg. Walker, 1974. Subj: Babies. Family life.

Steiner, Barbara. *But not Stanleigh* photos. by George and Ruth Cloven. Children's Pr., 1980. Subj: Animals – raccoons.

Steiner, Charlotte. *Birthdays are for everyone* ill. by author. Doubleday, 1964. Subj: Birthdays.

Charlotte Steiner's ABC ill. by author. Watts, 1946. Subj: ABC books.

The climbing book by Charlotte Steiner and Mary Burlingham; ill. by Charlotte Steiner. Vanguard, 1943. Subj: Format, unusual. Holidays – Christmas.

Daddy comes home ill. by author. Doubleday, 1944. Subj: Family life. Family life – fathers.

Five little finger playmates ill. by author. Grosset, 1951. Subj: Counting. Games. Participation.

A friend is "Amie" ill. by author. Knopf, 1956. Subj: Foreign languages. Friendship.

Kiki and Muffy ill. by author. Doubleday, 1943. Subj: Animals – cats. Family life – grandparents, great-grandparents.

Kiki is an actress ill. by author. Doubleday, 1958. Subj: Theater.

Kiki's play house ill. by author. Doubleday, 1962. Subj: Activities – playing.

Listen to my seashell ill. by author. Knopf, 1959. Subj: Noise, sounds. Sea and seashore.

Look what Tracy found ill. by author. Knopf, 1972. Subj: Activities – playing. Imagination.

Lulu ill. by author. Doubleday, 1939. Subj: Animals – dogs. Imagination – imaginary friends.

My bunny feels soft ill. by author. Knopf, 1958. Subj: Animals – rabbits.

My slippers are red ill. by author. Knopf, 1958. Subj: Concepts – color.

Pete and Peter ill. by author. Doubleday, 1941. Subj: Animals – dogs. Sports – hunting.

Pete's puppets ill. by author. Doubleday, 1952. Subj: Puppets.

Polka Dot ill. by author. Doubleday, 1947. Subj: Pets.

Red Ridinghood's little lamb ill. by author. Knopf, 1964. Subj: Animals – sheep. Elves and little people. Games.

The sleepy quilt ill. by author. Doubleday, 1947. Subj: Bedtime.

What's the hurry, Harry? ill. by author. Lothrop, 1968. Subj: Behavior – hurrying. Character traits – patience.

Steiner, Jörg. *The bear who wanted to be a bear* from an idea by Frank Tashlin; ill. by Jörg Müller. Atheneum, 1977. Subj: Animals – bears. Progress. Stores.

Rabbit Island ill. by Jörg Müller. Harcourt, 1978. Subj: Animals – rabbits. Character traits – freedom.

Steinmetz, Leon. *Clocks in the woods* ill. by author. Harper, 1979. Subj: Animals. Clocks. Time.

Stemp, Robin. *Guy and the flowering plum tree* ill. by Carolyn Dinan. Atheneum, 1981. Subj: Imagination. Trees.

Stephens, Karen. *Jumping* ill. by George Wiggins. Grosset, 1965. Subj: Activities – jumping.

Stephenson, Dorothy. *How to scare a lion* ill. by John E. Johnson. Follett, 1965. Subj: Animals – lions. Illness.

The night it rained toys ill. by John E. Johnson. Follett, 1963. Subj: Holidays – Christmas. Poetry, rhyme. Royalty. Toys.

Steptoe, John. *Birthday* ill. by author. Holt, 1972. Subj: Birthdays. Ethnic groups in the U.S. – Afro-Americans.

Daddy is a monster...sometimes ill. by author. Lippincott, 1980. Subj: Family life – fathers. Monsters.

Jeffrey Bear cleans up his act ill. by author. Lothrop, 1983. Subj: Animals – bears. School.

My special best words ill. by author. Viking, 1974. Subj: Ethnic groups in the U.S. – Afro-Americans. Family life. Language.

Stevie ill. by author. Harper, 1969. Subj: Ethnic groups in the U.S. – Afro-Americans. Friendship.

The story of jumping mouse: a Native American legend ill. by author. Lothrop, 1984. Subj: Animals – mice. Folk and fairy tales. Frogs and toads. Magic.

Uptown ill. by author. Harper, 1970. Subj: City. Ethnic groups in the U.S. – Afro-Americans. Poverty.

Sterling, Helen *see* Hoke, Helen L.

Stern, Elsie-Jean. *Wee Robin's Christmas song* ill. by Elsie McKean. Nelson, 1945. Subj: Birds – robins. Holidays – Christmas. Music. Songs.

Stern, Mark. *It's a dog's life* ill. by author. Atheneum, 1978. Subj: Animals – dogs. Character traits – freedom.

Stern, Peter. *Floyd, a cat's story* ill. by author. Harper, 1982. Subj: Animals – cats.

Stern, Ronnie. *Pop's secret* (Townsend, Maryann)

Stern, Simon. *Mrs. Vinegar* ill. by author. Prentice-Hall, 1979. Subj: Houses.

Stevens, Bryna. *Borrowed feathers and other fables* ill. by Freire Wright and Michael Foreman. Random House, 1978. Subj: Folk and fairy tales.

Stevens, Carla. *Hooray for pig!* ill. by Rainey Bennett. Seabury Pr., 1974. Subj: Animals. Animals – pigs. Sports – swimming.

Pig and the blue flag ill. by Rainey Bennett. Seabury Pr., 1977. Subj: Animals. Animals – pigs. School. Sports – gymnastics.

Stories from a snowy meadow ill. by Eve Rice. Seabury Pr., 1976. Subj: Animals. Character traits – kindness. Death. Friendship.

Stevens, Janet. *Animal fair* adapt. and ill. by Janet Stevens. Holiday, 1981. Subj: Animals. Dreams. Fairs. Poetry, rhyme.

The princess and the pea (Andersen, H C (Hans Christian))

Stevens, Margaret. *When grandpa died* ill. by Kenneth Ualand. Children's Pr., 1979. Subj: Death. Family life – grandparents, great-grandparents.

Stevenson, Drew. *The ballad of Penelope Lou...and me* ill. by Marcia Sewall. Crossing Pr., 1978. Subj: Character traits – bravery. Emotions – fear. Poetry, rhyme.

Stevenson, James. *The bear who had no place to go* ill. by author. Harper, 1972. Subj: Animals – bears. Emotions – loneliness.

Clams can't sing ill. by author. Greenwillow, 1980. Subj: Animals. Music. Noise, sounds. Sea and seashore.

"Could be worse!" ill. by author. Greenwillow, 1977. Subj: Family life. Family life – grandparents, great-grandparents. Farms. Monsters.

Grandpa's great city tour: an alphabet book ill. by author. Greenwillow, 1983. Subj: ABC books. Activities – flying. City.

The great big especially beautiful Easter egg ill. by author. Greenwillow, 1983. Subj: Eggs. Family life – grandparents, great-grandparents.

Howard ill. by author. Greenwillow, 1980. Subj: Behavior – lost. Birds – ducks. Friendship.

Monty ill. by author. Greenwillow, 1979. Subj: Animals – rabbits. Birds – ducks. Frogs and toads. Reptiles – alligators, crocodiles.

The Sea View Hotel ill. by author. Greenwillow, 1978. Subj: Activities – vacationing. Animals – mice. Hotels.

The terrible Halloween night ill. by author. Greenwillow, 1980. Subj: Family life – grandparents, great-grandparents. Holidays – Halloween.

We can't sleep ill. by author. Greenwillow, 1982. Subj: Animals. Bedtime. Family life – grandparents, great-grandparents. Sleep.

What's under my bed? ill. by author. Greenwillow, 1983. Subj: Bedtime. Emotions – fear. Family life – grandparents, great-grandparents.

Wilfred the rat ill. by author. Greenwillow, 1977. Subj: Animals – chipmunks. Animals – rats. Animals – squirrels. Friendship.

Winston, Newton, Elton, and Ed ill. by author. Greenwillow, 1978. Subj: Animals – walruses. Birds – penguins. Sibling rivalry.

The wish card ran out! ill. by author. Greenwillow, 1981. Subj: Behavior – wishing.

Worse than Willy! ill. by author. Greenwillow, 1984. Subj: Babies. Family life. Family life – grandparents, great-grandparents. Imagination. Sibling rivalry.

The worst person in the world ill. by author. Greenwillow, 1978. Subj: Friendship.

Yuck! ill. by author. Greenwillow, 1984. Subj: Magic. Witches.

Stevenson, Jocelyn. *Jim Henson's Muppets at sea* ill. by Graham Thompson. Random House, 1980. Subj: Boats, ships. Puppets. Sea and seashore.

Red and the pumpkins ill. by Kelly Oechsli. Holt, 1983. Subj: Food. Imagination. Puppets.

Stevenson, Robert Louis. *A child's garden of verses* ill. by Erik Blegvad. Random House, 1978. Subj: Poetry, rhyme.

A child's garden of verses ill. by Pelagie Doane. Doubleday, 1942. Subj: Poetry, rhyme.

A child's garden of verses ill. by Toni Frissell. U.S. Camera, 1944. Subj: Poetry, rhyme.

A child's garden of verses ill. by Gyo Fujikawa. Grosset, 1957. Subj: Poetry, rhyme.

A child's garden of verses ill. by Alice and Martin Provensen. Western Pub., 1951. Subj: Poetry, rhyme.

A child's garden of verses ill. by Tasha Tudor. Oxford Univ. Pr., 1947. Subj: Poetry, rhyme.

A child's garden of verses ill. by Brian Wildsmith. Watts, 1966. Subj: Poetry, rhyme.

The moon ill. by Denise Saldutti. Harper, 1984. Subj: Family life. Moon. Poetry, rhyme. Sports – fishing.

Stewart, Elizabeth Laing. *The lion twins* photos. by Marlin and Carol Morse Perkins. Atheneum, 1964. Subj: Animals – lions. Twins.

Stewart, Robert S. *The daddy book* ill. by Don Madden. American Heritage, 1972. Subj: Careers. Family life – fathers.

Stiles, Norman. *The Sesame Street ABC storybook* (Moss, Jeffrey)

Still, James. *Jack and the wonder beans* ill. by Margot Tomes. Putnam's, 1977. Subj: Folk and fairy tales. Giants.

Stinson, Kathy. *Red is best* ill. by Robin Baird Lewis. Firefly Pr., 1982. Subj: Concepts – color.

Stobbs, Joanna. *One sun, two eyes, and a million stars* by Joanna and William Stobbs; ill. by authors. Merrimack, 1983. Subj: Counting.

Stobbs, William. *Animal pictures* ill. by author. Bodley Head, 1982. Subj: Animals. Wordless.

A car called beetle ill. by author. Merrimack, 1979. Bodley Head, 1979. Subj: Automobiles.

The hare and the frogs (Æsop)

One sun, two eyes, and a million stars (Stobbs, Joanna)

There's a hole in my bucket ill. by author. Merrimack, 1983. Subj: Seasons – summer. Songs.

This little piggy ill. by author. Bodley Head, 1981. Subj: Animals – pigs. Counting. Nursery rhymes. Poetry, rhyme.

Stock, Catherine. *Sampson the Christmas cat* ill. by author. Putnam's, 1984. Subj: Animals – cats. Holidays – Christmas.

Sophie's bucket ill. by author. Lothrop, 1985. Subj: Family life. Sea and seashore.

Stoddard, Sandol. *Curl up small* ill. by Trina Schart Hyman. Houghton, 1964. Subj: Concepts – shape. Concepts – size. Family life. Imagination.

My very own special particular private and personal cat ill. by Remy Charlip. Houghton, 1963. Subj: Animals – cats. Pets. Poetry, rhyme.

The thinking book ill. by Ivan Chermayeff. Little, 1960. Subj: Family life. Imagination.

Stolz, Mary Slattery. *Emmett's pig* ill. by Garth Williams. Harper, 1959. Subj: Animals – pigs. Birthdays. Farms.

Stone, A. Harris. *The last free bird* ill. by Sheila Heins. Prentice-Hall, 1967. Subj: Birds. Ecology.

Stone, Bernard. *The charge of the mouse brigade* by Bernard Stone with Alice Low; ill. by Tony Ross. Pantheon, 1980. Subj: Animals – cats. Animals – mice. War.

Emergency mouse ill. by Ralph Steadman. Prentice-Hall, 1978. Subj: Animals – mice. Hospitals.

Stone, Jon. *Big Bird in China* photos. by Victor DiNapoli. Random House, 1983. Subj: Foreign lands – China. Puppets.

Stone, Lynn M. *Endangered animals* ill. with photos. Children's Pr., 1984. Subj: Animals. Nature.

Stone, Rosetta. *Because a little bug went ka-choo!* ill. by Michael K. Frith. Random House, 1975. Subj: Cumulative tales. Humor. Insects. Poetry, rhyme.

Stonehouse, Bernard. *Kangaroos* ill. with photos. Raintree, 1978. Subj: Animals – kangaroos.

Storm, Theodor. *Little John* (Orgel, Doris)

Storr, Catherine. *Clever Polly and the stupid wolf* ill. by Marjorie-Ann Watts. Faber, 1979. Subj: Animals – wolves. Character traits – cleverness.

Hugo and his grandma ill. by Nita Sowter. Merrimack, 1980. Subj: Activities – knitting. Family life – grandparents, great-grandparents.

Stott, Rowena. *The hedgehog feast* ill. by Edith Holden. Dutton, 1978. Subj: Animals – hedgehogs. Hibernation. Parties.

Stover, Jo Ann. *If everybody did* ill. by author. McKay, 1960. Subj: Behavior. Etiquette. Poetry, rhyme.

Why? Because ill. by author. McKay, 1961. Subj: Character traits – questioning.

Strachan, Margaret Pitcairn *see* Cone, Molly

Strahl, Rudi. *Sandman in the lighthouse* tr. and adapt. by Anthea Bell; ill. by Eberhard Binder. Children's Pr., 1967, 1969. Subj: Bedtime. Lighthouses. Sandman. Sea and seashore.

Straker, Joan Ann. *Animals that live in the sea.* National Geographical Soc., 1979. Subj: Sea and seashore.

Strand, Mark. *The planet of lost things* ill. by William Pène du Bois. Crown, 1983. Subj: Bedtime. Dreams. Noise, sounds.

Stratemeyer, Clara Georgeanna. *Frog fun* by Clara G. Stratemeyer and Henry Lee Smith, Jr.; ill. by Lucy Hawkinson. Harper, 1963. Subj: Frogs and toads.

Pepper by Clara G. Stratemeyer and Henry Lee Smith, Jr. Benziger, 1971. Subj: Animals. Animals – cats.

Tuggy by Clara Georgeanna Stratemeyer and Henry Lee Smith, Jr. Harper, 1971. Subj: Animals – dogs. Frogs and toads.

Strathdee, Jean. *The house that grew* ill. by Jessica Wallace. Oxford Univ. Pr., 1980. Subj: Family life. Houses. Moving.

Streatfield, Noel. *Sleepy Nicholas* (Brande, Marlie)

Stren, Patti. *Hug me* ill. by author. Harper, 1977. Subj: Animals – porcupines. Emotions – loneliness.

Mountain Rose ill. by author. Dutton, 1982. Subj: Character traits – appearance. Self-concept. Sports – wrestling.

Stroyer, Poul. *It's a deal* ill. by author. Astor-Honor, 1960. Subj: Activities – trading. Humor.

Struppi ill. by Ingrid Graichen. Imported Pubs., 1983. Subj: Animals. Format, unusual – cardboard pages. Wordless.

Stuart, Mary *see* Graham, Mary Stuart Campbell

Stubbs, Joanna. *Happy Bear's day* ill. by author. Elsevier-Dutton, 1979. Subj: Animals – bears. Behavior – solitude.

With cat's eyes you'll never be scared of the dark ill. by author. Dutton, 1983. Subj: Emotions – fear. Magic. Night.

Sturtzel, Howard A. *see* Annixter, Paul

Sturtzel, Jane Levington *see* Annixter, Jane

Suba, Susanne. *The monkeys and the pedlar* ill. by author. Viking, 1970. Subj: Animals – monkeys. Careers – peddlers. Humor.

Suben, Eric. *Pigeon takes a trip* ill. by Tiziana Zanetti; graphic design by Giorgio Vanetti. Golden Books, 1984. Subj: Activities – traveling. Birds – pigeons. Format, unusual – cardboard pages.

Sueyoshi, Akiko. *Ladybird on a bicycle* ill. by Viv Allbright. Faber, 1983. Subj: Insects – ladybugs. Sports – bicycling.

Sugita, Yutaka. *The flower family* ill. by author. McGraw-Hill, 1975. Subj: Flowers. Plants. Science.

Good night 1, 2, 3 ill. by author. Scroll Pr., 1971. Subj: Bedtime. Counting. Sleep.

Helena the unhappy hippopotamus ill. by author. McGraw-Hill, 1972. Subj: Animals – hippopotami. Behavior – needing someone. Emotions – loneliness. Emotions – sadness. Friendship.

My friend Little John and me ill. by author. McGraw-Hill, 1972. Subj: Animals – dogs. Wordless.

Suhl, Yuri. *The Purim goat* ill. by Kaethe Zemach. Four Winds Pr., 1980. Subj: Animals – goats. Character traits – helpfulness.

Simon Boom gives a wedding ill. by Margot Zemach. Four Winds Pr., 1972. Subj: Cumulative tales. Humor. Jewish culture. Weddings.

Sumiko. *Kittymouse* ill. by author. Harcourt, 1979. Subj: Animals – cats. Animals – mice.

Sundgaard, Arnold. *Jethro's difficult dinosaur* ill. by Stanley Mack. Pantheon, 1977. Subj: Dinosaurs. Eggs. Humor. Poetry, rhyme.

The Superman mix or match storybook ill. by Ross Andru and Joe Orlando. Random House, 1979. Subj: Format, unusual.

Supraner, Robyn. *Giggly-wiggly, snickety-snick* ill. by Stan Tusan. Parents, 1978. Subj: Concepts.

Would you rather be a tiger? ill. by Barbara Cooney. Houghton, 1973. Subj: Behavior. Imagination. Poetry, rhyme. Self-concept.

Supree, Burton. *Harlequin and the gift of many colors* (Charlip, Remy)

"Mother, mother I feel sick" (Charlip, Remy)

Surany, Anico. *Kati and Kormos* ill. by Leonard Everett Fisher. Holiday, 1966. Subj: Animals – dogs. Emotions – loneliness. Foreign lands – Hungary.

Ride the cold wind ill. by Leonard Everett Fisher. Putnam's, 1964. Subj: Boats, ships. Foreign lands – South America. Sports – fishing.

Sussman, Susan. *Hippo thunder* ill. by John C. Wallner. Albert Whitman, 1982. Subj: Bedtime. Emotions. Weather – storms.

Sutton, Eve. *My cat likes to hide in boxes* ill. by Lynley Dodd. Parents, 1973. Subj: Animals – cats. Cumulative tales. Participation. Poetry, rhyme.

Svendsen, Carol. *Hulda* ill. by Julius Svendsen. Houghton, 1974. Subj: Behavior. Poetry, rhyme. Trolls.

Swados, Elizabeth. *Lullaby* ill. by Faith Hubley. Harper, 1980. Subj: Bedtime. Songs.

Swayne, Samuel F. *Great-grandfather in the honey tree* by Samuel F. and Zoa Swayne; ill. by Zoa Swayne. Viking, 1949. Subj: Family life – grandparents, great-grandparents.

Swayne, Zoa. *Great-grandfather in the honey tree* (Swayne, Samuel F)

Swift, Hildegarde Hoyt. *The little red lighthouse and the great gray bridge* by Hildegarde H. Swift and Lynd Ward; ill. by Lynd Ward. Harcourt, 1942. Subj: Boats, ships. Bridges. Lighthouses.

Switzer, Robert E. *My friend the babysitter* (Watson, Jane Werner)

Sometimes I get angry (Watson, Jane Werner)

Sometimes I'm afraid (Watson, Jane Werner)

Syme, Daniel B. *I'm growing* (Bogot, Howard)

Szekeres, Cyndy. *Cyndy Szekeres' counting book, 1 to 10* ill. by author. Golden Pr., 1984. Subj: Animals – mice. Counting.

Long ago ill. by author. McGraw-Hill, 1977. Subj: Animals. U.S. history.

Taback, Simms. *Joseph had a little overcoat* ill. by author. Random House, 1977. Subj: Clothing. Format, unusual.

Tabberner, Jeffrey. *The endless party* (Delessert, Etienne)

Taber, Anthony. *Cats' eyes* ill. by author. Dutton, 1978. Subj: Animals – cats. Old age.

Taborin, Glorina. *Norman Rockwell's counting book* (Rockwell, Norman)

Tacher, Edith *see* Hurd, Edith Thacher

Tafuri, Nancy. *All year long* ill. by author. Greenwillow, 1983. Subj: Days of the week, months of the year.

Early morning in the barn ill. by author. Greenwillow, 1983. Subj: Farms. Morning.

Have you seen my duckling? ill. by author. Greenwillow, 1984. Subj: Birds – ducks. Caldecott award honor book. Character traits – individuality.

Tallarico, Tony. *At home* ill. by author. Tuffy Books, 1984. Subj: Family life. Houses.

Tallon, Robert. *Handella* ill. by author. Bobbs-Merrill, 1972. Subj: Activities – dancing. Problem solving. Theater.

Latouse my moose ill. by author. Knopf, 1983. Subj: Animals – dogs. Pets.

Talus, Taylor. *Animal hide-and-seek* (Tison, Annette)

Inside and outside (Tison, Annette)

Tamburine, Jean. *I think I will go to the hospital* ill. by author. Abingdon Pr., 1965. Subj: Hospitals.

Tan, Pierre Le *see* Le-Tan, Pierre

Tanaka, Hideyuki. *The happy dog* ill. by author. Atheneum, 1983. Subj: Animals – dogs.

Taniuchi, Kota. *Trolley* ill. by author. Watts, 1969. Subj: Cable cars, trolleys. Imagination.

Tapio, Pat Decker. *The lady who saw the good side of everything* ill. by Paul Galdone. Seabury Pr., 1975. Subj: Activities – traveling. Animals – cats. Character traits – optimism. Emotions – happiness. Humor. Weather – floods. Weather – rain.

Tarrant, Graham. *Rabbits* ill. by Tonny King. Putnam's, 1984. Subj: Animals – rabbits. Format, unusual.

Tarrant, Margaret. *Fairy tales* ill. with photos. Crowell, 1978. Subj: Folk and fairy tales.

Nursery rhymes ill. with photos. Crowell, 1978. Subj: Nursery rhymes.

Tate, Joan. *A Christmas book*

The giant fish and other stories (Otto, Svend)

Tatham, Campbell *see* Elting, Mary

Tax, Meredith. *Families* ill. by Marylin Hafner. Little, 1981. Subj: Family life.

Taylor, Edgar. *King Grisly-Beard* (Grimm, Jacob)

Taylor, John Edward. *Petrosinella* (Basile, Giambattista)

Taylor, Judy. *Sophie and Jack* ill. by Susan Gantner. Putnam's, 1983. Subj: Activities – picnicking. Animals – hippopotami. Family life.

Sophie and Jack help out ill. by Susan Gantner. Putnam's, 1984. Subj: Activities – gardening. Animals – hippopotami. Weather – storms.

Taylor, Mark. *The bold fisherman* ill. by Graham Booth. Golden Gate, 1967. Subj: Folk and fairy tales. Music. Sea and seashore. Songs. Sports – fishing.

The case of the missing kittens ill. by Graham Booth. Atheneum, 1978. Subj: Animals – cats. Animals – dogs. Behavior – lost. Problem solving.

Henry explores the jungle ill. by Graham Booth. Atheneum, 1968. Subj: Animals – tigers. Character traits – bravery. Circus. Seasons – summer.

Henry explores the mountains ill. by Graham Booth. Atheneum, 1975. Subj: Character traits – bravery. Fire. Helicopters. Seasons – fall.

Henry the castaway ill. by Graham Booth. Atheneum, 1972. Subj: Behavior – lost. Boats, ships. Seasons – spring. Weather – rain.

Henry the explorer ill. by Graham Booth. Atheneum, 1966. Subj: Animals – bears. Behavior – lost. Character traits – bravery. Seasons – winter.

"Lamb," said the lion, "I am here." ill. by Anne Siberell. Golden Gate, 1971. Subj: Animals. Religion.

Old Blue, you good dog you ill. by Gene Holtan. Golden Gate, 1970. Subj: Animals – dogs. Animals – possums. Folk and fairy tales. Friendship. Games. Music. Songs. Old age.

Taylor, Sydney. *The dog who came to dinner* ill. by John E. Johnson. Follett, 1966. Subj: Animals – dogs. Ethnic groups in the U.S. – Afro-Americans.

Teal, Valentine. *The little woman wanted noise* ill. by Robert Lawson. Rand McNally, 1946. Subj: Country. Farms. Noise, sounds. Senses.

Teleki, Geza. *Aerial apes: Gibbons of Asia* by Geza Teleki and others; ill. with photos. Coward, 1979. Subj: Animals – monkeys.

Telephones ill. by Christine Sharr. Wonder Books, 1971. Subj: Communication. Telephone.

Tellenbach, Margrit Haubensak *see* Haubensak-Tellenbach, Margrit

Tempest, P. *How the cock wrecked the manor* tr. from Lithuanian by Olimpija Armalyte; ill. by Albina Makūnaite. Imported Pub., 1982. Subj: Folk and fairy tales. Magic.

Tensen, Ruth M. *Come to the zoo!* Reilly, 1948. Subj: Animals. Zoos.

Terban, Marvin. *I think I thought: and other tricky verbs* ill. by Giulio Maestro. Houghton, 1984. Subj: Language. Poetry, rhyme.

Testa, Fulvio. *If you look around* ill. by author. Dial Pr., 1983. Subj: Concepts – shape.

If you take a paintbrush: a book of colors ill. by author. Dial Pr., 1983. Subj: Concepts – color.

If you take a pencil ill. by author. Dial Pr., 1982. Subj: Counting.

The land where the ice cream grows story and ill. by Fulvio Testa; told by Anthony Burgess. Doubleday, 1979. Subj: Food. Imagination.

Tester, Sylvia Root. *Chase!* ill. by author. Children's Pr., 1980. Subj: Animals.

Never monkey with a monkey: a book of homographic homophones ill. by John Keely. Children's Pr., 1977. Subj: Language.

Parade! ill. by author. Children's Pr., 1980. Subj: Circus.

What did you say? a book of homophones ill. by John Keely. Children's Pr., 1977. Subj: Language.

Tether, Graham. *The hair book* ill. by Roy McKié. Random House, 1979. Subj: Hair. Poetry, rhyme.

Skunk and possum ill. by Lucinda McQueen. Houghton, 1979. Subj: Activities – picnicking. Animals – possums. Animals – skunks. Friendship.

Thacher, Edith *see* Hurd, Edith Thacher

Thaler, Mike. *It's me, hippo!* ill. by Maxie Chambliss. Harper, 1983. Subj: Animals. Animals – hippopotami. Friendship.

Madge's magic show ill. by Carol Nicklaus. Watts, 1978. Subj: Magic.

Moonkey ill. by Giulio Maestro. Harper, 1981. Subj: Animals – monkeys. Friendship. Moon.

My puppy ill. by Madeleine Fishman. Harper, 1980. Subj: Animals – dogs. Imagination – imaginary friends. Pets.

There's a hippopotamus under my bed ill. by Ray Cruz. Watts, 1977. Subj: Animals – hippopotami.

The yellow brick toad: funny frog cartoons, riddles, and silly stories ill. by author. Doubleday, 1978. Subj: Humor. Riddles.

Thayer, Jane *see* Woolley, Catherine

Thelen, Gerda. *The toy maker: how a tree becomes a toy village* retold by Louise F. Encking; ill. by Fritz Kukenthal. Albert Whitman, 1935. Subj: Toys. Trees.

Things that go word book ill. by Hutchings. Rand McNally, 1977. Subj: Machines.

Thoburn, Tina. *A B See* (Ogle, Lucille)

I hear (Ogle, Lucille)

Thomas, Art. *Merry-go-rounds* ill. by George Overlie. Carolrhoda, 1981. Subj: Merry-go-rounds.

Thomas, Gary. *The best of the little books* ill. by Chris Cummings. Harvey House, 1980. Subj: Poetry, rhyme. Riddles. Tongue twisters.

Thomas, Ianthe. *Eliza's daddy* ill. by Moneta Barnett. Harcourt, 1976. Subj: Divorce. Ethnic groups in the U.S. – Afro-Americans. Seasons – summer.

Lordy, Aunt Hattie ill. by Thomas di Grazia. Harper, 1973. Subj: Ethnic groups in the U.S. – Afro-Americans. Seasons – summer.

Walk home tired, Billy Jenkins ill. by Thomas di Grazia. Harper, 1974. Subj: Activities – walking. City. Ethnic groups in the U.S. – Afro-Americans. Imagination.

Willie blows a mean horn ill. by Ann Toulmin-Rothe. Harper, 1981. Subj: Family life – fathers. Music.

Thomas, Katherine Elwes. *The real personages of Mother Goose.* Lothrop, 1930. Subj: Nursery rhymes.

Thomas, Kathy. *The angel's quest* ill. by Jacqueline Seitz. Living Flame Pr., 1983. Subj: Angels. Character traits – perseverance. Orphans. Religion.

Thomas, Patricia. *"Stand back," said the elephant, "I'm going to sneeze!"* ill. by Wallace Tripp. Lothrop, 1971. Subj: Animals. Humor. Poetry, rhyme.

"There are rocks in my socks!" said the ox to the fox ill. by Mordicai Gerstein. Lothrop, 1979. Subj: Animals – bulls, cows. Animals – foxes. Poetry, rhyme. Problem solving.

Thompson, Brenda. *Famous planes* by Brenda Thompson and Rosemary Giesen; ill. by Andrew Martin and Rosemary Giesen. Lerner, 1977. Subj: Airplanes, airports.

Pirates by Brenda Thompson and Rosemary Giesen; ill. by Simon Stern and Rosemary Giesen. Lerner, 1977. Subj: Pirates.

The winds that blow by Brenda Thompson and Cynthia Overbeck; ill. by Simon Stern and Rosemary Gieson. Lerner, 1977. Subj: Concepts – measurement. Sea and seashore. Weather – wind.

Thompson, Elizabeth. *The true book of time* (Ziner, Feenie)

Thompson, George Selden *see* Selden, George

Thompson, Harwood. *The witch's cat* ill. by Quentin Blake. Addison-Wesley, 1971. Subj: Animals – cats. Folk and fairy tales. Foreign lands – England. Witches.

Thompson, Susan L. *Diary of a monarch butterfly* graphic design by Sas Colby; ill. by Judy LaMotte. Walker, 1976. Subj: Insects – butterflies, caterpillars. Science.

One more thing, dad ill. by Dora Leder. Albert Whitman, 1980. Subj: Counting.

Thompson, Vivian Laubach. *Camp-in-the-yard* ill. by Brinton Turkle. Holiday, 1961. Subj: Problem solving. Sports – camping. Twins.

The horse that liked sandwiches ill. by Aliki. Putnam's, 1962. Subj: Animals – horses. Food.

Thomson, Pat. *Rhymes around the day* ill. by Jan Ormerod. Lothrop, 1983. Subj: Family life. Nursery rhymes.

Thomson, Ruth. *Peabody all at sea* ill. by Ken Kirkwood. Lothrop, 1978. Subj: Activities – vacationing. Animals – dogs. Boats, ships. Careers – detectives. Crime. Problem solving.

Peabody's first case ill. by Ken Kirkwood. Lothrop, 1978. Subj: Animals – dogs. Careers – detectives. Crime. Problem solving.

Thorne, Ian *see* May, Julian

Thorne, Jenny. *My uncle* ill. by author. Atheneum, 1982. Subj: Activities. Dreams. Family life. Sports – fishing.

The three bears. *Goldilocks and the three bears* adapt. and ill. by Lorinda Bryan Cauley. Putnam's, 1981. Subj: Animals – bears. Folk and fairy tales.

The story of the three bears ill. by L. Leslie Brooke. Warne, 1934. Subj: Animals – bears. Folk and fairy tales.

The story of the three bears ill. by William Stobbs. McGraw-Hill, 1964. Subj: Animals – bears. Folk and fairy tales.

The three bears (Hillert, Margaret)

The three bears ill. by Paul Galdone. Seabury Pr., 1972. Subj: Animals – bears. Folk and fairy tales.

The three bears adapted by Kathleen N. Daly; ill. by Feodor Rojankovsky. Golden Pr., 1967. Subj: Animals – bears. Folk and fairy tales.

The three little pigs. *The story of the three little pigs* ill. by L. Leslie Brooke. Warne, 1934. Subj: Animals – pigs. Animals – wolves. Character traits – cleverness. Folk and fairy tales.

The story of the three little pigs ill. by William Stobbs. McGraw-Hill, 1965. Subj: Animals – pigs. Animals – wolves. Character traits – cleverness. Folk and fairy tales.

The three pigs ill. by Tony Ross. Pantheon, 1983. Subj: Animals – pigs. Animals – wolves. Character traits – cleverness. Folk and fairy tales.

The three little pigs ill. by Erik Blegvad. Atheneum, 1980. Subj: Animals – pigs. Animals – wolves. Character traits – cleverness. Poetry, rhyme.

The three little pigs ill. by Lorinda Bryan Cauley. Putnam's, 1980. Subj: Animals – pigs. Animals – wolves. Character traits – cleverness. Folk and fairy tales.

The three little pigs: *in verse* ill. by William Pène Du Bois. Viking, 1962. Subj: Animals – pigs. Animals – wolves. Character traits – cleverness. Folk and fairy tales. Poetry, rhyme.

The three little pigs ill. by Paul Galdone. Seabury Pr., 1970. Subj: Animals – pigs. Animals – wolves. Character traits – cleverness. Folk and fairy tales.

The three little pigs ill. by Rodney Peppé. Lothrop, 1980. Subj: Animals – pigs. Animals – wolves. Character traits – cleverness. Folk and fairy tales.

The three little pigs retold by Margaret Hillert; ill. by Irma Wilde. Follett, 1963. Subj: Animals – pigs. Animals – wolves. Character traits – cleverness. Folk and fairy tales.

Thurber, James. *Many moons* ill. by Louis Slobodkin. Harcourt, 1943. Subj: Caldecott award book. Clowns, jesters. Illness. Moon. Royalty.

Thwaite, Ann. *The day with the Duke* ill. by George Him. World, 1969. Subj: Games.

Tierney, Hanne. *Where's your baby brother, Becky Bunting?* ill. by Paula Winter. Doubleday, 1979. Subj: Behavior – misbehavior. Family life. Sibling rivalry.

Ting. *Find the canary* (Morris, Neil)

Hide and seek (Morris, Neil)

Search for Sam (Morris, Neil)

Where's my hat? (Morris, Neil)

Tippett, James Sterling. *Counting the days* ill. by Elizabeth Tyler Wolcott. Harper, 1940. Subj: Holidays – Christmas. Poetry, rhyme.

Tison, Annette. *The adventures of the three colors* by Annette Tison and Talus Taylor. Collins-World, 1971. Subj: Concepts – color. Format, unusual.

Animal hide-and-seek by Annette Tison and Talus Taylor; ill. by authors. Collins-World, 1972. Subj: Activities – photographing. Animals. Format, unusual. Games. Insects.

Animals in color magic ill. by author. Merrill, 1980. Subj: Animals. Format, unusual.

Inside and outside by Annette Tison and Taylor Talus. Collins-World, 1972. Subj: Format, unusual. Houses.

Titus, Eve. *Anatole* ill. by Paul Galdone. McGraw-Hill, 1957. Subj: Animals – mice. Caldecott award honor book. Foreign lands – France.

Anatole and the cat ill. by Paul Galdone. McGraw-Hill, 1957. Subj: Animals – cats. Animals – mice. Caldecott award honor book. Character traits – bravery. Foreign lands – France. Problem solving.

Anatole and the piano ill. by Paul Galdone. McGraw-Hill, 1966. Subj: Animals – mice. Foreign lands – France. Music.

Anatole and the Pied Piper ill. by Paul Galdone. McGraw-Hill, 1979. Subj: Animals – mice. Foreign lands – France. Music. Problem solving.

Anatole and the poodle ill. by Paul Galdone. McGraw-Hill, 1965. Subj: Animals – dogs. Animals – mice. Foreign lands – France. Problem solving.

Anatole and the robot ill. by Paul Galdone. McGraw-Hill, 1960. Subj: Animals – mice. Foreign lands – France. Problem solving. Robots.

Anatole and the thirty thieves ill. by Paul Galdone. McGraw-Hill, 1969. Subj: Animals – mice. Crime. Foreign lands – France. Problem solving.

Anatole and the toyshop ill. by Paul Galdone. McGraw-Hill, 1970. Subj: Animals – mice. Foreign lands – France. Problem solving. Toys.

Anatole in Italy ill. by Paul Galdone. McGraw-Hill, 1973. Subj: Animals – mice. Foreign lands – Italy. Problem solving.

Anatole over Paris ill. by Paul Galdone. McGraw-Hill, 1961. Subj: Activities – flying. Animals – mice. Foreign lands – France. Kites.

Tobias, Tobi. *At the beach* ill. by Gloria Singer. McKay, 1978. Subj: Activities – vacationing. Family life. Sea and seashore.

Chasing the goblins away ill. by Victor G. Ambrus. Warne, 1977. Subj: Bedtime. Goblins. Night. Sleep.

The dawdlewalk ill. by Jeanette Swofford. Carolrhoda, 1983. Subj: Activities – walking.

Jane wishing ill. by Trina Schart Hyman. Viking, 1977. Subj: Behavior – wishing. Emotions – happiness. Family life. Humor. Self-concept.

Moving day ill. by William Pène du Bois. Knopf, 1976. Subj: Emotions. Moving. Toys – teddy bears.

Petey ill. by Symeon Shimin. Putnam's, 1978. Subj: Animals – gerbils. Death. Emotions. Pets.

Tobias catches trout (Hertza, Ole)

Tobias goes ice fishing (Hertza, Ole)

Tobias goes seal hunting (Hertza, Ole)

Tobias has a birthday (Hertza, Ole)

Todaro, John. *Phillip the flower-eating phoenix* by John Todaro and Barbara Ellen; ill. by John Todaro. Abelard-Schuman, 1961. Subj: Mythical creatures.

Todd, Kathleen. *Snow* ill. by author. Addison-Wesley, 1982. Subj: Activities – playing. Family life. Weather – snow.

Tolkien, J. R. R. (John Ronald Reuel). *The Father Christmas letters* ed. by Baillie Tolkien; ill. by author. Houghton, 1977. Subj: Communication. Holidays – Christmas.

Tolstoĭ, Alekseĭ Nikolaevich. *The great big enormous turnip* ill. by Helen Oxenbury. Watts, 1968. Subj: Cumulative tales. Farms. Folk and fairy tales. Foreign lands – Russia. Plants. Problem solving.

Tom Thumb. *Grimm Tom Thumb* by Jacob and Wilhelm Grimm; tr. by Anthea Bell; ill. by Svend Otto. Larousse, 1976. Translation of Tommeliden. Subj: Elves and little people. Folk and fairy tales.

Tom Thumb ill. by L. Leslie Brooke. Warne, 1904. Subj: Elves and little people. Folk and fairy tales.

Tom Thumb adapt. by Margaret Hillert; ill. by Dennis Hockerman. Follett, 1982. Subj: Elves and little people. Folk and fairy tales.

Tom Thumb by the Brothers Grimm; ill. by Felix Hoffmann. Atheneum, 1973. Translation of Der Daumling. Subj: Elves and little people. Folk and fairy tales.

Tom Thumb: *a tale* adapt. and ill. by Lidia Postma. Schocken, 1983. Based on a tale by Charles Perrault. Subj: Elves and little people. Folk and fairy tales.

Tom Thumb ill. by William Wiesner. Walck, 1974. Subj: Elves and little people. Folk and fairy tales.

Tom Tit Tot: *an English folk tale* ill. by Evaline Ness. Scribner's, 1965. Subj: Caldecott award honor book. Folk and fairy tales. Magic. Names.

Tomfool *see* Farjeon, Eleanor

Tomkins, Jasper. *The catalog* ill. by author. Green Tiger Pr., 1981. Subj: Animals. Humor.

Tompert, Ann. *Badger on his own* ill. by Diane de Groat. Crown, 1978. Subj: Animals – badgers. Birds – owls.

Charlotte and Charles ill. by John Wallner. Crown, 1979. Subj: Giants. Middle ages.

Little Fox goes to the end of the world ill. by John Wallner. Crown, 1976. Subj: Animals – foxes. Imagination.

Little Otter remembers and other stories ill. by John Wallner. Crown, 1977. Subj: Animals – otters. Family life – mothers.

Nothing sticks like a shadow ill. by Lynn Munsinger. Houghton, 1984. Subj: Animals – groundhogs. Animals – rabbits. Shadows.

Tord, Bijou Le *see* Le Tord, Bijou

Torgersen, Don Arthur. *The girl who tricked the troll* ill. by Tom Dunnington. Children's Pr., 1978. Subj: Farms. Trolls.

The troll who lived in the lake ill. by Tom Dunnington. Children's Pr., 1978. Subj: Ecology. Trolls.

Tornborg, Pat. *The Sesame Street cookbook* ill. by Robert Dennis. Platt, 1978. Subj: Activities – cooking. Puppets.

Totham, Mary *see* Breinburg, Petronella

Towle, Faith M. *The magic cooking pot: a folktale of India* ill. by author. Houghton, 1975. Subj: Folk and fairy tales. Food. Foreign lands – India. Magic.

Townsend, Anita. *The kangaroo* ill. by Michael Atkinson. Watts, 1979. Subj: Animals – kangaroos. Science.

Townsend, Kenneth. *Felix, the bald-headed lion* ill. by author. Delacorte, 1967. Subj: Animals – lions. Clothing. Emotions – embarrassment. Hair.

Townsend, Maryann. *Pop's secret* by Maryann Townsend and Ronnie Stern; ill. with photos. Addison-Wesley, 1980. Subj: Death. Family life – grandparents, great-grandparents.

Toye, William. *The fire stealer* ill. by Elizabeth Cleaver. Oxford Univ. Pr., 1980. Subj: Ethnic groups in the U.S. – Indians. Folk and fairy tales.

Tredez, Alain *see* Trez, Alain

Tredez, Denise *see* Trez, Denise

Trent, Robbie. *The first Christmas* ill. by Marc Simont. Harper, 1948. Subj: Holidays – Christmas. Poetry, rhyme. Religion.

Tresselt, Alvin R. *Autumn harvest* ill. by Roger Antoine Duvoisin. Lothrop, 1951. Subj: Holidays – Thanksgiving. Seasons – fall.

The beaver pond ill. by Roger Antoine Duvoisin. Lothrop, 1970. Subj: Animals – beavers. Ecology.

The dead tree ill. by Charles Robinson. Parents, 1972. Subj: Ecology. Trees.

The fisherman under the sea (Matsutani, Miyoko)

Follow the wind ill. by Roger Antoine Duvoisin. Lothrop, 1950. Subj: Poetry, rhyme. Weather – wind.

Frog in the well ill. by Roger Antoine Duvoisin. Lothrop, 1958. Subj: Frogs and toads.

Hide and seek fog ill. by Roger Antoine Duvoisin. Lothrop, 1965. Subj: Caldecott award honor book. Sea and seashore. Weather – fog.

How far is far? ill. by Ward Brackett. Parents, 1964. Subj: Concepts – distance. Science.

I saw the sea come in ill. by Roger Antoine Duvoisin. Lothrop, 1954. Subj: Behavior – solitude. Sea and seashore.

It's time now! ill. by Roger Antoine Duvoisin. Lothrop, 1969. Subj: City. Seasons.

Johnny Maple-Leaf ill. by Roger Antoine Duvoisin. Lothrop, 1948. Subj: Seasons. Seasons – fall. Trees.

The mitten: an old Ukrainian folktale ill. by Yaroslava. Lothrop, 1964. Adapted by Alvin Tresselt from the version by E. Rachev. Subj: Animals. Folk and fairy tales. Foreign lands – Ukraine.

Rabbit story ill. by Leonard Weisgard. Lothrop, 1957. Subj: Animals – rabbits.

Rain drop splash ill. by Leonard Weisgard. Lothrop, 1946. Subj: Caldecott award honor book. Cumulative tales. Science. Weather – rain.

Smallest elephant in the world ill. by Milton Glaser. Knopf, 1959. Subj: Animals – elephants. Character traits – smallness. Circus.

Sun up ill. by Roger Antoine Duvoisin. Lothrop, 1949. Subj: Farms. Sun. Weather.

What did you leave behind? ill. by Roger Antoine Duvoisin. Lothrop, 1978. Subj: Emotions.

White snow, bright snow ill. by Roger Antoine Duvoisin. Lothrop, 1947. Subj: Caldecott award book. Weather – snow.

The wind and Peter ill. by Garry McKenzie. Oxford Univ. Pr., 1948. Subj: Weather – wind.

The witch's magic cloth (Matsutani, Miyoko)

The world in the candy egg ill. by Roger Antoine Duvoisin. Lothrop, 1967. Subj: Eggs. Holidays – Easter. Magic.

Trez, Alain. *Good night, Veronica* (Trez, Denise)

The little knight's dragon (Trez, Denise)

Maila and the flying carpet (Trez, Denise)

Rabbit country (Trez, Denise)

The royal hiccups (Trez, Denise)

Trez, Denise. *Good night, Veronica* by Denise and Alain Trez; tr. by Douglas McKee; ill. by authors. Viking, 1968. Subj: Bedtime. Dreams. Sleep.

The little knight's dragon by Denise and Alain Trez; ill. by authors. Collins-World, 1963. Subj: Dragons. Knights.

Maila and the flying carpet by Denise and Alain Trez; tr. by Douglas McKee, ill. by authors. Viking, 1969. Subj: Activities – flying. Foreign lands – India. Magic. Royalty.

Rabbit country by Denise and Alain Trez; ill. by authors. Viking, 1966. Subj: Animals – rabbits.

The royal hiccups by Denise and Alain Trez; tr. by Douglas McKee; ill. by authors. Viking, 1965. Subj: Emotions – fear. Illness. Royalty.

Trimby, Elisa. *Mr. Plum's paradise* ill. by author. Lothrop, 1977. Subj: Activities – gardening. City.

Tripp, Paul. *The strawman who smiled by mistake* ill. by Wendy Watson. Doubleday, 1967. Subj: Emotions – happiness. Farms. Friendship. Scarecrows.

Tripp, Wallace. *My Uncle Podger* ill. by author. Little, 1975. Based on a passage from Three men in a boat (to say nothing of the dog) by Jerome Klapka Jerome. Subj: Animals – rabbits. Humor.

The tale of a pig: a caucasian folktale adapt. and ill. by Wallace Tripp. McGraw-Hill, 1968. Subj: Animals – pigs. Folk and fairy tales.

Trucks ill. by Art Seiden. Platt, 1983. Subj: Trucks.

Tsow, Ming. *A day with Ling* photos. by Christopher Cormack. Hamish Hamilton, 1983. Subj: Family life.

Tsultim, Yeshe. *The mouse king: a story from Tibet* ill. by Kusho Ralla. Penguin, 1979. Subj: Animals – mice. Folk and fairy tales. Foreign lands – Tibet.

Tucker, Nicholas. *Mother Goose abroad: nursery rhymes* ill. by Trevor Stubley. Crowell, 1974. Subj: Nursery rhymes.

Tudor, Bethany. *Samuel's tree house* ill. by author. Collins-World, 1979. Subj: Birds – ducks. Friendship. Houses. Toys. Trees.

Skiddycock Pond ill. by author. Lippincott, 1965. Subj: Birds – ducks. Boats, ships.

Tudor, Tasha. *Around the year* ill. by author. Walck, 1957. Subj: Days of the week, months of the year. Poetry, rhyme. Seasons.

Corgiville fair ill. by author. Crowell, 1971. Subj: Animals – goats. Fairs. Trolls.

The doll's Christmas ill. by author. Oxford Univ. Pr., 1950. Subj: Holidays – Christmas. Toys – dolls.

Junior's tune ill. by author. Holiday, 1980. Subj: Music. Sibling rivalry.

Mildred and the mummy ill. by author. Holiday, 1980. Subj: Libraries.

Miss Kiss and the nasty beast ill. by author. Holiday, 1979. Subj: Emotions – love.

1 is one ill. by author. Walck, 1956. Subj: Caldecott award honor book. Counting.

Snow before Christmas ill. by author. Oxford Univ. Pr., 1941. Subj: Holidays – Christmas. Seasons – winter. Weather – snow.

A time to keep: the Tasha Tudor book of holidays ill. by author. Rand McNally, 1978. Subj: Activities. Holidays.

Türk, Hanne. *Goodnight Max* ill. by author. Firefly Pr., 1983. Subj: Animals – mice. Bedtime. Wordless.

Happy birthday Max ill. by author. Alphabet Pr., 1984. Subj: Animals – mice. Birthdays. Wordless.

Max packs ill. by author. Alphabet Pr., 1984. Subj: Activities – traveling. Animals – mice. Wordless.

Max the artlover ill. by author. Alphabet Pr., 1983. Subj: Animals – mice. Art. Wordless.

Max versus the cube ill. by author. Alphabet Pr., 1982. Subj: Animals – mice. Problem solving. Riddles. Wordless.

Merry Christmas Max ill. by author. Firefly Pr., 1983. Subj: Animals – mice. Holidays – Christmas. Wordless.

Rainy day Max ill. by author. Alphabet Pr., 1983. Subj: Activities – walking. Animals – mice. Weather – rain. Wordless.

Raking leaves with Max ill. by author. Firefly Pr., 1983. Subj: Activities – working. Animals – mice. Wordless.

The rope skips Max ill. by author. Alphabet Pr., 1982. Subj: Activities. Animals – mice. Wordless.

Snapshot Max ill. by author. Alphabet Pr., 1984. Subj: Activities – photographing. Animals – mice. Wordless.

A surprise for Max ill. by author. Alphabet Pr., 1982. Subj: Animals – mice. Problem solving. Wordless.

Turkle, Brinton. *Deep in the forest* ill. by author. Dutton, 1976. Subj: Animals – bears. Folk and fairy tales. Wordless.

Do not open ill. by author. Dutton, 1981. Subj: Animals – cats. Behavior – trickery. Behavior – wishing. Monsters. Sea and seashore.

It's only Arnold ill. by author. Viking, 1973. Subj: Emotions – fear. Family life – grandparents, great-grandparents.

The magic of Millicent Musgrave ill. by author. Viking, 1967. Subj: Magic.

Obadiah the Bold; story and pictures by Brinton Turkle. Viking, 1965. Subj: Activities – playing. Behavior – growing up. Sea and seashore. U.S. history.

Rachel and Obadiah ill. by author. Dutton, 1978. Subj: Behavior – sharing. Money. Sibling rivalry.

The sky dog ill. by author. Viking, 1969. Subj: Animals – dogs. Imagination. Sea and seashore. Weather – clouds.

Thy friend, Obadiah ill. by author. Viking, 1969. Subj: Birds – sea gulls. Caldecott award honor book. Character traits – kindness to animals. Seasons – winter. U.S. history.

Turnage, Sheila. *Trout the magnificent* ill. by Janet Stevens. Harcourt, 1984. Subj: Behavior – dissatisfaction. Fish. Self-concept.

Turner, Josie *see* Crawford, Phyllis

Turpin, Lorna. *The sultan's snakes* ill. by author. Greenwillow, 1980. Subj: Behavior – hiding. Reptiles – snakes. Royalty.

Turska, Krystyna. *The magician of Cracow* ill. by author. Greenwillow, 1975. Subj: Character traits – ambition. Devil. Folk and fairy tales. Foreign lands – Poland. Magic. Moon.

The woodcutter's duck ill. by author. Macmillan, 1972. Subj: Birds – ducks. Character traits – kindness to animals. Folk and fairy tales. Foreign lands – Poland. Frogs and toads.

The turtle ill. by Charlotte Knox. Rourke, 1983. Subj: Reptiles – turtles.

Tusa, Tricia. *Libby's new glasses* ill. by author. Holiday, 1984. Subj: Glasses. Self-concept.

Tutt, Kay Cunningham. *And now we call him Santa Claus* ill. by author. Lothrop, 1963. Subj: Holidays – Christmas.

The twelve days of Christmas. English folk song. *Jack Kent's twelve days of Christmas* ill. by Jack Kent. Parents, 1973. Subj: Cumulative tales. Holidays – Christmas. Humor. Music. Songs.

The twelve days of Christmas ill. by Ilonka Karasz. Harper, 1949. Subj: Cumulative tales. Holidays – Christmas. Music. Songs.

The twelve days of Christmas ill. by Erika Schneider. Alphabet Pr., 1984. Subj: Cumulative tales. Format, unusual. Holidays – Christmas. Music. Songs.

Tworkov, Jack. *The camel who took a walk* ill. by Roger Antoine Duvoisin. Aladdin Books, 1951. Subj: Activities – walking. Animals. Animals – camels. Animals – tigers. Cumulative tales. Morning.

Uchida, Yoshiko. *The rooster who understood Japanese* ill. by Charles Robinson. Scribner's, 1976. Subj: Animals. Birds – chickens. Foreign languages.

Sumi's prize ill. by Kazue Mizumura. Scribner's, 1964. Subj: Character traits – ambition. Foreign lands – Japan. Kites.

Sumi's special happening ill. by Kazue Mizumura. Scribner's, 1966. Subj: Birthdays. Foreign lands – Japan. Old age.

Udry, Janice May. *Alfred* ill. by Judith S. Roth. Albert Whitman, 1960. Subj: Animals – dogs. Behavior – animals, dislike of. Emotions – fear.

Emily's autumn ill. by Erik Blegvad. Albert Whitman, 1969. Subj: Farms. Seasons – fall. Toys – dolls.

How I faded away ill. by Monica De Bruyn. Albert Whitman, 1976. Subj: Behavior – unnoticed, unseen. Emotions – embarrassment. Self-concept.

Is Susan here? ill. by Peter Edwards. Abelard-Schuman, 1962. Subj: Animals. Character traits – helpfulness. Family life – mothers. Imagination.

Let's be enemies ill. by Maurice Sendak. Harper, 1961. Subj: Behavior – fighting, arguing. Emotions – hate. Friendship.

Mary Ann's mud day ill. by Martha G. Alexander. Harper, 1967. Subj: Activities – playing. Ethnic groups in the U.S. – Afro-Americans.

Mary Jo's grandmother ill. by Eleanor Mill. Albert Whitman, 1970. Subj: Ethnic groups in the U.S. – Afro-Americans. Family life – grandparents, great-grandparents. Illness. Seasons – winter. Weather – snow.

The mean mouse and other mean stories ill. by Ed Young. Harper, 1962. Subj: Character traits – meanness.

The moon jumpers ill. by Maurice Sendak. Harper, 1959. Subj: Caldecott award honor book. Moon. Twilight.

"Oh no, cat!" ill. by Mary Chalmers. Coward, 1976. Subj: Animals – cats. Pets.

Theodore's parents ill. by Adrienne Adams. Lothrop, 1958. Subj: Adoption. Family life.

Thump and Plunk ill. by Ann Schweninger. Harper, 1981. Subj: Animals – mice. Family life – mothers. Sibling rivalry.

A tree is nice ill. by Marc Simont. Harper, 1956. Subj: Caldecott award book. Poetry, rhyme. Seasons. Trees.

What Mary Jo shared ill. by Eleanor Mill. Albert Whitman, 1966. Subj: Character traits – shyness. Ethnic groups in the U.S. Ethnic groups in the U.S. – Afro-Americans. Family life – fathers. School.

What Mary Jo wanted ill. by Eleanor Mill. Albert Whitman, 1968. Subj: Animals – dogs. Ethnic groups in the U.S. – Afro-Americans. Family life. Pets.

Ueno, Noriko. *Elephant buttons* ill. by author. Harper, 1973. Subj: Animals. Concepts – in and out. Concepts – size. Cumulative tales. Games. Humor. Participation. Wordless.

Uncle Gus *see* Rey, Hans Augusto

Ungerer, Jean Thomas *see* Ungerer, Tomi

Ungerer, Tomi. *Adelaide* ill. by author. Harper, 1959. Subj: Activities – traveling. Animals – kangaroos. Fire. Foreign lands – France.

The beast of Monsieur Racine ill. by author. Farrar, 1971. Subj: Behavior – trickery. Foreign lands – France. Humor. Monsters.

Christmas eve at the Mellops ill. by author. Harper, 1960. Subj: Animals – pigs. Holidays – Christmas.

Crictor ill. by author. Harper, 1958. Subj: Humor. Reptiles – snakes.

Emile ill. by author. Harper, 1960. Subj: Humor. Octopuses.

The hat ill. by author. Parents, 1970. Subj: Clothing. Foreign lands – Italy. Magic. Weather – wind.

The Mellops go diving for treasure ill. by author. Harper, 1957. Subj: Animals – pigs. Sea and seashore. Sports – skin diving.

The Mellops go flying ill. by author. Harper, 1957. Subj: Activities – flying. Airplanes, airports. Animals – pigs.

The Mellops go spelunking ill. by author. Harper, 1963. Subj: Animals – pigs. Caves. Character traits – perseverance.

The Mellops strike oil ill. by author. Harper, 1958. Subj: Animals – pigs. Fire. Oil.

Moon man ill. by author. Harper, 1967. Subj: Moon. Space and space ships.

No kiss for mother ill. by author. Harper, 1973. Subj: Animals – cats. Family life – mothers.

One, two, where's my shoe? ill. by author. Harper, 1964. Subj: Games. Wordless.

Orlando, the brave vulture ill. by author. Harper, 1966. Subj: Birds – vultures. Desert. Foreign lands – Mexico.

Rufus ill. by author. Harper, 1961. Subj: Animals – bats.

Snail, where are you? ill. by author. Harper, 1962. Subj: Games. Animals – snails. Wordless.

The three robbers ill. by author. Atheneum, 1962. Subj: Crime. Orphans.

Warwick's three bottles (Hodeir, André)

Zeralda's ogre ill. by author. Harper, 1967. Subj: Activities – cooking. Character traits – kindness. Giants. Monsters.

Untermeyer, Louis. *Æsop's fables* (Æsop)

The kitten who barked ill. by Lilian Obligado. Golden Pr., 1962. Subj: Animals – cats. Animals – dogs.

Upham, Elizabeth. *Little brown bear loses his clothes* ill. by Normand Chartier. Platt, 1978. Subj: Animals – bears. Behavior – losing things.

Usher, Margo Scegge *see* McHargue, Georgess

Uyeda, Frances. *Chōchō is for butterfly* (Sasaki, Jeannie)

Uysal, Ahmet E. *New patches for old* (Walker, Barbara K)

Vacheron, Edith. *Here is Henri!* by Edith Vacheron and Virginia Kahl; ill. by Virginia Kahl. Scribner's, 1959. Subj: Animals – cats. Foreign lands – France. Foreign languages.

Valens, Evans G. *Wingfin and Topple* ill. by Clement Hurd. Collins-World, 1962. Subj: Activities – flying. Fish.

Van Allsburg, Chris. *Ben's dream* ill. by author. Houghton, 1982. Subj: Dreams. Weather – rain.

The garden of Abdul Gasazi ill. by author. Houghton, 1979. Subj: Animals – dogs. Behavior – misbehavior. Caldecott award honor book. Imagination. Magic.

Jumanji ill. by author. Houghton, 1981. Subj: Caldecott award book. Games. Imagination. Jungle.

The mysteries of Harris Burdick ill. by author. Houghton, 1984. Subj: Imagination.

The wreck of the Zephyr ill. by author. Houghton, 1983. Subj: Boats, ships. Weather – storms.

Vance, Eleanor Graham. *Jonathan* ill. by Albert John Pucci. Follett, 1966. Subj: Character traits – questioning. Poetry, rhyme. Weather.

Van den Honert, Dorry. *Demi the baby sitter* ill. by Meg Wohlberg. Morrow, 1961. Subj: Activities – babysitting. Animals – dogs.

Van der Meer, Atie. *Oh Lord!* (Van der Meer, Ron)

Van der Meer, Ron. *Oh Lord!* by Ron and Atie van der Meer; ill. by authors. Crown, 1980. Subj: Humor. Religion.

Sailing ships (McGowan, Alan)

Vandivert, William. *Barnaby* photos. by author; story by Rita Vandivert. Dodd, 1963. Subj: Animals – kinkajous. Pets.

Van Horn, Grace. *Little red rooster* ill. by Sheila Perry. Abelard-Schuman, 1961. Subj: Birds – chickens. Farms.

Van Horn, William. *Harry Hoyle's giant jumping bean* ill. by author. Atheneum, 1978. Subj: Animals – cats. Animals – pack rats. Behavior – collecting things.

Twitchtoe, the beastfinder ill. by author. Atheneum, 1978. Subj: Problem solving.

Van Leeuwen, Jean. *Amanda Pig and her big brother Oliver* ill. by Ann Schweninger. Dial Pr., 1982. Subj: Animals – pigs. Behavior – growing up. Sibling rivalry.

The emperor's new clothes (Andersen, H C (Hans Christian))

More tales of Oliver Pig ill. by Arnold Lobel. Dial Pr., 1981. Subj: Animals – pigs. Family life.

Tales of Amanda Pig ill. by Ann Schweninger. Dial Pr., 1983. Subj: Animals – pigs. Family life. Sibling rivalry.

Tales of Oliver Pig ill. by Arnold Lobel. Dial, 1979. Subj: Animals – pigs. Family life.

Van Liew Foster, Doris *see* Foster, Doris Van Liew

Van Stockum, Hilda. *A day on skates: the story of a Dutch picnic* ill. by author. Hale, 1934. Subj: Activities – picnicking. Foreign lands – Holland. Sports – ice skating.

Van Woerkom, Dorothy. *Abu Ali: three tales of the Middle East* ill. by Harold Berson. Macmillan, 1976. Subj: Foreign lands – Turkey. Humor.

Alexandra the rock-eater: an old Rumanian tale retold ill. by Rosekrans Hoffman. Knopf, 1978. Subj: Dragons. Family life. Folk and fairy tales. Food. Foreign lands.

Becky and the bear ill. by Margot Tomes. Putnam's, 1975. Subj: Animals – bears. Character traits – bravery. U.S. history.

Donkey Ysabel ill. by Normand Chartier. Macmillan, 1978. Subj: Animals – donkeys. Humor.

The friends of Abu Ali: three more tales of the Middle East ill. by Harold Berson. Macmillan, 1978. Subj: Foreign lands – Turkey. Humor.

Harry and Shelburt ill. by Erick Ingraham. Macmillan, 1977. Subj: Animals – rabbits. Friendship. Reptiles – turtles. Sports – racing.

Hidden messages ill. by Lynne Cherry. Crown, 1980. Subj: Communication. Insects. Science.

The queen who couldn't bake gingerbread ill. by Paul Galdone. Knopf, 1975. Subj: Folk and fairy tales. Foreign lands – Germany. Humor. Royalty.

The rat, the ox and the zodiac: a Chinese legend ill. by Errol Le Cain. Crown, 1976. Subj: Animals. Animals – rats. Character traits – cleverness. Folk and fairy tales. Foreign lands – China. Zodiac.

Sea frog, city frog ill. by José Aruego and Ariane Dewey. Macmillan, 1975. Subj: Folk and fairy tales. Foreign lands – Japan. Frogs and toads.

Something to crow about ill. by Paul Harvey. Albert Whitman, 1982. Subj: Birds – chickens. Family life – fathers.

Tit for tat ill. by Douglas Florian. Greenwillow, 1977. Subj: Folk and fairy tales.

Varga, Judy. *Circus cannonball* ill. by author. Morrow, 1975. Subj: Circus.

The dragon who liked to spit fire ill. by author. Morrow, 1961. Subj: Dragons. Royalty.

Janko's wish ill. by author. Morrow, 1969. Subj: Behavior – wishing. Foreign lands – Hungary. Magic. Weddings.

The mare's egg ill. by author. Morrow, 1972. Subj: Animals – foxes. Behavior – trickery. Folk and fairy tales. Foreign lands – Russia.

Miss Lollipop's lion ill. by author. Morrow, 1963. Subj: Animals – lions. Circus. Pets.

The monster behind Black Rock ill. by author. Morrow, 1971. Subj: Animals. Behavior – gossip. Cumulative tales.

Varley, Dimitry. *The whirly bird* ill. by Feodor Rojankovsky. Knopf, 1961. Subj: Birds. Character traits – kindness to animals.

Varley, Susan. *Badger's parting gifts* ill. by author. Lothrop, 1984. Subj: Animals – badgers. Death. Friendship.

Varnum, Brooke Minarik. *Play and sing - it's Christmas!*

Vasiliu, Marcea *Everything is somewhere* ill. by author. John Day, 1970. Subj: Religion.

What's happening? ill. by author. John Day, 1970. Subj: Activities. City.

Vaughan, Eleanor K. *Timmy and the tin-can telephone* (Branley, Franklyn M)

Vecchio, Ellen Del *see* Del Vecchio, Ellen

Velthuijs, Max. *The painter and the bird* tr. by Ray Broekel; ill. by author. Addison-Wesley, 1975. Translation of Der Maler und der Vogel. Subj: Birds. Careers – artists. Imagination.

Venable, Alan. *The checker players* ill. by Byron Barton. Lippincott, 1973. Subj: Animals – bears. Behavior – fighting, arguing. Boats, ships. Friendship. Games. Reptiles – alligators, crocodiles.

Venino, Suzanne. *Animals helping people* ill. with photos. National Geographic Soc., 1983. Subj: Animals. Character traits – helpfulness.

Ventura, Marisa. *The painter's trick* (Ventura, Piero)

Ventura, Piero. *The painter's trick* by Piero and Marisa Ventura; ill. by Marisa Ventura. Random House, 1977. Subj: Careers – artists.

Piero Ventura's book of cities ill. by author. Random House, 1976. Subj: City.

Venturo, Betty Lou Baker *see* Baker, Betty

Vessel, Matthew F. *My goldfish* (Wong, Herbert H)

My ladybug (Wong, Herbert H)

My plant (Wong, Herbert H)

Our caterpillars (Wong, Herbert H)

Our earthworms (Wong, Herbert H)

Our tree (Wong, Herbert H)

Vevers, Gwynne. *Animal homes* ill. by Wendy Bramall. Merrimack, 1982. Subj: Animals. Houses.

Animal parents ill. by Colin Threadgall. Merrimack, 1982. Subj: Animals. Family life.

Animals of the dark ill. by Wendy Bramall. Merrimack, 1982. Subj: Animals. Night.

Animals that store food ill. by Joyce Bee. Merrimack, 1982. Subj: Animals. Food.

Animals that travel ill. by Matthew Hillier. Merrimack, 1982. Subj: Activities – traveling. Animals.

Vigna, Judith. *Anyhow, I'm glad I tried* ill. by author. Albert Whitman, 1978. Subj: Behavior – misbehavior. Character traits – kindness. School.

Couldn't we have a turtle instead? ill. by author. Albert Whitman, 1975. Subj: Animals. Babies. Emotions – envy, jealousy. Family life. Family life – mothers.

Daddy's new baby ill. by author. Albert Whitman, 1982. Subj: Divorce. Family life – fathers. Sibling rivalry.

Everyone goes as a pumpkin ill. by author. Albert Whitman, 1977. Subj: Family life – grandparents, great-grandparents. Holidays – Halloween.

Grandma without me ill. by author. Albert Whitman, 1984. Subj: Divorce. Family life – grandparents, great-grandparents.

The hiding house ill. by author. Albert Whitman, 1979. Subj: Behavior – hiding. Behavior – sharing. Friendship.

She's not my real mother ill. by author. Albert Whitman, 1980. Subj: Behavior – misbehavior. Divorce. Family life.

Villarejo, Mary. *The art fair* ill. by author. Knopf, 1960. Subj: Art.

The tiger hunt ill. by author. Knopf, 1959. Subj: Activities – photographing. Animals. Animals – tigers. Foreign lands – India.

Vincent, Gabrielle. *Bravo, Ernest and Celestine!* ill. by author. Greenwillow, 1982. Subj: Animals – bears. Animals – mice. Behavior – sharing. Money. Music.

Ernest and Celestine ill. by author. Greenwillow, 1982. Subj: Animals – bears. Animals – mice. Holidays – Christmas. Toys.

Ernest and Celestine's picnic ill. by author. Greenwillow, 1982. Subj: Activities – picnicking. Animals – bears. Animals – mice.

Smile, Ernest and Celestine ill. by author. Greenwillow, 1982. Subj: Activities – photographing. Animals – bears. Animals – mice.

Vinson, Pauline. *Willie goes to the seashore* ill. by author. Macmillan, 1954. Subj: Animals – mice. Sea and seashore.

Vinton, Iris. *Look out for pirates!* ill. by Herman B. Vestal. Random House, 1961. Subj: Boats, ships. Pirates.

Viorst, Judith. *Alexander and the terrible, horrible, no good, very bad day* ill. by Ray Cruz. Atheneum, 1972. Subj: Behavior – bad day. Family life.

Alexander, who used to be rich last Sunday ill. by Ray Cruz. Atheneum, 1978. Subj: Money.

I'll fix Anthony ill. by Arnold Lobel. Harper, 1969. Subj: Family life. Sibling rivalry.

My mama says there aren't any zombies, ghosts, vampires, creatures, demons, monsters, fiends, goblins, or things ill. by Kay Chorao. Atheneum, 1973. Subj: Bedtime. Emotions – fear. Family life – mothers. Imagination. Monsters.

Rosie and Michael ill. by Lorna Tomei. Atheneum, 1974. Subj: Friendship.

Sunday morning ill. by Hilary Knight. Harper, 1968. Subj: Activities – playing. Family life. Humor.

The tenth good thing about Barney ill. by Erik Blegvad. Atheneum, 1971. Subj: Animals – cats. Death. Careers – doctors. Pets.

Try it again, Sam: safety when you walk ill. by Paul Galdone. Lothrop, 1970. Subj: Activities – walking. Character traits – individuality. Safety.

Vipont, Charles *see* Foulds, Elfrida Vipont

Vipont, Elfrida *see* Foulds, Elfrida Vipont

A visit to a pond ill. with photos. Imported Pubs., 1983. Subj: Animals. Format, unusual – cardboard pages. Wordless.

Vogel, Carole Garbuny. *The dangers of strangers* by Carole Garbuny Vogel and Kathryn Allen Goldner; ill. by Lynette Schmidt. Dillon, 1983. Subj: Behavior – talking to strangers. Safety.

Vogel, Ilse-Margaret. *The don't be scared book: scares, remedies and pictures* ill. by author. Atheneum, 1964. Subj: Emotions – fear. Imagination. Poetry, rhyme.

Von Hippel, Ursula. *The craziest Halloween* ill. by author. Coward, 1957. Subj: Holidays – Halloween.

Von Jüchen, Aurel *see* Jüchen, Aurel von

Von Storch, Anne B. *see* Malcolmson, Anne

Vreeken, Elizabeth. *The boy who would not say his name* ill. by Leonard W. Shortall. Follett, 1959. Subj: Behavior – lost. Careers – police officers. Imagination. Names.

Henry ill. by Polly Jackson. Follett, 1961. Subj: Animals – mice. Pets.

One day everything went wrong ill. by Leonard W. Shortall. Follett, 1966. Subj: Behavior – bad day.

Waber, Bernard. *An anteater named Arthur* ill. by author. Houghton, 1967. Subj: ABC books. Animals – anteaters.

Bernard ill. by author. Houghton, 1982. Subj: Animals – dogs. Behavior – running away. Behavior – sharing.

But names will never hurt me ill. by author. Houghton, 1976. Subj: Names.

How to go about laying an egg ill. by author. Houghton, 1963. Subj: Birds – chickens. Eggs. Humor.

I was all thumbs ill. by author. Houghton, 1975. Subj: Octopuses. Sea and seashore.

Ira sleeps over ill. by author. Houghton, 1972. Subj: Activities – playing. Bedtime. Friendship. Sleep. Toys – teddy bears.

Just like Abraham Lincoln ill. by author. Houghton, 1964. Subj: U.S. history.

Lorenzo ill. by author. Houghton, 1961. Subj: Character traits – curiosity. Fish.

Lovable Lyle ill. by author. Houghton, 1969. Subj: Friendship. Reptiles – alligators, crocodiles.

Lyle and the birthday party ill. by author. Houghton, 1966. Subj: Birthdays. Emotions – envy, jealousy. Reptiles – alligators, crocodiles.

Lyle finds his mother ill. by author. Houghton, 1974. Subj: Family life – mothers. Reptiles – alligators, crocodiles.

Lyle, Lyle Crocodile ill. by author. Houghton, 1965. Subj: Character traits – helpfulness. Reptiles – alligators, crocodiles.

Mice on my mind ill. by author. Houghton, 1977. Subj: Animals – cats. Animals – mice.

Nobody is perfick ill. by author. Houghton, 1971. Subj: Behavior – mistakes. Friendship. Humor.

Rich cat, poor cat ill. by author. Houghton, 1963. Subj: Animals – cats.

The snake: a very long story ill. by author. Houghton, 1978. Subj: Format, unusual. Reptiles – snakes.

You're a little kid with a big heart ill. by author. Houghton, 1980. Subj: Behavior – growing up. Behavior – wishing. Magic.

Waddell, Helen. *The story of Saul the king* abridged by Elaine Moss from Helen Waddell's Stories from Holy Writ; ill. by Doreen Roberts. White, 1966. Subj: Religion.

Wade, Anne. *A promise is for keeping* ill. by Jon Petersson. Children's Pr., 1979. Subj: Friendship.

Wadsworth, Olive A. *Over in the meadow: a counting-out rhyme* ill. by Mary Maki Rae. Viking, 1985. Subj: Counting. Poetry, rhyme.

Waechter, Friedrich Karl. *Three is company* tr. by Harry Allard; ill. by author. Doubleday, 1980. Subj: Animals – pigs. Birds. Fish. Friendship.

Wagner, Elaine Knox *see* Knox-Wagner, Elaine

Wagner, Jenny. *Aranea: a story about a spider* ill. by Ron Brooks. Bradbury Pr., 1978. Subj: Spiders. Weather – rain.

The bunyip of Berkeley's Creek ill. by Ron Brooks. Bradbury Pr., 1977. Subj: Foreign lands – Australia. Monsters. Mythical creatures.

John Brown, Rose and the midnight cat ill. by Ron Brooks. Bradbury Pr., 1978. Subj: Animals – cats. Animals – dogs.

Wahl, Jan. *Button eye's orange* ill. by Wendy Watson. Warne, 1980. Subj: Handicaps. Toys.

Cabbage moon ill. by Adrienne Adams. Holt, 1965. Subj: Humor. Moon. Royalty.

Carrot nose ill. by James Marshall. Farrar, 1978. Subj: Animals – rabbits.

Doctor Rabbit's foundling ill. by Cyndy Szekeres. Pantheon, 1977. Subj: Animals – rabbits. Careers – doctors. Frogs and toads.

Dracula's cat ill. by Kay Chorao. Prentice-Hall, 1978. Subj: Animals – cats. Monsters.

The fishermen ill. by Emily Arnold McCully. Norton, 1969. Subj: Family life – grandparents, great-grandparents. Sports – fishing.

The five in the forest ill. by Erik Blegvad. Follett, 1974. Subj: Animals – rabbits. Eggs. Forest, woods. Holidays – Easter.

Follow me cried Bee ill. by John Wallner. Crown, 1976. Subj: Cumulative tales. Insects – bees. Poetry, rhyme. Weather – rain.

Frankenstein's dog ill. by Kay Chorao. Prentice-Hall, 1977. Subj: Animals – dogs. Monsters.

Hello, elephant ill. by Edward Ardizzone. Holt, 1964. Subj: Animals – elephants.

Jamie's tiger ill. by Tomie de Paola. Harcourt, 1978. Subj: Handicaps – deafness. Illness. Toys.

The Muffletump storybook ill. by Cyndy Szekeres. Follett, 1975. Subj: Toys – dolls.

The Muffletumps ill. by Edward Ardizzone. Holt, 1966. Subj: Toys – dolls.

The Muffletumps' Christmas party ill. by Cyndy Szekeres. Follett, 1975. Subj: Holidays – Christmas. Toys – dolls.

The Muffletumps' Halloween scare ill. by Cyndy Szekeres. Follett, 1977. Subj: Toys – dolls.

Old Hippo's Easter egg ill. by Lorinda Bryan Cauley. Harcourt, 1980. Subj: Animals – hippopotami. Animals – mice. Birds – ducks. Emotions – love. Family life.

Peter and the troll baby ill. by Erik Blegvad. Golden Pr., 1984. Subj: Activities – babysitting. Sibling rivalry. Trolls.

Pleasant Fieldmouse ill. by Maurice Sendak. Harper, 1964. Subj: Animals. Animals – mice.

The Pleasant Fieldmouse storybook ill. by Erik Blegvad. Prentice-Hall, 1977. Subj: Animals. Animals – mice.

Pleasant Fieldmouse's Halloween party ill. by Wallace Tripp. Putnam, 1974. Subj: Animals. Animals – mice. Holidays – Halloween.

Push Kitty ill. by Garth Williams. Harper, 1968. Subj: Activities – playing. Animals – cats.

Sylvester Bear overslept ill. by Lee Lorenz. Parents, 1979. Subj: Animals – bears. Circus. Family life. Sleep.

Tiger watch ill. by Charles Mikolaycak. Harcourt, 1982. Subj: Animals – tigers. Death. Foreign lands – India. Sports – hunting.

The woman with the eggs (Andersen, H C (Hans Christian))

Wakefield, Joyce. *Ask a silly question* ill. by Mike Venezia. Children's Pr., 1979. Subj: Poetry, rhyme. Riddles.

From where you are ill. by Tom Dunnington. Children's Pr., 1978. Subj: Concepts – perspective. Poetry, rhyme.

Walker, Barbara K. *New patches for old: a Turkish folktale* retold by Barbara K. Walker and Ahmet E. Uysal; ill. by Harold Berson. Parents, 1974. Subj: Behavior – mistakes. Folk and fairy tales.

Pigs and pirates: a Greek tale ill. by Harold Berson. White, 1969. Subj: Animals – pigs. Foreign lands – Greece. Pirates.

Teeny-Tiny and the witch-woman ill. by Michael Foreman. Pantheon, 1975. Subj: Character traits – cleverness. Foreign lands – Turkey. Witches.

Wallace, Daisy. *Ghost poems* ill. by Tomie de Paola. Holiday, 1979. Subj: Ghosts. Night. Poetry, rhyme.

Wallace, Ian. *Chin Chiang and the dragon's dance* ill. by author. Atheneum, 1984. Subj: Emotions – fear. Ethnic groups in the U.S. – Chinese-Americans. Family life – grandparents, great-grandparents. Holidays – Chinese New Year.

Wallas, Ada. *Clean Peter and the children of Grubbylea* (Adelborg, Ottilia)

Wallner, Alexandra. *Munch* ill. by author. Crown, 1976. Subj: Food. Poetry, rhyme.

Walsh, Jill Paton. *Lost and found* ill. by Mary Rayner. Deutsch (dist. by Dutton), 1985. Subj: Behavior – losing things. Character traits – luck. Family life – grandparents, great-grandparents.

Walt Disney Productions. *Tod and Copper.* Random House, 1981. Subj: Animals – dogs. Animals – foxes.

Tod and Vixey. Random House, 1981. Subj: Animals – dogs. Animals – foxes.

Walt Disney's Snow White and the seven dwarfs. Viking, 1979. Subj: Elves and little people. Emotions – envy, jealousy. Folk and fairy tales. Magic. Witches.

Walt Disney's The adventures of Mr. Toad. Random House, 1981. Subj: Animals – moles. Animals – rats. Frogs and toads.

Walter, Mildred Pitts. *My mama needs me* ill. by Pat Cummings. Lothrop, 1983. Subj: Emotions – loneliness. Ethnic groups in the U.S. – Afro-Americans. Family life.

Walter, Villiam Christian *see* Andersen, H. C. (Hans Christian)

Walters, Marguerite. *The city-country ABC: My alphabet walk in the country, and My alphabet ride in the city* ill. by Ib Ohlsson. Doubleday, 1966. The two stories are bound dos-á-dos. Subj: ABC books. City. Country. Format, unusual.

Warbler, J. M. *see* Cocagnac, A. M.

Ward, Andrew. *Baby bear and the long sleep* ill. by John Walsh. Little, 1980. Subj: Animals – bears. Hibernation. Seasons – winter.

Ward, Leila. *I am eyes, ni macho* ill. by Nonny Hogrogian. Greenwillow, 1978. Subj: Foreign lands – Africa. Nature.

Ward, Lynd. *The biggest bear* ill. by author. Houghton, 1952. Subj: Animals – bears. Caldecott award book. Character traits – kindness to animals. Foreign lands – Canada. Pets.

The little red lighthouse and the great gray bridge (Swift, Hildegarde Hoyt)

Nic of the woods ill. by author. Houghton, 1965. Subj: Animals. Animals – dogs. Foreign lands – Canada. Forest, woods.

The silver pony ill. by author. Houghton, 1973. Subj: Animals – horses. Dreams. Wordless.

Ward, May McNeer *see* McNeer, May Yonge

Ward, Nanda Weedon. *The black sombrero* ill. by Lynd Ward. Ariel, 1952. Subj: Animals. Clothing. Cowboys.

The elephant that ga-lumphed by Nanda Weedon Ward and Robert Haynes; ill. by Robert Haynes. Ariel, 1959. Subj: Animals. Animals – elephants. Foreign lands – India.

Ward, Nick. *Giant.* Oxford Univ. Pr., 1983. Subj: Behavior – misbehavior. Giants. Toys.

Warren, Cathy. *The ten-alarm camp-out* ill. by Steven Kellogg. Lothrop, 1983. Subj: Counting. Sports – camping.

Warren, Elizabeth *see* Supraner, Robyn

Warshofsky, Isaac *see* Singer, Isaac Bashevis

Wasmuth, Eleanor. *An alligator day* ill. by author. Grosset, 1983. Subj: Activities – playing. Reptiles – alligators, crocodiles.

The picnic basket ill. by author. Grosset, 1983. Subj: Activities – picnicking. Food. Reptiles – alligators, crocodiles.

Wasserberg, Esther. *Grandmother dear* (Finfer, Celentha)

Wasson, Valentina Pavlovna. *The chosen baby* ill. by Glo Coalson. Rev. ed. Lippincott, 1977. Subj: Adoption.

Watanabe, Shigeo. *How do I put it on?* ill. by Yasuo Ohtomo. Putnam's, 1979. Subj: Animals – bears. Clothing. Participation.

I can build a house! ill. by Yasuo Ohtomo. Putnam's, 1983. Subj: Animals – bears. Character traits – perseverance. Houses.

I can ride it! ill. by Yasuo Ohtomo. Putnam's, 1982. Subj: Activities – playing. Animals – bears. Character traits – perseverance.

I can take a walk! ill. by Yasuo Ohtomo. Putnam's, 1984. Subj: Activities – walking. Animals – bears.

I'm the king of the castle! ill. by Yasuo Ohtomo. Putnam's, 1982. Subj: Activities – playing. Animals – bears. Sand.

What a good lunch! ill. by Yasuo Ohtomo. Collins-World, 1980. Subj: Animals – bears. Food. Humor.

Where's my daddy? ill. by Yasuo Ohtomo. Putnam's, 1982. Subj: Animals – bears. Character traits – perseverance. Family life – fathers.

Watanabe, Yuichi. *Wally the whale who loved balloons* tr. from Japanese by D. T. Ooka; ill. by author. Heian, 1982. Subj: Animals – whales. Behavior – misbehavior. Toys – balloons.

Waterton, Betty. *A salmon for Simon* ill. by Ann Blades. Atheneum, 1980. Subj: Character traits – kindness to animals. Sports – fishing.

Watson, Carol. *Æsop's fables* (Æsop)

Opposites ill. by David Higham. Usborne, 1983. Subj: Concepts – opposites.

Shapes ill. by David Higham. Usborne, 1983. Subj: Concepts – shape.

Sizes ill. by David Higham. Usborne, 1983. Subj: Concepts – size.

Watson, Clyde. *Applebet: an ABC* ill. by Wendy Watson. Farrar, 1982. Subj: ABC books. Poetry, rhyme.

Catch me and kiss me and say it again ill. by Wendy Watson. Collins-World, 1978. Subj: Family life. Poetry, rhyme.

Father Fox's feast of songs ill. by Wendy Watson. Putnam's, 1983. Subj: Animals – foxes. Music. Poetry, rhyme.

Father Fox's pennyrhymes ill. by Wendy Watson. Crowell, 1971. Subj: Nursery rhymes.

Fisherman lullabies ed. and ill. by Wendy Watson; music by Clyde Watson. Collins-World, 1968. Subj: Bedtime. Music. Songs.

Hickory stick rag ill. by Wendy Watson. Crowell, 1976. Subj: Activities – picnicking. Humor. Poetry, rhyme. School.

How Brown Mouse kept Christmas ill. by Wendy Watson. Farrar, 1980. Subj: Animals – mice. Holidays – Christmas.

Midnight moon ill. by Susanna Natti. Collins-World, 1979. Subj: Activities – flying. Bedtime. Imagination. Moon.

Tom Fox and the apple pie ill. by Wendy Watson. Crowell, 1972. Subj: Animals – foxes. Behavior – sharing. Fairs. Food.

Watson, Jane Werner. *My friend the babysitter* by Jane Werner Watson, Robert E. Switzer and J. Cotter Hirschberg; ill. by Hilde Hoffmann. Golden Pr., 1971. Subj: Activities – babysitting.

Sometimes I get angry by Jane Werner Watson, Robert E. Switzer and J. Cotter Hirschberg; ill. by Hilde Hoffmann. Golden Pr., 1971. Subj: Emotions – anger.

Sometimes I'm afraid by Jane Werner Watson, Robert E. Switzer and J. Cotter Hirschberg; ill. by Hilde Hoffmann. Golden Pr., 1971. Subj: Emotions – fear.

The tall book of make-believe ill. by Garth Williams. Harper, 1950. Subj: Imagination. Poetry, rhyme.

Which is the witch? ill. by Victoria Chess. Pantheon, 1979. Subj: Holidays – Halloween. Witches.

Watson, Nancy Dingman. *The birthday goat* ill. by Wendy Watson. Crowell, 1974. Subj: Animals – goats. Birthdays. Crime. Fairs.

Sugar on snow ill. by Aldren Auld Watson. Viking, 1964. Subj: Food. Weather – snow.

Tommy's mommy's fish ill. by Aldren Auld Watson. Viking, 1971. Subj: Birthdays. Family life – mothers. Sports – fishing.

What does A begin with? ill. by Aldren Auld Watson. Knopf, 1956. Subj: ABC books. Farms.

What is one? ill. by Aldren Auld Watson. Knopf, 1954. Subj: Counting. Farms.

When is tomorrow? ill. by Aldren Auld Watson. Knopf, 1955. Subj: Sea and seashore. Time.

Watson, Pauline. *Curley Cat baby-sits* ill. by Lorinda Bryan Cauley. Harcourt, 1977. Subj: Activities – babysitting. Animals – cats.

Days with Daddy ill. by Joanne Scribner. Prentice-Hall, 1977. Subj: Family life. Family life – fathers.

Wriggles, the little wishing pig ill. by Paul Galdone. Seabury Pr., 1978. Subj: Animals – pigs. Behavior – wishing. Monsters.

Watson, Wendy. *The bunnies' Christmas eve* ill. by author. Putnam's, 1983. Subj: Animals – rabbits. Format, unusual. Holidays – Christmas.

Fisherman lullabies (Watson, Clyde)

Has winter come? ill. by author. Collins-World, 1978. Subj: Animals – groundhogs. Hibernation. Seasons – winter.

Lollipop ill. by author. Crowell, 1976. Subj: Animals – rabbits. Behavior – misbehavior.

Moving ill. by author. Crowell, 1978. Subj: Moving.

Watts, Bernadette *see* Bernadette

Watts, Mabel. *The day it rained watermelons* ill. by Lee Albertson. Lantern Pr., 1964. Subj: Behavior – indifference.

Something for you, something for me ill. by Abner Graboff. Abelard-Schuman, 1960. Subj: Activities – trading. Behavior – sharing.

Weeks and weeks ill. by Abner Graboff. Abelard-Schuman, 1962. Subj: Activities – photographing.

Watts, Marjorie-Ann. *Crocodile medicine* ill. by author. Warne, 1978. Subj: Behavior – boredom. Hospitals. Illness. Reptiles – alligators, crocodiles.

Zebra goes to school ill. by author. Elsevier-Dutton, 1981. Subj: Imagination – imaginary friends. School.

Weary, Ogdred *see* Gorey, Edward

Webb, Clifford. *The story of Noah* ill. by author. Warne, 1949. Subj: Religion – Noah.

Weber, Alfons. *Elizabeth gets well* ill. by Jacqueline Blass. Crowell, 1970. Translation of Elisabeth wird gesund. Subj: Hospitals. Illness.

Weelen, Guy. *The little red train* ill. by Mamoru Funai. Lothrop, 1966. Subj: Foreign lands – France. Trains.

Wegen, Ron. *The balloon trip* ill. by author. Houghton, 1981. Subj: Activities – ballooning. Family life. Wordless.

Billy Gorilla ill. by author. Lothrop, 1983. Subj: Behavior – trickery. Holidays – April Fools' Day.

The Halloween costume party ill. by author. Houghton, 1983. Subj: Holidays – Halloween. Parties.

Sand castle ill. by author. Greenwillow, 1977. Subj: Sea and seashore.

Sky dragon ill. by author. Greenwillow, 1982. Subj: Weather – clouds.

Where can the animals go? ill. by author. Greenwillow, 1978. Subj: Animals. Ecology.

Weihs, Erika. *Count the cats* ill. by author. Doubleday, 1976. Subj: Animals – cats. Counting.

Weil, Ann. *Animal families* ill. by Roger Vernam. Children's Pr., 1956. Subj: Animals.

Weil, Lisl. *The candy egg bunny* ill. by author. Holiday, 1975. Subj: Animals – rabbits. Holidays – Easter. Witches.

Gertie and Gus ill. by author. Parents, 1977. Subj: Careers – fishermen. Family life.

Gillie and the flattering fox ill. by author. Atheneum, 1978. Subj: Animals – foxes. Birds – chickens. Friendship.

Mother Goose picture riddles: a book of rebuses ill. by author. Holiday, 1981. Subj: Nursery rhymes. Rebuses.

Owl and other scrambles ill. by author. Dutton, 1980. Subj: Games. Participation.

The story of the Wise Men and the Child ill. by author. Atheneum, 1981. Subj: Holidays – Christmas. Religion.

To sail a ship of treasures ill. by author. Atheneum, 1984. Subj: Behavior – collecting things.

The very first story ever told ill. by author. Atheneum, 1976. Subj: Religion.

Weilerstein, Sadie Rose. *The best of K'tonton* ill. by Marilyn Hirsh. Jewish Pub. Soc., 1980. Subj: Jewish culture.

Weinberg, Florence. *Grandmother dear* (Finfer, Celentha)

Weiner, Beth Lee. *Benjamin's perfect solution* ill. by author. Warner, 1979. Subj: Animals – porcupines. Animals – possums. Behavior – mistakes. Self-concept.

Weisgard, Leonard. *The funny bunny factory* ill. by author. Grosset, 1950. Subj: Animals – rabbits. Holidays – Easter.

Mr. Peaceable paints ill. by author. Scribner's, 1956. Subj: Activities – painting. Careers – artists.

Silly Willy Nilly ill. by author. Scribner's, 1953. Subj: Animals – elephants. Behavior – forgetfulness.

Who dreams of cheese? ill. by author. Scribner's, 1950. Subj: Behavior – wishing. Dreams. Sleep.

Weiss, Ellen. *Clara the fortune-telling chicken* ill. by author. Dutton, 1978. Subj: Animals – sheep. Birds – chickens. Careers – fortune tellers. Seasons – winter.

Millicent Maybe ill. by author. Watts, 1979. Subj: Reptiles – alligators, crocodiles.

Pigs in space ill. by Alastair Graham. Random House, 1983. Subj: Animals – pigs. Puppets. Space and space ships.

Things to make and do for Christmas ill. by author. Watts, 1980. Subj: Holidays – Christmas.

You are the star of a Muppet adventure ill. by Benjamin Alexander. Random House, 1983. Subj: Puppets.

Weiss, Harvey. *My closet full of hats* ill. by author. Abelard-Schuman, 1962. Subj: Clothing.

The sooner hound: a tale from American folklore ill. by author. Putnam's, 1959. Subj: Animals – dogs. Careers – firefighters. Folk and fairy tales.

Weiss, Leatie. *Funny feet!* ill. by Ellen Weiss. Watts, 1978. Subj: Anatomy. Birds – penguins. Clothing.

Weiss, Miriam *see* Schlein, Miriam

Weiss, Nicki. *Maude and Sally* ill. by author. Greenwillow, 1983. Subj: Friendship.

Waiting ill. by author. Greenwillow, 1981. Subj: Character traits – patience.

Weekend at Muskrat Lake ill. by author. Greenwillow, 1984. Subj: Activities – vacationing. Family life.

Weissmann, Joe. *Hickory dickory duck:* (Patterson, Pat)

Welber, Robert. *Goodbye, hello* ill. by Cyndy Szekeres. Pantheon, 1974. Subj: Animals. Behavior – growing up. Poetry, rhyme. School.

Song of the seasons ill. by Deborah Kogan Ray. Pantheon, 1973. Subj: Seasons.

Welch, Martha McKeen. *Will that wake mother?* photos. by author. Dodd, 1982. Subj: Animals – cats.

Wellington, Anne. *Apple pie* ill. by Nita Sowter. Prentice-Hall, 1978. Subj: Seasons.

Wells, H. G. (Herbert George). *The adventures of Tommy* ill. by author. Knopf, 1967. Subj: Animals – elephants. Character traits – bravery. Character traits – kindness.

Wells, Rosemary. *Don't spill it again, James* ill. by author. Dial Pr., 1977. Subj: Animals – foxes. Poetry, rhyme. Trains. Weather – rain.

Good night, Fred ill. by author. Dial Pr., 1981. Subj: Behavior – misbehavior. Imagination. Sibling rivalry.

A lion for Lewis ill. by author. Dial Pr., 1982. Subj: Activities – playing. Imagination.

Max's breakfast ill. by author. Dial Pr., 1985. Subj: Animals – rabbits. Character traits – patience. Format, unusual – cardboard pages. Sibling rivalry.

Max's new suit ill. by author. Dial Pr., 1979. Subj: Animals – rabbits. Clothing. Format, unusual – cardboard pages.

Noisy Nora ill. by author. Dial Pr., 1973. Subj: Animals – mice. Behavior – needing someone. Poetry, rhyme.

Peabody ill. by author. Dial Pr., 1983. Subj: Sibling rivalry. Toys – dolls.

Stanley and Rhoda ill. by author. Dial Pr., 1978. Subj: Activities – babysitting. Animals – mice. Sibling rivalry.

Timothy goes to school ill. by author. Dial Pr., 1981. Subj: Animals – raccoons. Behavior – growing up. School.

Unfortunately Harriet ill. by author. Dial Pr., 1972. Subj: Behavior – bad day.

Wende, Philip. *Bird boy* ill. by author. Cowles, 1970. Subj: Activities – flying. Dreams.

Wenning, Elisabeth. *The Christmas mouse* ill. by Barbara Remington. Holt, 1959. Subj: Animals – mice. Holidays – Christmas. Music. Songs.

Werner, Jane *see* Watson, Jane Werner

Wersba, Barbara. *Amanda dreaming* ill. by Mercer Mayer. Atheneum, 1973. Subj: Dreams. Sleep.

Do tigers ever bite kings? ill. by Mario Rivoli. Atheneum, 1966. Subj: Animals – tigers. Character traits – kindness to animals. Poetry, rhyme. Royalty.

Werth, Kurt. *Lazy Jack* ill. by author. Viking, 1970. Subj: Character traits – laziness. Cumulative tales. Folk and fairy tales.

West, Emily *see* Payne, Emmy

West, Ian. *Silas, the first pig to fly* ill. by author. Grosset, 1977. Subj: Activities – flying. Animals – pigs.

West, James *see* Withers, Carl

Westcott, Nadine Bernard. *The giant vegetable garden* ill. by author. Little, 1981. Subj: Activities – gardening. Activities – picnicking.

Westerberg, Christine. *The cap that mother made* ill. by adapt. Prentice-Hall, 1977. Subj: Clothing. Folk and fairy tales. Foreign lands – Sweden.

Weston, Martha. *Peony's rainbow* ill. by author. Lothrop, 1981. Subj: Animals – pigs. Weather – rainbows.

Wetterer, Margaret. *Patrick and the fairy thief* ill. by Enrico Arno. Atheneum, 1980. Subj: Character traits – cleverness. Fairies. Family life – mothers.

Wexler, Jerome. *Find the hidden insect* (Cole, Joanna)

Weygant, Noemi. *It's autumn!* photos. by author. Westminster Pr., 1968. Subj: Poetry, rhyme. Seasons – fall.

It's summer! photos. by author. Westminster Pr., 1970. Subj: Poetry, rhyme. Seasons – summer.

It's winter! photos. by author. Westminster Pr., 1969. Subj: Poetry, rhyme. Seasons – winter.

Wezel, Peter. *The good bird* ill. by author. Harper, 1964. Subj: Behavior – sharing. Birds. Fish. Wordless.

The naughty bird ill. by author. Follett, 1967. Translation of Der freche Vogel Figaro. Subj: Animals – cats. Birds. Wordless.

What do you feed your donkey on? *Rhymes from a Belfast childhood* col. by Colette O'Hare; ill. by Jenny Rodwell. Collins-World, 1978. Subj: Foreign lands – Ireland. Nursery rhymes. Poetry, rhyme.

Wheeler, Cindy. *Marmalade's nap* ill. by author. Knopf, 1983. Subj: Animals – cats. Noise, sounds. Sleep.

Marmalade's picnic ill. by author. Knopf, 1983. Subj: Activities – picnicking. Animals – cats.

Marmalade's snowy day ill. by author. Knopf, 1982. Subj: Animals – cats. Weather – snow.

Marmalade's yellow leaf ill. by author. Knopf, 1982. Subj: Animals – cats. Seasons – fall.

Wheeler, M. J. *First came the Indians* ill. by James Houston. Atheneum, 1983. Subj: Ethnic groups in the U.S. – Indians.

Wheeler, Opal. *Sing in praise: a collection of the best loved hymns* ill. by Marjorie Torrey. Dutton, 1946. Subj: Caldecott award honor book. Music. Religion. Songs.

Sing Mother Goose ill. by Marjorie Torrey; music by Opal Wheeler. Dutton, 1945. Subj: Caldecott award honor book. Music. Nursery rhymes. Songs.

Wheeler, William A. *Mother Goose's melodies* (Mother Goose)

Wheeling, Lynn. *When you fly* ill. by author. Little, 1967. Subj: Activities – flying. Airplanes, airports. Poetry, rhyme.

White, Anne Terry. *Æsop's fables* (Æsop)

White, Florence Meiman. *How to lose your lunch money* ill. by Chris Jenkyns. Ritchie, 1970. Subj: Behavior – losing things. Behavior – misbehavior. School.

White, Laurence B. *Science toys and tricks* by Laurence B. White, Jr.; ill. by Marc Brown. Addison-Wesley, 1981. Subj: Science. Toys.

White, Paul. *Janet at school* photos. by Jeremy Finlay. Crowell, 1978. Subj: Handicaps. School.

Whitehead, Patricia. *Monkeys* ill. by Bert Dodson. Troll Assoc., 1982. Subj: Animals – monkeys.

Whiteside, Karen. *Lullaby of the wind* ill. by Kazue Mizumura. Harper, 1984. Subj: Bedtime. Weather – wind.

Whitlock, Ralph. *Penguins* ill. with photos. Raintree, 1978. Subj: Birds – penguins.

Whitney, Alex. *Once a bright red tiger* ill. by Charles Robinson. Walck, 1973. Subj: Animals – tigers. Character traits – pride.

The tiger that barks: the true picture story of Mohan and his friends photos. by Beverly Ecker. McKay, 1978. Subj: Animals – dogs. Animals – tigers. Family life.

Whitney, Alma Marshak. *Just awful* ill. by Lillian Hoban. Addison-Wesley, 1971. Subj: Careers – nurses. Illness. School.

Leave Herbert alone ill. by David McPhail. Addison-Wesley, 1972. Subj: Animals – cats. Character traits – kindness to animals.

Widdecombe Fair: *an old English folk song* ill. by Christine Price. Warne, 1968. Subj: Fairs. Folk and fairy tales. Foreign lands – England. Music. Songs.

Wiese, Kurt. *The cunning turtle* ill. by author. Viking, 1956. Subj: Reptiles – turtles.

The dog, the fox and the fleas ill. by author. McKay, 1953. Subj: Animals – dogs. Animals – foxes. Insects – fleas.

Fish in the air ill. by author. Viking, 1948. Subj: Caldecott award honor book. Foreign lands – China. Humor. Kites.

The five Chinese brothers (Bishop, Claire Huchet)

Happy Easter ill. by author. Viking, 1952. Subj: Animals – rabbits. Holidays – Easter.

The story about Ping (Flack, Marjorie)

The thief in the attic ill. by author. Viking, 1965. Subj: Animals. Trees.

You can write Chinese ill. by author. Viking, 1945. Subj: Caldecott award honor book. Foreign languages.

Wiesenthal, Eleanor. *Let's find out about Eskimos* by Eleanor and Ted Wiesenthal; ill. by Allan Eitzen. Watts, 1969. Subj: Ethnic groups in the U.S. – Eskimos.

Wiesner, William. *Happy-Go-Lucky: a Norwegian tale* ill. by author. Seabury Pr., 1970. Subj: Character traits – optimism. Cumulative tales. Farms. Foreign lands – Norway. Humor.

Noah's ark ill. by author. Dutton, 1966. Subj: Religion – Noah.

Tops ill. by author. Viking, 1969. Subj: Friendship. Giants. Violence, anti-violence.

The Tower of Babel ill. by author. Viking, 1968. "Based on the book of Genesis and on commentaries ... in the book Hebrew myths by Robert Graves and Raphael Patai." Subj: Language. Religion.

Turnabout: a Norwegian tale ill. by author. Seabury Pr., 1972. "This text has been adapted from the version of Edouard Laboulaye." Subj: Behavior – dissatisfaction. Foreign lands – Norway. Humor.

Wikland, Ilon. *Christmas in noisy village* (Lindgren, Astrid)

Wilcox, Daniel. *The Sesame Street ABC storybook* (Moss, Jeffrey)

Wild, Jocelyn. *The bears' ABC book* (Wild, Robin)

The bears' counting book (Wild, Robin)

Little Pig and the big bad wolf (Wild, Robin)

Spot's dogs and the alley cats (Wild, Robin)

Wild, Robin. *The bears' ABC book* by Robin and Jocelyn Wild; ill. by authors. Lippincott, 1978. Subj: ABC books. Animals – bears.

The bears' counting book by Robin and Jocelyn Wild; ill. by authors. Lippincott, 1978. Subj: Animals – bears. Counting.

Little Pig and the big bad wolf by Robin and Jocelyn Wild; ill. by authors. Coward, 1972. Subj: Animals – pigs. Animals – wolves. Character traits – cleverness. Holidays – Christmas. Poetry, rhyme.

Spot's dogs and the alley cats by Robin and Jocelyn Wild; ill. by authors. Lippincott, 1979. Subj: Animals – cats. Animals – dogs. Behavior – trickery.

Wildsmith, Brian. *Animal games* ill. by author. Oxford Univ. Pr., 1980. Subj: Animals. Games.

Animal homes ill. by author. Oxford Univ. Pr., 1980. Subj: Animals. Houses.

Animal shapes ill. by author. Oxford Univ. Pr., 1980. Subj: Animals. Concepts – shape.

Animal tricks ill. by author. Oxford Univ. Pr., 1980. Subj: Animals. Poetry, rhyme.

Bear's adventure ill. by author. Pantheon, 1982. Subj: Activities – ballooning. Animals – bears.

Brian Wildsmith's birds ill. by author. Watts, 1967. Subj: Birds.

Brian Wildsmith's circus ill. by author. Watts, 1970. Subj: Circus.

Brian Wildsmith's fishes ill. by author. Watts, 1968. Subj: Fish.

Brian Wildsmith's puzzles ill. by author. Watts, 1970. Subj: Games.

Brian Wildsmith's wild animals ill. by author. Watts, 1967. Subj: Animals.

Daisy ill. by author. Pantheon, 1984. Subj: Animals – bulls, cows. Behavior – running away.

Hunter and his dog ill. by author. Oxford Univ. Pr., 1979. Subj: Animals – dogs. Character traits – kindness to animals. Sports – hunting.

The lazy bear ill. by author. Watts, 1974. Subj: Animals – bears. Character traits – laziness. Friendship.

The little wood duck ill. by author. Watts, 1972. Subj: Birds – ducks.

The miller, the boy and the donkey (La Fontaine, Jean de)

The owl and the woodpecker ill. by author. Watts, 1971. Subj: Birds – owls. Birds – woodpeckers. Character traits – compromising.

Pelican ill. by author. Pantheon, 1983. Subj: Birds – pelicans. Sports – fishing.

Python's party ill. by author. Watts, 1975. Subj: Animals. Behavior – trickery. Reptiles – snakes.

Seasons ill. by author. Oxford Univ. Pr., 1980. Subj: Nature. Seasons.

The true cross ill. by author. Oxford Univ. Pr., 1977. Subj: Folk and fairy tales.

What the moon saw ill. by author. Oxford Univ. Pr., 1978. Subj: Animals. Concepts – opposites. Language. Moon. Sun.

Wilhelm, Hans. *A new home, a new friend* ill. by author. Random House, 1985. Subj: Animals – dogs. Family life. Friendship. Moving.

Wilkins, Mary Huiskamp Calhoun *see* Calhoun, Mary

Wilkinson, Sylvia. *Automobiles* ill. with photos. Children's Pr., 1982. Subj: Automobiles.

Will *see* Lipkind, William

Willard, Barbara. *To London! To London!* ill. by Antony Maitland. Weybright and Talley, 1968. Subj: Foreign lands – England.

Willard, Nancy. *The nightgown of the sullen moon* ill. by David McPhail. Harcourt, 1983. Subj: Moon. Night.

Simple pictures are best ill. by Tomie de Paola. Harcourt, 1977. Subj: Activities – photographing. Humor.

A visit to William Blake's inn: poems for innocent and experienced travelers ill. by Alice and Martin Provensen. Harcourt, 1981. Subj: Caldecott award honor book. Imagination. Poetry, rhyme.

Williams, Barbara. *Albert's toothache* ill. by Kay Chorao. Dutton, 1974. Subj: Illness. Reptiles – turtles. Teeth.

Chester Chipmunk's Thanksgiving ill. by Kay Chorao. Dutton, 1974. Subj: Animals – chipmunks. Holidays – Thanksgiving.

Hello, dandelions! photos. by author. Holt, 1979. Subj: Flowers. Plants.

I know a salesperson ill. by Frank Aloise. Putnam's, 1978. Subj: Careers. Stores.

If he's my brother ill. by Tomie de Paola. Harvey House, 1976. Subj: Character traits – questioning. Family life.

Jeremy isn't hungry ill. by Martha G. Alexander. Dutton, 1978. Subj: Activities – babysitting. Babies. Humor.

Kevin's grandma ill. by Kay Chorao. Dutton, 1975. Subj: Family life – grandparents, great-grandparents. Friendship.

So what if I'm a sore loser? ill. by Linda Strauss Edwards. Harcourt, 1981. Subj: Character traits – conceit. Family life.

Someday, said Mitchell ill. by Kay Chorao. Dutton, 1976. Subj: Behavior – wishing. Character traits – helpfulness. Character traits – smallness. Emotions – happiness.

Whatever happened to Beverly Bigler's birthday? ill. by Emily Arnold McCully. Harcourt, 1979. Subj: Behavior – misbehavior. Birthdays. Weddings.

Williams, Charles *see* Collier, James Lincoln

Williams, Garth. *The big golden animal ABC* ill. by author. Simon and Schuster, 1957. First published under the title: The golden animal A.B.C. Subj: ABC books. Animals.

The chicken book ill. by author. Delacorte Pr., 1970. Subj: Birds – chickens. Counting. Poetry, rhyme.

The rabbits' wedding ill. by author. Harper, 1958. Subj: Animals – rabbits. Weddings.

Williams, Gweneira Maureen. *Timid Timothy, the kitten who learned to be brave* ill. by Leonard Weisgard. Addison-Wesley, 1944. Subj: Food. Science. Emotions – fear.

Williams, Jay. *The city witch and the country witch* ill. by Ed Renfro. Macmillan, 1979. Subj: Activities – vacationing. City. Country. Witches.

Everyone knows what a dragon looks like ill. by Mercer Mayer. Four Winds Pr., 1976. Subj: Dragons. Foreign lands – China.

I wish I had another name by Jay Williams and Winifred Lubell; ill. by authors. Atheneum, 1962. Subj: Names. Poetry, rhyme.

Petronella ill. by Friso Henstra. Parents, 1973. Subj: Folk and fairy tales.

The practical princess ill. by Friso Henstra. Parents, 1969. Subj: Folk and fairy tales. Royalty.

School for sillies ill. by Friso Henstra. Parents, 1969. Subj: Character traits – cleverness. Humor. Royalty.

The surprising things Maui did ill. by Charles Mikolaycak. Four Winds Pr., 1980. Subj: Folk and fairy tales. Hawaii.

Williams, Jenny. *A wet Monday* (Edwards, Dorothy)

Williams, Leslie. *A bear in the air* ill. by Carme Solé Vendrell. Stemmer House, 1980. Subj: Animals – bears. Weather – clouds. Weather – rainbows.

Williams, Margery *see* Bianco, Margery Willimas

Williams, Vera B. *A chair for my mother* ill. by author. Greenwillow, 1982. Subj: Behavior – seeking better things. Caldecott award honor book. Family life.

Music, music for everyone ill. by author. Greenwillow, 1984. Subj: Family life. Family life – grandparents, great-grandparents. Illness. Music.

Something special for me ill. by author. Greenwillow, 1983. Subj: Birthdays. Family life.

Three days on a river in a red canoe ill. by author. Greenwillow, 1981. Subj: Boats, ships. Sports – camping.

Williamson, Hamilton. *Little elephant* ill. by Berta and Elmer Hader. Doubleday, 1930. Subj: Animals – elephants.

Monkey tale ill. by Berta and Elmer Hader. Doubleday, 1929. Subj: Animals – monkeys.

Williamson, Mel. *Walk on!* by Mel Williamson and George Ford; ill. by authors. Third Pr., 1972. Subj: City. Ethnic groups in the U.S. – Afro-Americans.

Williamson, Stan. *The no-bark dog* ill. by Tom O'Sullivan. Follett, 1962. Subj: Animals – dogs. Ethnic groups in the U.S. – Afro-Americans.

Willis, Jeanne. *The tale of Georgie Grub* ill. by Margaret Chamberlain. Holt, 1982. Subj: Activities – bathing. Character traits – cleanliness.

Willoughby, Elaine Macmann. *Boris and the monsters* ill. by Lynn Munsinger. Houghton, 1980. Subj: Animals – dogs. Monsters.

Wilson, Barbara. *ABC et/and 123* ill. by Gisèle Daigle. Fitzhenry and Whiteside, 1981. Subj: ABC books. Counting. Foreign languages.

Wilson, Christopher Bernard. *Hobnob* ill. by William Wiesner. Viking, 1968. Subj: Behavior – sharing.

Wilson, Joyce Lancaster. *Tobi* ill. by Anne Thiess. Funk and Wagnalls, 1968. Subj: Animals – cats.

Wilson, Julia. *Becky* ill. by John Wilson. Crowell, 1966. Subj: Character traits – honesty. Ethnic groups in the U.S. – Afro-Americans. Toys – dolls.

Winn, Marie. *The man who made fine tops* ill. by John E. Johnson; educational consultant: Helen F. Robison. Simon and Schuster, 1970. Subj: Careers.

Winston, Clara. *Thumbelina* (Andersen, H C (Hans Christian))

Winston, Richard. *Thumbelina* (Andersen, H C (Hans Christian))

Winter, Jeanette. *The girl and the moon man: a Siberian folktale* ill. by author. Pantheon, 1984. Subj: Animals. Folk and fairy tales. Foreign lands – Russia. Moon. Music.

Winter, Paula. *The bear and the fly* ill. by author. Crown, 1976. Subj: Animals – bears. Insects – flies. Wordless.

Sir Andrew ill. by author. Crown, 1980. Subj: Animals – donkeys. Character traits – vanity. Wordless.

Winteringham, Victoria. *Penguin day* ill. by author. Harper, 1982. Subj: Activities. Birds – penguins.

Winthrop, Elizabeth. *Bunk beds* ill. by Ronald Himler. Harper, 1972. Subj: Activities – playing. Bedtime. Family life. Imagination.

A child is born: the Christmas story adapt. from the New Testament; ill. by Charles Mikolaycak. Holiday, 1983. Subj: Holidays – Christmas. Religion.

I think he likes me ill. by Denise Saldutti. Harper, 1980. Subj: Family life. Sibling rivalry.

Katharine's doll ill. by Marylin Hafner. Dutton, 1983. Subj: Friendship. Toys – dolls.

Potbellied possums ill. by Barbara McClintock. Holiday, 1977. Subj: Animals – possums. Emotions – fear. Food. Night.

Sloppy kisses ill. by Anne Burgess. Macmillan, 1980. Subj: Animals – pigs. Friendship.

That's mine ill. by Emily Arnold McCully. Holiday House, 1977. Subj: Activities – playing. Behavior – fighting, arguing. Behavior – greed. Behavior – sharing. Sibling rivalry. Toys – blocks.

Tough Eddie ill. by Lillian Hoban. Dutton, 1985. Subj: Character traits – pride. School.

Wirt, Donna Aaron. *My favorite place* (Sargent, Susan)

Wirth, Beverly. *Margie and me* ill. by Karen Ann Weinhaus. Four Winds Pr., 1983. Subj: Animals – dogs. Pets.

Wisbeski, Dorothy Gross. *Pícaro, a pet otter* ill. by Edna Miller. Hawthorn, 1971. Subj: Animals – otters. Pets.

Wise, William. *The cowboy surprise* ill. by Paul Galdone. Putnam's, 1961. Subj: Cowboys. Glasses.

Nanette, the hungry pelican ill. by Winifred Lubell. Rand McNally, 1969. Subj: Birds – pelicans. Poetry, rhyme.

Wiseman, Bernard. *Doctor Duck and Nurse Swan* ill. by author. Dutton, 1984. Subj: Animals. Problem solving.

Don't make fun! ill. by author. Houghton, 1982. Subj: Animals – pigs. Behavior – misbehavior.

Little new kangaroo ill. by Robert Lopshire. Macmillan, 1973. Subj: Animals. Animals – kangaroos. Foreign lands – Russia. Poetry, rhyme.

Morris has a birthday party! ill. by author. Little, 1983. Subj: Animals – bears. Animals – moose. Behavior – misunderstanding. Parties.

Oscar is a mama ill. by author. Garrard, 1980. Subj: Animals – bulls, cows. Toys – dolls.

Tails are not for painting ill. by author. Garrard, 1980. Subj: Animals. Behavior – mistakes. Humor. School.

Withers, Carl. *The tale of a black cat* ill. by Alan E. Cober. Holt, 1966. Subj: Animals – cats. Games.

The wild ducks and the goose ill. by Alan E. Cober. Holt, 1968. Subj: Birds – ducks. Games. Sports – hunting.

Wittels, Harriet. *Things I hate!* by Harriet Wittels and Joan Greisman; ill. by Jerry McConnel. Behavioral Pub., 1973. Subj: Behavior. Emotions. Poetry, rhyme.

Wittman, Sally. *Pelly and Peak* ill. by author. Harper, 1978. Subj: Birds – peacocks, peahens. Birds – pelicans. Friendship.

Plenty of Pelly and Peak ill. by author. Harper, 1980. Subj: Birds – peacocks, peahens. Birds – pelicans. Friendship.

A special trade ill. by Karen Gundersheimer. Harper, 1978. Subj: Behavior – growing up. Friendship. Old age.

The wonderful Mrs. Trumbly ill. by Margot Apple. Harper, 1982. Subj: Friendship. School. Weddings.

Wodge, Dreary *see* Gorey, Edward

Wolcott, Patty. *Double-decker, double-decker, double-decker bus* ill. by Bob Barner Addison-Wesley, 1980. Subj: Friendship. Buses.

Wold, Jo Anne. *Tell them my name is Amanda* ed. by Caroline Rubin; ill. by Dennis Hockerman. Albert Whitman, 1977. Subj: Character traits – shyness. Names. Problem solving. Self-concept.

Well! Why didn't you say so? ill. by Unada. Albert Whitman, 1975. Subj: Animals – dogs. Behavior – lost. Behavior – misunderstanding. City.

Wolde, Gunilla. *Betsy and Peter are different* ill. by author. Random House, 1979. Translation of Annorlunda Emma och Per. Subj: Family life. Friendship.

Betsy and the chicken pox ill. by author. Random House, 1976. Translation of Emmas lillebror ar sjuk. Subj: Behavior – needing someone. Illness. Sibling rivalry.

Betsy and the doctor ill. by author. Random House, 1978. Translation of Emma hos doktorn. Subj: Careers – doctors. Hospitals. Illness.

Betsy and the vacuum cleaner ill. by author. Random House, 1979. Subj: Family life. Machines.

Betsy's first day at nursery school ill. by author. Random House, 1976. Translation of Emmas första dag på dagis. Subj: School.

Betsy's fixing day ill. by author. Random House, 1978. Subj: Character traits – helpfulness. Family life.

This is Betsy ill. by author. Random House, 1975. Translation of Emma tvärtimot. Subj: Emotions. Family life.

Wolf, Ann. *The rabbit and the turtle* ill. by author. Wonder Books, 1965. Subj: Animals – rabbits. Folk and fairy tales. Reptiles – turtles.

Wolf, Bernard. *Adam Smith goes to school* photos. by author. Lippincott, 1978. Subj: School.

Anna's silent world photos. by author. Lippincott, 1977. Subj: Handicaps – deafness.

Don't feel sorry for Paul photos. by author. Lippincott, 1974. Subj: Handicaps.

Michael and the dentist photos. by author. Four Winds Pr., 1980. Subj: Careers – dentists. Emotions – fear. Teeth.

Wolf, Janet. *The best present is me* ill. by author. Harper, 1984. Subj: Art. Family life – grandparents, great-grandparents.

Wolfe, Robert L. *The truck book* photos. by author. Carolrhoda, 1981. Subj: Trucks.

Wolff, Ashley. *The bells of London* ill. by author. Dodd, 1985. Subj: Birds – doves. Emotions – sadness. Foreign lands – England. Songs.

A year of birds ill. by author. Dodd, 1984. Subj: Birds. Days of the week, months of the year. Seasons.

Wolff, Robert Jay. *Feeling blue* ill. by author. Scribner's, 1968. Subj: Concepts – color.

Hello, yellow! ill. by author. Scribner's, 1968. Subj: Concepts – color.

Seeing red ill. by author. Scribner's, 1968. Subj: Concepts – color.

Wolkstein, Diane. *The banza: a Haitian story* ill. by Marc Brown. Dial Pr., 1981. Subj: Animals – goats. Animals – tigers. Character traits – bravery. Folk and fairy tales. Music.

The cool ride in the sky ill. by Paul Galdone. Knopf, 1973. Subj: Activities – flying. Animals – monkeys. Birds – buzzards. Birds – vultures. Character traits – cleverness. Folk and fairy tales.

The magic wings: a tale from China ill. by Robert Andrew Parker. Dutton, 1983. Subj: Activities – flying. Behavior – wishing. Cumulative tales. Folk and fairy tales. Foreign lands – China. Seasons – spring.

White wave: a Chinese tale ill. by Ed Young. Crowell, 1979. Subj: Folk and fairy tales. Foreign lands – China.

Wondriska, William. *Mr. Brown and Mr. Gray* ill. by author. Holt, 1968. Subj: Animals – pigs. Emotions – happiness. Money.

Puff ill. by author. Pantheon, 1960. Subj: Self-concept. Trains.

The stop ill. by author. Holt, 1972. Subj: Animals – horses. Character traits – kindness to animals. Desert. Emotions – fear. Ethnic groups in the U.S. – Indians.

The tomato patch ill. by author. Holt, 1964. Subj: Plants. Violence, anti-violence. Weapons.

Wong, Herbert H. *My goldfish* by Herbert H. Wong and Matthew F. Vessel; ill. by Arvis L. Stewart. Addison-Wesley, 1969. Subj: Fish. Pets. Science.

My ladybug by Herbert H. Wong and Matthew F. Vessel; ill. by Marie Nonast Bohlen. Addison-Wesley, 1969. Subj: Insects – ladybugs. Science.

My plant by Herbert H. Wong and Matthew F. Vessel; ill. by Richard Cuffari. Addison-Wesley, 1976. Subj: Plants. Science.

Our caterpillars by Herbert H. Wong and Matthew F. Vessel; ill. by Arvis L. Stewart. Addison-Wesley, 1977. Subj: Insects – Butterflies, caterpillars. Science.

Our earthworms by Herbert H. Wong and Matthew F. Vessel; ill. by Bill Davis. Addison-Wesley, 1977. Subj: Animals – worms. Science.

Our tree by Herbert H. Wong and Matthew F. Vessel; ill. by Kenneth Longtemps. Addison-Wesley, 1969. Subj: Science. Trees.

Wood, Audrey. *The napping house* ill. by Don Wood. Harcourt, 1984. Subj: Family life – grandparents, great-grandparents. Sleep.

Wood, Joyce. *Grandmother Lucy goes on a picnic* ill. by Frank Francis. Collins-World, 1976. Subj: Activities – picnicking. Activities – walking. Family life – grandparents, great-grandparents.

Grandmother Lucy in her garden ill. by Frank Francis. Collins-World, 1975. Subj: Family life – grandparents, great-grandparents. Foreign lands – England. Seasons. Seasons – spring.

Wood, Nancy C. *Little wrangler* ill. by Myron Wood. Doubleday, 1966. Subj: Cowboys.

Wood, Ray. *The American Mother Goose* ill. by Ed Hargis. Lippincott, 1940. Subj: Nursery rhymes.

Fun in American folk rhymes ill. by Ed Hargis; intro. by Carl Carmer. Lippincott, 1952. Subj: Nursery rhymes.

Woodcock, Louise Phinney. *The very little dog* (Skaar, Grace Marion)

Woolaver, Lance. *Christmas with the rural mail* ill. by Maud Lewis. Nimbus Pub., 1981. Subj: Foreign lands – Canada. Holidays – Christmas. Poetry, rhyme.

From Ben Loman to the sea ill. by Maud Lewis. Nimbus Pub., 1981. Subj: Behavior – running away. Poetry, rhyme. Sea and seashore. Seasons – spring.

Woolley, Catherine. *Andy and his fine friends* ill. by Meg Wohlberg. Morrow, 1960. Subj: Animals. Imagination – imaginary friends.

Andy and the runaway horse ill. by Meg Wohlberg. Morrow, 1963. Subj: Animals – horses. Traffic signs.

Andy and the wild worm ill. by Beatrice Darwin. Morrow, 1973, 1954. Subj: Animals – worms. Imagination.

The cat that joined the club ill. by Seymour Fleishman. Morrow, 1967. Subj: Animals – cats.

The clever raccoon ill. by Holly Keller. Morrow, 1981. Subj: Animals – raccoons. Behavior – trickery.

Gus and the baby ghost ill. by Seymour Fleishman. Morrow, 1972. Subj: Babies. Ghosts. Museums.

Gus was a friendly ghost ill. by Seymour Fleishman. Morrow, 1962. Subj: Friendship. Ghosts.

Gus was a gorgeous ghost ill. by Seymour Fleishman. Morrow, 1978. Subj: Clothing. Ghosts. Holidays – Halloween.

Gus was a real dumb ghost ill. by Joyce Audy dos Santos. Morrow, 1982. Subj: Ghosts. School.

The horse with the Easter bonnet ill. by Jay Hyde Barnum. Morrow, 1953. Subj: Animals – horses. Clothing. Holidays – Easter.

I like trains ill. by George Fonseca. Harper, 1965. Subj: Trains. Transportation.

Mr. Turtle's magic glasses ill. by Mamoru Funai. Morrow, 1971. Subj: Behavior – boredom. Glasses. Magic. Reptiles – turtles.

The popcorn dragon ill. by Jay Hyde Barnum. Morrow, 1953. Subj: Dragons. Food. Friendship.

The puppy who wanted a boy ill. by Seymour Fleishman. Morrow, 1958. Subj: Animals – dogs. Holidays – Christmas.

Quiet on account of dinosaur ill. by Seymour Fleishman. Morrow, 1964. Subj: Dinosaurs. Noise, sounds.

What's a ghost going to do? ill. by Seymour Fleishman. Morrow, 1966. Subj: Ghosts. Houses. Problem solving.

Worthington, Phoebe. *Teddy bear baker* by Phoebe and Selby Worthington; ill. by authors. Warne, 1980. Subj: Careers – bakers. Foreign lands – England. Toys – teddy bears.

Teddy bear coalman: a story for the very young by Phoebe and Selby Worthington; ill. by authors. Warne, 1980. Subj: Foreign lands – England. Toys – teddy bears.

Worthington, Selby. *Teddy bear baker* (Worthington, Phoebe)

Teddy bear coalman (Worthington, Phoebe)

Wright, Dare. *The doll and the kitten* photos. by author. Doubleday, 1960. Subj: Animals – cats. Toys – dolls. Toys – teddy bears.

Edith and Midnight photos. by author. Doubleday, 1978. Subj: Toys – dolls. Toys – teddy bears.

Edith and Mr. Bear photos. by author. Random House, 1964. Subj: Behavior – running away. Toys – dolls. Toys – teddy bears.

Edith and the duckling photos. by author. Doubleday, 1981. Subj: Birds – ducks. Eggs. Toys – dolls. Toys – teddy bears.

The lonely doll photos. by author. Doubleday, 1957. Subj: Toys – dolls. Toys – teddy bears.

The lonely doll learns a lesson photos. by author. Random House, 1961. Subj: Animals – cats. Pets. Toys – dolls. Toys – teddy bears.

Look at a calf photos. by author. Random House, 1974. Subj: Animals – bulls, cows. Farms.

Look at a colt photos. by author. Random House, 1969. Subj: Animals – horses. Farms.

Look at a kitten photos. by author. Random House, 1975. Subj: Animals – cats.

Wright, Josephine Lord. *Cotton Cat and Martha Mouse* ill. by John E. Johnson. Dutton, 1966. Subj: Animals – cats. Animals – mice. Behavior – sharing. Poetry, rhyme.

Wright, Martin. *Granny Stickleback* (Moore, John)

Wyler, Rose. *Spooky tricks* by Rose Wyler and Gerald Ames; ill. by Tālivaldis Stubis. Harper, 1968. Subj: Magic.

Wyndham, Robert. *The Chinese Mother Goose rhymes* (Mother Goose)

Wyse, Lois. *Two guppies, a turtle and Aunt Edna* ill. by Roger Coast. Collins-World, 1966. Subj: Family life. Fish. Problem solving. Reptiles – turtles. Telephone.

Yabuki, Seiji. *I love the morning* ill. by author. Collins-World, 1969 Subj: Emotions – happiness. Morning

Yaffe, Alan. *The magic meatballs* ill. by Karen Born Andersen. Dial Pr., 1979. Subj: Behavior – dissatisfaction. Family life. Magic.

Yagawa, Sumiko. *The crane wife* tr. from Japanese by Katherine Paterson; ill. by Suekichi Akaba. Morrow, 1982. Subj: Activities – weaving. Birds – cranes. Character traits – kindness to animals. Folk and fairy tales. Foreign lands – Japan.

Yamaguchi, Tohr. *Two crabs and the moonlight* ill. by Marianne Yamaguchi. Holt, 1965. Subj: Crustacea. Moon.

Yashima, Mitsu. *Momo's kitten* ill. by Tarō Yashima. Viking, 1961. Subj: Animals – cats. Ethnic groups in the U.S. – Japanese-Americans.

Plenty to watch ill. by Tarō Yashima. Viking, 1954. Subj: Foreign lands – Japan.

Yashima, Tarō. *Crow boy* ill. by author. Viking, 1955. Subj: Caldecott award honor book. Character traits – shyness. Emotions – loneliness. Foreign lands – Japan. School.

Momo's kitten (Yashima, Mitsu)

Seashore story ill. by author. Viking, 1967. Subj: Caldecott award honor book. Folk and fairy tales. Reptiles – turtles. Sea and seashore.

Umbrella ill. by author. Viking, 1958. Subj: Birthdays. Caldecott award honor book. City. Ethnic groups in the U.S. – Japanese-Americans. Umbrellas. Weather – rain.

The village tree ill. by author. Viking, 1953. Subj: Foreign lands – Japan. Seasons – summer. Trees.

The youngest one ill. by author. Viking, 1962. Subj: Character traits – shyness. Ethnic groups in the U.S. – Japanese-Americans. Friendship.

Yeoman, John. *The bear's water picnic* ill. by Quentin Blake. Macmillan, 1970. Subj: Activities – picnicking. Animals – bears. Animals – hedgehogs. Animals – pigs. Animals – squirrels. Frogs and toads.

Mouse trouble ill. by Quentin Blake. Macmillan, 1972. Subj: Animals – cats. Animals – mice. Friendship. Windmills.

The young performing horse ill. by Quentin Blake. Parents, 1979. Subj: Animals – horses. Theater. Twins.

Yezback, Steven A. *Pumpkinseeds* ill. by Mozelle Thompson. Bobbs-Merrill, 1969. Subj: Behavior – solitude. City. Ethnic groups in the U.S. – Afro-Americans.

Ylla. *Animal babies* by Ylla and Arthur S. Gregor; ill. by Ylla. Harper, 1959. Designed by Luc Bouchage. Subj: Animals.

I'll show you cats by Ylla and Crosby Newell Bonsall; ill. by Ylla. Harper, 1964. Planned by Charles Rado; designed by Luc Bouchage. Subj: Animals – cats.

Listen, listen! (Bonsall, Crosby Newell)

The little elephant by Ylla and Arthur S. Gregor; ill. by Ylla. Harper, 1956. Designed by Luc Bouchage. Subj: Animals – elephants.

Look who's talking by Ylla and Crosby Newell Bonsall; ill. by Ylla. Harper, 1962. Planned by Charles Rado; designed by Luc Bouchage. Subj: Birds – ostriches. Zoos.

Polar bear brothers by Ylla and Crosby Newell Bonsall; ill. by Ylla. Harper, 1960. Designed by Luc Bouchage. Subj: Animals – bears.

Two little bears ill. by author. Harper, 1954. Subj: Animals – bears. Behavior – lost.

Yolen, Jane. *The acorn quest* ill. by Susanna Natti. Crowell, 1981. Subj: Animals. Character traits – bravery. Character traits – selfishness. Dragons. Humor.

All in the woodland early: an ABC book ill. by Jane Breskin Zalben; music and lyrics by author. Collins-World, 1980. Subj: ABC books. Forest, woods.

Commander Toad and the big black hole ill. by Bruce Degen. Coward, 1983. Subj: Frogs and toads. Space and space ships.

Commander Toad and the planet of the grapes ill. by Bruce Degen. Coward, 1982. Subj: Frogs and toads. Illness. Space and space ships.

Commander Toad in space ill. by Bruce Degen. Coward, 1980. Subj: Frogs and toads. Space and space ships.

Dragon night and other lullabies ill. by Demi. Methuen, 1980. Subj: Animals. Bedtime. Sleep. Songs.

The emperor and the kite ill. by Ed Young. Collins-World, 1967. Subj: Caldecott award honor book. Character traits – smallness. Family life – fathers. Foreign lands – China. Kites. Royalty.

The giant's farm ill. by Tomie de Paola. Seabury Pr., 1977. Subj: Farms. Giants.

The giants go camping ill. by Tomie de Paola. Seabury Pr., 1979. Subj: Giants. Sports – camping.

The girl who loved the wind ill. by Ed Young. Crowell, 1972. Subj: Behavior – running away. Weather – wind.

The hundredth dove and other tales ill. by David Paladini. Crowell, 1977. Subj: Folk and fairy tales.

An invitation to the butterfly ball: a counting rhyme ill. by Jane Breskin Zalben. Parents, 1976. Subj: Animals. Counting. Poetry, rhyme.

Mice on ice ill. by Lawrence DiFiori. Dutton, 1980. Subj: Animals – mice. Animals – rats. Magic. Problem solving. Sports – ice skating. Theater.

Milkweed days photos. by Gabriel Amadeus Cooney. Crowell, 1976. Subj: Seasons – summer.

No bath tonight ill. by Nancy Winslow Parker. Crowell, 1978. Subj: Activities – bathing. Days of the week, months of the year. Family life – grandparents, great-grandparents.

The seeing stick ill. by Remy Charlip and Demetra Maraslis. Crowell, 1977. Subj: Foreign lands – China. Handicaps – blindness. Royalty.

Sleeping ugly ill. by Diane Stanley. Coward, 1981. Subj: Character traits – appearance. Folk and fairy tales. Magic.

Spider Jane ill. by Stefen Bernath. Coward, 1978. Subj: Behavior – sharing. Birds. Insects – flies. Spiders.

Yorinks, Arthur. *Louis the fish* ill. by Richard Egielski. Farrar, 1980. Subj: Careers – butchers. Fish. Imagination.

Youldon, Gillian. *Colors* ill. by author. Watts, 1979. Subj: Concepts – color. Format, unusual.

Counting ill. by James Hodgson. Watts, 1980. Subj: Counting. Format, unusual.

Numbers ill. by author. Watts, 1979. Subj: Counting. Format, unusual.

Shapes ill. by author. Watts, 1979. Subj: Concepts – shape. Format, unusual.

Sizes ill. by author. Watts, 1979. Subj: Concepts – size. Format, unusual.

Young animals in the zoo ill. with photos. Imported Pubs., 1983. Subj: Animals. Format, unusual – cardboard pages. Wordless.

Young domestic animals ill. with photos. Imported Pubs., 1983. Subj: Animals. Format, unusual – cardboard pages. Wordless.

Young, Ed. *The rooster's horns: a Chinese puppet play to make and perform* by Ed Young and Hilary Beckett; ill. by Ed Young. Collins-World, 1978. Subj: Folk and fairy tales. Foreign lands – China. Puppets.

The terrible Nung Gwama: a Chinese folktale ill. by author. Collins-World, 1978. Subj: Character traits – cleverness. Folk and fairy tales. Foreign lands – China. Monsters.

Up a tree ill. by author. Harper, 1983. Subj: Animals – cats. Trees. Wordless.

Young, Evelyn. *The tale of Tai* ill. by author. Oxford Univ. Pr., 1940. Subj: Behavior – lost. Foreign lands – China. Holidays – Chinese New Year.

Wu and Lu and Li ill. by author. Oxford Univ. Pr., 1939. Subj: Family life. Foreign lands – China.

Young, Helen. *A throne for Sesame* ill. by Shirley Hughes. Elsevier-Dutton, 1979. Subj: Behavior – growing up.

Young, Miriam Burt. *If I drove a bus* ill. by Robert M. Quackenbush. Lothrop, 1973. Subj: Buses. Careers – bus drivers. Transportation.

If I drove a car ill. by Robert M. Quackenbush. Lothrop, 1971. Subj: Automobiles. Transportation.

If I drove a tractor ill. by Robert M. Quackenbush. Lothrop, 1973. Subj: Machines.

If I drove a train ill. by Robert M. Quackenbush. Lothrop, 1972. Subj: Trains. Transportation.

If I drove a truck ill. by Robert M. Quackenbush. Lothrop, 1967. Subj: Careers – truck drivers. Transportation. Trucks.

If I flew a plane ill. by Robert M. Quackenbush. Lothrop, 1970. Subj: Activities – flying. Airplanes, airports. Careers – airplane pilots. Transportation.

If I rode a horse ill. by Robert M. Quackenbush. Lothrop, 1973. Subj: Animals – horses.

If I rode an elephant ill. by Robert M. Quackenbush. Lothrop, 1974. Subj: Animals – elephants.

If I sailed a boat ill. by Robert M. Quackenbush. Lothrop, 1971. Subj: Boats, ships.

Jellybeans for breakfast ill. by Beverly Komoda. Parents, 1968. Subj: Activities – playing. Imagination.

Miss Suzy's Easter surprise ill. by Arnold Lobel. Parents, 1972. Subj: Animals – squirrels. Holidays – Easter.

Please don't feed Horace ill. by Abner Graboff. Dial Pr., 1961. Subj: Animals – hippopotami. Zoos.

The sugar mouse cake ill. by Margaret Bloy Graham. Scribner's, 1964. Subj: Activities – cooking. Animals – mice. Careers – bakers. Food. Royalty.

The witch mobile ill. by Victoria Chess. Lothrop, 1969. Subj: Holidays – Halloween. Witches.

Yudell, Lynn Deena. *Make a face* ill. by author. Little, 1970. Subj: Anatomy. Emotions. Games. Participation.

Yulya. *Bears are sleeping* ill. by Nonny Hogrogian. Scribner's, 1967. Subj: Animals – bears. Hibernation. Music. Sleep. Songs.

Zacharias, Thomas. *But where is the green parrot?* by Thomas and Wanda Zacharias; ill. by Wanda Zacharias. Delacorte Pr., 1968. Translation of Und wo ist der grüne Papagei? Subj: Birds – parakeets, parrots. Concepts – color. Games.

Zacharias, Wanda. *But where is the green parrot?* (Zacharias, Thomas)

Zaffo, George J. *The big book of real airplanes* ill. by author. Grosset, 1951. Subj: Airplanes, airports. Helicopters. Transportation.

Big book of real fire engines text by Elizabeth Cameron; ill. by author. Grosset, 1950. Subj: Careers – firefighters.

The giant book of things in space ill. by author. Doubleday, 1969. Subj: Space and space ships.

The giant nursery book of things that go: fire engines, trains, boats, trucks, airplanes ill. by author. Doubleday, 1959. Subj: Airplanes, airports. Boats, ships. Transportation. Trucks.

The giant nursery book of things that work ill. by author. Doubleday, 1967. Subj: Machines. Tools. Transportation.

Zagone, Theresa. *No nap for me* ill. by Lillian Hoban. Dutton, 1978. Subj: Behavior – growing up. Sleep.

Zakhoder, Boris Vladimirovich. *How a piglet crashed the Christmas party* tr. by Marguerita Rudolph; ill. by Kurt Werth. Lothrop, 1971. Subj: Animals – pigs. Holidays – Christmas.

Rosachok tr. by Marguerita Rudolph; ill. by Yaroslava. Lothrop, 1970. Translation of Rusachok. Subj: Animals – rabbits. Behavior – dissatisfaction. Character traits – optimism. Frogs and toads.

Zalben, Jane Breskin. *Basil and Hillary* ill. by author. Macmillan, 1975. Subj: Animals. Animals – pigs. Farms.

Norton's nighttime ill. by author. Collins-World, 1979. Subj: Animals. Bedtime. Forest, woods. Night. Noise, sounds.

Oliver and Alison's week ill. by Emily Arnold McCully. Farrar, 1980. Subj: Activities. Friendship.

A perfect nose for Ralph ill. by John Wallner. Putnam's, 1980. Subj: Emotions – love. Toys – teddy bears.

Zallinger, Peter. *Dinosaurs* ill. by author. Random House, 1977. Subj: Dinosaurs. Science.

Zano, Gina Bell *see* Balzano, Jeanne

Zaslavsky, Claudia. *Count on your fingers African style* ill. by Jerry Pinkney. Crowell, 1980. Subj: Counting. Foreign lands – Africa.

Zelinsky, Paul O. *The lion and the stoat* ill. by author. Greenwillow, 1984. Subj: Animals – lions. Animals – weasels. Art. Friendship.

The maid and the mouse and the odd-shaped house ill. by author. Dodd, 1981. Subj: Animals – mice. Folk and fairy tales. Houses.

Zemach, Harve. *Duffy and the devil: a Cornish tale* ill. by Margot Zemach. Farrar, 1973. Subj: Caldecott award book. Devil. Folk and fairy tales. Foreign lands – England.

The judge: an untrue tale ill. by Margot Zemach. Farrar, 1969. Subj: Caldecott award honor book. Careers – judges. Monsters. Poetry, rhyme.

Mommy, buy me a China doll adapted from an Ozark children's song ill. by Margot Zemach. Follett, 1966. Subj: Music. Songs. Toys – dolls.

Nail soup: a Swedish folk tale ill. by Margot Zemach. Follett, 1964. Subj: Character traits – cleverness. Folk and fairy tales. Foreign lands – Sweden.

The tricks of Master Dabble ill. by Margot Zemach. Holt, 1965. Subj: Behavior – trickery. Humor. Royalty.

Zemach, Kaethe. *The beautiful rat* ill. by author. Four Winds Pr., 1979. Subj: Animals – rats. Folk and fairy tales.

Zemach, Margot. *It could always be worse: a Yiddish folk tale* ill. by author. Farrar, 1976. Subj: Caldecott award honor book. Folk and fairy tales. Humor. Jewish culture. Problem solving.

Jake and Honeybunch go to heaven ill. by author. Farrar, 1982. Subj: Animals – mules. Behavior – misbehavior. Ethnic groups in the U.S. – Afro-Americans. Folk and fairy tales.

The little tiny woman ill. by author. Bobbs-Merrill, 1965. Subj: Folk and fairy tales. Ghosts.

To Hilda for helping ill. by author. Farrar, 1977. Subj: Character traits – helpfulness. Emotions – envy, jealousy. Family life.

Zhitkov, Boris. *How I hunted for the little fellows* tr. from Russian by Djemma Bider; ill. by Paul O. Zelinsky. Dodd, 1979. Subj: Behavior – misbehavior. Character traits – curiosity. Foreign lands – Russia. Family life – grandparents, great-grandparents.

Ziefert, Harriet. *Sleepy dog* ill. by Norman Gorbaty. Random House, 1984. Subj: Animals – dogs. Sleep.

Ziegler, Ursina. *Squaps the moonling* tr. by Barbara Kowall Gollob; ill. by Sita Jucker. Atheneum, 1969. Translation of Squaps, der Mondling. Subj: Moon. Space and space ships.

Zijlstra, Tjerk. *Benny and his geese* ill. by Ivo de Weerd. McGraw-Hill, 1975. Translation of Bennie en zijn ganzen. Subj: Birds – geese. Folk and fairy tales. Wizards.

Zimelman, Nathan. *If I were strong enough...* ill. by Diane Paterson. Abingdon Pr., 1982. Subj: Behavior – growing up. Family life.

Mean Murgatroyd and the ten cats ill. by Tony Auth. Dutton, 1984. Subj: Animals – cats. Animals – dogs. Character traits – meanness.

Once when I was five ill. by Carol Rogers. Steck-Vaughn, 1967. Subj: Birthdays. Imagination.

Positively no pets allowed ill. by Pamela Johnson. Dutton, 1980. Subj: Animals – gorillas. Pets.

To sing a song as big as Ireland ill. by Joseph Low. Follett, 1967. Subj: Behavior – wishing. Foreign lands – Ireland. Elves and little people. Holidays – St. Patrick's Day. Music.

Zimmer, Dirk. *The trick-or-treat trap* ill. by author. Harper, 1982. Subj: Holidays – Halloween. Parties. Witches.

Zimmerman, Andrea Griffing. *Yetta, the trickster* ill. by Harold Berson. Seabury Pr., 1978. Subj: Foreign lands – Russia. Humor.

Zimmerman, Baruch. *A Japanese fairy tale* (Iké, Jane Hori)

Zimnik, Reiner. *The bear on the motorcycle* tr. by Cornelia Schaeffer; ill. by author. Atheneum, 1963. Translation of Der bär auf dem motorrad. Subj: Animals – bears. Behavior – running away. Circus. Motorcycles.

The proud circus horse ill. by author. Pantheon, 1957. Subj: Animals – horses. Behavior – running away. Character traits – pride. Circus.

Zindel, Paul. *I love my mother* ill. by John Melo. Harper, 1975. Subj: Emotions – loneliness. Emotions – love. Family life – mothers.

Ziner, Feenie. *Counting carnival* by Feenie Ziner and Paul Galdone; ill. by Paul Galdone. Coward, 1962. Subj: Activities – playing. Counting. Cumulative tales. Ethnic groups in the U.S. – Afro-Americans. Parades. Poetry, rhyme.

The true book of time by Feenie Ziner and Elizabeth Thompson; ill. by Katherine Evans. Children's Pr., 1956. Subj: Time.

Zion, Gene. *All falling down* ill. by Margaret Bloy Graham. Harper, 1951. Subj: Caldecott award honor book. Concepts – up and down.

Dear garbage man ill. by Margaret Bloy Graham. Harper, 1957. Subj: Careers – garbage collectors. City.

Harry and the lady next door ill. by Margaret Bloy Graham. Harper, 1960. Subj: Animals – dogs. Noise, sounds. Problem solving.

Harry by the sea ill. by Margaret Bloy Graham. Harper, 1965. Subj: Animals – dogs. Sea and seashore. Seasons – summer.

Harry, the dirty dog ill. by Margaret Bloy Graham. Harper, 1956. Subj: Activities – bathing. Animals – dogs. Behavior – running away.

Hide and seek day ill. by Margaret Bloy Graham. Harper, 1954. Subj: Behavior – hiding. City. Games.

Jeffie's party ill. by Margaret Bloy Graham. Harper, 1957. Subj: Games. Parties.

The meanest squirrel I ever met ill. by Margaret Bloy Graham. Scribner's, 1962. Subj: Animals – squirrels. Character traits – meanness. Friendship. Holidays – Thanksgiving.

No roses for Harry ill. by Margaret Bloy Graham. Harper, 1958. Subj: Animals – dogs. Clothing.

The plant sitter ill. by Margaret Bloy Graham. Harper, 1959. Subj: Plants.

Really spring ill. by Margaret Bloy Graham. Harper, 1956. Subj: Seasons – spring.

The summer snowman ill. by Margaret Bloy Graham. Harper, 1955. Subj: Holidays – Fourth of July. Seasons – summer. Snowmen. Weather – snow.

Zirbes, Laura. *How many bears?* ill. by E. Harper Johnson. Putnam's, 1960. Subj: Animals – bears. Counting.

Zola, Meguido. *The dream of promise: a folktale in Hebrew and English* ill. by Ruben Zellermayer. Kids Can Pr., 1981. Subj: Folk and fairy tales. Foreign languages. Jewish culture. Self-concept.

Only the best ill. by Valerie Littlewood. Watts, 1982. Subj: Emotions – love. Family life – fathers.

Zoll, Max Alfred. *Animal babies* tr. by Violetta Castillo; ed. by Hanns Reich; ill. by author. Hill and Wang, 1971. Translation of Tierkinder. Subj: Animals.

A flamingo is born tr. by Catherine Edwards Sadler; photos. by Winifried Noack. Putnam's, 1978. Subj: Birds – flamingos. Science.

Zolotow, Charlotte. *The beautiful Christmas tree* ill. by Ruth Robbins. Parnassus Pr., 1972. Subj: Holidays – Christmas. Trees.

Big sister and little sister ill. by Martha G. Alexander. Harper, 1966. Subj: Behavior – running away. Family life.

The bunny who found Easter ill. by Betty Peterson. Parnassus Pr., 1959. Subj: Animals – rabbits. Holidays – Easter.

But not Billy ill. by Kay Chorao. Harper, 1983. Subj: Babies. Behavior – growing up.

Do you know what I'll do? ill. by Garth Williams. Harper, 1958. Subj: Babies. Emotions – love. Family life.

Flocks of birds ill. by Ruth Lercher Bornstein. Crowell, 1981. Subj: Bedtime. Birds.

The hating book ill. by Ben Shecter. Harper, 1969. Subj: Behavior – gossip. Emotions – hate. Friendship.

Hold my hand ill. by Thomas di Grazia. Harper, 1972. Subj: Friendship. Weather – snow.

I have a horse of my own ill. by Yoko Mitsuhashi. Crowell, 1980. Subj: Animals – horses. Dreams. Night.

I know a lady ill. by James Stevenson. Greenwillow, 1984. Subj: Character traits – kindness. Old age.

If it weren't for you ill. by Ben Shecter. Harper, 1966. Subj: Family life. Sibling rivalry.

In my garden ill. by Roger Antoine Duvoisin. Lothrop, 1960. Subj: Plants. Seasons.

It's not fair ill. by William Pène Du Bois. Harper, 1976. Subj: Behavior – dissatisfaction. Emotions – envy, jealousy. Family life.

Janey ill. by Ronald Himler. Harper, 1973. Subj: Emotions – loneliness. Friendship. Moving.

May I visit? ill. by Erik Blegvad. Harper, 1976. Subj: Behavior – growing up. Emotions – love. Family life.

Mr. Rabbit and the lovely present ill. by Maurice Sendak. Harper, 1962. Subj: Animals – rabbits. Birthdays. Caldecott award honor book. Concepts – color. Family life – mothers. Holidays – Easter.

My friend John ill. by Ben Shecter. Harper, 1968. Subj: Friendship.

My grandson Lew ill. by William Pène Du Bois. Harper, 1974. Subj: Death. Family life. Family life – grandparents, great-grandparents.

The new friend ill. by Emily Arnold McCully. Crowell, 1981. Subj: Behavior – sharing. Friendship.

One step, two... ill. by Roger Antoine Duvoisin. Lothrop, 1955. Subj: Activities – walking. City. Counting.

Over and over ill. by Garth Williams. Harper, 1957. Subj: Holidays. Time.

The park book ill. by Hans Augusto Rey. Harper, 1944. Subj: Activities – playing. City.

The poodle who barked at the wind ill. by Roger Antoine Duvoisin. Lothrop, 1964. Subj: Animals – dogs. Noise, sounds. Pets.

The quarreling book ill. by Arnold Lobel. Harper, 1963. Subj: Behavior – fighting, arguing. Cumulative tales. Emotions – anger. Weather – rain.

River winding ill. by Kazue Mizumura. Crowell, 1978. Subj: Poetry, rhyme.

Say it! ill. by James Stevenson. Greenwillow, 1980. Subj: Activities – walking. Emotions – love. Family life – mothers. Nature. Seasons – fall.

The sky was blue ill. by Garth Williams. Harper, 1963. Subj: Emotions – love. Family life.

The sleepy book ill. by Vladimir Bobri. Lothrop, 1958. Subj: Bedtime. Sleep.

Some things go together ill. by Karen Gundersheimer. Rev. ed. Crowell, 1983. Subj: Family life – mothers. Poetry, rhyme.

Someday ill. by Arnold Lobel. Harper, 1965. Subj: Behavior – wishing. Dreams.

Someone new ill. by Erik Blegvad. Harper, 1978. Subj: Behavior – growing up. Family life.

The song ill. by Nancy Tafuri. Greenwillow, 1982. Subj: Nature. Seasons. Songs.

The storm book ill. by Margaret Bloy Graham. Harper, 1952. Subj: Caldecott award honor book. Emotions – fear. Weather. Weather – rain. Weather – rainbows.

Summer is... ill. by Ruth Lercher Bornstein. Crowell, 1983. Subj: Poetry, rhyme. Seasons – summer.

The summer night ill. by Ben Shecter. Harper, 1974. Published in 1958 under the title The night when mother was away. Subj: Activities – walking. Bedtime. Family life. Family life – fathers.

Three funny friends ill. by Mary Chalmers. Harper, 1961. Subj: Emotions – loneliness. Friendship. Imagination – imaginary friends.

A tiger called Thomas ill. by Kurt Werth. Lothrop, 1963. Subj: Character traits – shyness. Emotions – loneliness. Holidays – Halloween.

The unfriendly book ill. by William Pène Du Bois. Harper, 1975. Subj: Behavior – fighting, arguing. Friendship.

Wake up and good night ill. by Leonard Weisgard. Harper, 1971. Subj: Bedtime. Morning. Night.

When I have a son ill. by Hilary Knight. Harper, 1967. Subj: Behavior – growing up. Family life. Imagination.

When the wind stops ill. by Joe Lasker. Abelard-Schuman, 1962. Subj: Bedtime. Night. Weather – wind.

The white marble ill. by Lilian Obligado. Abelard-Schuman, 1963. Subj: Activities – playing. Friendship. Night.

William's doll ill. by William Pène Du Bois. Harper, 1972. Subj: Family life. Family life – grandparents, great-grandparents. Toys – dolls.

Zoo animals ill. with photos. Imported Pubs., 1983. Subj: Animals. Format, unusual – cardboard pages. Wordless.

Zusman, Evelyn. *The Passover parrot* ill. by Katherine Janus Kahn. Kar-Ben Copies, 1984. Subj: Birds – parakeets, parrots. Family life. Holidays – Passover. Jewish culture.

Zweifel, Frances. *Animal baby-sitters* ill. by Irene Brady. Morrow, 1981. Subj: Activities – babysitting. Animals. Nature.

Bony ill. by Whitney Darrow, Jr. Harper, 1977. Subj: Animals – squirrels. Pets.

Zwetchkenbaum, G. *The Peanuts shape circus puzzle book* ill. by author. Scholastic, 1983. Subj: Riddles.

The Peanuts sleepy time puzzle book ill. by author. Scholastic, 1983. Subj: Riddles.

The Snoopy farm puzzle book ill. by author. Scholastic, 1983. Subj: Riddles.

Snoopy safari puzzle book ill. by author. Scholastic, 1983. Subj: Riddles.

Title Index

Titles appear in alphabetical sequence with the author's name following in parentheses. For identical title listings, the illustrator's name is given to further identify the version. In the case of variant titles, both the original and differing titles are listed.

B

A child's garden of verses, ill. by Pelagie Doane (Stevenson, Robert Louis)
A child's garden of verses, ill. by Toni Frissell (Stevenson, Robert Louis)
A child's garden of verses, ill. by Gyo Fujikawa (Stevenson, Robert Louis)
A child's garden of verses, ill. by Alice and Martin Provensen (Stevenson, Robert Louis)
A child's garden of verses, ill. by Tasha Tudor (Stevenson, Robert Louis)
A child's garden of verses, ill. by Brian Wildsmith (Stevenson, Robert Louis)
A child's good morning book (Brown, Margaret Wise)
A child's good night book (Brown, Margaret Wise)
A child's grace (Burdekin, Harold)
Chin Chiang and the dragon's dance (Wallace, Ian)
The Chinese Mother Goose rhymes (Mother Goose)
The Chinese New Year (Cheng, Hou-Tien)
The Chinese story teller (Buck, Pearl S (Pearl Sydenstricker))
Ching-Ting and the ducks (Fribourg, Marjorie G)
A chipmunk lives here (Eberle, Irmengarde)
The chipmunk that went to church (Conger, Marion)
Chōchō is for butterfly (Sasaki, Jeannie)
Chocolate mouse and sugar pig (Hale, Irina)
Choo choo (Burton, Virginia Lee)
The chosen baby (Wasson, Valentina Pavlovna)
Chouchou (Seignobosc, Françoise)
The Christ Child (Petersham, Maud)
Christmas (Bruna, Dick)
The Christmas angel (Brown, Abbie Farwell)
The Christmas Anna angel (Sawyer, Ruth)
The Christmas birthday story (Laurence, Margaret)
A Christmas book
A Christmas book (Anglund, Joan Walsh)
The Christmas book (Bruna, Dick)
The Christmas bunny (Lipkind, William)
The Christmas camel (Parker, Nancy Winslow)
The Christmas cat (Holmes, Efner Tudor)
The Christmas cookie sprinkle snitcher (Partch, Virgil Franklin)
Christmas eve (Hurd, Edith Thacher)
Christmas eve at the Mellops (Ungerer, Tomi)
A Christmas fantasy (Haywood, Carolyn)
Christmas folk (Belting, Natalia Maree)
The Christmas grump (Low, Joseph)
Christmas in noisy village (Lindgren, Astrid)
Christmas in the barn (Brown, Margaret Wise)
Christmas in the chicken coop (Bond, Felicia)
Christmas in the stable (Lindgren, Astrid)
Christmas is a time of giving (Anglund, Joan Walsh)

Christmas moon (Cazet, Denys)
The Christmas mouse (Wenning, Elisabeth)
The Christmas pageant (De Paola, Tomie)
The Christmas party (Adams, Adrienne)
The Christmas piñata (Kent, Jack)
Christmas secrets (Schweninger, Ann)
A Christmas story (Chalmers, Mary)
Christmas surprise (Gordon, Sharon)
Christmas time (Schenk, Esther M)
The Christmas train (Gantschev, Ivan)
Christmas tree farm (Budbill, David)
Christmas tree on the mountain (Fenner, Carol)
Christmas trees and how they grow (Blough, Glenn O)
The Christmas whale (Duvoisin, Roger Antoine)
Christmas with the rural mail (Woolaver, Lance)
Chubby bear (Barto, Emily N)
Chubby's first year (Gág, Flavia)
Chun Ling in China (Fyson, Nance Lui) A family in China
The church cat abroad (Oakley, Graham)
The church mice adrift (Oakley, Graham)
The church mice and the moon (Oakley, Graham)
The church mice at bay (Oakley, Graham)
The church mice at Christmas (Oakley, Graham)
The church mice in action (Oakley, Graham)
The church mice spread their wings (Oakley, Graham)
The church mouse (Oakley, Graham)
Cinderella, ill. by Nonny Hagrogian (Grimm, Jacob)
Cinderella, ill. by Svend Otto (Grimm, Jacob)
Cinderella, ill. by Sheilah Beckett (Perrault, Charles)
Cinderella, ill. by Marcia Brown (Perrault, Charles)
Cinderella, ill. by Paul Galdone (Perrault, Charles)
Cinderella, ill. by Emanuele Luzzati (Perrault, Charles)
Cinderella, ill. by Phil Smith (Perrault, Charles)
Circles, triangles, and squares (Hoban, Tana)
El circo magico modelo (Everton, Macduff)
Circus (De Regniers, Beatrice Schenk)
Circus (Prelutsky, Jack)
Circus (Wildsmith, Brian) Brian Wildsmith's circus
The circus baby (Petersham, Maud)
Circus cannonball (Varga, Judy)
Circus! Circus! (Hopkins, Lee Bennett)
Circus cow (Scruton, Clive)
The circus in the mist (Munari, Bruno)
Circus magic (Baningan, Sharon Stearns)
Circus numbers (Peppé, Rodney)
Circus rucus (Lipkind, William)
The city (Florian, Douglas)

E

H

I

J

K

L

M

Mr. Pine's mixed-up signs (Kessler, Leonard P)

Mr. Pine's purple house (Kessler, Leonard P)

Mr. Pingle and Mr. Buttonhouse (MacGregor, Ellen)

Mr. Plum and the little green tree (Gilbert, Helen Earle)

Mr. Plum's paradise (Trimby, Elisa)

Mr. Rabbit and the lovely present (Zolotow, Charlotte)

Mr. Silver and Mrs. Gold (Fink, Dale Borman)

Mr. Simkin's grandma (Allen, Linda)

Mr. Skinner's skinny house (McGovern, Ann)

Mr. Squint (Partridge, Jenny)

Mr. Stripes the gopher (Fox, Charles Philip)

Mr. T. W. Anthony Woo (Ets, Marie Hall)

Mr. Tall and Mr. Small (Brenner, Barbara)

Mr. Turtle's magic glasses (Woolley, Catherine)

Mr. Willowby's Christmas tree (Barry, Robert E)

Mr. Wink and his shadow, Ned (Gackenbach, Dick)

Mr. Wren's house (Brock, Emma Lillian)

Mistletoe (McPhail, David)

Mitchell is moving (Sharmat, Marjorie Weinman)

The mitten (Tresselt, Alvin R)

Mittens (Newberry, Clare Turlay)

Mittens for kittens and other rhymes about cats (Blegvad, Lenore)

Mittens in May (Kumin, Maxine)

A mitzvah is something special (Eisenberg, Phyllis Rose)

Mix or match storybook (Scarry, Richard) Richard Scarry's mix or match storybook

The mixed-up chameleon (1975) (Carle, Eric)

The mixed-up chameleon (1984) (Carle, Eric)

Mog's Christmas (Kerr, Judith)

Moke and Poki in the rain forest (Funai, Mamoru)

The mole family's Christmas (Hoban, Russell)

Molly and Mr. Maloney (Morgan, Allen)

Molly and the slow teeth (Ross, Pat)

Molly Mullett (Coombs, Patricia)

Molly o' the moors (Keeping, Charles)

Molly Whuppie (De La Mare, Walter)

Molly's lies (Chorao, Kay)

Molly's Moe (Chorao, Kay)

Mom and dad and I are having a baby! (Malecki, Maryann)

Mommies (Carton, Lonnie Caming)

Mommies at work (Merriam, Eve)

Mommy and daddy are divorced (Perry, Patricia)

Mommy, buy me a China doll; (Zemach, Harve)

Momo's kitten (Yashima, Mitsu)

The monkey and the crocodile (Galdone, Paul)

Monkey and the white bone demon (Shi, Zhang Xiu)

Monkey in the jungle (Preston, Edna Mitchell)

Monkey in the middle (Bunting, Eve)

Monkey island (Reitveld, Jane Klatt)

Monkey see, monkey do (Oxenbury, Helen)

Monkey tale (Williamson, Hamilton)

The monkey that went to school (Meshover, Leonard)

Monkeys (Whitehead, Patricia)

The monkeys and the pedlar (Suba, Susanne)

Monroe's island (Brooks, Gregory)

Monsieur Bussy, the celebrated hamster (Claude-Lafontaine, Pascale)

Monster and the magic umbrella (Blance, Ellen)

Monster and the mural (Blance, Ellen)

Monster and the surprise cookie (Blance, Ellen)

The monster and the tailor (Galdone, Paul)

Monster at school (Blance, Ellen)

The monster behind Black Rock (Varga, Judy)

Monster birthday party (Freedman, Sally)

Monster buys a pet (Blance, Ellen)

Monster cleans his house (Blance, Ellen)

Monster comes to the city (Blance, Ellen)

The monster den (Ciardi, John)

Monster gets a job (Blance, Ellen)

Monster goes around the town (Blance, Ellen)

Monster goes to school (Blance, Ellen)

Monster goes to the beach (Blance, Ellen)

Monster goes to the circus (Blance, Ellen)

Monster goes to the hospital (Blance, Ellen)

Monster goes to the museum (Blance, Ellen)

Monster goes to the zoo (Blance, Ellen)

Monster has a party (Blance, Ellen)

The monster hunt (Newsham, Wendy)

The monster in the third dresser drawer and other stories about Adam Joshua (Smith, Janice Lee)

A monster is coming! A monster is coming! (Heide, Florence Parry)

Monster, Lady Monster and the bike ride (Blance, Ellen)

Monster looks for a friend (Blance, Ellen)

Monster looks for a house (Blance, Ellen)

Monster meets Lady Monster (Blance, Ellen)

Monster night at Grandma's house (Peck, Richard)

Monster on the bus (Blance, Ellen)

Monster poems

Monster tracks? (Delaney, A)

The Month-Brothers (Marshak, Samuel)

Monty (Stevenson, James)

Moo, baa, lalala (Boynton, Sandra)

Mooch the messy (Sharmat, Marjorie Weinman)

The moon (Asimov, Isaac)

The moon (Simon, Seymour)

The moon (Stevenson, Robert Louis)

N

O

Oh, riddlesticks! (Bishop, Ann)

Oh say can you say? (Seuss, Dr)

Oh, that koala! (Ruck-Pauquèt, Gina)

Oh, the thinks you can think! (Seuss, Dr)

Oh, were they ever happy! (Spier, Peter)

Oink and Pearl (Chorao, Kay)

Ol' Dan Tucker (Langstaff, John M)

Ola (Aulaire, Ingri Mortenson d')

Olaf reads (Lexau, Joan M)

Old Arthur (Skorpen, Liesel Moak)

The old ballad of the babes in the woods (The babes in the woods)

The old banjo (Haseley, Dennis)

The old barn (Carrick, Carol)

Old Black Witch (Devlin, Wende)

Old Blue (Hancock, Sibyl)

Old Blue, you good dog you (Taylor, Mark)

The old bullfrog (Freschet, Berniece)

Old Dame Trot and her comical cat (The moving adventures of Old Dame Trot and her comical cat)

The old-fashioned children's storybook

Old Father Frost (Odoyevsky, Vladimir)

Old hat, new hat (Berenstain, Stan)

Old Hippo's Easter egg (Wahl, Jan)

The old lady who ate people (Hinojosa, Francisco)

Old Lars (Magnus, Erica)

Old MacDonald had a farm, ill. by Mel Crawford

Old MacDonald had a farm, ill. by David Frankland

Old MacDonald had a farm, ill. by Abner Graboff

Old MacDonald had a farm, ill. by Tracey Campbell Pearson

Old MacDonald had a farm, ill. by Robert M. Quackenbush

Old MacDonald had an apartment house (Barrett, Judi)

The old man and the mule (Snyder, Anne)

The old man is always right (Andersen, H C (Hans Christian))

The old man of Lochnagar (Charles Prince of Wales)

Old man up a tree (Adamson, Gareth)

Old man Whickutt's donkey (Calhoun, Mary)

Old Mother Hubbard and her dog, ill. by Paul Galdone (Martin, Sarah Catherine)

Old Mother Hubbard and her dog, ill. by Evaline Ness (Martin, Sarah Catherine)

Old Mother Wiggle-Waggle (Jacobs, Joseph)

Old Mother Witch (Carrick, Carol)

Old Mrs. Billups and the black cats (Carroll, Ruth)

Old, older, oldest (Klein, Leonore)

Old-one-eye meets his match (Doty, Roy)

Old Sadie and the Christmas bear (Naylor, Phyllis Reynolds)

The old stump (Hawkinson, John)

Old Turtle's baseball stories (Kessler, Leonard P)

Old Turtle's winter games (Kessler, Leonard P)

The old witch and her magic basket (DeLage, Ida)

The old witch and the crows (DeLage, Ida)

The old witch and the dragon (DeLage, Ida)

The old witch and the ghost parade (DeLage, Ida)

Old Witch and the polka-dot ribbon (Devlin, Wende)

The old witch finds a new house (DeLage, Ida)

Old Witch rescues Halloween (Devlin, Wende)

The old woman and her pig

The old woman and her pig and 10 other stories (Rockwell, Anne F)

The old woman and the red pumpkin (Bang, Betsy)

The old woman and the rice thief (Bang, Betsy)

The oldest kid (Knox-Wagner, Elaine)

The O'Learys and friends (Berg, Jean Horton)

Oliver (Hoff, Syd)

Oliver and Alison's week (Zalben, Jane Breskin)

Oliver Button is a sissy (De Paola, Tomie)

Oliver's escape (Joerns, Consuelo)

On a summer day (Lenski, Lois)

On beyond zebra (Seuss, Dr)

On Christmas day in the morning (Langstaff, John M)

On Christmas Eve (Brown, Margaret Wise)

On divorce (Stein, Sara Bonnett)

On Market Street (Lobel, Arnold)

On mother's lap (Scott, Ann Herbert)

On my beach there are many pebbles (Lionni, Leo)

On the day Peter Stuyvesant sailed into town (Lobel, Arnold)

On the edge of the eastern ocean (Hall, Pam)

On the farm (Robinson, W W (William Wilcox))

On the go (Maestro, Betsy)

On the little hearth

On the other side of the river (Oppenheim, Joanne)

On the road (Scarry, Huck)

On the sand dune (Orgel, Doris)

On the town (Maestro, Betsy)

On to Widecombe Fair (Gauch, Patricia Lee)

On top of spaghetti (Glazer, Tom)

On wings of love (Agostinelli, Maria Enrica)

On your mark, get set, go! (Kessler, Leonard P)

Once a bright red tiger (Whitney, Alex)

Once a mouse... (Brown, Marcia)

Once in a wood (Æsop)

Once in royal David's city (Lines, Kathleen)

Once there was a tree (Busch, Phyllis S)

Once under the cherry blossom tree (Say, Allen)

P

Prize performance (Fisher, Aileen)

The prize pig surprise (Ernst, Lisa Campbell)

Professor Branestawn's building bust-up (Hunter, Norman)

Professor Bull's umbrella (Lipkind, William)

Professor Coconut and the thief (Gelman, Rita Golden)

A promise is for keeping (Wade, Anne)

The proud circus horse (Zimnik, Reiner)

The proud red rooster (Ehrhardt, Reinhold) Kikeri or, The proud red rooster

The proud white cat (Hürlimann, Ruth)

Psst, doggie (Keats, Ezra Jack)

Puddles and ponds (Busch, Phyllis S)

Puddums, the Cathcarts' orange cat (Parker, Nancy Winslow)

The pudgy book of toys

The pudgy fingers counting book

The pudgy pals

The pudgy pat-a-cake book

The pudgy peek-a-boo book

The pudgy rock-a-bye book

Puff (Wondriska, William)

Puffin (Lewis, Naomi)

Puffin book of nursery rhymes (Opie, Iona Archibald)

Pumpernickel tickle and mean green cheese (Patz, Nancy)

Pumpers, boilers, hooks and ladders (Fisher, Leonard Everett)

The pumpkin giant (Greene, Ellin)

The Pumpkin Heads (Abisch, Roz)

The pumpkin people (Cavagnaro, David)

The pumpkin smasher (Benarde, Anita)

The pumpkin sparrow (Fregosi, Claudia)

Pumpkinseeds (Yezback, Steven A)

Punch and Judy in the rain (Eaton, Su)

Punch's secret (Sarton, May)

A pup grows up (Foster, Sally)

The pup himself (Dennis, Morgan)

The pup went up (Blocksma, Mary)

Puppet party (Chernoff, Goldie Taub)

Puppet plays and puppet-making (Marks, Burton)

Puppet show (Peters, Sharon)

Puppies (Pfloog, Jan)

Puppies and kittens

Puppies for keeps (Lathrop, Dorothy Pulis)

A puppy called Spinach (Baker, Margaret)

A puppy named Gia (Machetanz, Sara)

The puppy who wanted a boy (Woolley, Catherine)

The puppy's new adventures (Ruby-Spears Enterprises)

Puptents and pebbles (Smith, William Jay)

The Purim goat (Suhl, Yuri)

Purple cow to the rescue (Cole, Ann)

Push Kitty (Wahl, Jan)

Push-pull, empty-full (Hoban, Tana)

Puss in boots, ill. by Marcia Brown (Perrault, Charles)

Puss in boots, ill. by Jean Claverie (Perrault, Charles)

Puss in boots, ill. by Hans Fischer (Perrault, Charles)

Puss in boots, ill. by Paul Galdone (Perrault, Charles)

Puss in boots, ill. by Julia Noonan (Perrault, Charles)

Puss in boots, ill. by Tony Ross (Perrault, Charles)

Puss in boots, ill. by William Stobbs (Perrault, Charles)

Puss in boots, ill. by Barry Wilkinson (Perrault, Charles)

Pussycat's Christmas (Brown, Margaret Wise)

Put me in the zoo (Lopshire, Robert)

Puzzles (Wildsmith, Brian) Brian Wildsmith's puzzles

Python's party (Wildsmith, Brian)

Q

Q is for crazy (Leander, Ed)

Q is for duck (Elting, Mary)

Quack? (Richter, Mischa)

The quangle wangle's hat (Lear, Edward)

The quangle wangle's hat (Lear, Edward) The pelican chorus and the quangle wangle's hat

The quangle wangle's hat (Lear, Edward) Two laughable lyrics The pobble who has no toes, [and] The quangle wangle's hat

The quarreling book (Zolotow, Charlotte)

The queen always wanted to dance (Mayer, Mercer)

The queen and Rosie Randall (Oxenbury, Helen)

The queen of Eene (Prelutsky, Jack)

The Queen of Hearts (Caldecott, Randolph)

The queen who couldn't bake gingerbread (Van Woerkom, Dorothy)

Quentin Blake's nursery rhyme book (Blake, Quentin)

Quick as a wink (Aldis, Dorothy)

The quicksand book (De Paola, Tomie)

The quiet evening (Hurd, Thacher)

The quiet house (Coontz, Otto)

The quiet noisy book (Brown, Margaret Wise)

Quiet on account of dinosaur (Woolley, Catherine)

Quiet! There's a canary in the library (Freeman, Don)

The quilt (Jonas, Ann)

Quilts in the attic (Fleisher, Robbin)

Quito express (Bemelmans, Ludwig)

R

Ra ta ta tam (Nickl, Peter)

The Rabbi and the twenty-nine witches (Hirsh, Marilyn)

Rabbit and pork (Lawrence, John)

The rabbit and the turtle (Wolf, Ann)
The rabbit catcher and other fairy tales (Bechstein, Ludwig)
Rabbit country (Trez, Denise)
A rabbit for Easter (Carrick, Carol)
Rabbit garden (Miles, Miska)
Rabbit Island (Steiner, Jörg)
Rabbit seeds (Le Tord, Bijou)
Rabbit story (Tresselt, Alvin R)
Rabbit tales (McCormack, John E)
Rabbit travels (McCormack, John E)
Rabbits (Henrie, Fiona)
Rabbits (Tarrant, Graham)
Rabbits in the meadow (Hess, Lilo)
Rabbits, rabbits (Fisher, Aileen)
Rabbits' search for a little house (Kwitz, Mary DeBall)
The rabbits' wedding (Williams, Garth)
The raccoon and Mrs. McGinnis (Miles, Miska)
Rachel (Fanshawe, Elizabeth)
Rachel and Obadiah (Turkle, Brinton)
The radish day jubilee (Bruce, Sheilah B)
A raft of riddles (Maestro, Giulio)
Railroad engineers and airplane pilots (Greene, Carla)
Rain (Kalan, Robert)
Rain (Ricketts, Michael)
Rain and hail (Branley, Franklyn M)
The rain cloud (Rayner, Mary)
Rain drop splash (Tresselt, Alvin R)
Rain makes applesauce (Scheer, Julian)
The rain puddle (Holl, Adelaide)
Rain! Rain! (Greene, Carol)
Rain rain rivers (Shulevitz, Uri)
The rainbow Mother Goose (Mother Goose)
A rainbow of my own (Freeman, Don)
Rainbow over all (Eastwick, Ivy O)
Raindrop stories (Bassett, Preston R)
The rainforest children (Pittaway, Margaret)
Rainy day Max (Türk, Hanne)
Rainy day together (Dragonwagon, Crescent)
Rainy rainy Saturday (Prelutsky, Jack)
Raking leaves with Max (Türk, Hanne)
Ralph rides away (Bishop, Bonnie)
Ralph's secret weapon (Kellogg, Steven)
Raminagrobis and the mice (Berson, Harold)
Rand McNally picturebook dictionary
The Randolph Caldecott treasury (Caldecott, Randolph)
Randolph Caldecott's favorite nursery rhymes (Caldecott, Randolph)
Randolph Caldecott's John Gilpin and other stories (Caldecott, Randolph)
Randolph Caldecott's picture book, no. 1 (Caldecott, Randolph)
Randolph Caldecott's picture book, no. 2 (Caldecott, Randolph)
The Random House book of poetry for children (Prelutsky, Jack)
Randy's dandy lions (Peet, Bill)
Rapunzel, ill. by Julia Ash (Grimm, Jacob)

Rapunzel, ill. by Bert Dodson (Grimm, Jacob)
Rapunzel, ill. by Trina Schart Hyman (Grimm, Jacob)
Rat is dead and ant is sad (Baker, Betty)
The rat race (McNaughton, Colin)
The rat, the ox and the zodiac (Van Woerkom, Dorothy)
The rats who lived in the delicatessen (Berson, Harold)
Read me a poem (Buell, Ellen Lewis)
Read one (Burningham, John)
Reading (Ormerod, Jan)
Ready, get set, go! (Peters, Sharon)
A real class clown (Coontz, Otto)
The real hole (Cleary, Beverly)
Real life monsters (Allen, Martha Dickson)
The real Mother Goose (Mother Goose)
The real personages of Mother Goose (Thomas, Katherine Elwes)
Really spring (Zion, Gene)
The reason for a flower (Heller, Ruth)
Rebecca Hatpin (Kraus, Robert)
Rebecka (Asch, Frank)
Red and the pumpkins (Stevenson, Jocelyn)
The red bantam (Fatio, Louise)
The red carpet (Parkin, Rex)
Red Fox and his canoe (Benchley, Nathaniel)
Red fox and the hungry tiger (Anderson, Paul S)
The red horse (Moeschlin, Elsa)
Red is best (Stinson, Kathy)
Red is never a mouse (Clifford, Eth)
Red legs (Goudey, Alice E)
Red light, green light (Brown, Margaret Wise)
Red mittens (Bannon, Laura)
Red Riding Hood (De Regniers, Beatrice Schenk)
Red Ridinghood's little lamb (Steiner, Charlotte)
Red rooster (Boutwell, Edna)
The red shoes (Andersen, H C (Hans Christian))
Red Tag comes back (Phleger, Fred B)
Red thread riddles (Jensen, Virginia Allen)
Redwoods are the tallest trees in the world (Adler, David A)
Regards to the man in the moon (Keats, Ezra Jack)
The remarkable egg (Holl, Adelaide)
The remarkable plant in apartment 4 (Maestro, Giulio)
The remarkable ride of Israel Bissell... as related to Molly the crow (Schick, Alice)
Remember the secret (Kübler-Ross, Elisabeth)
Reptiles (Harris, Susan)
Reptiles (Pluckrose, Henry)
The restless robin (Flack, Marjorie)
Rex (Sharmat, Marjorie Weinman)
A rhinoceros wakes me up in the morning (Goodspeed, Peter)
Rhymes around the day (Thomson, Pat)

S

Sand and snow (Kuskin, Karla)

Sand cake (Asch, Frank)

Sand castle (Wegen, Ron)

Sand dollar, sand dollar (Dos Santos, Joyce Audy)

The sand lot (Christian, Mary Blount)

Sandman in the lighthouse (Strahl, Rudi)

Sandpipers (Hurd, Edith Thacher)

Sandy at the children's zoo (Bolliger, Max)

Santa and Alex (Ephron, Delia)

Santa Claus and his elves (Kunnas, Mauri)

Santa Claus forever (Haywood, Carolyn)

Santa's crash-bang Christmas (Kroll, Steven)

Santa's favorite story (Aoki, Hisako)

Santa's moose (Hoff, Syd)

Santiago (Belpré, Pura)

Sara and the door (Jensen, Virginia Allen)

Sarah and the dragon (Coville, Bruce)

Sarah's unicorn (Coville, Bruce)

Sara's giant and the upside down house (Cunliffe, John)

Sasha and the samovar (Beim, Lorraine)

Sasha the cheetah (Irvine, Georgeanne)

Sasha the silly (Sharmat, Marjorie Weinman)

Saturday morning lasts forever (Bram, Elizabeth)

Save that raccoon! (Miklowitz, Gloria D)

Say it! (Zolotow, Charlotte)

A scale full of fish and other turnabouts (Bossom, Naomi)

Scareboy (Hart, Jeanne McGahey)

Scaredy cat (Krasilovsky, Phyllis)

Scaredy cats (Bonsall, Crosby Newell) The case of the scaredy cats

Scarlet Monster lives here (Sharmat, Marjorie Weinman)

The scary thing (Bannon, Laura)

Scenes from childhood (Sharon, Mary Bruce)

School (Baker, Eugene)

The school (Bruna, Dick)

School bus (Crews, Donald)

School daze (Keller, Charles)

School for sillies (Williams, Jay)

The school mouse and the hamster (Harris, Dorothy Joan)

Schoolmaster Whackwell's wonderful sons (Brentano, Clemens)

Science toys and tricks (White, Laurence B)

Scooter and the magic star (Gardner, Mercedes)

Scornful Simkin (Lorenz, Lee)

Scrambled eggs super! (Seuss, Dr)

Scrappy the pup (Ciardi, John)

The scribble monster (Kent, Jack)

The scribbler (Mendoza, George)

A scythe, a rooster and a cat (Domanska, Janina)

The sea dog (Dennis, Morgan)

Sea frog, city frog (Van Woerkom, Dorothy)

Sea full of whales (Armour, Richard Willard)

The sea monkey (Kaye, Geraldine)

Sea monsters of long ago (Selsam, Millicent E)

Sea otters (Shaw, Evelyn S)

Sea sums (Morse, Samuel French)

The Sea View Hotel (Stevenson, James)

The Sea World alphabet book

Seahorse (Morris, Robert A)

The seal

The seal and the slick (Freeman, Don)

The seamstress of Salzburg (Lobel, Anita)

Search for Sam (Morris, Neil)

The seashore noisy book (Brown, Margaret Wise)

Seashore story (Yashima, Tarō)

Seasons (Burningham, John)

The seasons (Lambert, David)

Seasons (Wildsmith, Brian)

The seasons of Arnold's apple tree (Gibbons, Gail)

The seaweed hat (Slobodkin, Louis)

Sebastian and the dragon (Kumin, Maxine)

Sebastian and the mushroom (Krahn, Fernando)

The secret birthday message (Carle, Eric)

The secret box (Cole, Joanna)

A secret for grandmother's birthday (Brandenberg, Franz)

The secret hiding place (Bennett, Rainey)

The secret in the dungeon (Krahn, Fernando)

The secret inside (Hayes, Geoffrey)

The secret life of Mr. Weird (Allen, Jeffrey)

The secret of the Sabbath fish (Aronin, Ben)

Secret places (Arneson, D J)

The secret seller (Lifton, Betty Jean)

The secret staircase (Barklem, Jill)

The secret three (Myrick, Mildred)

Secret tunnel (Chandler, Edna Walker)

The secret world of teddy bears (Prince, Pamela)

Secrets of a small brother (Margolis, Richard J)

See again, say again (Frasconi, Antonio)

See and say (Frasconi, Antonio)

See my lovely poison ivy, (Moore, Lilian)

See the bear (Bryant, Dean)

See the circus (Rey, Hans Augusto)

See what I am (Duvoisin, Roger Antoine)

See what I caught! (Piecewicz, Ann Thomas)

See you tomorrow (Cohen, Miriam)

The seed that peacock planted (Kepes, Juliet)

The seed the squirrel dropped (Petie, Haris)

Seeds and more seeds (Selsam, Millicent E)

Seeds of wind and water (Jordan, Helene J)

Seeds on the go (Fisher, Aileen)

Seeing is believing (Shub, Elizabeth)

Seeing red (Wolff, Robert Jay)

The seeing stick (Yolen, Jane)

Seeing things (Froman, Robert)

Seen any cats? (Modell, Frank)

Seesaw (Kahn, Joan)

Self-control (Gambill, Henrietta)

Send Wendell (Gray, Genevieve)

Too many babas (Croll, Carolyn)
Too many dogs (Dupré, Ramona Dorrel)
Too many rabbits (Parish, Peggy)
Too much noise (McGovern, Ann)
Too short Fred (Meddaugh, Susan)
Tool book (Gibbons, Gail)
The toolbox (Rockwell, Anne F)
Toolchest (Adkins, Jan)
Tooley! Tooley! (Modell, Frank)
Toot! Toot! (Kroll, Steven)
Tooth and claw (Freedman, Russell)
The tooth book (Seuss, Dr)
A tooth for the tooth fairy (Gunther, Louise)
Tooth-gnasher superflash (Pinkwater, Daniel Manus)
The top of the pizzas (Basso, Bill)
Tops (Wiesner, William)
Tops and bottoms (Conger, Lesley)
Topsy-turvies (Anno, Mitsumasa)
Topsys and turvys (Newell, Peter)
Tornado! (Adoff, Arnold)
The tortoise and the tree (Domanska, Janina)
Tortoise and turtle (Gendel, Evelyn)
Tortoise and turtle abroad (Gendel, Evelyn)
The tortoise's tug of war (Maestro, Giulio)
Tot Botot and his little flute (Cathon, Laura E)
Toto the timid turtle (Goldsmith, Howard)
The touch book (Moncure, Jane Belk)
The touch said hello (Forrester, Victoria)
Touch will tell (Brown, Marcia)
Touching (Allington, Richard L)
Tough Eddie (Winthrop, Elizabeth)
Tough Jim (Cohen, Miriam)
The Tower of Babel (Leeton, Will C)
The Tower of Babel (Wiesner, William)
Town and country (Provensen, Alice)
The town mouse and the country mouse, ill. by Lorinda Bryan Cauley (Æsop)
The town mouse and the country mouse, ill. by Paul Galdone (Æsop)
The town mouse and the country mouse, ill. by Tom Garcia (Æsop)
The town that moved (Finsand, Mary Jane)
Townsfolk and countryfolk (Sopko, Eugeh)
Towser and the terrible thing (Ross, Tony)
The toy maker (Thelen, Gerda)
The toy shop (Spier, Peter)
The toy trumpet (Grifalconi, Ann)
The tractor on the farm (Israel, Marion Louise)
Traffic (Maestro, Betsy)
The traffic stopper that became a grandmother visitor (Löfgren, Ulf)
The train (McPhail, David)
A train for the king (Karlin, Nurit)
Train whistle (Sattler, Helen Roney)
Trains (Broekel, Ray)
The traveling ball of string (Calhoun, Mary)
The traveling men of Ballycoo (Bunting, Eve)
Traveling to Tripiti (Steger, Hans-Ulrich)

The travels of Babar (Brunhoff, Jean de)
The travels of Ching (Bright, Robert)
The treasure (Shulevitz, Uri)
A treasure box of fairy tales (Jones, Olive)
A treasury of Peter Rabbit and other stories (Potter, Beatrix)
A treasury of songs for little children (Botwin, Esther)
The tree angel (Martin, Judith)
Tree house fun (Greydanus, Rose)
A tree is a plant (Bulla, Clyde Robert)
A tree is nice (Udry, Janice May)
A tree with a thousand uses (Fisher, Aileen)
A treeful of pigs (Lobel, Arnold)
Treehorn's treasure (Heide, Florence Parry)
Treehorn's wish (Heide, Florence Parry)
Trees (Gordon, Sharon)
The trees stand shining (Jones, Hettie, comp)
The tremendous tree book (Garelick, May)
Trick or treat (Slobodkin, Louis)
Trick or treat Halloween (Peters, Sharon)
The trick-or-treat trap (Zimmer, Dirk)
The tricks of Master Dabble (Zemach, Harve)
The trip (Keats, Ezra Jack)
The trip (Sharmat, Marjorie Weinman)
A trip through a school (Rowe, Jeanne A)
The trip to Panama (Janosch)
A trip to the yard (Cross, Genevieve)
The triplets (Seuling, Barbara)
The triumphs of Fuzzy Fogtop (Rose, Anne)
The troll book (Berenstain, Michael)
Troll country (Marshall, Edward)
The troll music (Lobel, Anita)
The troll who lived in the lake (Torgersen, Don Arthur)
Trolley (Taniuchi, Kota)
The trouble with mom (Cole, Babette)
The trouble with spider (Kraus, Robert)
Trout the magnificent (Turnage, Sheila)
The Troy St. bus (Charmatz, Bill)
Trubloff (Burningham, John)
Truck (Crews, Donald)
The truck book (McNaught, Harry)
The truck book (Wolfe, Robert L)
Truck drivers: what do they do? (Greene, Carla)
The truck on the track (Burroway, Janet)
Truck song (Siebert, Diane)
Trucks
Trucks (Broekel, Ray)
Trucks (Gibbons, Gail)
Trucks (Rockwell, Anne F)
Trucks and cars to ride (Baugh, Dolores M)
Trucks of every sort (Robbins, Ken)
The true book of time (Ziner, Feenie)
The true cross (Wildsmith, Brian)
The true Francine (Brown, Marc)
True or false? (Ruben, Patricia)
The truffle pig (Bishop, Claire Huchet)
Truffles for lunch (Berson, Harold)
Trumpet (Austin, Margot)
The truth about gorillas (Meyers, Susan)

U

UFO kidnap (Robison, Nancy)

Ugbu (Ayal, Ora)

The ugly book (Crowley, Arthur)

The ugly duckling, ill. by Adrienne Adams (Andersen, H C (Hans Christian))

The ugly duckling, ill. by Lorinda Bryan Cauley (Andersen, H C (Hans Christian))

The ugly duckling, ill. by Tadasu Izawa and Shigemi Hijikata (Andersen, H C (Hans Christian))

The ugly duckling, ill. by Johannes Larsen (Andersen, H C (Hans Christian))

The ugly duckling, ill. by Josef Palacek (Andersen, H C (Hans Christian))

Umbrella (Yashima, Tarō)

Uncle Eddie's moustache (Brecht, Bertolt)

Uncle Elephant (Lobel, Arnold)

Uncle Hugh (Gelman, Rita Golden)

Uncle Louie's fantastic sea voyage (Loof, Jan)

Uncle Roland, the perfect guest (Green, Phyllis)

Under the cherry tree (Mitchell, Cynthia)

Under the green willow (Coatsworth, Elizabeth)

Under the lemon tree (Hurd, Edith Thacher)

Under the ocean (Booth, Eugene)

Under the rowan tree (Brown, Abbie Farwell)

Under the shade of the mulberry tree (Demi)

Under the window (Greenaway, Kate)

The unexpected grandchild (Flory, Jane)

Unfortunately Harriet (Wells, Rosemary)

The unfriendly book (Zolotow, Charlotte)

The unicorn and the lake (Mayer, Marianna)

The unicorn and the plow (Moeri, Louise)

Unicorn moon (Cooper, Gale)

Unusual animals (Daly, Kathleen N)

Up a tree (Young, Ed)

Up and up (Hughes, Shirley)

Up day, down day (Hann, Jacquie)

Up high and down low (Slobodkin, Louis)

Up the alley with Jack and Joe (Kotzwinkle, William)

Up the down elevator (Farber, Norma)

Up there (Hill, Eric)

Uproar on Hollercat Hill (Marzollo, Jean)

Ups and down (Berkley, Ethel S)

Upside down (Johnson, Crockett)

The upside down riddle book (Phillips, Louis)

Upside-downers (Anno, Mitsumasa)

Upstairs and downstairs (Johnson, Ryerson)

Uptown (Steptoe, John)

Uptown, downtown (Bank Street College of Education)

Use your head, dear (Aliki)

Usha, the mouse-maiden (Gobhai, Mehlli)

V

Vagabul and his shadow (Marol, Jean-Claude)

Vagabul escapes (Marol, Jean-Claude)

Vagabul goes skiing (Marol, Jean-Claude)

Vagabul in the clouds (Marol, Jean-Claude)

The Valentine bears (Bunting, Eve)

Valentine cat (Bulla, Clyde Robert)

Valentine for a dragon (Murphy, Shirley Rousseau)

A valentine for Fuzzboom (Kelley, True)

The Valentine mystery (Nixon, Joan Lowery)

Valentine's Day (Guilfoile, Elizabeth)

Valerie and the good-night swing (Lobe, Mira)

The valiant little tailor (Grimm, Jacob)

The vanishing pumpkin (Johnston, Tony)

Vanka's donkey (Daugherty, Sonia)

The vegetable thieves (Moore, Inga)

The velveteen rabbit, ill. by Allen Atkinson (Bianco, Margery Williams)

The velveteen rabbit, ill. by Michael Hague (Bianco, Margery Williams)

The velveteen rabbit, ill. by William Nicholson (Bianco, Margery Williams)

The velveteen rabbit, ill. by Ilse Plume (Bianco, Margery Williams)

The velveteen rabbit, ill. by Tien (Bianco, Margery Williams)

Verity Mullens and the Indian (Belting, Natalia Maree)

Veronica (Duvoisin, Roger Antoine)

Veronica and the birthday present (Duvoisin, Roger Antoine)

Veronica's smile (Duvoisin, Roger Antoine)

Very far away (Sendak, Maurice)

The very first story ever told (Weil, Lisl)

The very hungry caterpillar (Carle, Eric)

The very little boy (Krasilovsky, Phyllis)

The very little dog (Skaar, Grace Marion)

The very little girl (Krasilovsky, Phyllis)

The very messy room (Stanton, Elizabeth)

A very mice joke book (Goundaud, Karen Jo)

A very special house (Krauss, Ruth)

The very tall little girl (Krasilovsky, Phyllis)

Victoria's castle (Holman, Felice)

The village tree (Yashima, Tarō)

Vim, the rag mouse (Daly, Niki)

The vingananee and the tree toad (Aardema, Verna)

The violin close up (Schaaf, Peter)

The VIP's mistake book (Partch, Virgil Franklin)

The vision of Francois the fox (Cunningham, Julia)

A visit from St. Alphabet (Morice, Dave)

A visit from St. Nicholas (Moore, Clement C)

A visit to a pond

Visit to the North Pole (Le-Tan, Pierre)

W

Wynken, Blynken and Nod (Field, Eugene)

Y

Yagua days (Martel, Cruz)
Yankee Doodle (Bangs, Edward)
Yankee Doodle (Schackburg, Richard)
A yard for John (Clymer, Eleanor Lowenton)
Yasu and the strangers (Slobodkin, Louis)
The year at Maple Hill Farm (Provensen, Alice)
A year in the forest (Hall, Bill)
A year of birds (Wolff, Ashley)
The year Santa went modern (Armour, Richard Willard)
Yellow and pink (Steig, William)
The yellow boat (Hillert, Margaret)
The yellow brick toad (Thaler, Mike)
Yellow, yellow (Asch, Frank)
Yet another big fat funny silly book (Hample, Stoo)
Yetta, the trickster (Zimmerman, Andrea Griffing)
Yoga for your children (Marshall, Lyn)
Yonie Wondernose (De Angeli, Marguerite)
You are special to Jesus (Dellinger, Annetta)
You are the star of a Muppet adventure (Weiss, Ellen)
You are what you are (McLenighan, Valjean)
You can go jump (McLenighan, Valjean)
You can write Chinese (Wiese, Kurt)
You can't catch me! (Rosen, Michael)
You can't make a move without your muscles (Showers, Paul)
You can't put braces on spaces (Richter, Alice Numeroff)
You know better than that (Smaridge, Norah)
You never can tell (Holland, Janice)
You ought to see Herbert's house (Lund, Doris Herold)
You read to me, I'll read to you (Ciardi, John)
You see the world around you (Selsam, Millicent E)
You think it's fun to be a clown! (Adler, David A)
You were born on your very first birthday (Girard, Linda Walvoord)
You will go to the moon (Freeman, Mae)
You will live under the sea (Phleger, Fred B)
You'll soon grow into them, Titch (Hutchins, Pat)
Young animals in the zoo
Young domestic animals

Young kangaroo (Brown, Margaret Wise)
The young man who wouldn't hoe corn (Schmidt, Eric von)
The young performing horse (Yeoman, John)
Young reader's color-picture dictionary (Parke, Margaret B)
The youngest one (Yashima, Tarō)
Your face is a picture (Clifford, Eth)
Your family, my family (Drescher, Joan)
Your first airplane trip (Ross, Pat)
Your first garden book (Brown, Marc)
Your own best secret place (Baylor, Byrd)
Your pet bear (Hamsa, Bobbie)
Your pet beaver (Hamsa, Bobbie)
Your pet camel (Hamsa, Bobbie)
Your pet elephant (Hamsa, Bobbie)
Your pet giraffe (Hamsa, Bobbie)
Your pet kangaroo (Hamsa, Bobbie)
Your pet penguin (Hamsa, Bobbie)
Your pet sea lion (Hamsa, Bobbie)
Your skin and mine (Showers, Paul)
Your turn, doctor (Robison, Deborah)
Your world let's visit the hospital (Pope, Billy N)
You're a little kid with a big heart (Waber, Bernard)
You're the greatest, Charlie Brown (Schulz, Charles M)
You're the scaredy cat (Mayer, Mercer)
Yours affectionately, Peter Rabbit (Potter, Beatrix)
Yuck! (Stevenson, James)
Yummers! (Marshall, James)

Z

Zebra goes to school (Watts, Marjorie-Ann)
Zebras (Goodall, Daphne Machin)
Zed and the monsters (Parish, Peggy)
Zeee (Enright, Elizabeth)
Zeek Silver Moon (Ehrlich, Amy)
Zeralda's ogre (Ungerer, Tomi)
Zoo animals
Zoo animals (Greeley, Valerie)
Zoo animals (Roosevelt, Michelle Chopin)
Zoo babies (Grosvenor, Donna)
The zoo book (Allen, Robert)
Zoo city (Lewis, Stephen)
A zoo for Mister Muster (Lobel, Arnold)
A zoo in her bed (Marcin, Marietta)
The zoo in my garden (Nakatani, Chiyoko)
The zoo that moved (Miklowitz, Gloria D)
Zoo, where are you? (McGovern, Ann)

Illustrator Index

Illustrators appear alphabetically in boldface followed by their titles. Names in parentheses are authors of the titles.

A

Abel, Ray. The new sitter (Abel, Ruth)

Abolafia, Yossi. Buffy and Albert (Pomerantz, Charlotte)
Harry's visit (Porte, Barbara Ann)
It's Valentine's Day (Prelutsky, Jack)
What I did last summer (Prelutsky, Jack)

Abrahams, Hilary. Pa's top hat (Corney, Estelle)
Sara's giant and the upside down house (Cunliffe, John)

Abrams, Kathie. Busy buzzing bumblebees (Schwartz, Alvin)

Accardo, Anthony. Ginger (Ronay, Jadja)

Ach, Michael E. I have feelings too (Berger, Terry)

Ackley, Telka. Please (Ackley, Edith Flack)
Thank you (Ackley, Edith Flack)

Adam, Barbara. The big big box (Adam, Barbara)

Adams, Adrienne. Arion and the dolphins (Anderson, Lonzo)
Bring a torch, Jeannette, Isabella
Cabbage moon (Wahl, Jan)
The Christmas party (Adams, Adrienne)
The day we saw the sun come up (Goudey, Alice E)
The Easter bunny that overslept (Friedrich, Priscilla)
The Easter egg artists (Adams, Adrienne)
Going barefoot (Fisher, Aileen)
The great Valentine's Day balloon race (Adams, Adrienne)
A Halloween happening (Adams, Adrienne)
The Halloween party (Anderson, Lonzo)
Hansel and Gretel (Grimm, Jacob)
Houses from the sea (Goudey, Alice E)
In the middle of the night (Fisher, Aileen)
Izzard (Anderson, Lonzo)
Jorinda and Joringel (Grimm, Jacob)
The littlest witch (Massey, Jeanne)
Mr. Biddle and the birds (Anderson, Lonzo)
The river bank (Grahame, Kenneth)
Snow White and Rose Red (Grimm, Jacob)
Summer's coming in (Belting, Natalia Maree)

Theodore's parents (Udry, Janice May)
Thumbelina (Andersen, H C (Hans Christian))
Two hundred rabbits (Anderson, Lonzo)
The ugly duckling (Andersen, H C (Hans Christian))
Where does everyone go? (Fisher, Aileen)
The white rat's tale (Schiller, Barbara)
A woggle of witches (Adams, Adrienne)
The wounded duck (Barnhart, Peter)

Adams, Pauline B. Picture book dictionary (MacBean, Dilla Wittemore)

Adams, Ruth Joyce. Fidelia (Adams, Ruth Joyce)

Adamson, Gareth. Old man up a tree (Adamson, Gareth)
What shape is it? (Hatcher, Charles)

Adamson, Joy. Elsa (Adamson, Joy)
Elsa and her cubs (Adamson, Joy)
Pippa the cheetah and her cubs (Adamson, Joy)

Addams, Charles. The Charles Addams Mother Goose (Mother Goose)

Adelborg, Ottilia. Clean Peter and the children of Grubbylea (Adelborg, Ottilia)

Adkins, Jan. The art and industry of sandcastles (Adkins, Jan)
Heavy equipment (Adkins, Jan)
Toolchest (Adkins, Jan)

Adler, David A. A little at a time (Adler, David A)

Agee, Jon. Ellsworth (Agee, Jon)

Agostinelli, Maria Enrica. I know something you don't know (Agostinelli, Maria Enrica)
On wings of love (Agostinelli, Maria Enrica)

Agre, Patricia. Clowns (Sobol, Harriet Langsam)
Jeff's hospital book (Sobol, Harriet Langsam)
My brother Steven is retarded (Sobol, Harriet Langsam)
We don't look like our mom and dad (Sobol, Harriet Langsam)

Ahlberg, Allan. The baby's catalogue (Ahlberg, Janet)
Burglar Bill (Ahlberg, Janet)
Each peach pear plum (Ahlberg, Janet)
Funnybones (Ahlberg, Janet)

The little worm book (Ahlberg, Janet)
Peek-a-boo! (Ahlberg, Janet)
Ahlberg, Janet. The baby's catalogue
    (Ahlberg, Janet)
  Burglar Bill (Ahlberg, Janet)
  Cops and robbers (Ahlberg, Allan)
  Each peach pear plum (Ahlberg, Janet)
  Funnybones (Ahlberg, Janet)
  The little worm book (Ahlberg, Janet)
  Peek-a-boo! (Ahlberg, Janet)
Aho, Jennifer J. Learning about sex (Aho,
    Jennifer J)
Aichinger, Helga. I never saw ... (Jerome,
    Judson)
  Jonah and the great fish (Bulla, Clyde
    Robert)
  Noah and the rainbow (Bolliger, Max)
  The shepherd (Aichinger, Helga)
  What shall I be tomorrow? (Blakeley,
    Peggy)
Aitken, Amy. I'm not moving! (Jones,
    Penelope)
  Kate and Mona in the jungle (Aitken,
    Amy)
  The one in the middle is the green
    kangaroo (Blume, Judy)
  Ruby! (Aitken, Amy)
  Ruby, the red knight (Aitken, Amy)
Akaba, Suekichi. The crane wife (Yagawa,
    Sumiko)
  Suho and the white horse (Otsuka, Yuzo)
Akino, Fuku. Sea sums (Morse, Samuel
    French)
Alain. Minette (Janice)
Alajalov, Constantin. Angels (Benét, William
    Rose)
Alanen, Erkki. The turtles' picnic and other
    nonsense stories (Berger, Terry)
Albertson, Lee. The day it rained
    watermelons (Watts, Mabel)
Alborough, Jez. Bare bear (Alborough, Jez)
Alcorn, John. Wonderful time (McGinley,
    Phyllis)
Alda, Arlene. Arlene Alda's ABC (Alda,
    Arlene)
  Matthew and his dad (Alda, Arlene)
  Sonya's mommy works (Alda, Arlene)
Alexander, Benjamin. You are the star of a
    Muppet adventure (Weiss, Ellen)
Alexander, Martha G. And my mean old
    mother will be sorry, Blackboard Bear
    (Alexander, Martha G)
  Big sister and little sister (Zolotow,
    Charlotte)
  Blackboard Bear (Alexander, Martha G)
  Bobo's dream (Alexander, Martha G)
  Charles (Skorpen, Liesel Moak)
  Elizabeth (Skorpen, Liesel Moak)
  The everyday train (Ehrlich, Amy)
  How my library grew by Dinah (Alexander,
    Martha G)
  I sure am glad to see you, Blackboard Bear
    (Alexander, Martha G)
  I'll be the horse if you'll play with me
    (Alexander, Martha G)
  I'll protect you from the jungle beasts
    (Alexander, Martha G)

Jeremy isn't hungry (Williams, Barbara)
Maggie's moon (Alexander, Martha G)
Marty McGee's space lab, no girls allowed
    (Alexander, Martha G)
Mary Ann's mud day (Udry, Janice May)
Maybe a monster (Alexander, Martha G)
Move over, Twerp (Alexander, Martha G)
No ducks in our bathtub (Alexander,
    Martha G)
Nobody asked me if I wanted a baby sister
    (Alexander, Martha G)
Out! Out! Out! (Alexander, Martha G)
Pigs say oink (Alexander, Martha G)
Sabrina (Alexander, Martha G)
The story grandmother told (Alexander,
    Martha G)
3 magic flip books (Alexander, Martha G)
We never get to do anything (Alexander,
    Martha G)
We're in big trouble, Blackboard Bear
    (Alexander, Martha G)
When the new baby comes, I'm moving out
    (Alexander, Martha G)

Alfonso, Carlos. Six in a mix (Richardson,
    Jack E)

Aliki. At home (Hautzig, Esther)
  At Mary Bloom's (Aliki)
  Aunt Nina and her nephews and nieces
    (Brandenberg, Franz)
  Aunt Nina's visit (Brandenberg, Franz)
  Cathy is company (Lexau, Joan M)
  Corn is maize (Aliki)
  Digging up dinosaurs (Aliki)
  Diogenes (Aliki)
  The eggs (Aliki)
  Everyone ready? (Brandenberg, Franz)
  Fossils tell of long ago (Aliki)
  Fresh cider and apple pie (Brandenberg,
    Franz)
  George and the cherry tree (Aliki)
  Go tell Aunt Rhody
  The horse that liked sandwiches
    (Thompson, Vivian Laubach)
  Hush little baby
  I wish I was sick, too! (Aliki)
  Is that a happy hippopotamus? (Morrison,
    Sean)
  It's not my fault (Brandenberg, Franz)
  June 7! (Aliki)
  Keep your mouth closed, dear (Aliki)
  The lazy little Zulu (Holding, James)
  Leo and Emily (Brandenberg, Franz)
  Leo and Emily and the dragon
    (Brandenberg, Franz)
  The listening walk (Showers, Paul)
  The long lost coelacanth and other living
    fossils (Aliki)
  The many lives of Benjamin Franklin
    (Aliki)
  Mummies made in Egypt (Aliki)
  My five senses (Aliki)
  My hands (Aliki)
  My visit to the dinosaurs (Aliki)
  Nice new neighbors (Brandenberg, Franz)
  No school today! (Brandenberg, Franz)
  Oh, Lord, I wish I was a buzzard
    (Greenberg, Polly)

The crooked colt (Anderson, C W (Clarence Williams))

Linda and the Indians (Anderson, C W (Clarence Williams))

Lonesome little colt (Anderson, C W (Clarence Williams))

A pony for Linda (Anderson, C W (Clarence Williams))

A pony for three (Anderson, C W (Clarence Williams))

The rumble seat pony (Anderson, C W (Clarence Williams))

Anderson, Douglas. Let's draw a story (Anderson, Douglas)

Anderson, Irv. The little runaway (Hillert, Margaret)

Anderson, Wayne. The magic circus (Logue, Christopher)

Andre, Evelyn M. Places I like to be (Andre, Evelyn M)

André, Rov. Lefty, the story of left-handedness (Lerner, Marguerite Rush)

Andru, Ross. The Superman mix or match storybook

Andrus, Carroll. Silly stories mix and match (Koelling, Caryl)

Angel, Marie. The tale of the faithful dove (Potter, Beatrix)

The tale of Tuppeny (Potter, Beatrix)

We went looking (Fisher, Aileen)

Angeli, Marguerite De *see* De Angeli, Marguerite

Angelia. The cozy little farm (Bonino, Louise)

Angelis, Nancy de *see* Angelo, Nancy Carolyn Harrison

Angelo, Nancy Carolyn Harrison. Camembert (Angelo, Nancy Carolyn Harrison)

Angelo, Nicholas. The vision of Francois the fox (Cunningham, Julia)

Angelo, Valenti. The acorn tree (Angelo, Valenti)

The candy basket (Angelo, Valenti)

Anglund, Joan Walsh. A is for always (Anglund, Joan Walsh)

A book of good tidings from the Bible (Anglund, Joan Walsh)

The brave cowboy (Anglund, Joan Walsh)

A child's book of old nursery rhymes (Mother Goose)

A Christmas book (Anglund, Joan Walsh)

Christmas is a time of giving (Anglund, Joan Walsh)

Cowboy and his friend (Anglund, Joan Walsh)

The cowboy's Christmas (Anglund, Joan Walsh)

Cowboy's secret life (Anglund, Joan Walsh)

A friend is someone who likes you (Anglund, Joan Walsh)

In a pumpkin shell (Mother Goose)

The Joan Walsh Anglund story book (Anglund, Joan Walsh)

Look out the window (Anglund, Joan Walsh)

Love is a special way of feeling (Anglund, Joan Walsh)

Love one another (Anglund, Joan Walsh)

Morning is a little child (Anglund, Joan Walsh)

Nibble nibble mousekin (Anglund, Joan Walsh)

Spring is a new beginning (Anglund, Joan Walsh)

Anno, Masaichiro. Anno's magical ABC (Anno, Mitsumasa)

Anno, Mitsumasa. Anno's alphabet (Anno, Mitsumasa)

Anno's animals (Anno, Mitsumasa)

Anno's Britain (Anno, Mitsumasa)

Anno's counting book (Anno, Mitsumasa)

Anno's counting house (Anno, Mitsumasa)

Anno's flea market (Anno, Mitsumasa)

Anno's Italy (Anno, Mitsumasa)

Anno's journey (Anno, Mitsumasa)

Anno's magical ABC (Anno, Mitsumasa)

Anno's U.S.A. (Anno, Mitsumasa)

Dr. Anno's midnight circus (Anno, Mitsumasa)

The king's flower (Anno, Mitsumasa)

Topsy-turvies (Anno, Mitsumasa)

Upside-downers (Anno, Mitsumasa)

Aoki, Hisako. Santa's favorite story (Aoki, Hisako)

Appell, Clara. Now I have a daddy haircut (Appell, Clara)

Appell, Morey. Now I have a daddy haircut (Appell, Clara)

Appelmann, Karl-Heinz. Be quite quiet beside the lake (Koenner, Alfred)

Apple, Margot. The bear in the bathtub (Jackson, Ellen B)

The blueberry bears (Lapp, Eleanor)

Cookie Becker casts a spell (Glazer, Lee)

Susie goes shopping (Greydanus, Rose)

The tale of Peter Rabbit (Potter, Beatrix)

The wonderful Mrs. Trumbly (Wittman, Sally)

Applebaum, Neil. Is there a hole in your head? (Applebaum, Neil)

Appleby, Ellen. Pets I wouldn't pick (Schmeltz, Susan Alton)

Where will the animals stay? (Calmenson, Stephanie)

Appleby, Leonard. Snakes (Appleby, Leonard)

Appleton, George S. Mother Goose in hieroglyphics (Mother Goose)

Appleyard, Dev. What you see is what you get (McLenighan, Valjean)

Archer, Peter. Nowhere to play (Emecheta, Buchi)

Ardizzone, Edward. Diana and her rhinoceros (Ardizzone, Edward)

Dick Whittington (Dick Whittington and his cat)

Hello, elephant (Wahl, Jan)

Johnny the clockmaker (Ardizzone, Edward)

The little fire engine (Greene, Graham)

The little girl and the tiny doll (Ardizzone, Edward)

Starbaby (Asch, Frank)

Turtle tale (Asch, Frank)

Asch, George. Linda (Asch, George)

Ash, Jutta. Chicken Licken (Chicken Little)

Rapunzel (Grimm, Jacob)

A week is a long time (Barton, Pat)

Ashby, Gwynneth. Take a trip to Japan (Ashby, Gwynneth)

Atene, Ann. The golden guitar (Atene, Ann)

Atene, Anna *see* Atene, Ann

Atkinson, Allen. The tale of Peter Rabbit and other stories (Potter, Beatrix)

The velveteen rabbit (Bianco, Margery Williams)

Atkinson, Michael. The kangaroo (Townsend, Anita)

Atkinson, Wayne. The miracles at Cana (Chase, Catherine)

Attenberger, Walburga. The little man in winter (Attenberger, Walburga)

Who knows the little man? (Attenberger, Walburga)

Atwood, Ann. The little circle (Atwood, Ann)

Sammy, the crow who remembered (Hazelton, Elizabeth Baldwin)

Auerbach, Marjorie. King Lavra and the barber (Auerbach, Marjorie)

Augarde, Stephen *see* Augarde, Steve

Augarde, Steve. Barnaby Shrew, Black Dan and... the mighty wedgwood (Augarde, Steve)

Barnaby Shrew goes to sea (Augarde, Steve)

Pig (Augarde, Steve)

Aulaire, Edgar Parin d'. Abraham Lincoln (Aulaire, Ingri Mortenson d')

Animals everywhere (Aulaire, Ingri Mortenson d')

Children of the northlights (Aulaire, Ingri Mortenson d')

Don't count your chicks (Aulaire, Ingri Mortenson d')

East of the sun and west of the moon (Aulaire, Ingri Mortenson d')

Foxie, the singing dog (Aulaire, Ingri Mortenson d')

The Lord's prayer (Aulaire, Ingri Mortenson d')

The Lord's prayer (Aulaire, Ingri Mortenson d')

Nils (Aulaire, Ingri Mortenson d')

Ola (Aulaire, Ingri Mortenson d')

Pocahontas (Aulaire, Ingri Mortenson d')

The terrible troll-bird (Aulaire, Ingri Mortenson d')

Too big (Aulaire, Ingri Mortenson d')

The two cars (Aulaire, Ingri Mortenson d')

Wings for Per (Aulaire, Ingri Mortenson d')

Aulaire, Ingri Mortenson d'. Abraham Lincoln (Aulaire, Ingri Mortenson d')

Animals everywhere (Aulaire, Ingri Mortenson d')

Children of the northlights (Aulaire, Ingri Mortenson d')

Don't count your chicks (Aulaire, Ingri Mortenson d')

East of the sun and west of the moon (Aulaire, Ingri Mortenson d')

Foxie, the singing dog (Aulaire, Ingri Mortenson d')

The Lord's prayer (Aulaire, Ingri Mortenson d')

The Lord's prayer (Aulaire, Ingri Mortenson d')

Nils (Aulaire, Ingri Mortenson d')

Ola (Aulaire, Ingri Mortenson d')

Pocahontas (Aulaire, Ingri Mortenson d')

The terrible troll-bird (Aulaire, Ingri Mortenson d')

Too big (Aulaire, Ingri Mortenson d')

The two cars (Aulaire, Ingri Mortenson d')

Wings for Per (Aulaire, Ingri Mortenson d')

Austin, Margot. Barney's adventure (Austin, Margot)

Growl Bear (Austin, Margot)

Manuel's kite string (Austin, Margot)

Trumpet (Austin, Margot)

Willamet way (Austin, Margot)

Auth, Tony. Mean Murgatroyd and the ten cats (Zimelman, Nathan)

Aver, Philip Van *see* Van Aver, Philip

Averill, Esther. The fire cat (Averill, Esther)

Jenny and the cat club (Averill, Esther)

Jenny's adopted brothers (Averill, Esther)

Jenny's birthday book (Averill, Esther)

Jenny's first party (Averill, Esther)

Jenny's moonlight adventure (Averill, Esther)

When Jenny lost her scarf (Averill, Esther)

Axeman, Lois. Everybody takes turns (Corey, Dorothy)

Happy healthkins (Moncure, Jane Belk)

The healthkin food train (Moncure, Jane Belk)

Healthkins exercise! (Moncure, Jane Belk)

Healthkins help (Moncure, Jane Belk)

Just like me (Neasi, Barbara J)

Katie did it (McDaniel, Becky Bring)

The look book (Moncure, Jane Belk)

Mine, yours, ours (Albert, Burton)

Sounds all around (Moncure, Jane Belk)

A tasting party (Moncure, Jane Belk)

Tomorrow you can (Corey, Dorothy)

The touch book (Moncure, Jane Belk)

What? (Reece, Colleen L)

What your nose knows! (Moncure, Jane Belk)

When? (Alden, Laura)

Where? (Moncure, Jane Belk)

Why? (Clark, Roberta)

Ayal, Ora. The adventures of Chester the chest (Ayal, Ora)

Ugbu (Ayal, Ora)

Ayer, Jacqueline. Little Silk (Ayer, Jacqueline)

Nu Dang and his kite (Ayer, Jacqueline)

The paper-flower tree (Ayer, Jacqueline)

Rumpelstiltskin (Grimm, Jacob)

A wish for little sister (Ayer, Jacqueline)

Ayer, Margaret. Paddy and Sam (Bothwell, Jean)

Some things you should know about my
dog (Batherman, Muriel)

Battaglia, Aurelius. Around the city (Bank
Street College of Education)

Bauer, Fred. The wooden man (Bolliger,
Max)

Baum, Joseph. One bright Monday morning
(Baum, Arline)

Baum, Willi. Birds of a feather (Baum, Willi)
The miracle of the mountain (Kipling,
Rudyard)

Baumli, Othmar. A duckling is born
(Isenbart, Hans-Heinrich)

Bayley, Nicola. La corona and the tin frog
(Hoban, Russell)
Crab cat (Bayley, Nicola)
Elephant cat (Bayley, Nicola)
Nicola Bayley's book of nursery rhymes
(Bayley, Nicola)
One old Oxford ox (Bayley, Nicola)
Parrot cat (Bayley, Nicola)
The patchwork cat (Mayne, William)
Polar bear cat (Bayley, Nicola)
Spider cat (Bayley, Nicola)
The tyger voyage (Adams, Richard)

Baynes, Pauline. A family book of nursery
rhymes (Opie, Iona Archibald)
Grasshopper and butterfly (Piers, Helen)
Puffin book of nursery rhymes (Opie, Iona
Archibald)

Baynton, Martin. Big John Turkle (Hoban,
Russell)
Jim Frog (Hoban, Russell)
Lavina bat (Hoban, Russell)

Beatty, Hetty Burlingame. Bucking horse
(Beatty, Hetty Burlingame)
Droopy (Beatty, Hetty Burlingame)
Little Owl Indian (Beatty, Hetty
Burlingame)
Moorland pony (Beatty, Hetty Burlingame)

Becker, Ron. My city (Bank Street College of
Education)
Uptown, downtown (Bank Street College
of Education)

Beckett, Sheilah. Cinderella (Perrault,
Charles)

Beckman, Per. Lisa cannot sleep (Beckman,
Kaj)

Bee, Joyce. Animals that store food (Vevers,
Gwynne)

Beerworth, Roger. Animal mix and match
(Koelling, Caryl)

Begay, Harrison. The little Indian basket
maker (Clark, Ann Nolan)

Behn, Harry. All kinds of time (Behn,
Harry)
Crickets and bullfrogs and whispers of
thunder (Behn, Harry)

Behr, Joyce. The funny songbook (Nelson,
Esther L)
The silly songbook (Nelson, Esther L)

Behrens, Paul. Grandmother Poppy and the
funny-looking bird (Allred, Mary)

Beisert, Heide Helene. Poor fish (Beisert,
Heide Helene)

Belenchia, Marc. Riddle me a riddle
(Moncure, Jane Belk)

Bellettati, Riccardo. The little sea horse
(Damjan, Mischa)

Bellville, Cheryl Walsh. Large animal
veterinarians (Bellville, Rod)
Round-up (Bellville, Cheryl Walsh)

Bellville, Rod. Large animal veterinarians
(Bellville, Rod)

Bemelmans, Ludwig. Hansi (Bemelmans,
Ludwig)
Madeline (Bemelmans, Ludwig)
Madeline and the bad hat (Bemelmans,
Ludwig)
Madeline and the gypsies (Bemelmans,
Ludwig)
Madeline in London (Bemelmans, Ludwig)
Madeline's rescue (Bemelmans, Ludwig)
Parsley (Bemelmans, Ludwig)
Quito express (Bemelmans, Ludwig)
Rosebud (Bemelmans, Ludwig)
Sunshine (Bemelmans, Ludwig)
Welcome home (Bemelmans, Ludwig)

Benarde, Anita. The pumpkin smasher
(Benarde, Anita)

Bendick, Jeanne. All around you (Bendick,
Jeanne)
Christmas trees and how they grow
(Blough, Glenn O)
What made you you? (Bendick, Jeanne)
Who lives in this meadow? (Blough, Glenn
O)
Why can't I? (Bendick, Jeanne)

Benjamin, Alan. Wings of rhyme
(Frankenberg, Lloyd)

Bennett, Rainey. After the sun goes down
(Bennett, Rainey)
The day is dancing and other poems
(Bennett, Rowena)
Hooray for pig! (Stevens, Carla)
Pig and the blue flag (Stevens, Carla)
The secret hiding place (Bennett, Rainey)

Benson, Patrick. The blue book of hob
stories (Mayne, William)

Bentley, Roy. The Groggs' day out (Bentley,
Anne)
The Groggs have a wonderful summer
(Bentley, Anne)

Benton, Robert. Little brother, no more
(Benton, Robert)

Benton, Sally. Don't ever wish for a 7-foot
bear (Benton, Robert)

Benvenuti. My everyday Spanish word book
(Kahn, Michèle)

Berelson, Howard. My friend Andrew
(Collins, Pat Lowery)

Berenstain, Jan. The bear detectives
(Berenstain, Stan)
The bears' almanac (Berenstain, Stan)
Bears in the night (Berenstain, Stan)
Bears on wheels (Berenstain, Stan)
The Berenstain bears and the messy room
(Berenstain, Stan)
The Berenstain bears and the missing
dinosaur bone (Berenstain, Stan)
The Berenstain bears and the sitter
(Berenstain, Stan)

Boxer, Deborah. 26 ways to be somebody else (Boxer, Deborah)

Boyer, Trevor. The penguin (Sheehan, Angela)

Boyle, Constance. The story of little owl (Boyle, Constance)

Boyle, Mildred. A yard for John (Clymer, Eleanor Lowenton)

Boynton, Sandra. A is for angry (Boynton, Sandra)
But not the hippopotamus (Boynton, Sandra)
The going to bed book (Boynton, Sandra)
Hester in the wild (Boynton, Sandra)
Hippos go berserk (Boynton, Sandra)
If at first... (Boynton, Sandra)
Moo, baa, lalala (Boynton, Sandra)
Opposites (Boynton, Sandra)

Bracken, Carolyn. Fast rolling fire trucks

Brackett, Ward. How far is far? (Tresselt, Alvin R)
One way is down (Fischer, Vera Kistiakowsky)
You will live under the sea (Phleger, Fred B)

Bradfield, Jolly Roger *see* Bradfield, Roger

Bradfield, Margaret. Dr. Trotter and his big gold watch (Gilbert, Helen Earle)
Mr. Plum and the little green tree (Gilbert, Helen Earle)
Nine hundred buckets of paint (Becker, Edna)

Bradfield, Roger. The flying hockey stick (Bradfield, Roger)
Giants come in different sizes (Bradfield, Roger)
A good night for dragons (Bradfield, Roger)

Brady, Irene. Animal baby-sitters (Zweifel, Frances)
Five fat raccoons (Freschet, Berniece)
Forest log (Newton, James R)
A mouse named Mus (Brady, Irene)
Wild mouse (Brady, Irene)

Bragg, Charles. Longbeard the wizard (Fleischman, Sid)

Bragg, Michael. King Nimrod's tower (Garfield, Leon)
The writing on the wall (Garfield, Leon)

Bram, Elizabeth. I don't want to go to school (Bram, Elizabeth)
One day I closed my eyes and the world disappeared (Bram, Elizabeth)
Saturday morning lasts forever (Bram, Elizabeth)
There is someone standing on my head (Bram, Elizabeth)
Woodruff and the clocks (Bram, Elizabeth)

Bramall, Wendy. Animal homes (Vevers, Gwynne)
Animals of the dark (Vevers, Gwynne)

Brande, Marlie. Sleepy Nicholas (Brande, Marlie)

Brandenberg, Aliki *see* Aliki

Brann, Esther. A book for baby (Brann, Esther)

'Round the world (Brann, Esther)

Brenner, Fred. A dog I know (Brenner, Barbara)
The drinking gourd (Monjo, F N)
The flying patchwork quilt (Brenner, Barbara)
The tremendous tree book (Garelick, May)

Brett, Jan. Annie and the wild animals (Brett, Jan)
Fritz and the beautiful horses (Brett, Jan)
In the castle of cats (Boegehold, Betty)
Inside a sandcastle and other secrets (Cuneo, Mary Louise)
St. Patrick's Day in the morning (Bunting, Eve)
Some birds have funny names (Cross, Diana Harding)
Some plants have funny names (Cross, Diana Harding)
The Valentine bears (Bunting, Eve)
You are special to Jesus (Dellinger, Annetta)

Brewster, Patience. Ellsworth and the cats from Mars (Brewster, Patience)
Good as new (Douglas, Barbara)
How do you do, Mr. Birdsteps? (Hamilton, Morse)
I met a polar bear (Boyd, Selma)
Nobody (Brewster, Patience)
Who's afraid of the dark? (Hamilton, Morse)

Brice, Tony. Baby animals (Brice, Tony)
The bashful goldfish (Brice, Tony)

Bridgman, Elizabeth. All the little bunnies (Bridgman, Elizabeth)
Nanny bear's cruise (Bridgman, Elizabeth)
A new dog next door (Bridgman, Elizabeth)

Bridle, Martin. Punch and Judy in the rain (Eaton, Su)

Bridwell, Norman. Clifford goes to Hollywood (Bridwell, Norman)
Clifford's good deeds (Bridwell, Norman)
Clifford's Halloween (Bridwell, Norman)
The witch grows up (Bridwell, Norman)
The witch next door (Bridwell, Norman)

Brierley, Louise. King Lion and his cooks (Brierley, Louise)

Briggs, Raymond. The elephant and the bad baby (Foulds, Elfrida Vipont)
Father Christmas (Briggs, Raymond)
Father Christmas goes on holiday (Briggs, Raymond)
Fee fi fo fum (Briggs, Raymond)
Jim and the beanstalk (Briggs, Raymond)
The Mother Goose treasury (Mother Goose)
Ring-a-ring o' roses (Briggs, Raymond)
The snowman (Briggs, Raymond)
The white land (Briggs, Raymond)

Bright, Robert. Georgie (Bright, Robert)
Georgie and the baby birds (Bright, Robert)
Georgie and the ball of yarn (Bright, Robert)
Georgie and the buried treasure (Bright, Robert)

Why the tides ebb and flow (Bowden, Joan Chase)
Wings on things (Brown, Marc)
Witches four (Brown, Marc)
Your first garden book (Brown, Marc)

Brown, Marcia. All butterflies (Brown, Marcia)
The blue jackal (Brown, Marcia)
The bun (Brown, Marcia)
Cinderella (Perrault, Charles)
Dick Whittington and his cat
Felice (Brown, Marcia)
The flying carpet (Arabian Nights)
Henry fisherman (Brown, Marcia)
How, hippo! (Brown, Marcia)
Listen to a shape (Brown, Marcia)
The little carousel (Brown, Marcia)
The neighbors (Brown, Marcia)
Once a mouse... (Brown, Marcia)
Peter Piper's alphabet (Brown, Marcia)
Puss in boots (Perrault, Charles)
Shadow (Cendrars, Blaise)
Skipper John's cook (Brown, Marcia)
Stone soup (Brown, Marcia)
Tamarindo! (Brown, Marcia)
The three billy goats Gruff (Asbjørnsen, P C (Peter Christen))
Touch will tell (Brown, Marcia)
Walk with your eyes (Brown, Marcia)

Brown, Palmer. Cheerful (Brown, Palmer)
Hickory (Brown, Palmer)
The silver nutmeg (Brown, Palmer)
Something for Christmas (Brown, Palmer)

Brown, Paul. Merrylegs, the rocking pony (Brown, Paul)

Brown, Richard Eric. Even the Devil is afraid of a shrew (Stalder, Valerie)
Gone fishing (Long, Earlene)
Mud fore sale (Nelson, Brenda)

Brown, Ruth. Crazy Charlie (Brown, Ruth)
A dark, dark tale (Brown, Ruth)

Browne, Anthony. Bear hunt (Browne, Anthony)
Gorilla (Browne, Anthony)
Hansel and Gretel (Grimm, Jacob)
Look what I've got! (Browne, Anthony)
Willy the wimp (Browne, Anthony)

Browne, Caroline. Mrs. Christie's farmhouse (Browne, Caroline)

Browne, Eileen. Halloweena Hecatee (Mitchell, Cynthia)

Browning, Colleen. Every man heart lay down (Graham, Lorenz B)

Bruna, Dick. Another story to tell (Bruna, Dick)
B is for bear (Bruna, Dick)
Christmas (Bruna, Dick)
The Christmas book (Bruna, Dick)
Farmer John (Bruna, Dick)
The fish (Bruna, Dick)
I can dress myself (Bruna, Dick)
I can read difficult words (Bruna, Dick)
I know more about numbers (Bruna, Dick)
Kitten Nell (Bruna, Dick)
Little bird tweet (Bruna, Dick)
Miffy (Bruna, Dick)
Miffy at the beach (Bruna, Dick)
Miffy at the playground (Bruna, Dick)
Miffy at the seaside (Bruna, Dick)
Miffy at the zoo (Bruna, Dick)
Miffy goes to school (Bruna, Dick)
Miffy in the hospital (Bruna, Dick)
Miffy in the snow (Bruna, Dick)
Miffy's bicycle (Bruna, Dick)
Miffy's dream (Bruna, Dick)
The orchestra (Bruna, Dick)
Poppy Pig goes to market (Bruna, Dick)
The sailor (Bruna, Dick)
The school (Bruna, Dick)
Tilly and Tess (Bruna, Dick)

Brunhoff, Jean de. Babar and Father Christmas (Brunhoff, Jean de)
Babar and his children (Brunhoff, Jean de)
Babar and Zephir (Brunhoff, Jean de)
Babar the king (Brunhoff, Jean de)
Babar's anniversary album (Brunhoff, Jean de)
The story of Babar, the little elephant (Brunhoff, Jean de)
The travels of Babar (Brunhoff, Jean de)

Brunhoff, Laurent de. Babar and the ghost (Brunhoff, Laurent de)
Babar and the Wully-Wully (Brunhoff, Laurent de)
Babar comes to America (Brunhoff, Laurent de)
Babar learns to cook (Brunhoff, Laurent de)
Babar loses his crown (Brunhoff, Laurent de)
Babar the magician (Brunhoff, Laurent de)
Babar visits another planet (Brunhoff, Laurent de)
Babar's ABC (Brunhoff, Laurent de)
Babar's anniversary album (Brunhoff, Jean de)
Babar's birthday surprise (Brunhoff, Laurent de)
Babar's book of color (Brunhoff, Laurent de)
Babar's castle (Brunhoff, Laurent de)
Babar's cousin, that rascal Arthur (Brunhoff, Laurent de)
Babar's fair will be opened next Sunday (Brunhoff, Laurent de)
Babar's mystery (Brunhoff, Laurent de)
Babar's picnic (Brunhoff, Laurent de)
Babar's visit to Bird Island (Brunhoff, Laurent de)
Gregory and Lady Turtle in the valley of the music trees (Brunhoff, Laurent de)
The one pig with horns (Brunhoff, Laurent de)
Serafina the giraffe (Brunhoff, Laurent de)

Brunner, Klaus. Sandy at the children's zoo (Bolliger, Max)

Brustlein, Daniel *see* Alain

Bruyn, Monica De *see* De Bruyn, Monica

Bryan, Ashley. Beat the story-drum, pum-pum (Bryan, Ashley)

Bryan, Marguerite. Friendly little Jonathan (Bryan, Dorothy)
Just Tammie! (Bryan, Dorothy)

C

Caldecott, Randolph. Hey diddle diddle, and Baby bunting (Caldecott, Randolph)
Hey diddle diddle picture book (Caldecott, Randolph)
The house that Jack built
Humpty Dumpty's favorite nursery rhymes (Cope, Dawn)
Panjandrum picture book (Caldecott, Randolph)
The Queen of Hearts (Caldecott, Randolph)
The Randolph Caldecott treasury (Caldecott, Randolph)
Randolph Caldecott's favorite nursery rhymes (Caldecott, Randolph)
Randolph Caldecott's John Gilpin and other stories (Caldecott, Randolph)
Randolph Caldecott's picture book, no. 1 (Caldecott, Randolph)
Randolph Caldecott's picture book, no. 2 (Caldecott, Randolph)
Sing a song of sixpence (Caldecott, Randolph)
The three jovial huntsmen (Caldecott, Randolph)

Calder, Nancy Edwards. Joseph and Anna's time capsule (Burstein, Chaya M)

Calleja, Gina. Peas again for lunch (Beech, Caroline)
The spaghetti word race (Etherington, Frank)

Calvert, Elinor H. *see* Lasell, Fen

Calvin, James. Thalia Brown and the blue bug (Dionetti, Michelle)

Cameron, John. If mice could fly (Cameron, John)

Cameron, Mary. Baby animals (Brown, Margaret Wise)

Cameron, Polly. The cat who thought he was a tiger (Cameron, Polly)
A child's book of nonsense (Cameron, Polly)
"I can't," said the ant (Cameron, Polly)

Campbell, Ann. Let's find out about boats (Campbell, Ann)
Let's find out about color (Campbell, Ann)

Campbell, Judy Piussi *see* Piussi-Campbell, Judy

Campbell, Rod. Look inside! All kinds of places (Campbell, Rod)
Look inside! Land, sea, air (Campbell, Rod)

Canning, Kate. A painted tale (Canning, Kate)

Cannon, Beth. Why worry? (Kimmel, Eric A)

Caparn, Rhys. Down the mountain (Bartlett, Margaret Farrington)

Capek, Jindra. The most beautiful song (Bolliger, Max)

Capelle, Erika Dietzsch *see* Dietzsch-Capelle, Erika

Caple, Kathy. Inspector Aardvark and the perfect cake (Caple, Kathy)

Caputo, Robert. More than just pets (Caputo, Robert)

Carigiet, Alois. Anton the goatherd (Carigiet, Alois)
A bell for Ursli (Chönz, Selina)
Florina and the wild bird (Chönz, Selina)
The pear tree, the birch tree and the barberry bush (Carigiet, Alois)
The snowstorm (Chönz, Selina)

Carle, Eric. Brown bear, brown bear, what do you see? (Martin, Bill (William Ivan))
Do bears have mothers too? (Fisher, Aileen)
Do you want to be my friend? (Carle, Eric)
Gravity at work and play (Engelbrektson, Sune)
The grouchy ladybug (Carle, Eric)
Have you seen my cat? (Carle, Eric)
The hole in the dike (Green, Norma B)
I see a song (Carle, Eric)
The mixed-up chameleon (1975) (Carle, Eric)
The mixed-up chameleon (1984) (Carle, Eric)
1, 2, 3 to the zoo (Carle, Eric)
Pancakes, pancakes (Carle, Eric)
The rooster who set out to see the world (Carle, Eric)
The secret birthday message (Carle, Eric)
The sun is a star (Engelbrektson, Sune)
The tiny seed (Carle, Eric)
Twelve tales from Æsop (Carle, Eric)
The very hungry caterpillar (Carle, Eric)
Walter the baker (Carle, Eric)
Watch out! A giant! (Carle, Eric)
Why Noah chose the dove (Singer, Isaac Bashevis)

Carlson, Nancy. Bunnies and their hobbies (Carlson, Nancy)
Harriet and the garden (Carlson, Nancy)
Harriet and the roller coaster (Carlson, Nancy)
Harriet and Walt (Carlson, Nancy)
Harriet's Halloween candy (Carlson, Nancy)
Harriet's recital (Carlson, Nancy)
Loudmouth George and the big race (Carlson, Nancy)
Loudmouth George and the cornet (Carlson, Nancy)
Loudmouth George and the fishing trip (Carlson, Nancy)
Loudmouth George and the new neighbors (Carlson, Nancy)
Loudmouth George and the sixth-grade bully (Carlson, Nancy)

Carpentier, Ralph. Fish out of school (Shaw, Evelyn S)
Octopus (Shaw, Evelyn S)

Carrick, Donald. The accident (Carrick, Carol)
Alex remembers (Griffith, Helen V)
Beach bird (Carrick, Carol)
Bear mouse (Freschet, Berniece)
Ben and the porcupine (Carrick, Carol)
The blue horse and other night poems (Fox, Siv Cedering)
The blue lobster (Carrick, Carol)

My animal Mother Goose (Cremins, Robert)

Crespi, Francesca. A treasure box of fairy tales (Jones, Olive)

Cretien, Paul D. Sir Henry and the dragon (Cretien, Paul D)

Crews, Donald. Blue sea (Kalan, Robert)
Carousel (Crews, Donald)
Eclipse (Branley, Franklyn M)
Freight train (Crews, Donald)
Harbor (Crews, Donald)
Light (Crews, Donald)
Parade (Crews, Donald)
Rain (Kalan, Robert)
School bus (Crews, Donald)
Ten black dots (Crews, Donald)
Truck (Crews, Donald)
We read A to Z (Crews, Donald)

Crichlow, Ernest. Galumpf (Lansdown, Brenda)
Two is a team (Beim, Lorraine)

Crichton, Michael *see* Douglas, Michael

Cristini, Ermanno. In my garden (Cristini, Ermanno)
In the pond (Cristini, Ermanno)
In the woods (Cristini, Ermanno)

Croll, Carolyn. The bear on the doorstep (Flory, Jane)
The big balloon race (Coerr, Eleanor)
Too many babas (Croll, Carolyn)
The unexpected grandchild (Flory, Jane)
We'll have a friend for lunch (Flory, Jane)

Cross, Peter. The Sesame Street ABC storybook (Moss, Jeffrey)

Croswell, Volney. How to hide a hippopotamus (Croswell, Volney)

Crowther, Robert. Hide and seek counting book (Crowther, Robert)
The most amazing hide and seek alphabet book (Crowther, Robert)

Croxford, Vera. All kinds of animals (Croxford, Vera)

Cruz, Ray. Alexander and the terrible, horrible, no good, very bad day (Viorst, Judith)
Alexander, who used to be rich last Sunday (Viorst, Judith)
The gorilla did it! (Hazen, Barbara Shook)
Horrible Hepzibah (Preston, Edna Mitchell)
I hate to go to bed (Barrett, Judi)
King Laurence, the alarm clock (Mann, Peggy)
There's a hippopotamus under my bed (Thaler, Mike)
What are we going to do about Andrew? (Sharmat, Marjorie Weinman)
What's wrong with being a skunk? (Schlein, Miriam)
The woman with the eggs (Andersen, H C (Hans Christian))
You think it's fun to be a clown! (Adler, David A)

Cuffari, Richard. How did numbers begin? (Sitomer, Mindel)
Little Yellow Fur (Hays, Wilma Pitchford)
My plant (Wong, Herbert H)

The wonderful box (Ames, Mildred)

Cummings, Chris. The best of the little books (Thomas, Gary)
The little book of fowl jokes (Lyfick, Warren)

Cummings, Pat. Just us women (Caines, Jeannette)
My mama needs me (Walter, Mildred Pitts)

Cummings, W. T. (Walter Thies). The kid (Cummings, W T (Walter Thies))
Miss Esta Maude's secret (Cummings, W T (Walter Thies))
Wickford of Beacon Hill (Cummings, W T (Walter Thies))

Cummings, William Lahey. Picture book theater (De Regniers, Beatrice Schenk)

Cummins, Jim. The Thanksgiving mystery (Nixon, Joan Lowery)
A tooth for the tooth fairy (Gunther, Louise)
The Valentine mystery (Nixon, Joan Lowery)
Who took the top hat trick? (Bowden, Joan Chase)

Cunningham, David. In the morning mist (Lapp, Eleanor)
The mice came in early this year (Lapp, Eleanor)

Curry, Peter. Animals (Curry, Peter)

Curtis, Cécile. Animals in danger (Kalman, Benjamin)

Cushman, Doug. Bicycle bear (Muntean, Michaela)
Giants (Cushman, Doug)
Haunted houses on Halloween (Patterson, Lillie)
Nasty Kyle the crocodile (Cushman, Doug)
Not counting monsters (Ross, H L)
Once upon a pig (Cushman, Doug)
The pudgy fingers counting book

D

Dabcovich, Lydia. The animal hedge (Fleischman, Paul)
Follow the river (Dabcovich, Lydia)
Nobody comes to dinner (Andrews, F Emerson (Frank Emerson))
Sleepy bear (Dabcovich, Lydia)
There once was a woman who married a man (Farber, Norma)

Daigle, Gisèle. ABC et/and 123 (Wilson, Barbara)

Dalrymple, De Wayne. The hunter I might have been (Mendoza, George)

Daly, Niki. Joseph's other red sock (Daly, Niki)
Vim, the rag mouse (Daly, Niki)

Da Rif, Andrea. The blueberry cake that little fox baked (Da Rif, Andrea)

Darling, Louis. Eric on the desert (Beim, Jerrold)
The swimming hole (Beim, Jerrold)
Waggles and the dog catcher (Cook, Marion B)

Delano, Jack. The emperor's new clothes (Andersen, H C (Hans Christian))

De Larrea, Victoria. Abracatabby (Hiller, Catherine)
The helping day (Herold, Ann Bixby)
Waiting for mama (De Regniers, Beatrice Schenk)

Delaunay, Sonia. Sonia Delaunay's alphabet (Delaunay, Sonia)

Delessert, Etienne. The endless party (Delessert, Etienne)
How the mouse was hit on the head by a stone and so discovered the world (Delessert, Etienne)
The secret seller (Lifton, Betty Jean)
Story number 1 (Ionesco, Eugene)

Delhumeau, Annick. Monsieur Bussy, the celebrated hamster (Claude-Lafontaine, Pascale)

DeLuna, Tony. Don't forget to come back (Harris, Robie H)
I wonder if Herbie's home yet (Kantrowitz, Mildred)
I'm not Oscar's friend any more (Sharmat, Marjorie Weinman)

Delving, Michael *see* Williams, Jay

Demarest, Chris L. Benedict finds a home (Demarest, Chris L)
Clemens' kingdom (Demarest, Chris L)
Hedgehog adventures (Stanovich, Betty Jo)
Pooks (Isele, Elizabeth)
Tree house fun (Greydanus, Rose)
World famous Muriel (Alexander, Sue)

Demi. The adventures of Marco Polo (Demi)
Dragon night and other lullabies (Yolen, Jane)
Fat Gopal (Singh, Jacquelin)
The shape of water (Goldin, Augusta)
Under the shade of the mulberry tree (Demi)
Where is it? (Demi)

Dennis, Morgan. Burlap (Dennis, Morgan)
The pup himself (Dennis, Morgan)
The sea dog (Dennis, Morgan)
Skit and Skat (Dennis, Morgan)

Dennis, Robert. The Sesame Street cookbook (Tornborg, Pat)

Dennis, Wesley. Flip (Dennis, Wesley)
Flip and the cows (Dennis, Wesley)
Flip and the morning (Dennis, Wesley)
Shoes for Punch (Arundel, Jocelyn)
Tumble, the story of a mustang (Dennis, Wesley)

De Paola, Thomas Anthony *see* De Paola, Tomie

De Paola, Tomie. Andy (that's my name) (De Paola, Tomie)
Authorized autumn charts of the Upper Red Canoe River country (Cohen, Peter Zachary)
Big Anthony and the magic ring (De Paola, Tomie)
Bill and Pete (De Paola, Tomie)
The carsick zebra and other riddles (Adler, David A)
The cat on the Dovrefell (De Paola, Tomie)

Charlie needs a cloak (De Paola, Tomie)
The Christmas pageant (De Paola, Tomie)
The cloud book (De Paola, Tomie)
The clown of God (De Paola, Tomie)
Country farm (De Paola, Tomie)
David's windows (Low, Alice)
Easter buds are springing (Hopkins, Lee Bennett)
The family Christmas tree book (De Paola, Tomie)
Fat magic (Kroll, Steven)
Fight the night (De Paola, Tomie)
Fin M'Coul (De Paola, Tomie)
Finders keepers, losers weepers (Lexau, Joan M)
Flicks (De Paola, Tomie)
Four scary stories (Johnston, Tony)
Four stories for four seasons (De Paola, Tomie)
Ghost poems (Wallace, Daisy)
The ghost with the Halloween hiccups (Mooser, Stephen)
The giant's farm (Yolen, Jane)
The giants go camping (Yolen, Jane)
The good giants and the bad Pukwudgies (Fritz, Jean)
Helga's dowry (De Paola, Tomie)
Hot as an ice cube (Balestrino, Philip)
The hunter and the animals (De Paola, Tomie)
I love you, mouse (Graham, John)
If he's my brother (Williams, Barbara)
Jamie's tiger (Wahl, Jan)
The knight and the dragon (De Paola, Tomie)
The Lady of Guadalupe (De Paola, Tomie)
The legend of Old Befana (De Paola, Tomie)
The legend of the bluebonnet (De Paola, Tomie)
Let's find out about houses (Shapp, Martha)
The little friar who flew (Gauch, Patricia Lee)
Marc the Magnificent (Alexander, Sue)
Marianna May and Nursey (De Paola, Tomie)
Mary had a little lamb (Hale, Sara Josepha)
Michael Bird-Boy (De Paola, Tomie)
Moon, stars, frogs and friends (MacLachlan, Patricia)
My daddy's mustache (Salus, Naomi Panush)
The mysterious giant of Barletta (De Paola, Tomie)
Nana upstairs and Nana downstairs (De Paola, Tomie)
Nicholas Bentley Stoningpot III (McGovern, Ann)
The night before Christmas (Moore, Clement C)
Noah and the ark (De Paola, Tomie)
Now one foot, now the other (De Paola, Tomie)
Old man Whickutt's donkey (Calhoun, Mary)
Oliver Button is a sissy (De Paola, Tomie)

Douglas, Stephanie. Three wishes (Clifton, Lucille)

Dowdy, Mrs. Regera *see* Gorey, Edward

Dowers, Patrick. One day scene through a leaf (Dowers, Patrick)

Dranko, Robert. The tractor on the farm (Israel, Marion Louise)

Drescher, Henrik. Looking for Santa Claus (Drescher, Henrik)
Simon's book (Drescher, Henrik)

Drescher, Joan. Follow that ghost! (Fife, Dale)
Horrible Hannah (Bottner, Barbara)
I'm in charge! (Drescher, Joan)
The marvelous mess (Drescher, Joan)
Nonna (Bartoli, Jennifer)
Tell me, grandma; tell me, grandpa (Newman, Shirlee)
Your family, my family (Drescher, Joan)

Drew, Patricia. Spotter Puff (Drew, Patricia)

Drew-Brook, Deborah. Casey visits the doctor (Marcus, Susan)

Drummond, Violet H. The flying postman (Drummond, Violet H)

Dubanevich, Arlene. Pigs in hiding (Dubanevich, Arlene)

Du Bois, William Pène. The alligator case (Du Bois, William Pène)
Bear circus (Du Bois, William Pène)
Bear party (Du Bois, William Pène)
Billy the barber (Kunhardt, Dorothy)
Elisabeth the cow ghost (Du Bois, William Pène)
Fierce John (Fenton, Edward)
The forbidden forest (Du Bois, William Pène)
Giant Otto (Du Bois, William Pène)
The hare and the tortoise and the tortoise and the hare (Du Bois, William Pène)
It's not fair (Zolotow, Charlotte)
Lazy Tommy pumpkinhead (Du Bois, William Pène)
Lion (Du Bois, William Pène)
Moving day (Tobias, Tobi)
My grandson Lew (Zolotow, Charlotte)
Otto and the magic potatoes (Du Bois, William Pène)
Otto at sea (Du Bois, William Pène)
Otto in Africa (Du Bois, William Pène)
Otto in Texas (Du Bois, William Pène)
The owl and the pussy-cat (Lear, Edward)
The planet of lost things (Strand, Mark)
The sick day (MacLachlan, Patricia)
The three little pigs
The unfriendly book (Zolotow, Charlotte)
We came a-marching...1, 2, 3 (Hobzek, Mildred)
Where's Gomer? (Farber, Norma)
William's doll (Zolotow, Charlotte)

Duchesne, Janet. Dinner ladies don't count (Ashley, Bernard)

Dugan, William. The ABC of cars, trucks and machines (Holl, Adelaide)

Duke, Kate. The guinea pig ABC (Duke, Kate)
Guinea pigs far and near (Duke, Kate)
Seven froggies went to school (Duke, Kate)

Dulac, Edmund. The snow queen and other stories from Hans Andersen (Andersen, H C (Hans Christian))

Dumas, Gerald. Time for Jody (Kesselman, Wendy)

Dumas, Philippe. Caesar, cock of the village (Dumas, Philippe)
Laura, Alice's new puppy (Dumas, Philippe)
Laura and the bandits (Dumas, Philippe)
Laura loses her head (Dumas, Philippe)
Laura on the road (Dumas, Philippe)
Lucy, a tale of a donkey (Dumas, Philippe)
Odette! (Fender, Kay)
The story of Edward (Dumas, Philippe)

Duncan, Riana. A nutcracker in a tree (Duncan, Riana)

Dunham, Meredith. In my treehouse (Schertle, Alice)

Dunn, Phoebe. The animals of Buttercup Farm (Dunn, Judy)
The little duck (Dunn, Judy)
The little goat (Dunn, Judy)
The little lamb (Dunn, Judy)
The little puppy (Dunn, Judy)
The little rabbit (Dunn, Judy)

Dunnington, Tom. The bears who came to breakfix (Jennings, Michael)
Bicycles (Baker, Eugene)
A computer went a-courting (Greene, Carol)
The elf in the singing tree (Bulette, Sara)
Fire (Baker, Eugene)
From where you are (Wakefield, Joyce)
The girl who tricked the troll (Torgersen, Don Arthur)
Home (Baker, Eugene)
I love cats (Matthias, Catherine)
I want to be a computer operator (Baker, Eugene)
Outdoors (Baker, Eugene)
A pet for Pat (Snow, Pegeen)
School (Baker, Eugene)
The thirteen days of Halloween (Greene, Carol)
The troll who lived in the lake (Torgersen, Don Arthur)
Wait, skates! (Johnson, Mildred D)
Water (Baker, Eugene)
Your pet bear (Hamsa, Bobbie)
Your pet beaver (Hamsa, Bobbie)
Your pet camel (Hamsa, Bobbie)
Your pet elephant (Hamsa, Bobbie)
Your pet giraffe (Hamsa, Bobbie)
Your pet kangaroo (Hamsa, Bobbie)
Your pet penguin (Hamsa, Bobbie)
Your pet sea lion (Hamsa, Bobbie)

Dunrea, Olivier. Eddy B, pigboy (Dunrea, Olivier)

Dunton, Mary Jane. A bunch of poems and verses (De Regniers, Beatrice Schenk)

Dunton, Sam. Lion Island (Bridges, William)
Ookie, the walrus who likes people (Bridges, William)

Duntze, Dorothée. Goodbye little bird (Damjan, Mischa)

E

I'll teach my dog 100 words (Frith, Michael K)

Robert the rose horse (Heilbroner, Joan)

Sam and the firefly (Eastman, P D (Philip D))

Snow (McKié, Roy)

Eaton, John. Fairy tales (Cummings, E E)

Eaton, Su. Punch and Judy in the rain (Eaton, Su)

Eaton, Tom. An animal for Alan (Ricciuti, Edward R)

Doghouse for sale (Pape, Donna Lugg)

Steven and the green turtle (Cromie, William J)

Where is my little Joey? (Pape, Donna Lugg)

Ebel, Alex. The moon (Asimov, Isaac)

Eberbach, Andrea. Willie the slowpoke (Greydanus, Rose)

Eckart, Frances. I want to be a carpenter (Greene, Carla)

Ecker, Beverly. The tiger that barks (Whitney, Alex)

Eckert, Horst see Janosch

Edman, Polly. Red thread riddles (Jensen, Virginia Allen)

Edwards, Gunvor. Snuffle to the rescue (Beresford, Elisabeth)

Edwards, Linda Strauss. The downtown day (Edwards, Linda Strauss)

So what if I'm a sore loser? (Williams, Barbara)

Edwards, Peter. Is Susan here? (Udry, Janice May)

Egielski, Richard. Louis the fish (Yorinks, Arthur)

Mary's mirror (Aylesworth, Jim)

Ehlert, Lois. Limericks by Lear (Lear, Edward)

What do you think I saw? (Sazer, Nina)

Ehrlich, Bettina see Bettina (Bettina Ehrlich)

Eichenauer, Gabriele. Once upon a rainbow (Lewis, Naomi)

Eichenberg, Fritz. Ape in cape (Eichenberg, Fritz)

Dancing in the moon (Eichenberg, Fritz)

A peaceable kingdom, and other poems (Coatsworth, Elizabeth)

The two magicians (Langstaff, John M)

Eidlitz, Barbara. Henry finds a home (St Pierre, Wendy)

Eitzen, Allan. Castles and mirrors and cities of sand (Bason, Lillian)

Let's find out about Eskimos (Wiesenthal, Eleanor)

My favorite place (Sargent, Susan)

Pick a raincoat, pick a whistle (Bason, Lillian)

What's that noise? (Kauffman, Lois)

Elgaard, Greta. You see the world around you (Selsam, Millicent E)

Elgin, Jill. Baby mouse goes shopping (Chase, Catherine)

Baby mouse learns his ABC's (Chase, Catherine)

Elgin, Kathleen. All ready for school (Adelson, Leone)

All ready for summer (Adelson, Leone)

All ready for winter (Adelson, Leone)

Speckles goes to school (Berquist, Grace)

Ups and down (Berkley, Ethel S)

Ellentuck, Shan. Did you see what I said? (Ellentuck, Shan)

A sunflower as big as the sun (Ellentuck, Shan)

Elliott, Gertrude. Nursery rhymes

Elliott, Ingrid Glatz. Hospital roadmap (Elliott, Ingrid Glatz)

Elliott, Miss. Mother Goose

Elson, Susan. Hello day (Aldis, Dorothy)

Elwell, Peter. The king of the pipers (Elwell, Peter)

Emberley, Ed. The big dipper (Branley, Franklyn M)

Columbus Day (Showers, Paul)

Drummer Hoff (Emberley, Barbara)

Ed Emberley's ABC (Emberley, Ed)

Ed Emberley's amazing look through book (Emberley, Ed)

Ed Emberley's big green drawing book (Emberley, Ed)

Ed Emberley's big orange drawing book (Emberley, Ed)

Ed Emberley's big purple drawing book (Emberley, Ed)

Ed Emberley's crazy mixed-up face game (Emberley, Ed)

Flash, crash, rumble and roll (Branley, Franklyn M)

Green says go (Emberley, Ed)

Klippity klop (Emberley, Ed)

Krispin's fair (Keller, John G)

Ladybug, ladybug, fly away home (Hawes, Judy)

London Bridge is falling down (Mother Goose)

Night's nice (Emberley, Barbara)

One wide river to cross (Emberley, Barbara)

The parade book (Emberley, Ed)

Rosebud (Emberley, Ed)

Simon's song (Emberley, Barbara)

Straight hair, curly hair (Goldin, Augusta)

Suppose you met a witch (Serraillier, Ian)

The wing on a flea (Emberley, Ed)

The Wizard of Op (Emberley, Ed)

Yankee Doodle (Schackburg, Richard)

Emberley, Edward Randolph see Emberley, Ed

Emberley, Michael. More dinosaurs! (Emberley, Michael)

Emberley, Rebecca. Drawing with numbers and letters (Emberley, Rebecca)

Emhardt, Erna. The story of Noah's ark (Haubensak-Tellenbach, Margrit)

Emmett, Fredrick Rowland. New world for Nellie (Emmett, Fredrick Rowland)

Endewelt, Jack. Green light, go (Bank Street College of Education)

Kwi-na the eagle (Jagendorf, Moritz A)

Endicott, James R. A tree with a thousand uses (Fisher, Aileen)

Flora, James. The day the cow sneezed (Flora, James)
Fishing with dad (Flora, James)
Grandpa's farm (Flora, James)
Grandpa's ghost stories (Flora, James)
Leopold, the see-through crumbpicker (Flora, James)
My friend Charlie (Flora, James)
Sherwood walks home (Flora, James)

Flora, Jane. A bouquet of littles (Krauss, Ruth)

Florian, Douglas. Airplane ride (Florian, Douglas)
A bird can fly (Florian, Douglas)
The city (Florian, Douglas)
People working (Florian, Douglas)
Tit for tat (Van Woerkom, Dorothy)

Foll, Alain Le *see* Le Foll, Alain

Fonseca, George. I like trains (Woolley, Catherine)

Fontana, Ugo. The rabbit catcher and other fairy tales (Bechstein, Ludwig)

Fontes, Marthe Seguin *see* Seguin-Fontes, Marthe

Forberg, Ati. The me I see (Hazen, Barbara Shook)
Mysteries in the garden (Fisher, Aileen)
Quilts in the attic (Fleisher, Robbin)

Ford, George. The best time of day (Flournoy, Valerie)
Walk on! (Williamson, Mel)

Ford, Lauren. The ageless story (Ford, Lauren)

Ford, Pamela Baldwin *see* Baldwin-Ford, Pamela

Foreman, Michael. Borrowed feathers and other fables (Stevens, Bryna)
Cat and canary (Foreman, Michael)
The crab that played with the sea (Kipling, Rudyard)
The general (Charters, Janet)
Land of dreams (Foreman, Michael)
Moose (Foreman, Michael)
Private zoo (McHargue, Georgess)
Teeny-Tiny and the witch-woman (Walker, Barbara K)
The tiger who lost his stripes (Paul, Anthony)
The two giants (Foreman, Michael)
War and peas (Foreman, Michael)

Forrai, Maria S. A look at birth (Pursell, Margaret Sanford)
A look at death (Anders, Rebecca)
A look at divorce (Pursell, Margaret Sanford)
A look at prejudice and understanding (Anders, Rebecca)

Forrest, Don. Creatures that look alike (Harris, Susan)

Forrester, Victoria. The magnificent moo (Forrester, Victoria)
Oddward (Forrester, Victoria)
The touch said hello (Forrester, Victoria)
Words to keep against the night (Forrester, Victoria)

Forsey, Christopher. Dinosaurs (Lambert, David)

Foster, Marian Curtis *see* Mariana

Foster, Sally. A pup grows up (Foster, Sally)

Fowler, Richard. Cat's story (Fowler, Richard)
Inspector Smart gets the message! (Fowler, Richard)

Fox, Charles Philip. Come to the circus (Fox, Charles Philip)
A fox in the house (Fox, Charles Philip)
Mr. Stripes the gopher (Fox, Charles Philip)

Fox, Dorothea Warren. Follow me the leader (Fox, Dorothea Warren)

Frame, Paul. Anna's snow day (Gunther, Louise)

Frances, Esteban. The thread soldiers (Heathers, Anne)

Francis, Anna B. Pleasant dreams (Francis, Anna B)

Francis, Frank. Grandmother Lucy goes on a picnic (Wood, Joyce)
Grandmother Lucy in her garden (Wood, Joyce)
The magic wallpaper (Francis, Frank)
Sing hey diddle diddle (Mother Goose)

Françoise *see* Seignobosc, Françoise

Frank, Dick. About dying (Stein, Sara Bonnett)
About handicaps (Stein, Sara Bonnett)
That new baby (Stein, Sara Bonnett)

Frankland, David. Old MacDonald had a farm

Frascino, Edward. Crystal is my friend (Gordon, Shirley)
Crystal is the new girl (Gordon, Shirley)
Gladys told me to meet her here (Sharmat, Marjorie Weinman)
Happy birthday, Crystal (Gordon, Shirley)
It'll all come out in the wash (Gray, Nigel)
The little mermaid (Andersen, H C (Hans Christian))
UFO kidnap (Robison, Nancy)

Frasconi, Antonio. The house that Jack built
How the left-behind beasts built Ararat (Farber, Norma)
See again, say again (Frasconi, Antonio)
See and say (Frasconi, Antonio)
The snow and the sun, la nieve y el sol (Frasconi, Antonio)

Fraser, Betty. A house is a house for me (Hoberman, Mary Ann)
Kenny's rat (Kouts, Anne)
Songs from around a toadstool table (Bennett, Rowena)

Fray, Rosalind. A baby starts to grow (Showers, Paul)

Frederick, Larry. Rain! Rain! (Greene, Carol)

Freedman, Russell. Farm babies (Freedman, Russell)
Hanging on (Freedman, Russell)
Tooth and claw (Freedman, Russell)

Freeman, Don. Add-a-line alphabet (Freeman, Don)
Beady Bear (Freeman, Don)
Bearymore (Freeman, Don)

Gackenbach, Dick. The adventures of
Albert, the running bear (Isenberg,
Barbara)
Amanda and the giggling ghost (Kroll,
Steven)
Annie and the mud monster (Gackenbach,
Dick)
Arabella and Mr. Crack (Gackenbach,
Dick)
A bag full of pups (Gackenbach, Dick)
Binky gets a car (Gackenbach, Dick)
Claude and Pepper (Gackenbach, Dick)
Claude the dog (Gackenbach, Dick)
Crackle, Gluck and the sleeping toad
(Gackenbach, Dick)
The dog and the deep dark woods
(Gackenbach, Dick)
Harry and the terrible whatzit
(Gackenbach, Dick)
Hattie be quiet, Hattie be good
(Gackenbach, Dick)
Hattie rabbit (Gackenbach, Dick)
I hate my brother Harry (Dragonwagon,
Crescent)
Ida Fanfanny (Gackenbach, Dick)
King Wacky (Gackenbach, Dick)
Little bug (Gackenbach, Dick)
Mr. Wink and his shadow, Ned
(Gackenbach, Dick)
The monster in the third dresser drawer
and other stories about Adam Joshua
(Smith, Janice Lee)
Mother Rabbit's son Tom (Gackenbach,
Dick)
One, two, three - ah-choo! (Allen, Marjorie
N)
Pepper and all the legs (Gackenbach, Dick)
The perfect mouse (Gackenbach, Dick)
The pig who saw everything (Gackenbach,
Dick)
Poppy the panda (Gackenbach, Dick)
The princess and the pea (Andersen, H C
(Hans Christian))
What's Claude doing? (Gackenbach, Dick)

Gág, Flavia. Chubby's first year (Gág, Flavia)
More once-upon-a-time stories (Dobbs,
Rose)

Gág, Wanda. ABC bunny (Gág, Wanda)
The funny thing (Gág, Wanda)
Gone is gone (Gág, Wanda)
Millions of cats (Gág, Wanda)
Nothing at all (Gág, Wanda)
Snippy and Snappy (Gág, Wanda)
Snow White and the seven dwarfs (Grimm,
Jacob)

Galdone, Paul. The adventures of Egbert the
Easter egg (Armour, Richard Willard)
The amazing pig (Galdone, Paul)
Amber day (Galdone, Joanna)
Anatole (Titus, Eve)
Anatole and the cat (Titus, Eve)
Anatole and the piano (Titus, Eve)
Anatole and the Pied Piper (Titus, Eve)
Anatole and the poodle (Titus, Eve)
Anatole and the robot (Titus, Eve)
Anatole and the thirty thieves (Titus, Eve)
Anatole and the toyshop (Titus, Eve)
Anatole in Italy (Titus, Eve)

Anatole over Paris (Titus, Eve)
Androcles and the lion (Galdone, Paul)
Animals on the ceiling (Armour, Richard
Willard)
The blind men and the elephant (Saxe,
John Godfrey)
The Bremen town musicians (Grimm,
Jacob)
A capital ship (Carryl, Charles Edward)
Cinderella (Perrault, Charles)
The cool ride in the sky (Wolkstein, Diane)
Counting carnival (Ziner, Feenie)
The cowboy surprise (Wise, William)
Dance of the animals (Belpré, Pura)
Edie changes her mind (Johnston,
Johanna)
The elves and the shoemaker (Grimm,
Jacob)
The first seven days (Galdone, Paul)
Gertrude, the goose who forgot (Galdone,
Joanna)
The gingerbread boy
The gorilla in the hall (Schertle, Alice)
Grandfather and I (Buckley, Helen
Elizabeth)
Grandmother and I (Buckley, Helen
Elizabeth)
The greedy old fat man (Galdone, Paul)
Hans in luck (Grimm, Jacob)
The hare and the tortoise (Æsop)
Henny Penny (Chicken Little)
Hereafterthis (Jacobs, Joseph)
High sounds, low sounds (Branley,
Franklyn M)
The history of Little Tom Tucker
The history of Mother Twaddle and the
marvelous achievements of her son Jack
Honeybee's party (Galdone, Joanna)
The horse, the fox, and the lion (Grimm,
Jacob)
The hungry fox and the foxy duck
(Leverich, Kathleen)
It does not say meow! (De Regniers,
Beatrice Schenk)
Jack-o'-lantern (Barth, Edna)
King of the cats (Galdone, Paul)
The lady who saw the good side of
everything (Tapio, Pat Decker)
The life of Jack Sprat, his wife and his cat
(Jack Sprat)
The little girl and the big bear (Galdone,
Joanna)
The little red hen
Little Red Riding Hood (Grimm, Jacob)
Little Tuppen
Look at your eyes (Showers, Paul)
The magic porridge pot (Galdone,
Paul)
Mr. Pingle and Mr. Buttonhouse
(MacGregor, Ellen)
Mr. Willowby's Christmas tree (Barry,
Robert E)
The monkey and the crocodile (Galdone,
Paul)
The monster and the tailor (Galdone,
Paul)
The moving adventures of Old Dame Trot
and her comical cat
Obedient Jack (Galdone, Paul)

Little truck (Gay, Michael)
Take me for a ride (Gay, Michael)
Gay, Zhenya. I'm tired of lions (Gay, Zhenya)
Look! (Gay, Zhenya)
Small one (Gay, Zhenya)
What's your name? (Gay, Zhenya)
Who's afraid? (Gay, Zhenya)
Wonderful things (Gay, Zhenya)
Geer, Charles. The wee little man (Berg, Jean Horton)
Gehr, Mary. Big store, funny door (Russell, Betty)
Run sheep run (Russell, Betty)
Three sides and the round one (Friskey, Margaret)
Geisel, Theodor Seuss *see* Seuss, Dr.
Geisert, Arthur. Pa's balloon and other pig tales (Geisert, Arthur)
Gekiere, Madeleine. The frilly lily and the princess (Gekiere, Madeleine)
Switch on the night (Bradbury, Ray)
Genia. Friend of Miguel (Miles, Miska)
Genji. In my garden (Dalmais, Anne-Marie)
Gentleman, David. The dancing tigers (Hoban, Russell)
George, Richard. Melinda's Christmas stocking (Jaynes, Ruth M)
Gerberg, Mort. Mr. Skinner's skinny house (McGovern, Ann)
Gergely, Tibor. Five little firemen (Brown, Margaret Wise)
The Giant little Golden Book of dogs (Daly, Kathleen N)
Wheel on the chimney (Brown, Margaret Wise)
Gerrard, Roy. The Favershams (Gerrard, Roy)
Matilda Jane (Gerrard, Jean)
Gerstein, Mordicai. Arnold of the ducks (Gerstein, Mordicai)
Follow me! (Gerstein, Mordicai)
Nice little girls (Levy, Elizabeth)
Prince Sparrow (Gerstein, Mordicai)
Roll over! (Gerstein, Mordicai)
The room (Gerstein, Mordicai)
Something queer at the ball park (Levy, Elizabeth)
Something queer at the haunted school (Levy, Elizabeth)
Something queer is going on (Levy, Elizabeth)
Something queer on vacation (Levy, Elizabeth)
"There are rocks in my socks!" said the ox to the fox (Thomas, Patricia)
Getz, Arthur. Humphrey, the dancing pig (Getz, Arthur)
Giacomini, Olindo. A hat for the queen (Bowden, Joan Chase)
Gianni, Peg. Alex, the amazing juggler (Gianni, Peg)
Gibbons, Gail. Boat book (Gibbons, Gail)
Clocks and how they go (Gibbons, Gail)
Department store (Gibbons, Gail)
Fire! Fire! (Gibbons, Gail)

Good junk (Enderle, Judith A)
Halloween (Gibbons, Gail)
Hot and cold (Chase, Catherine)
The missing maple syrup sap mystery (Gibbons, Gail)
The mouse in my house (Chase, Catherine)
My balloon (Chase, Catherine)
New road! (Gibbons, Gail)
Paper, paper everywhere (Gibbons, Gail)
Pete, the wet pet (Chase, Catherine)
The post office book (Gibbons, Gail)
The seasons of Arnold's apple tree (Gibbons, Gail)
Sun up, sun down (Gibbons, Gail)
Thanksgiving Day (Gibbons, Gail)
The too-great bread bake book (Gibbons, Gail)
Tool book (Gibbons, Gail)
Trucks (Gibbons, Gail)
Gibson, Myra Tomback. What is your favorite thing to touch? (Gibson, Myra Tomback)
Giese, Al. Circus (De Regniers, Beatrice Schenk)
Giesen, Rosemary. Famous planes (Thompson, Brenda)
Pirates (Thompson, Brenda)
The winds that blow (Thompson, Brenda)
Gilbert, Eliott. Mittens in May (Kumin, Maxine)
Gilchrist, Cathy. I never win! (Delton, Judy)
Giles, Ginger. How do we communicate? (Arnold, Caroline)
How do we have fun? (Arnold, Caroline)
How do we travel? (Arnold, Caroline)
What will we buy? (Arnold, Caroline)
Gili, Phillida. Fanny and Charles (Gili, Phillida)
Gill, Bob. A balloon for a blunderbuss (Gill, Bob)
Gill, Margery. The house where Jack lives (Crompton, Margaret)
The tale of the turnip (Hewett, Anita)
This little pig went to market (Montgomerie, Norah)
What did you dream? (Craig, M Jean)
Gilliam, Stan. Katie and the computer (D'Ignazio, Fred)
Giordano, Joe. The owl who loved sunshine (Carey, Mary)
Glaser, Milton. Rimes de la Mere Oie (Mother Goose)
Smallest elephant in the world (Tresselt, Alvin R)
Glass, Andrew. My brother tries to make me laugh (Glass, Andrew)
Spooky night (Carlson, Natalie Savage)
Terrible tyrannosaurus (Charlton, Elizabeth)
Gliewe, Unada G. *see* Unada
Glovach, Linda. The Little Witch's birthday book (Glovach, Linda)
The little Witch's black magic book of disguises (Glovach, Linda)
The little Witch's black magic book of games (Glovach, Linda)

The little Witch's Christmas book (Glovach, Linda)

The little Witch's Halloween book (Glovach, Linda)

The Little Witch's spring holiday book (Glovach, Linda)

The little Witch's Thanksgiving book (Glovach, Linda)

Gobbato, Imero. I am your misfortune (Rudolph, Marguerita)

Tops and bottoms (Conger, Lesley)

Gobhai, Mehlli. Lakshmi, the water buffalo who wouldn't (Gobhai, Mehlli)

Usha, the mouse-maiden (Gobhai, Mehlli)

Goble, Paul. Buffalo woman (Goble, Paul)

The friendly wolf (Goble, Paul)

The gift of the sacred dog (Goble, Paul)

The girl who loved wild horses (Goble, Paul)

Goffe, Toni. Toby's animal rescue service (Goffe, Toni)

Goffstein, M. B. (Marilyn Brooks). Across the sea (Goffstein, M B (Marilyn Brooks))

Family scrapbook (Goffstein, M B (Marilyn Brooks))

Fish for supper (Goffstein, M B (Marilyn Brooks))

Goldie the dollmaker (Goffstein, M B (Marilyn Brooks))

Laughing latkes (Goffstein, M B (Marilyn Brooks))

A little Schubert (Goffstein, M B (Marilyn Brooks))

Me and my captain (Goffstein, M B (Marilyn Brooks))

My Noah's ark (Goffstein, M B (Marilyn Brooks))

Natural history (Goffstein, M B (Marilyn Brooks))

Neighbors (Goffstein, M B (Marilyn Brooks))

Sleepy people (Goffstein, M B (Marilyn Brooks))

A writer (Goffstein, M B (Marilyn Brooks))

Goldman, Susan. Cousins are special (Goldman, Susan)

Grandma is somebody special (Goldman, Susan)

Goldsborough, June. An alphabet book (Chase, Catherine)

It happened on Thursday (Delton, Judy)

Who am I? (Raebeck, Lois)

Gomi, Taro. Coco can't wait! (Gomi, Taro)

Gonzales, Tomás. I can use tools (Kesselman, Judi R)

Goodall, John S.. The adventures of Paddy Pork (Goodall, John S)

The ballooning adventures of Paddy Pork (Goodall, John S)

Creepy castle (Goodall, John S)

An Edwardian Christmas (Goodall, John S)

An Edwardian summer (Goodall, John S)

Jacko (Goodall, John S)

The midnight adventures of Kelly, Dot and Esmeralda (Goodall, John S)

Naughty Nancy (Goodall, John S)

Paddy goes traveling (Goodall, John S)

Paddy Pork odd jobs (Goodall, John S)

Paddy Pork's holiday (Goodall, John S)

Paddy under water (Goodall, John S)

Paddy's evening out (Goodall, John S)

Paddy's new hat (Goodall, John S)

Shrewbettina's birthday (Goodall, John S)

The story of an English village (Goodall, John S)

The surprise picnic (Goodall, John S)

Goode, Diane. The adventures of Pinocchio (Collodi, Carlo)

The dream eater (Garrison, Christian)

The good-hearted youngest brother (Severo, Emöke de Papp)

Little pieces of the west wind (Garrison, Christian)

Peter Pan (Barrie, J M (James M))

The unicorn and the plow (Moeri, Louise)

When I was young in the mountains (Rylant, Cynthia)

Goodenow, Earle. The last camel (Goodenow, Earle)

The owl who hated the dark (Goodenow, Earle)

Gooding, Beverley. The open road (Grahame, Kenneth)

Goodman, Joan Elizabeth. The gingerbread boy

Goor, Nancy. All kinds of feet (Goor, Ron)

In the driver's seat (Goor, Ron)

Shadows (Goor, Ron)

Signs (Goor, Ron)

Goor, Ron. All kinds of feet (Goor, Ron)

Backyard insects (Selsam, Millicent E)

In the driver's seat (Goor, Ron)

Shadows (Goor, Ron)

Signs (Goor, Ron)

Goor, Ronald *see* Goor, Ron

Gorbaty, Norman. Sleepy dog (Ziefert, Harriet)

Gordon, Isabel. The shadow book (De Regniers, Beatrice Schenk)

Gordon, Margaret. The green children (Crossley-Holland, Kevin)

Jonah and the Lord (MacBeth, George)

Noah's journey (MacBeth, George)

A paper of pins

The pedlar of Swaffham (Crossley-Holland, Kevin)

The supermarket mice (Gordon, Margaret)

Wilberforce goes on a picnic (Gordon, Margaret)

Gordon, Mary Elizabeth. A pack of dreams (Greenwood, Ann)

Gorey, Edward. The dong with the luminous nose (Lear, Edward)

The monster den (Ciardi, John)

Red Riding Hood (De Regniers, Beatrice Schenk)

The shrinking of Treehorn (Heide, Florence Parry)

Treehorn's treasure (Heide, Florence Parry)

Treehorn's wish (Heide, Florence Parry)

The tunnel calamity (Gorey, Edward)

You read to me, I'll read to you (Ciardi, John)

Gorman, Terry *see* Powers, Richard M.

Gorsline, Douglas. North American Indians (Gorsline, Marie)
Nursery rhymes (Mother Goose)

Gorsline, Marie. North American Indians (Gorsline, Marie)

Goyder, Alice. Holiday in Catland (Goyder, Alice)
Party in Catland (Goyder, Alice)

Grabianski, Janusz. Androcles and the lion
Cats (Grabianski, Janusz)
Grabianski's wild animals (Grabianski, Janusz)
Horses (Grabianski, Janusz)

Graboff, Abner. Crystal magic (David, Eugene)
The daddy days (Simon, Norma)
The hungry goat (Mills, Alan)
I know an old lady (Bonne, Rose)
I want to whistle (Alexander, Anne)
Mr. Angelo (Schwalje, Marjory)
Mrs. McGarrity's peppermint sweater (Holl, Adelaide)
No-sort-of-animal (Palmer, Mary Babcock)
Noise in the night (Alexander, Anne)
Of course, you're a horse! (Radlauer, Ruth Shaw)
Old MacDonald had a farm
Please don't feed Horace (Young, Miriam Burt)
Something for you, something for me (Watts, Mabel)
The sun looks down (Schlein, Miriam)
Weeks and weeks (Watts, Mabel)

Graham, Alastair. Pigs in space (Weiss, Ellen)

Graham, Bob. Libby, Oscar and me (Graham, Bob)

Graham, Margaret Bloy. All falling down (Zion, Gene)
Be nice to spiders (Graham, Margaret Bloy)
Benjy and the barking bird (Graham, Margaret Bloy)
Benjy's boat trip (Graham, Margaret Bloy)
Benjy's dog house (Graham, Margaret Bloy)
Dear garbage man (Zion, Gene)
Harry and the lady next door (Zion, Gene)
Harry by the sea (Zion, Gene)
Harry, the dirty dog (Zion, Gene)
Hide and seek day (Zion, Gene)
Jeffie's party (Zion, Gene)
The meanest squirrel I ever met (Zion, Gene)
No roses for Harry (Zion, Gene)
The pack rat's day and other poems (Prelutsky, Jack)
The plant sitter (Zion, Gene)
Really spring (Zion, Gene)
The storm book (Zolotow, Charlotte)
The sugar mouse cake (Young, Miriam Burt)
The summer snowman (Zion, Gene)

Graham, Phyllis. Pip camps out (Brown, Myra Berry)

Graichen, Ingrid. Struppi

Grainger, Sam. The early words picture book (Gillham, Bill)

Gramatky, Hardie. Bolivar (Gramatky, Hardie)
Hercules (Gramatky, Hardie)
Homer and the circus train (Gramatky, Hardie)
Little Toot (Gramatky, Hardie)
Little Toot on the Mississippi (Gramatky, Hardie)
Little Toot on the Thames (Gramatky, Hardie)
Little Toot through the Golden Gate (Gramatky, Hardie)
Loopy (Gramatky, Hardie)
Nikos and the sea god (Gramatky, Hardie)
Sparky (Gramatky, Hardie)

Grammer, June Amos. Mary Anne (Dodge, Mary Mapes)

Granda, Sheila. Let's find out about the city (Pitt, Valerie)

Grant, Leigh. Isn't it a wonder! (Goddard, Carrie Lou)
The jolly witch (Burch, Robert)
The lion upstairs (Krensky, Stephen)
The smallest life around us (Anderson, Lucia)
What if a lion eats me and I fall into a hippopotamus' mud hole? (Hanlon, Emily)
Why couldn't I be an only kid like you, Wigger? (Hazen, Barbara Shook)

Grant, Vernon. Mother Goose

Grazia, Nick De *see* De Grazia, Nick

Grazia, Thomas Di *see* Di Grazia, Thomas

Greeley, Valerie. Farm animals (Greeley, Valerie)
Field animals (Greeley, Valerie)
Pets (Greeley, Valerie)
Zoo animals (Greeley, Valerie)

Green, Adam *see* Weisgard, Leonard

Green, Milton H. The Marcel Marceau counting book (Mendoza, George)

Green, Sheila Ellen *see* Greenwald, Sheila

Greenaway, Kate. A apple pie (Greenaway, Kate)
Marigold garden (Greenaway, Kate)
Mother Goose
The pied piper of Hamelin (Browning, Robert)
Under the window (Greenaway, Kate)

Greenleaf, Ann. No room for Sarah (Greenleaf, Ann)

Greenwald, Sheila. Brave Betsy (Dreifus, Miriam W)
Of course, you're a horse! (Radlauer, Ruth Shaw)

Gregg, Don. High Henry... the cowboy who was too tall to ride a horse (Doughtie, Charles)

Gregory, Dorothy Lake. All alone with daddy (Fassler, Joan)

Gretz, Susanna. Rilloby-rill (Newbolt, Henry John)
Teddy bears ABC (Gretz, Susanna)
Teddy bears go shopping (Gretz, Susanna)

H

Hansen, Carla. Barnaby Bear builds a boat (Hansen, Carla)
  Barnaby Bear vists the farm (Hansen, Carla)
Hansen, Jeff. Being a fire fighter isn't just squirtin' water (Hansen, Jeff)
Hansen, Vilhelm. Barnaby Bear builds a boat (Hansen, Carla)
  Barnaby Bear visits the farm (Hansen, Carla)
Hanson, Joan. Hurrah for Alexander (Marsh, Jeri)
  I don't like Timmy (Hanson, Joan)
  I won't be afraid (Hanson, Joan)
  I'm going to run away (Hanson, Joan)
  This is... (Patrick, Gloria)
Hanson, Peter E. Memorial Day (Scott, Geoffrey)
Ḥaqiqāt, Nāhid. Half for you (Azaad, Meyer)
Harada, Joyce. It's the ABC book (Harada, Joyce)
Hardcastle, Nick. Water (Leutscher, Alfred)
Hardy, Bert. A horse grows up (Richard, Jane)
Hare, Lorraine. Who needs her? (Hare, Lorraine)
Hargis, Ed. The American Mother Goose (Wood, Ray)
  Fun in American folk rhymes (Wood, Ray)
Harnoncourt, René D' see D'Harnoncourt, René
Harrison, Ted. A northern alphabet (Harrison, Ted)
Hart, Tom see De Hart, Tom
Hartelius, Margaret A. The chicken's child (Hartelius, Margaret A)
  Clay-dough, play-dough (Chernoff, Goldie Taub)
  Just a box? (Chernoff, Goldie Taub)
  Pebbles and pods (Chernoff, Goldie Taub)
  Puppet party (Chernoff, Goldie Taub)
Hartman, Laura. If it weren't for Benjamin (I'd always get to lick the icing spoon) (Hazen, Barbara Shook)
Hartman, Rosella. Big red barn (Brown, Margaret Wise)
Hartwell, Marjorie. A trip to the yard (Cross, Genevieve)
Harvey, Paul. Animals at night (Peters, Sharon)
  Big red fire engine (Greydanus, Rose)
  Dinosaurs in trouble (Gordon, Sharon)
  Happy birthday (Peters, Sharon)
  Happy Jack (Peters, Sharon)
  My secret hiding place (Greydanus, Rose)
  Pete the parakeet (Gordon, Sharon)
  Something to crow about (Van Woerkom, Dorothy)
  What is a reptile? (Kuchalla, Susan)
  What makes the weather (Palazzo, Janet)
  What's under the ocean? (Craig, Janet)
Haskins, Ilma. Color seems (Haskins, Ilma)
Hassall, Joan. The Oxford nursery rhyme book (Opie, Iona Archibald)
Hauman, Doris. The little engine that could (Piper, Watty)

Hauman, George. The little engine that could (Piper, Watty)
Hauptmann, Tatjana. A day in the life of Petronella Pig (Hauptmann, Tatjana)
Hauscherr, Rosmarie. Brothers are all the same (Milgram, Mary)
  When people die (Bernstein, Joanne E)
Havelock, Elaine. The crooked angel (Kavanaugh, James J)
Hawkins, Colin. Boo! Who? (Hawkins, Colin)
  Mig the pig (Hawkins, Colin)
  Pat the cat (Hawkins, Colin)
  What time is it, Mr. Wolf? (Hawkins, Colin)
Hawkins, Irene. The wild wood (Clewes, Dorothy)
Hawkins, Jacqui. Boo! Who? (Hawkins, Colin)
Hawkinson, John. Birds in the sky (Hawkinson, Lucy)
  Indian Two Feet and his eagle feather (Friskey, Margaret)
  Indian Two Feet and the wolf cubs (Friskey, Margaret)
  Indian Two Feet rides alone (Friskey, Margaret)
  The old stump (Hawkinson, John)
  Robins and rabbits (Hawkinson, John)
  What is a bird? (Darby, Gene)
  What is a butterfly? (Darby, Gene)
  What is a fish? (Darby, Gene)
  What is a plant? (Darby, Gene)
  What is a turtle? (Darby, Gene)
  Where the wild apples grow (Hawkinson, John)
Hawkinson, Lucy. Billy, the littlest one (Schlein, Miriam)
  Birds in the sky (Hawkinson, Lucy)
  Dance, dance, Amy-Chan! (Hawkinson, Lucy)
  Frog fun (Stratemeyer, Clara Georgeanna)
  Indian Two Feet and his eagle feather (Friskey, Margaret)
  Just one more block (Mayers, Patrick)
  Left, right, left, right! (Stanek, Muriel)
  What is a bird? (Darby, Gene)
  What is a butterfly? (Darby, Gene)
  What is a fish? (Darby, Gene)
  What is a plant? (Darby, Gene)
  What is a turtle? (Darby, Gene)
Hay, Dean. I see a lot of things (Hay, Dean)
  Now I can count (Hay, Dean)
Hayden, Chuck. Orange Oliver (Lasson, Robert)
Hayes, Geoffrey. Bear by himself (Hayes, Geoffrey)
  Elroy and the witch's child (Hayes, Geoffrey)
  Hocus and Pocus at the circus (Manushkin, Fran)
  Moon dragon (Manushkin, Fran)
  Patrick and Ted (Hayes, Geoffrey)
  The secret inside (Hayes, Geoffrey)
  When the wind blew (Brown, Margaret Wise)

Hayes, William D. (William Dimmity). Sebastian and the dragon (Kumin, Maxine)

Haynes, Robert. The elephant that ga-lumphed (Ward, Nanda Weedon)

Hazard, Eleanor. How to travel with grownups (Bridgman, Elizabeth)

Hearn, Lafcadio. The funny little woman (Mosel, Arlene)

Hechtkopf, H. David and Goliath (Brin, Ruth F)
Jonah's journey (Haiz, Danah)
The story of Esther (Brin, Ruth F)

Heckler, Bill. Red is never a mouse (Clifford, Eth)

Hedderwick, Mairi. Janet Reachfar and Chickabird (Duncan, Jane)
Katie Morag delivers the mail (Hedderwick, Mairi)

Heffernan, Ed. Coyote goes hunting for fire (Bernstein, Margery)
Earth namer (Bernstein, Margery)
How the sun made a promise and kept it (Bernstein, Margery)

Hefter, Richard. Some, more, most (Freudberg, Judy)
The strawberry book of shapes (Hefter, Richard)

Heine, Helme. Friends (Heine, Helme)
King Bounce the 1st (Heine, Helme)
Merry-go-round (Heine, Helme)
Mr. Miller the dog (Heine, Helme)
The most wonderful egg in the world (Heine, Helme)
The pigs' wedding (Heine, Helme)
Superhare (Heine, Helme)

Heins, Sheila. The last free bird (Stone, A Harris)

Heller, Linda. Alexis and the golden ring (Heller, Linda)
The castle on Hester Street (Heller, Linda)
Lily at the table (Heller, Linda)
A picture book of Hanukkah (Adler, David A)
A picture book of Jewish holidays (Adler, David A)
A picture book of Passover (Adler, David A)

Heller, Ruth. Animals born alive and well (Heller, Ruth)
Chickens aren't the only ones (Heller, Ruth)
Plants that never ever bloom (Heller, Ruth)
The reason for a flower (Heller, Ruth)

Henderson, Doris. Biddy and the ducks (Sondergaard, Arensa)

Henderson, Marion. Biddy and the ducks (Sondergaard, Arensa)

Hendricks, Don. My dad's a smokejumper (Hill, Mary Lou)

Hendrickson, June. Bantie and her chicks (Boreman, Jean)

Henkes, Kevin. All alone (Henkes, Kevin)
Clean enough (Henkes, Kevin)

Henrie, Marc. Cats (Henrie, Fiona)
Dogs (Henrie, Fiona)
Gerbils (Henrie, Fiona)
Rabbits (Henrie, Fiona)

Henstra, Friso. Petronella (Williams, Jay)
The practical princess (Williams, Jay)
School for sillies (Williams, Jay)
Wait and see (Henstra, Friso)

Herman, Vic. My days are made of butterflies (Martin, Bill (William Ivan))

Hermann, Fay. My zoo (Fay, Hermann)

Herrera, Velino. In my mother's house (Clark, Ann Nolan)

Herring, Ann. Peter and the wolf (Prokofiev, Sergei Sergeievitch)

Hertza, Ole. Tobias catches trout (Hertza, Ole)
Tobias goes ice fishing (Hertza, Ole)
Tobias goes seal hunting (Hertza, Ole)
Tobias has a birthday (Hertza, Ole)

Hess, Lilo. A cat's nine lives (Hess, Lilo)
The curious raccoons (Hess, Lilo)
Fawn in the woods (Eberle, Irmengarde)
Foxes in the woodshed (Hess, Lilo)
Rabbits in the meadow (Hess, Lilo)

Heuck, Sigrid. The little black hen (Hille-Brandts, Lene)

Hewett, Richard. Fly away free (Hewett, Joan)
The mouse and the elephant (Hewett, Joan)
Pets without homes (Arnold, Caroline)

Hewitt, Kathryn. Two by two (Hewitt, Kathryn)

Heymans, Margriet. Pippin and Robber Grumblecroak's big baby (Heymans, Margriet)

Hickson, Joan. The mysterious Baba and her magic caravan (Ainsworth, Ruth)

Hida, Keiko. The prancing pony (DeForest, Charlotte B)

Higa, James. Swords and daggers (Fisher, Aileen)

Higginbottom, J. Winslow. Baltimore orioles (Brenner, Barbara)
Billy's shoes (LeRoy, Gen)
The brothers Wrong and Wrong Again (Phillips, Louis)
Lucky Chuck (Cleary, Beverly)
Lucky stiff! (LeRoy, Gen)

Higham, David. Opposites (Watson, Carol)
Shapes (Watson, Carol)
Sizes (Watson, Carol)

Hijikata, Shigemi. The ugly duckling (Andersen, H C (Hans Christian))

Hildebrandt, Greg. The big city book (Ingle, Annie)
Dinosaurs (Daly, Kathleen N)
Today's biggest animals (Daly, Kathleen N)
Unusual animals (Daly, Kathleen N)

Hildebrandt, Tim. The big city book (Ingle, Annie)
Dinosaurs (Daly, Kathleen N)
Lilly, Willy and the mail-order witch (Bach, Othello)
Today's biggest animals (Daly, Kathleen N)
Unusual animals (Daly, Kathleen N)

Hill, Eric. At home (Hill, Eric)

Baby bear's bedtime (Hill, Eric)
Good morning, baby bear (Hill, Eric)
My pets (Hill, Eric)
The park (Hill, Eric)
Spot goes to school (Hill, Eric)
Spot's birthday party (Hill, Eric)
Spot's first walk (Hill, Eric)
Up there (Hill, Eric)
Where's Spot? (Hill, Eric)

Hill, Marjorie. The little red ferry boat (Potter, Russell)

Hillier, Matthew. Animals that travel (Vevers, Gwynne)

Hillman, Priscilla. A Merry-Mouse book of favorite poems (Hillman, Priscilla)
A Merry-Mouse book of months (Hillman, Priscilla)
The Merry-Mouse book of prayers and graces (Hillman, Priscilla)
A Merry-Mouse Christmas A B C (Hillman, Priscilla)
The Merry-Mouse schoolhouse (Hillman, Priscilla)
A mouse story (Holl, Adelaide)

Hillyer, Debra. Special delivery (Baker, Gayle)

Him, George. The day with the Duke (Thwaite, Ann)
Folk tales for reading and telling (Berg, Leila)
The giant Alexander (Herrmann, Frank)
The giant Alexander and the circus (Herrmann, Frank)
Squawky, the adventures of a Clasperchoice (Potter, Stephen)

Himler, Ronald. Allison's grandfather (Peavy, Linda)
Baby, come out! (Manushkin, Fran)
The best town in the world (Baylor, Byrd)
Bubblebath! (Manushkin, Fran)
Bunk beds (Winthrop, Elizabeth)
Bus ride (Jewell, Nancy)
Daddy (Caines, Jeannette)
Eye winker, Tom Tinker, chin chopper (Glazer, Tom)
The girl on the yellow giraffe (Himler, Ronald)
Janey (Zolotow, Charlotte)
The lion's tail (Davis, Douglas F)
Make a circle, keep us in (Adoff, Arnold)
Moon song (Baylor, Byrd)
Tornado! (Adoff, Arnold)
Wake up, Jeremiah (Himler, Ronald)
Wind Rose (Dragonwagon, Crescent)

Himmelman, John. Amanda and the witch switch (Himmelman, John)
Talester the lizard (Himmelman, John)

Hincks, Gary. Reptiles (Pluckrose, Henry)

Hines, Anna Grossnickle. Come to the meadow (Hines, Anna Grossnickle)
Maybe a band-aid will help (Hines, Anna Grossnickle)
Taste the raindrops (Hines, Anna Grossnickle)

Hippel, Ursula Von see Von Hippel, Ursula

Hippopotamus, Eugene H. see Kraus, Robert

Hipshman, Helen D. Adam's world, San Francisco (Fraser, Kathleen)

Hirsh, Marilyn. The best of K'tonton (Weilerstein, Sadie Rose)
Butchers and bakers, rabbis and kings (Greene, Jacqueline Dembar)
Captain Jiri and Rabbi Jacob (Hirsh, Marilyn)
Could anything be worse? (Hirsh, Marilyn)
The house on the roof (Adler, David A)
Leela and the watermelon (Hirsh, Marilyn)
One little goat (Hirsh, Marilyn)
The pink suit (Hirsh, Marilyn)
The Rabbi and the twenty-nine witches (Hirsh, Marilyn)
Wales' tale (Saunders, Susan)
Where is Yonkela? (Hirsh, Marilyn)

Hoban, Brom. Skunk Lane (Hoban, Brom)

Hoban, Lillian. Arthur's Christmas cookies (Hoban, Lillian)
Arthur's funny money (Hoban, Lillian)
Arthur's honey bear (Hoban, Lillian)
Arthur's pen pal (Hoban, Lillian)
Arthur's prize reader (Hoban, Lillian)
Attila the angry (Sharmat, Marjorie Weinman)
A baby sister for Frances (Hoban, Russell)
A bargain for Frances (Hoban, Russell)
Bee my Valentine! (Cohen, Miriam)
Best friends (Cohen, Miriam)
Best friends for Frances (Hoban, Russell)
The big hello (Schulman, Janet)
The big kite contest (Ruthstrom, Dorotha)
A birthday for Frances (Hoban, Russell)
Bread and jam for Frances (Hoban, Russell)
Charlie the tramp (Hoban, Russell)
The day the teacher went bananas (Howe, James)
Emmet Otter's jug-band Christmas (Hoban, Russell)
First grade takes a test (Cohen, Miriam)
Goodnight (Hoban, Russell)
Harry's song (Hoban, Lillian)
Harvey's hideout (Hoban, Russell)
Here come raccoons (Hoban, Lillian)
I don't care (Sharmat, Marjorie Weinman)
I'm telling you now (Delton, Judy)
In one door and out the other (Fisher, Aileen)
It's really Christmas (Hoban, Lillian)
Jim meets the thing (Cohen, Miriam)
Jim's dog Muffins (Cohen, Miriam)
Just awful (Whitney, Alma Marshak)
The laziest robot in zone one (Hoban, Lillian)
The little Brute family (Hoban, Russell)
Lost in the museum (Cohen, Miriam)
Mr. Pig and family (Hoban, Lillian)
Mr. Pig and Sonny too (Hoban, Lillian)
The mole family's Christmas (Hoban, Russell)
The new girl at school (Delton, Judy)
The new teacher (Cohen, Miriam)
No good in art (Cohen, Miriam)
No nap for me (Zagone, Theresa)
Nothing to do (Hoban, Russell)

The monkey that went to school
(Meshover, Leonard)
Slides (Baugh, Dolores M)
Supermarket (Baugh, Dolores M)
Swings (Baugh, Dolores M)
Trucks and cars to ride (Baugh, Dolores M)

Hoffmann, Felix. The bearskinner (Grimm, Jacob,)
A boy went out to gather pears
The four clever brothers (Grimm, Jacob)
Hans in luck (Grimm, Jacob)
The seven ravens (Grimm, Jacob)
The story of Christmas (Hoffmann, Felix)
Tom Thumb

Hoffmann, Hilde. The city and country Mother Goose (Mother Goose)
The green grass grows all around
My friend the babysitter (Watson, Jane Werner)
Sometimes I get angry (Watson, Jane Werner)
Sometimes I'm afraid (Watson, Jane Werner)

Hoffner, Pelagie Doane *see* Doane, Pelagie

Hoffnung, Gerard. The boy and the magic (Colette)

Hofstrand, Mary. Albion pig (Hofstrand, Mary)

Hogan, Inez. About Nono, the baby elephant (Hogan, Inez)
Epaminondas and his auntie (Bryant, Sara Cone)

Hogner, Nils. Seeds of wind and water (Jordan, Helene J)

Hogrogian, Nonny. Always room for one more (Alger, Leclaire)
The animal (Kherdian, David)
Arbor day (Fisher, Aileen)
Bears are sleeping (Yulya)
Billy Goat and his well-fed friends (Hogrogian, Nonny)
Carrot cake (Hogrogian, Nonny)
Cinderella (Grimm, Jacob)
The contest (Hogrogian, Nonny)
Country cat, city cat (Kherdian, David)
The devil with the green hairs (Grimm, Jacob)
The dog writes on the window with his nose, and other poems
The hermit and Harry and me (Hogrogian, Nonny)
I am eyes, ni macho (Ward, Leila)
One fine day (Hogrogian, Nonny)
One I love, two I love, and other loving Mother Goose rhymes (Mother Goose)
Right now (Kherdian, David)
Sir Ribbeck of Ribbeck of Havelland (Fontane, Theodore)

Hoguet, Susan Ramsay. I unpacked my grandmother's trunk (Hoguet, Susan Ramsay)

Holberg, Richard A. Wait for William (Flack, Marjorie)

Holden, Edith. The hedgehog feast (Holden, Edith)
The hedgehog feast (Stott, Rowena)

Holder, Heidi. Æsop's fables (Æsop)

Holdsworth, William Curtis. The gingerbread boy
The woman who lived in Holland (Howells, Mildred)

Hole, Quentin. The man from Ironbark (Paterson, Andrew Barton)

Holland, Janice. The blind men and the elephant (Quigley, Lillian Fox)
You never can tell (Holland, Janice)

Holland, Marion. A big ball of string (Holland, Marion)

Holland, Viki. We are having a baby (Holland, Viki)

Hollander, Edward S. Follow me, everybody (Bettinger, Craig)

Holling, Holling C. (Holling Clancy). The blot (Crawford, Phyllis)
Paddle-to-the-sea (Holling, Holling C (Holling Clancy))

Holm, Mayling Mack. A forest Christmas (Holm, Mayling Mack)

Holman, Nancé. The tent (Seymour, Dorothy Z)

Holt, Norma. Angelita (Kesselman, Wendy)
The secret seller (Lifton, Betty Jean)

Holtan, Gene. Old Blue, you good dog you (Taylor, Mark)

Hormann, Toni. What does the rooster say, Yoshio? (Battles, Edith)

Horn, William Van *see* Van Horn, William

Horvath, Maria. And me, coyote! (Baker, Betty)
Dancing turtle (Duff, Maggie)

Houser, Allan. The desert people (Clark, Ann Nolan)

Houston, James. First came the Indians (Wheeler, M J)
Kiviok's magic journey (Houston, James)

Houston, Judy. Listen! (Crume, Marion W)

Howard, Alan. Peter and the wolf (Prokofiev, Sergei Sergeievitch)

Howard, Jean G. Of mice and mice (Howard, Jean G)

Howe, Caroline Walton. Counting penguins (Howe, Caroline Walton)
Teddy Bear's bird and beast band (Howe, Caroline Walton)

Howe, Gertrude. Golden Kate (Bohanon, Paul)

Howell, Pat. Danbury's burning! (Grant, Anne)

Howell, Troy. Birds (Adoff, Arnold)
Breakfast with my father (Roy, Ronald)

Hubley, Faith. Lullaby (Swados, Elizabeth)

Huff, Vivian. Let's make paper dolls (Huff, Vivian)

Huffman, Tom. America's very own monsters (Cohen, Daniel)
Small plays for special days (Alexander, Sue)

Huggins, Susan. LeRoy's birthday circus (Dayton, Laura)

Hughes, Shirley. Alfie gets in first (Hughes, Shirley)

Alfie gives a hand (Hughes, Shirley)
Alfie's feet (Hughes, Shirley)
A cat's tale (Cate, Rikki)
David and dog (Hughes, Shirley)
George the babysitter (Hughes, Shirley)
Moving Molly (Hughes, Shirley)
Sally's secret (Hughes, Shirley)
A throne for Sesame (Young, Helen)
Up and up (Hughes, Shirley)

Hull, Helen S. The story of Barbara
(Chapman, Noralee)

Huntington, Will. Boats and ships from A to
Z (Alexander, Anne)
A little old man (Norton, Natalie)

Hurd, Clement. Bumble bugs and elephants
(Brown, Margaret Wise)
Caboose (Hurd, Edith Thacher)
Christmas eve (Hurd, Edith Thacher)
Come and have fun (Hurd, Edith Thacher)
The day the sun danced (Hurd, Edith
Thacher)
Engine, engine number 9 (Hurd, Edith
Thacher)
Goodnight moon (Brown, Margaret Wise)
Hello, Peter (Gipson, Morrell)
Hurry hurry! (Hurd, Edith Thacher)
Johnny Lion's bad day (Hurd, Edith
Thacher)
Johnny Lion's book (Hurd, Edith Thacher)
Johnny Lion's rubber boots (Hurd, Edith
Thacher)
Last one home is a green pig (Hurd, Edith
Thacher)
The lion on Scott Street (Siepmann, Jane)
The little brass band (Brown, Margaret
Wise)
Little dog, dreaming (Hurd, Edith
Thacher)
Monkey in the jungle (Preston, Edna
Mitchell)
The mother chimpanzee (Hurd, Edith
Thacher)
The mother kangaroo (Hurd, Edith
Thacher)
No funny business (Hurd, Edith Thacher)
The runaway bunny (Brown, Margaret
Wise)
The so-so cat (Hurd, Edith Thacher)
Stop, stop (Hurd, Edith Thacher)
Under the lemon tree (Hurd, Edith
Thacher)
What whale? Where? (Hurd, Edith
Thacher)
Wilson's world (Hurd, Edith Thacher)
Wingfin and Topple (Valens, Evans G)

Hurd, Edith Thacher. Two little miners
(Brown, Margaret Wise)

Hurd, Thacher. Hobo dog (Hurd, Thacher)
Mama don't allow (Hurd, Thacher)
Mystery on the docks (Hurd, Thacher)
The quiet evening (Hurd, Thacher)

Hürlimann, Ruth. The mouse with the daisy
hat (Hürlimann, Ruth)
The proud white cat (Hürlimann, Ruth)

Hurrell, David. Insects (Fields, Alice)

Hurt, Gerhardt. Scareboy (Hart, Jeanne
McGahey)

Hutchings. Things that go word book

Hutchins, Pat. The best train set ever
(Hutchins, Pat)
Changes, changes (Hutchins, Pat)
Clocks and more clocks (Hutchins, Pat)
Don't forget the bacon! (Hutchins, Pat)
Good night owl (Hutchins, Pat)
Happy birthday, Sam (Hutchins, Pat)
King Henry's palace (Hutchins, Pat)
One-eyed Jake (Hutchins, Pat)
1 hunter (Hutchins, Pat)
Rosie's walk (Hutchins, Pat)
The silver Christmas tree (Hutchins, Pat)
The surprise party (Hutchins, Pat)
The tale of Thomas Mead (Hutchins, Pat)
Titch (Hutchins, Pat)
The wind blew (Hutchins, Pat)
You'll soon grow into them, Titch
(Hutchins, Pat)

Hutchinson, William. Snoino mystery (Pape,
Donna Lugg)

Hutton, Kathryn. Self-control (Gambill,
Henrietta)

Hutton, Warwick. Beauty and the beast
(Hutton, Warwick)
Jonah and the great fish (Hutton,
Warwick)
Noah and the great flood (Hutton,
Warwick)
The nose tree (Hutton, Warwick)
The silver cow (Cooper, Susan)
The sleeping beauty (Grimm, Jacob)

Hyatt, Christine. Erik and the Christmas
horse (Peterson, Hans)

Hyman, Trina Schart. All in free but Janey
(Johnson, Elizabeth)
And a sunflower grew (Fisher, Aileen)
Curl up small (Stoddard, Sandol)
The enchanted forest (Hyman, Trina
Schart)
Epaminondas (Merriam, Eve)
How does it feel to be old? (Farber,
Norma)
Jane wishing (Tobias, Tobi)
Joanna runs away (La Farge, Phyllis)
A little alphabet (Hyman, Trina Schart)
Little Red Riding Hood (Grimm, Jacob)
Magic in the mist (Kimmel, Margaret
Mary)
On to Widecombe Fair (Gauch, Patricia
Lee)
Princess Rosetta and the popcorn man
(Greene, Ellin)
The pumpkin giant (Greene, Ellin)
Rapunzel (Grimm, Jacob)
Saint George and the dragon (Hodges,
Margaret)
The shy little girl (Krasilovsky, Phyllis)
The sleeping beauty (Grimm, Jacob)
Snow White (Grimm, Jacob)
Tight times (Hazen, Barbara Shook)

Hymes, James L. Oodles of noodles and
other rhymes (Hymes, Lucia)

Hymes, Lucia. Oodles of noodles and other
rhymes (Hymes, Lucia)

I

Ichikawa, Satomi. A child's book of seasons
(Ichikawa, Satomi)
Keep running, Allen! (Bulla, Clyde Robert)
Playtime (Mitchell, Cynthia)
Sun through small leaves (Ichikawa,
Satomi)
Suzanne and Nicholas at the market
(Ichikawa, Satomi)
Suzanne and Nicholas in the garden
(Ichikawa, Satomi)
Suzette and Nicholas and the seasons clock
(Mangin, Marie-France)
Under the cherry tree (Mitchell, Cynthia)
Iké, Jane Hori. A Japanese fairy tale (Iké,
Jane Hori)
Ilsley, Velma. Brownies - it's Christmas
(Adshead, Gladys L)
A busy day for Chris (Ilsley, Velma)
M is for moving (Ilsley, Velma)
The pink hat (Ilsley, Velma)
Ingraham, Erick. Cross-country cat
(Calhoun, Mary)
Harry and Shelburt (Van Woerkom,
Dorothy)
Hot-air Henry (Calhoun, Mary)
Old Blue (Hancock, Sibyl)
Ipcar, Dahlov. Animal hide and seek (Ipcar,
Dahlov)
The biggest fish in the sea (Ipcar, Dahlov)
Black and white (Ipcar, Dahlov)
Bright barnyard (Ipcar, Dahlov)
Brown cow farm (Ipcar, Dahlov)
Bug city (Ipcar, Dahlov)
The calico jungle (Ipcar, Dahlov)
The cat at night (Ipcar, Dahlov)
The cat came back (Ipcar, Dahlov)
A flood of creatures (Ipcar, Dahlov)
Hard scrabble harvest (Ipcar, Dahlov)
I like animals (Ipcar, Dahlov)
I love my anteater with an A (Ipcar,
Dahlov)
The land of flowers (Ipcar, Dahlov)
The little fisherman (Brown, Margaret
Wise)
Lost and found (Ipcar, Dahlov)
One horse farm (Ipcar, Dahlov)
Sir Addlepate and the unicorn (Ipcar,
Dahlov)
"The song of the day birds" and "The
song of the night birds" (Ipcar, Dahlov)
Stripes and spots (Ipcar, Dahlov)
Ten big farms (Ipcar, Dahlov)
Wild and tame animals (Ipcar, Dahlov)
World full of horses (Ipcar, Dahlov)
Irvine, Rex J. Clementine and the cage
(Heller, Wendy)
Isadora, Rachel. Backstage (Maiorano,
Robert)
Ben's trumpet (Isadora, Rachel)
City seen from A to Z (Isadora, Rachel)
Francisco (Maiorano, Robert)
Jesse and Abe (Isadora, Rachel)
A little interlude (Maiorano, Robert)
Max (Isadora, Rachel)

My ballet class (Isadora, Rachel)
No, Agatha! (Isadora, Rachel)
Opening night (Isadora, Rachel)
The Potters' kitchen (Isadora, Rachel)
Seeing is believing (Shub, Elizabeth)
Willaby (Isadora, Rachel)
Ishida, Takeo. In a meadow, two hares hide
(Bartoli, Jennifer)
Snow on bear's nose (Bartoli, Jennifer)
Ivanov, Anatoly. The demon who would not
die (Cohen, Barbara)
Ivenbaum, Elliot. Noah's ark (Chase,
Catherine)
Ives, Ruth. The bear who was too big
(Cooper, Letice Ulpha)
Ivory, Lesley Anne. A day in London (Ivory,
Lesley Anne)
A day in New York (Ivory, Lesley Anne)
Iwamatsu, Jun *see* Yashima, Tarō
Iwamura, Kazuo. Tan Tan's hat (Iwamura,
Kazuo)
Tan Tan's suspenders (Iwamura, Kazuo)
Ton and Pon big and little (Iwamura,
Kazuo)
Ton and Pon two good friends (Iwamura,
Kazuo)
Iwasaki, Chihiro. The birthday wish
(Iwasaki, Chihiro)
The red shoes (Andersen, H C (Hans
Christian))
Staying home alone on a rainy day
(Iwasaki, Chihiro)
What's fun without a friend? (Iwasaki,
Chihiro)
Will you be my friend? (Iwasaki, Chihiro)
Izawa, Tadasu. The ugly duckling
(Andersen, H C (Hans Christian))

J

Jackson, Pauline. Pip moves away (Brown,
Myra Berry)
Jackson, Polly. Henry (Vreeken, Elizabeth)
Jacobi, Kathy. Rose of Mother-of-Pearl
(Olujic, Grozdana)
Jacobs, Leslie. Mommies (Carton, Lonnie
Caming)
Somebody's slippers, somebody's shoes
(Brenner, Barbara)
Jacques, Faith. *see* Jaques, Faith
Jacquet, Jean-Pierre. Big Bird's copycat day
(Lerner, Sharon)
Jágr, Miloslav. The foolish frog (Seeger,
Pete)
James, Harold. How many blocks is the
world? (Blue, Rose)
I think I saw a snail (Hopkins, Lee
Bennett)
Jameson, Helen D. All together (Aldis,
Dorothy)
Janosch. Dear snowman (Janosch)
Hey Presto! You're a bear! (Janosch)
How does a czar eat potatoes? (Rose,
Anne)

The girl who wouldn't get married (Gross, Ruth Belov)

Hoddy doddy (Kent, Jack)

Jack Kent's happy-ever-after book (Kent, Jack)

Jack Kent's hokus pokus bedtime book (Kent, Jack)

Jack Kent's twelve days of Christmas (The twelve days of Christmas. English folk song)

Jack Kent's merry Mother Goose (Mother Goose)

Joey (Kent, Jack)

Knee-high Nina (Kent, Jack)

Laura's story (De Regniers, Beatrice Schenk)

Little Peep (Kent, Jack)

No one noticed Ralph (Bishop, Bonnie)

The once-upon-a-time dragon (Kent, Jack)

Piggy Bank Gonzalez (Kent, Jack)

Q is for duck (Elting, Mary)

Ralph rides away (Bishop, Bonnie)

Round Robin (Kent, Jack)

The scribble monster (Kent, Jack)

Silly goose (Kent, Jack)

Socks for supper (Kent, Jack)

There's no such thing as a dragon (Kent, Jack)

Kepes, Juliet. Cock-a-doodle-doo (Kepes, Juliet)

Five little monkeys (Kepes, Juliet)

Frogs, merry (Kepes, Juliet)

Lady bird, quickly (Kepes, Juliet)

Puptents and pebbles (Smith, William Jay)

Run little monkeys, run, run, run (Kepes, Juliet)

The seed that peacock planted (Kepes, Juliet)

The story of a bragging duck (Kepes, Juliet)

Kerr, Judith. Mog's Christmas (Kerr, Judith)

Kessler, Ethel. All aboard the train (Kessler, Ethel)

Do baby bears sit in chairs? (Kessler, Ethel)

Kessler, Leonard P. All aboard the train (Kessler, Ethel)

Animal doctors what do they do? (Greene, Carla)

Are we lost, daddy? (Kessler, Leonard P)

Be ready at eight (Parish, Peggy)

The big mile race (Kessler, Leonard P)

Big tracks, little tracks (Branley, Franklyn M)

Binky Brothers and the fearless four (Lawrence, James)

Binky Brothers, detectives (Lawrence, James)

A book of satellites for you (Branley, Franklyn M)

Colors, colors all around (Scott, Rochelle)

Cowboys what do they do? (Greene, Carla)

Deer in the snow (Schlein, Miriam)

Do baby bears sit in chairs? (Kessler, Ethel)

Doctors and nurses what do they do? (Greene, Carla)

Ducks don't get wet (Goldin, Augusta)

The ellipse (Charosh, Mannis)

Fast is not a ladybug (Schlein, Miriam)

Grandpa Witch and the magic doobelator (Kessler, Ethel)

Heavy is a hippopotamus (Schlein, Miriam)

Here comes the strikeout (Kessler, Leonard P)

A horse in the house (Crowell, Maryalicia)

It's about time (Schlein, Miriam)

Kick, pass, and run (Kessler, Leonard P)

Last one in is a rotten egg (Kessler, Leonard P)

Mr. Pine's mixed-up signs (Kessler, Leonard P)

Mr. Pine's purple house (Kessler, Leonard P)

Mrs. Pine takes a trip (Kessler, Leonard P)

Night story (Kessler, Ethel)

Old, older, oldest (Klein, Leonore)

Old Turtle's baseball stories (Kessler, Leonard P)

Old Turtle's winter games (Kessler, Leonard P)

On your mark, get set, go! (Kessler, Leonard P)

The pirates' adventure on Spooky Island (Kessler, Leonard P)

Railroad engineers and airplane pilots (Greene, Carla)

Riddles that rhyme for Halloween time (Kessler, Leonard P)

The silly Mother Goose (Kessler, Leonard P)

Soldiers and sailors what do they do? (Greene, Carla)

Soup for the king (Kessler, Leonard P)

Super bowl (Kessler, Leonard P)

Too many rabbits (Parish, Peggy)

Truck drivers what do they do? (Greene, Carla)

Two, four, six, eight (Kessler, Ethel)

What do they do? Policemen and firemen (Greene, Carla)

What have I got? (McClintock, Marshall)

What's inside the box? (Kessler, Ethel)

Kieffer, Christa. You were born on your very first birthday (Girard, Linda Walvoord)

Kilroy, Sally. Animal noises (Kilroy, Sally)

Babies' bodies (Kilroy, Sally)

Baby colors (Kilroy, Sally)

Copycat drawing book (Kilroy, Sally)

Noisy homes (Kilroy, Sally)

Kimura, Yasuko. Fergus and the sea monster (Kimura, Yasuko)

Kincade, Nancy. Even if I did something awful (Hazen, Barbara Shook)

King, R. A. Criss-cross applesauce (De Paola, Tomie)

King, Deborah. Look at seeds and weeds (Kirkpatrick, Rena K)

Puffin (Lewis, Naomi)

Sirius and Saba (King, Deborah)

King, Ernie. One is the engine (Meeks, Esther K)

King, Jessie M. Humpty Dumpty's favorite nursery rhymes (Cope, Dawn)

King, Tony. Rabbits (Tarrant, Graham)

L

Lantz, Paul. Patrick visits the library (Daly, Maureen)
When the cows got out (Koch, Dorothy Clarke)
Larrea, Victoria De *see* De Larrea, Victoria
Larrecq, John M. Broderick (Ormondroyd, Edward)
Eugene the brave (Conford, Ellen)
Just the thing for Geraldine (Conford, Ellen)
A single speckled egg (Levitin, Sonia)
Theodore (Ormondroyd, Edward)
Theodore's rival (Ormondroyd, Edward)
Larsen, Johannes. The ugly duckling (Andersen, H C (Hans Christian))
La Salle, Janet. Follett beginning to read picture dictionary (McIntire, Alta)
The little park (Fife, Dale)
Lasell, Fen. Fly away goose (Lasell, Fen)
Michael grows a wish (Lasell, Fen)
Lasker, Joe. All kinds of families (Simon, Norma)
Boxes (Craig, M Jean)
The boy who loved music (Lasker, David)
The cobweb Christmas (Climo, Shirley)
The do-something day (Lasker, Joe)
He's my brother (Lasker, Joe)
How do I feel? (Simon, Norma)
Howie helps himself (Fassler, Joan)
Lentil soup (Lasker, Joe)
Mothers can do anything (Lasker, Joe)
My house (Schlein, Miriam)
Nick joins in (Lasker, Joe)
The sun, the wind, the sea and the rain (Schlein, Miriam)
What do I do? (Simon, Norma)
What do I say? (Simon, Norma)
When the wind stops (Zolotow, Charlotte)
Laskowski, Janina Domanska *see* Domanska, Janina
Latham, Barbara. I like butterflies (Conklin, Gladys)
I like caterpillars (Conklin, Gladys)
Lathrop, Dorothy Pulis. An angel in the woods (Lathrop, Dorothy Pulis)
Animals of the Bible (Fish, Helen Dean)
The little mermaid (Andersen, H C (Hans Christian))
Puppies for keeps (Lathrop, Dorothy Pulis)
Who goes there? (Lathrop, Dorothy Pulis)
Lawrence, John. The giant of Grabbist (Lawrence, John)
The little store on the corner (Miller, Alice P)
Pope Leo's elephant (Lawrence, John)
Rabbit and pork (Lawrence, John)
Lawson, Robert. Four and twenty blackbirds (Fish, Helen Dean)
The hurdy-gurdy man (Bianco, Margery Williams)
The little woman wanted noise (Teal, Valentine)
The story of Ferdinand the bull (Leaf, Munro)
They were strong and good (Lawson, Robert)
Wee Gillis (Leaf, Munro)

Lazarevich, Mila. Do your ears hang low? (Glazer, Tom)
The fable of the fig tree (Gross, Michael)
The old man and the mule (Snyder, Anne)
Leaf, Anne Sellers. The book of favorite Muggins Mouse stories (Barrows, Marjorie Wescott)
Muggins' big balloon (Barrows, Marjorie Wescott)
Muggins Mouse (Barrows, Marjorie Wescott)
Muggins takes off (Barrows, Marjorie Wescott)
Leaf, Munro. Boo, who used to be scared of the dark (Leaf, Munro)
A flock of watchbirds (Leaf, Munro)
Gordon, the goat (Leaf, Munro)
Grammar can be fun (Leaf, Munro)
Health can be fun (Leaf, Munro)
How to behave and why (Leaf, Munro)
Manners can be fun (Leaf, Munro)
Noodle (Leaf, Munro)
Robert Francis Weatherbee (Leaf, Munro)
Safety can be fun (Leaf, Munro)
Leake, Don. Boo and the flying flews (Bowden, Joan Chase)
Of cobblers and kings (Sheldon, Aure)
Lear, Edward. ABC (Lear, Edward)
A book of nonsense (Lear, Edward)
Lebedev, V. In the van (Marshak, Samuel)
Lebedev, Vladimir Vasilievich *see* Lebedev, V.
Lebenson, Richard. Brownies - they're moving (Adshead, Gladys L)
Le Caine, Errol. Hiawatha's childhood (Longfellow, Henry Wadsworth)
Let's find out about Halloween (Cooper, Paulette)
Molly Whuppie (De La Mare, Walter)
Mrs. Fox's wedding (Grimm, Jacob)
The rat, the ox and the zodiac (Van Woerkom, Dorothy)
The snow queen (Andersen, H C (Hans Christian))
The three magic gifts (Riordan, James)
The twelve dancing princesses (Grimm, Jacob)
Leder, Dora. Agatha's alphabet, with her very own dictionary (Floyd, Lucy)
I know what I like (Simon, Norma)
I was so mad! (Simon, Norma)
One more thing, dad (Thompson, Susan L)
Where does my cat sleep? (Simon, Norma)
Why am I different? (Simon, Norma)
Lee, Alana. Puppet show (Peters, Sharon)
Lee, Doris. Gone is my goose (Koch, Dorothy Clarke)
Lee, Jared D. You can go jump (McLenighan, Valjean)
Lee, Jeanne M. The legend of the milky way (Lee, Jeanne M)
Lee, Manning. Boston Bells (Coatsworth, Elizabeth)
Lee, Russell. Noah and the ark (Ife, Elaine)
Stories Jesus told (Ife, Elaine)

Le Foll, Alain. The three trees of the Samurai (Cocagnac, A M (Augustin Maurice))

Leichman, Seymour. Shaggy dogs and spotty dogs and shaggy and spotty dogs (Leichman, Seymour)
The wicked wizard and the wicked witch (Leichman, Seymour)

Leigh, Tom. Sesame Street word book (Sesame Street)

Leisk, David Johnson *see* Johnson, Crockett

Lella, Barbara Di *see* Di Lella, Barbara

Lemerise, Bruce. Sheldon's lunch (Lemerise, Bruce)

Lemke, Horst. Places and faces (Lemke, Horst)

Lemoine, Georges. The emperor's nightingale (Andersen, H C (Hans Christian))

Lenski, Lois. Animals for me (Lenski, Lois)
At our house (Lenski, Lois)
Big little Davy (Lenski, Lois)
Cowboy Small (Lenski, Lois)
Davy and his dog (Lenski, Lois)
Davy goes places (Lenski, Lois)
Debbie and her dolls (Lenski, Lois)
Debbie and her family (Lenski, Lois)
Debbie and her grandma (Lenski, Lois)
Debbie goes to nursery school (Lenski, Lois)
A dog came to school (Lenski, Lois)
The donkey cart (Bulla, Clyde Robert)
I like winter (Lenski, Lois)
I went for a walk (Lenski, Lois)
Let's play house (Lenski, Lois)
The life I live (Lenski, Lois)
The little airplane (Lenski, Lois)
The little auto (Lenski, Lois)
The little family (Lenski, Lois)
The little farm (Lenski, Lois)
The little fire engine (Lenski, Lois)
The little sail boat (Lenski, Lois)
The little train (Lenski, Lois)
Lois Lenski's big book of Mr. Small (Lenski, Lois)
Mr. and Mrs. Noah (Lenski, Lois)
Mother Goose rhymes (Mother Goose)
Now it's fall (Lenski, Lois)
On a summer day (Lenski, Lois)
Papa Small (Lenski, Lois)
Policeman Small (Lenski, Lois)
Spring is here (Lenski, Lois)
A surprise for Davy (Lenski, Lois)
Susie Mariar (Lenski, Lois)

Lent, Blair. The angry moon (Sleator, William)
From King Boggen's hall to nothing-at-all
The funny little woman (Mosel, Arlene)
I stood upon a mountain (Fisher, Aileen)
John Tabor's ride (Lent, Blair)
The little match girl (Andersen, H C (Hans Christian))
Oasis of the stars (Economakis, Olga)
Pistachio (Lent, Blair)
The telephone (Chukovsky, Korney)
Tikki Tikki Tembo (Mosel, Arlene)
The wave (Hodges, Margaret)

Why the sun and the moon live in the sky (Dayrell, Elphinstone)

Leone, Sergio. Hooray for Henry (Bethell, Jean)

Lerner, Carol. Flowers of a woodland spring (Lerner, Carol)
The 100-year-old cactus (Holmes, Anita)
Sphinx (McClung, Robert)

LeSeig, Theo *see* Seuss, Dr.

Lesikin, Joan. Down the road (Lesikin, Joan)

Lester, Alison. Thing (Klein, Robin)

Le-Tan, Pierre. The afternoon cat (Le-Tan, Pierre)
Timothy's dream book (Le-Tan, Pierre)
Visit to the North Pole (Le-Tan, Pierre)

Le Tord, Bijou. Picking and weaving (Le Tord, Bijou)
Rabbit seeds (Le Tord, Bijou)

Lewin, Betsy. Animal snackers (Lewin, Betsy)
Cat count (Lewin, Betsy)
Hip, hippo, hooray! (Lewin, Betsy)
The strange thing that happened to Oliver Wendell Iscovitch (Olson, Helen Kronberg)

Lewin, Janetta. Look at weather (Kirkpatrick, Rena K)

Lewis, Bobby. Home before midnight

Lewis, Maud. Christmas with the rural mail (Woolaver, Lance)
From Ben Loman to the sea (Woolaver, Lance)

Lewis, Richard. Big Cowboy Western (Scott, Ann Herbert)

Lewis, Robin Baird. Red is best (Stinson, Kathy)

Lewis, Stephen. Zoo city (Lewis, Stephen)

Lewis, Tim. An apple a day (Barrett, Judi)

Leyden, Richard. Sometimes I like to cry (Stanton, Elizabeth)
The very messy room (Stanton, Elizabeth)

Lieberman, Frank. The fat baron (Boutell, Clarence Burley)

Liebman, Oscar. Frisky (Perera, Lydia)

Lignell, Lois. A tree is a plant (Bulla, Clyde Robert)

Lilly, Kenneth. Animal builders (Lilly, Kenneth)
Animal climbers (Lilly, Kenneth)
Animal jumpers (Lilly, Kenneth)
Animal runners (Lilly, Kenneth)
Animal swimmers (Lilly, Kenneth)
Animals at the zoo (Lilly, Kenneth)
Animals in the jungle (Lilly, Kenneth)
Animals of the ocean (Lilly, Kenneth)
Animals on the farm (Lilly, Kenneth)
The squirrel (Lane, Margaret)

Linch, Elizabeth Johanna. Samson (Linch, Elizabeth Johanna)

Lincoln, Patricia Henderson. And God bless me (Hopkins, Lee Bennett)

Lindberg, Jeffrey K. The Tower of Babel (Leeton, Will C)

Linden, Madelaine Gill. Bunny rabbit rebus (Adler, David A)

The comic adventures of Old Mother
Hubbard and her dog (Martin, Sarah
Catherine)
Days with Frog and Toad (Lobel, Arnold)
Dinosaur time (Parish, Peggy)
Dudley Pippin (Ressner, Phil)
Fables (Lobel, Arnold)
Frog and Toad all year (Lobel, Arnold)
Frog and Toad are friends (Lobel, Arnold)
Frog and Toad together (Lobel, Arnold)
Giant John (Lobel, Arnold)
Grasshopper on the road (Lobel, Arnold)
The great blueness and other predicaments
(Lobel, Arnold)
Gregory Griggs (Mother Goose)
Greg's microscope (Selsam, Millicent E)
Hildilid's night (Ryan, Cheli Durán)
A holiday for Mister Muster (Lobel,
Arnold)
I'll fix Anthony (Viorst, Judith)
Let's get turtles (Selsam, Millicent E)
Little runner of the longhouse (Baker,
Betty)
Lucille (Lobel, Arnold)
The man who took the indoors out (Lobel,
Arnold)
Martha, the movie mouse (Lobel, Arnold)
The mean old mean hyena (Prelutsky,
Jack)
Merry merry FIBruary (Orgel, Doris)
Ming Lo moves the mountain (Lobel,
Arnold)
Miss Suzy's Easter surprise (Young, Miriam
Burt)
More tales of Oliver Pig (Van Leeuwen,
Jean)
Mouse soup (Lobel, Arnold)
Mouse tales (Lobel, Arnold)
On the day Peter Stuyvesant sailed into
town (Lobel, Arnold)
Oscar Otter (Benchley, Nathaniel)
Owl at home (Lobel, Arnold)
Prince Bertram the bad (Lobel, Arnold)
The quarreling book (Zolotow, Charlotte)
The Random House book of poetry for
children (Prelutsky, Jack)
Red Fox and his canoe (Benchley,
Nathaniel)
Red Tag comes back (Phleger, Fred B)
Sam the minute man (Benchley, Nathaniel)
Seahorse (Morris, Robert A)
The secret three (Myrick, Mildred)
Small pig (Lobel, Arnold)
Someday (Zolotow, Charlotte)
The strange disappearance of Arthur
Cluck (Benchley, Nathaniel)
The tale of Meshka the Kvetch (Chapman,
Carol)
Tales of Oliver Pig (Van Leeuwen, Jean)
The terrible tiger (Prelutsky, Jack)
Terry and the caterpillars (Selsam,
Millicent E)
Tot Botot and his little flute (Cathon,
Laura E)
Uncle Elephant (Lobel, Arnold)
A zoo for Mister Muster (Lobel, Arnold)

Locke, Vance. The biggest family in the
town (Hoke, Helen L)

Locker, Thomas. Where the river begins
(Locker, Thomas)
Löfgren, Ulf. The boy who ate more than
the giant and other Swedish folktales
(Löfgren, Ulf)
The color trumpet (Löfgren, Ulf)
The flying orchestra (Löfgren, Ulf)
One-two-three (Löfgren, Ulf)
The traffic stopper that became a
grandmother visitor (Löfgren, Ulf)
The wonderful tree (Löfgren, Ulf)
Long, Olive M. Miss Muffet's Christmas
party (Crothers, Samuel McChord)
Longtemps, Kenneth. Our tree (Wong,
Herbert H)
Loof, Jan. Uncle Louie's fantastic sea voyage
(Loof, Jan)
Lopshire, Robert. Ann can fly (Phleger, Fred
B)
Big Max (Platt, Kin)
Big Max in the mystery of the missing
moose (Platt, Kin)
The biggest, smallest, fastest, tallest things
you've ever heard of (Lopshire, Robert)
How to make snop snappers and other fine
things (Lopshire, Robert)
I am better than you (Lopshire, Robert)
It's magic (Lopshire, Robert)
Little new kangaroo (Wiseman, Bernard)
The pig war (Baker, Betty)
Put me in the zoo (Lopshire, Robert)
Lord, John Vernon. Mr. Mead and his
garden (Lord, John Vernon)
The truck on the track (Burroway, Janet)
Lorentowicz, Irena. Lullaby (Bernhard,
Josephine Butkowska)
Mr. Bunny paints the eggs (Maril, Lee)
Nine cry-baby dolls (Bernhard, Josephine
Butkowska)
Lorenz, Lee. Big Gus and Little Gus (Lorenz,
Lee)
Pinchpenny John (Lorenz, Lee)
Scornful Simkin (Lorenz, Lee)
Sylvester Bear overslept (Wahl, Jan)
A weekend in the country (Lorenz, Lee)
Lorraine, Walter. The adventures of Isabel
(Nash, Ogden)
The armadillo who had no shell (Simon,
Sidney B)
David McCheever's twenty-nine dogs (Holt,
Margaret)
The dog who thought he was a boy
(Annett, Cora)
One snail and me (McLeod, Emilie
Warren)
Low, Joseph. Adam's book of odd creatures
(Low, Joseph)
Alex and the cat (Griffith, Helen V)
Benny rabbit and the owl (Low, Joseph)
Boo to a goose (Low, Joseph)
The Christmas grump (Low, Joseph)
Don't drag your feet... (Low, Joseph)
Five men under one umbrella (Low,
Joseph)
A Learical lexicon (Lear, Edward)
A mad wet hen and other riddles (Low,
Joseph)

Mice twice (Low, Joseph)
St. Nicholas and the tub (Burland, Brian)
Shrimps (Hawes, Judy)
Spider silk (Goldin, Augusta)
To sing a song as big as Ireland
(Zimelman, Nathan)
What if...? (Low, Joseph)

Lowery, Jo. A house for everyone (Miles, Betty)

Lowhar, Carmen. Butterflies and rainbows (Berger, Judith)

Lowitz, Anson. The pilgrims' party (Lowitz, Sadyebeth)

Lowman, Hubert A. Good times in the park (Bauer, Helen)

Lubell, Winifred. Here comes daddy (Lubell, Winifred)
I wish I had another name (Williams, Jay)
Nanette, the hungry pelican (Wise, William)
The pirates' bridge (Graham, Mary Stuart Campbell)
Rosalie, the bird market turtle (Lubell, Winifred)

Lubin, Leonard. Kevin's hat (Holland, Isabelle)

Lucas, Helen. The Christmas birthday story (Laurence, Margaret)

Luke, Kaye. Blessed Mother Goose (Mother Goose)

Luks, Peggy. The how (Boyd, Selma)
Two homes to live in (Hazen, Barbara Shook)

Luna, Tony De see DeLuna, Tony

Lupatelli, Anthony. Lupatelli's favorite nursery tales (Armitage, Marcia)

Lustig, Loretta. The best burglar alarm (Seabrooke, Brenda)
Mr. Simkin's grandma (Allen, Linda)
Mrs. Simkin's bed (Allen, Linda)

Luzzati, Emanuele. Cinderella (Perrault, Charles)

Lydecker, Laura. Hamilton (Peck, Robert Newton)

Lynch, Lorenzo. Big sister tells me that I'm black (Adoff, Arnold)

Lynch, Marietta. Mommy and daddy are divorced (Perry, Patricia)

M

Maas, Dorothy. The long and the short of it (Schurr, Cathleen)

Maas, Julie. Tom, Sue and the clock (Aiken, Conrad)

MacArthur-Onslow, Annette Rosemary. Minnie (MacArthur-Onslow, Annette Rosemary)

Macaulay, David. Castle (Macaulay, David)
Cathedral (Macaulay, David)

McBee, Jane. All about seeds (Kuchalla, Susan)

MacCabe, Lorin. Cable car Joey (MacCabe, Naomi)

MacCabe, Naomi. Cable car Joey (MacCabe, Naomi)

McCaffery, Janet. The goblin under the stairs (Calhoun, Mary)
The incompetent wizard (Oksner, Robert M)
Mrs. Dog's own house (Calhoun, Mary)
The pixy and the lazy housewife (Calhoun, Mary)
The runaway brownie (Calhoun, Mary)
The thieving dwarfs (Calhoun, Mary)
The traveling ball of string (Calhoun, Mary)
What makes a lemon sour? (Haines, Gail Kay)
The witch of Hissing Hill (Calhoun, Mary)

MacClain, George. I'm mad at you

McClintock, Barbara. Potbellied possums (Winthrop, Elizabeth)

McClintock, Deborah Derr. Let's count and count out

McCloskey, Robert. Bert Dow, deep-water man (McCloskey, Robert)
Blueberries for Sal (McCloskey, Robert)
Journey cake, ho! (Sawyer, Ruth)
Lentil (McCloskey, Robert)
Make way for ducklings (McCloskey, Robert)
The man who lost his head (Bishop, Claire Huchet)
One morning in Maine (McCloskey, Robert)
Time of wonder (McCloskey, Robert)

McClure, Gillian. Fly home McDoo (McClure, Gillian)
Prickly pig (McClure, Gillian)
What's the time, Rory Wolf? (McClure, Gillian)

McConnel, Jerry. Things I hate! (Wittels, Harriet)

McCord, Kathleen see Garry-McCord, Kathleen

McCrea, James. The king's procession (McCrea, James)
The magic tree (McCrea, James)
The story of Olaf (McCrea, James)

McCrea, Ruth. The king's procession (McCrea, James)
The magic tree (McCrea, James)
The story of Olaf (McCrea, James)

McCready, Lady see Tudor, Tasha

McCready, Tasha Tudor see Tudor, Tasha

McCue, Lisa. Corduroy's party (McCue, Lisa)
Corduroy's toys (McCue, Lisa)
Sprocket's Christmas tale (Gikow, Louise)

McCully, Emily Arnold. The bed book (Plath, Sylvia)
The black dog who went into the woods (Hurd, Edith Thacher)
Black is brown is tan (Adoff, Arnold)
The fishermen (Wahl, Jan)
For I will consider my cat Jeoffry (Smart, Christopher)
Friday night is papa night (Sonneborn, Ruth A)
Go and hush the baby (Byars, Betsy Cromer)

McMullan, Jim. Kangaroo and kangaroo (Braun, Kathy)

McNally, Bruce. Muppet babies through the year (Muntean, Michaela)
The tale of the dark crystal (Bass, Donna)

McNaught, Harry. Muppets in my neighborhood (Children's Television Workshop)
The truck book (McNaught, Harry)

McNaughton, Colin. At home (McNaughton, Colin)
At playschool (McNaughton, Colin)
At the park (McNaughton, Colin)
At the party (McNaughton, Colin)
At the stores (McNaughton, Colin)
Autumn (McNaughton, Colin)
The battle of Zormla (Hoban, Russell)
The flight of Bembel Rudzuk (Hoban, Russell)
The great gum drop robbery (Hoban, Russell)
The rat race (McNaughton, Colin)
Spring (McNaughton, Colin)
Summer (McNaughton, Colin)
They came from Aargh! (Hoban, Russell)
Walk rabbit walk (McNaughton, Colin)
Winter (McNaughton, Colin)

McPhail, David. Alligators are awful (and they have terrible manners, too) (McPhail, David)
Andrew's bath (McPhail, David)
The bear's bicycle (McLeod, Emilie Warren)
The bear's toothache (McPhail, David)
A big fat enormous lie (Sharmat, Marjorie Weinman)
Captain Toad and the motorbike (McPhail, David)
The cereal box (McPhail, David)
Fix-it (McPhail, David)
Great cat (McPhail, David)
Henry Bear's park (McPhail, David)
I want to be big (Iverson, Genie)
Leave Herbert alone (Whitney, Alma Marshak)
The magical drawings of Moony B. Finch (McPhail, David)
Mistletoe (McPhail, David)
The nightgown of the sullen moon (Willard, Nancy)
Pig Pig goes to camp (McPhail, David)
Pig Pig grows up (McPhail, David)
Pig Pig rides (McPhail, David)
Sisters (McPhail, David)
Snow lion (McPhail, David)
Stanley Henry Bear's friend (McPhail, David)
The train (McPhail, David)
A wolf story (McPhail, David)

McQueen, Lucinda. Hey! Don't do that! (Herz, Irene)
Kitty's new doll (Kunhardt, Dorothy)
Skunk and possum (Tether, Graham)

McToots, Rudi. The kid's book of games for cars, trains and planes (McToots, Rudi)

McVay, Tracy. The squirrel's tree party (DeLage, Ida)

Madden, Don. The daddy book (Stewart, Robert S)
Gravity is a mystery (Branley, Franklyn M)
Lemonade serenade or the thing in the garden (Madden, Don)
Me and my family tree (Showers, Paul)
No dogs allowed, Jonathan! (Christian, Mary Blount)
Nothing much happened today (Christian, Mary Blount)
The planets in our solar system (Branley, Franklyn M)
Why frogs are wet (Hawes, Judy)
The zoo that moved (Miklowitz, Gloria D)

Maddison, Kevin W. The pelican chorus and the quangle wangle's hat (Lear, Edward)
The pobble who has no toes (Lear, Edward)

Maestro, Betsy. On the go (Maestro, Betsy)
On the town (Maestro, Betsy)

Maestro, Giulio. Around the clock with Harriet (Maestro, Betsy)
Big city port (Maestro, Betsy)
Busy day (Maestro, Betsy)
Comets (Branley, Franklyn M)
Egg-ventures (Milgrom, Harry)
Fat polka-dot cat and other haiku (Maestro, Betsy)
Groundhog's Day at the doctor (Delton, Judy)
The guessing game (Maestro, Betsy)
Halloween howls (Maestro, Giulio)
Harriet at home (Maestro, Betsy)
Harriet at play (Maestro, Betsy)
Harriet at school (Maestro, Betsy)
Harriet at work (Maestro, Betsy)
Harriet goes to the circus (Maestro, Betsy)
Harriet reads signs and more signs (Maestro, Betsy)
I think I thought (Terban, Marvin)
Just enough Rosie (Maestro, Giulio)
Kitten from one to ten (Ginsburg, Mirra)
Leopard is sick (Maestro, Giulio)
Moonkey (Thaler, Mike)
Number ideas through pictures (Charosh, Mannis)
On the go (Maestro, Betsy)
On the town (Maestro, Betsy)
One more and one less (Maestro, Giulio)
Penny wise, fun foolish (Delton, Judy)
A raft of riddles (Maestro, Giulio)
The remarkable plant in apartment 4 (Maestro, Giulio)
Riddle romp (Maestro, Giulio)
Three friends find spring (Delton, Judy)
The tortoise's tug of war (Maestro, Giulio)
Traffic (Maestro, Betsy)
Where is my friend? (Maestro, Betsy)
Who said meow? (Polushkin, Maria)

Magagna, Anna Maria. Best-loved Bible verses for children
First prayers
Read me a poem (Buell, Ellen Lewis)

Magine, John. Christmas surprise (Gordon, Sharon)
Easter Bunny's lost egg (Gordon, Sharon)
Friendly snowman (Gordon, Sharon)
Sing me a song (Johnston, Mary Anne)

Magnus, Erica. Old Lars (Magnus, Erica)

Magnuson, Diana. The gazelle and the hunter (Foley, Bernice Williams)

Rudolph the red-nosed reindeer (May, Robert Lewis)

Mahood, Kenneth. Fifty million sausages (Benedictus, Roger)

The laughing dragon (Mahood, Kenneth)

Why are there more questions than answers, Grandad? (Mahood, Kenneth)

Maillard, Katharina. Circus magic (Baningan, Sharon Stearns)

Maitland, Antony. Dick Whittington (Dick Whittington and his cat)

Idle Jack (Maitland, Antony)

To London! To London! (Willard, Barbara)

Makie, Pam. Fat and skinny (Balestrino, Philip)

Makower, Sylvia. Samson's breakfast (Makower, Sylvia)

Makūnaite, Albina. How the cock wrecked the manor (Tempest, P)

Malecki, Maryann. Mom and dad and I are having a baby! (Malecki, Maryann)

Malvern, Corinne. Counting rhymes

Mandlin, Harvey. Benny's four hats (Jaynes, Ruth M)

Friends! friends! friends! (Jaynes, Ruth M)

Tell me please! What's that? (Jaynes, Ruth M)

That's what it is! (Jaynes, Ruth M)

Three baby chicks (Jaynes, Ruth M)

What do you say? (Crume, Marion W)

What is a birthday child? (Jaynes, Ruth M)

Manniche, Lise. The prince who knew his fate

Manson, Beverlie. The fairies' alphabet book (Manson, Beverlie)

Fairy poems for the very young

Maraslis, Demetra. The seeing stick (Yolen, Jane)

Marasmus, Seymour *see* Rivoli, Mario

Marceau, Marcel. The story of Bip (Marceau, Marcel)

Marche, Jim La *see* LaMarche, Jim

Margalit, Avishai. The Hebrew alphabet book (Margalit, Avishai)

Margie *see* Cooper, Margeria

Mari, Iela. Eat and be eaten (Mari, Iela)

The magic balloon (Mari, Iela)

Mariana. Doki, the lonely papoose (Mariana)

The journey of Bangwell Putt (Mariana)

Little Bear marches in the St. Patrick's Day parade (Janice)

Little Bear's Christmas (Janice)

Little Bear's New Year's party (Janice)

Little Bear's pancake party (Janice)

Little Bear's Sunday breakfast (Janice)

Little Bear's Thanksgiving (Janice)

Marino, Dorothy. Benjy's blanket (Brown, Myra Berry)

Buzzy Bear and the rainbow (Marino, Dorothy)

Buzzy Bear goes camping (Marino, Dorothy)

Buzzy Bear in the garden (Marino, Dorothy)

Buzzy Bear's busy day (Marino, Dorothy)

Company's coming for dinner (Brown, Myra Berry)

Edward and the boxes (Marino, Dorothy)

First night away from home (Brown, Myra Berry)

Good-bye thunderstorm (Marino, Dorothy)

Miss Hattie and the monkey (Olds, Helen Diehl)

Maris, Ron. Better move on, frog! (Maris, Ron)

My book (Maris, Ron)

Marokvia, Artur. Ching-Ting and the ducks (Fribourg, Marjorie G)

Follow the fall (Kumin, Maxine)

A French school for Paul (Marokvia, Merelle)

I caught a lizard (Conklin, Gladys)

If I were a bird (Conklin, Gladys)

Spring things (Kumin, Maxine)

We like bugs (Conklin, Gladys)

When insects are babies (Conklin, Gladys)

A winter friend (Kumin, Maxine)

Marol, Jean-Claude. Vagabul and his shadow (Marol, Jean-Claude)

Vagabul escapes (Marol, Jean-Claude)

Vagabul goes skiing (Marol, Jean-Claude)

Vagabul in the clouds (Marol, Jean-Claude)

Marshall, James. All the way home (Segal, Lore)

Bonzini! the tattooed man (Allen, Jeffrey)

Bumps in the night (Allard, Harry)

Carrot nose (Wahl, Jan)

The cut-ups (Marshall, James)

A day with Whisker Wickles (Jameson, Cynthia)

Dinner at Alberta's (Hoban, Russell)

The exploding frog and other fables from Æsop (McFarland, John)

Four little troubles (Marshall, James)

Four on the shore (Marshall, Edward)

Fox and his friends (Marshall, Edward)

Fox at school (Marshall, Edward)

Fox in love (Marshall, Edward)

Fox on wheels (Marshall, Edward)

George and Martha (Marshall, James)

George and Martha back in town (Marshall, James)

George and Martha encore (Marshall, James)

George and Martha one fine day (Marshall, James)

George and Martha rise and shine (Marshall, James)

George and Martha, tons of fun (Marshall, James)

The guest (Marshall, James)

I will not go to market today (Allard, Harry)

It's so nice to have a wolf around the house (Allard, Harry)

James Marshall's Mother Goose (Mother Goose)

MacGooses's grocery (Asch, Frank)

Mary Alice, operator number 9 (Allen, Jeffrey)

Outside my window (Skorpen, Liesel
Moak)
The queen always wanted to dance (Mayer,
Mercer)
Terrible troll (Mayer, Mercer)
There's a nightmare in my closet (Mayer,
Mercer)
Two moral tales (Mayer, Mercer)
What do you do with a kangaroo? (Mayer,
Mercer)
You're the scaredy cat (Mayer, Mercer)

Maynard, Barbara. Fraidy cat (Barrows,
Marjorie Wescott)

Mayo, Gretchen. Change (Greene, Laura)
Help (Greene, Laura)

Meddaugh, Susan. Maude and Claude go
abroad (Meddaugh, Susan)
Too short Fred (Meddaugh, Susan)

Meer, Atie Van der see Van der Meer, Atie

Meer, Ron Van der see Van der Meer, Ron

Megale, Marina. Safety zone (Meyer, Linda
D)

Melo, John. I love my mother (Zindel, Paul)

Mendoza, George. The alphabet boat
(Mendoza, George)

Merritt, Jane Hamilton see
Hamilton-Merritt, Jane

Merryweather, Jack. Cattle drive (Chandler,
Edna Walker)
Pony rider (Chandler, Edna Walker)
Secret tunnel (Chandler, Edna Walker)

Meryman, Hope. Akimba and the magic cow
(Rose, Anne)

Meyer, Elizabeth C. The blue china pitcher
(Meyer, Elizabeth C)

Meyer, Louis A. The clean air and peaceful
contentment dirigible airline (Meyer,
Louis A)

Michel, Guy. The butterfly book of birds
(Dalmais, Anne-Marie)

Mikolaycak, Charles. A child is born
(Winthrop, Elizabeth)
Johnny's egg (Long, Earlene)
The man who could call down owls
(Bunting, Eve)
Perfect crane (Laurin, Anne)
Peter and the wolf (Prokofiev, Sergei
Sergeievitch)
The surprising things Maui did (Williams,
Jay)
Tiger watch (Wahl, Jan)

Milhous, Katherine. The egg tree (Milhous,
Katherine)

Milius, Winifred Lubell see Lubell, Winifred

Mill, Eleanor. A button in her ear
(Litchfield, Ada B)
A cane in her hand (Litchfield, Ada B)
Mary Jo's grandmother (Udry, Janice May)
What Mary Jo shared (Udry, Janice May)
What Mary Jo wanted (Udry, Janice May)

Miller, Andrew. Nature's hidden world
(Selberg, Ingrid)

Miller, Bob. 2-B and the rock 'n roll band
(Paul, Sherry)
2-B and the space visitor (Paul, Sherry)

Miller, Don. The black B C's (Clifton,
Lucille)

Miller, Edna. Jumping bean (Miller, Edna)
Mousekin finds a friend (Miller, Edna)
Mousekin's ABC (Miller, Edna)
Mousekin's Christmas eve (Miller, Edna)
Mousekin's close call (Miller, Edna)
Mousekin's fables (Miller, Edna)
Mousekin's family (Miller, Edna)
Mousekin's golden house (Miller, Edna)
Mousekin's mystery (Miller, Edna)
Pebbles, a pack rat (Miller, Edna)
Pícaro, a pet otter (Wisbeski, Dorothy
Gross)

Miller, Grambs. Hummingbirds in the
garden (Gans, Roma)

Miller, J. P. (John Parr). Do you know color?
(Miller, J P (John Parr))
Dr. Squash the doll doctor (Brown,
Margaret Wise)
Learn about colors with Little Rabbit
(Miller, J P (John Parr))
Little turtle's big adventure (Harrison,
David Lee)
The wonderful house (Brown, Margaret
Wise)
The wonderful story book (Brown,
Margaret Wise)

Miller, Jane. Andrew the lion farmer (Hall,
Donald)
Birth of a foal (Miller, Jane)
Farm alphabet book (Miller, Jane)
Farm counting book (Miller, Jane)
Lambing time (Miller, Jane)
A part-time dog for Nick (Denison, Carol)
Scrappy the pup (Ciardi, John)
The wet world (Simon, Norma)

Miller, Marilyn. The people on Long Ago
Street (Budd, Lillian)
The pie wagon (Budd, Lillian)

Miller, Mitchell. One misty moisty morning
(Mother Goose)

Mills, Yaroslava Surmach see Yaroslava

Milne, Annabel. Look at flowers
(Kirkpatrick, Rena K)
Look at leaves (Kirkpatrick, Rena K)
Look at pond life (Kirkpatrick, Rena K)

Milord, Jerry. Maggie and the goodbye gift
(Milord, Sue)
Molly and the slow teeth (Ross, Pat)

Milord, Sue. Maggie and the goodbye gift
(Milord, Sue)

Minale, Marcello. Creatures great and small
(Flanders, Michael)

Mink, Norv. The funny hat (Barrows,
Marjorie Wescott)

Miracle, Veronica Mary. The two Georges
(Gunning, Monica)

Mitchell, Kurt. Jonah

Mitsuhashi, Yoko. I have a horse of my own
(Zolotow, Charlotte)
The silent concert (Leister, Mary)
Such is the way of the world (Elkin,
Benjamin)

Mitsui, Eiichi. Joji and the Amanojaku
(Lifton, Betty Jean)

Müller, Jörg. The bear who wanted to be a bear (Steiner, Jörg)
Rabbit Island (Steiner, Jörg)

Mullin, M. E. His mother's dog (Skorpen, Liesel Moak)

Mullins, Edward S. Animal limericks (Mullins, Edward S)

Mulready, William. The butterfly ball and the grasshopper's feast (Aldridge, Alan)

Munari, Bruno. ABC (Munari, Bruno)
Animals for sale (Munari, Bruno)
The birthday present (Munari, Bruno)
Bruno Munari's zoo (Munari, Bruno)
The circus in the mist (Munari, Bruno)
The elephant's wish (Munari, Bruno)
Jimmy has lost his cap (Munari, Bruno)
Tic, Tac and Toc (Munari, Bruno)
Who's there? Open the door (Munari, Bruno)

Munger, Nancy. My grandmother died but I won't forget her (Hogan, Bernice)

Munowitz, Ken. Noah (Mee, Charles L)

Munsinger, Lynn. Bear and Duck on the run (Delton, Judy)
Boris and the monsters (Willoughby, Elaine Macmann)
Don't tell me a ghost story (Eisenberg, Phyllis Rose)
Duck goes fishing (Delton, Judy)
How the alligator missed breakfast (Kinnell, Galway)
Martin by himself (Skurzynski, Gloria)
The mean, clean, giant canoe machine (Slate, Joseph)
Monkey in the middle (Bunting, Eve)
Nothing sticks like a shadow (Tompert, Ann)
A pet for Duck and Bear (Delton, Judy)
A very mice joke book (Goundaud, Karen Jo)
The wizard, the fairy and the magic chicken (Lester, Helen)

Murdocca, Sal. The bean boy (Bowden, Joan Chase)
The big cheese (Bunting, Eve)
The big strawberry book of questions and answers and facts and things (Malnig, Anita)
Have you seen Wilhelmina Krumpf? (Chasek, Judith)
1000 monsters (Benjamin, Alan)
Striding slippers (Ginsburg, Mirra)
Strong John (Bowden, Joan Chase)
Tuttle's shell (Murdocca, Sal)
Worthington Botts and the steam machine (Baker, Betty)

Murphy, Chuck. Winnie-the-Pooh (Milne, A A (Alan Alexander))

Murphy, Jill. Peace at last (Murphy, Jill)
What next, baby bear! (Murphy, Jill)

Murschetz, Luis. Mister Mole (Murschetz, Luis)

Musgrove, Margaret. Ashanti to Zulu (Musgrove, Margaret)

Myers, Amy. I know a monster (Myers, Amy)

Myers, Bernice. Charlie's birthday present (Myers, Bernice)
Herman and the bears and the giants (Myers, Bernice)

Myers, Bill. My friend William moved away (Hickman, Martha Whitmore)

Myers, Lou. The splendid belt of Mr. Big (Bulette, Sara)

Myller, Rolf. How big is a foot? (Myller, Rolf)
Rolling round (Myller, Rolf)

N

Nagel, Andreas Fischer see Fischer-Nagel, Andreas

Nagel, Heiderose Fischer see Fischer-Nagel, Heiderose

Nakano, Hirotaka. Elephant blue (Nakano, Hirotaka)

Nakatani, Chiyoko. The brave little goat of Monsieur Séguin (Daudet, Alphonse)
The day Chiro was lost (Nakatani, Chiyoko)
Fumio and the dolphins (Nakatani, Chiyoko)
The hippo boat (Kishida, Eriko)
The lion and the bird's nest (Kishida, Eriko)
My day on the farm (Nakatani, Chiyoko)
The zoo in my garden (Nakatani, Chiyoko)

Napoli, Guillier. Adventure of Mont Saint Michel (Napoli, Guillier)

Napoli, Victor Di see DiNapoli, Victor

Naprstek, Joel. Better, best, bestest (Diot, Alain)

Nardini, Sandro. The golden bird (Grimm, Jacob)

Nash, Linell. Custard the dragon and the wicked knight (Nash, Ogden)

Natti, Susanna. The acorn quest (Yolen, Jane)
The almost awful play (Giff, Patricia Reilly)
Dinosaurs and beasts of yore (Cole, William)
Frederick's alligator (Peterson, Esther Allen)
Helpful Hattie (Quin-Harkin, Janet)
I am three (Fitzhugh, Louise)
Midnight moon (Watson, Clyde)
Today was a terrible day (Giff, Patricia Reilly)

Negri, Rocco. The one bad thing about father (Monjo, F N)
Pampalche of the silver teeth (Ginsburg, Mirra)

Neill, Eileen Mueller. Out the door (Matthias, Catherine)

Ness, Evaline. All in the morning early (Alger, Leclaire)
Coll and his white pig (Alexander, Lloyd)
The devil's bridge (Scribner, Charles)
Do you have the time, Lydia? (Ness, Evaline)
Don't you remember? (Clifton, Lucille)

Everett Anderson's Christmas coming (Clifton, Lucille)
Exactly alike (Ness, Evaline)
Fierce the lion (Ness, Evaline)
The girl and the goatherd (Ness, Evaline)
The hand-me-down doll (Kroll, Steven)
Joey and the birthday present (Kumin, Maxine)
Josefina February (Ness, Evaline)
Josie and the snow (Buckley, Helen Elizabeth)
Josie's Buttercup (Buckley, Helen Elizabeth)
Kellyburn Braes (Alger, Leclaire)
Lonely Maria (Coatsworth, Elizabeth)
Old Mother Hubbard and her dog (Martin, Sarah Catherine)
Pavo and the princess (Ness, Evaline)
A pocketful of cricket (Caudill, Rebecca)
Sam, Bangs, and moonshine (Ness, Evaline)
Some of the days of Everett Anderson (Clifton, Lucille)
The steamroller (Brown, Margaret Wise)
Tom Tit Tot
The truthful harp (Alexander, Lloyd)
What color is Caesar? (Kumin, Maxine)
The wizard's tears (Kumin, Maxine)
The woman of the wood (Black, Algernon D)

Neuhart, Marilyn. Nabob and the geranium (Miller, Judith Ransom)

Neuhaus, David. His finest hour (Neuhaus, David)

Neustadt, Barbara. The first Christmas (Bible New Testament Gospels)

Nevett, Louise. Animals (Pitcher, Caroline)
Cars and boats (Pitcher, Caroline)
Dinosaurs and monsters
Masks and puppets

Nevins, Dan. Beneath your feet (Simon, Seymour)
Paper science (Milgrom, Harry)

Newberry, Clare Turlay. April's kittens (Newberry, Clare Turlay)
Barkis (Newberry, Clare Turlay)
Cousin Toby (Newberry, Clare Turlay)
Herbert the lion (Newberry, Clare Turlay)
The kittens' ABC (Newberry, Clare Turlay)
Lambert's bargain (Newberry, Clare Turlay)
Marshmallow (Newberry, Clare Turlay)
Mittens (Newberry, Clare Turlay)
Pandora (Newberry, Clare Turlay)
Percy, Polly and Pete (Newberry, Clare Turlay)
Smudge (Newberry, Clare Turlay)
T-Bone, the baby-sitter (Newberry, Clare Turlay)
Widget (Newberry, Clare Turlay)

Newell, Crosby see Bonsall, Crosby Newell

Newell, Peter. Topsys and turvys (Newell, Peter)

Newfeld, Frank. Alligator pie (Lee, Dennis)

Newland, Mary Reed. Good King Wenceslas (Newland, Mary Reed)

Newsham, Ian. The monster hunt (Newsham, Wendy)

Newsham, Wendy. The monster hunt (Newsham, Wendy)

Newsom, Carol. An Edward Lear alphabet (Lear, Edward)
Little owl leaves the nest (Leonard, Marcia)

Newton, Patricia Montgomery. The five sparrows (Newton, Patricia Montgomery)
Old Sadie and the Christmas bear (Naylor, Phyllis Reynolds)

Nichols, Marie C. One kitten too many (Bradbury, Bianca)

Nicholson, William, Sir. Clever Bill (Nicholson, William,)
The velveteen rabbit (Bianco, Margery Williams)

Nickl, Peter. Ra ta ta tam (Nickl, Peter)

Nicklaus, Carol. Alphabet cat (Black, Floyd)
Do armadillos come in houses? (Reed, Jonathan)
Hey, kid (Gelman, Rita Golden)
Hugh and Fitzhugh (Goodspeed, Peter)
Madge's magic show (Thaler, Mike)

Nicolas see Mordvinoff, Nicolas

Niemann, Gail. Rabbits, rabbits (Fisher, Aileen)

Nigognossian, Christine Willis. Thumbelina (Andersen, H C (Hans Christian))

Nikly, Michelle. The emperor's plum tree (Nikly, Michelle)

Niland, Deborah. ABC of monsters (Niland, Deborah)
The little goat (Fletcher, Elizabeth)
Mulga Bill's bicycle (Paterson, Andrew Barton)
What am I? (Fletcher, Elizabeth)
When the wind changed (Park, Ruth)

Niland, Kilmeny. The little goat (Fletcher, Elizabeth)
Mulga Bill's bicycle (Paterson, Andrew Barton)
What am I? (Fletcher, Elizabeth)

Nilsson, Lennart. How you were born (Cole, Joanna)

Ninon. ABC of cars and trucks (Alexander, Anne)
Scaredy cat (Krasilovsky, Phyllis)
The very little boy (Krasilovsky, Phyllis)
The very little girl (Krasilovsky, Phyllis)

Nister, Ernest. Little tales from long ago (Nister, Ernest)

Noack, Winifried. A flamingo is born (Zoll, Max Alfred)

Nobens, C. A. April Fools' Day (Kelley, Emily)

Noble, Trinka Hakes. Apple tree Christmas (Noble, Trinka Hakes)
Hansy's mermaid (Noble, Trinka Hakes)
Karin's Christmas walk (Pearson, Susan)
The king's tea (Noble, Trinka Hakes)
Will you take me to town on strawberry day? (Singer, Marilyn)
The witch who lost her shadow (Calhoun, Mary)

Nolan, Dennis. Witch Bazooza (Nolan, Dennis)
  Wizard McBean and his flying machine (Nolan, Dennis)
Nolden, Victor. The fox and the hare (Ginsburg, Mirra)
Noll, Sally. Off and counting (Noll, Sally)
Nonnast, Marie. Red legs (Goudey, Alice E)
Nook, Gerard. Have you seen roads? (Oppenheim, Joanne)
Noonan, Julia. Peter's pocket (Barrett, Judi)
  Puss in boots (Perrault, Charles)
Nordqvist, Sven. Pancake pie (Nordqvist, Sven)
Norelius, Einar. Jim, Jock and Jumbo (Bohman, Nils)
Norman, Vera Stone. Christmas time (Schenk, Esther M)
Northway, Jennifer. Dig away two-hole Tim (Agard, John)
Novak, Jiri Tibor. One big yo to go (Osborne, Valerie)
Numeroff, Laura Joffe. Amy for short (Numeroff, Laura Joffe)
  Emily's bunch (Numeroff, Laura Joffe)
  Phoebe Dexter has Harriet Peterson's sniffles (Numeroff, Laura Joffe)
  You can't put braces on spaces (Richter, Alice Numeroff)
Nussbaumer, Paul. Away in a manger (Nussbaumer, Marcs)
  Barry (Hürlimann, Bettina)
Nydorf, Seymour. One, two (DeCaprio, Annie)
Nygren, Tord. I'll take care of the crocodiles (Mählqvist, Stefan)

O

Oakley, Graham. The church cat abroad (Oakley, Graham)
  The church mice adrift (Oakley, Graham)
  The church mice and the moon (Oakley, Graham)
  The church mice at bay (Oakley, Graham)
  The church mice at Christmas (Oakley, Graham)
  The church mice in action (Oakley, Graham)
  The church mice spread their wings (Oakley, Graham)
  The church mouse (Oakley, Graham)
  Graham Oakley's magical changes (Oakley, Graham)
  Hetty and Harriet (Oakley, Graham)
Oberhänsli, Trudi. Sleep, baby, sleep
Oberländer, Gerhard. Joba and the wild boar (Baldner, Gaby)
Obligado, Lilian. The best Valentine in the world (Sharmat, Marjorie Weinman)
  A child's book of snakes, lizards and other reptiles (Daly, Kathleen N)
  Faint frogs feeling feverish and other terrifically tantalizing tongue twisters (Obligado, Lilian)

The kitten who barked (Untermeyer, Louis)
  Pickles and Jake (Chenery, Janet)
  The white marble (Zolotow, Charlotte)
O'Brian, William. The ear book (Perkins, Al)
O'Brien, John. Circus! Circus! (Hopkins, Lee Bennett)
Obrist, Jürg. Fluffy (Obrist, Jürg)
  The lonely prince (Bolliger, Max)
  The miser who wanted the sun (Obrist, Jürg)
  They do things right in Albern (Obrist, Jürg)
Oechsli, Kelly. A bear before breakfast (Clifford, Eth)
  The birthday car (Hillert, Margaret)
  The dog who insisted he wasn't (Singer, Marilyn)
  The dragon in the clock box (Craig, M Jean)
  The Easter bunny's secret (Darling, Kathy)
  Herbie's troubles (Chapman, Carol)
  The plaid peacock (Alan, Sandy)
  Red and the pumpkins (Stevenson, Jocelyn)
  Walter the wolf (Sharmat, Marjorie Weinman)
Ogan, Lewis A. The department store (Hastings, Evelyn Beilhart)
Ohlsson, Ib. The big yellow balloon (Fenton, Edward)
  Cat alley (Ohlsson, Ib)
  The city-country ABC (Walters, Marguerite)
Ohtomo, Yasuo. How do I put it on? (Watanabe, Shigeo)
  I can build a house! (Watanabe, Shigeo)
  I can ride it! (Watanabe, Shigeo)
  I can take a walk! (Watanabe, Shigeo)
  I'm the king of the castle! (Watanabe, Shigeo)
  What a good lunch! (Watanabe, Shigeo)
  Where's my daddy? (Watanabe, Shigeo)
O'Kelley, Mattie Lou. A winter place (Radin, Ruth Yaffe)
Olds, Elizabeth. Feather mountain (Olds, Elizabeth)
  Little Una (Olds, Elizabeth)
  Plop plop ploppie (Olds, Elizabeth)
Olfers, Sibylle Von. When the root children wake up (Fish, Helen Dean)
Olguin, John. Whalewatch! (Behrens, June)
Oliver, Dexter. I want to be... (Oliver, Dexter)
Oliver, Jenni. My name is Emily (Hamilton, Morse)
  Rabbit tales (McCormack, John E)
Olschewski, Alfred. We fly (Olschewski, Alfred)
  The wheel rolls over (Olschewski, Alfred)
O'Neill, Steve. Dinosaur do's and don'ts (Polhamus, Jean Burt)
  Doctor Dinosaur (Polhamus, Jean Burt)
Ono, Chiyo. The boy and the bird (Fujita, Tamao)

Onslow, Annette Rosemary MacArthur *see* MacArthur-Onslow, Annette Rosemary

Opgenoorth, Winfried. The snowman who went for a walk (Lobe, Mira)
Valerie and the good-night swing (Lobe, Mira)

Orbach, Ruth. Apple pigs (Orbach, Ruth)
Please send a panda (Orbach, Ruth)

Orlando, Joe. The Superman mix or match storybook

Orlando, Rosalie. I didn't want to be nice (Jones, Penelope)

Ormai, Stella. Bizzy Bones and Uncle Ezra (Martin, Jacqueline Briggs)
Mystery at mouse house (Hare, Norma Q)

Ormerod, Jan. Moonlight (Ormerod, Jan)
101 things to do with a baby (Ormerod, Jan)
Reading (Ormerod, Jan)
Rhymes around the day (Thomson, Pat)
Sunshine (Ormerod, Jan)

Ormsby, Virginia H. Twenty-one children plus ten (Ormsby, Virginia H)

Orr, Richard. Bears (Pluckrose, Henry)

Ortiz, Fran. Someone special, just like you (Brown, Tricia)

Osborn, Robert. I met a man (Ciardi, John)

Ostrovsky, Rose. Mumps! (Ostrovsky, Vivian)

O'Sullivan, Tom. The no-bark dog (Williamson, Stan)

Ott, Pepperl. Clelia and the little mermaid (Spang, Günter)

Ottie, Vanessa *see* Julian-Ottie, Vanessa

Otto, Svend. The brave little tailor (Grimm, Jacob)
A Christmas book
Cinderella (Grimm, Jacob)
The giant fish and other stories (Otto, Svend)
Grimm Tom Thumb (Tom Thumb)
The musicians of Bremen (Grimm, Jacob)
Taxi dog (Otto, Svend)
The wolf and the seven little kids (Grimm, Jacob)
The wonderful pumpkin (Hellsing, Lennart)

Overlie, George. Dear little mumps child (Lerner, Marguerite Rush)
The dentists' tools (Lapp, Carolyn)
Doctors' tools (Lerner, Marguerite Rush)
Merry-go-rounds (Thomas, Art)
Michael gets the measles (Lerner, Marguerite Rush)
Peter gets the chickenpox (Lerner, Marguerite Rush)

Owens, Gail. A bedtime story (Levine, Joan)
The eels' strange journey (Friedman, Judi)
Fog in the meadow (Ryder, Joanne)
Hurricane (McNulty, Faith)
I hate red rover (Lexau, Joan M)
The oldest kid (Knox-Wagner, Elaine)
Pooh's bedtime book (Milne, A A (Alan Alexander))
Spider in the sky (Rose, Anne)

Oxenbury, Helen. The animal house (Cutler, Ivor)
Beach day (Oxenbury, Helen)
The birthday party (Oxenbury, Helen)
Cakes and custard
The car trip (Oxenbury, Helen)
The checkup (Oxenbury, Helen)
The dancing class (Oxenbury, Helen)
The dragon of an ordinary family (Mahy, Margaret)
Eating out (Oxenbury, Helen)
Family (Oxenbury, Helen)
First day of school (Oxenbury, Helen)
Friends (Oxenbury, Helen)
Good night, good morning (Oxenbury, Helen)
The great big enormous turnip (Tolstoĭ, Alekseĭ Nikolaevich)
Helen Oxenbury's ABC of things (Oxenbury, Helen)
Monkey see, monkey do (Oxenbury, Helen)
Mother's helper (Oxenbury, Helen)
Numbers of things (Oxenbury, Helen)
Our dog (Oxenbury, Helen)
Pig tale (Oxenbury, Helen)
Playing (Oxenbury, Helen)
The quangle wangle's hat (Lear, Edward)
The queen and Rosie Randall (Oxenbury, Helen)
729 curious creatures (Oxenbury, Helen)
729 merry mix-ups (Oxenbury, Helen)
729 puzzle people (Oxenbury, Helen)
The shopping trip (Oxenbury, Helen)
Tiny Tim (Bennett, Jill)

Oxenham, Patrick. The porcupine

O'Young, Leoung. Hockey showdown (Kidd, Bruce)

P

Pache, Joycelyne. The fantastic story of King Brioche the First (Jenny, Anne)

Page, Don. Play ball, Kate! (Gordon, Sharon)
Tick tock clock (Gordon, Sharon)

Paladini, David. The hundredth dove and other tales (Yolen, Jane)

Palazzo, Anthony D. *see* Palazzo, Tony

Palazzo, Tony. Animal babies (Palazzo, Tony)
Animals 'round the mulberry bush (Palazzo, Tony)
Bianco and the New World (Palazzo, Tony)
Edward Lear's nonsense book (Lear, Edward)
Federico, the flying squirrel (Palazzo, Tony)
Noah's ark (Palazzo, Tony)
Songs for a small guitar (Graham, Al)
Timothy Turtle (Graham, Al)
Waldo the woodchuck (Palazzo, Tony)

Paleček, Josef. The little mermaid (Andersen, H C (Hans Christian))
The ugly duckling (Andersen, H C (Hans Christian))

Paling, John. Grey squirrel (Oxford Scientific Films)

Q

Reese, Ralph. The first crazy word book (Preiss, Byron)

Regniers, Beatrice De *see* De Regniers, Beatrice

Reich, Károly. Matt the gooseherd (Illyés, Gyula)

Reidel, Marlene. Jacob and the robbers (Reidel, Marlene)

Reidy, Kathleen. Alphabet sheep (Mendoza, George)
Silly sheep and other sheepish rhymes (Mendoza, George)

Reilly, Jack. You are what you are (McLenighan, Valjean)

Reiner, Traudl. Me and Clara and Baldwin the pony (Inkiow, Dimiter)
Me and Clara and Casimir the cat (Inkiow, Dimiter)
Me and Clara and Snuffy the dog (Inkiow, Dimiter)
Me and my sister Clara (Inkiow, Dimiter)

Reiner, Walter. Me and Clara and Baldwin the pony (Inkiow, Dimiter)
Me and Clara and Casimir the cat (Inkiow, Dimiter)
Me and Clara and Snuffy the dog (Inkiow, Dimiter)
Me and my sister Clara (Inkiow, Dimiter)

Reinl, Edda. The little snake (Reinl, Edda)

Reisman, Celia. Jeremy and the ghost (Charlton, Elizabeth)

Reiss, John J. Colors (Reiss, John J)
Numbers (Reiss, John J)
Shapes (Reiss, John J)

Reiss, Susan. Feet (Chase, Catherine)

Reitveld, Jane Klatt. Monkey island (Reitveld, Jane Klatt)

Remington, Barbara. The Christmas mouse (Wenning, Elisabeth)

Remington, Frederic. My very first book of cowboy songs (Moon, Dolly M)

Renfro, Ed. The city witch and the country witch (Williams, Jay)

Resko, John. The snowplow that tried to go south (Retan, Walter)

Rettich, Margret. The voyage of the jolly boat (Rettich, Margret)

Rey, H. A. *see* Rey, Hans Augusto

Rey, Hans Augusto. Anybody at home? (Rey, Hans Augusto)
Billy's picture (Rey, Margaret Elisabeth Waldstein)
Cecily G and the nine monkeys (Rey, Hans Augusto)
Curious George (Rey, Hans Augusto)
Curious George flies a kite (Rey, Margaret Elisabeth Waldstein)
Curious George gets a medal (Rey, Hans Augusto)
Curious George goes to the hospital (Rey, Margaret Elisabeth Waldstein)
Curious George learns the alphabet (Rey, Hans Augusto)
Curious George rides a bike (Rey, Hans Augusto)

Curious George takes a job (Rey, Hans Augusto)
Don't frighten the lion (Brown, Margaret Wise)
Elizabite, adventures of a carnivorous plant (Rey, Hans Augusto)
Feed the animals (Rey, Hans Augusto)
How do you get there? (Rey, Hans Augusto)
Humpty Dumpty and other Mother Goose songs (Rey, Hans Augusto)
Katy no-pocket (Payne, Emmy)
Look for the letters (Rey, Hans Augusto)
The park book (Zolotow, Charlotte)
Pretzel (Rey, Margaret Elisabeth Waldstein)
Pretzel and the puppies (Rey, Margaret Elisabeth Waldstein)
See the circus (Rey, Hans Augusto)
Spotty (Rey, Margaret Elisabeth Waldstein)
Tit for tat (Rey, Hans Augusto)
Where's my baby? (Rey, Hans Augusto)

Reyna, Marilyn De *see* Hafner, Marylin

Rice, Eve. Benny bakes a cake (Rice, Eve)
Ebbie (Rice, Eve)
Goodnight, goodnight (Rice, Eve)
New blue shoes (Rice, Eve)
Once in a wood (Æsop)
Papa's lemonade and other stories (Rice, Eve)
Sam who never forgets (Rice, Eve)
Stories from a snowy meadow (Stevens, Carla)
What Sadie sang (Rice, Eve)

Rice, James. Gaston goes to Texas (Rice, James)

Richards, Linda Rochester. A dog's life (Hopkins, Lee Bennett)

Richardson, Frederick. Mother Goose

Richter, Marianne. Little hedgehog (Ruck-Pauquèt, Gina)

Richter, Mischa. The deep dives of Stanley Whale (Benchley, Nathaniel)
Eric and Matilda (Richter, Mischa)
Quack? (Richter, Mischa)
The special string (Bakken, Harold)
To bed, to bed! (Richter, Mischa)

Ricketts, Michael. Fire
Rain (Ricketts, Michael)
Teeth (Ricketts, Michael)

Rieger, Shay. Honi and his magic circle (Gershator, Phillis)
The secret of the Sabbath fish (Aronin, Ben)

Rigie, Jane Chambless *see* Chambless-Rigie, Jane

Ringi, Kjell. My father and I (Ringi, Kjell)
The sun and the cloud (Ringi, Kjell)
The winner (Ringi, Kjell)

Rister, Claude *see* Marshall, James

Riswold, Gilbert. Brown rats, black rats (Annixter, Jane)

Rivoli, Mario. Do tigers ever bite kings? (Wersba, Barbara)

Roach, Marilynne K. Dune fox (Roach, Marilynne K)
Two Roman mice (Roach, Marilynne K)

Ross, Tony. The charge of the mouse
brigade (Stone, Bernard)
The enchanted pig (Ross, Tony)
The greedy little cobbler (Ross, Tony)
Hugo and Oddsock (Ross, Tony)
Hugo and the bureau of holidays (Ross,
Tony)
Hugo and the man who stole colors (Ross,
Tony)
Jack and the beanstalk
The pied piper of Hamelin (Ross, Tony)
Puss in boots (Perrault, Charles)
The three pigs (The three little pigs)
Towser and the terrible thing (Ross, Tony)
Rosselli, Colette. I went to the animal fair
(Cole, William)
Roth, Judith S. Alfred (Udry, Janice May)
Roth, Lazlo. The hill that grew (Meeks,
Esther K)
Roth, Susan L. Patchwork tales (Roth, Susan
L)
Rothe, Ann Toulmin see Toulmin-Rothe,
Ann
Roughsey, Dick. The giant devil-dingo
(Roughsey, Dick)
Rounds, Glen. Billy Boy
The boll weevil (Rounds, Glen)
Casey Jones (Rounds, Glen)
Contrary Jenkins (Caudill, Rebecca)
The day the circus came to Lone Tree
(Rounds, Glen)
Down in the boondocks (Gage, Wilson)
Elephant and friends (Freschet, Berniece)
Halfway up the mountain (Gilchrist, Theo
E)
Hush up! (Aylesworth, Jim)
I'm going on a bear hunt (Sivulich, Sandra
Stroner)
Lucky ladybugs (Conklin, Gladys)
Once we had a horse (Rounds, Glen)
Praying mantis (Conklin, Gladys)
The strawberry roan (Rounds, Glen)
Sweet Betsy from Pike (Rounds, Glen)
Three fools and a horse (Baker, Betty)
Rousseau, Henri. House of a hundred
windows (Brown, Margaret Wise)
Routh, Jonathan. The Nuns go to Africa
(Routh, Jonathan)
Rowand, Phyllis. Bears (Krauss, Ruth)
Every day in the year (Rowand, Phyllis)
George (Rowand, Phyllis)
George goes to town (Rowand, Phyllis)
The growing story (Krauss, Ruth)
It is night (Rowand, Phyllis)
Rowe, Eric. The childhood of Jesus (Ife,
Elaine)
Moses in the bulrushes (Ife, Elaine)
Rubel, Nicole. Alligator's garden (Muntean,
Michaela)
Aunt Bernice (Gantos, Jack)
Bruno Brontosaurus (Rubel, Nicole)
Greedy Greeny (Gantos, Jack)
The house that bear built (Muntean,
Michaela)
Me and my kitty (Rubel, Nicole)
The perfect pal (Gantos, Jack)
Rotten Ralph (Gantos, Jack)

Rotten Ralph's rotten Christmas (Gantos,
Jack)
Sam and Violet are twins (Rubel, Nicole)
Sam and Violet go camping (Rubel, Nicole)
Swampy alligator (Gantos, Jack)
The werewolf family (Gantos, Jack)
Woof, woof! (Kroll, Steven)
Worse than Rotten Ralph (Gantos, Jack)
Ruben, Patricia. Apples to zippers (Ruben,
Patricia)
True or false? (Ruben, Patricia)
Rubin, Eva Johanna. 3 X 3 (Krüss, James)
Ruby-Spears Enterprises. The puppy's new
adventures (Ruby-Spears Enterprises)
Rudinski, Richard. Eric needs stitches
(Marino, Barbara Pavis)
Rue, Leonard Lee. Hubert Hippo's world
(Lasher, Faith B)
Ruffins, Reynold. Light and darkness
(Branley, Franklyn M)
My brother never feeds the cat (Ruffins,
Reynold)
That's not fair (Sarnoff, Jane)
Ruggles, Gene. Learning about love (Jenkins,
Jordan)
Runyon, Anne Marshall. The spaghetti tree
(Fontaine, Jan)
Rupp, Jacques. The biggest house (Jaynes,
Ruth M)
Let me see you try (Crume, Marion W)
The littlest house (Curry, Nancy)
Rusling, Albert. The mouse and Mrs.
Proudfoot (Rusling, Albert)
Russell, Gertrude Barrer see Barrer-Russell,
Gertrude
Russell, Sandra Joanne. A farmer's dozen
(Russell, Sandra Joanne)
Russo, Marisabina. Easy-to-make spaceships
that really fly (Blocksma, Mary)
Russo, Susan. The ice cream ocean and
other delectable poems of the sea (Russo,
Susan)
The moon's the north wind's cooky
Ruthen, Marlene Lobell. The shofar that lost
its voice (Fass, David E)
Rutherford, Bill. Favorite poems for the
children's hour (Bouton, Josephine)
Rutherford, Bonnie. Favorite poems for the
children's hour (Bouton, Josephine)
Ryan, DyAnne DiSalvo see DiSalvo-Ryan,
DyAnne

S

Sage, Alison. Teddy bears cure a cold
(Gretz, Susanna)
Sahula, Peter. The zoo book (Allen, Robert)
St. Tamara. Chickaree, a red squirrel (St
Tamara)
Save that raccoon! (Miklowitz, Gloria D)
Sakai, Sanryo. Kappa's tug-of-war with the
big brown horse (Baruch, Dorothy)
Saldutti, Denise. I think he likes me
(Winthrop, Elizabeth)

The moon (Stevenson, Robert Louis)

Salek, Jaroslav. Patterns of nature (Baker, Jeffrey J W)

Salem, Mary Miller. Playland pony (Meeks, Esther K)

Salle, Janet La *see* La Salle, Janet

Saltzberg, Barney. It must have been the wind (Saltzberg, Barney)

Salvo-Ryan, DyAnne Di *see* DiSalvo-Ryan, DyAnne

Salzman, Yuri. The little hen and the giant (Polushkin, Maria)
The man who entered a contest (Krasilovsky, Phyllis)
Two homes for Lynn (Noble, June)

Salzmann, Laurence. A family Passover (Rosen, Anne)

Sambin, Michele. Caught in the rain (Ferro, Beatriz)
Francie's paper puppy (Bröger, Achim)

Samsa, Ermanno. The lazy beaver (Gallo, Giovanni)

Samuels, Barbara. The bananas move to the ceiling (Manes, Esther)
Faye and Dolores (Samuels, Barbara)

Sanchez, Carlos. Perez and Martina (Belpré, Pura)

Sandberg, Lasse. Come on out, Daddy! (Sandberg, Inger)
Little Anna saved (Sandberg, Inger)
Little ghost Godfry (Sandberg, Inger)
Nicholas' favorite pet (Sandberg, Inger)

Sanderson, Ruth. Five nests (Arnold, Caroline)
We remember Philip (Simon, Norma)

Sandin, Joan. Crocodile and hen (Lexau, Joan M)
Daniel's duck (Bulla, Clyde Robert)
Hill of fire (Lewis, Thomas P)
It all began with a drip, drip, drip (Lexau, Joan M)
The long way to a new land (Sandin, Joan)
The secret box (Cole, Joanna)
Small Wolf (Benchley, Nathaniel)
Time for Uncle Joe (Jewell, Nancy)
Woodchuck (McNulty, Faith)

Sandland, Reg. The town that moved (Finsand, Mary Jane)

San Souci, Daniel. The brave little tailor (Grimm, Jacob)
Song of Sedna (San Souci, Robert D)

Sant, Laurent Sauveur. Dinosaurs (Sant, Laurent Sauveur)

Santoro, Christopher. Animals build amazing homes (Nussbaum, Hedda)
Prehistoric mammals (Miller, Susanne Santoro)

Santos, Joyce Audy Dos *see* Dos Santos, Joyce Audy

Sasaki, Isao. Snow (Sasaki, Isao)

Sasaki, Jeannie. Chōchō is for butterfly (Sasaki, Jeannie)

Satorsky, Cyril. My daddy and I (Alexander, Anne)

Savitt, Sam. Springfellow (Kraus, Robert)

Sawada, Hajime. The missing button adventure (Marcus, Susan)

Saxon, Charles D. Don't worry about Poopsie (Saxon, Charles D)
Gabriel Wrinkles, the bloodhound who couldn't smell (Doughtie, Charles)

Say, Allen. The bicycle man (Say, Allen)
How my parents learned to eat (Friedman, Ina R)
The lucky yak (Lawson, Annetta)
Magic and the night river (Bunting, Eve)
Once under the cherry blossom tree (Say, Allen)

Scarry, Huck. Huck Scarry's steam train journey (Scarry, Huck)
Looking into the Middle Ages (Scarry, Huck)
My first picture dictionary (Howard, Katherine)
On the road (Scarry, Huck)

Scarry, Richard. The adventures of Tinker and Tanker (Scarry, Richard)
Egg in the hole (Scarry, Richard)
The great big car and truck book (Scarry, Richard)
Is this the house of Mistress Mouse? (Scarry, Richard)
Nonsense alphabets (Lear, Edward)
Peasant Pig and the terrible dragon (Scarry, Richard)
Richard Scarry's ABC word book (Scarry, Richard)
Richard Scarry's animal nursery tales (Scarry, Richard)
Richard Scarry's best Christmas book ever! (Scarry, Richard)
Richard Scarry's best counting book ever (Scarry, Richard)
Richard Scarry's best first book ever (Scarry, Richard)
Richard Scarry's best Mother Goose ever (Mother Goose)
Richard Scarry's best story book ever (Scarry, Richard)
Richard Scarry's best word book ever (Scarry, Richard)
Richard Scarry's busiest people ever (Scarry, Richard)
Richard Scarry's busy busy world (Scarry, Richard)
Richard Scarry's busy houses (Scarry, Richard)
Richard Scarry's cars and trucks and things that go (Scarry, Richard)
Richard Scarry's favorite Mother Goose rhymes (Mother Goose)
Richard Scarry's funniest storybook ever (Scarry, Richard)
Richard Scarry's great big air book (Scarry, Richard)
Richard Scarry's great big mystery book (Scarry, Richard)
Richard Scarry's great big schoolhouse (Scarry, Richard)
Richard Scarry's hop aboard! Here we go! (Scarry, Richard)
Richard Scarry's Lowly Worm word book (Scarry, Richard)

Granny, the baby and the big gray thing
(Parish, Peggy)
Teach us, Amelia Bedelia (Parish, Peggy)
What is a fish? (Eastman, David)

Swerger, Lisbeth. Little red cap (Grimm,
Jacob)

Swift, Tony. Bees and wasps (Pluckrose,
Henry)

Swofford, Jeannette. The dawdlewalk
(Tobias, Tobi)

Szasz, Suzanne. A tiny baby for you
(Langstaff, Nancy)

Szekeres, Cyndy. Argentaybee and the
boonie (Hiller, Catherine)
Brimhall comes to stay (Delton, Judy)
Cyndy Szekeres' counting book, 1 to 10
(Szekeres, Cyndy)
Doctor Rabbit's foundling (Wahl, Jan)
The girl who was a cowboy (Krasilovsky,
Phyllis)
Goodbye, hello (Welber, Robert)
Goodnight orange monster (Lifton, Betty
Jean)
Here's Pippa again! (Boegehold, Betty)
Hurray for Pippa! (Boegehold, Betty)
Jumper goes to school (Parish, Peggy)
Ladybug and dog and the night walk
(Berends, Polly Berrien)
Little chick's story (Kwitz, Mary DeBall)
Little Richard and Prickles (Scarry, Patsy)
Long ago (Szekeres, Cyndy)
The Muffletump storybook (Wahl, Jan)
The Muffletumps' Christmas party (Wahl,
Jan)
The Muffletumps' Halloween scare (Wahl,
Jan)
No! No! (Myller, Lois)
Patsy Scarry's big bedtime storybook
(Scarry, Patsy)
Pippa Mouse (Boegehold, Betty)
Pippa pops out! (Boegehold, Betty)
Small Bear builds a playhouse (Holl,
Adelaide)

Szilagyi, Mary. This year's garden (Rylant,
Cynthia)

Szumski, Richard. Let's take a trip (Baugh,
Dolores M)

T

Taback, Simms. Euphonia and the flood
(Calhoun, Mary)
Fishy riddles (Hall, Katy)
Joseph had a little overcoat (Taback,
Simms)
Too much noise (McGovern, Ann)

Taber, Anthony. Cats' eyes (Taber, Anthony)

Tafuri, Nancy. Across the stream (Ginsburg,
Mirra)
All asleep (Pomerantz, Charlotte)
All year long (Tafuri, Nancy)
Coconut (Dragonwagon, Crescent)
Early morning in the barn (Tafuri, Nancy)
Have you seen my duckling? (Tafuri,
Nancy)

If I had a Paka (Pomerantz, Charlotte)
My hands can (Holzenthaler, Jean)
The Piney Woods peddler (Shannon,
George)
The song (Zolotow, Charlotte)

Taggart, Tricia. My sister says (Baker, Betty)

Takahashi, Haruo. Tuxedo Sam (Nichols,
Cathy)

Talbot, Nathan. My sister's silent world
(Arthur, Catherine)

Tallarico, Tony. At home (Tallarico, Tony)

Tallon, Robert. ABCDEF...
Handella (Tallon, Robert)
Latouse my moose (Tallon, Robert)

Talus, Taylor. The adventures of the three
colors (Tison, Annette)
Animal hide-and-seek (Tison, Annette)

Tamburine, Jean. I think I will go to the
hospital (Tamburine, Jean)
It's nice to be little (Stanley, John)

Tan, Pierre Le see Le-Tan, Pierre

Tanaka, Hideyuki. The happy dog (Tanaka,
Hideyuki)

Taniuchi, Kota. Trolley (Taniuchi, Kota)

Tateishi, Shuji. Baby owl (Funazaki, Yasuko)

Taylor, Elizabeth Watson. The animals who
changed their colors (Allamand, Pascale)

Taylor, Jody. The old witch and the ghost
parade (DeLage, Ida)

Taylor, Scott. Fiesta! (Behrens, June)

Tenggren, Gustaf. Mother Goose
The night before Christmas (Moore,
Clement C)
Thumbelina (Andersen, H C (Hans
Christian))

Tenniel, John. The nursery "Alice" (Carroll,
Lewis)

Tenny, Eric. Lions and tigers (Pluckrose,
Henry)

Testa, Fulvio. The butterfly collector (Lewis,
Naomi)
If you look around (Testa, Fulvio)
If you take a paintbrush (Testa, Fulvio)
If you take a pencil (Testa, Fulvio)
The land where the ice cream grows
(Testa, Fulvio)
Leaves (Lewis, Naomi)
The paper airplane (Baumann, Kurt)

Tester, Sylvia Root. Chase! (Tester, Sylvia
Root)
Parade! (Tester, Sylvia Root)

Thaler, Mike. The yellow brick toad (Thaler,
Mike)

Thatcher, Frances. Percival's party (Hynard,
Julia)
Snowy the rabbit (Hynard, Stephen)
Snuffles' house (Faunce-Brown, Daphne)

Theobalds, Prue. Marvella's hobby
(Cushman, Jerome)

Thiess, Anne. Tobi (Wilson, Joyce Lancaster)

Thollander, Earl. The hullabaloo ABC
(Cleary, Beverly)
Jump frog jump (Miles, Miska)
No, no, Rosina (Miles, Miska)

U

One, two, where's my shoe? (Ungerer, Tomi)

Orlando, the brave vulture (Ungerer, Tomi)

Rufus (Ungerer, Tomi)

Seeds and more seeds (Selsam, Millicent E)

Snail, where are you? (Ungerer, Tomi)

The sorcerer's apprentice (Hazen, Barbara Shook)

That pest Jonathan (Cole, William)

The three robbers (Ungerer, Tomi)

Warwick's three bottles (Hodeir, André)

What's good for a four-year-old? (Cole, William)

Zeralda's ogre (Ungerer, Tomi)

Unwin, Nora Spicer. The good rain (Goudey, Alice E)

Urbanowich, Evelyn. A treasury of songs for little children (Botwin, Esther)

Uyeda, Frances. Chōchō is for butterfly (Sasaki, Jeannie)

V

Vaës, Alain. The steadfast tin soldier (Andersen, H C (Hans Christian))

Vallario, Jean. A lion under her bed (Hawkins, Mark)

Vallier, Jean. The king, the mice and the cheese (Gurney, Nancy)

Van Allsburg, Chris. Ben's dream (Van Allsburg, Chris)

The garden of Abdul Gasazi (Van Allsburg, Chris)

Jumanji (Van Allsburg, Chris)

The mysteries of Harris Burdick (Van Allsburg, Chris)

The wreck of the Zephyr (Van Allsburg, Chris)

Van Aver, Philip. Twenty nursery rhymes (Mother Goose)

Van Bilsen, Rita. Jack and the magic stove (Beresford, Elisabeth)

Vanderlinden, Kathy. I love my cat! (Schaffer, Marion)

Van der Meer, Atie. Oh Lord! (Van der Meer, Ron)

Van der Meer, Ron. Oh Lord! (Van der Meer, Ron)

Vandivert, Rita. Barnaby (Vandivert, William)

Vandivert, William. Barnaby (Vandivert, William)

Vanecek, Kveta. The cats' opera (Dillon, Eilis)

Van Horn, William. Harry Hoyle's giant jumping bean (Van Horn, William)

Twitchtoe, the beastfinder (Van Horn, William)

Van Pelt, Harold L. A motor holiday (Greene, Carla)

Van Sciver, Ruth. The boy who couldn't roar (Berquist, Grace)

Let's go to a post office (Buchheimer, Naomi)

Let's go to a school (Buchheimer, Naomi)

Van Severen, Joe. Learning about monsters (Gilleo, Alma)

Van Stockum, Hilda. A day on skates (Van Stockum, Hilda)

Van Westering, Francien. The lady of Stavoren (Bouhuys, Mies)

Varga, Judy. Circus cannonball (Varga, Judy)

The dragon who liked to spit fire (Varga, Judy)

Janko's wish (Varga, Judy)

The mare's egg (Varga, Judy)

Miss Lollipop's lion (Varga, Judy)

The monster behind Black Rock (Varga, Judy)

Varley, Susan. Badger's parting gifts (Varley, Susan)

Vasiliu, Marcea. Everything is somewhere (Vasiliu, Marcea)

What's happening? (Vasiliu, Marcea)

Velez, Walter. How the Ewoks saved the trees (Howe, James)

Velthuijs, Max. The painter and the bird (Velthuijs, Max)

The wolf and the kid (Damjan, Mischa)

Vendrell, Carme Solé. A bear in the air (Williams, Leslie)

Venezia, Mike. Ask a silly question (Wakefield, Joyce)

Sometimes I worry... (Gross, Alan)

What if the teacher calls on me? (Gross, Alan)

Veno, Joseph. Horace the friendly octopus (Drdek, Richard E)

Ventura, Marisa. The painter's trick (Ventura, Piero)

Ventura, Piero. Piero Ventura's book of cities (Ventura, Piero)

Ten brothers with camels (Cretan, Gladys Yessayan)

Vernam, Roger. Animal families (Weil, Ann)

Jungle animals (Buck, Frank)

Vestal, Herman B. Look out for pirates! (Vinton, Iris)

Veyrac, Robert De *see* De Veyrac, Robert

Vial, Yves. Sprig the tree frog (Pursell, Margaret Sanford)

Vidal, Beatriz. Bringing the rain to Kapiti Plain (Aardema, Verna)

Vigna, Judith. Anyhow, I'm glad I tried (Vigna, Judith)

Couldn't we have a turtle instead? (Vigna, Judith)

Daddy's new baby (Vigna, Judith)

Everyone goes as a pumpkin (Vigna, Judith)

Grandma without me (Vigna, Judith)

The hiding house (Vigna, Judith)

She's not my real mother (Vigna, Judith)

Villarejo, Mary. The art fair (Villarejo, Mary)

The tiger hunt (Villarejo, Mary)

Villemain, Patricia. Linda's airmail letter (Bell, Norman)

Vincent, Gabrielle. Bravo, Ernest and Celestine! (Vincent, Gabrielle)

Ernest and Celestine (Vincent, Gabrielle)

Ernest and Celestine's picnic (Vincent, Gabrielle)

Smile, Ernest and Celestine (Vincent, Gabrielle)

Vinson, Pauline. Willie goes to the seashore (Vinson, Pauline)

Visscher, Peter. Air (Lloyd, David)

Vo-Dinh Mai. First snow (Coutant, Helen)

The happy funeral (Bunting, Eve)

A thousand pails of water (Roy, Ronald)

Vogel, Ilse-Margaret. The don't be scared book (Vogel, Ilse-Margaret)

Vojtech, Anna. The star husband (Mobley, Jane)

Von Hippel, Ursula. The craziest Halloween (Von Hippel, Ursula)

W

Waber, Bernard. An anteater named Arthur (Waber, Bernard)

Bernard (Waber, Bernard)

But names will never hurt me (Waber, Bernard)

How to go about laying an egg (Waber, Bernard)

I was all thumbs (Waber, Bernard)

Ira sleeps over (Waber, Bernard)

Just like Abraham Lincoln (Waber, Bernard)

Lorenzo (Waber, Bernard)

Lovable Lyle (Waber, Bernard)

Lyle and the birthday party (Waber, Bernard)

Lyle finds his mother (Waber, Bernard)

Lyle, Lyle Crocodile (Waber, Bernard)

Mice on my mind (Waber, Bernard)

Nobody is perfick (Waber, Bernard)

Rich cat, poor cat (Waber, Bernard)

The snake (Waber, Bernard)

You're a little kid with a big heart (Waber, Bernard)

Waechter, Friedrich Karl. Three is company (Waechter, Friedrich Karl)

Wahl, Richard. I want to be a librarian (Baker, Donna)

I want to be a pilot (Baker, Donna)

I want to be a police officer (Baker, Donna)

Walker, David. The sleeping beauty (Perrault, Charles)

Wallace, Ian. Chin Chiang and the dragon's dance (Wallace, Ian)

Wallace, Jessica. The house that grew (Strathdee, Jean)

Walles, Dwight. The wonderful way that babies are made (Christenson, Larry)

Wallner, Alexandra. The friends of Charlie Ant Bear (Hall, Malcolm)

Munch (Wallner, Alexandra)

Wallner, John. Charlotte and Charles (Tompert, Ann)

Follow me cried Bee (Wahl, Jan)

Frizzy the fearful (Sharmat, Marjorie Weinman)

Good night to Annie (Merriam, Eve)

Grandma's secret letter (Davis, Maggie S)

Hippo thunder (Sussman, Susan)

A January fog will freeze a hog

Little Fox goes to the end of the world (Tompert, Ann)

Little Otter remembers and other stories (Tompert, Ann)

The Macmillan picture wordbook (Daly, Kathleen N)

The night Stella hid the stars (Radley, Gail)

One tough turkey (Kroll, Steven)

A perfect nose for Ralph (Zalben, Jane Breskin)

Rumpelstiltskin (Grimm, Jacob)

Snow White and Rose Red (Grimm, Jacob)

The terrible thing that happened at our house (Blaine, Marge)

Tonight's the night (Aylesworth, Jim)

When the dark comes dancing (Larrick, Nancy)

Winter (Allington, Richard L)

Walsh, John. Baby bear and the long sleep (Ward, Andrew)

Walters, Audrey. Just like you (Klein, Leonore)

Walton, Tony. Witch's holiday (Low, Alice)

Ward, Keith. Timothy Tiger (Barrows, Marjorie Wescott)

Ward, Lynd. America's Ethan Allen (Holbrook, Stewart)

The biggest bear (Ward, Lynd)

The black sombrero (Ward, Nanda Weedon)

Little Baptiste (McNeer, May Yonge)

The little red lighthouse and the great gray bridge (Swift, Hildegarde Hoyt)

My friend Mac (McNeer, May Yonge)

Nic of the woods (Ward, Lynd)

The silver pony (Ward, Lynd)

Warren, Betsy. Speedy gets around (Price, Dorothy E)

Warren, Elizabeth Avery *see* Warren, Betsy

Warshaw, Jerry. The case of Og, the missing frog (Harrison, David Lee)

Chicken riddle (Bishop, Ann)

The Ella Fannie elephant riddle book (Bishop, Ann)

Hey riddle riddle (Bishop, Ann)

Merry-go-riddle (Bishop, Ann)

Mrs. Periwinkle's groceries (Snow, Pegeen)

Noah riddle? (Bishop, Ann)

Oh, riddlesticks! (Bishop, Ann)

The riddle ages (Bishop, Ann)

Riddle-iculous rid-alphabet book (Bishop, Ann)

Wild Bill Hiccup's riddle book (Bishop, Ann)

Wasmuth, Eleanor. An alligator day (Wasmuth, Eleanor)

The picnic basket (Wasmuth, Eleanor)

Watanabe, Yuichi. Wally the whale who loved balloons (Watanabe, Yuichi)

Noisy book (Brown, Margaret Wise)
On the sand dune (Orgel, Doris)
Penguin's way (Johnston, Johanna)
Peter's brownstone house (Colman, Hila)
The quiet noisy book (Brown, Margaret Wise)
Rabbit story (Tresselt, Alvin R)
The raccoon and Mrs. McGinnis (Miles, Miska)
Rain drop splash (Tresselt, Alvin R)
Red light, green light (Brown, Margaret Wise)
Salt boy (Perrine, Mary)
The seashore noisy book (Brown, Margaret Wise)
Señor Baby Elephant, the pirate (Joslin, Sesyle)
Silly Willy Nilly (Weisgard, Leonard)
Sir Kevin of Devon (Holl, Adelaide)
Something for now, something for later (Schlein, Miriam)
The summer noisy book (Brown, Margaret Wise)
Sylvester Jones and the voice in the forest (Miles, Miska)
Timid Timothy, the kitten who learned to be brave (Williams, Gweneira Maureen)
Try and catch me (Jewell, Nancy)
Valentine cat (Bulla, Clyde Robert)
Wake up and good night (Zolotow, Charlotte)
Watch that watch (Colman, Hila)
Whale's way (Johnston, Johanna)
What is for my birthday? (Eberstadt, Isabel)
When a boy wakes up in the morning (McNulty, Faith)
When I go to the moon (Lewis, Claudia Louise)
Where does the butterfly go when it rains? (Garelick, May)
Whistle for the train (Brown, Margaret Wise)
Who dreams of cheese? (Weisgard, Leonard)
Weiss, Ellen. Clara the fortune-telling chicken (Weiss, Ellen)
Funny feet! (Weiss, Leatie)
Millicent Maybe (Weiss, Ellen)
Things to make and do for Christmas (Weiss, Ellen)
The vingananee and the tree toad (Aardema, Verna)
Weiss, Harvey. The amazing Mr. Pelgrew (Schlein, Miriam)
Here comes night (Schlein, Miriam)
Herman McGregor's world (Schlein, Miriam)
Looking for Alexander (DeJong, David Cornel)
My closet full of hats (Weiss, Harvey)
My family (Schlein, Miriam)
Olaf reads (Lexau, Joan M)
The pile of junk (Schlein, Miriam)
The sooner hound (Weiss, Harvey)
3D, 2D, 1D (Adler, David A)
Weiss, Nicki. Maude and Sally (Weiss, Nicki)
Waiting (Weiss, Nicki)

Weekend at Muskrat Lake (Weiss, Nicki)
Weissman, Bari. Golly Gump swallowed a fly (Cole, Joanna)
The magic guinea pig (Springstubb, Tricia)
No place for a goat (Sattler, Helen Roney)
Weissman, Mottke. Numbers a first counting book (Allen, Robert)
Weissman, Sam Q. School daze (Keller, Charles)
Welch, Martha McKeen. Will that wake mother? (Welch, Martha McKeen)
Wells, H. G. (Herbert George). The adventures of Tommy (Wells, H G (Herbert George))
Wells, Rosemary. Don't spill it again, James (Wells, Rosemary)
Good night, Fred (Wells, Rosemary)
Impossible, possum (Conford, Ellen)
A lion for Lewis (Wells, Rosemary)
Max's breakfast (Wells, Rosemary)
Max's new suit (Wells, Rosemary)
Noisy Nora (Wells, Rosemary)
Peabody (Wells, Rosemary)
Stanley and Rhoda (Wells, Rosemary)
Tell me a Trudy (Segal, Lore)
Timothy goes to school (Wells, Rosemary)
Unfortunately Harriet (Wells, Rosemary)
Wende, Philip. Bird boy (Wende, Philip)
Why can't I be William? (Conford, Ellen)
Wennerstrom, Genia Katherine *see* Genia
Wenzel, Gregory C. More about dinosaurs (Cutts, David)
Werth, Kurt. Dick Whittington and his cat
How a piglet crashed the Christmas party (Zakhoder, Boris Vladimirovich)
How Mrs. Santa Claus saved Christmas (McGinley, Phyllis)
Lazy Jack (Werth, Kurt)
Meet Miki Takino (Copeland, Helen)
One dark night (Preston, Edna Mitchell)
One mitten Lewis (Kay, Helen)
A tiger called Thomas (Zolotow, Charlotte)
Tony's birds (Selsam, Millicent E)
West, David. Airplanes (Cave, Ron)
Automobiles (Cave, Ron)
Motorcycles (Cave, Ron)
West, Ian. Silas, the first pig to fly (West, Ian)
Westcott, Nadine Bernard. The emperor's new clothes (Andersen, H C (Hans Christian))
The giant vegetable garden (Westcott, Nadine Bernard)
Westerberg, Christine. Bouncy baby bunny finds his bed (Bowden, Joan Chase)
The cap that mother made (Westerberg, Christine)
Westering, Francien Van *see* Van Westering, Francien
Weston, Martha. Lucky porcupine! (Schlein, Miriam)
Peony's rainbow (Weston, Martha)
Westphal, Peggy. Quick as a wink (Aldis, Dorothy)
Wexler, Jerome. The amazing dandelion (Selsam, Millicent E)

Wilkinson, Barry. Puss in boots (Perrault, Charles)

Wilks, Mike. In granny's garden (Harrison, Sarah)

Williams, Barbara. Hello, dandelions! (Williams, Barbara)

Williams, Garth. Amigo (Baylor, Byrd)
Bedtime for Frances (Hoban, Russell)
The big golden animal ABC (Williams, Garth)
Chester Cricket's pigeon ride (Selden, George)
The chicken book (Williams, Garth)
Do you know what I'll do? (Zolotow, Charlotte)
Emmett's pig (Stolz, Mary Slattery)
Fox eyes (Brown, Margaret Wise)
The little fur family (Brown, Margaret Wise)
The little giant girl and the elf boys (Minarik, Else Holmelund)
Over and over (Zolotow, Charlotte)
Push Kitty (Wahl, Jan)
The rabbits' wedding (Williams, Garth)
The sky was blue (Zolotow, Charlotte)
The tall book of make-believe (Watson, Jane Werner)
Three little animals (Brown, Margaret Wise)
Wait till the moon is full (Brown, Margaret Wise)

Williams, Jay. I wish I had another name (Williams, Jay)

Williams, Jenny. The boy with two shadows (Mahy, Margaret)
Let's find out about babies (Shapp, Martha)
A lion in the meadow (Mahy, Margaret)
Rooms for rent (Mahy, Margaret)
A wet Monday (Edwards, Dorothy)

Williams, Vera B. A chair for my mother (Williams, Vera B)
Hooray for me! (Charlip, Remy)
Music, music for everyone (Williams, Vera B)
Ostrich feathers (Brenner, Barbara)
Something special for me (Williams, Vera B)
Three days on a river in a red canoe (Williams, Vera B)

Williamson, Mel. Walk on! (Williamson, Mel)

Wilson, Dagmar. Benny and the bear (Carleton, Barbee Oliver)
Gertie the duck (Georgiady, Nicholas P)
More poems to read to the very young (Frank, Josette)
While Susie sleeps (Schneider, Nina)

Wilson, Dick. "Why am I going to the hospital?" (Ciliotta, Claire)

Wilson, John. Becky (Wilson, Julia)

Wilson, Maurice. Horses (Pluckrose, Henry)
Lions and tigers (Pluckrose, Henry)

Wilson, Rowland B. Tubby and the lantern (Perkins, Al)
Tubby and the Poo-Bah (Perkins, Al)

Winborn, Marsha. Sir William and the pumpkin monster (Cuyler, Margery)

Winter, Jeanette. The girl and the moon man (Winter, Jeanette)
Harry (the monster) (Cameron, Ann)
Hinny Winny Bunco (Greene, Carol)
Hush little baby
More Witch, Goblin, and Ghost stories (Alexander, Sue)
Witch, Goblin, and Ghost in the haunted woods (Alexander, Sue)
Witch, Goblin and Ghost's book of things to do (Alexander, Sue)
Witch, Goblin and sometimes Ghost (Alexander, Sue)

Winter, Paula. The bear and the fly (Winter, Paula)
Sir Andrew (Winter, Paula)
Where's your baby brother, Becky Bunting? (Tierney, Hanne)

Winteringham, Victoria. Penguin day (Winteringham, Victoria)

Wiseman, Bernard. Doctor Duck and Nurse Swan (Wiseman, Bernard)
Don't make fun! (Wiseman, Bernard)
Morris has a birthday party! (Wiseman, Bernard)
Oscar is a mama (Wiseman, Bernard)
Tails are not for painting (Wiseman, Bernard)

Wiser, Guy Brown. Timothy turtle (Davis, Alice Vaught)

Witt, Patricia De see DeWitt, Patricia

Witt, Robin De see DeWitt, Robin

Wittman, Sally. Pelly and Peak (Wittman, Sally)
Plenty of Pelly and Peak (Wittman, Sally)

Wodge, Dreary see Gorey, Edward

Wohlberg, Meg. Andy and his fine friends (Woolley, Catherine)
Andy and the runaway horse (Woolley, Catherine)
Demi the baby sitter (Van den Honert, Dorry)
The smallest boy in the class (Beim, Jerrold)

Wolcott, Elizabeth Tyler. Counting the days (Tippett, James Sterling)

Wolde, Gunilla. Betsy and Peter are different (Wolde, Gunilla)
Betsy and the chicken pox (Wolde, Gunilla)
Betsy and the doctor (Wolde, Gunilla)
Betsy and the vacuum cleaner (Wolde, Gunilla)
Betsy's first day at nursery school (Wolde, Gunilla)
Betsy's fixing day (Wolde, Gunilla)
This is Betsy (Wolde, Gunilla)

Wolf, Ann. The rabbit and the turtle (Wolf, Ann)

Wolf, Bernard. Adam Smith goes to school (Wolf, Bernard)
Anna's silent world (Wolf, Bernard)
Don't feel sorry for Paul (Wolf, Bernard)
Michael and the dentist (Wolf, Bernard)

Wolf, Janet. The best present is me (Wolf, Janet)

Wolfe, Robert L. The truck book (Wolfe, Robert L)

Wolff, Ashley. The bells of London (Wolff, Ashley)
A year of birds (Wolff, Ashley)
Wolff, Barbara. Egg to chick (Selsam, Millicent E)
Wolff, Robert Jay. Feeling blue (Wolff, Robert Jay)
Hello, yellow! (Wolff, Robert Jay)
Seeing red (Wolff, Robert Jay)
Wondriska, William. Mr. Brown and Mr. Gray (Wondriska, William)
Puff (Wondriska, William)
The stop (Wondriska, William)
The tomato patch (Wondriska, William)
Wood, Don. The napping house (Wood, Audrey)
Wood, Leslie. The story of the little red engine (Ross, Diana)
Wood, Myron. Little wrangler (Wood, Nancy C)
Wood, Owen. Answer me that (Dennis, Suzanne E)
The owl and the pussy-cat (Lear, Edward)
Woodcock, Louise Phinney. The very little dog (Skaar, Grace Marion)
Woodroffe, Paul. Thirty old-time nursery songs (Mother Goose)
Woodward, Hildegard. Roger and the fox (Davis, Lavinia)
The wild birthday cake (Davis, Lavinia)
Worth, Jo. Look at trees (Kirkpatrick, Rena K)
Worthington, Phoebe. Teddy bear baker (Worthington, Phoebe)
Teddy bear coalman (Worthington, Phoebe)
Worthington, Selby. Teddy bear baker (Worthington, Phoebe)
Teddy bear coalman (Worthington, Phoebe)
Wright, Blanche Fisher. The real Mother Goose (Mother Goose)
Wright, Dare. The doll and the kitten (Wright, Dare)
Edith and Midnight (Wright, Dare)
Edith and Mr. Bear (Wright, Dare)
The lonely doll (Wright, Dare)
The lonely doll learns a lesson (Wright, Dare)
Look at a calf (Wright, Dare)
Look at a colt (Wright, Dare)
Look at a kitten (Wright, Dare)
Wright, Dave. Edith and the duckling (Wright, Dare)
Wright, Freire. Borrowed feathers and other fables (Stevens, Bryna)
Wright, Joe. The Archery contest (Saddler, Allen)
The king gets fit (Saddler, Allen)
Wright, Martin. Granny Stickleback (Moore, John)
Wright, Walter. Star wars
Wright-Frierson, Virginia. Big boy, little boy (Stanovich, Betty Jo)
Wrigley, Elsie. Baby Jumbo (DuBois, Ivy)
Mother fox (DuBois, Ivy)

Wronker, Lili Cassel see Cassel-Wronker, Lili
Wurmfeld, Hope. Black is beautiful (McGovern, Ann)
Feeling mad, feeling sad, feeling bad, feeling glad (McGovern, Ann)
Wyman, Cherie R. Brimhall turns detective (Delton, Judy)

Y

Yabuki, Seiji. I love the morning (Yabuki, Seiji)
Yajima, Yasugi. Peter and the wolf (Prokofiev, Sergei Sergeievitch)
Yamaguchi, Marianne. Two crabs and the moonlight (Yamaguchi, Tohr)
Yanagihara, Ryohei. The sorcerer's apprentice (Dukas, P (Paul Abraham))
Yap, Weda. Stories for little children (Buck, Pearl S (Pearl Sydenstricker))
Yaroslava. An egg is for wishing (Kay, Helen)
How a shirt grew in the field (Rudolph, Marguerita)
Ivanko and the dragon (Rudchenko, Ivan)
The mitten (Tresselt, Alvin R)
Rosachok (Zakhoder, Boris Vladimirovich)
A stocking for a kitten (Kay, Helen)
Yashima, Tarō. Crow boy (Yashima, Tarō)
Momo's kitten (Yashima, Mitsu)
Plenty to watch (Yashima, Mitsu)
Seashore story (Yashima, Tarō)
Soo Ling finds a way (Behrens, June)
Umbrella (Yashima, Tarō)
The village tree (Yashima, Tarō)
The youngest one (Yashima, Tarō)
Ylla. Animal babies (Ylla)
The duck (Brown, Margaret Wise)
I'll show you cats (Ylla)
Listen, listen! (Bonsall, Crosby Newell)
The little elephant (Ylla)
Look who's talking (Ylla)
Polar bear brothers (Ylla)
The sleepy little lion (Brown, Margaret Wise)
They all saw it (Brown, Margaret Wise)
Two little bears (Ylla)
Yokoi, Daisuke. Cars and trucks
Youldon, Gillian. Colors (Youldon, Gillian)
Numbers (Youldon, Gillian)
Shapes (Youldon, Gillian)
Sizes (Youldon, Gillian)
Young, Ed. Bo Rabbit smart for true (Jaquith, Priscilla)
The Chinese Mother Goose rhymes (Mother Goose)
The emperor and the kite (Yolen, Jane)
The girl who loved the wind (Yolen, Jane)
High on a hill
The lion and the mouse (Æsop)
The mean mouse and other mean stories (Udry, Janice May)
The rooster's horns (Young, Ed)
The terrible Nung Gwama (Young, Ed)